A Kannada-English School-dictionary

A

KANNAḌA-ENGLISH

SCHOOL-DICTIONARY

CHIEFLY BASED ON THE LABOURS OF THE

REV. DR. F. KITTEL

BY THE

Rev. J. BUCHER.

ಕನ್ನಡ ಮತ್ತು ಇಂಗ್ಲಿಷ್

ಶಾಲಾನಿಘಂಟು

MANGALORE
BASEL MISSION BOOK & TRACT DEPOSITORY
1899

PRINTED AT THE BASEL MISSION PRESS, MANGALORE.

PREFACE.

The present work is designed to form a companion volume to the well known and much appreciated English-Canarese School-Dictionary, compiled by the Rev. F. Ziegler. The publication of a Kannada-English School-Dictionary has for a long time been a deep-felt desideratum, as the two smaller editions hitherto extant have but insufficiently served their purpose. The stupendous work of the Rev Dr. Kittel, the eminent lexicographer of the Kannaḍa language, whose unremitting labours have set a permanent literary monument to the language, standing out in bold features of historical, etymological and philological, critical researches for guidance and instruction to *litterateurs* striving after Kannaḍa embellishment and scholarship, held out promising inducements and marked facilities to undertake this work which is chiefly based upon it

Plan and arrangement: To add to the usefulness of the work and to facilitate its use, I deemed it fit to indicate the principles that have been adopted in arranging the matter and when launching on new methods I have attempted rather to err on the side of cautious adherence than on the side of hasty innovation.

I. Orthography: *a* **Obsolete Letters.** These are ಱ and ೞ, now universally represented by ರ and ಳ, and have been put in parantheses immediately after the words in which they occur to give an insight into their different origin and meaning.

N. B. The double consonant ಕ್ಷ has been brought to its proper place and is invariably to be looked up under the letter ಕ್ಷ.

b **Sonnĕ.** The method of using **bindu** or **sonnĕ** indiscriminately before classified (*vargíya*) and unclassified (*avargíya*) letters sanctioned by former lexicographers, grammarians and time-honoured [illegible] it variance with the laws of etymology. These laws have not seldom to give way to usage and well-established practice. But, though this convenient mode of representing by sonně the letters n, n and m, when followed by consonants of their own class, and the nasals n, and ń has been adhered to, the alphabetical order of words has been maintained uninfringed Words in which the sonně occurs, appear now in their proper place in the alphabet This may at the beginning occasion a little embarrassment to those who are accustomed to look up this class of words at the head of each letter, but all difficulty will with practice disappear

c **Orthography proper** is yet a neglected field of study' The colloquial language, legitimately abounding with provincial peculiarities, dialectical whimsicalities and vulgar inelegancies, must ever differ from the written language The *lingua litera* should possess a uniform system of spelling, which it has in some respects not yet accepted, but approving of various spellings as authors think fit. The four short vowels ă, ĕ, ĭ, ŭ, for instance promiscuously interchange in words like ಮದುವೆ. ಮದಿವೆ, ಮದೆವೆ, ಮದವೆ, ಮದುಮೆ, *etc* ...or ಕಿತ್ತಳಿ, ಕಿತ್ತಳೆ, ಕಿತ್ತಿಳಿ, ಕಿತ್ತಿಳೆ, *etc* or ಅಂಗಳ, -ಳು, -ಳಿ, -ಳೆ, *etc* or ಅಫಿಮು, ಅಫೀಮು, ಅಫಮು, ಅಫು, *etc.* ..or ಚಗತಿ, ಚಗತಿ, ಚಿಗತಿ, ಚಿಗೆತಿ. *etc* As most of these forms occur in books, newspapers and documents, they demand the same attention of being embodied in the vocabulary which is a mere encumbrance to the student. Hence a standard orthography is greatly desired.

II. Compounds. This class of words is very numerous in the Kannaḍa language and materially contributes to its copiousness The largest number of compounds has been received from the ductile, flexible and infinitely copious Samskrita language, so peculiarly adapted to form numberless compounds All compounds, irrespective of their origin, whether of pure Kannada, of Samskrita, of Tadbhava or of any other tongue, have been treated alike, and subordinated to leading words—a hyphen denoting the division of the members of the compound

ಚಿನ್ನಟ್ಟು, ಚೆಂಬಲ, etc., had in many instances to be introduced as independent words when the euphonic changes effected in combining the separate parts would involve too great a task to recognise them. Both **Saṁskrita** noun-compounds, as of ಅಗ್ನಿ, ಆತ್ಮ, ಕರ್ಮ, ನೀತಿ, etc., as well as adjectival and adverbial compounds, as of ಅತಿ, ಪರ, ಅಷ್ಟ, ಸು, etc , have been treated in this manner, provided the phonetic changes caused by the sandhi of the two words remained unmodified Where a phonetic change or an elision or a permutation of letters took place the compound was treated as a separate word.

III. Derivatives: *a.* **Unusual Derivatives.** It should be borne in mind that there is, logically speaking, a vast class of derivatives formed by adding to a primary root etymological terminations, inflectional affixes, *etc.*, .. *e. g.* ಪು added to ನೆನ=ನೆನಪು, ಹೊಳೆ=ಹೊಳಪು; or ಸು added to ನೆನೆ=ನೆನಸು, ತಿಳಿ=ತಿಳಿಸು, or ಇಕೆ added to ನಂಬು=ನಂಬಿಕೆ, ಅಂಜು=ಅಂಜಿಕೆ, ಉಡು=ಉಡಿಕೆ; or ಮೆ added to ತಾಳು=(ತಾಳುಮೆ) ತಾಳ್ಮೆ, ಬಲ=ಬಲ್ಮೆ; etc. These being difficult to trace to their original constituent parts have, of course, been considered as underived and treated accordingly.

b **Proper derivatives** of *abstract* and *personal* nouns, where no hazy uncertainty is felt, terminating in -ತನ, -ತ್ವ, -ತೆ, -ವಂತ, -ಗಾರ, -ಗಾತಿ, -ಬೋರ, -ಇಷ್ಟ, -ದಾರ, *etc.* have consistently been added on to the primary word. In incorporating these derivatives the same method has been employed as with the compound.

Verbal Derivatives of unfrequent occurrence terminating in -ಇಸು, as ಕೋಪಿಸು, ಸಂತೋಷಿಸು, ಸ್ನೇಹಿಸು, *etc.* have been exhibited under the primary words ಕೋಪ, ಸಂತೋಷ, ಸ್ನೇಹ, *etc.*, however with the alteration of writing the whole word in full to avoid ambiguity and confusion Verbs of great importance and frequent usage, as: ಇಳಿಸು, ಕಲಿಸು, ನಡಿಸು, ಬೋಧಿಸು, *etc.*, have been introduced as independent words

IV. Homonyms, of which the Kannaḍa language embosoms a good number, have occasionally been split up under two or three heads, when they obviously and intelligibly belong to different roots bearing the characteristic of distinct derivation.

Homonymous roots involving the sense of a noun, of a verb and even eventually of an adverb, as ಕಟ್ಟು, ತಪ್ಪು, ನೆಟ್ಟನೆ, ತೊನಕು, ಹೊರ, *etc* have been treated under one head with their respective grammatical signs.

V. Grammatical significations. For a School-Dictionary it is a most important feature to indicate the parts of speech, the determination of which cannot be left to the discretion of the pupil The abbreviated grammatical signs have been added after the Kannada word The treatment of the Saṁskrita different verbal derivations that have not yet assumed a definite part of speech in Kannaḍa has been made subject to the same method adopted by reliable Saṁskṛita lexicographers. The abbreviation for *"causative verb"*, with which the Kannaḍa language can be marvellously enriched, has been expelled as fallen into disuse and where necessary substituted by *v. t.* The grammatical signs are only added to the *leading word* and not to compounds or derivatives being in most cases self-evident

VI. English equivalents. Special attention has been paid to the rendering of the English equivalents. Brevity and conciseness have systematically been aimed at in order to give a ready-made coin. Considerable pains have also been taken to contract and condense the equivalents into as few groups as practicable to facilitate comprehension. Another effort has been made while arranging the several meanings in order to indicate their actual growth and development, beginning, if possible, with the primitive meaning suggested by etymology It has also been found recommendable not to adduce too many English equivalents to facilitate the choice of the most appropriate one.

VII. Origin of words. The Kannaḍa language is one of the principle representatives of the Dravidian language-family in South-India spoken by upwards of 10 millions It is however to be remembered that the language, as in fact all languages, being in constant transition and permutation, does not only comprise [illegible] -n-
gredient [illegible] ve

and constructive factor in the language is the *Dravidian* which forms the solid groundwork determining the declensional and conjugational and other inflections and supplying the more common, homely and familiar words, as ಬರು, ಕೇಳು, ನೋಡು, ಹೋಗು, ಒಳ್ಳೆ, ಕೆಟ್ಟ, ಚಲೋ: ಮನೆ, ಕೆಲಸ ಮೇಲೆ, ಕೆಳಗೆ, *etc.* Next we have the **Saṁskṛita** element which has had a great influence upon the language in enriching its vocabulary, in augmenting its synonyms and in ennobling its composition. The introduction of Saṁskrita words dates back to the contact of the Dravidians with the Aryans and supplied the language with almost all its abstract, religious and scientific terms. The Dravidian words are for every day events and natural feelings, while the Samskrita are elegant, dignified and artificial, fitted for rhetoric, subtle disputation and the profound expressions of philosophy. Many have retained their unaltered Saṁskrita form, whereas others have changed so as to suit the Kannaḍa tongue. The latter class are called Tadbhavas Next we have a good number of **Hindustâni** and **Mahraṭi** words, chiefly relating to feudalism *and* militia, whose introduction is due to the Moghul and Mahratta conquests of Kannaḍa districts. Some few Portuguese expressions have found their way into the language too, as ಇಂಗ್ರೇಜಿ. ಕುಮೀಜು. *etc.* from the Portuguese period Finally the **English** language has also commenced to contribute its mite mainly relating to education, jurisprudence and revenue. Some have already become home-words and, as time advances and a smattering of mispronounced English diffuses into the masses, it is but natural that this process of assimilation continues at even a more extensive rate.

To bring out this feature conspicuously it has been thought desirable to mark with the initials of the respective language the words migrated from. The carrying out of this principle has sometimes met with considerable difficulty with regard to words, doubtless of Saṁskritic origin, but which had come into Kannaḍa through the medium of another Indian language, as **s.** ದಸರಾತ್ರಿ = **h.** ದಸರಾ = **k.** ದಸರೆ **s.** ಮರ್ಕಟ = **m.** ಮಂಕಡ = **k.** ಮಂಗ; **s.** ಕರ್ಪಟ = **h.** ಕಪ್ಡಾ = **k.** ಕಪಡೆ In such cases the greatest probability lies

always carried the decision, as no comparative philological studies could be made It has been the compiler's aim to attain to utmost accuracy with pure Kannada and pure Samskrita words, whereas with Tadbhavas such an exactitude was unattainable

As ancient classical literature is extensively read in schools and colleges a considerable number of obsolete and obolescent words principally occurring in Jaimini Bhârata and other poetical works proscribed have been inserted and marked by the letters **a. k.**

VIII. Fusion of elements. The foreign words that have come into the language do not stand by themselves as an independent class but have become Kannadasised subject to Kannaḍa laws and analogies But, notwithstanding this metamorphosis the borrowed words, taken as a class, have a peculiar character which separates them even to the feeling of an uneducated Kannaḍa man from the Dravidian stock, thus giving to the language a somewhat heterogeneous aspect. But a still more serious disadvantage is the necessity of expressing new ideas either with the help of Saṁskrita or English. The expressiveness and suggestiveness of these terms are hidden from those who are unacquainted with Saṁskrita and English, and thus the language suffers in its power of quickening and originating thought

IX. Conclusion. To secure the greatest possible accuracy and perfection the manuscript copy was, before its print, placed into the hands of R Ry. Bh. Shiva Rau, the experienced and learned corrector of the Basel Mission Press, whose thorough acquaintance with the great work of Dr. Kittel in having carried it through the press has enabled him to make some valuable suggestions and not a few additions, for whose liberal services the author is under great obligation My thanks are also due to the Kanarese Pandit B Rama Krishnaya, Munshi of the G. M. High School Mangalore, who assisted in reading the proc [illegible], G. M.

High School, for a list of legal terms The printer and publisher deserve also a vote of thanks.

In conclusion the author desires to express his profound admiration for the supreme Kannaḍa scholarship of Dr. Kittel's work

Though the compiler is more sensible of the deficiencies and shortcomings of this work than any other person can be, he does not hesitate to confidently commend it to the public, for whom it will prove both instructive and useful, and he will be amply rewarded for his night-labours bestowed upon it by its appreciative and extensive use

Hints and suggestions for improvement and enhanced efficiency will readily and thankfully be received.

Mangalore, January 1899.

J. Bucher.

List of Abbreviations.

a. = adjective.
abl. = ablative.
acc. = accusative.
ad. = adverb.
a. k. = ancient Kannaḍa.
arith. = arithmetic.
chr., *christ.* = Christian.
cf. = confer, compare.
conj. = conjunction.
Cpd. = compound or *Cpds.* compounds.
dat. = dative.
decl. = declension.
dem. = demonstrative.
dupl., *dpl.* = a couple of words used to make the idea more impressive, *as:* ಕಾಡುಮೇಡು, ಮನಃಪೂರ್ವಕ, *etc.*
e. = English.
e. g. = *exempli gratia* (for example).
esp. = especially.
etc. = *et caetera* (and so on).
f. = words of foreign derivation, *i. e.* Tamil, Telugu, Malayalam, Portuguese, Latin, Greek, *etc.*
f. = feminine.
fig. = figuratively.
fr. = from.
fut. = future.
gen. = genitive.
g., *gram.* = grammar.
h. = Hindustani, Persian, and Arabic.
hon. = honorific.
i. e. = *id est* (that is).
imp. = imperative.
int. = interjection.
inter. = interrogative
lit. = literally.
loc. = locative.
k. = (pure) Kannaḍa.
m. = Mahratti words.
N. = Name; proper name.
n. = noun.
neg. = negative.
P. p. = Past participle (*P. ps.* = Past participles).
pl. = plural.
pref. = prefix.
prep. = preposition.
pres. = present.
pro. = pronoun.
q. v. = *quod vide* (which see).
reit. = reiteration, *i. e.* a couple of words, the first of which is rendered more impressive and powerful by the second one which is however meaningless by itself, *e. g.* ಉಪ್ಪು ಸಪ್ಪು, ಅಗಸಗಿಸ, *etc.*
rep. = repetition, *i. e.* the act of repeating the same word twice or thrice, *e. g.* ಅಂತೆಂತು, ಎಲ್ಲೆಲ್ಲಿ, ಬಿಟ್ಟುಬಿಟ್ಟು, ಒರೆದವನು, ಮೆತ್ತ ಮೆತ್ತ, ಸಣ್ಣ ಸಣ್ಣ, *etc.*
s. = (pure) Saṁskṛita.
s. = *sub*, under.
sing. = singular.
tb. = tadbhava.
v. i. = verb intransitive.
v. t. = verb transitive.
= equal (in meaning).
& = and.
-. = hyphen, indicating that the principal word is to be prefixed in the case of compounds and derivatives.

A

KANNAḌA-ENGLISH
SCHOOL-DICTIONARY.

ಕನ್ನಡ ಮತ್ತು ಇಂಗ್ಲಿಷ್
ಶಾ ಲಾ ನಿ ಘ ಂ ಟು.

ಅ

ಅ. The first letter of the alphabet. 2, a short vowel inherent in every consonant. 3, a termination denoting etymological functions in declensions and conjugations, *as a 1st pers pl imp* ಹೋಗುವ, *b gen. sing.* ನೀರ, *etc.* 4, a negative prefix to nouns derived from Sanskrit, *as* ಅಯೋಗ್ಯ unworthy (*fr* ಯೋಗ್ಯ). Before a vowel ಅ becomes ಅನ್, thus ಅ-ಅಂತ = ಅನಂತ endless.

ಅಂ. A termination used in declension and conjugation in ancient Canarese. 2, *cop. conj.* both, and, also.

ಅಂಶ, ಅಂಶೆ s. *n* A part, share, portion. 2, a fraction *(anth)* 3, a degree of latitude or longitude. -ಚಕ್ರ. An astrological diagram

ಅಂಶಕ s. *n.* A part. 2, a kinsman, coheir.

ಅಂಶಾಂಶ s. *n* A part of a portion, a [sub-division.

ಅಂಶು (= ಅಂಚು 2) s *n* A ray of light. 2, the sun. 3, light, splendour. 4, a point. -ಜಾಲ. A collection of rays -ಧರ. The sun -ಮತ್ಫಲೆ. The plantain. -ಮಾಲಿ, -ಹಸ್ತ. The sun. -ಮಾಲೆ. Halo.

ಅಂಶುಕ s *n* Cloth, dress. 2, fine cloth.

ಅಂಸ s. *n* The shoulder, shoulder-blade. -ಕೂಟ. A bull's hump.

ಅಂಸಲ s. *a.* Strong, stout, lusty

ಅಃ k *int* expressing admiration, contempt or jest

ಅಕ s. *n* Pain, trouble, sin.

ಅಕಚ s. *a.* Bald-headed

ಅಕಟ, ಅಕಟಕಟ, ಅಕಟಾ k. *int* Alas! oh!

ಅಕಟವಿಕಟ k. *a* Frightful. 2, adverse, contrary.

ಅಕಟಾಯಿಸು k. *v i* To become warped (leather).

ಅಕರ s *a.* Handless, maimed.

ಅಕರ್ತವ್ಯ s. *a.* Not to be done, improper.

ಅಕರ್ಮ s. *a* Without work. *n.* Crime. -ಕ. Neuter or intransitive (verb, *g*).

ಅಕಲಂಕ s. *a* Stainless, spotless, pure.

ಅಕಲ್ಮಷ s. *n.* Purity, innocency

ಅಕಸಾಲಿ, ಅಕಸಾಲಿಗ ಅಕಸಾಲೆಗ k n A gold or silver smith
ಅಕಸ್ಮಾತ್ ಅಕಸ್ಮಾತ, ಅಕಸ್ಮಾತ್ತು s. ad By chance, suddenly, unexpectedly
ಅಕಳಸಕಳ k n Excessive tickling a. Too much 2, disrespectful
ಅಕಾರ s. n The letter ಅ.
ಅಕಾರಣ s a Causeless
ಅಕಾರತು h. a. Vain, useless
ಅಕಾರಾಂತ s n A term with final ಅ
ಅಕಾರ್ಯ s n An improper act.
ಅಕಾಲ s. n Inauspicious time. a. Unseasonable. -ಫಲ. Fruit out of season -ಮರಣ. Untimely death
ಅಕಿಂಚನ s. a Very poor
ಅಕುಟಿಲ s a Not crooked, upright, honest
ಅಕುಪ್ಯ s. n Gold silver
ಅಕೂಪಾರ s. n The ocean 2, the king of tortoises supposed to uphold the world, a big tortoise.
ಅಕೃತ್ಯ s a Undone 2, criminal. n. What ought not to be done 2 a crime
ಅಕೃಷ್ಣಕರ್ಮ s. a Guiltless
ಅಕೊ = ಅಗೋ
ಅಕ್ಕ k n An elder sister -ತಂಗಿಯರು Elder and younger sisters.
ಅಕ್ಕಚ್ಚಿ, ಅಕ್ಕಮ್ಮ k n An affectionate mode of addressing an elder sister.
ಅಕ್ಕಜ k n Wonder, surprise. 2, envy a. Wonderful, curious.
ಅಕ್ಕಟ = ಅಕಟ.
ಅಕ್ಕಡಿ, ಅಕ್ಕಡೆ k. n A furrow between two others of a main crop
ಅಕ್ಕಡಿತಕ್ಕಡಿ n Deceit in words, etc
ಅಕ್ಕನಿ k n The close adhesion of the woof and warp in the web of a loom
ಅಕ್ಕದಾಮ, ಅಕ್ಕಮಾಲೆ tb of ಅಕ್ಷಮಾಲೆ.
ಅಕ್ಕಬ k n Wonder, surprise
ಅಕ್ಕಯ್ಯ = ಅಕ್ಕಚ್ಚಿ q v
[illegible]

ಅಕ್ಕರ, ಅಕ್ಕರತೆ, ಅಕ್ಕರಿಕೆ, ಅಕ್ಕರು (ರ=ಱ) k n Attachment, affection, love
ಅಕ್ಕರೆ ಅಕ್ಕರು (ರ=ಱ) k. n. Necessity 2, occasion, need, want 3, desire
ಅಕ್ಕಲಕರೆ k n Anthemis pyrethrum, used for coughs, asthma, etc
ಅಕ್ಕಲು = ಹಕ್ಕಲು.
ಅಕ್ಕಸ k n Love, passion.
ಅಕ್ಕಸಾಲಿಗ = ಅಕಸಾಲಿಗ, q v.
ಅಕ್ಕಸಾಲೆ f. n The workshop of a goldsmith 2, a goldsmith
ಅಕ್ಕಳಿಸು, ಅಕ್ಕುಳಿಸು k v. i The muscles of the stomach to contract from hunger 2, to fear. 3, to flinch.
ಅಕ್ಕಾಡು a k v i To ooze, flow, run down, as tears, etc
ಅಕ್ಕಿ k n Raw rice deprived of its husk, -ಗಚ್ಚು. Rice-water; for cpds see ಎಲಕ್ಕಿ, ಕುಸಲಕ್ಕಿ, ಸಣ್ಣಕ್ಕಿ, ದಪ್ಪಕ್ಕಿ. etc
ಅಕ್ಕಿಸು a k v t To digest.
ಅಕ್ಕು, ಅಕ್ಕುಂ a k. v i. To subdue. 2, to seize. 3, fut of ಆಗು, it will become.
ಅಕ್ಕುಡಿಸು a k v. i To become small
ಅಕ್ಕುಳಿಸು = ಅಕ್ಕಳಿಸು. [come.
ಅಕ್ಕೆ past gerund of ಅಕ್ಕು. May it be-
ಅಕ್ರಮ s. n Confusion, irregularity, sin
ಅಕ್ರೂರ a Gentle. n. Krishna's uncle and friend.
ಅಕ್ರೋಡ (tb. of ಆಕ್ಷೋಟ) n A large, nut-bearing tree
ಅಕ್ಷ s n A die for gambling 2, the axle of a wheel 3, the eye 4, an organ of sense. 5 knowledge 6, the soul 7, a lawsuit -ತೃತೀಯ. N of a festival -ಮಾಲೆ. A rosary
ಅಕ್ಷತ, ಅಕ್ಷತೆ, ಅಕ್ಷಂತೆ s. a Not crushed, whole n Raw rice generally mixed with turmeric and used for religious ceremonies
ಅಕ್ಷಯ s a Imperishable, inexhaustible -ಪಾತ್ರೆ An inexhaustible vessel. [illegible] indu cycle

ಅಕ್ಷರ s. n. A letter of the alphabet. 2, eternal beatitude 3 penance 4, the sky.

ಅಕ್ಷಿ s n. The eye -ರೋಗ. Eye-disease. -ರೋಮ Eyelash

ಅಕ್ಷೌಹಿಣಿ s. n. A large army consisting of elephants, chariots, horse and foot

ಅಖ್ k int expressing abhorrence or disgust.

ಅಖಂಡ s. a. Undivided, entire, whole.

ಅಖಂಡನ s. n Non-refutation. 2, time

ಅಖಂಡಿತ s a Unbroken. 2, continuous 3, unrefuted.

ಅಖಾತ s. a Not dug. n A natural pond.

ಅಖಾದ್ಯ s. a Uneatable, unfit to be eaten

ಅಖಿನ್ನ s a Not distressed, not wearied.

ಅಖಿಲ s a. Without a gap, entire, whole all

ಅಗ s a Not moving. n A tree, a mountain.

ಅಗಚು k v. t. To press firmly, compress, squeeze down

ಅಗಜಾತೆ s n Pârvatî, the daughter of Himâlaya.

ಅಗಡು k n Viciousness, meanness a Wild, untamed -ತನ Mischievousness.

ಅಗಣಿ (tb of ಅಗ್ಗಲ) n A wooden bolt to fasten a native door

ಅಗಣಿತ s a Uncounted. 2, innumerable.

ಅಗತ, ಅಗತೆ k n The act of digging.

ಅಗತ್ಯ s n Necessity, want, need. a Wanted, necessary -ವಾಗಿ. Necessarily, urgently, positively.

ಅಗದ s a Free from disease, healthy n A medicine ಅಗದಂಕಾರ A physician.

ಅಗದಿ m. a Altogether, wholly; quite

ಅಗಧರ s. n The mountain supporter, Vishnu.

ಅಗಪೆ k. n A ladle of cocoanut shell

ಅಗಭೇದಿ s. n The mountain-splitter Indra 2, a hatchet.

ಅಗಮ s. a No[illegible] 2, mountain

ಅಗಮ್ಯ s. a Inaccessible, unattainable.

ಅಗರು 1 k n Dandruff.

ಅಗರು 2 s n The balsam tree which yields Bdellium, *Amyris agallocha* -ಗಂಧ. A yellow fragrant wood.

ಅಗಲ k n Expansion, space, extent. 2, width, breadth 3, far distance. a Broad.

ಅಗಲಿಕೆ k n. Separation

ಅಗಲಿಸು (fr ಅಗಲು) k. v t To remove 2, to separate, disunite

ಅಗಲು k v i To separate from, quit, part, leave n = ಅಗಲ

ಅಗಲ್ಚು (= ಅಗಲಿಸು) k v t. To spread out, to abandon.

ಅಗಸ, ಅಗಸಿಗ k n A washerman -ಗಿತ್ತಿ, ಅಗಸತಿ A washerwoman

ಅಗಸಾಲ, ಅಗಸಾಲಿಗ = ಅಕಸಾಲ, etc q v

ಅಗಸೆ 1, -ಬಾಗಲು k n A town-gate, the gate of a fort

ಅಗಸೆ 2. (tb. of ಅತಸಿ) n Common flax, *Linum usitatissimum* 2, (tb of ಅಗಸ್ತ್ಯ) a tree with scarlet flowers, *Sesbania grandiflora* -ಎಣ್ಣೆ Lin-seed oil. -ಹೂ. Lin-flower

ಅಗಸ್ತ್ಯ s. n. N. of a rishi, son of Mitra and Varuna by Urvasî. 2, the regent of the star Canopus.

ಅಗಳತ, ಅಗಳತೆ, ಅಗಳ್ತೆ (ಳ = ೞ) k n A fort ditch, trench, moat

ಅಗಳಾಡಿಸು k v. t To cause to swing, to wave. ಅಗಳಾಡು v. i To swing, shake

/ಅಗಳ (ಳ = ೞ) = ಅಗುಳ.

ಅಗಳು 1. k n A grain of boiled rice. 2, food

ಅಗಳು 2 (ಳ = ೞ) k v t & i To dig, burrow. 2, to tear off. n. A fort ditch, moat

ಅಗಾಡಿ h. n The front, van ad In front

ಅಗಾಧ s. n A hole chasm. a Deep, bot[illegible]

ಅಗಿ k. v. t. To dig, burrow. 2, to chew, champ. v. i. to tremble, shake, fear. 2, to be glad.

ಅಗಿಣಿ k. n. Water (a word only used by educated Lingaits).

ಅಗಿಲು (= ಅಗರು 2, q. v.) s. n. Fragrance.

ಅಗಿಸು k. v. t. To cause to dig.

ಅಗುಚು. = ಅಗಚು, q. v.

ಅಗುಂಪಲೆ k. n. Extensiveness, greatness. a. Great.

ಅಗುರು s. a. Not heavy, light. n. A fragrant aloe wood, *agallochum*.

ಅಗುಬುರ್, ಅಗುರ್ವು k. n. Terror, amazement.

ಅಗುರ್ವಿಸು k. v. t. To terrify.

ಅಗುಲು k. v. t. To shake, move. v. i. To become loose.

ಅಗುಸೆ = ಅಗಸೆ, q. v.

ಅಗುಳಿ (ಳಿ = ಱಿ) (*tb. of* ಅಗರ್ಲ) n. A bolt, a bar for locking a door.

ಅಗುಳು 1. = ಅಗಳು.

ಅಗುಳು 2. (ಳು = ಱು) k. v. t. To dig.

ಅಗೆ 1 = ಅಗಿ k. v. t. To dig. See ಅಗಿ.

ಅಗೆ 2 k. n. A seedling, a germ, bud, shoot, *cf.* ಮೊಳಕೆ. 2, a suffix to form adverbs, *e. g.* ನೆಟ್ಟಗೆ, ಸುಮ್ಮಗೆ. -ಕಟ್ಟು, -ಮಾಡು To raise seedlings.

ಅಗೋ (= ಅಕೋ) k. *int.* Lo! behold!

ಅಗೋಚರ s. a. Invisible, imperceptible, wondrous.

ಅಗ್ಗ 1 (*tb. of* ಅರ್ಘ) n. Cheapness. a. Cheap, low, mean.

ಅಗ್ಗ 2. *tb. of* ಅಗ್ರ, q. v.

ಅಗ್ಗಲಿಸು = ಅಗ್ಗಳಿಸು, q. v.

ಅಗ್ಗವಣಿ (= ಅಗಿಣಿ) k. n. Water. 2, an offering of water.

ಅಗ್ಗಳಿಕೆ k. n. Greatness, great power.

ಅಗ್ಗಳಿಸು (= ಅಗ್ಗಲಿಸು) k. v. t. & i. To be or become pre-eminent, to make great efforts, to excel.

ಅಗ್ಗಳೆ k. n. A powerful man.

ಅಗ್ಗಿ (...) Fire.

ಅಗ್ಗಿಟಿಗೆ, ಅಗ್ಗಿಷ್ಟಿಕೆ, ಅಗ್ಗಿಷ್ಟಕೆ (*tb. of* ಅಗ್ನಿಷ್ಟ, *etc.*) n. A potsherd used as a fire-pan or chafing dish.

ಅಗ್ನಿ s. n. Fire. 2, the god of fire, Agni. 3, the guardian of the south-east. 4, bile. 5, gold. -ಕಣ, -ಕಿಡಿ, -ಬಿಂದು A spark. -ಕಾರ್ಯ Feeding the sacrificial fire with ghee. -ಕಾಷ್ಠ. Firewood, *Agallochum*. -ಕುಂಡ. A firehole. -ಚಿತ್ One who arranges a sacrificial fire-place. -ಜ್ವಾಲೆ. Flame of fire, a plant bearing red blossoms used by dyers. -ತಾರೆ The Pleiades. -ದೀಪನ. Stimulating digestion. -ದೇವಿ The Pleiades. -ನಯನ, -ನೇತ್ರ. Śiva with an eye of fire. -ಫಲ. A diamond. -ಬಾಣ. A fiery arrow, a rocket. -ಬಾಧ Damaging with fire. -ಭೂ Born of fire, Śiva's son. -ಮಥನ, -ಮಂಥ. Production of fire by friction. -ಮಂಥ The tree *Premna spinosa*. -ಮಾಂದ್ಯ Languor of the digestive power. -ಮಿತ್ರ. The fire's friend, the wind. -ಮುಖ A deity: Brahmâ. -ಮುಖಿ The marking nut. -ರಕ್ಷಣೆ Preservation of the sacred fire. -ವರ್ಣ. N. of a prince. -ಶಿಖ. Having a crest of fire, saffron, safflower; a lamp, a rocket; an arrow. -ಶಿಖೆ A flame, the plant *Gloriosa superba*. -ಷ್ಟೋಮ Praise of Agni, a peculiar sacrifice in spring. -ಸಂಸ್ಕಾರ. The consecration of fire, any rite in which the application of fire is essential. -ಸಖ. The wind. -ಸ್ತಂಭನ. The (magical) quenching of fire. -ಹೋತ್ರ An oblation to Agni. -ಹೋತ್ರಿ Practising the agni-hôtra; maintaining the sacrificial fire, one who has prepared the sacrificial fire-place. ಅಗ್ನೀಧ್ರ The priest who kindles the fire.

ಅಗ್ನ್ಯುತ್ಪಾತ s. n. A meteor, comet.

ಅಗ್ರ 1 k. n. The thrush, a sore mouth.

ಅಗ್ರ 2 (= ಅಗ್ಗ 2) s. n. A top, point, summit. 2, the front. 3, the beginning. 4, ... prai... , multitude.

7. aim, resting place. *a* Prominent, excellent, best, chief, first. -ಗಣ್ಯ. Foremost, principal. -ಜ, -ಜನ್ಮ First-born, an elder brother; a Brâhmana. -ಣಿ Foremost, excellent. -ತಃ In front of. -ತಾಂಬೂಲ The first present of betel leaf at an assembly. -ಪೂಜೆ. The first act of reverence rendered to the principal man at assemblies -ಬಲ An advance-force -ಮಾಂಸ The heart -ಸಾಲೆ The cooking hall of a temple -ಹಾರ Villages assigned to Brâhmanas for their maintenance. -ಹಾರಿಕ. A man belonging to an agrahâra.

ಅಗ್ರಾಮ್ಯ s. *a.* Not rustic -ತೆ Unvulgarity.

ಅಗ್ರಾಹ್ಯ s *a.* Unacceptable, inadmissible.

ಅಗ್ರಿಮ s. *a* Foremost. 2, best. 3, elder, eldest.

ಅಗ್ರಿಯ, ಅಗ್ರೀಯ s. *a* Principal, best *n.* An elder brother.

ಅಗ್ರೇದಿಧಿಷು s *n.* A man who marries a widow at his first marriage

ಅಗ್ರೇಶ್ವರ s. *n.* The supreme lord.

ಅಗ್ರೇಸರ s. *a* Preceding. 2, best. *n* A leader, headman

ಅಗ್ರೋದಕ s. *n.* Water used for the worship of an idol.

ಅಗ್ರ್ಯ s *a* Foremost, first; best 2, intent.

ಅಘ s. *n.* Sin crime 2, pain. 3 passion.

ಅಘಟನ s *a* Difficult, impossible

ಅಘಟಿತ s *a* Not happened. 2, improbable, unlikely. *n* Any wonder.

ಅಘನ s. *a* Liquid, not dense.

ಅಘಮರ್ಷಣ s *a* Expiatory. *n* A daily expiatory prayer, reciting a particular passage from the Vêdas.

ಅಘಾಟ s *n* A wonder, excess.

ಅಘೋರ s. *a* Not terrific 2, terrible *n* A euphemistic title of Śiva

ಅಂಕ s *n* A hook 2, the lap, thigh 3, the side or flank. 4, the body. 5, a mark 6, a numerical figure 7, a fault. 8, a war 9, proximity. 10, place -ಡೊಂಕು Excessive crookedness. -ಮಾಲೆ. A list of titles -ವೀರ A valiant man

ಅಂಕಗಣಿತ s *n* Arithmetic.

ಅಂಕಣ f *n.* The space between two pillars or beams.

ಅಂಕನ s. *n.* Marking, stamping.

ಅಂಕಿತ s. *a* Marked *n* A sign, signature 2, a word. 3, a dedication. -ನಾಮ. A proper name.

ಅಂಕಿಸು s. *v t* To mark look at

ಅಂಕುರ s. *n* A sprout, shoot. 2, hair. 3, blood. ಅಂಕುರಿಸು. To sprout, to rise, to happen

ಅಂಕುಶ (*tb* ಅಂಕುಸ) s. *n* A hook, esp. for driving an elephant.

ಅಂಕೆ 1 k *n* An order, command; control, restraint, check. 2, (= ಆನಿಕೆ) leaning against; a lever. 3, trust

ಅಂಕೆ 2. *n* (*tb. of* ಅಂಕ). A numerical figure; an account.

ಅಂಕೋಠ, ಅಂಕೋಲ, (-ಲು -ಲೆ) s. *n* The plant *Alangium hexapetalum.*

ಅಂಗ 1. a k. *n.* Way, manner, mode

ಅಂಗ 2 s *n* A limb, member 2, the body. 3, the mind. 4, an expedient. 5, a verse-line. 6, N. of Bengal proper. *int.* Indeed, true; please. -ಚಿತ್ತ. The heart's wish. -ಚೇಷ್ಟೆ. Gestures of the body. -ನ್ಯಾಸ Ceremony of touching certain parts of the body. -ಪರೀಕ್ಷೆ, -ಶೋಧನೆ Anatomy. -ಪ್ರದಕ್ಷಿಣ. Rolling one's body round a temple. -ರಕ್ಷ, -ರಕ್ಷಣೆ, -ರಕ್ಷೆ Protection of the body, also an amulet. -ರಕ್ಷಕ A body-guard -ರಾಗ. Unguents for the body, perfuming the body. -ವಸ್ತ್ರ. A small cloth, an upper garment -ವಿಕಾರ. Change of bodily appearance, fainting. -ವಿಕ್ಷೇಪ, -ಹಾರ Gesticulation -ಸಂಸ್ಕಾರ. Embellishment of body -[illegible] Mutilated, incorporeal - [illegible] Mutilation.

ಅಂಗಜ s. n. (born from the body) The son [illegible] Káma [illegible] a son [illegible]

ಅಂಗಜನ್ಮ s. n. Káma. [illegible] The [illegible] of Káma [illegible].

ಅಂಗಜಾತ s. = [illegible] q. v.

ಅಂಗಡಿ k. n. A shop, a stall. -ಬೀದಿ A market-street. -ಕಾರ, -ಗಾರ, -ಯವ A shopkeeper. -ಮನೆ A house with a shop. -ಸಾಮಾನು A shop drug. -ಸರಕು The goods of a shop. -ಹಾಕು, -ಇಡು To open a shop.

ಅಂಗಣ (tb. of ಅಂಗನ) n. A court, a yard, esp. in front of a house, an area.

ಅಂಗತ, ಅಂಗತೆ (= ಅಂಗಾತ) k. ad. Back-ways, on the back.

ಅಂಗದ s. n. A bracelet worn on the upper arm. 2. N. of a son of Váli.

ಅಂಗನೆ, ಅಂಗನಾ s. n. A woman, female.

ಅಂಗಳ. tb. of ಅಂಗಣ q. v.

ಅಂಗರಖಾ h. n. A long coat.

ಅಂಗಲ, ಅಂಗಲು, ಅಂಗಲಂಗಲು k. a. Separate, apart.

ಅಂಗಲಾಚು (-ಚಿದ) k. v. i. To weep, grieve, lament. ಅಂಗಲಾಚಿಕೆ. Grief.

ಅಂಗವಣೆ m. n. Habitude; power, vigour.

ಅಂಗಯಿಸು k. v. i. To come together, meet, crowd. v. t. To lay hold of, seize.

ಅಂಗಳ, (-ಳು) ಅಂಗಳಿ, (-ಲು, -ಳೆ) k. n. The palate of the mouth. 2, (tb. of ಅಂಗಣ) a courtyard.

ಅಂಗಾಂಗಿ s. n. Limb and limb related to another.

ಅಂಗಾತ k. = ಅಂಗತ etc., q. v.

ಅಂಗಾರ (= ಇಂಗಾಲ) k. n. Charcoal. 2, Mars.

ಅಂಗಾರಕ (= ಅಂಗಾರ 1-2) s. n. 3, a sectarian mark made with charred wood. -ಧಾನಿ. A portable fire-place. -ವಾರ Tuesday.

ಅಂಗಾಲು k. n. The sole of the foot.

ಅಂಗೀಕಾರ s. n. Assent, [illegible] Accepting, agreeing, accepting, acceptance.

ಅಂಗೀಕರಿಸು s. v. t. To agree to, to accept, adopt.

ಅಂಗುಟ, [illegible] = ಅಂಗುಷ್ಠ q. v.

ಅಂಗುಲಿ, -ಲೀ s. n. A finger. 2. the thumb. 3. a finger's breadth. ಅಂಗುಲಿತ್ರಾಣ A finger-protector used whilst shooting arrows. ಅಂಗುಲಿನಿರ್ದೇಶ Pointing at with the finger. ಅಂಗುಲಿಸ್ಫೋಟನ Cracking the fingers.

ಅಂಗುಲೀಯಕ s. n. A finger-ring.

ಅಂಗುಷ್ಠ s. n. The thumb. 2. the great toe.

ಅಂಗುಸ್ತಾನ h. n. A thimble.

ಅಂಗುಟ, -ಠ, -ಷ್ಠ = ಅಂಗುಷ್ಠ etc.

ಅಂಗೂರ h. n. The grape.

ಅಂಗೈಯು. ಅಂಗೈ k. n. The palm of the hand.

ಅಂಗೋಪಾಂಗ s. n. The body and its members.

ಅಂಗೋಷ್ಠ. tb. of ಅಂಗುಷ್ಠ q. v.

ಅಂಘ್ರಿ s. n. A foot. 2. the root of a tree. -ಜ The foot-born: a śûdra.

ಅಕಠೋರ s. a. Gentle, tractable.

ಅಕುಶಲ s. a. Not dexterous (f. ಕುಶಲ).

ಅಚಂಚಲ s. a. Unmoveable, steady. -ತೆ Steadiness.

ಅಚರ s. a. Immoveable.

ಅಚಲ s. a. Immoveable, fixed. 2, eternal. n. A mountain, the earth. 2 an ascetic.

ಅಚಲೆ s. n. The earth.

ಅಚಾತುರ್ಯ s. n. Want of ability.

ಅಚ್ಚೆಚ್ಚೆ k. n. Impurity, filth.

ಅಚಿಂತ್ಯ s. a. Incomprehensible.

ಅಚಿರ s. a. Not long, short, brief, recent. -ಪ್ರಭೆ, ಅಚಿರಾಂಶು. Lightning.

ಅಚೇತ s. a. Unconscious, very poor.

ಅಚೇತನ s. n. Unconsciousness. a. Insensible, fainting.

[illegible] s. n. Unconsciousness, igno-

[illegible] 1. = [illegible] k. a. -[illegible] = [illegible]). Proper boundary: suitable order, size, etc.

[illegible] 2 tb. of [illegible] 1. Pure, clear; unmixed, real. 2. = [illegible]. -[illegible]. Pure Kannada. -[illegible]. Pure and fresh water. [illegible]. [illegible]. *N.*

[illegible] a. k. n. Bewilderment.

[illegible] r. of [illegible]. = [illegible]. [illegible] r. A warm cotton cloth to cover at night.

[illegible] tb. of [illegible]. q. v.

[illegible] tb. of [illegible]. q. v.

[illegible] tb. of [illegible]. q. v.

[illegible] tb. of [illegible]) n. Wonder, surprise.

[illegible]. [illegible] ad. Unmeaningly; foully (in eating).

[illegible] k. n. A firm, strong man. [illegible]. Firmness of a man.

[illegible] k. n. Bread (used only by young children). 2. mother: a Malayala woman. 3. a pap.

[illegible] 2. tb. of [illegible] q. v.

[illegible] k. n. Paying unjustly.

[illegible] tb. of [illegible].

[illegible] 1. = [illegible]) k. n. Firmness: (bodily) strength. 2. a well-defined boundary. 3. a mould: an impression. 4. a type, stamp. 5. a weaver's reed. -[illegible]. A printed letter. -[illegible]. = [illegible]. -[illegible]. A printing press. -[illegible]. A cake of jaggery. -[illegible]. Firm devotion. -[illegible]. To print, seal. -[illegible]. To seal, impress firmly.

[illegible] 1. k. v. t. To pay unjustly, as rent for failed crop. n. Intimacy, love. 2. tb. of [illegible], a die: an axle. 3. the soul.

[illegible] 3. f. n. A Pegu pony.

[illegible]. [illegible] a. k. n. An attendant, guard.

[illegible] = [illegible] k. n. [illegible]

[illegible] k. n. [illegible]

[illegible] = [illegible] s. 1. Pure, clear, transparent. -[illegible]. A white bear.

[illegible] s. a. Unbroken, uninjured. 2. new. 3. defectless.

[illegible] s. 1. Uncut, uninjured, inseparable.

[illegible] s. 1. Firm, imperishable. 2. Vishnu. -[illegible]. Permanence.

[illegible] s. 1. Unborn. n. Brahmâ. 2. Vishnu. 3. Śiva. 4. the sun. 5. rain. 6. a driver, leader. 7. a ram: a he-goat. 8. the sign Aries.

[illegible]. [illegible], [illegible] s. n. Śiva's bow.

[illegible] s. n. A huge serpent. *Boa constrictor.*

[illegible] s. 1. Not sewed, as a cloth.

[illegible] s. 1. Unpeopled. n. A desert. 2. an insignificant person. 3. driving.

[illegible] s. a. Unfit to be born. n. A phenomenon foreboding evil.

[illegible] k. n. Goods and chattels, tools, baggage.

[illegible] k. n. Rough calculation, an. Aboni.

[illegible]. [illegible] s. n. Bishop's weed *Ligusticum ajwain.* 2. common carraway. *Carum carui.*

[illegible] s. 1. Unconquerable, invincible. n. Defeat. 2. Vishnu.

[illegible] 1. = [illegible] a. k. n. The Indigo [plant.

[illegible] 2. s. a. Ageless, undecaying.

[illegible] s. 1. Indigestible: undecaying. n. Friendship.

[illegible] s. n. Goat's horn: the shrub *Odina wodier.*

[illegible] s. a. Not to be injured. 2. continual.

[illegible] s. a. Not awake. n. A common weed. *Eclipta alba.*

[illegible] s. n. The state of being not wakeful. 2. carelessness.

ಅಜಾಗೃತೆ = ಅಜಾಗರೂಕತೆ

ಅಜಾಜಿ s. n. Cumin seed

ಅಜಾಣ (*tb* *of* ಅಜ್ಞಾನ) n A foolish man.

ಅಜಾಂಡ s n. Brahmâ's egg the universe.

ಅಜಾತ s *a*. Unborn, not existent -ಶತ್ರು One who has no enemies

ಅಜಾಮುಲ, ಅಜಾಮೋದ = ಅಜಮೋದ, *q. v.*

ಅಜಿಗಜಿ k *n* Ground lime.

ಅಜಿತ s *a* Unconquerable 2, unsurpassed *n* Vishnu.

ಅಜಿನ s. *n*. The skin. 2, the skin of an antelope. -ಪತ್ರ. A bat. -ಯೋನಿ An antelope, a deer.

ಅಜಿರ s *a* Agile, quick *n* A court, yard 2, an object of sense. 3, air

ಅಜಿವಾನ h. *n*. Bishop's weed

ಅಜಿಹ್ಮ s *a* Not crooked, straight *n* A fish, a frog.

ಅಜೀರ್ಣ s *a* Undigested *n*. Indigestion.

ಅಜುರ. = ಅಜರ, *q. v*

ಅಜೆ s *n* Nature 2, illusion.

ಅಜೇಯ s *a* Invincible.

ಅಜ್ಜ 1. k. *n*. Opportunity. 2, the dry filaments

ಅಜ್ಜ 2 (*tb of* ಆರ್ಯ) *n*. A grandfather.

ಅಜ್ಜಿ (*tb. of* ಆರ್ಯಾ) *n*. A grandmother. -ಕಥೆ An idle story

ಅಜ್ಜಿಗೆ, ಅಜ್ಜುಗೆ (*tb of* ಅರ್ಜಕ). *n*. A great-flowered jasmine.

ಅಜ್ಜುಗುಜ್ಜು k. *n*. The state of being thin and small. -ಪ್ರಾಯ. The age of debility

ಅಜ್ಞ s *a*. Not knowing, ignorant. 2, foolish. -ತೆ. Ignorance.

ಅಜ್ಞಾನ s. *n*. Ignorance. 2, mâyâ. -ತನ. Ignorance.

ಅಜ್ಞಾನಿ s *a* Ignorant. unwise. *n* A stupid person.

ಅಂಚಲ, ಅಂಚಳ s *n* The end or border of a cloth.

ಅಂಚಿತ s. *a*. Bent 2. honoured 3.

ಅಂಚು 1 (= ಹಂಚು *q. v.*) k. *v. t* To divide. 2, (= ಹೊಂಚು, *q v*) to lurk.

ಅಂಚು 2. (*tb. of* ಅಂತ) *n* Edge, border, brim, selvage, skirt, bank, shore, side. -ಕಟ್ಟು. To construct a bank, to form a selvage.

ಅಂಚೆ 1 k. *n* A postal road, a stage, the post (= ಟಪಾಲು) -ಕಚೇರಿ, -ಕಟ್ಟೆ A post office. -ಕಾರ. A postal officer. -ಯವ A post runner.

ಅಂಚೆ 2. (= ಆಚೆ) *ad*. In that side. *n* (*tb. of* ಹಂಸ) A swan -ತುಪ್ಪಳ Goose-down.

ಅಂಜನ s *n* Anointing. 2, a black collyrium applied to the eye-lashes 3, magic ointment. 4, ink. 5, night. -ಕ್ರಿಯೆ Anointing

ಅಂಜನಿಕೆ s *n* A species of lizard. 2, a small mouse

ಅಂಜಲಿ (= ಅಂಜುಲಿ) s. *n* The cavity formed by hollowing the palms together, when raised towards the forehead it is a salutation to superiors. 2, a measure of corn -ಪುಟ = ಅಂಜಲಿ, No 1.

ಅಂಜಿಕೆ k *n*. Fear

ಅಂಜಿಸು k. *v. t* To frighten.

ಅಂಜು (= ಅಳರು) k. *v i*. To fear, feel anxiety, to be afraid of. *n* Fear. -ಕುಳಿ, -ಗುಳಿ. A coward

ಅಂಜುಲಿ = ಅಂಜಲಿ *q v*.

ಅಂಜೂರ h. *n*. A fig, a fig-tree

ಅಟ 1, ಅಟೆ k *n*. Motion, play, speech. -ಮಟ. Trickery, fraud, escape -ಮಟಿಸು, -ಮರಿಸು To play tricks, deceive

ಅಟ 2 m *n* Obstruction, a bar lever. -ಕಟ. Weariness -ಗೋಲು A pole for lifting sacks.

ಅಟಕಾಯಿಸು h *v. t* To stop, hinder, check

ಅಟಕಾವ್, ಅಟಕೆ h *n* Obstruction, restraint

ಅಟಕಿಸು. = ಅಟಕಾಯಿಸು, *q v*

ಅಟರುಷ, ಅಟರೂಷ f. *n* The shrub *Justicia adhatoda*

ಅಟವಣಿ. ಅಟವಣೆ f *n*. Addition and sub-

ಅಟವಿ (= ಅಡವಿ) s. *n.* A wood, forest.

ಅಟೋಪ, ಅಟೋಪು f. *n.* Control, power.

ಅಟ್ಟ s *a* High, lofty, *n.* A garret or upper loft in a house. 2, a tower, buttress. 3, a scaffold -ಹಾಸ = ಅಟ್ಟಾಸ A loud laughter: a pomp, parade. 4, (*fr.* ಅಡು) cooked.

ಅಟ್ಟವೆ (= ಅಟ್ಟೆ) s. *n.* A structure of poles put on stones. 2, *tb.* *of* ಅಷ್ಟಮಿ, *q v.*

ಅಟ್ಟಳೆ *tb.* *of* ಅಟ್ಟಾಲ *q. v*

ಅಟ್ಟಾಲ, ಅಟ್ಟಾಲಕ s *n* An apartment on the roof. 2, a palace. 3, a bastion.

ಅಟ್ಟಾಸ (*tb* *of* ಅಟ್ಟಹಾಸ) *n.* *see s.* ಅಟ್ಟ.

ಅಟ್ಟಿಸು k. *v. t* To take possession of. 2, to cause to pursue. 3, to cause to evaporate or to be wasted.

ಅಟ್ಟು k. *v t.* To keep close to, follow. 2, to pursue, chase, drive away 3, to send. 4, to put. *v. i* To evaporate, to be wasted. *n* Closeness. 2, putting. -ಕುಳಿ, -ಗುಣಿ N. of a game in which cowries are put from hole to hole on a wooden board.

ಅಟ್ಟುಂಬಳಿ k *n.* Gifts to the bride and bridegroom.

ಅಟ್ಟುಳಿ a k *n* A crowd, multitude. 2, annoyance

ಅಟ್ಟೆ k. *n.* A headless trunk 2, a sole, sandal, skin, bark 3, a leech.

ಅಟ್ಣು k. *n.* Mud. 2, (*tb* *of* ಅಟ್ಟಾಲ) a stand on poles.

ಅಡ k. *n.* = ಅಡ್ಡ 1. -ಗಟ್ಟು. = ಅಡ್ಡಗಟ್ಟು.

ಅಡಕ k. *n.* Compacture. 2, piling, storing, a pile. 3, hiding one's self. 4, becoming obedient. 5, abridgment. -ಗೊಳಿಸು To compress

ಅಡಕು (= ಅಡ್ಕು) k. *v t* To press, as cotton. 2, to pile, as pots, grass, *etc.* 3, to put. 4, to subdue, control

ಅಡಕೆ (= ಅಡಿಕೆ) k. *n* The areca palm, its nut.

ಅಡಕೊತ್ತು, -ಗತ್ತರಿ k. *n.* A betel-nut cutter.

ಅಡಗಣಿಸು k. *v. t.* To thwart, obstruct.

ಅಡಗಿಸು k. *v t* To cause to hide, to conceal, hide 2, to suppress. 3, to appease.

ಅಡಗು (= ಅಡಂಗು) k. *v. i* To conceal one's self, to disappear 2, to be quenched, humbled, contained in 3, to crouch *n* (a k.) Flesh, meat (= ಮಾಂಸ). 2, becomingness, agreeableness

ಅಡಗೆ (= ಅಡಿಗೆ etc.) k *n.* Cooking

ಅಡಂಗು (= ಅಡಗು *q. v*) a. k *n.* A fort.

ಅಡಚಣೆ f *n* Difficulty, distress

ಅಡಚು (*cf.* ಅಗಚು, ಅಡಕು, ಅಣಚು, *etc*) k *v. t.* To pack up, close, to stuff, press down, to humble 2, to hush, silence. 3, to rap, cuff. [clothes.

ಅಡದಿ k. *n.* Clothes to be washed; hired

ಅಡಪ (= ಹಡಪ) k. *n* A barber's dressing case, a betel-pouch -ವಳ (-ವಳ್ಳ) One who carries a betel-pouch

ಅಡವು (= ಅಡಹು) k. *n.* A pledge, pawn.

ಅಡಬಡ k *ad* Rashly, *e. g* -ತಿನ್ನು.

ಅಡಬಳ a k *n* A cook 2, flesh

ಅಡಂಬರ (*tb* *of.* ಆಡಂಬರ) *n.* Ostentation, display.

ಅಡಯಾಳ k *n.* A mark, sign

ಅಡರಾಟ k *n.* A scuffle 2, vying, rivalry

ಅಡರು k *v. t.* To climb, mount, to pounce upon, rush at. *v. i.* To be united with, to appear; to amass *n* An attack, an attempt ಅಡರಿಸು To cause to ascend, *etc.*

ಅಡರ್ಚು k *v. t.* To bring together, to set in readiness

ಅಡಲು k *v i.* To be shaken, to be afraid, to grieve. *n* Tremor, confusion; fear 2, mud.

ಅಡವಿ (*tb.* *of* ಅಟವಿ) *n* A forest, wood, jungle. -ಗಿಚ್ಚು. Fire in forests -ಪಾಲು. A miserable lot. -ಬೀಳು To go astray

ಅಡವು (= ಅಡಪು) k. *n* Suitableness; closeness, thickness 2, a pawn pledge deposit 3, An impediment

ಅಡಸಟ್ಟು h n. Estimate, computation

ಅಡಸಲ, ಅಡಸಾಲ tb of ಅಟರೂಪ q v

ಅಡಸು (= ಅಡರು) k v t To attack, trouble 2, to enter 3, to put into, stuff into. 4, to hold firmly, to cover v. i To be stern; to be filled in

ಅಡಹು k. a. see ಅಡವು No. 2

ಅಡಾಡಿ k n Rashness, haste ad Quickly.

ಅಡಾಗೆ f n Unremunerated and forced labour or service 2 a foreigner

ಅಡಾಯಿಸು f. v t. To stop, arrest, to put before (cf ಅಡ್ಡಯಿಸು)

ಅಡಾಯುಧ k-s n. A scimitar.

ಅಡಾವುಡಿ k n Alarm, uproar, quarrel, (riot

ಅಡಿ (= ಅಂ) k. n The foot, the measure of a foot. (ಅಡಿಗಳ ಮೇಲೆ ಬೀಳು, to fall down at the feet, ಅಡಿಕೆಡು, to become slow) 2, a verse-line. 3, a step, pace (ಅಡಿಗಡಿಗೆ, from step to step; ಅಡಿಯಿಡು, to step, walk) 4 the bottom of any thing. (-ಕಾಣು, to see the bottom, -ತುಂಡು, the lower piece of anything, -ಪಟ್ಟಿ, a door-sill) 5, (= ಅಡು) cooking

ಅಡಿಕೆ (= ಅಡಿಗೆ) k n Cooking 2, (= ಅಡಕೆ, q. v.) the areca palm

ಅಡಿಗಬ್ಬು k n. Firewood.

ಅಡಿಗಲ್ಲು k. n An anvil

ಅಡಿಗೆ (= ಅಡಗೆ) k. n. Cooking, boiling, maturing, dinner. -ಮನೆ, -ಸಾಲೆ. A kitchen -ಒಲೆ. A fire-place. -ಮಾಡು To cook. -ಮಾಡುವವ, -ಯವ. A male cook. -ಯಾಗು To be cooked. -ಸಾಮಾನ Cooking utensils.

ಅಡಿಮೆ a k n Slavery.

ಅಡಿಯ k n A slave

ಅಡಿವಿ = ಅಡವಿ q v

ಅಡು k v. t. To cook, boil, dress; to prepare a meal; to mature n Cooking, etc -ಗಬ್ಬು Fuel -ಕೂಳು Boiled rice -ಗೂಲಜ್ಜಿ, -ಗೋಲಜ್ಜಿ. A woman who cooks for strangers -ಬಾಣಲೆ. A f .

ಅಡುಕು = ಅಡಕು, q. v

ಅಡುಸು k n. Clay mud.

ಅಡೆ 1 (= ಒಡೆ) a k If, when, e.g ಕೇಳಿಸುವಡೆ, ಕೊಡುವಡೆ, etc

ಅಡೆ 2 (= ಪಡೆ) k. v.t. To obtain get, have, to shut up, enclose, confine 2, (= ಅಗೆ) to strike, throw. v i To be enclosed, barred. n A wood on which artisans put their working articles 2 a sticky mass of tamarind, sugar, etc 3, cowdung. 4, a thin cake of rice flour. 5. the border of a cloth 6, a k Trust. -ಗಲ್ಲು. An anvil. -ಹಬ್ಬ. Cake-feast.

ಅಡ್ಡ 1. (= ಅಡ) k. n. The state of being across, obstacle. a Crosswise, horizontal -ಕಟ್ಟು To fasten across, to thwart, stop, arrest -ಕಟ್ಟು. -ಕಟ್ಟೆ A dam in rice-fields. -ಕಸಬು, -ಕಸುಬಿ A profession contrary to custom. -ಕಾಲು The leg put crosswise, as obstacle. -ಕಾವಲಿ, -ಕಾಲುವೆ A by-channel -ಕಾವಡಿ A kâvaḍi carried on the neck -ಕೀಲಿ. A transverse bolt. -ಕೂಸು A child carried in the arms -ಕೈ. The hand placed transversely. -ಕೆಲಸ Extra work -ಕೋಲು A transverse bar -ಕಟ್ಟಿಗೆ. A wooden cross bar -ಅಗಲ Distance across, width. -ಗೀಚು To cross out. -ಗೀಟು, -ಗೆರೆ A cross line -ಕೊಂಬು A cross branch. -ಗೋಡೆ A partition or curtain wall ಅಡ್ಡಂಕೆ. A figure written from left to right; the total. -ಚಾಟು. A shelter. -ಚೌಕ An oblong frame, the Linga box -ಅಂಚು, ಅಡ್ಡಂಚು The breadth of the foot -ಅಣಿ, ಅಡ್ಡಣಿ The woof that crosses the warp in a loom. -ತಲೆ, -ದಲೆ. An ill-formed head -ತಾಕು To touch, thwart, interfere with. -ತಿಡ್ಡ, -ತಿಡ್ಡಿ, ಅಡ್ಡಾತಿಡ್ಡಿ Awkwardness, clumsiness, awkwardly -ತಿರುಪು To turn aside -ತೊಡರು To thwart, interfere. -ದಂಡಿ, -ದಂಡಿಗೆ A scale beam, a bamboo pole

it. -ದಪ್ಪೆ.

A slit bamboo put crosswise. -ತೊಲೆ. A transverse beam -ನಗೆ A half-suppressed laugh -ನಾಮ A surname, a sectarian crossmark on the forehead of Smârtas -ನಾಲಿಗೆ. A lying or opposing tongue -ನಿಲುವು Breadth and height. -ನುಡಿ Contradiction -ಪಂಕ್ತಿ A side-row of people at dinner -ಪಟ್ಟಿ The upper or lower part of a door-frame. -ಪಲ್ಲಕಿ A palankeen carried crosswise. -ಬರು. To come in the way. -ಬೀಳು To fall across, to prostrate -ಮರ A cross bar -ಮಾತು Gainsaying, an evasion -ಮಾರ್ಗ. A cross way, by-path. -ಮುಡಿ A knot of hair -ಪಾಗು. To be cross, -ಪಾಗಿ, transversely, across, broadwise. -ಇಡು, -ವಿಡು To oppose -ಸಾಲು (=-ಪಂಕ್ತಿ) A transverse line or furrow -ಸುಳಿ To pass by. -ಹಚ್ಚು To apply horizontally, as sectarian mark. -ಹಾಕು. To put crosswise, to put before for obtaining a blessing or pardon. -ಹಾದಿ =-ಮಾರ್ಗ. -ಹಾಯು To pass by, to thwart. -ಹೆಸರು. =-ನಾಮ. -ಆಡು, ಅಡ್ಡಾಡು. To walk about, promenade -ಆಸು, ಅಡ್ಡಾಸು. To recline. lean on -ಇಕ್ಕು To put across or before ಅಡ್ಡೈಸಗು To make hostile efforts. ಅಡ್ಡೇಟು A shot beside the mark ಅಡ್ಡೊಕ್ಕಲು. A new tenant, fresh comer ಅಡ್ಡೋಟ An indirect course

ಅಡ್ಡ 2. k. n. Seven duddus, two anas and four pies 2, a weight=$\frac{1}{18}$th of a varaha

ಅಡ್ಡಗಿಸು. = ಅಡ್ಡಯಿಸು, q. v.

ಅಡ್ಡಣಿಗೆ k n A three-legged stand.

ಅಡ್ಡನೆ (= ಅಡನೆ) k. ad. Across, transversely.

ಅಡ್ಡಯಿಸು (= ಅಡ್ಡಗಿಸು) k. v. t. To move obliquely. 2, to obstruct. 3, to intervene, conceal

ಅಡ್ಡಲು k. n. An obstacle ad Across. ಅಡ್ಡಲಾಗು (-ಆಗು). To become an obstacle; to oppose.

ಅಡ್ಡವಿಸು (= ಅಡ್ಡಯಿಸು) a. k v t To obstruct.

ಅಡ್ಡಾತಿಡ್ಡಿ = ಅಡ್ಡತಿಡ್ಡಿ, q v

ಅಡ್ಡಾನ k. a. Broad

ಅಡ್ಡಿ k. n. An obstacle, opposition, delay. -ಮಾಡು To oppose, hinder.

ಅಡ್ಡಿಕೆ k n. A necklace.

ಅಡ್ಡೆ k. n A bamboo by which one or two persons carry burdens suspended from its midst or both ends. -ಹೊರು To carry it

ಅಡ್ಡಾಡಿ (= ಅಡನಾಡಿ) k. n. A perverse or stubborn person

ಅಡ್ಲಿಗೆ k n A flat basket or earthen vessel

ಅಡ್ಲು k. n Mud

ಅಣ k A suffix used in the formation of a verbal noun, or 1st pers. pl imperat., e g ಮಾಡುವಣ, ನಡೆಯುವಣ.

ಅಣಂ (= ಅಣಂ) a. k. ad Whatsoever, howsoever. a Small

ಅಣಕ k n Mockery, derision 2, (= ಅಡಕ) closeness, firmness.

ಅಣಕಿಸು k v. t To mock, deride

ಅಣಗಿಸು. = ಅಡಗಿಸು, q v

ಅಣಗು = ಅಡಗು, q. v.

ಅಣಜಾಣ k. n. A very clever man.

ಅಣಬಿಗೆ k. n A pitcher or water jar.

ಅಣಬೆ, ಅಣಂಬೆ k n A mushroom

ಅಣಲು k. n The under part of the mouth 2, a squirrel

ಅಣಸು k n A ferrule. 2, a throng.

ಅಣಾ (= ಆಣೆ) h n. An anna.

ಅಣಿ (=ಅಡಗು) k n. Joining together of threads in a loom 2, fitness, beauty; order. 3, an array, a body of soldiers. -ಕಟ್ಟು To join a certain number of threads, etc -ತುಳಿ. To move the loom's treadle

ಅಣಿಗೆ (= ಹಣಿಗೆ) k n A comb

ಅಣಿಮ s. n Minuteness 2, the power of becoming an atom.

ಅಣಿಯರ a k *n*. Fitness, nicety; greatness

ಅಣಿಲೆ k. *n* (= ಅಳಲೆ) Ink-nut, *Terminalia chebula.*

ಅಣು s *a*. Minute. *n*. An atom. 2, Śiva.

ಅಣುಗ k. *n*. A son ಅಣುಗಿ, ಅಣುಗೆ. A daughter

ಅಣುಂಕು a. k *v t* To humble, to ruin, destroy.

ಅಣೆ 1. k *int used in calling a woman* ho! ho!

ಅಣೆ 2 (= ಅಣಿ) k *v. i* To touch, come in contact 2, to be quenched. *v t* To strike, push. 2, to embrace. *n*. Approach. 2, a dam, dike -ಕಟ್ಟು, -ಕಟ್ಟೆ A dam.

ಅಂಟರಳೆ (= ಅಂಟುವಾಳ) f *n* The soap-nut tree.

ಅಂಟುಬಿಕೆ k *n* A prickly climbing shrub, *Acacia intsia*

ಅಂಟುರಿಸು k *v t*. To evaporate

ಅಂಟು k *v. i* To come in contact with, touch, to be contagious *v. t* To touch, to embrace. 2, (= ಅಟ್ಟು, No. 1) to follow, pursue. *n*. Contagion, impurity 2, gum, paste. 3, a grafted branch, a young plant. -ರೋಗ. A contagious disease

ಅಂಡ s. *n*. An egg (ಮೊಟ್ಟೆ) -ಜ. Egg-born, a bird, a fish, *etc.*

ಅಂಡಲೆ a k. *v. t*. To oppress, trouble, hurt. *n* Oppression, trouble.

ಅಂಡಿಸು k *v i* To go near, to resort to.

ಅಂಡು k *n* An approach. 2 a buttock.

ಅಂಡೆ k. *n*. A vessel made of bamboo. 2, (a k) nearness, vicinity.

ಅಣ್ಣ k *n* An elder brother, an elderly male. 2, an affectionate mode of addressing boys, *as* ಅಣ್ಣಾ! *f*. ಅಣ್ಣೆ -ತಮ್ಮಂದಿರು Brothers

ಅಣ್ಣಾಲಿಗೆ k. *n* The uvula

ಅಣ್ಣೆ k. *n*. Excellence, purity. -ಪಾಲು Pure milk -ಕಲ್ಲು A pebble tossed in

ಅಣ್ಪಿತ a k. *n* Friendship

ಅತಂತ್ರ s. *a*. Unrestrained, useless, waste.

ಅತರ್ಕ್ಯ s. *a* Invincible

ಅತಲ s. *n* N. of a hell. (*lit* bottomless)

ಅತಲಕುತಲ k. *n* Tumult, confusion

ಅತಸಿ s *n* Common flax, *Linum usitatissimum*

ಅತಿ s. *ad*. Over, beyond. 2, exceedingly, much, very 3, surpassing. -ಕರ್ಮ. A great sin -ಕರ್ಮಿ. A great sinner -ಕಾಟ Great trouble -ಕಾಟಕ. A very troublesome man -ಕಾಯ. Gigantic, a son of Râvana -ಕೊಂಕು Very crooked -ಕ್ರಮ. -ಕ್ರಮಣ Going over, transgression, trespass, surpassing; neglect, imposition. -ಕ್ರಮಿಸು To surpass; trespass; to let pass away; to become excessive -ಗಳೆ, -ಕಳೆ To disregard, contemn, to deny; to spend (time). -ಗ್ರಾಹಕ Smart. -ಜಡ Very cold, very stupid -ಜವ Great speed. -ಜಾಗರ Very wakeful; the black curlew. -ದಪ್ಪ Very thick. -ದಾಹ. Great heat, great thirst -ದುಃಖ Great affliction. -ನಿಷ್ಠುರ. Very fierce. -ಪಾತ Lapse, transgression. -ಪಾಪ. A heinous sin. -ಬಂಧನ. Close confinement. -ಬಲ Very strong -ವೇಗ Very swift -ಮಧುರ Very sweet -ಮಾತ್ರ Beyond measure, excessive -ಯಾಶೆ = ಅತ್ಯಾಶೆ -ಯುದ್ಧ. A great fight. -ರಸ Full of juice or essence; rich in poetical taste; a sweet cake -ರಿಕ್ತ. -ರೇಕ Excessive. -ರೂಢ. Commonly known -ವಾದ Talkativeness -ವಾಸ Fast on the day before performing the Śrâddha. -ವೇಳೆ Excessive -ಶಯ Excellence, surprise; trouble, superior, abundant, wonderful -ಶಯಿಸು. To become great, to wonder. -ಸಣ್ಣ. Minute -ಸರ್ಜನ Liberality; a gift. -ಸಾರ Great charm diarrhoea, dysentery. -ಸ್ವಲ್ಪ.

Very little. -ಹಾಸ. Great laughter. -ಹೆಡ್ಡು. Great stupidity.

ಅತಿಥಿ s. n. An invited guest -ಪೂಜನ. Hospitality -ಸತ್ಕಾರ Civilities to guests.

ಅತೀತ s. a. Gone by, past, gone beyond 2, passed away. 3, having neglected -ಕಾಲ Past time. -ಕ್ರಿಯೆ A neglected business

ಅತೀಂದ್ರಿಯ s a. Going beyond the senses n The mind.

ಅತೀವ s ad Exceedingly, very.

ಅತೀವ್ರ s a Not sharp, blunt. 2, slow

ಅತುಕು a k. v. t. To join, cement. v. i. To be joined, united.

ಅತುಲ s. a. Unequalled

ಅತುಷಾರ s. a. Not cold or dewy

ಅತುಷ್ಟಿ s n Dissatisfaction.

ಅತ್ತ, ಅತ್ತಲು k ad In that direction or place, aside, beyond. -ಕಡೆ = ಅತ್ತ. ಅತ್ತತ್ತಲು, etc. Far beyond. ಅತ್ತಣ. Of that side or place. ಅತ್ತಿತ್ತ. Here and there.

ಅತ್ತರು f. n Attar of roses, perfume, essence

ಅತ್ತರಿ k n. A carpenter's plane.

ಅತ್ತಿ k n. The red-wooded fig-tree, Ficus racemosa.

ಅತ್ತಿಗೆ (tb of ಅತ್ತಿಕೆ) n An elder brother's wife.

ಅತ್ತು k. (p p. of ಅಳು) Having wept.

ಅತ್ತೆ s. n. A mother-in-law. 2, (= ಸೋದರತ್ತೆ) a father's sister.

ಅತ್ಯಧಮ s. a. Exceedingly low or mean

ಅತ್ಯಂತ s. a. Beyond limit; excessive 2, endless. 3, absolute. -ದುಃಖ. Very great affliction

ಅತ್ಯಯ s. n Going over or beyond; surpassing. 2, death, sin. 3, danger; distress

ಅತ್ಯರ್ಥ s. a Excessive.

ಅತ್ಯಾಶೆ s n. Extravagant desire or hope

ಅತ್ಯಾಶ್ಚರ್ಯ s. n. A great marvel

ಅತ್ಯುತ್ತಮ s a. Exceedingly good.

ಅತ್ಯುನ್ನತ s a Very high.

ಅತ್ಯುಷ್ಣ s a. Very hot.

ಅತ್ರಿ s n N of a rishi and a star in the Great Bear. -ಜಾತ Born from Atri the moon.

ಅಥ s. An auspicious particle, used in stuti, mangala, etc. ad Now, then, what? how? moreover, rather, but, else.

ಅಥರ್ವ s. n The fourth vêda.

ಅಥವಾ s. ad. Or.

ಅದ k. *The termination of the relative negative participle, as* ಮಾಡದ, ತಿನ್ನದ

ಅದಕು (= ಅಗಚು, ಅದಪು, ಅಮುಕು etc.) k. v t To press, squeeze, cram 2, to be bruised n. A bruise in a metal vessel

ಅದಟ a. k n A very firm or persevering man

ಅದಟು a. k. v. t To scold, reprimand, to subdue v. i (= ಅದರು) To tremble. n Self-will, boldness, pride

ಅದದ h a. Of counting or numeration

ಅದನಾ h a. Low, mean, vulgar.

ಅದಪು (= ಅದಕು) k. v t To squeeze 2, (a. k) to upbraid, reprove

ಅದಬು h. n. Respect, regard.

ಅದರು (= ಅದಟು) k. v. i To tremble n Trembling, tremor. -ಗುಂಡಿಗೆ Faint-heartedness. -ಬೆದರು. Shaking and quaking -ವಾಯು The palsy. ಅದರಿಸು. To make shake.

ಅದರ್ಶನ s n. Non-vision, disappearance. a Invisible

ಅದಲಾಬದಲು, ಅದಲುಬದಲು f n. Exchanging.

ಅದಲು = ಅದರು

ಅದಾತಾರ (tb. of ಅದಾತೃ) a. Not giving. n A miser.

ಅದಾನು (3rd pers. sing pres. of ಆಗು) k He may be. ಅಪಾಸೆ. He is

ಅದಾಲತು h n Justice, a court of justice.

ಅದಾವತ್ h n. Enmity, hatred

ಅದಿತಿ s n The mother of the gods 2, the earth

ಅದಿಮು = ಅದಕು, q v

ಅದಿರು (= ಅದರು) k v. i To tremble, shiver, fear.

ಅದಿಗರಂತಿ, ಅದಿಮುರ್ತ್ತೆ k n The creeper *Gaertnera racemosa*

ಅದಿರ್ಪು a k n Trembling, fear.

ಅದೀಪನ s a Indigestive n Bad digestion.

ಅದು k pro That, it. 2, the affix of the 3rd person singular neuter of the negative mood, *as* ಮಾಡದು, ಹೋಗದು, ಹುಟ್ಟದು

ಅದುಕು = ಅತುಕು, k. q v

ಅದುಗು k v i. To become soft by pressing ಅದುಗಿಸು To make soft by pressing.

ಅದುಗೋ (= ಅಕೋ) k. int Lo! behold!

ಅದುರು (= ಅದರು) k v i To tremble. n Native metal 2, dandruff

ಅದುಹು a k. v. i To be perplexed

ಅದೃಢ s a Unstable. 2, irresolute.

ಅದೃಶ್ಯ s a Invisible, not fit to be seen.

ಅದೃಷ್ಟ s. a Unseen, invisible, unknown n Unforeseen danger, destiny, fate. -ವಂತ, -ಶಾಲಿ A lucky (or unlucky) man

ಅದೆ 1. k A termination of the negative participle *as* ತಿನ್ನದೆ, ಉಣ್ಣದೆ

ಅದೆ 2. int Lo! look there v i It is, there is. ಅದೇ. That very thing

ಅದೋ k int Ah! oh!

ಅದ್ಗಣಿ. ಅದ್ವಗಣಿ k. n An anvil

ಅದ್ದಿಕೆ k. n. Immersion, dipping, dying clothes

ಅದ್ದು k. v. t To immerse, dip, to dye. 2 = ಅದು, *as in* ದೂರವಾದದ್ದು ಬೇಕಾದದ್ದು, ಹೊಡೆದದ್ದು *etc*

ಅದ್ದೆ f a. Acting. -ಕೆಲಸ. Acting work.

ಅದ್ಭುತ s a. Wonderful n. A marvel

ಅದ್ಯ ad Now, to-day -ತನ Referring to to-day --ಭೂತ The aorist (imperfect)

ಅದ್ವಯ s. a Not two, without a second, unique. n Non-duality 2, identity.

ಅದ್ರಿ s n. A stone, a mountain. 2 a tree 3, the sun -ಕನ್ಯೆ -ಜೆ Pârvati -ಕೀಲೆ. The earth. -ತಟ Tableland -ಭೇದನ India -ರಾಜ Himâlaya -ಸಾರ Iron

ಅದ್ವೈತ s. a. Destitute of duality unique n The doctrine of the identity of the Brahma and the universe, pantheism

ಅಧನ s a Destitute of wealth or property.

ಅಧಮ s a Lowest 2, vile, bad

ಅಧರ s a Lower 2. low vile n. The lower lip; the lip

ಅಧರ್ಮ s n Unrighteousness, irreligion; wickedness ಅಧರ್ಮಿ An unrighteous or wicked man

ಅಧಿ s. ad. Above, over and above; besides, upon

ಅಧಿಕ s. a Additional, abundant, intercalated 2, surpassing, superior, excellent n Abundance -ತರ Very much. -ಮಾಸ. An intercalar month

ಅಧಿಕರಣ s n Supremacy. 2, a receptacle 3 a topic 4, a category. 5, the locative case ಅಧಿಕರಿಸು To aim at, to master

ಅಧಿಕಾಧಿಕ s. a. Over and above very much

ಅಧಿಕಾರ s. n Authority; government, rule, right 2, privilege. 3, the use of royal insignia, royalty 4, an office -ಕೊಡು To empower -ಸ್ಥ, ಅಧಿಕಾರಿ A man in authority, an officer.

ಅಧಿಗತ s a Found, obtained 2 learned

ಅಧಿದೇವತೆ, ಅಧಿದೇವಿ, ಅಧಿದೈವತ s n A presiding deity

ಅಧಿನಾಯಕ, ಅಧಿಪ, ಅಧಿಪತಿ s n. A ruler

ಅಧಿರಾಜ s. n. A supreme king

ಅಧಿವಾಸ s. *n* An abode, house.

ಅಧಿಷ್ಠಾನ s *n*. Standing by, abiding 2, an abode, a basis, site; a settlement. 3, authority. ಅಧಿಷ್ಠಿಸು To govern

ಅಧೀನ s. *a*. Subject to, dependent upon

ಅಧೀಶ s. *n* A lord, master -ತ್ವ Authority, power.

ಅಧೃಷ್ಟ s. *a* Not bold, modest

ಅಧೇಲಿ f. *n* A half-rupee

ಅಧೈರ್ಯ s *n* Want of courage, timidity. -ಗೊಳ್ಳು To become timid

ಅಧೋಗತಿ s. *n*. Downward movement, perdition

ಅಧೋಭಾಗ s *n*. The lower part.

ಅಧೋಮುಖ s. *ad* Bending the head, upside down.

ಅಧೋಲೋಕ s *n*. The lower world.

ಅಧ್ಯಕ್ಷ s *a*. Observable, supervising. *n* An inspector -ತನ. Superintendence

ಅಧ್ಯಯನ s *n* Reading, *esp.* the Vêdas

ಅಧ್ಯಾತ್ಮ s *n* The supreme soul.

ಅಧ್ಯಾಪಕ s. *n*. A teacher.

ಅಧ್ಯಾಪನ s. *n*. Instruction, *esp.* on the Vêdas

ಅಧ್ಯಾಯ s. *n*. A lesson, chapter. 2, a reader

ಅಧ್ರುವ s. *a*. Unfixed, uncertain.

ಅಧ್ವ s *n*. A road. 2, time. 3, sky.

ಅಧ್ವರ s. *n* A sacrifice

ಅಧ್ವಾನ s *a* Devoid of sound *n*. A wilderness. 3 misfortune

ಅನ್ = ಅನ್ನು, ಅಂತ, ಅಂದರೆ, *q v*

ಅನ s. *n*. Breath.

ಅನಕ, ಅನಕಾ k *prep* Till, until 2, meanwhile

ಅನಘ s. *a*. Sinless, faultless.

ಅನಂಗ s. *a*. Incorporeal. *n*. Kâma. 2 the ether

ಅನಚ್ಛ s. *a*. Unclear, turbid

ಅನಡುಹ, ಅನಡ್ವಾಹ s. *n*. A bull ಅನಡುಹಿ, ಅನಡ್ವಾಹಿ A co[illegible]

ಅನತಿಶಯ s *a*. Not [illegible]

ಅನದ್ಯತನಭೂತ s. *n*. The pluperfect tense (*g*).

ಅನನುಕೂಲ s *a*. Adverse, unfavourable

ಅನಂತ s. *a*. Endless, infinite, eternal. *n* Vishnu, Krishna or Śiva 2, the sky. 3, the earth 4, the snake king -ತ್ವ Eternity, boundlessness

ಅನಂತರ s. *a*. Having no interval 2, following, next *ad*. Afterwards. ಅನಂತರದಲ್ಲಿ, afterwards.

ಅನನ್ಯ s. *a* Not different. 2, unique. 3, fixed on one object

ಅನಪಕಾರಿ s. *a*. Harmless, innocuous.

ಅನಪರಾಧಿ s. *a*. Innocent *n* An innocent man.

ಅನರ್ಗಲ s. *a* Unfettered, free; haughty.

ಅನರ್ಘ್ಯ s. *a*. Priceless.

ಅನರ್ಥ s. *a*. Worthless, useless; unhappy. 2, meaningless. *n*. Nonsense

ಅನಲ, ಅನಲು s. *n* Fire, the god of fire. 2, digestive power

ಅನವದ್ಯ s. *a* Irreproachable, faultless

ಅನವಧಾನ s. *a*. Inattentive *n* -ತೆ Inattention.

ಅನವಧಿ s *a*. Unlimited.

ಅನವರತ s. *a* Incessant.

ಅನವಸರ s. *a*. Having no leisure.

ಅನವು (= ಅನು) k. *n* Suitable place, room

ಅನಶನ s *n* Fasting.

ಅನಸೂಯ s. *n*. Unenviousness, freedom from spite. 2, the wife of Atri

ಅನಹಿತ s *n* Disadvantage, loss

ಅನಾಕಾರ s. *a*. Shapeless, deformed.

ಅನಾಚಾರ s *a*. Regardless of custom, unprincipled *n* Irreligion; incivility

ಅನಾಥ s. *a* Fatherless, helpless, poor. -ನಾಥ. A friend of the friendless ಅನಾಥೆ A widow, helpless woman

ಅನಾದರ, ಅನಾದರಣೆ s *n* Disrespect, slight

ಅನಾದಿ s. *a*. Without beginning, eternal *n* Heaven. -ವಾರ್ತೆ Tradition.

[illegible] s *a* Dis[illegible] despised

[illegible] s. *a* [illegible]

ಅನಾಧಾರತೆ s. n The state of having no support.

ಅನಾಮಕ, ಅನಾಮಿಕ s. a. Nameless, infamous.

ಅನಾಮಿಕೆ, ಅನಾಮಿ s n The ring-finger.

ಅನಾಯಕ s. a Without a leader. ad Disorderly

ಅನಾಯಾಸ s. n. Absence of exertion, ease. a. Easy

ಅನಾರ್ಯ s. a. Not-respectable, vulgar, un-Aryan

ಅನಾವೃಷ್ಟಿ s. n Want of rain, drought.

ಅನಾಸು f. n. The pine-apple, *Ananas sativus*

ಅನಿಚ್ಛೆ s n. Absence of desire, indifference.

ಅನಿತು (= ಅನಿತ್ತು) a k. *pro. (remote)* That much, that time, so much; so many a. All, the whole. ಅನಿಬರು. All persons

ಅನಿತ್ಯ s a. Not everlasting, transient, unstable

ಅನಿಮಿತ್ತ, ಅನಿಮಿತ್ಯ s. a Causeless, groundless.

ಅನಿಮಿಷ s. a Not winking. vigilant. n Not a moment 2, a god.

ಅನಿಯಮಿತ s. a. Lawless; irregular.

ಅನಿಲ s n. Wind or air· the deity of wind

ಅನಿವಾರ a. Refractory; excessive

ಅನಿವಾರ್ಯ a Inavertible n. Calamity.

ಅನಿಶ s. a. Nightless, sleepless, continuous.

ಅನಿಷ್ಟ s a. Unwished, disagreeable n Ill-luck; crime, hatred.

ಅನಿಸು k. v. t. To cause to say.

ಅನೀತಿ s. n. Injustice, immorality -ವಂತ An unjust man

ಅನೀಶ s. n. One who has no protector or superior a Powerless

ಅನು 1. k n. (*cf.* ಅನವು, ಅನುವು) Fitness, propriety, loveliness 2, worth. 3, [illegible] 5 [illegible] 7 occurrence; opportunity, leisure. -ಗೊಳಿಸು. To make ready, prepare -ವಾಗು. To be ready or fit, an occasion to happen

ಅನು 2 = ಅನ್ನು, q v.

ಅನು 3 s ad Afterwards then prep Along; with, severally, each by each, towards, like, according to.

ಅನುಕಂಪ s. n Sympathy, compassion, tenderness.

ಅನುಕರಣ s. n. Imitation, resemblance. -ಪದ, -ಶಬ್ದ An imitative word. ಅನುಕರಿಸು. To imitate 2. to accept 3, to make ready

ಅನುಕರ್ಷ s n. Attraction

ಅನುಕೂಲ s. a Favourable, agreeable n. (=-ತೆ) Good-will, suitableness of circumstances, convenience, favour, help -ಮಾಡು, ಅನುಕೂಲಿಸು To be favourable; to help -ಪಡೆಯು To agree; to obtain

ಅನುಕ್ರಮ s. n Succession, method.

ಅನುಕ್ರಮಣ s. n Methodical arrangement

ಅನುಕ್ರಮಣಿಕೆ s n A table of contents; a preface.

ಅನುಗ s a Going after n A companion, a servant

ಅನುಗತ s. a Gone after n. A follower.

ಅನುಗತಿ s. n. Succession, order.

ಅನುಗಮನ s. a. Following. n. Sati.

ಅನುಗಾಮಿ s n A follower, companion

ಅನುಗುಣ s. a. Congenial with -ತ್ವ. Congeniality.

ಅನುಗ್ರಹ s n. Conferring benefits, favour, kindness, aid. -ಹೊಂದು, -ಪಡೆ To gain favour

ಅನುಗ್ರಹಿಸು s v. t. To favour, grant, vouchsafe.

ಅನುಚಿತ s. a Improper; wrong

ಅನುಜ, ಅನುಜಾತ s a. After-born n. A younger brother.

[illegible] s. [illegible] Living [illegible]). n. A [illegible]

ಅನುಜ್ಞೆ s. n. Assent, permission, leave to depart. 2, an order.

ಅನುತಾಪ s. n Repentance 2, sorrow ಅನುತಾಪಿ Penitent

ಅನುತ್ತಮ s a. Highest, best, excellent.

ಅನುತ್ತರ s a Highest, best, excellent 2, low, inferior. 3, silent, without any reply

ಅನುದಿನ s ad. Every day, daily

ಅನುನಯ s. n Salutation, courtesy. 2, entreaty. 3, conduct, discipline

ಅನುಪತ್ಯ s. n Absence of the means of subsistence, need.

ಅನುಪಪತ್ತಿ s n. Non-accomplishment, insufficiency.

ಅನುಪಪನ್ನ s. a. Non-accomplished, deficient [best

ಅನುಪಮ s. a Incomparable, peerless,

ಅನುಪಲ್ಲವಿ s. n. The response in a chorus.

ಅನುಪ್ರಾಸ s n Alliteration.

ಅನುಬಂಧ s. n. Binding, connection. 2, an uninterrupted series. 3, consequence, result. 4, motive 5, an indicatory letter 6, commencement -ಕ್ರಿಯೆ. An auxiliary verb (*as* ಕೊಳ್ಳು *in* ಕಂಡುಕೊಳ್ಳು).

ಅನುಬಿಂಬ s. n A reflection ಅನುಬಿಂಬಿಸು. v. i. To be reflected

ಅನುಭವ s. n. Knowledge from observation, enjoyment, experience. 2, apprehension, understanding -ಮಾಡಿ ಕೊಳ್ಳು. To make one's self acquainted with

ಅನುಭವಿಸು s. v t. To experience· to enjoy, suffer, undergo.

ಅನುಭಾವ s n. Dignity, authority. 2, resolution

ಅನುಭೋಗ s. n. Enjoyment. 2, experience, undergoing.

ಅನುಭೋಗಿಸು s. v. t. To enjoy. 2, to experience.

ಅನುಮತ s. a. Approved, permitted, allowed. n. = ಅನುಮತಿ.

ಅನುಮತಿ (= ಅನುಮತ n.) s. n. Assent, permission; approbation.

ಅನುಮತಿಸು s. v t To assent, agree 2, to persuade

ಅನುಮಾನ s. n Hesitation, doubt, suspicion 2, inference (*in logic*) -ಬೀಳು, -ಪಡು To doubt, *etc*

ಅನುಮಾನಿಸು s. v t To doubt, hesitate, to suspect

ಅನುಮೇಯ s a. Inferable. ಅನುಮೇಯಿಸು. To infer.

ಅನುಮೋದ s n. Pleasure from sympathy; assent, acceptance. ಅನುಮೋದಿಸು v. i. To feel sympathetic joy, to assent

ಅನುಯೋಗ s. n. A question. 2, reproof.

ಅನುಯೋಜನ s n. A question 2, attachment ಅನುಯೋಜಿಸು v i To attach, join

ಅನುರಕ್ತಿ, ಅನುರಾಗ s. n. Affection, love, devotion ಅನುರಕ್ತಿಸು, ಅನುರಾಗಿಸು i. t. v. i To love; to be fond of.

ಅನುರಾಧೆ s. n. The seventeenth lunar mansion

ಅನುಲಾಪ s n. Tautology. ಅನುಲಾಪಿಸು v. t. To repeat the same word.

ಅನುಲೇಪನ s n. Ointment, anointing. ಅನುಲೇಪಿಸು v. t. To anoint.

ಅನುವರ್ತನ s. n. Following; concurring. 2, compliance, obedience 3, continuance 4, consequence. ಅನುವರ್ತಿಸು v. t To refer or apply. 2, to follow

ಅನುವಾದ s. n. Repetition, confirmation. 2, slander. ಅನುವಾದಿಸು v i. To reason, argue

ಅನುವು (= ಅನು) -ತನುವು k n Preparation for setting out 2, refreshment.

ಅನುವೃತ್ತಿ s. n Complying with. 2, reverting to. 3, imitating, conformity.

ಅನುವೇಸು. = ಅನ್ವಯಿಸು s. ಅನ್ವಯ.

ಅನುಶಯ s n Close connection. 2, evil result. 3, repentance. 4, wrath.

ಅನುಶಾಸನ s. n Regulating, instruction, direction.

ಅನುಷ್ಠಾನ s. n Undertaking; performance practice business ಅನು[illegible]ಸು v t. To perform.

ಅನುಸಂಧಾನ s n. Investigation 2, plan, scheme. ಅನುಸಂಧಿಸು v t. To join, connect; to meet

ಅನುಸರಣ, ಅನುಸಾರ s. n Following, imitating. 2, conformity to. ಅನುಸಾರವಾಗಿ According to

ಅನುಸರಿಸು s. v t To act in like manner, to follow.

ಅನುಸಾರಿ s n A follower

ಅನುಸಾರಿಣಿ s. n (lit She who follows) N of the second string of a lute

ಅನುಸ್ವಾರ s. n After-sound, the nasal sound represented by ಂ (g).

ಅನೂಕ s n. The spine 2, race. 3, temperament

ಅನೂನ s a. Undiminished, not less, whole.

ಅನೂರು s. a Thighless n Aruna, the dawn

ಅನೃಜು s a Not straight 2, wicked

ಅನೃತ s a. Untrue. n Falsehood, lie. 2, agriculture.

ಅನೆ k. *Suffix to form adverbs, as* ಸಟ್ಟನೆ, ಉಸಿಕನೆ, ಸುಮ್ಮನೆ

ಅನೆಯ, ಅನೇ k. *Suffix to denote ordinals, as* ಮೊದಲನೇ, ಎರಡನೇ, ಮೂರನೇ, *etc*

ಅನೇಕ s. a Not one, many, several. -ವಿಧ In different ways, various. -ಆವರ್ತಿ. Many times.

ಅಂತ 1. (= ಅಂಥ, *q v.*) k *ad.* Such, such a one 2, *p p of* ಅನ್ನು

ಅಂತ 2. s. n. End, limit, boundary. 2, completion, death, decay. 3, a final syllable *(g)* 4, certainty. 5, disposition. 6, nearness. 7, inside

ಅಂತಃ (= ಅಂತರ್) s *ad.* Within, in the middle 2, between. -ಕರಣ The inner organ the heart, conscience, soul 2, *(fig.)* favour, love, mercy (= ದಯ, ಪ್ರೀತಿ) -ಕರಣವಡು To have mercy -ಕರಣಶುದ್ಧ A man whose mind is pure -ಕಲಹ Inner strife -ಪುರ The inner or female apartment, gynaeceum -ಶುದ್ಧಿ Inward purity -ಸಾರ. Having internal

ಅಂತಃಸ್ಥ (*cf* ಅಂತಸ್ಥು) s a Being amidst. n A semi-vowel.

ಅಂತಕ s a Making an end. n. Death, Yama

ಅಂತಪ್ಪ *See s* ಅಂತು.

ಅಂತರ್ = ಅಂತಃ, *q v*

ಅಂತರ s a. Inner, interior. 2, near, related. 3, distant; different. 4, surpassing. n The interior 2, the soul (ಅಂತರಾತ್ಮ) 3, interval, distance; difference 4, a variety. 5, period of time, occasion 6, respect 7, a surety 8, great height. 9, obstacle (ಅಂತರಾಯ) 10. *at the end of cpds.* different, another, *as* ದೇಶಾಂತರ, another country, ಜನ್ಮಾಂತರ, ಮಾನಸಾಂತರ, ಲೋಕಾಂತರ, *etc* ಅಂತರಾತ್ಮ. The soul.

ಅಂತರಂಗ s n. The inner part, mind, heart. 2, secrecy.

ಅಂತರಗಂಗೆ s n A water-plant, *Pistia stratiotes*

ಅಂತರಂತರ s a Leaving a proper distance when sitting at meals, or space between hills, *etc*

ಅಂತರಾಂತರ s n The inner soul 2, difference.

ಅಂತರಾಯ s. n. Obstacle, impediment.

ಅಂತರಾಲ s n. Intermediate space or time

ಅಂತರಿಕ್ಷ s n Atmosphere, sky.

ಅಂತರಿಸು s v t To leave a space between 2, to put off. v i To disappear

ಅಂತರಿಂದೆ (ರಿ = ಈ) k *prep.* Afterwards

ಅಂತರಿಂದ್ರಿಯ k. n An internal organ, manas, buddhi, ahankāra and chitta.

ಅಂತರ್ಗತ s a. Included in. 2, hidden, forgotten.

ಅಂತರ್ಧಾನ s n Disappearance

ಅಂತರ್ಭೂತ s a Internal inner.

ಅಂತರ್ಮಂದಿರ, ಅಂತರ್ಗೃಹ s. n. An inner apartment.

ಅಂತರ್ಮುಖ s. n Continual attention of

ಅಂತರ್ಯ s *n* The interior. 2, a hidden thought.

ಅಂತರ್ಯಾಮಿ s. *n* The supreme soul.

ಅಂತಸ್ತಾಪ s. *n*. Inward heat, distress

ಅಂತಸ್ತು (*tb of* ಅಂತಃಸ್ಥ) *a*. Being between *n*. A story of a building 2, degree of rank

ಅಂತಸ್ಥ s *n* A secret.

ಅಂತಹ a. k = ಅಂತು, *q v*

ಅಂತಾ (= ಅಂಥ, *q. v*) *ad*. Such. 2, = ಅನ್ನತ್ತಾ [*etc*. (*g*.)

ಅಂತಾನೆ, ಅಂತಿ, *etc*. = ಅನ್ನುತ್ತಾನೆ, ಅನ್ನುತ್ತಿ,

ಅಂತಿಕ s *ad* Near *n* Vicinity 2, end.

ಅಂತು k. *ad* In that manner, thus, so *n* The whole, total ಅಂತಪ್ಪ, ಅಂತಹ. Such, such a one. ಅಂತಿಂತು (= ಅಂತು-ಇಂತು). Either so or thus, at any rate ಅಂತೂ. And so, as for, *as* ಹೊಸವು ಅಂತೂ ತೋರಲಿಲ್ಲ, as for new ones they did not appear.

ಅಂತುಟು = ಅನಿತು

ಅಂತೆ 1, ಅಂತೇ k. *ad*. Even so, just like, just as (ಹಾಂಗೆ).

ಅಂತೆ 2. k. *d i*. It is said, *see s*. ಅನ್ನು.

ಅಂತ್ಯ s. *a* Last, final. 2, lowest. *n*. The end -ಜ, -ಜನ್ಮ. Lowest born, a Śûdra.

ಅಂತ್ಯೇಷ್ಟಿ s *n*. Funeral ceremonies.

ಅಂತ್ರ *tb of* ಅಂತರ, *q v. as* ದೇಶಾಂತ್ರ, ಮುಖಾಂತ್ರ, *etc* 2, entrail, gut.

ಅಂಥ, ಅಂಥಾ (= ಅಂತಾ) k *ad* Such, of that kind, *as* ತಕ್ಕಂಥ, ಹುಟ್ಟಿದಂಥಾ, ಇರುವಂಥಾದ್ದು, *etc* ಅಂಥಂಥಾ. Such and such

ಅಂದ (= ಅಸು 1) k *n*. Fitness, beauty 2, manner 3, nature, faculty 4, true state -ಗೆಡಿಸು. To spoil, ruin -ಗೆಡು To become ugly. -ಗೇಡಿ. An ugly creature -ಗೊಳಿಸು To cause to look nice -ವಡೆ. To be beautiful -ಗಾರ. A handsome man, *f*. -ಗಾರಳು, -ಗಾತಿ.

ಅಂದಣ, ಅಂದಳ (*tb. of* ಆಂದೋಲ) *n*. A litter, palankeen

ಅಂದರೆ (*f* ಅನ್ನು) k. [illegible] to say. ಸಂಧಿ ಅಂದರೆ [illegible]

ಅಂದಾಜು h *n*. Proportion, estimate. ಕಟ್ಟು. To make an estimate

ಅಂದಿಪ್ಪನಾರು k. *n*. An evergreen tree, *Carallia integerrima*.

ಅಂದಿಹುಳ k. *n*. A small insect that infests grain.

ಅಂದು 1. k *ad* At that time, then ಚಿಕ್ಕಂದು. Childhood ಅಂದಿನಿಂದ. Since then ಅಂದಿಗೆ. Then ಅಂದೆಂದು Always

ಅಂದು 2 k *v t* To suffer, to get at, to obtain *v i*. To reach, arrive

ಅಂದುಕ s. *n*. A chain, fetter. 2, an anklet.

ಅಂದುಗು k. *n* The clearing nut plant, *Strychnos potatorum*

ಅಂದ್ರೆ. = ಅಂದರೆ, *q v*.

ಅಂಧ s. *a*. Blind. *n* Darkness. 2, turbid water. ಅಂಧಾದರಬಾರು h. A bad government.

ಅಂಧಕ s. *a*. Blind. *n* A blind man. 2, darkness 3, water.

ಅಂಧಕಾರ s *n* Darkness -ಕವಿ, -ಮುಚ್ಚಿಕೊಳ್ಳು Darkness to cover

ಅಂಧ್ರ f *n* The Telugu country, a Telugu man.

ಅನ್ನ 1 (= ಅನ್ನೆ) a. k. *ad* That time, meanwhile -ಬರ, -ಬರೆ So long as, until.

ಅನ್ನ 2. s. *n*. Food, *esp* boiled rice. 2, the sun; water -ಋಣ One's allotment to eat rice. -ಕಂಟಕ. One who hinders another's living -ಕುದಿಸು, -ಬೇಸು To boil rice -ಗತ. Depending on food -ಛತ್ರ A building in which food is distributed. -ದಾತ, -ದಾನಿ. A giver of food -ದಾನ. Giving of food -ದ್ವೇಷ. Want of appetite -ಪಚನೆ. Digestion. -ಪದಾರ್ಥ Rice and curry. -ಪಾನ. Meat and drink -ಪ್ರಾಶನ. The ceremony of putting rice into a child's mouth for the first time. -ಭೇದಿ Green vitriol. -ವಸ್ತ್ರ Food and clothing. -ಶಾಂತಿ Feeding the hungry. ಅನ್ನಾಭಾವ. [illegible]

-ಹೋಗು To have an appetite ಅನ್ನಾ ಥಿ A beggar

ಅನ್ನು k v t To say, speak, name ಅನ್ನಿಸು To cause to say, *etc.* ಅನ್ನಿಸಿಕೊಳ್ಳು To be called, to pass for. (*P ps.* ಅಂದು, ಅಂತ, ಅಂತಾ, having said, *for which often* ಎಂದು, *etc. are used) The verb* ಅನ್ನು, *like* ಎನ್ನು, *is used to introduce words and sentences, as* ಎಲ್ಲಿಗೆ ಹೋಗಲಿ ಅಂತ ಕೇಳಿದನು, he asked "where shall I go?" ಅಂತೆ. Having said, it is said ಅಂದರೆ That is to say *(explanatory)* ಅನ್ನುವಿಕೆ. Saying.

ಅನ್ನು (= ಅನ್ನ 1) a k. *ad.* Meanwhile, until 2, truly certainly

ಅನ್ಯ, ಅನ್ಯಕ s. *a.* Other, another, different, foreign -ಜಾತಿ Another caste. -ದೇಶ A foreign country. -ಪಾಕ Cooked by others -ಭಾವ. The mind of another -ಭಾಷೆ Another language

ಅನ್ಯತರ s *a* Either of the two.

ಅನ್ಯತ್ರ s. *ad* Elsewhere.

ಅನ್ಯಥಾ s. *ad* Otherwise, in a different manner.

ಅನ್ಯಾಯ s. *n* Unlawfulness, injustice. -ಗಾರ. An unjust man

ಅನ್ಯೋನ್ಯ s *a* Mutual. *n* Reciprocity 2, intimacy, friendship, amity -ಭಾವ Mutual affection -ವಾಗು. To become reconciled. -ಸಲ್ಲಾಪ. Conversation -ಸ್ನೇಹ Mutual friendship.

ಅನ್ವಯ s. *n* Succession; connection 2, race, family 3, grammatical construction of a sentence *(g.)* 4, drift, purport. ಅನ್ವಯಿಸು To construe, to arrange words in order

ಅನ್ವರ್ಥ s *a* Intelligible, clear -ನಾಮ. A word of self-evident meaning.

ಅನ್ವವಾಯ s *n* Family, race.

ಅನ್ವಾಹಿತ s *a.* Deposited 2, renewed, as a sacred fire

ಅನ್ವಿತ s. *a* Connected, understood

ಅನ್ವೇಷಣ s. *n* Searching, investigation

ಅ

ಅಪ 2 s *ad* Away 2, negatively, contradictorily. 3, without

ಅಪಕಾರ s *n.* Wrong, offence harm 2, wickedness ಅಪಕಾರಿ An offender

ಅಪಕೀರ್ತಿ s *n* Reproach 2, disgrace, infamy -ಹೊಂದು To be disgraced. -ತಂದುಕೊಳ್ಳು To incur disgrace

ಅಪಕೃತ್ಯ s *n.* A wrong act; damage, injury.

ಅಪಕ್ರಮ s *n* Going away 2, flight 3, (= ಅಕ್ರಮ) disorder.

ಅಪಕ್ವ s *a.* Uncooked, raw. 2, unripe.

ಅಪಖ್ಯಾತಿ s. *n.* Injured reputation, disgrace

ಅಪಗತ s. *a.* Gone, departed. 2, deceased ಅಪಗತಿ. Low condition.

ಅಪಚಾರ s *n.* Improper conduct, offence, mistake 2, defect.

ಅಪಚಿತಿ s *n* Honour, respect 2, loss 3, expense.

ಅಪಜಯ s *n.* Defeat, reverse, loss -ಪಡಿಸು To defeat -ಹೊಂದು To be defeated.

ಅಪಜ್ಞಾನ s *n* Concealment of knowledge

ಅಪತ್ನೀಕ s *a.* Wifeless *n* A widower.

ಅಪತ್ಯ s. *n* Offspring a child

ಅಪಥ್ಯ s. *a* Unfit, unwholesome. *n* Bad diet 2, a lie.

ಅಪಪೂರು (ರು = ಱು) k. *n* Slander, calumny; disgrace -ಇಡು, -ಮಾಡು, -ಹಾಕು To calumniate. -ಪಡು To be disgraced. [state.

ಅಪಬದಿ (*tb of* ಅಪದಶೆ) *n.* A low miserable

ಅಪದೇಶ s *n* A pretence 2, a butt, mark. 3, fame. 4, quarter.

ಅಪಧ್ವಂಸ s. *n* Falling away; degradation

ಅಪನಂಬಿಕೆ, ಅಪನಂಬಿಗೆ, ಅಪನಂಬುಗೆ k. *n* Distrust, mistrust, unbelief

ಅಪನಿಂದೆ s. *n.* Abuse, reproach -ಹೊರಿಸು To accuse falsely

ಅಪಪ್ರಯೋಗ s. *n* Misapplication.

s. *n* In... ...uage.

ಅಪಮಾನ (= ಅವಮಾನ) s. n Disrespect, dishonour, disgrace. -ಮಾಡು To disgrace

ಅಪಮೃತ್ಯು s n. A sudden or violent death 2. a minor death, i.e a desperate sickness.

ಅಪರ s a Hinder, later 2, following 3, other. 4, different, distant. n. The hind foot of an elephant. 2, the future 3, the west.

ಅಪರಂಜಿ f. n Pure gold

ಅಪರಪಕ್ಷ s. n The latter or dark half of the month 2, the other side, defendant

ಅಪರರಾತ್ರಿ, ಅಪರಾತ್ರಿ s n The latter half of the night. [Śiva.

ಅಪರಾಜಿತ s. a Unconquered. n. Vishnu,

ಅಪರಾದ್ಧ s a Sinned; guilty.

ಅಪರಾಧ s n Offence, crime, 2, penalty, punishment. 3, fault, mistake. -ಕ್ಷಮಿಸಿಬಿಡು. To pardon an aparâdha. -ಕೊಡು To pay a fine. -ಮಾಡು. To commit an aparâdha -ಹೊರು. To charge an aparâdha upon.

ಅಪರಾಧಸ್ಥ, ಅಪರಾಧಿ s n A guilty person, criminal

ಅಪರಾಹ್ಣ n The afternoon.

ಅಪರಿಮಿತ s a. Unmeasured, unlimited

ಅಪರೂಪ (tb. ಅಪೂರೂಪ) s a. Ugly 2, uncommon, rare

ಅಪಲಾಪ s. n. Denial. abnegation; hiding. 2, an outcry. ಅಪಲಾಪಿಸು. To deny; to cry out

ಅಪವಾದ s. n. Evil speaking, blame 2, refutation 3, exception

ಅಪವಿತ್ರ s a Impure, unclean.

ಅಪಶಕುನ s. n. A bad omen.

ಅಪಶಬ್ದ s n. A harsh word. 2, incorrect language.

ಅಪಸದ s. n. An outcaste.

ಅಪಸರ tb of ಅಪಸ್ವರ, q. v.

ಅಪಸಾಕ್ಷಿ s. n False witness.

ಅಪಸಿದ್ಧಾಂತ s n An erroneous conclusion.

ಅಪಸ್ಮಾರ s. n Forgetfulness, unconsciousness. 2, epilepsy.

ಅಪಸ್ವರ s. n An unmusical sound. 2, a hoarse voice.

ಅಪಹರಣ s. n Taking away; stealing

ಅಪಹರಿಸು s v. t. To take away, to rob, plunder

ಅಪಹಾರ s n. Taking away. 2, stealing. ಮಾನಾಪಹಾರ. Defamation.

ಅಪಹಾಸ್ಯ s. n Ridicule, scorn, mockery -ಮಾಡು To mock at

ಅಪಾಂಗ s a Deformed. n. The outer corner of the eye. 2, a sectarian mark

ಅಪಾತ್ಯಯ s. n. Concealment of knowledge

ಅಪಾತ್ರ s. a Unworthy, unfit.

ಅಪಾದಾನ s n. The ablative case (g.)

ಅಪಾಪೋಲಿ k. a. Stray, as cattle, disorderly, as a man, ill-done

ಅಪಾಯ s. n. Going away 2, destruction. 3, evil. 4, peril, danger

ಅಪಾರ s. a. Shoreless, unbounded, immense. [ment.

ಅಪಾರ್ಥ s a. Unmeaning n. False argu-

ಅಪಾಶ್ರಯ s n. A refuge 2, a fence, hedge. a. Helpless.

ಅಪಿ s prep. On; near to ad. Moreover 2, though. 3, certainly. 4, perhaps

ಅಪಿಧಾನ s. n. Covering. 2, a cover

ಅಪುತ್ರ s. a Sonless.

ಅಪುನರ್ಭವ s. n Exemption from further transmigration (= ಮುಕ್ತಿ).

ಅಪುಷ್ಪ s. a. Not flowering

ಅಪೂಪ s. n A cake of flour, etc.

ಅಪೂರ್ವ s a. Unprecedented. 2, extraordinary, wonderful, unparalleled

ಅಪೇಕ್ಷಿಸು s v. t. To desire, wish for, to expect.

ಅಪೇಕ್ಷೆ s. n Desire, wish; hope -ಹುಟ್ಟಿಸು. To excite desire, etc

ಅಪೋಹ s. n Removal of doubt 2, arguing

[illegible] becoming, being, [illegible]

ಗುದಿ ಅಪ್ಪಂತೆ As well as possible ಅಪ್ಪಂದವ An agreeable or fit man. ಅಪ್ಪದು = ಆಗುವದು

ಅಪ್ಪ 2. k n Father, cf ಚಿಕ್ಕಪ್ಪ, ದೊಡ್ಡಪ್ಪ, etc. 2, an affix to proper name, as ಪೊನ್ನಪ್ಪ 3, (tb of ಅಪೂಪ) a rice cake

ಅಪ್ಪಟ f. a. Pure, unmixed

ಅಪ್ಪಟಿ k. n Flatness

ಅಪ್ಪಣೆ (tb of ಅಜ್ಞಾಪನ) n Order, command, law 2, permission, leave -ಕೇಳು To ask permission -ಕೊಡು To give permission, to order. -ತಕ್ಕೊಳ್ಳು, -ಹೊಂದು. To take leave -ಮಾಡು To order.

ಅಪ್ಪನ (tb of ಅರ್ಪಣ) n Tax, rent

ಅಪ್ಪಯಿಸು k v t To embrace, to seize eagerly

ಅಪ್ಪರಿಸು k. v t. To lift up and throw [down

ಅಪ್ಪಳಿಸು k v t. To strike against, to slap. 2, = ಅಪ್ಪರಿಸು.

ಅಪ್ಪಿಗ (= ಅಪ್ಪುಗೆ) k. n. Joining cementing. 2, a patch

ಅಪ್ಪು 1 k v t. To join, unite 2, to embrace. n An embrace (ಆಲಿಂಗನ) ಅಪ್ಪಿಕೊಳ್ಳು. To embrace, clasp. ಅಪ್ಪಿಕೊಳುಹ, ಅಪ್ಪಿಕೊಳ್ಳುವಿಕೆ. An embrace

ಅಪ್ಪು 2. (tb of ಅಪ್) n Water.

ಅಪ್ಪುಗೆ, ಅಪ್ಪುವಿಕೆ k n An embrace.

ಅಪ್ರಕಾಶ s a. Not shining, hidden

ಅಪ್ರತಿ, ಅಪ್ರತಿಮ s a Unequalled, incomparable

ಅಪ್ರತಿಷ್ಠೆ s. n Instability 2. ill-fame, dishonour -ಮಾಡು To disgrace

ಅಪ್ರತೀತಿ s. n Unjust imputation

ಅಪ್ರತ್ಯಕ್ಷ s a Invisible, imperceptible

ಅಪ್ರಬುದ್ಧ s a Stupid, dull

ಅಪ್ರಮಾಣ s a Unlimited, unproved, unauthorised, dishonest. n A lie

ಅಪ್ರಮಾಣಿಕ (= ಅಪ್ರಾಮಾಣಿಕ) s a Unproved, unwarranted, unworthy of being believed -ತೆ Untruthfulness, dishonesty. [table

ಅಪ್ರ

ಅಪ್ರಯೋಜಕ s a Unserviceable, useless

ಅಪ್ರಸಿದ್ಧ s a. Unknown, obscure. ಅಪ್ರಸಿದ್ಧಿ n The state of being unknown, obscurity

ಅಪ್ರಸ್ತುತ s a Unpraised, irrelevant, unsuitable, accidental.

ಅಪ್ರಾಮಾಣಿಕ. = ಅಪ್ರಮಾಣಿಕ, q. v

ಅಪ್ರಿಯ s a Disagreeable, disliked

ಅಪ್ರೀತಿ s. n Want of love, disaffection, dislike

ಅಪ್ರೌಢ s a. Modest, unlearned. -ತೆ Ignorance

ಅಪ್ಸರ, ಅಪ್ಸರಸ್, ಅಪ್ಸರಸಿ, ಅಪ್ಸರೆ s. n A celestial nymph.

ಅಫಲ s a. Unfruitful 2, barren, useless.

ಅಫಿನಿ, ಅಫಿಮು, ಅಫೀಮು, ಅಫು h. n. Opium -ಖೋರ. An opium eater.

ಅಬಕಾರಿ = ಅಬುಕಾರಿ, q. v.

ಅಬಕ್ಕನೆ k ad Hastily

ಅಬದ್ಧ s a. Unbound. 2, wrong n A lie, falsehood -ಖೋರ, -ಗಾರ A liar -ಭಾಷಣ. Lying -ಸಾಕ್ಷಿ False witness

ಅಬಂದರ, ಅಬಂದರೆ (tb. of ಅಭದ್ರ) n Disorder confusion waste.

ಅಬಲ s a Weak, feeble n Weakness ಅಬಲೆ. A woman.

ಅಬಾದು f. a Valueless, futile. n. Tare in weighing. ಅಬಾದ, -ಮನುಷ್ಯ. A man of monstrous circumference. -ಅಂಗಿ A very wide jacket -ಕಟ್ಟು, -ತೂಕ ಮಾಡು To tare

ಅಬಾಸ, ಅಬಾಸು f. n Incongruity. 2, disagreeableness (= ಅಸಹ್ಯ)

ಅಬುಕಾರಿ (= ಅಬಕಾರಿ) h n Revenue derived from intoxicating liquors.

ಅಬುಜ tb. of ಅಬ್ಜ, q v

ಅಬ್ಜ (tb ಅಬುಜ) s a. Born in water. n The moon 2, a lotus. 3, a pearl. -ಕರ. A lotus-like hand. -ಗರ್ಭ, -ಜ, -ಭವ. Offspring of the lotus Brahmâ -ಬಂಧು, -ಸಖ. The sun. -ವಾಸಿನಿ. Lakshmî -ವೈರಿ, ಅಬ್ಜಾರಿ, ಅಬ್ಜಾಹಿತ. The moon.

ಅಭ್ರ s n A cloud 2, a tear -ಪುಲ್ಲು.

ಬ್ಧಿ s. *n* The ocean 2, pure knowledge (ಕೇವಲಜ್ಞಾನ) 3, right behaviour (ನೀತಿ) -ಜ, -ನಂದನ The moon -ಶಯನ, -ಶಾಯಿ Vishnu

ಬ್ಬ, ಅಬ್ಬಬ್ಬ, ಅಬ್ಬಾ k *int.* Ha! 2, ah, alas!

ಬ್ಬರ, ಅಬ್ಬರಣೆ k *n* A loud cry; sound, report, noise 2, desire.

ಬ್ಬರಿಸು k *v i* To cry aloud, to bark, howl 2, to desire

ಬ್ಬಳಿಕೆ k. *n.* Eructation or belching.

ಬ್ಬುಜೆ k. *n* Soot, mould

ಬ್ಬೆ k. *n.* A plant from which pens are made 2, (*tb of* ಅಂಬೆ) mother.

ಬ್ರು h *n.* Honour, reputation.

ಭಕ್ತ s. *a* Undevout, unbelieving.

ಭಂಗ s. *a* Not breaking; without destruction

ಭಯ s. *a.* Unfearful, fearless *n* Fearlessness, peace, safety. -ಈ, -ಕೊಡು. To give assurance of security -ದಾತ, -ಪ್ರದಾನ Giving safety

ಭವ s. *a* Unborn

ಭಾಗ್ಯ s. *a.* Unfortunate, poor, wretched.

ಭಾಜನ s *a* Improper *n* Impropriety

ಭಾವ s *n* Non-existence, absence 2, omission 3, death -ಕ್ರಿಯೆ The negative mood (*g*)

ಭಿ s *ad* On 2, towards 3, in presence of. 4, intensely [term.

ಭಿಖ್ಯ, ಅಭಿಖ್ಯೆ s. *n* A name, a word,

ಭಿಗಮನ s. *n* Coming near 2, adoration (of idols) at noon.

ಭಿಘಾತ s. *n.* Attack; injury, loss.

ಭಿಘಾರ s *n* Ghee put on food or oblation.

ಭಿಚರ s. *n* A servant

ಭಿಚಾರ s *n* Incantation, sorcery

ಭಿಜನ s. *n* Race, family, ancestors. 2, fame; a badge of honour.

ಭಿಜಾತ s. *a* Well-born, noble 2, proper 3, learned

ಭಿಜಿತ s *a* Victorious (ly.)

ಅಭಿಜ್ಞ s. *a.* Knowing, clever -ತೆ, ಅಭಿಜ್ಞಾನ Knowledge

ಅಭಿಧಾನ, ಅಭಿಧೆ s. *n.* A name. 2, speech; a word 3, sense, meaning 4, a vocabulary.

ಅಭಿನಯ s *n* Indication of a passion by look or gesture 2, dramatic representation ಅಭಿನಯಿಸು. To represent dramatically; to imitate

ಅಭಿನವ s. *a* Quite new; fresh, young. ಅಭಿನವಿಸು To become new.

ಅಭಿನಿವೇಶ s. *n.* Inclination, attachment 2, determination.

ಅಭಿನ್ನ s *a.* Unbroken, undivided 2, unaltered; identical

ಅಭಿಪ್ರಾಯ s. *n.* Aim, purpose, intention, opinion, meaning. -ಮಾಡು. To interpret

ಅಭಿಮತ s *a.* Assented to. 2, wished *n* Desire, wish ಅಭಿಮತಿಸು To assent to, approve of

ಅಭಿಮಂತ್ರಣ s *n.* Calling, inviting. 2, consecrating by a formula (ಮಂತ್ರ) ಅಭಿಮಂತ್ರಿಸು To consecrate, to charm

ಅಭಿಮನ್ಯು s. *n.* A son of Arjuna

ಅಭಿಮಾನ s. *n* Conceit, pride 2, noble feeling, affection, love, self-respect -ಹಿಡಿ To love -ಗಿತ್ತಿ A proud female.

ಅಭಿಮಾನಿ s *n.* A person of noble feelings. *a.* Proud

ಅಭಿಮಾನಿಸು s. *v t* To honour; to love, to shelter, protect.

ಅಭಿಮುಖ s. *a.* Facing, fronting. 2, approaching

ಅಭಿಯೋಗ s. *n* Application; exertion 2, an attack, fight; a charge

ಅಭಿರಾಮ s *a* Pleasing, delightful, beautiful

ಅಭಿರುಚಿ s. *n.* Desire, taste, pleasure.

ಅಭಿರೂಪ s *a.* Pleasing, handsome.

ಅಭಿಲಾಷ, ಅಭಿಲಾಷೆ s. *n.* Desire, wish. ಅಭಿಲಾಷಿಸು To desire, wish.

ಅಭಿವಂದನ, ಅಭಿವಾದ, ಅಭಿವಾದನ s. *n.* A respectful salutation. -[illegible]. To salute respectfully.

ಅಭಿವೃದ್ಧಿ s n Increase, prosperity, success, progress.

ಅಭಿಶಾಪ s. n. Curse, calumny.

ಅಭಿಷಂಗ s n. Union 2, attachment. 3, debt. 4, a curse

ಅಭಿಷಿಕ್ತ s a Sprinkled over, inaugurated, enthroned.

ಅಭಿಷೇಕ s. n Sprinkling over, consecration, inauguration 2, the liquid used for sprinkling. 3, purifying an idol with ablutions. ಪಟ್ಟಾಭಿಷೇಕ Coronation of a king -ಮಾಡು, ಅಭಿಷೇಕಿಸು. To sprinkle over; to inaugurate

ಅಭಿಸರಣ s. a Going towards, dispersion, following.

ಅಭಿಹತಿ s n. A stroke, injury.

ಅಭಿಹಾರ s. n Seizing, robbing. 2, an attack 3, reversion 4, exertion

ಅಭೀಕ್ಷಿಸು s. v. i. To look towards.

ಅಭೀಷ್ಟ s. a. Wished, desired. 2, acceptable -ಸಿದ್ಧಿ Gaining of a desired object

ಅಭೇದ s. n. Absence of difference, identity.

ಅಭೇದ್ಯ s a Impenetrable, indivisible

ಅಭ್ಯಂಗ, ಅಭ್ಯಂಗನ, ಅಭ್ಯಂಜನ s. n Smearing the body with unctuous substances 2. an unguent.

ಅಭ್ಯನುಜ್ಞೆ s n Permission, order.

ಅಭ್ಯಂತರ s n The interior 2, an obstacle, impediment -ಮಾಡು, ಅಭ್ಯಂತರಿಸು To hinder

ಅಭ್ಯರ್ಚನ s n Worship, reverence

ಅಭ್ಯಸ್ತ s a Practised, studied

ಅಭ್ಯಾಗತ s a Come, arrived n An uninvited guest

ಅಭ್ಯಾಗಮ s. n Arrival; visit.

ಅಭ್ಯಾಸ s. n Use, habit. 2, study, learning 3, practice, exercise -ನಡಿಸು, ಅಭ್ಯಾಸಿಸು To study, practise. *cpds* ವಿದ್ಯಾಭ್ಯಾಸ, ಶರೀರಾಭ್ಯಾಸ.

ಅ… … hm

ಅಭ್ಯುತ್ಥಾನ, ಅಭ್ಯುದಯ s. n. Rising, elevation; increase, prosperity.

ಅಭ್ರ s n A cloud 2, sky, atmosphere. 3, the eye 4 talc, mica -ಕೇಶ N of Śiva -ಗರ್ಜನೆ Thunder -ಮಣಿ Heaven's gem the sun, moon -ಮಾಲೆ. Succession of clouds.

ಅಭ್ರಕ s n The sedge *Cyperus rotandus.* 2, talc, mica.

ಅಮಕು = ಅದಕು ಅಮುಗು.

ಅಮಕ್ಕಳ k n. Tumult

ಅಮಗ k n. A fit opportunity, festive occasion. 2, season.

ಅಮಗು (=ಅಮಕು) k. v t To squeeze. *etc.*

ಅಮಂಗಲ s. a Inauspicious, unlucky. -ಕರ. Causing ill-luck -ಕಾರಿ One who causes ill-luck -ಹಾರಿ One who averts ill-luck ಅಮಂಗಲೆ A widow.

ಅಮಂಗುರ k n A medicinal shrub, *Physalis flexuosa*

ಅಮಟೆ (*tb of* ಆಂಬಷ್ಠ), -ಕಾಯಿ n. A hog-plum

ಅಮತ s a Unfelt, imperceptible

ಅಮತಿ s n. Unconsciousness, ignorance

ಅಮನುಷ್ಯ s. a. Not human n. A demon.

ಅಮಮ k. *int. of surprise and pain* Ha! alas!

ಅಮರ s a Immortal n A god. 2, quicksilver -ದಬಳ್ಳಿ. A shrubby creeper. -ಕೋಶ. N of the Samskrita dictionary by Amarasimha -ಗಂಗೆ, -ನದಿ The celestial Ganges. -ತ್ವ Immortality -ಪತಿ. Indra. -ಲೋಕ Heaven. ಅಮರಿ, ಅಮರೆ A female deity.

ಅಮರಾದ್ರಿ s n. The mountain of the gods. Méru.

ಅಮರಾವತಿ s. n The abode of the gods.

ಅಮರಿಕೆ. ಅಮರ್ಕೆ k n Fitness, suitableness

ಅಮರು k v i To be closely united, to be linked to 2 to arise, appear. 3, to be fit, to fit. 4, to fall upon, to climb 5 to embrace ಅಮರಿಸು. To

o reprove

ಅಮರ್ಚು (=ಅಮರಿಸು) k. v t To join 2, to apply. 3, to put on 4, to seize 5, to prepare, to perform. ಅಮರ್ಚಿಸು. To cause to join

ಅಮರ್ತ್ಯ s a Immortal. n. A god.

ಅಮರ್ದು (tb of ಅಮೃತ, q. v) n. Ambrosia. ಅಮ್ಮರ್ದುಣಿ. A god. -ಗದಿರ The moon.

ಅಮರ್ಯಾದೆ s. n Disrespect, rudeness, impropriety.

ಅಮರ್ಷ s n. Non-endurance. 2, impatience, passion.

ಅಮಲ್, ಅಮಲು 1. h n. Intoxication, drunkenness -ಆಗು, -ಏರು, -ಹತ್ತು. To be drunk. -ಗಾರ A drunkard.

ಅಮಲ್, ಅಮಲು 2 h. n Business. 2, rule, reign 3, an office. 4, collection of revenue. -ದಾರ. A native revenue collector.

ಅಮಲ s. a Stainless, clean n. Talc -ತೆ, -ತ. Stainlessness.

ಅಮಲಿನ s. a. Stainless

ಅಮಸಾಲು h a Unclaimed, heirless. -ಜಿಂದಿಗೆ. An unclaimed property of a person dying without heirs which reverts to the government.

ಅಮವಾಸೆ. tb of ಅಮಾವಾಸ್ಯೆ, q. v.

ಅಮಳ (tb of ಯಮಲ) n A pair, twin.

ಅಮಾಂಸ s. a. Without flesh; feeble, thin

ಅಮಾತ್ಯ s. n A minister, counsellor.

ಅಮಾನತು h. n. A deposit. charge. 2, suspension.

ಅಮಾನಿ h. n What is in charge of a collector on the part of government in opposition to that which is rented out to tenants of the soil

ಅಮಾನುಷ s. a. Inhuman; monstrous.

ಅಮಾರ್ಗ s. a. Pathless. n. A wrong road. 2, a bad man

ಅಮಾವಾಸೆ, ಅಮಾಸೆ tb of ಅಮಾವಾಸ್ಯೆ.

ಅಮಾವಾಸ್ಯೆ s. n. The first day of the first quarter on which the moon is invisible

ಅಮಿತ s a. Unmeasured, boundless, infinite.

ಅಮಿತ್ರ s n An enemy

ಅಮೀನ h n. A petty revenue officer. 2, the lowest executive officer of a civil court

ಅಮುಕು, ಅಮುಗು, ಅಮುಚು (= ಅದಕು) k. v t To press down.

ಅಮೂಲ್ಯ s a Priceless, precious, inestimable

ಅಮೃಣಾಲ s. n The root of a fragrant grass, Kaskas

ಅಮೃತ (tb. ಅಮರ್ದು, q. v.) s a Immortal. n. Immortality 2, ambrosia, food of the gods. 3 anything sweet, e g. water, milk, juice of sôma 4, quicksilver. 5, a ray. 6, N. of several plants -ಕರ. The moon, a physician. -ತ್ವ Immortality -ಫಲ. The custard-apple. -ಬಳ್ಳಿ The heart-leaved moonseed. ಅಮೃತಾಂಧ. A deity

ಅಮೇಧ್ಯ s a. Impure; unholy. n Excrement, faeces

ಅಮೇಯ s a Immeasurable

ಅಮೋಘ s a. Unfailing, efficacious, productive

ಅಮೋಲಿಕ (tb of ಅಮೌಲ್ಯಕ) a Invaluable, excellent.

ಅಮೌಲ್ಯ s. a. Priceless, excellent, invaluable.

ಅಂಪಕ k n An entertainment given to friends at their departure

ಅಂಬ. =ಅನ್ನುವ, p. p. of ಅನ್ನು, q. v

ಅಂಬಕ s n. An eye.

ಅಂಬಕಳ (tb. of ಅಮ್ಲ) n A kind of pap mixed with buttermilk.

ಅಂಬಟೆ = ಅಮಟೆ, q v.

ಅಂಬರ s n. Clothes, apparel 2, the sky, atmosphere 3, cotton. 4, talc. 5, a perfume, Ambergris. -ಮಣಿ. The sun ರಕ್ತಾಂಬರ A purple cloth

ಅಂಬರೀಷ s. n A frying-pan. 2, the sun. 3, Šiva, Vishnu. 4, war. 5, remorse.

ಅಂಬಲ k n. A public hall.

ಅಂಬಲಿ (*tb of* ಆಮ್ಲ. = ಅಂಬಳ, *q. v.*) *n.* A kind of porridge

ಅಂಬಾ s *n.* The cry of a cow

ಅಂಬಾಡಿಯೆಲೆ k *n* A whitish and fragrant kind of betel leaf

ಅಂಬಾರ h *n.* A heap of thrashed straw -ಖಾನೆ A granary

ಅಂಬಾರಿ h *n* A howdah on an elephant

ಅಂಬಾರೆ k *n* A kind of insect. ಅಂಬಾರುಣ್ಣಿ. An insect infesting cattle

ಅಂಬಿ k *n* A boat -ಗಾರ. = ಅಂಬಿಗ, *q v*

ಅಂಬಿಕಾ, ಅಂಬಿಕೆ s *n* A mother. 2, Durgâ.

ಅಂಬಿಗ, ಅಂಬಿಗಾರ k *n* A boatman

ಅಂಬಿಲ = ಅಂಬಲಿ, *q v*

ಅಂಬು 1 k *n* An arrow -ಗಾರ An archer. ಅಂಬಿನ ಹದ, ಅಂಬಿನ ಹೊದೆ. A quiver ಬಿಲ್ಲಂಬು. A bow and arrow.

ಅಂಬು 2 a. k *v i* To dry, fade

ಅಂಬು 3 s *n* Water -ಚರ Aquatic -ಜ. Water-born a lotus -ಜಮಿತ್ರ The sun -ಜೋದ್ಭವ Brahmâ -ದ, -ಧರ. A cloud -ನಿಧಿ, -ರಾಶಿ The ocean -ವಾಹ A cloud -ಸರಣಿ. The bed of a stream

ಅಂಬುಗರಿಕೆ k *n.* The creeping bent grass *Agrostis stolonifera*

ಅಂಬುಧಿ s. *n.* The ocean.

ಅಂಬೆ 1 (= ಅಂಬಾ) s. *n* A mother. 2, Durgâ

ಅಂಬೆ 2 = ಅಂಬಾ, *q. v*

ಅಂಬೆ 3. = ಆಮ್ಲ. -ಹಳದಿ Scented turmeric

ಅಂಬೆಗಾಲು k. *n* The crawling knees. ಅಂಬೆಗಾಲಾಡು, ಅಂಬೆಗಾಲಿಕ್ಕು, ಅಂಬೆಗಾಲಿಡು. To crawl on hands and knees.

ಅಂಭ, ಅಂಭಸ್ s *n* Water

ಅಂಭೋಜ, ಅಂಭೋಜಾತ, ಅಂಭೋರುಹ s. *n.* A lotus

ಅಂಭೋಧಿ, ಅಂಭೋನಿಧಿ s. *n* The ocean.

ಅಮ್ಮ (*tb of* ಅಂಬೆ) *n* A mother. 2, a respectful title for females (*as* ಅಮ್ಮನವರು). a respectable woman 3, a gr (Durgâ). 5, the smallpox *See* ಚಿಕ್ಕಮ್ಮ, ದೊಡ್ಡಮ್ಮ, ಕಲ್ಲಮ್ಮ ಅಮ್ಮಗಳು Widows ಅಮ್ಮಣ್ಣಿ. An affectionate name for a female; a coward. ಅಮ್ಮನ ಬೇನೆ Cholera

ಅಮ್ಮವ್ಮಾ, ಅಮ್ಮಲಾಲಾ (= ಅವ್ವ, *q v*) *int of pain or weariness* Ah! alas!

ಅಮ್ಮಣ್ಣೆ k *n.* A nipple, teat

ಅಮ್ಮಾಲೆ k *n.* A game of throwing hand-balls in the air

ಅಮ್ಮು a. k *v i* To be able, to wish, desire. *n* Desire.

ಅಮ್ಲ s. *n* Sourness, acidity 2, vinegar.

ಅಮ್ಲಾನ s *n* The globe amaranth. *Gomphrena globosa*

ಅಮ್ಲಿ, ಅಮ್ಲಿಕೆ s. *n* The tamarind tree, *Tamarindus indica.*

ಅಯ್ 1 ಅಯ್ಯ k *n.* Sir. -ಗಳು A schoolmaster.

ಅಯ್ 2 (= ಅಯ್ದು 2) k *a.* Five -ನೂರು. Five hundred. -ಮಡಿ, -ವಡಿ Five fold -ವಣ್ಣ Five colours. -ವತ್ತು Fifty -ಸಾಸಿರ Five thousand. -ಸರ A five fold string (of pearls).

ಅಯನ s. *n* Going. 2, road path 3, half a solar year ಅಯನಿಸು To move as the sun.

ಅಯಸ್ s *n* Iron, steel, metal

ಅಯಾನ s. *a* Not moving; stopping. 2, without a vehicle.

ಅಯಿದು k *a* Five

ಅಯಿನು h *a* Original, principal, prime

ಅಯಿಂದಾ h *ad.* Hereafter; in future

ಅಯಿಬು h *n.* A flaw, fault, defect.

ಅಯಿದೆ (*tb of* ಅವಿಧವಾ) *n* A wife whose husband is alive

ಅಯಿಲು (= ಅಮಲು *q v*) k. *n* Bewilderment, madness

ಅಯಿರಾವತ. = ಐರಾವತ

ಅಯಿವಜು h. *n* Property, wealth, cash, money.

ಅಯುಕ್ತ s. *a* Unfit, unsuitable, impro-

ಅಯುತ f n A myriad.

ಅಯೋಗ್ಯ s a Unfit, unsuitable, unworthy. -ತನ, -ತೆ. Unfitness, disqualification, unworthiness

ಅಯೋಧ್ಯೆ s n Oude, the capital of Râma.

ಅಯ್ಕುಳ್ a. k. n Cold, coldness, frost, snow. 2, the cold season

ಅಯ್ತು (fr ಅಹುದು- ಎ 3) = ಅದೆ k It certainly is, it is

ಅಯ್ದು 1 k v i To go to, to join 2. to approach (ಬರು). 3, to obtain (-ಹೊಂದು) ಅಯ್ದಿಸು To cause to go to, etc ಅಯ್ದೆ. Exceedingly, greatly, then, even

ಅಯ್ದು 2. (=ಅಯಿದು) k a. Five. -ವರೆ Five and a half. -ರಸ Five liquids

ಅಯ್ಯ s n A master, sir 2, a father 3, a Jangama 4, a teacher. -ತನ. The state of being an Ayya or Jangama -ಂಗಾರ An epithet of respect among Śrîvaishnavas cpds. ಅಕ್ಕಯ್ಯ, ಅಣ್ಣಯ್ಯ, ಅಪ್ಪಯ್ಯ, ಅಮ್ಮಯ್ಯ, ಮಾವಯ್ಯ, ಭಾವಯ್ಯ.

ಅಯ್ಯಯ್ಯೋ, ಅಯ್ಯೋ k int of grief: Alas' 2, of surprise Aha'

ಅಯ್ರಾಣಿ f. n A small vessel or vase used at weddings.

ಅಯ್ರು f n A disease of the eye

ಅಯ್ವತ್ತು k see ಅಯ್

ಅಯ್ಸು (=ಅನಿತು, q v) a k. ad. That [much.

ಅರ 1 (=ಅರ್ಗ) k n. A file

ಅರ 2 (=ಅರ 2) k a A half. -ಕಾಪೊತ್ತು The half ರ when written as ೯ -ಕ್ಷಣ Half a moment -ಗಣ್ಣು A purblind eye -ಗಾಯ A slight wound -ಗಾವು. Slight heat -ಗೋಡೆ A low wall. -ಗೋರು Half of the produce of a field -ಚಣ್ಣ Breeches covering the buttocks. -ತಾವು Half a sheet of paper. -ದಲೆ. Half the head. -ಪಾವು. Three rupees' weight -ಮಣ Half a maund -ಮನಸ್ಸು Reluctance. -ಮರೆ Partial screening, want of ... half -ಸೇರು. ...

ಅರ 3. abbrev of ಅರಸು, q v. -ಗಿಣಿ A parrakeet -ನೆಲ್ಲಿ The country gooseberry. -ಮಗ. A king's son -ಮನೆ A palace; a court -ಸ್ಥಾನ A royal council.

ಅರಕ k. n Washing rice 2, the state of broken or injured, as a tile. ಅರಕಂಚಟ್ಟಿ A brass basin.

ಅರಕು h n. Spirit, juice, essence; toddy.

ಅರಕೆ k n The half

ಅರಗು 1. k. n A border, margin. 2, vicinity.

ಅರಗು 2 k v i To decay, to be digested.

ಅರಗು 3. (tb. of ಲಾಕ್ಷೆ) n Gumlac, sealing-wax. ಅರಗಿನ ಕಡ್ಡಿ A stick of lac. ಅರಗಿನ ಮಸಿ, -ಶಾಯಿ A superior ink made from lac, etc ಮುದ್ರೆ- Sealing wax.

ಅರಚನೆ s. n. Disorder.

ಅರಚು (ರ= ಱ) = ಅರಿಚು

ಅರಟೆ k n = ಹರಟೆ. 2, a reel

ಅರಡು (= ವರಡು) k. v i To be extended, etc.

ಅರಣ k. n A nuptial present.

ಅರಣಿ s n. The wood of the Ficus religiosa used for kindling fire by attrition [lizard.

ಅರಣೆ (=ರಾಣೆ) k. n A greenish kind of

ಅರಣ್ಯ s n A wood, forest, wilderness (=ಕಾಡು, ವನ, ಅಡವಿ).

ಅರತ 1. k. n The act of grinding

ಅರತ 2 s a Indifferent to.

ಅರತ್ನಿ s n The elbow. 2, a cubit.

ಅರದ s a Toothless

ಅರದಳ, ಅರದಾಳ, ಅರಿದಳ, ಅರಿದಾಳ (tb. of ಹರಿತಾಳ) n Yellow orpiment.

ಅರದೇಶಿಪರದೇಶಿ s n A mendicant, pilgrim.

ಅರನಾರಿ k n. Paralysis; also -ಜೀನೆ. 2, one-sidedness

ಅರಬು, ಅರಬಿ f n An Arab. -ಸ್ಥಾನ, -ದೇಶ. ...

ಅರಮನೆ (*see* s ಅರ 2) n. A palace, a court. 2, government

ಅರಮಾಯಿಷಿ ಪರಮಾಯಿಷಿ h n A gift of rare value

ಅರಮೆ a. k *ad.* To some extent, here and there. [aha!

ಅರರ s. *int of wonder* Well done!

ಅರಲು, ಅರಳು k v i. To expand, open (*as* flowers) n A flower. -ಅರಲ ಮಾಡು, ಅರಲಿಸು. To cause to blossom. -ಪಡಿಗ, -ವಡಿಗ. A florist

ಅರವ, ಅರವು k. n. Tamil -ಭಾಷೆ. The T language. -ದೇಶ The T country -ಗಿತ್ತಿ A Tamil woman

ಅರವಟಿಕೆ, ಅರವಟಿಗೆ, ಅರವಟ್ಟಿಗೆ, ಅರವೊಟ್ಟಿಗೆ (ರ=ಱ) k. n A shed on the roadside in which water, buttermilk, *etc.* are distributed gratis ಅರವಟ್ಟಿಗ. A of founder an aravarigĕ.

ಅರವತ್ತು (ರ=ಱ) k n Sixty

ಅರವಾಸಿ, ಅರವಾಶಿ *See* s. ಅರ 2.

ಅರವಿಂದ s n. A lotus. -ನೇತ್ರೆ. A lotus-eyed woman -ಬಂಧು, -ಸಖ. The sun.

ಅರವು (ರ=ಱ) k. n Knowledge.

ಅರವೆ (ರ=ಱ) k n Indigestion 2, cloth

ಅರಸ, ಅರಸು (*tb. of* ರಾಜ) n A king, lord. ಅರಸತಿ A queen. -ಧರ್ಮ. A king's duty. -ಗುಣ, -ಮಗ, *etc.* -ತನ. Kingship, royalty. -ಹುಣ್ಣು. A carbuncle.

ಅರಸಿ (*tb of* ರಾಜ್ಞಿ) n. A queen

ಅರಸಿನ, ಅರಸಿಣ (*tb. of* ಹರಿದ್ರಾ) n Turmeric

ಅರಸು (ರ=ಱ) k. v t. To inquire after seek, search n. Research, enquiry

ಅರಸೆಮರ = ಅರಳಿ, q v

ಅರಳ k. n. Amazement, perplexity

ಅರಳಿ (= ಅರಸೆಮರ) k. n. The poplar-leaved fig-tree, *Ficus religiosa.*

ಅರಳು (= ಅರಲು, q. v.) k v i To bloom. n A flower 2, parched grain.

ಅರಳೆ 1 k. n Dressed cotton. 2, a post, pillar.

ಅರಳೆ 2. (= ಅಣಲೆ) k. n. The gall nut T...

ಅರಳೆಲೆ k. n A forehead ornament for young children. 2, a fig leaf.

ಅರಾಜಕ s *a* Anarchical

ಅರಾತಿ s n An enemy, foe

ಅರಾಲ s. *a.* Bent, crooked, curved

ಅರಿ 1 (= ಹರಿ) k v. t To cut or lop off. n Cutting off, gnawing.

ಅರಿ 2 (= ಅರೆ) k v t To grind on a slab. -ಸು To cause to grind

ಅರಿ 3. k. n A mass of unthrashed corn 2, excess in corn measure. 3, a disease of the eye (-ಗಣ್ಣು)

ಅರಿ 4. (ರಿ=ಱಿ) k. v. i & t To learn to know, to know, understand *P ps.* ಅರಿದು, ಅರಿತು. ಅರಿಯದಿರು, ಅರಿಯದೆ ಹೋಗು To be ignorant of. ಅರಿಯದವ >< ಅರಿದವ, ಅರಿತವ ಅರಿಸು To make known, inform.

ಅರಿ 5 s. n. An enemy.

ಅರಿಕೆ, ಅರಿತ, ಅರಿಹ, ಅರಿಹು (ರಿ=ಱಿ) k. n. Knowledge, understanding, information. ಅರಿಕೆ ಮಾಡು To inform

ಅರಿಚು (ರಿ=ಱಿ) a. k. v. i. To bawl, scream [tree

ಅರಿಟಾಳ (*tb. of* ಅರಿಷ್ಟ) n The soapnut

ಅರಿತ್ರ s n An oar, a rudder.

ಅರಿದು a. k. *a* Impossible, inexplicable.

ಅರಿಮೆ (ರಿ=ಱಿ). = ಅರಿಕೆ, q v.

ಅರಿಲ್ (ರ=ಱ) a. k n. A star 2, mud.

ಅರಿವು. = ಅರಿಕೆ, q v

ಅರಿವೆ, ಅರಿವಿ (ರಿ=ಱಿ) = ಅರವೆ.

ಅರಿಷ್ಟ s *a* Unhurt n Good or bad luck, misfortune 2, buttermilk 3, the neem tree 4, the soap-nut tree, *Sapindus trifoliatus.* ಕೆಟ್ಟರಿಷ್ಟ. A very heavy calamity.

ಅರಿಸಮಾಸ s. n An unsuitable composition of words.

ಅರಿಸಿನ. = ಅರಸಿನ, q. v.

ಅರಿಸು k v. t. To cause to cut off 2, to cause to grind 3 (ರಿ=ಱಿ) to in-

ಅರಿಸೆ (*tb. of* ಅರ್ಶಸ್) *n.* Piles.

ಅರು 1 (ರು=ಱು) = ಆರು k *a* Six. -ಪಡಿ. Six-fold -ವತ್ತು. Sixty.

ಅರು 2 (ರು=ಱು) a. k. *v. i* To be cut asunder; to cease.

ಅರುಗು = ಅರಗು 1, *q v.*

ಅರುಚಿ s. *n* Aversion, dislike; disgust

ಅರುಚು = ಅರಿಚು, *q v*

ಅರುಣ s *a.* Yellow, ruddy. *n* Aruna, the dawn 2, a ray -ಸಾರಥಿ The sun ಅರುಣೋದಯ Sunrise.

ಅರುಂಧತಿ s *n.* N of the wife of Vasishtha. 2, N. of a star -ನಾಥ Vasishtha

ಅರುಪು (ರ=ಱ,) *see s* ಅರಿ 4) a k *v. t.* To make known

ಅರುಬುತ. *tb. of* ಅದ್ಭುತ, *q. v.*

ಅರುಮೆ a k *n.* Love, affection

ಅರುಂಬು a k. *n* A flower-bud.

ಅರುಲು (ರು=ಱು) k *n.* Mud -ಗದ್ದೆ A muddy paddy-field

ಅರುಲುಮರುಲು, ಅರುಳುಮರುಳು k. *n.* Bewilderment, dotage.

ಅರುವು (ರು=ಱು.=ಅರಿಕೆ) k *n.* Knowledge. -ಮರುವು Silliness, dotage

ಅರುಹು (ರ=ಱ) k. *v. t* To make known. *n.* Knowledge.

ಅರೂಪ s *a* Formless; ugly.

ಅರೆ 1 k *v t* To grind, pulverize 2, (ರೆ=ಱೆ) to strike, beat. *n.* The plant *Grislea tomentosa.* 2, a. k stone, rock 3, the back. -ಯಟ್ಟು To pursue.

ಅರೆ 2 (= ಅರ *q v*) k *n* A half 2, a little -ಗಡಿ To cut into halves. -ಗಂಟು. A loose knot of hair -ಗುಂಡಿಗೆ. Half-heartedness, timidity. -ಗೆಲಸ Unfinished work -ದೆರೆ. To open half. -ನುಡಿ Indistinct utterance -ನೋಟ A leer, side glance. -ಪಾಲು. Half a part. -ಬೇವು. The Persian lilac -ಬಿರಿ To be half opened, *as* a flower. -ಮರುಳ. A half-mad man. -ಮನೆ. Hesitation, doubt. -ಮೈ Half the body -ಮಾದಲು ಗಿಡ, -ಮಾವಳದ ಗಿಡ. A spinous shrub, *Randia dumetorum.* -[illegible] To leave unfinished. -[illegible]. The half moon

ಅರೋಗ s. *n.* Health ಅರೋಗಿ A healthy person

ಅರೋಚಕ, ಅರೋಚಿಕೆ s. *n.* Want of appetite, disgust, indigestion. *a.* Insipid

ಅರ್ಕ s *n* Radiance 2, the sun 3, crystal. 4, Indra 5, swallow wort, *Calotropis gigantea.* -ವಾರ Sunday

ಅರ್ಕೆ k *n.* Weeping, lamentation.

ಅರ್ಗಲ, ಅರ್ಗಲೆ (*tb* ಅಗಳಿ) s. *n* An impediment, a bolt, lock.

ಅರ್ಗಳ a k *n.* Greatness, a great man

ಅರ್ಘ s. *n.* Price, cost 2, an offering to gods, *etc.*

ಅರ್ಘ್ಯ s *a* Valuable; venerable *n* A reverential offering to gods or venerable men.

ಅರ್ಚ s. *n* Invocation, worship. -ಕ. A worshipper. -ನೆ Worship, homage ಅರ್ಚಿಸು To worship

ಅರ್ಚಿಸ್ s. *n.* Flame. 2, shine, lustre

ಅರ್ಚು (= ಅರಿಚು, *q v*) k. *v. i.* To cry aloud.

ಅರ್ಜಿ, (ಅರ್ಜು) h. *n* A written petition. -ಬರೆಯು, -ಹಾಕು, -ಕೊಡು, -ಮಾಡು, *etc.* To petition -ದಾರ A petitioner.

ಅರ್ಜಿಸು s. *v. t.* To acquire, gain.

ಅರ್ಜುನ s *a* White *n* Silver. 2, the tree *Terminalia arjuna.* 3, the son of Indra and Kuntī.

ಅರ್ಣ s *a.* Moving *n.* Water. -ವ. The ocean

ಅರ್ತಿ k. *n* Love, desire. 2, pleasure, fun. -ಗೆಡಿಸು To spoil a wish -ಕಾರ. A man of pleasure. -ಸು To be pleased with

ಅರ್ತೊಲೆ (*fr* ಅರೆ-ತೊಲೆ) k *n* The weight of half a rupee

ಅರ್ಥ s *n* Aim, purpose, cause, reason 2, meaning. 3, advantage, utility. 4, a request. 5, manner, sort. 6, wealth -ಕಾರಿ Useful -ಕೊಡು. To mean; to confer riches -ನಿಶ್ಚಯ. Ascertainment. -ವಂತ A man of property. -ವಾದ Explanatory remark.

-ವಿಸು To explain expound -ಶಾಸ್ತ್ರ The science of polity -ಶ್ಲೇಷ. Pun. -ಹೀನ Meaningless, poor, failing -ಹೇಳು. To interpret. ಅರ್ಥಾಂತರ A different meaning. ಅರ್ಥಾಪತ್ತಿ. An inference

ಅರ್ಥಿ s. *a* Desiring. *n* A beggar. 2, a plaintiff -ತ್ವ Entreaty. -ಸು. To desire, to ask for

ಅರ್ಧ s *a* Half, halved. *n* A half. -ಆಣೆ Half an Anna -ಗೋಳ A hemisphere. -ಚಂದ್ರ A crescent -ದೃಷ್ಟಿ Purblind -ರಾತ್ರಿ Midnight. -ವಿರಾಮ A semicolon. ಅರ್ಧಾಂಗ Half the body -ಯಿಸು, ಅರ್ಧಿಸು. To halve.

ಅರ್ನ (=ಅರ) k. *n* A file

ಅರ್ನೂರು, = ಅರುನೂರು, *q v*

ಅರ್ಪಣ s *n* Placing upon 2, offering, delivering consigning. ಅರ್ಪಿಸು To offer, deliver consign

ಅರ್ಬಿ a. k *n*. A torrent checked in its course ಅರ್ಬಿಸು To roar

ಅರ್ಬು k. *n* Crying ಅರ್ಬಾಟ Crying aloud.

ಅರ್ಬುದ s *n* A serpent 2 a hundred millions. 3, swelling, polypus.

ಅರ್ಭಕ s *a*. Small, weak *n* A child, the young of any animal.

ಅರ್ಬು (=ಅರುಬು, *q v*) k. *n*. Mud, clay.

ಅರ್ವ s *a* Vile, low. *n*. A horse. -ತಿ. A mare

ಅರ್ವತ್ತು. *See* s. ಅರು.

ಅರ್ಶಸ್ s *n*. Piles

ಅರ್ಹ s. *a* Deserving, worthy. 2, proper, fit. *n* A Jaina saint. -ಣೆ Worship -ತ್ Venerable, a Jaina saint.

ಅಲ್ a k *n* That place, direction, *as in* ಅತ್ತಲ್ (ಅತ್ತ-ಅಲ್), ಎತ್ತಲ್ (ಎತ್ತ-ಅಲ್). 2 state or condition, in verbal nouns *as* ಉಣಲ್, ಒಯ್ಯಲ್. *v i* To be fit, right or sufficient

ಅಲ (=ಅಲಾ) k *int. of assent* Indeed. *of*

ಅಲಕ s *n* A curl, hair-lock

ಅಲಕಾಪುರ s *n*. Kubêra's residence.

ಅಲಕು, = ಅಲುಗು, ಒಲುಗು, *q v*

ಅಲಕ್ತಕ s. *n* Red lac

ಅಲಕ್ಷಣ s. *n* An inauspicious sign *a*. Unfortunate. ಅಲಕ್ಷಿತ Unseen, unobserved.

ಅಲಕ್ಷಿಸು s *v. t* To disregard, slight

ಅಲಕ್ಷ್ಯ s *n* Disregard, contempt. *a* Insignificant

ಅಲಗರ್ದ s *n* A water-snake

ಅಲಗು (= ಅಲಕು) k *v. i* To move about, to be agitated *n* The blade of a knife, sword, *etc*

ಅಲಘು s. *a* Not light, weighty, solemn

ಅಲಂಕರಣ s *n*. Adorning

ಅಲಂಕರಿಸು s. *v. t*. To ornament, decorate

ಅಲಂಕಾರ s. *n* Ornament. 2, elegance. 3 a rhetorical expression. -ಶಾಸ್ತ್ರ. A text-book of rhetoric. -ಮಾಡು = ಅಲಂಕರಿಸು, *q v* ಅಲಂಕೃತ Ornamented.

ಅಲಂಗ f *n* A rampart

ಅಲಂಘ್ಯ s. *a* Insurmountable, inviolable

ಅಲತಗೆ, ಅಲತಿಕೆ *(tb. of* ಅಲಕ್ತಕ*)* *n* Lac, used as red ink

ಅಲಪು, ಅಲಪಟೆ k. *n*. Weariness, fatigue

ಅಲಬು k. *n* N of different species of *Alysicarpus* (casual

ಅಲಭ್ಯ s *a* Unattainable. 2, rare,

ಅಲಂಪು a. k *n* Beauty, ornament, pleasure

ಅಲರು (= ಅರಲು, *q v*) k *v i* To spread, to open blossom, bloom. *P p*. ಅಲರ್ದು. *n* A flower bloom ಅಲರ್ಗಣ್ಣು A flower-like eye. -ತೋರಣ A festoon of flowers -ವಕ್ಕಿ The large black bee ಅಲರ್ವಾಸ. A bed of flowers -ಬಳ್ಳಿ. A flowering creeper ಅಲರಿಸು, ಅಲರ್ಚು. To cause to blossom

[illegible] h. *n* Pay given before-

ಅಲವಿಕೆ, ಅಲವು (= ಅಲಪು) k n Fatigue, weariness

ಅಲಸ s a. Lazy, idle, weary, faint -ತ್ವ Idleness.

ಅಲಸಂದಿ, ಅಲಸಂದಿಗೆ k. n A species of pulse, *Vigna catjang*

ಅಲಸಿಕೆ, ಅಲಸು k n Fatigue, idleness. -ಆಗು, -ಪಡು. To be tired

ಅಲಸು k v i To become weary, tired, vexed. v. t To shake, agitate, as in water. n. Weariness, idleness -ಗಾರ A lazy man.

ಅಲಾತ s. n A fire brand 2, a rope, cord

ಅಲಾಬು h n. Mahammadans' Moharam festival. 2, the bottle-gourd

ಅಲಾಯಿದ, ಅಲಾಹಿದ h. a. Distinct, apart.

ಅಲಾಯಿಬಲಾಯಿ h. n An affectionate greeting, embrace.

ಅಲಿ (= ಅಲ್ಲಿ) k ad. There, as ತುಪ್ಪದಲಿ, ಸಭೆಯಲಿ, ನಿಮ್ಮಲಿ. v i = ಅಲಿಂ. Must, may. 2, pr. imper as ಆಗಲಿ, ಇರಲಿ, ಉಣ್ಣಲಿ, ತಕ್ಕೊಳ್ಳಲಿ, ತರಲಿ, ಸಾರಲಿ.

ಅಲಿಕ s n The forehead

ಅಲಿಗಿನ ಗಿಡ k n An aquatic plant, *Aeshynomene aspera.*

ಅಲಿಂಗ s a. Genderless (g).

ಅಲಿಂದ s n. A terrace before a house-door.

ಅಲುಕು, ಅಲುಗು, ಅಲುಂಗು k v i To be agitated, shaky or loose, to shake ಅಲುಗಾಡು To shake, tremble ಅಲುಕಿಸು, ಅಲಂಗಿಸು v. t. To skake

ಅಲುಗೋಜಿ h n A whistle, pipe.

ಅಲುಬು a. k. v t. To wash with water

ಅಲೆ k v i To move about, shake. 2, to roam, wander; to dangle v t To shake n A wave, billow

ಅಲೇಖ s n. A blank book 2, a deity.

ಅಲೇಮಾನಿ f. n. Allemagne, Germany, Europe -ಕತ್ತಿ. A dragoon sword. -ತುರುಪು A dragoon troop.

ಅಲೊಪಂ, ಅಲೊ... [illegible]
ಬರಲೊಪಂ, ಪ್ರ... [illegible]

ಅಲೋಕ s n. Not the world, the spiritual world

ಅಲೌಕಿಕ s. a Not worldly, not secular, unusual. -ತನ Unworldliness, unusualness

ಅಲ್ಕಾಬು h n A title, titles, honors

ಅಲ್ಪ s. a. Small, little, insignificant, mean. -ತನ Smallness. -ದಿನ A few days. -ಪ್ರಾಣ An unaspirated letter. -ಬುದ್ಧಿ. Weak-mindedness -ಮತಿ Weak-minded, stupid -ವೃಷ್ಟಿ. Small rain. -ಸ್ವಲ್ಪ. Rather little ಅಲ್ಪಾಯುಷ್ಯ A short life ಅಲ್ಪಿಷ್ಟ Very small

ಅಲ್ಮೈರ f. n. An almira, a chest of drawers, wardrobe.

ಅಲ್ಲ 1. (fr. ಅಲ್ No. 2, q v) k ad Not, no, its opposite is ಹೌದು -ಗಳೆ. To reject, deny. ಅಲ್ಲವೆ int Is it not? ಅಲ್ಲದ Being not good, fit -ವನು A useless or bad man ಅಲ್ಲದೆ Besides, except, unless ಇದಲ್ಲದೆ. Moreover ಅಲ್ಲೆನ್ನು. To deny.

ಅಲ್ಲ 2. k. n Green ginger.

ಅಲ್ಲಕಲ್ಲೋಲ (= ಅಲ್ಲೋಲಕಲ್ಲೋಲ) k n. Great agitation (as of water or mind), confusion, disorder, tumult.

ಅಲ್ಲಗಳೆ k v. t To deny, reject, refuse.

ಅಲ್ಲಣೆ, ಅಲ್ಲಣೆಗೆ a k n. Mirth, merry-making, jest.

ಅಲ್ಲರ k n. Separation of lovers or friends.

ಅಲ್ಲರಿ k. n. Trouble, disturbance, harass

ಅಲ್ಲಾಟ, ಅಲ್ಲಾಡಿಕೆ k n Moving about

ಅಲ್ಲಾಡು k. v. i To move, shake, swing, to be loose. ಅಲ್ಲಾಡಿಸು v. t. To shake, move about.

ಅಲ್ಲಿ (= ಅಲಿ) k ad There, in that place -ಹೋಗು. Go there ಅಲ್ಲಲ್ಲಿ. Here and there ಅಲ್ಲಿಗಲ್ಲಿಗೆ Here and there. -ತನಕ. So far as that place, till then 2, used to form the loc., as ಮನೆಯಲ್ಲಿ, etc 3, also added to rel part, as [illegible]

ಅಲ್ಲು k. *v. t* To join, knit, plait, braid.

ಅಲ್ಲೋಲಕಲ್ಲೋಲ = ಅಲ್ಲಕಲ್ಲೋಲ, *q v*.

ಅವ1, ಅವನು k *pro*. He, that man, *f*. ಅವಳು, *pl* ಅವರು. ಅವರಿಬ್ಬರು. Both of them

ಅವ2 s. *ad* Off, away, down *(implying disrespect)*

ಅವಕಾಶ s *n* Place, opportunity, leisure, interval.

ಅವಕೃಪೆ s. *n* Displeasure disfavour

ಅವಕ್ರ s. *a* Not crooked, upright, straight

ಅವಗಡ f *n*. An obstruction; jeopardy. 2, inaccessibility 3, monstrosity. 4, impossibility ಅವಗಡಿಸು. To depress, slight, suppress 2, to hurry, hasten, become impetuous

ಅವಗಣಿತ s *a*. Disregarded, despised

ಅವಗತ s. *a* Gone near. 2, known, understood ಅವಗತಿ Knowledge.

ಅವಗಮನ s *n*. Understanding, comprehension

ಅವಗಾಹ, ಅವಗಾಹನ s *n*. Diving into, bathing. 2, comprehension. ಅವಗಾಹಿಸು, ಅವಗಹಿಸು. To dive into, to enter into, to comprehend

ಅವಗುಣ s. *n*. A vice, an evil effect

ಅವಗ್ರಹ, ಅವಗ್ರಾಹ s. *n* Separation. 2, obstacle 3, drought ಅವಗ್ರಹಿಸು To lay hold on, attain

ಅವಘಾತ s *n* Striking, killing 2, a violent blow

ಅವಚು (= ಅಗಚು, ಅದಕು) k. *v. t* To press, to confine, embrace. 2, to hide

ಅವಚ್ಛಿನ್ನ s *a* Cut off, broken. 2, predicated

ಅವಚ್ಛೇದ s *n* Any thing cut off, portion. 2, distinction. 3 discrimination.

ಅವಜ್ಞತೆ s. *n*. Negligence

ಅವಜ್ಞೆ s. *n* Disregard, disrespect, contempt

ಅವತಂಸ s. *n* A garland of flowers 2.

ಅವತರಣ s. *n*. Descending 2, annotation ಅವತರಣಿಕೆ = ಅವತಾರಿಕೆ.

ಅವತರಿಸು s. *v. i*. To descend, to become incarnate

ಅವತಾರ s *n* Descent 2, incarnation -ಎತ್ತು, -ತಕ್ಕೊಳ್ಳು To become incarnate

ಅವತಾರಿಕೆ s. *n*. A preamble or preface

ಅವತೆ *tb. of* ಅವಸ್ಥೆ, *q. v*.

ಅವದಶೆ s *n* Misfortune

ಅವದಾತ s. *a*. White 2, pure; beautiful

ಅವದಾನ s *n* A great act, achievement.

ಅವದೂರು = ಅಪದೂರು, *q v*.

ಅವದ್ಯ s *a* Low, inferior; disagreeable

ಅವಧರಿಸು s *v. t* To think upon, listen to

ಅವಧಾನ s *n* Attention; care, devotion. ಅವಧಾನಿ Attentive, careful, a title. ಅವಧಾನಿಸು To mind, pay attention.

ಅವಧಾರಣ (-ಣೆ) s. *n*. Affirmation, emphasis. ಅವಧಾರಿಸು To ascertain.

ಅವಧಿ s. *n*. A limit, period, time 2, opportunity. 3, engagement. 4 extremity; misfortune

ಅವಧೂತ s. *a* Shaken off, rejected, separated from worldliness *n* A virakta.

ಅವಧ್ಯ s. *a*. Inviolable.

ಅವನ s *n*. Favour 2, joy. 3, satisfaction -ತಿ. Prostration.

ಅವನಿ s. *n*. The earth. -ಜೆ, -ಸುತೆ Sîtâ -ಧರ A mountain -ಪ, -ಪತಿ, -ಪಾಲಕ, ಅವನೀಶ A king -ರುಹ A tree.

ಅವಪಥ್ಯ s. *n* An error in diet.

ಅವಭೃಥ s. *a* Removing. *n*. Purification by bathing, *as* after sacrifice or marriage

ಅವಮತಿ s. *n* Dislike, disregard.

ಅವಮನ್ನಣೆ (*tb. of* ಅವಮಾನನೆ). = ಅವಮರ್ಯಾದೆ

ಅವಮರ್ಯಾದೆ s *n* Incivility, disrespect.

ಅವಮಾನ (= ಅಪಮಾನ) s *n* Disrespect, dishonour. -ಮಾಡು. -ಪಡಿಸು To treat

ಅವಯವ s. n A limb, member, part. -ಸಂಬಂಧ The relation of membership

ಅವಯೋಗ s n An inauspicious omen

ಅವರ 1 s a Inferior, low; posterior, following. -ಜ. A younger brother.

ಅವರ 2. k pro Their

ಅವರೂಪಿತ s. a. Misshapen, deformed.

ಅವರೆ (tb. of ಆಮರೆ) n. A species of pulse, *Phaseolus radiatus.*

ಅವರೋಧ s. n. Obstruction 2, seraglio of a palace.

ಅವರೋಹ s n. A shoot of a plant, a pendent branch. 2, the climbing of a creeper

ಅವರ್ಗ s. n A non-class. a Unclassified ಅವರ್ಗೀಯ Not belonging to the classified consonants (g).

ಅವರ್ಜ f. n. A day book, ledger.

ಅವರ್ಷಣ s n. Drought.

ಅವಲಕ್ಕಿ k. n Rice scalded, dried, fried, and flattened by beating it in a mortar.

ಅವಲಕ್ಷಣ s n An unlucky sign.

ಅವಲಗ್ನ s. a. Hanging down n. The waist

ಅವಲಂಬ, ಅವಲಂಬನೆ s. n. Resting on, dependence, support, a prop, stay ಅವಲಂಬಿಸು. v. t To hang on; to depend on. ಅವಲಂಬಿತ. Supported.

ಅವಲೀಲೆ s n Sport, play. ad Easily, readily

ಅವಲು k n. Pounding in a mortar; cf ಅವಲಕ್ಕಿ.

ಅವಲೋಕ, ಅವಲೋಕನ s. n. Seeing, looking 2, sight (ನೋಟ). 3 observation ಅವಲೋಕಿಸು To look at (ನೋಡು)

ಅವಶ s. a. Uncontrolled. 2, necessary

ಅವಶಕುನ, = ಅಪಶಕುನ, q v

ಅವಶಾತ್ (fr ಅವಶ) ad. Unawares, suddenly

ಅವಶಿಷ್ಟ s a. Left, remaining n Remainder.

ಅವಶ್ಯ s a Inevitable. n Necessity, urgency. ad Necessarily certainly. -ಬೀಳು To become necessary

ಅವಷ್ಟಂಭ s. n. Relying on 2, self-confidence. 3, a pillar ಅವಷ್ಟಂಭಿಸು. To lean upon.

ಅವಸರ s n Occasion, opportunity 2, haste, speed, urgency, hurry. -ಪಡಬೇಡ Don't be in a hurry. ಕಟ್ಟವಸರ Great hurry ಅವಸರಿಸು To make haste, be eager.

ಅವಸಾನ s n Conclusion, termination, end; death; limit

ಅವಸಾಯ s n. Conclusion, certainty. 2, remainder

ಅವಸ್ಥೆ s n State, condition (as ಬಾಲ್ಯಾವಸ್ಥೆ, childhood; ಯೌವನಾವಸ್ಥೆ, manhood, ವೃದ್ಧಾವಸ್ಥೆ, old age) 3, trouble, strait. -ಬೀಳು To come into troubles.

ಅವಹೇಲ, ಅವಹೇಲನ s n Disrespect, contempt.

ಅವಳಿ, (tb of ಯಮಲಿ) ಅವಳಿಜವಳಿ n. A pair. -ಮಕ್ಕಳು Twins

ಅವಳು k. pro. She

ಅವಾಕ್ಸ್ವರ s n. A mispronunciation

ಅವಾಚಿ s n. The south.

ಅವಾಚ್ಯ s a Improper to be uttered, obscene.

ಅವಾಜು f n. Voice, sound; report.

ಅವಾಂತರ s. a. Intermediate. n. Incursion, havoc.

ಅವಾಯಿ f n. A report or rumour. 2, bustle, alarm

ಅವಾರ s n The near bank of a river.

ಅವಿ 1. k v. t To hide, conceal 2, (= ಅಳಿ) v. i To rot, perish; to go out, be extinguished

ಅವಿ 2 s. n A sheep 2, the sun. 3, a mountain

ಅವಿಕಲ s a. Perfect, entire. 2, consistent.

ಅವಿಘ್ನ s. a. Unhindered. n Safety.

ಅವಿಚಾರ, ಅವಿಚಾರಣೆ s. n. Inconsideration, inadvertance, promptitude ಅವಿಚಾರಿ. Inconsiderate, an indiscriminate person [illegible] Prejudice

[illegible] s. a. Unshaken, unmoved

ಅವಿಚು (= ಅವಿಸು, ಅವುಚು) k. v. t. To hide, conceal

ಅವಿಚ್ಛಿನ್ನ, ಅವಿಚ್ಛೇದ s. a. Unseparated, undivided; entire, incessant

ಅವಿದ್ಯ s. a. Unwise, foolish. ಅವಿದ್ಯೆ n. Ignorance. 2, illusion

ಅವಿಧಿ s. n. Irregularity. 2, misfortune, trouble

ಅವಿಧೇಯ s. a. Disobedient. -ತ್ವ Disobedience.

ಅವಿಭಕ್ತ s. a. Undivided, joint.

ಅವಿಭಾಗ s. a. Undivided. n. Undivided condition

ಅವಿಮುಕ್ತ s. a. Unloosed. n. N. of a tîrtha near Benares

ಅವಿರಲ, ಅವಿರಳ s. a. Close, thick, compact. 2, not rare

ಅವಿರುದ್ಧ s. a. Unobstructed, proper, consistent with

ಅವಿಲಂಬ, ಅವಿಲಂಬನ s. a. Not delaying, quick

ಅವಿವೇಕ s. n. Want of discrimination; ignorance, indiscretion. ಅವಿವೇಕಿ Inconsiderate, short-sighted

ಅವಿಶೇಷ s. a. Uniform, alike. n. Uniformity, equability.

ಅವಿಶ್ವಾಸ s. n. Distrust, unbelief (= ಅಪನಂಬುಗೆ, q. v.). ಅವಿಶ್ವಾಸಿ An unbeliever, infidel.

ಅವಿಸು = ಅವಿಚು

ಅವಿಹಿತ s. a. Unprescribed. 2, improper

ಅವೀರೆ s. n. A woman who has neither husband nor son

ಅವು, ಅವುಗಳು k. pro. They; pl. of ಅದು

ಅವುಕು, ಅವುಗು, ಅವುಂಕು (= ಅವಕು, ಅವಚು.) k. v. t. To press, squeeze. ಅವುಕಿಸು. To cause to press, etc.

ಅವುಚು. = ಅವಿಚು. 2, to hold firmly.

ಅವುಡಲ, ಅವುಡಲು (tb. of ಆಮಂಡ) n. The castor-oil plant, *Ricinus communis*.

ಅವುಡು k. v. i. To chew, champ. n. The jaw. 2, the lower lip

ಅ[illegible] (= [illegible]) k. n. An invitation to [illegible]

ಅವುತೆ k. n. A coat of mail.

ಅವೆ k. pl. of ಅದೆ. (They) are. *Cpds.* ಆಗುತ್ತವೆ, ಕಾಣುತ್ತವೆ, *etc.*

ಅವೇದ್ಯ s. a. Unascertainable

ಅವೈದಿಕ s. a. Not vêdic. n. A man not versed in the vêda

ಅವ್ಯಕ್ತ s. a. Indistinct, imperceptible. 2, inarticulate. n. The soul.

ಅವ್ಯಥೆ s. n. Ease, happiness (= ಸುಖ)

ಅವ್ಯಯ s. a. Unchangeable, imperishable. n. An indeclinable word, a particle. 2, heaven. -ಕ್ರಿಯಾಪದ. A form of verb used for all genders, numbers, and tenses.

ಅವ್ಯವಸ್ಥೆ s. n. Disorder, confusion

ಅವ್ಯವಹಿತ s. a. Adjoining, contiguous. -ಪೂರ್ವಕಾಲ The time just past.

ಅವ್ಯಾಪಾರ s. n. Recess from work

ಅವ್ಯಾಪ್ಯ s. a. Peculiar. 2, not pervading

ಅವ್ವ, ಅವ್ವೆ (tb. of ಅಂಬೆ) n. A mother. 2, a feminine title of respect and love. 3, an elderly woman. ಅವ್ವವ್ವಚ್ಚಿಯಾಟ. A kind of children's sport.

ಅವ್ವವ್ವ. = ಅಮ್ಮಮ್ಮ, q. v.

ಅವ್ವಳಿಸು a. k. v. i. To jump up or upon

ಅವ್ವಾ k. Imitation of the note of the cuckoo

ಅಶಕ್ತ s. a. Unable, incompetent; weak. -ತನ, -ತೆ, ಅಶಕ್ತಿ Inability, weakness

ಅಶಕ್ಯ s. a. Impossible.

ಅಶನ s. n. Eating. 2, food

ಅಶನಾರ್ಥ s. n. Maintenance, ration.

ಅಶನಾರ್ಥಿ s. n. One who is desirous of or asks for food

ಅಶರೀರ s. a. Bodiless. n. The sky. 2, Kâma. -ವಾಕ್ಯ, -ವಾಣಿ An oracle voice from heaven.

ಅಶಾಸ್ತ್ರ, ಅಶಾಸ್ತ್ರೀಯ s. a. Unscriptural, heterodox

ಅಶಿಕ್ಷಿತ s. a. Untrained, unlearnt.

ಅಶುಚಿ s. *a* Impure. *n* Impurity, *also* -ತ್ವ [Impurity.

ಅಶುದ್ಧ s *a* Impure, incorrect ಅಶುದ್ಧಿ

ಅಶುಭ s. *a* Inauspicious *n*. Ill-luck.

ಅಶೇಷ s. *a*. Without remainder, entire. 2, infinite, endless

ಅಶೋಕ s *a* Sorrowless. *n* A deity 2 the tree *Jonesia asoka*.

ಅಶೋಧಿತ s *a* Unpurified, unrevised, unrefined.

ಅಶೋಭಿತ s *a*. Not beautiful [ness.

ಅಶೋಭೆ s *n* Absence of beauty, comeli-

ಅಶೌಚ s *n* Impurity.

ಅಶ್ಮ s *n*. A stone. 2 a cloud. -ಕಾರಕ. A stone mason -ಗರ್ಭ An emerald. -ರಿ The disease of the gravel -ಸಾರ. Iron.

ಅಶ್ಮಾರೋಪಣ s. *n* A ceremony at marriages.

ಅಶ್ರದ್ಧೆ s. *n*. Unbelief, distrust 2, dislike.

ಅಶ್ರಾಂತ s. *a*. Unwearied, continual

ಅಶ್ರು s. *n* A tear

ಅಶ್ರುತ s. *a* Unheard; inaudible

ಅಶ್ಲೀಲ s *a*. Ugly, vulgar

ಅಶ್ವ s *n*. A horse. -ಗಂಧ, -ಗಂಧಿ. The plant *Physalis flexuosa*. -ತರ A mule -ಪಾಲ A groom -ಮೇಧ. The horse-sacrifice -ರಥ A carriage drawn by horses -ರಾಜ. A royal horse. -ಲಕ್ಷ್ಮೀ Richness in horses -ವೈದ್ಯ A veterinary surgeon. -ಶಾಲೆ A stable ಅಶ್ವಾರೋಹ. A horseman. ಅಶ್ವೆ. A mare

ಅಶ್ವತ್ಥ s. *n*. The holy fig-tree *Ficus religiosa*

ಅಶ್ವತ್ಥಾಮ s. *n*. N of Drôna's son.

ಅಶ್ವಿನಿ s. *n*. A goddess, mother of the twin sons. 2, the first of the 28 nakshatras [rank

ಅಷರಾಫ್ h. *n*. Noblemen, persons of

ಅಷ್ಟ s. *a* Eight. -ಕ. Eightfold. -ಕಷ್ಟ The eight troubles, much trouble -ಕೋಣ, -ದಲ An oc... ...n. -ಗಂಧ. The eight perfumes. -ತಾಳ A mode of beating time in music. -ದಿಕ್ಕು, -ದಿಶ್ The eight cardinal points of the compass. -ಪದ N. of a Kannada metre, N of a poem -ಪಾದ Spider -ಭಾಗ್ಯ. The eight requisites to the regal state, *as* ರಾಜ್ಯ, ಭಂಡಾರ, ಸೈನ್ಯ, ಆನೆ, ಕುದುರೆ, ಛತ್ರ, ಚಾಮರ, ಆಂದೋಲನ -ಭೋಗ The eight pleasures, *as* ಮನೆ, ವಸ್ತ್ರ, ಆಭರಣ, *etc* -ಮ The eighth -ಮದ The eight kinds of pride, viz of ಅನ್ನ, ಅರ್ಥ, ವಿದ್ಯೆ, ಕುಲ, ರೂಪ, *etc* -ಮೂರ್ತಿ Eight-formed: Siva. -ವಸು Eight demigods, *as*: ಆಪ, ಧ್ರುವ, ಸೋಮ, ಅನಿಲ, ಅನಲ, *etc* -ವಿಧಪೂಜೆ. Worship of an idol with eight things ಗಂಧ, ದೀಪ, ಧೂಪ, *etc*. -ವಿವಾಹ The eight kinds of marriage. ಅಷ್ಟಾಂಗ Eight parts of the body for performing obeisance *as:* hands, breast, forehead, eyes, throat and middle of the back ಅಷ್ಟಾಂಗಯೋಗ. The eight stations of yôga, *as* ಯಮ, ನಿಯಮ, ಆಸನ, ಪ್ರಾಣಾಯಾಮ, ಪ್ರತ್ಯಾಹಾರ, ಧಾರಣ, ಧ್ಯಾನ, ಸಮಾಧಿ

ಅಷ್ಟಮಿ s. *n* The eighth lunar day of either fortnight

ಅಷ್ಟಾರ್ಚನೆ s. *n* Eight daily observances to the household gods, *as* ಸ್ನಾನ, ವಸ್ತ್ರಾಭರಣ, ಗಂಧ, ಅಕ್ಷತೆ, ಪುಷ್ಪ, ಧೂಪ, ದೀಪ, ನೈವೇದ್ಯ

ಅಷ್ಟಾದಶ s *a* Eighteen -ಜಾತಿ. Eighteen castes -ಪರ್ವ Eighteen books of Mahâbhârata. -ಪುರಾಣ. The eighteen Purânas. ಅಷ್ಟಾಪದ. A spider ಅಷ್ಟಾವಕ್ರ Greatly deformed, ugly, N. of a saint ಅಷ್ಟಾವಿಧಾನ Eight kinds of service to an idol after the pûjĕ.

ಅಷ್ಟು k. *n*. That measure *pro*. That much so much ಅಷ್ಟರೊಳಗೆ, ಅಷ್ಟರೊಳು. Meanwhile ಅಷ್ಟರು So many persons ಆದಷ್ಟು, ಹೇಳಿದಷ್ಟು, ಎರಡಷ್ಟು, *etc*. ಅಷ್ಟೇ. Even that much. -ಒಂದು, ಅಷ್ಟೊಂದು At all events, a little. ಅಷ್ಟೋತ್ತರಶತಕ One hundred and eight

ಅಷ್ಠಿ s. *n* Seed, a kernel, stone.

...a k. *n* Slenderness weakness. 2 fitness; order; strength -ಗಲ

...

ದಸ. An energetic man. -ಗೊರೆ, -ವಳಿ Strength to fail, be exhausted -ವಸ Haste, speed

ಅಸಂಶಯು s n Doubtlessness, certainty.

ಅಸಂಸ್ಕಾರ s. n. The state of being uninitiated.

ಅಸಂಹ್ಯ tb. of ಅಸಹ್ಯ

ಅಸಂಹಿಸು = ಅಸಹಿಸು, q v

ಅಸಗ k. n A washerman 2, N. of a Kannada author

ಅಸಂಖ್ಯ ಅಸಂಖ್ಯಾತ, ಅಸಂಖ್ಯೇಯು s a. Innumerable.

ಅಸಂಗತಿ s. n Non-attachment 2, impropriety, incongruity a Not attached.

ಅಸಂಗತ s a. Unassociated 2, uneven. 3 inconsistent 4, imperishable.

ಅಸಡ k. n A stupid man. ಅಸಡಿ A stupid woman [ದುರೆ, etc.

ಅಸಡು k n. Stupidity, stubbornness -ಕು

ಅಸಡ್ಡಾಳ (tb. of ಅಶ್ರದ್ಧೆ) n Contemptibleness, ugliness.

ಅಸಡ್ಡೆ (tb. of ಅಶ್ರದ್ಧೆ) n Dislike, contempt, scorn -ಮಾಡು. To despise, slight

ಅಸತಿ s n An unfaithful wife.

ಅಸತ್ಯ s. a Untrue n. Untruth, falsehood

ಅಸದಳ (tb of ಅಸಾಧ್ಯ) n. Impossibility

ಅಸಂತುಷ್ಟ s a Displeased, not content ಅಸಂತುಷ್ಟಿ Discontent.

ಅಸಂತೃಪ್ತಿ s n Dissatisfaction, discontent. [tent

ಅಸಂತೋಷ s. n. Displeasure, discon-

ಅಸಂದರ್ಭ s. n Hinderance, inconvenience. [vulgar

ಅಸಭ್ಯ s. a Unfit for an assembly,

ಅಸಮ s a. Unequal, uneven 2, odd

ಅಸಮಯು s. n Unfit time.

ಅಸಮರ್ಥ s a Powerless, feeble, incompetent.

ಅಸಮಶರ s. n The five-arrowed Kâma

ಅಸಮಾಧಾನ s. n. Displeasure, discontent indisposition [equalled.

ಅ . . . nequal . . . r

ಅಸಮಾನಗಿರಿ h n A ceiling cloth. 2, an ornamental brush of peacock's feathers.

ಅಸಮಾಪ್ತ s a Unfinished, incomplete. -ಕ್ರಿಯೆ. A participle (g), as, ಹೋಗಿ, ನಡೆದು etc.

ಅಸಂಪೂರ್ಣ s a. Incomplete imperfect.

ಅಸಂಬಂಧ s. n. Non-connection

ಅಸಂಭವ s a. Inconsistent, improbable, unlikely n An extraordinary event.

ಅಸಂಭಾವ್ಯ s a Incomprehensible. -ತ್ವ. Incomprehensibleness. [from.

ಅಸಮ್ಮತ s a Disapproved, differing

ಅಸಮ್ಮತಿ s n. Dissent, disapproval

ಅಸಯ್ಯ tb of ಅಸಹ್ಯ, q. v

ಅಸಲು h a. Original, legitimate, wellborn, exactly copied n. The principal, an original

ಅಸಹಾಯು s. a Friendless, lonely

ಅಸಹಿಸು s v. i To be intolerant, to be disgusted with.

ಅಸಹ್ಯ s a Unbearable, disgustful n Disgust -ಪಡು To be disgusted

ಅಸಾಧಾರಣ s. a Uncommon, peculiar, distinguished

ಅಸಾಧ್ಯ (= ಅಸದಳ) s a. Impossible, incurable

ಅಸಿ 1 k int of disgust Fy!

ಅಸಿ 2 k v t To scatter, disperse v. i. To shake, move n That which is laid on the ground 2 (a k) thinness. -ಕಲ್ಲು The lower stone for grinding curry-stuff. -ದು That is thin -ನಡು. A tender waist -ಹೂ. A delicate flower -ಬೆರಳು A thin finger.

ಅಸಿ 3 s. n A sword, knife. -ಪತ್ರ. The blade of a sword [glio

ಅಸಿಕ್ನಿ s n A female servant in a sera-

ಅಸು s. n Life. -ಈ, -ಕೊಡು. To give life -ಬಿಡು, -ವಳಿ To give up one's life, die. -ಧಾರಣ. Existence -ಆಘ. Escaping with life.

. . . k . agitate

ಅಸುರ್ a. k v i To feel disgusted, to be impatient n Fatigue.
ಅಸುರ s n The sun 2, a demon, an Asura -ರಿಪು, -ವೈರಿ, -ಹರ, ಅಸುರಾರಿ. Vishnu, Krishna.
ಅಸೂಯ, ಅಸೂಯೆ s n. Displeasure. 2, envy, jealousy. 3, aversion -ಪಡು. To bear malice.
ಅಸೆ = ಅಸಿ [disease.
ಅಸೌಖ್ಯ s. n. Ailment, indisposition.
ಅಸೌಮ್ಯ s a Ugly, disagreeable -ಸ್ವರ Having a croaking voice.
ಅಸ್ತ s a Disappeared n Sunset -ಮನ, -ಮಯ, -ಮಾನ. Disappearance; setting, as a heavenly body, sunset. -ನ್ಯಸ್ತ Disordered ಅಸ್ತಮಿಸು To set
ಅಸ್ತರು, ಅಸ್ತ್ರಿ h. n Lining of a garment
ಅಸ್ತಿಭಾರ, ಅಸ್ತಿವಾರ s. n A foundation.
ಅಸ್ತು s. int Be it so, let it be
ಅಸ್ತ್ರ s n A missile weapon. 2, a bow -ಗೃಹ An arsenal. -ಜೀವ A soldier ಅಸ್ತ್ರಿ A bowman.
ಅಸ್ಥಿ s n. A bone. -ಗತ. Seated in the bones -ಪಂಜರ A skeleton -ಪಾತ್ರ An urn. -ಶೇಷ. A skeleton. -ಸ್ರಾವ. A kind of consumption.
ಅಸ್ಥಿರ s a Unsteady, uncertain. -ತ್ವ. Unsteadiness.
ಅಸ್ಪಷ್ಟ s a Indistinct
ಅಸ್ರು (= ಅಶ್ರು) s. a. A tear. 2, water. 3, an eye. 4, blood
ಅಸ್ವತಂತ್ರ s a Dependant subject
ಅಸ್ವಭಾವಿಕ s. a Unnatural.
ಅಸ್ವರ s. a. Indistinct, having a disagreeable voice n A consonant (g)
ಅಸ್ವಸ್ಥ s n. Illness, sickness. ailment.
ಅಸ್ವಾರಸ್ಯ s a Sapless, insipid.
ಅಸ್ವಾರ್ಥ s. n. Disinterestedness, generosity.
ಅಹ (= ಅವ್ವ q v, ಅಗುವ) a k ಅಹುದು, ಹೌದು. Yes ಅಹುದಾಗು To be yes or true. ಅಹುದೆನ್ನು To say yes; to assent, affirm. [thu
ಅಹಗೆ (= ಹಾಗೆ) a. k ad Th... ...

ಅಹಂಕಾರ ಅಹಂಕೃತಿ, ಅಹಂಕ್ರಿಯೆ s n. The sense of self, egotism, pride, haughtiness ಅಹಂಕರಿಸು. To be egotistic or proud ಅಹಂಕಾರವಂತ, ಅಹಂಕಾರಿ. A proud man [manner
ಅಹಂಗೆ (= ಹಾಗೆ, q v) a. k. ad That
ಅಹನಿ (Dual day and night) s. n A day ಅಹನ್ಯಹನಿ Day by day, daily
ಅಹಮ್ s pron. I -ಅಹಮಿಕೆ. Conceit. -ಭಾವ High notion of one's own superiority. -ಮತಿ. Conceit
ಅಹರ್, ಅಹಸ್ s n A day. ಅಹರ್ನಿಶ Day and night
ಅಹಲೆಕಾರ h. n A public servant.
ಅಹವಾಲು h n. State, circumstances, condition
ಅಹಷಾಂ h n Attendance, retinue. 2, a number of coolies.
ಅಹಹ, ಅಹಹಾ s int of joy or sorrow.
ಅಹಿ s n. A serpent 2, the demon Vritra -ಕಟಕ. A number of serpents. -ಕಾಂತ, -ಪ, -ಪತಿ The lord of serpents: Śēsha -ಭೂಷಣ. Śiva -ಶಯ್ಯೆ. A couch of snakes.
ಅಹಿತ s a Not beneficial, unfriendly. n. An enemy, damage -ಕರ. Adverse, unwholesome -ತ್ವ. Enmity.
ಅಹುದು See s ಅಹ. [less
ಅಹೇತು s. n Causelessness -ಕ Causeless
ಅಹೋರಾತ್ರ, ಅಹೋರಾತ್ರಿ s. n Day and night, from sunrise to sunrise
ಅಳ a. k. n Contact, nearness. 2, fitness, propriety, comeliness 3 power, strength 4, possibility. -ವಡಿಕೆ Joining, bringing about. -ವಡಿಸು To join, to tie, to attach, to bring about -ವಡು To be closely joined; to be at hand -ವಳಿ To be depressed, to faint
ಅಳಕ k. a. Neither thick nor thin (fluids)
ಅಳಕು k. v i To fear 2, (= ಅಳುಕು) to prick, throb. 3 (= ಅಲಕು) to move about n Fear 2, the pricking of [illegible]
[illegible]

ಅಳಟು (ಳ=ೞ) k v i To be in anguish.

ಅಳತೆ k n Measure, extent; measurement -ಮಾಡು. To measure

ಅಳರು (ರು=ಱು) a. k v i To fear. n Fear, anguish ಅಳರಿಸು To frighten

ಅಳಲು (ಳ=ೞ) a. k v i To grieve, be afflicted n Grief, sorrow, affliction. ಅಳಲಿಸು To grieve harass.

ಅಳಲೆ k. n A squirrel. 2, = ಅಣಿಲೆ, q v

ಅಳವಿ (= ಅಳ, q v) a. k n Nearness 2. strength 3, combat 4, trust.

ಅಳವು k n Measure -ಗೋಲು A measuring rod.

ಅಳವೆ (ಳ=ೞ) k. n The bar, the ebbing of the tide in a river-mouth

ಅಳವೇಲಿ = ಅಳುವೇರಿ, ಆಳುವೇರಿ, q. v

ಅಳಸು k. v t To measure or cause to be measured 2, (= ಅಳಿಸು) to efface

ಅಳಿ (ಳಿ=ೞಿ) k. v i. To be ruined, to perish, decay, to disappear; to die v t To ruin 2, (= ಅಳೆ) to measure n. Ruin, waste, damage 2, remainder of liquids 3, a void, nought (expressed by the sign ೦) -ಕಣ್ಣು. A bad eye. -ಗಬ್ಬ Miserable poetry -ಗವಿ, -ಗಬ್ಬಿಗ A bad poet -ಜಪ Useless prayers -ಯಾಸೆ Vain hope

ಅಳಿಕಿಸು k v. t To oppose, to harass 2, to frighten 3, (ಳಿ = ೞಿ) to efface, erase

ಅಳಿಗೆ k n. An earthen vessel

ಅಳಿಪು 1 a k v. i To be addicted to, to long for n Desire, attachment love

ಅಳಿಪು 2 (ಳಿ=ೞಿ) k v t To destroy v i To be destroyed. n. Ruin, destruction, death

ಅಳಿಯ k n A son-in-law, a nephew. -ಸಂತಾನ The law of inheritance according to which a man's property descends to his sister's son. -ತನ. Being an ಅಳಿಯ

ಅಳಿಲು (= ಅಳಲೆ) k n A squirrel.

ಅಳಿಸು (ಳಿ=ೞಿ) k v. t To ruin, destroy,

ಅಳು (ಳು=ೞು) k v i To weep, cry. -ವಿಕೆ, -ವು. Weeping -ಗೂಸು. A cross child -ಕುಳಿ. -ಬುರುಕ A crying or fretful person, f. -ಬುರುಕಿ. ಅಳಿಸು To make weep

ಅಳುಕಿಸು = ಅಳಿಕಿಸು

ಅಳುಕು ಅಳ್ಕು k v i To fear, be afraid n Fear

ಅಳುಗು (ಳು=ೞು) a k v i. To decay v t. To love

ಅಳುಂಬ a. k. n. Excess, greatness, excellence.

ಅಳುಲು (= ಅಣಿಲು) k n. A squirrel

ಅಳುವೇರಿ. = ಅಳವೇರಿ, q v.

ಅಳೆ (= ಅಳಿ No. 3) k. v t To measure n Measure. 2 buttermilk -ದು ಕೊಡು. To measure out -ದು ತುಂಬಿಕೊಡು. To give heaped measure. -ದು ನೋಡು To ponder. -ಯುಂಬ. A Gŏlla.

ಅಳ್ಕಜ (ಳ್ಕ = ೞ್ಕ) k n. Envy, jealousy. -ಕಾರ. An envious man.

ಅಳ್ಕನೆ k ad. Suddenly.

ಅಳ್ಕರು (ಳ್ಕರು = ೞ್ಕಱು) a k v t To love. 2, to fear. n Love.

ಅಳ್ಕು 1. = ಅಳುಕು.

ಅಳ್ಕು 2. (ಳ್ಕ = ೞ್ಕ) a k v. i. To be worn out, digested. n The state of being worn out or digested.

ಅಳ್ಕೆ k n An embrace 2, (ಳ್ಕೆ = ೞ್ಕೆ) weeping. 3, boiling

ಅಳ್ಗು (ಳ್ಗ = ೞ್ಗ) k v i. To be dissolved to decay.

ಅಳ್ತಿ (ಳ್ತಿ = ೞ್ತಿ = ಅತಿ) k. n Love 2, pleasure -ವಡು To feel love -ಕಾರ A lover.

ಅಳ್ದು (ಳ್ದು = ೞ್ದು) a. k v i To wither fade. 2, to die. 3, (= ಅದ್ದು) to dip

ಅಳ್ಳು k n Shaking, trembling. ಅಳ್ಳಾಡು (= ಅಲ್ಲಾಡು). To move, shake, tremble

ಅಳ್ಳೆ k n What is shaking 2, th sides of the abdomen, the weak spot tenderness. 3 the flank of an anima -ಗೊಬ್ಬು. Feebleness -ಗೊಂಬು.

ಆ

ಆ. 1. k The second letter of the alphabet 2 *a remote pronominal adjective* That, those, *as*: ಆ ಮನುಷ್ಯ That man ಆ ಕಡೆ. That side ಆ ಕಾರಣ Therefore. ಆ ಕ್ಷಣ Instantly. ಆ ಬಗ್ಗೆ On that account ಆ ಬಳಿಕ Thereafter. ಆ ಮೇಲೆ. Afterward ಆ ವರೆಗೆ Until then ಆವಾಗ Then 3, *a final particle in friendly conversation, as.* ಹಾ, ರಾಮಾ! ಮಕ್ಕಳಿರಾ! 4, *an interrogative affix, as* ಬಂದಿರಾ? ಹೋಗುತ್ತೀರಾ?

ಆ 2. s *ad* From 2, towards 3, all around 4, till, as far as.

ಆಂ (= ನಾ, ನಾನು) a k *pro* I

ಆಃ k *int of surprise and sorrow*

ಆಕರ s. *n.* A multitude 2 a mine. 3, a place.

ಆಕರಣ, ಆಕರಣೆ s *n* Calling; a challenge. ಆಕರಿಸು To accept, to challenge.

ಆಕರ್ಣನ s *n.* Hearing, listening. ಆಕರ್ಣಿಸು To hear, listen (*cf* ಆಲಿಸು, ಕೇಳು)

ಆಕರ್ಷ s *n* Drawing, attraction towards one's self (= ಆಕರ್ಷಣ). 2, a die or dice, playing with dice, *etc.* 3, temptation, allurement. -ಕ. A magnet ಆಕರ್ಷಿಸು To attract, draw.

ಆಕಸ್ಮಿಕ s. *a* Sudden *ad* Suddenly, instantly

ಆಕಳ, ಆಕಳು k *n.* A cow. -ಕರು. A cow's calf. -ಮಂದೆ A herd of cattle -ಹಟ್ಟಿ A cowpen

ಆಕಳಾಸ k *n* Disgust

ಆಕಳಿಕೆ (= ಆಕುಳಿಕೆ) k *n.* Yawning, gaping ಆಕಳಿಸು *v. i.* To yawn, gape.

ಆಕಾಂಕ್ಷೆ s *n* Desire, wish 2, requiring of a word to complete the sense 3, suspicion ಆಕಾಂಕ್ಷಿಸು To desire, wish

ಆಕಾರ s *n* Form, shape 2, a hint, sign 3, the vo [illegible]
ಪೂಜೆ -ಗುಟ್ಟು, - [illegible]

ಆಕಾರಣ s. *n* Calling; challenging

ಆಕಾಶ (*tb* ಆಕಾಸ, ಆಗಸ) s *n* The sky or atmosphere, an empty space. 2 the ether. -ಗಂಗೆ. A cascade -ಗೂಡು, -ದೀಪ. A lamp hung on a pole. -ಬಾಣ A sky-rocket -ಬಿಲ್ಲು. The rainbow -ವಾಣಿ An aerial voice.

ಆಕಾಸ *tb of* ಆಕಾಶ, *q v*

ಆಕೀರ್ಣ s. *a.* Scattered, crowded, confused

ಆಕು a k. *n* A leaf, a herb, filament. -ರಾಯಿ A file

ಆಕುಂಚನ s. *n.* Bending, contraction; curving ಆಕುಂಚಿತ. Bent, contracted

ಆಕುಲ, ಆಕುಲಿತ s *a* Filled with, full, confused, bewildered

ಆಕುಳಿಕೆ = ಆಕಳಿಕೆ, *q v*

ಆಕೃತಿ s. *n.* Form, shape. 2, the body 3 tribe, species

ಆಕೆ 1. k. *pro* That woman, she. 2, she, the married wife (*hon*).

ಆಕೆ 2 a k *n* Power, valour -ವಾಳ. A valiant man

ಆಕ್ರಂದನ s. *n* Lamentation, weeping ಆಕ್ರಂದಿಸು To weep, lament

ಆಕ್ರಮಣ s. *n* Approaching 2, attacking, seizing, grasping. 3, overpowering [To rise

ಆಕ್ರಮಿಸು s *v. t* To seize, grasp *v. i.*

ಆಕ್ರಾಂತ s. *a.* Possessed, obtained 2, subjected overpowered *Cpds* ದುಃಖಾಕ್ರಾಂತ, ಮಂದಾಕ್ರಾಂತ, *etc*

ಆಕ್ರೋಶ s *n* Calling aloud. 2. reviling, abusing

ಆಕ್ಷೇಪ s. *n.* Tossing. 2, abuse, taunt; reproach 3, objection, doubt -ಮಾಡು, ಆಕ್ಷೇಪಿಸು. To reproach, to object

ಆಖರಿ h *n.* The end ಆಖರು = ಆಖೈರು.

ಆಖಾತ s *n.* A natural pond

[illegible]

ಆಖೇಟ s n Chase, hunting 2, fright.

ಆಖೈರು h. a. Last, final. n. The end

ಆಖ್ಯ s. a. Named 2, making known. n = ಆಖ್ಯೆ

ಆಖ್ಯಾತ s. a Made known, famous 2, conjugated. n A verb, predicate (g) -ಪದ An inflected verb (g) -ವಿಭಕ್ತಿ. An affix of conjugation (g)

ಆಖ್ಯಾತಿ s n. Fame, name -ಸು. To make known

ಆಖ್ಯಾನ s n Saying 2, a tale 3, a word.

ಆಖ್ಯೆ s n An appellation, fame, a name

ಆಗ, ಆಗಲು, ಆಗ್ಗೆ k ad That time, then ಆಗಾಗ, ಆಗಾಗ್ಗೆ, ಆಗಿಂದಾಗ್ಗೆ From time to time, occasionally. ಆಗಿನ Of that time.

ಆಗಡ a k. n. Sport, fun, mockery -ಕಾರ A scoffer, teaser

ಆಗಡು (= ಆಗ) a k ad Then

ಆಗತ s. a Come, received. -ಸ್ವಾಗತ. Reception, welcome ಆಗತಿ. Arrival, return, income; chance

ಆಗಮ s n. Arrival. 2, precept; a work on sacred science. 3, an augment (g.). 4, knowledge, science. -ನ. Coming ಆಗಮಾಮ್ನಾಯ. The Śâstras and vêdas ಆಗಮಿಸು To arrive

ಆಗರ (tb. of ಆಗಾರ) n. An abode, asylum 2, a garden 3, a saltpan

ಆಗಲ್, ಆಗಲು = ಆಗ, q v

ಆಗಲಿ See s ಆಗು

ಆಗಸ (tb of ಆಕಾಶ) -ಮಣಿ The sun

ಆಗಳು (= ಆಗ) a. k ad. Always. 2, that time.

ಆಗಾಗ, ಆಗಾಗ್ಗೆ See s ಆಗ.

ಆಗಾಢ s. n. Pretence of agony or injury.

ಆಗಾಮಿ s a Coming, future. -ಕ್ರಿಯೆ The future tense (g.). ಆಗಾಮಿಕ Relating to future.

ಆಗಾರ (= ಆಗರ) s n. A house, dwelling.

ಆಗ[illegible] To come into [illegible] t

4, to become 5. to be 6, to be done or finished 7, to come under. 8, to be suitable, fit, to agree 9, to be possible, to be related. ಅವನು ನನಗೆ ಏನೂ ಆಗುವದಿಲ್ಲ, he is not related to me ಆದದ್ದು ಆಯಿತು, what is done is done ಆಗಗೊಡು To allow to happen ಆಗದ Not coming about impossible ಆಗದವನು An unfriendly man, ಕೆಲಸಕ್ಕೆ ಆಗದವನು, an incompetent man ಆಗದು It is unfit or forbidden, as ಮಾಡಲಾಗದು ಆಗಲಿ (3rd pr. sing imp.) May become or be, be it (so) (ಹಾಗಾಗಲಿ, be it so) *Rep. to express* whether—or, either- or, *as* ಇದಾಗಲಿ ಅದಾಗಲಿ, either this or that, ಬಡವನಾಗಲಿ ಐಶ್ವರ್ಯವಂತನಾಗಲಿ, whether poor or rich. ಆಗುವ (pr p) Possible practicable ಆಗುವಂತೆ ಮಾಡು, ಆಗುವ ಹಾಗೆ ಮಾಡು To accomplish, bring about ಆಗಿ. (p p) Having become, happened, being finished, etc 1. *affixed to adjectives or nouns it is used to form adverbs, as* ಚೆನ್ನಾಗಿ, ಮೃದುವಾಗಿ, ಸಲುವಾಗಿ, ಸಂತೋಷವಾಗಿ, *etc* 2, *it is used to convey the idea of* "voluntarily" 'of itself", *as* ಅವನಾಗಿ or ತಾನಾಗಿ ಬಂದನು, he came of his own accord 3 *with the Dative it signifies* for, on account of, in behalf of, *as* ನಿನಗಾಗಿ, ತಂದೆಯ ಮಾತಿಗಾಗಿ ಮಾಡುವದಕ್ಕಾಗಿ, ಮಾಡಿದಕ್ಕಾಗಿ, ಮಾಡದಕ್ಕಾಗಿ, ಇದ್ದದ್ದಕ್ಕಾಗಿ 4, *it signifies a state or quality, as* ಅಪರಂಜಿಯಾಗಿರುವ ಬಂಗಾರ, ಬಹಳ ಅಧಿಕವಾಗಿರುವದು. ಆಗಿ ಹೋಗು. To be finished, to die. ಆದರೂ (ಆದಡೆಯು, ಆದೊಡೆಯು) Though, soever ಆದರೆ If it be, if so. ಆಗು *is also used to form a kind of passive, as* ಹೇಳೋಣವಾಯಿತು, ಕೊಡೋಣವಾಯಿತು. ಆಗಿಸು. To bring about, perform. ಆಗುವಿಕೆ Becoming, happening

ಆಗ k *ad* In into.

ಆಗ್ = ಆಗ q v.

ಆಗ್ನೇಯ s a Relating to fire n The

ಆಗ್ಯೆ (= ಆಗ, *q. v*) k. *ad* Then ಆಗಿಂದಾಗ್ಯೆ From time to time ಆಗ್ಯೂ Also, then, notwithstanding, though, *as,* ಮಾಡಿದಾಗ್ಯೂ. Though he did it

ಆಗ್ರಹ s *n.* Seizing 2, earnest solicitation. 3, violence (ಬಲಾತ್ಕಾರ). 4, anger. ಆಗ್ರಹಿಸು To become angry

ಆಘ್ರಾಣ s. *n.* Smelling ಆಘ್ರಾಣಿಸು. To smell.

ಆಂಗಿರಸ s *n.* Brihaspati 2, the 6th year in the cycle of sixty.

ಆಚಂದ್ರಾರ್ಕ s. *a* As long as moon and sun endure.

ಆಚಮನ s *n* Rinsing the mouth or sipping water at a religious ceremony.

ಆಚರಣೆ s *n* Observing 2, conduct, practice, performance. -ಮಾಡು, ಆಚರಿಸು To perform, observe

ಆಚಾರ s. *n.* Conduct, good behaviour. 2, an established rule of conduct, custom, usage, practice. *Cpds* ವ್ರತಾಚಾರ, ಕುಲಾಚಾರ, ದೇಶಾಚಾರ, ಲೋಕಾಚಾರ, *etc*

ಆಚಾರಿ (*tb. of* ಆಚಾರ್ಯ) *n* A title assumed by Brahmin cooks, idol-makers, smiths, artificers, house-pûjâris, *etc.*

ಆಚಾರ್ಯ s. *n.* A spiritual guide. 2, a conductor of religious ceremonies. 3, a title of learned men.

ಆಚೆ k. *ad* That side, beyond. 2, after, afterwards, *as* ಆಚೆಯ ಹೊಲ, ಆಚೆಬೀದಿ. -ಕಡೆ That side

ಆಚ್ಛಾದನ s. *n* Covering, concealing, a covering ಆಚ್ಛಾದಿಸು To cover, conceal

ಆಜ s. *n* Relating to goats -ಕ. A flock of goats

ಆಜಿ s. *n.* Going, running 2, war, battle. 3, level ground

ಆಜೀವ, ಆಜನ್ಮ s. *n* Livelihood. *ad* As long as life endures.

ಆಜ್ಞಾಪನ s. *n.* Ordering ಆಜ್ಞಾಪಿಸು To order, command

ಆಜ್ಞೆ (*tb* ಆಣೆ) s *n* An order, command. 2, permission [illegible] ment. -ನಿರ್ಣ [illegible]

-ಕೊಡು To order; to allow. -ತೆಗೆದುಕೊಳ್ಳು To take leave. -ಮಾಡು. To order, to condemn, punish. -ಮೀರು To transgress a command ಆಜ್ಞಾಧಾರಕ Obedient.

ಆಟ k *n* Motion 2, play, sport, amusement, jest 3, a dance, stage performance, gambling. 4, sound. *Cpds:* ಕಳ್ಳಾಟ, ಕೊಂಡಾಟ, ಕೋಲಾಟ, ತೋಳಾಟ, ನೀರಾಟ, ಹುಡುಗಾಟ, ಹೋರಾಟ. -ಆಡು. To play, to act, perform. -ಕಾತಿ, -ಗಾತಿ A dancing girl. -ಗಾರ, -ಗುಳಿ, -ಂಗುಳಿ A player, a gambler -ಪಾಟ *dupl* -ವಿಕ A player, an actor; a cheat, (s.) a woodman.

ಆಟಂಕ s. *n* Obstruction, obstacle. ಆಟಂಕಿಸು. To hinder

ಆಟಾಳಿ k *n* A person given to play.

ಆಟಾಳು f *n* An extra servant

ಆಟಿ k *n* A player. -ಕೆ, -ಗೆ (*cf* ಆಡಿಕೆ). Play ಆಟಿಸು To long for, desire.

ಆಟು k *n.* Motion, play (f) *a* Minor, extra.

ಆಟೋಪ s. *n.* Ostentation, pomp. 2, control, power.

ಆಡಂಗಿ k *n* A female

ಆಡಂಬರ s. *n* A drum 2, roaring. 3, thunder. 4, pomp, display. 5, expanse; a heap

ಆಡಳಿತ, ಆಡಳಿತೆ k. *n* Administration, management.

ಆಡಿ k *n* That moves or plays ಆಡಿಕೆ. A holding, motion, play, a holiday ಆಡಿಗ An actor. -ತನ. Moving, playing

ಆಡು 1. k. *v i.* To be in motion, to wag, wave, shake 2, to play, sport. 3, to dance, act 4, to speak, utter, sound 5, to abuse *Cpds* ಅಲ್ಲಾಡು, ಈಡಾಡು, ಕುಣಿದಾಡು, ಕೊಂಡಾಡು, ತಿರಿಗಾಡು, ಬೀಸಾಡು, ಹೊರಳಾಡು, ಹೋರಾಡು, *etc.* *n* Motion. -ಕುಳಿ. A playful person -ವಿಕೆ, -ಹ, ಆಡಿಕೆ Moving, playing ಆಡಿಸು To cause to move, play, dance, *etc.* [illegible]

-ಮುಟ್ಟದ ಗಿಡ, -ಸೋಗೆ. A shrub, *Justicia adhaloda*

ಆಡೇಲು k n A screech owl.

ಆಢಕ s. n. A measure of grain.

ಆಢಕಿ s. n A kind of pulse.

ಆಢ್ಯ s a Rich, wealthy n. Arrogance

ಆಣ್ (= ಆಳ್) k a. Male n Priority

ಆಣತಿ 1 k n Singing, praising

ಆಣತಿ 2 (*tb of* ಆಜ್ಞಪ್ತಿ) n. An order, command

ಆಣಿ 1. k. n Roundness. 2, excellency, preciousness -ಮುತ್ತು A costly pearl

ಆಣಿ 2 s n The linch-pin, a nail 2, a limit -ಕಲ್ಲು The base of a pillar. -ಕಾರ A nail-maker

ಆಣಿಸು k v i To crack or burst

ಆಣೆಕಲ್ಲು k n. A hailstone

ಆಣೆ 1 (*tb of* ಆಜ್ಞೆ) n Command. 2, oath -ಇಡು -ಕಟ್ಟು, -ಮಾಡು, -ಹಾಕು To swear -ಬಿಡಿಸು To free from an oath ದೇವರಾಣೆ By God ಮಗನಾಣೆ By my son

ಆಣೆ 2 k. n. A crack -ಬಿಡು To crack, burst

ಆಂಡಿ k. n A Śaiva religious mendi- [cant.

ಆಣ್ಬ, ಆಣ್ಮ (*fr* ಆಣೆ) a k. n A ruler, lord, master.

ಆತ, ಆತಂ k. *dem pro* That man, he

ಆತಂಕ (= ಅಟಂಕ) s. n Obstacle, hindrance (ಅಡ್ಡಿ) 2, disease 3, fear ಆತಂಕಿಸು To hinder

ಆತತಾಯಿ s n An assailant, felon, murderer

ಆತಪ s. n Sunshine ಆತಪ್ತ *a* Heated.

ಆತಪತ್ರ s n A parasol

ಆತಿಥ್ಯ s n Hospitality 2, a guest. -ಕೊಡು, -ಮಾಡು. To entertain a guest

ಆತೀರ್ಣ s a. Crossed, passed over

ಆತು, = ಆಂತು k. *p. p. of* ಆನು, *q v*

ಆತುರ s. n Longing for. 2, excitement, haste. -ತೆ. Desire -ಪಡು, -ಬೀಳು, -ಪಡ
ಸು. To be hasty ... To feel

ಆತುಷ್ಟಿ s. n Complete satisfaction.

ಆತೆ, ಆತೆಹುಳ k. n. A cockroach.

ಆತ್ಮ s. n. The soul 2, the self. 3, nature. character 4, intellect, mind 5, the soul of the universe. 6 effort. 7, wind, air -ಕ (*in cpds.*) Having the nature of. -ಘಾತಕ. Suicide -ಜ, -ಜಾತ, -ಭವ A son -ಜೆ, -ಜಾತೆ, -ಭವೆ A daughter -ಜ್ಞ. Self-knowing; a sage. -ದ್ರೋಹಿ Fretful, miserable -ನಿವೇದನ, ಆತ್ಮಾರ್ಪಣ Offering one's self as a sacrifice -ನೇಪದ. The middle voice of a verb (*g*). -ಭೂ Self-born; Brahmâ. -ವಂಚಕ Self-deceiver -ವಂಚನೆ Self-delusion. -ವಿದ್ Self-knowing, a sage. -ಸ್ತುತಿ. Self-praise ಆತ್ಮಾರ್ಥ. One's own sake, reflexive (*g*). *Cpds* ಪರಮಾತ್ಮ, ಜೀವಾತ್ಮ, ಪುಣ್ಯಾತ್ಮ, ಪಾಪಾತ್ಮ, ದುರಾತ್ಮ, *etc*

ಆತ್ಮಿಕ (= ಆತ್ಮಕ, *q v*) s *a*. Having the nature of.

ಆತ್ಮೀಯ s *a* Own relating to self

ಆತ್ರೇಯ s n Durvâsa 2, the moon

ಆದ k (*rel p p of* ಆಗು, *q v*). *Affixed to nouns it converts them into adjectives, as* ಭಾರವಾದ, heavy, ವಿಸ್ತಾರವಾದ extensive, *etc.* -ಕಾರಣ, -ದರಿಂದ. Therefore ಆದಾನು He may become. ಆದೀತು. It may be, yes.

ಆದರ, ಆದರಣೆ s n Reverence, homage. 2, kind treatment, kindness, consolation. ಆದರಿಕ. A helper in trouble ಆದರಿಸು. To respect; to treat kindly

ಆದರೂ (*fr.* ಆಗು) k *conj*. Either, or 2, any (ಯಾರಾದರೂ, any one, ಏನಾದರೂ, something, ಎಲ್ಲಾದರೂ, anywhere). 3, at least (ಈಗಲಾದರೂ, at least now). 4, though (ಮಾಡಿದರೂ, though he did)

ಆದರೆ (*fr* ಆಗು) *cond conj* If, if it be (ಹಾಗಾದರೆ, if it be so) 2, but

ಆದರ್ಶ s n A mirror -ನ Showing, a mirror.

ad, front.

ಆದಾಯ s n. Gain, income, profit, advantage.

ಆದಿ s. n Beginning a. First, prior. (ಅನಾದಿ, without beginning; ಅನಾದಿಯಿಂದ, from eternity) con. And so on, etc. -ಕಾರಣ A primary cause. -ದೇವ. The creator. -ಶೇಷ The sovereign of the serpent race. Cpds ಅನಾದಿ, ಯುಗಾದಿ, ದಿನಾದಿ, ಜಗದಾದಿ.

ಆದಿತ್ಯ s n. The sun -ವಾರ. Sunday.

ಆದಿಮ s a First, prior, original

ಆದೀಕ s. n Profit, gain, income.

ಆದು = ಆಯ್ದು P. p. of ಆಯು, q v.

ಆದೇಯ s. n A gift.

ಆದೇಶ s. n Information 2, precept. 3, an order. 4 a substitute.

ಆದ್ಯ s. a First, initial. -ಕವಿ N. of Vâlmîki.

ಆಧಾನ s. n Placing, depositing 2, a deposit, pledge, a surety. 3, a receptacle.

ಆಧಾರ s n Support, aid. 2 authority. sanction, foundation. 3, a receptacle. -ಸ್ಥ, ಆಧಾರಿ A man of property -ವಿಲ್ಲದವನು, ನಿರಾಧಾರಿ, a destitute man

ಆಧಿ s. n Location 2, a deposit 3, thought, care, anxiety, cf. ವ್ಯಾಧಿ.

ಆಧಿಕ್ಯ s. n. Excess, abundance; superiority.

ಆಧಿಪತ್ಯ s. n. Supremacy, authority.

ಆಧೀನ s. a Subjected, dependent. n. Subjection control, charge. Cpds. ಸ್ವಾಧೀನ, ಪರಾಧೀನ, ದೈವಾಧೀನ

ಆನ = ಆದ Rel p p. of ಆನು, q v

ಆನಕ s. n A large drum beaten at one end 2, a tambourine

ಆನತ s a. Bent, bowed, humbled, submissive

ಆನನ s n The mouth, face

ಆನಂದ s n Happiness, joy, delight 2, the 48th year of the cycle. -ಕರ, -ಕಾರಕ Gladdening. -ಜಲ. Tears of joy. -ಪಡು. To rejoice. -ಭೈರವಿ. A kind of tune ಆನಂದಿಸು. To rejoice.

ಆನಮ s n. Bending. ಆನಮಿಸು To salute reverently.

ಆನಿಕಲ್ಲು (= ಆಣಿಕಲ್ಲು) k. n A hailstone

ಆನು k. v t. To touch, join 2, to rest on, to recline on, to lean 3, to lay hold of, put on, to receive, to bear, endure v i To be slow (P. p ಆತು). ಆತುಹೋಗು To burn slowly ಆನಿಸು To cause to touch, etc. n = ಆನಿಕೆ Leaning on

ಆನುಕೂಲ್ಯ s n Suitableness, conformity

ಆನುಗುಣ್ಯ s. n Congeniality

ಆನೆ 1. k n. An elephant (=ಗಜ, ಕರಿ, ನಾಗ). Cpds· ಕಾಡಾನೆ, ಸೀರಾನೆ, ಬೆಳ್ಳಾನೆ, ಹೆಣ್ಣಾನೆ, etc. -ಕಾಲು The Cochin leg, elephantiasis. -ಕಾಸು, -ದುಡ್ಡು. An old copper coin so called -ಗಜ್ಜಿ A troublesome kind of itch -ದಂತ Ivory -ಬಾಗಲು. The entrance gate of a palace. -ಮುಯ್ಲಿ. A bad kind of small-pox. -ಮುಸುಡಿನ ನೆಗಳು The long-nosed alligator -ಹೆಜ್ಜೆ The foot-print of an elephant -ಗೊಲಿ. An elephant-killer. -ಹಳ್ಳಿ, -ಗೂಳ್ಳಿ. A pit for catching wild elephants.

ಆನೆ 2. (= ಹಾನೆ) He is. 2, aff for 3rd pers sing. masc present; as: ಇರುತ್ತಾನೆ, ಬರುತ್ತಾನೆ, etc.

ಆಂತರ್ಯ (fr ಅಂತರ) s n The inside, heart, the mind, secrecy

ಆಂತು (=ಆತು) k P. p. of ಆನು, q v.

ಆಂತ್ರ s. n The bowels, entrails -ವಾಯು, -ವೃದ್ಧಿ Ingual hernia, rupture. [owl

ಆಂದೆಗ (=ಆಡೀಲು) k. n The white screech

ಆಂದೋಲ, ಆಂದೋಲನ s. n. Swinging

ಆಂದೋಲಿಕ s. n A palankeen (ಪಾಲಕಿ)

ಆಂಧಸಿಕ s n. A cook

ಆಂಧ್ರ s. n Telugu -ದೇಶ T. country.

ಆಪ 1. k Rel. pres p of ಆಗ್ Being strong, able or possible. -ನಿತು, ಆಪಾಟು As much as possible. ಆಪುದು. It will be possible.

ಆಪ 2 s. n Water.

ಆಪಗೆ s. n A river, stream

ಆಪಣ s n A shop 2, a market ಆಪಣಿಕ. A shop-keeper, merchant

ಆಪತು, ಆಪತ್ತು. ಆಪದ (tb of ಆಪದ್) n. Trouble, misfortune, calamity, distress. -ಪಡು, -ಬೀಳು To be in distress. ಆಪತ್ಕಾಲ A time of trouble ಆಪದ್ಧರ್ಮ. Practice allowable in time of distress

ಆಪನ್ನ s. a Gained, acquired. 2, distressed

ಆಪಾತ s n Rushing on; throwing down, happening 2, the instant

ಆಪಾದ, ಆಪಾದನ s n. Accusation, punishment ಆಪಾದಿಸು To charge, punish.

ಆಪಾನ s n A drinking-party

ಆಪು k. n. An object to lean upon, refuge, protection 2, a kind of bulrush, *Typha elephantina*

ಆಪೂರ್ಣ s a Full. -ತೆ Fulness

ಆಪೇಕ್ಷಕ s a Expecting, wishing. ಅಪೇಕ್ಷಿತ a. Wished.

ಆಪೇಕ್ಷೆ. = ಅಪೇಕ್ಷೆ

ಆಪೋಶನ s n. Sipping of water at the beginning and end of meals

ಆಪ್ತ s a Obtained reached, apt, fit 2, trustworthy n A friend.

ಆಪ್ತಾಗಿರಿ f n. An ornamental umbrella borne over râjas (tude

ಆಪ್ತಿ s. n Reaching, obtaining, apti-

ಆಪ್ಯ s a. Watery; consisting of water 2, obtainable.

ಆಪ್ಯಾಯನ s a. Causing fulness, satisfying n. Satisfaction, pleasure

ಆಪ್ಲವ, ಆಪ್ಲವನ s n Bathing ablution -ವ್ರತಿ. A Brâhmana who has taken the bath after his period of study.

ಆಬರು, ಆಬುರು. ಆಬ್ರು h n Honour, character, renown. -ಗೇಡಿ A man without honour or character

ಆಬಾದು h. a Flourishing, cultivated

ಆಬಾಸ (*tb of* ಆಭಾಸ) n Fallacy, failure, defect.

ಆಬ್ದಿಕ s a Annual, yearly.

ಆಭರಣ s n An ornament

ಆಭಾ

ಆಭಾಷಣ s. n. Addressing, speaking

ಆಭಾಸ s. n. Splendour, light, appearance, reflection

ಆಭೀರ s n A cowherd

ಆಭ್ಯಂತರ (*fr* ಅಭ್ಯಂತರ, *q v*) s a Internal n. Obstacle.

ಆಮ 1. s. a Raw, uncooked, unripe. n. Constipation, passing unhealthy excretions (mucus), sickness -ರಕ್ತ, -ಶಂಕೆ. Dysentery. -ಸೋಲು A sour sauce or seasoning made of tamarind

ಆಮ 2 k n A potter's kiln

ಆಮದು h. n Coming, income, import.

ಆಮಂತ್ರ, ಆಮಂತ್ರಣ s n Welcome. 2, invitation.

ಆಮಯ s n Sickness, disease

ಆಮಲಕ s n The plant *Emblic myrobalan* (= ನೆಲ್ಲಿ).

ಆಮವಡೆ (*tb. of* ಆಮವಟಿ) n. A kind of cake made of split pulse mixed with spices fried in ghee or oil and soaked in curds.

ಆಮಾತ್ಯ s. n A minister, counsellor.

ಆಮಾಶಯ s. n The stomach.

ಆಮಿಷ s. n Flesh. 2 a bribe 3, a gift. 4, desire.

ಆಮಿಸ. = ಆಮಿಷ, *q v.*

ಆಮಿಲ h. n. A native revenue officer

ಆಮುಷ್ಮಿಕ s. a Belonging to the other world

ಆಮೂಲ s. ad By the root entirely

ಆಮೆ k. n. A tortoise, turtle.

ಆಮೋದ s a Gladdening. n Pleasure, joy. 2, fragrance ಆಮೋದಿಸು. To be glad, to smell at

ಆಂಬರ (*tb* ಆಮ್ಲ) n Pepper water with tamarind.

ಆಂಬೋಡೆ *See* ಆಮವಡೆ.

ಆಮ್ಲ, ಆಮ್ಲಿಕೆ s n. The tamarind tree. 2 sourness, acidity

ಆಯ 1 a. k n The inside; the vital

articu-

erness.

ಆಯ 2. k. n Measure, dimension, extent, rule, order, fitness. 2, craftiness, deceit. -ಕಟ್ಟು Properness, suitableness, measure, extent -ಗಾರ A clever man -ಕಟ್ಟುಗಾರ A man who does his work properly

ಆಯ 3. s. n Revenue 2, profit -ಸಾಮ್ಯ, -ಸ್ವಾಮ್ಯ. Corn given by the villagers to the hereditary servants of the village as their established fees of office. -ಗಾರ. A hereditary village servant

ಆಯತ 1., ಆಯತ್ತ 1 k. n. Fitness. 2, readiness. 3, ease [diffuse

ಆಯತ 2. s a. Checked 2, extended,

ಆಯತನ s n A place, seat, home. 2, an altar 3, a temple.

ಆಯತ್ತ 2 s a Dependent on 2, docile

ಆಯಾಸ s. n. Effort, exertion, trouble. 2, fatigue -ಗೊಳ್ಳು, -ಪಾಗು, -ಪಡು To become weary.

ಆಯಿ 1 h. n. A mother

ಆಯಿ 2, ಆಯು 1 k n Collecting v t To collect, gather, to select. P p. ಆದು -ಕೆ, -ವಿಕೆ Selecting. ಆದುಕೊಳ್ಳು. To select for one's self ಆಯಿಸು To cause to choose -ಕುಳಿ A beggar

ಆಯಿತು, ಆಯಿತ್ತು k (3rd pers sing past t of ಆಗು). It became, it is done. etc.

ಆಯು 2, ಆಯುಷ್ಯ, ಆಯುಸ್ s. n Life, age, duration of life -ವಂತ, ಆಯುರ್ವಂತ Long-lived ಆಯುರಾರೋಗ್ಯ. Long life and health. ಆಯುಪರ್ಯಾಯ The term of life. -ಹೀನ, ಆಯುಹೀನ. Short-lived

ಆಯುಧ s. n. A weapon 2, a tool. -ಶಾಲೆ An arsenal -ಪಾಣಿ, -ಧಾರಿ, -ಸ್ಥ, ಆಯುಧಿಕ A soldier -ಧರಿಸು. To arm.

ಆಯುರ್ವೇದ s. n. Medicine. ಆಯುರ್ವೇದಿ A physician.

ಆರ (Inf. of ಆರ್ to be filled, teem) k. aff. To the full, as ಕಣ್ಣಾರ, ಕಿವಿಯಾರ, ಮನಸ್ಸಾರ, etc -ಗಾಡು A perfect wild, a place never cultivated.

ಆರಡಿ a k n Publicity, infamy, scandal

ಆರಣ್ಯ s a. Relating to a forest n. A forest -ಕ. A woodman

ಆರತಿ, ಆರ್ತಿ (tb of ಆರಾತ್ರಿಕ) n The ceremony of waving (around an idol or person) a burning lamp Cpds: ದೀಪಾರತಿ, ಧೂಪಾರತಿ, ಮಂಗಳಾರತಿ. -ಎತ್ತು, -ಬೆಳಗು, -ಮಾಡು Ârati to wave. -ಕೊಡು. Â to offer

ಆರಬ್ಧ s. a Begun. n Beginning ಆರಭ್ಯ. Beginning from

ಆರಂಬ, ಆರಂಬು k. n. Tillage, cultivation -ಗಾರ A cultivator, farmer.

ಆರಂಭ s. n. Beginning, commencement. 2, effort -ವಾಗು, ಆರಂಭಿಸು To begin

ಆರಯಿಸು, ಆರೈಸು k v t To expect, look for, take care of

ಆರಯು, ಆರಯ್ಯು k. v. t To search; to investigate, consider, to look to, to nourish. ಆರಯ್ಕೆ. Searching, fostering.

ಆರವಾರ k n. Bawling 2, (f) a mortgage with possession

ಆರಾಟ (ರ = ಱ) a k n The anxiety of a sick man.

ಆರಾತಿ s n. An enemy.

ಆರಾಧಕ s. n A worshipper

ಆರಾಧನೆ s. n Service, worship. ಆರಾಧಿಸು. To worship, adore (ಪೂಜಿಸು)

ಆರಾಧ್ಯ s a. To be worshipped or served. n A class of Śaiva Brâhmanas.

ಆರಾಮ s n Repose 2, pleasure. 3, a grove, garden

ಆರಿಕೆ k n The Indian millet, *Panicum italicum*

ಆರಿದ್ರ tb. of ಆರ್ದ್ರ.

ಆರಿಸು k. v t. To collect, gather, to pick out, choose. 2, (ರ = ಱ) to quench, allay; to heal

ಆರು 1 k. n. Fullness, abundance ad. Fully Cpds ನೂರಾರು, ಸಾವಿರಾರು.

ಆರು 2 = ಯಾರು

ಆರು 3 k. n A pair of oxen yoked to the plough. 2, a frame put on the neck of cattle v i. To cry aloud -ಹೂಡು, -ಕಟ್ಟು To yoke oxen to a plough.

ಆರು 4 (ರು=ಬು) k v i To go out, be extinguished 2, to grow cool 3, to dry. 4, to heal. ಆರಿಹೋಗು To dry up, etc ಆರಬಿಡು ಒರಿಡು, ಆರಿಕ್ಕು To put out to dry.

ಆರು 5. (ರು=ಱು) k a Six. ಆರಡಿ Six feet. the dark blue bee. ಆರನೆಯ Sixth Cpds -ಗಂಟು, -ದಳಿ, -ವಾಡೆ -ನೂರು, -ರುತು, -ವರ್ಣ, -ಸಾವಿರ, etc

ಆರೂಢ s a Mounted, ascended

ಆರೆ 1 k. n A shrub, *Bauhinia racemosa*.

ಆರೆ 2. f n. A shoemaker's knife. 2, Mahratta -ಕಾರ A Mahratta man.

ಆರೆ 3. = ಆರ 2, pl of ಆನೆ 1.

ಆರೋಗಣೆ k. n. Eating, a meal (= ಭೋಜನ). -ಮಾಡು, ಆರೋಗಿಸು. To eat.

ಆರೋಗ್ಯ s n Health a Wholesome -ಗೊಳಿಸು To make healthy. -ಕರ, -ಕಾರಕ Healthy, wholesome.

ಆರೋಪ, ಆರೋಪಣ s n An accusation, charge ಆರೋಪಿ. An accused person. -ತರು, ಆರೋಪಿಸು To apply, ascribe, to accuse.

ಆರೋಹ, ಆರೋಹಣ s n. Rising, mounting, ascending, a ladder. ಆರೋಹಿಸು. To ascend

ಆರ್ಚು k. v i To cry aloud. 2, (=ಆರಿಸು No 2) to quench.

ಆರ್ಜನೆ s n Acquiring. ಆರ್ಜಿಸು To acquire

ಆರ್ಜವ s n. Honesty, rectitude. 2, [flattery

ಆರ್ತ s. a Afflicted, distressed; unhappy, full of desire. -ವ. Seasonable. -ಸ್ವರ. Cry of pain.

ಆರ್ತಿ s. n Pain, sickness. 2, desire. 3, = ಆರತಿ, q v

ಆರ್ದ್ರ s a Wet, moist, fresh; soft. -ಕ. Green ginger -ಕ. Green ginger -ಗೊಳಿಸು. To moisten -ತ್ವ -ಭಾವ Moisture

ಆರ್ದ್ರೆ s n. The sixth lunar mansion.

ಆರ್ಭ... [illegible]

ಆರ್ಬು, ಆರ್ಬಟ k. n Crying aloud, roaring. ಆರ್ಬಟಿಸು, ಆರ್ಬರಿಸು. To cry aloud

ಆರ್ಯ s n A respectable venerable man, an Ârya 2, a man of good family. 3, an elder ಆರ್ಯಾವರ್ತ. The abode of the Âryas, the country between the Himâlaya and the Vindhya mountains

ಆರ್ಷ s n A certain form of marriage ಆರ್ಷೇಯ Venerable, very ancient

ಆಲ k n The Banian, *Ficus indica;* ಆಲದ ಮರ. 2, the red water-lily 3, (s) animal poison

ಆಲಂಬ, ಆಲಂಬನೆ s. n Depending on. 2, support, assistance -ಮಾಡು, ಆಲಂಬಿಸು To lean upon, support. -ಕೊಡು. To give support -ಹಚ್ಚಿಕೊಳ್ಳು To patronize ಆಲಂಬಿತ Supported.

ಆಲಂಭ s n Seizing; killing

ಆಲಯ s n. An abode, house, an asylum. Cpds ದೇವಾಲಯ, ಹಿಮಾಲಯ, etc.

ಆಲಯಿಸು, ಆಲಯ್ಸು k. v i. & t. To listen, attend to, mind

ಆಲವಾಲ s. n A trench for water round the foot of a tree

ಆಲಸ್ಯ s. n Idleness, indolence, weariness, languor. -ಗಾರ A lazy man, sickly man -ತನ = ಆಲಸ್ಯ -ವಾಗು. To be slow -ಮಾಡು. To delay.

ಆಲಾಪ, ಆಲಾಪನೆ s. n Speech, conversation 2, lamentation. 3 the prelude in music ಆಲಾಪಿಸು To converse, to lament

ಆಲಿ 1. k n The pupil of the eye 2, an inflammation of the eye -ಕಲ್ಲು (=ಆಣಿಕಲ್ಲು) A hailstone.

ಆಲಿ 2. s. n A bee 2, a female friend. 3, desire. 4, a line. 5, a bridge, dike

ಆಲಿಂಗನ s n Embracing clasping, an embrace. -ಮಾಡು, ಆಲಿಂಗಿಸು. To embrace.

ಆಲಿಸು = ಆಲಯಿಸು, q. v

ಆಲು... [illegible] 2, an [illegible] *nulatum*.

3, one who possesses, *as* ಕರುಣಾಲು, ದಯಾಲು -ಗಡ್ಡೆ. A potato

ಆಲೆ k. *n* A sugar-cane mill. 2, the lobe of the ear

ಆಲೋಕ, ಆಲೋಕನ s. *n* Looking, sight, aspect. 2, light, lustre. ಆಲೋಕಿಸು To behold. ಆಲೋಕಿತ Seen

ಆಲೋಚನೆ s *n* Thought; opinion, intention, counsel. -ಮಾಡು, ಆಲೋಚಿಸು To think, consider. -ಕೊಡು, -ಹೇಳು To give one's opinion.

ಆಲೋಡನ s *n* Mixing, stirring 2, acquaintance, experience.

ಆವ, ಆವಂ (= ಯಾವ) a k *pro*. What? which? ಆವನಾನೊಬ್ಬ. Whoever ಆವಲ್ಲಿ (= ಎಲ್ಲಿ) Where? ಆವಾಗ. When? ಆವುದಾನೊಂದು. Whatsoever ಆವುದು What?

ಆವಗಂ a. k *ad*. Whenever, always 2, further.

ಆವರಣ s *a*. Covering; veiling, enclosing. *n*. A fence, railing, a bolt. ಆವರಿಸು To cover, conceal, enclose.

ಆವರಿ = ಆವಿ 1, *q v*.

ಆವರ್ಜಾ, ಆವರ್ಜೆ h. *n*. A head in the ledger.

ಆವರ್ತ s. *n*. Turning, revolving 2, a whirlpool.

ಆವರ್ತನ s. *n* Turning, repeating.

ಆವರ್ತಿ s. *n* A turn, time. -ಮಾಡು. To repeat, as a lesson.

ಆವಲಿ, ಆವಳಿ s. *n*. A row, range, line. 2, a series 3, a heap

ಆವಶ್ಯಕ s *a*. Necessary, inevitable *n*. Need.

ಆವಾಗ (*fr*. ಆವ) k. *ad* When.

ಆವಾಪ s *n*. Scattering 2, a trench for water at the root of a tree (= ಆಲವಾಲ). 3, a bracelet

ಆವಾಸ s *n*. An abode, dwelling

ಆವಾಹನ s. *n* Inviting; invoking a deity to occupy an image.

ಆವಿ (= ಆವರಿ) k. *n*. Steam, vapour; heat 2, a potter's kiln.

ಆವಿರ್ಭಾವ s. *n*. Becoming manifest ಆವಿರ್ಭವಿಸು. To be manifest, to be born.

ಆವಿರ್ಭೂತ s *a* Become visible.

ಆವು k *n* A cow *pro* We

ಆವುತಿ *tb* of ಆಹುತಿ, *q v*

ಆವೃತ s. *a* Enclosed, covered. ಆವೃತಿ Covering 2, an edition, *as* of a book.

ಆವೃತ್ತ s *a*. Turned round, averted.

ಆವೃತ್ತಿ s. *n*. Repetition. 2, revolution. 3, an edition, *as*, of a book.

ಆವೆ (= ಆಮೆ) k. *n*. A turtle, tortoise. -ಚಿಪ್ಪು. A tortoise shell

ಆವೇಗ s. *n* Hurry; agitation

ಆವೇಶ s *n* Entering, taking possession of. 2, demoniacal frenzy, excitement 3, pride. -ತುಂಬು, -ಬರು, -ಆಗು To be possessed by a demon

ಆವೇಷ s *n*. Pervading, visiting.

ಆವೇಷ್ಟನ s. *n*. Surrounding, wrapping, a wrapper, an enclosure. ಆವೇಷ್ಟಿಸು To surround, wrap.

ಆಶ *tb of* ಆಶೆ, *q. v*

ಆಶಂಸನ s *n* Wishing 2, declaring. ಆಶಂಸೆ. Wish, desire, hope, declaration.

ಆಶಯ s. *n* A resting place, an asylum; a receptacle. 2, meaning, intention 3, will 4, property

ಆಶಾಪಾಶ, ಆಶಾಬಂಧ s. *n*. The snare of lust.

ಆಶಾಭಂಗ s. *n* Disappointment.

ಆಶಿಸು s. *v. t* To desire, wish 2, to bless.

ಆಶೀರ್ವಚನ, ಆಶೀರ್ವಾದ s. *n* A blessing, benediction. -ಕೊಡು, -ಮಾಡು, ಆಶೀರ್ವದಿಸು. To bless.

ಆಶು s *a* Quick, fast. *n*. Haste -ಗ The wind, the sun

ಆಶೆ s. *n* Wish, desire, expectation, hope -ಗೊಳ್ಳು, -ಪಡು, -ಮಾಡು. To desire. -ಕೊಡು, -ತೋರಿಸು. To hold out hopes -ಕೆಡಿಸು. To disappoint. -ನಿಂತು ಹೋಗು To despair.

ಆಶೌಚ (*fr*. ಅಶುಚಿ) s *n* Impurity

ಆಶ್ಚರ್ಯ s *a*. Curious marvellous. *n*. Wonder, surprise, astonishment

-ಗೊಳ್ಳು, -ಪಡು. To be surprised. -ಕರ Surprising

ಆಶ್ಮ (*fr* ಅಶ್ಮ) s *a* Stony, made of stone

ಆಶ್ರಮ s *n* A hermitage 2, one of the four religious orders *i e* ಬ್ರಹ್ಮಚಾರಿ, ಗೃಹಸ್ಥ, ವಾನಪ್ರಸ್ಥ, ಸನ್ಯಾಸಿ

ಆಶ್ರಯ (*tb* ಆಸರ, ಆಸರೆ) s *n*. Depending on, a support shelter, refuge, protection -ಕೊಡು. To afford help -ಗೊಳ್ಳು To have recourse to for shelter ಆಶ್ರಯಿಸು To join, to obtain, to follow, to approach for protection

ಆಶ್ರವ s *n* Stream, flow 2, distress. 3 a promise *a*. Obedien . compliant

ಆಶ್ರಿತ s *a* Resorting to, having sought the protection of, protected, being dependant on *n* A dependant

ಆಶ್ಲೇಷ s. *n* An embrace 2 N of the 9th lunar mansion

ಆಶ್ವಯುಜ. ಆಶ್ವಿನ. ಆಶ್ವೀಜ s. *n* The 7th lunar month (September-October)

ಆಶ್ವಾಸ s *n* Breathing. 2, encouraging, consolation, *also* -ನ 3, a chapter of a book. ಆಶ್ವಾಸಿಸು To breathe to comfort.

ಆಷಾಢ s *n* The 4th lunar month (June-July) 2, an ascetic s staff. -ಭೂತಿ. A cheat, scamp

ಆಸಾರಿ (*tb* ಆಸರಿ) s *n* The plant *Asparagus racemosus*

ಆಸಕ್ತ s *a* Devotedly attached to 2, zealously pursuing.

ಆಸಕ್ತಿ s. *n* Attachment, diligence, zeal ಆಸಕ್ತನಾಗಿರು To be ardently devoted to

ಆಸರಿ *tb of* ಆಸಾರಿ, *q v*.

ಆಸನ s *n*. Sitting, sitting as devotees in peculiar postures 2, a seat, stool, chair *Cpds:* ಪದ್ಮಾಸನ, ಗರುಡಾಸನ ಪದ್ಮಾಸನ ಸಿಂಹಾಸನ *etc*

ಆಸನ್ನ s *a* Sat down, closely united near. [disease

ಆಸಮಾಕ (*tb of* ಅಸ್ಮಾಕ) *n* Aphthous

ಆಸಾದನ s *n*. Gasping, panting.

ಆಸು (ಉ = ಊ) k *v i*. To be weary or fatigued *P. p* ಆಸತ್ತು *n*. Weariness, fatigue -ಬೇಸರ *dupl* Fatigue. -ಆರು To be tired ಆಸಾರಿಸು. To remove fatigue, to rest.

ಆಸವ s. *n*. Distilling 2, spirituous liquor

ಆಸಾದನ s. *n* Laying down meeting with: obtaining

ಆಸಾಮಿ h *n* A person or individual.

ಆಸಾರ s *n* Incursion. 2 a heavy fall of rain 3 provision, food. -ಮಳೆ A kind of hail

ಆಸು k. *n* The sâl tree, *Shorea robusta*

ಆಸುರ 1 a k. *n*. Increase, abundance, strength 2, annoyance, trouble

ಆಸುರ 2. (*fr* ಅಸುರ) s *a* Relating to evil spirits. *n*. A form of marriage

ಆಸೆ (*tb of* ಆಶಾ. *q v*.) -ಗೊಳ್ಳು To shelter, protect -ತೋರಿಸು To allure -ಬುರುಕತನ Avarice. -ಪಡು To desire. -ಗಾರ, -ಬುರುಕ. A covetous man.

ಆಸೇವನ. ಆಸೇವೆ s *n*. Attending to assiduous practice, commerce.

ಆಸ್ತರಣ s *n* Spreading 2, a carpet 3 a layer.

ಆಸ್ತಿ s *n* Property, wealth. -ಪಾಸ್ತಿ *rel*. -ಕ A believer in God and another world, a theist. a man of property; pious, faithful -ಕ್ಯ. Theism. -ಗಾರ, -ವಂತ. A man of property.

ಆಸ್ಥಾನ s *n* Place site. 2, an assembly. ಆಸ್ಥಾನಿಕ A courtier

ಆಸ್ಥೆ s. *n*. An assembly 2. care 3 effort 4, condition.

ಆಸ್ಪತ್ರಿ f. *n* The English "hospital"

ಆಸ್ಪದ s. *n* Place. 2, position. 3, business 4. basis occasion opportunity -ಕೊಡು To allow

ಆಸ್ಫೋಟ. ಆಸ್ಫೋಟನ s. *n*. Moving to and fro, flapping, clapping the arms: knocking as at a door ಆಸ್ಫೋಟಿಸು

[illegible] s. m. The mouth; the face. [illegible] Sore mouth. [illegible] Spitting saliva.

[illegible] Tasting, eating: flavour. [illegible] To taste, to enjoy. [illegible]

[illegible] Known. [illegible] Noted for good qualities.

[illegible] s. m. [illegible] To take [illegible]

[illegible] s. m. [illegible] To discharge. [illegible] A warm [illegible]

[illegible] s. m. Taking food. [illegible] food. [illegible] To take food. [illegible] Digestion. [illegible] The eating. [illegible]

[illegible] s. m. Oblations offering: an oblation in the sacred fire. [illegible] To offer an oblation. [illegible] To receive an offering.

[illegible] s. m. Calling; summoning.

[illegible] surprise.

[illegible] s. a. Daily. s. A religious ceremony to be performed every day.

[illegible] s. m. Joy of mind. Gladness. [illegible] To be glad. [illegible] To make glad.

[illegible] s. m. Depth. [illegible] To sound the depth. [illegible] A deep tank.

[illegible]

[illegible] s. m. A mushroom.

[illegible]

[illegible]

[illegible] s. m. Depth. [illegible] To lessen. [illegible]

[illegible] s. m. Contempt, disgrace. [illegible] To despise.

[illegible]

[illegible]

[illegible]

[illegible] *P* [illegible]

[illegible] s. m. A servant, a soldier, a messenger. [illegible] Manly strength.

[illegible]

[illegible] s. m. A measure of a fire.

[illegible]

[illegible] s. m. The third letter of the alphabet [illegible]

respectively, as: ಗುರುವಿನ, ಗೋವಿನ, ಲೇಸಿಂಗೆ, ಗುರುವಿಂಗೆ, ಮಾತಿನೊಳ್, ಕರ್ತೃವಿನೊಳ್, ಗುರುವಿನಲ್ಲಿ, ಊರಿನಲ್ಲಿ, *and to form the instrumental sing and plur, either following the shorter or the common longer form of the genitive, as* ರೂಪಿನಿಂದ, ಕಾಲಿನಿಂದ, ವಿದ್ವಾಂಸರಿಂದ, *etc.*

ಇರ್ (= ಇಚ್, ಇತ್, ಇಮ್, *etc*) a. k Two. ಇಕ್ಕಟ್ಟು Two ways or parties; narrowness, strait, dilemma. ಇಕ್ಕಟ್ಟುಮುಕ್ಕಟ್ಟು. Many difficulties. ಇಕ್ಕಡೆ, ಇಕ್ಕೆಲ Both sides. ಇಕ್ಕಣ್ಣು. Both eyes. ಇಕ್ಕರೆ Both banks. ಇಕ್ಕಾಲು. Both legs. ಇಕ್ಕೈಯ್. Both arms.

ಇಕಾರ s The letter ಇ

ಇಕೆ 1 k *An affix for the formation of neuter nouns, as* ಹುಡುಗಾಟಿಕೆ, ಬುದ್ಧಿವಂತಿಕೆ, ಹೆಚ್ಚಿಕೆ. *etc*

ಇಕೆ 2. (= ಇಕ್ಕೆ) k. *An affix to form the dative of the infinitive with final* ಅಲು, *as:* ಮಾಡಲಿಕೆ, ಹೋಗಲಿಕೆ, ಹೇಳಲಿಕೆ *etc.*

ಇಕೊ, ಇಕೋ, ಇಗೋ k *int* Look here! lo! behold!

ಇಕ್ಕಟ್ಟು (*see s* ಇರ್) k *n* Strait, dilemma. ಇಕ್ಕಟ್ಟಿನ ಸ್ಥಳ. A narrow passage. ಇಕ್ಕಟ್ಟಾಗು To be strait

ಇಕ್ಕರಿಸು k *v i.* To sound. *v. t.* To kill.

ಇಕ್ಕುಳ (ಳ = ೞ) k. *n* Tongs, pincers

ಇಕ್ಕು k. *v t* To put, place, to beat; to serve, *as* food, to give, *as* money, alms, *etc*, to abandon, to be put. 2, to kill. ಇಕ್ಕಡು, ಇಕ್ಕರಿಸು To put aside, lay by. ಇಕ್ಕಿಸು To cause to put, *etc.* ಇಕ್ಕುಹ. Putting, *etc*

ಇಕ್ಕೆ 1. k *n* Abiding, an abode, a place of rest or refuge (= ಆಶ್ರಯ).

ಇಕ್ಕೆ 2 (= ಇಕೆ 2) k *An affix of infinitive, as:* ಮಾಡಲಿಕ್ಕೆ, ಹೋಗಲಿಕ್ಕೆ, *etc.*

ಇಕ್ಕೇರಿ k. *n* The residence of the kings of Bidanûr. -ವರಹ. A gold coin of that name

ಇಕ್ಕೋ. = ಇಕೋ, *etc. q v*

ಇಕ್ಷು s. *n* The sugar-cane, *also* -ದಂಡ

ಇಕ್ಷ್ವಾಕು s *n* A bitter gourd. 2, N. of the first king of the solar dynasty.

ಇಗ k *An affix to form masculines, as* ಗಾಣಿಗ, ಪಾಂಡಿಗ, ಬಾಳಿಗ, ಹೂವಡಿಗ

ಇಗರು k *v i* To be evaporated, dried up. 2, to shoot, sprout. *n.* A sprout, germ. 2, the gums

ಇಗರ್ಜಿ (= ಇಂಗ್ರೇಜಿ No 2) f *n.* A church.

ಇಗೋ. = ಇಕೋ *etc., q v*

ಇಂ, ಇಮ್ k *n* Sweetness; agreeableness. ಇಂಗಡಲ್. The sea of milk. ಇಂಗೋಲು The sugar-cane.

ಇಂಕಾರು h *n* Refusal, denial, abnegation, disdain; *also* ಇನ್ಕಾರು. -ಮಾಡು, ಇಂಕರಿಸು. To deny, refuse.

ಇಂಚು k *n* A little

ಇಂಗಡ (*tb of* ವಿಘಟ = ಪಿಂಗಡ, *q. v*) s *n.* Separateness. ಇಂಗಡಿಸು To separate.

ಇಂಗಲಿಕ, ಇಂಗಲೀಕ, ಇಂಗುಲಿಕ (*tb of* ಹಿಂಗುಲ) *n* Vermilion

ಇಂಗಳ (*tb. of* ಅಂಗಾರ) *n.* Heated charcoal, fire. -ಗಣ್ಣ Śiva. ಇಂಗಳಂಗೊಳ್ಳು To catch fire

ಇಂಗಿತ s *n* A hint, sign. 2, aim, intention, covert purpose. -ಜ್ಞ. Understanding signs, *etc*

ಇಂಗು 1 k *v i.* To be imbibed, to soak into. 2, to dry up. 3, to boil away. 4, to give. ಇಂಗಿಸು. To evaporate, to cause to give

ಇಂಗು 2. (*tb. of* ಹಿಂಗು) *n.* A perennial plant, *Ferula asafoetida.* -ಹಚ್ಚು, -ಹಾಕು To deceive

ಇಂಗ್ರೇಜಿ ಇಂಗ್ಲೀಷು f. *n.* English. 2, (= ಇಗರ್ಜಿ) an "église" a Roman Catholic church

ಇಜ a. k. *An affix to form masculines denoting* "born of" *as,* ಅಲರಿಜ (flower-born), Brahmâ

ಇಚ್ಚ = ಇಚ್ಛೆ. ಇಚ್ಚಂಕೆ A random figure the third term in the rule of three.

ಇಚ್ಚಕ, ಇಚ್ಚಗ (*tb. of* ಇಷ್ಟಕ) *n* Coaxing, ... Flatter- ... oax.

ಇಚ್ಛಯಿಸು (*tb. of* ಇಚ್ಛಯಿಸು) *v. t.* To desire, wish, covet.

ಇಚ್ಚೆ (*tb of* ಇಚ್ಛೆ, *q v*) -ಗೊಳಿಸು. To allure. -ಕಾರ, -ಗಾರ. One who wishes or wills; a willing man; *f.* -ಗಾತಿ. -ತೀರು A wish to be gratified.

ಇಚ್ಛೆ (*tb* ಇಚ್ಚೆ) s. *n* Wish, desire, inclination 2, a question in mathematics ಇಚ್ಛಾನುಸಾರ According to one's wish. ಇಚ್ಛಾಪೂರ್ತಿ Full gratification of one's desires.

ಇಜ್ k. *a* Two -ಜತೆ, -ಜೊತೆ, -ಜೋಡು. Unlikeness, dissimilarity, oddness.

ಇಜಾಫೆ h *n.* Increase, augmentation.

ಇಜಾರ, ಇಜಾರು h. *n.* Trowsers, breeches.

ಇಜಾರೆ h. *n* A contract, monopoly. ಇಜಾರದಾರ A contractor, monopolist

ಇಟಕು (=ಇಡಕು) k. *n* Narrowness, straitness *v i.* To come within reach

ಇಟ್ಟಣೆ, ಇಟ್ಟಳ a k. *n.* A crowd, throng, abundance 2 hindrance, strait. ಇಟ್ಟಣಿಸು, ಇಟ್ಟಳಿಸು To be close, crowded; to throng

ಇಟ್ಟಿ, ಇಟ್ಟಂಗಿ k *n.* The vomit-nut tree, *Strychnos nux vomica.* 2, (*tb. of* ಯಷ್ಟಿ) a spear, lance

ಇಟ್ಟಿಗೆ (*tb of* ಇಷ್ಟಕ) *n.* A brick -ಅಚ್ಚು A brick mould. -ಗೂಡು, -ಬಟ್ಟಿ. A brick kiln -ಮಾಡು. Brick to make -ಯವ. A brick-maker

ಇಟ್ಟೆಡೆ, ಇಟ್ಟಿಡೆ k. *n.* Narrowness; a strait, obstacle.

ಇಡಕು k *v. t* To pinch, to press, beat, cuff *n* (=ಇಟಕು, *q. v.*) Narrowness; trouble

ಇಡರು (=ಎಡರು) k. *n.* Hindrance, obstacle 2, trouble. 3, enmity *v i* (ರು=ಱು) To stumble.

ಇಡಿ k *v. i.* To be close, heaped, to crowd; to abound. 2, to be powdered; to crumble *v t* To pound *n* The state of being close. 2, the whole. 3, a collection, mass. 4, cement -ಗಂಟು A treasure. -ಸು. To cause to powder, to cause to put erect, *etc*

ಇಡು k *v t* To put down, to throw. 2, to put, place, to give, as a name; to set, plant 3, to put on, to lay by, keep; to preserve 4, *at the end of certain words* to produce, make, *etc* *n.* (=ಇಡುವಿಕೆ) Putting, planting ಇಟ್ಟುಕೊಳ್ಳು To take into one's employ; to lay by, *as* money, *etc*, to put on, keep *Cpds.* ಆಣೆಯಿಡು, to adjure; ಕೂಗಿಡು, to cry, ತೂಗಿಡು, to amass; ಮನಸ್ಸಿಡು, to mind, ಮೊರೆಯಿಡು, to invoke, ಮುದ್ದಿಡು, to kiss, ಆನಿಡು, to prop

ಇಡುಕು, ಇಡುಗು (=ಇಡಕು) k *n* Narrowness 2, a cattle-disease. 3, freedom *v t.* To unloose, set free. ಇಡುಕಿರು A throng, crowd. -ಮುಡುಕು, ಇಡುಮುಡುಕು A narrow curve or passage -ತೊಡಗು Full of difficulties

ಇಡುಗೆ k *n.* Putting on 2, an ornament

ಇಡುಪು k. *n* A crack, hole.

ಇಡೆ 1. = ಎಡೆ 1, *q v.*

ಇಡೆ 2 f *n* The earth 2, heaven 3, an oblation, food. 4, a cow. 5, speech.

ಇಡ್ಡಲಿ, ಇಡ್ಡಲಿಗೆ, ಇಡ್ಡಳಿಗೆ k. *n.* A kind of sour pudding.

ಇಣಚಿ k. *n* A squirrel.

ಇಣೆ, ಇಣಿ k *n* An ox's hump

ಇಂಡೆ a. k. *n* A crack; a piece, lump 2, a wreath, garland.

ಇತ್ k *a* Two. ಇತ್ತಟ್ಟು Both sides ಇತ್ತಡಿ Both banks. ಇತ್ತಂಡ Both portions ಇತ್ತರ. Two lines, both sides ಇತ್ತಲೆ Two or both heads

ಇತಬಾರಿ h *a.* Trustworthy

ಇತರ s *a.* Other, different 2, low, vulgar -ತ್ರ. At an other place ಇತರೇತರ. Mutual ಇತರೇತರಕ್ರಿಯೆ An action of two or more persons

ಇತಿ 1. ಇತ್ತಿ k *An affix to form feminines, as* ಜಾಣಿತಿ, ಮುದಲಿಗಿತ್ತಿ, ಒಕ್ಕಲಗಿತ್ತಿ, *etc.*

ಇತಿ 2. s *conj.* Therefore 2, in conclusion, here ends. -ಹ Thus indeed

ಇತಿಹಾಸ s. *n.* A legend, traditional account -ಕಾರ A historian, narrator.

ಇತು k *A termination of the third pers sing neuter of the imperfect, as.* ಮಾಡಿತು, ಮುರಿಯಿತು, ಹೇಳಿತು *etc*

ಇತ್ತ (*pron of* ಅತ್ತ) k. *ad* This side; in this direction or place, after this, further, *also* ಇತ್ತಲು -ಅತ್ತ To and fro -ಕಡೆ This side ಇತ್ತಿತ್ತ *rep* Nearer, in course of time -ಕಾಗಿ, -ಲಾಗೆ To this side, afterwards, lately, recently. [it was

ಇತ್ತು k *P p of* ಈ Having given. 2,

ಇತ್ಯರ್ಥ s *n* The whole matter, settlement, decision

ಇತ್ಯಾದಿ s *ad.* And so on etc

ಇದ. ಇದಕೋ, ಇದಿಗೋ k *int* Lo' look here!

ಇದಿರು (= ಎದುರು, *q v.*) k *n* That which is opposite, the front, opposition. ಇದಿರಾಗು To face. ಇದಿರಿಕ್ಕು, ಇದಿರಿಡು To put in front, to oppose ಇದಿರುತ್ತರ Contradiction -ನೋಡು To look straight, to expect ಇದಿರೊಡ್ಡಣ The hostile army ಇದಿರೊಡ್ಡು To oppose. ಇದಿಗೊಳ್ಳು To come to meet out of respect or love.

ಇದಿರಿಸು (= ಎದುರಿಸು) ಇದಿರ್ಚು k. *v t* To face, to oppose, withstand.

ಇದು k *prox dem pro* This, it

ಇದುರು = ಇದಿರು -ವಾದಿ A defendant. -ವಾದಿಸು To contradict, to contend.

ಇದೆ k *3rd pers sing pres neut of* ಇರು It is, there is. 2, lo' just now

ಇದ್ದಲಿ, ಇದ್ದಲು k *n* Charcoal

ಇದ್ದು, (ಇರ್ದು) k *P p. of* ಇರು, to be *By means of* ಇದ್ದು *a subjunctive mood is formed, as* ಇದ್ದರೆ, if ಇದ್ದಕಿದ್ದಹಾಗೆ. Just as it was; without any apparent cause

ಇನ್ (= ಇರ್ *etc*) k *n* Two 2, sweetness ಇನ್ನೂರು Two hundred.

ಇನ s. *n* A master king 2, the sun. 3, a husband -ಕುಮಾರ. Saturn; Yama, Karna; Sugriva -ವಿಷ Râhu assigned either in favour or charity, or in compensation of the duties of hereditary office -ದಾರ A holder of an inâm.

ಇನಾಯತು h *n* Favour, grace, a grant. -ನಾಮೆ A letter of favour.

ಇನಿ a. k *n.* Sweetness; loveliness ಇನಿದು. That is sweet, ambrosia.

ಇನಿತು, ಇನಿಸು (= ಇಷ್ಟು) k *pror dem pro* This much, this measure. 2, all this or these 3, a little, a trifle ಇನಿಬರು So many persons (as these)

ಇಂತ 1 ಇಂತಾ, k *An affix of comparison.* Than, *as* ಅದಕ್ಕಿಂತ, ಮುಂಚಿಗಿಂತ, *etc*

ಇಂತ 2, ಇಂತಹ. = ಇಂಥ

ಇಂತಿ, ಇಂತು k. *ad* Thus, so, in this manner, (*at the end of letters*) in conclusion, *as* ಇಂತಿ ಬಿನ್ನಪ ಇಂತಿ ನಮಸ್ಕಾರ. ಇಂತಪ್ಪ, ಇಂತಹ = ಇಂಥ Being of this kind, such ಇಂತಿಷ್ಟು So and so many or much, very much

ಇಂಥ, ಇಂಥಾ (= ಇಂತಹ) k *ad.* Such, like this, of this kind ಇಂಥಿಂಥ Such and such

ಇಂದ (= ಇಂ) k. *An affix to form the instr or abl. case, as* ಅವನಿಂದ, ನನ್ನಿಂದ, ಮನುಷ್ಯರಿಂದ ನನ್ನ ದೆಸೆಯಿಂದ, *etc.*

ಇಂದಿರ (*tb of* ಇಂದ್ರ. *q.v*) ಇಂದಿರಾ, ಇಂದಿರೆ Lakshmi

ಇಂದೀವರ s *n* The blue lotus

ಇಂದು 1 k *ad.* This time, to-day ಇಂದಿಗೆ For to-day. -ತನಕ, -ವರೆಗೆ. Till to-day ಇಂದಿನಿಂದ From to-day

ಇಂದು 2 s *n* The moon -ಕಳೆ, -ರೇಖೆ A digit of the moon -ಕಾಂತ. The lunar gem -ಜನಕ The ocean -ಮಂಡಲ. The disk of the moon -ವಾರ Monday

ಇಂದ್ರ (*tb* ಇಂದಿರ) s. *n* Indra, the deity of svarga, and the regent of the East quarter 2, a prince. *a.* Best, excellent -ಕೀಲ. N of a mountain -ಕೋಶ. A platform, terrace -ಗೋಪ The cochineal insect the firefly. -ಜಾಲ raud, trick, or of Indra' a son of Râvana -ಧನುಸ್, -ಚಾಪ A rainbow. -ನೀಲ A sapphire -ಪುರ, -ಲೋಕ Heaven. ಇಂದ್ರಾಣಿ Indra's wife

ಇಂದ್ರಿಯ s. n Relating to Indra 2, power, faculty. 3, an organ of sense. -ನಿಗ್ರಹ Restraint of the organs of sense -ನಿಗ್ರಹ ಮಾಡು. To restrain them -ನಿಗ್ರಹಿ One who restrains them *Cpds* ಜ್ಞಾನೇಂದ್ರಿಯ, ಕರ್ಮೇಂದ್ರಿಯ, *etc*

ಇಂಧನ s n. Kindling 2, fuel.

ಇನ್ನು k *ad.* Further, yet, still, moreover; hereafter *n* The current time ಇನ್ನಷ್ಟು. So much more. ಇನ್ನಿಲ್ಲ. No more, no longer; not yet. -ಮುಂದೆ, -ಮೇಲೆ. Henceforth, hereafter ಇನ್ನೆಲ್ಲಿ. Where else? ಇನ್ನೊಂದು Another thing. ಇನ್ನೊಬ್ಬ. Another man ಇನ್ನೊಮ್ಮೆ Once more, again.

ಇಪ್ಪ a k. (= ಇರುವ) *Pres. rel. part. of* ಇರು Being, *etc*

ಇಪ್ಪತ್ತು k *a* Twenty. *Cpds.* ಇಪ್ಪತ್ತೊಂದು, ಇಪ್ಪತ್ತೆರಡು *etc.*

ಇಪ್ಪೆ, ಇಪ್ಪೆಯ ಮರ k. *n* The tree *Bassia latifolia.*

ಇಬ್ (= ಇರ್). k *a* Two. ಇಬ್ಬಗೆ Two divisions. ಇಬ್ಬಂದಿ Mongrel of low descent; double-tongued ಇಬ್ಬರು. Two persons. ಇಬ್ಬಳ. Two balas. ಇಬ್ಬಾಯಿ Two mouths, double edge ಇಬ್ಬಿಬ್ಬರು. Two and two persons

ಇಬಡಿ, ಇಬ್ಬಡಿ k. *n* A kind of blackwood tree.

ಇಬನಿ, ಇಬ್ಬನಿ k. *n.* Fog, mist. dew

ಇಬ್ಭಾಗ (*fr* ಇಬ್-ಭಾಗ) k. *n* Two parts

ಇಭ s. *n.* An elephant. -ಪುರ = ಹಸ್ತಿನಾಪುರ.

ಇಮ್ 1 (= ಇನ್) k. *a* Sweet. ಇಮ್ಮಾವು A sweet mango. ಇಮ್ಮೊರೆ. An entreaty in sweet, humble words.

ಇಮ್ 2. k *a* Two ಇಮ್ಮಡಿ, ಇರ್ಮಡಿ Two fold, double ಇಮ್ಮಡಿ ಮಾಡು, ಇಮ್ಮಡಿಸು To double ಇಮ್ಮಿಗಿಲ್. Twice as much ಇಮ್ಮೆಯ್. Two sides, *as* of a cloth.

ಇಮರು. ಇವಿರು, [illegible] To eva-porate, dry up, to wane [illegible]

ಇಮಾರತು h *n* An edifice, a palace

ಇಮೆ a k *n* The eyelid.

ಇಂಪು, ಇಮ್ಮು k *n* Sweetness; agreeableness, pleasantness. -ಪಡೆ To become nice ಇಂಪಾಗಿ, ಇಮ್ಮನೆ Sweetly (ಕಿವಿಗಿಂಪಾಗಿ, melodiously)

ಇಂಬ k *n.* Expansion, width, breadth

ಇಂಬು 1 k. *n.* A resting place; a home, a place, space, room (ಆಶ್ರಯ) ಇಂಬಾಗು To become a shelter; to give room. -ಗೊಡು To give place, to afford shelter -ಗೊಳಿಸು To place.

ಇಂಬು 2. (= ಎಂಬು) k *n.* A saying, word.

ಇಮ್ಮನೆ k. *ad* In a sweet agreeable or proper manner.

ಇಮ್ಮು (= ಇಮ್ 1, ಇಂಪು, *q v*) k. *n.* Sweetness, ambrosia.

ಇಮ್ಮೆ k *a* Twice

ಇಯತ್ತೆ f. *n* Quantity.

ಇರಕು, ಇರುಕು, ಇರುಂಕು (ರ = ಱ) k *v i.* To be compressed, squeezed (= ಇರಕಿಸು) *v. t* To press, squeeze. *n.* The state of being squeezed 2, butting.

ಇರಚಲು (ರ = ಱ) k *n* A driving rain.

ಇರಟು. = ಇರಳು, *q v*

ಇರವಂತಿಗೆ k. *n.* A kind of jasmine, *Jasminum sambac*

ಇರವು a k *n.* Being, staying, support; condition, system.

ಇರಸಾಲು h *n* A remittance to the treasury

ಇರಸು, ಇರಿಚು k *n.* An iron axle-tree.

ಇರಳು (= ಇರುಳು, *q. v*) k. *n.* Night

ಇರಾದಾ, ಇರಾದೆ h *n* Purpose, design, intention, accord

ಇರಿ 1 k *A honorific affix, employed in addressing a superior, as* ಬೇಡಿರಿ, ಹೋದಿರಿ, ಸಾಕಿರಿ, *etc.* 2, *an affix of the 2nd pers pl past, fut, imper, and neg, as* ಮಾಡಿದಿರಿ, ಮಾಡುವಿರಿ, ಮಾಡದಿರಿ, ಮಾಡಿರಿ, *etc*

[illegible] 2 ([illegible]) k [illegible] strike, to pierce, stab, to butt, to kill [illegible] fling -ಮಾಡು To stab mutually. ಇರತ, ಇರಿತೆ, ಇರಿವು Piercing, stabbing, *etc*

ಇರಿಜಲು = ಇರಚಲು *q v*

ಇರಿವೆ, ಇರುವೆ ಇರುಂಬೆ, ಇರುಪೆ, (ರು=ಱು) k *n* An ant -ಗೂಡು, -ಹುತ್ತು. An ant hill.

ಇರಿಸಿಲು (ರಿ=ಱಿ) k *n* A pit-fall to catch elephants, *etc*

ಇರಿಸು k *v t.* To cause to be or to stay; to place, put, deposit.

ಇರು k *v i* To be, to exist, to remain, stay, to hesitate, delay *n* (ರು=ಱು). Goring, butting *P. p* ಇರ್ದು (=ಇದ್ದು, *q. v.*) ಇರಗೊಡು To allow to be ಇರಬೇಡ Do not be! *With a dative or locative case, it expresses possession, as* ನನಗೆ ಮನೆ ಇದೆ, I have a house. ಇರಲು Being, remaining. ಇರುವಿಕೆ, ಇರುಹ Being, existing, *etc* ಇರ ಇರುತ್ತ, ಇರುತ್ತಿರುತ್ತ. In course of time, gradually

ಇರುಕು (=ಇರಕು, *etc. q. v.* ರು=ಱು) k *v t* To compress, *etc* *n.* A narrow place, thicket

ಇರುಬು (ರು=ಱು) = ಇರಿಸಿಲು.

ಇರುಬೆ (ರು=ಱು) k. *n* A throng, crowd.

ಇರುವಾಯಿಕಟ್ಟು (*fr* ಎರಡು ಬಾಯಿ ಕಟ್ಟು) k. *n.* Constipation and stoppage of urine

ಇರುವಾರ k *n* Two shares both the landlord's and cultivator's share of the produce.

ಇರುಳು (=ಇರಳು) k *n* Night ಇರುಳರಸು The moon -ಕಳವಾರ A night-watchman -ಹಗಲು. Night and day. -ಹೊತ್ತು Night time.

ಇರ್ (=ಇರ್) k *a* Two ಇರ್ಕಟ್ಟು=ಇಕ್ಕಟ್ಟು, *q. v* ಇರ್ಕಾಲು = ಇಕ್ಕಾಲು, *q. v* ಇರ್ಕಿವಿ Both ears ಇರ್ಕೆಯ್ (=ಇಕ್ಕೆಯ್) Both hands ಇರ್ತಲೆ (=ಇತ್ತಲೆ). Two heads, two generations -ತಲೆಗೊಜ್ಜು, -ತಲೆಗೊಜ್ಜ A grandfather ಇರ್ಬಲ Both forces. ಇರ್ಪಾಳಿ. The second cultiva- [illegible]

ಇರ್ಕಿಸು (=ಇಕ್ಕಿಸು) k *v t.* To cause to put; to cause to kill

ಇರ್ಕು (=ಇಕ್ಕು) k *v. t.* To put down 2, to destroy *n.* Killing, destroying

ಇರ್ಪು a k *n* Loveliness, desire, charm. *a.* (=ಇರ್ಮೆ) Twice.

ಇರ್ವಾರು (=ಉರ್ವಾರು) *n* A sort of cucumber.

ಇಲಾಖೆ h. *n* A claim a village under a township 2, department; district, presidency

ಇಲಾಚಿ h *n* Cardamoms

ಇಲಾಜು h *n* A remedy; a resource; a means. -ಮಾಡು To attempt.

ಇಲಾಲು h. *n.* A large torch.

ಇಲಿ k *n* A rat, a mouse. -ಕಿವಿ Rat-ear a small-leafed vegetable. -ಪಾಷಾಣ. Rat's bane, arsenic. -ಬಲೆ, -ಬೋನು A rat-trap -ಯಾಲ, -ಪಾಲ An aquatic plant, *Salvinea cucullata*

ಇಲಿಕು k *v. i* To be squeezed bruised

ಇಲಿಚಿ k. *n* The jujube tree.

ಇಲಿಮಿಂಚಿ k. *n* A lemon the lemon tree.

ಇಲುಕು k *n.* Cramp, sprain

ಇಳೆ (ಇಳಾ), ಇಳೆ s. *n* The earth. 2, a cow. 3, speech 4, Budha's wife ಇಳಾತಲ Earth's surface. ಇಳಾಧಿಪ, ಇಳಾಧೀಶ, ಇಳೇಶ A king ಇಳಾಪುತ್ರ The planet Mars, a Śudra. ಇಳಾಪುತ್ರಿ Sitā

ಇಲ್ಲ k (*fr. defective verb* ಇಲ್, to be) *Third person of the neg. mood, used for all persons, genders, and numbers:* It, he, she is not or exists not, *etc.*, there does not occur or come 2 not, no, *as.* ಗುರುವಿಲ್ಲ, ಮಗನಿಲ್ಲ, ಹಿತವರಿಲ್ಲ, ಸವಿಯಿಲ್ಲ, ಮಾಡುವವಿಲ್ಲ, ಬೇಕಾಗಿಲ್ಲ, ನೋಡಿಲ್ಲ or ನೋಡಲಿಲ್ಲ; ಬಂದಿದ್ದಿಲ್ಲ, ಮಾತಾಡಲಿಕ್ಕಿಲ್ಲ, *etc* ಇಲ್ಲದೆ *Part neg* Not being, not existing, without. ಇಲ್ಲದ. *Rel part. neg.* ಇಲ್ಲದತನ Nothingness, poorness. ಇಲ್ಲದವನು A poor [illegible] To destroy [illegible] To cease to exist, fail, disappear ಇಲ್ಲವೆ, ಇಲ್ಲವೇ Is there not? or not? or. ಇಲ್ಲವೇ ಇಲ್ಲ. Certainly not. ಇಲ್ಲವೋ, ಇಲ್ಲೋ Or not? is it not? ಇಲ್ಲೆನ್ನು To say no.

ಇಲ್ಲಣ k. *n* Soot.

ಇಲ್ಲದೆ, ಇಲ್ಲವೆ, ಇಲ್ಲಾ. *See s.* ಇಲ್ಲ

ಇಲ್ಲಾಮಲ್ಲಿ k *n* A tell-tale, backbiting -ತನ Scandal

ಇಲ್ಲಿ k *ad.* In this place, here, this place (*opp of* ಅಲ್ಲಿ). -ಗಲ್ಲಿಗೆ From here to there -ತನಕ. So far as this, up to this. -ದ, -ಯವನು. A man of this place

ಇವ k. *prox dem. pro* This man, he, *also* -ನು. -ಳು This woman, she. ಈತ *and* ಈಕೆ *are used as substitutes for* ಇವ *and* ಇವಳು *respectively when speaking of a respectable person, cf* ಈತ *and* ಈಕೆ.

ಇವು, ಇವುಗಳು k. *pl. of* ಇದು, *q. v*

ಇವೆ k *pl of* ಇದೆ

ಇಶಾರೆ f *n* A sign or signal, a hint.

ಇಷು s. *n* An arrow. -ಧಿ. A quiver

ಇಷ್ಟ s. *a.* Wished, desired, agreeable; dear, beloved. *n.* Wish, desire, love 2, a husband 3, sacrificing -ಕಾರಿ. A person who confers what is desired or agreeable -ಗಂಧ Fragrant, a fragrant substance -ದೇವತೆ. A tutelary deity. -ಮಿತ್ರರು Friends and acquaintances, beloved friends -ಶಿಷ್ಟರು. Dear good people -ಸಿದ್ಧಿ, ಇಷ್ಟಾಪೂರ್ತಿ The fulfilment of one's desire. ಇಷ್ಟಾರ್ಥ. Anything desired or agreeable

ಇಷ್ಟು (= ಇನಿತು) k *prox dem. n. & pro.* This much, so much as this, thus much or many, *etc.* ಇಷ್ಟಷ್ಟು. This much and that much ಅವನ ಕಷ್ಟ ಇಷ್ಟಷ್ಟಲ್ಲ, his trouble is excessive ಇಷ್ಟೊತ್ತು, *etc.* ಇಷ್ಟೊಂದು So much as this, little, much

ಇಸಕೊಳ್ಳು k *v t* To take *imp.* ಇಸಕೋ!

ಇಸಬು h *n* An itch which attacks the wrists. -ಗೋಲು. An annual plant, fleawort.

ಇಸಮು h *n* A name, an individual. -ವಾರ. Name by name. -ವಾರವಟ್ಟಿ An individual account [an era.

ಇಸವಿ h *a* Christian. *n* The Christi-

ಇಸು 1. (= ಎಸು, *q v*) k *v. t.* To throw, shoot, as an arrow.

ಇಸು 2. k. *Affix joined 1, to Samskrita, tadbhava (and Hindusthâni) themes to form verbs, and 2, to Kannada themes to form (transitive or) causative verbs, as* ಅಂಗೀಕರಿಸು, ಅನುಕರಿಸು, ಬದಲಾಯಿಸು, ಭಾವಿಸು, ಭಾಗಿಸು, ಪಾಲಿಸು, ಪರಿಹರಿಸು, ರಕ್ಷಿಸು, ಪೂಜಿಸು, ನಡೆಯಿಸು, ನೋಯಿಸು, ಮೇಯಿಸು, ಮಾಡಿಸು, ಅಡಿಸು, ಮುತ್ತಿಸು, ಕಾಣಿಸು, ತರಿಸು, ಬರಿಸು, ರಂಗಿಸು, *etc.*

ಇಸ್ತಕಬಾಲು h *n* Reception, meeting and receiving a visitor

ಇಸ್ತಿಹಾರ್ h. *n* Proclamation -ನಾಮೆ. A written notice, advertisement

ಇಸ್ತ್ರೀ h. *n* A smoothing iron, ironing.

ಇಸ್ವಿ. = ಇಸವಿ

ಇಸ್ಸಿ k. *int* Fie! ಇಸ್ಸಿಸ್ಸಿ *rep*

ಇಹ 1 (= ಇಪ್ಪ, ಇರುವ, *etc pres rel p of* ಇರು, to be) a. k *n* Being; stay. ಇಹದು. = ಇರುವದು, ಇಪ್ಪದು, *etc*

ಇಹ 2. s. *ad* Here; at this time. *n* The present state, present world. -ಪರ. Earth and heaven -ಲೋಕ. This world.

ಇಹಗೆ, ಇಹಂಗೆ (= ಹೀಗೆ, *etc*, *q. v*) a. k. *ad.* In this manner, thus.

ಇಳ (ಳ = ಐ) k. *n* Coming down, descending. -ತರ. A going down, declining, *as* in age; subsiding, *as* anger, disease, *etc*, reduction, a slope. -ವರೆ, -ವಾರೆ A slope. -ಹೊತ್ತು. Midday to sunset.

ಇಳಕು (ಳ = ಐ) k *v t.* To cause to go down, to lower. *v i.* To go down, incline. ಇಳಕಲ, ಇಳಕಲು. Sloping, a sloping ground.

ಇಳಿತ, ಇಳಿಕೆ (ಳ = ಱ) k. n. Descending, descent. 2, ebb.

ಇಳಿ (ಳ = ಱ) k. v. i. To come down, descend, alight; to set, as the sun; to become less; to subside; to be abated, as anger; to be dispelled; to slope. -ಜಾರು. A declivity, slope; to slip down. -ಸ್ವಾಧೀನ, -ಭೋಗ್ಯ. A mortgage with possession. -ಬೀಳು. To fall downwards; to fly away. -ಯಲಿಕ್ಕು. To suspend. -ಬಿಡು. To let down. -ಮುಳುಗು. To dive completely. -ಯುವಿಕೆ. Descending. -ಕೆ. Descent etc.; fading; degraded condition. -ಗೊಳ್ಳು. To humble one's self.

ಇಳಿಪು, ಇಳಿಸು 1. (ಳ = ಱ) k. v. t. To cause to descend; to let down, lower; to take down, etc.; to dispel.

ಇಳಿಸು (ಳ = ಱ) 2. k. n. Stopping, thwarting. -ಹಾಕು. To thwart, oppose.

ಇಳೆ (= ಇಳಾ) s. n. The earth (ಭೂಮಿ). 2, water (ಜಲ). 3, food (ಅನ್ನ). 4, sound (ಶಬ್ದ).

ಈ

ಈ. The fourth letter of the alphabet. 2, contraction of ಇಯು: (1) in the acc. sing., as: ಬಾವೀ ತೋಡು, ಗಾಳೀ ತಪ್ಪಿಸ್ಕೊ; (2) in the gen. sing., as: ಸೆಲ್ಲೀ ಕಾಯಿ, ತಾಯಿಯ ಜೊತೆ; (3) in the loc. sing., as: ಹಂತೀಲಿ, ಹಾದೀಲಿ. 3, contraction of ಇದು: (1) in the imperat., as: ನಡೀರಿ! ಹೋಗೀರಿ! (2) in the third pers. sing. impf., as: ಮುಗೀತು, ಮುರೀತು.

ಈ 2. dem. pro. (substitute of ಇದು). This; these. -ವಾರಿ, -ಸಾರಿ. This time. ಈ ಕಾರಣ. This cause, on this account. ಈ ತರ, ಈ ಪ್ರಕಾರ, ಈ ಬಗ್ಗೆ, ಈ ರೀತಿ, ಈ ಮೇರೆ. In this manner. ಈ ವರಿಗೆ, -ವರೆಗೆ. Till now, thus far. ಈವಾಗ. Now, this time. ಈಹೊತ್ತು, -ದಿವತ್ತು. Today.

ಈ 3. k. v. t. To give, bestow; to allow. P. p. ಇತ್ತು. v. i. (= ಈಯು, ಈನ್, q. v.) To bring forth. ಈಯಲಾಗು. To be brought forth. ಈಯಿಸು. To cause to give; to cause to bring forth.

ಈಕಾರ s. The letter ಈ.

ಈಕೆ k. hon. pro. This woman, she; cf. ಇವಳು.

ಈಕ್ಷಕ s. n. A spectator, beholder.

ಈಕ್ಷಣ s. n. Seeing; sight. 2, the eye. ಈಕ್ಷಣಿಕ. A male fortune-teller; f. ಈಕ್ಷಣಿಕೆ.

ಈಕ್ಷಣೆ s. n. Looking.

ಈಕ್ಷಿತ s. a. Seen, regarded, considered.

ಈಕ್ಷಿಸು s. v. t. d'i. To see, behold, look at; to consider. -ವಿಕೆ. Seeing.

ಈಕ್ಷೆ s. n. Sight, viewing.

ಈಗ, ಈಗನು, ಈಗಲು, ಈಗಳ್ k. ad. Now; at this time. ಈಗಲೂ. Also now. ಈಗಲೇ. Just now. Cpds.: ಈಗಿನವನು, ಈಗಿನವರು, etc. ಈಗ್ಗೆ. For the present; now. ಈಗನ್ನು. Still now.

ಈಚಲ, ಈಚಲು 1, ಈಚಲೆ, ಈಚಿಲ k. n. The wild date tree. -ನೀರು. Toddy. -ಗಾರ. A toddy-drawer or -seller; f. -ಗಾತಿ.

ಈಚಲು 2. k. n. The white ant when winged.

ಈಚು 1. k. n. Dryness, saplessness, witheredness. -ಹೋಗು. To become sapless.

ಈಚು 2. (tb. of ಈಷೆ) n. The pole or shaft of a plough, cart, etc. -ಕಯ್. The staff or handle in the shaft of a plough.

ಈಚೆ k. ad. This side; on this side. ಈಚೆಗೆ, ಈಚೆಗೆ. To this side; afterwards, later.

ಈಜು, ಈಜಾಡು (=ಈಸು) k v i To swim. n. Swimming, *also* ಈಜಾಟ.

ಈಟಂಗಿ. = ಇಟ್ಟಿಗೆ, q v.

ಈಟಿ f n A lance, spear, javelin

ಈಟು. = ಇಪ್ಪು, q v

ಈಡಿ k. n Toddy. -ಗ. A man of the toddy-drawers' caste, f. -ಗಿತ್ತಿ.

ಈಡಿತ s a Praised

ಈಡು 1 *(fr* ಇಡು) k. n. Putting, throwing ಈಡಾಗು. To be exposed to, to become an object for, to incur ಈಡಾಡು. To scatter, disperse, expose

ಈಡು 2 k n Increase, strength; means 2, proportion; a prop, support, fitness, equality; an equivalent, compensation, a pawn, pledge, security -ಕಾರ, -ಗಾರ A powerful man ಈಡಾಗು To become equal; to suffice, to become bail or bondsman -ಇಡು, -ಕಟ್ಟು, -ಹಾಕು To pledge. -ಜೋಡು. A good match -ಮಾಡು. To make equal.

ಈಡೇರು *(fr.* ಈಡು-ಏರು) k. v. i To be fulfilled. ಈಡೇರಿಸು. To fulfil

ಈಂಟು a. k v t. To drink, sip.

ಈತ k *hon. pro.* This person, he *Rel past part of* ಈ 3, v. i.

ಈತಿ s n Calamity from rain, drought, locusts, *etc*

ಈತು k. *An affix for 3rd pers sing neut. pres of uncertainty or possibility, as* ಬಂದೀತು, ಬಿಟ್ಟೀತು.

ಈದು k *P p of* ಈ 3, *v. i. and* ಈನ್, *q v.* -ಎಕೆ Bringing forth

ಈನು (= ಈ 3, *v. i*) k. v. i To bring forth young, yean, cub.

ಈಪಿ k n. The dung of flies, a nit.

ಈಪ್ಸೆ s. n. Desire, wish ಈಪ್ಸಿತ Desired

ಈಬು f. n. Difference.

ಈಯು = ಈ, q. v.

ಈರ್ (= ಇರ್, *etc*) k *a.* Two. ಈರಡಿ. Two feet ಈರಯ್ದು. Ten ಈರಯ್ದುಸಾಸಿರ Ten thousand. ಈರಾರು. Twelve. ಈರಾರು ರಾಶಿ The twelve signs of the zodiac. ಈರೇಳು. Fourteen

ಈರು k v t To pull 2, to comb out nits n A nit 2, (ರು=ಱು) the gums

ಈರಣಿಗೆ k. n A comb for removing nits

ಈರುಳ್ಳಿ (= ನೀರುಳ್ಳಿ) k. n An onion

ಈರ್ಷೆ, ಈರ್ಷ್ಯೆ s. n. Envy, spite, malice

ಈಲಿ t. n A sort of weapon· a short sword, a cudgel

ಈಲು k n. Attachment, *as* that of animals or children [ago

ಈವರು (ರು=ಱು) a k *ad* A little while

ಈವಾಗ (= ಈಗ) k. *ad* Now, at this time.

ಈಶ s. n. An owner, lord, master. 2t Śiva (ಈಶ್ವರ) -ತ್ವ Supremacy

ಈಶಾನ s. n Śiva, the regent of the north-east quarter 2, the sun. ಈಶಾನ್ಯ The north-east quarter.

ಈಶ್ವರ *(tb* ಈಸರ) s. n. A lord. 2, Śiva. 3, the 11th year of the cycle. 4, the universal soul. -ಬಳ್ಳಿ, -ಬೇರು A twining shrub, Indian birthwort. ಈಶ್ವರಿ, ಈಶ್ವರೆ. Durgâ ಈಶ್ವರೇಶ್ವರ The lord of lords Śiva

ಈಷಣ s n. Desire, wish -ತ್ರಯ The three dominant desires ದಾರೇಷಣ, ಪುತ್ರೇಷಣ, ವಿತ್ತೇಷಣ, the desire after a wife, a son and riches

ಈಷತ್ s *ad.* Slightly n A little. ಈಷದ್ಭೇದ A slight difference.

ಈಷೆ *(tb.* ಈಚು, ಈಸು) s n The pole or shaft of a plough or carriage

ಈಸರ *tb. of* ಈಶ್ವರ, q v

ಈಸು 1 (= ಈಜು) k v. i To swim. n. Swimming ಈಸಗಲಿಸು. To teach to swim ಈಸಾಡು = ಈಸು -ಕುಂಬಳಕಾಯಿ A dried pumpkin used in swimming.

ಈಸು 2, ಈಯಿಸು *(fr* ಈ) k v t To cause to give 2, to yield, allow. 3, to cause to calve. ಈಸಿಕೊಳ್ಳು. To take

ಈಸು 3 (= ಇನಿತು, *q v*) k *pro* So much as this, this much

ಈಸು 4. *tb of* ಈಷೆ, *q v.*

ಈಹ, ಈಹೆ s. *n* Effort, exertion, wish, desire

ಈಹಾಮೃಗ s. *n.* A wolf

ಈಳಿಗೆ (*tb of* ಈಲಿಕ) *n* A sickle 2, a blade set in a stock for slitting up vegetables. -ಕತ್ತಿ, -ಮಣೆ. The stock wherein the blade is set.

ಈಳಿಗೆ (ಳ=ಱ) k *n* Disentanglement, freedom

ಈಳೆ k *n.* An orange, *etc., cf.* ಕಿತ್ತಿಳೆ, ದೊಡ್ಡಿಳೆ.

ಉ

ಉ The fifth letter of the alphabet 2, *the final of many Kannada words, as:* ಕರು, ಕಾವು, ಕಳವು ಕೊಡು, ನೋಡು, ಎರಡು, *etc* 3, *an auxiliary letter added to words ending in a consonant in classical language, as:* ಬಿಲ್ಲು, ಕಲ್ಲು, ಹೇಳು, ಕೇಳು, *etc* 4 *an auxiliary letter to form tadbhavas, as* ರಜ್ಜು, ತೇಜಸ್ಸು, ಮನಸ್ಸು, *etc* 5, *an auxiliary to form the nominative of nouns ending in* ಇ *or* ಎ, *as* ಸಭೆಯು, ವಿದ್ಯೆಯು, ಗಿಳಿಯು, ಹೇಡಿಯು, *etc*

ಉಂ 1. k *conj.* = ಅಂ

ಉಂ 2 k *int of displeasure*

ಉಃ k. *int of joy* hey! ah!

ಉಕ k *An affix to form masc. nouns, as* ಕಟ್ಟುಕ, ತಟ್ಟುಕ, *etc.*

ಉಕಾರ s *n* The letter ಉ

ಉಕ್ಕಡ k *n.* The outermost part of a town or village 2, an entrenchment about a camp, a match, a guard-house 3 a piece of rope tied to the end of a well-rope, for fastening the vessel.

ಉಕ್ಕಂದ k. *n* Swell abundance. 2, a narrow board or piece of bamboo tied between two beams used for hanging clothes *etc.* on

ಉಕ್ಕಿವ, ಉಕ್ಕೆವ k *n* Cunning, fraud

ಉಕ್ಕು 1 k *v i* To rise, swell, *as* the sea, to come up in boiling, to foam, to boil, *as* rage, to be elated. *n* Rising [illegible] 4, power -ಇಸು To lose one's power. -ವಿಕೆ. Rising ಉಕ್ಕೇರು. To rise up, effervesce

ಉಕ್ಕು 2 k *n* Steel. -ಸುಣ್ಣ Ashes of calcined iron

ಉಕ್ಕೆ k *n* Ploughing 2, remainder -ಹೊಡೆ To plough.

ಉಕ್ತಿ s. *n* Speech, a word, expression. -ಸು. To speak

ಉಕ್ಷ s *n.* An ox, bull. -ಗ One who rides on an ox Śiva -ಪತಿ, -ರಾಜ Śiva

ಉಖೆ s. *n* A pot, caldron

ಉಗನಿಬಳ್ಳಿ k *n* A shrubby creeper, the heart-leaved moonseed, *Cocculus cordifolius.* 2, the creeper *Lettsomia aggregata.*

ಉಗಮ (*tb of* ಉದ್ಗಮ) *n* Source, origin

ಉಗರಿಸು k *v i* To gasp, breathe hard

ಉಗಾದಿ. *tb. of* ಯುಗಾದಿ, *q v.*

ಉಗಿ 1 k. *v t.* To pull, draw off or out 2, to hurt, rend, slit, break 3 to fear. *n.* Pulling.

ಉಗಿ 2. (= ಉಗುಳು) k *v. i* To spit, spirt out.

ಉಗಿ 3 k *n* Steam, vapour or reek. -ಕಾವು The heat of steam -ಕಾಸು To warm by steam -ಕೊಡು To foment -ಯಂತ್ರ. A steam-engine

ಉಗು k *v i* To become loose, to flow, trickle, to be shed, to let loose, to throw ಉಗಿಸು To let loose, spill

ಉಗುರ್, ಉಗುರು k *n* A nail, a claw - [illegible] -nail.

-ನಂಜು. Poison caused by scratching. -ಬೆಚ್ಚಗೆ Luke-warm. -ಸುತ್ತು. A whitlow. ಉಗುರಿಸು. To scratch asunder.

ಉಗುಳು (ಳು=ಱು) k v i To spit out, to sputter n. Spittle, saliva. ಉಗುಳಿಸು To cause to spit. -ರೋಗ Salivation

ಉಗ್ಗ k n A rope or cord attached to anything, as a handle.

ಉಗ್ಗಡ, ಉಗ್ಗಡಣೆ a. k. n Repeated sounds, as in dancing or music, noise, clamour. ಉಗ್ಗಡಿಸು. To sound, to cry out, proclaim

ಉಗ್ಗಾರ tb of ಉದ್ಗಾರ, q v.

ಉಗ್ಗಿ k = ಹುಗ್ಗಿ

ಉಗ್ಗು k v i To stammer, falter in speaking v. t To throw as water. n. Stammering.

ಉಗ್ರ s a Terrific 2, cruel 3, hot, sharp. 4, angry n Śiva *Cpds* -ಕೋಪ, -ಬಿಸಲು, -ಬುದ್ಧಿ, -ಶಕ್ತಿ, *etc* -ಗಂಧ Bishop's seed, caraway -ತೆ Violence, passion, anger -ಶಾಸನ A severe command -ಸೇನ N of Kaṁsa's father.

ಉಗ್ರಾಣ k n. A storehouse, granary; a treasury

ಉಗ್ರಾಣಿ, ಉಗ್ರಾಣಿಕ k. n A store-keeper 2, a village-peon.

ಉಘೆ k *int* Hurra! huzza!

ಉಂಚಿ k. n The warp spread and starched.

ಉಂಕಿಸು k v t To consider, to observe

ಉಂಗುಟ tb of ಅಂಗುಷ್ಟ q v

ಉಂಗರ. ಉಂಗುರ k n A ring -ಗೂದಲು. A ringlet. -ಬೆರಳು The ring-finger ಮುದ್ರೆಯುಂಗುರ. A seal-ring.

ಉಚಾಯಿಸು s. v. i To go beyond, to overstep; to transgress, to pass or elapse, as time, *etc*.

ಉಚಿತ s a. Delightful, agreeable 2, usual 3, right, proper, convenient, suitable. n. A gift, present. -ಜ್ಞ. Knowing what is proper -ವಾಗಿ. Gratuitously

ಉಚ್ಚ (= ಉನ್ನ) s a High, lofty, elevated, tall, deep n The apex of a planet's orbit.

ಉಚ್ಚರಣೆ s n Uttering, pronunciation.

ಉಚ್ಚರಿಸು s. v. i. & v t. To utter, pronounce, speak

ಉಚ್ಚಲಿಸು, ಉಚ್ಚಳಿಸು k v i To come forth, proceed 2, to separate 3, to penetrate. 4, to run over, as water

ಉಚ್ಚಾಟನ s n. Scaring, expelling, removing by means of magical incantations

ಉಚ್ಚಾಪತಿ f n Taking of goods upon credit -ಆಗಿ On credit

ಉಚ್ಚಾರ, ಉಚ್ಚಾರಣೆ s. n Utterance, pronunciation, articulation

ಉಚ್ಚಿ k. n. The top or crown of the head -ಬಾಯಿ. The fontanel.

ಉಚ್ಚಿಕೆ s n. Diarrhoea

ಉಚ್ಚು k. v. t. To pull out, draw, as a sword. 2, to untie, loosen v. i To become loose, to fly off, as an arrow. 2, to become free 3, to be purged. n Looseness, *etc*. -ಗಂಟು. A loose knot. ಉಚ್ಚಿ ಬಿಡು, ಉಚ್ಚಿ ಹಾಕು. To strip off. ಉಚ್ಚಾಗು, ಉಚ್ಚಿ ಬರು, ಉಚ್ಚಿ ಬೀಳು To become loose

ಉಚ್ಚೆ k. n. Urine. -ಕಟ್ಟು Stoppage of urine. -ಚೀಲ The bladder. -ಜಾಡ್ಯ, -ಪೀಡೆ, -ರೋಗ A urinary disease, diabetes -ಬಿಡು, -ಹೊಯ್ಯು To void urine

ಉಚ್ಚೈಶ್ರವಸ್ s n. Indra's horse.

ಉಚ್ಚೈರ್ಘೋಷ s n Neighing.

ಉಚ್ಛಿಷ್ಟ s. a Left, rejected n. Leavings, orts, remainder

ಉಚ್ಛೋಷಣ s. n Drying up, making dry

ಉಚ್ಛ್ವಾಸ s n. Breathing, breath.

ಉಜಾಡು h a Desolate, depopulated.

ಉಜೂರು h. n Deference, respect

ಉಜ್ಜಯನಿ s. n. N. of a city in Mâlava, Oujein.

ಉಜ್ಜು k v t To rub n Rubbing -ಕಂಬಳಿ A kind of blanket -ಕಲ್ಲು. A smoothing stone -ಕೊರಡು, -ಗೊರಡು. A carpenter's plane.

ಉಜ್ಜುಗ tb of ಉದ್ಯೋಗ, q. v

ಉಜ್ಜ್ವಲ s. a Blazing up, bright, clear, beautiful, lovely -ತೆ Splendour ಉಜ್ಜ್ವಲಿಸು To flame, shine

ಉಂಚ 1. k n A bamboo basket used for covering poultry.

ಉಂಚ 2 = ಉಚ್ಚ.

ಉಟ s n Leaves grass, etc used in thatching -ಜ A hut made of leaves

ಉಟಾಯಿಸು f v t. To raise

ಉಟ್ಟಿ k n A net-work sling for suspending pots, etc 2, (= ಹುಟ್ಟಿ) a honeycomb.

ಉಟ್ಟು 1 k. n An anchor 2, (= ಹುಟ್ಟು) a paddle.

ಉಟ್ಟು 2 = ಹುಟ್ಟು k 2, P. p of ಉಡು, q v.

ಉಟ್ಲೋಟ, ಉಟ್ಲುಬಡಿ k. n A play in which any eatables or vessels containing them are suspended and swung and persons attempt to get them

ಉಡ = ಉಡಿ 2 k. -ದಾರ (= ಉಡಿದಾರ). A waist-string or zone; a woman's girdle.

ಉಡಗಿಸು. = ಉಡುಗಿಸು

ಉಡಗು. = ಉಡುಗು

ಉಡಚು k n. A venereal boil.

ಉಡಪು k n. Clothes, garments.

ಉಡಾಫೆ h. n Denial, rejection, scorn.

ಉಡಾಯಿಸು h v t. To reject contemptuously.

ಉಡಾಸ h n Causing to fly or wave. -ಪಾವಡ, -ರುಮಾಲು A silk cloth used as a fan in ceremonial processions.

ಉಡಿ 1 k v i To be shattered to pieces, to crush, bruise, to pull asunder, as dough, to twist, as a wick.

ಉಡಿ 2. k n. A pouch made by females (or males) by folding the front part of their garment for putting in eatables, money ...

-ಸಾಲು. = ಉಡಸಾಲ, q. v) 3, (= ಉಡಿಕೆ) a garment 4. a kind of disease.

ಉಡಿಕೆ, ಉಡಿಗೆ k n Putting on clothes, wearing, clothing, raiment -ತೊಡಿಗೆ Apparel and ornaments

ಉಡಿಲು. = ಉಡಿ 2, q v.

ಉಡು 1 k v. t. To wrap round the waist; to put on the lower garment, as the sîrĕ, dôtra, etc P p ಉಟ್ಟು n. (= ಉಡಿ) The waist. 2 a garment, clothes -ಗೆರೆ, -ಗೊರೆ A present of sîrĕ, etc to the bride and bridegroom at the celebration of their marriage or on any auspicious occasion -ದಾರ = ಉಡದಾರ

ಉಡು 2 k n An iguana, *Lacerta monitor.*

ಉಡು 3 s n A star 2, water -ಪ, -ಪತಿ, -ರಾಜ The moon

ಉಡುಕಿಸು k. v t To straighten, tighten, compress, to vex

ಉಡುಗು (= ಉಡಗು) k v. i. To shrink, shrivel, to abate, to fade, to disappear, to desist, to stop, to remove, to leave, quit v t To sweep ಉಡುಗಿಸು To cause to shrink, sweep, etc.

ಉಡುಗೆ. = ಉಡಿಕೆ, q v

ಉಡುತೆ k n A squirrel

ಉಡುಪ s n The moon (s ಉಡು 3) 2, a raft, float. 3, the bird called câtaka. 4, a serpent.

ಉಡುಪು = ಉಡಪು, q v

ಉಡುರು k n. The bellowing of an ox or a bull

ಉಡುವೆ k. n A jungle.

ಉಡೆ (= ಉಡಿ 2, q. v.) k n The waist

ಉಡ್ಡಿ k n Any set of three, as marbles, seeds, etc with a fourth set on the top. -ಇಕ್ಕು, -ಇಡು, -ಹಾಕು To set thus

ಉಣಾಂಕಿ a. a Inferior, lower

ಉಣಿ, (ಉಣಿಗ) k n. A person who feeds on. -ಕೆ Taking a meal -ಸು A meal,

ಉಂಟು 1 k (Third pers sing. of the ... it is

etc 2, that exists. 3, *with the dative it expresses possession (as*: ಅವನಿಗುಂಟು, he has) *n*. Existence ಉಂಟಾಗು To become, to happen, to be born, to accrue to ಉಂಟಾಗುವಿಕೆ. Becoming, *etc* -ಮಾಡು. To cause to be, to create, produce -ಮಾಡುವಿಕೆ. Creating

ಉಂಟು 2. k. = ಉರುಟು. ಉಂಟಾಡು To roll

ಉಂಡಲಿಗೆ k *n*. A kind of rice cake

ಉಂಡಿಗ s. *n* A single, solitary man

ಉಂಡಿಗೆ k *n* A stamp 2, a pass, a ticket for free passage

ಉಂಡು k *P. p of* ಉಣ್ಣು, *q v*

ಉಂಡೆ k *n*. A ball of anything, *as* of raw sugar, tamarind, *etc*. -ಗಟ್ಟು. To form a ball.

ಉಣ್ಣೆ k. *n* Taking a meal, a meal. 2, a tick.

ಉಣ್ಣು k. *v t*. To eat a meal (or ûta), *as* anna (kûl), hôlige, *etc* 2, to enjoy, as riches. *P p* ಉಂಡು. ಉಣ್ಣಬಡಿಸು, ಉಣ್ಣಲಿಕ್ಕು, ಉಣ್ಣಲಿಡು To serve up a meal ಉಂಡಾಡಿ, -ಗ. A glutton ಉಣ್ಣವಳಿಯದು Much, further, in vain ಮೊಲೆಯುಣ್ಣು. To suck.

ಉಣ್ಣೆ *(tb of* ಊರ್ಣ) *n*. Wool

ಉಣ್ಮು a k *v. i* To go up, to break forth, to issue.

ಉತಾರು s *n*. Subsiding, alleviation, diminution, descent, cheapness

ಉತಾವಳಿ f *n*. Haste, impatience

ಉತ್ಕಟ s. *a* Excessive, important, superior, high. 2, proud 3, mad, furious 4, difficult. *n*. Eagerness, affliction

ಉತ್ಕಂಠಿತ s *a* Desiring, longing for, distressed

ಉತ್ಕಂಠೆ s. *n* Longing; regretting, anxiety, regret

ಉತ್ಕರ್ಷ s *a* Raising, drawing out. *n* Excellence. 2, joy; pleasure

ಉತ್ಕಲಿಕೆ s *n* [illegible] 2, [illegible] 3, a wave

ಉತ್ಕೃಷ್ಟ s *a*. Excellent, eminent, superior -ತೆ Excellence.

ಉತ್ಕ್ರಮ, ಉತ್ಕ್ರಮಣ s *n*. Going out or astray, transgression. ಉತ್ಕ್ರಮಿಸು To depart, *as* life; to exceed, transgress, *as* an order

ಉತ್ತ, ಉತ್ತಾ, ಉತ್ತಂ k *A termination of the pres participle, as*: ನಡಗುತ್ತ, ಜೀವಿಸುತ್ತ, ನೋಡುತ್ತಾ, ಬರುತ್ತಂ, *etc*

ಉತ್ತ, ಉತ್ತಲ್ k *ad* To or in the middle side or direction, *cf*. ಅತ್ತ *and* ಇತ್ತ

ಉತ್ತಂಸ s. *n* A gold necklace worn by women

ಉತ್ತತ್ತಿ. = ಉತ್ತುತ್ತೆ, *q v*.

ಉತ್ತಮ s *a* Uppermost, chief, best, excellent *n*. The first person *(g)* -ಪುರುಷ An excellent man; the first person *(g)*. -ಶ್ಲೋಕ A man well spoken of. ಉತ್ತಮಾಂಗ. The head. ಉತ್ತಮಾಧಮ Good and bad. ಉತ್ತಮಿಕೆ Excellence, superiority ಉತ್ತಮೋತ್ತಮ The very best.

ಉತ್ತರ 1 s *a*. Higher, upper 2, superior, excellent. 3, northern 4, left, posterior 5, subsequent, following, latter. *n* An answer, reply, a mandate 2, a defence, rejoinder. 3, future consequence -ಆಡು, -ಕೊಡು, -ಈ, -ಹೇಳು. To give an answer. -ನಿಲ್ಲಿಸು To silence. -ಕಡೆ. The northern direction -ಕರ್ಮ, -ಕ್ರಿಯೆ Funeral rites -ಕಾಶಿ Benares -ಧ್ರುವ. The north pole. -ಪಕ್ಷ A defendant, the dark half of the month -ಪೂಜೆ Worship at the close of a ceremony. -ವಾದಿ. A defendant. ಉತ್ತರಾಧಿಕಾರಿ. A successor, an heir. ಉತ್ತರಾಯಣ. The summer solstice ಉತ್ತರೋತ್ತರ More and more, success, welfare. ಉತ್ತರಿಸು To answer; to order

ಉತ್ತರ 2 s *a* Crossing over, coming out, escaping from -ಣ Crossing over

ಉತ್ತರಣೆ k. *n* A common weed, *Achyranthes aspera*

[illegible] s *a* Relating to the north [illegible]

ಉತ್ತರಾಭಾದ್ರ s. *n.* The twenty-sixth lunar mansion.

ಉತ್ತರಾಷಾಢ s *n* The twenty-first lunar mansion

ಉತ್ತರಿಸು s *v t* To cross, to come out; to escape, *cf* ಉತ್ತರ 2

ಉತ್ತರೀಯ, -ಕ s. ಉತ್ತರಿಗೆ (*its tb.*) *n.* An upper garment

ಉತ್ತರೆ s *n.* The north 2, the twelfth lunar mansion 3, N of Virâta's daughter.

ಉತ್ತಾನ s. *a.* Lying on the back. 2, shallow -ಪಾದ. N. of a star, N of a king

ಉತ್ತಾ = ಉತ್ತ, *etc., q v*

ಉತ್ತಾರ s. *n* Rescuing 2, remission, giving back 3, land given rent-free by government to an individual (śânabhôga, gauda, *etc*) as a reward for services

ಉತ್ತಾಲ, ಉತ್ತಾಳ s. *a* Formidable, arduous, difficult, speedy; high, tall

ಉತ್ತೀರ್ಣ s *a.* Crossed, rescued, liberated, released

ಉತ್ತು (= ಉತ್ತುರ್) *P. p of* ಉರು, *q. v.* 2, *p p. of* ಉಳು.

ಉತ್ತುತ್ತೆ (= ಉತ್ತತ್ತಿ) k *n* Dried dates.

ಉತ್ತ k. *An affix for forming third pers sing neut as:* ಆಗುತ್ತೆ (= ಆಗುತ್ತದೆ), ಇರುತ್ತೆ (= ಇರುತ್ತದೆ), *etc*

ಉತ್ತೇಜಕ s *a.* Stimulating, stimulant

ಉತ್ತೇಜನ s *n* Incitement; an incentive, inducement, stimulant.

ಉತ್ಥಾನ s *n* Rising, resurrection. 2, manly exertion. 3, starting on an expedition 4, a courtyard (ಅಂಗಳ) 5, joy -ದ್ವಾದಶಿ A feast of the 12th day in the month of ಕಾರ್ತಿಕ.

ಉತ್ಪತ್ತಿ s *n* Birth, production, origin; produce, profit. -ಸ್ಥಾನ The source of anything

ಉತ್ಪಥ s *n* Error, evil 2, the air, sky

ಉತ್ಪನ್ನ s *a* Born, produced *n.* Produce, [illegible]

ಉತ್ಪಲ s *n.* The blue lotus, *Nymphaea caerulea* -ಮಾಲೆ N of a vritta. -ಮಿತ್ರ The moon

ಉತ್ಪಾತ s *n* A portent, prodigy or phenomenon, any public calamity, *as* earthquake, eclipse, *etc* -ಕ Perverse

ಉತ್ಪಾದ s *n.* Coming forth, producing. -ನ Bringing forth

ಉತ್ಪಾದಿಸು s. *v t* To produce

ಉತ್ಪ್ರೇಕ್ಷೆ s *n* Overlooking, indifference. 2, a simile, comparison.

ಉತ್ಸರ್ಗ s *n.* Emission 2, excretion. 3 quitting 4, gift 5 a general precept.

ಉತ್ಸರ್ಜನ s. *n* Letting loose, quitting, gift

ಉತ್ಸರ್ಜಿಸು s *v t* To let loose; to quit, abandon.

ಉತ್ಸವ s. *n.* Elevation. 2, joy. 3, a festival; a festive procession. 4, a libation ಉತ್ಸವಿಸು. To make merry, be glad *Cpds* ದೀಪೋತ್ಸವ, ರಥೋತ್ಸವ

ಉತ್ಸಹ (*tb. of* ಉತ್ಸಾಹ, *q. v.*) *n* A feast, a festive procession

ಉತ್ಸಾಹ s *n.* Effort, perseverence, energy. 2, joy, happiness. 3, heroism. -ಧ್ವನಿ A sound of delight. ಉತ್ಸಾಹಿ Active, persevering, a happy person ಉತ್ಸಾಹಿಸು To rejoice.

ಉತ್ಸುಕ s. *a* Restless 2, eager 3, longing for 4, regretting for. *n.* Ardent desire. -ತೆ Zeal, affection, regret.

ಉದ, ಉದಕ s *n* Water. ಉದಜ. The lotus.

ಉದಧಿ s *n.* A reservoir for water, the ocean

ಉದಯ s *n* Rising 2, the eastern mountain behind which the sun is supposed to rise 3, light 4, creation, production. 5 becoming visible. -ಕಾಲ. The time of sunrise -ರಾಗ The dawn; a morning carol ಉದ [illegible]

ಉದಯಾದಿತ್ಯ The rising sun. ಉದಯಿಸು. To rise, to be born

ಉದರ s n The belly, womb. -ನಿರ್ವಾಹ. Sustenance of life -ಪೂರ Till the belly is full. -ಪೋಷಣೆ Feeding the belly -ಶೂಲೆ The colic

ಉದರಿ s n Having a belly 2, = ಉದ್ದರಿ.

ಉದರಿಸು k. v t To cause to fall or drop down.

ಉದರು, ಉದುರು k. v. i To fall, drop down n Falling 2 the state of boiled rice or pulse not sticking to one another.

ಉದಾತ್ತ s. a. Elevated high 2, generous, illustrious. -ಚರಿತ A man of noble behaviour

ಉದಾನ s n Breathing upwards -ವಾಯು The vital air which rises up the throat and passes into the head.

ಉದಾರ s a Lofty, exalted, generous, liberal, proper, right -ತನ, -ತೆ Liberality, generosity. -ಶೀಲ. Generous-minded. ಉದಾರಿ A liberal, generous person.

ಉದಾರು h n Debt, credit, cf. ಉದ್ದರಿ.

ಉದಾಸ s. n Indifference, apathy

ಉದಾಸೀನ s. a Indifferent, neutral 2, despised n Indifference; contempt, disregard. -ಮಾಡು. To disregard, disrespect

ಉದಾಹರಣೆ s n. Saying, declaration 2, an example, illustration, instance 3, a reply 4, an opposite argument ಉದಾಹರಿಸು To declare, explain

ಉದಿತ s. a Bound 2, said, spoken. 3, sprung up born.

ಉದಿಸು. = ಉದಯಿಸು.

ಉದು a. k. dem pro. (cf ಅದು ಇದು) This (between the two)

ಉದಿರು, ಉದುರು (= ಉದರು, q v.) k i i To fall down, drop, as fruits or leaves. ಉದುರಿಸು, ಉದಿರ್ಚು = ಉದರಿಸು

ಉದೋ k. int. Behold (what is between the two)! ho! halloo!

ಉದ್ಗಮ (= ಉಗಮ) s n Rising, source origin; production a flower ... ಮಂಜರಿ A flower bunch -ಮಾಲೆ A flower-wreath ಉದ್ಗಮಿಸು. To rise; to ascend, to be born

ಉದ್ಗಾರ s n Spitting out vomiting 2, eructation. 3, an ejaculation, an interjection. -ವಾಚಕಚಿಹ್ನೆ The sign of exclamation

ಉದ್ಘಟ s n A kind of vessel -ನ Unfastening, revealing

ಉದ್ಘಾಟ s n. Watch or guard-house -ಕ. An opener, a key -ನ (= ಉದ್ಘಟನ). Opening, revealing, raising lifting up

ಉದ್ಘೋಷಣ s. n Crying out; sounding. ಉದ್ಘೋಷಿಸು To cry out, sound.

ಉದ್ದ (tb. of ಊರ್ಧ್ವ) n Height, tallness; length, depth a. Long, tall ಉದ್ದಗಲ Length or height and breadth. Cpds : -ಕಾಲು, -ಕೂದಲು, -ಗಿಡ, -ದಾವಿ, etc. -ಮಲಗು. To lie down lengthwise ಉದ್ದಳತೆ Height, length. ಉದ್ದುರುಟು Very proud behaviour

ಉದ್ದಂಡ s a Having a raised staff 2, powerful, violent, proud -ತನ. Pride.

ಉದ್ದನ ಉದ್ದನ್ನ s. a. High, tall -ಗೋಣು A long neck

ಉದ್ದಮಿ = ಉದ್ದಿಮಿ, q v.

ಉದ್ದರಿ = ಉದ್ದಿರಿ, q v

ಉದ್ದಿ k n. A low ridge in a field for irrigation purposes -ಗೆ. The pole of a carriage

ಉದ್ದರಿ, ಉದ್ರಿ (tb. of ಉದ್ಧಾರ) n Credit, purchase on credit -ಕೊಡು. To give on credit

ಉದ್ದಮಿ, ಉದ್ದಿಮಿ, ಉದ್ದಿಮೆ (tb. of ಉದ್ಯಮ) n. Business, profession. -ಗಾರ, -ದಾರ A trader, a farmer

ಉದ್ದಿಶ್ಯ s prep. Aiming at, with regard to, on account of.

ಉದ್ದೀಪ, -ನ s n. Inflaming, exciting, animating, stimulating

ಉದ್ದೀಪ್ತ s. a. Lighted, shining, inflamed.

ಉದ್ದು 1 (= ಉಜ್ಜು, q. v.) k v t To rub

ಉದ್ದು 2 k *n* A common pulse, *Phaseolus mungo*, *also* ಉದ್ದಿನ ಪೇಳು

ಉದ್ದೇಶ s. *n* Object motive, purpose, meaning, intention. 2, an assignment, a previous statement ಉದ್ದೇಶಿಸು. To aim at, intend.

ಉದ್ಧಟ s *a* Rude, impudent. *n* Rudeness

ಉದ್ಧರಣ s *n* Raising, lifting. 2, delivering, rescuing 3, final emancipation

ಉದ್ಧರಿಸು s. *v t.* To lift up 2, to rescue, deliver save, release

ಉದ್ಧರ್ಷ s. *n* Great joy, a festival

ಉದ್ಧಾರ s *n.* Raising 2, deliverance, redemption 3, obligation -ಕ. A deliverer -ಮಾಡು = ಉದ್ಧರಿಸು

ಉದ್ಧೂತ s. *a* Roused up 2 exalted, high

ಉದ್ಧೃತ s *a.* Drawn up 2, raised, elevated.

ಉದ್ಭವ s. *n* Birth, production, origin, existence, manifestation ಉದ್ಭವಿಸು To be born, to exist

ಉದ್ಭಾಸ s. *n.* Radiance, splendour

ಉದ್ಭಿಜ್ಜ s. *a.* Sprouting, germinating *n* A plant or vegetable -ಕೋಟಿ The vegetable kingdom

ಉದ್ಭಿನ್ನ s. *a* Opened, budded 2 different

ಉದ್ಭ್ರಮ s *n* Whirling; agitation, anxiety ಉದ್ಭ್ರಮಿಸು. To be perplexed.

ಉದ್ಯಮ (*tb* ಉದ್ದಮ *etc*) s *n.* Undertaking, exertion; business.

ಉದ್ಯಮಿ s *a* Active, diligent -ಸು To undertake anything

ಉದ್ಯಾನ s. *n* A garden, park 2, motive, purpose -ವನ. A beautiful garden.

ಉದ್ಯಾಪನ s *n* Accomplishing 2, the concluding ceremony of any religious observance

ಉದ್ಯುಕ್ತ s *a* Zealously active.

ಉದ್ಯೋಗ s *n* Business, an occupation, profession -ನಡಸು To follow a profession. -ಮಾಡು To work, to exercise an office -ಪರ್ವ. N of the fifth book of the Mahâbhârata -ಸ್ಥ A man of profession, an official. ಉದ್ಯೋಗಿ Active, diligent, a person in office. ಉದ್ಯೋಗಿಸು To undertake anything, to be busy.

ಉದ್ರ s *n* An otter

ಉದ್ರಿ. = ಉದ್ದರಿ, *q v*

ಉದ್ರೇಕ s. *n.* Excess, increase, abundance 2, enjoyment 3, forwardness ಉದ್ರೇಕಿಸು To be excited.

ಉದ್ವರ್ತನ, -ನ s. *n.* Going up, 2, rubbing and cleansing the body with unguents.

ಉದ್ವಹನ s. *n* Lifting up 2, carrying 3, leading home, marrying

ಉದ್ವಾರ್ಚನೆ s *n* Concluding ceremonies of an idol-worship

ಉದ್ವಾಹನ s *n* That which raises. ಉದ್ವಾಹಿಕ Matrimonial ಉದ್ವಾಹಿಸು. To marry

ಉದ್ವೇಗ s. *n* Rashness, agitation, anxiety, fear. ಉದ್ವೇಗಿಸು To go swiftly

ಉನಿ k. *v i* To be soaked; to soak. -ಯ ಹಾಕು, ಉನಿಸು To soak.

ಉನಿತು a. k. *a.* So much as this.

ಉಂತು k *ad.* In this (intermediate) manner.

ಉಂದು k *ad* This (or at this intermedi-ate) time

ಉನ್ನತ s *a* Raised, elevated, high, eminent *n* Elevation, altitude. -ತ್ವ, -ತಿ Height, sublimity greatness; eminence, majesty ಉನ್ನತೋನ್ನತ. Very high the highest

ಉನ್ನರು. = ಹುನ್ನರು.

ಉನ್ನಿಸು a k *v i* To think, consider

ಉನ್ಮತ್ತ 1, ಉನ್ಮದ s *a* Intoxicated; mad, furious 2, haughty, arrogant ಉನ್ಮತ್ತತೆ, ಉನ್ಮಾದ Madness, intoxication, pride. [*metel Datura*

ಉನ್ಮನ, -ಸ್ s. a. Excited in mind, longing for.

ಉನ್ಮಾದ s. n. Madness, extravagance, arrogance.

ಉನ್ಮೀಲನ s. n. Winking, awaking, expanding.

ಉಪ s. ad. Under, inferior, towards, on, near to, with, etc. 2, *prefixed to verbs or nouns it denotes approach, vicinity or inferiority, as.* -ಕ್ರಮ, -ಗ್ರಾಮ, -ಪುರಾಣ, *etc.*

ಉಪಕಥೆ s. n. A short story related in a long one.

ಉಪಕರಣ s. n. Helping. 2, an implement, instrument, a means.

ಉಪಕಾರ. s. n. Help, assistance; benefit, a favour, kindness; *also* ಉಪಕೃತಿ. -ಅರಿ, -ನೆನಸು, -ಸ್ಮರಿಸು To be grateful. -ಮಾಡು, ಉಪಕರಿಸು To benefit, help; to do a favour. -ಸ್ಮರಣೆ Gratitude. -ಹೊರಿಸು. To put under obligation, to oblige. ಉಪಕಾರಿ Gracious, a benefactor. ಉಪಕಾರಿಣಿ. A protectress, a palace.

ಉಪಕ್ರಮ s. n. Approach. 2, commencement. 3, a design. 4, a means. ಉಪಕ್ರಮಿಸು. To commence.

ಉಪಕ್ಷಮ s. n. Patience, forbearance.

ಉಪಗತ s. a. Gone to, approached, occurred, granted.

ಉಪಗೃಹ s. n. An inner apartment.

ಉಪಗ್ರಹ s. n. Confinement. 2, a minor planet.

ಉಪಘಾತ s. n. Injury, damage, hurt.

ಉಪಚಯ s. n. Collecting, accumulation, quantity, heap.

ಉಪಚರಣ, ಉಪಚಾರ s. n. Service; attendance; homage, attention, courtesy, civility. 2, pretext, metaphor. 3, physicking. ಉಪಚಾರಿ. Serving, a polite person. ಉಪಚರಿಸು To wait on, to treat kindly.

ಉಪಜೀವನ s. n. Living, subsistence, livelihood, maintenance. -ಸಾಗಿಸು. To maintain one's existence. ಉಪಜೀವಕ Living upon; a dependant. ಉಪಜೀವಿಸು. To live upon, to get one's livelihood, to live.

ಉಪಟಳ (*tb. of* ಉಪದ್ರ) n. Annoyance, trouble.

ಉಪತಾಪ s. n. Heat. 2, pain, trouble. 3, disease. ಉಪತಾಪಿಸು To feel pain, to be sorrowful.

ಉಪದೇಶ s. n. Instruction, teaching, information, advice; initiation in a mantra. -ಕ ಉಪದೇಶಿ A teacher; a spiritual guide. -ಕೊಡು, -ಮಾಡು, ಉಪದೇಶಿಸು. To instruct, teach, advise. -ತಕ್ಕೊಳ್ಳು To take advice.

ಉಪದ್ರ (*tb. of* ಉಪದ್ರವ) n. A calamity, disaster, trouble, annoyance, a disease or affliction; a national distress. -ಕೊಡು, -ಮಾಡು, -ಪಡಿಸು. To trouble, afflict.

ಉಪಧೆ s. n. Imposition, fraud. 2, a penultimate letter (*g*).

ಉಪನಗರ s. n. A suburb.

ಉಪನಯನ s. n. Investiture with a thread to be worn over the left shoulder and under the right.

ಉಪನಿಷದ್ s. n. The knowledge of Brahmâ as the only existent. 2, the sections of the vêdas which treat of this knowledge.

ಉಪನೇತ್ರ s. n. Spectacles.

ಉಪನ್ಯಾಸ s. n. A statement, suggestion. 2, an introduction. 3, lecturing.

ಉಪಪತ್ತಿ s. n. Production, gaining; a theory; proof, means.

ಉಪಪನ್ನ s. a. Produced, gained, proved; suited to the occasion.

ಉಪಪಾತಕ s. n. A sin in the second degree, *as* killing a cow, *etc.*

ಉಪಭೋಗ s. n. Enjoyment, use. 2, pleasure. ಉಪಭೋಗಿಸು. To enjoy, *etc.*

ಉಪಮಾನ s. n. Comparison, analogy, illustration, a simile.

ಉಪಮೆ s. n. Resemblance, similarity, a simile, comparison. ಉಪಮಿಸು. To compare.

ಉಪಯುಕ್ತ s. a. Adapted, suitable, convenient, useful. -ತನ A proper behaviour

ಉಪಯೋಗ s. n. Application, use, service, utility. ಉಪಯೋಗಿಸು To make use of, to use.

ಉಪರತಿ s n. Ceasing, stopping, refraining from sensual enjoyment

ಉಪರಿ s ad Above; upon; besides; beyond, after.

ಉಪರೋಧ s. n. Hindering, obstruction; impediment -ಕ One who hinders, etc. ಉಪರೋಧಿಸು To hinder, etc

ಉಪಲಬ್ಧ s a Obtained; perceived, well known

ಉಪವನ s. n A grove, garden in the [suburbs

ಉಪವಾಸ s n A fast, fasting -ಇರು, -ಬೀಳು, -ಮಾಡು To fast ಉಪವಾಸಿ. One who fasts

ಉಪವಿಶೇಷಣ s n A word used to modify an adjective, an adverb (g)

ಉಪವೀತ s. n. The sacrificial thread worn by the three first classes

ಉಪವೇದ s. n. Writings subordinate to the vêdas, as on medicine, music, etc.

ಉಪಶಮ, ಉಪಶಮನ s n Calmness, composure, patience 2, quieting, appeasing. 3, anodyne ಉಪಶಮಿಸು To abate, become calm or refreshed, to take rest -ಮಾಡು. To calm. appease

ಉಪಶಾಂತಿ s. n. Calmness. composure, tranquillity.

ಉಪಸರ್ಗ s. n Connection, nearness 2, trouble, misfortune. 3 a calamity 4, a preposition, a prefix (g)

ಉಪಸರ್ಪಣೆ s n Approaching (for help). ಉಪಸರ್ಪಿಸು To approach, to have recourse to.

ಉಪಸಾಗರ s. n. A bay.

ಉಪಸ್ಥಿತ s. ad Approached, near, at hand.

ಉಪಹತಿ s n. Destruction, vexation distu[illegible]

ಉಪಹಾರ s. n. An oblation; a tribute, present, gift

ಉಪಾಕರ್ಮ s n A ceremony performed once a year before reciting the vêdas

ಉಪಾಗಮ s. n. Approach, agreement. 2, a minor âgama

ಉಪಾದಾನ s. n Abstraction, withdrawing the organs of sense and perception from the outer world. 2, material cause -ಕಾರಣ. Immediate or proximate cause

ಉಪಾಧಿ s. n Virtuous reflection 2, deception disguise 3, a peculiarity 4, an attribute, epithet 5, the natural character of species, quality or action.

ಉಪಾಧ್ಯ s n Teacher 2, a priest that conducts the ceremonies, etc

ಉಪಾಧ್ಯಾಯ s. n A schoolmaster, a preceptor ಉಪಾಧ್ಯಾಯಿ, ಉಪಾಧ್ಯಾಯೆ A female teacher, a teacher's wife.

ಉಪಾಯ s n A means, expedient, way, scheme, stratagem -ಗಾರ, -ಶಾಲಿ A schemer, an expert -ಹೇಳು. To point out means. -ಕಲ್ಪಿಸು, -ಮಾಡು. To devise, contrive

ಉಪಾಸ. tb. of ಉಪವಾಸ, q. v. ಉಪಾಸಿ. = ಉಪವಾಸಿ

ಉಪಾಸನೆ s n Service, worship, adoration -ಮಾಡು, ಉಪಾಸಿಸು To worship.

ಉಪಾಸ್ತಿ s. n Worship, meditation

ಉಪೇಕ್ಷೆ s n Disregard, neglect, indifference. ಉಪೇಕ್ಷಿಸು. To disregard, disdain, neglect.

ಉಪೇಂದ್ರ s. n. Vishnu or Krishna 2, a king 3, N. of a man.

ಉಪೋದ್ಘಾತ s n. An example. 2. a beginning 3, analysis

ಉಪೋಷಣ -ಷ್ಯ s n. A fast, fasting.

ಉಪ್ಪತ k n Salted and dried vegetables

ಉಪ್ಪರ (tb of ಉಪರಿ) n Height, loftiness

ಉಪ್ಪರಿಗೆ (tb. of ಉಪಕಾರಿಕೆ) n. A palace; an upstair house, the upper story of [illegible] ouse

ಉಪ್ಪರಿಸು k. v. i To rise, as the soul, to jump up v. t. To extend, increase, spread

ಉಪ್ಪಲಿಗ k n One of the salt-maker's caste

ಉಪ್ಪಲಿಗೆ k n A small tree, *Macaranga indica*

ಉಪ್ಪಾರ (ರ=ಱ) k n A bricklayer, stone-mason 2, a salt-maker, f -ತಿ ಉಪ್ಪಾರಿಕೆ The business of a bricklayer or a salt-maker.

ಉಪ್ಪು k. n Salt. 2, doting affection 3, a game at which the women play ಉಪ್ಪಗಚಿ. A thorny climbing shrub *Monetia*. ಉಪ್ಪಿನ ಕಟ್ಟೆ. A salt pan or depôt. ಉಪ್ಪಿನ ಕಲ್ಲು Rock-salt ಉಪ್ಪಿನ ಕಾಯಿ. Pickles -ಕಾರ. Salt and other spicery. -ಗಡ್ಲೆ. Bengal gram parched and seathed in salt. ಉಪ್ಪಿಟ್ಟು. A kind of cake with various ingredients. -ಉಣ್ಣು, -ತಿನ್ನು. To be in one's employ. -ಮಡಿ. A salt—bed -ಮಣ್ಣು Salt earth. ಉಪ್ಪೂಡು. To salt

ಉಬ್ಬಟೆ a.k. n Swelling, elation, power, boldness, heroism 2, crying aloud

ಉಬ್ಬಣಿ k n A wooden beam for locking a door. 2, a kind of weapon; a club

ಉಬ್ಬರ k. n. Swelling, increase, abundance. ಉಬ್ಬರಿಸು. To swell, be swollen, to rise, to be full, to be elated, to be joyful.

ಉಬ್ಬಲು (=ಉಮ್ಮಿ, ಉಯ್) k. n The husk of paddy. 2 fallen hair or wool.

ಉಬ್ಬಸ, ಉಬ್ಬುಸ k n Asthma 2, fretfulness, envy 3, difficulty, trouble -ಪಡು, -ಬೀಳು To become asthmatic

ಉಬ್ಬಳಿಕೆ k n Nausea, qualm, eructation. ಉಬ್ಬಳಿಸು To nauseate

ಉಬ್ಬು k v. i To swell, to rise, to be puffed up n The state of being swollen; elation, pride 2, crying -ವಿಕೆ, ಉಬ್ಬಿಕೆ Swelling. -ಗುಂದು. Pride to fade -ಗೊಬ್ಬು. Excessive pride -ತಗ್ಗು Hill and dale; unevenness. -ಹೊಳೆ A swollen ri..., ... To cause to swell ...

ಉಬ್ಬೆ k n. Heat; steam. 2, rain -ಗೆ ಹಾಕು. To expose to steam -ಮನೆ. A washerman's hut where dirty clothes are steamed.

ಉಬ್ಬೇಗ (tb. of ಉದ್ವೇಗ) n Anxiety, fear, distress

ಉಭಯ s a. Both -ಕರ್ತೃಕ Two agents -ತರು, -ತ್ರರು Persons of both sides, both persons. -ತ್ರ. In both places or times. -ಪಾರ್ಶ್ವ. Both sides -ಭಾಷೆ Both languages Samskrita and Kannada -ಲಿಂಗ. A word of common gender -ಲೋಕ This and the other world. ಉಭಯಾನುಮತ. Mutually agreed to or accepted ಉಭಯಾನುಮತಿ Mutual agreement.

ಉಮಾ, ಉಮೆ s. n. Lin, flax, *Linum usitatissimum* 2, Śiva's wife ಉಮಾಪತಿ, ಉಮೆಯೊಡೆಯ Śiva.

ಉಮೇದ, ಉಮೇದು h n. Confidence, assurance, aptitude, inclination -ವಾರ. A candidate, volunteer. -ವಾರಿ Expectancy, volunteering.

ಉಂಬಳಿ, ಉಂಬುಳಿ (ಳಿ=ೞಿ) k. n An enjoyment-gift · the rent-free grant of a land -ಗಾರ. The holder of an umbali.

ಉಂಬು k *A vulgar form of* ಉಣ್ಣು, q. v.

ಉಮ್ಮತ್ತ. tb. of ಉನ್ಮತ್ತ q v.

ಉಮ್ಮಲು k n Phlegm, mucus. 2, difficult breathing.

ಉಮ್ಮಳ (tb of ಉಷ್ಮನ್) n. Heat; grief, trouble, anxiety. ಉಮ್ಮಳಿಕೆ. Heat, distress, anxiety, fatigue. ಉಮ್ಮಳಿಸು. To be hot, to grieve, be distressed.

ಉಮ್ಮಿ, ಉಯ್. = ಉಬ್ಬಲು, q v.

ಉಮ್ಮಿಗೆ, ಉಮ್ಮುಗೆ k n Milky grains of wheat or barley fried for eating.

ಉಮ್ಮೆ k n A stone used to remove juice 2, (tb of ಊಷ್ಮ) heat, steam

ಉಯ್ k v t. To restrain, check, bind

ಉಯ್ಯಾಲು, ಉಯ್ಯಾಲು, ಉಯ್ಯಾಲೆ k. n. A swing. ಉಯ್ಯಾಲೋತ್ಸವ A festival in which the idol of Vishnu is ... un

ಉರ (*tb of* ಉರಸ್) *n.* The breast
ಉರಗ s *n* A snake -ಭೂಷಣ. A mungoose, a peacock. -ಶಯನ Vishnu -ಪತಿ, ಉರಗೇಂದ್ರ The king of snakes
ಉರಟ = ಉರುಟು.
ಉರಟಣೆ k *n* Rolling-play a play of a newly married couple
ಉರಟಾ h. *a* Inverse upside down. -ಯಿಸು To reject, deceive
ಉರಟು (= ಉರುಟು) k *v i* To roll *n* Coarseness, *as* of cloth, thread, hair, *etc*, thickness. -ತೊಗಲು. A coarse skin -ನೂಲು Stout thread.
ಉರತ (= ಉರುತ) k *n* Burning, irritation
ಉರಪು (= ಉರುಪು) k *v. i* To inflame, burn *n* Burning
ಉರಲು 1. (= ಉರುಲು) k. *n* A running knot, a noose, snare 2, rolling, crumbling. -ಗಡ್ಡೆ The potato
ಉರಲು 2, ಉರವಲ k *n* Fuel.
ಉರವಣೆ k *n.* Crying aloud.
ಉರವಣೆ k. *n.* Haste, rashness, impulse, urgency. ಉರವಣಿಸು To act hastily or presumptuously
ಉರಳಿ k *n* A ball, *as* of dough, *etc.* 2, a bulb 3, a round vessel
ಉರಳು = ಉರುಳು, *q v*
ಉರಿ 1 k *v. i.* To burn, blaze, glow, to burn from rage, envy, fever, *etc.* *n* Burning; flame, blaze. *etc* -ಆರಿಸು, -ಕೆಡಿಸು, -ನೊಂದಿಸು. To quench a flame. -ಕಜ್ಜಿ A burning itch -ಕಿಡಿ A glowing spark. -ಕೆ, -ತ Burning. -ಕೆಂಡ A burning coal. -ಗಣ್ಣು An inflamed eye -ಗಿಚ್ಚು, -ಬೆಂಕಿ A flaming fire -ಚೇಳು A reddish kind of scorpion -ನಂಜು Morbid humours of the body -ನಾಲಿಗೆ A fiery tongue. -ಮಾರಿ. The furious Durga, a passionate woman -ಬತ್ತಿ, -ವತ್ತಿ A burning wick -ಮೂತ್ರ, -ಯುಚ್ಚೆ. Morbidly heated urine, strangury, gravel. -ಮಾತು, -ವಾತು A sharp word -ಹಚ್ಚು, -ಹತ್ತಿಸು To kindle a fire -ಸು, -ಸು To cause to burn
ಉರಿ 2 (ರಿ = ಱಿ) k *n* A coarse network for suspending pots and other vessels.
ಉರು 1. s *a* Great much, excessive, eminent, precious -ತರ Greater, wider
ಉರು 2. (ರು = ಱು) a k. *v i.* To be, to stay, stop, to hesitate, to come about
ಉರುಕ.(ರು = ಱು) k *n* Standing, stopping
ಉರುಗು 1. k *n.* Passion, anger
ಉರುಗು 2 (ರು = ಱು) a k *v i* To be crooked, distorted *n* Crookedness -ಕಾಲು A crooked leg. -ಬಾಯಿ A wry face. -ಬೆರಳು A crooked finger
ಉರುಟು (= ಉರಟು) k. *v i* To go beyond, to be overbearing 2, to roll. *n* Pride 2, coarseness *as* of cloth, *etc* 3, rolling, roundness, a plain ring ಉರುಟಾಣಿ = ಉರಟಣೆ, *q v.*
ಉರುತ, ಉರುಪು = ಉರತ, ಉರಪು
ಉರುಬು (ರು = ಱು) k *n* Violence, rapidity, force
ಉರುಬೆ, ಉರುವು (ರು = ಱು) k *n* Mass. multitude, excess, excellence
ಉರುಲು (= ಉರಲು) k. *n* A noose, snare, gin -ಹಾಕಿಕೊಳ್ಳು To hang one's self
ಉರುವಣೆ = ಉರವಣೆ, *q v.*
ಉರುಸು h *n* Offerings at the shrine of a Muhammadan saint
ಉರುಳು k. *v i.* To roll, to be turned over, to revolve *n.* Rolling. 2, a noose ಉರುಳಾಡು To roll about. ಉರುಳಿಸು To cause to roll, *etc.* -ಸೇವೆ. A religious vow or penance which consists in rolling one's self round a temple.
ಉರೆ (ರೆ = ಱೆ) k *ad* Abundantly, well, nicely fully, much. *n.* Abundance
ಉರೇ k *int* Bravo! well done!
ಉರ್ಕು. = ಉಕ್ಕು. *q v*
ಉರ್ಚು = ಉಚ್ಚು, *q. v.*
ಉರ್ಮು = ಉಮ್ಮು, *q. v*
ಉರ್ಬು = ಉಬ್ಬು, *q v.*

ಉಲಕು k. v. i. To start up, *as* a tiger. 2, to flash on the mind, painful thoughts to arise. 3, to be sprained. *n.* A sprain

ಉಲಿ k. v. i. To sound, to cry, utter, speak. *n.* A sound, a cry. -ವ, -ಪು, -ವು. A sound; a cry

ಉಲಿಪೆ. = ಉಲುಫೆ, *q. v.*

ಉಲುಕು, ಉಲ್ಕು = ಉಲಕು, *q. v.*

ಉಲುಟು. = ಉರುಳು, *q. v.*

ಉಲುಫೆ (= ಉಲಿಪೆ) h. *n.* Gratuitous supplies or presents given to great persons on a journey

ಉಲೂಕ s. *n.* An owl

ಉಲ್ಕ, ಉಲ್ಕೆ s. *n.* A flame, a meteor. 2, a firebrand. ಉಲ್ಕಾಪಾತ Falling of a star.

ಉಲ್ಲಂಗಿ k. *n.* A snipe

ಉಲ್ಲಂಘನೆ s. *n.* Passing over; transgression. ಉಲ್ಲಂಘಿಸು. To cross, to transgress.

ಉಲ್ಲಟ, ಉಲ್ಲಟಪಲ್ಲಟ (= ಉರಟಾ) f. *a.* Inverse, upside down, topsyturvy, out of order.

ಉಲ್ಲಸ. = ಉಲ್ಲಾಸ, *q. v.* ಉಲ್ಲಸಿಸು. = ಉಲ್ಲಾಸಿಸು.

ಉಲ್ಲಾಪ s. *n.* An outcry. 2, change of voice in grief, sickness, *etc*

ಉಲ್ಲಾಸ s. *n.* Sport, joy, delight. -ಗಾರ. A gay man. ಉಲ್ಲಾಸಿಸು (= ಉಲ್ಲಸಿಸು). To delight, be merry.

ಉಲ್ಲಿ k. *ad.* In this intermediate place.

ಉಲ್ಲೇಖ, ಉಲ್ಲೇಖನ s. *n.* Scraping, writing, description. ಉಲ್ಲೇಖಿಸು To write

ಉಲ್ಹಾಸ. *tb. of* ಉಲ್ಲಾಸ. *q. v*

ಉವ k. *An affix of the present rel. part. of the future, and of the imp., as* ಸಾಯುವ, ಬರುವ, ಕೇಳುವ. *ad.* This (intermediate) man.

ಉಶನಸ (*tb. of* ಉಶನಸ್) *n.* The planet Venus. 2, Sukra.

ಉಶ್ವಾಸ (*tb. of* ಉಚ್ಛ್ವಾಸ) *n.* Breathing, inhaling, breath. -ನಿಶ್ವಾಸ. Inhaling and exhaling.

ಉಷ, ಉಷಸ್ s. *n.* Morning light, dawn. ಉಷಃಕಾಲ The dawn, daybreak

ಉಷ್ಟ್ರ s. *n.* A camel. 2, an "ostrich". ಉಷ್ಟ್ರ, -ಕೆ A she-camel

ಉಷ್ಣ s. *a.* Hot, warm. 2, passionate, sharp. *n.* Heat, warmth, *also* -ತೆ. -ಉದಕ, ಉಷ್ಣೋದಕ. Hot water.

ಉಸಲಿ h. *n.* Boiled pulse seasoned with salt, chilli, *etc*

ಉಸಬು, ಉಸುಕು, ಉಸುಬು k. *n.* Sand.

ಉಸಲು. = ಉಸುರು *q. v.*

ಉಸಾಬರಿ f. *n.* Business, affair.

ಉಸುರು k. *v. i.* To speak, say, (to breathe). *n.* Breath, life. 2 taking breath. ಉಸುರಾಡಿಸು, ಉಸುರಿಕ್ಕು, ಉಸುರಿಡು, ಉಸುರ್ಗರೆ, ಉಸುರ್ವಿಡು To breathe. -ಕಟ್ಟು, -ಹಿಡಿ. To hold the breath. -ಕಟ್ಟಿಸು. To choke. -ಕಳೆ, -ಬಿಡು. To exhale, to expire

ಉಹೂ k. *int.* A sound used by cattle drivers in calling their cattle. *ad.* No, no!

ಉಳ್ k. *v. t.* To have, possess. *v. i.* To be. *Pres. rel. past* ಉಳ್ಳ. Being, possessing, *affixed to nouns it turns them into adjectives, as* ಕೆಲಸವುಳ್ಳ, employed, ಬುದ್ಧಿಯುಳ್ಳ, wise, ಜ್ವರವುಳ್ಳ, feverish, ಪ್ರೀತಿಯುಳ್ಳ, lovely, *etc.*

ಉಳ (ಳ = ಱ) (= ಉಳಿ 2) k. *n.* Remaining, remnant. -ಕೊಳ್ಳು. To remain, stop, to escape. -ಗಡೆ, -ಪಡಿ, -ವು, -ಹು. The remainder. -ಿ. Remaining

ಉಳಿ 1. k. *v. i.* To conceal one's self. *n.* A thief. 2, a chisel, an awl. 3, hiding; an ambush, a hunter's hut.

ಉಳಿ 2 (ಳ = ಱ) k. *v. i.* To leave, quit. 2. to be left, to remain. 3, to be left out. 4, to be saved. 5, to remain behind. *P. p.* ಉಳಿದು ಉಳಿತು. *n.* Remaining, remnant. -ಕೆ. Remainder. [illegible] kind of omen. -[illegible], -[illegible]. To [illegible] save, keep alive

ಉಳು (ಳು = ಡು) k. v. t. To plough, P. p. ಉತ್ತು. ಉತ್ತಭೂಮಿ, ploughed land. -ತ, -ಮೆ, -ವಿಕೆ. Ploughing.

ಉಳುಗು (ಳು = ಡು) k. v. i. To be attached. ಉಳ್ಕೆ. Attachment.

ಉಳ್ಳು k. v. i. To shine; to blaze. n. A shining substance, a meteor. 2, = ಉಲ್ಕೆ.

ಉಳ್ಳಿ k. n. A bulb; an onion. *Cpds.*: ಕಾರುಳ್ಳಿ, ಸೀರುಳ್ಳಿ, ಬೆಳ್ಳುಳ್ಳಿ. -ಗಡ್ಡೆ. An onion.

ಊ

ಊ The sixth letter of the alphabet. 2, *a copulative conjunction signifying:* and; and...and; also; at any rate; even; though. ಎಲ್ಲಿಯೂ, everywhere; ಎಂದೂ, always.

ಊಕಾರ s. The letter ಊ.

ಊಕೆ, ಊಂಕೆ k. n. The warp of a loom spread and starched.

ಊಚ, ಊಚು (*tb. of* ಉಚ್ಚ) a. Superior, costly. -ಅರಿವೆ. Costly cloth. -ನೀಚ. Superior and inferior.

ಊಜಿ k. n. An insect that infests grain.

ಊಟ (*fr.* ಉಣು) k. n. A meal; taking a meal. -ಕೂಟ. A dinner party. -ಕೊಡು. To give a dinner. -ಕ್ಕೆ ಕರೆ. To invite to a meal. -ಗೀಟ. *redt.* -ಮಾಡು. To take a meal. -ಮಾಡಿಸು. To give a meal. -ಗಾರ. A great eater; *f.* -ಗಾರಳು, -ಗಾರ್ತಿ.

ಊಟು h. n. Rising. -ಬೈಸು. Rising and sitting down, *as* on haunches in quick succession.

ಊಟೆ k. n. A natural spring of water.

ಊಡು k. v. t. To give to eat, make eat. 2, to join, yoke. 2, to smear. v. i. To eat. ಊಡಿಸು. To cause to eat: *cf.* ಊಟ.

ಊತ (*fr.* ಊರು) k. n. Firmness.

ಊದ, ಊದು h. n. Frankincense. -ಬತ್ತಿ, -ಕಡ್ಡಿ. A stick covered with frankincense, pastille.

ಊದರೆ k. n. A kind of corn-tares, *Paspalum pilosum*.

ಊದಾ, [illegible] h. [illegible]

ಊದು k. v. t. To blow. 2, to refine metal. v. i. To be puffed up; to swell. n. Blowing; swollen state; *also:* ಊದಲು, ಊದಿಕೆ. -ಗೊಳವೆ, -ಗೋಲು. A blow-pipe. -ಗಲ್ಲ. A swollen cheek. -ಗಾಲು. A swollen leg. ಊದಿ ಹೇಳು. To say distinctly.

ಊನ s. a. Lessened, deficient; maimed; defective. n. A defect, maim; deduction; *also* -ತೆ. -ಮಾಡು. To maim or injure.

ಊಬಲು = ಉಬ್ಬಲು, *q. v.*

ಊಬು k. n. The awn of barley. -ಹುಲ್ಲು. A common fodder grass.

ಊಮೆ k. n. A dumb man; a taciturn man.

ಊರು 1. k. n. A village; a town. -ಬಾಗಲು, ಊರಗಸೆ. A town gate. ಊರವ, ಊರಿನವ. A villager, townsman; *f.* ಊರವಳು. ಊರಾಳು. A villager; village-people. -ಕಟ್ಟೆ. A raised seat round a tree in front of a village. -ಕೇರಿ, -ಗೇರಿ. A village street. -ಜನರು, -ಮಂದಿ. Townsfolk. -ಹತ್ತಿರ. The neighbourhood of a village. -ಗ. A rustic, vulgar man. -ಗನುಡಿ. A vulgar expression.

ಊರು 2. (ರು = ಱು) v. t. To lean on, *as* a stick. 2, to put down, fix, set firmly; to plant (ಬೇರೂರು, to root). v. i. To be, exist; to settle; to stay. 2, to leak out, to spring, *as* water. 3, to be soaked. n. Leaning, *etc.* -ಕೋಲು. A walking stick. ಕಾಲೂರಿ ನಿಂತುಕೊಳ್ಳು. To stand firmly. ಊರಿಸು. To cause to lean on, penetrate. [illegible]

ಊರ್ಜ s. n Power, energy, effort ಊರ್ಜಿತ. Powerful; well established, mighty, excellent, much.

ಊರ್ಧ್ವ s. a High, raised up n Elevation. -ಗತಿ. Going upwards, ascent, môksha. -ಪುಂಡ್ರ. A perpendicular line on the forehead of a Vaishnava. -ಲೋಕ. Heaven. -ಶ್ವಾಸ. Expiration

ಊರ್ಮಿ s n A wave. 2, a fold in a garment -ಳೆ Janaka's daughter and wife of Lakshmana

ಊಷ, ಊಷರ s n Salt ground

ಊಷ್ಮ s n Heat, steam, passion.

ಊಸರವಳ್ಳಿ, ಊಸರುಳ್ಳಿ k. n. A kind of lizard, the Indian monitor.

ಊಹೆ (*tb. of* ಊಹ) n. A guess, conjecture 2, reasoning, reflection. -ಮಾಡು, ಊಹಿಸು. To suppose, reason, infer

ಊಳಿಗ (ಳ = ಱ) k n Work, business; service -ದವ, ಊಳಿಗ A male servant -ಗಿತ್ತಿ A female servant -ತನ. Service

ಊಳು a. k v. i To call, to cry out; to howl (*p p.* ಊಳ್ದು, ಊಳಿ) n. A howl.

ಋ

ಋ. The seventh letter of the alphabet.

ಋಕಾರ s. The letter ಋ.

ಋಕ್ಕು. *tb. of* ಋಚ್, *q. v.*

ಋಗ್ವೇದ s. n. The ṛigvêda, the first of the four vêdas.

ಋಚ್ (*tb* ಋಕ್ಕು) n. The ṛigvêda 2, a verse of the ṛigvêda

ಋಜು s *a.* Straight, right; honest, upright -ವೀರ. An honest hero.

ಋಣ s n Guilt. 2, debt; obligation -ಕೊಡು To lend money. -ತೀರಿಸು, -ಪರಿಹರಿಸು To pay a debt -ಮಾಡು. To borrow. -ಹೊರು. To incur debt. -ಗಾರ. A debtor. -ಬಾಧೆ The trouble from debt -ವಿಮುಕ್ತ. Released from debt -ಮುಕ್ತಿ, -ಮೋಕ್ಷ. Discharge of a debt -ಸ್ಥ. A creditor, a debtor ಋಣಾನುಬಂಧ The connection of indebtedness in some preceding birth for certain sufferings or enjoyments.

ಋತ s. *a.* True, right. n Truth 2, gleaning 3, an ascetic. 4, the sun, moon 5, water

ಋತು s n A period, an epoch, a period or season consisting of two months: ವಸಂತ, ಗ್ರೀಷ್ಮ, ವರ್ಷ, ಶರದ್, ಹೇಮಂತ, ಶಿಶಿರ. -ವೃತ್ತಿ A year

ಋತ್ವಿಜ್ s n. A priest who officiates at sacrifices

ಋದ್ಧಿ s n. Growth; prosperity, welfare. 2, excellence, *cf.* ವೃದ್ಧಿ, *q. v.*

ಋಭುಕ್ಷ s. n. Indra. ṛbhukṣa

ಋಶ್ಯ s. n The white-footed antelope.

ಋಷಭ = ವೃಷಭ, *q v*

ಋಷಿ s n An inspired poet, sage, saint, hermit, seven principal ṛishis are enumerated, *see* ಸಪ್ತರ್ಷಿ. 2, the seven principal stars of the great bear.

ಋಷ್ಯ (= ಋಶ್ಯ) s n. The white-footed antelope. -ಮೂಕ. A mountain in the Dekhan, known as the temporary abode of Râma with Sugrîva. -ಶೃಂಗ. N. of a personage in the first book of the Râmâyana

ಋ ೠ ಌ

The eighth, ninth and tenth letters of the alphabet No words begin with these letters and the use of them is extremely rare

ಎ

ಎ. The eleventh letter of the alphabet. 2, the final *(a) of nouns, (b) of verbs, and (c) of adverbs, as* ಆನೆ, ಎಡೆ, ಒಲೆ, ತೆಗೆ, ತೊಳೆ, ಪಡೆ, ಮತ್ತೆ, ಮೇಲೆ, ಮೆಲ್ಲನೆ, ಒಳಗೆ, ಕೆಳಗೆ, *etc* 3, *a particle of emphasis or vocative, as* ನಾಲ್ಕೆ, ಆತನೆ ತಾನೆ, ಕೇಳಿರೆ, ಕರೆಯಿರೆ, *etc*; ದೇವರೆ, ರಾಮನೆ, ಮಗನೆ, *etc.* 4, *a particle used in doubtful questions, as,* ಬಂದರಾಯಿತೆ? ಸಾಕೆ? 5, *termination of the 1st a. p sing of the future and impf and of the neg verb, as* ಮಾಡುವೆ (= ಮಾಡುವೆನು), ಮಾಡಿದೆ (= ಮಾಡಿದೆನು); ಮಾಡೆ (=ಮಾಡೆನು)

ಎಂ a. k *A termination of the 1st p. sing. pres fut and impf and of the neg verb, as* ಬಾಳ್ದಪೆಂ, ಬಾಳ್ದೆಂ, ಬಾಳ್ವೆಂ, ಬಾಳೆಂ

ಎಕತ್ಯಾರು h *n* Authority, control, [power.

ಎಕರಾರು h. *n* A confession, a deposition.

ಎಕಾರ s. *n*. The letter ಎ

ಎಕ್ಕ *tb. of* ಏಕ. -ಟಿ Alone, in private, a single person -ಟಿಕರೆ. To call aside. -ತಾಳ = ಏಕತಾಲ, *q. v.*

ಎಕ್ಕಟಿಗ k. *n* A superior, noble man

ಎಕ್ಕಟಿ k *n* Greatness, wonder.

ಎಕ್ಕಡ, ಎಕ್ಕವಡ f *n* A kind of leathern sandal

ಎಕ್ಕತಾಳಿ k *n* Ridicule mockery jest -ಮಾಡು. To mock, jest.

ಎಕ್ಕರಿಸು k. *v t* To mock, deride, make faces at.

ಎಕ್ಕಲ a k *n* A wild hog *a* High tall, ...

ಎಕ್ಕಸಕ್ಕ, ಎಕ್ಕಸೆಕ್ಕ k *n* Confusion, doubt. 2, ridicule, mockery

ಎಕ್ಕಿ k *n* A piece of timber forming one side of a cot-frame.

ಎಕ್ಕು k. *v t* To divide, to dress cotton, to card wool *v i* To come up, stand on tiptoe 2, to purge ಎಕ್ಕಿಸು To cause to dress cotton *etc*

ಎಕ್ಕೆ (*tb of* ಅರ್ಕ) *n*. The swallow-wort, *Calotropis gigantea. Cpds* · -ಕಾಯಿ, -ಗಿಡ, -ನಾರು -ಹಾಲು

ಎಗಚಿ k. *n* The jujube tree, *Zizyphus jujuba.*

ಎಗರು k *v. i.* To rise, to fly, to jump. 2, to fly away, to be spent, *as* money to wear off, *as* gilt. paint *etc.*, to be ruined, *as* commerce. ಎಗರಿಸು. To cause to rise, *etc*, to pilfer

ಎಗಸು k *n* Rising, embarkation -ಮತಿ Dues for embarking

ಎಗ್ಗ, ಎಗ್ಗಳ a k *n*. A rude, rustic, low man -ತನ Rudeness. stupidity

ಎಗ್ಗಳ = ವೆಗ್ಗಳ

ಎಗ್ಗು k *n* Shame. 2 disgrace, blame; harm -ಳ A bashful person -ಳತನ Bashfulness -ಹಿಡಿ To find fault with

ಎಂಗ k *n* A stupid, silly person 2, fraud, deceit. -ನಾಣ್ಯ. A counterfeit coin

ಎಚ್ಚು k *v t* To shoot arrows, to expel, *as* water through a syringe.

ಎಚ್ಚತ್ತು k. *P p of* ಎಚ್ಚರು, *q v*

ಎಚ್ಚರ, ಎಚ್ಚರಿಕೆ (ರ = ಱ) k *n* Wake- ... precaution, care. -ಗೇಡಿ An inattentive or negligent person. -ಗೇಡಿತನ Inattention, negligence -ಗೊಳಿಸು To awaken -ಗೊಳ್ಳು To be awake; to make provision -ತಪ್ಪು, -ಮರೆ. To lose one's self ಎಚ್ಚರದಿಂದ ಇರು. To be watchful -ವಡು To be cautious. -ಆಗು, -ವಾಗು To be awake -ಕೊಡು. To call attention, to give caution.

ಎಚ್ಚರು (ರು = ಱು) k i i To awake ಎಚ್ಚರಿಸು To awaken, wake; to caution, forewarn, to put in mind

ಎಜಮಾನ. = ಯಜಮಾನ, q v.

ಎಜ್ಜ (tb. of ವೇಧ) n. A bore, hole.

ಎಂಜಲ, ಎಂಜಲು k n Food or drink which has come in contact with the mouth and regarded as impure, spittle, saliva. -ಮಾತು A past word, repeating another's words. -ಹುಳ An insect living in orts. -ಮಾಡು, ಎಂಜಲಿಸು To defile

ಎಟಕು k i i To come within reach. 2, to be sufficient ಎಟಕಿನೋಡು. To peep standing on tiptoe. ಎಟಕಿಸು. To stand on tiptoe to reach anything

ಎಟ್ಟ k. n A bush-harrow. ಎಟ್ಟಾ ಹೊಡೆ. To roll or flatten sown field.

ಎಟ್ಟಿ k n. An obstinate person -ತನ Obstinacy

ಎಟ್ಟು k i i. To be accessible n A blow.

ಎಡ 1. (= ಎಡೆ) k. n Place, ground. -ತಾಕು. To go and come frequently to frequent

ಎಡ 2 k n The left, the left side *Cpds.* -ಗಡೆ, -ಗಣ್ಣು, -ಗಾಲು, -ಗಿವಿ, -ಮಗ್ಗುಲು, -ಕೆಗಲು, *etc* -ಬಲ Left and right. -ಮುರಿ. To turn to the left -ಚ A left-handed man

ಎಡ 3 (= ಎಡೆ) k n. Place between, interval, inferiority. -ಕುಂಟೆ A smaller kind of weeding machine -ತಡೆ An obstacle -ತರ A middling sort, mediocrity. -ಪಟ್ಟು, -ವಟ್ಟು. Bad state or character; stupidity. [speaking

ಎಡಕು k n. Difficulty, especially in

ಎಡರಾಳಿ k n. A foe, adversary.

ಎಡರು 1 k n Strait, trouble 2, an impediment, obstacle.

ಎಡರು 2. (ರು = ಱು) a k n Poverty, ruin. 2, crookedness. v i. To be crooked, to be dishonest. 2, to stumble, trip

ಎಡವು, ಎಡಹು (cf. ಎಡರು 2, v. i) k. v i To stumble, trip to strike with the foot against

ಎಡೆ 1. (= ಎಡ) k. n A place, spot, ground 2, room, interval, distance 3, inferiority. -ಗ A good-for-nothing man -ಬಿಡದೆ Uninterruptedly -ಕಟ್ಟು. A small dam. -ಗೆಡೆ To fall down -ಗೆಡೆಗೆ rep Here and there -ಗೊಡು. To give way, submit -ಗೊಳ್ಳು To take place, occur, to come to a stand, to obtain, to resort to -ಪ್ರಾಯ, -ಹರೆಯ The middle age -ಆಡು, -ಯಾಡು. To move, wander, roam -ಉಡುಗು, -ಯುಡುಗು To leave room, to stop, cease -ಒತ್ತು, -ಯೊತ್ತು To compress, squeeze. -ಸೆಳೆ The inner velocity of a river. -ಹೊತ್ತು The time between sunrise and sunset

ಎಡೆ 2. (tb of ಇಡೆ) n An offering, meal. 2, the leaf, *etc.* on which food is placed -ಇಕ್ಕು, -ಇಡು, -ಕೊಡು, -ಮಾಡು, -ಹಾಕು. To present food to a deity or man

ಎಡ್ಡ k. n. A cheat, liar 2, (= ಹೆಡ್ಡ) a stupid man -ತನ Falsehood, stupidity -ತಿ A stupid woman ಎಡ್ಡಿಸು To abuse; to mock, to cheat. ಎಡ್ಡು Cheating, stupidity

ಎಣಿಕೆ k n. Counting, reckoning 2, thinking, thought, notice, observation, opinion -ಕೈಗೂಡು. Thinking to succeed -ಗೆಯ್. To think, *etc.*

ಎಣಿಸು k. v t To add together, to count, to reckon, to estimate, to consider, to compare i i. To think of. ಎಣಿಸಿ ನೋಡು To number

ಎಣೆ 1 k. n A couple pair connexion, fellowship; equality similarity i match -ಕಳೆ, -ಗಳೆ To become loose. -ಗಂಟು A woman's braid of hair. -ಗೊಳ್ಳು To become equal, to face -ವಕ್ಕಿ, -ವಕ್ಕಿ. The ruddy goose

ಎಣೆ 2 = ಪೆಣೆ.

ಎಂಟು 1. k *n* Arrogance.

ಎಂಟು 2. k *a*. Eight ಎಂಟನೆ. Eighth. ಎಂಟಾನೆಂಟು. About eight. ಎಂಟೂವರೆ Eight and a half. ಎಂಟೆಂಟು Eight and eight, eight times eight. -ದಿಕ್ಕು, -ದೆಸೆ. The eight points of the compass -ಕೋಣ, -ಮೂಲೆ. An octagon.

ಎಣ್ಣಿಸು. = ಎಣಿಸು, *q v*

ಎಣ್ಣು k. *v. i.* To count; to think

ಎಣ್ಣೆ k *n* Oil -ಕಾಸು To heat oil. -ಗೆಂಪು Dark brown -ತೆಗೆ. To extract oil -ಬಿಡು, -ಹಾಕು, -ಹೊಯ್ಯು. To pour oil, to spoil *as* another's affairs -ಹಚ್ಚಿಕೊಳ್ಳು. To anoint one's self with oil -ಗಾಣ. An oil-mill -ಗಸಿ, -ಕದಳು The sediment of oil

ಎಣ್ಬರು k *pro.* Eight persons.

ಎತ್ತ 1. ಎತ್ತಲು k *ad* Where? which place or direction? -ಕಡೆ Whither? ಎತ್ತಲುಂ Everywhere ಎತ್ತಾನುಂ In whatsoever direction, occasionally ಎತ್ತೆತ್ತಲುಂ Everywhere.

ಎತ್ತ 2. (*cf* ಎತ್ತು) k. *n.* Lifting up. 2, undertaking, finding out an item in an account. 3, deceit, cunning -ಗಡೆ A means. device, a trick

ಎತ್ತರ, ಎತ್ತರು k. *n.* Height, tallness -ಗದ್ದೆ An elevated rice-field.

ಎತ್ತು 1. k *v. t* To lift, raise, take up, to collect, *as* money, alms, *etc*, to assume, *as* a form (avatâra), to mention, *as* the name of another *n* = ಎತ್ತ 2 ಎತ್ತಿಕೆ. Lifting, *etc.* ಎತ್ತಿ ಬರೆ. To copy, *as* a manuscript. ಎತ್ತಿಕೊಂಡು ಹೋಗು. To take away ಎತ್ತಿ ಹೋಗು. To go to attack ಮೇಲೆತ್ತು, ಮೇಲಕ್ಕೆತ್ತು. To lift up ಎತ್ತಿಸು To cause to raise, *etc* -ಗಡೆ. = ಎತ್ತಗಡೆ -ಗಲ್ಲು. Lift-stone -ಬಾಡಿ [illegible] that [illegible] ಎತ್ತೊಲೆ A moveable stove -ವಿಕೆ. Lifting, raising, *etc.*

ಎತ್ತು 2. k *n.* An ox, bullock. *Cpds* · -ಗಾಡಿ, -ಘಂಡಿ, -ಸವಾರಿ, *etc* -ನಾಲಿಗೆ Bullock's tongue, *Trichodesma indicum.*

ಎತ್ತುವಳಿ k *n.* Collecting money

ಎತ್ನ. *tb of* ಯತ್ನ, *q. v*

ಎದರು, ಎದಿರು, ಎದುರು (= ಇದಿರು *q. v.*) k *n.* The front; that which is opposite -ಆಡು, ಎದುರಾಡು To outbid; to contradict ಎದುರಾಯಿಸು To oppose, contradict ಎದುರಾಳಿ An antagonist -ಗೊಳ್ಳು, ಎದುಗೊಳ್ಳು. -ಬರು To meet. -ನುಡಿ, -ಮಾತು, -ಎದುರುತ್ತರ. A contradiction. -ಹೇಳು, ಎದುಖಂಡಿಸು To contradict -ವ್ಯಾಜ್ಯ A counter-claim. ಎದುಚೀಟು, ಎದುಸುಗಡಿ A document given by the purchaser of land stipulating to give it back on repayment of the purchase money within a definite term, a counterpart. ಎದುವಗಳ್ಳಿ A note of hand given for another that is lost, the counterpart of a deed or lease

ಎದೆ k *n* The chest, breast, courage -ಆರು. The breast to become dry, courage to be quenched -ಒಡೆ The heart to break. courage to fail -ಕರಗು The heart to melt -ತು, -ಕೊಡು. To become courageous -ಕುಂದು, -ಗುಂದು, -ಗೆಡು. Courage to fail. -ಗುಂಡಿಗೆ. The pit of the stomach. -ಗೊಟ್ಟು ನಿಲ್ಲು To stand boldly. -ತಚ್ಚು, -ಗಿಚ್ಚು. Heartache. -ಗಾರ. A bold man -ಗುದಿ. The heart to be agitated; violent mental agitation, fear -ಗುಂದು Courage to fail. -ಗೆಡಿಸು To dishearten -ಗೊಯಿಕ, -ಬಡಕ A man who disheartens another -ಮುರಿ To labour to weariness, fag hard -ಉರಿ, -ಯುರಿ. The heart-burn -ಪೂಡಕ. A coward -ಹಾರು. The heart to palpitate

ಎದ್ದು k *P p of* ಏಳು.

ಎನಿತು, ಎನಿತ್ತು a. k *pro* How much? [illegible] many?

ಎನಿಬರು a. k *pro.* How many persons?

ಎನು k *aff.* *The common form of* ಎಂ *for the 1st pers. sing past, fut., and neg, as* ಮಾಡಿದೆನು, ಮಾಡುವೆನು, ಮಾಡೆನು.

ಎಂತ 1. =ಅಂತ, *q. v.* *A common p p. of* ಎನ್ನು, *q v.*

ಎಂತ 2. ಎಂತಹ, ಎಂತಾ = ಎಂಥ, *q v*

ಎಂತು k. *pro* In what manner or way? how? ಎಂತುಂ By all means.

ಎಂತುಟು = ಎನಿತು, *q v.*

ಎಂಥ, ಎಂಥಾ (=ಎಂತ 2) k. *pro.* What kind or sort? *int.* What a kind! how! *as:* ಎಂಥ ದೊಡ್ಡ ಮನೆ! ನೋಡು, ದೇವರು ಎಂಥಾ ಜ್ಞಾನಿಯು, ಎಂಥಾ ಸಮರ್ಥನು ಎಂಥಾ ಒಳ್ಳೆಯವನು!

ಎಂದು 1 k (*p p. of* ಎನ್ನು) Having said *Used to introduce a sentence, when it is equivalent to* 'that", *as* ಬಂದರು ಎಂದು ಹೇಳಿದನು, he said 'they came" ಎಲ್ಲಿ ಹೋಗಲಿ ಎಂದು ಕೇಳಿದನು, "where shall I go?" he asked

ಎಂದು 2 k *ad* What time? when? ಎಂದೂ, ಎಂದಿಗೂ, ಎಂದೆಂದಿಗೂ. For ever and ever, always, continually. ಎಂದಿಗಾದರೂ At any time soever. once. ಎಂದಿನಂತೆ, ಎಂದಿನಪೊಲ್, ಎಂದಿನ ಹಾಗೆ As usual ಎಂದುಂ, ಎಂದೂ Ever, always.

ಎನ್ನ (= ನನ್ನ) a k. *pro* Of me, my. ಎನ್ನದು Mine.

ಎನ್ನು (= ಅನ್ನು) k. *v t* To say, speak; to call. *P. ps.* ಎಂದು, ಎಂತ, *pres. p.* ಎಂಬ. ಎಂದರೆ, (ಎಂದೊಡೆ) = ಅಂದರೆ

ಎಪ್ಪತ್ತು k. *a* Seventy ಎಪ್ಪತ್ತನಾಲ್ಕು, ಎಪ್ಪತ್ತನಾಲ್ಕು 74

ಎಬಡ k *n.* A foolish, silly man. -ತನ. Silliness.

ಎಬ್ಬಿಸು k. *v. t.* To rouse, awaken, to lift up, to raise, to enliven, give life ಕೋಪವೆಬ್ಬಿಸು To provoke.

ಎಬ್ಬು a. k *v i* To rise. ಎಬ್ಬಟ್ಟು. To follww, pursue, to harass.

ಎಮ 1. (= ಎಮ್ಮ, *q v*) k. *int.* Well, indeed.

ಎಮ 2. k. *pro.* Our. ಎಮಗೆ To us. ಎಮತು Ours

ಎಮಕೆ, ಎಮಿಕೆ k. *n* A bone. 2, an ornament.

ಎಮೆ, ಎವೆ k. *n.* An eyelash, eyelid. -ಇಕ್ಕು To shut the eyelids

ಎಂಬು k *v t* To say. -ಕೆ Saying ಎಂಬ, -ವ (*pres. rel part. of* ಎನ್ನು) That is or are called. ಎಂಬುದಾಗಿ (ಎಂಬುದು-ಆಗಿ) *used as* ಎಂದು, *q v.*

ಎಂಬತ್ತು k *a* Eighty

ಎಮ್ಮ k *pro* Of us, our. ಎಮ್ಮದು. Ours.

ಎಮ್ಮೆ k. *n.* A female buffalo -ಚೇಳು. A large black scorpion -ಬಳ್ಳಿ. The plant *Convolvulus argenteus.* -ಹೋರಿ (-ವೋರಿ). A male buffalo-calf.

ಎಯ್ಯು a k. *n.* A porcupine. -ಮುಳ್ಳು. A porcupine quill

ಎರಕ k. *n.* Any metal infusion, molten state. -ಹೊಯಿ. To pour melted metal into a mould, to cast.

ಎರಕೆ (ರ = ಱ) k. *n* A wing, a fin, an arm.

ಎರಗು (ರ = ಱ) k *v i* To bow, to make obeisance to; to alight, perch; to fall upon, to join, to accrue to *n.* A bow, an obeisance.

ಎರಚು (ರ = ಱ) k *v t.* To sprinkle, to scatter; to strew, to sow. -ಕೆ. Strewing.

ಎರಡು k *a* Two ಎರಡಕ್ಕೆ ಹೋಗು. To go to void excrement. -ಆಗು, ಎರಡಾಗು. To become separated. -ನಾಲಿಗೆಯವ. A double tongued, deceitful man, liar -ನುಡಿ. To speak two things to be insincere -ಬಗೆ To play tricks, act deceitfully, two ways -ಮಾಡು To split -ವರೆ. Two and a half. -ಹೊತ್ತು. Morning and evening ಎರಡೆರಡು. Two and two, two times two ಎರಡೂ Both.

ಎರಲ್, ಎರಲು (= ಹೆರಳ್) a k *n.* 2, wind, air. 3, playing

ಎರಲೆ, ಎರಳೆ k *n* An antelope, deer

ಎರವು k. *n.* An object of desire; a thing borrowed, *as* a book, *etc.*, a loan 2, difference; damaging, deficiency, harm -ಇಕ್ಕು, ಎರವಿಕ್ಕು. To grant an object of desire, to lend. -ಬೇಡು To ask a loan. -ಮುಟ್ಟು, ತಕ್ಕೊಳ್ಳು. To borrow

ಎರುಬು k. n. Dung, muck

ಎರೆ 1. k. n A dark-brown colour 2, black grease for wheels 3, black soil (= -ನೆಲ -ಭೂಮಿ, -ಮಣ್ಣು, -ಹೊಲ) 4, a worm that lives in orts, a bait 5, food for animals 6, = ಹೆಗೆ

ಎರೆ 2 a k. v. t To beg, ask, solicit -ವ A beggar.

ಎರೆ 3. (ರೆ = ಱೆ) k v. t To pour out, to cast, as metal, to cover with water v. i To bathe. n. Pouring. 2, a master, f ಎರತಿ. ಎರೆಯಪ್ಪ A sweet pancake

ಎರ್ದೆ = ಎದೆ, q v

ಎಲಚಿ k n The jujube. -ಬಳ್ಳಿ The bottle-gourd

ಎಲಬು, ಎಲುಬು, ಎಲುವು k. n A bone

ಎಲರು a k. n. Wind, air breath -ಉಣಿ, ಎಲರುಣಿ Air-eater: a serpent.

ಎಲವ k. n The silk-cotton tree, *Bombax heptaphyllum*

ಎಲವೋ k int (strong, rough) Ho! o! oh!

ಎಲು. ಎಲುಬು, ಎಲುವು = ಎಲಬು q. v

ಎಲಾ, ಎಲೇ k. int (familiar and friendly) O! oh!

ಎಲೆ k n A leaf; the blade of a knife 2, the betel leaf, a leaf-plate ಎಲೆಯ ಮೇಲೆ ಕೂತಿರು To sit at dinner. -ಅಡಿಕೆ, ಎಲಡಿಕೆ Betel leaf and areca nut ಎಲಡಿಕೆ ಹಾಕಿಕೊಳ್ಳು To chew ĕladikĕ -ಗಾರ A betel-seller, f. -ಗಾತಿ. -ಕಾವು. A fomentation with a heated leaf -ಕಳ್ಳಿ, -ಗಳ್ಳಿ. A thorny and milky shrub, *Euphorbia nivulia* -ತುಂಬು, -ತೊಟ್ಟು. The stem of a leaf -ತೋಟ A betel garden -ನಾಗರ A small dangerous snake found on leaves -ಬಿಡು To sprout -ಮಿಡತೆ A green locust. -ವಸ್ತ್ರ A coloured handkerchief -ವನಿ, -ಹನಿ A drop on a leaf

ಎಲೋ k. int O! etc.

ಎಲ್ಲ, ಎಲ್ಲವು. ಎಲ್ಲಾ k n. All, everything, the whole ಎಲ್ಲಮ್ಮ N. of a goddess ಎಲ್ಲರೂ All persons ಎಲ್ಲವೂ All things. ಎಲ್ಲಾಗ ,

ಎಲ್ಲಿ k ad In what place? where? whither? -ಯವ A man of what place? -ಯದು A thing of what place? -ಯಾದರೂ Wheresoever, everywhere

ಎಲ್ಲೆ k n A limit, boundary, also -ಕಟ್ಟು. -ಕಲ್ಲು A boundary stone

ಎವು k. Termination of the first pers pl of past, fut, and neg., as ಕೇಳಿದೆವು, ಕೇಳುವೆವು, ಕೇಳೆವು

ಎವೆ = ಎಮೆ, q v

ಎಷ್ಟು (= ಎನಿತು) k inter pro How much? how many? ಎಷ್ಟಂತ To what extent? ಎಷ್ಟರ, ಎಷ್ಟರಲ್ಲಿ, ಎಷ್ಟರೊಳಗೆ, ಎಷ್ಟಕ್ಕೆ, etc -ಮಟ್ಟಿಗೆ, ಎಷ್ಟರ ಮಟ್ಟಿಗೆ. To what extent? how long or far? ಎಷ್ಟೋ How (very) many (one does not know)

ಎಸಕ (fr. ಎಸೆ) a. k n Shine, splendour, beauty, form, delight.

ಎಸಗು a. k v. t To engage in, undertake, to do, perform; to commence

ಎಸಗೆ, ಎಸಿಗೆ (fr ಎಸೆ 1) k n. A throw, shot

ಎಸರು k n. The boiling water in a cooking pot the water strained from boiled vegetables etc, pepper water

ಎಸಳು k. n A flower-leaf, petal, a small twig with leaves

ಎಸಳೆ k. n N of a jungle tree

ಎಸು, ಎಸೆ 1 k v. t To shoot an arrow, to throw P ps ಎಸದು, ಎಸೆದು, ಎಸ್ತು. n A shot, a throw· also ಎಸುಗೆ

ಎಸೆ 2. k. v i To shine, to be brilliant, beautiful, distinguished; to appear, to become manifest.

ಎಹಗೆ, ಎಹಂಗೆ (= ಹ್ಯಾಗೆ, ಹ್ಯಾಂಗೆ) a k ad. In what manner? how?

ಎಳ 1 = ಎಳೆ, q v

ಎಳ 2, ಎಳತು ಎಳದು k P ps of ಎಳೆ, q v That is tender, young, etc

ಎಳಗ k n A species of sheep, the ram used by boys for riding.

ಎಳಚಿ = ಎಲಚಿ, q v

ಎಳದು, ಎಳೆದು k n Unsteadiness, fickle-

ಎಳಸು a. k. *i. t.* To desire long for, to take pleasure in. *n* Desire, *etc.*

ಎಳೆ 1 (= ಎಳ) k *n* Tenderness, youth, weakness, moderation, lightness in colour, *etc* *a* Tender, young, *etc* -ಗಂದಿ, -ಗಂದು, -ಗಂದೆ A newly calved cow, a milch cow -ಗಾಯಿ A tender fruit -ಗಾಳಿ. Gentle wind -ಗೂಸು. A tender infant -ಕೆಂಪು, -ಗೆಂಪು A light red, the colour of the dawn -ಜೊನ್ನ Faint moonshine -ತನ. Tenderness, youth. -ತಳಿರ್, -ದಳಿರ್ Tender foliage -ನಗೆ. A smile -ನಾರು A tender fine fibre. -ನೀರು The water of a tender cocoanut -ಪ್ರಾಯ Youth -ಬಣ್ಣ. A faint colour. -ಬಿಸಿಲು, -ವಿಸಿಲು A morning or evening, sunshine. -ಮಾವು A tender mango. -ಯುವ. A young man, a boy -ಯುಳು A young woman, a girl -ಹುಲ್ಲು Tender grass

ಎಳೆ 2. (ಳೆ = ಱ³) k *v t.* To pull, draw, drag, to seize, take forcibly *P ps.* ಎಳೆದು, ಎಳತು, ಎಳದು ಎಳಕೊಳ್ಳು. To pull towards one's self, to lay hold of, to absorb. ಎಳದಾಡು To pull mutually ಎಳವು Pulling, drawing; spasm, cramp ಎಳಸು, ಎಳಿಸು To cause to drag, to put off; to thwart.

ಎಳ 3 (ಳೆ = ಱ³) k *n.* Thread ಎಳೆಯನ್ನು ತೆಗೆ To spin.

ಎಳ್ಬು k *v i* To go upwards, rise

ಎಳ್ಳು k *n* The gingely-oil seed of *Sesamum indicum* ಎಳ್ಳಗಸೆ. A blackish kind of linseed -ಚಟ್ಣಿ. A chatney of sesamum. -ನೀರು Sesamum seeds and water offered to departed ancestors -ಬೆಲ್ಲ. A mixture of sesamum and jaggory given as an auspicious present -ಎಣ್ಣೆ, ಎಳ್ಳೆಣ್ಣೆ, -ತೈಲ Sesamum oil. -ದೇವಡಿ A sweetmeat of sesamum and sugar -ಹುಗ್ಗಿ. A dish of milk rice, and sesamum

ಏ

ಏ. The twelfth letter of the alphabet 2, *a particle of emphasis, as* ಶಂಕರನು ನೀವೇ! ಒಮ್ಮೆಲೇ, ತಪ್ಪದೇ ಬಾ, ನಮ್ಮ ಹಿತದ ಸಲುವಾಗಿಯೇ 3, *a contraction of* ಎಯು *a, in the genitive, as* ಮನೇ ಬಾಗಲು, ಸಾಲೇ ಮನೆ, *b. in the locative, as* ಕಡೇಲಿ, *etc*, *c, in the affix* ಅನೆಯ, *as* ಎರಡನೇ ಪುಸ್ತಕ, *d, in the infinitive, as* ಕರೇ ಕಳುಹಿಸು 4, = ಏನು, *etc.*, *q v.* ಏಗೆಯು What to do? ಏವೇಳು. What to say?

ಏಕ s *a* One, alone. solitary. 2, unique, pre-eminent 3, one of two or more. -ಕಾಲ. The same time -ಗೃಹಕೃತ್ಯ. An undivided family -ಚಕ್ರವರ್ತಿ, -ಚ್ಛತ್ರಾಧಿಪತಿ. A supreme sovereign -ಜಾತಿ. Once-born. a Śūdra -ತರ. One of two or many. -ತಾಲ Keeping time, harmony -ತ್ರ In one place together. -ತ್ವ Oneness, unity. -ದಾ At once -ದೇಶಿ. Of one or the same country. -ದೇಹ Having only one body, closely united in friendship -ಪತ್ನಿ Only one wife -ಮತಿ, -ಮನಸ್ಸು One mind, unanimous -ಮತ್ಯ Concord -ರಸ Perfect assimilation -ವಚನ. The singular number (*g*). -ವಾಕ್ಯತೆ Agreement of meaning -ಸಪ್ತತಿ 71 -ಸ್ಥ Standing together, unanimous -ಸ್ಥಾನ. The place of a unit ಏಕಾ ಏಕಿ. Suddenly all at once ಏಕಾಕಿ Alone, solitary. ಏಕಾಕ್ಷರ A monosyllable ಏಕಾಕ್ಷಿ One-eyed; a crow ಏಕಾಗ್ರ Intent upon one object ಏಕಾಂಗಿ Of one member, solitary, alone ಏಕಾದಶ. Eleven the eleventh . ಾದ The eleventh [illegible] of the waxing or waning moon on which Brahmanas use to wake and fast. ಏಕಾಧಿಪತಿ. A sole monarch; an astrological term ಏಕಾಂತ A lonely place, solitude, secrecy; a secret, alone, secret, hidden. ಏಕಾಂತವಾಸ. A hermitage, a harem. ಏಕಾಬ್ದಿ A heifer one year old ಏಕಾರ್ಥ One meaning; synonym. ಏಕಾಶ್ರಯ The protection of one deity only ಏಕಾಹ The period of one day; a ceremony performed on the eleventh day in the course of funeral rites

ಏಕಾರ s n The letter ಏ

ಏಕೀನ h. n. Honesty, uprightness.

ಏಕೀಭಾವ s. n. Becoming one, association. ಏಕೀಭವಿಸು To become one

ಏಕೂನು f n. Sum total.

ಏಕೋದ್ದಿಷ್ಟ s. n The śrâddha performed for one deceased individual.

ಏಟು k. n A blow; a throw. 2, a kind of gambling with dice. -ಗಾರ A shooter -ಕೊಡು, -ಬಡಿ, -ಹೊಡಿ. To strike a blow.

ಏಡಿ k. n A crab. 2, a coward

ಏಡಿಸು k. v. i To speak ill, to mock.

ಏಣ s. n A kind of deer or antelope; f ಏಣಿ.

ಏಣಿ k. n. A ladder -ದೀವಿಟಿಗೆ A number of flambeaux fixed on a horizontal ladder and carried in a procession or before persons of distinction -ಏರು, -ಹತ್ತು To mount a ladder

ಏಣು k. n. An edge, border

ಏತ (fr. ಏರು) k n. Ascent; rise. 2. a lever for raising water, picotta. 3, an instrument for pounding rice -ಕೋಲು The bamboo by which the bucket hangs.

ಏತಕೆ. = ಯಾತಕೆ, see s ಏನು

ಏತಾದೃಶ s ad Such like, of this kind. similar.

ಏದು k. n. A porcupine. v i To pant.

ಏನಿಕೆ k , ~ " ^

ಏನು k. inter pro What? dat ಏತಕ್ಕೆ, instr ಏತರಿಂದ, gen ಏತರ, etc ಏನಾಗು To become what? ಏನಾದರೂ, ಏನಾನುಂ Whatsoever it may be, anything. ಏನಿಲ್ಲನ್ನು. To say it is nothing ಏನೋ. O what?

ಏನೆ k. aff for the 1st pers. sing pres, e g ತರುತ್ತೇನೆ, ಮುಗಿಸುತ್ತೇನೆ, ನಡಿಯುತ್ತೇನೆ, etc.

ಏಬ್ರಾಸಿ = ಎಬ್ರಾಸಿ, q. v.

ಏಯ್. = ಏನು, q. v.

ಏರಂಡ s. n The castor-oil plant, Palma Christi

ಏರಿ k. n. A raised bank, the bank of a tank, etc, also ಕಟ್ಟೆ.

ಏರು 1. (= ಆರು) k n A pair of oxen yoked to the plough -ಕಂದಾಯ -ಸುಂಕ Plough-tax

ಏರು 2. (ರು = ಱು) k. v t. To ascend, mount, climb. v i. To rise, to increase P p ಏರಿ. ಏರುತ್ತ, ಏರುವಿಕೆ, ಏರಿಕೆ Rising, mounting, etc. ಏರ ಕಟ್ಟು To tie on high, hang down ಏರುಬ್ಬಸ Hard breathing ಏರಹಾಕು To pile. ಏರಹೊತ್ತು. The time from sunrise to midday ಏರವೇರು Poison to take effect ಏರಿಸು To raise, to place upon, etc ಏರಿ ಬರು. To ascend.

ಏರ್ಪಡು k. v. i To be arranged, settled fixed, established ಏರ್ಪಡಿಸು. To arrange, to set in order ಏರ್ಪಾಟು, ಏರ್ಪಾಡು Arrangement, decision.

ಏಲಕ್ಕಿ f n Large cardamoms -ಗಿಡ. The cardamom plant

ಏಲಾಂ h n An auction, public sale.

ಏಲು k. v i To hang, dangle. ಏಲಾಡು. To swing

ಏವ k n Disgust, dislike; ugliness

ಏವಂ s ad. Thus, certainly; even.

ಏವು k pl of ಏನು

ಏವೆ k pl of ಏನೆ

ಏಷಣ s n Seeking, wish, desire.

ಏಸು 1. k *v. t.* To throw *n* A throw, shot. ಏಸಾಡು. To shoot arrows

ಏಸು 2 (= ಎನಿತು) k *pro.* What quantity? *etc.*

ಏಳಿಸು (= ಏಡಿಸು) k *v t.* To censure, reprove, to throw into shade ಏಳಿದ. Contempt, blame.

ಏಳಿಗೆ, ಏಳ್ಗೆ (ಳ = ೞ) k. *n.* Rising; growth, increase, greatness, magnificence, glory, haughtiness

ಏಳು 1. (ಳು = ೞು) k. *v i.* To stand up to get up, rise *P p* ಎದ್ದು. ಎದ್ದುಹೋಗು Get up and go away. ಏಳಿಸು To raise -ವಿಕೆ, ಏಳ್ವಿಕೆ Rising ಏಳುತ್ತ ಬೀಳುತ್ತ Rising and falling. ಏಳೇಳು, ಎದ್ದೇಳು. Rise, rise! arise

ಏಳು 2 (ಳು = ೞು) k *a* Seven. ಏಳನೆ. Seventh ಏಳೆಂಟು Seven or eight, seven times eight. ಏಳೆಳೆಕಟ್ಟಾಣಿ A necklace of gold beads composed of seven strings

ಐ

ಐ. The thirteenth letter of the alphabet. *The initial ಐ in Kannada words has arisen from ಅಯ್, ಅಯಿ, and those words may also be looked up under this spelling*

ಐ s. *int*, *as* ಐಸಾಕು O! enough.

ಐಕಮತ್ಯ s *n* Unanimity, agreement

ಐಕಾರ s. *n* The letter ಐ.

ಐಕ್ಯ s *n* Oneness, unity harmony, identity -ಭಾವ Oneness

ಐಗಳು (= ಅಯ್ಗಳು) k *n* A Jangama 2, a school-master

ಐತರು (= ಅಯ್ತರು) k. *v i* To come, approach

ಐತಿಹ್ಯ s *n.* Oral tradition, a legend, tale.

ಐದು 1 (= ಅಯ್ದು, *q v.*) k *a* Five

ಐದು 2 (= ಅಯ್ದು) k *v. i.* To join, to draw near, to reach, obtain get

ಐದುತನ. = ಅಯ್ದೆತನ, *q v.*

ಐನಾ k. *n.* A mirror; spectacles

ಐನೋರು (= ಅಯ್ನೋರು) k. *n.* A school-master. 2, a respectful mode of addressing a Brâhmana.

ಐರದಾಳಿ (= ಅಯ್ರದಾಳಿ) k *n* The marriage badge tied round a female's neck.

ಐರಾಣಿ = ಅಯ್ರಾಣಿ, *q v*

ಐರಾವತ s *n.* Indra's male elephant; *f* ಐರಾವತಿ.

ಐಲವಿಲ s. *n.* Kuvêra.

ಐವಜಿ h. *ad.* Instead of

ಐವಜು h. *n* Property wealth. cash or goods

ಐವತ್ತು (= ಅಯ್ವತ್ತು) k. *n* Fifty

ಐಶ್ವರ್ಯ s *n* Power, might, wealth, riches, opulence -ವಂತ A rich man; *f* -ವಂತೆ.

ಐಸಿರಿ. *tb of* ಐಶ್ವರ್ಯ, *q. v*

ಐಸು = ಅಯಿಸು, *q v*

ಐಹಿಕ (*fr.* ಇಹ) s *a* Relating to this world, temporal secular

ಒ

ಒ. The fourteenth letter of the alphabet 2, *a particle employed in common as well as doubtful questions, e g.* ಆನೆಯೊ? 3, *in admonition and calling, as* ಸ್ನಾನ ಮಾಡಿದೊ! ಬಾರೊ! ಒ ಕಾಳಪ್ಪ!

ಒಂಬು k *n* The cry of buffaloes.

ಒಕ್ k *a* One 2, *short p p of* ಒಗೆ. ಒಕ್ಕಟ್ಟು One bond; unanimity, concord, harmony ಒಕ್ಕಣ್ಣ A one-eyed man. ಒಕ್ಕೊಡು. To throw, cast away; to wash and give.

ಒಕಾರ k. *n*. The letter ಒ.

ಒಕ್ಕಣೆಕೆ, ಒಕ್ಕಣೆ s *n*. The honorific address at the top of a letter, *etc* 2 style of composition. ಒಕ್ಕಣಿಸು. To tell say, to describe

ಒಕ್ಕರಿಸು k *v i* To spit out, vomit 2, to retire.

ಒಕ್ಕಲ, ಒಕ್ಕಲಮಗ, ಒಕ್ಕಲಿಗ k *n* A farmer, husbandman, *f* ಒಕ್ಕಲಗಿತಿ, ಒಕ್ಕಲಿತಿ

ಒಕ್ಕಲಿಕ್ಕು k *v. t* To thrash down, destroy; to trouble greatly

ಒಕ್ಕಲು k *n*. Residing, tenancy, a home, residence 2 a tenant, farmer, a subject ಒಕ್ಕಲಾಗು To become a tenant, *etc*. -ತನ. Husbandry farming. ಒಕ್ಕಲ ಮನೆ, ಒಕ್ಕಲಟಿ A tenant's house, a farmhouse

ಒಕ್ಕು k *i t*. To tread out corn, to thrash *n* Thrashing. 2, an omen -ಗೋಲು. A thrashing stick.

ಒಕ್ಕೆರೆ (*tb of* ಪುಷ್ಕರ) *n* A pond

ಒಕ್ಕುಳಿಸು k *i i*. To belch

ಒಗಟು, ಒಗಟೆ k. *n* A riddle, enigma

ಒಗಡಿಕೆ (= ಓಕರಿಕೆ) k *n* Vomiting

ಒಗಡಿಸು = ಒಕ್ಕರಿಸು, *q v*

ಒಗತ k *n* Washing. 2 throwing

ಒಗತನ k *n* The harmonious life of husb[illegible] management of household affairs, the affairs of life

ಒಗಮು. = ಒಗೆದು, *p p of* ಒಗೆ.

ಒಗರು k *n* An astringent taste.

ಒಗಿ = ಒಗೆ 2, *q v*

ಒಗು a k *n* Running over, excess. 2, (= ಪೊಗು) to enter -ಮಿಗೆ Abundance.

ಒಗೆ 1. a. k *v. i*. To come forth, be born, originate.

ಒಗೆ 2 k *v t* To beat wet clothes on a stone for cleaning them, to wash 2, to throw *P. ps* ಒಗದು, ಒಗದು

ಒಗ್ಗ k *n* A follower of the mailâra linga.

ಒಗ್ಗರ k. *n* A heap, mass.

ಒಗ್ಗರಣೆ k *n*. A kind of seasoning. ಒಗ್ಗರಿಸು To season, spice.

ಒಗ್ಗು k *v i* To become one, unite with. 2, to agree with one's constitution, *as* water, *etc* 3, (= ಬೊಗ್ಗು) to bow; to be submissive *v t* To join *n*. An assemblage, heap, mass

ಒಂಟಿ k *n* A hook 2, a gold armlet worn by females

ಒಜ್ಜತ a k *n* Equality, harmony, agreeableness; pleasure

ಒಜ್ಜಯು. ಒಜ್ಜೆಯು a k *n*. Disgrace, impropriety, contempt

ಒಜನ h *n* Gravity, dignity, influence.

ಒಜ್ಜರ a k *n*. A spring, fountain.

ಒಜ್ಜೆ (= ವಜ್ಜೆ) f *n* A weight load, burden

ಒಟ (= ವಟ) m *int* An imitative sound --ಮಾತಾಡು, -ಗುಟ್ಟು To talk much, to prate, gabble

ಒಟಾರ f *n* The compound round a house

ಒಟ್ಟ (= ವಟ್ಟ) h *n* Discount.

ಒಟ್ಟಜಿ, ಒಟ್ಟಲು k *n* A heap, mass. abundance

[illegible] = [illegible] *q v*

ಒಟ್ಟು k. v. t To make one join, to put together, pile up v. i To come together, assemble; to become a mass, be united n. Union, a heap, pile, sum total 2, the close adhering of a lump of clay. ಒಟ್ಟಿಗೆ (dat.), ಒಟ್ಟಾರೆ, all together, on the whole -ಆಗು, -ಕೂಡು. To come together, convene, to become one in mind. -ಆಗಿರು. To be united, as a family. -ಕೂಡಿಸು, -ಮಾಡು To join together, to add up. -ತೇರೀಜು The whole amount -ಲೆಕ್ಕ Sum total ಒಟ್ಟಿಕೆ. Heaping

ಒಟ್ಟೆ k n. A crack, hole -ಬೀಳು To be cracked, to get a hole

ಒಟ್ಟೈಸು, ಒಟ್ಟಿಸು k v t To collect, join, to heap together, to convene. v i To become one, to come together

ಒಡ k. n. Union; being together, company. -ಗೂಡು To join, be united with, to be obtained, to happen, to obtain ಒಡಗೂಡಿಸು To cause to be united with, etc -ಗೂಟ Close union. -ಹುಟ್ಟು. To be born by the same parents, birth as brothers and sisters, brothers or sisters -ಬಡು. = ಒಡಂಬಡು.

ಒಡಕ, ಒಡಕು k. n. The state of being cracked or broken, a fracture, crack, disunion. -ಧ್ವನಿ. A broken voice -ಬಾಯವ One who cannot keep secrets.

ಒಡಕಲ k. n Broken state, broken paddy or split pulse with chaff or husk.

ಒಡತಿ k n. A mistress.

ಒಡದು. = ಒಡೆದು. P p. of ಒಡೆ.

ಒಡನೆ (fr. ಒಡ) k. prep. With, together with. ad Forthwith, immediately. ಒಡನಾಟ Company, intercourse. ಒಡನಾಡಿ. A companion, friend ಒಡನಾಡಿತನ Companionship, friendship ಒಡನಾಡು To associate with. ಒಡನೊಡನೆ All at once, etc

ಒಡಂಬಡು (= ಒಡಬಡು) k v i To agree, assent, to consent, to covenant. ಒಡಂಬಡಿಸು To cause to agree; to persuade, convince ಒಡಂಬಡಿಕೆ, ಒಡಂಬಡಿಕೆ A covenant, agreement, bond, treaty, compact.

ಒಡರಿಸು. ಒಡರ್ಚು k v. t To join, to put to v i. To enter into, engage in, undertake, begin, to perform, to endeavour, try

ಒಡಲು k n The body; the belly, stomach. ಒಡಲುರಿ Burning of the belly; internal grief.

ಒಡವೆ, ಒಡಿವೆ k. n A thing, substance, possession, a jewel, property, wealth.

ಒಡಿ 1. ಒಡೆ 1. k v i. To be broken, to crack, burst, to break forth, as a bud, etc, to bud, to turn, as milk, to fail, as courage; to branch off 2, to trickle through, ooze, sink. v t To break -ಗಟ್ಟು, -ಯಕಟ್ಟು To strain off, filter through a cloth -ಗಲಸು. To break, to destroy; a broken mass. -ಬಡಿ, -ಮುರಿ To bruise -ಸು. To cause to break, etc.

ಒಡಿ 2. k. n. Heat.

ಒಡೆ 3 a k aff If; when, to, as ಉಳ್ಳೊಡೆ, ಬಂದೊಡೆ, ರಾಜನೊಡೆ.

ಒಡೆ 3. k n. Possession, ownership; rule, sway, also -ತನ. -ಯ An owner; a lord, master, a chief, leader, a ruler, king -ಯರೊಡೆಯ Lord of lords

ಒಡ್ಡ 1 k n. A class of people who cut stones, dig tanks and wells and speak a Tĕlugu patois

ಒಡ್ಡ 2, ಒಡ್ಡಣ 1. k n A pile, heap 2, an assembly, an army.

ಒಡ್ಡಣ 2 = ಒಡ್ಯಾಣ.

ಒಡ್ಡಂತಿ (tb. of ವರ್ಧಂತಿ, q. v) n. A birthday festivity

ಒಡ್ಡು k v t To place, put, lay, to fix, set, to catch; to array. 2, to oppose, resist 3, (= ಒಟ್ಟು) to heap up n A heap, pile, mass, a bank, a large gathering, a stake at play, host, army. ಒಡ್ಡಿಸು To cause to place, etc. -ಓಲಗ, ಒಡ್ಡೋಲಗ A great assembly, a royal audience, darbâr

ಒಡ್ಯಾಣ k. n. A gold or silver belt or zone.

ಒಣ k *a* Dry. 2, sapless, profitless, empty, false. -ಕ An emaciated man -ಕೆಲಸ Useless business -ಗಾಯಿ. Dry fruit. -ಮಾತು A senseless word -ಮೋರೆ. A sad countenance. -ರಗಳೆ, -ಹರಟೆ Useless talk. -ಸಂಶಯ Groundless suspicion -ಹೆಮ್ಮೆ Vain pride.

ಒಣಗು k *v i* To dry, become dry, to wither. ಒಣಗಿಲು Dryness. ಒಣಗಿಸು To dry.

ಒಂಟಿ 1 k *a* One, single, alone *Cpds*. -ಜೋತ್ರ, -ಗಣ್ಣು, -ತೋಳು, *etc* -ಎಲುವಿನವ, ಒಂಟೆಲುವಿನವ. A man of mere bones a weak man. -ಗ. A single man -ಗತನ, -ತನ. Loneliness, solitude. -ಗಿತ್ತಿ. A solitary woman.

ಒಂಟಿ 2. k *n* A gold earring.

ಒಂಟು k *v i* To agree with one's health, *as* water.

ಒಂಟೆ (*tb. of* ಉಷ್ಟ್ರ) *n* A camel.

ಒಂಡು k *n* Sediment, deposit, dregs mud in rivers, tanks, *etc*, turbidness

ಒತ್ತಟ್ಟು k *n* The nightmare

ಒತ್ತಟ್ಟು k *n*. One side. *ad*. Aside.

ಒತ್ತಡ, ಒತ್ತಲ k *n*. Fomentation

ಒತ್ತರ k *n*. Impetuousness, force, speed. 2, one layer or division. ಒತ್ತರಿಸು To increase, to be or become lofty, haughty, impetuous, quick. *i t* To join closely, to subdue

ಒತ್ತಾಯ k *n* Force, violence, compulsion, impetus.

ಒತ್ತಾಸೆ k *n* Help, assistance. -ಗಾರ A helper, assistant

ಒತ್ತು k *i. t* To press, squeeze, to shampoo, to press down; to impress, *as* a seal, to overpower, to trouble, to use unusual force or power, *as* in speaking, calling, *etc*, to stress, emphasize 2, to foment. *v i* To give way, step aside. *n*. Closeness, thickness, a pile, vicinity, pressure 2, an ... letter ... Pressing ಒತ್ತಿಸು ...

ಕ್ಕರ, ಒತ್ತಕ್ಕರ A double consonant. -ಗೊಡು To prop -ಉಂಗರ, ಒತ್ತುಂಗರ A thin finger-ring or toe-ring to tighten other rings

ಒತ್ತೆ k *n*. A pledge, pawn. 2, a single or one of a pair. -ಈ, -ಕೊಡು, -ಹಾಕು, -ಇರಿಸು, ಒತ್ತಿಡು To pledge pawn -ಬಿಡಿಸು To redeem a pawn -ತೆಗೆದುಕೊಳ್ಳು. To take a pawn

ಒತ್ತೆರ k. *n* One kind or sort

ಒದಗು k *v i* To come to hand, be got, to be effected, to be ready for, to be at hand, to be of use, to thrive, increase 2 to give way, step aside. *n* That is at hand ಒದಗಿಸು. To cause to be obtained, to make ready, *etc*; to fulfil

ಒದಮೆ k *n* The lip

ಒದರು (ರು=ಱು) k. *i t*. To shake, to cry aloud, shout, shriek, howl, to shake, move to and fro *n*. Shaking, *etc*. -ವಿಕೆ, ಒದರಾಟ Crying with great noise. -ಆಡು, ಒದರಾಡು To shout with great noise ಒದರಿಸು. To cause to shout, howl, *etc*.

ಒದವು. = ಒದಗು, *q v*. 2, to gain, obtain

ಒದಿ, ಒದೆ k. *i. t*. To kick, to spur. *P. ps*. ಒದೆದು, ಒದದು, ಒದ್ದು ಒದ್ದಿಕೆ A kick ಒದ್ದಾಟ Mutual kicking, kicking in pain; struggle, trouble, hardship. ಒದ್ದಾಡು To kick mutually, to kick in pain, to struggle in difficulty or distress

ಒಡ್ಡಿಕೆ k *n* Union, concord, friendship.

ಒದ್ದೆ k *n* Wetness, dampness, moisture *a*. Damp wet *Cpds* -ತಲೆ, -ನೆಲ, -ಬಟ್ಟೆ

ಒನ್ k. *a*. One -ದೆಸೆ One direction.

ಒನಕೆ, ಒನಿಕೆ k. *n* A large wooden pestle.

ಒನಪು = ಒಲಪು, *q v*

ಒನೆ k. *i t* To winnow, fan corn. ಒನಲಿ. A sieve

ಒಂತು k *n* A turn rotation, time 2 a share -ಗೊಳು -ಹಾಕಿಸು To take ... miss one's turn -ತೀರಿಸು. To finish one's turn. ಒಂತಿನವ. One who takes his turn

ಒಂದಿಕೆ, ಒಂದಿಗೆ k. *prep.* Together with ಅವನೊಂದಿಗೆ, *etc.*

ಒಂದು 1 (= ಹೊಂದು) k. *v. i.* To be one or united; to be linked to; to come to meet, to be fit, suitable *v. t.* To obtain, to get; to use ಒಂದಿಸು To join, to place or fix on, to grant.

ಒಂದು 2. (ಒಪ್) k. *a.* One; a, an, a certain thing. ಒಂದಕ್ಕೆ ಹೋಗು To go to make water. ಒಂದನೆಯ First. ಒಂದರೆ, ಒಂದೂವರೆ One or one and a half ಒಂದರಂತೆ Like one; at the rate of one, per one. -ಆಗು, ಒಂದಾಗು To become one; to unite. ಒಂದಾನೊಂದು. Some or other, a certain—; once upon a time. ಒಂದಿನಿತು, ಒಂದಿಷ್ಟು A little. -ಗೂಡು To be joined -ತರ, -ಪ್ರಕಾರ, -ಬಗೆ One sort or mode, an unusual manner. -ಬಾರಿ, -ಸಲ, -ಸಾರಿ, ಒಂದಾವರ್ತಿ. One time, once -ಮಾಡು. To join, unite -ವೇಳೆ. One time, once, perhaps. -ಹೊತ್ತು, ಒಪ್ಪೊತ್ತು From morning till midday, or from midday till evening. ಒಂದೂ ಮುಕ್ಕಾಲು. One and three-fourths -ಇಲ್ಲ, ಒಂದೂ ಇಲ್ಲ Nothing. ಒಂದೆ One only. -ಎರಡು, ಒಂದೆರಡು. One or two, a few. -ಎಲಗ, ಒಂದೆಲಗ. A herb, *Hydrocotile asiatica.* ಒಂದೊಂದು *rep* One — the other, one another, separate, own, each by itself

ಒಪ್ಪ k. *n.* Fitness, properness, neatness, elegance, beauty, lustre, polish, correctness. -ಮಾಡು To bestow the last honours (on a deceased person) -ಇಡು, -ವಿಡು, -ಇಕ್ಕು, -ವಿಕ್ಕು To embellish, polish. -ಹಾಕು To sign

ಒಪ್ಪಂದ k. *n.* An agreement, a contract, a treaty, a covenant -ಮಾಡು. To make an agreement, *etc.*

ಒಪ್ಪಯಿಸು = ಒಪ್ಪಿಸು, *q. v.*

ಒಪ್ಪಾನೆ k. *n.* Fitness, propriety. *ad* Fitly.

ಒಪ್ಪಿಕೆ, ಒಪ್ಪಿಗೆ, ಒಪ್ಪಿತ k. *n.* Consent, agreement; admission ಒಪ್ಪಿತ ಹಾಕು. To sign.

ಒಪ್ಪಿಸು k. *v. t.* To deliver over, give in charge, commit, to give. 2, to deliver 3, to prevail on. ಒಪ್ಪಿಸಿಕೊಳ್ಳು To take over a charge: to comply with. ಒಪ್ಪಿಸಿ ಕೊಡು. To give over a charge, *as* ಲೆಕ್ಕ-, ಪಾರ-, ಉದ್ಯೋಗ-, *etc*

ಒಪ್ಪು k. *v. i.* To suit, be fit, proper, agreeable 2, to agree to, assent, consent, to admit. 3, to be manifested *n.* Fitness, consent, beauty; elegance. ಒಪ್ಪಂತೆ In a suitable manner -ಆಚಾರ, ಒಪ್ಪಾಚಾರ An agreement. -ಗೊಳಿಸು To persuade -ಎಸೆ, ಒಪ್ಪೆಸೆ. To appear to great advantage. -ವಿಕೆ Aggreeing, *etc*; *cf* ಒಪ್ಪಿಕೆ.

ಒಬ್ಬ k. *a.* One (*m or f.*), a, an. *n.* A certain man. ಒಬ್ಬನೆ Only one, he alone. ಒಬ್ಬರು. Some, *the honorific plural*, somebody ಒಬ್ಬರೊಬ್ಬರು. These —the others, one another, these and others, every, each, *also* ಒಬ್ಬರನ್ನೊಬ್ಬರು, ಒಬ್ಬರಿಗೊಬ್ಬರು. ಒಬ್ಬಳು, ಒಬ್ಬಾಕೆ. One woman, a woman ಒಬ್ಬಾನೊಬ್ಬ A certain (man or woman). ಒಬ್ಬೊಬ್ಬ. *rep.* Every or each (man or woman). ಒಬ್ಬೊಬ್ಬರು They mutually; every one or each of them; they one by one. ಒಬ್ಬಂಟಿಗ, ಒಬ್ಬಟಿಗ A single solitary man

ಒಬ್ಬಟ್ಟು k. *n.* A sweet cake, hôlıgĕ

ಒಬ್ಬಿ = ಒಮ್ಮೆ *q. v.*

ಒಬ್ಬೆ k. *n.* A bush thicket.

ಒಮ್ k. *a* One. ಒಂಬತ್ತು. Nine ಒಮ್ಮನ. One mind, unanimity.

ಒಮ್ಮೆ k. *ad.* Once, one time or turn, together. ಒಮ್ಮಿಗೆ All at once ಒಮ್ಮಿಂದೊಮ್ಮೆ Suddenly; at some time or other, sometimes. ಒಮ್ಮೆಲೆ Together ಒಮ್ಮೊಮ್ಮೆ. *rep* Now and then, occasionally, by turns.

ಒಯ್. ಒಯಿ. ಒಯ್ಯು (- ವಯ್ಯು, *q. v.*) k. To carry off to conduct, convey P p ಒಯ್ದು. ಒಯ್ತು. Conveying, etc

ಒಯಾಳಿ, ಒಯ್ಯಾಳಿ (= ವಯ್ಯಾಳಿ, tb of ವಾಹ್ಯಾಳಿ, n A ride on horseback. -ಗ A rider on horseback -ಬಯಲು. A plain used for horse-races.

ಒಯ್ಯನೆ k ad Slowly, gently, leisurely

ಒಯ್ಯಾರ (= ವಯ್ಯಾರ, tb of ವಿಹಾರ) n Parade, coquetry 2, beauty, grace -ಗಾತಿ, -ಗಿತ್ತಿ A coquette -ಗಾರ, ಒಯ್ಯಾರಿ A showy man. -ತನ Showiness -ಮಾಡು To be dandy or foppish.

ಒಯ್ಯು = ಒಯ್, q v.

ಒರಗು (ರ = ಱ) k v i To be bent, to recline, lean upon, to lie or fall down, to rest n A bend 2, a cushion ಒರಗಿಸು. To cause to recline.

ಒರಟು (= ಉರಟು, q v.) k. n Pride, gruffness 2, coarseness ಒರಟ A rough man ಒರಟಾಡು To speak gruffly.

ಒರತೆ (ರ = ಱ) k. n A spring, fountain, a flow, a fluid.

ಒರಲು 1 = ಒರಳು, q. v.

ಒರಲು 2, ಒಱಲ್ (ರ = ಱ) a k. v i To cry out or scream from pain, etc n. An outcry, scream ಒರಲಿಸು To cause to cry out etc

ಒರಲೆ (ರ = ಱ) k n Soreness with watery humour -ಗಣ್ಣಿನವ A blear-eyed man -ಗಾಲು A foot affected with elephantiasis

ಒರಸು, ಒರಿಸು k. v t To rub gently, stroke, to scour, brush, to wipe, to rub off or out, to blot out, efface 2, to annoy; to crush 3, to separate by friction, as grain from the ears. n Rubbing, friction. 2, teasing, destroying

ಒರಳು (= ಒರಲು) k n A large mortar ಕಲ್ಲು-. A stone mortar.

ಒರುಷ. = ವರುಷ, q v

ಒರೆ 1. k v. t To rub, smear. 2, to rub on a ... 3, to ... examine 4, to ...

pull v. i To come in contact, to touch. 2, to sound, to utter, speak. n. Rubbing, etc 2, a word, an expression -ಗಲ್ಲು A touch-stone. -ಗಲ್ಲಿಗೆ ಹಚ್ಚು To apply to a touch-stone

ಒರೆ (ರೆ = ಱೆ) 2 k v i To ooze, spring, drip, flow; to be wet, moist.

ಒರೆ (ರೆ = ಱೆ) 3 k n A sheath, scabbard. -ಗಳೆ, -ಕಳಚು, -ತೆಗೆ. To draw a sword -ಗಾರ A sheathmaker -ಗೊಳಿಸು To sheath

ಒಬರ್, ಒವರ್. = ಒಬ್ಬ, q v

ಒಮ್ಮೆ = ಒಮ್ಮೆ, q v

ಒಲಪು k n Affectation in walking, foppishness, coquetry -ಗಾರ A fop, dandy -ಗಾರಳು, -ಗಾತಿ A coquette.

ಒಲವು (= ಒಲುಮೆ, ಒಲ್ಮೆ) k n Pleasure; kindness, favour. ಈಶ್ವರನ- The grace of God -ಆಗು, ಒಲವಿತ್ತು To be pleased.

ಒಲಸೆ = ವಲಸೆ, q v.

ಒಲಿ k. v. i To be pleased, favourable; to like, love, to be apt, fit -ಮೆ, ಒಲುಮೆ (= ಒಲವು, ಒಲ್ಮೆ). Pleasure; affection, love, favour, royal protection -ಸು To please

ಒಲೆ 1 k. v. i To swing, to shake, tremble, to move. 2 to hang or bend to one side, as a wall, etc v t To shake ಒಲೆದಾಡು To swing or move about.

ಒಲೆ 2 k n A fire-place furnace, an oven, hearth -ಗುಂಡು The three stones of which an ŏlĕ consists -ಇಡು, -ಮಾಡು, -ಹಾಕು, -ಹೂಡು To form an ŏlĕ. -ಹೊತ್ತಿಸು. To kindle a fire -ಗೆ ಬೆಂಕಿ ಹಾಕು. To put fire into an ŏlĕ

ಒಲ್ಮೆ. = ಒಲಿಮೆ s ಒಲಿ, q v.

ಒಲ್ಲಿ k n. A small dôtra

ಒಲ್ಲು k (d v. To will, to like, love). ಒಲ್ಲೆ 1st pers s. neg., as ಮಾಡಲೊಲ್ಲೆ, ಹೋಗಲೊಲ್ಲೆ I will not do etc Neg ... ಒಲ್ಲದ ... ಯಾರಾಗವೊಲದು. (vlg. ... W].

ಒಸಗೆ k n. Joy; feast, festival 2, speech, news. -ಕಳುಹಿಸು. To send news

ಒಸಡಿ, ಒಸಡು k n The gums.

ಒಸರು (cf. ಒರೆ 2) k v i. To ooze, trickle, flow gently. n Oozing etc ಒಸರ್ಗಲ್ A kind of crystal -ನೀರು Trickling water.

ಒಸಿ (=ವಸಿ) f. n A little.

ಒಳ್ 1. (=ಉಳ್) k. n. That is true, good, nice, etc *Its final is doubled before a following vowel.* ಒಳ್ಗುಣ. A good quality -ತೊಲೆ, -ದೊಲೆ A beautiful beam -ನುಡಿ, -ಮಾತು A true, good word. -ಮುತ್ತು A real pearl -ಬೆಳಗು, -ವೆಳಗು. Beautiful lustre -ಎಣ್ಣೆ ಒಳ್ಳೆಣ್ಣೆ Good, eatable oil.

ಒಳ್ (=ಒಳ, q v.) 2. k. *prep.* In, into, among, at, with, *as* ದೇವರೊಳ್, ಮನೆಯೊಳ್, ಕವಿಯೊಳ್, ನೀರೊಳ್, ದಿನದೊಳ್, *etc* -ಅಂಕೆ, ಒಳಂಕೆ Control -ಅಟ್ಟೆ. ಒಳಟ್ಟೆ The inner sole of a shoe.

ಒಳ k n. The inside. a. Inner, subordinate -ಕಲಮು. A subordinate paragraph. -ಕೆಯ್ The palm of the hand. -ಗಡೆ The inner side, inside, meanwhile, afterwards, later. -ಗುಟ್ಟು A secret -ಗುಡಿ. The inner part of a temple. -ಡೊಂಕು. Bending inward, concave. -ದಾರಿ. A bye-path. -ದೇಶ, -ನಾಡು, -ಸೀಮೆ An inland country -ಪಡು. To yield, to be subject to; to be merged. -ಪಡಿಸು. To make subordinate, to inclose; to seduce. -ಭಾಗ. An inner part, a subdivision -ಮೈ. The inner side, *as* of a cloth. -ಸಂಚು. A plot, intrigue -ಸಂಚುಗಾರ An intriguer, plotter. -ಸಾಲ A secret debt. -ಸೆರಗು. The tail end of a woman's cloth. -ಹೊಟ್ಟೆ. The inside of the belly, the stomach ಒಳಾಯ. Intermediate space

ಒಳಗು k. n The inside, inner part. *prep* (=ಒಳಗೆ, q v.) Within, in, into. -ಆಗು, ಒಳಗಾಗು. To get into the power of, to submit one's self, to be subject; to incur. ಒಳಗಿಂದೊಳಗೆ Secretly, privately. -ಗೊಡು, -ದೋರು. To give out a secret.

ಒಳಗೆ (=ಒಳಗು) k *prep* Inside, within, in, into; *as·* ಉಡಿಯೊಳಗೆ, ನೆಲದೊಳಗೆ, ನೀರೊಳಗೆ, *etc.* -ಇರು, ಒಳಗಿರು To be inside or in -ಸೇರು. To go inside, to sink, *as* an eye ಒಳಗೊಳಗೆ. *rep.*

ಒಳವು k. n The inside, a secret. 2, control.

ಒಳಿತು, ಒಳ್ಳಿತು k n That is good, nice, handsome, excellent, well. ಒಳಿತಾಗಿ ಮಾಡು To do a thing well

ಒಳ್ಳಿದ k n A good, nice man

ಒಳ್ಳೆ k. n Goodness, handsomeness, *etc.* (*see* ಒಳಿತು) a. Good, nice, fine, excellent, proper; *gen.* ಒಳ್ಳೆಯ *or* ಒಳ್ಳೇ. *Cpds* -ಕೆಲಸ, -ಗುಣ, -ನಡತೆ -ದು = ಒಳಿತು, q v. ಒಳ್ಳೇದು Very good, well. -ಯವನು. A good man -ತನ. Goodness, good conduct, propriety, *etc*

ಓ

ಓ. The fifteenth letter of the alphabet. 2, *a contraction of* ಉವ, *as* ಆಗೋದು, ಹೋಗೋದು, ಹೂಡೋದು, ಬಿತ್ತೋದು, *etc.* 3, *interrog affix, as·* ಮುತ್ತಿದನೋ? ಬಿದ್ದನೋ? ಹೋಗುತ್ತೀಯೋ? [illegible] *etc* 4, *int. of admiration,* [illegible] *as in* [illegible] ಕೆಟ್ಟವನೋ, ನೀನು! ಮಂಗಗಳು ಎಷ್ಟೋ ಕೆಲಸ ಮಾಡುತ್ತವೆ! 5, *int.* ಓ ಓ (=ಓಹೋ), o, oh! 6, *int of calling, as* ಓ ತಮ್ಮಾ, ಓ ದೇವರೆ v i To be attached to, fond of *P. p.* ಓತು. [illegible] A beloved man husband, *f.* ಓವಳ್

ಓಕರಿ k *n.* Vomiting -ಸು (= ಒಕ್ಕರಿಸು, *etc*). To vomit, retch, spit out; to emit. -ಕೆ Vomiting

ಓಕಳಿ, ಓಕುಳಿ k *n* A red liquid of turmeric and chunam sprinkled upon persons at the hôli feast or other auspicious occasions -ಆಡು To sprinkle the ôkuli on one another.

ಓಕಾರ s *n* The letter ಓ.

ಓಗಟ. = ಒಗಟು, *q v*

ಓಗರ k *n* Boiled rice, *also* ಓಗರದ ಗಂಜಿ. *Cpds* ಮೇಲೋಗರ, ಹಾಲೋಗರ *etc.*

ಓಘ s *n* A stream, current 2, a heap, multitude.

ಓಂಕಾರ s. *n.* The mystic syllable ôm

ಓಜ k. *n* A teacher, guru. 2, a carpenter blacksmith

ಓಜಸ್, ಓಜಸ್ಸು s. *n* Strength, energy. 2, light, splendour 3, manifestation.

ಓಜೆ a k *n* A row, line, range; regularity, order.

ಓಟ (*fr* ಓಡು) k. *n.* Running, a run, race, speed. -ಗಾರ. A runner, racer; *f.* -ಗಾರಳು, -ಗಾತಿ

ಓಟೆ 1 k *n* The tree *Garcinia pictoria* 2, a jungle reed 3, a crack, hole

ಓಟೆ 2. k *n* A half of a cocoa-nut shell 2, the shell, *as* of the wood-apple, almonds, *etc.*

ಓಡ k *n* A boat, ferry boat -ಗಾರ A boatman

ಓಡು 1 k *n* A fragment, potsherd; an earthen pan, the skull

ಓಡು 2. k *v. i.* To run, to flee. ಓಡಿ ಹೋಗು To go quickly, decamp ಓಡಾಟ, ಓಡ್ಯಾಟ. Running about. ಓಡಾಡು, ಓಡ್ಯಾಡು To run about, skip. ಓಡಾಟ. Running about ಓಡಿಸು. To cause to run, to drive away. ಓಡಿಸಿಬಿಡು. To drive off -ವಿಕೆ, ಓಡಿಕೆ Running

ಓಡೆ k. *n* An earthen hoop used for walling the inside of wells; a large store-vessel. 2, a fried cake.

ಓಣ k *A verbal affix, as* ಹೋಗೋಣ, ನಡೆಯೋ[illegible] 2. *aff.* [illegible] *noun* *as* ಬೊಗಳೋಣ, ಗುಣುಗುಟ್ಟೋಣ, ನಮ್ಮ ಇರೋಣವು 3, *aff. of the 1st p pl. imp, as* ಓಡೋಣ' ಹೋಗೋಣ' ನೋಡೋಣ' *etc* Let us run' *etc.*

ಓಣಿ k *n* A line, row 2, a lane, alley.

ಓತಿ k. *n* A kind of lizard or chameleon, blood-sucker.

ಓದು (*of* ಓದು) k *n* Reading, study

ಓದು k. *v t.* To read; to recite; to study. ಓದಿಕೆ, -ವಿಕೆ. Reading, *etc.* ಓದಕಲಿ. To learn to read ಓದಗೊಡು, ಓದಗೊಡಿಸು To let read ಓದಿ ಬಿಡು To read off. ಓದಬರು To be able to read ಓದುವ ಹುಡುಗ. A pupil ಓದಿಸು. To cause to read, to instruct. ಓದಾಳಿ. A reader, a learned man.

ಓನಾಮ s *n* The name or mantra that begins with ಓ, *i e* ಓ ನಮಃ ಶಿವಾಯ. 2, a N of the alphabet

ಓಪಾದಿ k *n.* Likeness, similarity.

ಓಮ, ಓಮು, ಓವ, ಓವು k *n.* Bishop's weed, *Ligusticum ajwaen*

ಓಯಿ k *int* O! ho! hallo!

ಓರ (= ಓರೆ, *q v*) k *n.* Declivity, sloping 2, side, edge, margin.

ಓರಗಿತ್ತಿ (= ವಾರಗಿತ್ತಿ) k *n* A husband's brother's wife

ಓರಗೆ k *n* Equality; similarity, a match. -ಯವ A man of the same age

ಓರದಿ k *n.* Sloping, declivity; variance

ಓರಣ a k. *n* A line, row ಓರಣಿಸು To be or put in a row.

ಓರು k *n* A hole. *v. i.* To think, ponder, to consider

ಓರೆ k. *n* Leaning, sloping, bending, declivity, crookedness *a* Slant, oblique, crooked. -ಕೋರೆ *rep.* -ಗಟ್ಟು. A tie bending to one side, a way of tying the turban. -ಗಣ್ಣು. A squint-eye, a side-glance. -ಚಪ್ಪರ A pent-roof. *Other cpds* -ಕಿವಿ, -ಕೈ, -ಮೂಗು, -ಮೋರೆ, *etc.* -ಯಾಗು To become [illegible]

ಓಲಗ (= ವಾಲಗ) f. *n* Service, homage, an assembly, an audience, a durbar. 2, a haut-boy -ಈ, -ಕೊಡು. To hold a public levee, to pay homage -ಶಾಲೆ A hall of audience

ಓಲಗಿಸು, ಓಲಯ್ಸು, ಓಲವಿಸು f. *v. t* To serve, to assemble, to bring together.

ಓಲಾಟ k *n* Affection, friendship 2, swinging.

ಓಲಾಡು k. *v. t.* To love *v. i* To sport in water, to swim, bathe

ಓಲು k *n* A bail, security, pledge; a hostage -ಆಗು, ಓಲಾಗು. To become bail. -ಇಕ್ಕು, -ಇರಿಸು, -ಕೊಡು, ಓಲಿಡು. To give as a pledge, security, or hostage -ಗಾರ A bondsman, *f* -ಗಾತಿ

ಓಲೆ k *n*. A leaf of a palmyra-tree, a cadjan leaf used to write on with an iron style 2, an ear-ornament of gold or of palm-leaves. -ಚಂದ್ರಿಕೆ A coil of palm-leaf. -ಚಳತುಂಬು. A pendent of an ôlĕ ear-ring. -ತಿರಗಣಿ. The screw of an ear-ring -ಪುಸ್ತಕ A book of cadjan leaves -ಭಾಗ್ಯ. A female's good fortune to wear an ôlĕ as a sign of her husband being alive. ಓಲೆಯ ಮರ. The palmyra tree

ಓಲೆಕಾರ k. *n*. A government servant who carries letters, *etc*. a porter.

ಓಷಧಿ s *n*. A plant, herb. 2, an annual plant

ಓಷ್ಠ s *n* A lip. ಓಷ್ಠ್ಯ. A labial

ಓಸರ k *a* Sloping, slanting *n*. An unsatisfactorily balanced burden.

ಓಸರಿಸು k. *v i* To go to one side; to turn aside, to give way, yield, to go away, to hesitate

ಓಸ್ಕರ (a k ಓಸುಗ) k *n* Cause, reason sake *prep* On account of ಕಟ್ಟುವದಕ್ಕೋಸ್ಕರ, ನನಗೋಸ್ಕರ, ಒಳ್ಳೇದಕ್ಕೋಸ್ಕರ

ಓಹೋ, ಓಹೋಹೋ k *int of wonder, admiration, etc.* Ho! stop! oho!

ಓಳಿ (= ಓಣಿ) k *n*. A continuous line, a row, succession

ಔ

ಔ The sixteenth letter of the alphabet *In Kannada words it is another form of* ಅವು, *or of* ಅವ *(as* ಅವುತಲ= ಔತಲ, ಅವುತಣ= ಔತಣ, ತವರು= ತೌರು), *and therefore for all Kannada and Tadbhava words with initial* ಔ *not found below see under initial* ಅವ *or* ಅವು

ಔಕಾರ s. *n* The letter ಔ.

ಔಕು (= ಅವುಕು) k *v t* To press down, squeeze, shampoo.

ಔಗು (= ಅವುಗು) k *v. t* To yield to pressure, *as* a ripe fruit.

ಔಚಿತ್ಯ (*fr* ಉಚಿತ) s *n* Fitness, propriety; pleasure, delight.

ಔಜಸ s. *n* Lustre, shine; gold.

ಔಚು. = ಅವುಚು. *q. v*

ಔತಲ (= ಅವುತಲ, *tb of* ಅಮಂಡ) *n* The castor-oil plant

ಔತಣ (= ಅವುತಣ) k *n*. A festive dinner 2, an invitation to dinner -ಮಾಡು. To make a feast

ಔತುಕೊಳ್ಳು (= ಅವುತುಕೊಳ್ಳು, *fr*. ಅವಿ) k *v. t* To hide one's self

ಔತ್ಸುಕ್ಯ (*fr* ಉತ್ಸುಕ) s. *n* Anxiety, uneasiness, eagerness, zeal.

ಔದಾರ್ಯ (*fr* ಉದಾರ) s *n* Generosity, nobility, greatness

ಔದಾಸೀನ್ಯ (*fr*. ಉದಾಸೀನ) s. *n* Indifference. apathy

ಔನ್ನತ್ಯ (*fr*. ಉನ್ನತ) s. *n* Height, greatness, haughtiness.

ಔಪಾಸನ (*fr* ಉಪಾಸನ) s *n*. A kind of adoration of Agni. *a* Devotional.

ಔರ (= ಹಪ್ಪರ) k *n*. Lightness.

ಔರಸ s. *a* Legitimate *n*. A legitimate son.

ಔಷಧ s. *n* Medicine, drug; a herb. -ಕೊಡು To administer medicine. -ಮಾಡು. To prepare medicine, apply remedies

ಔಷ್ಟ್ರಕ s *n* A herd of camels

ಂ ಃ

The seventeenth and eighteenth letters of the alphabet. *The first is generally called* anusvâra *or* sŏunĕ, *and the second called visarga, is found only in Samskrita words. There is no word beginning with either of these letters.*

ಕ್

ಕ್. The nineteenth letter of the alphabet ಕ. The letter ಕ್ pronounced with the short a.

ಕ, ಕಂ s. *n* Brahmâ 2, the soul. 3, the sun 4, the head 5, water 6, pleasure

ಕಂಯಿ = ಕಹಿ, *q. v*

ಕಂಸ s. *n* Brass 2, a metal vessel, a goblet 3 a king of Mathurâ killed by Krishna. 4, a bracket, an arc

ಕಂಸಾಳ (*tb of* ಕಾಂಸ್ಯತಾಲ) *n* A gong; a triangle. -ಕ. A gold- or silversmith, *f* -ಗಿತ್ತಿ

ಕಕಾರ s *n*. The letter ಕ

ಕಕುದ s *n*. A peak, summit. 2, a bull's hump. *a*. Pre-eminent, chief

ಕಕುಭ s *n* A region, quarter. 2, the tree *Terminalia arjuna* *a* Chief, pre-eminent.

ಕಕುಲತೆ, ಕಕುಲಾತೆ k. *n*. Love; compassion, vain desire

ಕಕ್ಕ f *n* A father's younger brother

ಕಕ್ಕಡ f. *n* A piece of twisted cloth dipped in oil, lighted, and used as a light

ಕಕ್ಕಡೆ k *n*. N. of a weapon.

ಕಕ್ಕಬಿಕ್ಕರಿ, ಕಕ್ಕರಿಬಿಕ್ಕರಿ k. *n*. Crookedness.

ಕಕ್ಕಲಾತೆ = ಕಕುಲತೆ, *q. v*.

ಕಕ್ಕಸ 1 k *n* Trouble (heavy breathing, *etc*) arising from an overloaded stomach, from running, *etc*

ಕಕ್ಕಸ 2 *tb of* ಕರ್ಕಶ, *q v* -ಗಾರ A cruel man; *f* -ಗಾತಿ

ಕಕ್ಕಸು (= ಕಕ್ಕೊಸು) f *n* A cac-hus a privy.

ಕಕ್ಕಾಬಿಕ್ಕೆ k *n*. An affrighted or timid man -ರಿ, ಕಕ್ಕಾಬಿಕ್ಕಿ, ಕಕ್ಕಾಬಿಕ್ಕು. Fear, alarm

ಕಕ್ಕಿ (*cf* ಕಕ್ಕ) s *n*. A mother's younger sister, uncle's wife; step-mother.

ಕಕ್ಕು 1 (= ಕಡಿಕು) a. k *n* A notch, dent, the rough or toothed part of a millstone, file or saw, roughness, sharpness. 2, a splinter, shiver.

ಕಕ್ಕು 2 k *v. i* To vomit *n* Vomiting. ಕಕ್ಕಿಸು. To cause to vomit.

ಕಕ್ಕುಬಿಕ್ಕು = ಕಕ್ಕಾಬಿಕ್ಕರಿ, *q v*

ಕಕ್ಕೆ k *n* The pudding-pipe tree, *Cassia* ...

ಕಕ್ಕೋಲ s n. N of a plant bearing a berry containing waxy and aromatic substance, a perfume made of its berries, *also* -ಕ.

ಕಕ್ಕೋಸು = ಕಕ್ಕಸು, *q. v.*

ಕಕ್ಷ (= ಕಚ್ಚೆ) s. *n.* The hem of a garment tucked into the waist-band 2, a girdle. 3, the armpit, *also* -ಮೂಲ. 4, a forest. 5, an objection or reply in argument -ಪಾಲ. A bag carried under the armpit.

ಕಕ್ಷಿ s. *n.* One party as opposed to another; objection, contention. -ಗಾರ A party (in a civil or criminal case)

ಕಗ (= ಕಡು *q. v.*) k. *n* Hardness, strength, *etc.* -ಗಂಟು (= ಕಡುಗಂಟು). A fast knot that cannot be easily untied, a hard knot in wood. -ಗತ್ತಲೆ Thick darkness -ಕಲ್ಲು, ಕಗ್ಗಲ್ಲು. A very hard stone. -ಕಾಡು, ಕಗ್ಗಾಡು. An impervious jungle. -ಕಾಯಿ, ಕಗ್ಗಾಯಿ. An unripe fruit -ಕಾರು, ಕಗ್ಗಾರು Great dryness, drought -ಕಾಲ, -ಕಗ್ಗಾಲ. Famine. -ಕುಂಬಳ, ಕಗ್ಗುಂಬಳ. A hard gourd

ಕಗ್ಗ k. *n.* A long, tedious speech or literary composition.

ಕಂ (= ಕಣ್ಣು) k. *n* The eye -ಕಣ. An eye-drop, tear -ಕಡೆ, ಕಂಗಡೆ A side-glance, leer. -ಕಾಣು, -ಗಾಣು To perceive -ಕೆಡು, ಕಂಗೆಡು To be blinded, confused, vexed; to be afraid. -ಗೆಡಿಸು To blind, bewilder, confuse

ಕಂಕಣ, ಕಂಕಳ s. *n.* An ornament of the wrist, bracelet 2, a waist-tie 3, a crest, trinket -ಕಾರ Borax -ಗ್ರಹಣ. A partial eclipse -ಬದ್ಧ. A man tying a kankana round his wrist for any auspicious rites.

ಕಂಕರೆ h *n* Gravel, a pebble.

ಕಂಕಳು. = ಕಂಕುಳ, *q v.*

ಕಂಕಾಲ s. *n.* A skeleton. -ಧರ Who carries the backbone of Vishnu. Śiva

ಕಂಕಿ k. *n* An ear of corn stripped of its grain. -[illegible] To thrash out corn

ಕಂಕುಳ (ಳ = ೞ) k *n* The armpit.

ಕಂಗಳ, ಕಂಗಾಳ k *n* A blind man

ಕಂಗಾರು k. *n* Displeasure, anger.

ಕಂಗಾಲ್ h *a* Poor; poverty-stricken, weak ಕಂಗಾಲ A pauper. -ತನ. Pauperism, wretchedness

ಕಂಗು. = ಕಂಗಾರು, *q. v.* 2, the heart-pea. 3, the Indian millet -ಆಗು, ಕಂಗಾಗು To become angry or annoyed

ಕಂಗೆಡು, *see s.* ಕಂ.

ಕಂಗೋರೆ m. *n* An ornamental cordon, groove, *etc.*

ಕಚ s. *n.* The hair of the head 2, matted hair. 3, a binding, a band

ಕಚಕ್ಕನೆ k *ad* Smartly, forcibly 2, with the sound of treading or anything falling into mud.

ಕಚಫು k. *n.* A dish of boiled vegetables or fruits seasoned with salt, pepper, *etc.*

ಕಚರಾ h *n* Rubbish, dirt, straw. -ಕೆಲಸ Worthless business -ತೆರಿಗೆ Municipal tax

ಕಚೇರಿ (= ಕಚ್ಚೇರಿ) h. *n.* A hall of audience, a court for administration of public business; an office. -ಮಾಡು. To open a court or office for business. *Cpds* -ಕೆಲಸ, -ಚಾಕರಿ, -ಉದ್ಯೋಗ

ಕಚೋರ f. *n.* The long Zedoary, *Curcuma zerumbet.*

ಕಚ್ಚಡ (= ಕಚ್ಚರ) h *n* Filth, rubbish.

ಕಚ್ಚಡಿ k *n.* A kind of vegetable dish.

ಕಚ್ಚಳಿ (ಳಿ = ೞಿ) a k. *n.* An honorary arm-ring.

ಕಚ್ಚಾ h. *a.* Unripe, green; raw, rude, rough, tender, minor, less -ಸೇರು A seer of only 20 or 24 rupees' weight. -ಕೆಲಸ. A clumsy affair -ಮನುಷ್ಯ. A mean man -ಲೆಕ್ಕ. A rough account.

ಕಚ್ಚು k *v t* To bite, to sting 2, to gripe, ache, *as* the stomach. *v. i* To join *n.* Biting, a bite, an incision; a notch, a wound 2, washing, water in which rice has been washed

-ಆಟ, ಕಚ್ಚಾಟ Quarrel -ಆಡು, ಕಚ್ಚಾಡು. To bite one another, *as* dogs, to quarrel -ಕಚ್ಚಿಸು. To cause to bite.

ಕಚ್ಚೂರ f *n*. A leafless plant, *Kaempferia galanga*

ಕಚ್ಚೆ (*tb of* ಕಕ್ಷ & ಕಚ್ಛ) *n* The hem of a garment tucked into the waist-band. 2, a female's cloth. 3, a girdle.

ಕಚ್ಚೇರಿ = ಕಚೇರಿ, *q. v.*

ಕಚ್ಛ (= ಕಚ್ಚೆ no 1) s. *n*. 2, marshy ground. 3, the bank of a river 4, a tree -ಶುದ್ಧಿ Chasteness.

ಕಚ್ಛೋರ = ಕಚೋರ, *q. v.*

ಕಜಾಕ್ h. *n* The sash worn by peons or sepoys

ಕಜೂರ (= ಖರ್ಜೂರ) f *n* The date fruit

ಕಜ್ಜ. *tb of* ಕಾರ್ಯ, *q. v.* = ಕೆಲಸ, ಉದ್ಯೋಗ.

ಕಜ್ಜಲ s. *n*. Lamp-black, a collyrium

ಕಜ್ಜಾಯ *f n* Bread. 2, a kind of sweet cake.

ಕಜ್ಜಿ (*tb of* ಖರ್ಜು) *n*. Scab (the disease), itch. -ಬುರುಕ One infected with the itch and always scratching it; *f.* -ಬುರುಕಿ -ಹುಳ Parasite in the itch.

ಕಂಚಾ k *n* A marble -ಆಡು. To play marbles.

ಕಂಚಿ 1. k *n* A kind of bitter and sour orange.

ಕಂಚಿ 2 (*tb of* ಕಾಂಚಿ) *n* The town Conjeveram -ಮೇಕೆ A small white goat.

ಕಂಚಿನಿ h. *n*. A dancing girl

ಕಂಚಿವಾಳ s *n* The mountain ebony, *Bauhinia variegata*.

ಕಂಚು (*tb of* ಕಾಂಸ್ಯ) *n* White brass, bell-metal, a vessel made of it. -ಮಿಂಚಾಗು To appear or come suddenly or like a flash. -ಉರುಳಿ, -ರುಳಿ A round vessel of ಕಂಚು

ಕಂಚುಕ s. *n*. A bodice, jacket, an armour.

ಕಂಜ s. *a*. Water-born. *n* A lotus. 2, Bra[illegible]

ಕಂಜೋದರ Vishnu. -ಜ -ಜನ, -ಉದಯ, ಕಂಜೋದಯ Brahmâ. -ವೈರಿ The moon -ಸಖ, ಕಂಜಾಪ್ತ The sun.

ಕಟ 1. (= ಕಡೆ) k. *n*. End, corner -ವಾಯಿ, -ಬಾಯಿ. The two corners of the mouth, a cheeck

ಕಟ 2. s. *n* A twist of straw, a mat 2, time, season. 3, the hip 4, the temples of an elephant 5, excess.

ಕಟಕ 1. k. *n* A butcher.

ಕಟಕ 2 (*tb.* ಕಡಗ) s *n*. A bracelet, anklet 2, the side of a hill, table-land. 3, an army. 4, the ocean. 5, a tusk.

ಕಟಕಟಾ. = ಅಕಟ, *q. v*

ಕಟಕಟಿ, ಕಟಕಟೆ 1 k. *n* Trouble, annoyance, grievance, distress.

ಕಟಕಟೆ 2. k *n* A railing, balustrade

ಕಟಕರೋಹಿಣಿ, ಕಟಂಬರೆ s *n* The medicinal plant *Helleborus niger*

ಕಟಕಿ k *n* Irony, derision 2, a shrew.

ಕಟಕು 1 k *n* A sort of white or reddish clay. 2, dryness, crispness, *as* of bread.

ಕಟಕು 2 (*tb. of* ಕಟಕ) *n*. An ear-ring set with precious stones or pearls.

ಕಟಪಿಟಿ (= ಕಟಕಟಿ) k. *n* Annoyance, teasing 2, gabble

ಕಟಾಕ್ಷ s. *n*. A side-glance 2, kind regard, favour ಕಟಾಕ್ಷಿಸು To look at, to favour, regard.

ಕಟಾಂಜನ s. *n*. A railing to lean against.

ಕಟಾಯಿಸು h. *v. t.* To reap *as* corn. 2, to deduct, to finish. ಕಟಾವು Cutting, reaping

ಕಟಾರಿ (= ಕಠಾರಿ) h. *n* A sort of dagger.

ಕಟಾಹ (= ಕಡಾಯಿ) s. *n* A boiler for oil or butter; a frying pan 2, a hemisphere. 3, nearness. 4, opportunity, season.

ಕಟಿ 1, ಕಟೆ k *v. t.* To cut a stone with a chisel. 2, to keep the mind awake.

ಕಟಿ 2 s. *n*. The hip, loins -ಬಂಧ A [illegible] zone of the earth -ವಾತ.

Lumbago. -ಸೂತ್ರ. A waist-band worn by females

ಕಟಿಕ = ಕಟಕ, q. v.

ಕಟು, ಕಟುಕ s. a. Pungent, strong-scented, biting, bitter, fierce. 2, disagreeable. n. A pungent taste -ಕರೋಹಿಣಿ. = ಕಟುಕರೋಹಿಣಿ, q. v.

ಕಟೋರ h. n A bowl or cup.

ಕಟ್ಟ (= ಕಟ 1, ಕಡೆ 1) k. n. End -ಕಡೆ The farthest end; at the very end. -ಉತ್ತರ, ಕಟ್ಟುತ್ತರ A final answer.

ಕಟ್ಟಡ, ಕಟ್ಟಣ k n. A building

ಕಟ್ಟಲೆ, ಕಟ್ಟಳೆ (fr ಕಟ್ಟು) k n An order, command, rule, rate, a case. 2, a weight used by goldsmiths or jewellers 3, thick butter-milk. -ಚೀಲ. A bag for keeping weights, etc -ಮಾಡು To order ದಿನ- Daily.

ಕಟ್ಟಿಗೆ (tb. of ಕಾಷ್ಠಿಕೆ) n. Wood or timber, fuel, a stick -ಗಿಟ್ಟಿಗೆ red. -ಗಾರ, -ಯವ. A wood-seller -ಗುಣ, -ಮನಸ್ಸು. A hard heart, obstinacy -ಕಡಿ To cut wood

ಕಟ್ಟು 1 (= ಕಡು, q v) k n. Intensity; excess, etc. ಕಟ್ಟಡವಿ, ಕಟ್ಟರಣ್ಯ A thick jungle. ಕಟ್ಟಂಬಲಿ A thick kind of porridge. ಕಟ್ಟಲೆ, ಕಟ್ಟಳೆ, see separately. ಕಟ್ಟಾಜ್ಞೆ. A strict order. ಕಟ್ಟಾಯ. A firm resolution ಕಟ್ಟಾಳು. A strong man ಕಟ್ಟಾಳ್ತನ. Great valor ಕಟ್ಟುತ್ತರ A strict order. ಕಟ್ಟುತ್ತಾರ Remission of land-revenue on account of loss by failure of rain, etc -ಮಸ್ತಿ Excessive pride. -ಮಸ್ತು. Strength -ಉಬ್ಬು, ಕಟ್ಟುಬ್ಬು A great noise. -ಹುಳಿ. A strong acid -ಉಳಿಗ, ಕಟ್ಟುಳಿಗ A hard task.

ಕಟ್ಟು 2. k v. t. To bind, tie; to affix, to yoke, to construct, build, form, to dam in, as water, to shut up, as a door, to lay by, deposit, as money, to restrain, to apply to, to determine, as price, to collect, to obtain, to bewitch, charm v i To be checked, stopped, formed (ಕಟ್ಟಿಕೊಳ್ಳು. To embrace ಪುಣ್ಯ ಕಟ್ಟಿಕೊಳ್ಳು. To obtain merit ಕಟ್ಟಿಕೊಂಡು ಹೋಗು. To conduct away with one's self. ಕಟ್ಟಿಹಾಕು = ಕಟ್ಟು 1, v t ಕಟ್ಟಿಸು To cause to bind, etc -ವಿಕೆ. Tying) n Binding, fastening, restraint. 2, a band, tie, a boundary. 3, a pack, bundle. 4, a frame. 5, build, form 6, a regulation rule. 7, a fiction 8, bewitching. Cpds. ಇಕ್ಕಟ್ಟು, ಕಣ್ಣುಕಟ್ಟು, ಚೌಕಟ್ಟು, ತಲೆಕಟ್ಟು, ನಡುಕಟ್ಟು, ನೆಲೆಗಟ್ಟು, ಮಣಿಕಟ್ಟು, etc ಕಟ್ಟುಪಡಕ. A binding written agreement. ಕಟ್ಟನ್ನ. Boiled rice tied up for a journey. ಕಟ್ಟಾಗು. To become a rule; to stop, to be shut, as school. ಕಟ್ಟಾಗಿ Rightly, positively. ಕಟ್ಟಾಣಿ, ಕಟಾಣಿ A necklace of small gold beads. -ಕಥೆ A fiction -ಮಾಡು To bind, tie, to restrain, to regulate; order -ಮುಟ್ಟು Great embarrassment, strength. -ವಾಸ. A wrapper or cover. -ಶಬ್ದ. A fictitious term -ಕಟ್ಟೊಡೆ To break a rule; an association to be dissolved. -ಕ. A man who ties; a fiction.

ಕಟ್ಟು 3. k. n. Soup of any pulse ಕಟ್ಟನ್ನ. Boiled rice mixed with it (cf. s. ಕಟ್ಟು). -ರಸ, -ಸಾರು. Such soup seasoned with salt, pepper, etc

ಕಟ್ಟೆ k. n. A structure, a guard-house. 2, a dam, dike. 3, a bridge 4, a basin round the foot of a tree (= ಆಲವಾಲ, q v.) 5, a pond Cpds. ಅಣೆ-, ಟಪಾಲು-, ನೀರ-, ಸುಂಕದ-, etc

ಕಟ್ಲೆ. = ಕಟ್ಟಳೆ, q v. 2, a law-suit, case

ಕಠಾರಿ. = ಕಟಾರಿ, q v.

ಕಠಿಣ, ಕಠಿನ s a Hard, stiff, inflexible, violent, cruel, harsh. -ತೆ, -ತ್ವ Hardness, cruelty. -ಹೃದಯ A hard heart; hard-hearted, cruel. -ಬುದ್ಧಿ, -ಮನಸ್ಸು. A cruel disposition -ರೋಗ. A dangerous sickness -ಮಾಡು To harden, to vex.

ಕಠೋರ s a. Hard, stiff, sharp, cruel 2, full. -ತನ. Hardness, severity. Cpds -ಮಾತು. -ವಾಕ್ಯ, -ಶಬ್ದ.

ಕಡ 1 k *n.* A debt. 2, a loan -ಬೀಳು. To incur debt -ಗಾರ A debtor.

ಕಡ 2 k. *n.* A ferry, ford.

ಕಡ 3 (=ಕಡೆ) k *n* End, corner.

ಕಡ 4 (=ಕಡು) k. *n.* Churning 2, cutting -ಗೋಲು A churning stick -ಕತ್ತಿ, -ಗತ್ತಿ A chopper-bill, a small crescent knife.

ಕಡಗು, ಕಡಂಗು k *n* A channel leading water to a tree, a ditch

ಕಡಜ k *n.* A wasp, hornet

ಕಡತ (*cf.* ಕಡಿ) k *n* A book made of folded cloth covered with charcoal paste 2, cutting, a cut, incision

ಕಡದು (*fr* ಕಡಿ) k. *a* Steep, upright. 2, hard, rough, severe, firm. *n.* Steepness, uprightness, hardness, *etc.* -ಗಾರ A powerful man, a harsh man

ಕಡದು *P p of* ಕಡಿ *or* ಕಡೆ.

ಕಡಂದುರು. = ಕಡಜ, *q v.*

ಕಡಬ, ಕಡವ k *n.* A species of deer

ಕಡಬು, ಕಡುಬು k. *n* A cake boiled in steam

ಕಡಮೆ. = ಕಡಿಮೆ, *q v.*

ಕಡಲು k. *n.* The sea, an ocean. -ಅಣುಗ, ಕಡಲಣುಗ. The moon. -ತೆರೆ. A wave of the sea. -ನಾಲಿಗೆ. Cuttle-fish bone.

ಕಡಲೆ = ಕಡ್ಲೆ, *q v*

ಕಡವಸ = ಕಡಾಸು, *q v*

ಕಡವೆ (= ಕಡಬ) k. *n.* An elk; the Indian stag.

ಕಡಸು k. *n* A young cow or buffalo not yet calved.

ಕಡಾಕಡಿ (= ಖಡಾಖಡಿ) f *n.* Strictness, accuracy

ಕಡಾಣಿ = ಕಡಿವಾಣ, *q. v.*

ಕಡಾಯಿ (*tb. of* ಕಟಾಹ) *n* A large, round boiler.

ಕಡಾವಿಗೆ, ಕಡಾವು s *n* Wooden shoes 2, a lathe, turning

ಕಡಾಸು k. *n* A skin (to sit or lie on); *also* ಕಡಾಸನ.

ಕಡಿ k *v. t.* To bite, bite or cut off, to sting, [illegible] stomach, to gnash, *as* the teeth. 2, to cut, hack, to chop; to dig, *as* a well, to pull. *v i.* To itch, *as* the body *P. ps.* ಕಡ, ಕಡದು, ಕಡಿದು. ಕಡ ದಾಟಿ. Altercation ಕಡದಾಡು. To cut down, to fight, wrangle ಕಡಿ, ಕಡಿತ, ಕಡತ A cut, bite, a chip, piece, bit, a potsherd, an oblong roll of cotton thread. -ತಲೆ A leather-shield. -ಮೆಟ್ಟು The impression of a horse's hoof. -ಯಕ್ಕಿ Grits of rice.

ಕಡಿಮೆ (= ಕಡಮೆ) k *n* Deficiency; want, defect, inferiority -ಮಾಡು. To make less, decrease. -ಯಾಗು. To become less -ಬೀಳು To fall short ಹೆಚ್ಚು- More or less; difference.

ಕಡಿವಾಣ, ಕಡಿಯಾಣ, ಕಡಿಯಣ k. *n.* A bit, bridle. -ಹಾಕು To bridle -ಎಳೆ, -ಬಿಗಿಹಿಡಿ To pull in the reins.

ಕಡು (= ಕಟ್ಟು) k *n* Firmness, intensity; vehemence, swiftness; abundance, excess. *ad* Greatly, swiftly. -ಕಷ್ಟ Great trouble. -ಕಳ್ಳ A great thief. -ಕೇಡು. A heavy loss -ಕೋಪ, -ಗೋಪ. Great wrath -ಕತ್ತಲೆ, -ಗತ್ತಲೆ Great darkness. -ಗಲಿ A great hero -ಗಾಸಿ Great trouble. -ಕುದುರೆ, -ಗುದುರೆ. A swift horse -ಗೇಡಿ A very mischievous person. -ಚಳಿ Severe cold -ನಾಲಿಗೆ. A talkative tongue -ನೋವು. Acute pain. -ಪಾತಕ, -ಪಾಪ A heinous sin -ಪಾಪಿ A notorious sinner -ಮೂರ್ಖ. A big fool. -ವೇಗ Great swiftness. -ಶೋಕ Great grief. -ಹೆಡ್ಡ A very stupid man

ಕಡುಕು k. *n* A cut, piece, a bit, a headless trunk.

ಕಡುಪು k. *n* Force, vehemence; severity; pride, great valor

ಕಡುಬು = ಕಡಬು, *q v.*

ಕಡೆ 1 (=ಕಟೆ 1) k. *n* End, termination; limit, direction, place *a.* Last, low, ulterior, inferior -ಗಣಿಸು. To look upon as inferior, slight, to end -ಗಾ [illegible] To the very last, totally. -ಗೆ Aside, towards; in the end, at last, finally ಕಡೆಗೆ ತೆಗೆ. To rescue -ಗೆ ಹೋಗು. To go last, to go aside. -ತನಕ. Until the end. -ನೋಟ A side glance. -ಹಾಟಿಸು, -ಹಾಯಿಸು To cause to pass by, through or over: to save -ಗೂಸು, -ಹುಟ್ಟು. The youngest child ಕಡೇಲಿ A common form of ಕಡೆಯಲ್ಲಿ. ಎಡಗಡೆ The left side ಬಲಗಡೆ. The right side.

ಕಡೆ 2 k. v. t To churn, to stir; to rub together, as two pieces of wood to excite fire. 2, to turn in a lathe. 3, to pass over, to get through. v i. To fall down, sink ಮೊಸರ- To churn curds. n Churning. -ಗೋಲು = ಕಡಗೋಲು s ಕಡ 4. -ಚಲು Turning a lathe; also ಕಡಾವು

ಕಡ್ಡ k n A clown, blockhead, an unpolite man 2, a pitfall to catch elephants -ಮಾಡು To make a dolt of one ಕಡ್ಡಾಟ Obstinacy, pertinacity, stupidity

ಕಡ್ಡಾಯು k n. Force, compulsion, exaction. -ಗಾರ. An outrageous man. -ಮಾಡು. To force, constrain.

ಕಡ್ಡಿ (tb of ಕಾಷ್ಠ) n A small stick, fibre of a leaf or a bit of a haulm -ಅರಗು, -ಯರಗು Stick lac, a stick of sealing wax

ಕಡ್ಲೆ (= ಕಡಲೆ) k. n The Bengal gram or chicken-pea, *Cicer arietinum*.

ಕಣ್ (= ಕಣ್ಣು, q. v) k n The eye, a mesh. -ಕಾಡಿಗೆ, -ಕಪ್ಪು. A collyrium for the eye -ಕುಣಿ The socket of the eye -ಕುಣಿಕೆ. The inner or outer corner of the eye -ಗೆಡಿಸು, ಕಂಗೆಡಿಸು To blind, bewilder, confuse. -ಸೊಲ್ಲ A smile of the eye -ಜಾಡೆ A faint notice ಕಣ್ಣಾರ, ಕಣ್ಣಾರೆ Distinctly, clearly ಕಣ್ಣಿಡು. To fix the eyes. ಕಣ್ಣೀರು Tears. ಕಣ್ಣುಬ್ಬು. An eye-brow. ಕಣ್ಣುರಿ Smarting of the eye, envy. ಕಣ್ಣೆವೆ, ಕಣ್ಣವೆ An eye-lash, eyelid -ಪರೆ A web or film of the eye -ತೆರೆ -... To open the eyes. -ಮುಚ್ಚು. To shut the eyes -ಸನ್ನೆ, -ಸಯ್ಗೆ. A wink

ಕಣ 1. s. n. A grain, single seed, a particle, a granule, an atom 2, a drop, spark a Small.

ಕಣ 2. k n. A piece of cloth for a female's bodice, as ರವಕೆ.

ಕಣ 3 (tb of ಖಲ) n A thrashing floor, a battle-field, a misty halo round the moon.

ಕಣಕ k. n Dough, especially of wheaten flour

ಕಣಕಪ್ಪಟಿ (= ಕಣುಕಪ್ಪಟೆ) k. n A flittermouse, bat

ಕಣಗಲ, ಕಣಗಿಲು k n A shrub yielding Tapioca, the bitter *cassava* plant

ಕಣಗಿಲೆ k n. Fragrant oleander, *Nerium odorum*.

ಕಣಜ s n. A corn-bin, i e. a cylindrical structure for storing grain, a granary, barn. -ಹುಳ. A wasp. -ಹಾಕು To store grain.

ಕಣವೆ (=ಕಣಿವೆ, ಕಣಿವೆ) k. n. A hill-pass, gap, ditch.

ಕಣಾ k. int. Lo! indeed!

ಕಣಿ 1 k. n. Sight, spectacle; ominous sight, divination, sooth. -ಕೇಳು To ask for a divination -ಹೇಳು To divine. -ಗಾರ A fortune teller; f. -ಗಾತಿ.

ಕಣಿ 2 k n A knot, tie 2, a stone.

ಕಣಿ 3 (tb of ಖನಿ) n A ditch; a mine.

ಕಣಿ 4 f. n An atom, grits, a trifle

ಕಣಿಕೆ k n The stalk of the great millet deprived of its ear

ಕಣಿವೆ, ಕಣಿವೆ. = ಕಣವೆ, q v.

ಕಣುಕಪ್ಪಟಿ = ಕಣಕಪ್ಪಟಿ, q v.

ಕಣೆ k n. A stick, an arrow. 2, a wooden roller of an oil-mill

ಕಂಟ (tb of ಕಂಠ) n. An iron style for writing on palm-leaves 2, the neck of a vessel.

ಕಂಟಕ s. n A thorn, the point of a needle. 2. a foe 3, annoyance, obstacle; danger 4, a hunter -ಫಲ A jack fruit. ಕಂಟಕಿ. An awn, a troublesome woman.

ಕಂಟಕಾರಿ, -ಕೀ. s. n. A sort of prickly nightshade, *Solanum jacquini*.

ಕಂಟಲೆ, ಕಂಟ್ಲೆ k. n A double bag carried across a beast

ಕಂಟಿ s n A species of *Solanum*. 2 the *Acacia catechu* 3, any thorny shrub 4, a kind of gold ornament for the breast *a* Thorny, annoying.

ಕಂಟು k. n An offset in the wall of a well or at the foot of a wall, a flight of stairs leading to a well.

ಕಂಠ (*tb.* ಕಂಟಿ) s n The throat. 2, the neck of a vessel 3, an iron style for writing 4, guttural sound. 5, the body. -ಪಾಠ Learning by heart. -ಮಾಲೆ A necklace -ಲಗ್ನ Embracing -ಶೋಷ. Vain talk. -ಸೂತ್ರ The thread worn by wives round their neck; the sacrificial thread. ಕಂಠೋಷ್ಠ್ಯ. The vowels ಉ, ಊ, and ಓ

ಕಂಠಿ s n A collar; a necklace. ಕಂಠೀರವ. Roaring from the throat, a lion. ಕಂಠೀರವರಾಯ N of a Mysore king. ಕಂಠೀರವರಾಯನ ಹಣ A gold fanam (4 ⅔ Anas)

ಕಂಡ 1. k n Flesh, meat

ಕಂಡ 2 (*p a. of* ಕಾಣು). Seen, he saw

ಕಂಡ 3 (*tb. of* ಖಂಡ, *q v*) -ತುಂಡು ಮಾತಾಡು To speak so that further argument becomes futile. -ಸಕ್ಕರೆ Sugar-candy.

ಕಂಡನೆ k n Final settlement, treaty. *Cpds* -ಪತ್ರ, -ಹಣ, *etc.*

ಕಂಡೆಲಿ k n A kind of bill-hook or cleaver

ಕಂಡಿ 1 k n A chink, a hole, an opening, gap.

ಕಂಡಿ 2 f n. A measure of capacity and weight. 2, a certain timber-measure

ಕಂಡಿಕೆ k n. A ball of thread put into the w... ... 2 ... a piec

ಕಂಡಿತ (= ಖಂಡಿತ, *fr* ಕಡು) k n Firmness, positiveness, strictness, certainty. -ಮಾತು. A decisive word.

ಕಂಡಿಸು (= ಖಂಡಿಸು) k *v. t.* To settle, *as* the price of a thing

ಕಂಡು k *P p of* ಕಾಣು, *q. v.*

ಕಂಡುಗ k n A measure of capacity equal to twenty kŏlagas

ಕಂಡೆಯ k. n. A kind of sword. 2, large extent

ಕಂಡೋಲ f n. A basket for holding grain, a store-room 2, a weight from 20 to 28 maunds

ಕಣ್ಣಿ k n A rope, cord, a neck-rope.

ಕಣ್ಣೀರು k. n Tears -ಸೋರು. Tears to flow. -ಇಡು, -ತರು, -ಸುರಿಸು. Tears to shed. *See s* ಕಣ್

ಕಣ್ಣು (= ಕಣ್, *q. v.*) k. n The eye, an eye-like knot in sticks, *etc*, a small hole, an orifice, a mesh -ಕಟ್ಟು To shut or bewitch the eyes, to deceive; jugglery -ಕಟ್ಟಿನವ A juggler -ಕಾಣು The eye to see. -ಕಿಸಿ To assume an angry look. ಕಣ್ಗೆಸುರು An evil eye -ಕುಕ್ಕು The eye to be dazzled, *as* by the rays of the sun -ಗತ್ತಲೆ. Fainting, swoon. -ಗುಡ್ಡೆ. The eye-ball -ಗೊಂಬೆ. The pupil of the eye. -ನೋವು, -ಬೇನೆ Pain of the eye. -ಪಿಚ್ಚು, -ಪಿಸರು, -ಪಿಳ್ಳು. Rheum of the eye. -ಮಂಜು, -ಮಬ್ಬು Dimness of sight. -ಮುಚ್ಚಾಲೆ A kind of blindman's buff -ಸನ್ನೆ. A sign made with the eye, a wink. -ಹುಬ್ಬು The eyebrow. -ಹುಬ್ಬು ಗಂಟು ಹಾಕಿಕೊಳ್ಳು To frown. -ಹೂವು. A white spot on the eye-ball. -ಹೋಗು. To lose the eye-sight -ಎತ್ತು ಕಣ್ಣೆತ್ತು. To lift up the eyes. -ಮರೆ ಮಾಡು. To hide from view -ಹೊಡೆ To twinkle the eye

ಕಣ್ಣುಕಪ್ಪಟಿ = ಕಣಕಪ್ಪಟಿ, *q. v*

ಕಣ್ಣೆ k n A clot, lump, *as* of jaggory, flesh, *etc.*

... Strych-

ಕತಬೆ h. n. A writ of agreement, written bond.

ಕತಚೆರ (=ಕದಚೆರ) h. n. Strife, contention; controversy.

ಕತಿ (=ಖತಿ) k n. Anger, wrath.

ಕತ್ತರಿ (=ಕತ್ರಿ, *tb. of* ಕರ್ತರಿ) *n* Scissors, shears; a rat-trap. -ಗಳ್ಳ. A pickpocket -ಬಾವುಲಿ A gold ornament worn near the top of the ear -ಸು. To cut with scissors; to cut; to shear, to pick, steal

ಕತ್ತಲೆ (ಕತ್ತಲು) k *n* Darkness. ಮುಂಗತ್ತಲೆ. Darkness after sunset. ಹಿಂಗತ್ತಲೆ. Darkness before dawn -ಆಗು. To be dark

ಕತ್ತಾಳೆ k. *n* The Barbadoes aloe 2, the small aloe.

ಕತ್ತಿ (*tb. of* ಕರ್ತ್ರಿ) *n* A knife, a razor, a sword. -ಕಟ್ಟು. To gird on one's sword, to be hostile -ಮತ A religion established by the sword or force -ಸಾಧಕ, -ಸಾಧನ Sword exercise. ಬಿಚ್ಚು- A naked sword -ಬಿಚ್ಚು. To draw a sword. -ಮುಡುಕು, -ತಿವಿ To pierce with a sword.

ಕತ್ತು 1. k. *n* The neck, throat. -ಕೊಯ್ಯು. To cut the throat.

ಕತ್ತು 2 k *v. t* To inflame, kindle.

ಕತ್ತು 3 h *n* Writ, a writing 2, a kind of hand-writing

ಕತ್ತೂರಿ *tb of* ಕಸ್ತೂರಿ, *q. v.*

ಕತ್ತೆ k. *n.* An ass, donkey -ಕಿರುಬ, -ಕುರುಬ The hyæna; a kind of deer.

ಕತ್ರಿ. =ಕತ್ತರಿ, *q v.*

ಕಥನ s. *n.* Telling, relating, narration, tale ಕಥಿಕ. A story-teller

ಕಥೆ s *n.* A speech; a tale, story, narrative. 2, affair. -ಹೇಳು, ಕಥಿಸು. To relate a story. ಕಥಾಂತರ. The course of a story or conversation

ಕದ k *n.* The leaf of a door, a door.

ಕದಕದ k *int* Ha! ha! ha! -ನಗು. To laugh loudly. [illegible] sh[illegible] be agitate[illegible]

ಕದಡು k *v. i* To be shaken, stirred, troubled, to become turbid, muddy, impure *v. t.* To stir *n.* Turbidness; mud. 2, commotion, tumult.

ಕದನ s. *n.* War, fight -ಗಲಿ. A hero in battle.

ಕದಂಬ (=ಕಡಂಬ) s. *n* The tree *Nauclea cadamba.* 2, a multitude 3, mustard seed, turmeric

ಕದರು k *n* A spindle. 2, lustre.

ಕದಚೆರ =ಕತಚೆರ, *q v*

ಕದಲಿ s *n.* The plantain tree or banana, *Musa sapientum.* 2, a flag, banner. 3 Śiva 4, an elephant

ಕದಲು (=ಕದಡು, *q. v.*) k. *v. i* To move, shake ಕದಲಾಡು To move about, shake, be unsteady ಕದಲಿಕೆ. Motion ಕದಲಿಸು. To cause to move or shake, to cause to become turbid.

ಕದಿ k *v. t* To steal *P p.* ಕದ್ದು. -ಕ, -ಗ A thief, *f.* -ಕಿ.

ಕದಿರು, ಕದರು k *n* A spike of corn, ear. 2, a spindle. 3, splendour

ಕದೀಮು h *a.* Old, ancient ಕದೀಮ. An old servant, veteran. ಕದೀಮಿ Long standing.

ಕದುಬು a k *v. t.* To press, to distress, trouble

ಕದುರು. =ಕದರು, *q v*

ಕದೆ a. k *v i* To join, approach.

ಕದ್ದು k *P p. of* ಕದಿ.

ಕದ್ರು s. *a.* Brown, tawny *n* N. of Kaśyapa's wife.

ಕನ್ k *n* Blackness. ಕನ್ನಡ The black country. Kannada (Canarese), the country and its language, Canara, the Carnatic ಕನ್ನಡಭಾಷೆ Canarese language

ಕನಸು k *n* A dream. -ವರಿಕೆ Talking in one's sleep. -ವರಿಸು. To talk in sleep

ಕನಕ s *n* Gold. 2, the thorn-apple, *Datura metel* and *fastuosa.* 3, a N [illegible] N. [illegible] [illegible]e [illegible] mposed many [illegible]s.

-ವೃಷ್ಟಿ. A shower of gold ಕನಕಾಭಿಷೇಕ Honouring a venerable person by pouring gold-coins on his feet or head.

ಕನಡಿ = ಕನ್ನಡಿ, q. v.

ಕನಡಕ k. n A pair of spectacles

ಕನರು k n. A disagreeable smell, as that of burning oil

ಕನಲು k v i. To chafe, be angry n Anger

ಕನಸು (= ಕನ) k. n A dream, vision. -ಕಾಣು, -ಕಂಡುಕೊಳ್ಳು, -ಬೀಳು To dream.

ಕನಿ k n. Tender-heartedness, pity, kindness -ಕರ. Pity, compassion. -ಕರ ಪಡು, -ಕರಿಸು. To have compassion on

ಕನಿಷ್ಠ s n The smallest or least, the last or worst; inferior, base 2, the youngest. -ಕೆ, ಕನಿಷ್ಠೆ. The little finger

ಕಂತ, ಕಂತು h n A fixed term of payment, instalment (ವಾಯಿದ).

ಕಂತು 1. k v. i To set, as the sun, etc ಕಂತಿಸು. To extinguish.

ಕಂತು 2. s a. Happy n. The heart. 2, a granary

ಕಂತೆ k. n. A bundle, as of straw, etc

ಕಂಥೆ s n A rag, patched garment, a thick cloth made of quilted rags

ಕಂದ 1 k. n. A young child, a term of endearment for grown-up children

ಕಂದ 2. s n. A bulbous or esculent root, bulb 2, a lump, swelling. 3, a kind of metre. -ಮೂಲ A radish and other esculent roots

ಕಂದಕ h n A ditch, trench.

ಕಂದರ s n A cave, glen, a valley

ಕಂದಲು k n A small earthen water-vessel.

ಕಂದಾಚಾರ h n Military; police.

ಕಂದಾಯ h n Tribute, tax, land-tax. 2, a space of four months.

ಕಂದಿ k. n A cow that has calved a Dust-coloured

ಕಂದಿಕೆ k. n Fading, faded state.

ಕಂದು 1 k v i To be burnt or scorched. to turn [illegible] fade, wither, wane n Discoloration by scorching, blackness; want of lustre. 2, lowness of spirits, sorrow. -ಕುಂದು Stains and deficiencies -ಬೆಳ್ಳಿ. Impure silver.

ಕಂದು 2 k n. A calf. 2, young plantain trees 3, the foetus of beasts.

ಕಂದು 3. f. n An iron plate for baking cakes.

ಕಂದೋಟಿ h n A money-bag, purse

ಕನ್ನ k n A hole made by burglars in a house-wall -ಕಳವು, -ಚೋರಿ. Burglary. -ಗತ್ತರಿ A burglar's instrument. -ಗಾರ, ಕನ್ನೋಜ A burglar. -ಕೊರೆ, -ಹಾಕು To break a hole in a wall for burglary.

ಕನ್ನತೆ = ಕನ್, q v

ಕನ್ನಡಿ (= ಕನಡಿ) k n. A looking-glass, mirror; a pair of spectacles

ಕನ್ನಡಿಗ k n. A man of Kannada country, f. ಕನ್ನಡಿಗಿತಿ

ಕನ್ನಡಿಸು k v t. To translate into Kannada 2, to mirror

ಕನ್ನಿಕೆ, ಕನ್ಯಕೆ = ಕನ್ಯೆ, q v

ಕನ್ನೆ tb of ಕನ್ಯೆ, q v

ಕನ್ಯೆ s n A girl, maiden, virgin 2, the sign of the zodiac Virgo -ತನ Maidenhood ಕನ್ಯಾಕುಮಾರಿ Cape Comorin ಕನ್ಯಾದಾನ Giving a girl in marriage ಕನ್ಯಾವ್ರತ. A vow of virginity

ಕಪಟ s. n Fraud, deceit, hypocrisy, disguise, dissimulation -ಗಾರ, -ಸ್ಥ, ಕಪಟಿ. A deceitful man, hypocrite -ತನ, -ತ್ವ. Deceitfulness. -ವೇಷ. Disguise ನಿಷ್ಕಪಟ. Sincerity

ಕಪಡೆ h n. An article of apparel, cloth.

ಕಪನಿ f. n A sort of cloak dyed with kâvi and worn by lingâyita priests or ascetics.

ಕಪಲಿ, ಕಪಿಲೆ k n. An apparatus for raising water, consisting of pulley, rope and leathern bucket, worked by oxen -ಬಾನೆ The leathern bucket -ಹೊಡಿ,

ಕಪಾಟ s. n The leaf of a door, a door. 2, an almira

ಕಪಾಲ s. n The skull. 2, a cup, jar, pot; a lid. 3, a potsherd.

ಕಪಿ s. n A monkey. -ಮುಷ್ಟಿ. A firm grasp. -ಮುಷ್ಟಿಗಾರ. An obstinate fellow

ಕಪಿತ್ಥ s. n The wood-apple tree, *Feronia elephantum*.

ಕಪಿಲ s n Brown, tawny. n N of a rishi, the founder of the sânkhya philosophy. ಕಪಿಲೆ A brown coloured cow

ಕಪಿಶ s a. Brown. n. Incense

ಕಪೋತ k n A dove, pigeon

ಕಪೋಲ s. n A cheek

ಕಪ್ಪ1. k. n. Tribute, *also* -ಕಾಣಿಕೆ.

ಕಪ್ಪ2 k n A ring of wire for the wrist or feet.

ಕಪ್ಪಟ (*tb. of* ಕರ್ಪಟ) n. A tattered cloth.

ಕಪ್ಪರ (*tb of* ಕರ್ಪರ) n. A large potsherd.

ಕಪ್ಪು 1 k. v t To dig n A hole in the ground, pit. -ಕುಳಿ A hole for catching elephants.

ಕಪ್ಪು 2. k. n. Blackness, the black colour, collyrium a Black

ಕಪ್ಪು 3.= ಕಪ್ಪ 1, *q v.*

ಕಪ್ಪುರ. *tb of* ಕರ್ಪೂರ, *q. v.*

ಕಪ್ಪೆ k n. A frog -ಕಣ್ಣು Very large eyes -ಕುರ A frog-shaped boil. -ಚಿಪ್ಪು. A bivalve shell. -ಹುಣ್ಣು A spreading sore in the palm of the hand or sole of the foot.

ಕಫ s. n. Phlegm.

ಕಬ್ k n. Blackness. 2, a stone ಕಬ್ಬಕ್ಕಿ. A rose-finch ಕಬ್ಬಸುರಿ The wave-leafed fig-tree, *Ficus infectoria*

ಕಬಕ್ಕನೆ k. *ad.* In a snatching manner. -ಕಚ್ಚು To bite snatchingly, *as* a dog. -ನುಂಗು To gulp quickly, *as* beasts

ಕಬಂಧ s n. Water. 2, a cloud. 3, a headless trunk.

ಕಬರ h n. A Muhammadan tomb.

ಕಬರಿ s. n. A knot of braided hair.

ಕಬರು h n. News, information. 2, attention. -ದಾರ A careful or strict man -ದಾರ್. Take care! mind! -ದಾರಿ Carefulness, strictness

ಕಬಲ (*tb of* ಕವಲ) n A mouthful, a bolus, pill. ಕಬಲಿಸು To eat, devour.

ಕಬಾತ f n A bullock or horse-load of grass, *etc.* ಕಬಾಡಿ, -ಗ A person who brings and sells it, a milk-man

ಕಬೂಲು h n. Agreeing to; consent. agreement, *also* ಕಬೂಲಿ -ಆಗು. To consent.

ಕಬೋಡಿ k. n. A blind man

ಕಬ್ಬ *tb. of* ಕಾವ್ಯ, *q v.*

ಕಬ್ಬಕ್ಕಿ k. n. A rose-finch, starling, *see s.* ಕಬ್.

ಕಬ್ಬಿಗ (*tb of* ಕವಿ) n. A poet

ಕಬ್ಬಿಣ, ಕಬ್ಬುನ k. n Iron. -ಕಿಟ್ಟ Rust of iron, dross.

ಕಬ್ಬು k n Sugarcane. ಕಬ್ಬಿನ ಹಾಲು. Juice of sugarcane

ಕಮಟು, ಕಮುಟು h n. Rancidity, smell of burnt oil or ghee.

ಕಮಂಡಲ, ಕಮಂಡಲು s. n An ascetic's water-pot

ಕಮನೀಯ s. a. Desirable; lovely, pleasing.

ಕಮರು k. v. i To be burnt, scorched. n. Scorchedness, the disagreeable smell arising from burnt oil, *etc*, *also* ಕಮರಿಕೆ, -ಗೆ

ಕಮಲ s. n The lotus, *Nelumbium speciosum* 2, water 3, the moon. -ಅಕ್ಷ, ಕಮಲಾಕ್ಷ Vishnu, lotus seed -ನಾಥ, ಕಮಲೇಶ. Vishnu -ಗರ್ಭ, -ಜ, -ಭವ, ಕಮಲೋದ್ಭವ Brahmâ. -ಬಾಂಧವ, -ಮಿತ್ರ, -ಸಖ The sun. -ವೈರಿ The moon ಕಮಲಾಲಯೆ, ಕಮಲೆ Lakshmî.

ಕಮಾನು h n A bow; an arch, a vault, a spring, *as* of a watch; a fiddle-stick.

ಕಮಾಯಿಷಿ m. n. Collection of the revenues -ದಾರ A sea-custom superintendent, a toll-collector.

ಕಂಪ, ಕಂಪನ, ಕಂಪಾಯಮಾನ s. n. Trembling, tremor, quaking. ಕಂಪಿಸು. To tremble, *etc.*

ಕಂಪ್ಪು k n. A bad smell. 2, fragrance.

ಕಂಬ tb. of ಕಂಭ, q v

ಕಂಬನಿ k n An eye-drop tear -ತೊಡೆ To wipe tears -ಇಡು, -ಇಕ್ಕು, -ಗರಿ, -ಸುರಿ. To shed tears, weep.

ಕಂಬಲ, ಕಂಬಳಿ s n. A blanket, cumley 2, a dew-lap -ಹುಳ A caterpillar

ಕಂಬಳ k n Daily hire or wages -ಗಾರ. A day-labourer

ಕಂಬಿ k n Wire, an iron band, a bar, rail, the bridge of the nose 2, a stripe running parallel with the border of a cloth 3, a thick bamboo laid across the shoulder for carrying burdens. 4, a club, mace -ಗ A mace bearer, doorkeeper. -ಕಾರ. A kambi bearer. -ಯುಚ್ಚು, ಕಂಬುಚ್ಚು. A plate with holes for drawing wire

ಕಂಭ (tb. of ಸ್ತಂಭ) n A post, pillar. -ಪೂಜೆ. Worship paid to the first pillar when erecting a building

ಕಮ್ಮಗಾರ = ಕಮ್ಮಾರ, q v.

ಕಮ್ಮಗೆ, ಕಮ್ಮನೆ k ad. Fragrantly, deliciously

ಕಮ್ಮಟ k n. Coinage, mint ಕಮ್ಮಟಿ A coiner.

ಕಮ್ಮರು h. n The loins, waist. -ಬಂದ. A waistband, belt

ಕಮ್ಮಾರ (tb. of ಕರ್ಮಕಾರ) n. A blacksmith -ಸಾಲೆ The workshop of a blacksmith

ಕಮ್ತಿ h n. Deficiency. -ಜಾಸ್ತಿ More or less

ಕಮ್ಮು k n. Fragrance. v. i Breath to be fragrant

ಕಯ್ 1 (= ಕೆಯ್) k v. t. To do.

ಕಯ್ 2. (= ಕೆಯ್, ಕೈ) k n The hand

ಕಯ್ 3, ಕಯಿ (ಕಹಿ, q. v) k n. Bitterness, also ಕಯ್ಪು. -ಬೇವು Neem or margosa tree, also ಬೇವು.

ಕರ 1 k. P. p of ಕರೆ. -ಕೊಳ್ಳು. = ಕರೆದು ಕೊಳ್ಳು -ಕೊಂಡುಬರು To bring along with one's self. -ಕೊಂಡು ಹೋಗು To conduct away with one's self. -ತರು. To cal

ಕರ 2 s n Doing, making (ಕೃತ್ಯ) 2, the hand (ಹಸ್ತ, ಕೆಯ್) 3, the elephant's trunk. 4, tax, royal revenue. 5, a ray of light. 6, a cloud

ಕರಕರೆ k n. Grief, trouble; worrying, annoyance -ಮಾಡು To vex ಕರಕರಿಸು To feel remorse, to be grieved.

ಕರಕು k. n. Cinder; the crust formed on cooking pots 2, calcined drugs.

ಕರಗ (tb of ಕರಕ) n A kind of water-jar

ಕರಗಸ (=ಗರಗಸ, tb of ಕ್ರಕಚ) n A saw. -ದ ಹಲ್ಲು. The teeth of a saw.

ಕರಗು k. v. i To be dissolved, to melt; to melt away, to become softened to pity or love; to wane, as the body, to pine away for grief, to languish ಕರಗಿಸು To cause to be dissolved, to melt.

ಕರಜಿಕಾಯಿ k n A small pancake

ಕರಟ s n The shell of a cocoanut.

ಕರಟಕ s n A crow 2, N of a jackal in the Hitôpadêśa; a backbiter.

ಕರಡ k. n Dried fodder-grass.

ಕರಡಿ k n. A bear -ಮರಿ. A bear's cub.

ಕರಡಿಗೆ (tb of ಕರಂಡಕ) n A basket or covered box, a casket or small box of metal or wood.

ಕರಡು 1. k a. Rough, uneven, hard, waste, useless -ಕಾಗದ. A waste paper -ಬರೆ. To write roughly -ಮುತ್ತು. Rough, inferior pearl

ಕರಡು 2. f a Rough, as an account. n. A day-book, scrawling, a scrawl.

ಕರಣ s. n. Making, causing 2, an instrument, means. 3, an organ of sense, also ಕರಣೇಂದ್ರಿಯ 4, cause motive 5, a scribe 6, a rhythm, dramatic action.

ಕರಣಿ s n. Doing. 2, = ಕರಣಿಕ. 3 a mason's trowel, also ಕರಣಿಕೆ.

ಕರಣಿಕ, ಕರಣೀಕ s n A writer, a village clerk, the head native official

ಕರಣೆ 1. k. *n.* A clot, lump. 2, a ball made of iron filings, and rice flour and rubbed on tambours to make them sound well

ಕರಣೆ 2. h *n* The large brass trumpet which sounds the bass.

ಕರಂಡ, ಕರಂಡಕ = ಕರಡಿಗೆ, *q v*

ಕರತಲ s. *n* The palm of the hand

ಕರತಾಲ, -ಳ s *n* A cymbal. 2, beating time by clapping the hands.

ಕರದು *P. p of* ಕರೆ 1

ಕರಪೀಠ s. *n.* A flat piece of wood for cripples to rest their hands on.

ಕರಬೂಜು h. *n.* The musk-melon.

ಕರರುಹ s. *n.* A finger-nail

ಕರವೀರ s *n.* A fragrant oleander

ಕರಸು = ಕರಿಸು, s ಕರಿ, *q v*

ಕರಹ k. *n.* Calling, inviting.

ಕರಳು. = ಕರುಳು, *q. v.*

ಕರಾಚೂರಿ f. *n* A sword. 2, a man of positive speech. ಕರಾಚೂರು. Positiveness

ಕರಾಡ s. *n* A class of Brâhmanas.

ಕರಾರ, ಕರಾರು h. *n* A promise, an agreement -ನಾಮೆ. A written contract

ಕರಾಲ, ಕರಾಳ s *a* Great, large. 2, formidable, dreadful. 3, crooked.

ಕರಾಲಂಬನ, ಕರಾವಲಂಬನ s. *n.* A helping hand, helping, support.

ಕರಾವಳಿ k. *n* The seacoast region or that of the banks of a river.

ಕರಿ 1 s. *v i* To be scorched, burnt. 2, to fry, roast. 3, to dig *P ps.* ಕರಿದು, ಕರಿತು. ಕರಿಸು. To cause to fry or roast.

ಕರಿ 2 (= ಕರೆ) k *n.* Blackness; a dark-blue colour. 2, charcoal *Gen* ಕರಿಯ or ಕರೀ -ಕ, -ಗ. A black man, *f.* -ಕೆ, -ಗಿ. -ಜಾಲಿ. A thorny shrub with fragrant flowers, *Acacia farnesiana*, the babool tree, *Acacia arabica*. -ಜಗೆ A dis[illegible] of [illegible] -ಜೀರಿಗೆ. A [illegible] otherb, [illegible] -ತುಂಬೆ The Malabar cat-mint, *Anisomeles malabarica* -ತುಳಸಿ. A small shrub, the holy basil, *Ocimum sanctum* -ದಿವಸ. An unpropitious day. -ದು That is black -ನೆಕ್ಕಿ. A wild shrub, *Gendarussa vulgaris* -ಬೇವು The curry-leaf tree, *Murraya koenigii*. -ಮಣಿ A black bead worn by married women -ಮರ The ebony tree. -ಯುತ್ತರಾಣಿಗಿಡ. A Jamaican plant, *Stachytarpheta jamaicensis* -ಯುಪ್ಪು A kind of black sea-salt -ಹತ್ತಿ The American cotton-plant. -ಹರಿ. To tear (*i e.* do away with) unpropitiousness.

ಕರಿ 3 s *n.* An elephant. -ಮುಖ, -ವದನ. Ganêśa.

ಕರಿ 4. (= ಕಱ) k. *n.* Vegetables of any kind. 2, flesh, curry.

ಕರಿ 5 = ಕರೆ, *q v.*

ಕರಿತು *P p. of* ಕರಿ 1, *q. v.*

ಕರಿಕೆ (ರಿ = ಱ) k. *n.* The Huriallee [grass

ಕರೀರ s. *n* A tender shoot of bamboo 2, a thorny shrub, *Capparis aphylla*.

ಕರು 1. k *n* Embossed work, bass-relief, a puppet

ಕರು 2. (ರು = ಱು) k *n.* A calf, *also* ಕರ

ಕರುಣ, ಕರುಣೆ s *n* Pity, compassion, mercy. 2, favour; pardon *a* Merciful. -ವಂತ Compassionate, pitiable, a compassionate man ಕರುಣಾತುರ. Pitiful. -ಕರ, ಕರುಣಾಳು. A person who possesses pity, compassionate ಕರುಣಾಕರ, ಕರುಣಾಬ್ಧಿ, ಕರುಣಾಂಬು, ಕರುಣಾಕರನಿಧಿ, ಕರುಣಾಸಾಗರ, ಕರುಣಾಸಮುದ್ರ, ಕರುಣಾಸಿಂಧು An ocean of mercy ಕರುಣಿಸು To be merciful, to show mercy to.

ಕರುಳು k *n.* An entrail, the bowels. 2 love, pity -ತೋರಿಸು. To be openhearted, to show mercy -ಎಳೆ Bowels to yearn -ಕಟ್ಟು To restrain the bowels.

ಕರುಬು, ಕರುಂಬು (ರು = ಱು) k *v. t.* To envy *n* Envy.

[illegible]

To send one person to call another. ಕರಸು, ಕರಿಸು, ಕರೆಯಿಸು, ಕರೆಸು. To cause to call, send for. -ಯುವಿಕೆ. Calling.

ಕರೆ 2. k. n. A bank, shore; a boundary. 2, the border of a cloth or blauket. 3, a cow-house.

ಕರೆ 3. (= ಕರಿ, q. v.) k. n. Blackness; a dark-blue colour; *also* ಕರ್ರಗೆ. *Cpds.:* -ಬೆಕ್ಕು, -ಕರಡಿ, -ಕೂದಲು, -ಚಿಕ್ಕೆ, -ಚಿಗರಿ, -ತೋಳ, -ಬಣ್ಣ, -ಮುಷ್ಟೆ, -ಮುಪ್ಪು, -ಮೆಣಸು, -ಹಲ್ಲಿ, *etc.* -ವ್ವ. The black dame: a household-goddess.

ಕರೆ 4. (ರೆ = ಱೆ) k. v. t. To milk; to cause to flow, to rain; to give milk.

ಕರೋಡ h. n. A crore, lakh.

ಕರ್ಕಟ, ಕರ್ಕಾಟಕ s. n. A crab: the sign Cancer.

ಕರ್ಕಶ s. a. Hard, firm. 2, rough, harsh, severe, violent; unkind. -ತೆ. Hardness, harshness.

ಕರ್ಕೋಟ s. n. N. of a serpent; *also* -ಕ.

ಕರ್ಜಿ. = ಕಜುರ, ಖಜುರ, q. v.

ಕರ್ಜಿಕಾಯಿ. = ಕರಜಿಕಾಯಿ, q. v.

ಕರ್ಜೂರ (= ಕಜೂರ) f. n. The fruit of the date tree.

ಕರ್ಣ s. n. The ear. 2, a helm, rudder. 3, the sun. 4, N. of a hero. -ಗತ. Come to the ear. -ಪಿಶಾಚ. A demon forced to communicate by whispering in the ear. -ಶೂಲೆ. Ear-ache. ಕರ್ಣೇಂದ್ರಿಯ. The organ of hearing.

ಕರ್ಣಾಟ (= ಕನ್ನಡ) s. n. The Karṇâṭa country. -ಕ. Belonging to K.; the K. language; (*also* -ಭಾಷೆ); the Karṇâṭa man. -ತೋಪು. A matchlock. -ವ್ಯಾಕರಣ. A grammar of K. language. -ದೇಶ. K. country. -ಧಾತು. A K. verbal root.

ಕರ್ಣಿ, ಕರ್ಣಿಕೆ. *tb.* of ಕರಣಿ, ಕರಣಿಕ, q. v.

ಕರ್ತ. *tb.* of ಕರ್ತೃ, q. v.

ಕರ್ತರಿ (= ಕತ್ತರಿ, ಕತ್ರಿ, q. v.) s. n. Scissors.

ಕರ್ತವ್ಯ s. a. Fit to be done. n. Obligation, duty, task.

ಕರ್ತೃ s. A [illegible] creator; a master. 2, an agent, the active noun, subject (*g.*). -ತ್ವ. Agency.

ಕರ್ಪಾಸ s. n. Cotton.

ಕರ್ಪುರ, ಕರ್ಪೂರ s. n. Camphor. -ಬಳ್ಳಿ. Thick-leaved lavender, *Lavendula carnosa.* -ಶಿಲಾಜತು, -ಶಿಲಾಧಾತು. A crystallized gypsum.

ಕರ್ಮ s. n. An act, action; performance, business; duty. 2, the accusative; the objective noun (*g.*); the idea of the passive voice (*g.*). 3, any religious action. 4, sin. -ಕಾರ. An artisan, mechanic. -ಗತಿ. Fate. -ಠ. Skilful in work; scrupulously exact in performance of a religious rite. -ದೋಷ. Sin, vice. -ಧಾರಯ. N. of a class of compounds. -ಮಾರ್ಗ. The way of works. -ವಿಪಾಕ. The consequences of actions. -ಸಾಕ್ಷಿ. The sun. -ಸಿದ್ಧಿ. Success. ಕರ್ಮಾಂತರ. Funeral rites. ಕರ್ಮಿ. Acting; a sinner. ಕರ್ಮಿಷ್ಠ. Very active; very sinful. ಕರ್ಮೇಂದ್ರಿಯ. The organ of action.

ಕರ್ಮಣಿ s. n. A verb in the passive voice (*g.*).

ಕರ್ಷ, ಕರ್ಷಣ s. n. Drawing, dragging.

ಕರ್ಳು. = ಕರುಳು, q. v.

ಕಲ್ (= ಕಲ್ಲು) k. n. A stone. -ಕುಟಿಗ. A mason. -ತೊಟ್ಟಿ. A stone-trough. -ನಾರು. The bastard aloe. -ಗಣಿ. A stone quarry. -ಮಳೆ. Hail.

ಕಲ s. a. Dumb. n. Gold. 2, a musical time; a melodious tone, *as* humming, *etc.* -ಕಂಠ. The cuckoo (ಕೋಗಿಲೆ); a bee; a swan; a pleasing tone. -ಕಲ. A confused noise. -ಕಲಾಟ. Twittering of birds. -ರವ. A low sweet tone.

ಕಲಕ, ಕಲ್ಕ k. n. Mixture; a mixture of unboiled ingredients; infusion (*med.*).

ಕಲಕಾಲ k. n. A very long time. *ad.* At all times, permanently.

ಕಲಕು k. v. i. To be agitated, shaken, turbid, *etc.* v. t. To agitate, shake; [illegible] up [illegible] iness.

-ಮಾಡು, ಕಲಕಾಡು. To make turbid. ಕಲಕಿಸು. To disturb, stir.

ಕಲಂಕ s *n* A stain, spot, mark. 2, a fault, blemish. 3, fierceness

ಕಲಗಚ್ಚು k. *n* The water in which raw rice and other vegetables have been washed and mixed with strained rice-water, *etc.* and given to cattle

ಕಲಂಗಡಿ f *n* The water-melon.

ಕಲತ್ರ s *n.* A wife

ಕಲಬತ್ತು h *n.* A mortar and pestle.

ಕಲಬೆರಿಕೆ k. *n.* Mixture, *as* of cold and hot water

ಕಲಮ f *n* White rice growing in deep [water.

ಕಲಮು, ಕಲಂ h *n.* A reed pen, a painter's brush. 2, a paragraph; a distinct head, item. 3, a graft -ದಾನಿ A standish.

ಕಲಲು h. *n.* Ruin, loss.

ಕಲಶ s. *n* A water-vessel, jar, pitcher, vase. 2, an ornamental or rounded pinnacle on the top of a temple; a dome. -ಪೂಜೆ The rite of worshipping a water-pot. -ಪ್ರತಿಷ್ಠೆ. The rite of fixing a dome on the top of a temple, *etc.* -ಸ್ಥಾಪನೆ. A rite preliminary to ಕಲಶಪೂಜೆ.

ಕಲಸು k. *v t.* To mix, mingle. *n.* Mixed state. ಕಲಸನ್ನ. Boiled rice mixed with tamarind, chillies, salt, *etc.*

ಕಲಹ s *n* Quarrel, strife, war, battle. ಕಲಹಿಸು. To quarrel

ಕಲಹಂಸ s. *n* A kind of goose or [swan.

ಕಲಾಕಾಂತ s *n* The moon

ಕಲಾಕೌಶಲ್ಯ s. *n* Cleverness in the elegant arts, *as* singing, dancing, *etc.*

ಕಲಾಪ s. *n.* Quarrel, contention. 2, a collection. 3, an ornament. 4, a quiver

ಕಲಾಬತು h *n.* Silken thread covered with gold or silver.

ಕಲಾಯು, ಕಲಾಯಿ h. *n* The tinning of brass and other vessels -ಗಾರ. A tinner of vessels.

ಕಲಾಲ h. *n.* A distiller or vendor of spirituous liquors.

ಕಲಾಸಿ h. *n* A seaman, lascar

ಕಲಿ 1 k. *v. t* To learn, study *v i.* To be mixed; to come together, to meet. *P. p* ಕಲಿತು *n* A learned man -ಕೆ, -ತ. Learning, skill. ಕಲಿಸು To teach, to mix, *also* ಕಲಸು, *q v.*

ಕಲಿ 2 s. *n.* A warrior, hero 2, the fourth age of the world, the age of sin, *also* -ಯುಗ -ತನ. Valor, heroism -ಕಾಲ. A time of sin and misery, the age of vice.

ಕಲಿತು. *P. p. of* ಕಲಿ, *q. v.*

ಕಲುಷ s. *a* Turbid, muddy. *n.* Sin.

ಕಲೆ 1 k. *n* The scar, a stain, taint

ಕಲೆ 2, ಕಲಾ s. *n* A small part, a sixteenth of the moon's orb. 2, a measure of time. 3, a fine art (there are 64). 4, skill. 5, grace, lustre.

ಕಲ್ಕ s. *n.* Dirt, filth, a kind of paste. 2, sin; pride.

ಕಲ್ಕಿ s. *n.* N of Vishnu in his tenth and last avatâra yet to come.

ಕಲ್ಪ s. *n* A precept, injunction 2, one of the six vêdângas which prescribes rituals. 3, a day of Brahmâ or the period of a thousand yugas. -ತರು, -ದ್ರುಮ, -ವೃಕ್ಷ. One of the trees (-ಲತೆ, a creeper) of svarga granting all desires.

ಕಲ್ಪನೆ s. *n.* Making, fabrication, invention 2, a fancy, idea, an imagination ಕಲ್ಪಿತ. Fabricated, artificial, invented.

ಕಲ್ಪಿಸು s. *v. t.* To make, to fabricate, invent; to assume, feign, to give a precept

ಕಲ್ಮಷ s. *n.* A stain, a blemish, sin, dirt

ಕಲ್ಯಾಣ s. *a* Beautiful, happy, auspicious, lucky. *n.* Good fortune, prosperity, welfare 2, a marriage festival. ಕಲ್ಯಾಣಿ. Sarasvatî. Pârvati,

Lakshmî; ೨. of a tune -ಸಾಯಿ. A kind of sweetmeat

ಕಲ್ಲಂಗಡಲೆ k. n A shrubby plant, *Sida rhombifolia*

ಕಲ್ಲಂಗಡಿ = ಕಲಂಗಡಿ, q v

ಕಲ್ಲಿ k n. A kind of coarse net-work, a bag made of it.

ಕಲ್ಲು k n A stone. -ಅಣಬೆ, ಕಲ್ಲಣಬೆ. A mushroom growing in rocks. -ಇದ್ದಲಿ Mineral coal -ಕಣಿ, ಕಲ್ಲಕಣಿ. A quarry -ಕುಟಿಗ A stone-cutter or mason. -ಗುಂಡು. A boulder -ನಾರು (=ಕಲ್ನಾರು). Asbestus -ಬಂಡೆ A rock -ಬಾಳೆ. A wild plantain tree. -ಮಳೆ Hail -ಮುಳ್ಳು Stones and thorns -ಮೆಟ್ಲು. Stone steps. -ಸಕ್ಕರೆ Sugar-candy -ಸುಂಟಿ Wild ginger -ಸುಣ್ಣ. Stone-lime. -ಹಾಕು To throw a stone down, to destroy another's business. -ಹೂವು. Lichen on stones -ಎದೆ, ಕಲ್ಲೆದೆ. A stone-like or firm heart. ಕಲ್ಲೆದೆಯವ A man who has an unfeeling heart. -ಎಸೆ, ಕಲ್ಲೆಸೆ. To throw stones, *also* -ಒಗೆ, -ಹೊಡೆ, a stone's throw -ಒತ್ತು, ಕಲ್ಲೊತ್ತು Stone pressure; a kind of hard boil on the heel.

ಕಲ್ಲೋಲ s n. A surge, billow, wave

ಕವ k. *An imitative sound of anger* - - ಮಾಡು To scold.

ಕವಚ s. n. Armour, coat of mail; a jacket 2, an amulet.

ಕವಚು. = ಕವಿಚು, q v

ಕವಗ (*tb. of* ಕವಟ) -ಕಂಟಕ An ugly-looking puppet of dough -ಗಂಟಿಕ A great cheat.

ಕವಡಿ, ಕವಡೆ (*tb. of* ಕಪರ್ದ) n. A cowrie.

ಕವಡಿಕೆ k n. An ornamental, stitched binding of a dôtra.

ಕವಡು k n. A bifurcation -ಮಾತು. A word out of place.

ಕವಣೆ k n. A sling for throwing stones. -ಕಲ್ಲು ಹೊಡಿ, - - ಎಸೆ. To sling a stone

ಕವದಿ = ಕವುದಿ, q v

ಕವನ s n. Composing a poetical composition, ... -ಗಾರ ... poet

ಕವಲ, ಕವಳ (= ಕಬಲ) s n A mouthful, morsel, bolus 2, a gargle.

ಕವಲು k v i. To become forked, to branch off n A forked branch or stick, divided state a couple, pair -ಒಡೆ, ಕವಲೊಡೆ. To get branches

ಕವಲೆ. *tb. of* ಕಪಿಲೆ, q. v.

ಕವಳಿ k n A swoon. 2, = ಕವಳೆ. 3, = ಕವಳಿಗೆ 2

ಕವಳಿಗೆ 1. (*tb. of* ಕಪಾಲಿಕೆ) n. Śiva's alms-pot, a skull. 2, a metal vessel

ಕವಳಿಗೆ 2 f. n A pack or bundle of betel or plantain-leaves -ಮನೆ A house with a gable-roof.

ಕವಳೆ f n. A spinous shrub, bearing black eatable berries, *Carissa carandas.*

ಕವಾಟ = ಕಪಾಟ, q v.

ಕವಾಡ = ಕಬಾಡ, q. v. ಕವಾಡಿಗ. A cow-herd; *f.* -ಗಿತ್ತಿ.

ಕವಾತು, ಕವಾಯಿತು h. n. Military manoeuvres, parade

ಕವಿ 1, k v. t. & i. i. To come upon, to attack; to cover, overspread (*P ps* ಕವ, ಕವಿ, ಕವಿದು). n. A rush. -ಚು, -ಸು. To put upon.

ಕವಿ 2 s n. A wise man; a poet 2, Śukra. 3, water. -ಕೌಶಲ. The cleverness of a poet. -ತೆ, -ತ್ವ Poesy, poetic style -ರಾಜ, ಕವೀಶ್ವರ A very eminent poet. ನರ- A taught poet. ವರ- A born poet.

ಕವಿಚು k. v i To be turned upside down, to be upset.

ಕವಿಯ s n. The bit of a bridle

ಕವಿಲೆ. *tb of* ಕಪಿಲೆ, q. v

ಕವುಂಕುಳು, = ಕಂಕುಳ, q v.

ಕವುಜು, ಕವುಜುಗ f n The wood or the oriental partridge.

ಕವುದಿ k n. A quilted cover for the night; quilted rags.

ಕವ್ಯ s. n. An oblation of food to ancestors

... s A whip ... [illegible]

ಕಶ್ಮಲ s. *n* Consternation, alarm; fainting. *a* Foul, dirty.

ಕಶ್ಯಪ s. *n*. A tortoise. 2, N. of a rishi.

ಕಷಾಯ s *a* Astringent 2, fragrant *n* An infusion, decoction of medicinal herbs. -ಕಾಸು To decoct

ಕಷ್ಟ s *n*. Trouble, misery, woe. 2, bodily exertion, toil, hard work. 3, difficulty *a* Bad, evil; severe. -ಕೊಡು To give trouble. -ಪಡು To suffer trouble. -ಪಡಿಸು To afflict, annoy -ಮಾಡಿಸಿಕೊಳ್ಳು To get one's self shaved. -ಮಾಡು To toil; to shave. -ಸಹಿಸು, -ಸೋಸು Patiently to bear trouble. ಕಷ್ಟಾಳು. Painstaking.

ಕಸ 1 k *n* Rubbish, sweepings, off-scourings, impurities in the body; a weed. -ಕಣ್ಣು. An inflamed eye. -ಗುಡಿಸು, -ಹೊಡೆ. To sweep. -ಕೆಲು, -ಬರಿಗೆ, -ಬರಲು. A broom -ದವ. A scavenger

ಕಸ 2. k *P p. of* ಕಸಿ. -ಕೊಳ್ಳು To take away by force, snatch away

ಕಸಕಸೆ h. *n* Poppy-seed. -ಗಿಡ The opium poppy, *Papaver somniferum*

ಕಸಗಾಯಿ k. *n*. A hard, unripe fruit.

ಕಸಬು h. *n*. Business, trade, profession

ಕಸಬೆ h. *n*. The chief town of a district or tâluk; *also* ಕಸಬಾ.

ಕಸರು 1. k *n* Astringency 2, unripeness 3, bad humours in the body. 4, dust.

ಕಸರು 2 h *n*. Deficiency, defect, profit or loss on the exchange of coins.

ಕಸವಿಸಿ, ಕಸಿವಿಸಿ k *n*. Uneasiness, as in the bowels; disquiet

ಕಸಾಬ, ಕಸಾಯ, ಕಸಾಯಿ h. *n* A butcher.

ಕಸಾರಿಕೆ f *n*. Indisposition

ಕಸಿ 1 k. *v. i*. To slip down from; to fall. 2, to ooze, trickle. *n*. Fine rain, drizzling

ಕಸಿ 2 h. *a*. Pruned, castrated. *n*. Pruning, castration. -ಮಾಡು To prune, castrate.

ಕಸುಗಾಯಿ. = ಕಸಗಾಯಿ, *q v*

ಕಸುವು f. *n*. Strength, power; the nutrimental principle, *as* of soils, *etc*.

ಕಸೂತಿ h. *n*. Embroidery -ತೆಗೆ -ಹಾಕು. To embroider

ಕಸೆ f *n* The tie of an angi, *etc* -ಪಾವಡೆ A petticoat with strings attached.

ಕಸ್ತಿ h. *n*. Violence, force, annoyance

ಕಸ್ತು h. *n*. Cares, trouble, fuss, ado. -ಗಾರ A painstaker. -ತಗಾದೆ. A peremptory demand for payment.

ಕಸ್ತೂರಿ s. *n*. Musk. 2, a scented mark put on the forehead -ಅರಿಸಿನ. A kind of scented turmeric. -ಕಡ್ಡಿ. A stick covered with musk -ಗೊಬ್ಬಳಿ A kind of Acacia with fragrant flowers. -ಮೃಗ The musk-deer.

ಕಹಳೆ *(tb. of* ಕಹಲೆ) *n*. A metal trumpet.

ಕಹಿ k. *n*. Bitterness, *also* -ಪು -ಗಿಡ A bitter shrub. -ಪಲ್ಯ Bitter greens. -ಸೋರೆ. A kind of bitter gourd

ಕಳ 1 k. *a Sound in weeping 2, a sound in boiling, as of rice 3, sound indicating agitation* -ಕಳ. *rep*. -ಕಳನೆ ಅಳು To weep and sob. -ವಳ. Agitation, distress, anxiety. -ವಳಗೊಳ್ಳು, -ವಳಪಡು, -ವಳಿಸು To be agitated; to grieve, to be anxious, perplexed

ಕಳ 2. (= ಕಳ್ಳ) k. *n* A thief, rogue 2, a battle field.

ಕಳ 3. *P. p. of* ಕಳೆ, *q v* -ಕೊಳ್ಳು. To put off, let drop, to spend, to lose, to get rid of; to break, *as* a promise (ಮಾತು), to give up, *as* a friendship (ಸ್ನೇಹ).

ಕಳ 4. (*tb. of* ಖಲ) *n* A threshing floor.

ಕಳಂಕ. = ಕಲಂಕ, *q. v.*

ಕಳಚು s. *v. t*. To put off, let drop. 2, to shake off, to pull off *v i* To become loose.

ಕಳತ (ಳ = ಱ) k. *n*. Purging.

ಕಳತ್ರ. = ಕಲತ್ರ, *q v.*

ಕಳದು *P. p. of* ಕಳೆ, *q. v*

ಕಳವು = ಕಲವು, q. v.

ಕಳವು k. n. Theft.

ಕಳವೆ h. a. Rejected, adulterated; base (as coin, fruits, etc.).

ಕಳಸ tb. of ಕಲಶ, q. v.

ಕಳಸಿಗೆ f. n. A water-pot. 2, a corn-measure equal to ⅓ of a mudi.

ಕಳಹು = ಕಳುಹಿಸು, q. v.

ಕಳಿ (ಳಿ = ಱಿ) 1. k. v. t. & v. i. To end, die. 2, to loosen, to remove. 3, to purge. n. A great distance. 2, sour gruel.

ಕಳಿ 2. k. v. i. To ripen well (P. p. ಕಳಿತು). n. Ripeness. -ಹಣ್ಣು A ripe fruit.

ಕಳಿಂಗ f. n. A cunning, bad man.

ಕಳಿಲೆ (tb. of ಕರೀರ) n. A tender bamboo shoot used for pickles.

ಕಳಿಸು, ಕಳಿಹಿಸು, ಕಳುಹಿಸು, ಕಳುಹು k. v. t. To send, despatch, delegate; to dismiss. ಕಳುಹಿಸಿ ತರಿಸು To send for. ಹೇಳಿ- To send word. ಕರೆ-. To send one to call another.

ಕಳು a. k. v. t. To steal.

ಕಳೆ (= ಕಳಿ) k. v. t. To throw away; to abandon, leave; to reject, pull off, to leave out, to get rid of, to subtract, deduct; to spend, as time or money; to draw out, as a sword; to remove, do away with, destroy, to extinguish, as a lamp; to lose. v. i. To become loose, to go, pass, be spent (P. ps. ಕಳೆ, ಕಳದು, ಕಳೆದು) n. Removal. -ನೊಗ The yoke fastened round the neck of the bullocks. -ದ ಕೀಲು. The pegs used to fasten the yoke.

ಕಳೆ 2. k. n. Weed. -ಕೀಳು, -ತೆಗಿ. To weed.

ಕಳೆ 3. (tb. of ಕಲಾ) n. Shine, lustre, a ray, beauty. 2, the fine arts. 3, a part, a digit. 4, the number sixteen. -ಗಳೆ To lose one's lustre. -ಗುಂದು, -ಕೆಡು Lustre to fade.

ಕಳ್ಳ (= ಕಳ2) k. n. A thief; a rogue, bad fellow. f. -ತಿ, ಕಳ್ಳಿ. -ಕಾಗದ, -ಚೀಟು, -ಪತ್ರ A forged document. -ಕಿ- A hole made by burglars. -ಕುಣಿಕೆ. The hollow above the chest between the larynx and trachea. -ಗಂಟು. A sham-bundle, a puzzle-knot. -ಜನ. Thieves. -ದನ. Thievish straying cattle. -ದಾರಿ. A thieves' path. -ಮಾತು A lie. -ರುಜು A forged signature. -ವೇಷ A disguise. -ಸಾಕ್ಷಿ False witness. -ಹುಂಡಿ. A forged cheque. -ಹೊನ್ನು A counterfeit coin. -ಉಸುಬು, ಕಳ್ಳುಸುಬು. Quicksand. -ಆಟ, ಕಳ್ಳಾಟ, -ತನ Thievishness; theft.

ಕಳ್ಳಿ k. n. The milk-hedge, *Euphorbia tirukalli*. 2, a wicked person.

ಕಳ್ಳು k. n. Toddy.

ಕಾ, = ಕಾಯು, q. v.

ಕಾಂಸ್ಯ s. n. White brass, bell-metal, any amalgam of zinc and copper.

ಕಾಕ (tb. ಕಾಗೆ) s. n. A crow. 2, an impudent fellow. 3, N. of a râkshasa. -ಜ್ವರ A quartan ague. -ಪಕ್ಷ Three or five locks of hair left over the temples at the time of tonsure. -ಬಲಿ Offering of food to crows. -ಬುದ್ಧಿ Insolent notions. -ಭಾಜನ The crow's portion, waste, ruin.

ಕಾಕಂಬಿ, ಕಾಕವಿ f. n. Molasses.

ಕಾಕಮಾರಿ s. n. A twining shrub, *Cocculi indici*.

ಕಾಕಲಿ s. n. A soft, sweet sound.

ಕಾಕಾ (= ಕಕ್ಕ) h. n. A paternal uncle.

ಕಾಕಿ (= ಕಾಗಿ) s. n. A (female) crow. -ಗಿಡ. A common spinous shrub, *Canthium parviflorum*.

ಕಾಕು 1. k. n. Overheat, excitement, tiredness from the effects of sun, trouble, etc. 2, sharp smell, as of onion.

ಕಾಕು 2. s. n. Change of voice, as in fear, anger, grief, etc. 2, sarcasm; perversity. 3, stress. 4, patois. -ಮತಿ. A perverse mind. -ಮಾತು. A perverse word.

ಕಾಕುದ s. n. The palate.

ಕಾ[illegible] k. [illegible] ... of forests.

ಕಾಕೋದರ s n. A serpent -ಶಾಯಿ Vishnu.

ಕಾಗಡಿ k n. = ಕಾವಡಿ 2, a kind of cradle

ಕಾಗದ h. n. Paper, a letter, note, document -ಪತ್ರ. Letters and notes correspondence. -ಬರೆ. To write a letter -ತಲಪು A letter to arrive -ಹಚ್ಚು. To affix a public notice

ಕಾಗಿ, ಕಾಗೆ (tb. of ಕಾಕ) n. A crow -ಗಣ್ಣು. Small eyes, as those of a crow -ಬಣ್ಣ A black colour -ಬಂಗಾರ Talc mineral. -ರೋಗ A disease (consumption) by which the face becomes black.

ಕಾಗುಣಿತ k. n Spelling, putting letters together.

ಕಾಂಕೆ (= ಕಾಕು) k. n Heat of any kind.

ಕಾಂಕ್ಷೆ s. n Wish, desire. 2, a disease of the eyes -ತೀರಿಸಿಕೊಳ್ಳು To fulfill one's desire ಕಾಂಕ್ಷಿಸು. To desire, wish.

ಕಾಚ (= ಕಾಜು, ಗಾಜು) s n Glass; alkaline ashes. 2, a sling for suspending things. -ಲವಣ A medicinal salt. -ಹುಲ್ಲು. A fragrant grass.

ಕಾಚಿ = ಕಾಮಂಚಿ. -ಗಿಡ. The plant *Solanum indicum* -ಹುಲ್ಲು. = ಕಾಂಚಿಹುಲ್ಲು.

ಕಾಚು k. n. Cashoo, catechu, solidified juice of *Acacia catechu*

ಕಾಜವಾರ (= ಕಾಸರಕ) k. n. The tree bearing the *nux vomica*

ಕಾಜಿ h n A Muhammadan priest, a judge

ಕಾಜು tb of ಕಾಚ, q v

ಕಾಂಚನ s n Gold. 2, a tree with fragrant blossoms, *Mesua ferrea.*

ಕಾಂಚಿ s. n. A girdle, a woman's zone.

ಕಾಂಚಿ ಹುಲ್ಲು (cf ಕಾಚಿಹುಲ್ಲು) k n. Lemon grass, *Andropogon shoenanthus*

ಕಾಂಚಿವಾಳ. = ಕಂಚಿವಾಳ, q. v

ಕಾಂಜಿರ k n = ಕಾಜವಾರ, q v 2, a species of gourd

ಕಾಟ (fr. ಕಾಡು 1) k n Trouble, annoyance, plague. 2, a forester 3. a strong smell, as that of tobacco, chillies, etc -ಆಚಾರ, ಕಾಟಾಚಾರ Good behaviour to avoid annoyance. -ಕ. A forester or fowler, a troublesome man (f. ಕಾಟಕಿ); trouble -ಕತನ. Annoyance

ಕಾಟಕಾಯಿ, ಕಾಟಕಾಯಿ, ಕಾಟಗಾಯು k. n Plundering, marauding, pillaging.

ಕಾಟು k n. A bite, cut.

ಕಾಟಿ k n. A kind of fermented pap of jôla or râgi

ಕಾಠಿಣ್ಯ s n Hardness, firmness; severity

ಕಾಡ. = ಕಾಡು 2, q. v. *Cpds.*: -ಗಿಚ್ಚು, -ಎಮ್ಮೆ, -ಕೋಣ, -ನಾಯಿ, -ಸೊಣ, -ಬಸವಣ್ಣ, *etc.*

ಕಾಡಿ f. n. A blade of grass, a bit of straw, etc ; a stick. -ಕಾರ. Caustic.

ಕಾಡಿಗ k n A troublesome man 2, a duck.

ಕಾಡಿಗೆ h n Lampblack, a collyrium prepared from it. -ಜೋಳ. A blackish jôla -ಬಣ್ಣ Black colour.

ಕಾಡು 1. k v. t To treat harshly; to give trouble; to tease; to plague ಕಾಡಿಸು. To trouble, plague

ಕಾಡು 2 (= ಕಾವ) k n A forest, a jungle. a. Wild *Cpds.*. -ಕುದುರೆ, -ಕುರಿ, -ಕುರುಬ, -ಕೋಣ, -ಗತ್ತೆ, -ಗಿಚ್ಚು, -ಗೆಣಸು, -ಜನ, -ನಾಯಿ, -ಸೊಣ, -ಬೆಕ್ಕು, -ಬೆಳ್ಳುಳ್ಳಿ, -ಮನುಷ್ಯ, -ಮೃಗ, -ರೋಗ, -ಹಂದಿ, -ಹಾಗಲ, -ಹೆಸರು, etc Wild or jungle—, *etc.*

ಕಾಡೆ 1 f n A decoction.

ಕಾಡೆ 2. (tb of ಕಾಂಡ) n. A stalk

ಕಾಣ k. n. One who does not see 2, a crow. a One-eyed.

ಕಾಣಿ 1. k n A sixty-fourth fractional part ($\frac{1}{64}$) of any coin (cpds · ಅರೆ-, ಗಿಡ್ಡಗಾಣಿ, ದುಗ್ಗಾಣಿ, ಮುಕ್ಕಾಣಿ) 2, gift, property, hereditary right. ಕಾಣಾಚಿ. Hereditary right to lands, etc

ಕಾಣಿ 2. s. n Unevenness of scales. 2, that which is put to counterpoise. -ಕಟ್ಟು. To make scales even -ತೂಕ. A weight put to balance scales

ಕಾಣಿಕೆ k. n A present, gift. 2, sight. -ಕೊಡು. To make presents -ಇಟ್ಟು ಕೈ ಮುಗಿ. To give a present and worship

ಕಾಣಿಸು k. v. t To show. 2, to show one's self v. i. To become visible, to appear.

ಕಾಣು k v. t To see, regard, perceive v. i To appear, to be apparent. P. p ಕಂಡು ಕಾಣಗೊಡು. To let appear. ಕಾಣಬರು, ಕಂಡುಬರು To appear, come in sight. ಕಾಣೆ (for f.), ಕಾಣೋ (for male) emph. See ' lo ' ಕಂಡು ಹೋಗು To visit ಕಂಡು ನೋಡು To examine ಕಂಡು ಮಾಡು. To imitate. ಕಂಡು ಮಾತಾಡು To have an interview with. ಕಾಣುವಿಕೆ, ಕಾಣ್ಕೆ Seeing, appearing. ಕಾಣಿಕೆ, ಕಾಣ್ಕೆ. Sight, a present, gift. ಕಾಣ್ಕೆ. Great valour

ಕಾಂಡ s. n. A stalk, stem. 2, an arrow. 3, a part, the section of a book. 4, a bundle 5, season. 6, water. -ಪಟ A curtain, screen.

ಕಾಂಡಾಲ s. n A granary constructed of bamboos.

ಕಾಂಡಿಗೆ s. n. N. of a plant; a kind of a gourd, *Cucumis utilissimus*

ಕಾತರ, ಕಾತಳ s a. Confused, agitated, perplexed. 2, timid, afraid. n. Confusion, perplexity; also ಕಾತರತೆ. 2, alarm, fright; ಕಾತರಿಸು. To be agitated, perplexed.

ಕಾತರಿ (ಖಾತರಿ) h. n Assurance, guarantee

ಕಾತಿ a k n. Coir, cord made of it. 2, anger.

ಕಾತು, = ಕಾಯ್ದು, P p of ಕಾಯು.

ಕಾದಲ್, ಕಾದಲ್ಕೆ a k n Affection, love ಕಾದಲ A dear man, a paramour ಕಾದಲೆ. A sweetheart

ಕಾದು 1, ಕಾದಾಡು k v t To war, fight ಕಾದಾಟ A fight, quarrel

ಕಾದು 2 P p of ಕಾ & ಕಾಯು

ಕಾನ h n. Ear -ಬಾವಲಿ. An ear ornament

ಕಾನನ s . . . . . .

ಕಾನೂನು h. n. A rule, regulation.

ಕಾಂತ s. a. Dear, beloved; beautiful, agreeable. n. A lover, husband. 2, a stone 3, a house 4, the moon. ಕಾಂತೆ A lovely woman, wife.

ಕಾಂತಾರ s. n A forest. 2, a difficult road. 3, a kind of sugarcane, also -ಕ.

ಕಾಂತಿ s. n Wish; loveliness, beauty, splendour, lustre, personal decoration -ತಪ್ಪು, -ಮುಚ್ಚು Lustre to be obscured -ಗುಂದು Lustre to decrease.

ಕಾಪಟ್ಯ (fr. ಕಪಟ) s. n. Dishonesty, fraud.

ಕಾಪಾತು, see s ಕಾಪು

ಕಾಪಾಲ s a Relating to the skull ಕಾಪಾಲಿಕ. A religious mendicant; Śiva's worshipper.

ಕಾಪಿ 1. h. n. Coffee -ಗಿಡ. The coffee-tree.

ಕಾಪಿ 2. f. n. N. of a tune.

ಕಾಪಿ 3. f. n. A copy.

ಕಾಪು k n. Guarding, preserving, protection. 2, a preservative ceremony on the 7th day after a child's birth ಕಾಪಾಡಿಸು To make watch or guard ಕಾಪಾಡು. To guard, protect, take care of, defend, nourish ಕಾಪಾಡುವಿಕೆ. = ಕಾಪು.

ಕಾಮ s. n. Wish, desire, love, lust. 2, the god of love -ನ ಬಿಲ್ಲು. The rainbow -ನ ಸುಡುವದು. The burning of an effigy of Kâma at his annual festival. -ನ ಹುಣ್ಣಿಮೆ. Kâma's annuae festival, the hôli. -ಚರ Following one's own inclinations -ಕಸ್ತೂರಿ Sweet Basil. -ಕ್ರೋಧ ಲೋಭ ಮೋಹ ಮದ ಮತ್ಸರ. The six vices. -ಜನಕ. Vishnu or Krishna -ಧೇನು The cow of plenty. -ಪತ್ನಿ. Rati the wife of Kâma. -ಬಾಣ The (five) arrows of Kâma. -ವಿಕಾರ Unnatural desire. ಕಾಮಾಕ್ಷಿ. Durgâ, a kind of lute -ಆತುರ, ಕಾಮಾತುರ. Excited by lust -ವೈರಿ, ಕಾಮಾರಿ Śiva ಕಾಮಿ. Lustful, a libidinous man. ಕಾಮಿತ Wished, desired; a wish, desire. ಕಾಮಿತಾ . . A desired object ಕಾಮಿನಿ. A loving woman, a woman in general ಕಾಮಿಸು To wish, desire. ಕಾಮ್ಯ Desirable, agreeable, optional ಕಾಮ್ಯಾರ್ಥ. An advantage desired from observances or rites

ಕಾಮಗಾರಿ f. n Work, workmanship. -ಶಿಕ್ಷೆ Imprisonment with hard labour.

ಕಾಮಂಚ k. n. The lemon grass, *Andropogon schoenanthus* [jaundice.

ಕಾಮಣಿ, ಕಾಮಲೆ, ಕಾಮಿಲೆ k. n. A kind of

ಕಾಮಾಟಿ f. n. Labour (for wages). 2, a day-labourer, *also* ಕಾಮಾಟ

ಕಾಯ s. n. The body 2, a multitude -ಜ. -ಜಾತ A son, Kâma.

ಕಾಯಂ h a Fixed, permanent, confirmed. -ಮಾಡು. To confirm.

ಕಾಯಕ s n. Work, profession, pursuit, rite. *a.* Relating to the body

ಕಾಯದೆ, ಕಾಯಿದೆ h. n A rule, regulation

ಕಾಯಿ 1. = ಕಾಯು, *q. v.*

ಕಾಯಿ 2 k n. An unripe fruit in hard or nearly full-grown state, any nut, pod 2, hardness, callosity. -ಆಗು, ಕಾಯಾಗು. Fruit to grow -ಕಟ್ಟು, -ಗಟ್ಟು To form or become hard, *as* a boil. -ಕಸರು, -ಕಸಿ Various vegetables -ಪಲ್ಯ, -ಪಲ್ಯೆ, -ಸೊಪ್ಪು. Pod and leaf vegetables. -ಬಿಡು To get fruits. -ಹಾಲು. The milk of a cocoanut.

ಕಾಯಿಲೆ h. n. Sickness.

ಕಾಯಿಸು k. v. t To boil, make hot, *also* ಕಾಸು 2, to watch

ಕಾಯು 1 (= ಕಾ, ಕಾಯಿ, *q v.*) k. v. t To guard, protect, to take care of, to tend, to watch; to keep in check v i. To wait. *P. ps* ಕಾದು, ಕಾಯ್ದು.

ಕಾಯು 2. k. v. i. To grow hot, be heated, to become angry. *P. ps.* ಕಾದು, ಕಾಯ್ದು

ಕಾಯ್ಪು (= ಕಾವು) k. n Heat. 2, wrath.

ಕಾರ್ k *a.* Black n Blackness. 2, rainy season. -ಗತ್ತಲೆ, -ಪೊಬ್ಬು. Sable darkness. -ಮುಗಿಲು A black cloud -ಇರುಳು, ಕಾರಿರುಳು. A dark night. -ಎಳ್ಳು, ಕಾರೆಳ್ಳು. A mole.

ಕಾರ 1. (*tb of* ಕ್ಷಾರ) n Pungency, hotness of taste; a pungent, hot substance 2, an alkali, *as* soda or potash 3, wrath. ಸಾರಾಯಿ A kind of vermicelli

ಕಾರ 2. s n. Making, causing. 2, a maker, doer 3, *a term used to designate the sound of a letter, as* ಅಕಾರ, ಇಕಾರ, *etc*

ಕಾರಕ s. *a.* Making. n An agent -ಪದ. A noun on which the case of an adjective depends *(g.).*

ಕಾರಕೂನ h n. A clerk, a tollman

ಕಾರಖಾನೆ, ಕಾರ್ಖಾನೆ h n A manufactory, work-shop

ಕಾರಗೃಹ, ಕಾರಾಗೃಹ s. n A jail

ಕಾರಂಜಿ f n A playing fountain

ಕಾರಣ s n Cause; reason; motive, origin, a means. 2, agency, instrumentality 3, need of *ad.* For, on account of. -ಪುರುಷ A deity; a great man -ಬೀಳು. To be necessary. ಕಾರಣಿಕ. Causal, investigating the cause, an examiner, performance

ಕಾರಣಿ k. n. The red stripes or painting upon the walls of a house.

ಕಾರಭಾರ h. n Business, affairs; government. -ಮಾಡು To manage. ಕಾರಭಾರಿ. A superintendent, manager.

ಕಾರವಿ h. n. A kind of red cotton cloth.

ಕಾರಿ 1 k. n A backwater, an arm of the sea. 2, a ford

ಕಾರಿ 2. s n. Making, causing, *etc* 2, an artist, artificer, actor. -ಕೆ A female who does, a doing, a business; a comment, gloss

ಕಾರೀಕ f. n. The dried date-fruit.

ಕಾರು 1. k. n. Blackness. -ಗತ್ತಲೆ. Sable darkness

ಕಾರು 2 = ಕಾರ್. -ಹುಣ್ಣಿಮೆ. A feast in the third month. -ಹುಲ್ಲು. Grass in the rainy season. -ಗದ್ದೆ. Wet cultivation. -ಬೆಳೆ The wet-season crop

ಕಾರು 3 (ರು = ಱು) k v i To vomit. n. Vomiting ಕಾರಿಕೆ Vomiting ಕಾರಿಸು. To cause to vomit.

ಕಾರುಣ್ಯ s n. Compassion kindness. -ನಿಧಿ. A treasure of compassion -ಸಾಗರ An ocean of compassion.

ಕಾರುಬಾರು. = ಕಾರಭಾರ, q. v.

ಕಾರೆ 1 k. n The spinous shrub *Webera tetandra*. *Cpds.* -ಗಿಡ, -ಮುಳ್ಳು, -ಹಣ್ಣು.

ಕಾರೆ 2. f n. Confinement, a prison (*cf.* ಕಾರಗೃಹ). 2, pain 3, a gold collar.

ಕಾರೆ 3 *tb of* ಕಾರ್ಯ, *q v* -ಗಾರ A workman. -ಗಾರಿಕೆ Workmanship.

ಕಾರ್ಖಾನೆ, = ಕಾರಖಾನೆ, q. v.

ಕಾರ್ಗತ್ತಲೆ, *see s* ಕಾರು 1

ಕಾರ್ತಿಕ s n N. of the 8th lunar month (October-November).

ಕಾರ್ಪಣ್ಯ (*fr.* ಕೃಪಣ) s. n. Poverty, imbecility; pity; parsimony, niggardliness -ಪಡು. To be in distress.

ಕಾರ್ಪಾಸ s. *a* Made of cotton n. Cotton; cotton-cloth.

ಕಾರ್ಯ (= ಕಾರೆ) s. n Affair, business, act 2, object, purpose 3, cause, origin. -ವಾಸಿ. A good state of affairs -ಭಾಗ. A division of a work, plot, intrigue. -ಸಾಧಿಸು To accomplish a business. -ಸಿದ್ಧಿ Success, fulfilment of an object -ಸಿದ್ಧಿಸು. Work to be accomplished

ಕಾಲ s n. Time, the proper time. 2, a period of time, season, life-time. 3, death, Yama. 4, fate. 5, power. 6, tense of a verb -ಕಳೆ. To spend time. -ಕ್ಷೇಪ. Spending the time; delay; livelihood. -ಕೂಟ. Deadly poison. -ಖಂಡ The liver -ಗಣನ Calculation of time -ಗಣನವಿದ್ಯೆ Astronomy. -ಗತಿ. The lapse of time. -ಚಕ್ರ. The wheel of time, vicissitude of life. -ಜ್ಞ An astrologer -ಜ್ಞಾನ. Knowledge of time or futurity -ಜ್ಞಾನ ಹೇಳು. To foretell -ಜ್ಞಾನಿ A prophet. -ತ್ರಯ. The three times· past, present, and future, or morning, noon and evening -ತುಂಬು Time to be fulfilled; death to come. -ದರ್ಶ. A seer. -ಪುರುಷ, -ಮೂರ್ತಿ [illegible] -ರುದ್ರ. A terrible form of Śiva. -ಮಾನ. Measurement of time -ವಶ, ಕಾಲಾಧೀನ Subject to time or death -ವಾಚಕ A term expressing time. -ಹರಣ. Passing away time, delay ಕಾಲಾನುಕಾಲ From season to season; once. ಕಾಲಾನುಸಾರ, ಕಾಲಾನುಸರಣೆ. Conformity to the times ಕಾಲಾಂತರ Interval; period, process of time. ಕಾಲಾವಧಿ. Fixed time; the end of a year.

ಕಾಲಾಟ, ಕಾಲಾಡಿ, -ಡಿಸು, *see s.* ಕಾಲು.

ಕಾಲಿ (= ಕಾಳಿ) s n Blackness 2. Durga; *also* ಕಾಲಿಕಾದೇವಿ. -ದಾಸ. N. of a celebrated poet.

ಕಾಲಿಂಗ (= ಕಾಳಿಂಗ) s n N of a country or people 2, the black snake.

ಕಾಲಿಂದಿ s n The river Yamuna. 2, fem. name.

ಕಾಲಿವೆ, ಕಾಲುವೆ k n. A water-course, channel.

ಕಾಲು k. n. The foot, leg 2, a strand or lock of hair. -ಅಟ್ಟ, ಕಾಲಟ್ಟ A bench ಕಾಲಾಡು. To take a walk; *caus* ಕಾಲಾಡಿಸು -ಆಡಿ, ಕಾಲಾಡಿ A fast walker, a wanderer, roamer. -ಆಳು, ಕಾಲಾಳು. A foot-soldier. -ಇಕ್ಕು, -ಇಡು, -ಊರು, ಕಾಲಿಕ್ಕು, ಕಾಲಿಡು, ಕಾಲೂರು. To take a step; to walk. -ಕಟ್ಟು, ಕಾಲ್ಗಟ್ಟು To tie the leg; to embrace one's feet, a shackle, marriage. -ಕಡಗ A plain anklet -ಕುಪ್ಪಸ, -ಕುಬುಸ. Trowsers -ಉಂಗರ, ಕಾಲುಂಗರ A ring worn on the second toe. -ಗಡ. A ford. -ಚೀಲ. Stockings -ತೆಗೆ, ಕಾಲ್ತೆಗೆ To retreat, flee -ದಾರಿ, -ವಟ್ಟೆ A footpath. -ದೂಳು Dust of the feet an evil (*as* belly-ache) supposed to have occasioned from contact with one's feet-dust. -ನಡಿಗೆ, -ನಡೆ. Walking on foot. -ಬಲ. Foot-soldiers -ಬೀಳು. To fall at one's feet. -ಮುಡಿ To bend the leg, *i e* to make water, urine -ಮುರಿ, -ಮೆಟ್ಟು A sandal or shoe -ಮಾಡು. To make for begin. -ಸರಪಣಿ. A chain [illegible] ...es.

ಕಾಲು 2 k n A quarter or fourth part

ಕಾಲುವೆ = ಕಾಲಿವೆ, q v

ಕಾಲುಷ್ಯ (fr ಕಲುಷ) s n Foulness, filth, sin. 2, want of harmony.

ಕಾಲೋಚಿತ s a Opportune, in season, suitable to the time n. A suitable time

ಕಾವಂಚಿ k. n. The lemon grass, *Andropogon schoenanthus*.

ಕಾವಡಿ k. n A bamboo pole with slings at each end for carrying burdens across the shoulder

ಕಾವಣಿ a. k. n A shed, pandal

ಕಾವಂದ h. n. Lord, master, owner

ಕಾವರ a. k n Passion, anger, wrath

ಕಾವಲ, ಕಾವಲು k n. Guarding, watching, a guard, watch, custody. 2, a pasture ground. -ಗಾರ, -ದವ, -ದ A guard, sentinel.

ಕಾವಲಿ k n A frying or baking pan.

ಕಾವಲೆ. = ಕಾಲಿವೆ, q v

ಕಾವಳ k. n. Darkness

ಕಾವಿ k. n. A red earth or ochre

ಕಾವು 1 (= ಕಾಯ್ಪು, etc.) k. n. Heat, glow. 2, cauterization -ಕೊಡು, -ಹಾಕು To cauterize, foment.

ಕಾವು 2. k n A stalk, stem; a handle.

ಕಾವೆ h. n. Ringing and turning of a horse whilst at full speed. -ತಿರುಗಿಸು. To longe a horse

ಕಾವೇರಿ s n N of a river, N. of a fem.

ಕಾವ್ಯ (fr ಕವಿ) s n Poetry, a poetical composition -ಕರ್ತಾರ, -ಕರ್ತೃ. A poet. -ರಚನೆ Composition of a piece of poetry

ಕಾಶಿ (= ಕಾಸಿ) s. n. Benares. 2, N. of a people ದಕ್ಷಿಣ-. Hampe near Bellary. ಉತ್ತರ-. Benares -ಕಾಗದ Good white paper. -ತಾಲಿ A marriage badge attached to a female's necklace. -ಪಟ್ಟೆ. Fine silk. -ಭಾಗೀರಥಿ. Water brought from Benares.

ಕಾಶ್ಮೀರ s. n. N. of a country. 2, saffron.

ಕಾಷಾಯ s. a Red. n. A red cloth; *also* -ವಸನ

ಕಾಷ್ಠ s n A piece of wood, a stick; dry wood. 2, a blockhead. -ವ್ಯಸನ. Vain grief. ಕಾಷ್ಠಿಕೆ. = ಕಟ್ಟಿಗೆ.

ಕಾಷ್ಠೆ s n A region of the world. 2, place, site. 3, a measure of time. 4, excellence.

ಕಾಸ s n Cough, catarrh 2, asthma -ಮರ್ದ. A cough-medicine, *Cassia sophora*. [groom

ಕಾಸಗಾರ, ಕಾಸದಾರ, ಕಾಸ್ತಾರ h. n A

ಕಾಸಗಿ h a Private, not public, own

ಕಾಸರ, ಕಾಸರ್ಕ, ಕಾಸಂರಕ (= ಕಾಜವಾರ. tb of ಕಾರಸ್ಕರ) n. The tree *Strychnos nux vomica*

ಕಾಸಾ h a Good, fine; legitimate, own.

ಕಾಸಿ 1. = ಕಾಶಿ, q. v. -ದಾವಳಿ. A soft woollen dâvali.

ಕಾಸಿ 2 (tb of ಕಾಶಾ) n A cloth for girding the loins.

ಕಾಸು 1 (= ಕಾಯಿಸು) k v t. To warm, make hot, to boil, to bake *as* bread, *etc*.

ಕಾಸು 2. k. n. The smallest copper coin, a cash; a coin in general.

ಕಾಳ s. a. Black -ಗತ್ತಲೆ. Sable darkness. -ಜೀರಿಗೆ. Black cummin -ರಾತ್ರಿ A dark night.

ಕಾಳಗ k. n Fight, battle, war.

ಕಾಳಂಜಿ k n A spittoon 2, a vessel from which scented water is sprinkled.

ಕಾಳಿ (= ಕಾಲಿ) s. n Durgâ. -ಅಮ್ಮ, ಕಾಳಮ್ಮ. N -ನಾಥ Śiva.

ಕಾಳಿಂಗ s. n The black cobra, *Naga tripudians*.

ಕಾಳಜ, ಕಾಳಿಜ f n. The liver. 2. the breast, heart.

ಕಾಳು (ಳು = ಡು) k n. A coin, single grain, seed, a pea; a bean 2, (= ಕಾಡು) a forest, *etc*. -ಆಗು, ಕಾಳಾಗು. To be ruined, to become troublesome or hostile -ಭೈರವ. A ferocious Bhairava

ಕಿಕ್ಕರಿಸು k v. t. To make small, to reduce v. i. To be closely united or thickset, *as* fruits or leaves on a tree.

ಕಿಕ್ಕಿರಿ k *v i* To be close together, dense *n* A crowd, throng

ಕಿಗ್ಗಟ್ಟು k *n* A small tie or band.

ಕಿಂಕರ s *n*. A servant, slave. -ತೆ, -ತ್ವ. Servitude, destitution.

ಕಿಚ, ಕಿಚಿ k *An imitative sound* -ಗುಟ್ಟು, -ಅನ್ನು. To chirp, chatter.

ಕಿಚಡಿ, ಕಿಚ್ಚಡಿ h. *n*. A mixture of boiled rice and pulse.

ಕಿಚ್ಚು k *n* Fire -ಮೋರೆ A wrathful countenance. ಹೊಟ್ಟೆ-. Envy.

ಕಿಂಚಿತ s. *a*. Somewhat. 2, a little.

ಕಿಟಕಿ, ಕೆಟಕಿ, ಕಿಡಕಿ h. *n*. A window, a wicket -ಬಾಗಲು The window-opening. -ಬಾವಲಿ. An ear-ornament. -ತೆರೆ To open a window.

ಕಿಟ್ಟ 1 k. *n*. A gajuga *(Molucca bean)*

ಕಿಟ್ಟ 2. s *n*. Secretion, excrement, dross of iron; rust, *etc*, cowdung kept in a pit.

ಕಿಟ್ಟಿ k. *n*. A kind of torture in which the hand, ear, or nose is pressed between two sticks

ಕಿಡಿ k *n* A spark -ಕಿಡಿ *rep* -ಕಿಡಿಯಾಗು. To be enraged -ಗಣ್ಣು. A fiery, red eye. -ಕೆಂಕಿ A little fire.

ಕಿಡಿಗೇಡಿ k. *n*. A mischievous boy -ತನ Mischievousness.

ಕಿಣಿ k *An imitative sound* -ಎನ್ನು, -ಗುಟ್ಟು To tinkle, tingle

ಕಿಂಡಿ k *n*. A chink, gap, cleft.

ಕಿತಾಬು h. *n*. A title. 2, a book

ಕಿತ್ತಡಿ k *n*. An ascetic, a rishi.

ಕಿತ್ತಳೆ, -ಹಣ್ಣು k *n* An orange

ಕಿತ್ತಾ h *n* A time, turn -ವಾರ In fragments

ಕಿತ್ತಾಟ (=ಕಚ್ಚಾಟ) k. *n*. Strife, quarrel.

ಕಿತ್ತಾನ್, ಕಿಂತಾನ್ h *n* Canvas, linen.

ಕಿತ್ತು k *v. t.* To pluck out 2, *p. p of* ಕೀಳು.

ಕಿನಕಾಪು, ಕಿನಕಾಬು h. *n*. Silk stuff interwoven with gold or silver thread, brocade.

ಕಿವಾರ, ಕಿ [illegible]

ಕಿನ್ನರ s. *n* A human figure with a horse's head, a demigod serving Kuvêra. -ಪತಿ Kuvêra.

ಕಿನ್ನರಿ s. *n*. A lute. 2, *f. of* ಕಿನ್ನರ.

ಕಿಫಾಯತಿ m *n* Profit, gain.

ಕಿಬ್ಬೆರಳು, ಕಿಬ್ಬೊಟ್ಟೆ k *n* The little finger.

ಕಿಂಪುರುಷ = ಕಿನ್ನರ, *q v*

ಕಿಮ್ಮತು h. *n*. Price, value

ಕಿರಣ s. *n* A ray of light.

ಕಿರಡು (ದ=ಱ), *see s.* ಕಿರಿ 2, *q. v*

ಕಿರಬ, ಕಿರಬು (ರ=ಱ) k. *n* A hyena; a leopard.

ಕಿರಮಂಜಿ f *n* Cochineal; cochineal colour.

ಕಿರಾಣಿ m. *n*. Grocery, *as* sugar, spices, *etc*

ಕಿರಾತ s. *n* N. of a savage tribe inhabiting woods and mountains.

ಕಿರಾಯ h *n* Rent, hire, fare.

ಕಿರಿ 1 k. *v i* To grin

ಕಿರಿ 2 (ರ=ಱ) = ಕಿರು 1. k *a*. Small, little,, short, young trifling, junior -ಕುಲ = ಕಿರುಕುಲ *Cpds* -ಗಂಟೆ, -ಗಣ್ಣು, -ಗಿವಿ, -ಗೂದಲು, -ಗೆಯ್, -ತಂಗಿ, -ತಮ್ಮ -ದು, ಕಿರಮು, ಕಿದುನ. A small insignificant affair or state. -ನುಡಿ To use mean language, a disrespectful word -ನೆಲ್ಲಿಗಿಡ The plant *Flacourtia cataphracta*. -ನೋಟ. A leer -ಬೆರಳು, -ಬೊಟ್ಟು. The little finger. -ಯನು. A young man, a junior, *f.* ಕಿರಿಯಳು. -ಮಗ The youngest son -ಹೊಟ್ಟೆ The abdomen

ಕಿರಿಕಿಜೋಡು (ರಿ=ಱಿ) k. *n*. A pair of creaking shoes

ಕಿರಿಕಿರಿ h *n*. Annoyance, trouble.

ಕಿರಿಗೆ (ರಿ=ಱಿ) k. *n* A small sîrĕ worn by girls.

ಕಿರಿದು, *see s* ಕಿರಿ.

ಕಿರಿಯಾತು f *n* A kind of gentian, *Agathotes chirayta*

ಕಿರೀಟ s. *n*. A diadem, crown, tiara. ನವರತ್ನ- A crown of nine sorts of

- .

ಕಿರು 1. = ಕಿರಿ, *q. v* -ಕಸಲೆ, -ಕುಸಾಲೆ A kind of potherb. -ಕುಲ, ಕಿರಕುಳ. A low or inferior caste or kind -ಗತ್ತಲೆ Slight darkness -ಗತ್ತಿ A short sword. -ಗೊರಳು. A short neck. -ದೊಡೆ The shank, lower or upper part of the leg -ನಗೆ. A smile. -ನಾಲಿಗೆ. The uvula. -ಬೆರಳು = ಕಿರಿಬೆರಳು, *s.* ಕಿರಿ -ತುರುಚಿ A plant that stings like a nettle, *Tragia cannabina.*

ಕಿರು 2. (ರು=ಱು) k *An imitative sound.* -ಗುಟ್ಟು. To cry, scream, to creak, *as* a door.

ಕಿರ್ದ h. *n.* An account of receipts and disbursements

ಕಿಲಬು = ಕಿಲುಬು, *q. v.*

ಕಿಲ, ಕಿಲಿ k. *int. An imitative sound.* --ನಗು. To titter from pleasure.

ಕಿಲುಬು, ಕಿಲುವು (= ಕಿಲಬು) k. *n.* Rust, verdigris. *v t.* To get corroded or covered with verdigris.

ಕಿಲ್ಬಿಷ s. *n.* Fault, offence, sin; disease.

ಕಿಲ್ಲೆ h. *n* A fort. -ದಾರ. The commander of a fort.

ಕಿವಚು k. *v. t* To crush and squeeze with the hand.

ಕಿವಡು k *n* Deafness; *also* -ತನ. ಕಿವಡ. A deaf man; *f* ಕಿವಡಿ

ಕಿವಿ k. *n.* The ear (ಕರ್ಣ, ಶ್ರೋತ್ರ, ಶ್ರವಣ), the touch-hole of a cannon; a handle, *as* of a frying pan. -ಕೊಡು To listen, pay attention to. -ಕೊಟ್ಟುಕೇಳು. To hear attentively -ತೂತು. A perforation in the auricle -ತೂತು ಮಾಡು To bore the ear -ತೆರೆ. To open the ears -ಮಾತು. A whispered word. -ಮುಚ್ಚು. To shut the ears -ಯ ಮೇಲೆ ಇಡು, -ಯ ಮೇಲೆ ಹಾಕು. To make known, to communicate -ಯಾರೆ Attentively -ಹರಕ A man whose auricle is rent, *f.* -ಹರಕಿ -ಹಿಂಡು, -ತಿರಿಗಿಸು. To twist the ear

ಕಿವುಡು. = ಕಿವಡು, *q v.*

ಕಿಸ k *n.* Putting astride, grinning. -ಗಾಲು. The legs put astride (in walking) -ಬಾಯಿ A grinning mouth. -ವಾಯ A grinner, simpleton.

ಕಿಸಕ್ಕನೆ k *ad.* Suddenly, unawares 2, sneeringly.

ಕಿಸಮು h. *n* Kind, sort -ವಾರು. Sorted.

ಕಿಸಿ k *v t* To put astride *v i* To grin

ಕಿಸು k *n* Redness, a dark-red colour. 2, = ಕಿಸ, *q. v*

ಕಿಸುರು k. *v. i.* To be disagreeable. *n* Disagreeableness, disgustfulness, strife, quarrel.

ಕಿಸೆ h *n* A pocket

ಕಿಸ್ತಿ, ಕಿಸ್ತು h *n* An instalment, payment by instalments, *as* of assessment -ಬಂದಿ. Settlement of revenue by instalments. -ಬಾಕಿ. Arrears of instalments

ಕಿಳಿರು a. k *v. i* To neigh.

ಕೀ 1 k. *int An imitative sound.* ಕೀ ಕೀ The cry of certain birds. -ಚಕ್ಕ The curlew

ಕೀ 2 k. *v. i* To become pus.

ಕೀಚಕ s. *n* A hollow bamboo whistling in the wind. 2, a chief of Virâtarâja's army.

ಕೀಟ, ಕೀಟಕ s. *n* A worm, insect. ಕೀಟ ಕತನ. Mischief-making

ಕೀಟಲೆ k *n.* Mischief-making trouble

ಕೀನಾಶ s. *a.* Poor, wretched; small, little. 2, sick

ಕೀರ k. *n* The mungoose 2, (f) a parrot 3, (*tb of* ಕ್ಷೀರ) milk

ಕೀರು 1. (ರು=ಱು) k. *v i.* To scream. 2, to rage, fume. *v t* To scrape, scratch

ಕೀರು 2 f. *n* A dish composed of rice, wheat, *etc*

ಕೀರ್ತನೆ s. *n* A praise, song of praise, eulogium. 2, fame, glory

ಕೀರ್ತಿ s *n.* Fame, glory, renown, report 2, praise, worship. -ಗಳಿಸು. To acquire fame -ವಂತ. A famous man -ವಡಿಸು, -ಸು. To praise, laud

ಕೀಲ. = ಕೀಲು, *q. v.*

ಕೀಲಕ s *n* A pin, bolt, wedge, *etc.* 2. the forty-second year in the Hindu cycle.

ಕೀಲಿ s n. A lock, the spring of a watch -ಕೈಯ್ The key of a lock -ತೆಗೆ To unlock

ಕೀಲು (tb. of ಕೀಲ) n A pin, peg, bolt, bar, wedge joint, etc. 2, device, contrivance; a secret. ಕೀಲಿಸು. To bind, fasten, fix, pin.

ಕೀವು (f) ಕೀ) k n Pus, matter of a sore

ಕೀಸು a. k. v. t To make thin, scrape 2, to pull out or off. n Scraping, scratching 2, a coil of palm leaf put in the ear-hole.

ಕೀಳು 1. (ಳು = ಐು) k n. Lowness, meanness 2, a low, inferior, base, mean man. 3, a veranda. -ಜಾತಿ A low caste -ಮನುಷ್ಯ, ಕೀಳ A low man -ತನ. Lowness, inferiority -ತರ. An inferior kind -ಮೇಲು. Evil and good. -ಮಾತು, -ನುಡಿ A low, improper word.

ಕೀಳು 2. k. v t. To pull out; to pluck out or up, to uproot, eradicate. P. p ಕಿತ್ತು.

ಕು s. *A particle implying inferiority, wickedness, etc*

ಕುಕಿಲು k n The cuckoo. v i To cry as a cuckoo

ಕುಕೂಲ s. n A smoking fire

ಕುಕ್ಕಡಿ f. n The quantity of thread spun in one ball 2, the ball-like swelling produced on the upper arm from being struck. -ಏಳು. To swell thus.

ಕುಕ್ಕರಿಸು k. v. t. To put down with violence or destroy, as vessels, 2, to squat

ಕುಕ್ಕಿಬಳ್ಳಿ k. n. A creeper running wild, *Passiflora foetida*

ಕುಕ್ಕು 1 k v. t. To peck, to strike in a pecking manner, to hack, dig up 2, (*fig*) to urge. 3, to beat gently, as a cloth in washing. v. i To wink, be dazzled by the sunlight, etc

ಕುಕ್ಕು 2 k. n A heron, crane 2, shaking

ಕುಕ್ಕುಟ s n. A cock. ಕುಕ್ಕುಟಿ A hen. ಕುಕ್ಕುಟಾಸನ A certain posture of an ascetic during religious meditation

ಕುಕ್ಕುರ s n A dog 2, a vegetable perfume.

ಕುಕ್ಕೆ k. n A small basket

ಕುಕ್ಕೋಟ k. n Trot, as of a horse

ಕುಕ್ಷಿ s n A cavity. 2, the belly. ಕುಕ್ಷಿಂಭರಿ. Selfish, greedy.

ಕುಗು k v. i To become low be depressed, to crouch; to decrease; to cease or stop, as voice or speech ಕುಗ್ಗಿಸು. To cause to be depressed, etc.

ಕುಗ್ರಾಮ s n. A hamlet -ವಾಸಿ. A petty villager

ಕುಂಕುಮ s n Saffron, *Crocus sativus*. 2, crimsoned saffron-powder applied by married women to their foreheads; a kind of cosmetic -ಕೇಸರಿ. The saffron flower.

ಕುಂಕೆ k n The nape of the neck. 2, the shoulder.

ಕುಂಗು = ಕುಗ್ಗು, q v

ಕುಚ s n The female breast; a nipple.

ಕುಚಾಳಿ f. n A bad disposition, jeering, mockery.

ಕುಚು k n. Whispering. --ಮಾತಾಡು. To whisper

ಕುಚೇಷ್ಟೆ s n An evil design, wicked contrivance, reviling and defaming, wild tricks

ಕುಚೋದ್ಯ s. n. Ridicule, derision, mockery, an evil thought. -ಗಾರ. A mocker, reviler

ಕುಚ್ಚಿತ. tb of ಕುತ್ಸಿತ, q v.

ಕುಚ್ಚು 1 k v. t To boil -ಅಕ್ಕಿ Rice made from paddy slightly boiled and dried.

ಕುಚ್ಚು 2 (tb of ಕೂರ್ಚ. = ಕುಂಚ, q v) n. A bunch, bundle, cluster, a tassel; a brush.

ಕುಜ s. a Earth-born, low-born n. The earth's son: the planet Mars. -ವಾರ Tuesday.

ಕು... [illegible] An unripe jack-fruit.

ಕುಂಚ (=ಕುಚ್ಚು 2) s. n A bunch, cluster, tassel; a brush used by weavers; *also* ಕುಂಚಿಗೆ

ಕುಂಚಿ s n. A hooded cloak for children

ಕುಂಚಿಗೆ (*tb of* ಕೂರ್ಚಕ) n A brush used by weavers for cleaning the warp.

ಕುಂಜ s. n A place overgrown with creepers, a bower.

ಕುಂಜರ s n An elephant. a. Pre-eminent, excellent.

ಕುಟಂಕ (*tb.* ಕೊಟ್ಟಿಗೆ) n A roof; hut

ಕುಟರು (*tb* ಗುಡಾರ) n A tent.

ಕುಟಾಂಯಿಸು h. v. t. To mix

ಕುಟಿ s A curve 2, a hut 3, a nosegay.

ಕುಟಿಕ, ಕುಟಿಗ k. *aff*. One who beats, *etc. Cpds* ಕಲ್ಲು-, ಮರ-, ಚೆಂಬು-, *etc.*

ಕುಟಿಲ s a Bent, crooked, curved 2, curly. 3, dishonest, fraudulent. n. Insincerity, dishonesty. -ತನ, -ತೆ, -ತ್ವ. Dishonesty

ಕುಟೀರ s n. A hut, cottage

ಕುಟುಕು k v t To gulp, swallow 2, to sting n A draught, morsel

ಕುಟುಂಬ s n. A household, family; a wife -ಸ್ಥ. A housefather ಕುಟುಂಬಿ. A householder, *f.* ಕುಟುಂಬಿನಿ

ಕುಟ್ಟಣಿ k n A metal mortar to pound betel-nuts

ಕುಟ್ಟನಿ, ಕುಟ್ಟನಿ (= ಕಂಟಣಿ) s n A bawd, procuress.

ಕುಟ್ಟು k. v. t. To beat, strike, pound, bruise. 2, to throw. 3, to prick, ache 4, (*at the end of cpds*) to utter, *etc.*, to do (*as*. ಗುಣುಗುಟ್ಟು, ಬುಸುಗುಟ್ಟು, ಸೊಪ್ಪುಗುಟ್ಟು, *etc.*). n A blow; a piercing pain in the bowels -ವಿಕೆ, ಕುಟ್ಟಿಕೆ Beating.

ಕುಟ್ಟೆ k. n. Decay the state of being pulverised by wood-worms

ಕುಠಾರ, ಕುಠಾರಿ s. n. An axe. -ಧರ Ganapati, Parasurâma

ಕುಡ k n. A staff-like iron roller for clearing cotton from the seed 2, a cauterising iron. 3, a stick of sealing wax.

ಕುಡಕ, ಕುಡಿಕ k. n A drinker, drunkard.

ಕುಡತ, ಕುಡಿತ k. n. Drinking, a draught.

ಕುಡತಾ, ಕುಡತಿ f. n A jacket.

ಕುಡತೆ, ಕುಡಿತೆ k n. The hollowed palm of the hand. 2, a liquid measure in S. C. = ½ sheer

ಕುಡವ s n A measure of capacity = ¼ ಪ್ರಸ್ಥ

ಕುಡಿ 1. k v. t. & i. To drink, to inhale. n. Drinking -ಸು To cause to drink. -ನೀರು Drinking water

ಕುಡಿ 2. k. n. A point, top; a bamboo shoot, the end of a lamp's wick, the lash of a whip, the point of a flame 2, a flag -ನೋಟ A side glance. -ಮೀಸೆ. A mustache with pointed extremities -ಸೆರಗು The extreme point of a cloth.

ಕುಡಿಕೆ k. n A small vessel, an inkstand, bottle, *etc* -ಬಿರುಸು. A kind of firework.

ಕುಡು 1. (= ಕೊಡು) a. k. v. t To give, *etc.*

ಕುಡು 2 k n Croockedness. -ಗಲು, -ಗೋಲು. A sickle -ಮಿಂಚು. A zigzag lightning.

ಕುಡುಕು k. v t To wash (a cloth) gently 2, to peck.

ಕುಡುಪು k n. A stick for beating drums, *etc*, a fiddle-stick.

ಕುಣಿತ (= ಕುಣಿತ) k. n. Dancing.

ಕುಣಿ 1. k. n. A hole, a pit, a grave-pit. -ಗಣ್ಣು. A sunken eye. -ನರಿ. A fox.

ಕುಣಿ 2, ಕುಣಿಯು ಕುಣಿದಾಡು k v. t. To dance, to jump, frisk, hop. -ತ, -ದಾಟ, -ಯುವಿಕೆ. Dancing

ಕುಣಿ 3. s a Crooked-armed, having a withered or crippled arm. -ಕ. A cripple

ಕುಣಿಕೆ k n. A loop, noose; a clasp; a link, knot. 2, a hollow, cavity. 3, a finger 4, a corner.

ಕುಣಿತ, ಕುಣಿಹ. = ಕುಣತ q. v.

ಕುಂಟ k n A cripple, lame man, f ಕುಂಟಿ 2, tb of ಕುಂಠ -ಗಾಲು. A lame foot -ನಿಕೆ Hopping -ನಿಕೆಯಾಟ. A hop-scotch

ಕುಂಟಣ (tb. of ಕುಟ್ಟಿಣಿ, q v.) k. n. A procurer, whoremaster, also -ಗ; f. -ಗಿತ್ತಿ.

ಕುಂಟು k n Lameness, hopping, a hop. v i. To limp, halt, hop

ಕುಂಟೆ k. n. An instrument for levelling ploughed ground and removing noxious weeds 2, the web-beam in a loom. 3, a pool, pond 4, a broom-stick.

ಕುಂಠ s a Blunt, dull; indolent, weak; foolish, cf. ಕುಂಟ ಕುಂಠಿತ. Blunted, lazy, stupid; confounded

ಕುಂಡ s. n. A pit. 2, a pot 3, a pool, pond. 4, a son born in adultery, also -ಗೋಳಕ

ಕುಂಡರು. = ಕುಂದ್ರು, q v ಕುಂಡರಬೀಳು. To fall or sink down

ಕುಂಡಲ s n. An ear-ring, also one worn as a badge of honour by Panditas, etc , brackets. 2, an astrological diagram, also ಗ್ರಹ-. -ಪಂಡಿತ A scholar who wears a pair of such a badge

ಕುಂಡಲಿ s a. Circular, spiral n A snake. 2, the herb *Mollugs cerviana*

ಕುಂಡೆ k. n. Buttocks, the posteriors, the bottom of a vessel -ಚಣ್ಣ Tight breeches

ಕುಂದ್ರು (= ಕುಂಡರು, ಕೂಡ್ರು, etc) k v. i. To sit down ಕುಂದ್ರಿಸು. = ಕುಳ್ಳಿರಿಸು

ಕುತಣಿ, ಕುತನಿ, ಕುತ್ತನಿ h. n Satin

ಕುತಂತ್ರ s. n. A wicked design -ಗಾರ. A man of wicked devices

ಕುತರ್ಕ s n Fallacious argument, fallacy, sophism.

ಕುತು f n. A leathern oil-bottle

ಕುತುಕ f n Eagerness, desire, curiosity

ಕುತುಬಿ h. n The Muhammadan Friday sermon and blessing

ಕುತೂಹಲ s. n Eagerness; curiosity, desire 2, sport, amusement

ಕುತ್ತು k [illegible] sickness, trouble, adversity. danger ಕುತ್ತೆ. A sickly female.

ಕುತ್ತಿಗೆ k. n The throat; the neck.

ಕುತ್ತು k v. t. To beat, strike, bruise; to push. n. A stroke; that is small -ಅಡಿ, ಕುತ್ತಡಿ. A small foot -ಗೆ. Striking ಕುತ್ತಿಸು. To cause to beat.

ಕುತ್ಸಿತ s a Reviled, despised, contemptible, vile.

ಕುದಕಲು. = ಕುಚ್ಚು, q v

ಕುದರು. ಕುದುರು k n Low ground, a hollow, the bed of a stream

ಕುದರೆ = ಕುದುರೆ, q v.

ಕುದಿ k v i To boil, bubble up 2, to suffer pain, to grieve (P ps. ಕುದಿದು, ಕುದ್ದು). n Boiling, grief. ಕುದಸು, -ಸು. To boil, etc

ಕುದುಕು a k v i To trot. n Trotting

ಕುದುರು k. v i To recover from illness, be set, arranged, etc.; to come to hand, to fit, to become quiet, firm, to prosper, succeed n Settlement, symmetry, health, family 2, a garden-bed. 3, a rim of a mortar -ಪಾಟು Success, as of a business. -ಮಾಡು To fix, establish

ಕುದುರೆ k n. A horse. 2, the cock of a gun 3, a knight at chess. -ಕಿವಿಗನ ಮರ The tree *Terminalia tomentosa* -ಗಾರ -ಯವ A horsekeeper. -ಜಿಪಿ. The hair of a horse's tail -ಮಸಾಲೆ. A perennial fodder plant, the *Lucerne* grass. -ಮುಖ N of a sanitarium on the Western Ghauts -ಮುಸುಡಿನ ಗಳು. A kind of crocodile -ರಾವುತ A horseman -ಏರು, -ಹತ್ತು. To mount a horse.

ಕುದೆ a. k n A fetter.

ಕುದ್ದಾಲ (tb ಗುದ್ದಲಿ) s n A hoe, a kind of spade 2, mountain ebony.

ಕುದ್ದು. P p of ಕುದಿ, q. v.

ಕುದ್ರಿಗೇಡಿತನ k. n Envy

ಕುನಸು h n. Rancour spite.

ಕು[illegible] k [illegible] stoop

n A curved ground. -ಚೀಲ A sack, bag -ತ್ವ. Crookedness, insolence.

ಕುಂತಲ s n. Hair, cf ಕೂದಲು. 2, a mode of dressing the hair. 3, N. of a country.

ಕುಂತಿ s. n N. of the daughter of the Yâdava prince Śûra and mother of the Pândavas.

ಕುಂತು = ಕುಳಿತು, ಕೂತು, etc (P p of ಕುಳಿರು). Having sat down.

ಕುಂದ 1 k. n. A pillar of bricks, etc.

ಕುಂದ 2 s. n A kind of jasmine. 2, Olibanum, a resin 3, one of Kubêra's treasures.

ಕುಂದಕ k n. Defect, hindrance.

ಕುಂದಣ k. n. Setting a precious stone with gold. 2, fine gold.

ಕುಂದಣಿಗೆ, ಕುಂದಳಿಗೆ k. n The rim of a mortar.

ಕುಂದು k n. To become lean; to wane, decrease, fail, sink; to faint, cease n. Decrease, deficiency, defect, want; fault, emaciation; grief -ಇಡು, -ತರು, ಕುಂದಿಡು. To find fault with ಕುಂದು ಎಣಿಕೆ. ಕುಂದುಹ. Decreasing, decline. ಕುಂದಿಸು. To cause to decrease, etc

ಕುನ್ನಿ k. n A cub, puppy, etc, a young dog

ಕುಪಿತ s a Provoked, angry n. Anger -ಮತಿ A passionate person

ಕುಪ್ಪಟಿ, ಕುಪ್ಪಡಿಗೆ k n A portable furnace.

ಕುಪ್ಪರಿಸು. = ಕುಪ್ಪಳಿಸು, q v

ಕುಪ್ಪಸ (tb. of ಕೂರ್ಪಾಸ) n A bodice; a jacket, a cuirass.

ಕುಪ್ಪಳಿಸು k. v i To heap, to be numerous, to jump over. 2, to be injured or scalded, to blister v t To amass, heap.

ಕುಪ್ಪಿ (tb of ಕೂಪಿ) n A vial, flask [bottle

ಕುಪ್ಪು k v t To heap, lay up v. i (= ಕುಪ್ಪಳಿಸು) To leap, jump n. A kind of disease ಕುಪ್ಪಿಸು To cause (an animal) to jump, to jump with joined feet

ಕುಪ್ಪೆ k. n. A pile, heap, a dunghill.

ಕುಬಕು k v. t. To dig up the ground slightly.

ಕುಬುದ್ಧಿ s n. Evil-mindedness

ಕುಬುಸ, ಕುಬ್ಸ = ಕುಪ್ಪಸ, q. v

ಕುಬೇರ = ಕುವೇರ, q. v

ಕುಬೋಧಕ s. n. A bad teacher. ಕುಬೋಧನೆ. Bad instruction.

ಕುಬ್ಜ s a Hump-backed, dwarfish, f. ಕುಬ್ಜೆ.

ಕುಮಕಿ, ಕುಮಕು, ಕುಮ್ಮಕ್ಕು h. n. Help, assistance

ಕುಮತಿ s. n. Evil-mindedness, weak intellect.

ಕುಮರಿ k n. A piece of forest land cleared of its trees and cultivated for one or two years only

ಕುಮಾರ s. n A boy, youth, son. 2, the heir apparent 3, Skanda, the god of war. -ಗುರು. Śiva -ವಾಲ್ಮೀಕಿ. The author of Kannada Râmâyana. -ವ್ಯಾಸ. The author of Kannada Bhârata. -ಸ್ವಾಮಿ. Skanda

ಕುಮಾರಿ, ಕುಮಾರತಿ, ಕುಮಾರ್ತೆ s. n. A young girl, maiden; a daughter. ಕುಮಾರೀಭೂತಿರ Cape Comorin.

ಕುಮುಕು. = ಕುಮಕಿ, q v.

ಕುಮುಟು k. n Nauseousness, mustiness, damp smell.

ಕುಮುದ s. n. The white water-lily, *Nymphaea esculenta*. 2, the blue lotus 3, the elephant of the south-west quarter. 4, the moon 5, camphor. a. Brown, tawny. -ಗಡ್ಡೆ. A fragrant garden flower, *Kaempferia rotunda*. -ಪ್ರಿಯ, -ಬಂಧು, -ಬಾಂಧವ, ಕುಮುದಿನೀ ಕಾಂತ The moon. -ವೈರಿ, ಕುಮುದಾರಿ. The sun

ಕುಂಪಣಿ f n Company

ಕುಂಬಳ (tb of ಕೂಷ್ಮಾಂಡ) n The pumpkin gourd. -ಕಾಯಿ. A pumpkin -ಬಳ್ಳಿ. The pumpkin-creeper

ಕುಂಬಾರ (ರ = ಱ) (tb of ಕುಂಭಕಾರ) n. A potter. f. -ಗಿತ್ತಿ. -ಅ -ವಾ... -ತಿಗ...

A potter's wheel. -ತನ ಕುಂಬಾರಿಕೆ The business of a potter.

ಕುಂಬು k. n Bowing down, an obeisance 2, decay

ಕುಂಟೆ k n A wall on a roof that serves for a balustrade

ಕುಂಭ s n A water-jar, pot, the sign of the zodiac *Aquarius* 2, N of a demon. 3, a grain measure. -ಕ. Stopping the breath in yôga -ಕರ್ಣ. N of a râkshasa -ಕಾರ A potter. -ಕೋಣ. N. of a town in Tanjore.

ಕುಂಭಿನಿ s. n. The earth

ಕುಂಭೀಪಾಕ s n A hell in which the wicked are baked like potter's vessels, *etc.*

ಕುಮ್ಮು k v t To beat with a pestle, pound n Pounding

ಕುಯಿಲು k. n. Cutting, reaping. 2, a tenon -ಆಳು, ಕುಯಿಲಾಳು A reaper

ಕುಯುಕ್ತಿ s. n A wicked device

ಕುರಗ f n An instrument of goldsmiths, *etc*, a sort of anvil

ಕುರಂಗ s. n An antelope, deer.

ಕುರಚಿ (ರ=ಱ). = ಕುರುಚು, q v

ಕುರಂಜಿ (*tb. of* ಕುರುವಿಂದ) n The corundum-stone, *Spatum adamanticum*, used for cutting diamonds

ಕುರಟಿಕೆ, ಕುರಟಿಗೆ = ಕುರುಟಿಕೆ q v

ಕುರಡ = ಕುರುಡ, q v.

ಕುರಬ = ಕುರುಬ, q v.

ಕುರರ s n. An osprey; f ಕುರರಿ.

ಕುರಾಣ = ಖುರಾನು, q. v

ಕುರಿ 1 (ರಿ=ಱಿ) k n A mark, aim, an object of aim v t. To mark, to take note of, regard, mind. *P. p.* ಕುರಿತು *(used as a particle)* With a view to, respecting, regarding, *etc* ಕುರಿಪು. A mark, *etc*

ಕುರಿ 2. (ರಿ=ಱಿ) k n. A sheep, ram. -ಕಾಲು, -ತುಪ್ಪಟ್ಟ Wool -ಕಾವ, -ಗಾವ. A shepherd -ಗಿಡ. A creeper said to be an antidote for snake-bites -ತನ A sheepish disposition ... ...

A flock of sheep -ಮರಿ. A lamb -ಹಟ್ಟಿ A sheepfold

ಕುರಿಚಿ (=ಕುರ್ಚಿ) h n. A chair.

ಕುರಿತು, *see s.* ಕುರಿ 1 q. v

ಕುರು 1 k n A protuberance on the body, a boil 2, smallness.

ಕುರು 2 s n The ancestor of the Pândus and Dhritarâshtra -ಕ್ಷೇತ್ರ. N of the field of battle between the Kurus and Pândus near Delhi. -ವೈರಿ. Bhîma

ಕುರುಗಣೆ (ರು=ಱು) k n The state of being diminished. 2, the serum of the ear, ear-wax

ಕುರುಚು (ರು = ಱು) (= ಕುರಚಿ) k n Smallness, dwarfishness a Small, dwarfish

ಕುರುಜು k n An artificial frame-work used to put idols in, *etc.*

ಕುರುಟಿಕೆ, ಕುರುಟಿಗೆ h n A plant used as medicine for the eyes, *Odina wodier*.

ಕುರುಡ (= ಕುರಡ) k a Blind n A blind man, f ಕುರುಡಿ -ತನ, ಕುರುಡು Blindness. ಕುರುಡು ಬೀಳು To become blind

ಕುರುಂಜಿ = ಕುರಂಜಿ, q. v

ಕುರುಪು (ರು = ಱು) k. n. A mark, sign, a characteristic, acquaintance. -ಇಡು, ಕುರುಪಿಡು To mark, define, to consider

ಕುರುಬ (ರು = ಱು) k. n A shepherd 2, a foolish man, f -ತಿ, -ಗಿತ್ತಿ -ನ ಗಡ್ಡೆ. A perennial creeping plant, *Lepidagathis cristata*. -ತನ The profession of a shepherd foolishness

ಕುರುಂಬ (ರು = ಱು) k. n A caste of mountaineers; f ಕುರುಂಬಿತಿ.

ಕುರುಬೆ k n A tender, young cocoanut

ಕುರುವಕ s n A crimson sort of amaranth. 2, a species of barleria 3, the red cedar

ಕುರುವಿಂದ (= ಕುರಂಜಿ, q v) s n. The fragrant grass *Cyperus rotundus* 2, ...

ಕುರುಹು (ರು=ಱು) (=ಕುರುಪು) k n A sign, mark, *etc*

ಕುರುಳು, ಕುರುಳ್ k n. A curl or lock of hair. 2, a cake of dried cow-dung.

ಕುರೂಪ s *a* Ugly, deformed. *n*. Ugliness. ಕುರೂಪಿ. An ugly person.

ಕುರ್ಚಿ (=ಕುರಿಚಿ) h. *n*. A chair.

ಕುರ್ಚಿಗೆ k. *n*. A weeding hook

ಕುಲ s *n*. A race, family, tribe caste. 2, a crowd, herd troop, multitude 3, a noble family. 4, a house. -ಕ. =-ಜ. -ಕರ್ಣಿ. A village clerk or accountant. -ಕ್ಷಯ. Extinction of a race or caste. -ಕಾಯಕ. =-ವೃತ್ತಿ. -ಗೆಡಕ. A spoiler of caste, one whose caste is spoiled, *also* -ಗೇಡಿ, a bad rude fellow -ಗೆಡು Caste to be spoiled. -ಗೇಡಿತನ. The act of spoiling caste; an act disgraceful to one's family. -ಗೋತ್ರ. Caste and family. -ಜ Well-born, ancestral. -ದೇವತೆ, -ದೈವ. The tutelar deity of a caste or family. -ಧರ್ಮ, ಕುಲಾಚಾರ Duty peculiar to a race or caste -ನಾರಿ, -ಸ್ತ್ರೀ. A woman of a good family. -ಪುತ್ರ A son of a noble family -ಭ್ರಷ್ಟ. An outcast -ವಿಹೀನ, -ಹೀನ. A man of low birth. -ವೃತ್ತಿ. Caste profession. -ಶ್ರೇಷ್ಠ. Eminent by birth -ಸಂಬಂಧ Family connection -ಸ್ಥ. Belonging to a good family, *f*. -ಸ್ಥೆ ಕುಲಾಚಾರ. The established practices of caste. ಕುಲೋದ್ಧಾರಕ. A man who elevates a race or family.

ಕುಲಕು =ಕುಲುಕು, *q v*

ಕುಲಾಯಿ, ಕುಲಾಯಿ, ಕುಲಾವಿ h *n*. A little cap

ಕುಲಾಯಿಸು h *v. t.* To open, expand, to increase, *also* ಖುಲಾಯಿಸು

ಕುಲಾಲ s. *n* A potter; *f*. ಕುಲಾಲಿ. -ಚಕ್ರ. A potter's wheel.

ಕುಲಾಸ =ಖುಲಾಸ, *q v.*

ಕುಲಿಕು. =ಕುಲುಕು, *q v.*

ಕುಲಿಮೆ. =ಕುಲುಮೆ. *q. v.*

ಕುಲೀನ s. *a*. Of high descent well-born.

ಕುಲುಕು k *v. i* To shake, *as* a vessel, body or voice. *n* Shaking, a shake, trotting ಕುಲುಕಿಸು. To cause to shake; to agitate. -ಗಾತಿ. A coquette. ಕುಲುಕೋಟ Trottings, trot.

ಕುಲುಮೆ, ಕುಲ್ಮೆ k *n*. A fire-pit or furnace.

ಕುಲ್ h *n* A male buffalo.

ಕುಲ್ಮಾಷ s. *n* Sour gruel 2, a sort of phaseolus. 3, a species of dolichos, *Dolichos biflorus*

ಕುಲ್ಯ s. *n*. A canal. 2, a ditch; a dyke. 3, a river. 4, a bad habit. *a*. Of a good family, well-born

ಕುಲ್ಲಾ h. *a*. Expanded, opened, *also* ಖುಲ್ಲಾ.

ಕುಲ್ಲು h. *n* The whole.

ಕುವರ 1. *tb of* ಕುಮಾರ, *q v.*

ಕುವರ 2. k. *n*. A potter. 2, a veil.

ಕುವಲಯ s. *n*. Any water-lily.

ಕುವಾಕ್, ಕುವಾಚ್ s. *n*. Speaking ill of any one.

ಕುವಿಂದ, -ಕ s. *n*. A weaver.

ಕುವೇರ (=ಕುಬೇರ) s. *n*. The god of wealth and regent of the north.

ಕುವ್ವೆ. =ಕೂಪೆ, *q v.*

ಕುಶ s. *n* The sacrificial grass 2, a son of Râmacandra. ಕುಶಾಗ್ರ. Point of kuśa-grass. ಕುಶಾಗ್ರಬುದ್ಧಿ, -ಮತಿ. Acumen, shrewd, intelligent

ಕುಶಲ s. *a*. Right, proper; prosperous, clever, expert *n* Cleverness. 2, well-being. 3, virtue -ಗಾರ A clever man, *f* -ಗಾತಿ, ಕುಶಲಿ -ತನ, -ತೆ Cleverness, ability -ಪ್ರಶ್ನೆ. A friendly enquiry after one's welfare

ಕುಶಾಲು h. *n* Ease; fun, frolic, pleasure. -ಫಿರಂಗಿ. Salute firing. -ಮಾಡು. To rejoice

ಕುಶಿ, ಕುಷಿ h *n* Pleasure; will

ಕುಶಿನಿ f *n* Kitchen -ಗಾರ A cook

ಕುಷ್ಕಿ h *n*. Dry land not artificially irrigated.

ಕುಷ್ಠ s. *n*. Leprosy, *also* -ರೋಗ.

ಕುಸಕು. = ಕುಸುಕು, *q v*

ಕುಸಕುಸು k *n*. Whispering -ಮಾತಾಡು, ಕುಸುಗುಟ್ಟು. To whisper

ಕುಸಂಧಿ s. *n* An improper union of letters 2, an unlucky conjunction of stars 3, a narrow space.

ಕುಸಿ k. *v. i*. To bend, stoop, to sink, give way, to tumble *n* Bending, sinking 2, the peg or pin of a door -ಬೀಳು To give way as a wall, *etc*.

ಕುಸುಕು k *v t*. To strike. 2, (= ಕುಕ್ಕು) to wash by slightly beating

ಕುಸುಬು k *v t*. To wash (= ಒಗಿ) clothes by beating them on a stone

ಕುಸುಮ s. *n* A flower. -ಷಟ್ಪದಿ N of a metre.

ಕುಸುಂಬರಿ (= ಕೋಸಂಬರಿ) f *n* Raw fruits, *etc* preserved as a seasoning

ಕುಸುಂಬೆ (*tb of* ಕುಸುಂಭ) *n*. Dried flowers of safflower 2, the red dye prepared from them -ದುಪ್ಪಟಿ A deep red cloth -ಬಣ್ಣ. A deep red colour

ಕುಸುಂಭ (= ಕುಸುಂಬೆ) s. *n* The safflower *Carthamus tinctorius* 2, a student's water-pot.

ಕುಸುರಿ, ಕುಸುರು k. *n* The pulp or soft part of some vegetables and fruits 2, the sticky filament of flowers. -ಗಾಯಿ. A very young unripe fruit

ಕುಸ್ತಿ h. *n*. Wrestling. -ಬಿಡು. To set on to wrestle. -ಯಾಡು, -ಹಿಡಿ To wrestle

ಕುಸ್ತುಂಬರಿ, ಕುಸ್ತುಂಬರು = ಕೊತ್ತುಂಬರಿ, *q. v*

ಕುಹಕ (= ಕುಯುಕ) s. *n* A cheat, rogue, a juggler, (*f* ಕುಹಕಿ). deception, legerdemain

ಕುಳ 1. (= ಕುಲ, *q v*) s *n*. Family, race 2, a tenant 3, a tax-payer. -ವಾಡಿ An inferior village-servant -ವಾಡಿಕೆ, -ವಾಡಿತನ The business of a kulavâdi. -ವಾರು. A settlement made with the farmers individually.

ಕುಳ 2 (ಳ = ೞ) k *n* Confusion 2, a plough-[illegible]

ಕುಳಿ 1 k *n*. *An affix for the formation of nouns, as*. ಬಡ-, ಮರು-, *etc*

ಕುಳಿ 2 (ಳಿ = ೞಿ) k. *n* A hollow, a hole; a pit *v t* To dig, make a hole

ಕುಳಿತು (*P p of* ಕುಳಿರು) k Seated, sat down -ಕೊಳ್ಳು. To sit down

ಕುಳಿರು 1. (= ಕುಂತ್ರು, ಕುಳ್ಳಿರು, ಕೂಡ್ರು) k *v i* To sit down, squat, to stoop

ಕುಳಿರು 2 k *n* Coolness, coldness, cold, snow. ಕುಳಿರ್ಗಾಳಿ. A cool wind. ಕುಳಿರ್ವೆಟ್ಟು The snow-mountain Himâlaya

ಕುಳ್ಳ k. *n*. A dwarf, *f*. ಕುಳ್ಳಿ

ಕುಳ್ತು = ಕುಳಿತು *q v*.

ಕುಳ್ಳಿರು (= ಕುಳಿರು) k *v i* To sit down ಕುಳ್ಳಿರಿಸು To cause to sit down

ಕುಳ್ಳು k. *n* A cake of dried cow-dung. 2, shortness -ತಾಳಿ A pile of kullu for cooking -ಬಾನ A stack of kullu

ಕೂರೆಣೆ, ಕೂಗಟೆ, ಕೂಗಣೆ k *n*. Ear-wax.

ಕೂಗು k. *v i* To cry aloud, to cry out (*also* -ಹಾಕು, ಕೂಗಾಡು, ಕೂಗಿಡು). *n*. A cry, clamour, shout. ಕೂಗಳತೆ. The distance at which a loud cry can be heard -ವಿಕೆ. Crying aloud.

ಕೂಚು 1 k *n* A post in a wall for the support of beams 2, smallness -ಗಿಡ A small stunted tree

ಕೂಚು 2. h. *n* March or decampment of troops or people

ಕೂಜ (= ಹೂಜೆ) h. *n*. An earthen water-jug; a goglet.

ಕೂಟ 1. (*fr* ಕೂಡು) k *n* A junction, union, an assembly, crowd, a quantity, company -ಕೂಡು To assemble.

ಕೂಟ 2. s. *n*. The summit of a mountain, any prominence 2, a plot, fraud, conspiracy. 3, an astrological term.

ಕೂಟಸ್ಥ s. *n*. The male representative of a family 2, eternally the same, *as* space, soul, *etc*.

ಕೂಡ, ಕೂಡಾ (*inf. of* ಕೂಡು) k. *prep*. Together with, along with; with 2, also likewise -[illegible]. To [illegible]

ಕೂಡಲು, ಕೂಡ್ಲು k n A junction, confluence. ಕೂಡಲೆ, ಕೂಡ್ಲೆ. At the very moment, forthwith

ಕೂಡಿಕೆ k. n Joining, meeting. 2, marrying a widow -ಗಂಡ. A man who has married a widow -ಹೆಂಡತಿ A remarried widow.

ಕೂಡಿಸು k. v. t To join, to mix, to add, to amass. -ವಿಕೆ. Adding, addition

ಕೂಡು k v i. To join, unite; to meet, come together, to be possible; to take place. 2, to be fit v. t To join, add, *as* numbers. ಕೂಡ, *inf.* ಕೂಡ ಬೀಳು To be accumulated. -ಹಾಕು. To heap up. ಕೂಡಿ ಬರು. To come together, to prosper, *as* a business, to assemble and come to a place, to astrologically agree, *as* the horoscopes.

ಕೂಡೆ k *prep* With, together with; at the same time, further, also ~ಕೂಡೆ Mutually, all together.

ಕೂತ್ರು (=ಕುಳ್ಳಿರು) k v i To sit down. ಕೂತ್ರಿಸು. To cause to sit down

ಕೂಡ್ಲೆ =ಕೂಡಲೆ, *q. v.*

ಕೂತು k *P. p of* ಕುಳಿರು, *q v*

ಕೂದಲು k n Hair of the head or bòdy.

ಕೂನು k v. i To bend, stoop. n A hump 2, a mark, sign. ಕೂನ. A hump-backed man, *f.* ಕೂನಿ

ಕೂಪ s. n A hole, a well. 2, a mast

ಕೂರಿಗೆ (ರಿ=ಱಿ) k. n A sowing machine

ಕೂರು 1 k. n Sharpness, acuteness, *also* ಕೂರಿಕೆ. ಕೂರಾಳು. A brave soldier. ಕೂರಪ. A sharp, acute or brave man.

ಕೂರು 2. k. n. A tenon

ಕೂರು 3 k v. i. To mind, be attached to, to love. ಕೂರ್ಪ, ಕೂರ್ಪವನು A lover; beloved man, a husband. ಕೂರ್ಪು Love

ಕೂರು 4. k. v. i To sit down.

ಕೂರೆ (ರೆ=ಱೆ) k. n A kind of cloth-louse.

ಕೂರ್ಚ s. n. A bunch, bundle 2, the space between the eyebrows. 3, the beard, mustaches. -ಕ, ಕೂರ್ಚಿಕೆ A brush.

ಕೂರ್ಪಾಸ =ಕುಪ್ಪಸ, *q. v.*

ಕೂರ್ಮ s. n. A tortoise, turtle 2, the second incarnation of Vishnu, *also* ಕೂರ್ಮಾವತಾರ. -ಪುರಾಣ The purâna of the said incarnation ಕೂರ್ಮಾಸನ. A stool in the form of a tortoise back.

ಕೂರ್ಮೆ a. k. n. Attachment, love.

ಕೂಲಂಕಷ, ಕೂಲಂಕುಷ s. n The whole, from first to last

ಕೂಲಿ k n. Hire, wages, esp. daily cooly 2, a day-labourer, a cooly -ಕೆಲಸ Daily labour -ಮಾಡು, -ಕೆಲಸ ಮಾಡು. To work as a day-labourer. -ಕಾರ -ಯವ, -ಯಾಳು A cooly, *f.* -ಕಾರ್ತಿ, -ಯವಳು, -ಯಾಕೆ.

ಕೂಲು 1 k. v. i. To fall down; to be overturned, ruined. ಕೂಲಿಸು To cause to fall

ಕೂಲು 2. k n. A tenon 2, a sloping flight of stairs leading down to the water of a tank

ಕೂವ (*tb of* ಕೂಪ) n. A mast, *also* -ಕಂಬ

ಕೂವೆ (=ಕುವ್ವೆ) k n The East-Indian arrowroot, *Curcuma angustifolia.*

ಕೂಷ್ಮಾಂಡ s n. The pumpkin gourd.

ಕೂಸು k n. An infant, babe. ಕೂಸಾಟ Children's play ಕೂಸಾಡು. To play like children. ಕೂಸಾಡಿಸು. To amuse a child. -ತನ. Childhood. ಕೂಸಾಳು. A weak, useless person

ಕೂಳ (ಳ=ೞ) k. n A vulgar, rude, stupid, vile man, *f.* ಕೂಳಿ. *a.* Vulgar, *etc.* -ತನ. Rudeness, meanness.

ಕೂಳಿ, ಕೂಳೆ 1 k n. A basket for fishing.

ಕೂಳು (ಳು=ೞು) (*tb. of* ಕೂರು) n Boiled rice, food -ಬಕ್ಕ, -ಬೊಕ್ಕ, ಕೂಳ್ಬಣಿಗ A glutton. -ಸೀರೆ. Food and clothing.

ಕೂಳೆ 2. k. n The stump of jôla, stubble in general.

ಕೃಚ್ಛ್ರ s. n. Distress. 2, difficulty. 3

pain *a.* Bad, miserable. -ಮೂತ್ರಪು ರೀಷತ್ವ Difficulty in the evacuations

ಕೃತ s. *a* Done, made, wrought *n* Deed, action, accomplishment. 2, the first of the four yugas of the world. 3, a kind action, benefit -ಕ. Made, artificial, simulated, false; hypocrisy -ಕೃತ್ಯ Contented, satisfied. -ಘ್ನ Ungrateful. -ಘ್ನತೆ. Ingratitude -ಜ್ಞ Grateful. -ಜ್ಞತೆ, -ಜ್ಞತ್ವ. Gratitude. -ಯುಗ = ಕೃತ No 2. -ವರ್ಮ, -ಹಸ್ತ Dexterous, skilful ಕೃತಾಕೃತ Done and not done. ಕೃತಾರ್ಥ. Successful; satisfied; clever.

ಕೃತಿ s *n*. Doing, action; a literary work, poem. -ಪತಿ An author, a poet

ಕೃತ್ತಿ s *n*. Hide, skin. 2, the birch tree

ಕೃತ್ತಿಕೆ s *n* The third lunar mansion containing six stars called the *Pleiades*

ಕೃತ್ಯ s *a* To be done, proper *n* Action, act, deed; business, duty.

ಕೃತ್ಯೆ s *n* An act, deed 2, a female deity.

ಕೃತ್ರಿಮ s. *a* Artificial 2 false deceitful. *n*. Guile, deceit 2, bewitchment, witchcraft. ಕೃತ್ರಿಮಿ A deceitful person

ಕೃದಂತ s. *n* A word ending with a ಕೃತ್ affix.

ಕೃಪಣ s. *n* Pitiable, miserable, poor. 2, avaricious -ತನ, -ತ್ವ Wretchedness; avarice.

ಕೃಪಾ s. *n*. Pity, tenderness, compassion, mercifulness, kindness; *also* ಕೃಪೆ -ಕಟಾಕ್ಷ, -ದೃಷ್ಟಿ. A kind look, the eye of favour. -ನಿಧಿ, -ಸಾಗರ An ocean of tenderness. -ಳು Compassionate, merciful. -ಹೀನ Pitiless.

ಕೃಮಿ (= ಕ್ರಿಮಿ) s *n* A worm, insect 2, a spider. -ಘ್ನ. A vermifuge, *Erycibe paniculata*

ಕೃಶ s *a*. Lean, emaciated, thin, slender

ಕೃಷಿ s *n*. Agriculture, husbandry -ಕ, ಕೃಷೀವಲ A husbandman

ಕೃಷ್ಟ *tb of* ಕೃಷ್ಣ, *q v*

ಕೃಷ್ಣ (= ಕೃಷ್ಟ, ಕ್ರಿಷ್ಣ) s. *a* Black; wicked. *n* The dark half of the lunar month 2, one of the incarnations of Vishnu. 3, a crow. 4, the black antelope. 5, Indra 6, a river so called. -ಕರ್ಮ. An evil deed, criminal. -ಜಯಂತಿ. Krishna's birthday -ಪಕ್ಷ. = ಕೃಷ್ಣ *n*. No. 1. -ಪಾಡ್ಯ. The first day of the moon's wane -ಪಕ್ತ Black-faced. -ಸನ್ನಿ A disease in which the tongue turns black -ಸರ್ಪ. The black cobra -ಹೃದಯ A wicked disposition ಕೃಷ್ಣಾಗರು A black variety of *Agallochum* or aloe wood ಕೃಷ್ಣಾಜಿನ. The skin of the black antelope ಕೃಷ್ಣಾವತಾರ An incarnation of Krishna.

ಕೆ (= ಅಕೆ, ಅಕ್ಕೆ, ಅಗೆ, ಇಕೆ, ಇಕ್ಕೆ, *etc*) k *A suffix to form the dative sing*, *as* ವನಕೆ, ಮರಕ್ಕೆ, *etc* 2 *a nominal or pronominal suffix, as* ಬಾಳಿಕೆ, ಮತಿಕೆ, ಹರಿಕೆ, ಅಕೆ, ಈಕೆ, *etc*

ಕೆಕ್ಕರಬಳ್ಳಿ k *n* The melon vine ಕೆಕ್ಕರಿಕೆ. The musk-melon.

ಕೆಕ್ಕಸ k *n* Insult, insulting language

ಕೆಕ್ಕಳಿಸು k *v i* To be excited from fear

ಕೆಂ, ಕೆಂಜ (= ಕೆಙ್ ಕೆನ್, ಕೆಮ್) k *n* Redness. *a* Red -ಕಣ್ Red or fiery eye. -ಕಿಡಿ A red spark. -ಗುಡಿ The red sprout coral -ಗೆಂಡ. A shining live coal.

ಕೆಚ್ಚನೆ (= ಕೆಂ, *q v*) k. *ad*. Redly. *n*. Redness.

ಕೆಚ್ಚಲ, ಕೆಚ್ಚಲು k *n* The udder of beasts.

ಕೆಚ್ಚು 1. k. *v t* To join the ends of two threads by twisting them with the fingers. *n*. The knot formed by twisting

ಕೆಚ್ಚು 2 k. *n*. Core, the heart of a tree, essence, strength 2, pride. -ಗಟ್ಟು. To become strong. ಕೆಚ್ಚೊಳಗಾಗಿ. Pieces [illegible]

ಕೆಂ, ಕೆಞ್ಚ್ k n Redness; *also* -ಚಗೆ, -ಚನೆ, -ಚು. ಕೆಂಚ. A red or brown man; *f.* ಕೆಂಚಿ -ಜಗ -ಜಗೆ A kind of red ant

ಕೆಟ್ಟ (*past rel part. of* ಕೆಡು) k *a* Wicked, bad, foul, rotten 2, mischievous, injurious 3, abominable 4, fierce. -ತನ. A bad, wicked disposition

ಕೆಟ್ಟು. *P p. of* ಕೆಡು, *q v*

ಕೆಡಕ k *n.* A mischief-maker, a bad. wicked, mean man; *f* ಕೆಡಕಿ -ತನ. A bad, depraved nature or conduct.

ಕೆಡಕು k *n* Corruption, ruin, foulness, evil. -ತನ = ಕೆಡಕತನ

ಕೆಡಪು (= ಕೆಡವು, ಕೆಡಹು) k *v t* To make fall down, to fell; to throw to the ground, to pull down.

ಕೆಡವು = ಕೆಡಪು. *q. v* 2, to pierce through, *as* a hole

ಕೆಡಹು = ಕೆಡಪು, *q. v.*

ಕೆಡಿಸು (*fr* ಕೆಡು) k *v t* To destroy, ruin, to spoil; to deflower; to extinguish, *as* a lamp. *Cpds* ಎಡೆ-, ಕಾಲ್-, ಗತಿ-, ನಡೆ-, *etc.*

ಕೆಡು k. *v. i* To be ruined, spoiled to become foul, bad, vicious, vile, low, to be extinguished. *P. p.* ಕೆಟ್ಟು. *Cpds* ಗತಿ-, ದೆಸೆ-, ನೆಲೆ-, ಮತಿ-, *etc* ಕೆಟ್ಟುಹೋಗು = ಕೆಡು. -ಕು. = ಕೆಡಕು, *q v* -ವಿಕೆ, -ಹ. Ruin, destruction.

ಕೆಡೆ a. k *v i* To fall down, drop, sink *v. t* To let fall *n.* The act of dropping (words) thoughtlessly. -ನುಡಿ To speak thoughtlessly, a thought less word or speech.

ಕೆಣಕು k. *v. t.* To irritate or provoke ಕೆಣಕಾಟ. Provocation. ಕೆಣಕಿಸು. To cause provocation

ಕೆಂಡ k. *n.* A live coal. -ಗಣ್ಣು. A fiery or red eye -ರೊಟ್ಟಿ. Bread baked on coals. -ಸಂಪಿಗೆ. A red sort of sampigĕ -ಸೇವೆ. The ceremony of walking over burning coals

ಕೆತ್ತನೆ (= ಕೆತ್ತಿಕೆ, ಕೆತ್ತಿಗೆ) k *n* The act of setting, *as* precious stones, *etc*, engraving

ಕೆತ್ತು k *v t* To chisel, carve, engrave, cut, to scrape, to chip, *as* grass, plank, *etc*, to make thin. 2, to enclose, set *as* precious stones ಕೆತ್ತಿಸು. To cause to carve, engrave. ಕೆತ್ತಿಕೆ, ಕೆತ್ತಿಗೆ. The act of setting, engraving, carving, *etc* ಕೆತ್ತಿಗೆ ಸರಪಣಿ. A chain set with precious stones.

ಕೆತ್ತೆ k. *n* A chip, paring

ಕೆದಕು k *v. t.* To stir, scratch

ಕೆದರು (ರು = ಱು) k. *v i.* To scatter, be scattered about, to disperse, to swing about; to scratch, *as* fowls, dogs, *etc.*

ಕೆನ್ (= ಕೆಂ, *q v*) Red. *Cpds.* -ದಾವರೆ, -ದಾಳೆ, -ನಾಲಿಗೆ, -ನೀರು, -ನೆತ್ತರು, -ನೆಯ್ದಿಲೆ, -ನೆಲ, *etc.*

ಕೆನೆ k. *n.* The cream of milk 2, beauty. -ಕಟ್ಟು Cream to set. -ಗಂಜಿ. The scum of boiled rice -ಮೊಸರು. Creamy curds.

ಕೆಂದು (= ಕೆನ್) k *n* Redness.

ಕೆನ್ನೆ k *n* The upper cheek.

ಕೆಮ್ (= ಕೆನ್ *etc, q. v.*) k *a* Red. *Cpds* -ಬಟ್ಟೆ, -ಬಣ್ಣ, -ಬೆಳಗು, -ಮಣ್ಣು, -ಮ್ಮೋರೆ, *etc.*

ಕೆಂಪಗೆ k *a.* Red. *ad* Redly.

ಕೆಂಪು k. *n* Redness, red colour; a ruby; *also* -ಕಲ್ಲು -ಕುಂಟಾಲಗಿಡ A medicinal shrub, *Gomphia angustifolia* -ಗೋರಟೆ. The red species of Barleria -ಜಂಬುನೇರಲು. The fruit of the tree *Eugenia malaccensis* -ನೆಲಗುಂಬಳ. A water-plant, *Polygonum glabrum.* -ಬಂಗಡಬಳ್ಳಿ. The creeping plant, *Ipomaea biloba.* -ಬಸಳೆ The vegetable *Basella rubra* -ಮಂದಾರ. The red flower of *Bauhinia variegata* -ಲಾವಗ The rock bush-quail, *Perdicula argoondah* -ಹುಲಿಗಿಡ. A small shrub, *Phyllanthus rhamnoides.*

ಕೆಂಬಾರ k. *n* The redness of evening

ಕೆಮ್ಮು k *n* A cough, coughing, *also* ಕೆಮ್ಮಲು. *v. i.* To cough ಕೆಮ್ಮಿಸು. To cause to cough.

ಕೆಯ್ = ಕೈ, *q v. and its cpds* -ಕೆ, -ತೆ, -ಮೆ. An act, performance; deceit, fraud.
ಕೆಯ್ದು. = ಕೈದು -ಕಾರ A soldier
ಕೆಯಿ. (= ಕೈ, *q v*) k *n* A field
ಕೆರ 1. ಕೆರವು k *n*. A leather sandal, a shoe
ಕೆರ 2 = ಕೆರದು. *P p of* ಕೆರೆ *in* ಕೆರಕೊಳ್ಳು
ಕೆರಕು k *n*. Roughness (*as* of stone) 2, scab
ಕೆರಂಟು a k *v i* To scratch
ಕೆರಸೆ (= ಗೆರಸೆ) k *n* A flat bamboo basket.
ಕೆರಳು k *v i* To cry, shout. 2, to become angry. 3, to increase, *as* pain, *etc*, to spread, *as* a sore.
ಕೆರೆ 1 k *v t* To scratch, scrape 2, to shave
ಕೆರೆ 2 (ರೆ = ಱೆ) k. *n* A tank. -ಕಟ್ಟೆ The bank of a tank -ಯೊಡಲು The inner part of a tank. -ಕಾಲುವೆ. The channel of a tank. -ತೂಬು The sluice of a tank. -ಹಾವು. A water snake
ಕೆಲ 1 a. k *n*. Side, vicinity, the right or left side. -ಕೆಲ *rep*. Both sides -ಸಾಗು (-ಆಗು). To go aside -ಸಾರು To get out of the way, retire
ಕೆಲ 2. k *a*. Some, several, a few -ಬರು, -ವರು Some or a few persons -ವು, -ಉು Some or a few things
ಕೆಲಸ k *n* Work; occupation, business; affair, employment, act; use -ಕ್ಕೆ ಬರು, -ಕ್ಕೆ ಬೀಳು To come to work, to be serviceable -ಗಳ್ಳ. A lazy man; *f*. -ಗಳ್ಳತಿ, -ಗಳ್ಳೆ -ತಕ್ಕೊಳ್ಳು To exact work. -ಹೇಳು To order a work
ಕೆಲಸಿ k *n* A barber and hair-dresser; *also* -ಗ. 2, a person who works.
ಕೆಲೆ k. *v i*. To cry for joy. 2, to cry out abusively -ತ Abusive vociferation
ಕೆಲ್ಲೆ k. *n* A shiver, splinter
ಕೆಸರು (ರು = ಱು) k *n* Wet soil, mud, mire. -ಗಲ್ಲು A foundation stone ಕೆಸರಿಗೆ. [illegible]

ಕೆಸವು k *n*. A mushroom
ಕೆಸು k *n*. A stemless plant with large leaves and eatable tubers, the *Cocco, Arum colocasia*.
ಕೆಳ (= ಕೆಳಗು, *q. v*) k. *a* Lower -ಗಡೆ, -ತಟ್ಟು The lower side, downwards, beneath -ತನಕ To the bottom -ತುಟಿ The lower lip. -ದವಡೆ. The molars of the lower jaw -ಭಾಗ The lower part -ಹೊಟ್ಟೆ. The abdomen pelvis
ಕೆಳಗು, ಕೆಳಗೆ (= ಕೆಳ) k *n* The state of being under, below, down or inferior; the bottom. *ad* Under, down *Decl*. ಕೆಳಗಿನಿಂದ, ಕೆಳಕ್ಕೆ, ಕೆಳಗಿನ, *etc*. ಕೆಳಗಿಡು To lay down ಕೆಳಗಿಳಿ To descend. -ಬೀಳು. To fall to the ground -ಮೇಲು ಮಾಡು To make the lower side upper; to turn -ಮೇಲೆ Topsyturvy
ಕೆಳದಿ (= ಗೆಳತಿ) k *n*. A female companion
ಕೆಳರ್ (ಕೆರಳು) a k *v. i* To gape, to open, expand, to blossom 2 to cry out, to dispute, wrangle.
ಕೆಳೆ (= ಗೆಳೆ) a. k *n*. Union, friendship, a companion, friend -ಯ A male companion -ತನ. Companionship
ಕೇಕರ s. *a* Squint-eyed. *n* A leer
ಕೇಕರಿಸು k. *v i*. To hawk in spitting. ಕೇಕರಿಕೆ. Hawking in spitting
ಕೇಕು, ಕೇಗು k *v i*. To cry as a peacock *n*. The cry of a peacock
ಕೇಡಿ k. *n* One who ruins or is ruined; *also* -ಗ, ಕೇಡುಗ. *Cpds*. ಕುಲ-, ತಿಳಿ-, ಬಾಯ್-, ಬುದ್ಧಿ-, ಮತಿ-, ವಿಚಾರ-, ವ್ರತ-, *etc*. -ಗತನ, -ತನ Destructiveness, impairedness.
ಕೇಡು k. *n*. Ruin, destruction; mischief, disaster; loss -ಗಾಲ A disastrous period. ಕೇಡಾಳಿ A mischief-maker.
ಕೇಣಿ k. *n*. Envy, grudge, anger 2, deliberation. -ಕಾರ A grudger -ಸರ. Envy, stubbornness
ಕೇತಕಿ s *n* The fragrant screw-pine, *Pandanus odoratissimus*.
ಕೇತನ s. *n*. Summons, invitation, *also* ಕೇತ. 2, business 3, a place. 4, [illegible]

ಕೇತು s n A ray of light; brightness. 2, a comet. 3, the descending node 4, a flag

ಕೇದಗೆ, ಕೇದಿಗೆ. *tb of* ಕೇತಕಿ, *q v*

ಕೇದಾರ s. n A field; a park 2, a temple 3, the body. -ಗೌಳ. N. of a tune

ಕೇಂದ್ರ s n. The centre of a circle 2, a planet's distance from the first point of its orbit

ಕೇಪಲ k. n. A shrub with red or white flowers, *Ixora coccinea.*

ಕೇಪು f. n A periodical supply of merchandise.

ಕೇರ m. n. Rubbish, refuse, *etc.* *a* Inferior. -ಮಾವು An inferior mango.

ಕೇರಲ, ಕೇರಳ s n. The Malabar country.

ಕೇರಿ k n. A street, lane.

ಕೇರು 1 k n. The tree *Semecarpus anacardium*, which produces the marking nut. -ಬೀಜ The marking-nut.

ಕೇರು 2 (ರು=ಱು) k v i To winnow

ಕೇರೆ k. n The rat-snake, *Ptyas mucosus*, *also* -ಹಾವು

ಕೇಲು k n A large earthen water-jar

ಕೇವಲ s. a. Alone, only, mere 2, entire, whole, all 3, pure, unmingled.

ಕೇಶ s n The hair of the head. -ಮಾರ್ಜನಿ A comb ಕೇಶಿ, ಕೇಶಿಕ Having much hair

ಕೇಶವ s. n. Krishna, Vishnu. 2, N of the author of the Śabdamanidarpana, *also* ಕೇಶಿರಾಜ

ಕೇಸರ s n The filament of flowers. 2, the plant *Mimusops elengi* 3, saffron. 4, the mane of a horse or lion

ಕೇಸರ-ಈ-ಹಿಂದ್ h. n. The empress of Hindusthân, title of Queen Victoria

ಕೇಸರಿ s. a. Having a mane. 2, saffron coloured n. A lion. 2, a horse. -ಭತ್ತ. A kind of paddy -ಭಾತು. Rice seasoned with saffron, sugar, *etc*

ಕೇಸು a. k. n Redness. ಕೇಸಕ್ಕಿ A red kind of rice. ಕೇಸುರಿ A red flame. ಕೇಸುಳ್ಳಿ. An onion.

ಕೇಳಿ (ಳಿ=ೞಿ) a k n. A line, series; a group

ಕೇಳು k v. i To hear, to listen to, to heed, mind v. t To hear, mind 2, to ask, beg, to demand *P p* ಕೇಳಿ, ಕೇಳ್ದು. -ವಿಕೆ, ಕೇಳಿಕೆ. Hearing; asking, hearsay. ಕೇಳಿಸು. To cause to hear or listen, to be heard, to hear, to sound.

ಕೈ (=ಕೆಯ್) k. n. The hand (ಹಸ್ತ) 2, an elephant's trunk 3, a branch, spathe 4, a staff, a handle, a key 5, means, instrumentality. 6, handiness ಕೈಯ *is used for the genitive or dative*, ಕೈಯಿಂದ *instrumental, and* ಕೈಯಲ್ಲಿ, *locative or dative, as* ನನ್ನ ಕೈಯ ಕೆಳಗೆ, under me, ಅವನ ಕೈಯ ಹೇಳು, tell him, ಅವನ ಕೈಯಿಂದಾಯಿತು, it was done by him, ಅವನ ಕೈಯಲ್ಲಿ ಹೇಳಿದೆ, I told him; ನಿನ್ನ ಕೈಯಲ್ಲಿ ಏನದೆ what have you got? *etc.* -ಕಟ್ಟು. A kind of ornamental bracelet. -ಕರಣ A medical treatment. -ಕಷ್ಟ, -ಕೆಲಸ. Handicraft -ಕಾಗದ. A note of hand, a bond -ಕಾಲು. Hands and feet -ಕಾಲು ಕಟ್ಟಿಕೊಳ್ಳು To make obeisance -ಕಾಲು ಬೀಳು. To fall to one's feet. -ಕೂಲಿ Working as a day-labourer, wages for such work -ಕೂಲಿಗಾರ A day-labourer -ಕೂಸು. A child in arms -ಕೆಳಗೆ Under one's control or authority. -ಕೊಡಲಿ A small axe. -ಕೊಡು To help, to deceive. -ಕೊಳ್ಳು To seize, to receive, obtain, accept, adopt, to undertake, to mind (ಸ್ವೀಕರಿಸು, ಅಂಗೀಕರಿಸು. *etc*). -ಕೋಲು A walking stick -ಕೆಂಡ್ಳ. Hand-stock -ಗಡ A temporary loan given without bond or interest -ಗಂಟು. A purse of money for one's own use. -ಗತ್ತಿ. A small knife. -ಗಡಕ. A male pilferer, *f* -ಗಡಕಿ. -ಗಾಣಿಕೆ. A present given with the hand. -ಗಾಯು To protect -ಗಾರ A clever man -ಗಾರಿಕೆ The arts of industry, manufacture. -ಗುದ್ದಲಿ A small hoe -ಗುರುತು A person's signature. -ಗೂಡಿಸು. To accomplish. -ಗೂಡಿಬರು, -ಗೂಡು. To be obtained; to succeed. -ಗೆಡು. To lose, be defeated. -ಗೊಡು. To give the hand; to stretch the hand for help or promise. -ಚಪ್ಪರ. A shrine wherein idols are carried about. -ಚಪ್ಪಳಿ, -ಚಪ್ಪಳೆ. Clapping the hands. -ಚಳಕ. Dexterity, sleight of hand. -ಚಳಕು. Cramp in the hand. -ಚಾಚು. To stretch out the hand. -ಚಿಟಿಕೆ, -ಚಿಟುಕು. A snap with the fingers. -ಚೀಟು. A note of hand. -ಚೀಲ. A glove; a small bag. -ಜೋಡಿಸು, -ಮುಗಿ. To join the hands in greeting. -ತಟ್ಟು. To clap the hands; to touch pieces of money in counting; to beckon. -ತಪ್ಪು. A mistake; a slip of the pen; to fall from the hand. -ತಾಳ. A kind of cymbal. -ತಾಳು. An instrument to move the inner latch of a door from out-side. -ತುತ್ತು. A handful of food. -ತೊಡಿಗೆ. Ornaments of the hand. -ದಸ್ತು. A deal of cards for games. -ದುರುಕು. To grasp; to thrust the hand into; seizing. -ದೊಡ್ಡದು ಮಾಡು. To be liberal in giving alms. -ನೀಡು. To stretch out the hand. -ನೀರು. Water poured over the hands of the marrying couple. -ನೆರವು. Help, assistance. -ಪಾವಡ. A handkerchief: *also* -ಪಟ್ಟಿ, -ವಸ್ತ್ರ. -ಪಿಡಿ. A handle; a looking glass; a handbook. -ಬಟ್ಟಲು. A small cup; a scoop. -ಬದಲು. A loan (of money). -ಬರಹ. Handwriting. -ಬಳೆ. A bracelet. -ಬಾಚಿ. A small adze. -ಬಾಳು. A sickle. -ಬಿಡು. To let loose one's hand; to cease to assist; to desert. -ಮಗ್ಗ. A hand-loom. -ಮರೆ. To be confounded or amazed; an attitude in dancing. -ಮಸಕು. Black dirt on the hand; a slow poison. -ಮಾಟ. A hand-gesture. -ಮಾಡು. To make signs with the hand; to rebel; to brandish; to bargain. -ಮಾರು. A fathom; offering of goods for sale at the [illegible]

excessive. -ಮೀರು. To exceed, surpass, go beyond; to get out of one's power. -ಮುಟ್ಟು. To touch with the hand; small utensils. -ಮುರಿ. The hand to break; *fig.* a plain bracelet, *also* -ಮುರಿಗೆ. -ಯಕ್ಷರ (-ಅಕ್ಷರ). Writ, hand-writing; signature. -ಯಾಡಿಸು. To move with the hand; to rub gently; to stroke. -ಯಾರೆ. With full and open hands; with a prompt hand. -ಯಾರೈಕೆ. Nursing with one's own hand, supporting by one's own means. -ಯಾಸೆ (-ಆಸೆ). Bribery; a bribe. -ಯಾಳು (-ಆಳು). An assistant, servant. -ಯೆಣ್ಣೆ. Oil extracted by hand. -ಯೆತ್ತು. To raise the open hand. -ಯೊಡ್ಡು (-ಒಡ್ಡು). To hold out the open hands to receive anything. -ಲಾಗು (-ಆಗು). To be produced by the hand; to be practicable; to be able, useful. -ವಶ. Actual possession. -ವಶವಾಗು. To come into one's power or possession. -ವಾರ. A pair of compasses; praise, eulogy. -ವಾರಿಸು. To praise. -ಬೀಸು. To swing the arms when walking. -ಸನ್ನೆ. A sign made with the hand. -ಸಾಗು. To be possible. -ಸಾಲೆ. A veranda. -ಸೂರೆ. Spoil, plunder. -ಸೆರೆ. Arrest, captivity. -ಸೊಡರು. A small lamp. -ಹಚ್ಚು, -ಹಾಕು. To put the hand to. -ಗೆ ಬರು. To be obtained; to become useful. -ಯಲ್ಲಿ. In the hand, *etc.* -ಯೊಳಗೆ. In or into the power; under the control.

ಕೈ 2. k. *n.* Bitterness.

ಕೈಕೊಳ್ಳು *see s.* ಕೈ.

ಕೈಂಕರ್ಯ (*fr.* ಕಿಂಕರ) s. *n.* Service; servitude.

ಕೈದಿ h. *n.* A prisoner.

ಕೈದು 1. k. *n.* A weapon.

ಕೈದು 2. h. *n.* Imprisonment; restraint; arrest. -ಖಾನೆ. A prison. -ಮಾಡು. To put a stop to; to arrest.

ಕೈಫಿಯತು h. *n.* Statement; an affair, [illegible]

ಕೈಲಾಸ s n N. of a mountain in the Himâlaya range, the seat of Kuvêra and paradise of Šiva -ಗತ A lost debt -ವಾಸಿ A deceased worshipper of Šiva.

ಕೈವಲ್ಯ (*fr* ಕೇವಲ) s n Perfect exemption from further transmigration, absorption in the supreme soul 2, pureness.

ಕೊಕ್ಕರಿಬಿಕ್ಕರಿ (= ಕಕ್ಕರಿಬಿಕ್ಕರಿ) k n Crookedness, *as* in writing.

ಕೊಕ್ಕರಿಸು k v i To chuckle, giggle 2, (*fr* ಕುತು) to shrink, shrug *as* from cold, fear, *etc.* 3, to menace, abuse.

ಕೊಕ್ಕರೆ k. n. A crane

ಕೊಕ್ಕು (*fr* ಕೊಂಕು) k. n. The beak or bill

ಕೊಕ್ಕೆ k n Crookedness, a crook, a hook. -ಕೋಲು A hook, a walking stick with a bent handle. -ಮನುಷ್ಯ. A perverse man -ಮೊಳೆ A hooked nail.

ಕೊಗ್ಗ (= ಕೊಂಗ) k n. Crookedness 2, a man with uncouth voice

ಕೊಗ್ಗಿ, ಕೊಗ್ಗಲಿ, ಕೊಗ್ಗೆ k. n. A very common under-shrub, *Tephrosia purpurea*

ಕೊಂಕಣ k n. The Concan country of the western coast -ಸ್ಥ, ಕೊಂಕಣಿ, ಕೊಂಕಣಿಗ. A Concan Brâhmana.

ಕೊಂಕು k. v i To be bent, crooked, curved, deformed; to become perverse, untrue, *etc* n Crookedness, *etc.* -ಕೊರತೆ. Wrongs and defects. -ಗುರುಳು, -ಗೂದಲು Curled hair -ನುಡಿ An altered voice or speech.

ಕೊಂಕುಳು (= ಕಂಕುಳು) k n The armpit.

ಕೊಂಗ = ಕೊಗ್ಗ, *q v* -ಮಂಗ A buffoon -ತನ. Buffoonery.

ಕೊಂಗೆ (= ಕೊಂಬೆ) k n. The branch of a tree

ಕೊಚ್ಚಿ k n Cochin on the Malabar coast.

ಕೊಚ್ಚು 1. k. v. t To sift flour on a small fan. 2, (= ಕೊಯ್ಯು) to cut up, to chop. n. Cuttings, chips. 2, powder, dust. ಕೊಚ್ಚಿಕೆ The act of cutting.

ಕೊಚ್ಚು 2. k. v i To speak much, prattle, brag

ಕೊಚ್ಚೆ k. n. Mud, mire.

ಕೊಜ್ಜ h. n A eunuch

ಕೊಂಚ k n A little, littleness, inferiority -ದವ An insignificant man

ಕೊಟಾರ (= ಕೊಟ್ಟಾರ) k. n. A threshing floor

ಕೊಟಿಗೆ. = ಕೊಟ್ಟಿಗೆ, *q v.*

ಕೊಟ್ಟು 1. (= ಗೊಟ್ಟು) k n A bamboo tube 2, an extremity -ಕೊನೆ. The extreme point.

ಕೊಟ್ಟು 2 f. n A fort. -ಗಾರ A man of a fort

ಕೊಟ್ಟಗೆ (= ಕೊಟಿಗೆ, ಕೊಟ್ಟಿಗೆ. *tb of* ಕುಟಂಕ) n. A stall, out-house, a barn, room, *etc.*

ಕೊಟ್ಟಣ (*fr* ಕುಟ್ಟು) k n. Beating the husk from paddy, *etc.*

ಕೊಟ್ಟಾರ (*tb of* ಕೋಷ್ಠಾಗಾರ) n A threshing floor. ಕೊಟ್ಟಾರಿ. The officer in charge of a granary, a steward

ಕೊಟ್ಟಿ h. a False, counterfeit, forged, vicious, bad -ಕತಬೆ. A forged bond -ನಡತೆ A bad conduct -ರೂಪಾಯಿ A counterfeit rupee.

ಕೊಟ್ಟಿಗೆ. = ಕೊಟ್ಟಗೆ, *q. v*

ಕೊಟ್ಟು 1. *P. p. of* ಕೊಡು.

ಕೊಟ್ಟು 2. k. n. A point, a nipple, a crest, a head-ornament.

ಕೊಟ್ಟೆ k n The stone or kernel of fruit.

ಕೊಠಡಿ h n. A chamber, room

ಕೊಡ (*tb. of* ಕುಟ) n. A pitcher, pot. -ಪಾನ. A kŏda of copper or brass

ಕೊಡಕೆ, ಕೊಡಂಕೆ a. k. n The ear. -ಮುರು An ear-ring.

ಕೊಡಗು k. n The Coorg country -ಕತ್ತಿ. A Coorg-knife, a broad sword ಕೊಡಗ A Coorg man

ಕೊಡಗೆ k n A gift, grant

ಕೊಡಚೆಗಿಡ k. n. A large prickly shrub, *Zizyphus xylopyrus.*

ಕೊಡಚು k *v. t* To remove, rub off, *as* ear-wax or impurities

ಕೊಡತ k *n.* The pain of a sore 2, severe itching. 3, a stick tied to a dog's neck

ಕೊಡತಿ (*f.* ಕುಡು) k. *n.* A wooden hammer

ಕೊಡವು, ಕೊಡವು k *v. t.* To scatter or throw about, to shake

ಕೊಡಲಿ (= ಕೊಡ್ಲಿ *tb of* ಕುಠಾರ) *n.* An axe, hatchet

ಕೊಡಸಿಗೆ k. *n.* The small tree *Clutia collina.* 2, (*tb of* ಕುಟಜಕ) the medicinal tree *Wrightia antidysenterica*

ಕೊಡಿ k *n* Strength, stoutness -ಕಲ್ಲು. Stone-like firmness in one's health

ಕೊಡಿಗೆ. = ಕೊಡಗೆ, *q v.* -ಮಾನ್ಯ Land free of rent

ಕೊಡು (*cf* ಕುಡು) k *v. t* To give, to present bestow, grant. *P.p.* ಕೊಟ್ಟು. ಕೊಡು *is often added to other verbs without altering their meaning, as* ತಳುಹಿಸಿಕೊಡು. = ತಳುಹಿಸು, ವಿಭಾಗಿಸಿಕೊಡು = ವಿಭಾಗಿಸು, *etc. Affixed to infinitive forms of other verbs it denotes* to allow, permit, *as* ಮಾಡಗೊಡು, ಬರಗೊಡು, to allow to do, come, *etc.* ಕೊಡಿಸು. To cause to give ಕೊಡು. -ವಿಕೆ. Giving. -ಕೊಳ್ಳುವದು Giving and receiving.

ಕೊಡೆ k. *n* An umbrella, a parasol *v t* To hollow, scrape scoop. 2, to ache

ಕೊಡ್ಡ k *n.* A stupid man, a clown

ಕೊಡ್ಲಿ = ಕೊಡಲಿ, *q. v*

ಕೊಣ (= ಕೊಳ) k *n.* A pond, tank

ಕೊಣಕ k *n.* A club swung in the hands for exercise.

ಕೊಣಬಿಗೆ k *n* A round wooden dish to knead dough *etc.* in

ಕೊಂಡ 1 k *n* A hill, mountain. -ಮುಸುಡಿ A large black-faced monkey

ಕೊಂಡ 2 *tb. of* ಕುಂಡ, *q. v.* -ಹಬ್ಬ. A feast in honour of Vîrabhadra

ಕೊಂಡಾಡು (*see s* ಕೊಳ್ಳು) k. *v t.* To applaud, praise, glorify

ಕೊಂಡಿ k [illegible]

lock 2, the sting of a scorpion -ಸು To slander, defame

ಕೊಂಡು. *P.p of* ಕೊಳ್ಳು, *q v*

ಕೊಂಡೆ k. *n.* A chaplet of pearls. 2, a tassel.

ಕೊಂಡೆಗ, ಕೊಂಡೆಯ k. *n* Calumny, slander, defamation 2, a slanderer, defamer, *also* -ಗಾರ, *f.* ಕೊಂಡೆಗಿತ್ತಿ

ಕೊತ್ವಾಲ h. *n.* The chief officer of a town police. 2, the overseer of a travellers' bangalow

ಕೊತ್ತಳ k *n* A bulwark, bastion

ಕೊತ್ತಿ k. *n* A cat

ಕೊತ್ತು k. *v t.* To chop, mince *n.* A bunch, cluster 2, a mark for a liquid measure.

ಕೊತ್ತುಂಬರಿ (*tb. of* ಕುಸ್ತುಂಬುರಿ) *n* Coriander seed

ಕೊದಲು k. *v. i* To hesitate in speaking, to stammer, to mutter. *n.* Stammering

ಕೊನರು a k *v i.* To sprout; to arise, extend *n* A shoot, sprout; the film of a lotus

ಕೊನೆ k *v. i* To succeed in an object. *n* An extremity, a point, a top, an end; a branch *Cpds* ಮರದ- ಪಾದದ-, ತುಟಿಯ-, ಬಿಲ್ಲಿನ-, *etc* -ಗಾಣಿಸು To accomplish -ಗಾಣು To be accomplished.

ಕೊಂತ (*tb of* ಕುಂತ) *n.* A spear, lance. -ಕಾರ A spearman.

ಕೊಂದು *P p. of* ಕೊಲ್ಲು, *q v*

ಕೊಂದೆ k. *n* The tree *Cassia fistula*

ಕೊಪ್ಪ, ಕೊಪ್ಪಲ k *n.* A hamlet, village, *affixed to village-names*

ಕೊಪ್ಪರಿಗೆ (*tb of* ಕರ್ಪರ) *n.* A metal boiler

ಕೊಪ್ಪು k *n.* The notched extremity of a bow or horn 2, a woman's knot of hair 3, an ear-ornament.

ಕೊಪ್ಪೆ k *n* The hoed made of a cumbly

ಕೊಬರಿ, ಕೊಬ್ಬರಿ k *n* The kernel of the cocoanut. -ಚಟ್ನಿ A kind of chatney [illegible] ಚ್ನಿ.

Half of a cocoanut kernel. -ಎಣ್ಣೆ. Cocoanut oil.

ಕೊಬ್ಬು k v i To grow fat, thick, *etc*, to be rank, luxuriant, to become proud, insolent. *n*. Fat; luxuriance; pride. ಕೊಬ್ಬಿಗ A proud man.

ಕೊಮೆ k. *v. i*. To begin to burn, *as* fire or anger.

ಕೊಂಪೆ 1 k. *n*. A small bundle or load of thorny twigs. 2, a thorn bush.

ಕೊಂಪೆ 2 k *n*. A small hamlet, *cf* ಕೊಪ್ಪ.

ಕೊಂಬು 1 k. *v t* To seize, take ಕೊಂಬ.= ಕೊಳ್ಳುವ, *q v* ಕೊಂಬೋಣ Taking

ಕೊಂಬು 2. k *n*. A horn of animals; a tusk. 2, ಉ or its embodied form ು. 3, a branch of a tree, *also* ಕೊಂಬೆ

ಕೊಂಬೆ k *n* A branch.

ಕೊಮ್ಮೆ k *n* A corn-bin 2, hog-weed, *Boerhavia procumbens*.

ಕೊಯಿ, ಕೊಯ್ಯು k. *v. t*. To cut; to pluck, *as* fruit, *etc*. *v i* To crop, reap *P ps*. ಕೊಯಿದು, ಕೊಯ್ದು. ಕೊಯಿಕ A cutter. ಕೊಯಿಕತನ, ಕೊಯಿತ. Cutting -ಲು Reaping, plucking ಕೊಯಿಸು. To cause to cut.

ಕೊರ 1 k *n*. *The sound produced by hoarseness*, the pur, *as* of a cat (*see* ಕೊತ್ತಿ). -ಎನ್ನು, -ಗುಟ್ಟು To pur.

ಕೊರ 2. (ರ=ಱ *cf*. ಕೊರೆ 1) k *n* Cutting. -ಕಲ್ಲು. A rugged stone.

ಕೊರಕಲು (ರ=ಱ) k *n*. A cut, channel, the bed of a stream ಕೊರಕು. To bite

ಕೊರಗಣೆ k. *n*. Sorrow.

ಕೊರಗು k *v. i*. To become sapless; to shrivel; to wane, to sorrow. *n* Sorrow. ಕೊರಗಿಸು To cause to be sapless.

ಕೊರಚ (ರ=ಱ) k *n*. A thievish wandering hill-tribe.

ಕೊರಚು, ಕೊರಚಾಡು (ರ=ಱ) k *v. t* To upbraid, revile; to speak much and uselessly ಕೊರಚಾಟ Upbraiding, mocking, reviling, useless talk

ಕೊರಟು k. *n* The state of being stunted or checked in growth. -ಬೀಳು. To get stunted.

ಕೊರಡು k *n* The trunk of a lopped tree, a stump, lop. 2, a clod-crusher.

ಕೊರಡೆ (ರ=ಱ) f. *n* A whip.

ಕೊರತೆ (ರ=ಱ) k *n* Deficiency; want loss; defect; fault -ಪಡು. To feel a want to be poor. -ಬರು, -ಬೀಳು Deficiency or loss to come about

ಕೊರನಾರಿಗಡ್ಡೆ k *n*. A kind of sedge, *Cyperus hexastachyus*.

ಕೊರಪ k. *n* A curry-comb.

ಕೊರಲು. = ಕೊರಳು, *q v*.

ಕೊರಲೆ (ರ=ಱ) k *n* A kind of millet. *Panicum italicum* 2, a kind of ant.

ಕೊರವ (ರ=ಱ) k. *n* A man of a tribe so called who make baskets, mats, *etc*, *f* -ತಿ, *and* ಕೊರವಂಜಿ, who is also a fortune-teller

ಕೊರಳು k *n* The throat, the neck, voice. -ಕಟ್ಟಿಕೊಳ್ಳು To embrace one's neck from love. -ಕೊಯಿಕ A cut-throat -ಪಟ್ಟಿ A collar

ಕೊರಿ, ಕೊರೆ 1 (ರಿ, ರೆ=ಱಿ ಱೆ) k *v. t*. To cut, *as* wood, letters, *etc*., to break, bore, *as* a hole, to excavate, *as* running water the soil, to pierce *as* cold 2, to diminish 3, to whirl, rave. *n* Cutting; a cut off piece -ತ, ಕೊರತ Cutting, piercing of cold.

ಕೊರಿಪಿರಿ f *n*. Annoyance, trouble

ಕೊರೆ 2. (ರೆ=ಱೆ) k *n* Smallness, deficiency defect 2, rest, remainder. 3, a rambler *P. p*. -ದು, ಕೊರದು. -ದಿನ A day of absence. -ಪ್ರಾಣ. The point of death -ಸಂಬಳ. The rest of pay.

ಕೊಲಿಕೆ k. *n* A clasp, hook, *etc*.

ಕೊಲಿಮೆ, ಕೊಲುಮೆ =ಕುಲಿಮೆ k *n*. A forge.

ಕೊಲು = ಕೊಲ್ಲು, *q v*.

ಕೊಲೆ k *n* Killing, murder, slaughter -ಗ, -ಗಡಿಕ, -ಗೆಡುಕ, -ಗಾರ. A murderer. -ಪಾತಕ Manslaughter

ಕೊಲ್ಲಟಿಗ k *n* A pole-dancer, ropedancer, *f* ಕೊಲ್ಲಟಿಗತ್ತಿ.

ಕೊಲ್ಲಣಿಗೆ a. k. *n* Playing, play, performance

ಕೊಲ್ಲಾರ, ಕೊಲ್ಲಾರಿ, ಕೊಲ್ಲಾರು k *n.* A cart drawn by oxen

ಕೊಲ್ಲಿ k *n.* A bend, curve, a nook, a gulf, bay ಕೊಲ್ಲಿ Bend

ಕೊಲ್ಲು k *v. t* To kill, slay, murder *P p* ಕೊಂದು -ವಿಕೆ Killing -ವವ, -ಇ A murderer.

ಕೊಸರು k *v. i* To spread, *as* a sore, to become overbearing, to disentangle one's self forcibly from another's hold *v t* To desire, to demand an article gratis or into the bargain. *n* Anything given to boot in buying.

ಕೊಳ (=ಕೊಣ) k *n* A pond.

ಕೊಳಕು (ಳ=ೞ) k *n* The state of decay, rottenness putridity. ಕೊಳಕ. A dirty man, a decrepit man, *f* ಕೊಳಕಿ. -ಮಂಡಲ, -ಹಾವು The chain viper. -ತನ Filthiness.

ಕೊಳಕೆ, ಕೊಳ್ಕೆ k *n* The third crop of rice.

ಕೊಳಗ 1 k *n* A measure of grain = 4 ballas 2, a large metal vessel

ಕೊಳಗ 2. k *n.* The hoof of a beast.

ಕೊಳಗುಳಿಕೆ, ಕೊಳವಳಿಕೆ k *n* A spiny herb *Barleria longifolia*

ಕೊಳಚೆ, ಕೊಳಚೆ (ಳ=ೞ) (*cf* ಕೊಳಕು) k. *n* The state of being impure, stinking, muddy, *etc.,* soft mud

ಕೊಳತು. =ಕೊಳೆತು (ಳ = ೞ) *P p of* ಕೊಳೆ.

ಕೊಳಲು (ಳ=ೞ) k *n* A flute, fife.

ಕೊಳವಿ, ಕೊಳವೆ (ಳ=ೞ) k *n* A tube blow-pipe.

ಕೊಳಸು. =ಕೊಳಿಸು, *q. v*

ಕೊಳು =ಕೊಳ್ಳು, *q. v.*

ಕೊಳೆ (ಳೆ=ೞೆ) k *v i* To wear out, *as* cloth, to decay, rot, spoil, to spoil, become putrid, to wither, to become lean. *P. ps* ಕೊಳೆತು, ಕೊಳತು *n* Dirt, impurity, mud, bodily exeretion, hinderance, detention -ಹಾಕು. To rot; to detain ಕೊಳಸು, ಕೊಳಿಸು To cause t . .

ಕೊಳ್ಳ k. *n* A depth, the cleft of a rock, cave, *etc*

ಕೊಳ್ಳಿ k *n.* A fire-brand. -ದೆವ್ವ, -ಪಿಶಾಚ An *ignis fatuus*

ಕೊಳ್ಳು k *v. t* To seize, to take, to accept; to take for one's own use or benefit, to obtain; to buy, to undertake *P p* ಕೊಂಡು *Imp. sing* ಕೋ. *Pres part.* ಕೊಳ್ಳುತ್ತ, ಕೋತ ಕೊಳ್ಳು *as the second member of a compound* to get, obtain acquire, hold on, *as rel. pr part* ಬರ-, ಮಾಡಿ-. ಕೊಂಡು-. To buy ಕೊಂಡು ಬರು To bring ಕೊಂಡು ಹೋಗು To take away ಕೊಂಡಾಟ. Praise ಕೊಂಡಾಡು To praise, reverence. ಕೊಳ್ಳುವಿಕೆ Taking, *etc*

ಕೊಳ್ಳೆ k. *n* Pillage, plunder. -ಗಾರ. A plunderer.

ಕೋ k *An imp. sing. of* ಕೊಳ್ಳು

ಕೋಕನದ s. *n.* The red lotus.

ಕೋಕಿಲ =ಕೋಗಿಲೆ, *q v.*

ಕೋಗಿಲೆ (*tb. of* ಕೋಕಿಲ) *n* The Indian cuckoo, *Cuculus indicus* -ಗಿಡ A plant of which the leaves are used for plates, *etc.*

ಕೋಗೀರು h *n.* A cushion used as a saddle

ಕೋಚು (=ಕೋಸು) k *n* -ಭಟ್ಟ. A foolish stupid bhatta, a N.

ಕೋಟ s. *n* Crookedness. 2, a shed, hut. 3, a fort -ಡಿ. A room; *also* ಕೊಟ್ಟಡಿ

ಕೋಟರ s. *n* The hollow of a tree.

ಕೋಟಲೆ k. *n.* Trouble, affliction, pain -ಪಡು. To suffer pain ಕೋಟಲಿಗ. A troublesome man

ಕೋಟಿ s *n.* A crore or ten millions. 2, the point or extreme part 3, the edge of a sword 4, an angle. 5, a countless number. -ಪಾತ್ರ. A rudder. ಕೋಟೀರ A crest ಕೋಟೀರ A harrow. ಕೋಟ್ಯನುಕೋಟಿ, ಕೋಟ್ಯಂತರ Countless

ಕೋಟೆ (*tb of* ಕೋಟ) *n.* A wall round . . . ತನೆ,

-ಕೊಂಬೆ The battlements of a fort -ಗಸ್ತು. A fort patrole. -ಗಾವಲು. A fort-guard

ಕೋಟ್ಟಾರ f. *n.* A stronghold of thieves. 2, the steps of a pond

ಕೋಠಿ f *n* A granary, a factory, warehouse

ಕೋಡಗ k *n* A monkey, ape. -ಚೇಷ್ಟೆ. An apish trick

ಕೋಡಂಗಿ k. *n* An apish man, a buffoon. -ತನ. Buffoonery

ಕೋಡಬಳೆ k *n* A *kind of fried cake* in the form of a ring

ಕೋಡಿ 1 k. *n.* An outlet or weir of a tank -ಕಟ್ಟು To stop the outlet -ಕಡಿ. To open the outlet.

ಕೋಡಿ 2. k *n* Deficiency, defect, want. 2, number 20

ಕೋಡಿ 3 k *n.* A kind of a flag with an image of a demi-god set up on a post before a temple. -ಹಬ್ಬ. A festival in connection with it.

ಕೋಡು 1 a. k *v t* To be cool. 2, to tear. 3, to shrink. *n.* Coldness. 2, fear. 3, shrinking.

ಕೋಡು 2. k *n* A horn of animals, a tusk 2, the peak of a hill 3, a branch. -ಕಳ್ಳಿ The milkhedge. -ಗಲ್ಲು. The peak of a hill. -ಮುರುಕಬಳ್ಳಿ. The creeper *Cynanchum pauciflorum.*

ಕೋಡೆ k *n* West wind, the hot season. -ಗದ್ದೆ. A field yielding crop in the hot season.

ಕೋಣ 1. k. *n* A male buffalo 2, a foolish man. -ದ ಬಳ್ಳಿ. A leafless, shrubby creeper, *Sarcostemma intermedium.* -ತಿದ್ದು, -ಸಾಧಕ ಮಾಡು. To train a buffalo.

ಕೋಣ 2 s *n* An angle a corner

ಕೋಣೆ k *n* An inner apartment or chamber, room 2, a kitchen.

ಕೋತ k. *n.* N. of a low-caste tribe on the Nilagiri. 2, (f) deficiency, reduction -ಗಿರಿ. N. of one of the Nilagiri hills.

ಕೋತಂಬರಿ (*tb of* ಕುಸ್ತುಂಬುರಿ) *n.* Coriander

ಕೋತಲು h *n* Saving, laying up -ಸಂಬಳ. An extra pay.

ಕೋತಿ k *n* A monkey, ape -ಚೇಷ್ಟೆ. A monkey's trick

ಕೋತು m *n* Farming, tenanting 2, (= ಬಾರಕೋತು) barracks.

ಕೋದಂಡ k *n* A rope for punishment, suspended in schools, on which a boy is tied up with his hands clasped and which he is not permitted to loose.

ಕೋನ (*tb. of* ಕೋಣ 2) *n.* An angle, corner. ಕೋನೇರಿ, ಕೋನೇರು A stone built tank with steps on all sides

ಕೋಪ s. *n* Passion, wrath, anger -ಗಾರ. A passionate man, *f.* -ಗಾತಿ ಕೋಪಿಷ್ಠ. Very passionate, an irascible man; *f* ಕೋಪಿಷ್ಠಳು -ಶಾಂತ ಮಾಡು. To pacify, appease ಕೋಪಿಸು To become angry ಕೋಪೋದ್ರೇಕ Excess of passion.

ಕೋಮಟಿ k. *n* A Vaiśya shopkeeper. 2, a miser; *also* -ಗ, *f.* -ಗಿತ್ತಿ -ತನ. A Kômati's profession; covetousness

ಕೋಮಲ s *a.* Tender, soft, sweet, pleasing -ತೆ Softness, *etc*

ಕೋಯಷ್ಟಿ s. *n* The lapwing; the paddy bird.

ಕೋರ = ಖೋರ, *q v*

ಕೋರಕ s. *n.* A bud

ಕೋರಂಗಿ s *n.* Small cardamoms

ಕೋರಂಬು f *n.* A frontlet of idols.

ಕೋರಯಿಸು k. *v t* To be dazzled

ಕೋರಾ f. *n.* Unbleached cotton cloth. *a.* New. ಕೋರಾನ್ನ. Undressed corn.

ಕೋರಿ (ರಿ=ಱಿ) k *n.* A rag, a worn out blanket -ಸೆಟ್ಟಿ. A Lingâyta hawker or tradesman. -ಹಣ್ಣು. A ripe mulberry. -ಹುಳ. A caterpillar.

ಕೋರಿಕೆ (ರಿ=ಱಿ) k. *n* Wish, desire, longing, hope -ಈಡೇರು, -ತೀರು, -ನೆರವೇರು A wish to be gratified.

ಕೋರು 1 (ರು=ಱು) k. *v. t* To wish, desire, hope

ಕೋೞರು 2 (*fr*. ಕೊಱೆ) k *n* A part, portion, share in cultivation, *etc*

ಕೋೞೆ 1 k. *n*. Crookedness, perverseness. -ಪಟ A small flag

ಕೋೞೆ 2 (ಠ = ಱ³, *fr*. ಕೊಱೆ) k *n* Cutting, sharpness 2, a tusk, a long tooth, fang -ದಾಡೆ, -ಹಲ್ಲು A pointed tooth -ಮೀಸೆ. Pointed whiskers -ರುಮಾಲು A turban with pointed foldings.

ಕೋೞ್ಟು f. *n* A court

ಕೋೞಲ k *n* Decoration; figure, form, *as* of masks, dresses, *etc*., as used in devil dances. 2, public procession.

ಕೋೞಾರ k. *n*. Colar. -ತಟ್ಟು A country pony.

ಕೋೞಾಹಲ s. *n* A loud noise, an uproar

ಕೋೞಲಿ k. *n*. A stubble of jôla.

ಕೋೞು k *n* A stick, staff, rod, a measure of length. ಕೋೞರಗು. A stick of sealing wax ಕೋೞಾಟ A children's play with alternate motions and mutually striking small sticks. ಕೋೞಾಡು To play as above -ಊರು. To lean on a stick -ಕುದುರೆ A stick on which boys ride, a crutch -ಗಳ್ಳಿ A species of leafless milk-hedge.

ಕೋೞುಕಾರ k *n*. A peon.

ಕೋೞವ a. k *n*. A potter.

ಕೋೞವಿ k. *n*. A tube 2, a gun, matchlock -ಹಾರಿಸು. To shoot.

ಕೋೞವಿದ s. *a* Skilled, experienced, wise, *f*. ಕೋೞವಿದೆ

ಕೋೞವೆ 1 k *n* Dyspepsy. 2, a boil on the head of children. 3, the climbing plant *Bryonia grandis* with red fruit 4, a crucible [milk.

ಕೋೞವೆ 2 h *n* A kind of condensed

ಕೋೞಶ, ಕೋೞಷ s *n* A case, a sheath, scabbard, a pod. 2, a storehouse, treasury. 3, a vocabulary, dictionary, *cf* ಅಮರ- -ಗೃಹ. A treasury

ಕೋೞಷ್ಠ s. *n*. The intestines 2, an apartment, a granary 3, (= ಕುಷ್ಠ) leprosy. 4, a square *as* in tables of calcul[illegible]

ಕೋೞಸಂಬರಿ.= ಕೋೞಸುಂಬರಿ, *q v*

ಕೋೞಸು 1 k. *n* The state of being crooked or curved, *as* that of a wall, road, *etc*. -ಗಣ್ಣು. A squint eye

ಕೋೞಸು 2 h *n* Cabbage 2, (*tb of* ಕ್ರೋಶ) a distance of 3 miles

ಕೋೞಸುಂಬರಿ f. *n* Raw fruit, *etc*, preserved *as* a seasoning

ಕೋೞಳ k. *n*. Stocks for criminals.

ಕೋೞಳಿ (ಳ = ಱ¹) k *n* A cock, a hen; a fowl in general -ಕಟ್ಟು To set cocks a fighting -ಕೋೞಡು Calicut -ಗರಿ A quill. -ಗೂಡು. A hen's nest -ತತ್ತಿ. A fowl's egg. -ಹುಂಜ A cock

ಕೋೞಳು k *n* Seizure, pillage, calumny.

ಕೋೞಳೆ (ಳ = ಱ³) k. *n*. Thick phlegm

ಕೌ. *For words beginning with this letter and not found below, see under* ಕವ *or* ಕವು.

ಕೌಂಗು (*tb of* ಕ್ರಮುಕ) *n* The betel-nut tree, *Areca catechu*.

ಕೌಟಿಲ್ಯ s. *n*. Crookedness, falsehood, deceit *etc*, *also* ಕೌಟಿಲ್ಯತೆ

ಕೌಂಡನ್ಯ, ಕೌಂಡಿನ್ಯ s *n* N. of a sage, N of a grammarian.

ಕೌತುಕ (*fr*. ಕುತುಕ) s *n*. Curiosity, a wonder, surprise, astonishment 2, eagerness 3, joy, pleasure, sport, gaity

ಕೌತೂಹಲ (*fr* ಕುತೂಹಲ) s. *n* Eagerness, vehemence; curiosity.

ಕೌಂತೇಯ (*fr*. ಕುಂತಿ) s *n* N of Sahadêva, Yudhishthira Bhîma, and Arjuna

ಕೌಪೀನ s *n*. A small piece of cloth worn over the privities 2, a wrong act.

ಕೌಮಾರ (*fr*. ಕುಮಾರ) s. *a* Juvenile *n*. Childhood

ಕೌಮುದಿ (*fr* ಕುಮುದ) s. *n* Moonlight

ಕೌರವ s *n* A descendant of Kuru

ಕೌಲಿಕ (*fr* ಕುಲ) s *a* Belonging to a family; ancestral *n* A heretic, impostor. 2, (=ಕೌಲೀನ) rumour report.

ಕೌಲೀನ s *a* Belonging to a noble [illegible]

ಕೌಲು h. *n* Agreement. 2, safeguard to pass, *as* granted to an enemy 3, stipulated tribute. -ಕರಾರು An agreement.

ಕೌಶಲ (*fr*. ಕುಶಲ) s *n*. Well-being, happiness 2, skilfulness, cleverness

ಕೌಶಿಕ s *n* Indra. 2, N. of Viśvâmitra 3, a snake-catcher. 4, an owl

ಕೌಸಲ್ಯೆ s *n* The wife of Daśaratha and mother of Râma

ಕೌಸ್ತುಭ s. *n* The jewel suspended on Vishnu's or Krishna's breast

ಕೌಳಿಕ (*tb. of* ಕೌಟಿಕ) *n*. A butcher. 2. deceit.

ಕ್ಕೆ k. *A dative affix, as* ದನಕ್ಕೆ, ಮರಕ್ಕೆ, ಆದಕ್ಕೆ, *etc*

ಕ್ಯಾಕರಿಸು.=ಕೇಕರಿಸು, *q v*

ಕ್ರತು s. *n*. Sacrifice, offering. -ಧ್ವಂಸಿ. Śiva -ಪುರುಷ. Vishnu.

ಕ್ರಂದನ s *n* Crying out, calling. 2, weeping.

ಕ್ರಮ s. *n*. A step; the foot. 2, order, series, regular course 3, method, manner 4. a sacred precept -ಣ. Going, proceeding, advancing. *Cpds* · ಅತಿ-, ಅನು-, ಕಾಲ-, *etc*. -ತಪ್ಪು Order to be missed. ಕ್ರಮಿಸು To go, walk, to cross.

ಕ್ರಮಾಗತ s *a* Descended regularly or lineally.

ಕ್ರಮೇಣ s. *a* By degrees, gradually, in order.

ಕ್ರಯ s. *n* Price, value. 2, buying. -ಇಡು, -ಕಟ್ಟು. To fix a price. -ಕೊಡು To pay for. -ಬೀಳು Price to fetch, to cost -ವಿಕ್ರಯ. Trade, traffic -ಚೀಟು, -ಶಾಸನ. A deed of sale. ಕ್ರಯಿಕ. A purchaser.

ಕ್ರವ್ಯ s *n* Raw flesh. ಕ್ರವ್ಯಾದ. Carnivorous, a râkshasa

ಕ್ರಾಂತಿ s *n*. Going, the sun's course on the globe, the ecliptic, *also* -ಚಕ್ರ, -ವೃತ್ತ.

ಕ್ರಿಮಿ (=ಕೃಮಿ) s *n*. An insect worm. -ಜ Produced by worms silk.

ಕ್ರಿಯಾತ್ಮಕ s. *a*. Having the nature of a verb.

ಕ್ರಿಯಾ (ಕ್ರಿಯೆ) s. *n*. Action, work, business, an act 2, time tense, a verb. 3, a literary work. 4, bodily action 5, a religious ceremony 6, expiation. 7, a means; an instrument. -ಪದ. A verb -ಫಲ. Consequence of acts. -ಮಾಲೆ The conjugation of a verb. -ಅರ್ಥ The meaning of a verb -ವಂತ An active man; a truthful man. -ವಾಚಕ. A verbal noun. -ವಿಭಕ್ತಿ An inflection of the persons of a tense. -ವಿಶೇಷಣ That which defines an action an adverb. -ಸಮಾಸ. A verbal compound

ಕ್ರಿಷ್ಣ, ಕ್ರಿಷ್ಟಣ. *tb. of* ಕೃಷ್ಣ, *q v*.

ಕ್ರಿಸ್ತ *n*. Christ. -ಶಕ. The era of Christ ಕ್ರಿಸ್ತಿ. Christian. ಕ್ರಿಸ್ತಿಯ A Protestant Christian, *f*. -ಳು

ಕ್ರೀಡೆ s. *n*. Play, sport, amusement. ಕ್ರೀಡಿಸು To play, sport ಕ್ರೀಡಾವನ. A pleasure garden, park.

ಕ್ರುಪೆ. *tb of* ಕೃಪೆ, *q. v*

ಕ್ರೂಜೆ f *n*. A cross -ಗೆ ಜಡಿ, ಕ್ರೂಜಿಸು To crucify

ಕ್ರೂರ s. *a*. Cruel. fierce, pitiless; hot; sharp; harsh, terrible. *n*. A scoundrel. -ಕರ್ಮಿ. A person who performs pitiless deeds. -ಚಿತ್ತ. A cruel-minded man. -ತನ, -ತ್ವ Cruelty

ಕ್ರೇತವ್ಯ, ಕ್ರೇಯ s. *a*. Purchasable

ಕ್ರೈಸ್ತ f. *n*. A Christian *a*. Christian. -ತ್ವ, -ಧರ್ಮ. Christianity.

ಕ್ರೋಡ s. *n* The chest, breast, bosom. 2, Saturn. -ರೂಪಿ. Vishnu ಕ್ರೋಡೀಕರಿಸು To abridge, write briefly

ಕ್ರೋಧ s *n*. Anger, wrath, passion

ಕ್ರೋಧನ s. *n*. The fifty-ninth year of the cycle.

ಕ್ರೋಧಿ s. *a*. Angry. passionate. *n*. The thirty-eighth year of the cycle.

ಕ್ರೋಶ s *n* Calling out; a cry, shout 2, a measure of distance. a kos $\frac{1}{4}$ yôjana.

ಕ್ರೌಂಚ s. n A curlew 2, a mountain in the Himâlaya 3, one of the divisions of the world.

ಕ್ರೌರ್ಯ (fr ಕ್ರೂರ) s n Cruelty, fierceness

ಕ್ಲಿಷ್ಟ s a Fatigued, tired. 2, put to shame. 3, contradictory

ಕ್ಲೀಬ s a. Idle, slothful, mean, miserly n The neuter gender

ಕ್ಲುಪ್ತ (tb of ಕ್ಲೃಪ್ತ), a Arranged, fixed

ಕ್ಲೇಶ s n Affliction, pain, distress, -ಪಡು. To suffer pain, to grieve.

ಕ್ವಚಿತ್ s ad. Anywhere, somewhere. 2, sometimes 3, very little

ಕ್ಷಕಾರ s n. The syllable ಕ್ಷ.

ಕ್ಷಣ s n A moment 2, a measure of time equal to 4 minutes or ⅕ second. 3, leisure. 4, season. -ದ Leisure-giving; night -ಪ್ರಭೆ. Lightning -ಭಂಗುರ Transient, perishable ಕ್ಷಣಾರ್ಧ Half a moment. ಕ್ಷಣಿಕ Momentory, transient.

ಕ್ಷತ್ರ, ಕ್ಷತ್ರಿಯ s n. A man of the military caste, Kshatriya; f ಕ್ಷತ್ರಿಯೆ.

ಕ್ಷಪಣ s n. Fasting. 2, A Buddha or Jaina mendicant.

ಕ್ಷಮ s. a. Patient, enduring, putting up with 2, adequate, competent.

ಕ್ಷಮಿಸು s. v t. To endure, bear patiently, to put up with, to pardon, forgive. ಪಾಪ ಕ್ಷಮಿಸಿ ಬಿಡು. To pardon sin.

ಕ್ಷಮೆ (ಕ್ಷಮಾ) s n Patience, forbearance, indul- gence, long-suffering; pardon, forgiveness.

ಕ್ಷಯ s. n. Wane, decrease, diminution, consumption, loss, destruction 2, pulmonary consumption. 3, sixtieth year of the cycle. -ತಿಥಿ A lunar day beginning after sunrise and ending before that of the next. -ಪಕ್ಷ The fortnight of the waning moon. -ರೋಗ. Consumption in general ಕ್ಷಯಿಸು. To wane, decrease.

ಕ್ಷರ s. a. Perishable.

ಕ್ಷಾಂತ s a Enduring, patient. ಕ್ಷಾಂತಿ. Patience, forbearance.

ಕ್ಷಾಮ s a. Scorched, emaciated, wasted, thin. n Emaciation, debility; famine.

ಕ್ಷಾರ s. a. Salty, biting, acid, pungent. n. Salt, any saline substance, alkali; soda, nitre, saltpetre, essence

ಕ್ಷಾಲ, ಕ್ಷಾಲನ s. n. Washing. ಕ್ಷಾಲಿತ. Washed, cleansed.

ಕ್ಷಿತಿ s n An abode. 2, the earth, a field. 3, decrease, wane, loss. ಕ್ಷಿತ. Decreased, wasted -ಕಾಂತ, -ನಾಥ, -ಪ, -ಪತಿ, -ಪಾಲ, -ರಮಣ, ಕ್ಷಿತೀಶ. A king.

ಕ್ಷಿಪ್ರ s. a. Quick, swift, speedy

ಕ್ಷೀಣ s. a Wasted, worn away; emaciated, thin, slender, miserable. -ತ್ವ Wasting, diminution, decay.

ಕ್ಷೀರ s n Milk 2, water -ಜ Curds. -ನೀರ. Milk and water. -ಸ Essence of milk. -ಸಮುದ್ರ, ಕ್ಷೀರಾಬ್ಧಿ. The sea of milk ಕ್ಷೀರಾಗಾರ A dairy. ಕ್ಷೀರಾಗಾರಿ A dairy-man

ಕ್ಷುದ್ರ s a. Small, little. 2 poor, miserable 3, low, vile. 4, avaricious, niggardly. n. A fault, slander -ಕ, -ಗಾರ A slanderer. ಕ್ಷುದ್ರಿ A slanderous person.

ಕ್ಷುಧೆ (ಕ್ಷುಧಾ) s. n. Hunger. ಕ್ಷುಧಾರ್ತ, ಕ್ಷುಧಿತ. Hungry.

ಕ್ಷುರ s. n A razor. -ಕ, -ಮರ್ದಿ, ಕ್ಷುರಿ. A barber.

ಕ್ಷುಲ್ಲಕ (= ಕ್ಷುದ್ರ, ಕ್ಷುದ್ರಕ) s a. Little; thin. 2, poor, indigent. 3, avaricious. n A man of the lowest extraction.

ಕ್ಷೇತ್ರ s n. A field 2, place, country; a place of pilgrimage 3, the body 4, a diagram -ಜೀವ A husbandman -ಜ್ಞ. Experienced, skilful; the soul -ಪಾಲ A deity protecting the fields Bhairava. -ಫಲ Area, quotient

ಕ್ಷೇಪ s. n Casting, pushing, depressing; passing away. Cpds ಕಾಲ-, ದಿ-, ಸಂ-

ಕ್ಷೇಮ s n Well-being, weal, happiness; health -ಕರ Promoting well-being. -ಸಮಾಚಾರ. News regarding a person's welfare.

ಕ್ಷೋಣಿ s. n. The earth; a field 2, a certain high number -ಪತಿ A king

ಕ್ಷೋಭ s n Agitation, commotion, disturbance, emotion, alarm.

ಕ್ಷೌರ (fr. ಕ್ಷುರ) s n. Shaving -ಮಾಡಿಸಿಕೊಳ್ಳು. To get one's self shaved. -ಕತ್ತಿ. A razor -ಕ. A barber

ಖ

ಖ. The twentieth letter of the alphabet.

ಖ s. n. The sky. 2, an organ of sense (ಇಂದ್ರಿಯ) 3, perception (ಬುದ್ಧಿ) 4, mind (ಮನಸ). -ಗ, -ಚರ Moving in the air the sun, a bird, an arrow. -ಗಪತಿ, -ಗೇಶ್ವರ. Garuda. -ಗೋಲ The celestial sphere, astronomy.

ಖಚಿತ s. a Bound, inlaid, studded. 2, joined. 3, positive, true.

ಖಜ s n Stirring, churning 2, a ladle. -ಕ An awning, canopy

ಖಜಾಕೆ s. n. A ladle. spoon.

ಖಜಾನೆ h. n. A treasury; treasure. ಖಜಾಂಚಿ. A cashkeeper

ಖಜ್ಜಾ h. n Quarrelling -ಖೋರ. A quarrelsome man.

ಖಟ್ವ, ಖಟ್ವಾ s n. A bedstead, cot. 2, a hammock.

ಖಡ್ಗ s n. A sword. 2, a rhinoceros, also -ಮೃಗ ಖಡ್ಗಾಖಡಿ, etc. Sword to sword, a sword-fight; also ಖಡಾಖಡಿ.

ಖಂಡ (=ಕಂಡ) s a Broken, divided. n A fragment, part, piece, a section. 2, a division of the terrestrial globe

ಖಂಡಣೆ, ಖಂಡನ s n Dividing, reducing to pieces; refuting.

ಖಂಡಿತ 1. (=ಕಂಡಿತ, q v) k n. Firmness, strictness, certainty.

ಖಂಡಿತ 2 s. a. Cut, taken to pieces, refuted.

ಖಂಡಿಸು s. v. t To break, crush, cut, to disappoint, etc., to refute (in argument).

ಖತಾವಣಿ m. n. The paper on which the items of the day-book are abstracted.

ಖತಿ (=ಕತಿ) k. n. Anger, wrath, rage.

ಖದಿರ s. n The tree *Acacia catechu*, its resin called *catechu*

ಖದ್ಯೋತ s n A fire-fly; the sun

ಖನಕ s n. A digger, miner, a house-breaker 2, a rat.

ಖನನ s n. Digging; burying.

ಖನಿ (=ಕಣಿ) s. n. A mine, quarry -ಜ. A mineral. -ತ್ರ A spade

ಖಪುರ s n. The betel-nut tree, *Areca catechu* 2, the mouth. 3, a buffalo. 4, disgrace.

ಖರ s. a Hard, sharp, pungent. n. The twenty-fifth year of the cycle. 2, an ass 3, N of a râkshasa -ಕರ Hot-rayed; the sun. -ಶಾಣ A grind-stone, a sharp saw.

ಖರಡೆ h. n A foul copy; a day-book; a scrawl, also ಕರಡು.

ಖರಾರು h n A curry comb

ಖರೀದಿ h n. A purchase, price, cost.

ಖರೆ 1 f a True, correct. -ಹೇಳು. To speak truly.

ಖರೆ 2. s. n The grass *Andropogon serratus*

ಖರ್ಚು (=ಕರ್ಚು, q. v) h. n. Expenditure, expense, costs. -ವೆಚ್ಚ dupl -ದಾರ. A spendthrift -ಬೀಳು, -ಹಿಡಿ To cost money.

ಖರ್ಜು s n Itch, scab.

ಖರ್ಜೂರ (=ಕಜೂರ, etc) s. n The date-tree, *Phoenix dactylifera*.

ಖರ್ವ s *a*. Maimed; shoit, low *n* A dwaif 2, ten thousand millions.

ಖರ್ಬೂಜ (=ಕರ್ಬೂಜ) s *n*. The water-melon

ಖಲ s *n* A rogue, scoundrel. 2, a threshing floor 3, sediment, dregs. 4, contest, battle 5, a mortar. *a*. Low, base -ಕರಣ Threshing corn. -ತಿ Bald-headed. -ಪು A sweeper.

ಖಲ್ಲ s. *n*. A leaf or paper rolled into a cup.

ಖಳ. = ಖಲ, *q* *v*

ಖಳಿಲನೆ (ಳಿ = ಱ) k *ad* Loudly, roughly

ಖಾಡ. = ಖಡ್ಡ, *q* *v* ಖಾಡಾಖಾಡಿ A wrestling match.

ಖಾಣ h *n* Food fodder.

ಖಾತರಿ = ಕಾತರಿ, *q* *v*

ಖಾತೆ 1 s *n* An artificial pond.

ಖಾತೆ 2. f *n* An account on the day-book 2, province, depaitment.

ಖಾದನ s. *n* Eating; food ಖಾದಿತ Eaten.

ಖಾದಿ f *n* A thick cotton-stuff.

ಖಾನ h *n* A prince, chief, a title borne by Mohammadan nobles.

ಖಾನೆ h. *n* A place, house, *as in* ಕಾರಖಾನೆ, ಮೇಜುವಾನೆ. 2, a sliding box, drawer. -ಸುಮಾರಿ. A census of the population.

ಖಾಮಖಾ h *ad* Positively, certainly

ಖಾರಿ f. *n* A measure of capacity equivalent to about three bushels.

ಖಾಲಿ h. *a*. Empty, vacant 2, unemployed 3, useless -ಆಗು To become vacant, to be disappointed.

ಖಾಸಾ. = ಕಾಸಾ, *q* *v* -ಸ್ವಾರಿ. The equipage or procession of a chieftain, the chieftain in person.

ಖಿಜಮತ h. *n*. Service, attendance

ಖಿನ್ನ s *a*. Depressed, distressed, wearied.

ಖಿಲ s *n* A piece of waste land 2 a supplement. 3, anything empty or fruitless.

ಖಿಲಾತು h *n*. A robe of honour.

ಖುದ f *n*. God

ಖುದ್ದ h. *a* Own, in person, self.

ಖುರ (=ಕುರ) f *n*. A hoof.

ಖುರಾಕು f *n*. Rich, nutritive diet

ಖುರಾನು (=ಕುರಾನ) h *n* The Koran.

ಖುರ್ದಬುರ್ದ h. *n* Embezzlement

ಖುರ್ನಾಸ, ಖುರ್ನೀಸು h *n*. Obeisance, reverence.

ಖುಲಾಸ h. *n* Openness; emptiness, evidence, clearness, freedom *a* Open.

ಖುಲ್ಲ s *a* Small, low, mean, wicked. 2, (h) = ಕುಲ್ಲ -ತನ Meanness

ಖುಷಾಮತು f. *n*. Flattery, fawning

ಖುಷಾಲು. = ಕುಶಾಲು, *q*. *v*.

ಖುಷಿ = ಕುಶಿ, *q* *v*

ಖೂನ h *n* An indication, sign

ಖೂನಿ h. *n*. Murder. -ಖೋರ, -ಗಾರ. A murderer

ಖೂಬು h *ad*. Well, finely; copiously.

ಖೇಚರ (*fr* ಖ) s. *a*. Moving in the air *n* A bird; a deity.

ಖೇಟಯು, ಖೇಟ್ಯ s *n*. A shield.

ಖೇದ s *n* Sorrow, grief, distress, despondency. -ಗೊಳ್ಳು, ಖೇದಿಸು To feel grieved.

ಖೇಪ s *n* A single time, turn.

ಖೇಲ s *n* Moving to and fro; *also* -ನ. ಖೇಲಿ. Play, sport

ಖೋಡಿ s. *n* An evil disposition; a vice; a mean, miserable wretch. *a*. Ill-disposed, having a bad habit. -ತನ. An evil disposition.

ಖ್ಯಾತ s. *a*. Well known. famous, *also* ಪ್ರ-. ಖ್ಯಾತಿ. Fame, celebrity, gloiy.

ಗ

ಗ. The twenty-first letter of the alphabet.

ಗ 1. k *An affix to form words denoting time, as* ಆಗ, ಈಗ, *etc.* 2, *an affix to form masculine nouns, as* ಹುಡುಗ, ಪಾರಿಗ, ಮಗ, *etc*

ಗ 2. s. *a.* Going, moving

ಗಕಾರ s. *n* The letter ಗ

ಗಕ್ಕನೆ k *ad* Quickly, suddenly.

ಗಗನ s *n.* The sky, atmosphere. -ಮಣಿ. The sun -ಚರ A bird, a planet

ಗಗ್ಗರ k. *n* A hollow silver ornament filled with pebbles for jingling

ಗಗ್ಗರಿ k *n* A hollow ring of brass containing bits of metal, *etc.* to produce a jingling noise

ಗಂಗದೊವಲು f *n* The dowlap of an ox or bull.

ಗಂಗಾ (= ಗಂಗೆ, *q v*) s *n.* The Ganges. -ಜಮುನಾ. The Ganges and Yamuna rivers, a cloth with different coloured border on each side -ದೇವಿ A water-goddess -ಧರ, -ಧರೇಶ್ವರ, -ಧೀಶ, -ವತಂಸ Śiva. -ನಂದನ, -ಪುತ್ರ, -ಸುತ. Bhîshma -ಯಾತ್ರೆ Pilgrimage to the Ganges -ಸ್ನಾನ Bathing in the Ganges. ಗಂಗೋದಕ. Ganges water

ಗಂಗಾಳ s *n.* A circular metal vessel for holding water, *etc* 2, a metal plate for eating from.

ಗಂಗೆ s *n* The river Ganges 2, Satyavatî, the boatman's daughter who became Bhîshma's mother. -ದೊಗಲು = ಗಂಗದೊವಲು

ಗಚ್ಚಿ h *n.* A chunammed floor -ಎಣ್ಣೆ Varnish

ಗಚ್ಚು h. *n.* Mortar, plaster, cement.

ಗಜ 1 s *n.* An elephant 2, N. of a râkshasa. -ಕರ್ಣ. Ringworm -ದಂತ. Elephant's tusk. -ನಗರಿ, -ಪುರ Delhi -ಪ್ರಾಸ A kind of alliteration. -ಮುಖ, -ವದನ, ಗಜಾನನ. Ganêśa -ಲಕ್ಷ್ಮಿ A picture of Lakshmî with elephants on her sides -ವೈರಿ, ಗಜಾರಿ A lion ಗಜೇಂದ್ರ A large stately elephant.

ಗಜ 2 h *n.* A measure of three feet; a yard 2, a ramrod

ಗಜಗ. = ಗಜುಗ, *q v.*

ಗಜನಿ k. *n.* Poor rice lands.

ಗಜರು (ರು = ಱು) a. k. *v t.* To roar, to scold. *n.* A loud sound or speech.

ಗಜಾಲು f. *n.* Loud idle talk. -ಗಾರ. A chatterer, *f* -ಗಾತಿ.

ಗಜಿಬಿಜಿ k *n.* Confusion, disorder, intricacy -ಬರಹ An illegible writing -ಮಾರ್ಗ. A rough road. -ಮಾಡು To confuse.

ಗಜುಗ, ಗಜ್ಜಿಗ, ಗಜ್ಜುಗ k. *n* A prickly climbing shrub, the Molucca bean, *Guilandina bonducella.* 2, a protuberance from the eye-ball.

ಗಜ್ಜರಿ f *n* A sweet carrot

ಗಜ್ಜಿ. = ಕಜ್ಜಿ, *q v*

ಗಜ್ಜೆ. = ಗೆಜ್ಜೆ, *q v*

ಗಂಜ f *n.* A store-room, treasury 2, a mine.

ಗಂಜಲ, ಗಂಜಳ k *n* The urine of cattle, *etc* -ದ ಹುಲ್ಲು. A species of coarse grass, *Eleusine indica*

ಗಂಜಿ (*tb of* ಕಾಂಜಿ) *n.* Conjee, rice gruel, starch. -ಕಸ. A creeping plant, *Indigofera linifolia* -ಬಟ್ಟೆ A starched cloth. -ರಟ್ಟು A cloth used in straining boiled rice.

ಗಂಜೀಫ h *n* A pack of round cards.

ಗಂಜು f *n.* A set of round vessels that are put one within another in the form of a cone

ಗಟಕ (*tb. of* ಘಟಕ) *n.* A powerful, able man

ಗಟ್ಟ k. *n.* A ghaut, mountain-range.

ಗಟ್ಟಣೆ (*tb. of* ಘಟ್ಟನ) *n* Beating down, *as* roads; loading a gun.

ಗಟ್ಟಿ k *n* Firmness, hardness, the state of (fluids, *etc*) being thick, solid, strength, ability. 2, a lump 3, an ingot. 4, smartness, fineness. 5, a strong, smart person *a* Firm, strong, solid -ಆಳು. A strong, able person -ಕೆಲಸ. A strong work. -ಗ. A strong, energetic man -ಮೊಸರು. Thick curds. -ಹಾಲು. Thick milk -ವಳ್ತಿ A toilet woman.

ಗಟ್ಟಿಸು (= ಘಟ್ಟಿಸು) f. *v. t.* To strike, beat 2, (k.) to make effort (to speak loud).

ಗಟ್ಟು (=ಗಡ್ಡಿ) f *n*. A bundle, ream of [paper.

ಗಡ 1. = ಗಡು, *q v.*

ಗಡ 2 h *n*. A small fort. 2, a liquid measure

ಗಡ 3 k *int expressing quick motion or disorder* -ಗಡ. Quickly (used of walking, reading, eating, *etc*) -ಗಡ ಎನ್ನು. To rattle, *as* thunder, carts, *etc.* -ಬಡ, -ಬಡಿ, -ಬಿಡಿ Bustle, confusion, tumult, ado.

ಗಡ 4. = ಗಡು, *q. v.*

ಗಡಗಂಚಿ h. *n*. A stand, shelf

ಗಡಂಗ h *n* A godown, store-room; a spirit-shop

ಗಡಚು. =ಗಡುಸು, *q v*

ಗಡಣ a. k. *n*. A mass, heap, a multitude ಗಡಣಿಸು To join, heap, pile.

ಗಡಣೆ (*tb. of* ಗಣನೆ) *n*. Reckoning, meaning, sense. -ಗೊಳ್ಳು. To regard, care for, *etc*

ಗಡತರ (=ಗಡುತರ) k. *n*. Massiveness, stoutness, strength. *a.* Massive, *etc*

ಗಡದ, ಗಡಸು f. *a* Thick, *as* darkness, sound, deep, *as* sleep, study, *etc*

ಗಡಪು h. *n* Disappearance, hiding

ಗಡವು. = ಗಡು, *q. v.*

ಗಡಸರಿ k *n* A stout, robust person

ಗಡಾಯಿಸು f *v t* To hide or fix firmly in the earth

ಗಡಾರಿ h *n* An iron crow-bar

ಗಡಿ 1. (=ಗಡ) k. *n*. A term, limit, a frontier; a place -ಕಲ್ಲು A boundary-stone -ಠಳ್ಳೆ, -ಕೋಟೆ, -ದುರ್ಗ. A hill fort -ಪಾರು ಮಾಡು. To banish.

ಗಡಿ 2 (*tb. of* ಘಟಿ) *n* An hour of 24 minutes; a gong.

ಗಡಿಗೆ (*tb. of* ಘಟಿಕಾ) *n* An earthen vessel.

ಗಡಿಬಿಡಿ (*see s.* ಗಡ 3) k. *n*. Confusion; vexation

ಗಡಿಯಾರ, ಗಡಿಯಾಲ h *n* An hour-glass; a gong; a watch, clock.

ಗಡು k *n* A limit, a period, term, instalment, *also* -ಬ, -ವು

ಗಡುತರ. =ಗಡತರ, *q v*

ಗಡುದು. =ಗಡದ, *q v*

ಗಡುಸು (=ಗಡಚು) k *n* Hardness, brittleness, *as* of iron, difficulty, *as* of work, heaviness, *as* of rain.

ಗಡೆ 1 k. *n*. A bamboo pole 2, match; comparison. -ಕಾರ A man who carries a pole with a flag; an oarsman

ಗಡೆ 2 (*tb of* ಘಟ) *n* A wheel for raising water

ಗಡ್ಡ k. *n* The beard, the chin. -ಇಡು, -ಬಿಡಿಸು, -ಬೆಳಸು To let the beard grow. -ಬೋಳಿಸು To have the beard shaved

ಗಡ್ಡಿ. = ಗಟ್ಟು, *q v.*

ಗಡ್ಡೆ k *n*. A mass, a lump, clump 2, any bulbous root 3, the root of the ear 4, an island; *also* ನಡು- -ಕಟ್ಟು. To freeze, congeal, to grow in clumps, *as* grass ಗೆಣಸಿನ-. A sweet potato. ಮೊಸರಿನ- A clot of curdled milk

ಗಣ s. *n* A flock, multitude, troop, tribe. 2, a body of troops equal to 27 chariots, 27 elephants, 81 horses and 135 foot 3, the attendants of Śiva 4, a syllable foot in prosody 5 a number. 6, a group of lunar mansions. -ಕ, ಗಣಿಕ. An arithmetician; an accountant, an astrologer; *f* -ಕಿ -ತಿ [illegible] Reckoning, counting, [illegible] -t [illegible]ing.

-ಪತಿ, ಗಣಾಧಿಪ, ಗಣಾಧೀಶ Ganêśa; Śiva -ಯಿಸು, ಗಣಿಸು To count, reckon, to consider, regard.

ಗಣಾಜಿಲೆ k. n Hogweed, *Boerhavia procumbens* 2, the chicken-pox

ಗಣಿಲು (=ಗಣೆ) k. n A knuckle of the fingers; a knot or joint in a cane.

ಗಣಾರ್ಚನೆ s n The homage paid by the Lingavantas to the Jangamas

ಗಣಿಕೆ (=ಗಣಿಲು) k n A knot, joint -ಹುಣ್ಣು. A sore on the finger joints.

ಗಣಿತ s. n. Calculating, the science of computation, arithmetic. a Counted -ಗಾರ, -ಜ್ಞ. An astrologer. -ವಿದ್ಯೆ, -ಶಾಸ್ತ್ರ The science of computation, comprising arithmetic, algebra and geometry. ಗಣಿತಿಸು, ಗಣಿದಿಸು. To count, to consider

ಗಣೆ k n The stalk of an onion

ಗಣೆಗಾರ k. n A boatman, a tumbler

ಗಣೇಶ, ಗಣೇಶ್ವರ s n Pârvati's son Ganêśa

ಗಂಟಡಿ h. n A small bundle, parcel

ಗಂಟಲ, ಗಂಟಲು, ಗಂಟ್ಲು k. n. The throat

ಗಂಟೆ k n A kind of small gold earring.

ಗಂಟು (tb of ಗ್ರಂಥಿ) n The knot or joint of a reed, bamboo or a cane 2, a knot. 3, a bundle, parcel 4, money, wealth; capital in trade 5, swelling and hardening of the veins ಗಂಟಾಸೆ. The desire of becoming rich -ಗಳ್ಳ. One who falsely assumes the appearance of poverty, one who does not return a loan. -ಗೊಯ್ಕ. A pick-pocket. -ತುಂಬೆ The herb *Leucas urticaefolia* -ಬಾರಂಗಿ An under-shrub, *Clerodendron serratum* -ಬೀಳು To get knotted, close connection to spring up; union or harmony to take place; to run counter to, to attack. -ಮೋರೆ A frowning look or countenance -ವ್ಯಾಜ್ಯ A difficult lawsuit. -ಹಾಕು. To make a knot; to knit, as the eye-brows, to employ capital.

ಗಂಟೆ (tb of ಘಂಟೆ) n An English hour. -ಬಾರಿಸು, -ಹೊಡೆ To ring a bell.

ಗಂಟ್ಲು. =ಗಂಟಲು, q v

ಗಂಡ 1 k n A strong, male person, a husband (pl. ಗಂಡರು, ಗಂಡಂದಿರು) 2, (=ಗಂಡು)strength, greatness. -ಕ, -ಮೃಗ. A rhinoceros -ಗಲಿ A strong hero -ಗೂಸು, ಗಂಡುಗೂಸು A male person. -ಮೆಣಸು. The Pimento tree, *Eugenia acris* -ಹೆಂಡರು, -ಹೆಂಡತಿಯರು Husband and wife

ಗಂಡ 2. s. n. The cheek. 2, a boil. 3, the force of any disease, rain, wind, *etc*, the baneful influence of a star (*cf* ಗಂಡಾಂತರ) a Chief, best, excellent. -ಮಾಲೆ, ಗಂಡಮಾಲೆ. Scrofula of the throat. -ಸ್ಥಲ The temples of an elephant.

ಗಂಡಸ, ಗಂಡಸು k n. A male person. -ತನ Virility -ಮಕ್ಕಳು Male persons.

ಗಂಡಾಗುಂಡಿ h. n. Impudence; audacity.

ಗಂಡಾಂತರ s. n. Danger, peril, jeopardy (*cf. s.* ಗಂಡ 2).

ಗಂಡಾಮಾಲೆ. *See s.* ಗಂಡ 2, *q v.*

ಗಂಡು k n Strength; manliness; firmness; bravery. 2, the male sex; a male a. Male, manly. ಗಂಡಕ್ಷರ. An aspirate ಗಂಡಾಡು A he-goat. ಗಂಡಾಳು A male cooly. -ಕೆಲಸ A superior work. -ಕೇಸಲ. The shrub *Memecylon amplexicaule.* -ಗೊಳ್ಳು To become impetuous. -ಬಿದರು A solid bamboo -ಗತನ Manliness, valour. *Other cpds* -ಗೂಸು, -ಗೋಗಿಲೆ, -ಜಾತಿ, -ಜಂಕೆ, -ಪಶು, -ಮಕ್ಕಳು, -ಮರಿ, -ಮೃಗ, -ಸಿಂಹ, -ಹುಳ, -ಹುಡುಗ. A boy.

ಗಂಡೂಷ s n Rinsing the mouth.

ಗಣ್ಣ h n A division of paddy land

ಗಣ್ಯ s. a Calculable, numerable, worthy of esteem

ಗತ s. a Gone, departed, past, disappeared, arrived at, gone to any state, belonging to; relating to. -ಗೋಷ್ಠಿ. Stale words, indefinite postponement, *as* of a law-suit ಗತಾನುಗತಿಕ Successive, in rotation; following custom, imitating ಗತಾರ್ಥ. Unmeaning, nonsensical, deprived of an object

ಗತಿ s *n*. Going, motion, gait; march, progress 2, a path, way; refuge, resource, an expedient, means, course of events, condition, happiness 3, the diurnal motion of a planet in its orbit 4, transmigration 5, deliberation; knowledge. 6, sin, vice. -ಗೆಡು Progress, state, *etc* to be destroyed -ಗೆಡಿಸು. To destroy the course, condition, *etc*, to check. -ಗೇಡಿ A person destroying his own or others welfare. -ಗೇಡು Ruin of welfare, *etc* -ಸು. To go, to die, to pass, *as* time. -ವಿಹೀನ, -ಹೀನ. Remediless, forlorn ಸದ್ಗತಿ Good fortune, heaven ದುರ್ಗತಿ Misfortune, poverty, hell

ಗತ್ತು (*tb. of* ಗತ) *n* Beating time in music for dancers. -ಗಾರ A time-server.

ಗತ್ಯಂತರ s *n* Another remedy or resource; a way of avoiding.

ಗದ 1. s. *n*. Speaking, speech.

ಗದ 2. s. *n*. Disease, sickness.

ಗದ 3 k *n* Shaking, quick motion. -ಗದ ನಡುಗು, -ಗದನೆ ನಡುಗು (*v i*) To shake, tremble violently, *also* -ಗದಿಸು

ಗದಸು k *n* The smell of cattle-urine, burning chillies, *etc*

ಗದರು (ರು = ಱು) k *v i* To thunder, roar, cry, to menace, to exhort earnestly. ಗದರಿಸು To exhort earnestly, to scare frighten ಗದರಿಕೆ. Reproof, exhortation

ಗದಾ, ಗದೆ s *n* A mace, club. ಗದಾಧರ. Krishna.

ಗದು k. *n* A swelling, tumour

ಗದ್ಗದ, ಗದ್ಗದಿಕೆ s *n* Stammering, indistinct utterance, *as* sobbing, *etc*.

ಗದ್ದ k *n* The chin

ಗದ್ದರಿಸು = ಗದರಿಸು, *q. v* *v. i*. To thunder, roar

ಗದ್ದಲ k. *n*. Noise; din.

ಗದ್ದಿಗೆ, ಗದ್ದುಗೆ k *n*. A throne, a seat, a tomb monument of Jangamas. 2, a basis.

ಗದ್ದೆ k *n* A field, paddy-land. -ತೆವರು, -ಬದ A ridge between rice-fields. -ಮಡಿ. A paddy-field -ಮಡಿರುಮಾಲೆ. A turban-cloth with square stripes

ಗದ್ಯ s *a* To be spoken *n*. Prose -ಪದ್ಯ. Prose and verse

ಗದ್ಯಾಣ s *n*. A silver weight equal to about a farthing 2, a small gold coin.

ಗನ *tb of* ಘನ, *q. v*.

ಗಂತು s *n*. A way, course. 2, moving about.

ಗಂದ *tb. of* ಗಂಧ, *q. v*. -ಪಟ್ಟಿಗೆ, -ವಟ್ಟಿಗೆ. The cross bars fastening the planks of a door -ಪುಡಿ, -ವುಡಿ Perfumed powder. -ಗಂದಿಗ A perfume-seller; an oculist.

ಗಂಧ (= ಗಂದ) s *n*. Smell, odour. 2, a perfume 3, sandal-wood 4, arrogance. -ದ ಎಣ್ಣೆ Sandal oil -ಕಚೋರ Zedoary, *Curcuma zedoaria* -ಬೇವು. The curry leaf-tree, *Murraya koenigii*. -ಮೆಣಸು Cubeb, *Piper cubeba* -ಸರಕು Spicery, perfumery, scented drugs. -ಕಸ್ತೂರಿ. Scented musk -ದ ತೈಲ Sandal oil. -ನ Fragrance; perseverance, manifestation, intimation -ಫಲಿ A medicinal plant and perfume. -ಮಾಲ್ಯ A fragrant garland. -ಮೂಷಿ, -ಮೂಷಿಕೆ The musk rat -ರಸ Myrrh. -ವತಿ The earth, a kind of perfume -ವಾಹ The wind -ಲೀಡ. Black salt ಗಂಧಾಕ್ಷತೆ. The pigment called akshatĕ and sandal-paste.

ಗಂಧಕ s *n*. Sulphur. -ಘೃತಿ Sulphuric acid. -ಶುದ್ಧಿ Prepared sulphur

ಗಂಧರ್ವ s. *n*. A celestial musician 2, a singer. 3, a ghost. 4, a kind of deer -ವಿವಾಹ. A marriage on mutual agreement of the parties

ಗಪ್‌ಚಿಪ್ h a Silent, still *int* Silence!

ಗಪಗಪ. ಗಪಗಪನೆ, ಗಪ್ಪಗಪ್ಪ, *etc* k. *ad* Quickly, greedily.

ಗಪ್ಪನೆ (=ಕಪ್ಪನೆ) k *ad*. Suddenly, all at once -ಹಿಡಿ. To seize suddenly.

ಗಪ್ಪಿ h. *n*. A lie, falsehood

ಗಪ್ಪು h. *n*. Deceit falsehood 2, invisibleness. 3, stillness, muteness.

ಗಬಗಬ =ಗವಗವ. *etc*, *q v*.

ಗಬ್ಬ. *tb of* ಗರ್ಭ, *q v*. -ವಾಗು To become pregnant (used of cattle)

ಗಬ್ಬಿ (*tb. of* ಗರ್ವ) *a* Proud, haughty.

ಗಬ್ಬು k. *n* A bad smell, stench

ಗಭೀರ (=ಗಂಭೀರ) s *a* Deep, profound, grave, solemn

ಗಮ 1 k *n*. Strong scent, fragrance -ಗಮ ನಾರು, -ಗಮಿಸು To smell sweetly.

ಗಮ 2 s *n* Going, march 2, flightiness, thoughtlessness, rashness.

ಗಮಕ s *a* Making clear. *n* An evidence 2 a kind of consecutive compound 3, = ಗಮ 2, No 2, loftiness, exertion.

ಗಮನ 1 k. *n*. Odour, fragrance.

ಗಮನ 2 s *a*. Going, walking, march. ಗಮನಿಸು, ಗಮಿಸು. To go; to walk.

ಗಂಪೆ k. *n*. A basket.

ಗಂಭೀರ (= ಗಭೀರ, *q v*.) s. *a*. Deep, solemn -ತೆ Depth, profoundness, sagacity

ಗಮ್ಮತ್ತು h. *n*. Game play; amusement, fun

ಗಮ್ಮನೆ k *ad* Quickly

ಗಮ್ಯ s *a* Accessible; attainable, intelligible, suitable.

ಗಯ, ಗಯೆ s *n*. N. of a place of pilgrimage in Behar. ಗಯಾವಳ A begging Brâhmana at Gayâ, an extortioner ಗಯುಳ A weak-minded or vain man. ಗಯ್ಯಾಳಿ. A shrew, scold, vixen.

ಗರ 1 s *n*. A drink, poison, venom. 2, an astrological division of the day; *see* ಗರಜವಾಕರಣ

ಗರ 2 (*tb. of* ಗ್ರಹ, *q v*) *n*. A planet, an evil spirit -ಬಡೆ, -ಹೊಡೆ. An evil spirit to smite any one -ವಟಿಗೆ, -ವಟ್ಟಿಗೆ Possession, frenzy, torment. -ವಟಿಸು. To become possessed with an evil spirit, to rave, wander -ಹಿಡಿ. An evil spirit to seize.

ಗರಕು k *n* Unevenness, roughness

ಗರಗ, ಗರುಗ k *n* A common weed, *Eclipta alba*

ಗರಗತ್ತಿ k *n* The tree *Ficus asperrima*

ಗರಗರ (ರ=ಱ) k *ad* Whirlingly, smartingly, quickly -ನೆ ತಿರುಗು. To turn around, *as* a millstone, *etc*

ಗರಗರಿಕೆ a. k *n*. Pleasantness, beauty.

ಗರಗಸ (*tb of* ಕ್ರಕಚ) *n*. A saw. -ದ ಮರ. A tree with rough leaves, *Ficus conglomerata*

ಗರಗು (ರ=ಱ=ಗರುಗು) k. *n* The state of being scorched by heat. *a*. Fragile, brittle, dry, *as* flowers leaves, *etc*.

ಗರಜವಾಕರಣ, ಗರಜೆ s *n*. The fifth of the eleven astrological divisions of the day.

ಗರಜು h *n*. Need, necessity, pressing business

ಗರಡಿ = ಗರುಡಿ, *q. v*

ಗರತಿ (*tb. of* ಗೃಹಪತಿ) *n*. A decent and reputable woman.

ಗರಮು h. *a* Hot *n* Heat. ಗರಮಿ Heat.

ಗರಲ s *n* Poison, venom -ಗ್ರೀವ, -ಧರ, ಗರಲಾಶನ Śiva. -ಪೂರ. A serpent

ಗರಸು (= ಗರುಸು) k. *n* Gravel.

ಗರಸೆ k *n* A measure (of salt) equal to 400 marakâls

ಗರಾಣೆದಾರ h *n*. A respectable man.

ಗರಿ (ರಿ=ಱಿ) k *n*. A feather, a wing, the feather-like leaf of a palm, *etc*. -ಗಟ್ಟು. To get strength; to improve. -ಮರ The two side-portions of a wheel of an idol-car

ಗರಿಕೆ. = ಕರಿಕೆ, *q. v*

ಗರಿಮ, ಗರಿಮೆ, ಗರಿಮೆ s. *n* Heaviness, weight. 2, dignity, worth.

ಗರೀಬ h. a Poor

ಗರೀಯಸ್ (fr. ಗುರು) s a Heavier; dearer.

ಗರುಡ s n The feathered vehicle of Vishnu, an eagle, kite. 2, a building shaped like Garuda 3, a military array. -ಕಂಬ, -ಗಂಬ. A pillar before a temple on which at festivals an image of Garuda or Nandi is set up. -ಪಾತಾಳ. A medicinal herb, *Ophiorrhiza mungos*, said to be an antidote to snake-bites -ಪುರಾಣ. N of a small purâna by Garuda. -ಫಲ. The tree *Hydnocarpus venenata* -ವಾಹನ A kind of idol-conveyance

ಗರುಡಿ (= ಗರಡಿ) k n An abode. 2, a fencing-school, gymnasium; *also* -ಮನೆ -ಸಾಧಕ, -ಸಾಧನೆ Gymnastic exercises

ಗರುವಲಿ (= ಗಾಳಿ) a. k. n. Wind

ಗರುಸು = ಗರಸು, q. v

ಗರ್ಜನೆ k n A sound in loud belching or in creaking.

ಗಗ್ಗರಿ (tb of ಘರ್ಘರಿ) n. A churn -ಗಿಡ. A medicinal herb, *Wedelia calendulacea*

ಗರ್ಜನೆ s n. Roaring; rumbling. 2, wrath; reproach -ಮಾಡು, ಗರ್ಜಿಸು To roar

ಗರ್ಜಿ k n. N. of a tree of which the sour fruits are used for pickles.

ಗರ್ತಿ = ಗರತಿ, q v.

ಗರ್ದಭ s. n. An ass

ಗರ್ಧನೆ s n. Greediness.

ಗರ್ಭ (= ಗಬ್ಬ) s. n. The womb 2, an embryo. 3, a child. 4, the inside, interior -ಗುಡಿ, -ಗೃಹ A lying-in chamber, the sanctuary of a temple -ಧರಿಸು To conceive -ಧಾರಣ. Pregnancy, gestation. -ವತಿ. A pregnant female -ಶ್ರೀಮಂತ Born to riches and honour. -ಸಂಸ್ಕಾರ A purificatory rite observed by pregnant females. ಗರ್ಭಿಣಿ. Pregnant, a pregnant woman ಗರ್ಭಿತ Pregnant, inclosed. ಗರ್ಭೀಕರಿಸು ... [illegible]

ಗರ್ವ (= ಗಬ್ಬ) s. n. Pride, arrogance, conceit. -ಹೀನ. Prideless. ಗರ್ವಿ Proud, haughty. ಗರ್ವಿಷ್ಠ. Most haughty. ಗರ್ವಿಸು To become proud.

ಗರ್ವು. tb. of ಗರ್ವ, q v.

ಗಲಗಲ (= ಕಲಕಲ) s n Clamour, confused chatter. -ಮಾಡು. To chatter loudly.

ಗಲಗು 1 k n A kind of reed for pens.

ಗಲಗು 2. k. n. Loud chatter.

ಗಲತಿ = ಗಲ್ಲತ್ತು, q v

ಗಲಬರಿಕೆ k. n Rinsing ಗಲಬರಿಸು To rinse

ಗಲಬಿಲಿ = ಗಲಿಬಿಲಿ, q. v

ಗಲಟೆ f. n Hubbub, uproar, clamour

ಗಲಮಿಸೆ h n Mustaches curling over the cheeks.

ಗಲಸೋಧನೆ s. n. A kind of jugglery consisting in swallowing stones, *etc*

ಗಲಿಬಿಲಿ k. n Disorder, confusion.

ಗಲೀಜು h. a. Dirty, filthy

ಗಲುಹು k n. Tinkling, jingling.

ಗಲೇಪು h. n A case, *as* of a pillow, sofa, *etc*

ಗಲ್ಪಟ್ಟಿ s n. A wrapper round the throat, neck-tie

ಗಲ್ಲ k n The cheek. -ತಗ್ಗು A dimple in the cheek [ಗಲತಿ

ಗಲ್ಲತ್ತು h a Astray; misplaced, *also*

ಗಲ್ಲಾ h. n. Corn 2, = ಗಲ್ಲೆ, q. v

ಗಲ್ಲಿ s n A lane, alley

ಗಲ್ಲಿಸು k v t To shake, *as* the boiled contents of a pot, *etc*, or *as* corn, *etc*, on a fan 2, to trouble annoy. v i. To be troubled, *etc*

ಗಲ್ಲು f n Hanging, *as* a culprit. ಗಲ್ಲಾಗು To be hanged ಗಲ್ಲಿಗೆ ಕೊಡು, -ಹಾಕು To hang on the gallows ಗಲ್ಲಿನ ಶಿಕ್ಷೆ Punishment by hanging -ಮರ A gallows.

ಗಲ್ಲೆ k. n. A lump, clot 2, (= ಗಲ್ಲಾ) a money-hole in the shop of shroffs and [illegible]

ಗವ k. n. Smart itching -ಗವ ಎನ್ನು. To itch very much

ಗವತ. = ಗವುಡ, q v.

ಗವನ k n. Attention, care, heed. ಗವನಿಸು. To heed, mind

ಗವಯ s n A species of ox, the Gayal.

ಗವರಿಗ (ರ=ಱ) a. k n. A basket-maker

ಗವಲು. = ಗವುಲು, q. v.

ಗವಸಣೆ, -ಕೆ, -ಗೆ k n A cover, wrapper, case, sack.

ಗವಳಿ 1. = ಗವುಳಿ, q v

ಗವಳಿ 2. ಗವಳಿಗ (=ಗೌಳಿಗ, ಗೋವಳಿಗ. tb. of ಗೋಪಾಲಿ, -ಕ) n A man of the cowherd caste; f ಗವಳಿಗಿತ್ತಿ

ಗವಾಕ್ಷ s n A small round-window; an air-hole.

ಗವಾರ h a. Rustic, clownish.

ಗವಿ k. n. A cave, cell. 2, covering -ಸು To heed, pay attention.

ಗವುಜಿ k. n Noise, hubbub

ಗವುಡ (=ಗೌಡ) s n. The chief officer of a village. 2, a title of honour among peasants; f. -ಗಿತ್ತಿ, -ಸಾನಿ -ತನ, ಗವುಡಿಕೆ. A Gavuda's business ಗವುಡಿ A maidservant.

ಗವುಲಿ f n. A flour-paste made into threads and cut into small bits.

ಗವುಲು (=ಗವಲು) k n. A fetid smell

ಗವುಳಿ k. n The house lizard

ಗವ್ಯ s a. Belonging to a cow. milk, cheese, butter, urine and dung; also ಪಂಚ-.

ಗಸಗಸ k. n A sound like quick rubbing -ತಿಕ್ಕು. To rub, as the teeth, clothes on a stone, etc.

ಗಸಣಿ k n Care, concern, grief.

ಗಸಿ k. n The sediment or dregs of oil, melted butter, or pickles.

ಗಸ್ತಿ h. n. A patrol, going the rounds; also -ಪಹರೆ

ಗಹಗಹ k. n The sound of laughter. ಗಹಗಹಿಸು. To laugh merrily. ಗಹಗಹಿಕೆ. Hilarity

ಗಹನ s a. Deep, dense; inaccessible. 2, difficult of comprehension, profound. n. A thicket, a wood 2, a mystery, secret.

ಗಹ್ವರ s a. Deep 2, contiguous. n A thicket 2, an abyss; a cave. 3, a deep secret. 4, a jungle. 5, hypocrisy

ಗಳ 1. (=ಗಲ) s. n The neck, throat. -ದೊಡಿಗೆ A neck-ornament -ಗಾಳ. A hook for the throat

ಗಳ 2. (=ಗಱ) k n Quick motion. -ಗಳನೆ Quickly

ಗಳಪು (ಳ=ೞ) k v. i To chatter, prate. n Idle talk ಗಳವ. A loquacious, lying man ಗಳವತ್ತು Idle prattle.

ಗಳಗೆ, ಗಳಿಗೆ 1. (tb of ಘಟಿಕೆ) n A high bamboo-basket for storing corn

ಗಳಂತಿಗೆ f. n An inner chamber.

ಗಳಿಕೆ (ಳಿ=ೞಿ) f. n. Acquirement, acquisition, gain.

ಗಳಿಗೆ 2. (tb. of ಘಟಿಕೆ) n A fold, as of cloth.

ಗಳಿಗೆ 3. (ಳ=ೞ) (tb. of ಘಟಿಕೆ) n. A period of twenty-four minutes; a short time

ಗಳಿಸು (tb of ಘಟಿಸು) v t. To procure; to acquire, obtain, gain.

ಗಳು k. An affix of the plural, as ಮನೆ-, ಮರ-, ಕಾಲು-, ಇವು-, etc.

ಗಳೆ (ಳೆ=ೞೆ) k n. A bamboo rod, a pole, staff, a churning stick.

ಗಳೇವು h n A complete agricultural apparatus, a set of implements.

ಗಾಗಳ k n Noise; hubbub.

ಗಾಂಗೇಯ (fr. ಗಂಗಾ) s. a. Belonging to the Ganges. n. Karna 2, Bhishma.

ಗಾಜು (tb of ಕಾಚ, q v) n. Glass

ಗಾಂಜಿ (= ಗಂಜ) s n The dried heads of the hemp-plant. -ಗಿಡ The hemp-plant, Cannabis sativa

ಗಾಟ, ಗಾಟು (=ಕಾಟು) k. n A sharp, strong smell as of tobacco, burnt chillies, etc.

ಗಾಡಿ m. n A load-cart, a carriage. -ಚಟ್ಟು. The inner seat of a cart -ಸತ್ತು

A round nose-ring. -ಗಾರ. -ಯವ. A cart-driver.

ಗಾಡಿಗ (= ಗಾರುಡಿಗ) s. n A juggler.

ಗಾಢ s a Hidden or absorbed in 2, tight, close, firm, compact, deep, sound, *as* sleep; intense. 3, excessive, much -ನಿದ್ರೆ A sound sleep ಗಾಢಾಂಧಕಾರ Thick darkness.

ಗಾಣ k n An oil-mill; a sugarcane-mill. 2, (= ಗಾಳ) a hook; a fish-hook. -ಆಡಿಸು. To work a mill

ಗಾಣಿಗ k n An oil-miller, *f.* ಗಾಣಗಿತ್ತಿ.

ಗಾಂಡಿವ, ಗಾಂಡೀವ s. n. Arjuna's bow ಗಾಂಡಿವಿ, ಗಾಂಡೀವಿ. Arjuna.

ಗಾಂಡು m. n The posteriors -ಗುಡಿಗೆ. A bump with the knee upon a boy's posteriors; an aching fever. [ಘಾತ.

ಗಾತ (*tb. of* ಖಾತ) n. Depth 2, *tb. of*

ಗಾತರ, ಗಾತ್ರ 1. (=ಗಡತರ, *q. v.*) k. n Stoutness; thickness.

ಗಾತಿ (= ಗಾತೀ) s. *A fem affix of nouns, as*· ತಚ್ಚಿ-, ಕೋಪ-, ಜಗಳ-, ವಿನೋದ-, *etc.*

ಗಾತ್ರ 2. s. n A limb of the body 2, the body [proverb

ಗಾಥೆ (= ಗಾದೆ) s. n. A song; a saying,

ಗಾದರಿ k n The mark left by a whip, by the bite of a musquito, *etc*

ಗಾದಿ h n Cushion 2, the seat of an eminent personage.

ಗಾದೆ (*tb. of* ಗಾಥೆ) n. A saying, proverb, *also* -ಮಾತು [*cf.* ಆ-

ಗಾಧ s a. Fordable, shallow. n Bottom.

ಗಾನ s n. Singing, a song

ಗಾಂಧಾರ s n. The third of the seven primary notes of music. 2, Candahar and its people

ಗಾಂಧಾರಿ s n N of the wife of Dhritarâshtra 2, N of a râga.

ಗಾಬರ, ಗಾಬರಿ (=ಘಾಬರ) h. a. Overcome by terror, grief, *etc* n Terror, consternation

ಗಾಬು k n Fear, alarm.

ಗಾಂಪ k n A rustic, simpleton -ತನ The behaviour of a rustic. ಗಾಂಪು. Stupidity

ಗಾಂಭೀರ್ಯ s. n Deepness, profundity, earnestness, sagacity

ಗಾಯ (= ಘಾಯ) k. n. A hit, bruise, wound 2, (*tb of* ಗಾಲ) straining, sifting

ಗಾಯಕ s. n A singer, musician

ಗಾಯತ್ರಿ s. n A song 2, N. of a type of metres 3, the vedic verse repeated by every Brâhmana.

ಗಾಯನ s n Singing, song. -ಗಾರ A singer, musician.

ಗಾರ s *A masc affix of nouns denoting* agency, profession, *etc*, *as*· ಕಂಚು-, ಕುದುರೆ-, *etc.*

ಗಾರಡ, ಗಾರಡಿ *tb. of* ಗಾರುಡ, *q. v.*

ಗಾರಣ a k. n. Tale-bearing, calumniating.

ಗಾರಿಗೆ k n A flat cake made of wheat or black gram and fried in ghee or oil. ಗಾರಿಸು. To fry.

ಗಾರು k. n. A sharp eruption on the body from internal heat. -ಬೊಕ್ಕೆ. A rash

ಗಾರುಡ (*fr* ಗರುಡ) s a. Relating to garuda. n A charm against poison. 2, jugglery -ತನ, ಗಾರುಡಿ Jugglery ಗಾರುಡಿಗ A conjurer, juggler, a poison doctor

ಗಾರೆ m n Lime, plaster, mortar. -ಕೆಲಸ. A plastering work. -ಗಾರ. A plasterer

ಗಾರ್ದಭ s a. Asinine. n An ass.

ಗಾಲ (= ಗಾಯ No. 2) s n. Flowing; straining, swallowing.

ಗಾಲಿ k. n. A wheel.

ಗಾಲಿತ s. a Strained, sifted. [hurry

ಗಾಲುಮೇಲು m n Disorder, commotion,

ಗಾವದ, ಗಾವುದ (*tb of* ಗವ್ಯೂತ) n An Indian league

ಗಾಸಿ (=ಘಾಸಿ) k. n. Trouble, annoyance, fatigue, pain.

ಗಾಳ k n A fish-hook

ಗಾಳಿ (= ಘಾಳಿ, *q v*) k. n Wind, air; emptiness, a demon. *Cpds* : ಒಳ-, ತಂ-,

[illegible] ಟು

A mass of lies. -ತಕ್ಕೊಳ್ಳು. To take an airing. -ಪಟ A paper kite -ಪೂಜೆ Demon worship. -ಬಿಡು. Wind to begin to blow. -ಮಾತು. An empty word, abuse, slur. -ಸುದ್ದಿ. A false report -ಹಾಕು. To fan.

ಗಾಳಿಸು s. v t To strain, to sift

ಗಿಜ್ಜಿ k n Pegging one top into another -ಹೊಡೆ To peg likewise

ಗಿಜಿ k. *A sound denoting confusion* -ಗಿಜಿ The state of being crowded -ಗುಟ್ಟು To be crowded -ಬಿಜಿ. The chirping of birds, confusion, disorder

ಗಿಂಜು k. n Being full of seeds and disagreeable taste

ಗಿಟಕ, ಗಿಟಕು k n. The kernel of the cocoanut when still in the nut

ಗಿಟ್ಟು (=ಕಿಟ್ಟು) k. v. i. To be obtained 2, to be closely pressed ಗಿಟ್ಟದವ A useless man.

ಗಿಡ k n. A plant; a small tree, shrub. -ಗಡ್ಡ, -ಗಂಟಿ *dupl* -ಮೂಲಿಕೆ Medicinal plants and roots, a herbal medicine.

ಗಿಡಗ, ಗಿಡುಗ k n A hawk, a falcon

ಗಿಡಿ k v t To devour by mouthfuls. n. An imitative sound -ಬಿಡಿ A small drum like an hour-glass

ಗಿಡು =ಗಿಡ, *q. v.*

ಗಿಡ್ಡ k n A short, small man, a dwarf. -ನೆ Short, small *Cpds:* -ಕಾಲು, -ಕೈ -ನಾಯಿ, *etc.*

ಗಿಡ್ಡು k n. Shortness, smallness.

ಗಿಣಿ (=ಗಿಳಿ) k n A parrot -ಮೂಗು A parrot's beak, a Roman nose.

ಗಿಂಟ k n Gingham, stout cloth.

ಗಿಂಡಿ k. n A small round water-vessel with or without a spout.

ಗಿಣ್ಣ, ಗಿಣ್ಣು 1. k n The milk of a lately calved cow or buffalo.

ಗಿಣ್ಣೆ k n A cancerous disease destroying toes and fingers

ಗಿಣ್ಣು 2. (=ಗೆಣ್ಣು) k. n A knot, joint, *as* of a sugarcane, finger, *etc.*

ಗಿತ್ತಿ k *A fem affix of nouns, as:* ಕುಟಿಲ-, ಕುಂಬಾರ-, ಡೊಂಬರ-, *etc.*

ಗಿದ್ದ k n A quarter ($\frac{1}{4}$). -ಕಾಣಿ. $\frac{1}{4}$ of a kâni. -ನ The fourth part of a sôlige.

ಗಿರ =ಗಿದ್ದ -ಕಾಲು. $\frac{1}{16}$ part -ಪಾವು $\frac{1}{4}$ part of a measuring seer

ಗಿರಕು (ರ=ಱ) k n Being close, strait, narrow.

ಗಿರಗಿ, ಗಿರಿಗಿ k. n. The ankle.

ಗಿರಣಿ f. n. A cotton-press

ಗಿರದಿ f. n. A round cushion

ಗಿರಬ್ದಾರಿ h. n. Distress, penury; fate.

ಗಿರಾಕಿ h. n A buyer, a customer. a. Saleable

ಗಿರಾಸತಿ (*tb. of* ಗೃಹಗತಿ) n. One's private affairs.

ಗಿರಾಯಿಸು =ಗೇರಾಯಿಸು, *q. v*

ಗಿರಿ 1 s. n. A mountain, hill. a. Respectable, venerable -ಕಣಿಕೆ A species of Achyranthes -ಜಾ, -ಜಾತೆ, -ಜೆ, -ಸುತೆ Mountain-born · Pârvati. -ಧರ. Krishna; Vishnu in the form of a tortoise. -ರಾಜ The Himâlaya -ಶೃಂಗ. A mountain peak.

ಗಿರಿ 2. h. *Aff denoting office, business or profession, as* ದಿವಾನ-, ಸಿಪಾಯಿ-, ಮುನಿಸಿ-

ಗಿರಿ 3. (ರಿ=ಱಿ) k n Whirling, buzzing. -ಗಿಟ್ಟಿ. A kind of rattle-box -ಗಿರಿತಿರುಗು To turn round with speed

ಗಿರು (ರು=ಱು) k n Creaking -ಗಟೆ. A sort of castanets, a child's turning rattle -ಗುಟ್ಟು To creak, *as* a door.

ಗಿರ್ರನೆ k ad Quickly, speedily; with a whirl.

ಗಿಲಕು k n. Tinkling, rattling, *etc.*, a jingle -ಗಿಲಕು. *rep.* The sound emitted by the gejje

ಗಿಲಾಯ, ಗಿಲಾಯಿ h n. A plaster of lime, water and sand.

ಗಿಲಿ k. n Fear. -ಹಿಡಿ. To be afraid

ಗಿಲಿಕೆ k. n. A child's rattle-box.

ಗಿಲಿಬಿಲಿ =ಗಲಿಬಿಲಿ, *q. v.*

ಗಿಲ್ಲಾ h n A complaint, slander.

ಗಿಳಿ (=ಗಿಣಿ) k n A parrot

ಗೀಂಕಾರ k n The roaring of an elephant, also ಘೀಂಕಾರ

ಗೀಚಲುಬಾಚಲು (=ಗೀಚುಬಾಚು) k n Scrawl scribble

ಗೀಚು, ಗೀಜು, ಗೀರು k v t. To scrape, to scratch, scrawl, to draw lines with a pen, to erase v i To scribble. n A scratch; scrawling, a furrow -ಬಾಚು = ಗೀಚಲು ಬಾಚಲು, q v

ಗೀಜಗ, ಗೀಜುಗ k. n. The bottle-bird, *Ploceus baya.*

ಗೀಟು (=ಗೀರು, q v) k n A line, stroke

ಗೀತ, ಗೀತೆ s. n A song, hymn. ಗೀತಿ Singing; a song. 2, the Bhagavadgîtâ.

ಗೀಮು k n. A house, abode

ಗೀರು (=ಗೀಚು, ಗೀಜು, q v.) k v t. To scrape or rub off, *as* butter; to draw. *as* lines n A scratch, a line, streak, stripe, groove ಗೀರ ಚಿಪ್ಪು, -ಸಿಂಪಿ A striped shell -ಗಂಧ Sandal streaks on the body. -ನಾಮ A sectarian line of gôpi on the forehead. -ಬಳೆ A fluted gold bracelet.

ಗೀರ್ವಾಣ s. n A god, deity -ಭಾಷೆ Samskrita

ಗುಂಯಿ k. n. Whizzing, buzzing. -ಗುಂಯಿ rep *The sound of some insects*

ಗುಕ್ಕು 1. k. v t To draw a deep breath whilst speaking. ಗುಕ್ಕು ಮಾತಾಡು To falter in speaking

ಗುಕ್ಕು 2 k. n. An inarticulate sound. 2, a mouthful. 3, palpitation of the heart.

ಗುಗ್ಗರಿ k. n Grain boiled and seasoned. 2, shrinking 3, =ಗುಗ್ಗುರಿ -ಕಸ An annual weed, *Hedyotis aspera* -ಗೋಣಿಲು. A mode of punishing boys by tying the hands round the knees in a sitting posture and fixing a stick between them

ಗುಗ್ಗಳ (=ಗುಗ್ಗುಲು) s. n. The fragrant gum bdellium, a powder made of it.

ಗುಗ್ಗುರಿ k n Curling, bristling, *as* the hair of the body. 2, =ಗುಗ್ಗರಿ -ಗೊಳ್ಳು. To become erect, horripilate, bristle.

ಗುಗ್ಗುಲು, ಗುಗ್ಗುಳ. =ಗುಗ್ಗಳ, q v 2, the tree *Amyris agallochum.* 3, *Moringa hyperanthera*

ಗುಂಗಾತೆ, ಗುಂಗಾಡಿ, ಗುಂಗಾಣಿ k n. A musquito

ಗುಂಗಿ k n A large black bee, *also* -ಹುಳ

ಗುಂಗು k. n. The husk of paddy.

ಗುಂಗುರು 1. k n. Curling -ಕೂದಲು. = ಉಂಗುರ ಕೂದಲು. Curled hair

ಗುಂಗುರು 2 k n An eye-fly. 2, a musquito, gnat

ಗುಚ್ಛ s. n A bundle, tassel. bunch, *as* of flowers; a cluster 2, a bush 3, a necklace of 32 strings

ಗುಜರಾಥ (=ಗುಜ್ಜರಾಷ್ಟ್ರ, *tb. of* ಗುರ್ಜರರಾಷ್ಟ್ರ) n. The district of Gujarât ಗುಜರಾಥಿ. An inhabitant or language of Gujarât.

ಗುಜರಾನು h. n. Livelihood, subsistence

ಗುಜರಿ (=ಗುಜ್ಜರಿ) f. n. The evening market

ಗುಜಸ್ತ h a. Past, *as* a year, *etc*

ಗುಜುಗುಜು k. n *A sound in whispering;* whispering -ಮಾತಾಡು, ಗುಜುಗುಜಿಸು. To whisper

ಗುಜುರು, ಗುಜ್ಜ 1 a. k. n Shortness, smallness.

ಗುಜ್ಜ 2. k. n A dwarf.

ಗುಜ್ಜರಾಷ್ಟ್ರ. = ಗುಜರಾಥ, q v. -ಪಟ್ಟೆ Fine cloth from Gujarât.

ಗುಜ್ಜರಿ. = ಗುಜರಿ, q. v.

ಗುಜ್ಜಾರಿ k n. A dwarf; *f.* ಗುಜ್ಜಿ.

ಗುಜ್ಜು k n. A small perpendicular post, to raise short beams, a queen-post. 2, shortness, smallness

ಗುಂಜಾಯಿಷಿ h n. Illicit profit, excess of the area of the land under assessment.

ಗುಂಜಾಲಾಡು s n. A sweetmeat of Bengal gram-dough formed like Abrus seeds.

ಗುಂಜಿ s n. The seed of *Abrus precatorius, also* ಗು[illegible]

ಗುಂಜು k v i. To be entangled, *as* thread. 2, to pull, contract, *as* muscles. *n.* Particles of cotton sticking to one's cloth, nap. 2, the coir of cocoanuts.

ಗುಟಕು, ಗುಟುಕು k *n* A single gulp or draught of any liquid ಗುಟುಕರಿಸು. To drink in a single gulp. ಗುಟುಗುಟು ಕುಡಿ, ಗುಟುಕಿಸು. To drink in gulps ಗುಟುಕ್ಕನೆ With a single gulp.

ಗುಟಗರೆ k *v i* To grunt, bellow, *as* a bull.

ಗುಟಿಕೆ s *n.* A pill, bolus.

ಗುಟ್ಟ. = ಗುಡ್ಡ, *q. v.*

ಗುಟ್ಟಿ k *n* A mixture of medicine for babies.

ಗುಟ್ಟು k. *n* A secret, a hidden thought, one's private affairs

ಗುಡ s *n* A ball, globe 2, molasses, jaggory -ಪಾನ. A beverage made of jaggory, *etc.*

ಗುಡಸಲು, ಗುಡುಸಲು, *etc* k. *n* A hut with a thatched roof.

ಗುಡಸು k. *n* A round thing 2, (=ಗುಡಿಸು) the round mark ᵒ used for the vowel ಓ, *and* the round mark ⁻ used for the vowel ಉ.

ಗುಡಾಕು f *n* A preparation of tobacco for smoking or snuff.

ಗುಡಾಣ k *n* A large water-vessel, caldron.

ಗುಡಾರ s *n* A tent 2, a thick coarse cloth

ಗುಡಿ 1. (=ಗುಡಸು No 1) k *n* A circle; a halo 2, a mass, cluster. -ಕಟ್ಟು A halo to form round the sun or moon, to form a ring; to come together, *as* people.

ಗುಡಿ 2. (*tb of* ಕುಟಿ) *n* A house, a temple -ಗಟ್ಟು. A group of houses -ಗಾರ A turner and cabinet-maker.

ಗುಡಿಗೆ h *n.* Breeches -ಚಣ್ಣ A sort of breeches.

ಗುಡಿಸು k. *v t* To sweep. 2, to heap up. ಗುಡಸಲು, ಗುಡಿಸಲು. Sweeping

ಗುಡುಗು 1. k. *v i* To run when playing at tip-cat or ball. ಗುಡುಗಾಡು. To run about

ಗುಡುಗು 2 k *v i* To thunder *n.* Thunder, roar, *etc*

ಗುಡುಗುಡಿ m *n.* A smoking pipe; a hubble-bubble.

ಗುಡುಗುಡಿಸು k. *v i* To grumble, to roar, to growl, grunt.

ಗುಡುಸಲು. = ಗುಡಸಲು, *q. v.*

ಗುಡ್ಡ 1 k *n.* A boy, pupil, a dwarf. 2, shortness

ಗುಡ್ಡ 2. k *n* A mountain, a hill. -ಗಾಡು. *dpl.* -ಗಾಡುಜನ Jungle-people -ದ ಗೋಣಿಜೇ ಮರ. A shrub, *Alangium lamarkii* -ಪನ್ನೇರಳು A small tree, *Eugenia zeilanica.* -ರಂಜಿಪ್ರ. The tree *Elaeocarpus serratus.*

ಗುಡ್ಡು k. *n* The eye-ball. 2, an egg, spawn 3, shortness, smallness

ಗುಡ್ಡೆ k *n.* A heap, pile 2, a piece of cloth used by men

ಗುಣ s *n.* A cord, string. 2, quality, property 3, the three fundamental qualities. satva, rajas, tamas 4, a good quality, virtue, merit, excellence, wisdom, energy, dignity; goodness; temperance, recovery from sickness, favourable issue, benefit. 5, political wisdom 6, flavour, taste. 7, multiplication. 8, a secondary gradation of a vowel, the vowels a, ê, ô. 9, joy. 10, protection. 11, *at the end of a compound* fold, times. -ಕ (*math*) Multiplier -ಕರ, -ಕಾರ. Profitable. -ಗ್ರಾಹಿ One who appreciates good qualities -ಜ್ಞ. A scholar. -ತ್ವ. Dependence, virtue. -ದೋಷ. Virtue and vice -ಧರ್ಮ The virtue or duty incidental to certain qualities, *as.* clemency is the virtue of royalty -ನ (*math*) Multiplication. -ನಾಮ A name that expresses the nature of a thing, person, *etc* -ನಿಧಿ. An ocean of virtues -ಮಣಿ.

A jewel of virtues -ಯಿಸು = ಗುಣಿಸು -ವಚನ, -ವಾಚಕ (*g.*) An adjective -ವಂತ. A good man, *f.* -ವಂತೆ -ಶ್ರೇಷ್ಠ Pre-eminent in virtues ಗುಣಾಕಾರ. (*math.*) Multiplication ಗುಣಿ Endowed with good qualities ಗುಣಿತ (*math.*) Multiplied, multiplication

ಗುಣಿ (= ಕುಣಿ) k *n* A hole, pit. -ಗಣ್ಣು A sunken eye -ಗಲ್ಲ. A sunken cheek.

ಗುಣಿಸು s. *v t* To multiply, to enumerate, to calculate

ಗುಣಿಕೆ *tb of* ಗುಟಿಕೆ, *q v*

ಗುಣುಗುಟ್ಟು k. *v i* To murmur, grumble, mutter.

ಗುಂಟ 1 k *n.* Proximity. *ad.* Near; along, *as* ದಾರಿ-, ಮನೆ.

ಗುಂಟ 2 (= ಗೂಟ) k *n* A peg, plug

ಗುಂಟೆ f *n* The $\frac{1}{40}$ part of an acre.

ಗುಂಡ (= ಗುಂಡಿ, ಗುಂಡು) k. *n* Roundness, hollowness and deepness 2, a N.; a servant. -ಬಾವಿ. A temporary well sunk in the dry bed of a stream -ಬಟ್ಟಲು A small round and deep metal vessel -ಗೆ. Of a round, globular form. -ಲಿಗೆ. A round water-vessel.

ಗುಂಡಾಂತರ k *n* A foundation. -ಮಾಡು. To lay a foundation, to ruin completely

ಗುಂಡಿ (= ಗುಂಡ) k. *n.* A hole, pit hollow 2, = ಗುಂಡಿಗೆ, *q v* 3, a large round vessel -ಕಾಯಿ The physical heart.

ಗುಂಡಿಗೆ k *n* The pit of the stomach 2, the thorax, heart; courage

ಗುಂಡು 1 a k *n* A heap, mass, a crowd, *etc*

ಗುಂಡು 2 k *n* Anything round, *as* a boulder, a stone for grinding or constructing an ôlĕ, a globe, a ball, marble, a bullet, cannon ball. -ಅರ, ಗುಂಡರ A round file -ಕಲ್ಲು A grinding stone. -ಮಲ್ಲಿಗೆ. A kind of jasmine. -ಮುಳುಗ A diving water-bird -ಹಾರಿಸು -ಹೊಡೆ To shoot a bullet, to fire a gun.

ಗುಣ್ಯ s *a* Endowed with qualities *n* The mu[illegible]

ಗುತ್ತ k. *n.* Closeness; tightness -ಬಳೆ A tight bracelet. -ನೆ Closely, tightly.

ಗುತ್ತಾ. ಗುತ್ತೆ. = ಗುತ್ತಿಗೆ, *q v*

ಗುತ್ತಿ a k *n* A bunch or cluster of flowers. 2, a bush

ಗುತ್ತಿಗೆ ಗುತ್ತೆ k *n* An exclusive right of sale, farm, monopoly 2, rental on land.

ಗುದಗ k *n.* A fat, stout man, *f.* ಗುದಗಿ. 2, a prop behind a door to keep it shut

ಗುದಗೆ. = ಗುದಿಗೆ, *q v*

ಗುದಿ 1 k *n* A rope for the feet used in climbing palm trees. 2 a bunch.

ಗುದಿ 2 k *v i* To jump, to stamp.

ಗುದಿಗೆ, ಗುದುಗೆ (= ಗುದಗೆ) k *n* A club, cudgel

ಗುದ್ದಲಿ, ಗುದ್ಲಿ (*tb. of* ಕುದ್ದಾಲ) *n* A kind of pickaxe, hoe

ಗುದ್ದ k. *n* A clog tied to the neck of cattle

ಗುದ್ದು 1. k. *n.* A hole, *as* of a mouse snake fox, *etc*

ಗುದ್ದು 2 k *v t* To strike with the fist, fist, cuff, box, to pound. *n* A blow with the fist. ಗುದ್ದಾಗುದ್ದಿ Fisticuffs ಗುದ್ದಾಡು To box -ಮೊಳ. A short cubit. -ವಿಕೆ Fisting, pounding

ಗುನಿ k *n* A small crest on the grain of jôla 2, the husk of paddy

ಗುಜ್ಜು k *n.* Smallness 2, a raised spot ಗುಜ್ಜಾನೆ A dwarfish elephant.

ಗುಜ್ಜಾಂಪಟ್ಟಿ k *n* Paper gilt with tinsel

ಗುಪ್ತ s *a* Concealed, hidden, secret 2, guarded, preserved. -ಚ A spy. ಗುಪ್ತಿ Concealment, protection, a sword-stick

ಗುಪ್ಪನೆ k. *ad* Silently.

ಗುಬರು, ಗುಬುರು k *n* Thickness, *as* of a foliage 2, veiling, covering -ಕಟ್ಟು, -ಗಟ್ಟು To become thick in foliage, a cover over the head a cloak

ಗುಬಾರು k *n* Noise of a crowd. 2, a [illegible]

ಗುಬ್ಬಿ 1. k n A knob, protuberance. 2, a button. -ಮೊಳೆ A stout nail with a pommelled head.

ಗುಬ್ಬಿ 2. k. n. A sparrow; *also* ಗುಬ್ಬಚ್ಚಿ. -ಬೆಳಸೆ A small grass whose seeds stick to one's clothes, *Lappago aliena* -ಹುಲ್ಲು. A common grass, *Sporobolus diander*

ಗುಮಗುಮಾಯಿಸು k v. t. To send forth a fragrant odour, *also* ಗುಮಗುಮ ಅನ್ನು.

ಗುಮುಟ, ಗುಮ್ಮಟ h. n A copula or dome 2, a huge figure of stone, representing a Jaina saint.

ಗುಮುರಿ f n Fight of children.

ಗುಮಸ್ತ =ಗುಮಾಸ್ತ, q v.

ಗುಮಾನ h. n. Heed, care, consideration; suspicion, surmise ಗುಮಾನಿ. Suspicious; suspected.

ಗುಮಾಸ್ತ h n An agent, deputy, an accountant. -ಗಿರಿ The post of a gumâsta.

ಗುಂಪು k. n. A mass, heap, crowd, number. -ಕೂಡು, -ಗೊಳ್ಳು To assemble

ಗುಂಫ s. a Stringing together, arranging. -ನ Winding, arranging. ಗುಂಫಿತ. Strung together; arranged.

ಗುಂಬ 1 k n. Mysteriousness, obscurity 2, reservedness.

ಗುಂಬ 2. (*tb of* ಕುಂಭ) n. A pot 2, the nave of a wheel

ಗುಮ್ಮ k. n. A bugbear, devil.

ಗುಮ್ಮಟ. = ಗುಮುಟ, q. v.

ಗುಮ್ಮನ. = ಗುಂಬ 1., q. v -ಗುಸುಕ *dupl.* Reservedness, a reserved man, f. -ಗುಸುಕಿ

ಗುಮ್ಮನೆ k. *ad.* Quickly.

ಗುಮ್ಮು k. v. t To cuff, box, to strike v i To push one's self along, *as* a baby. n. A push forward, *as* in swimming 2, recoil ಗುಮ್ಮಿಕ್ಕು To recoil

ಗುಮ್ಮುಟ = ಗುಮುಟ, q v

ಗುರಕೆ (ರ=ಐ) k. n. Snoring, growling ಗುರಕಾಯಿಸು To growl snarl at, *as* a dog, *etc*; to turn upon one in anger

ಗುರಕು (ರ=ಐ) = ಗುರುತ

ಗುರಾಣಿ s. n A shield.

ಗುರಿ (ರಿ=ಐ) k n An aim 2, a mark, butt -ಕಾರ A man skilled in archery, a headman -ಇಡು, -ನೋಡು, -ಹಿಡಿ. To take aim. -ತಾಕು. To hit the mark. -ಯಾಗು. To become the butt of, to fall into, *as* into sin, to be stricken, *as* with sorrow. -ಹೊಡೆ To aim and shoot; to hit the mark

ಗುರು 1. s a Heavy, weighty; venerable. n Any venerable person, a religious teacher. 2, Brihaspati (Jupiter), the preceptor of the gods. -ಕುಲವಾಸ. Stay in the house of gurus. -ಕುಲವಾಸಿ. A disciple, pupil. -ತರ. Heavier, larger, more important -ತ್ವ. Weight, dignity, worth, a teachership -ದಕ್ಷಿಣೆ. A present to a teacher. -ಭಕ್ತಿ. Devotedness to one's teacher -ಮಠ A guru's residence. -ಮಂತ್ರ. The counsel of a guru -ಮೂರ್ತಿ The visible shape of a teacher, N. -ವಾರ Thursday. -ಶೇಷ The orts of a guru's meal. -ಶೇಷಪ್ರಸಾದ Distribution of the orts of a guru's meal to his devotees -ಹಸ್ತ. A Lingavanta -ಹಿರಿಯರು *dpl.* Preceptors and ancestors.

ಗುರು 2 (ರು=ಐು) k. n A sound in snoring or purring; *also* ಗುರುಕು -ಗುಟ್ಟು, -ಗುರಿಸು, -ಗುರೆನ್ನು To snore; to pur -ಗುಮ್ಮನೆ Silently

ಗುರುಕು. = ಗುರಕೆ, q v.

ಗುರುಗಂಜಿ (= ಗುಲಗಂಜಿ) k n The creeper *Abrus precatorius,* wild liquorice and its seeds

ಗುರುತ, ಗುರುತು (ರ=ಐ) k n A mark, sign, a characteristic mark, any sign used by illiterate persons for their signature 2, knowledge ಗುರುತಿನವ A male acquaintance ಗುರುತಿಲ್ಲದವ. An unacquainted man, a stranger -ಹಚ್ಚು To point out, to note, record. -ಹಿಡಿ, -ಹಿಡಿ To note the peculiar features of a person or thing, to recognise. -ಹೇಳು. To tell the peculiar feature of a person or thing

ಗುರ್ರುಗುಟ್ಟು (=ಗುರುಕಾಯಿಸು & ಗುರಕೆ) k. v i To growl, snarl as dogs, etc.

ಗುರ್ತು. = ಗುರುತು, q v

ಗುರ್ಜಿ k n. The camboge tree, Garcinia pictoria

ಗುರ್ಜರ s n Gujarât -ಪಟ್ಟೆ Woven silk or fine cloth from G

ಗುರ್ವಿ, ಗುರ್ವಿಣಿ s n A pregnant woman

ಗುಲಗಂಜಿ = ಗುರುಗಂಜಿ, q v

ಗುಲಾಬಿ h n. A rose; also -ಹೂ a Rose-coloured. -ಗಿಡ. A rose bush -ಬಣ್ಣ. Rose colour.

ಗುಲಾಮ h. n. A slave, menial -ತನ. Slavery, bondage

ಗುಲಾಲು m. n. The red powder which the Hindus throw about at the hóli feast

ಗುಲ್ಮ s. n A shrub, bush, a thicket. 2, a disease of the spleen 3, a body of troops consisting of 9 elephants, 9 chariots, 27 horses, and 45 foot. -ವೃದ್ಧಿ. Ague-cake-

ಗುಲ್ಲು k n. A loud noise, hubbub.

ಗುಸಗುಸ = ಕುಸಕುಸ, q v.

ಗುಹೆ (=ಗವಿ) s n A cave, cavern.

ಗುಹ್ಯ s a. Private, secret n. A secret, mystery.

ಗುಳ 1. = ಗುಡ, q v.

ಗುಳ 2 (ಳ=ಡ) k n. A horse's or elephant's trappings. 2, (=ಕುಡ) a bar of iron

ಗುಳಿ k. affix for the formation of nouns, as ಆಟ-, ಬಂಚ-.

ಗುಳಿಕ (tb of ಕುಲಿಕ) n N of Kétu

ಗುಳಿಗೆ (tb of ಗುಟಿಕೆ, q v) n A ball, pill, bolus.

ಗುಳುಗುಳು k. n The murmuring sound produced by rippling water.

ಗುಳೆ, ಗುಳ್ಯೆ k n People leaving a place en masse from invasion or famine -ತೆಗೆ, -ಹೋಗು. People to remove en masse, etc -ಗುಳೇದಗುಡ್ಡ N of a place in the Bijapur district

ಗುಳ್ಳ k. n A stout herb, Solanum ferox. 2, a round kind of brinjal

ಗುಳ್ಳಿ, ಗುಳ್ಳೆ k n. A bubble, a blister, a small round shell

ಗೂಗಿ, ಗೂಗೆ (=ಗೂಬೆ) k n An owl

ಗೂಟ (=ಗೂಂಟ) k. n A peg, pin

ಗೂಡು k n A nest, a dove-cot, a fowl-house; a recess, niche, a cage, trap, the pit of the stomach; the hollow in bones; a frame.

ಗೂಡೆ k n A basket.

ಗೂಢ s a. Covered hidden; invisible, secret private, occult -ಚಾರಿ, -ಪುರುಷ. A spy. ಗೂಢಾಂಗ. A tortoise.

ಗೂಂಟ = ಗೂಟ q. v.

ಗೂದೆ 1 k n The love-apple or tomato

ಗೂದೆ 2 k n Prolapsus of the anus

ಗೂನು k. n. A hump -ಬೆನ್ನು A hump-back ಗೂನ A man with a hump, f ಗೂನಿ

ಗೂಬೆ (=ಗೂಗಿ, etc) k. n. An owl -ಗಣ್ಣು. A rolling eye, or one of deficient sight -ಬಾಳು. An idle life, longevity.

ಗೂರಲು, ಗೂರು k. n An asthmatic disease, also ಗೂರುಬ್ಬಸ

ಗೂರು (ರು=ಱು) k v t To root up the earth with horns.

ಗೊವ್ವೆನ್ನು k. v i To murmur or roar, as the water, to sound.

ಗೂಳಿ k. n A bull 2, a big louse -ಬಸವ, -ಹೋರಿ A bull allowed to roam at liberty and dedicated to a deity

ಗೂಳೆ. = ಗುಳೆ, q v

ಗೃಂಜನ s n Garlic

ಗೃಧ್ರ s a Greedy n A vulture.

ಗೃಹ s. n A house. -ಕಲಹ Domestic dissensions. -ಕೃತ್ಯ. Domestic duties, household matters -ಕ್ಷಯ The ruin of a house -ಚ್ಛಿದ್ರ A family folly, a private foible. -ಪತಿ, -ಮೇಧಿ A householder a Brâhmana who is married and settled. -ಪ್ರವೇಶ The ceremony of occupying a newly built house, [illegible] her husband's house -ಮಾತೆ. A mother-in-law. -ಮೇಧ A domestic sacrifice -ಶಾಂತಿ Purificatory ceremonies of a house -ಸ್ಥ, ಗೃಹಾಧಿಪ A householder, a gentleman, patrician -ಸ್ಥಾಶ್ರಮ. The second of the four religious stages of a Brâhmana. -ಸ್ಥಿಕೆ. Politeness, gentlemanliness. -ಣಿ A housewife, a matron ಗೃಹಾವಗ್ರಹಣಿ The threshold. ಗೃಹಿಣಿ. The mistress of a house, a wife.

ಗೃಹ್ಯ, ಗೃಹ್ಯಕ s a. Domestic, domesticated, tame. -ಸೂತ್ರ. A class of ritual works containing directions for domestic ceremonies.

ಗೆ k. *A suffix for the dative, as* · ಅರಸಿಗೆ, ನಾಳೆಗೆ, ಆತಗೆ, ಅಕೆಗೆ, *etc.*

ಗೆಜ್ಜೆ (= ಗಜ್ಜೆ) k. n. A spherical jingling bell 2, the groin -ಗೋಲು A stick to which gĕjjĕs are attached, used in music or by post-runners. -ಹುಲ್ಲು A common grass, *Andropogon aculatus* -ಗಾರ A maker of small bells

ಗೆಡ್ಡೆ (= ಗಡ್ಡೆ, *q v*) k n. Any bulbous root

ಗೆಣತಿ k. n A female companion, *also* ಗೆಣೆಗಾತಿ

ಗೆಣಸು, ಗೆಣೆಸು k n. A bulbous root. a species of *Yam dioscorea;* the sweet potato, *Batatas edulis*

ಗೆಣೆತನ, ಗೆಣತನ, ಗೆಳೆತನ k. n. Companionship, friendship

ಗೆಣ್ಣು. = ಗಿಣ್ಣು, *q v*

ಗೆದಲು (= ಗೆದ್ದಲೆ, *q. v.*) k. n. The white ant, termite

ಗೆದಿ (= ಗೆಲಿ) k *v t* To conquer, to gain

ಗೆದ್ದಲು = ಗೆದಲು, *q v*

ಗೆದ್ದು. = ಗೆಲಿದು, ಗೆಲ್ದು. *P p. of* ಗೆದಿ, ಗೆಲ್ಲು

ಗೆಯಿ, ಗೆಯು k. *v t* To perform, do, to prepare, to work till. *Cpds* . ಕೆಲಸಂ-, ಕ್ಷೇಮ-, ಸಿದ್ಧ-, ಪುಣ್ಯಂ-, ಮುದ್ದು-, *etc.* -ಸು To cause to perform, *etc.* ಗೆಯ್ವೊಕ್ಕಲಿಗ A husbandman

ಗೆರಸೆ, ಗೆರಿಸೆ (= ಕೆರಸೆ, *q. v.*) k n A basket.

ಗೆರೆ k. n A scratch, a line; a streak. -ಹಾಕು To rule, to mark; to draw a line over.

ಗೆಲವು, ಗೆಲುವು k. n. Gain; victory. 2, a happy, sprightly air. -ಸೋಲು Gain and loss

ಗೆಲಿ, ಗೆಲು, ಗೆಲ್ಲು k. *v. t.* To win, gain, to overcome, conquer, to triumph. *P p.* ಗೆಲ್ದು, ಗೆದ್ದು, ಗೆಲುಮೊಗ A winning countenance ಗೆಲುಗೆ, ಗೆಲುವಿಕೆ. Winning ಗೆಲಿಸು, ಗೆಲ್ಲಿಸು. To cause to win, *etc*

ಗೆಳತಿ (= ಕೆಳದಿ, *etc*) k n. A female friend

ಗೆಳೆ (= ಕೆಳೆ, *q v*) k n A friend, companion. -ತನ. Friendship, companionship, *etc*

ಗೇ k. *v. t.* To perform, *etc P p* ಗೇದು.

ಗೇಣಿ k n. Rent, contract. -ಚೀಟು. A lease ಮೂಲ-. A permanent lease ಚಾಲ- Annual lease ವಾಯಿದೆ-. A lease for a fixed time

ಗೇಣು k n A span -ಹೊಟ್ಟೆ The stomach that is only a span in length or breadth

ಗೇಂಡ, ಗೇಂಡಾಮೃಗ f n Rhinoceros.

ಗೇನ. *tb of* ಜ್ಞಾನ, *q. v.*

ಗೇಟೆ k. n A morbid swelling. -ಮೋರೆ A swollen face -ಹೊಟ್ಟೆ. A swollen belly.

ಗೇಮೆ k n. Work. -ಕರಾರು. A labour contract

ಗೇಯು. = ಗೆಯ್ಯು, *q. v.*

ಗೇರಾಯಿಸು h. *v. t.* To surround, hem in.

ಗೇರಿ f n Giddiness.

ಗೇರು 1 k. n *A phlegmatic sound produced in the chest.*

ಗೇರು 2. k. n. The marking-nut tree; the cashew-nut tree. -ಬೀಜ. The marking nut, *Semecarpus anacardium;* the cashew-nut tree.

ಗೇಲಿ k. n Ridicule, derision. -ಮಾಡು. To ridicule.

ಗೈ = ಗೆಯಿ, *etc, as* · ನಿದ್ದೆಗೈ, to sleep. ಯೋಚನೆಗೈ, to reflect, *etc.*

ಗೈರ, ಗೈರು h *pref* Dis-, un-, extra, out of. -ಖರ್ಚು. Extra expense. -ಮಾಮೂ

ಲು That is against custom or usage. -ವಾಜಿಬಿ. Unreasonable, improper. -ವಿಲೆ Out of order; lost -ಹಾಜರು Absent

ಗೊಂಗಡಿ h n A cloak or blanket worn over the head and face. 2, a cumbly

ಗೊಂಗೆ a. k n A mass, heap 2, the large grey babbler.

ಗೊಜಗು k. v i To speak indistinctly. n Indistinct speech.

ಗೊಜ್ಜಲು k. n Mud, mire

ಗೊಜ್ಜು k. n A thick mess of boiled brinjals, mangoes, *etc* mixed with tamarind, chillies, *etc* 2, acidity, sourness.

ಗೊಜ್ಜೆ k n. Putridity, mud, mire

ಗೊಂಚಲು k n. A bunch, cluster, *as:* ಹೂವಿನ-, ಹಣ್ಣಿನ-, ಮುತ್ತುಗಳ-, ಕಾಯಿ-, *etc.*

ಗೊಟಕು. = ಗುಟುಕು, *etc*, *q v.*

ಗೊಟರು k. n. A hole, hollow -ಬೀಳು A hollow to be formed

ಗೊಟ್ಟ k n A bamboo tube for administering food or medicine to cattle. 2, a mango-stone 3, a corner.

ಗೊಟ್ಟು k. n Scarcity 2, dryness 3, obstinacy -ಕಾಲ Drought.

ಗೊತಗು = ಗೊಟರು, *q v.*

ಗೊತವೆ k. n. Connexion, intercourse, concern with, care about.

ಗೊಡ್ಡು (*cf.* ಗೊಟ್ಟು) k. n Barrenness, sterility, saplessness. -ಆಕಳು A barren cow -ಆಟ, ಗೊಡ್ಡಾಟ Nonsense -ಕೆಲಸ Useless work -ಮರ A barren tree -ಮಾತು A vain word. -ಸಾರು. A broth without strength. -ಹರಟೆ. Useless talk.

ಗೊಣಗು k v i To nasalize. n Nasalization 2, grumbling, murmuring. ಗೊಣಗ One who nasalizes, *f* ಗೊಣಗಿ.

ಗೊಣಸು k. n. A link of a chain 2, a loop 3, a bunch of 5 pearls.

ಗೊಂಡೆ k n A cluster, a tuft, a tassel 2, a thickset state 3, an amaranth, *Gomphrena globosa* ಗೊಂಡಾರಣ್ಯ An impervious jungle.

ಗೊಣ್ಣೆ k n Mucus of the nose 2, a blot of ink.

ಗೊತ್ತು (= ಗುರುತು, *q v*) k n A mark, sign, token 2, knowledge, acquaintance 3, appointment, regulation, order, a place of resort or shelter -ಗಾರ. A male acquaintance; a person of distinction; a headman. -ಮಾಡು, -ಹಚ್ಚು, -ಹತ್ತಿಸು To find out ಗೊತ್ತಾಗು. To be known, to be found out

ಗೊದಕು, ಗೊದಗು k n Mud, mire.

ಗೊದಗೊದ k. n Thickness, *as* of ambali, *etc*

ಗೊದಮು k. n A bat used in leading the course of an idol-car.

ಗೊದ್ದ k n. A large black ant.

ಗೊದ್ದೆ k. n Pig's dung

ಗೊನೆ k n A cluster or bunch of fruit, *as* of cocoanuts, plantains, mangoes, *etc*

ಗೊಂದಣಿ, ಗೊಂದಣೆ a k n A mass an assemblage, a crowd, throng. ಗೊಂದಣಿಸು. To assemble, *etc*, to be plentiful

ಗೊಂದಲ f n. Confusion, bustle, tumult

ಗೊಂದಿ k. n An alley, lane 2, a strait.

ಗೊಬ್ಬರ k n Manure 2, the measles

ಗೊಂಬೆ (= ಬೊಂಬೆ) k n. An image, idol, a puppet, doll, the pupil of the eye. -ಮದುವೆ A sham-marriage made by children with dolls

ಗೊರಕು (ರ = ಱ) k n Snoring

ಗೊರಗು k n A kind of hood made of leaves or grass

ಗೊರಜಿ k n N. of a plant -ಪಲ್ಯ A common potherb, *Digera arvensis.*

ಗೊರಲೆ (ರ = ಱ) k n A kind of termites

ಗೊರವ k n. A class of Śaiva beggars, *f* -ತಿ, ಗೊರವಿತಿ.

ಗೊರವಂಕ k n The common Maina, *Acridotheres tristis*

ಗೊರವಿ k. n An evergreen tree which makes good torches, *Ixora parviflora.*

ಗೊರಸು, ಗೊರಿಸೆ, ಗೊರುಸು k n. A hoof

ಗೊಲೆ k n. The notched extremity of a bow 2, a cluster

ಗೊಲ್ಲ (*tb. of* ಗೋಪಾಲ) *n.* A cowherd, *f.* -ತಿ 2, an assistant cashkeeper

ಗೊಳಗೊಳಕೆ k. *n* The yellow thistle, *Argemone mexicana.*

ಗೊಳಲಿ k *n.* Husk, chaff. 2, the rind of a tamarind fruit.

ಗೋ (= ಗೋವು) s. *n* A cow. 2, a bull 3, a ray of light (ಕಿರಣ) 4, heaven. 5, the earth 6, water 7, Sarasvatî -ಕರ್ಣ. A cow's ear, a place of pilgrimage in North Kanara -ಕುಲ A herd of kine, a cow-house; a village on the river Yamunâ, Krishna's residence -ಕುಲಾಷ್ಟಮಿ The birthday of Krishna -ಕ್ಷುರ. The plant *Asteracantha longifolia.* -ಜಾತಿ Cattle, cattle-like nature. -ದಾನ. Gift of a cow -ಧನ. Property in cattle. -ಪಥ. A cattle path. -ಪುಚ್ಛ. A cow's tail; a necklace of 2 or more strings. -ಮಯ. Cowdung -ಮಾಂಸ Beef -ಮಾರಿ A disease of cattle -ಮುಖ A cow's mouth, a round platter with a snout used for placing idols on. -ಮುಖವ್ಯಾಘ್ರ "A wolf in sheep's clothing" -ಮೇಧ Sacrifice of a cow. -ರಕ್ಷ, -ರಕ್ಷಕ. A cowherd -ರಸ Cow's milk, buttermilk -ಶಾಲೆ A cowpen. -ವತ್ಸ. A calf.

ಗೋಗರೆ k *v t* To beg loudly *n* Bellowing sound of a bull-frog.

ಗೋಚರ s. *n* Range (*lit.* field for cattle) *a* Being within range or reach of, accessible, attainable, perceivable by the mind, sense, or the eye -ವಾಗು, ಗೋಚರಿಸು. To become perceptable; to appear

ಗೋಚಿ f *n* A cloth to cover the privities.

ಗೋಜು k *n* Interference, entanglement 2, intercourse. 3, embarrassment, trouble.

ಗೋಟು 1. k. *n* Fringe, ribbon, edging, trimming 2 a stunted tamarind fruit. 3, the state of being full grown, but hard, *as* ಗೋಟಡಕೆ. A hard, inferior kind of areca nut.

ಗೋಟು 2 h *n.* The border or hem of a garment. 2, a cloak of broadcloth

ಗೋಡು k *n.* Sediment from the bottom of wells, tanks, *etc*

ಗೋಡೆ (*tb. of* ಕುಡ್ಯ) *n* A wall -ಗನ್ನ. A hole made by burglars in a wall. ಹಾಳು- A dilapidated wall.

ಗೋಣ k *n* = ಗೋಣು 2, a man with a neck. -ಗೊಯ್ಕ. A cut-throat; *f.* -ಗೊಯ್ತಿ

ಗೋಣಿ 1 k *n* A sack, pack-sack; *also* -ಚೀಲ. 2, a confluent kind of small-pox, *also* -ದಡಾರ -ಚೀಲ, -ತಟ್ಟು. Sackcloth.

ಗೋಣಿ 2 (= ಗೋಳಿ) k. *n.* The tree called *Ficus elastica.*

ಗೋಣು k. *n* The nape, neck, throat. -ಗೊಯ್ಕ. A cut-throat -ಮುರಿದು ಬೀಳು. To drop the head and fall, *as* in dying.

ಗೋತ 1 k. *n.* The fetid urine of cattle.

ಗೋತ 2 k. *n.* A ruinous business, loss. -ಹಾಕು. To die.

ಗೋತ್ರ s *n.* A cow-pen 2, family, race, lineage; kin, offspring. 2, the family-name -ಜ A relation

ಗೋದಣಿ, ಗೋದಲಿ, ಗೋದಲೆ k. *n* A crib for cattle.

ಗೋದಾವರಿ s *n* The Godavery river.

ಗೋದಿ (*tb of* ಗೋಧೂಮ) *n.* Wheat, *Triticum vulgare* -ಕಾಳು A grain of wheat, wheat -ನಾಗರ *Naga tripudians* -ರವೆ, -ಸಜ್ಜಿಗೆ Granulated wheaten flour, rolong -ಹಿಟ್ಟು Wheaten flour.

ಗೋಧೂಳಿ s *n* Dust raised by cattle on the road when coming home. 2, evening twilight. -ಲಗ್ನ. Marriage performed at gôdhûli

ಗೋಧಿ s *n* The forehead. 2, an iguana

ಗೋಧಿಕೆ, ಗೋಧೆ s. *n* A large kind of lizard; an iguana

ಗೋನಾಳಿ a. k *n.* The throat, neck

ಗೋಂದ, ಗೋಂದು h n Gum

ಗೋಪ s n A cowherd. 2, the head of a district, a king. 3, Krishna. -ತಿ A bull -ನ Guarding, protection -ವಾಹನ Indra's vehicle Airâvata, Brahmâ's vehicle the hamsa, Vishnu's vehicle Garuda. -ಸ್ತ್ರೀ. A herd's-woman

ಗೋಪಾಲ (= ಗೋವ, *q v*) s. n A cowherd, a caste of Vaishnava mendicants 2, alms 3, a N. -ಬುಟ್ಟಿ. A mendicant's bamboo basket

ಗೋಪಿ s n. A cowherd's wife, Krishna's foster-mother, a milkmaid -ಚಂದನ A species of white clay used by Vaishnavas for making sectarian marks.

ಗೋಪು (*tb of* ಗೋಪ) n N 2, a neck-ornament

ಗೋಪುರ s n A town-gate, gate; a tower over the gate of a city or temple

ಗೋಪ್ಯ s. a Secret, hidden.

ಗೋಮನಾಳಿ, ಗೋಮಾಳೆ, *etc* k. n. The neck or throat with Adam's apple.

ಗೋಮಯ s n. Cowdung.

ಗೋಮಾಂತಕ s n Goa.

ಗೋಮು f. n A bad mark in a horse.

ಗೋಮೇದಕ, ಗೋಮೇಧಿಕ s n A precious stone of a reddish colour

ಕೋರಟೆ, ಗೋರಂಟ, ಗೋರಂಟೆ (*tb. of* ಕುರಂಟ) n. The prickly flower-plant *Lawsonia spinosa*

ಗೋರಾ h a White, of fair complexion.

ಗೋರಿ 1. h n A grave, tomb

ಗೋರಿ 2 k. n. Drawing together, attracting, decoy 2, a kind of rake -ಕಾಯಿ *Dolichos fabaeformis*

ಗೋರು 1 k v t. To draw; to gather pile, to fish with a net, *etc* 2, to scratch. n. Drawing, *etc* -ಮಣೆ A kind of rake

ಗೋರು 2. f. n Trouble, annoyance.

ಗೋರೆ k n A shovel.

ಗೋರೋಚನ (*tb* ಗೋರೋಜನ) s. n. A yellow [illegible] prepared from the urine or bile of a cow or found in its head

ಗೋಲ (= ಗೋಲು, ಗೋಳ) s n A ball globe, circle sphere -ರಸ Gum-myrrh. ಗೋಲಾಕಾರ Globular. ಗೋಲಾರ್ಧ A hemisphere.

ಗೋಲಕ h n. A money-box, till 2, a ball

ಗೋಲಕೊಂಡ s n Golconda near Hydrabad

ಗೋಲಿ s n A small ball -ಕಲ್ಲು A marble

ಗೋಲು (*tb of* ಗೋಲ, *q. v*) n A circle, ring, a globe. ಗೋಲುಂಗರ A plain finger-ring.

ಗೋವಗಿಡ k n The guava tree, *Psidium guaiava.*

ಗೋವರ್ಧನ s n A hill in Vṛindâvana.

ಗೋವಳ. *tb of* ಗೋಪಾಲ, *q v*

ಗೋವಿಂದ s n A chief-herdsman. 2, Krishna, Vishnu

ಗೋವು = ಗೋ, *q v*

ಗೋವೆ s n Goa

ಗೋಷಾ h n A veil, cover used by Mohammadan women when appearing in public.

ಗೋಷ್ಟಿ m n A word, a story

ಗೋಷ್ಠ s n A cow-pen

ಗೋಷ್ಠಿ s n An assembly 2, a conversation, discourse.

ಗೋಷ್ವಾರೆ h n An abstract, summary

ಗೋಸಾಯಿ, ಗೋಸಾವಿ. *tb of* ಗೋಸ್ವಾಮಿ. *q v.*

ಗೋಸುಂಬೆ k n. A chameleon.

ಗೋಸ್ಕರ. = ಒಸ್ಕರ, *q v*

ಗೋಸ್ವಾಮಿ (= ಗೋಸಾಯಿ) s. n. The master of cows. 2, a religious mendicant

ಗೋಳ (*tb. of* ಗೋಲ, *q v*) n A ball, a globe. 2, (k) clamour, tumult.

ಗೋಳಾಡು k v i To bewail, lament. ಗೋಳಾಟ Lamentation weeping. ಗೋ[illegible]

ಗೋಳಿ k. *n* Any kind of fig tree which bears no apparent flowers, the banyan tree, *Ficus bengalensis* 2, a small potherb of the genus *Portulaca* -ಹಕ್ಕಿ A teal, water-duck

ಗೌಡ 1. (=ಗವುಡ, *q. v*) k *n* The headman of a village, *f.* -ಗಿತ್ತಿ

ಗೌಡ 2 s *n* Sweetmeats 2, the district of Gaur in Bengal -ಮಾರ್ಗ, -ರೀತಿ. The gauda style. -ಬಂಗಾಳಿ Trickery

ಗೌಣ s. *a* Subordinate, secondary.

ಗೌತಮ s *n*. N of Buddha or Sâkyamuni, the founder of the Buddhist sect.

ಗೌರಮ್ಮ, ಗೌರವ್ವ s. & k *n* Pârvati.

ಗೌರವ (*fr* ಗುರು) s *a* Relating to a guru *n* Weight, gravity 2, importance 3, dignity, respectability

ಗೌರಿ s. *n*. A virgin 2, Pârvatî 3, a yellow pigment -ಕಾಂತ, -ಪತಿ Śiva. -ಪಾಷಾಣ. A kind of mineral. -ಪುತ್ರ. Ganapati.

ಗೌಲಿ (=ಗವುಲಿ. *q. v*) f *n* A paste of wheaten flour cut into threads

ಗೌಳಿ (=ಗವಳಿ, ಗವಳಿಗ) k *n* A milkman.

ಗ್ನಾನ. *tb. of* ಜ್ಞಾನ, *q v*

ಗ್ರಂಥ s. *n* Binding. 2, a book or composition in prose or verse, a code, a religious treatise. 3, wealth 4, great knowledge. -ಕರ್ತ, -ಕಾರ An author. -ಲಿಪಿ. One of the characters used in writing.

ಗ್ರಂಥಿ s *n* A knot, a tie, a joint gland

ಗ್ರಸ್ತ s. *a* Devoured, eaten, seized. 2, imperfectly pronounced

ಗ್ರಹ s *n* A planet 2, an imp, evil spirit, demon -ಚಾರ The bad influence of unpropitious stars, fate, destiny. -ಪತಿ The sun -ಪೀಡೆ, -ಬಾಧೆ. Trouble from unpropitious stars or demons. -ಮಾಲೆ The planets -ಶಾಂತಿ. Propitiation of the planets by offerings

ಗ್ರಹಣ s. *n* Seizing, taking, accepting 2. seizure of the sun or moon an eclipse 3, understanding, comprehension.

ಗ್ರಹಣಿ s *n* Diarrhœa, dysentery 2, rickets, marasmus.

ಗ್ರಹಸ್ತ *tb of* ಗೃಹಸ್ಥ, *q. v.*

ಗ್ರಹಿಕೆ s *n* Understanding, comprehension.

ಗ್ರಹಿಸು s *v. t.* To accept, acknowledge; to comprehend, understand.

ಗ್ರಾಚಾರ. *tb. of* ಗ್ರಹಚಾರ *s.* ಗ್ರಹ, *q v*

ಗ್ರಾಮ s *n* A village 2, a multitude collection. -ಕಂಟಕ Village vermin, a mischief-maker. -ಣಿ The headman of a village -ದೇವತೆ The deity of a village. -ಮುನಸೀಪ A Gavuda, a village-munsif -ವಾಸಿ. A villager; tame -ಶಾಂತಿ Purification of a village from infesting devils, *etc.* -ಸ್ಥ. A villager

ಗ್ರಾಮ್ಯ s *a* Rustic, vulgar, coarse, rude *n* A villager, an uneducated man. -ಪಶು. A domestic beast -ಭಾಷೆ. A vulgar dialect -ಶಬ್ದ A vulgar term

ಗ್ರಾಸ s. *n*. A mouthful, morsel. 2, food, nourishment. ಗ್ರಾಸೋಪಾಯ. Means of subsistence

ಗ್ರಾಹಕ s *a* Seizing, receiving, accepting, perceiving -ಶಕ್ತಿ The faculty of comprehension

ಗ್ರಾಹಿ s. *a* Seizing, accepting. *etc*, holding; perceiving

ಗ್ರಾಹ್ಯ s *a*. Perceivable; acceptable, comprehensible

ಗ್ರೀಷ್ಮ, -ಕಾಲ s *n* The hot season from the middle of May to the middle of July, heat, warmth.

ಘ್

ಘ್. The twenty-second letter of the alphabet.

ಘಕಾರ s. n. The letter ಘ.

ಘಟ s. a. Coming to, reaching, joining. n. Collection. 2, a troop of elephants. 3, the body. 4, an earthen water-vessel. -ಸರ್ಪ. A large serpent.

ಘಟಕ s. a. Strong, powerful; forming a constituent part. n. A manager between parties.

ಘಟನೆ s. n. Joining, junction; arranging, effecting, effort, exertion, accomplishment, success.

ಘಟಿ s. n. A small water-jar. 2, a period of 24 minutes. 3, a gong. 4, a sinking cup for measuring time. -ಯಂತ್ರ. A machine for raising water.

ಘಟಿಕೆ (= ಗಳಿಗೆ 3, q. v.) s. n. A period of 24 minutes.

ಘಟಿತ s. a. Joined, united; planned, devised, occurred. ಘಟಿತಾರ್ಥ. Practicableness.

ಘಟಿಸು (= ಗಳಿಸು, q. v.) s. v. i. To be gained, to happen, etc., also ಘಟಿಯಿಸು.

ಘಟೆ s. n. Effort, endeavour. 2, an assemblage, collection.

ಘಟ್ಟ (= ಗಟ್ಟ q. v.) k. n. A range of mountains, ghaut, defile. ಸೋಪಾನ-. A staircase.

ಘಟ್ಟನೆ s. n. Beating down, as a road, folding by beating gently.

ಘಟ್ಟನ (= ಘಟ್ಟನೆ) s. n. Touching, rubbing, beating, striking, compressing, practice.

ಘಟ್ಟಿ (= ಗಟ್ಟಿ, q. v.) k. a. Firm. 2, loud. 3, solid. 4, able, clever. -ಗ. A strong, able man. -ತನ. Strength, energy, ability.

ಘಟ್ಟಿಸು = ಗಟ್ಟಿಸು, q. v.

ಘಟಾ (tb. of ಘಟ) n. A drum formed of an earthen ...

ಘಡಾಯಿಸು = ಗಡಾಯಿಸು q. v.

ಘಡಾರಿ = ಗಡಾರಿ, q. v.

ಘಡಿಯಾರ, ಘಡಿಯಾಲ = ಗಡಿಯಾರ, q. v.

ಘಂಟಾ, ಘಂಟೆ (= ಗಂಟೆ) s. n. A bell, a gong. ಘಂಟಾಕರ್ಣ. An attendant on Śiva. ಘಂಟಾನಾದ, ಘಂಟಾರವ The sound of a bell.

ಘನ s. a. Compact, solid, hard, dense, full, large, great, much, auspicious. n. Any compact substance. 2, respect, honour, dignity, greatness. 2, an assemblage, solidity. -ಅಳತೆ. A cubic measure. -ತರ Uncommonly hard, thick, great, etc. -ತೆ, -ತ್ವ Firmness, solidity, greatness, excellence. ಘನೀಭೂತ Thickened, compact. -ರಸ Water, a decoction, camphor.

ಘಮ, = ಗಮ 1 q. v.

ಘರಟ್ಟ s. n. A grindstone.

ಘರ್ಮ (= ಗರಮು) s. n. Heat, sunshine; the hot season. 2, sweat, perspiration; also -ಜಲ.

ಘರ್ಷಣ s. n. Rubbing, grinding, friction, furbishing.

ಘಳಿಗೆ = ಗಳಿಗೆ 2, 3, q. v.

ಘಳಿಲ್ ಘಳಿಲನೆ (ಳಿ = ಱಿ) a. k. ad. Quickly.

ಘಾಟ, ಘಾಟೆ s. n. The nape of the neck.

ಘಾಡಾ h. a. Thick, coarse, as cloth.

ಘಾತ s. n. Striking, wounding, killing. 2, destruction, ruin, a blow. -ಕ Killing, felonious, a murderer, f. -ಕಿ. -ನ Killing, striking. ವಿಶ್ವಾಸ- Breach of trust. ಘಾತಿ Killing, a killer. ಘಾತಿಸು To strike, to slay, etc.

ಘಾತುಕ s. a. Killing, destructive, mischievous.

ಘಾಬರಿ = ಗಾಬರಿ. q. v.

ಘಾಯ (= ಗಾಯ. q. v.) k. n. A wound. -ವಾಗು. To be wounded.

ಘಾರಿಗೆ = ಗಾರಿಗೆ q. v.

ಘಾಸಿ (=ಗಾಸಿ, *q v*) k *n*. Harass, distress, fatigue; pain, hurt

ಘಾಳಿ (=ಗಾಳಿ, *q. v*) k. *n* Wind, air ಬಿರು-. A hurricane. ತಂ- A cool breeze. -ತಕ್ಕೊಳ್ಳು, -ತಿನ್ನು To take an airing. -ವಾರ್ತೆ, -ಸುದ್ದಿ A false report, a rumour

ಘೀಂಕಾರ (=ಗೀಂಕಾರ, *q v*) k *n* The roaring of an elephant

ಘುಟಿಕೆ s *n*. The ankle.

ಘೃಣೆ, ಘೃಣಿ s *n*. Heat, ardour, tenderness, disgust

ಘೃತ s. *n* Clarified butter, ghee

ಘೇರು f *n*. A circumference.

ಘೋರ s. *a* Terrific, frightful, terrible, awful, vehement. -ತರ Very terrible. -ಮೂರ್ತಿ. Bhairava

ಘೋಷ s *n*. Sound, noise, cry, roar. 2, a station of herdsmen -ಣೆ Speaking loud, crying -ವರ್ಣ, ಘೋಷಾಕ್ಷರ A sonant letter ಘೋಷಿಸು. To make a great noise, to cry out, proclaim

ಘ್ರಾಣ s *n*. Smell, odour, the nose. -ತರ್ಪಣ Fragrant substance, a perfume. ಘ್ರಾಣಿಸು To smell ಘ್ರಾಣೇಂದ್ರಿಯ. The organ of smell

ಙ

ಙ. The twenty-third letter of the alphabet. *No words begin with it*

ಚ

ಚ. The twenty-fourth letter of the alphabet.

ಚಕಚಕ (=ಝಗಝಗ) s *ad*. Glitteringly

ಚಕಡಾ (*tb of* ಶಕಟ) =ಚಕ್ಕಡಿ, *q v*

ಚಕಮುಕಿ, ಚಕ್ಕಮುಕ್ಕಿ h. *n* A flint and steel for striking fire. -ಹತ್ತಿ. Silk-cotton tinder

ಚಕಾರ s *n* The letter ಚ. -ಶಬ್ದ A word.

ಚಕಿತ s *a* Shaking, afraid, timid

ಚಕೋತ (*tb of* ಚಕ್ರವರ್ತ), ಚಕೋತು. =ಚಕ್ಕೋತ, *q v*.

ಚಕೋರ s. *n* The bartavelle or Greek partridge 2, =ಚಕ್ಕೋತ

ಚಕ್ಕಚೌಕ (=ಚಚ್ಚೌಕ) *tb*. *a* Square.

ಚಕ್ಕಡಿ (=ಚಕಡಾ *tb. of* ಶಕಟ) *n* A cart, a travelling cart

ಚಕ್ಕನೆ a. k. *ad* Quickly, suddenly.

ಚಕ್ಕಂದ k. *n*. Idle talk, happiness, pleasure

ಚಕ್ಕರ *tb of* ಚಕ್ರ, *q v*

ಚಕ್ಕಲಗುಳಿ, ಚಕ್ಕಳಗುಳಿ k. *n* Tickling another. -ಮಾಡು To tickle

ಚಕ್ಕಲಿ, ಚಕ್ಕುಲಿ (*tb of* ಶಷ್ಕುಲಿ) *n* A cake made in the form of a ring and fried in ghee or oil

ಚಕ್ಕವಕ್ಕಿ =ಚಕ್ರವಾಕ *s*. ಚಕ್ರ, *q v*.

ಚಕ್ಕಳ 1. k *n* A cot or seat of cane or bamboo -ಬಕ್ಕಳ, -ಮುಕ್ಕಳಿ Sitting cross-legged

ಚಕ್ಕಳ 2 f *n*. Skin, leather

ಚಕ್ಕುಬಂದಿ h. *n* Defining of the boundaries of an estate, jurisdiction

ಚಕ್ಕೆ (=ಚೆಕ್ಕೆ, ಸಕ್ಕೆ. *tb. of* ಶಲ್ಕ) *n*. A chip of wood or of stone

ಚಕ್ಕೋತ, ಚಕ್ಕೋತು (=ಚಕೋತ, *etc. tb. of* ಚಕ್ರವರ್ತ) *n* The pumplemose or shaddock, *Citrus decumana* 2, an esculent vegetable, goose-foot

ಚಕ್ರ (=ಚಕ್ಕರ) s *n* A wheel. 2, a potter's wheel 3, a discus 4 a circle, diagram. 5 a plaything for children 6, a realm, rule. 7, a circuit 8, a multitude, a form of military array. 9, the horizon 10, an ancient coin, a quarter rupee -ಧರ, -ಪಾಣಿ. Vishnu or Krishna -ವರ್ತಿ =-ವಾಕ. -ವರ್ತಿ A sovereign, emperor. -ವರ್ತಿನಿ An empress -ವರ್ತಿಸೊಪ್ಪು. The pot-herb, *Chenopodium album*, the goose-foot. -ವಾಕ. The ruddy goose ಚಕ್ರಾಂಗ. A gander. ಚಕ್ರಾಂಗಿ A goose.

ಚಕ್ಲಿ k *n* A cultivated tree, the Manilla tamarind, *Pithecolobum dulce*.

ಚಕ್ಷು s *n* The eye. -ರಿಂದ್ರಿಯ. The sense of seeing

ಚಗಚೆ (=ಚೊಗಚೆ) k. *n* The plant *Cassia tora*

ಚಂಗ =ಚಂಗ್ಯ, *q. v.*

ಚಂಗದಿರ =ಚೆಂಗದಿರ, *q v*

ಚಂಗನೆ k *ad* In bounds, with agility.

ಚಂಗಲಕೋಷ್ಟ k *n* A sort of *Costus*.

ಚಂಗು 1. k *n* A jump, leap, *etc*, agility *v. i* To jump *etc.* -ಚಂಗನೆ ಹಾರು. To jump with agility

ಚಂಗು 2. h. *n* A Jew's harp

ಚಂಗೂಲಿ k. *n* A day-labourer

ಚಂಗ್ಯ (=ಚಂಗ) k *n* Crookedness, perverseness -ಮುಂಗ್ಯತನ. Apish pranks, frolics, sport.

ಚಚ್ಚರ (=ಚೆಚ್ಚರ) k *n* Haste. 2, wakefulness care.

ಚಚ್ಚು =ಚಿಚ್ಚು, *q v*

ಚಚ್ಚೌಕ (=ಚಕ್ಕಚೌಕ, *q v*) f *a* Square

ಚಜ್ಜಿ k *n* A kind of grain, *Holcus spicatus*

ಚಂಚಲ s *a* Shaking, unsteady, fickle, capricious. *n.* The wind -ತನ, -ತ್ವ Unsteadiness, fickleness. -ಮನಸ್ಸು Fickle-mindedness.

ಚಂಚಲಿ k *n* A small cultivated tree, *Flacou*[illegible]

ಚಂಚಲೆ s. *n* Lightning, fortune

ಚಂಚಿ m. *n.* A bag with pockets for betel, *etc*

ಚಂಚು s *n* The beak of a bird

ಚಂಜಿ = ಸಂಜೆ, *q v*

ಚಟ s *n* A taste, taking, an acquired liking or fondness, an ill-habit -ತೀರಿಸಿ ಕೊಳ್ಳು. To eradicate a habit.

ಚಟಕ k *n.* A ceremony in honor of the departed ancestors, *also* -ಶ್ರಾದ್ಧ. 2, a sparrow, *f.* ಚಟಕೆ

ಚಟಕಾಯಿಸು (=ಚಟಾಯಿಸು) h *v. t* To cut or knock off, cut short.

ಚಟಕು =ಚಿಟಕು, *q v*

ಚಟಕ್ಕನೆ k *ad.* All at once suddenly

ಚಟಚಟ k *n.* A snapping or crashing sound 2, (f) fretting and grieving. *ad* Quickly

ಚಟಪಟಿಕೆ f. *n* Quickness, smartness, sharpness, briskness.

ಚಟಾಕು h. *n.* The sixteenth part of a pakkâ sêr.

ಚಟಾಯಿಸು =ಚಟಕಾಯಿಸು, *q. v.*

ಚಟಿಗೆ (*cf.* ಚಟ್ಟಿ) k *n.* A small earthen pot with a broad mouth.

ಚಟುಪಟಿಕೆ = ಚಟಪಟಿಕೆ, *q. v.*

ಚಟ್ಟ 1. (=ಚಟ್ಟು) k *n* Flatness. 2, the frame or bottom of a cart, bedstead, chair, *etc.* 3, a bier or litter.

ಚಟ್ಟ 2 k *n* Order, regulation (*in law*), neatness, fineness.

ಚಟ್ಟನೆ k. *ad.* Suddenly, all at once

ಚಟ್ಟಿ (=ಚಿಟ್ಟಿ) k *n.* An earthen pot

ಚಟ್ಟು 1. =ಚಟ್ಟ 1, *q v* 2, (=ಚತ್ತು) the flat cloth-cover over a palankeen 3, the seedless pod of beans, *etc.*

ಚಟ್ಟು 2 k *n.* Impurity 2, destruction -ಮಾಡು To kill, to ruin.

ಚಟ್ಟು 3 k. *n.* The dried fruit of nĕlli

ಚಟ್ಟಿ k *n.* Flatness, levelness 2, European dress -ಕಾರ. A man dressed [illegible]

ಚಟ್ಣಿ h. n. A seasoning prepared of chopped chillies, *etc.*, chutney
ಚಡತಿ h. n. Jealousy
ಚಡಾಯಿಸು h. v. t. To tighten, fasten 2, to increase, raise, to lay on, to lash.
ಚಡಾವು h. n. Ascent, rise; increase, *as* of assessment, value, *etc.* 2, a kind of shoes
ಚಡಿ 1. f. n. A dovetail (*in carpentry*).
ಚಡಿ 2 h. n. A cane. 2, a staircase
ಚಡುಪುಗನೆ k. *ad.* Quickly, rapidly
ಚಡ್ಡಿ k. n. Breeches reaching to the thighs.
ಚಣಕ s. n. The chick-pea, Bengal gram 2, = ಚಡ್ಡಿ, *q. v.*
ಚಣಿಗ k. n. A sort of pulse or lentil, *Cicer lens*
ಚಂಡ s. *a.* Hot, fiery; passionate, wrathful, impetuous, mischievous. n. Heat; passion. 2, Śiva, N. of a demon
ಚಂಡವಾಳ f. n. Earnest money, a handsel.
ಚಂಡಾಲ s. n. An outcaste; a man of the lowest and most despised of the mixed tribes
ಚಂಡಿ 1 s. n. A passionate and violent female. 2, an obstinate or mischievous man. 3, obstinacy, *etc.* 4, Durgâ, N. of a female. -ಕಾ, -ಕೆ Durgâ. -ತನ Obstinacy. -ಸು. To be obstinate or angry.
ಚಂಡಿ 2. (= ತಂಡಿ) k. n. Wetness. *a.* Wet, moist
ಚಂಡಿಕೆ k. n. A tuft, a crest, a tuft of hair left on the head at the tonsure -ಬಿಡು. To leave a tuft on the head
ಚಂಡು 1 (= ಚೆಂಡು) k. n. A ball to play with, a bunch or cluster of flowers. ಚಂಡಾಡು To play at ball -ಮಲ್ಲಿಗೆ A variety of jasmine. -ಹೂವು. A flower like marigold, *a Chrysanthemum.*
ಚಂಡು 2 k. n. The nape of the neck, neck
ಚಂಡೆ s. n. Durgâ, *also* ಚಂಡಿ, -ಕೆ. 2, a certain perfume. ಚಂಡೇಶ, ಚಂಡೇಶ್ವರ Śiva
ಚಣ್ಣ k. n. Short breeches
ಚತುಃ.=ಚತುರ 1. -ಪದ, -ಪಾದ. A quadruped
ಚತುರ 1 s. *a.* Four. -ಕಳ್ಳಿ. The triangular spurge, *Euphorbia antiquarum.* -ಧಪತಿ A commander of four districts or of constituents of an army. -ಶ್ರ Quadrangular, a square, a boundary. ಚತುರಾನನ, ಚತುರಾಸ್ಯ. Four-faced Brahmâ. ಚತುರೋಪಾಯ The four expedients or means of success. ಚತುರಂಗ. Four-membered chess. ಚತುರಂಗಬಲ, ಚತುರ್ಬಲ A complete army comprising elephants, chariots, cavalry and infantry.
ಚತುರ 2. (= ಚದರ, ಚದುರ, *etc.*) s. *a.* Dexterous, clever, ingenious. 2, charming. n. Skilfulness, dexterity, shrewdness. *also* -ತೆ, -ತನ
ಚತುರ್ಥ s. *a.* Fourth, the fourth. ಚತುರ್ಥೀ. The fourth case, the dative, the fourth day in a lunar fortnight
ಚತುರ್ದಶ s. *a.* Fourteen. ಚತುರ್ದಶಿ The fourteenth day in a lunar fortnight
ಚತುರ್ದಿಶೆ s. n. The four points of the compass
ಚತುರ್ಭುಜ s. *a.* Four-armed. n. Vishnu, Krishna
ಚತುರ್ಮುಖ s. n. Brahmâ; Śiva
ಚತುರ್ಯುಗ s. n. The four yugas or ages of the world
ಚತುರ್ವರ್ಣ s. n. The four castes
ಚತುರ್ವಿಂಶತಿ s. *a.* Twenty-four.
ಚತುರ್ವಿಧ s. *a.* Four-fold.
ಚತುರ್ವೇದ s. n. The four vêdas
ಚತುಷ್ಟಯ s. *a.* Four-fold. n. An aggregate of four
ಚತುಷ್ಕೋಣ s. *a.* Square, quadrangular. n. A square.
ಚತುಷ್ಪದ, ಚತುಷ್ಪಾದ, ಚತುಷ್ಪಾದ s. *a.* Four-footed. n. A quadruped.

ಚತ್ತರಿಗೆ *tb. of* ಛತ್ರಿಕೆ. = ಛತ್ರಿ, *q v.*

ಚತ್ತು m. *n* A ceiling; a covering in general

ಚತ್ರಿ, -ಗೆ (*tb of* ಛತ್ರಿ) *n* An umbrella, parasol

ಚತ್ವರ s. *n* A quadrangular place

ಚತ್ವಾರಿ s *n*. Four ಚತ್ವಾರಿಂಶತ Forty.

ಚದರ (*tb of* ಚತುರ) *a* Square.

ಚದರು (ರು=ಱು) k *v i* & *t*. To scatter, disperse. ಚದರಿಸು *v t* To scatter, disperse

ಚದುರ. *tb of* ಚತುರ, *q. v.*

ಚಂದ 1. (*tb of* ಛಂದ) *a*. Pleasing, beautiful, lovely. *n*. Fitnees, niceness, beauty 2, appearance, shape, form; manner -ಗೆಡು Beauty to be gone -ಗೇಡಿ. A mannerless person.

ಚಂದ 2 (*tb. of* ಚಂದ್ರ) *n*. The moon, *also* -ಪ್ಪ, -ಮಾಮ.

ಚಂದನ, ಚಂದಲ s. *n*. Sandal, *Sirium myrtifolium*· either the tree, the wood, or its preparation.

ಚಂದಿ f *n* A gable-wall.

ಚಂದಿರ. *tb of* ಚಂದ್ರ, *q v*

ಚಂದ್ರ 1 s. *a* Glittering, excellent. *n*. The moon 2 gold 3, the red colour. 4, camphor 5, excellence -ಕಾಂತ The moon-stone, a fabulous gem -ಕಾಂತಿ Moonlight, the moon-flower *Ipomaea grandiflora* -ಕೋಲು A head-ornament of gold -ಗ್ರಹಣ. An eclipse of the moon -ಜ್ಯೋತಿ Moonlight, a kind of firework. -ತಾರಾಬಲ Propitiousness of the moon and stars -ಬಿಂಬ, -ಮಂಡಲ The lunar disk -ಭಾಗೆ The Chenab river. -ಲೋಕ The sphere of the moon -ವಂಶ The lunar race of kings -ಶಾಲೆ An upper room -ಸೂರ್ಯ. Moon and sun -ಹಾರ A necklace of moonlike gold beads -ಹಾಸ N of a prince.

ಚಂದ್ರ 2. k *n* Red lead, *minium* -ಕಾಳಿ ಸೀರೆ, -ಗಾಪಿಸೀರೆ A kind of sîrĕ -ಬಾಳೆ A reddish kind of plantain. -ಮಾವು A reddi[illegible] ...an...

ಚಂದ್ರಿಕೆ s. *n* Moonlight, elucidation 2, a coil of written palm-leaf.

ಚಂದ್ರೋದಯ s *n* Moon rise. -ಮಾತ್ರೆ. A cooling bolus.

ಚನ್ನ k *n* A beautiful, handsome man. 2, N, *also* -ಪ್ಪ, -ಯ್ಯ -ಪಟ್ಣ Madras -ಬಸವ N, son of Basava's sister. -ಬಸವಪುರಾಣ. A poetical Kannada work about Čannabasava.

ಚನ್ನಾಗಿ k *ad*. Nicely, well, *see s* ಚನ್ನು.

ಚನ್ನಿಗ k. *n* A handsome, fine man, *f* -ಳು.

ಚನ್ನು k *n* Beauty, grace, niceness, excellence. *Cpds* ಚನ್ನುಛತ್ರಿ, ಚನ್ನಮಗ, ಚನ್ನ ಮಾತು, *etc* ಚನ್ನಾಗಿ Nicely, well, properly; correctly.

ಚನ್ನೆ k. *n* A beautiful female. ಚನ್ನಕ್ಕ, ಚನ್ನವ್ವ. N

ಚಪ್ h. *int* Hush! silent!

ಚಪಟಿ = ಚಪ್ಪಟೆ, *q v.*

ಚಪಲ s *a*. Moving to and fro, wavering unsteady, fickle, wanton 2, active quick, agile, swift. 3, inconsiderate 4, momentary. -ತನ, -ತೆ, -ತ್ವ Fickleness, inconstancy, smartness. ಚಪಲೆ. A fickle woman, lightning.

ಚಪಾಟಿ m *n*. A slap. -ಬಡಿ To slap with open hands

ಚಪಾತಿ h *n* A hand-made cake

ಚಪಾಯಿಸು h. *v t* To hide

ಚಪಾವಣೆ, ಚಪಾವು h. *n* Hiding, concealment.

ಚಪ್ಪಗೆ k *n* Insipidness, tastelessness. *ad* Insipidly

ಚಪ್ಪಟೆ 1 k *n* Flatness *a* Flat -ಮೂಗು. A flat nose -ಕಲ್ಲು A flat stone.

ಚಪ್ಪಟೆ 2. (= ಚಪಾಟಿ) h *n* A smart slap -ಬಡಿ, -ಕೊಡೆ To slap with the palm

ಚಪ್ಪಡಿ (*cf* ಚಪ್ಪಟೆ 1) k. *n*. A large flat stone 2 a dodge, trick -ಎಳೆ, -ಹಾಕು To drag or put a flat stone (on another's business) to ruin

ಚಪ್ಪರ (= ಚಪ್ಪ) k. *n* A shed. 2, a [illegible] ...iled

roof 4, a trellis 5, the canopy of a bedstead *Cpds:* ಮದಿವೆ-, ಬಿಸಲು-, ಹುಲ್ಲು-, ಹಂಚಿನ-, *etc* -ಮಂಚ. A canopied bedstead. -ಮನೆ. A shed. -ಹಾಕು To put up a thatch

ಚಪ್ಪರಣೆ k. *n* A smacking of the lips used by peasants to stop their cattle

ಚಪ್ಪರಿಸು 1 k. *v i* To chuckle or cluck *to an animal* 2, *to* smack the lips, to chew with a noise. 3, to chirp.

ಚಪ್ಪರಿಸು 2. (= ಚಪ್ಪಳಿಸು) k. *v t.* To slap, pat.

ಚಪ್ಪಲಿ h *n.* A shoe or sandal

ಚಪ್ಪಳಿ = ಚಪ್ಪಟೆ 2, *q. v.*

ಚಪ್ಪಾಳೆ k *n* Clapping the hands -ಇಕ್ಕು, ಚಪ್ಪಳಿಕ್ಕು. To clap the hands

ಚಪ್ಪೆ 1. k. *n.* The hip-bone. 2, insipidness.

ಚಪ್ಪೆ 2 f. *n* An impression, seal, stamp

ಚಪ್ರ = ಚಪ್ಪರ, *q. v.*

ಚಬಕು. ಚಬುಕು h *n.* A horse-whip -ಹೊಡೆ, -ಕಳೆ. To whip -ಮರ. The Casuarina tree

ಚಮಕಾಯಿಸು, ಚಮಕಿಸು f *v t* To lash soundly, to frighten, rebuke. 2, to make to flash or brandish

ಚಮಟಿಕೆ, ಚಮಟಿಗೆ = ಚಮ್ಮಟಿಗೆ, *q. v.*

ಚಮಡ h. *n* The skin.

ಚಮತ್ಕಾರ, ಚಮತ್ಕೃತಿ, s *n* Astonishment, surprise, a show, spectacle, a wonder, skilfulness, cleverness 2, wit, eloquence -ದ ಒಕ್ಕಣೆ Ambiguous style

ಚಮರ s. *n* The yak or *bos grunniens.* 2, the chowry or long brush made of the yak's tail, *also* ಚಮರಿ.

ಚಮು, ಚಮೂ s *n* An army 2, a division of an army consisting of 129 elephants, 129 cars, 2187 horses, and 3685 foot -ಪ, -ಪತಿ A general

ಚಮ್ಚ h. *n.* A spoon

ಚಂಪಕ s. *n* A yellow fragrant flower, *Michelia champaca.*

ಚಂಬು (= ಚೊಂಬು *q v*) k. *n.* Copper. 2, a globular vessel used for drinking; *cf* ತಂಬಿಗೆ -ಕುಟಿಗ A coppersmith.

ಚಮ್ಮಟಿಗೆ (= ಚಮಟಿಕೆ *tb. of* ಚರ್ಮಪಟ್ಟಿಕೆ, ಚರ್ಮಯಷ್ಟಿಕೆ) 3 a whip 2, a sledge-hammer 3, a leather backgammon board, *also* ಚಮ್ಮಟ್ಟಿಗೆ

ಚಮ್ಮಾರ (*tb of* ಚರ್ಮಕಾರ) *n* A shoemaker; a worker in leather.

ಚರ 1 k *An imitative sound* -ಕ್ಕನೆ With the sound of ಚರ ಚರಚರ *rep* The sound of scratching with the nails or with a pen, *etc* ಚರಚರನೆ. With the sound of ಚರಚರ.

ಚರ 2 s *a* Moving, walking, movable; living. *n.* Locomotive any animal. 2, a spy; *cf.* ಚಾರ ಚರಸುರಡಿ (*i. e* ಚರರ ಸುದ್ದಿ) News brought by spies. -ಕ. A wanderer; a spy; witchcraft -ಆಸ್ತಿ, -ಸೊತ್ತು. Movable property -ಬಂಡವಲ. Live stock, capital employed in business -ಯಿಸು. To walk about

ಚರಣ s *n.* Moving 2, a foot 3, a sect, school. 4, a verse-line -ತಲ. The sole. -ಯುಗ Both the feet

ಚರಂತಿ s. *n* A jangama who has taken the vow of celibacy

ಚರಬಾಗಿಸು s. & k. *v i* To go away (*used in lingavanta mathas*)

ಚರಬಿ (= ಚೆರ್ಬಿ) h. *n.* Fat, suet

ಚರಮ s *a.* Last, final, ultimate, western

ಚರವಿಗೆ, ಚರಿವಿಗೆ k. *n* A large copper or brass pot for carrying water

ಚರಾಚರ s. *a.* Movable and immovable. *n* Animals and plants, all created things

ಚರಾಯಿ f. *n* Pasture; pasture-ground.

ಚರಿಗೆ. = ಚರವಿಗೆ, *q v*

ಚರಿತ s. *n* Going, course, conduct, practice, deeds; story. ಚರಿತಾರ್ಥ Attaining one's object, successful. *n* Accomplishment, welfare.

ಚರಿತ್ರ s. *n* Walk, behaviour, exploits, story history or account of one's deeds, *etc*, nature, disposition -ಗಾರ A historian.

ಚರಿತ್ರೆ. = ಚರಿತ್ರ, *q. v.*

ಚರಿಸು (*cf.* ಚರ) s. *v. i.* To move about, to walk, to wander, roam, to behave, to set about.

ಚರು s *n* A caldron, pan, pot 2, (=ಚರುವು) an oblation of rice, *etc.* to the gods or manes.

ಚರುಗ k *n* An offering to Dêmavva.

ಚರುವು = ಚರು No. 2, *q. v.*

ಚರ್ಚೆ s *n* Reflection, consideration. 2, investigation, reasoning, inquiry, logic. 3 a word 4, idle slander, ridicule 5, a quarrel, dispute. 6, perfuming the body. ಚರ್ಚಿಸು. To consider, to investigate, to discuss.

ಚರ್ಮ s. *n* Skin, leather, hide, bark, *etc.* 2 a shield -ಕಾರ A shoemaker. -ಚಕ್ಷು. The material, physical eye. -ಪಟ್ಟಿಕೆ. = ಚಮ್ಮಟ್ಟಿಗೆ, *q. v.*

ಚರ್ಯೆ s *n* Going, behaviour, conduct, practice, occupation

ಚರ್ವಣ s *n.* Chewing, masticating, solid food.

ಚಲ 1 s *a.* Moving, stirring; unsteady, movable *n* Agitation

ಚಲ 2 (*tb. of* ಛಲ) *n* Firmness of character, resoluteness, obstinacy, self-will -ಗಾರ An obstinate man, A resolute speaker; an obstinate person

ಚಲನ, ಚಲನೆ s *a* Moving, wandering *n* Going away, setting out, departing

ಚಲಮೆ, ಚಲಿಮೆ s *n.* A small pit, a spring of water or a fountain head, brook.

ಚಲಾಯಿಸು (*fr.* ಚಲ). *v. t* To make go, to execute *v. i* To go beyond; to be finished.

ಚಲಾವಣೆ, ಚಲಾವಣಿ f *a* Current *as* coin, *etc* *n* Currency, practice

ಚಲಿತ s *n* Moving, trembling, marching.

ಚಲಿಸು s *v. t.* To move, to stir, to tremble; to go [illegible]

ಚಲುವಿಕೆ, ಚಲುವು (= ಚೆಲುವು, ಚಲ್ವು) k *n.* Beauty, handsomeness, elegance, grace, niceness. ಚಲುವ, ಚಲ್ವ A handsome man, *f* ಚಲುವಿ, ಚಲುವೆ, ಚಲುವತಿ

ಚಲೋ, ಚಲೋಕ k *a* Beautiful, nice, elegant; *also* ಚಲೊ ಚಲೋದು That is nice well, *etc* *Cpds* · -ಬುದ್ಧಿ, -ಮನಸ್ಸು, -ಚಿತ್ತ, -ಗುಣ, -ನಡತೆ, -ಮಾತು, *etc*

ಚಲ್ಲ 1 k *n* Fun, amusement, pleasure, smile. ಚಲ್ಲಮಾಡು To sport gambol ಚಲ್ಲಾಟ. Sport, fun ಚಲ್ಲಾಟಮಾಡು.= ಚಲ್ಲಮಾಡು -ವತ್ತ A jocose man, a man who gets his living by coaxing.

ಚಲ್ಲ 2. (*inf of* ಚಲ್ಲು. *q v.*). -ಬಡಿ. To drive off, disperse scatter ಚಲ್ಲಾಪಲ್ಲಿ, ಚಲ್ಲಾ ಪಿಲ್ಲಿ Disorderly, confusedly.

ಚಲ್ಲನ್ f. *n* A challan, voucher, an invoice

ಚಲ್ಲಣ (= ಚಣ್ಣ) k *n* Breeches of different length

ಚಲ್ಲಾಟ. *see s* ಚಲ್ಲ 1 *and s.* ಚಲ್ಲು 1

ಚಲ್ಲು 1. (= ಚೆಲ್ಲು, *q v*) k *v t.* To scatter about, to pour out, spill, *as* milk, to squander, to throw away, to sow, *as* seed ಚಲ್ಲಾಟ Throwing about ಚಲ್ಲಾಡು To throw about. ಚಲ್ಲಿಬಿಡು. To spill throw away ಚಲ್ಲಿಹೋಗು. To be spilt.

ಚಲ್ಲು 2 k *n* An idle person, a gadabout. -ತನ Idleness.

ಚಲ್ವ, ಚಲ್ವಿಕೆ, ಚಲ್ವು = ಚಲುವ, ಚಲುವಿಕೆ, *q v*

ಚವಕಿ (= ಚೌಕಿ) h. *n* A low seat, stool. 2, a guard-house, a matha, the inner veranda of a house.

ಚವಡಿಕೆ (= ಚೌಡಿಕೆ *tb. of* ಚಮುಂಡಿಕೆ) *n.* A kind of lute

ಚವರ = ಚಮರ, *q v.*

ಚವರಿ (= ಚೌರಿ) s. *n* A kind of head-ornament made of the hair of the yak's tail

ಚವಲ f *n* Two Anas; *cf.* ಚವ್ವಲಿ.

ಚವುಕ = ಚೌಕ, *q v* 2, cheap

ಚವುಕಸಿ (= ಚೌಕಸಿ) h *n* Careful inquiry; investigation

ಚವುಕಳಿ (*fr* *tb.* ಚೌಕ) *n.* An ear-ring with four pearls. 2, a chequered cloth.

ಚವುಕಾರ f. *n.* Soap

ಚವುಡಿ, ಚವುಂಡಿ (*tb of* ಚಾಮುಂಡಿ) *n* N of a female demon worshipped by Śûdras.

ಚವುತಿ. *tb of* ಚತುರ್ಥಿ. = ಚೌತಿ, *q v*

ಚವುದರಿ (= ಚೌದರಿ) f. *n.* A village officer. 2, the officer of a royal guard.

ಚವುಲ. = ಚವಲ. *q. v.* 2, = ಚೌಲ.

ಚವುಳು (= ಚೌಳು) k. *n.* Brackishness -ಉಪ್ಪು, ಚವುಳುಪ್ಪು, -ಕಾರ. Soda-saltpetre-

ಚಹಾ (= ಚಾ, ಚಾಹ) h. *n* Tea.

ಚಹರೆ f. *n* Features, complexion. 2, green fodder.

ಚಳಕ a. k *n* Expertness, dexterity, skill

ಚಳಕು (= ಚಳುಕು) k *n* The cramp, rheumatic pains. *v i* To be painfully contracted, *as* a muscle of the body

ಚಳತುಂಬು f *n* A kind of ear-drop

ಚಳಿ 1. k *v. i* To become tired or fatigued; the feet to pain from walking -ಸು. To cause to be fatigued; to trouble.

ಚಳಿ 2. k. *n.* Coldness, cold, chill, frost, snow, *etc* -ಗಾಲ The cold season -ಜ್ವರ Ague. -ನಾಡು. A cold country. -ಆಗು, -ಬೀಳು. To become cold. -ಹಿಡಿ To catch cold

ಚಳುಕು = ಚಳಕು, *q v*

ಚಳೆ k. *v i.* To abound, *as* fruits on a tree, *etc* *n* Sprinkling, *also* ಚಳೆಯ -ಕೊಡು, -ಹಾಕು To sprinkle.

ಚಳ್ಳು k *n* A long flexible twig. ಚಳ್ಳವರೆ. A cultivated pulse, *Dolichos lablab*

ಚಳ್ಳೆ. (*tb. of* ಶೇಲು) *n* The Sepistan plum of a gummy character; *also* -ಮರ.

ಚಾ = ಚಹಾ, *q v*

ಚಾಕ್ e *n* Chalk

ಚಾಕ f. *n.* Neat, tidy, trim -ಚಕ್ಯ Acuteness, agility, speed

ಚಾಕರ h. *n.* A servant, *f* -ಳು

ಚಾಕರಿ h. *n.* Service; employment. -ಚಾಕರಿ *rest* -ಯವ. A servant, *f.* -ಯವಳು

ಚಾಕು h. *n* A penknife.

ಚಾಚು k. *v t.* To stretch out, hold out, extend, *also* ಚಾಚಿಬಿಡು. ಚಾಚಿಸು. To cause to stretch out.

ಚಾಂಚಲ್ಯ (*fr.* ಚಂಚಲ) s. *n.* Fickleness, unsteadiness

ಚಾಟಕ s *n* Jugglery, incantation, *also* -ಮಂತ್ರ, -ವಿದ್ಯೆ

ಚಾಟಿ k. *n* A whip

ಚಾಟು 1 k *n.* A refuge; a shelter.

ಚಾಟು 2 s. *n* Pleasing discourse, flattery, clear speech -ತನ Agreeableness, flattery.

ಚಾಡಿ h. *n.* Slander, backbiting -ಕಾರ, -ಕೋರ, -ಗ, -ಗಾರ, ಚಾಡ. A slanderer, a talebearer.

ಚಾಣ. = ಚಾನ, ಚೇಣ, *q. v.*

ಚಾಂಡಾಲ. = ಚಂಡಾಲ, *q v.*

ಚಾತಕ s *n* The bird *Cuculus melanoleucus* (supposed to live upon raindrops).

ಚಾತಾಳಧವ k *n* A so-called Sarternee, a man of a Śûdra caste that worships Vishnu.

ಚಾತುರ (*fr* ಚತುರ) s. *a* Dexterous clever, ingenious. -ತನ, ಚಾತುರ್ಯ. Dexterity, cleverness, shrewdness, pleasantness.

ಚಾತುರ್ಥಿಕ (*fr.* ಚತುರ್ಥ) s *a* Quartan, *as* ague

ಚಾದರ h *n* A cotton or silk sheet or a dôtra worked with gold or silver threads

ಚಾನ (= ಚಾಣ) k *n* A small chisel

ಚಾಂದಣಿ, ಚಾಂದನಿ h *n.* An awning

ಚಾಂದ್ರ (*fr* ಚಂದ್ರ) s *a* Lunar -ಮಾನ Lunar measurement of time -ಮಾಸ. A lunar month -ಮಾನವರ್ಷ, -ಸಂವತ್ಸರ. The lunar year ಚಾಂದ್ರಾಯಣ An expiatory observance regulated by moon's phases

ಚಾಪ 1. s. *n.* A bow. 2, a rainbow.

ಚಾಪ 2. = ಚಾಪೆ 2, *q v* 2, = ಚಾಪು 2, *q v*.

ಚಾಪಲ, ಚಾಪಲ್ಯ (*fr* ಚಪಲ) s. *n*. Mobility, unsteadiness, fickleness, agility.

ಚಾಪಿಸು h *v t*. To stamp, to print, *also* ಛಾಪಿಸು

ಚಾಪು 1 k. *n* Stretch, length, extent.

ಚಾಪು 2 h. *n*. The cock of a gun.

ಚಾಪೆ 1. k *n*. A mat.

ಚಾಪೆ 2 (= ಚಾಪ) h. *n*. A stamp, a type, an impression -ಖಾನೆ A printing office

ಚಾಮರ (= ಚಮರ) s *n*. A chowry the bushy tail of the *Bos grunniens* used as a fan

ಚಾಮುಂಡಿ s *n* Durgâ; *also* ಚಾಮುಂಡೇಶ್ವರಿ.

ಚಾಯು (*tb of* ಛಾಯೆ) *n*. Colour, shade, *etc*, *also* ಚಾಯಿ 2, the madder plant.

ಚಾರ 1 s *n*. Course, motion 2, a spy, messenger. 2, a prison. -ಚಿಪ್ಪು. A privy.

ಚಾರ 2 f *n* Green fodder of cattle.

ಚಾರ 3. (ರ = ಱ) k *n* A line, streak

ಚಾರಣ s *n* Wandering; a strolling actor, bard; a celestial singer.

ಚಾರಿ s *n* Acting 2, course 3, a way, manner, method 4, stratagem 5, intention, mind. 6, cheapness.

ಚಾರಿತ್ರ s *n* Conduct, behaviour, a ceremony

ಚಾರಿಸು k. *v t* To grind, triturate, *as* sandal, to mix by rubbing, *as* medicine

ಚಾರು 1 s. *a* Agreeable, lovely, beautiful.

ಚಾರು 2 (ರು = ಱು) k. *n* Sap, juice, broth

ಚಾರ್ಖಾನ f *n* A square -ಸೀರೆ A female's cloth with small coloured squares in it

ಚಾರ್ಮಾಡಿ f *n*. N of a ghaut

ಚಾರ್ವಾಕ s *n*. An atheist or materialist, a sceptic

ಚಾಲ s. *a* Movable, changing -ಗೇಣಿ (Movable rent), rent for one year -ತಿ, ಚಾಲ್ತಿ . . . . . .

ಚಾಲಕ್, ಚಾಲಾಕ್ h *a* Smart dexterous, clever

ಚಾಲನ s *n* Causing to move or pass through, sifting, making loose. ಚಾಲನಿ A sieve, strainer

ಚಾಲು (= ಚಾಲ, *q. v*) s. *n* Moving, custom, manner 2, currency, *as* of a coin, order, *etc* 3, a pace, *as* of a horse.

ಚಾವಡಿ h *n* A court; a village-hall; a veranda.

ಚಾವಣಿ h *n* Cantonments, temporary erections for troops 2, a roof, roofing

ಚಾವಿ h *n* A key -ಕೊಡು To wind, *as* a clock or watch

ಚಾಳಕ f. *a*. Mischievous. *n*. A man full of tricks and pranks

ಚಾಳಿ (*tb of* ಚಾಲ) *n* Conduct, practice, habit, a silly habit. -ಸು. To be fickle, *etc*. 2, to sift

ಚಾಳಿಸು (*fr* ಚಾಲ) *n* Dimness of vision. 2, the age of 40 ಚಾಳೀಸು. A pair of spectacles

ಛಿಃ (= ಚೀ, ಛೀ) k *int* Fie! for shame! pshaw!

ಚಿಕಣಿ h *a* Hard, thick, rich -ಅಡಿಕೆ, -ಯಡಿಕೆ A fine kind of betel-nut

ಚಿಕಿತ್ಸೆ s *n* The science of medicine, therapeutics ಚಿಕಿತ್ಸಕ A physician.

ಚಿಕೀರ್ಷೆ s *n* Will, design.

ಚಿಕ್ಕ k *a* Little, small, young -ಅಕ್ಕ, ಚಿಕ್ಕಕ್ಕ. A younger of the elder sisters. -ಅಣ್ಣ, ಚಿಕ್ಕಣ್ಣ. A younger of the elder brothers -ತಂದೆ = ಚಿಕ್ಕಪ್ಪ, *q v* -ತಮ್ಮ. The youngest brother. -ತಾಯಿ An aunt, a step-mother. ಚಿಕ್ಕದು That is small. ಚಿಕ್ಕಂದು. Childhood ಚಿಕ್ಕಪ್ಪ. An uncle -ಪ್ರಾಯ Age between the 7th and 16th year -ಮಕ್ಕಳು Small, young children -ಮಾತು An insignificant word ಚಿಕ್ಕಮ್ಮ, ಚಿಕ್ಕವ್ವ = -ತಾಯಿ. -ತನ = ಚಿಕ್ಕಂದು, *q v*

ಚಿಕ್ಕಣ k *n* A small bodice

ಚಿಕ್ಕಣ್ಣ, ಚಿಕ್ಕಪ್ಪ, ಚಿಕ್ಕಮ್ಮ ಚಿಕ್ಕವ್ವ *see s.* ಚಿಕ್ಕ.

ಚಿಕ್ಕಾಸು, ಚಿಕ್ಕಾಡಿ k *n* A flea

ಚಿಕ್ಕಿ, ಚಿಕ್ಕೆ 1 k. n. A spot, speck, dot, *as* that of a cat, cloth, *etc* 2, a star 3, an aunt. -ಬೊಟ್ಟು A black dot applied to the forehead between the eye-brows

ಚಿಕ್ಕೆ 2. k. n. A flat-nosed woman 2, a mouse. 3, a betel-nut

ಚಿಗತು. = ಚಿಗಿತು. *P. p of* ಚಿಗಿ

ಚಿಗರಿ, ಚಿಗರೆ k. n. An antelope

ಚಿಗರು = ಚಿಗುರು. *q v*

ಚಿಗರೆ. = ಚಿಗರಿ, *q v*

ಚಿಗಳಿ k n A ball made of fried gingely oil-seed mixed with jaggory.

ಚಿಗಿ 1 k. *v t.* To throw with the fingers.

ಚಿಗಿ 2. (=ಚಿಗುರು). k *v i* To sprout, shoot 2, (= ಜಿಗಿ) to jump.

ಚಿಗುರು (= ಚಿಗರು) k *v i* To sprout, shoot; to bud, blossom *n* A sprout, shoot. ಚಿಗುರೆಲೆ A young betel leaf; a fresh leaf

ಚಿಟಕಾಯಿಸು h *v t* To loosen a thorn in the flesh with a needle, to cause pain.

ಚಿಟಕಿ. = ಚಿಟಿಕೆ 1, 2 *q v*

ಚಿಟಕು (= ಚಿಟುಕು) k *n.* Cracking of the finger-joints 2, a quantity of thread wound upon a reel. a skein -ಮುರಿ To crack the finger-joints.

ಚಿಟಗುಟ್ಟು k. *v. i* To throb, *as* the head

ಚಿಟಿ k *n* Smallness, littleness -ಕೊಳಗು. The hind hoofs of cattle

ಚಿಟಿಕೆ 1 k. *n.* A snap with finger and the thumb 2, a little, a pinch, *as* of snuff, *also* ಚಿಟಿಕಿ 3, a castenet -ಹಾಕು To snap with the fingers.

ಚಿಟಿಕೆ 2 k. *n.* Cauterising in any part of the body to cure particular diseases -ಹಾಕು To cauterise for that purpose

ಚಿಟುಕು. = ಚಿಟಕು, *q v*

ಚಿಟ್ಟನೆ k *ad* With a scream

ಚಿಟ್ಟಾಮುಟ್ಟಿ k *n* A perennial plant, *Pavonia zeylanica*

ಚಿಟ್ಟಿ k *n.* A measure of grain, equal to four seru or -olh.. .

ಚಿಟ್ಟು (= ಚಿಟಿ) k. *n* Smallness shortness. 2, disgust ಚಿಟ್ಟಿಲಿ A small rat, a mouse -ಹರಳು. A herbaceous shrub, *Sida cordifolia*, a small kind of eastor-oil seed ಚಿಟ್ಟೋಳಿಗ A small work.

ಚಿಟ್ಠಾ h. *n* A roll of lands under cultivation

ಚಿಟ್ಟಿ (= ಚಿಟ್ಠಿ) h *n.* A rough daybook

ಚಿಡಾಯಿಸು f *v t.* To excite, provoke

ಚಿಣಿ, ಚಿಣ್ಣೆ (= ಚಿಟಿ) k *n* Smallness 2, the bat in the game of tip-cat, *also* -ಕೋಲು. -ಕೋಲಾಟ, -ಯಾಟ. The game of tip-cat.

ಚಿಣ್ಣ k *n.* A little one, a boy

ಚಿತಾ, ಚಿತಿ, ಚಿತೆ s *n* A funeral pile ಚಿತಾಭಸ್ಮ. The ashes of a funeral pile

ಚಿತ್ತ s. *a.* Perceived *n* Thought, intention, aim, wish, will. 2, the heart, the mind -ಗೊಡು To agree to. -ಭೇದ Inconsistency of purpose or will -ಭ್ರಮೆ, -ವಿಭ್ರಮೆ Madness -ವೃತ್ತಿ Disposition of mind, feeling, the mind, the attention -ಶುದ್ಧಿ. Purity of mind ದೇವರ ಚಿತ್ತ. God's will.

ಚಿತ್ತಯಿಸು, ಚಿತ್ತಯ್ಸು, ಚಿತ್ತವಿಸು s. *v t.* To attend to, notice, consider

ಚಿತ್ತರ. *tb of* ಚಿತ್ರ, *q. v.*

ಚಿತ್ತಾರ (*tb of* ಚಿತ್ರಕಾರ) *n.* A portrait, any picture. ಚಿತ್ತಾರಿಗ A painter

ಚಿತ್ತಿನಿ s *n* An intelligent woman

ಚಿತ್ತು h. *n.* A blot, obliteration, correction in writing

ಚಿತ್ತ *tb. of* ಚಿತ್ರೆ, *q. v*

ಚಿತ್ರ (= ಚಿತ್ತರ) s *a* Perceptible; bright-coloured, variegated *n.* An ornament. 2, a painting, picture, sketch 3, variegated colour 4, a wonder, marvel; *also* ವಿ- (ಅದ್ಭುತ, ಆಶ್ಚರ್ಯ) 5, a mark on the forehead -ತೆಗೆ, -ಬರೆ. To draw a picture. -ಕ A painter; a leopard or chita -ಕಾಯ A tiger, panther. -ಕಾರ -ಗಾರ A painter -ಕೂಟ. N of a hill -... N of the ... order of the vices and virtues of mankind in Yama's world -ಪಟ A picture, painting. -ಭಾನು The sixteenth year of the cycle of sixty -ಮೂಲ, -ಮೂಲಿಕೆ. An under-shrub, the Ceylon leadwort -ಲೇಖೆ A portrait, N of a daughter of king Vâna's minister. -ವಧೆ Horrid torture. -ವಿಚಿತ್ರ Variegated, multiform. ಚಿತ್ರಾಕಾರ = ಚಿತ್ರಾರ

ಚಿತ್ರಾನ್ನ s n Boiled rice mixed with various condiments.

ಚಿತ್ರಾಪುರ s n N of a place in North [Kanara

ಚಿತ್ರಾಸನ s n A square carpet of a variegated colour.

ಚಿತ್ರಿ, ಚಿತ್ರಿಕ s n. A painter. ಚಿತ್ರಿತ Variegated, painted ಚಿತ್ರಿಸು. To draw, to paint.

ಚಿತ್ರೆ s n The fourteenth lunar mansion *Spica virginis* 2, a sort of cucumber, *Cucumis madraspatanus*.

ಚಿದಕು k v t To peel the skin of soaked avarĕ pulse by squeezing n. Peeling of the skin, *as* of soaked pulse

ಚಿದಂಬರ s n N of a place of pilgrimage

ಚಿದಾನಂದ s n. Intellectual happiness. -ಮೂರ್ತಿ, -ರೂಪ Śiva.

ಚಿದ್ರೂಪ s a Intelligent, thoughtful, amiable, good-hearted n Krishna

ಚಿದ k n. Small pieces. -ಕಡಿ To mince.

ಚಿನಾಯಿ s a. Relating to or coming from China.

ಚಿನಿವಾರ, ಚಿನಿವಾಲ k. n. A money-changer, a jeweller

ಚಿನುಕುರುಳಿ k n Soaked and germinated gram seasoned with salt and chillies and fried

ಚಿಂತನ, ಚಿಂತನೆ s n Thinking, consideration, reflecting upon, anxious thought.

ಚಿಂತಾಕುಲ s a. Anxious, solicitous.

ಚಿಂತಾಕ್ರಾಂತ s a. Overcome by anxiety or care, f ಚಿಂತಾಕ್ರಾಂತೆ

ಚಿಂತಾಮಣಿ s n The philosopher's stone. 2, N of a work in Kanarese -ಪುಸ್ತಕ. A book on omens. -ಯಂತ್ರ A talisman

ಚಿಂತಾಲು h. n Large scales for weigh- [ing

ಚಿಂತಿತ s. a. Thought, reflected upon. n Care; intention

ಚಿಂತಿಸು s. v t To think about, reflect upon v i To be anxious, sorrowful

ಚಿಂತೆ (ಚಿಂತಾ) s n Sad or sorrowful thought care, anxiety; reflection ಚಿಂತಿಲ್ಲ. Never mind -ಗೆಯ್ಯು, -ಗೊಳ್ಳು, -ಮಾಡು To be anxious -ಮಾಡು To reflect, consider. ಚಿಂತ್ಯ To be thought of, reflected

ಚಿಂದಿ f n. A shred, strip, a rag.

ಚಿನುಮಯ. = ಚಿನ್ಮಯ, q. v.

ಚಿನ್ನ k. n. Gold 2, smallness. -ವರದ (=ಚಿನಿವಾರ, q v). A dealer in gold, a shroff

ಚಿನ್ನಿವಾರ = ಚಿನಿವಾರ, q v

ಚಿನ್ಹೆ, ಚಿಹ್ನ (tb of ಚಿಹ್ನ) n A sign, token, mark.

ಚಿನ್ಮಯ s a. Full of knowledge n All-intelligence

ಚಿಪ್ಪಿಗ 1 (tb of ಶಿಲ್ಪಿಕ) n An artisan, mechanic.

ಚಿಪ್ಪಿಗ 2 (=ಚಿಂಪಿಗ, fr. s. ಸಿವ್ to sew) n A tailor.

ಚಿಪ್ಪು k n A shell, cockle crust, hard covering, the skull -ಗಟ್ಟು. The shell to form, *as* of a coconnut

ಚಿಬ್ಬಲ, ಚಿಬ್ಬಲು k n A bamboo lid

ಚಿಬ್ಬು (tb of ಸಿಧ್ಮ) n. A reddish or blackish spot on the body, freckle

ಚಿಮುಕು. ಚಿಮುಕಿಸು (= ಚಿಮಿಕಿಸು, ಚಿಮುಕಿಸು) k v. t. To sprinkle

ಚಿಮುಟ, ಚಿಮುಟಿಗೆ f. n. A pair of tweezers, pincers

ಚಿಮಣಿ e. n. A chimney.

ಚಿಮಿಚಿಮಿಸು k. v. i To prattle, *as* children 2, welter, wallow.

ಚಿಮಿಕಿಸು, ಚಿಮುಕಿಸು = ಚಿಮುಕಿಸು, q v.

ಚಿಮುಟಿ f n Nippers. -ಕ್ಷೌರ Plucking out hairs with nippers.

ಚಿಮುಟು k v i. To twinkle, wink. 2, (f.) to squeeze, pinch

ಚಿಂಪಿಗ (=ಚಿಪ್ಪಿಗ, fr. s. ಸಿವ್) n A tailor

ಚಿಮ್ಮು k v t To propel with the finger 2, to push forward; to cast, fling, to butt or toss with horns 3, to squirt 4, to break forth, to gush out; to fly off 5, to brandish a weapon.

ಚಿಯೋನ್ f. n Zion; the Church of God

ಚಿರ s. a Long, lasting a long time. -ಂಜೀವ, -ಜೀವಿ, -ಂಜೀವಿ. Long-lived, a term used in epistles when addressing or referring to a younger relative. -ತರ. Uncommonly long.

ಚಿರತೆ (ರ=ಱ) k. n. A cheeta or hunting leopard

ಚಿರಾಕು h. n A lamp.

ಚಿರಾಯಿತ (ರಾ=ಱಾ) k. n A kind of gentian, *Agathotes chirayta.*

ಚಿರಾಯು s. a. Long-lived n. A crow ಚಿರಾಯ For a long time, a long time

ಚಿರ್ತೆ =ಚಿರತೆ, q v

ಚಿಲಕ k n A hasp or small chain for fastening a door.

ಚಿಲವಾನ k n The odd money over a round sum.

ಚಿಲಿಕೆ k n. Small pieces of wood used for building a flat roof. 2, the pot-herb *Hingtsha repens*

ಚಿಲಿಮೆ h. n The bowl of a hukka

ಚಿಲ್ಪಟಿ m n A very irritable person

ಚಿಲ್ಮಿಷ (=ಕಿಲ್ಮಿಷ) s n Malice, roguery. -ಗಾರ A mischievous fellow

ಚಿಲ್ಲ 1. k n The clearing-nut tree, *Strychnos potatorum.*

ಚಿಲ್ಲ 2 f a Blear-eyed n The Bengal kite. -ಗಣ್ಣು. A bleared eye

ಚಿಲ್ಲರ, ಚಿಲ್ಲರೆ (ರ=ಱ) k n Smallness, pettiness, trifling; cash under one rupee -ಖರ್ಚು. Petty expenses. -ಜನಸು, -ಸಾಮಾನು. Sundry small articles of commerce, as grain, etc -ಮಾತು A trifling word. -ರೊಕ್ಕ. Small money, change.

ಚಿಲ್ಲಾ. = ಚಲ್ಲಾ, q v. ಚಿಲ್ಲಾಪಿಲ್ಲಿ = ಚಲ್ಲಾಪಿಲ್ಲಿ, q v

ಚಿಲ್ಲು k. n. A piece of wood holding a spindle

ಚಿವಟು = ಚಿಮುಟು, q v.

ಚಿವರು. = ಚಿವುರು, q v.

ಚಿವುಟು 1 k v. t. To cut off, pluck off or pinch off with the nails

ಚಿವುಟು 2. = ಚಿಮುಟು, q v

ಚಿವುರು (= ಚಿವರು) k. v. t. To scratch with the nails or claws. n Scratching. -ಗಾಯ. A wound made by scratching.

ಚಿವ್ವು k. v t. To shave or scrape, to peel or bark, to trim, to smooth or polish.

ಚೀ (= ಛಿ, q v) k int Fie! shame! ಚೀ ಚೀ rep Fie, fie!

ಚೀಟಿ, ಚೀಟು 1. h n Printed cotton, chintz. -ಪಾಟಿ. rcl

ಚೀಟಿ, ಚೀಟು 2 h n A chit, note, a bill, bond, a lot, ticket. ಅಂಗಡಿ- A note to a shopkeeper ಕಳ್ಳ-. A forged note of hand. ರಹದಾರಿ- A passport -ಹಾಕು. To cast lots.

ಚೀಡೆ k n A fried sweetmeat in the form of a marble

ಚೀನ f. n. China, Chinese 2, a kind of cloth. -ದೇಶ China ಚೀನಿ Chinese. ಚೀನಿಕಾಯಿ. The squash-gourd ಚೀನಿ ಸಕ್ಕರೆ Granulated white sugar ಚೀನಿ ಬೆಳ್ಳಿ. Pure silver without alloy

ಚೀಪು 1 k v t To suck.

ಚೀಪು 2. f. n. A piece of stone or wood used as a supporting prop.

ಚೀರಣಿ k. n. A small chisel

ಚೀರು 1 = ಚಿವರು, q v.

ಚೀರು 2. (ರು=ಱು) k v i To scream, cry out n Screaming 2, raging, fierceness.

ಚೀಲ k n A bag, sack

ಚುಕಾಣಿ, ಚುಕ್ಕಾಣಿ h. n. The helm of a ship or boat

ಚುಕಾಯಿಸು h v. t. To settle, adjust, to fix, as the price, to discharge

ಚುಕ್ಕಿ (*tb. of* ಶುಕ್ರ) *n* Śukra, the planet Venus 2, = ಚಿಕ್ಕೆ, *q v*

ಚುಕ್ಕೆ (= ಚಿಕ್ಕೆ) k *n* A small mark, dot, spot.

ಚುಂಗಡಿ k *n.* Pettiness: small money, change, a trifling sum 2, interest on money.

ಚುಂಗಾಣಿ k *n* A small smoking pipe.

ಚುಂಗು k *n.* The end of a turban; a dangling tatter. 2, the fibrous tuft, *as* of a pealed cocoanut.

ಚುಚ್ಚು k. *v. t.* To insert. 2, to pierce into, *as* with a knife, thorn, *etc.*, to pierce or bore, *as* the ears 3, to incite, *as* to quarrel *n* Piercing ಚುಚ್ಚಿಸು To cause to pierce

ಚುಂಚ, ಚುಂಚು 1 k *n* A bird's beak ಚುಂಚಿಲಿ A musk-rat

ಚುಂಚು 2 k. *a* A projecting ledge on a house. 2, the hair curling round the forehead 3, red or brown colour.

ಚುಟುಕು h. *n* Shortness brevity

ಚುಟುಕ್ಕನೆ k. *ad* Fiercely, painfully, *as* a scorpion stings

ಚುಟ್ಟ, ಚುಟ್ಟಿ k. *n* A cheeroot, cigar

ಚುದ್ರ (*tb. of* ಕ್ಷುದ್ರ) *n.* Slander. -ತನ Slandering

ಚುನಾಬ್ h. *n.* Side 2 majesty, excellency

ಚುನಾಯಿಕೆ, ಚುನಾವಣೆ h *n.* Choosing, selection.

ಚುನಾಯಿಸು h *v. t* To choose 2, to plait, fold

ಚುನ್ನ a. k. *n.* Blame, censure, abuse; scorn -ನುಡಿ A word of abuse -ಮಾಡು To blame, censure.

ಚುಮುಚುಮು k *rep. int* With intense brilliancy, used of the rising of the sun. *n* Throbbing or smarting sensation.

ಚುಂಬನ s. *n* Kissing, a kiss ಚುಂಬಕ. A loadstone

ಚುಂಬಿಸು s *v t* To touch lightly or [softly

ಚುರಚಿ = [illegible]

ಚುರುಕು (ರು = ಱು), ಚುರುಕ k *n* Quickness, speed, haste; heat; keenness smartness, sharpness 2, force, vehemence 3, dearness *a* Quick, sharp -ಬುದ್ಧಿ Quick understanding -ತನ. Keenness, smartness.

ಚುರುಚುರು k *ad* With violent smarting. -ಗುಟ್ಟು, -ಎನ್ನು To smart violently

ಚುಲಕ, ಚುಲುಕು k *n* Lightness of temper or conduct, levity, *also* -ಬುದ್ಧಿ, -ತನ [with.

ಚುಳಕೆ k *n* A stout stick to beat cotton

ಚೂಟಿ k. *n* Aim 2 a device, scheme, expedient; *also* ಚೂಟು. -ಗಾರ A contriver, schemer

ಚೂಡ, ಚೂಡಾ, ಚೂಡೆ s *n* A single lock or tuft of hair left on the head at tonsure 2, a crest, plume 3, a kind of bracelet. ಚೂಡಾಕರ್ಮ The rite of tonsure. ಚೂಡಾಮಣಿ A jewel worn in a crest, any person or thing pre-eminently excellent

ಚೂಣಿ a k. *n.* The foremost part, front, van

ಚೂಪು a. k *n.* Sight; a look, glance, the eye 2, pointedness, *as* of a pen

ಚೂರಣ *tb of* ಚೂರ್ಣ, *q v.*

ಚೂರಿ (*tb. of* ಛುರಿ) *n* A penknife, a knife, a table-knife.

ಚೂರು 1 k *n* A frame thrown over houses to form the roof.

ಚೂರು 2 k *n* A part, portion, piece, fragment ಚೂರಡಿಕೆ Betel-nut in small bits -ಚೂರು *rep* Bits and pieces

ಚೂರುಮುರಿ (= ಚುರುಮುರಿ) f *n* Cleaned rice, soaked and parched.

ಚೂರ್ಣ (= ಸುಣ್ಣ) s. *n* Powder, dust, crumbs 2, chunam or lime 3, = ಸೂರ್ಣ. *a.* Powdered pulverised

ಚೂರ್ಣಿಕೆ s *n* A kind of easy prose

ಚೂಲಿಕೆ s *n* The comb or crest of a cock 2, the front.

ಚೆಕ್ಕು. = ಚಕ್ಕು, *q. v* 2, an oil-press, sugar-mill

ಚೆಕ್ಕೈ. = ಚಕ್ಕೈ, q. v

ಚೆಂಗು (= ಚಂಗು q v) k v i To jump, skip, caper, to run away. n. A jump.

ಚೆಚ್ಚರ (= ಚಚ್ಚರ, q v) k. n Quickness. 2, certainty. 3, carefulness ಚೆಚ್ಚರಿಗ A zealously active man

ಚೆಚ್ಚು (= ಜಜ್ಜು, q v.) k v. t To crush, grind, etc.

ಚೆಟ್ಟ = ಚಟ್ಟ2, q v.

ಚೆಟ್ಟೆ k. n A hen-sparrow. 2, = ಚಟ್ಟೆ.

ಚೆಟ್ಟು. = ಚಟ್ಟು, q. v

ಚೆಂಡಿಕೆ. = ಚಂಡಿಕೆ, q v.

ಚೆಂಡು (= ಚಂಡು, q v) k n A play-ball.

ಚೆದರು = ಚದರು, q v

ಚೆಂದ = ಚಂದ 1, q v

ಚೆಂದರ, ಚೆಂದಿರ. = ಚಂದ್ರ 1, q. v

ಚೆನ್ನು. = ಚನ್ನು, q v ಚೆನ್ನಾಗಿ = ಚನ್ನಾಗಿ

ಚೆಂಬಿಗೆ (= ತಂಬಿಗೆ) k n. A brass vessel, used for drinking water, etc.

ಚೆರಬಿ = ಚರಬಿ, q v

ಚೆರಿಗೆ = ಚರಿಗೆ, q v

ಚೆರ್ಚೆ (tb. of ಚರ್ಚೆ, q. v.) s. n Ridicule, etc.

ಚೆರ್ಬಿ. = ಚರಬಿ, q v

ಚೆಲುವು, ಚೆಲೊ. = ಚಲುವು, ಚಲೊ, etc, q v

ಚೆಲ್ಲಾಟ = ಚಲ್ಲಾಟ, q. v

ಚೆಲ್ಲು (= ಚಲ್ಲು 1, q v) k. v. t. To scatter about, shed, spill, etc ಚೆಲ್ಲಿಸು. To cause to scatter about, etc.

ಚೆಲ್ವ, ಚೆಲುವ = ಚಲ್ವ, etc., q v.

ಚೇಗು k n The heart or core of a tree, essence.

ಚೇಚೇ f. int. Fie! shame! 2, not so!

ಚೇಟ, ಚೇಟಕ s. n. A servant, slave, f. ಚೇಟಿ

ಚೇಡ f n. A goblin summoned to harrass people. -ಮಾಡು. To practise black-art

ಚೇತನ (fr. ಚಿತ್) s. a Conscious, intelligent; alive; living. n. The mind, soul, a living and sentient being 2, power, strength.

ಚೇತನ್ಯ (tb of ಚೈತನ್ಯ) n. Power

ಚೇತರಿಸು (i e ಚೇತನಿಸು, fr ಚೇತನ) v. i To re- cover consciousness ಚೇತರಣೆ. Con- sciousness, strength

ಚೇತಸ್ s. n Consciousness, intelligence; the mind, intellect.

ಚೇಪು k n A gush, as of milk

ಚೇರ k n The Cêra or Kongu country.

ಚೇಲ s n Cloth; a garment

ಚೇಷ್ಟೆ s n Gesture, grimaces, action; exertion. 2, mischievous tricks, derision ಈ-. A ridiculous grimace -ಗಾರ A man full of tricks and pranks

ಚೇಳು (ಳು = ಚು) k. n. A scorpion -ಕೊಂಡಿಗಿಡ, -ಬಾಲದಗಿಡ The Indian turnsole, Heliotropium indicum. -ಬಾಣ A rocket resembling a scorpion in its movements -ಕುಟುಕು, -ಬಡಿ A scorpion to sting -ಕೊಂಡಿ A scorpion's sting

ಚೈತನ್ಯ (= ಚೇತನ) s n Intelligence, consciousness; sensation, the soul 2, power, strength. 3, N of a Vaishnava reformer. -ಸ್ಥ A rich man.

ಚೈತ್ಯ (fr. ಚಿತಾ) s a. Relating to a funeral pile. n A monument, tombstone, temple 2, (fr ಚಿತ್) the mind

ಚೈತ್ರ s n. The first month of the lunar year (March-April).

ಚೊಕ್ಕ k n Niceness, elegance, beauty, charm, etc. 2, purity, cleanness. -ಊಟ An excellent meal. -ಚಿನ್ನ. Pure gold. -ನೀರು Pure water. -ಬೆಳ್ಳಿ Pure silver.

ಚೊಕ್ಕಟ, -ಟು, ಚೊಕ್ಕಳಿಕೆ. = ಚೊಕ್ಕ, q v.

ಚೊಗಟೆ k. n The annual herb Cassia occidentalis.

ಚೊಂಗ (= ಚೊಂಚ, ಚೊಂಚು) k. n Crookedness perverseness. 2, a perverse man, f ಚೊಂಗಿ Cpds. -ಕಾಲು, -ಗೆಯ್, etc.

ಚೊಚ್ಚಲು, ಚೊಚ್ಚಿಲು k n The first birth; the first offspring. -ಮಗ A first-born son -ಮಗಳು. A first-born daughter.

ಚೊಂಚ, ಚೊಂಚು = ಚೊಂಗ, q v

ಚೊಟ್ಟು = ಕೊಂಗ, q. v

ಚೊಲ್ಲಣ. = ಚಲ್ಲಣ, *q. v.*

ಚೋಜಿಗ (= ಸೋಜಿಗ. *tb. of* ಚೋದ್ಯ) *n.* Surprise, wonder; a marvel, wonder.

ಚೋಟು **k.** *n.* A span. ಚೋಟಗಲ. A span's breadth. ಚೋಟಳತೆ. A span's measure. ಚೋಟುದ್ದ. A span's length. ಚೋಟೆತ್ತರ. A span's height.

ಚೋದ್ಯ (= ಚೋಜಿಗ, *etc.*) **s.** *n.* Surprise, astonishment, wonder.

ಚೋಪದಾರ **f.** *n.* A mace-bearer.

ಚೋರ **s.** *n.* A thief, robber. -ತನ, -ತ್ವ, ಚೋರಿ. Theft, robbery.

ಚೋಲಿ, -ಕೆ **s.** *n.* A short jacket; bodice.

ಚೋಲಿ **s.** *n.* A kind of chignon made of some hair of the čamari.

ಚೋಳ **k.** *n.* The coast of Coromandel; N. of its people. -ದೇಶ, -ಮಂಡಲ. The Čôḷa country.

ಚೌಕ (= ಚವುಕ. *tb. of* ಚತುಷ್ಕ) *a.* Four-sided, square. *n.* A four-sided linga-box. 2, a square handkerchief. 3, four rupees. 4, a square in a town where four roads meet; a square in the centre of a temple or house. 5, the number four on a die. 6, prolixity, worthlessness (*as in* ಚೌಕದ ಮಾತು).

ಚೌಕಟ್ಟು **h.** *n.* A frame.

ಚೌಕಸುದ್ಧ (*tb. of* ಚತುಷ್ಕ & **s.**) *n.* Whole square.

ಚೌಕಸಿ. = ಚವುಕಸಿ, *q. v.*

ಚೌಕಳಿ. = ಚವುಕಳಿ, *q. v.*

ಚೌಕಿ (= ಚವಕಿ, ಚವುಕಿ, *q. v.*) *n.* A group of four houses. 2, the square in the centre of a house.

ಚೌಕೀದಾರ **h.** *n.* A watchman.

ಚೌಕು. = ಚೌಕ, *q. v.* -ವ. Four castes.

ಚೌತಿ (= ಚವುತಿ. *tb. of* ಚತುರ್ಥಿ) *n.* The fourth lunar day.

ಚೌದರಿ. = ಚವುದರಿ, *q. v.*

ಚೌಪದ (*tb. of* ಚತುಷ್ಪದ) *n.* A class of metres.

ಚೌರ. *tb. of* ಕ್ಷೌರ, *q. v.*

ಚೌರಿ (= ಚವರಿ. *tb. of* ಚಾಮರ) *n.* A chowry.

ಚೌಲ **s.** *n.* The tonsure of a child. 2, (= ಚವಲ) a silver coin of two Aṇas.

ಚೌಳು. = ಚವುಳು, *q. v.*

ಛ

ಛ. The twenty-fifth letter of the alphabet.

ಛಕಾರ **s.** *n.* The syllable ಛ.

ಛಟ **k.** *int. An imitative sound.* -ಛಟ. *rep.* The sound of snapping or clashing.

ಛಡಾಛಡಿ **h.** *ad.* Quickly.

ಛತ್ರ 1. (= ಚತ್ರ) **s.** *n.* A parasol, umbrella. -ಕ. A mushroom. -ಪತಿ. A regal title.

ಛತ್ರ 2. **s.** *n.* A choultry, inn.

ಛದ, -ನ **s.** *n.* A covering. 2, a wing. 3, a leaf.

ಛದಿಸ್ **s.** *n.* A covering. 2, the thatch or roof of a house.

ಛದ್ಮ **s.** *n.* Disguise, fraud, deceit, trick.

ಛಂದ. = ಚಂದ 1, *q. v.*

ಛಂದಸ್ಸು **s.** *n.* Metrical science, prosody. 2, the vedic hymns.

ಛರ್ದಿ **h.** *n.* Sickness, vomiting.

ಛಲ **s.** *n.* Fraud, deceit, deception, disguise; pretext; device. 2, (= ಚಲ 2) firmness. -ವಾದಿ. An obstinate man.

ಛವಿ **s.** *n.* Skin. 2, colour; beauty. 3, light, lustre.

ಛಾನಸ (*tb of* ಛಾಂದಸ) *n.* Loitering, delay -ಗಾರ A loiterer

ಛಾಂದಸ (*fr* ಛಂದಸ್) s *a* Relating to prosody. *n.* A Brâhmana conversant with the vêdas, *also* ಛಾಂದಸಿಕ

ಛಾಯೆ, ಛಾಯಾ (= ಚಾಯೆ) s *n.* Shade, shadow. 2, reflection 3 a screen, protection, respect 4, splendour 5, faint appearance. ಛಾಯಾತನಯ, ಛಾಯಾನಂದನ. The son of čhâyâ the planet Saturn ಛಾಯಾಯಂತ್ರ Shadow-instrument. a sundial

ಛಿದ್ರ s. *n.* A hole, slit, rent, a defect, flaw, fault. ಛಿದ್ರಾನ್ವೇಷಣ. Searching for faults

ಛಿನ್ನ s. *a* Cut, divided, torn, broken -ಛಿನ್ನ, -ಭಿನ್ನ Shattered, piecemeal

ಛೂರಿ = ಚೂರಿ, *q v.*

ಛೇಕ s. *a.* Tame. 2, shrewd, clever *n.* A kind of alliteration

ಛೇದ s *n* Cutting, chopping, tearing off, a section, piece. 2, a divisor, denominator of a fraction, *also* -ನ. -ಮಾಡು, ಛೇದಿಸು. To cut, make an incision, to cut asunder.

ಜ್

ಜ್. The twenty-sixth letter of the alphabet

ಜ s. *a* Born. *n* A son, *as*· ಅಗ್ರಜ, ಆತ್ಮಜ, ಇಂದ್ರಜ, ಉದ್ಭಿಜ, *etc.*

ಜಕಾತಿ h *n.* Customs, excise

ಜಕಾರ s. *n* The letter ಜ

ಜಕೀರೆ h. *n.* An old store or hoard

ಜಕ್ಕ (*tb of* ಯಕ್ಷ, *q. v*) ಜಕ್ಕಣ, ಜಕ್ಕಪ್ಪ. N., *f.* ಜಕ್ಕವ್ವ

ಜಕ್ಕಣೆ = ಜಕ್ಕಿಣಿ, *q v*

ಜಕ್ಕಲು k. *n.* Obsequiousness, fawning.

ಜಕ್ಕಿಣಿ (*tb of* ಯಕ್ಷಿಣಿ) *n.* A woman who dies in the matron state and receives divine honours, *i e.* sîrĕs are dedicated to her, *etc*

ಜಕ್ಕಿಸು (= ಜಗ್ಗಿಸು) k *v. t* To pull with effort 2, to press down. *v. i* To be rude

ಜಕ್ಕುಲಿ k. *v.* Ticklishness (*cf* ಚಕ್ಕಲಗುಳಿ). -ಸು. To amuse, divert; to jeer at, deride, to tickle, to touch, to play about

ಜಗ 1 (= ಝಗ) s *n* Glittering, notoriety. -ಜಗ, -ಜಗನೆ Sparkingly, brightly. -ಜಗಹೊಳೆ To shine brilliantly -ಜಗಿಸು. To glitter, shine.

ಜಗ 2. (*tb of* ಜಗತ್) *n* The world -ಜ್ಜನ. Mankind. -ಜ್ಜ್ಯೋತಿ The ligh. of the world the sun -ದೊಡೆಯ The lord of the world -ಬಂಡ. The greatest liar in the world, the most shameless man -ಮೊಂಡ The most stupid man in the world.

ಜಗತಿ, ಜಗತ್ತು (= ಜಗ) s *n.* The world, universe. ಜಗತ್ಕರ್ತ, ಜಗತ್ಕರ್ತೃ. The creator of the world, Brahmâ ಜಗತ್ತ್ರಯ The three worlds svarga, bhûmi, and pâtâla ಜಗದೀಶ, ಜಗದೀಶ್ವರ The Lord of the universe. ಜಗದ್ಗುರು. The guru of the world; Jesus Christ; an eminent guru. ಜಗದ್ರಕ್ಷಕ. The Saviour of the world Christ. ಜಗನ್ನಾಥ. The Lord of the world. God, N. of a town near Cuttack ಜಗನ್ನಾಯಕ. The governor of the world. God. ಜಗನ್ಮಾತೆ. Durgâ, Lakshmî

ಜಗತಿ 1 = ಜಗಲಿ, *q v*

ಜಗತಿ 2. (= ಜಗತ್ತು) s. *n.* The earth. 2, the world, universe 3, the king and his subjects -ವಲಯ. Earth's circumference, the terrestrial globe.

ಜಗತ್ಯ. *tb of* ಜಗತ್, *q v*

ಜಗಲಿ (= ಜಗತಿ) k. *n* A raised, open veranda, a seat of mud *etc*

ಜಗಳ k. *n.* A quarrel, fight, war. -ಗಂಟ, -ಗಾರ A quarrelsome man; *f.* -ಗಾತಿ. -ತರು To rouse a quarrel. -ತೆಗೆ To pick a quarrel -ಮಾಡು. To create a quarrel ಜಗಳಾಡು, -ಮಾಡು. To quarrel

ಜಗಳೆ (= ಜಾಗಟೆ) *tb* *n* A gong.

ಜಗಿ (= ಜಗಿ) k *v t.* To chew *as* betel

ಜಗುಳು (ಳು = ಱು) a k *v i* To go off, to slip, to drop down

ಜಗ್ಗಿಸು. = ಜಕ್ಕಿಸು, *q v*

ಜಗ್ಗು 1. k *v. i* To bend down, *as* a tree with fruit, to sink, *as* a wall, to hang down *n* Bending

ಜಗ್ಗು 2. k *v. t* To pull, drag, draw

ಜಂಕಿಸು a k. *v t.* To scold, chide, to despise *v i.* To cry ಜಂಕಣೆ Scolding ಜಂಕೆ. Crying out

ಜಂಗಮ s. *a.* Movable, locomotive, living *n* A Lingavanta; *f* -ಗಿತ್ತಿ -ಪ್ರಸಾದ Any favour from a Jangama. -ಲಿಂಗ A Jangama, a linga worn by him

ಜಂಗಲ, ಜಂಗಲು h *n.* A forest, jungle

ಜಂಗಾಲ್ 1 f *n* A platform with railings placed on two boats, used at ferries

ಜಂಗಾಲ್ 2. h *n* Zangar, a greenish blue dye

ಜಂಗು k *n* A bell worn by a Jangama mendicant

ಜಂಗುಳಿ k. *n* A mass, assemblage, herd, *etc*

ಜಂಗೆ k *n* A stride

ಜಂಘೆ s *n.* The shank or lower part of the leg the leg ಜಂಘಾನಿಲ. A swift wind. ಜಂಘಾಬಲ Power of legs ಜಂಘಾಲ Running, fleet, swift, a runner, courier

ಜಜ್ಜರಿತ. *tb. of* ಜರ್ಜರಿತ, *q v*

ಜಜ್ಜು k. *v. t* To bruise, crush squash. *n* A bruise

ಜಂಜರ h *a* General consecutive, not specific ... cutive number -ಬಂದಿ Running numbers or papers

ಜಂಜಡ, ಜಂಜಾಟ f *n.* Trouble, bother, plague

ಜಂಜಾಲು h *n* A swivel gun

ಜಟಕಾಯಿಸು f. *v t.* To scorn, treat scornfully, *also* ಜಟಕರಿಸು.

ಜಟಪಟ f *ad* Smartly, quick. ಜಟಪಟಿ, ಜಟಾಪಟಿ Strife, scuffle, angry discussion [hair

ಜಟಾಜೂಟ s. *n* A quantity of twisted.

ಜಟಾಮಾಂಸಿ s *n* A herb growing on the Himâlaya, the Indian spikenard

ಜಟಾಯು s *n.* N of a fabulous vulture.

ಜಟಿ, ಜಟಾ (= ಜಡೆ, *q v*) s *n* Twisted and matted hair, a tress of hair· 2 a pendent root from the banyan. *etc* 3, the fibrous root of trees. ಜಟಾಧಾರಿ Wearing matted or braided hair

ಜಟ್ಟಿ (= ಜೆಟ್ಟಿ) f *n.* A professional wrestler -ಮಲ್ಲ *dpl* An athlete among wrestlers -ಕಾಳಗ, -ಕುಸ್ತಿ, -ಗುದ್ದಾಟ, -ಯುದ್ಧ. A wrestling match. -ಮುಳ್ಳು Steel of boxers

ಜಠರ s. *n* The belly. *a* Hard, firm. ಜಠರಾಗ್ನಿ The gastric juice.

ಜಡ s *a.* Cold, frigid, chilly 2, slow, dull, apathetic, stupid, foolish 3, hard, solid *n.* Cold 2, (= ಜಡ್ಡು) indisposition, illness -ಕಾಲ The cold season -ಗುಣ A sluggish disposition -ಹೋಗು To be difficult

ಜಡಜ (= ಜಲಜ) s. *a* Water-born. *n* A lotus

ಜಡತ (*f*. ಜಡಿ) k *n* Beating, driving in, *as* a nail. -ಮಾಡು To drive in, *etc.*

ಜಡತಿ f. *n* A close and narrow search.

ಜಡತೆ, ಜಡತ್ವ s *n* Coldness; apathy, stupidity, inertness

ಜಡಾಯಿಸು (= ಜಡಾಯಿಸು, *q v*) k *v t* To drive in, to fasten or bolt, *as* a door

ಜಡಿ 1. k. *v. t* To threaten, menace, to ... on.

2, to wave, brandish, *as* a sword, *etc.* 3, to beat, to pound. 4, to beat into, to drive in, *as* a nail -ಸು To cause to beat

ಜಡಿ 2 k. *n.* A long-continued, fine, small rain; *also* -ಮಳೆ

ಜಡೀಭಾವ (*fr* ಜಡ) s *n.* Dulness apathy, insensibility

ಜಡುಪು f. *n.* A flap (attached to a paper kite).

ಜಡೆ *tb.* *of* ಜಟೆ, *q v* -ಕಳ್ಳಿ A kind of Euphorbia, triangular spurge. -ಕುಚ್ಚು. An ornament attached to a tress of hair of women -ನಾಗರ, -ಬಿಲ್ಲೆ Ornaments worn by women over their plaited hair

ಜಡ್ಜಿ e. *n.* The judge.

ಜಡ್ಡು 1. (= ಜಡ್ಡು) k *n.* A callous spot; a wart, scar. 2, the disagreeable smell of sheep's milk, *etc.*

ಜಡ್ಡು 2. (*tb* *of* ಜಡ) *n* Slight indisposition sickness; dulness; *also* -ತನ -ಬುದ್ಧಿ. A dull understanding

ಜಂಟಿ h *n.* Joining, meeting, partnership. -ಗಾರ A partner -ಪಟ್ಟೆ Title-deeds in the name of two persons. -ಮಾಡು, -ಹಾಕು To join, tie -ಸು To join, to annex

ಜಂಡೆ h. *n* A flag, banner.

ಜತನ (=ಯತನ *tb* *of* ಯತ್ನ) *n* Care, heed

ಜತಿ (*tb* *of* ಯತಿ) *n* An ascetic. 2, harmony in music.

ಜತೆ (= ಜತ್ತು, ಜೊತ್ತು *tb* *of* ಯುತಿ) *n.* Union; intercourse, company; a pair; a fellow. -ಗಾರ A male companion, *f.* -ಗಾತಿ -ಬೀಳು To pair, accompany.

ಜತ್ತಕ a k. *n.* Fraud, deceit hypocrisy; disguise

ಜತ್ತಿಗೆ = ಜೊತ್ತಿಗೆ, *q v*

ಜತ್ತು (=ಜತೆ) *tb.* *n.* Intercourse, friendship

ಜನ s. *n* Man, mankind, people, a person in general. -ಜನಿತ Known to all -ತೆ People, mankind, birth. -ನಾಥ, -ಪ, -ಪತಿ. -ನಾಯಕ. A king -ರಂಜನ Gratifying people -ಪದ A community, people, an empire, -ವಾರ್ತೆ. Rumour, report.

ಜನಕ s *n.* A progenitor, father, Sitâ's father -ಜೆ, -ತನಯೆ, ಜನಕಾತ್ಮಜೆ Sitâ

ಜನನ (=ಜನ್ಮ) s *n* Birth production 2, race, lineage -ಪತ್ರ, -ಪತ್ರಿಕೆ Horoscope ಜನನಿ A mother

ಜನಮೇಜಯ s *n* N. of a king, Parikshit's son

ಜನಾಂಗ s *n* A nation, tribe

ಜನಾನಿ h *a* Made for women *n.* A seraglio, harem.

ಜನಾಂತ s. *n* An uninhabited place. 2, a region, country

ಜನಾರ್ದನ s *n.* Vishnu, Krishna

ಜನಿ 1. s. *n* Birth, production. 2, a woman 3, a daughter-in-law -ತ. Born, begotten. -ಯಿಸು To be born or produced.

ಜನಿ 2. k. *v. i* To flow, to drop.

ಜನಿವಾರ (= ಜನ್ನಿವಾರ *tb* *of* ಯಜ್ಞೋಪವೀತ) *n.* The sacrificial thread

ಜನೆ a. k *n* The yolk of an egg

ಜಂತ *tb* *of* ದಂತ, *q v.*

ಜಂತು s *n.* A creature, living being 2, any animal

ಜಂತೆ f *n* A short small beam or rafter

ಜಂತ್ರ. *tb* *of* ಯಂತ್ರ, *q v*

ಜನ್ನ (*tb* *of* ಯಜ್ಞ) *n.* A sacrifice

ಜನ್ನಗೆ (*tb* *of* ಯಾಜ್ಞಿಕ) *n* That belongs to sacrifice.

ಜನ್ನಿವಾರ = ಜನಿವಾರ, *q. v*

ಜನ್ಮ (= ಜಲ್ಮ) s *n.* Birth, production, origin, existence, life -ಕೊಡು To give birth to -ತಕ್ಕೊಳ್ಳು, -ಎತ್ತು To be born -ದೇಶ Native country. -ನಕ್ಷತ್ರ. The natal star -ಪತ್ರ, -ಪತ್ರಿಕೆ. Horoscope -ಪಾಪ. Original sin -ಭೂಮಿ Birthplace. -ರಾಶಿ The sign of the zodiac that contains the natal star ಜನ್ಮಿಸು = ಜನಿಸು

ಜನ್ಮಾಂತರ s *n.* Another state of existence, transmigration

ಜನ್ತಿ s n A creature, man

ಜನ್ಯ s. a. Born, produced. n Rumour, report 2 war, combat

ಜಪ s n. Muttering, muttering a vedic verse, names of a deity, charms, prayers -ಮಾಡು ಜಪಿಸು To perform japa -ಮಾಲಿಕೆ, -ಮಾಲೆ, -ಸರ A rosary.

ಜಪ್ತಿ h. n. Seizure, confiscation, attachment (law).

ಜಪ್ಪಿಸು f. v t To wait and watch patiently, to lurk

ಜಬರ, ಜಬರು h n Powerful. -ದಸ್ತು Oppression, force, violence

ಜಬರಿಸು k. v l. To chide, scold

ಜಬಾಬು = ಜವಾಬು, q v

ಜಬ್ಬಲ k n The state of being weak, infirm or frail from old age, etc.

ಜಬ್ಬು 1. (= ಜಬ್ಬಲ) k n Weakness; softness; slackness

ಜಬ್ಬು 2 (= ಜಬರಿಸು) k. v. t. To scold, abuse. 2, to suck. n. Weakness, frailty; softness, slackness

ಜಮಖಾನೆ h n. A sitting carpet.

ಜಮದಗ್ನಿ s n Blazing fire. 2, N. of Paraśurâma's father

ಜಮಾ (= ಜಮೆ) h. n Receipts, income; collection -ಖರ್ಚು Receipts and disbursements -ಬಂದಿ. Settlement of assessments -ಯಿಸು. To assemble, to collect, to succeed, as a business -ವಸೂಲು -ಬಾಕಿ. The collections and the outstanding balances

ಜಮೇದಾರ h n A commander of a body of troops, the head peon.

ಜಮೀನದಾರ (=ಜಮೀನುದಾರ) h n A zemindar, landholder

ಜಮೀನು h n. Land or ground -ದಾರ = ಜಮೀನದಾರ, q. v [ದಾರ, q v

ಜಮೆ. = ಜಮಾ, q v ಜಮೇದಾರ = ಜಮಾ

ಜಂಪು f n. Drowsiness, sleepiness

ಜಂಪೆತಾಳ f. n Slow time in music, andante.

ಜಂಬ (=ಡಬ್ಬು, ಡಂಭ tb of ದಂಭ) n. Ostentation, pomp -ಗಾರ A man of ostentat

ಜಂಬರ k n Affair, business

ಜಂಬೀರ s n A lemon.

ಜಂಬು 1 k n Length 2, a kind of reed, *Typha angustifolia*.

ಜಂಬು 2. s n. The rose apple, *Eugenia jambolana* -ದ್ವೀಪ The central division of the world, including India; India

ಜಂಬುಕ s. n A jackal

ಜಂಬುಖಾನೆ. = ಜಮುಖಾನೆ, q. v

ಜಂಭ s n A lemon 2, N. of a demon destroyed by Indra. 3, the jaws; a tooth, tusk

ಜಯ s n Victory, conquest, winning 2. the twenty-eighth year of the cycle. -ಜಯ rep. Hurra! bravo! all hail! glory unto! -ಹೊಂದು To gain victory. -ಘೋಷ -ಧ್ವನಿ A shout or cry of victory -ಪತ್ರ A record of victory. -ಮಂಗಳ A cheer of victory -ಲಕ್ಷ್ಮಿ, -ಶ್ರೀ. The goddess of victory. -ವಂತ, -ಶಾಲಿ, -ಶೀಲ A conqueror. -ಸು = ಜಯಿಸು, q v

ಜಯಂತಿ s. n. A flag, banner 2 the day on which a deity assumed an incarnation 3, the plant *Sesbania aegyptiaca*

ಜಯಮಿನಿ tb of ಜೈಮಿನಿ q v.

ಜಯಸು, ಜಯಿಸು s. v. t To conquer, defeat, overcome

ಜರ 1. k n Sliding -ಕುಂಡಿ, ಜರಗುಂಡಿ Sliding on the posteriors, as children do.

ಜರ 2. tb. of ಜ್ವರ, q. v ಚಳಿ- Ague -ಗೆಂಡೆ Ague-cake

ಜರ 3. h n Brocade 2, a little, somewhat.

ಜರ 4 (= ಜರೆ 1) s. n Growing old, decaying, wasting.

ಜರಗು (= ಜರುಗು) k v i To slip, slide; to roll down as sand from a heap, to pass, elapse as time, to be done as a business n Loose texture as that of cloth ಜರಗಿಸು To cause to sl... as ... k

ಜರಠ h. *a* Worn out; old, hard, solid 2, bent, drooping. 3 harsh, cruel. *n.* Old age 2, mud, mire.

ಜರತು k *n* Unsubstantiality, uselessness.

ಜರಡೆ (= ಜಲ್ಲಡೆ) k. *n* A sieve.

ಜರಣ s *a* Waxing old 2, promoting digestion *n* Cumin-seed.

ಜರತಾರ, ಜರತಾರೆ h *n* Silver wire covered with gold ಜರತಾರಿ Worked with jaratâra

ಜರದು (= ಜರಿದು) *P p of* ಜರಿ 1.

ಜರಬು (= ಜರುಬು) h. *n.* Terribleness, awe

ಜರಾಯು s *n* The womb 2, the afterbirth. -ಜ Born of the womb

ಜರಿ 1 (=ಸರಿ) k *v. i* To slip or fall, to slide or slip down, to shrink back. 2, to fall away, to lose flesh *n* A ravine worn by a stream. -ಗಿಡ A fern. ಹಿಂಜರಿ To retreat, retire ಮುಂಜರಿ To advance.

ಜರಿ 2. h. *n.* Gold or silver threads. *a.* Worked with such threads. ಜರೀಪಟಕ A laced belt, a grand flag

ಜರಿ 3 (ರಿ = ಱಿ) k. *n.* A centipede.

ಜರಿ 4 (ರಿ = ಱಿ) = ಜರೆ 2, *q v*

ಜರೀಪ h *n* A giraffe

ಜರೀಬು h *n* A land-measure. 2, measurement.

ಜರುಗು. = ಜರಗು, *q. v.*

ಜರುಟು (ರು = ಱು) k *v. i.* To talk much, to be loquacious *n* Garrulity, vain talk

ಜರುಬು. = ಜರಬು, *q. v.*

ಜರೂರು h. *ad.* Necessarily, urgently, at all events.

ಜರೆ 1. (= ಜರ 4, ಜರಾ) s. *n.* Old age, decrepitude, grey hair.

ಜರೆ 2. (ರೆ = ಱೆ) k. *v. t* To rebuke, abuse; to disgrace, disdain, jeer at *P. ps.* ಜರದು, ಜರೆದು.

ಜರ್ಜರ s. *a* Old, infirm, decayed 2, broken, shattered. ಜರ್ಜರಿತ (= ಜಜ್ಜರಿತ). Torn, broken in pieces, infirm ಜರ್ಜರಿಸು To become infirm

ಜಬ್ಬರ್ k *v t* To scold, rebuke.

ಜಲ (= ಜಳ) s. *n* Water (ಉದಕ, ನೀರು). 2, fraud, hypocrisy. -ಕ Relating to water, a bath, bathing -ಕಣ A water-drop -ಕಂಟಕ. A crocodile, danger from water. -ಕನ್ಯೆ A water-nymph. -ಕ್ರೀಡೆ Sporting in water, bathing for pleasure -ಕ್ಷಾಲನ Washing or cleansing with water. -ಗಾರ One who searches for gold in drains, *etc.* -ಗ್ರಹ. A shark or crocodile. -ಚರ Aquatic, a fish -ಜ, -ಜಾತ A lotus; a shell -ಜಂತು An aquatic animal -ಜಾರಿ The moon. -ತರಂಗ. A wave, harmonicon -ದ, -ಧರ. A cloud, a fragrant grass, *Cyperus rotundus* -ದಾರಿ A drain, kennel -ದ್ರೋಣಿ A bucket -ಧಿ, -ನಿಧಿ The ocean -ಪಕ್ಷಿ A water-bird -ಪತಿ Varuna. -ಪದ್ಧತಿ A water-course, a gutter -ಪುಷ್ಪ. An aquatic flower, a fish -ಪ್ರಲಯ A deluge -ಪ್ರವಾಹ The current of water -ಬುದುಬುದ A water-bubble -ಮಯ Watery. -ಯಂತ್ರ A syringe, a water-engine. -ರಾಶಿ The ocean -ರುಹ. A lotus -ರುಹರಿಪು The moon. -ವಾಯಸ. The diver-bird. -ಶಂಕೆ. Fear arising from water, making water -ಶುಕ್ತಿ A bivalve shell -ಸಂಧಿ. Straits -ಹರಿ A small vessel with a channel for conveying water ಜಲಾಧಾರ A reservoir

ಜಲದಿ (= ಜಲ್ದಿ) h *ad* Quickly

ಜಲಾಯಿಸು s. *i. t.* To burn.

ಜಲಾಲಿ h. *n.* A sort of masquerade at the Moharam.

ಜಲಾವರ್ತ s. *n.* A whirlpool, eddy

ಜಲಾಶಯ, ಜಲಾಶ್ರಯ (*f*. ಜಲ) s *n.* A lake or pond.

ಜಲೂಕೆ s. *n.* A leech.

ಜಲೋದರ s *n* Dropsy

ಜಲ್ದಿ. = ಜಲದಿ, *q v*

ಜಲ್ಪ, ಜಲ್ಪನ s. n Talk, chatter, discussion ಜಲ್ಪಾಕ. Talkative; a chatterer, f. ಜಲ್ಪಾಕಿ

ಜಲ್ಕ tb of ಜನ್ತು q v

ಜಲ್ಲಡಿ, ಜಲ್ಲಡೆ = ಜರಡೆ, q v

ಜಲ್ಲನೆ k ad. With a start.

ಜಲ್ಲಿ 1 (= ಜಲ್ಲಿ) k n A round bamboo basket used for storing coin

ಜಲ್ಲಿ 2 k n Broken stone. 2, falsehood, lie 3, tassels, hangings -ಕೊಡು, -ಹೊಡೆ To lie

ಜಲ್ಲಿಸು k. v t. To sift

ಜಲ್ಲು f. n. A boatman's pole. 2, the state of being torn, as cloth or leaves

ಜಲ್ಲೆ k. n. A bamboo pole.

ಜವ 1 s. n Speed, velocity, swiftness. -ಗೆಡು. Velocity to be impaired.

ಜವ 2 tb of ಯಮ, q v

ಜವಕಾರ (tb of ಯವಕ್ಷಾರ) n Saltpetre.

ಜವನಿಕೆ (tb. of ಯವನಿಕೆ) n. A curtain, screen, veil

ಜವಳಿ 1 k n. Cloth of any kind -ಕ, -ಕಾರ A cloth-seller

ಜವಳಿ 2. (tb of ಯಮಲಿ) n A pair, twins; sameness. -ನುಡಿ Two words

ಜವಳು, = ಜವುಗು, etc, q. v

ಜವಾಜಿ, ಜವಾದಿ (= ಜವ್ವಾಜಿ) h. n Civet 2, musk. -ಬೆಕ್ಕು A civet cat.

ಜವಾನ h. n A peon

ಜವಾಬು (= ಜವಾಬು) h. n. An answer, reply -ದಾರ. A responsible man. -ದಾರಿ Responsibility

ಜವಾರಿ f a Produced in one's own country, as cloth, wool, etc

ಜವಾಹೀರು h n A jewel, jewelry

ಜವಿ k n. The hair of a horse's tail.

ಜವುಗು, ಜವುಳು (= ಜವಳು) k. n Swampy ground, a swamp.

ಜವೆ. tb of ಯವ, q v -ಗೋಧಿ. Barley, Hordeum vulgare.

ಜವ್ವನ tb. of ಯೌವನ, q v.

ಜವ್ವಾಜಿ =

ಜವ್ವಾಲೆ (= ಉಯ್ಯಾಲೆ, ಜೋಕಾಲೆ) f n. A swing

ಜಸ. tb of ಯಶ, q v

ಜಹಗೀರು (= ಜಾಗೀರು) h. n An assignment by government of lands or revenues. -ದಾರ. The holder of a jahagiru

ಜಹಜು h. n. A ship.

ಜಹ್ನು s n N of a king who adopted Ganges as his daughter -ತನಯ, ಜಾಹ್ನವಿ The Ganges

ಜಳ s. n. Heat, hot vapour. -ಜಳ. Shining brightly

ಜಳಕ (= ಜಲಕ, s ಜಲ) s n A bath, bathing -ಮಾಡು. To bathe.

ಜಳ್ಳು (= ಜರಡು, q v) k n Emptiness, hollowness. -ಕಾಳು An empty grain of corn. -ಮಾತು A vain word -ಎಳ್ಳು, ಜಳ್ಳೆಳ್ಳು Barren sesamum.

ಜಾ, ಜಾಕಾಯಿ = ಜಾಜಿ, ಜಾಜಿಕಾಯಿ, q v

ಜಾಗ h. n. A place, spot, room.

ಜಾಗಟೆ (tb of ಜಯಘಂಟೆ) n. A gong used by religious mendicants, in temples, etc.

ಜಾಗರ, ಜಾಗರಣ (= ಜಾಗ್ರತೆ) s n Waking, wakefulness, keeping a vigil

ಜಾಗರೂಕ s a Wakeful -ತೆ Wakefulness.

ಜಾಗೀರು. = ಜಹಗೀರು, q. v.

ಜಾಗು a. k n Silence, taciturnity.

ಜಾಗ್ರತ s a Awake, attentive, also ಜಾಗ್ರತ n. = ಜಾಗ್ರತೆ. -ಇಡು. To pay attention

ಜಾಗ್ರತೆ s n. Wakefulness, attention, carefulness -ಗೊಳ್ಳು, -ತೆಕೊಳ್ಳು. To take care -ಮಾಡು, -ಇಡು To be attentive.

ಜಾಂಗಲಿಕ, ಜಾಂಗುಲಿಕ s n. A snake-catcher juggler.

ಜಾಜಿ (tb of ಜಾತಿ) n Nutmeg mace. 2, Jasminum grandiflorum. -ಕಾಯಿ Nutmeg. -ಪತ್ರೆ. Mace. -ಮಲ್ಲಿಗೆ, -ಹೂವು. Jasmine

ಜಾಜು k n. Red colour.

ಜಾಜ್ವಲ್ಯಮಾನ s a Shining resplen-

ಜಾಠರ s a. Stomachic, abdominal

ಜಾಡ (= ಜೇಡ) k. n A weaver, f -ಗಿತ್ತಿ, -ತಿ 2, a spider, also -ಹುಳ -ನ ಗೂಡು A spider's nest

ಜಾಡಣೆ (= ಝಾಡಣೆ) f n Shaking, sweeping, throwing, discharging; diarrhoea

ಜಾಡಮಾಲಿ h. n. A sweeper

ಜಾಡಾ h. n A general clearance of accounts, also ಜಾಡೆ

ಜಾಡಿ 1 h n. A discharge; a flood, an outburst, as of tears wrath, etc.

ಜಾಡಿ 2 k n A common cumbly.

ಜಾಡಿ 3. h. n A jar

ಜಾಡಿಸು f v t To sweep, to dust. 2, to shake off, as dust from cloth, etc., to jerk or throw out, as an arm, etc, to purge. 3, to reprove

ಜಾಡೆ k n The mark of a footstep, track, trace; wink, hint

ಜಾಡ್ಯ (fr ಜಡ) s. n. Coldness, apathy, indisposition, disease.

ಜಾಣ (tb of ಜ್ಞಾನ) n. A skilful, knowing, or clever man, f -ಳು, ಜಾಣೆ -ತನ, ಜಾಣಿಮೆ, ಜಾಣ್ಮೆ Cleverness, knowledge, understanding.

ಜಾತ s a. Born, brought forth, produced, possessing, manifest n. A son, birth, a creature, a race, kind, sort, species, a mass -ಕ A horoscope. -ಕರ್ಮ A ceremony performed on the birth of a child

ಜಾತಾಬಾಕಿ h n. Balance, remainder after deductions.

ಜಾತಿ s. n Birth 2 lineage, race, family; tribe, caste 3, kind, sort, species. 4, superior breed 5, (= ಜಾಜಿ) nutmeg 6, the great-flowered jasmine. ಉತ್ತಮ-, ಒಳ್ಳೇ-, ಮೇಲು-. A high caste; a good family ಕೀಳು-, ಕೆಟ್ಟ-, ನೀಚ-, ಹೀನ- A low caste -ದ್ವೇಷ Enmity with one's caste. -ಧರ್ಮ The law or usage of caste. -ಭೇದ. A distinction of castes -ಭ್ರಷ್ಟ An outcast. -ವಂತ Of high birth or rank -ಸಂಕರ. A medley of castes. -ಹೀನ = -ಭ್ರಷ್ಟ, q v.

ಜಾತ್ಯ s a Belonging to a family, or caste, of noble descent

ಜಾತ್ರೆ tb of ಯಾತ್ರೆ. q v.

ಜಾದೂಗಿರಿ h. n Magical arts

ಜಾನಕೀ s n. Sîtâ, the wife of Râma. -ಪತಿ, -ರಮಣ Râma.

ಜಾನು s n The knee.

ಜಾನ್ಹವಿ = ಜಾಹ್ನವಿ. q v.

ಜಾಪಾಳದ ಕಾಯಿ f n The croton-seed. ಜಾಪಾಳದ ಗಿಡ *Croton tiglium* plant

ಜಾಪ್ಯ (tb. of ಯಾಪ್ಯ) n. Loitering, laziness. 2, a sluggard, lazy man. a. To be muttered -ಗಾರ A sloth, sluggard.

ಜಾಬಿತ, ಜಾಬಿತಾ h n A passport; a memorandum, an inventary, catalogue

ಜಾಬು (= ಜವಾಬು) h n An answer, a letter of correspondence.

ಜಾಮು = ಜಾವ, q. v

ಜಾಮಾತೃ s n A son-in-law.

ಜಾಮೀನ, ಜಾಮೀನು h n A bail, security; surety, sponsor. -ದಾರ, ಜಾಮೀನ್ದಾರ. A surety, bondsman. -ದಸ್ತಾವೇಜು Surety-bond.

ಜಾಮೇಯ s. n A sister's son

ಜಾಂಬ f n A sort of goblet

ಜಾಂಬವ s a. Belonging to the jambu tree 2, = ಜಾಂಬವಂತ.

ಜಾಂಬವಂತ s n. N of the chief of the bears. ಜಾಂಬವತಿ. His daughter.

ಜಾಯಮಾನ s a. Being born.

ಜಾಯಾ s n. Loss, injury, damage

ಜಾಯಿ. = ಜಾಜಿ, q. v.

ಜಾಯು s. n. A medicament, medicine

ಜಾರ s n A paramour, an adulterer. -ತ್ವ Adultery -ಪುರುಷ = ಜಾರ -ಸ್ತ್ರೀ, ಜಾರೆ An adulteress, harlot

ಜಾರಿ h. n Relieving from a state of sequestration, as land. 2, currency. 3. enforcement, execution. -ಮಾಡು. to execute

ಜಾರು (ರು=ಱು) k v i To slip, slide 2, to steal away, to withdraw, retire. 3, to go off, to run away 4, to flow down 5, to become loose, *as* a knot *n* Slipping, disappearance, a slide -ವಿಕೆ Sliding, *etc*, flowing

ಜಾಲ s *n* A net, snare, a web; a net-work. 2, a lattice, loophole 3, deception, illusion; conjuring 4, pride 5, a pretext 6, a multitude. 7, a cover, covering, film 8, an unblown flower 9, an organ of sense. 10, the sky -ಗಾರ (=ಜಲಗಾರ) A deceiver, conjurer, a fisherman, *f* -ಗಾತಿ.

ಜಾಲಕ s *n* A woven texture, a web. 2, a loophole; *cf* ಜಾಲಿಕೆ

ಜಾಲರಿ h *n* Net-work, fringe

ಜಾಲಾರಿ k *n*. A tree yielding a kind of lac, *Shorea laliura*

ಜಾಲಿ 1 k. *n*. The thorny babool tree, *Acacia arabica* 2, the thorny shrub, *Acacia farnesiana*

ಜಾಲಿ 2. s. *n* A species of cucumber, *Trichosanthes dioeca*. 2, a fisherman.

ಜಾಲಿಕ s. *n* A fisherman 2, a spider. 3, a conjurer, juggler. 4, = ಜಾಲಿಕೆ Nos 1 & 2

ಜಾಲಿಕೆ s *n* A net 2, a chain-armour 3, a leech 4, woollen cloth; *cf*. ಜಾಲಕ ಜಾಲಿಸು (= ಜಾಳಿಸು) To cleanse rice *etc* by washing in water

ಜಾವ (*tb of* ಯಾಮ) *n* A night-watch, the eighth part of a day, *also* ಜಾಮ

ಜಾವಳ (*tb. of* ಸಾಮಾನ್ಯ) *a* Common, vulgar, insignificant

ಜಾವಗೆ f. *n* The match of a matchlock

ಜಾವು = ಜಾವ, *q. v*

ಜಾಸ್ತಿ h *n* Excess, oppression, force *a* More than, additional, extra

ಜಾಹೀರಾತು h *n* Proclamation.

ಜಾಹೀರು h *a* Published, public -ನಾಮೆ A written proclamation.

ಜಾಹ್ನವಿ (*fr*. ಜಹ್ನು) s. *n*. The daughter of Jahnu the Ganges

ಜಾಳ = ಜಾಲ, *q. v* -ಅರಿವೆ Cloth of a thin texture. -ಕ. = ಜಾಲಕ, *q v*

ಜಾಳಿಗೆ 1 (*tb of* ಜಾಲಕ or ಜಾಲಿಕಾ) *n* A net 2, a lattice-window 3, a purse 4, an assemblage.

ಜಾಳಿಗೆ 2 (ಳಿ=ಱಿ) k. *n* Cloth, raiment.

ಜಾಳು = ಜತಡು, *q v* -ನುಡಿ, -ಮಾತು. An empty, vain speech

ಜಿಗಟು (= ಜಬಟು) k *n*. Stickiness 2, gum 3 birdlime

ಜಿಗಣೆ, ಜಿಗಳೆ, ಜಿಗಳ f. *n*. A leech.

ಜಿಗಿ 1 k *n* Thickness, viscidity. 2, a kind of blight or mildew falling on the cotton plant 2, gum.

ಜಿಗಿ 2 k *v i* To jump. 2, (= ಜಗಿ) to chew, *as* betelnut, bread, *etc*

ಜಿಗುಪ್ಸೆ *tb. of* ಜುಗುಪ್ಸೆ, *q v*.

ಜಿಂಕೆ k. *n* An antelope

ಜಿಂಗಿ s *n* Intoxication. 2, the plant *Rubia munjista*, madder

ಜಿಜ್ಞಾಸೆ s. *n* Desire of knowing; inquiry, investigation.

ಜಿಟ್ಟೆ k *n* A grasshopper 2, a sty

ಜಿಡ್ಡಿ = ಡಿಡ್ಡಿ, *q v*.

ಜಿಡ್ಡು k. *n* A greasy or oily substance. 2, rancidity.

ಜಿಣುಗು, ಜಿಣುಂಗು = ಜಿನುಗು, *q v*

ಜಿತ 1. s *a*. Subdued, overcome, won. -ಕಾಮ. One who has subdued desire, lust, *etc*, an ascetic, *f* -ಕಾಮೆ -ಶತ್ರು One who has conquered his enemies. ಜಿತಾಕ್ಷ, ಜಿತೇಂದ್ರಿಯ One who has conquered his passions

ಜಿತ 2. (*tb of* ಸ್ಥಿತ) *a* Fixed, firm, stable. -ಪಡಿಸು To make firm; to commit to memory. -ಪಡು. To become firm, to be mastered, *as* a lesson. -ಮಾಡು = -ಪಡಿಸು. -ಬುದ್ಧಿ A firm mind

ಜಿದ್ದು h. *n*. Affront, contention. 2, spite, hatred

ಜಿನ s *a* Victorious, steady, brave. *n*. A saint of the [illegible] sect, a

Jaina saint. -ಪ್ರಬುದ್ಧಿ Jaina doctrine -ಮುನಿ, -ಯತಿ A Jaina saint, ascetic, monk

ಜಿನಗು (= ಜಣಗು) k n Fineness, *as* of texture, thread, *etc*

ಜಿನಸು (= ಜೀನಸು) h n. An article, wares, goods

ಜಿನಿಗಿಸು k i i. To become insensible, to faint. i. t To liquefy, melt, *as* butter

ಜಿನುಗು 1 = ಜನಗು, *q v*.

ಜಿನುಗು 2 k i i. To drizzle 2, to mutter, hum. 3, to melt, *as* butter, ghee, *etc* n Drizzling rain

ಜಿಂದಗಿ, ಜಿಂದಿಗಿ h. n Goods and chattels, one's estate, (movable) property.

ಜಿಪಣ, ಜಿಪುಣ (*tb of* ಕೃಪಣ) n A miserly, avaricious man, *f*. ಜಿಪುಣಿ

ಜಿಬಟು = ಜಿಗಟು, *q v*

ಜಿಬರು k. n Rheum of the eye

ಜಿಬಳ. = ಜಿಬ್ಬು. ಜಿಬಳಡಿಕೆ. Tender areca-nut, cut into pieces, boiled and dried

ಜಿಬ್ಬು k n Stickiness, sliminess.

ಜಿಮ್ಖಾನ f & h. n Gymkhana, an association for the competition in gymnastics and sports

ಜಿಮ್ಮಿ k n. A prickly tree, *Zanthoxylon rhetsa*

ಜಿಮ್ಮೆ h n Charge, trust of a thing.

ಜಿರಾಯಿತು h n Land fit for agriculture 2, cultivation

ಜಿರಲೆ (ರ = ಱ) k n. A centipede 2, a cockroach. 3, a kind of earwig.

ಜಿಲಿಬಿಲಿ, ಜಿಲೇಬಿ h n. A sort of sweetmeat

ಜಿಲೇವು f n. Glitter, gloss, shine

ಜಿಲ್ಲಾ, ಜಿಲ್ಲೆ h n A district -ದಾರ. The governor of a district

ಜಿಲ್ಲು k n. The sensation produced by touching cold water ಜಿಲ್ಲೆನ್ನು That sensation to be produced.

ಜಿಷ್ಣು s a. Victorious, triumphant. n. An arhat 2, Indra. 3, Vishnu. 4, Śiva

ಜಿಹ್ವೆ, ಜಿಹ್ವಾ s n The tongue. 2, the flame of fire ಜಿಹ್ವಾಮೂಲ The root of the tongue. ಜಿಹ್ವಾರವ A word

ಜೀಕಳಿ k n. A squirt, syringe

ಜೀಟು k n A prop, stay, *as* for a wall

ಜೀತ (*tb of* ಜೀವಿತ) n Living, salary, wages, work -ಗಾರ A paid servant.

ಜೀನ 1 (*tb. of* ದೀನ) n A niggardly, miserly man, *f* ಜೀನಿ. *a* Decayed, old -ತನ Niggardliness.

ಜೀನ 2 h n A saddle -ಗಾರ. A saddler.

ಜೀನಸು = ಜಿನಸು, *q v*

ಜೀನಿ, ಜೀನು. = ಜೀನ 2, *q v*

ಜೀಬಿ h n The area between the inner and outer walls

ಜೀಯ f n Sir, master, a particle expressing assent.

ಜೀರಿಗೆ (*tb of* ಜೀರಕ) n. The cumin seed. -ಮಾವು A kind of fragrant mango. -ಸಣ್ಣಕ್ಕಿ, -ಸಾಲೆ. A superior kind of rice.

ಜೀರು (ರು = ಱು) k. n. Screaming, shrilling; *cf* ಚೀರು -ಜಂಟೆ A kind of bee

ಜೀರ್ಕೊಳವಿ (= ಜೀಕಳಿ) k. n A syringe

ಜೀರ್ಣ s. *a*. Grown old; worn out, consumed, digested. -ಕೋಶ. The stomach. -ವಸ್ತ್ರ. Old, tattered cloth. ಜೀರ್ಣಿಸು To be digested. ಜೀರ್ಣೋದ್ಧಾರ Repairing of what is worn out.

ಜೀವ s. *a*. Living n A living being, a creature 2, existence, life 3, (= ಜೀವಾತ್ಮ) the principle of life, the living soul 4, (= -ನ) livelihood. 5, Brihaspati. 6, water. -ಆ. A servant; a usurer. -ಕಳೆ. The glow of life, life. -ಕೊಡು To give up one's life. -ಗಳ್ಳ. A coward -ತೆಗೆ To kill. -ದ ಗೆಳೆಯ. A very dear friend. -ದ ಭಯ Fear to lose one's life. -ದ ಮೇಲಿನ ಆಶೆ, -ದಾಶೆ. Love of one's life. -ದ ಹಂಗು Obligation with regard to one's life -ದಾನ The gift of life. -ದಿಂದ ಇರು. To be alive. -ದಿಂದ ಉಳಿ. To remain alive -ಧನ. Live stock, cattle -ಮಾನ. Life-time, life -ರಾಶಿ The animal kingdom -ಹಿಂಸೆ Destroying life -ಸ್ಥಾನ A vital organ ಜೀವಾಕ್ಷರ A vowel

ಜೀವತ್, ಜೀವಂತ s. a Living, alive.

ಜೀವನ s n. Life, existence, means of subsistence, livelihood. 2, water. -ದಾದ A cloud ಜೀವನಾಂಶ, ಜೀವನಾಧಾರ. Maintenance, livelihood ಜೀವನೋಪಾಯ Means of livelihood.

ಜೀವನ್ಮುಕ್ತಿ s. n Liberation from further births and from ritual acts ಜೀವನ್ಮುಕ್ತ A man purified by knowledge of Brahma

ಜೀವಾತ್ಮ. = ಜೀವ No. 3, q v

ಜೀವಾಳ (tb of ಜೀವಲ) n. A vital member or organ 2, a chip put in the mouthpiece of a musical pipe or drone. 3, substance, pith essence.

ಜೀವಿ s n A living being a. Living, alive -ತ. Living; life, existence; wages. -ತ ಕಾಲ. Lifetime. -ಸು To live, exist, to live by.

ಜುಕಾಯಿಸು h v. i To stoop, bend, to reel. stagger.

ಜುಗಾರು f n Gambling

ಜುಗುಪ್ಸೆ s n Censure, reproach 2, aversion, disgust.

ಜುಂಜು k. n. The comb of a cock.

ಜುಟ್ಟು k n. The tuft of hair left on the crown of the head at tonsure, a crest, as of a cock -ಬಿಡಿಸು. To produce a juttu at tonsure

ಜುಟ್ಲೆ k n A kind of pigeon

ಜುಡುಪು h n A bush, a thicket

ಜುಣುಗು k. v i To shrink, contract; to withdraw n Shrinkage

ಜುಮಕಿ h. n. The pendant of an earring.

ಜುಮಲಾ = ಜುಮ್ಲಾ, q v.

ಜುಮ್ಮನೆ k. ad Quickly. 2, with horripilation.

ಜುಮ್ಮಾಮಸೀದಿ h n A mosque that is visited on Fridays.

ಜುಮ್ಲಾ h. ... ...

ಜುರಮಾನ, ಜುಲಮಾನ (= ಜುಲುಮಾನು, ಜುಲ್ಮಾನೆ) h. n. A fine, penalty, punishment.

ಜುಲಮೆ = ಜುಲುಮೆ, q. v.

ಜುಲಾಬು h n A purgative, a purge. 2, diarrhoea.

ಜುಲಾಯಿ f n A weaver 2, (e) July (7th month of the year)

ಜುಲಿಪೆ h n. Small locks of hair kept on children's head as ornament.

ಜುಲುಮಾನು = ಜುಲಮಾನ, q v

ಜುಲುಮೆ (= ಜುಲಮೆ, ಜುಲ್ಮೆ) h n. Oppression, tyranny, injustice, compulsion

ಜುಲ್ಮಾನೆ = ಜುಲಮಾನ, q v

ಜುವ್ವಿಮರ k n The wavy-leafed figtree, Ficus infectoria

ಜೂಗಳಿಸು (= ತೂಕಡಿಸು) k v i To nod, doze, to move on or proceed slowly, as vehicles or work.

ಜೂಗು = ತೂಗು, q v ಜೂಗಾಡು (= ತೂಗಾಡು) To waddle

ಜೂಜು (tb. of ದ್ಯೂತ) n Gambling, game. ಜೂಜಾಡು To gamble, game -ಕಟ್ಟು. To wager -ಗಾರ. A gambler.

ಜೂಟ1 (tb of ಜುಡಿತ) n The matted or clotted hair of an ascetic. 2, bodily strength of children

ಜೂಟ2 h n A lie

ಜೂಡಿ f n A favourable quit-rent on inâm lands

ಜೂತಿ h n. A shoe 2, (f) impulse, energy

ಜೂನು e. n. June (6th month of the, [year).

ಜೂಪರ k n Thin, drizzling rain.

ಜೂಲು1 k n A tatter -ನಾಯಿ. A dog with long hair [etc.

ಜೂಲು2 h n A body-cloth of horses,

ಜೂಳಿ k. n The spout of a vessel

ಜೆ s a. Born (f) n A daughter, as ಆತ್ಮ- etc

ಜೆಗ್ಗು = ಜಗ್ಗು, q v

ಜೆಂಗ್ h a Relating to war n Petulance, dunning; besieging -ಸರಂಜಾ ... ...

ಜಿಟ್ಟಿ = ಜಟ್ಟಿ, q v

ಜಿಡೆ = ಜಡೆ, q v

ಜಿನುಯೆರಿ e n January (1st month of the year).

ಜೇಗಟೆ. = ಜಾಗಟೆ, q. v.

ಜೇಡ. = ಜಾಡ, q v

ಜೇಡಿ k n A sort of pipe-clay, chalk.

ಜೇನು k. n Honey, also -ತುಪ್ಪ. -ನೊಣ, -ಹುಳ. A honey-bee -ಹುಟ್ಟು, -ಗೂಡು A honey-comb. -ಮೇಣ. Wax

ಜೇಬು h n A pocket

ಜೇರು 1 h a Feeble, exhausted. n. Weakness, indisposition.

ಜೇರು 2. k. n A wall -ಗಂಡಿ, -ಗಿಂಡಿ. An embrasure for guns, a loophole -ಮುತ್ತಿಗೆ A close siege

ಜೇವಣಿಗೆ k. n. Sweetness pleasantness.

ಜೇಷ್ಠಮಧು s. n. Liquorice

ಜೈನ (fr ಜಿನ) s n. A Jaina

ಜೈಮಿನಿ s. n N of a rishi and philosopher -ಭಾರತ A Kannada metrical translation of a Samskrita poem

ಜೊಟ್ಟಿ = ಜರಡು, q. v

ಜೊಂಡಿಗ k. n A cockroach.

ಜೊಂಡು k n The scurf of the head, dandruff 2, a filthy mass of scum floating on water 3, the elephant-grass

ಜೊತೆ (= ಜತೆ tb of ಯುತ) n Union, company, pair. -ಗೊಳಿಸು. To join -ಗಾರ. = ಜತೆಗಾರ, q v.

ಜೊತ್ತು = ಜತ್ತು, q. v.

ಜೊನ್ನವಕ್ಕಿ (tb. of ಜ್ಯೋತ್ಸ್ನಪಕ್ಷಿ) n. The Greek partridge.

ಜೊಂಪ a. k n A cluster, bunch

ಜೊಂಪಿಸು a. k. v. t To cause to tremble v. i. To tremble, to be aroused 2 to get intoxicated, stupefied.

ಜೊಂಪು a. k. n. Inebriation, stupor, paralisation.

ಜೊಲ್ಲು k n Saliva, slaver.

ಜೊಳ್ಳು (= ಜಳ್ಳು, q v) k. n. Emptiness.

ಜೋ k. int Hush! ಜೋ ಜೋ Hush, hush! used in lulling infants; cf. -ಗಳ.

ಜೋಕಾಲೆ = ಜವ್ವಾಲೆ, q v.

ಜೋಕು m n. An affected manner of speaking, walking, dressing, etc; a scheme, trick -ಗಾರ A man of affected manners; f. -ಗಾತಿ.

ಜೋಕೆ k. n Attention, caution, care. 2, beauty, harmony. -ಮಾಡು. To take care, protect. -ಯಾಗಿರು To be attentive, cautious, to be safe, well protected

ಜೋಗ. tb of ಯೋಗ, q. v. -ತಿ. A female beggar dedicated to Ellamma.

ಜೋಗಳ (= ಜೋಗುಳ) k. n A lullaby.

ಜೋಗಿ tb. of ಯೋಗಿ, q. v.

ಜೋಗು k n. A waterfall. 2, benumbed sensation of a limb

ಜೋಗುಳ = ಜೋಗಳ, q v

ಜೋಡಣೆ f n. Joining, junction, preparation, readiness

ಜೋಡಿ f n. A pair or couple. 2, a sheet of paper.

ಜೋಡಿಸು f. v t To join, unite, to put to, to collect.

ಜೋಡು f. n. Junction, union, company, a pair or couple, a match. 2, a pair of shoes 3, a suit of armour. 4, close connection ಜೋಡಕ್ಷರ A double letter, diphthong.

ಜೋತಿ tb. of ಜ್ಯೋತಿ, q v

ಜೋತಿಷ. = ಜ್ಯೋತಿಷ, q v

ಜೋತು = ಜೋಲ್ದು P. p of ಜೋಲು, q v.

ಜೋದ (tb. of ಯೋಧ) n. An elephant-driver.

ಜೋನಿ k n. Fluidity, as of jaggory; also -ಬೆಲ್ಲ -ಗ One of a Śûdra caste.

ಜೋಪಡಿ f. n A hut; a cottage.

ಜೋಪಾನ f n. Taking care of, looking after, fostering -ಮಾಡು. To take care of.

ಜೋಬ, -ದ್ರ k. n A dull, lazy man.

ಜೋಮಾಲೆ k. n A gold necklace

ಜೋಯಿಸ *tb of* ಜ್ಯೋತಿಷ, *q v.*

ಜೋರಾವರಿ (= ಜೋರು 2, *q v*) h *n* Violence, force

ಜೋರು 1 (= ಸೋರು) k *v i* To trickle, drip, leak *n* Trickling, a flow. -ಗಟ್ಟು To tie up in a cloth for straining, *as* curds. -ಹಾಕು To strain, *as* soaked grain

ಜೋರು 2 h *n* Strength, force, violence, stress, oppression, compulsion -ವಸೂಲು Dunning hard for payment

ಜೋಲಿ 1 f *n* Concern, business, affair 2, connexion, intercourse

ಜೋಲಿ 2. f. *n.* Hanging, dangling, oscillation, evasion, delay. -ಮಾಡು To delay -ಗಾರ A loiterer

ಜೋಲು k *v i* To hang down from, to move to and fro, to swing, oscillate, dangle, to droop; (*also* ಜೋಲಾಡು *P ps* ಜೋಲ್ದು, ಜೋತು) *n.* Hanging down, slackness, looseness. -ಗಿವಿ A long, flapping ear. -ಬಾವಲಿ. A kind of ear-ornament -ಬೀಳು To hang down, *etc.* -ಮುಖ. A downcast countenance ಜೋಲ್ದುರುಬು. A loose tuft of hair

ಜೋಳ (*tb. of* ಯವನಾಲ) *n.* One of the several species of millet. 2, (*tb. of* ಯುಗಲ) union, pair -ವಾಳಿ. An associate, a partner.

ಜೋಂಳಿಗೆ (*tb of* ಝೌಲಿಕ) *n* A small bag for receiving alms, a wallet

ಜ್ಞ s *a.* Knowing, intelligent. -ತೆ, -ತ್ವ. Knowledge of

ಜ್ಞಪ್ತಿ s *n.* Knowing. understanding, apprehension.

ಜ್ಞಾತ s *a* Known, understood. -ಸಿದ್ಧಾಂತ. Versed in any science or śâstra

ಜ್ಞಾತಿ s. *n.* A paternal relation, kinsman

ಜ್ಞಾನ s *n* Knowledge, cognizance; intelligence, religious knowledge -ಚಕ್ಷು, -ದೃಷ್ಟಿ The eye of intelligence, intellectual vision. -ಮಂಟಪ A prison (*ironically*) -ಮಾರ್ಗ. The path of wisdom -ವಂತ. A wise man, *f* -ವಂತೆ. -ವೃದ್ಧ Advanced in knowledge

ಜ್ಞಾನಿ s *n* A wise person sage 2 an astronomer or astrologer -ತೆ Knowledge, perception -ಸು To consider, reflect ಜ್ಞಾನೇಂದ್ರಿಯ An organ of perception, the skin, tongue, eye, ear, and nose

ಜ್ಞಾಪಕ s *n.* Bearing in mind, remembrance, recollection ಜ್ಞಾಪಿಸು To indicate notify.

ಜ್ಞೇಯ s *a* Cognizable perceptible

ಜ್ಯೇಷ್ಠ s *a.* Most excellent, oldest; elder-born *n* An elder brother 2, the third lunar-month

ಜ್ಯೇಷ್ಠೆ s. *n* An elder sister 2, the eighteenth lunar mansion.

ಜ್ಯೋತಿ (= ಜೋತಿ, ಜ್ಯೋತಿಸ್) s *n* Light; brightness, clearness. 2, fire. 3, a ray of light. 4, a star 5, the eye. -ಶ್ಶಾಸ್ತ್ರ. The science of astronomy (or astrology)

ಜ್ಯೋತಿಷ (= ಜೋಯಿಸ, *q v*) s *n.* Astronomy; astrology 2, an astronomer, astrologer; *also* ಜ್ಯೋತಿಷಿಕ, ಜ್ಯೋತಿಷ್ಕ.

ಜ್ಯೋತಿಸ್ = ಜ್ಯೋತಿ, *q v*

ಜ್ಯೋತ್ಸ್ನ s *n* A moonlight night, *also* ಜ್ಯೋತ್ಸ್ನೆ 2, a species of cucumber

ಜ್ವರ s *a* Heated, inflamed *n* Fever. 2, mental pain, grief.

ಜ್ವಲ s *n.* Flame, blaze. -ತ್ Burning, blazing -ತ್ಪರ್ವತ. A volcano -ನ. Shining, burning ಜ್ವಲಿತ Kindled, blazing ಜ್ವಲಿಸು. To burn, flame

ಜ್ವಾಲೆ, ಜ್ವಾಲಾ s *n* A blaze, flame. 2, fire ಜ್ವಾಲಾಮುಖಿ A volcano

ಝ್

ಝುಕ್. The twenty-seventh letter of the alphabet. *It occurs only in a limited number of Kannada and Tadbhava words*

ಝುಕಾರ s. n. The letter ಝು.

ಝುಗೆ f n. A robe extending to the feet

ಝುಂಕಾರ (= ಝೇಂಕಾರ) s. n. Buzzing or humming, *as* of bees, *etc.*

ಝುಂಝಾವಾತ s n A violent storm with rain.

ಝುಣಝುಣ s n The jingling or tinkling of ornaments, *also* -ತ್ಕಾರ, -ತ್ಕೃತಿ.

ಝುಲ್ಲರಿ s. n. A sort of drum or cymbal 2, a curl lock or hair. 3, tassels, fringes; *cf.* ಜಾಲರಿ

ಝುಲ್ಲಿ k. n. Tassels, fringes, hangings

ಝುಷ s n. A fish.

ಝುಳಪಿಸು s. v t To make glitter or shine 2, to brandish, *as* a sword.

ಝುಾಯಿ s. n A sort of drum, *also* ಜಾಯಿ

ಝಿಂಟಿ s n The shrub *Barleria cristata.*

ಝಿಲ್ಲಿಕೆ, ಝಿಲ್ಲೀಕೆ, ಝೀರುಕೆ s n A cricket

ಝೇಂಕಾರ. = ಝುಂಕಾರ, *q. v* ಝೇಂಕರಿಸು. To hum, buzz.

ಞ

ಞ. The twenty-eighth letter of the alphabet.

ಟ

ಟ The twenty-ninth letter of the alphabet.

ಟಕಾಯಿಸು f v. t. To put in mind, remind. 2, to deceive, cheat v i To be exhausted

ಟಕಾರ s. n. The letter ಟ

ಟಕ್ಕ (= ಠಕ್ಕ) h. n. A cunning fellow, rogue

ಟಕ್ಕಿಸು = ಟಕಾಯಿಸು, *q v.*

ಟಕ್ಕು (= ಠಕ್ಕು) f. n. Cunning, trickery, hypocrisy. -ತನ Cunning, deceitful behaviour. -ಟವಳಿ *dpl*

ಟಗರು k. n A ram

ಟಂಕ s. n A stone-mason's hammer 2, pride, conceit. 3, a stamped coin -ಶಾಲೆ A mint

ಟಂಕಣ s n Borax, *also* -ಕಾರ.

ಟಂಕಾರ, ಟಂಕೃತಿ s. n Howling, a sound, clang, the twang of a bow-string

ಟಂಕೆ k n A staff 2, (s.) the leg

ಟಂಗು h. n. A saddle girth. -ಹರಿ. To be reduced to poverty.

ಟಣಕಲಿ k n An aquatic plant, *Aeschynomene aspera.*

ಟಣಕ್ಕನೆ k. *ad* With a bounce in leaping.

ಟಣಾಯಿಸು h v. t. To stop, detain.

ಟಪಾಲು. = ಟಪ್ಪಾಲು. *q v.*

ಟಪ್ಪಾ h. n = ಟಪ್ಪೆ, *q. v.* 2, a variety in song.

ಟಪ್ಪಾಲು h. n. The post, mail. ಟಪ್ಪಾಲಿಗೆ ಹಾಕು To post ಟಪ್ಪಾಲಿನವ The postman -ಕಟ್ಟೆ. A post-office ಟಪ್ಪಾಲ್ಗಾಡಿ. A post-coach.

ಟಪ್ಪೆ h n. A stage, a halting place. -ಕುದುರೆ. A relay-horse.

ಟರಾಯಿಸು h. v t. To settle, fix, decide

ಟರಾವಣೆ, ಟರಾವು h. n Settlement, decision.

ಟಲಾಯಿಸು f. v. t. To lead, as a horse v. i To walk about

ಟಲಾಸು = ತಲಾಸು, q. v

ಟವಣೆ k n Simple and compound addition

ಟವಳಿ m. n Guile, trick, deceit. -ಗಾರ A deceiver

ಟವುಳಿ (= ಟಾಳಿ) k n Armour, mail

ಟಾಕಣ h. n. A pony

ಟಾಕಾ f n. A stitch, also ಟಾಕು

ಟಾಕು 1 f n The nib of a pen, a steel-pen -ಕೊಡು To nib a pen

ಟಾಕು 2 k n A support, a vault -ಗೂಡು. Arches with niches on the walls surrounding big temples

ಟಾಕುಟೀಕು f ad Orderly, neatly n Neatness, order

ಟಾಕೋಟಾಕು f. ad Speedily

ಟಾಣ, ಟಾಣಾಯ = ಠಾಣಾ, q v

ಟಾವು (= ಠಾವು) f n. A place, room an abode. ಟಾವಿಕೆ Knowledge, acquaintance with

ಟಿಕಾಣೆ f n A place, spot, an abode, seat, destination 2, means, opportunity

ಟಿಟ್ಟಿಭ s n The bird *Parra jacana,* the lapwing

ಟಿಪಾಯಿಸು h. v t To shuffle, as cards

ಟಿಪ್ಪಣ, ಟಿಪ್ಪಣೆ f n A gloss, comment, commentary. 2, a note, memorandum -ಗಾರ A commentator

ಟಿಸಲು k n. A forked or lateral branch.

ಟೀಕು 1. s. n. A commentary, a gloss, also ಟೀಕಾ, ಟೀಕೆ. ಟೀಕಾಕಾರ A commentator ಟೀಕಿಸು To explain, interpret.

ಟೀಕು 2. (= ಠೀಕು) h. n Right, just, proper.

ಟೀಕೆ f. n. A necklace of gold wire 2 a gem. 3, = ಟೀಕು 1.

ಟುಮುಕಿ f n. A tom-tom

ಟೆಕ್ಕೆ 1 k. n. A banner or standard

ಟೆಕ್ಕೆ 2. (= ತಕ್ಕೆ) k n. An embrace 2. wood, etc. grasped in arms.

ಟೆಂಕ = ಟೊಂಕ, q v

ಟೆಂಕಲು = ತೆಂಕಲು, q v

ಟೆಪಾರಿಕೆ f n A lid 2, striking off excess of grain in a measure

ಟೊಂಕ k n The hip and loins; the waist.

ಟೊಂಗೆ (= ಕೊಂಗೆ) k n The branch of a tree.

ಟೊಣಪ f. n A fat dolt, blockhead.

ಟೊಣಪೆ f n. A cudgel, mace. 2, stoutness.

ಟೊಣೆ a k v t To cheat, deceive

ಟೊಣ್ಣೆ f n. A stout dull woman

ಟೊಪ್ಪರ, ಟೊಪ್ಪಿ, ಟೊಪ್ಪಿಗೆ (= ತೋಪಿ, q v) f. n A cap; a hat

ಟೊಳ್ಳು (= ತೊಳ್ಳು) k n Hollowness, emptiness -ಮಾತು A vain speech -ಮಾಡು, -ಕೊರೆ To scoop out.

ಟೊಳ್ಳೆ k n A hollow, cavity, a fistula 2, a perished eye-socket.

ಟೋಕು h. a Whole or round, as a number; wholesale, also ತೋಕು

ಟೋಪಿ = ಟೊಪ್ಪಿ, q v.

ಟ್ರಾಳಿ = ಟವುಳಿ, q v

ಠ

ಠ. The thirtieth letter of the alphabet.

ಠಕಾರ s. *n* The letter ಠ

ಠಕ್ಕ = ಟಕ್ಕ, *q v*

ಠಕ್ಕು = ಟಕ್ಕು, *q v*

ಠಸ್ಸೆ h. *n* A stamp.

ಠಾಕೂರ s *n* An object of reverence, an honorific title

ಠಾಣ್ಯ, ಠಾಣೆ (*tb of* ಸ್ಥಾನ) *n* The head station of a district, an encampment; a police station, a garrison -ಗೆ ಹಾಕು To capture -ದಾರ The officer in charge of a thâṇâ

ಠಾವಿ. = ಟಾವಿಕೆ, *s.* ಟಾವು, *q v*

ಠಾವು. = ಟಾವು, *q. v.*

ಠಿಕಾಣಿ = ಟಿಕಾಣಿ, *q v*

ಠೀಕು = ಟೀಕು 2 *q v.*

ಠೀವಿ f *n* Style, fashion, grandeur, ornament 2, an air, manner

ಠೇವಣಿ, ಠೇವು f *n* A stock (of money) 2, a deposit (*as* security)

ಡ

ಡ. The thirty-first letter of the alphabet

ಡಕಾರ s. *n* The letter ಡ.

ಡಕಾಯಿತಿ = ಡಾಕಾಯಿತಿ, *q. v.*

ಡಕ್ಕೆ (*tb. of* ಢಕ್ಕೆ 2) = ಡಂಕ, q. v.

ಡಗೆ (= ದಗೆ) f. *n.* Deceit 2, heat, sultriness.

ಡಂಕ (= ಡಕ್ಕೆ) *s. n.* A pretty large double drum

ಡಂಗರ, ಡಂಗುರ f *n* A public proclamation by beat of tom-tom -ಬಡಿ, -ಹೊಡೆ, -ಹೊಯ್. To proclaim by beat of tom-tom

ಡಂಗುರುಚಾಟ k. *n* A kind of 'hide and seek' play

ಡಂಗೆ (= ದಂಗೆ) h *n* Tumult, uproar; dunning -ಕೂತುಕೊಳ್ಳು, -ಮಾಡು. To dun. -ಗಾರ. An uproarious man.

ಡಬದ್ದಾಳಿಕೆ h. *n.* Showiness, an empty display of greatness or authority, an imposing air.

ಡಬರಿ f *n.* A cylindrical saucepan.

ಡಬಾಣಿ f. *n* A pair of kettle-drums.

ಡಬೀರಿ h. *n.* A moonshee, writer

ಡಬ್ಬ 1 = ಡಬ್ಬಿ. *q. v.*

ಡಬ್ಬ 2, ಡಬ್ಬನೆ k *ad* Suddenly, *used of vessels, etc falling from above.*

ಡಬ್ಬಿ h. *n* A small box, *as* a snuff-box, pill-box, offering-box, *etc*

ಡಬ್ಬು 1 (= ದೊಬ್ಬು) k *v t* To shove, push, thrust. 2, = ಡಬ್ಬ 2. ಡಬ್ಬಗವಚು. ಡಬ್ಬಹಾಕು. To put upside down.

ಡಬ್ಬು 2 f. *n.* A kind of drum.

ಡಬ್ಬು 3. f. *n* Showiness, ostentation, bragging, falsehood, lie 2, a dub or copper coin. four pies. -ಗಾರ A showy man.

ಡಬ್ಬೆ h. *n* A large tin box.

ಡಮರ s *n* A riot, tumult, turmoil, distress

ಡಮರುಕ s *n* A kind of drum

ಡಮಾಮಿ, ಡಮಾರ f. *n.* A pair of kettle-drums.

ಡಂಬ, ಡಂಭ (= ದಂಬ. *tb. of* ದಂಭ) *n.* Pomp, ostentation, show ಡಂಬಾಚಾರ. Vain display. -ಕ. Arrogance, pride, an ostentatious man, a deceiver. -ಗಾರ A showy man.

ಡಯನ s *n* Flying in the air.

ಡರಕಿ, ಡರಕು (ರ= ಱ) k. *n* A belch.

ಡಲಾಯಿತ h *n* A peon of a district office

ಡವಕೆ a. k *n* A spittoon.

ಡವಣೆ f. *n* A kind of drum shaped like an hour-glass

ಡವಾಲಿ h *n.* A peon's belt

ಡವಿಗೆ k *n* A thick bamboo. 2, a skeleton's skull, *also* ಡವುಗೆ

ಡವುಡು (= ದವುಡು) h *n* A race or run

ಡವುಲು (= ಡೌಲು) h. *n* Shape, form; way, manner; indications, appearance 2, estimated revenue, probable produce 3, a pompous air, empty display -ಕೊಚ್ಚು. To brag, boast -ಜಾಸ್ತಿ Too high an estimate -ಗಾರ An ostentatious man -ಮಾಡು To make a show

ಡಾಕಾಯಿತಿ (= ಡಕಾಯಿತಿ) h *n.* Dacoity, gang-robbery

ಡಾಕಿಣಿ k *n.* The sword of a female demon.

ಡಾಕಿನಿ k *n* A kind of female demon attending Kâli. 2, = ಡಾಕಿಣಿ, *q v.*

ಡಾಕು, ಡಾಗು h. *n.* A spot, stain, inoculated cow-pox 2, an attack. 3, dawk, post-office

ಡಾಗಲಿ a k *n* An anvil.

ಡಾಗಿಸೆ. = ಪಾಗಿಸೆ, *q v*

ಡಾಣ (= ದಾಣ *tb of* ಧಾನ್ಯ) *n* Horse-gram

ಡಾಣೆ, ದಾಣೆ a k *n* A staff, club

ಡಾಬು 1 (*tb. of* ದಾಮ) *n.* A woman's girdle.

ಡಾಬು 2 k. *n* Intimidation, menacing, awfulness; *also* -ಜರಬು

ಡಾಮರ = ಡಮರ, *q v.* 2, dammer.

ಡಾಂಬಿಕ (*tb of* ದಾಂಭಿಕ) *a.* Deceitful, proud

ಡಾಲು (*tb of* ಢಾಲ) *n* A shield, buckler.

ಡಾವಣಿ (*tb of* ದಾಮನಿ) *n* A long rope for tying cattle in a row. -ಕಟ್ಟು To tie cattle in a row

ಡಾವರಿಸು a k *v. i.* To whirl about, to flicker, [illegible]

ಡಾವು h *n* Spite, malice, hatred, revenge. 2, (= ಡಾವುರ) desire -ತೀರಿಸು. To revenge one's self

ಡಾವುರ (= ದಾವರ) f *n* Burning thirst; desire, need, want.

ಡಾವೆ = ಡಾವು, *q v*

ಡಾಳ, ಡಾಳ f *n* Lustre, beauty, gracefulness. -ಯಿಸು, ಡಾಳಿಸು To shine, to be beautiful

ಡಾಳಿಮ, ಡಾಳಿಂಬ, ಡಾಳಿಂಬೆ = ದಾಡಿಮ, *q. v.*

ಡಿಕ್ಕಾ, ಡಿಕ್ಕಿ k *n* A push, butt ಡಿಕ್ಕಾಡಿಕ್ಕಿ, ಡಿಕ್ಕಾಮುಕ್ಕಿ *dpl* -ಕೊಡು, -ಹೊಡೆ To butt.

ಡಿಂಗರ s *n* A servant slave, *also* ಡಿಂಗರಿಗ 2, a rogue 3, a fat man

ಡಿಂಡಿಮ s. *n.* A kind of small drum.

ಡಿಂಬ s *n* A scuffle, turmoil 2, calamity arising from excessive rain, drought, locusts, *etc* 3, a globe, an egg. 4, a child.

ಡಿಂಬು k *n* A lamp-stand

ಡಿಂಭ s. *n* A new-born child, young animal 2, a fool

ಡಿಳ್ಳ a k *n* Tottering state, agitation of mind, fear

ಡಿಲ್ಲಿ, ಡಿಳ್ಳಿ s *n.* The town of Delhi.

ಡೀಲ, ಡೀಲಿ h *a.* Loose, slack *n* Delay. -ಬಿಡು To slacken, to delay

ಡುಬರಿ (= ಡುಬ್ಬ, ಡುಬ್ಬು) k. *n* The hump on a camel's back 2, curvedness, roundness.

ಡುಬಾಯಿಸು f *v t* To immerse, to ruin.

ಡುಬ್ಬ, ಡುಬ್ಬು = ಡುಬರಿ, *q v*

ಡುರಕಿ (ರ = ಱ) k. *n* The bellowing of bulls and oxen. -ಹಾಕು To bellow

ಡೆಂಕಣ, ಡೆಂಕಣಿ a. k *n.* The flag-staff on a bastion

ಡೆಂಕೆ = ಡಂಕ, *q v.*

ಡೆಂಡಣಿಸು f *v i* To be overcome or stupefied, *as* by grief, terror, *etc.*

ಡೆಬ್ಬೆ (= ಡಬ್ಬೆ) k. *n* A blow.

ಡೇಗೆ k *n* A hawk, falcon

ಡೇರಾ, ಡೇರೆ h. *n.* A tent.

ಡೊಕ್ಕರ 1. a k *n.* Thumping striking; a [illegible]

ಡೊಕ್ಕರ 2 = ಡೊಗರು, *q v*.

ಡೊಕ್ಕರಿಸು k *v t*. To choke, stifle

ಡೊಕ್ಕೆ k *n* The body -ಯೆಲುಬು. A rib

ಡೊಗರು (ರು=ಱು) k. *n* A hollow, hole, *as* in a wall, *etc*

ಡೊಗೆ k *v t* To make a hole.

ಡೊಗ್ಗೆ k *n* Thickness, *as* of butter-milk

ಡೊಂಕ, ಡೊಂಕು k. *n* Crookedness, a bend, curve -ಕಾಲು. A bent leg -ಗೋಣು A bent neck -ತನ = ಡೊಂಕ

ಡೊಂಗರ f. *n* A steep rock, a precipice.

ಡೊಣೆ k. *n*. A small pond in rocks 2, a hollow, hole 3, a quiver -ಗಣ್ಣು A sunken eye

ಡೊಣ್ಣೆ k. *n* A cudgel, club 2, a chameleon -ಕಾಟಿ N of several kinds of Agames -ಮೂಗು A huge nose -ಮೆಣಸಿನ ಕಾಯಿ A large kind of chilli. -ಹುಳ. An insect living in cowdung

ಡೊಬ್ಬು = ದೊಬ್ಬು, *q v*

ಡೊಂಬ, ಡೊಂಬರ f. *n*. A caste of tumblers, *f* -ಗಿತ್ತಿ.

ಡೊಂಬಿ k *n* A mass, multitude, crowd, mob.

ಡೊಳ್ಳಾಸ a k *n*. Trick, fraud, a fantastic form

ಡೊಳ್ಳು (= ಬೊಳ್ಳು) k. *n*. Hollowness, a huge belly, *also* -ಹೊಟ್ಟೆ. *a* Hollow, huge -ಗಾರ A boaster. -ಮಾತು. An empty speech

ಡೋಕಾ h *n*. Danger, peril, injury, loss in trade -ರಿ. One who cries out when he is not hurt.

ಡೋಣಿ (=ದೋಣಿ *tb of* ದ್ರೋಣಿ) *n* A tub, trough, *etc*, a boat

ಡೋರ h *n*. A man who colours leather.

ಡೋರಿಯ h. *n* A sort of striped cloth

ಡೋಲಿ h *n* A dooly or litter -ತೊಟ್ಟಿಲು. A swinging cradle.

ಡೋಲು (*tb of* ಢೋಲ) *n* A large drum.

ಡೌಲು = ಡವುಲು, *q v*.

ಢ

ಢ. The thirty-second letter of the alphabet

ಢಕಾರ s *n* The letter ಢ

ಢಕ್ಕಾಮುಕ್ಕಿ h. *n*. Shoving and cuffing, *also* ಧಕ್ಕಾಮುಕ್ಕಿ.

ಢಕ್ಕೆ 1 h *n* A sudden push, a shock, damage, harm. -ಪಡು, -ಬೀಳು. To receive a shock.

ಢಕ್ಕೆ 2 s *n* A double drum.

ಢಾಲ = ಡಾಲು *q. v*.

ಢಾಳು f *n* Cast, mould, way, style. ಢಾಳ. A clever fellow.

ಢೆಂಕಣೆ = ಡೆಂಕಣಿ, *q v*.

ಢೋಲ = ಡೋಲು, *q. v*.

ಣ

ಣ. The thirty-third letter of the alphabet *It stands as final in many Kannada and some Tadbhava words, as* ಉಣ್, ಕಣ್, ಕಾಣ್, ಗೇಣ್, ಜೇಣ್, *etc*

ಣಕಾರ s *n*. The letter ಣ

ತ

ತ. The thirty-fourth letter of the alphabet.

ತಮಸ್ಸುಕು h. n. A note of hand, bond.

ತಕ್ (= ತೆಗೆದು). *P. p. of* ತೆಗೆ, *in* ತಕ್ಕೊಳ್ಳು, ತಕ್ಕೊಂ (= ತೆಗೆದುಕೊಳ್ಳು), *etc.*

ತಕಡಿ. = ತಕ್ಕಡಿ, *q. v.*

ತಕರಾರು, ತಕರೀರು h. *n.* Starting objections; making difficulties, contesting. -ಅರ್ಜಿ. An appeal; a counter-petition.

ತಕಸೀರು (= ತಕ್ಸೀರು) h. *n.* An offence, fault. -ಗಾರ. An offender.

ತಕಾರ s. *n.* The letter ತ.

ತಗಾವಿ h. *n.* Advances made to cultivators from the public treasury.

ತಕ್ಕ (*P. p. rel. of* ತಗು) k. *a.* Fit, proper; right, suitable, good; worthy, deserving. *n.* A good man, friend. ತಕ್ಕದು. That is fit, *etc.*; anything proper. ನೀನು ಹೋಗ ತಕ್ಕದು, you ought to go. ತಕ್ಕಂತೆ, ತಕ್ಕ ಹಾಗೆ. As is or was fit. -ನಿತು, -ಷ್ಟು. As much as is suitable.

ತಕ್ಕಡಿ f. *n.* A balance or pair of scales. -ಕಲ್ಲು, -ಕಟ್ಟು. Scale weights. -ಬಟ್ಟಲು, -ತಟ್ಟೆ. The scale-pan.

ತಕ್ಕರಿಸು k. *v. t.* To sprinkle, *as* water.

ತಕ್ಕುಬಿತ್ತಿ h. *n.* Fraud, dishonest doings.

ತಕ್ಕಾಳಿ k. *n.* The tomato or love-apple, *Lycopersicum esculentum.*

ತಕ್ಕು a. k. *n.* Greatness, largeness. 2, love, affection, desire. -ಮೆ. Fitness.

ತಕ್ಕೆ (= ತೆಕ್ಕೆ 2) k. *n.* Embracing. 2, wood, *etc.* that can be once grasped with the arms. 3, joining; a mate. 4, an accumulation, heap. 5, a number of persons, *etc.* assembled together. [*etc.*

ತಕ್ಕೊಳ್ಳು (*fr.* ತಕ್, *q. v.*) *v. t.* To take,

ತಕ್ತಾ h. *n.* A tabular statement, *etc.*; an account, *as* of receipts, expenses, *etc.*

ತಕ್ಯ h. *n.* A pillow, cushion, pad.

ತಕ್ರ s. *n.* Buttermilk.

ತಕ್ಷಕ s. *n.* A cutter, carpenter; *also* ತಕ್ಷ. 2, the principal serpent of pâtâla.

ತಕ್ಷಣ. *tb. of* ತತ್ಕ್ಷಣ, *q. v.*

ತಕ್ಸೀರು. = ತಕಸೀರು, *q. v.*

ತಗಚೆ k. *n.* The under-shrub *Cassia occidentalis.* 2, the Indian mulberry tree, *Morinda citrifolia.*

ತಗಡು f. *n.* A flat piece or sheet of metal; a metal plate.

ತಗಣೆ, ತಗಣಿ k. *n.* A bug. -ಹಿಡಿ. To have bugs.

ತಗರ (= ತವರ. *tb. of* ತಮರ) *n.* Tin.

ತಗರು (= ಟಗರು) k. *n.* A ram.

ತಗಲು, ತಗುಲು 1. k. *v. i.* To come in contact with; to touco, hit.

ತಗಲು, ತಗುಲು 2. f. *n.* Trick, fraud; *also* ದಗಲು. -ಗಾರ. A cheat.

ತಗಹು a. k. *n.* An obstacle. 2, connection; continuous line; order.

ತಗಾದೆ h. *n.* Urging for payment. 2, a claim, dispute; a suit.

ತಗು a. k. *v. i.* To be fit or proper; *see* ತಕ್ಕ.

ತಗುಳು a. k. *v. i.* To be joined together; to approach; to commence. *v. t.* To chase, pursue; to drive away; to push back.

ತಗುಳ್ಚು a. k. *v. t.* To join. 2, to get to. 3, to undertake; to employ. 4, to set on fire.

ತಗೆ a. k. *v. t.* To stop, arrest; to stun. *n.* Stopping.

ತಗೀರು h. *n.* Dismissal.

ತಗ್ಗ 1. k. *n.* N. of a tree. 2, a large shrub, *Clorodendron phlomoides.*

ತಗ್ಗ 2. h. *n.* Thuggee; the practice of kidnapping.

ತಗ್ಗಿಸು k. *v. t.* To make low; to bow, *as* the head; to lessen; to appease.

ತಗ್ಗು k v. i To be low, depressed, to stoop, to be humble; to decrease, to be appeased, etc n. Low ground, a declivity, a hole, a valley, decrease, scarcity ತಗ್ಗಾಳು A dwarf -ಗದ್ದೆ. A low paddy-field -ದವಸ Dear grain. -ದಿನ್ನೆ Dale and hill -ನೆಲ, -ಭೂಮಿ Low ground -ಮುಗ್ಗು Ups and downs

ತಂಗದಿರು a k n A cool ray ತಂಗದಿರ. The moon

ತಂಗಳು k n Any cold or stale food, as rice, bread, etc., also ತಂಗಳನ್ನ

ತಂಗಾಳಿ k n A cool breeze.

ತಂಗಿ k n A younger sister 2, an epithet of endearment for a female younger than one's self

ತಂಗು k v. i To stop, to stay, sojourn n. Halt: a day's journey

ತಂಗುಡೆ k n A horse's or elephant's trappings

ತಂಗೇಡಿ k. n. The plant *Cassia auriculata.*

ತಜವಿಜೆ, ತಜವೀಜು h n Investigating, planning, arranging.

ತಂಜಾವೂರು k n. Tanjore

ತಟ s n A declivity 2, a bank or shore 3, a field 4, the sky, horizon. -ಸ್ಥ. Standing still; awaiting intently; indifferent.

ತಟಕು k. n A drop, as of water, etc, a small quantity

ತಟಕ್ಕನೆ k ad In drops 2, quickly, suddenly

ತಟಗುಟ್ಟು (fr ತಟ, -ಕುಟ್ಟು) k. v t. To hammer. v. i. To wander about

ತಟವಟ k n Fraud, trickery. -ಗಾರ A deceitful man liar

ತಟಾಯಿಸು (i. e ತಟ್ಟಿಹಾಯಿಸು) k. v. i To pass by or over, as a river, etc. 2, to pass right through.

ತಟಾರನೆ = ತಟಕ್ಕನೆ, q v

ತಟಿತ್ತು s n. Lightning

ತಟ್ಟ a. k n Flatness, levelness 2, a thin, emaciated fellow.

ತಟ್ಟನೆ (= ತಟಕ್ಕನೆ, q. v.) k ad. Suddenly, all at once.

ತಟ್ಟಿ (= ತಡಿಕೆ, q v.) k. n A frame-work of bamboos, plaited palm-leaves or straw, a tatty 2 matting

ತಟ್ಟು 1. k v t. To tap, to touch, to pat, to strike, to clap, to knock, to drive, to remove n A slap or pat, a blow 2, (fig) a blow, as of disease, danger, etc, fatigue 3, the measles 4, flatness -ಮುಟ್ಟು A great strait or dilemma

ತಟ್ಟು 2 k. n Side, direction

ತಟ್ಟು 3. h. n A pony or tattoo

ತಟ್ಟು 4 f n. Sackcloth.

ತಟ್ಟೆ 1. (= ತಟ್ಟ, etc) k n Flatness. 2, a flat, lid-like basket 3, a platter, plate 4, a flat, beanless pod.

ತಟ್ಟೆ 2. k. n. A bamboo split in two.

ತಟ್ಳೆ k n A woman's shoe

ತಡ (cf. ತಡಪು, ತಡೆ) k. n Check, obstacle. 2, delay. 3, perplexity, confusion -ಗಟ್ಟು. To stop, as water, to charm, as snakes, etc -ತ Stopping, restraining, lasting wearing well, as cloth. -ವಡಿಸು To impede; to perplex, to turn the wrong way. -ಮಾಡು To delay, to be slow, loiter; to delude, perplex -ವಾಗು. Delay to occur

ತಡಕು k v. t. To grope for, seek ತಡಕಿಸು To cause to seek

ತಡಗಣಿ k. n. The pulse *Vigna catjang.*

ತಡಪು k n Hindrance 2, a small cloth like apron

ತಡವರಿಸು k. v. t To grope, to seek.

ತಡವು k. v t To touch or rub gently. 2, (=ತಡವರಿಸು) to grope. 3, to stop. n Delay

ತಡವೆ k. n A time, turn

ತಡಸಲು f n A water-fall

ತಡಸು a. k v i. To stay, wait v t. (=ತಡಿಸು) To stop, hinder n Impeding, hindering.

ತಡಹು k n. Stop, cessation v t. To stroke

ತಡಾಕಿ f n Smartness, shrewdness

ತಡಿ 1. k n A thick staff, cudgel

ತಡಿ 2. k n A saddle made of woollen or cotton cloth, a mattress

ತಡಿ 3. k a Damp wet -ವೃಡಿ Imperfectly moistened, as clay

ತಡಿ 4 (tb of ತಟ) n A bank, shore.

ತಡಿಕೆ (=ತಟ್ಟಿ) k n A frame of bamboos, straw or leaves used as a screen, tatty, etc

ತಡಿಸು k v. t To stop, to detain, to keep off.

ತಡೆ k. v i To delay lose time, to loiter to wait 2, to last. as cloth. v t To stop, to detain check, to endure, bear. n. (= ತಡ, q v.) An obstacle, hindrance, impediment, a charm, delay. -ಕಟ್ಟು. = ತಡಗಟ್ಟು, s ತಡ q v -ಗಟ್ಟಿ A dam -ಹಾಕು. To stop, to raise objections

ತಣಕಾಯಿಸು (fr. ತಸು) h v t. To inquire after.

ತಣಲು k n Glowing coals

ತಣಸು k. n Coldness, coolness, wetness, also ತಣವು.

ತಣಿ k v i To grow cool; to be refreshed, to be calmed or appeased 2, to get feeble. (P. p ತಣಿತು, ತಣಿದು). n Shame, modesty -ಸು. To cool, refresh, appease

ತಣಿವು, ತಣಿವು, ತಣುವು k n. Coolness, calmness, appeasement, satiation

ತಣಾಳಿ = ತಂಗಾಳಿ, q v.

ತಂಟೆ h n A quarrel, dispute, trouble, annoyance 2 connection, interference -ಗಾರ, -ಕೋರ A quarrelsome man. -ಮಾಡು To annoy. -ಮಾರಿ A troublesome person, also ತಂಟ್ಲಮಾರಿ

ತಂಡ k. n A mass a multitude; a crowd, a party ತಂಡೋಪತಂಡ Crowds upon crowds

ತಂಡಸ f. n Pincers tongs

ತಂಡಿ (= ಥಂಡಿ) k n Cold, wetness

ತಂಡುಲ s n. Rice cleaned from the husk.

ತಂಡೆ k n A foot-ornament of women

ತಂಡೇಲ f n The master of a boat a tindal.

ತಣ್ಣ k n Coolness, cold -ಗೆ, -ನೆ Cold, cool, cooling, refreshing, calm

ತಣ್ಣಸ = ತಣಸು, q v

ತಣ್ಣೀರು k n Cool or cold water -ತಳಿ To sprinkle cold water

ತಣ್ಣೆರಲು, ತಣ್ಣೆಲರು k n Cool breeze.

ತಣ್ಣೆಳಲು k n A cool shade

ತಣ್ಪು = ತಂಪು, q v

ತಣ್ಬಿಸಿಲು k n Assuaged sunshine or heat

ತತ s. a Extended, spread n A stringed musical instrument

ತತಿ 1 s n Extent, a series, range a crowd, troop.

ತತಿ 2. (tb of ತತ್ತಿ) n A proper time or season

ತತ್ಕಾಲ s n. That time, present time ad Directly, immediately.

ತತ್ಕ್ಷಣ s n. The same moment. ad. Instantly, forthwith

ತತ್ತರ 1 f n Trembling, shuddering. -ಗುಟ್ಟು, -ಗೊಳ್ಳು ತತ್ತರಿಸು To tremble.

ತತ್ತರ 2. (ರ=ಱ) a k. n Perplexity, confusion.

ತತ್ತಿ (= ತತ್ತಿ) k. n. An egg.

ತತ್ಪರ s a Intent upon, wholly devoted to. -ತೆ. Entire devotion

ತತ್ಪುರುಷ s n The supreme soul 2, a class of compounds (g.)

ತತ್ಪೂರ್ವ s a Prior, former

ತತ್ರ s. ad There, thither, therein, then

ತತ್ವ s. n. The true or real state, reality, truth, essential nature the very essence, a principle, Brahmâ -ಜ್ಞ Knowing the true nature of anything, understanding the principles of a science. -ಜ್ಞಾನ. Knowledge of the truth. -ಜ್ಞಾನಿ A philosopher. -ಶಾಸ್ತ್ರ Ph[illegible]

ತತ್ಸಾರ s n Want, lack

ತತ್ಸಮ s a The same with it. n A word that exists in Kannada as well as in Samskrita

ತಥಾ s ad So, thus 2, it is so. -ಸ್ತು May it be so.

ತಥ್ಯ s a True genuine. n. Truth

ತಪಕು k v t To strike, beat n Striking, beating

ತದನಂತರ s a Next to that ad Thereupon, then

ತದಲು, ತಪ್ಲ k n. A frame of thorns, etc, used as a gate in a hedge

ತದಾರಭ್ಯ s ad Thence, since then

ತದಿಸು, ತದುಕು k n The gum olibanum tree, *Boswellia thurifera.*

ತದಿಗಿಣ k *int Sounds used in beating time in music*

ತದಿಗೆ *tb of* ತೃತೀಯ, *q v*

ತದ್ದಿನ s n That day 2 the day of mourning for deceased relations.

ತದ್ಧರ್ಮ s. n That business, that religion.

ತದ್ಧಿತ s n *An affix to form nouns, or a noun formed by it,* a derivative noun (*g*).

ತದ್ಭವ s n A word corrupted from Saṁskrita or any other language.

ತದ್ವತ್ s *ad* So, in that manner, also, likewise

ತನ k. *An affix for forming true Kannada words, as:* ಒಕ್ಕಲು-, ಕಲಿ-, ಕಳ್ಳ-, ಬಡ-, ಮನೆ-. *etc.*

ತನಕ k. *prep* Till, until, as far as

ತನಿಕಿ h n. Ascertaining, examination

ತನಯ s n A son, *f.* ತನಯೆ. A daughter.

ತನಿ a k. *v. i* To thrive, develop *P p* ತನಿತು. *n* The state of having thriven, full, developed, matured, *etc* -ಗಂಪು A rich fragrance -ಗಬ್ಬು. Juicy sugarcane. -ಬೆಲ್ಲ Delicious jaggory. -ರಸ. Essence, excellent flavour -ವೀರರಸ. Great heroism -ಸುಖ. Great pleasure or joy -ಸೊಬಗು Great beauty -ಹರಕೆ Great blessing

ತನು 1 s *a.* Thin, slender, small, delicate. *n.* The body 2, the skin -ಜ, ಜಾತ, -ಭವ A son, *f* -ಜಾತೆ, -ಜೆ -ಮನಧನ Body, mind, and property.

ತನು 2 = ತಂಪು, *q v*

ತನೆ k *n* Pregnancy of beasts

ತಂತರ *tb of* ತಂತ್ರ, *q v.*

ತಂತಿ (*tb of* ತಂತ್ರಿ) *n.* A string, cord, a wire, *as* of a lute -ಟಪ್ಪಾಲು The telegraph. -ವಾದ್ಯ A stringed instrument -ವರ್ತಮಾನ A telegram

ತಂತು 1. (= ತಂದಿತು) k *Third pers singl. impf. of* ತರು

ತಂತು 2 s *n* A thread, string, a filament, a wire -ಕರಣ Weaving, spinning. -ಪಟ Cotton cloth -ವಾದ್ಯ. Any stringed instrument -ವಾಯ A weaver, a spider, a loom -ಹಾರುವ. A thread Brâhmana

ತಂತು 3. *tb of* ತಂತ್ರ, *q v* -ಗಾರ. A cunning man.

ತಂತ್ರ s. *n* A thread. 2, a loom, vesture 3, a system, ritual 4, an established doctrine 5, magical and mystic formularies 6, a charm 7, a design, cunning. trick, intrigue, plot 8, a curse; plotting -ಗಾರ (= ತಂತುಗಾರ) A cunning, crafty man -ಬಂತ್ರ ಮಾಡು. To contaminate, adulterate

ತಂತ್ರಿ s *n* = ತಂತಿ. 2, a pûjâri -ಸು. To use an expedient

ತಂದಲ್ a k *n* Water-drops, spray

ತಂದು *P. p. of* ತರು, *q v*

ತಂದೆ k *n.* Father. -ಗೆ ತಂದೆ. A paternal grandfather. -ತಾಯಿ Father and mother -ತಾಯಿಗಳು Parents -ವಾದಿ Relationship by father's side.

ತಂದ್ರಿ s. *n* Fatigue, sleepiness, exhaustion.

ತನ್ನ k *pro. Gen of* ತಾನು, *q v, dat.* ತನಗೆ, *acc.* ತನ್ನನ್ನು; *abl* ತನ್ನಿಂದ

ತನ್ನಿ k *2nd pers pl imp of* ತರು

ತನ್ಮಧ್ಯ s *ad* Meanwhile

ತಪ s *n* Heat, burning 2, the hot season. 3, austerity, penance 4, a demon. -ಗೆಯ್ಯು To perform a penance. -ನ Heating, burning, the sun; mental distress ತಪೋಧನ Rich in penance, ascetic, pious, an ascetic, devotee ತಪೋಲೋಕ. One of the seven Hindu worlds inhabited by devotees

ತಪಕ್ಕನೆ k *ad.* All at once

ತಪಟೆ f *n* A tambourine beaten with sticks

ತಪರಾಖು h. *n.* A slap on the check

ತಪಲೆ *f. n* A round metallic cooking vessel.

ತಪಶೀಲು h *n* Details, minute description.

ತಪಶ್ಚರಣ, ತಪಶ್ಚರಣೆ, ತಪಶ್ಚರ್ಯೆ (*fr.* ತಪ) s *n* The practice of penance.

ತಪಸ್, ತಪಸ್ಸು (*fr* ತಪ) s *n* Heat 2, austerity, penance

ತಪಸಿ 1, ತಪಸ್ವಿ (*tb of* ತಪಸ್ವಿ) *n* An ascetic, religious mendicant, *f* -ನಿ

ತಪಸಿ 2. f *n.* The wild mangosteen. *Diospyros embryopteris*, *also* -ಗಿಡ. 2, the plant *Caesalpinia bonducella*

ತಪಾಲು = ಟಪಾಲು, *q. v.*

ತಪಿತ s *a.* Heated, burnt

ತಪಿಸು s. *v i* To be hot, to burn, to suffer pain

ತಪ್ತ s. *a* Heated, burnt, afflicted

ತಪ್ಪ = ತರುವ, ತರ್ಪ. *Pres. rel part of* ತರು

ತಪ್ಪಟೆ = ತಪಟೆ, *q v*

ತಪ್ಪನೆ k *ad* Quickly, all at once.

ತಪ್ಪಲ, ತಪ್ಪಲು k. *n.* The level ground on the top of a mountain, table-land

ತಪ್ಪಲೆ = ತಪಲೆ, *q v*

ತಪ್ಪಸಿಗಿಡ. = ತಪಸಿಗಿಡ *q v.*

ತಪ್ಪಿತ = ತಪ್ಪು, *q v.*

ತಪ್ಪಿಸು k. *v t.* To cause to miss or pass by, to let slip; to avert, to evade, to avo[illegible]

ತಪ್ಪು k *v i* To make a false step, to slip; to mistake or blunder, to be missed or lost, to fail, to disappear; to miss. *n* Slipping, erring. 2, a slip, error, mistake, blunder, an impropriety, a fault, misdemeanour. ತಪ್ಪಡಿ. A false step -ಒಪ್ಪಿಕೊಳ್ಳು To acknowledge one's fault. -ಕಾಣಿಕೆ. A gift to make amends for a misdeed -ಕೆಲಸ. A misdeed -ಕ್ಷಮಿಸು, -ಸಯ್ರಿಸು. -ಗಾಣಿಸು To overlook a fault -ಗಂಟು. A wrong knot or connection -ದಾರಿ. A wrong road -ದೊರು. A mistake to occur -ಮಾಡು To make a mistake. -ತಿದ್ದು To correct a mistake -ಸಾಧಿಸು To charge (a man) with a fault -ಹಿಡಿ To find fault with -ಹೆಜ್ಜೆ = ತಪ್ಪಡಿ -ಹೊರಿಸು. To accuse (one) of a fault. -ವಿಕೆ Erring, missing ತಪ್ಪಿ ಹೋಗು To be lost, *as* an employment, to go astray

ತಫಾವತು h. *n.* Difference, deviation, variance, *as* of accounts, failure; shortcoming

ತಬಕ, ತಬಕು h. *n* A plate for betel-leaf, *etc*

ತಬಟೆ = ತಪಟೆ, *q. v.*

ತಬಲಕು h. *n* A packet of papers 2, a string which binds a packet

ತಬೀಯತು h *n* Constitution, disposition.

ತಬೇಲಿ h. *n.* A stable.

ತಬ್ಬರಿಸು k *v i* To be overcome by terror, grief, *etc*, to be amazed. 2, to slip stumble

ತಬ್ಬಲಿ = ತಬ್ಬಿಲಿ, *q v* -ಕೂಸು An orphan, child -ಕೆಲಸ Vile action -ಮನುಷ್ಯ, A vile man

ತಬಿಬ್ಬು k *n.* Bewilderment, maze.

ತಬ್ಬಿಲಿ (= ತಬ್ಬಲಿ) k *n* A child's bereavement of its mother or parents 2, a wretched, mean or inferior person or thing.

ತಬ್ಬು k *v t.* To embrace 2. to clasp [illegible] ...ood.

etc *n* An embrace -ಹುಲ್ಲು An armful of grass ತಬ್ಬಿಸು. To cause to embrace or clasp.

ತಬ್ದೀಲಿ h *n*. Exchange, transfer; arrangement

ತಮ s *aff of superl*. Most.

ತಮ, ತಮಸ್ =ತಮಸ್ಸು, *q v*.

ತಮಗೆ k *pro*. (*dat of* ತಾವು) To them.

ತಮತು, ತಮುತ್ತು, ತಮ್ಮದು k *pro* Theirs, yours (*honorif*)

ತಮರ =ತಪರ *q v*.

ತಮಸೂಕು h *n*. A note of hand, bond

ತಮಸ್ಸು (*tb of* ತಮಸ್) *n*. Darkness, gloom 2, mental darkness; sin, ignorance. 3, Rāhu

ತಮಾಮು h. *n*. The whole. *ad*. Wholly, entirely.

ತಮಾಷೆ h *n*. A farce, tricks of conjurers, sport, fun, a pantomime -ಗಾರ A showman, buffoon

ತಮಿಳ k. *n* The Tamil language; Tamil

ತಂಪು (=ತಣ್ಪು) k *n*. Coolness, coldness, wetness; a cooling, gratifying or refreshing quality or thing. *a* Cool *ad* Coolly -ಮಾಡು, ತಂಪಿಸು To cool to extinguish *as* fire or a light -ಗಾಳಿ. A cool wind ತಂಪಿನ ಮರ A shady tree.

ತಂಬತ್ತಿಜಾಲಿ k. *n*. A shrub with long thorns and fragrant yellow flowers, *Acacia eburnea*.

ತಂಬಳ (ಳ=ೞ). =ತಮಿಳ, *q. v*.

ತಂಬಾಕೆ, ತಂಬಾಕು h *n*. Tobacco

ತಂಬಿ h *n* Chastisement, beating.

ತಂಬಿಗೆ =ಚೆಂಬಿಗೆ, *q v*.

ತಂಬಿಟ್ಟು k *n*. The flour of fried rice mixed with milk or water, jaggory, *etc*

ತಂಬು h. *n* A tent.

ತಂಬುಲ *tb of* ತಾಂಬೂಲ, *q v*

ತಂಬುಳಿ k. *n* Vegetables ground with cocoanut scrapings, mixed with curds, salted and seasoned to taste

ತಂಬೂರ h *n*. A kind of guitar with three to five strings, *also* ತಂಬೂರಿ

ತಮ್ಮ 1 k. *pro* (*gen of* ತಾವು) Their, your (*honorif*) -ದು Theirs, yours *Acc* ತಮ್ಮನ್ನು, *instr* ತಮ್ಮಿಂದ, *loc* ತಮ್ಮಲ್ಲಿ.

ತಮ್ಮ 2 k *n* A younger brother, also a word of endearment, *pl* ತಮ್ಮಂದ್ಯರು, ತಮ್ಮಂದಿರು

ತಮ್ಮಟೆ (=ತಪಟೆ, *q v*) k *n*. A tambourine.

ತಮ್ಮಡಿ k *n*. An attendant on an idol

ತಮ್ಮೆ k *n*. The lobe of the ear or gristle of the nose -ಗಿಡ A cultivated pulse, *Dolichos lablab*.

ತಯಾರ, ತಯಾರು h *a* Prepared, made ready, waiting to do, *etc*. ತಯಾರಿ. Readiness, preparation -ಮಾಡು ತಯಾರಿಸು To make ready, prepare.

ತರ 1 (=ತರಹ, ತರಾ) h. *n* Kind, manner, fashion, rank, class, sort, succession, order, equality 2, a layer, stratum, a heap. -ಗತಿ Classification, sort, kind, condition, grade, class. -ಗಾರ. A bricklayer -ತರ *rep* Varieties. ಕೀಳ್-. Low rank, inferior sort ಮೇಲ್- High rank, good sort

ತರ 2. k *An imitative sound*. -ಗುಟ್ಟು To tremble. -ತರ =ತರತರ.

ತರ 3 s. *aff of comp. degree* More, *as*: ಅಧಿಕ-, ಪ್ರಿಯ-, ಲಘು-, *etc*.

ತರ 4 s *n*. Passing, crossing, *also* -ಣ

ತರಕಲು (=ತರಕು, ತರಸು 2) k. *n*. Roughness, unsmoothness, unevenness, *as*: -ಕಂಬಳಿ, -ಕಲ್ಲು, -ನೆಲ, -ಮೈ, *etc*

ತರಕಾರಿ h *n*. Esculent vegetables

ತರಕು. =ತರಕಲು, *q v*

ತರಗಸಿ k *n*. *Cassia tora*, *cf*. ತಗಚೆ

ತರಗು 1. (=ತಗ್ಗು) k *n* Diminishing; wastage. 2, customary deduction; brokerage, commission. ತರಗಿನಂಗಡಿ. A broker's shop

ತರಗು 2 (ರ=ಱ) k *n* That which is dried dry or dead leaves said to be eaten by ascetics. ತರಗೆಲೆ A dry leaf

ತರಂಗ s. *n* A wave, billow, surge ತರಂಗಿಣಿ A river

ತರಳ, ತರಟು a k *n*. Baldness -ದಲೆ. -ಮಂಡೆ. A bald head.

ತರಣ s *a* Crossing over ತರಣಿ A float boat, the sun, the plant *Aloe perfoliata*, a kind of rose

ತರತರ, -ನೆ k *ad* Tremblingly quakingly. -ನಡುಗು To tremble, quake

ತರದೂದು h *n*. Getting ready, improving, effort, labour, exertion

ತರಪು k *n* An inferior stone like a diamond, *also* ತರಪ

ತರಫು h. *n* Side, direction, party, a division of a district

ತರಬು (= ತರುಬು. ರ = ಱ) k *v. i* To stay, stop

ತರಬೇತು h *n* Education, training

ತರಲ s. *a*. Moving to and fro, unsteady, fickle 2, liquid 3, sparkling. *n* A child, infant. 2, the central gem of a necklace -ತೆ, -ತ್ವ Unsteadiness ತರಲೆ Rice-gruel.

ತರವಾರ, ತರವಾರಿ (= ತಲವಾರ) f. *n*. A sword, scymitar.

ತರಸ s *n* Meat, flesh

ತರಸು 1 = ತರಿಸು, *q v*

ತರಸು 2 (= ತರಕಲು) k *n* A field lying waste or fallow.

ತರಹ = ತರ 1, *q v*.

ತರಹದ k *n*. The exercise of patience, forbearance, *also* ತರಹರಿಕೆ. ತರಹರಿಸು To be patient, to bear patiently

ತರಳ = ತರಲ, *q v*.

ತರಳು k *n*. A ripe dried fruit, *as* a cocoanut

ತರಳೆ (ರ = ಱ) h. *n* A useless business -ಮನುಷ್ಯ A good-for-nothing man. -ಮಾತು A useless word

ತರಾ (= ತರ 1) -ತರ *rep* Various kinds or ways, differences of rank -ವಳಿ. Various kinds

ತರಾತುರಿ (*tb of* ತ್ವರಾ-ತ್ವರಿ) *n* Speed, haste

ತರಾಸು (= ತ್ರಾಸು) h *n* A balance, scales

ತರಿ 1 (= ತರಕಲು) k *n* Roughness, grit

ತರಿ 2 (ರಿ = ಱಿ) k *v. t*. To strip or cut off th[illegible]

to pluck to cut *v. i* To be chafed or grazed. -ಸು To cause to cut

ತರಿಸು s *v. i*. To cross over, to float, swim

ತರು 1 k. *v t* To bring, to give *P p*. ತಂದು, *neut sing past* ತಂದಿತು, ತಂತು *imper 2nd pers. sing*. ತಾ, *pl* ತನ್ನಿ, ತನ್ರಿ ತರಿಸು To cause to lead or bring. -ವಳಿ. Bringing home, *as* a girl for marriage -ವಿಕೆ. Bringing, fetching.

ತರು 2 (ರು = ಱು) a k *v. i*. To join, to approach, to engage in *n*. The state of being joined, fit. or settled -ವಾಯ, *q v*

ತರು 3 s *n* A tree -ಕಾಟ A squirrel -ಬೊಡ್ಡೆ The foot of a tree

ತರುಣ 1 s *a* Young, tender, juvenile, fresh, lively. *n* A young man, a boy, *f* ತರುಣಿ -ತೆ, -ತ್ವ Tenderness, youth, juvenility

ತರುಣ 2 (ರು = ಱು) k *a* Fit or proper time

ತರುಪು = ತರಪು, *q v*

ತರುಬು = ತರಬು, *q v*.

ತರುವಾಯ (*fr* ತರು 2, *q v*.) k. *ad* Afterwards subsequently.

ತರ್ಕ s *n* Supposition, conjecture. 2, reasoning, speculation. 3, deliberation, dispute, discussion 4, doubt 5, logic 6, wish 7, motive -ಕ, ತರ್ಕಿಕ. A logician, disputant, reasoner -ವಾದ Disputation -ವಿದ್ಯೆ, -ಶಾಸ್ತ್ರ The science of logic. ತರ್ಕಿಸು. To reason, to speculate, dispute

ತರ್ಜನ s *n* Threatening, pointing at in ridicule, putting to shame, wrath ತರ್ಜನಿ The forefinger ತರ್ಜಿಸು To threaten

ತರ್ಜುಮೆ h *n* A translation, an abstract.

ತರ್ಪಣ s. *n*. Satisfying, pleasing, satisfaction, an oblation to the manes or gods, a libation ತರ್ಪಿಸು. To please, satisfy, to offer an oblation to the [illegible]

ತರ್ಲೆ (= ತರಳೆ) k *n* Idle talk

ತರ್ಷ, ತರ್ಷಣ s *n*. Thirst; desire.

ತಲ 1 (= ತಳ) s *n*. A level surface 2, the palm of the hand 3, depth, the lower part, base, a pit, pond, the ground 4, the palmyra tree. 5, cause, origin, motive ತಲಾತಲ One of the seven divisions of hell

ತಲ 2 = ತರ 1, *etc*, *q v* -ತಲಾಂತರ (= ತಲ-ತಲ-ಅಂತರ) Generations upon generations ತಲಾಂತರ A generation

ತಲಪು k *v i* To reach, come to hand, to arrive ತಲಪಿಸು. To cause to reach, *etc*

ತಲಬು h *n* Pay, wages, a summons

ತಲವಾರ (= ತರವಾರ) f *n* A sword

ತಲಾರಿ = ತಳವಾರ, *q v*

ತಲಾವು h *n* A tank

ತಲಾಸು h *n* Search, quest -ಮಾಡು To make inquiry into; to get, obtain

ತಲೆ k. *n* The head, a generation, that which is uppermost or principal -ಕಟ್ಟು A head-tie, the head or top-dash of a letter; an adjoining field -ಕೆಳಗು, -ಕೆಳಗೆ The head downwards, topsyturvy. -ಕೊಟ್ಟಮಾರಿ. A brawler -ಗಡಿ. To behead -ಗಾಯು. To protect. -ಗಿಂಬು A pillow. -ಗೆಡಹು (= ಗಡಿ) To decapitate -ಗೇರು. To rise to the head, to affect it, *as* poison -ಗೊಡು To risk one s life in. -ಗೊಯ್ಯು To decapitate. -ಗೊಯ್ಕ. A murderer, a ruffian, a cheat -ತಿರುಗು. To become giddy. -ತೂಗು To nod, a nod. -ದಿಂಬು = -ಗಿಂಬು -ದೋರು. To spring up, appear. -ನೋಯು, -ಸಿಡಿ The head to ache -ನೋವು, -ಸಿಡಿತ The headache. -ಪಟ್ಟಿ A piece of wood over a door -ವಟ್ಟು An application for headache. -ಬಾಗಲು. The entrance door -ಬುರುಡೆ. The skull -ಬಿಲಗು The ridge-pole -ಬೇನೆ = ತಲೆನೋವು -ಬೇಸರ Tiresomeness -ಬೋಳಿಸು To shave the head -ಬೋಳಿಸಿಕೊ -ಬಾಗಿಸಿಕೊಳ್ಳು To get the head shaved -ಯ ಮೇಲೆ ಕೂಡ್ರು. To trouble, to be forward -ಯ ಮೇಲೆ ಹೊತ್ತುಕೊಳ್ಳು. To take upon one s self -ಯಾದವ A chief, headman. -ಯಾರು. A kind of yoke for cattle -ಯೆತ್ತು To rise from a poor condition -ಸೋಡು. The skull -ಬಾಗಿಸು. To bend the head, obey -ಬಾಗು The head to bend -ಶೂಲೆ = -ನೋವು -ಹಂಚು. A ridge tile -ಹಿಡಿ To affect the head, as a strong smell, *etc.* -ಹೋಕ. A very dissolute man -ಹೊರೆ A load carried upon the head

ತಲ್ಪ s. *n* A bed; a couch. 2, an upper [story.

ತಲ್ಲಣ, ತಲ್ಲಳ k *n* Agitation, alarm, fear; grief, *etc* ತಲ್ಲಣಿಸು To be agitated, alarmed, to be anxious about

ತವ s *pro* Of thee, thine, thy

ತವಕ s *n* Love; desire; eagerness; haste, hurry ತವಕಿಸು To be eager; to hasten.

ತವಕ್ಷೀರ (*tb* of ತ್ವಕ್ಕ್ಷೀರ) *n* Manna of bamboo. 2, an extract from wheat, *etc.*

ತವಟು (= ತವುಟು) k *v. t* To sift pounded grain, *etc*, on a bamboo fan

ತವಡು, ತವುಡು k. *n*. Bran.

ತವರ, ತವರು 1 f *n* Tin

ತವರು 2. k *n*. The house of a woman's own people, *also* -ಮನೆ.

ತವಾಯಿ h *n*. A fine, ill-luck, great trouble. 2, detention

ತವು a k *v. i* To decrease, to waste away; to perish *v t*. To diminish *n* Decrease, ruin ತವಿಸು To cause to decrease, to destroy.

ತವುಟು = ತವಟು *q v.*

ತವುಟೆಗಿಡ k. *n*. The gooseberry bush, the red myrtle, *Rhodomyrtus tomentosa*

ತವೆ 1 = ಸವೆ, *q v*

ತವೆ 2. a k. *ad* Abundantly, wholly, further

ತವೆ 3 h *n* A metal lid of cooking vessels

ತಸಕೀಲು, ತಸಕು f n Cheating, trickery

ತಸದೀಕು (= ತಸ್ತೀಕು) h n A fixed allowance paid by government to a pagoda, mosque, etc, in lieu of assumed lands

ತಸಬೀರು h. n A picture

ತಸ್ಕರ s n A thief robber, theft, f ತಸ್ಕರೆ

ತಸ್ಕಲು = ತಸಕಲು, q v.

ತಸ್ತೀಕು = ತಸದೀಕು, q v

ತಸ್ತು h n A metal water-vessel, an ewer

ತಹ 1 a k. *Rel pres. part of* ತರು

ತಹ 2 h n Peace, agreement of opinion -ನಾಮೆ A written treaty, agreement

ತಹಕೀಕು h. a Correct, true.

ತಹತಹ k. n Anxiety, distress, eagerness

ತಹಶೀಲು (= ತಾಸೀಲು) h n Collection of the revenue -ದಾರ A Tahsildâr, a native collector, the head of a talook

ತಳ (= ತಲ 1 q v) s n The bottom, *etc*, the hand. -ಹಲ್ಲು. The lowest step, *as* of a ladder. ತಳಾರಿಸು To dry what is at the bottom, to rest the feet after much walking

ತಳಕು k n Shine, glitter, flash 2, coquetry. 3, = ತಕ್ಕೆ. -ಹಾಕು. To tie two beasts together

ತಳತಳ k n. Brightness, gleam, glitter -ಗುಟ್ಟು, ತಳತಳಿಸು To glitter, flash, shine

ತಳಪ, ತಳಪು k n Splendour, lustre, shine, a dye to colour the hair

ತಳಮಳ, ತಳವಳ k n Agitation, alarm, fear -ಗುಟ್ಟು, ತಳಮಳಿಸು To be agitated, alarmed.

ತಳರ್ a. k. v i To move, to totter; to set out, depart n Moving, tottering

ತಳವರ, ತಳವಾರ (*tb of* ಸ್ಥಲವಾರ) n A watchman, beadle -ನ ಬಳ್ಳಿ. A climbing herb *Vitis setosa.*

ತಳಹದಿ, ತಳಾದಿ f n The foundation of a building

ತಳಿ 1 k v t To strew sprinkle n. Strewing sprinkling ತಳಿಸು To cause to sprir

ತಳಿ 2 k v i To shoot, sprout 2, to unfold, to appear n A race, family; a stock or breed.

ತಳಿ 3 k n. A fence; an asylum, a choultry for travellers

ತಳಿ 4. (ಳ = ೞ) k n A clog, cudgel, a palisade.

ತಳಿಗೆ f n A metal plate turned up at the rim

ತಳಿರು a k. v. i. To sprout, put forth leaves. n. A young shoot sprout ತಳಿರ್ದುಟಿ A bud-like lip ತಳಿರ್ದೋರಣ A festoon of young leaves ತಳಿರ್ಬಿಡು. To put forth shoots -ತಳಿರ್ವಸೆ A bed of tender leaves

ತಳಿಸು (*cf s* ತಳಿ 1) k v t To pound, beat

ತಳುಗು (= ತಂಗು) k v i To stay, halt.

ತಳುವು (= ತಡವು) a k v i To stay, delay, to be slow, to be bewildered n Stop, delay

ತಳೆ 1 a k v t To hold, to bear, to carry, support, to obtain. get. n. A tie, halter fetters.

ತಳೆ 2 (ಳ = ೞ) k. n A parasol an umbrella

ತಳ್ಚು k. v t To smear the body with an unguent n Anointing, lustre

ತಳ್ಕು (ಳ್ಕು = ೞ್ಕು) = ತಗ್ಗು. q v

ತಳ್ಳಂಕ a k n. Embarrassment, fear. *etc.*

ತಳ್ಳಿ k n. Connexion, association. company, intimacy 2, raising quarrels; slander, calumny -ಕೋರ A slanderer -ಮಾಡು To calumniate -ಅರ್ಜಿ. An anonymous petition

ತಳ್ಳು (= ತೆಳ್ಳು) k v. t To push. shove away, thrust, drive, to dismiss reject n Pushing, *etc.*, dismissal, *also* -ವಿಕೆ, ತಳ್ಳಿಕೆ.

ತಾ 1, ತಾಂ = ತಾನು, q v

ತಾ 2. k. 2nd *pers sing imp. of* ತರು. Bring.

ತಾಕೀದಿ, ತಾಕೀದು h. *n* Injunction, direction 2, a letter from a superior to a subordinate government officer.

ತಾಕು (= ತಾಗು) k. *v. i* To join, touch. *v. t* To come in contact with, to hit, strike or dash against, to collide with, to attack *n* Touching, hitting -ತೋಕು Wear and tear ತಾಕಿಸು To make touch, *etc*

ತಾಕುಳ. = ತಾಗುಳ, *q v*

ತಾಗಾಯತಿ h *prep.* Until, up to

ತಾಗು. = ತಾಕು, *q. v.*

ತಾಗುದಿ a. k *n* An ambush, lurking place.

ತಾಗುಳ (= ತಾಕುಳ) a. k. *n* Ardour, passion, formidableness

ತಾಜಾ, ತಾಜೀ h *a.* Fresh, green, new -ಕಲಮ್. A fresh para, a postscript

ತಾಜೀಂಮು h. *n.* Treating with ceremony and respect

ತಾಟ h *n* A dining plate 2, stiffness, tightness, pride *also* ತಾಟೆ -ಗಿತ್ತಿ A quarrelsome, wicked woman

ತಾಟಕಿ, ತಾಟಕೆ s. *n* A female fiend, a vixen, a hideous woman -ತನ. A wicked, quarrelsome disposition.

ತಾಟು 1 k *v t* To strike against, touch, come in contact with. 2, to strike. *n.* Striking against, *etc* -ಹೊಡಿ To knock one against another

ತಾಟು 2 f *n* The sloping frame of a roof.

ತಾಟು 3 = ತಾಟ, *q. v.*

ತಾಟು 4 h *n.* Pomp, show. -ಗಾರ. A showy man -ಮಾಡು To make fine.

ತಾಡನ s. *n.* Beating, striking. ತಾಡಿಸು To beat.

ತಾಣ *tb of* ಸ್ಥಾನ, *q v.*

ತಾಂಡವ s. *n* A wild dance, esp of the god Śiva

ತಾಂಡವಾಳ k. *n.* Cast iron, *also* ತಂಡವಾಳ

ತಾತ (= ತಂದೆ) s *n.* A father. 2, a grand-father.

ತಾತಾತೂತು k *n.* Full of holes.

ತಾತಿ = ತಾಯಿತಿ, *q v*

ತಾತ್ಕಾಲಿಕ (*fr* ತತ್ಕಾಲ) s *a.* Contemporary, instantly appearing, immediate

ತಾತ್ಪರ್ಯ s *n.* Aim, object. purpose, intent. 2. meaning, purport, drift. 3, explanation

ತಾತ್ಸಾರ f *n* Slight, disrespect, contempt

ತಾದೃಶ s *ad.* Such like, such a one

ತಾನ s *a.* Drawn, stretched *n* Expanse, a thread: a tone, the key-note in music.

ತಾನು 1 k *pro.* He, she, it, *in the reflexive or reciprocal sense* *pl* ತಾವು, ತಾನಾಗಿ Of himself, *etc*, voluntarily

ತಾನು 2 h *n* A web or piece of cloth

ತಾಂತ್ರಿಕ s *a* Relating to tantras. *n* A man versed in any science or system, a scholar

ತಾಪ s *n* Heat, torment; distress. -ಜ್ವರ A burning fever -ತ್ರಯ The three sorts of affliction, *i e* âdhidaivika, âdhibhautika and âdhyâtmika

ತಾಪಾಳು k. *n* A bar, bolt.

ತಾಪಿ s *a* Oppressed by heat. -ತ. Heated, distressed, pained.

ತಾಪಿಸು s *v. i.* To be hot, to burn, to suffer pain *v. t.* To warn, admonish

ತಾಫು k. *n* A pimp's house

ತಾಫೆ h *n.* A set of dancing girls and musicians

ತಾಫ್ತಾ h. *n* A kind of silk cloth

ತಾಬೂತು h *n* A bier carried about at the Moharam by Muhammadans

ತಾಬೆ h *n* Dependance, charge. -ದಾರ. A dependant

ತಾಬೇಲು (= ತಾಂಬೇಲು) k *n* A turtle

ತಾಮರೆ (= ತಾವರೆ) a. k *n* A lotus. 2, the ring-worm.

ತಾಮಸ (*fr.* ತಮಸ್) s *a.* Of darkness. *n.* Slothfulness, slowness, darkness. 2, a villain -ಗಾರ A sloth, sluggard. ತಾಮಸಿ Night, a vicious man

ತಾಂಬಾಣ f *n.* A metal dish

ತಾಂಬೂಲ (=ತಂಬುಲ) s. n A betel-leaf roll with its ingredients betelnut spices and lime 2, the areca-nut

ತಾಂಬೇಲು, = ತಾಪೇಲು, q v

ತಾಮ್ರ s n. Copper a Coppery red -ಭಸ್ಮ Oxide of copper -ಕುಟ್ಟಕ A coppersmith -ತಗಡು Sheet-copper -ಪರ್ಣಿ N of a river or a town -ಮು ಖಿ A European

ತಾಯಿ k. n Mother -ತಂದೆ. Mother and father, pl -ತಂದೆಗಳು Parents

ತಾಯಿತಿ f. n A small box or tube containing an amulet and worn on any part of the body

ತಾರ್ k. v t The base for the neg of ತರ್, as ತಾರ (He) won't bring ತಾರದ Not brought, etc.

ತಾರ 1 f n. A copper coin of 2 kâsu.

ತಾರ 2. s a. Crossing, floating 2, high, as a note in music. 3, clear, white, good, excellent n The ether, sky. 2, a mountain 3, a star. 4, the pupil of the eye ತಾರಾಬಲ The influence of stars ತಾರಾಮಂಡಲ The stairy region, zodiac, a large well, a kind of fire-work.

ತಾರ 3. h n. Tare (in trade). -ತಕ್ಕಡಿ. Fraud, deceit -ತಕ್ಕಡಿಗ A deceiver

ತಾರಕ s. n One who helps another through a difficulty, a protector. 2, a star 3, daitya, also ತಾರಕಾಸುರ

ತಾರಣ s n One that enables to cross, crossing 2, the 18th year of the cycle.

ತಾರತಮ್ಯ (fr ತರ more, and ತಮ most) s n Gradation, discrimination

ತಾರಯ್ಸು, ತಾರವಿಸು f. v. t. To sing in soprano, to exercise the voice before singing

ತಾರಸಿ h n. Work done with bricks and gârĕ

ತಾರಿ = ತಾರೆ 2, q v

ತಾರೀಖು, ತಾರೀಕು h. n. A date

ತಾರೀಫು h n Praise applause. 2 fun

ತಾರು (ರು = ಱು) k v i To become dry, to wither, wane n Dryness 2, a bunch of areca-nuts -ಗದ A double door. -ಮಾರು Disorder, confusion

ತಾರುಣ್ಯ s. n Youth youthfulness

ತಾರೆ 1. = ತಾರ 2, q v 2, Vâli's wife 3, Brihaspati's wife.

ತಾರೆ 2. (ರೆ = ಱೆ) k n A large timber tree, the Beleric myrobalan

ತಾರ್ಕಣೆ s n Personal observation 2, demonstration

ತಾರ್ಕಿಕ (fr ತರ್ಕ) s n A sophist, a disputant

ತಾಲ 1. (= ತಾಳ) s n. Clapping the hands 2 beating time in music, musical time 3, a cymbal. 4, a short span, the palm of the hand.

ತಾಲ 2 (= ತಾಲಿ 3, ತಾಳೆ 2) s. n The palmyra tree, Borassus flabelliformis -ಪತ್ರ A palmyra leaf -ಮಧು Toddy

ತಾಲವ್ಯ (fr ತಾಲು). s a. Palatal ತಾಲ ವ್ಯಾಕ್ಷರ A palatal letter

ತಾಲಿ 1 (= ತಾಳಿ 3) k n A golden neck-ornament, as a marriage-badge

ತಾಲಿ 2 (tb of ಸ್ಥಾಲಿ) n A kind of metal vessel

ತಾಲಿ 3 (= ತಾಳೆ 2) s. a. The talipot or fan-palm Corypha laliera. 2, = ತಾಲ 2.

ತಾಲೀಮು h n Gymnastic instruction, a gymnasium, also -ಖಾನೆ

ತಾಲು s. n. The palate.

ತಾಲೂಕು h n A talook, division of a district

ತಾವಡ k n A necklace of lotus beads

ತಾವರೆ (= ತಾಮರೆ. tb of ತಾಮರಸ) n The lotus. Cpds ಅಡಿದಾವರೆ, ಕೆಂಪು-, ನೆಲ-, ಬಿಳಿ-, ಬೆಟ್ಟ-, ಮರ-, etc -ಕಂದ Brahmâ -ಗಡ್ಡೆ The bulbous root of a lotus. -ಗಣ್ಣ Vishnu. -ಮಣಿ A lotus seed often used as a bead

ತಾವು 1. k pro (pl of ತಾನು) They 2, you (honorif)

ತಾವು 2 (= ಠಾವು, q v) k n A place, etc.

h. n A [illegible] pipe

ತಾಸೀಲು = ತಹಸೀಲು, *q v*

ತಾಸು h. *n.* An hour -ಬಡಿ, -ಬಾರಿಸು To strike the hour -ಹೊತ್ತು An hour's time

ತಾಸೆ f. *n* A flat drum -ದವ A drummer

ತಾಳ. = ತಾಲ 1, No 2 *etc*, *q v* -ಗತಿ A mode of beating time in music. -ಧರ A time-keeper in a musical performance.

ತಾಳದ k *n* Boiled and seasoned vegetables

ತಾಳಿ 1 k *n* A pile of dried cakes of cowdung

ತಾಳಿ 2. (*tb. of* ತಾಲ 2) *n.* The palmyra tree, *Borassus flabelliformis.*

ತಾಳಿ 3 = ತಾಲಿ 1, *q v*

ತಾಳಿ ೆ. = ತಾಳಿಮೆ, *q v*

ತಾಳಿಮೆ k *n* Patient endurance, patience, forbearance, *also* ತಾಳ್ಮೆ

ತಾಳಿಸು k. *v t* To season food. 2, to temper, sharpen.

ತಾಳು 1 k *v t* To hold, to take, get, undergo *v i.* To suffer patiently, endure, to wait, to wear well; to bear with *P p.* ತಾಳಿ, ತಾಳ್ದು ಕೋಪ- To get angry; to suppress anger; to pardon

ತಾಳು 2 (ಳು = ಱು) k. *n.* The bar or bolt of a door 2, a corn-stalk. 3, the bottom

ತಾಳುಮೆ = ತಾಳಿಮೆ, *q v*

ತಾಳೆ 1 f *n* Tallying, agreement, *as* of accounts *etc* -ನೋಡು, -ಹಾಕು To compare together. -ಬೀಳು. To agree with tally

ತಾಳೆ 2 = ತಾಲ 2, *q v* -ಮರ = ತಾಳಿ 2 -ಯೋಲೆ, -ವಾಲೆ, -ವೋಲೆ A hollow coil of palm leaf worn by married women into the lobe of their ears

ತಾಳೆ 3 (ಳೆ = ೞೆ) k. *n* The fragrant screwpine, *Pandanus odoratissimus.*

ತಾಳ್ಮೆ = ತಾಳಿಮೆ, *etc*, *q v*

ತಾಳ್ವರಿ (*fr* ತಾಳು 2) k *n* The bottom of a tree or hill

ತಿಕಟಿ, ತಿಕ್ಕಟಿ f *n* A mason's level, an instrument used in spinning thread.

ತಿಕ್ಕಲು k *n* Confused mind (*cf.* ದಿಗಿಲು). 2, stuttering stammering. ತಿಕ್ಕಲಾಟ. Confused behaviour -ತಿಕ್ಕಲಾಗಿ ಮಾತಾಡು To stutter.

ತಿಕ್ಕು k *v t* To rub, scour, to wipe. 2, to treat harshly, annoy ತಿಕ್ಕಾಟ, ತಿಕ್ಕಾಟ Rubbing, scouring, annoying

ತಿಕ್ತ s *a* Sharp, bitter *n.* Pungency, bitterness -ಕ Bitter, the plant *Trichosanthes dioeca*

ತಿಗಟು, ತಿಗಟೆ, ತಿಗಡು, ತಿಗುಡು k *n* Rind, bark.

ತಿಗಡಿ h *n.* Fraud -ಬಿಗಡಿ *dpl*

ತಿಗಡೆ (*tb of* ತ್ರಿಪುಟೆ) *n* Indian jalap -ಬಳ್ಳಿ Its creeper, *Ipomoea turpethum.*

ತಿಗಳ, ತಿಗುಳ k. *n.* A Tamil man, *esp* an emigrant, *f.* -ಗಿತ್ತಿ ತಿಗಳತಿ.

ತಿಗುರಿ k *n* A potter's wheel

ತಿಗುರು (*cf.* ತಿಕ್ಕು) a. k *v t* To rub, to annoy *n.* An unguent, perfume

ತಿಗ್ಗಾಮುಗ್ಗಾ k *ad* In a very rough manner

ತಿಂಗಳು k *n* The moon, a month ತಿಂಗಳವರೆ. A kind of avarĕ bearing every month. -ಬೆಳಕು. Moonlight.

ತಿಟ್ಟು k *n* Rising ground, hillock. 2, abuse. *v t* To abuse, scold.

ತಿಣಕು ತಿಣುಕು k *v i* To strain 2, to undergo trouble *v. t* To press, to make violent efforts.

ತಿಂಡಿ k *n* Food 2, itch -ಕೋರ, -ಪಾಕ, -ಪೋಕ, -ಹೋತ A glutton, *f.* -ಗಾತಿ -ಇಡು, -ಹಾಕು To set food before one

ತಿಣ್ಣ a k *n* Thickness, greatness, weight, excess

ತಿತಿಕ್ಷೆ s *n* Forbearance, patience, resignation

ತಿತ್ತಿ (= ತಿದಿ *tb. of* ದೃತಿ) *n* A leather bag 2, bellows

ತಿತ್ತಿರಿ s *n* The francoline partridge

ತಿಥಿ s *n* A lunar day. 2 an annual ceremony performed by Brâhmanas for their deceased ancestors

ತಿದಿ (= ತಿತ್ತಿ *tb of* ದೃತಿ) *n* A pair of bellows -ಊದು To blow bellows

ತಿದ್ದು k *v t* To make straight; to correct, rectify, mend, to improve, to reform, to train; to break 2, to settle a debt *n* Correction, *etc* -ಪಡಿ, -ಪಾಟ, -ಪಾಟು. A corrected state, improvement. ತಿದ್ದಿದ Corrected, trained, *as* -ಕುದುರೆ -ಎತ್ತು, -ಮನೆ ತಿದ್ದಿಸು To cause to correct, train, *etc.*

ತಿನಸ, ತಿನಸು 1. ತಿನಿಸು k *n* Food. -ಗೂಳಿ A glutton

ತಿನಸು 2 k *n* Irritation in the skin, itching, the itch, irritability

ತಿನಸು3, ತಿನಿಸು2, ತಿನ್ನಿಸು (*cf* ತಿನ್ನು) k *v. t* To make eat, feed

ತಿನು. = ತಿನ್ನು *q v* *P p* ತಿಂದು

ತಿಂತಿಣಿ k *n* A crowd, multitude, a row -ಸು To be crowded

ತಿಂದು *P p. of* ತಿನ್ನು

ತಿನ್ನಾಳಿ k *n* A glutton, gourmand

ತಿನ್ನು k *v t* To eat, *as* things requiring biting 2, to suffer or undergo, as blows, *etc* 3, to take, *as* bribes *P. p* ತಿಂದು, *part neg* ತಿನ್ನದೆ; *rel part.* ತಿನ್ನುವ, ತಿಂದ, ತಿಂಬ. *3rd pers neut. sing. imp.* ತಿಂತು

ತಿಪ್ಪಲಿ k *n* *Piper longum*

ತಿಪ್ಪೆ (= ತಿಟ್ಟು, *q v*) k *n* A heap, hillock, a pile, a dung-hill -ಕುಣಿ, -ಕಳ್ಳ A dung-hole.

ತಿಬ್ಬಳಿ (= ತಿಳವಳಿಕೆ) k *n* Understanding, knowledge, sense

ತಿಬ್ಬಿ h *n* A manner of stitching.

ತಿಬ್ಬು k *n* The string of a bow.

ತಿಮರ, ತಿಮುರು, ತಿಮ್ಮುರು k. *n* Irritation in the skin, itching

ತಿಮಿ 1. = ತಿಮಿ, *q v*

ತಿಮಿ 2, ತಿಮಿಂಗಿಲ s *n* A large fabulous [fish

ತಿಮಿರ s *n* Darkness, dimness of the eyes 2. ignorance. 3, sorrow 4, Râhu. -ರಿಪು, -ವೈರಿ The sun

ತಿಮಿರು k *v t* To rub and clean the skin.

ತಿಂಬು (= ತಿನ್ನು, *q v*) k *In the pres and fut*,. *as* ತಿಂಬುತ್ತದೆ ತಿಂಬೋಣ, *etc* -ವಿಕೆ Eating

ತಿರಕ = ತಿರುಕ, *q v*

ತಿರಗಣಿ (= ತಿರುಗಣಿ ತಿರುಗುಣಿ) k *n* Turning, a wheel for raising water a windlass roller, a screw.

ತಿರಗು = ತಿರಿಗು, ತಿರುಗು *q v*

ತಿರಪ, ತಿರಪೆ = ತಿರುಪೆ, *q v*

ತಿರಸ್ಕರಿಸು s *v t* To put aside, disrespect, disdain, scorn

ತಿರಸ್ಕಾರ s. *n* Setting aside, disregard, disdain, reproach, abuse

ತಿರಳು (= ತಿರುಳು, ತಿಳಲು, *q v*) k *n* Pith, core, pulp, kernel, essence.

ತಿರಿ k. *v i* To turn round, to wander about 2, to beg alms. ತಿರಿದುಣ್ಣು, ತಿರಿದುಂಬು To live by alms

ತಿರಿಗಿ k. *ad* Again once more ತಿರಿ-. Again and again

ತಿರಿಗಿಸು (= ತಿರಗಿಸು) k *v t.* To turn, to twist

ತಿರಿಗು (= ತಿರುಗು, *q. v.*) k *v i* To go round; to turn, to roll, to go back; to change or shift *as* the wind to cease *as* a disease, to wander or ramble about ತಿರಿಗಾಟ Wandering about, *also* ತಿರಿಗಾಡುವಿಕೆ. ತಿರಿಗಾಡು To walk or wander about ತಿರಿಗಿಕೊಳ್ಳು To turn round ತಿರಿಗಿ ಬರು To return ತಿರಿಗಿ ಬೀಳು To turn round and fall upon. to affront, to revolt. ತಿರಿಗಿ ಮಾತಾಡು. To contradict

ತಿರಿಚು k. *v. t.* To twist, *as* a string, *etc.*, to wring off, *as* the neck of a bird

ತಿರು 1 k *n* Turning, a bow-string 2, (= ತಿರಪ, *etc*) begging -ಬೋಕಿ A beggar, a mendicant's bowl -ಮುರು. Turnings and windings, reverse order, deceit.

ತಿರು 2. (*tb of* ಶ್ರೀ) *a* Holy sacred -ಕೂಳು Holy, *i e* sacrificial food. -ಚೂರ್ಣ Coloured powders used for the sectarian mark by votaries of [illegible] in the Arcot district. -ಮಣ್ಣು Sacred clay to make sectarian marks to the right and left of the forehead. -ಚೂರ್ಣ, -ಮಲೆ The sacred hill with the Vaishnava fane at Tirupati -ಮಾಳಿಗೆ A guru's house. -ಮುಡಿ A holy tuft of hair at the back of the head. -ವಾಂಕೋಡು Travancore.

ತಿರುತ = ತಿರು, q v.

ತಿರುಕ (= ತಿರಕ) k. n A wanderer, a [beggar

ತಿರುಗಣೆ, ತಿರುಗುಣೆ = ತಿರಗಣೆ, q v.

ತಿರುಗು = ತಿರಿಗು, q. v.

ತಿರುಪು k n A screw 2, changing ತಿರುಪಿನ ಓಲೆ A gold ear-ornament with a screw -ಹೂ, ತಿರುಪಿನ ಹೂ A head-ornament with a screw.

ತಿರುಪೆ (= ತಿರಪೆ) k n Wandering about (for alms), begging, alms -ಎತ್ತು, -ಬೇಡು To beg.

ತಿರುವು k v t To turn, as the head, key, screw stone in a mortar n Turning, a bow-string

ತಿರುಹು = ತಿರುವು, q. v

ತಿರುಳು = ತಿರಳು q v

ತಿರೋಹಿತ s. a Covered, hidden, lost

ತಿರ್ಯಕ್ s a Going horizontally. n An amphibious animal, a bird -ಪುಂಡ್ರ. A horizontal sectarial line on the forehead of a Śaiva -ಜಂತು, -ಜೀವ An animal -ಯೋನಿ The animal creation -ಲೋಕ The earth

ತೀರ್ವೆ f. n Assessment, duty, tax. -ದಾರ A person paying assessment.

ತಿಲ s. n The *Sesamum* plant and its seed -ಘಾತಕ An oilman

ತಿಲಕ s n. A freckle. 2, a sectarian or ornamental mark made on the forehead with coloured earth, *etc*

ತಿಲೋಣಿ s. n A strong smelling annual herb, *Gynandropsis pentaphylla.*

ತಿಲ್ಲಾನ k n A series of sounds used in humming a tune.

ತಿವಿ (= ತಿವು 1) k v t To strike with the fist, box ... pierce stab n Piercing, *etc*, *also* -ತ. ತಿವಿಸು. To cause to strike

ತಿಷ್ಠೆ s n. Staying, standing -ಹಾಕು To stay, lodge

ತಿಳ, ತಿಳು (= ತಿಳದು, ತಿಳಿದು) *P. p. of* ತಿಳಿ *in* ತಿಳಕೊಳ್ಳು, ತಿಳುಕೊಳ್ಳು

ತಿಳಲು = ತಿರಳು, q v

ತಿಳಿ k. v i. To become clear, pure. 2, to be plain or known v t. To know, understand, perceive, learn, to feel as pain ನನಗೆ ತಿಳಿಯುತ್ತದೆ I understand, know, *etc*, ನನಗೆ ತಿಳಿಯಿತು. I understood, *etc* -ಯಗೊಡು To let know -ಯಪಡಿಸು. To make known. -ಯಬರು = ತಿಳಿ, No 2 -ಯುವಿಕೆ, -ವಳಿಕೆ, -ವಿಕೆ, ತಿಳುವಳಿಕೆ, ತಿಳುವಿಕೆ. Knowledge, understanding, intelligence -ಹೇಳು, -ಯ ಮಾಡು. = -ಸು q v

ತಿಳಿ 2 k n Clearness, pureness 2, knowledge, understanding, *also* -ವು. 3, clear substances, *as* conjee water, *etc.* -ಗೇಡಿ A stupid person -ಗೇಡಿತನ. Ignorance, stupidity. -ನಿದ್ರೆ A light sleep. *Other cpds* -ನೀರು, -ಬಣ್ಣ, -ರಸ, -ಸುಣ್ಣ, *etc*

ತಿಳಿಸು k. v. t To make clear or known; to let know, to inform

ತಿಳುಹು, ತಿಳುಹಿಸು k v. t To make known, to let know

ತೀ k n. Fire v t. To burn.

ತೀಕ್ಷ್ಣ s a Sharp, hot, pungent, fiery; harsh, zealous, energetic n. Sharpness, heat, haste. 2, poison. -ಬುದ್ಧಿ. A keen mind

ತೀಟೆ k n Itching, irritation, an itching desire, lust, lasciviousness -ಕೆರೆ. To scratch an irritation in the skin. -ಜಗಳ Useless quarrel -ಬಾಯಿ A blabber -ಹತ್ತು, -ಹಿಡಿ To be affected with the itch

ತೀಡು k v. t To press, squeeze, rub, to scour, to smear on, *as* unguents on the body, to sharpen, to rub out, *as* insects, to strike with the palm of the hand. v i To touch, *as* air 2, to blow, *as* the wind.

ತೀನಿ k. n. Food, feeding ತೀನಾಳಿ A glutton

ತೀರ 1. s n A shore, bank, margin, brink, edge

ತೀರ 2, ತೀರಾ (fr ತೀರು 1) k ad Fully, quite, very.

ತೀರಿಕೆ (= ತೀರ್ಕೆ) k n Conclusion, end, decision. 2, leisure -ಮಾಡು To finish complete ನ್ಯಾಯ- The judgment

ತೀರು 1 k v i To be finished, come to an end, to end cease; to be done, accomplished 2 to cease to live, die 3, to be paid, liquidated, settled -ವಿಕೆ End, termination ತೀರಿಸು To finish, to accomplish carry out, execute, to fulfill, to settle decide, to clear off, liquidate pay, as ಉಪಕಾರ-, ಕಾಂಕ್ಷೆ-, ದಾವೆ-, ಬತ್ತಿ-, ಮುಯ್ಯಿಕ್ಕೆ ಮುಯ್ಯಿ-, ನ್ಯಾಯ-, ನೀರಡಿಕೆ-, ವ್ಯಾಜ್ಯ- ಸಾಲ-, ಸಿಟ್ಟು-ಹಗೆ- etc ತೀರಿಸಿಬಿಡು, ತೀರಿಸಿ ಹಾಕು To finish off ತೀರಿತು. Ended ತೀರದು Can't be finished

ತೀರು 2. k n. Conclusion 2, settlement 3, finish, beauty, manner, mode, peculiar habit, also ತೀರ -ಗಡೆ End, completion. -ವಳಿ, -ವಾಟು Leisure, opportunity -ಮಾನ. Conclusion, settlement, decision, sentence -ಮಾನಿಸು To finish determine, decide

ತೀರುವೆ k. n Dues fees, customs, tax

ತೀರ್ಚು = ತೀರಿಸು, q v

ತೀರ್ಥ s n A passage ford 2 a holy place in the vicinity of streams. 3, sacred water 4, a sacred object; a school of philosophy 5, a worthy person. 6, an ascetic. -ಕರ A Jina -ಪಾದ, -ರೂಪ A title for a venerable man. -ಯಾತ್ರೆ A pilgrimage -ಶ್ರಾದ್ಧ Funeral ceremonies observed at a place of pilgrimage.

ತೀರ್ಪು (fr ತೀರು) k n Settlement, decision, sentence -ಆಗು To be decided

ತೀರ್ವಕೆ ([illegible]

ತೀರ್ವೆ = ತೀರುವೆ q v

ತೀವು a k. v i To become full, to abound v t To fill

ತೀವ್ರ s a Strong, severe, fierce, sharp; rash, quick, excessive, much -ಗೊಳ್ಳು, -ಪಡು To be quick -ತೆ, -ತ್ವ Sharpness, severity; -ಬುದ್ಧಿ A keen mind.

ತುಕಡಿ, ತುಕ್ಕಡಿ h n A bit, a bit of bread, detachment. 2, a district, province. -ದಾರ The headman of a district

ತುಕ್ಕು 1 a k. v i To crowd, throng

ತುಕ್ಕು 2. k n Rust of iron, canker.

ತುಂಗ 1 s. a High, lofty, prominent, chief -ಭದ್ರೆ The river Tungabhadre in the Mysore territory

ತುಂಗ 2, ತುಂಗೆ k n A species of grass. -ಗಡ್ಡೆ, -ಮುಸ್ತೆ The bulb of *Cyperus rotundus* -ಹುಲ್ಲು The *Cyperus* grass

ತುಚ್ಛ s a. Trifling, contemptible, low, mean ತುಚ್ಛೀಕಾರ Contempt -ತುಚ್ಛೀಕರಿಸು. To contemn, disdain

ತುಟಾರ f. n Inconsideration. indiscretion ತುಟಾರಿಸು To be indiscreet

ತುಟಿ k. n The lip. -ಜಾರಿದ ಮುತ್ತು A slip of the tongue. ಗಡಸು-, ಹಂಡಿ-, ದೊಣ್ಣೆ- A large lip -ಸೇವೆ Lip-service, hypocrisy

ತುಟ್ಟಿ (tb of ತ್ರುಟಿ) n Dearness a Dear. ad Dearly; at a high rate. -ಧಾರಣೆ A high price -ಸು To decrease in, strength or power.

ತುಡಗ, = ತುಡುಗ, q v.

ತುಡು (= ತೊಡು, q v) v. t To join, put on as clothes, to cover

ತುಡುಕು a. k. v. t To grasp quickly, seize, snatch n Grasping quickly -ಉಳಿ. A grasping thief, cf ಕೈಮುಡುಕು

ತುಡುಗ (= ತುಡಗ) k n A thief, rascal, f. ತುಡುಗಿ -ಆವು, ದನ A thievish cow -ತನ Theft thievishness -ಬುದ್ಧಿ A wicked mind

ತುಡುಗು k n Theft, stealth rascality, a stolen thing. -ಮಾಡು To steal

ತುಡುಪು k n An oar, a flat wooden

ತುಣಕ, ತುಣಕು 1, ತುಣುಕು 1. a. k *n* A fragment piece, bit ಅರಿವೇ-, ರೊಟ್ಟಿ-, *etc*

ತುಣಕು 2, ತುಣುಕು 2 (= ತುಳಕು, ತುಳುಕು, *etc*) k *v i* To shake or be agitated, *as* water.

ತುಣಿ = ತುಳಿ, *q. v*

ತುಂಟ k *n* A mischievous, wicked, insolent, lewd man, rogue, *etc.*, *f* ತುಂಟಿ -ಕುದುರೆ. A wicked horse -ಹುಡುಗ. A wicked boy. -ಕೆಲಸ A mischievous business -ತನ, ತುಂಟಾಟ Wickedness, mischief, impudence, *also* ತುಂಟು -ಬುಂಟು. *rep.*

ತುಂಡ s *n*. A beak, a snout, the point of an instrument

ತುಂಡಿ s. *n*. A beak, the mouth; the navel.

ತುಂಡಿಸು k *v t* To cut or break into pieces, make piece-meal *etc.*

ತುಂಡು k *n* A fragment, piece, a bit, a little. ತುಂಡಂಗಿ. A small jacket; a cockroach -ಕಾಲು A maimed leg. -ತುಂಡು *rep* -ದೊರೆ, -ಪಾಳೆಗಾರ A petty chieftain. -ಮಾಡು. To cut into pieces. -ಬಟ್ಟೆ A rag -ತುಂಡಾಗಿ ಬೀಳು To fall to pieces -ತನ = ತುಂಟತನ

ತುತೂರಿ, ತುತ್ತೂರಿ f. *n* A long trumpet -ಊದು. To blow the trumpet

ತುತ್ತ = ತುದಿ, *q v* -ತುದಿ The very point.

ತುತ್ಥ (*tb of* ತುತ್ಥ) *n* Blue vitriol, sulphate of copper

ತುತ್ತು k *n* A mouthful of food, a morsel, food *v t* To take by mouthfuls

ತುದಾ (= ಸುದಾ?) s *ad* Or, perhaps however.

ತುದಿ k *n* An extremity, end, point, top, tip *Cpds* ಮರದ-, ಮೊಳೆಯ-, ಬೆಟ್ಟದ-, ಸುಂಡಿಲ-, ಬಿಲ್ಲ-, ಕೆಲಸದ-, ಭುಜದ-, *etc* -ಕಾಲ್ Tiptoe -ಕುಂಡೆ The hip, loins -ಗಮ್ಮು. To be hazardous -ಗುಂಡು. A summit -ಗೆ ಬರು To be nearly ready -ನಾಲಿಗೆ The tip of the tongue -ಬಾಲ The end of a tail -ಮುಟ್ಟ. To the end, completely -ಮೂಗು The tip of the nose. -ಮೊದಲು The foremost point, the very beginning, beginning and end.

ತುಂತುರು (ರು=ಱು) k. *n*. Drizzling, spray, a drop -ಮಳೆ A fine drizzling rain -ಮುಯ್ಯು Vapour, fog. -ಹನಿ Spray

ತುಂದ s *n* The belly ತುಂದಿ Gorbellied, corpulent, *also* ತುಂದಿಕ, ತುಂದಿಲ.

ತುನ್ನ s *a* Hit, stung, hurt -ವಾಯ. A tailor

ತುಪರಿಬಳ್ಳಿ k *n* A creeping plant much cultivated, *Luffa aegyptiaca*

ತುಪಾಕಿ h *n* A musket, matchlock gun -ಕುಂದ, -ಕಟ್ಟಿಗೆ. A gun-stock -ಚಾಪು. A gun-lock. -ಕಿವಿ The touch-hole of a gun. -ಚಾಪಿನ ಕೀಲು The trigger -ಜಡಿ To load a gun -ಹಚ್ಚು, -ಹಾರಿಸು, -ಹೊಡಿ To fire a gun. -ಬಾವಿಗೆ The match of a matchlock

ತುಪಾನು h *n* A storm, typhoon, slander, calumny -ಹಾಕು, -ಹೊರಿಸು To accuse falsely

ತುಪ್ಪ k *n* Clarified butter, ghee *Cpds* ಹೊಸ-, ಕಾಸಿದ-, ಕರಗಿಸಿದ-, ಜೇನ-, *etc.* -ಗೆಣಸು A species of sweet potato. -ಹೀರೆ, ತುಪ್ಪೀರೆ A kind of Luffa

ತುಪ್ಪಟ, ತುಪ್ಪಳ k *n* A feather; the soft plumage or down of birds, the soft hair of rabbits, *etc.*

ತುಬಾಕಿ. = ತುಪಾಕಿ, *q v*

ತುಬ್ಬು k *v t* To point out a thief *v i* To be found out *n* Detection. -ಮಾಡು To detect find out

ತುಮಕಿ k *n* The wild mangosteen tree, *Diospyros embryopteris*, *also* ತುಮರಿ

ತುಮುಲ s *n* Uproar, tumult

ತುಂಬ = ತುಂಬಾ, *q. v* *s.* ತುಂಬು.

ತುಂಬಿ 1. (= ದುಂಬಿ) k *n* A large black bee *Cpds* ಎಳೆ-, ಕೆಂಪು-, ಮಾಲೆ-, *etc*

ತುಂಬಿ 2 f *n* A kind of long gourd, *Lagenaria vulgaris*.

ತುಂಬಿ 3. = ತುಂಬೆ, *q v*

ತುಂಬು 1 k *v i* To become full, be filled up, to abound, to get plump

2. to possess, as a demon. v. t. To fill. n. Becoming full, etc. -ಯೌವನ Blooming youth. ತುಂಬ, ತುಂಬಾ Fully, all over, much. ತುಂಬಿಕೆ. Repletion, etc. ತುಂಬಿಸು To fill, to cause to fill.

ತುಂಬು 2. k. n. The foot-stalk of a leaf, flower or fruit, stalk.

ತುಂಬು 3 (= ತೂಬು) a. k. n. A tube, the wheel-nave through which the axle passes. 2, an outlet, sluice, also ತೂಬು.

ತುಂಬುರ, ತುಂಬುರು 1. s. n. N. of a Gandharva.

ತುಂಬುರು 2. k. n. The wild mangosteen, Diospyros embryopteris.

ತುಂಬೆ k. n. The herb Phlomis indica. 2, the very common weed Leucas linifolia.

ತುಯ್ಯು k. v. t. To pull, draw, stretch. -ತ Pulling.

ತುಯ್ಯಾಲು k. n. A dish of rice, milk and sugar.

ತುರ s. a. Quick, swift.

ತುರಕ = ತುರುಕ, q. v.

ತುರಗ s. a. Going quickly. n. A horse.

ತುರಂಗ 1. = ತುರಗ, q. v. -ಶಕ್ತ್ರ. -ವದನ Horse-faced, a Kinnara.

ತುರಂಗ 2. f. n. A prison.

ತುರಂಗಿ s. n. A horseman, rider, a groom.

ತುರಚೆಗಿಡ (ರ = ಱ) k. n. An annual plant, stinging like nettles, cowhage.

ತುರಂಜಿ h. n. A tree so called. a. Excellent.

ತುರತ (tb. of ತ್ವರಿತ) n. Haste, urgency. ad. Quickly, soon.

ತುರಾಯಿ, ತುರಾಯಿ h. n. An ornament for the turban, a plume, crest, a tufted head of certain flowers. -ಮರ A cypress.

ತುರಿ 1 (ರಿ = ಱಿ) k. n. Itching, scratching, the itch, lust. -ಕಜ್ಜಿ, -ಗಜ್ಜಿ Scab, herpes. -ಕೆ Itching, scratching. -ಕೆಗಿಡ ... heterophylla. -ಸು, -ಸು To scratch, itch.

ತುರಿ 2 k. n. Grating. 2, scraping.

ತುರಿತ = ತುರತ, q. v.

ತುರು (ರು = ಱು) a. k. n. A cow, kine. -ಪಳ್ಳಿ, -ಹಟ್ಟಿ A cowpen. -ಮಂದೆ -ಹಿಂಡು. A herd of kine. -ಗಾರ, -ವಳ A cowherd; f. -ಗಾತಿ, -ವಳ್ತಿ.

ತುರುಕ (= ತುರಕ) h. n. A Turk, a Mussulman. a. Turkish.

ತುರುಕು (ರು = ಱು) k. v. t. To force into, cram, stuff, also ತುರುಬು.

ತುರುಗ (ರು = ಱು) a. k. n. A throng, crowd, also ತುರುಗಲ್.

ತುರುಗು (ರು = ಱು) a. k. v. i. To be crammed, crowded, amassed. n. A throng, crowd.

ತುರುಪು e. n. A "troop", a trump or winning card.

ತುರುಬು (ರು = ಱು) k. v. t. To tuck in, as flowers in the hair, also ತುರುಕು, q. v. n. The bundle of hair of the head.

ತುರುವು k. v. t. To scrape, bore, hollow, as fruits or kernel out of its shell. n. Grating, scraping.

ತುರುವೆ (ರು = ಱು) k. n. The country mallow, Sida indica.

ತುರುಷ್ಕ s. n. A Mahomedan, a foreigner. 2, olibanum, Indian incense.

ತುರುಸು = ತುರಿಸು, q. v.

ತುರ್ತ. = ತುರತ, q. v.

ತುಲನ s. n. Lifting, raising, weighing.

ತುಲಸಿ (= ತುಳಸಿ) s. n. A small shrub, the holy basil, Ocymum sanctum. -ಕಟ್ಟೆ. A square pedestal in which the holy basil is planted. -ಪೂಜೆ Worship of the basil shrub. -ಮಾಲೆ. A garland of the basil shoots.

ತುಲೆ, ತುಲಾ (= ತೊಲೆ, ತೋಲ) s. n. A balance, scales. 2, weight. 3, the sign of the zodiac Libra. 4, equality. 5, the beam of a balance. 6, a ... ight of gold, jewels, *etc*, against one's person and distributed to Brâhmanas

ತುವರಿ = ತೊಗರಿ, *q v*

ತುವಾಲ e *n* A towel.

ತುಷ s. *n*. The husk of grain

ತುಷಾರ s *a* Cold, frigid, dewy *n* Cold, frost dew.

ತುಷ್ಟ s *a* Satisfied, contented, glad, *etc*.

ತುಷ್ಟಿ s *n* Satisfaction; pleasure -ಪಡಿಸು. To satisfy, gratify, appease -ಪಡು. To be satisfied or contented

ತುಸ, ತುಸು k *n* A little -ತುಸ *rep*

ತುಹಿನ s *n* Mist, dew, cold 2, moonlight 3, camphor. -ಗಿರಿ The Himâlaya

ತುಳಕು, ತುಳುಕು (= ತುಣುಕು) k *v i* To be agitated, to shake, as water, *etc* to be scattered in drops, to run over, *also* ತುಳಕಾಡು

ತುಳಸಿ = ತುಲಸಿ *q v*

ತುಳಿ (ಳಿ = ೞಿ) k *v t* To tread on, trample, to crush to pieces with the feet. 2, to annoy, harass. *v i* To be trodden down, to be abject *P ps* ತುಳದು, ತುಳಿದು *n* Treading, trampling, *etc*, *also* ತುಳಿದಾಟ.- ಗೆಂಡ Walking on fire. ತುಳಿತ. Treading, *etc*

ತುಳಿಲ್ (ಳಿ = ೞಿ) a k. *n* A salutation, obeisance. 2, valour. 3, work, servitude ತುಳಿಲಾಳು. A valorous man. ತುಳಿಲ್ವೆಲ್ To be valorous, to be a servant

ತುಳು k. *n* Tulu, N of a country on the western coast of South-India. -ವ. Relating to Tulu, a Tulu man.

ತುಳುಕು = ತುಳಕು, *q v*.

ತುಳ್ಳು a. k *v. i*. To roll, to jump, *also* ತುಳ್ಳಾಡು

ತೂ k *int* *An imitative sound of spitting or of flouting* -ತೂ *Flouting with fie! hoot!* -ತೂ ಎನ್ನು. To say fie

ತೂಕ (= ತೂಗು 2) k *n*. Weight; worth; the weight of gold varaha -ದ ಕಲ್ಲು The measure of weight. -ಮಾಡು, -ಹಾಕು. To weigh -ಮಾಡಿಸು To get weighed

ತೂಕು k *n* Weight 2, nodding. ತೂಕಡಿಕೆ. Drowsiness, lassitude. ತೂಕಡಿಸು To doze

ತೂಗು 1. k *v t* To weigh. 2, to swing or rock, *as* a cradle, to wag, *as* the head, to hang up ತೂಗಾಡು. To hang down, swing, to rock, *as* a cradle, to waddle ತೂಗಿ ನೋಡು To weigh and examine ತೂಗಿಸು To cause to weigh, rock, *etc*

ತೂಗು 2 (= ತೂಕ, ತೂಕು) k *n* Weighing, swinging, *etc* ತೂಗಡಿಸು. = ತೂಕಡಿಸು -ಕೋಲು. A kind of balance. -ದೀವಿಗೆ A hanging lamp -ಮಂಚ A swinging cot -ಮಣೆ A swing -ಮರ. A gallows -ತಲೆ A nodding head

ತೂತು k. *n* A hole ತೂತಾಗು. To get a hole. -ಕೆಡಪು To pierce a hole through. -ಕೊರೆ, -ತೆಗೆ, -ಮಾಡು To bore a hole -ಬೀಳು. To become holed, be spoiled

ತೂಪರೆ, ತೂಬರೆ k. *n* The wild mangosteen tree.

ತೂಬು k *n* The nave of a wheel 2, the sluice of a tank 3, the hole of an axe, hoe, *etc*, into which the handle goes -ಮುಚ್ಚು To shut up a flood-gate. -ತೆರೆ To open it

ತೂರು 1 (ರು = ಱು) k *v t* To winnow *v i* To be shaken off 2, to run, bolt away *n*. Winnowing.

ತೂರು 2 (ರು = ಱು) k. *v i* To enter, to go through a hole, as a thread, *etc*, to penetrate 2, to drizzle. *n*. Drizzling 2, penetrating

ತೂರ್ಣ s. *a*. Quick, fleet *n* Rapidity, quickness

ತೂರ್ಯ s. *n* A musical instrument. 2, a bugle

ತೂಲ s *n* Cotton; the down of birds

ತೂಳು a k *v i*. To go off, to recoil 2, to rush forward, to chase 3, to attack *n*. Attacking.

ತೃಣ s *n* Any gramineous plant, grass, a reed, straw -ಕುಟಿ. A thatched hut -ಗ್ರಾಹಿ Amber -ಧ್ವಜ A bamboo. -ಪ್ರಾಯ Worth a straw, worthless -ರಾಜ. The palmyra tree, the cocoanut tree, bamboo, sugarcane

ತೃತೀಯ s *n* The third. 2, chunam (being the third ingredient of tâmbûla) -ವಿಭಕ್ತಿ The instrumental case ತೃತೀಯೆ The 3rd day of a lunar fortnight

ತೃಪ್ತ s *a* Satisfied, contented, pleased.

ತೃಪ್ತಿ s *n* Satisfaction, contentment; pleasure, gratification -ಗೊಳ್ಳು, -ಪಡು To get satisfied, pleased. -ಪಡಿಸು, -ಮಾಡು To satisfy, please

ತೃಷಿತ, ತೃಷ್ಣಕ s *a*. Thirsty

ತೃಷೆ s *n* Thirst 2 desire

ತೆಕ್ಕನೆ a k *ad* Greatly, very much

ತೆಕ್ಕೆ, ತೆಕ್ಕೆ k *n* An embrace 2, a coil -ಬೀಳು To clasp in the arms -ಹಾಕು To embrace.

ತೆಗದು, ತೆಗೆದು k *P. p of* ತೆಗಿ ತೆಗೆ ತೆಗದು ಕೊಳ್ಳು To take, receive -ಹಾಕು To put away, remove, dismiss

ತೆಗಸು = ತೆಗಿಸು, *q v*

ತೆಗಳ್ (ಳ್=ೞ್) a k *v t* To rebuke, to blame, abuse. *n* Blame, abuse

ತೆಗಿ, ತೆಗೆ k *v t* To take, to buy; to take away, steal, to seize, to exact, to put out, to prolong *as* a note in music, to obtain, to open, *as* a door, to undertake, to pick up, *as* a quarrel, to assume, *as* a birth, to employ, *as* a grammatical form, to vaccinate (ಮುಯ್ಲಿ-), to draw, *as* a line, map, *etc* (ಗೆರೆ-), to bore, *as* a hole, to find out, *as* a means, to ask about, to dig, *as* a channel, *etc* *v i* To be taken away, to become less, to disappear 2 to retreat, flee *P. p* ತೆಗದು, ತೆಗದು ತೆಗೆದುಕೊಂಡು ಬರು. To bring ತೆಗೆದುಕೊಂಡು ಹೋಗು To take away ತೆಗೆದುಹಾಕು (*see s* ತೆಗದು) To throw down; to raise *as* a siege - - To allow to ...

ಹಿಂದಕ್ಕೆ-, ಹಿಂದೆಗೆ To draw back, retreat, retire. ಮಾಚಕೇ- To dishonour one -ಸು, -ಯಿಸು To cause to take, *etc*

ತೆಗೆ 2 k *v t* To grind *as* sandalwood on a stone

ತೆಂಕ, ತೆಂಕಣ k *n* The south, *also* ತೆಂಕಲು, -ಗಾಳಿ, ತೆಂಗಾಳಿ South wind -ದೇಶ, *etc* -ದೆಸೆ The southern quarter

ತೆಂಕು k *v i*. To float, swim

ತೆಂಗಲೆ k *n* A certain Vaishnava mode of putting the nâma

ತೆಂಗು k *n*. The cocoanut palm *Cocos nucifera* ತೆಂಗಿನ ಕಾಯಿ. A cocoanut ತೆಂಗಿನ ಮರ. = ತೆಂಗು ತೆಂಗಿನ ನಾರು. The coir or fibre of the cocoanut *Other cpds* ತೆಂಗಿನ ಎಣ್ಣೆ, ತೆಂಗಿನ ಗಡ್ಡೆ, ತೆಂಗಿನ ಗರಿ, ತೆಂಗಿನ ಚಿಪ್ಪು, *etc*

ತೆಂಟು a k. *v t* To winnow

ತೆಂಡೆ k *n* A small bundle *as* of grass, *etc* -ಸುತ್ತು. To tie together, *as* growing sugarcanes

ತೆತ್ತಿ = ತತ್ತಿ, *q v*

ತೆತ್ತಿಗ a. k *n* A servant 2, a connection, friend

ತೆತ್ತಿಸು a k *v. t* To bring into close connection, to insert, to pierce through

ತೆತ್ತು 1. *P p of* ತೆರು

ತೆತ್ತು 2 k *v t* To twist *v i* To be twisted, connected

ತೆನಿಸು e *n*. Tennis a play in which a ball is kept in motion (ಚೆಂಡಾಟ)

ತೆನೆ k *n* A spike, ear of corn 2, the coping of a wall, the top of a rampart, a merlon of a fort -ಗಜ The Indian millet

ತೆಪ್ಪ k. *n* A float, raft -ತೇಲು To float a raft -ಬತ್ತು, -ನೂಕು To push a raft

ತೆಪ್ಪಗೆ, ತೆಪ್ಪನೆ k *ad*. At leisure, at ease, well

ತೆಪ್ಪರಿಸು (ರಿ=ಱಿ) k. *v i* To become conscious, to start up awake (*with* ...

ತೆರ 1 (ರ=ಱ) a k n An opening, a way course, manner sort ತೆರಂ. In a manner, etc

ತೆರ 2 (ರ=ಱ) = ತೆರದು, ತೆರೆದು P. p of ತೆರೆ in ತರಕೊಳ್ಳು, to open

ತರ 3. (ರ=ಱ) = ತೆರವು q. v

ತೆರಗೆ = ತೆರಿಗೆ, q v

ತೆರಟು k v t To tuck up (a garment when passing a river), to join, unite

ತೆರಪು (ರ=ಱ) k n An opening, a gap, an interval, room, place. 2, cessation as of rain 3, leisure 4, opportunity 5, the state of being empty, as a house, box, etc -ಗೊಳ್ಳು To occupy more place, to leave room (for others)

ತೆರವು (ರ=ಱ) = ತೆರಪು, q v 2, the price paid for a wife; also ತೆರ -ಮಾಡು To empty.

ತೆರಳು 1 a k v i To move, stir, to tremble, quiver, to proceed, to set out depart ತೆರಳ್ಕೆ. Moving, quivering, setting out

ತೆರಳು 2 a. k v. i To join, to assemble ತೆರಳ್ಕೆ. A mass, multitude.

ತೆರಳೆ k n A round lump 2, sap, pith -ಯ ಹುಳ A silk-worm, an insect in fruits

ತೆರಿಗೆ (ರಿ=ಱಿ) k n Tribute, tax, also ತೆರಗೆ. -ಎತ್ತು To levy taxes -ಕಟ್ಟು To impose a tax -ಕಾಗದ A written lease -ಕೊಡು To pay taxes. -ಬಿಡು To free from taxes.

ತೆರಿ = ತೆರೆ, q v

ತೆರಿಸು (ರಿ=ಱಿ) k. v. t To cause to open, etc. 2, to cause to pay, as taxes, etc

ತೆರು (ರ=ಱ) k v t To pay P p ತೆತ್ತು -ವಿಕೆ Paying

ತೆರೆ 1. (ರೆ=ಱೆ) k v. i To be uncovered; to open v. t To open, to uncover; to unfold. P ps ತೆರದು, ತೆರೆದು, ತೆರೆದು. n Opening, tribute, tax

ತೆರೆ 2. k n A wave, billow 2, a fold, a wrinkle 3, a curtain, screen -ಕೊನೆ The crest of a wave. -ತಗೆ To remove a curtain -ಬಿಡು To let down a curtain -ಯುಲಿ The roar of waves. -ಬಡಿ -ಹೊಡಿ The waves to beat

ತೆಲಗ, ತಲುಗು k n Telugu, the Tĕlugu language ತೆಲುಗ, ತೆಲುಂಗ A Tĕlugu man; f ತೆಲಗಿತಿ, ತಲುಗಿತಿ, ತೆಲುಂಗಿತಿ

ತೆಲೆಗ್ರಾಮು e n A telegram, a message by wire to a distance (ತಂತಿವರ್ತಮಾನ).

ತೆಲೆಗ್ರಾಫ e n. Telegraph (ತಂತಿಟಪ್ಪಾಲು).

ತಲೆಫೋನು e n Telephone an apparatus for transmitting sound to a distance.

ತಲ್ಲಟ a k n A gift, present, esp to the bride and bridegroom at their marriage; also ತೆಲ್ಲಟು

ತೆವಟು = ತವಟು, q v

ತೆವಡೆ k n. A small dam in a field 2, = ತೆಂಪೆ

ತೆವರಿ, ತೆವರು k n. A hillock, a balk. v. t To rub, to tease 2, to rob, steal [desire.

ತೆವಲು, ತೆವುಲು (=ತಿನುರ) k n An itching

ತವಳು k v i. To creep along

ತೆಳು (=ತಿಳಿ 2) k n Thinness, fineness, delicateness -ಕಾಗದ. Thin paper. -ಗನ್ನಡ Fine or perspicuous Kannada. -ನೀರು Clear water -ಪು, -ವು Thinness, watery state -ಬಟ್ಟೆ Fine cloth. -ಬಣ್ಣ A light colour. -ವೆಲರ್ A gentle breeze

ತೆಳ್ಳಗೆ, ತೆಳ್ಳನೆ k a. Thin, delicate, etc ad Thinly, etc n Thinness

ತೆಳ್ಳು = ತಳ್ಳು, q v

ತೇ = ತೇಯು, q. v

ತೇಗು 1. k n The teak tree, Tectona grandis.

ತೇಗು 2. k. v. i To belch. n A belch -ವಿಕೆ Belching

ತೇಜ s. n Radiance, splendour, brilliance 2, power, might. energy 3, majesty, glory, fame 4, the sun, also ತೇಜಸ್ -ಪುಂಜ A mass of lustre; a learned or virtuous man -ಸ್ವಿ Brilliant, powerful. ತೇಜ A horse. ತೇಜೋಮಯ. Full of light, energy, etc. ತೇಜೋವಂತ A bright-faced man

ತೇಟು h n Genuine, pure

ತೇಟೆ k n. Purity, clearness, *as* of water -ವಡಿಸು, -ಮಾಡು To clear up

ತೇಪೆ (= ತ್ಯಾಪೆ) k n. A patch.

ತೇಮ (= ತೇವ, ತ್ಯಾವ) s n Wetness, damp, moisture -ನ. Moistening, a sauce

ತೇಮಾನ k n Loss in assaying metals. 2, waste from want of work

ತೇಯು (= ತೇ, *q v*) k v t To grind or macerate in water on a slab *P ps.* ತೇದು, ತೇಯ್ದು

ತೇರು 1 k n. A chariot, an idol car. ತೇರಾಟ An idol car-festival -ಎಳೆ, -ಹಿಡಿ To draw a car in procession

ತೇರು 2. k. v i. To reach. 2, to be successful. 3, to recover from illness, *as* ಸುಖ-, ರೋಗ-, ಕಷ್ಟ- -ಗಡೆ Success, *as* in an examination

ತೇಲು k v.i To be afloat, to float 2, to slip, glide off. 3 to become loose, *as* the roots of young plants *P ps* ತೇಲಿ, ತೇಲ್ದು ತೇಲಕಟ್ಟು To suspend ತೇಲಾಡು To float about ತೇಲಿಸು. To make float, to open the eyes wide, stare

ತೇಲಿ (*tb of* ತೈಲಿ) n An oilman

ತೇವ, ತೇವು (*tb of* ತೇಮ) n Wetness, moisture

ತೇವುಳಿ k n A disease of falling off of the hair

ತೈನಾತಿ h a. Stipendiary, placed at the command of, assigned

ತೈಲ s n Sesamum oil, oil in general -ಪರ್ಣೀ. Sandal, turpentine -ಪಾಕ Any article of food fried in oil -ತಿಕ್ಕು, -ಪೂಸು, -ಹಚ್ಚು To apply oil, anoint ತೈಲಿಕ. An oilman

ತೈಲಿ h n A bag, purse s = ತೇಲಿ

ತೊಕ್ಕು k n Fruits pounded and mixed with salt, chillies, *etc*

ತೊಗಟು. ತೊಗಟೆ k n Bark, rind, peel, a pod

ತೊಗರಿ (*tb of* ತುವರಿ, *q v*) n The pigeon-pea

ತೊಗರು ...

ತೊಗಲು k. n The skin, a hide, leather, peel, *as* of an orange ತೊಗಲುಬಾವಲಿ. The flying fox -ಬೊಂಬೆ A leathern puppet. -ಸುಲಿ To flay, skin

ತೊಗೆ k n A dish of boiled split pulse

ತೊಂಗಲ್ a k n A cluster, a bundle, bunch, tassel, *also* ತೊಂಗೆ.

ತೊಂಗು k. v. i. To hang down, swing. 2, to stoop (*as in* ತೊಂಗಿ ನೋಡು)

ತೊಟ್ಟಿಲು (= ತೊಟ್ಲು) k. n A cradle

ತೊಟ್ಟಿ k n. A trough, font, tub.

ತೊಟ್ಟು 1. *P.p of* ತೊಡು, *q v*

ತೊಟ್ಟು 2 k n A nipple. 2, the foot-stalk of a fruit, flower or leaf

ತೊಟ್ಟು 3. (= ತಟುಕು) k n A drop

ತೊಟ್ಟೆ k n. A bees' empty cell

ತೊಟ್ಲು = ತೊಟ್ಟಿಲು, *q v.*

ತೊಡಕು k. v. i. To get entangled, *as* thread, a horn in a tree *etc* 2, to engage, *as* in work 3, to be in opposition. *v t* To commence (= ತೊಡಗು), to entangle, to hinder, interfere n Entanglement, impediment, hindrance, objection, perplexity -ಬೀಳು To become entangled, to be hindered ತೊಡಕಾಗು To be hindered, *as* work.

ತೊಡಗು (= ತೊಡಕು, *v. t*) k v t To engage, *as* in work to begin; to undertake *v i.* To be begun ತೊಡಗಿಸು. To cause to commence or undertake

ತೊಡಂಬೆ a k n A cluster, a bundle, bunch

ತೊಡರು k. v. i To be linked to, connected with, *etc*, to join, to fall in with, to be arrested, checked, to be caught *v t* To encircle *as* creepers round a tree n. Connection; a badge of honour, an impediment, a check.

ತೊಡರಿಸು, ತೊಡಚು k v t. To tie, link, insert, fasten, fix.

ತೊಡವು, ತೊಡಹು k. n Apparel, clothing, an ornament 2, the beginning, the ...

ತೊಡಸು k v t. To wipe away, to efface, destroy 2, to cause to smear, as chunam, cowdung, etc; also ತೊಡಿಸು ತೊಡಯಿಸು, ತೊಡೆಯಿಸು

ತೊಡಿಗೆ k. n Apparel, clothing, an ornament

ತೊಡು (= ತುಡು) k. v. t To put on, as clothes, ornaments etc P p ತೊಟ್ಟು ತೊಡಿಸು To dress another = ತೊಡಸು, q v

ತೊಡೆ 1. k. v. t To smear, anoint, rub on as oil, unguents, to whitewash. 2, to wipe, as tears 3, to efface, destroy

ತೊಡೆ 2. k n The thigh. -ವಾಳ A bubo

ತೊಣಚಿ, ತೊಣಚೆ k n A gadfly, dogfly

ತೊಣೆ a. k n Likeness, equality.

ತೊಂಡಲು k n. A chaplet of pearls 2, (f) = ಸುಂಡಲು, q v.

ತೊಂಡು k. n Insolence 2, straying 3, chatter, prate -ಜುಲುವಾನೆ A fine for the trespass of stray cattle -ದನ Stray cattle -ತನ Strolling, straying

ತೊಂಡೆ 1 k n. A chameleon 2 the upper part of a sugarcane

ತೊಂಡೆ 2 (tb of ತುಂಡಿ) n The tiny gourd *Momordica monadelpha* Cpds ಕಾಗೆ-, -ಕಾಯಿ -ಬಳ್ಳಿ, ಹುಚ್ಚು-.

ತೊಂಡ್ಲು = ತೊಂಡಲು, q v.

ತೊತ್ತು k n A female servant, a mean woman ತೊತ್ತಿನ ಮಗ The son of a maid-servant

ತೊದ k n A Tōda of the Nilgiris

ತೊದಲು k v i To stammer, falter n. Stammering, faltering, speaking indistinctly 2, untruth -ನುಡಿ, -ಮಾತು Stammering speech. -ನಾಲಿಗೆ A stammering tongue

ತೊನೆ a. k. v. i To swing, wave to and fro

ತೊಂತು k v t To wind one's self round 2 to instigate one (to quarrel)

ತೊಂದರೆ. ತೊಂದ್ರೆ k n. Intricacy, embarrassment, difficulty, trouble, vexation, impediment, drawback -ಗೊಳ್ಳು -ಪಡು -ಬೀಳು To [illegible] embarrassed [illegible] -ಗೊಳಿಸು To embarrass, etc -ಕೆಲಸ, -ಕಾರ್ಯ A troublesome affair

ತೊನ್ನು k. n Leprosy, white leprosy

ತೊಪ್ಪಲು k n. All small leaves of plants in general.

ತೊಪ್ಪೆ k n Fresh cow-dung

ತೊಂಬತ್ತು k a Ninety.

ತೊಂಟೆ a k n A cluster. 2, a host, multitude. 3, a large bamboo basket.

ತೊಯು, ತೊಯ್ಯು (= ತೋಯು) k v i To become wet or moist. v t. To moisten P p ತೊಯಿದು ತೊಯಿಸು, ತೊಯ್ಯಿಸು To make wet, to steep in water.

ತೊರಡು (ರ = ಱ) k n A hook for taking down fruits from trees

ತೊರಳೆ k n The spleen

ತೊರೆ 1. k. v i Milk to form in the breast a Mature, ripe

ತೊರೆ 2. (ರೆ = ಱೆ) k. v t To put away, quit, give up, reject. P. ps. ತೊರದು, ತೊರೆದು

ತೊರೆ 3 (ರೆ = ಱೆ) k n A hollow, hole, a cave 2, a stream, river -ಮಾವು A mango-tree near a river -ಮಂಜಿ. An undershrub, *Indigofera trita*.

ತೊರೆಯ k n. A salt-maker.

ತೊಲಗು k v i To go away, depart; to go aside, to retire, to be separated; to fail ತೊಲಗಿ ಹೋಗು To forsake. ತೊಲಗಿಸು. To separate, cause to go away.

ತೊಲೆ (tb of ತುಲಾ) n A beam of wood. 2, a balance 3, a rupee's weight.

ತೊಳ (= ತೊಳದು, ತೊಳೆದು) P. p of ತೊಳೆ, in ತೊಳಕೊಳ್ಳು

ತೊಳಗು a k. v. i To shine, be bright. n. Splendour.

ತೊಳಲು (ಳ = ೞ) a k. v i. To move round 2, to roam or wander about 3, to get perplexed v. t To roll n Moving, roaming ತೊಳಲಿ Moving round. ತೊಳಲಿಕಲ್ಲು A wooden hand-mill ತೊಳಲಿಕೆ. ತೊಳಲುವಿಕೆ. Roaming or wandering about

ತೊಳಸಲು k *n* Pounding ತೊಳಸಲಕ್ಕಿ. Rice cleared of its bran

ತೊಳಸು 1 k. *v. t* To beat, pound *as* rice so as to deprive it of its bran. 2, to box, fight 3, to cause to wash, to get washed *n* Pounding, boxing. 2, entanglement

ತೊಳಸು 2 (ಳ=ಋ) k *v. t* To turn round. *v i* To nauseate *n* Revolving, rolling, wandering

ತೊಳೆ, ತೊಳೆ 1 k *v. t* To wash. *P ps* ತೊಳದು, ತೊಳೆದು

ತೊಳೆ 2 k *n*. A hole 2, one of the divisions in an orange, jack fruit, *etc* -ಮಾಡು. -ಹಾಕು. To bore a hole

ತೊಳ್ತು = ತೊತ್ತು.

ತೊಳ್ತುಳಿ (ಳ್ತುಳಿ=ಋ್ತುಋ) a k. *n* Poor, miserable, dejected

ತೊಳ್ಳೆ k *n*. A hollow, hole, cavity 2, deficit, debt.

ತೋ = ತೋಯು *q v*

ತೋಕೆ a k *n*. A tail

ತೋಚು (= ತೋರು) k *v i*. To appear, seem occur to the mind ಹೀಗೆ ತೋ ಚುತ್ತದೆ So it seems ತೋಚಿಕೆ Appearing, occurring to the mind

ತೋಟ k. *n* A garden -ಗಾರ, ತೋಟಿಗ A gardener, florist.

ತೋಟಿ k *n* An inferior village servant, sweeper, scavenger, *etc* 2, a scuffle; a quarrel

ತೋಟೆ h *n* A cartridge; *also* ತೋಟಾ.

ತೋಡ k *n*. A kind of white rat that infests crops

ತೋಡಿ k. *n* N of a tune.

ತೋಡು 1 k *v i* To go out. *v. t* To bale out water, to wind thread from one spool upon another 2, to dig excavate, to burrow. *n* A water-course

ತೋಡು 2. k. *n*. An expedient

ತೋಡೆ h *n* A ring of gold, *etc*, for the wrist or ankle

ತೋಂಟ — ತೋಟ *q v*

ತೋತಾಯ f *n* A counterfeit, an imposter.

ತೋಮ k *n* An expedient. 2, *p. p of* ತೋ -ಗಾರ A man clever in expedients

ತೋಪ, ತೋಫ = ತೋಫು, *q v*

ತೋಪಡೆ k *n* A carpenter's plane

ತೋಪಿ. = ಟೋಪ್ಪಿ, *q v*

ತೋಪು k *n* A clump of trees, grove, wood.

ತೋಫು h *n* A cannon -ಖಾನೆ A depôt of artillery stores. -ಹಾರು A gun to be fired -ಸುಡು, -ಹಾರಿಸು. To fire a gun.

ತೋಬರಿ f. *n*. A horse's mouth-bag.

ತೋಯ s *n*. Water -ಜ A lotus -ಜ ನಾಭ -ಜಾಕ್ಷ Vishnu -ಜಮಿತ್ರ The sun -ಜಾರಿ The moon. -ನಿಧಿ The ocean. ತೋಯಾಶಯ. A lake.

ತೋಯು k *v i* To become wet or moist *P p* ತೋಯ್ದು. ತೋಯಿಸು. To moisten wet, to soak, steep

ತೋರ k. *n* Bigness largeness stoutness, greatness, a stout man -ತಲೆ A large head. -ಹನಿ, -ಹನಿ A big drop -ಹ, ತೋರಿಹ Being large.

ತೋರಂಜಿ f *n* The pumplemose or shaddock tree, *Citrus decumana*

ತೋರಣ s *n*. A festoon suspended across gateways, streets, *etc*

ತೋರಿಕೆ (ರ=ಱ) k *n* Appearance, sight. 2, conjecture, opinion 3, exhibition, *also* ತೋಱಿಕೆ

ತೋರು (ರು = ಱು) k *v i* To appear, seem, be visible, to come into existence, to occur *v t* To show, exhibit, to evince. *n* Appearing, showing ತೋರಡವು. A mortgage without possession -ಬೆರಳು The fore-finger ತೋರಿಸು To show, to evince ತೋರಿಸಿ ಕೊಡು. To point out ತೋರಿಸುವಿಕೆ. Showing. -ವಿಕೆ. = ತೋರಿಕೆ.

ತೋಲ s. *n* Weight, a weight of gold or silver amounting to 210 grains. [illegible] Tŏla

ತೋಲು k a Much, plenty n A way, road
ತೋಲೆ k. n A cataract.
ತೋವೆ = ತೊಗೆ, q. v.
ತೋಷ s n Satisfaction, contentment, joy, pleasure, *also* -ಣ ತೋಷಿಸು. To be delighted, pleased.
ತೋಷೇಖಾನೆ h n A treasury
ತೋಸ್ದಾನು h. n A leather pouch.
ತೋಸ್ಟು e n A toast ತೋಸ್ಟಿನ ರೊಟ್ಟಿ. A toasted bread
ತೋಹು a. k n Deceit, a lurking place; an ambush. 2, decoying. 3, a hedge; a thicket, a crowd.
ತೋಳ k n. A wolf
ತೋಳು k n The arm -ಎತ್ತಿತೂಗು. To dandle a child in the arms. ತೋಳ ತೊಡಿಗೆ, -ಬಂದಿ An arm-bracelet. -ಬಲ. Strength of the arm -ಬೀಸು. To swing the arm.
ತೌ *For words with this initial see s* ತವ *or* ತವು
ತೌರು. = ತವರು, q. v
ತ್ಯಕ್ತ s. a. Left, forsaken, thrown away.
ತ್ಯಜನ s n Leaving, abandoning.
ತ್ಯಜಿಸು s. v t. To leave, quit, renounce, to dismiss, to shun
ತ್ಯಾಗ 1. (= ತೇಗ) k. n. Teak.
ತ್ಯಾಗ 2. s. n Abandoning, renouncing, resigning; gift, donation, generosity. -ಭೋಗ Generosity and enjoyment. ತ್ಯಾಗಿ. Leaving, liberal, a donor, a hero
ತ್ಯಾಜ್ಯ s a To be left, avoided, abandoned, shunned n An unlucky hour. 2, giving up, resigning.
ತ್ಯಾಪೆ = ತೇಪೆ, q v
ತ್ಯಾವ = ತೇವ, q v ತ್ಯಾವಿಸು. To moisten, *etc*
ತ್ರಯ s. a Triple, threefold n. A triad ತ್ರಯೋದಶ Thirteenth ತ್ರಯೋದಶಿ. The thirteenth day of the lunar fortnight.

ತ್ರಸ s. a Movable, moving. n. Animals.
ತ್ರಸರ s. n A weaver's shuttle
ತ್ರಾಣ s n Protection, defence; help 2, strength, vigour, might, ability. 3, capacity. -ಗುಂದು. Power to be impaired -ಗುಂದಿಸು To impair power. -ಗೊಳ್ಳು, -ಹೊಂದು To become strong.
ತ್ರಾಣಿ One who is strong or powerful ಸರ್ವತ್ರಾಣಿ Almighty; the Almighty, God.
ತ್ರಾತ s. a Protected, saved.
ತ್ರಾಸ s. n Fear, anxiety; vexation, annoyance -ಕೊಡು. To vex, harass. -ಗೊಳ್ಳು To be vexed
ತ್ರಾಸು (= ತರಾಸು) f n. A balance -ಮುಳ್ಳು The needle of a scale beam.
ತ್ರಾಹಿ s *int.* Protect! save!
ತ್ರಿ s. a. Three -ಕರಣ (= ಕರಣತ್ರಯ). Mind, speech and action. -ಕರಣಶುದ್ಧಿ. Purity of mind, speech and action. -ಕಾಲ Past, present and future, morning, noon and evening. -ಕೋಣ Triangular; a triangle. -ಗುಣ The three qualities of nature, i e satva, rajas and tamas, threefold, thrice. -ಜಗತ್ Heaven, earth and the lower region. -ತಯ A triad. -ತಾಪ = ತಾಪ ತ್ರಯ. -ದಂಡ. The triple staff of a mendicant Brâhmana who has renounced the world. -ದರ್ಶಿ Seeing the past, present and future, omniscient. -ದಶ Thirty. -ದೋಷ. Disorder of the three humours of the body, vitiation of the bile, blood and phlegm -ದೋಷಹರ Removing the tridôsha -ನಾಮ. = ಮೂರು ನಾಮ, q v -ಪಥ. The three paths; the sky, earth, and lower region. -ಗಾಮಿನಿ, -ಪಥೆ. The Ganges. -ಪದಿ. N of a metre, a tripod -ಪುಟಿ. Triangular, a musical tâla that requires three beatings. -ಪುಂಡ್ರ A sectarian mark consisting of three lines made on different parts of the body by Śaivas and Vaishnavas. -ಪುರ Three strong cities. -ಪುರುಷ

Brahmâ, Vishnu and Śiva; three generations -ಭುವನ Heaven, earth and the lower region -ಮತ Three systems of religion smârta or advaita, mâdhva or dvaita, râmânuja or visishtâdvaita -ಮೂರ್ತಿ The triad of Brahmâ, Vishnu and Śiva -ಯಂಬಕ = ತ್ರ್ಯಂಬಕ -ರತ್ನ. The three gems Buddha, the law, and the congregation -ರಾತ್ರಿ Three nights -ಲಿಂಗ Having three genders: an adjective -ಲೋಕ = ತ್ರಿಭುವನ, *q v.* -ವರ್ಗ Three objects of life religion or virtue, wealth, and pleasure -ವಿದ್ಯೆ The three branches of knowledge -ವೇಣಿ Triple braid, the junction of the Ganges, the Yamunâ and the Sarasvatî. -ಶೂಲ A trident -ಸಂಧಿಗ್ರಾಹಿ One who understands and remembers a slôka hearing it three times

ತ್ರೇತಾ, ತ್ರೇತೆ s *n* A triad. 2, the second of the four ages of the world. ತ್ರೇತಾಗ್ನಿ The three sacred fires collectively

ತ್ರೈಕಾಲಿಕ (*fr* ತ್ರಿಕಾಲ) s. *a* Relating to the three times, *i. e* past, present, and future

ತ್ರೈರಾಶಿಕ s *n*. The rule of three

ತ್ರ್ಯಂಬಕ (= ತ್ರಿಯಂಬಕ) s. *a* Triocular. *n* Śiva 2 N of a town

ತ್ರ್ಯಾಹಿಕ s *a* Tertian, quartan, *as* fever

ತ್ವಕ್, ತ್ವಚ್ s. *n* Skin 2, bark, rind, husk

ತ್ವಕ್ಕ್ಷೀರೆ (ತವಕ್ಷೀರ) f *n* Manna of bamboo, tabâshîr.

ತ್ವರಿತ s. *a*. Quick swift, speedy

ತ್ವರ (*tb of* ತ್ವರೆ) *n*. Haste, speed, velocity -ಪಡು To be quick, hasty, *etc*

ತ್ಸಾಪ್ಸ್ಟ್ರು s. *n*. A man of very dirty, nasty habits

ಥ

ಥ್. The thirty-fifth letter of the alphabet *In Kannada it occurs only in few words*

ಥಕಾರ s. *n* The letter ಥ

ಥಟ್ಟು a k *n*. A mass, host, army -ರಿ. (=-ಉರಿ) To blaze up

ದ

ದ್. The thirty-sixth letter of the alphabet.

ದ *The termination of the affirmative and negative relative participles, as:* ಕೇಳಿದ, ಮಾಡಿದ, ಹೇಳಿದ, ಹೋದ, ತಿಂದ *etc*, ಕೇಳದ, ಮಾಡದ, ಹೇಳದ, ಹೋಗದ, ತಿನ್ನದ, *etc*

ದಂಶ s *n* A bite, sting 2, a tooth, 3, a gad-fly. -ಕ. Biting, any thing fit to be chewed, *as* pickles

ದಂಷ್ಟ್ರ s *n* A large tooth, tusk, fang

ದಂಷ್ಟ್ರಿ [illegible] wild [illegible]

ದಕಾರ s *n* The letter ದ

ದಕ್ಷಿಣ, ದಕ್ಕಿಣ (*tb. of* ದಕ್ಷಿಣ) *n*. The south, the upper Dekhan

ದಕ್ಕು k *v i* To be obtained, got, acquired, to remain as in one's possession. 2, to remain, to be saved, to become well *n* Acquirement, possession, property ನನಗೆ ದಕ್ಕಿತು I have obtained it. -ಮಾಡಿ ಕೊಳ್ಳು To obtain possession. ದಕ್ಕಿಸಿಕೊಳ್ಳು To appropriate to [illegible] each.

ದಕ್ಷ s a Skilful, able, intelligent n. N. of a son of Brahmâ 2, ability, fitness. -ಕನ್ಯೆ Durgâ. -ತೆ. Cleverness, ability

ದಕ್ಷಿಣ (= ದಕ್ಕಣ) s. a Right, not left 2, straightforward, sincere, upright n The south, country of the south, the Dekhan. -ಧ್ರುವ. The south-pole. ದಕ್ಷಿಣಾಯನ. The sun's progress south of the equator, winter solstice. ದಕ್ಷಿಣೋತ್ತರ. The south and the north, right and left

ದಕ್ಷಿಣೆ (= ದಖಿಣಾ) s n. The south 2, (money) presents given to Brâhmanas 3, a fee, gift.

ದಖಣ, ದಖ್ಖಣ, ದಖನ (tb of ದಕ್ಷಿಣಾ) n. The upper Dekhan. ದಖಣಿ, ದಖನಿ. The Hindusthâni language

ದಗಡಿ f n. A rude woman

ದಗಲು h. n Trick, fraud. -ಬಾಜ Roguery; a dishonest person, also ದಗಾಖೋರ.

ದಗಲೆ h n. Armour, a coat of mail

ದಗಾ, ದಗೆ h n Deceit, fraud, imposture. ದಗಾಖೋರ A dishonest man -ಖೋರತನ Deceiving.

ದಗೆ f n Heat, glow.

ದಗ್ಗನೆ k ad With a blaze -ಉರಿ. To burn brightly.

ದಗ್ಧ s a Burnt, scorched. -ಹಸ್ತ. A luckless man

ದಂಗೆ (= ತಂಗೆ) h n Tumult and confusion, as of a mutiny. -ಏಳು To become rebellious -ಮಾಡು, -ಬೀಳು To rebel

ದಜ್ಜಿ k. n. Half of a split tamarind seed -ಬಾರ A kind of backgammon

ದಟ್ಟ k. a. Thick, stout, robust, crowded together, thick-set, dense. n Quilted rags -ಕೂದಲು Thick, bushy hair -ಗೆ Densely. -ಣೆ The state of being thick, crowded together, close, etc -ಯಿಸು, -ಯ್ಸು. To grow thick, close, dense. -ಸ್ತ Thick, dense, etc.

ದಟ್ಟಿ k n A waist-band· a sash

ದಟ್ಟಿಸು k. v t. To rub out, obliterate, to efface 2, (f.) to scold, menace

ದಟ್ಟು k n Stumbling ದಟ್ಟಡಿ A tottering, waddling step

ದಡ 1 *A sound imitating the rattling of thunder, etc, trembling, quivering, palpitation* -ದಡ, -ಬಡ rep. -ದಡ, -ದಡನೆ In hurry and flurry. -ಬಡ ಮಾತಾಡು. To speak rapidly.

ದಡ 2 (tb of ತಟ) n. A bank, shore

ದಡಂಬಡಿಕೆ k n Impetuousness, force

ದಡಾರ (tb. of ದದ್ರು) n Measles

ದಡಿ 1 (= ದಂಡಿ) k n A staff, a cudgel. -ಗ A clubman

ದಡಿ 2. f. n The border of a cloth

ದಡೂತಿ f. n Of close texture, as cloth 2, respectability; wealth.

ದಡೆ h n. A weight of ten sêrs and equal to ¼ of a maund. 2, a weight to counterbalance.

ದಡ್ಡ k n A blockhead, a stupid, ignorant man, f -ಳು, ದಡ್ಡಿ 2, a double consonant, also -ಕ್ಕರ. *Cpds* -ಕೆಲಸ, -ಗುಣ, -ಮಗ, etc -ತನ. Stupidity, ignorance.

ದಡ್ಡಿ (= ತಡಿಕೆ) k. n. A tatty, screen 2, a cage. 3, a stable.

ದಡ್ರಂಡೆ k n. A profligate woman

ದಣ (= ದಣಿದ) k P p of ದಣಿ, in ದಣ ಕೊಳ್ಳು.

ದಣವು k. n Fatigue, weariness, exhaustion. -ಆರಿಸು, -ತೀರಿಸು To take rest -ಆಗಿರು To be weary -ಗೊಳ್ಳು To be fatigued

ದಣಿ 1. k v i To be fatigued or tired. 2, to be satiated. ದಣಿಸು To cause to be fatigued, to satiate.

ದಣಿ 2. tb. of ಧನಿ, q v.

ದಣಿವು, ದಣು, ದಣುವು = ದಣವು q v

ದಂಟು k n A stalk *Cpds* ಜೋಳದ-ತಾವರೆಯ-, ಸೂರಣದ-, etc

ದಂಡ (= ದಂಡು) s. n. A stick, staff, rod. 2, a stalk. 3, a staff or sceptre 4, the oar of a boat 5, punishment, a fine imprisonment 6, a t of military array, an army, *also* ದಂಡು -ಕಟ್ಟು To set a fine on. -ಕೊಡು. To pay a fine -ಬೀಳು A fine to be imposed upon -ಕ N of a vritta, a pole. -ನೀತಿ. Administration of justice, ethics -ಯಾತ್ರೆ. A bridal procession, conquest of a region -ಪ್ರಣಾಮ, -ಪ್ರಣಾಮು, -ವತ್ಪ್ರಣಾಮು A prostration of the body

ದಂಡನ s. n Beating, punishing, inflicting punishment, torment, *also* ದಂಡನೆ -ಪತ್ರ A penalty-clause in a document

ದಂಡಿ 1. k n. Greatness, might, abundance, excess. 2, anger 3, cruelty

ದಂಡಿ 2 s. n. A doorkeeper, porter. 2, a religious mendicant carrying a staff, an ascetic

ದಂಡಿಗೆ (*tb of* ದಂಡಿಕೆ) n The beam of a balance. 2, a kind of palankeen

ದಂಡಿಸು s v t To punish, chastise, to mortify

ದಂಡು (*tb of* ದಂಡ) n An army -ಇಡು, -ಇಟ್ಟುಕೊಳ್ಳು. To keep an army -ಕೂಡಿಸು. To assemble an army. -ಬಿಡು To encamp an army. ದಂಡೆತ್ತು To levy an army. ದಂಡಿಗೆ ಹೋಗು. To enlist in the army

ದಂಡೆ 1 s n A string; a garland, wreath 2, a kind of gymnastic exercise of the body

ದಂಡೆ 2. (*tb. of* ತಟಿ) n. A bank, shore. -ಗುಂಟ Along the shore

ದಂಡೋರ = ಡಂಗರ, *q v* -ಹಾಕಿಸು To be proclaimed by beat of drum

ದತ್ತ s a Given, granted, made over -ಪುತ್ರ. An adopted son ದತ್ತಾಪಹಾರ. The resumption of a gift ವಾಗ್ದತ್ತ A promise.

ದತ್ತೂರ, ದತ್ತೂರಿ (*tb of* ಧತ್ತೂರ) n. The thorn-apple, *Datura alba*

ದದ್ದು 1 k n Being cracked, *as* an earthen vessel

ದದ್ದು 2. (*tb of* ದದ್ರು) n. Cutaneous eruption, h..., ..ra-h.. ringworm.

ದಧಿ s n Curds -ಫಲ Wood-apple. -ಸಾರ Butter.

ದನ (*tb of* ಧನ) n Cattle, a cow, bullock. -ಗಾಯುವವ A herdsman -ದ ಮಂದೆ, -ದ ಹಿಂಡು. A herd of cattle

ದನಿ (*tb of* ಧ್ವನಿ) n. A sound, voice -ಗೊಡು, -ಗೊಳ್ಳು To echo

ದನು s a N of Daksha's daughter and Kaśyapa's wife -ಜ. A Dânava. -ಜಮಥನ -ಜಹರ, -ಜಾರಿ Krishna

ದಂತ s n A tooth, a tusk fang. 2, an elephant's tusk ivory. 3, an elephant -ದೋಲೆ An ôlĕ of ivory. -ಧಾವನ Cleaning the teeth. -ಮೂಲ. The root of a tooth -ವಕ್ರ N of a Dânava -ಶಠ Acidity, sourness -ಶಠೆ Wood sorrel -ಹೀನ Toothless.

ದಂತಿ s a Having teeth n. An elephant. 2, the croton plant, *Croton tiglium*; *also* -ಕೆ -ಮುಖ. Ganapati

ದಂತ್ಯ s. a Dental, as a letter

ದಂದಲೆ h n Vexation, chicanery.

ದಂದುಗ k n Intricacy trouble, annoyance -ಗೊಳ್ಳು, -ಪಡೆ (-ಬಡೆ). To fall into trouble

ದಪ್ಪ k. n Thickness, stoutness, coarseness *Cpds* · -ಕ್ಕೈ, -ನೂಲು -ನೀರುಳ್ಳಿ. -ಎಲೆ, -ತುಟಿ, *etc* -ನೆ -ನ್ನ Thick, coarse

ದಫನು h n Burial

ದಫಾ, ದಫೇ h. n Time, turn. 2, a party of peons ದಫೇದಾರ. A head peon.

ದಫ್ತರ h. n. A record, register, a bundle of records. -ದಾರ A head native revenue officer of a collectorate

ದಬದಬ k n *A sound imitating the palpitation of the heart or any heavy fall.* -ಅನ್ನು To palpitate. ದಬದಬಿ A waterfall

ದಬಾದುಬಿ f. n. Unfair dealing, cheating.

ದಬಾಯಿಸು f. v. t. To force down; to menace, to slam, *as* a door.

ದಬ್ಬಣ, ದಬ್ಬಳ f. n A pack-needle.

ದಬ್ಬು (= ದೊಬ್ಬು, ತೊಬ್ಬು) k v t To push

ದಬ್ಬೆ (=ಡಬ್ಬೆ) k. n A slip, split, strip, esp of bamboo 2, (f) a blow.

ದಮ s. a Taming. n Self-restraint, subduing the passions, *also* -ನ

ದಮಡಿ (=ದಮ್ಮಡಿ) h n A kâsu, the fourth part of a duddu. 2, a small tambourine

ದಮನಕ s. n N of jackal

ದಮಯಂತಿ s. n N of Nala's wife.

ದಮಾನು h n. The large sail of a boat. *a.* Leeward.

ದಮಾಸು h. n. Damask. 2, a wooden leveller

ದಮಿತ s *a* Subdued, conquered -ಅಘ, ದಮಿತಾಘ. One whose sin is subdued.

ದಂಪತಿ s n The master of the house 2, (*dual*) man and wife -ಗಳನ್ನು ಕೂಡಿಸು To join in marriage by repeating certain formulas

ದಂಭ s n Arrogance, ostentation, pride 2, deceit, fraud, hypocrisy -ಕ Arrogant, *etc.* ದಂಭಾಚಾರ, -ಶೀಲ. Arrogant, ostentatious behaviour.

ದಮ್ಮ. *tb.* of ಧರ್ಮ, *q. v.* ದಮ್ಮಯ್ಯ. Generous master!

ದಮ್ಮಡಿ = ದಮಡಿ, *q. v*

ದಮ್ಮು h n Breath, panting; asthma -ಕಟ್ಟು, -ಹಿಡಿ To suspend one's breath, breath to be choked

ದಯೆ (*tb of* ದಯಾ) n. Sympathy, compassion, tenderness, pity, mercy, clemency, love. -ಪಾಲಿಸು To take pity on, to grant graciously -ಮಾಡು. To be kind, considerate, to grant graciously. -ವಂತ A compassionate man. ದಯಾಕಟಾಕ್ಷ. A side-glance full of mercy, kindness, *etc* ದಯಾಧಾರ. A very compassionate man. ದಯಾಗುಣ. The quality of compassion, *etc.* ದಯಾರಸ. The feeling of compassion ದಯಾಂಬುಧಿ, ದಯಾಸಮುದ್ರ, ದಯಾಬ್ಧಿ. Ocean of compassion. ದಯಾಳು, -ಳು Pitiful, merciful, kind, *etc.*

ದರ f. n Rate [illegible]

ದರಕು k n. Roughness, hoarseness.

ದರಖಾಸ್ತು h. n. An application, offer for a rent or farm

ದರಗ h. n. A Mohammadan place of worship

ದರಜಾಸ್ತಿ h n An extra tax.

ದರಜಿ (=ದರ್ಜಿ) h n A tailor.

ದರಣ (*tb. of* ಧರಣ) n The weight and value of one-fourth of a varaha. 11 anĕs 8 kâsus.

ದರದು h. n. Care, regard; need

ದರಬಾರ, ದರಬಾರು h. n A royal court, a hall of audience, a levee-room 2, the people assembled 3, government, rule 4, pomp, show

ದರಮಹಾ h. n. Monthly pay *a* Monthly

ದರವಾಜಾ h n A gate or door, a gateway.

ದರಿ s. n. A cave, a hole. 2, a valley

ದರಿಂವಿಲ್ಲಾ h *ad.* In this case, at this time, hereinafter.

ದರಿದ್ರ s. a. Poor, needy, distressed n. A poor man, *f.* -ಳು. 2, poverty, want, *also* -ತನ, -ತ್ವ

ದರಿಯಾಪ್ತಿ (=ದರ್ಯಾಫ್ತಿ) h. n Investigation

ದರುವು (*tb. of* ಧ್ರುವ) n. A song in peculiar metre

ದರುಶನ *tb of* ದರ್ಶನ, *q v.*

ದರೆ s. n. A cave. 2, barren soil. 3, a wall

ದರೋಗ h. n The chief native officer in the department of abkâri, salt, sandal, *etc.*

ದರೋಬಸ್ತು h n All without exception

ದರ್ಜೆ, ದರ್ಜೆ h n Rank, order, grade

ದರ್ಜಿ = ದರಜಿ, *q v.*

ದರ್ಪ s n. Pride, arrogance 2, boldness

ದರ್ಪಣ s n A looking-glass, mirror

ದರ್ಬಾರು = ದರಬಾರು, *q v.*

[illegible] s. [illegible] grass, *Poa cynosuroides.*

ದಯಾರ್ಪ್ತಿ. = ದರಿಯಾಪ್ತಿ, q v

ದರ್ಶ s. n Looking at, viewing, sight, view -ಕ. A spectator, an exhibitor, a savant; showing, displaying. -ಕ ಸರ್ವನಾಮ A demonstrative pronoun

ದರ್ಶನ s n Seeing 2, sight, vision, appearance, observation; perception 3, exhibition 4, a visit 5, view, theory. 6, a system of philosophy -ಕೊಡು To favour one with a visit -ತೆಗೆ, -ಮಾಡು To visit

ದರ್ಶಿ s n Seeing, showing; a seer, spectator, f -ನಿ -ತ Seen, shown, apparent -ಸು To see

ದಲ್ a. k ad Certainly, to be sure, indeed

ದಲಿ = ದಳ3, q v

ದಲನ s n Splitting, breaking to pieces, bursting

ದಲಾಲಿ, ದಲ್ಲಾಳಿ h n Brokerage, commission. 2, a broker -ತನ A broker's business

ದವ s n Fire 2, a wood on fire 3, a forest conflagration, also ದವಾನಲ

ದವಡು. = ದವುಡು, q v

ದವಡೆ k n. The jaw bone, mandible. -ಹಲ್ಲು The molars

ದವತಿ, ದವುತಿ, ದೌತಿ h n An inkstand

ದವನ (tb of ದಮನ) n The plant *Artemisia indica* and its flower

ದವಸ (tb of ಯವಸ) n Corn, grain. -ಧಾನ್ಯ rett

ದವಳ s n A conch-shell used for blowing 2, tb of ಧವಳ, q. v

ದವಾ h n Medicine. -ಖಾನೆ A medicine-shop, dispensary

ದವಾಲಿ = ದವಾಳಿ, q v.

ದವುಡು (= ದವಡು, ದಾಡು) h. n A race, run 2, a military excursion, expedition

ದಶ s a Ten. -ಕ Tenfold, a decade -ಕಂಠ, -ಗ್ರೀವ -ಮುಖ, -ವದನ, -ಶಿರ Râvana. -ಗುಣ Tenfold, penalty for not affixing a stamp to an official document -ದಾನ . . , ti . . w , land . . mum gold ghee, raiment, betel, grain jaggory, daughters in marriage -ದಿಕ್ಕು The eight points of the compass and the earth and sky -ಮ Tenth -ಮಾಂಶ Decimal. -ಮಿ The tenth lunar day -ರಥ. N of Râma's father ದಶಾಂಶ. Ten parts, the tenth part ದಶಾಂಗ Ten members, an incense composed of ten ingredients ದಶಾವತಾರ The ten incarnations of Vishnu ದಶೇಂದ್ರಿಯ The ten organs of perception and action.

ದಶೆ s n The skirt, edge or hem of a garment, the wick of a lamp 2, age, period 3, state or condition of life 4, fate ದಶಾವಂತ A fortunate man ದಶಾಹೀನ An unfortunate man.

ದಸಕತ್ತು h n. Hand-writing, signature

ದಸಕು k. n A thin dust-like coating on certain grains, as jôla, rági, etc, a kind of husk

ದಸನು e n A dozen, 12 pieces, also ಡಜನು

ದಸಮಾಹೆ s n. Ten months' pay given for twelve

ದಸರ, ದಸರೆ (tb. of ದಶರಾತ್ರಿ) n The tenth day of the śuklapaksha of the seventh month (âśvina), the last day of the navarâtri, also -ಹಬ್ಬ

ದಸಿ k n A stake, a wooden peg

ದಸಿ. tb of ದಶೆ, q v.

ದಸ್ಕತ್ತು. = ದಸಕತ್ತು. q v

ದಸ್ತಾವೇಜು, ದಸ್ತೈವಜು h n A document, a bond.

ದಸ್ತು h n A quire of paper 2, a pack of 3 cards 3 money withheld by government to an official

ದಸ್ತೂರಿ h n Custom, fashion 2, customary fees, postage, tax

ದಹನ s n. Consuming by fire, burning 2, fire, Agni -ಸಂಸ್ಕಾರ The rites of cremation ದಹಿಸು To burn up

ದಳ1 (ಳ = ಲ) a k. n An army contain- . . . . and

chariots -ಪತಿ, -ಮುಖ್ಯ, -ನಾಯಿ A general -ಮುಖ The van of an army.

ದಳ 2. f. n Thickness, solidity. -ಸರ. Thickness, compactness

ದಳ 3 (=ದಲ) f. n A leaf, petal. 2, a part, fragment

ದಳಾಳಿ. = ದಲಾಲಿ, q v

ದಳೆ k v t To seam v i To become abundant, as fruits etc, to spread, as small-pox, etc

ದಾಕ್ತರು e n A doctor, European physician

ದಾಕ್ಷಾಯಣಿ s n N of any of the daughters of Daksha -ಪುತ್ರ Ganêśa.

ದಾಕ್ಷಿಣ್ಯ (fr. ದಕ್ಷಿಣಾ) s n Civility, courtesy, politeness, honesty, candour, obsequiousness -ಗಾರ, -ವಂತ, -ಶಾಲಿ An obsequious man

ದಾಖಲಾತು h n. Proof, documentary evidence

ದಾಖಲು h. a Entered, as into an account, etc. n Entry of an item in an account or register -ಮಾಡು To enter as a name into a register, etc.

ದಾಗಡಿಬಳ್ಳಿ k. n A winding half shrubby plant, Cocculus villosus

ದಾಗಿನ h. n. Jewels worn on the body, personal property.

ದಾಗುಜೂಜಿ h n Repairing, doing up.

ದಾಟಿಸು k v. t To make cross, etc

ದಾಟು k v t. To cross, ford, to pass, to go beyond, to escape v i To die, to expire or pass away, elapse, as time n Stepping, passing over, etc. -ಕಥೆ A summary. -ಕಾಲು. A far-stepping foot. -ಹೊಲಿಗೆ. Sewing with long stitches

ದಾಡಿ h. n The beard

ದಾಡಿಮ, ದಾಡಿಂಬ s n. The pomegranate tree and its fruit, Punica granatum.

ದಾಡೆ (tb of ದಂಷ್ಟ್ರ) n A tusk, a fang, a molar. 2, a jawbone

ದಾನ (tb of ಧಾನ್ಯ) n Grain. 2, (= ದಾವಣಿ) a rope

ದಾಣಾ f n Thickness, stoutness -ದಡಿ. A very stout man, cf. ದಾಂಡಿಗ

ದಾಂಟು = ದಾಟು, q v.

ದಾಂಡಿಗ f n A stout, strong man. -ತನ. Rudeness

ದಾತ, ದಾತಾರ tb of ದಾತೃ, q. v.

ದಾತೃ s. n A giver, donor -ತ್ವ Liberality

ದಾದ (tb of ತಾತ, q v) n A respectful term of address for an elderly man.

ದಾದಿ (tb of ಧಾತ್ರಿ) n A nurse

ದಾನ s n Giving, a gift, present, donation -ಈಯು, -ಮಾಡು. To make gifts, etc -ಗುಣ A liberal disposition -ತೆ Liberality. -ಧರ್ಮ. Almsgiving, charitable acts -ಪತ್ರ, -ಶಾಸನ A deed of gift -ಪಾತ್ರ A presented vessel, an object of charity -ವಸ್ತ್ರ. A presented cloth -ಶೀಲ, -ಶೂರ A generous person.

ದಾನವ s. n Danu's descendant, a giant.

ದಾನಿ s. n A donor.

ದಾಂತ s a Subdued, enduring. 2, ending in ದ. ದಾಂತಿ Self-restraint

ದಾಂದಲೆ = ದಂದಲೆ, q. v.

ದಾಪು k. n Stretch, etc, the measure of a stride -ಹಾಕು To measure by strides.

ದಾಬಣಿಕಾರಿ f. n. A certain border of a cloth.

ದಾಬು = ಡಾಬು 1, 2, q v

ದಾಮ (= ಡಾಬು 1, q. v) s. n. A string, cord, thread 2, a girdle. 3, a chaplet, wreath for the forehead. -ನಿ. = ದಾವಣಿ.

ದಾಮಾಷಾ h. n Proportionate distribution, equitable allotment, dividends.

ದಾಮೋದರ s a. Having a cord round the belly. n. Krishna

ದಾಂಭಿಕ (fr ದಂಭ) s a. Deceitful; ostentatious. proud n Ostentatiousness; also ದಾಂಭಿಕ.

ದಾಯ s n A gift, present. 2, a part, partition. 3, share, inheritance, patrimony. 4, property. 5. a throw of dice 6, an opportunity, fit moment, a means -ಕ A giver, heir, kinsman. -ವಿಭಾಗ. A portion of inheritance

ದಾಯಾದಿ (*tb of* ದಾಯಾದ್ಯ) *n* A descendant from a male stock

ದಾಯಿ (*tb. of* ಧಾತ್ರಿ) *n* A wet nurse. 2, (s) giving granting

ದಾಯಿಗ (*tb. of* ದಾಯಕ) *n* A remote kinsman. 2, = ದಾಯಾದಿ.

ದಾರ 1 s *n* A rent, cleft, hole 2, a wife -ಕ. A child

ದಾರ 2 *tb. of* ದ್ವಾರ, *q v*

ದಾರ 3 (*tb. of* ಧಾರ) *n* A string, thread 2, (*aff*) holder, possessor, *as* ಅಮಲ-, ದಾವಾ-, *etc*

ದಾರಣೆ f *n* Rate, market price

ದಾರಬಂದ, ದಾರವಂದ (*tb. of* ದ್ವಾರಬಂಧ) *n.* A doorframe 2 the panel of a door.

ದಾರಿ k. *n* A way, road, path -ಕಟ್ಟು. To block up a way. -ಕೊಡು To let pass. -ಗೊಳ್ಳು To start, to make a way for one's self, *as* water -ನಡೆ. To go on foot, to travel. -ನೋಡು. To look out for, wait for -ಬಿಡು To go out of the way -ಹೋಕ. A stroller -ಕಾರ, -ಗ A traveller

ದಾರಿದ್ರ, ದಾರಿದ್ರ್ಯ s *n* Poverty, indigence distress

ದಾರು s *n.* A piece of wood, timber. 2, = ದೇವದಾರು -ಹಸ್ತ, -ಹಸ್ತಕ. A wooden spoon or ladle.

ದಾರುಣ s *a* Cruel, horrible, hard rough *n* Cruelty, horror

ದಾರೆ 1, -ಹುಳಿ k *n* The fruit of *Averrhoa carambola*

ದಾರೆ 2. *tb of* ಧಾರೆ, *q. v.*

ದಾರ್ಢ್ಯ s *n* Stability, strength, energy.

ದಾಲಚಿನ್ನಿ, ದಾಲ್ಚಿನಿ f. *n* Cinnamon

ದಾಲು h *n* Split pulse, dhâl.

ದಾವ 1. = ಯಾವ, *q v*

ದಾವ 2 (= ದವ) s *n* A forest conflagration, *also* ದಾವಾಗ್ನಿ, ದಾವಾನಲ 2, a forest.

ದಾವಣಿ (*tb of* ದಾಮನಿ) *n* A rope for tying cattle

ದಾವತಿ f *n* Labour, toil, exertion, trouble -ಗೊಳ್ಳು, -ಪಡು. To toil, *etc.* -ಪಡಿಸು To give trouble. -ಮಾಡು. To take pains.

ದಾವರ f *n* Thirst, desire, need, want; *also* ದಾವು.

ದಾವಾ, ದಾವೆ (= ದಾವು) h *n.* Enmity, spite, a suit. complaint -ಸೊತ್ತು Property in litigation -ದಾರ A prosecutor; complainant, plaintiff

ದಾಶ s. *n* A fisherman 2, a servant.

ದಾಶರಥಿ (*fr.* ದಶರಥ) s *n* Râma

ದಾಷ್ಟೀಕ (*tb of* ಧಾರ್ಷ್ಟಿಕ) *n.* A bold and influential man, boldness -ತನ Boldness

ದಾಸ s *n* A male servant, slave, a devotee *f.* ದಾಸಿ -ಗೆಲಸ Servile work. -ಭಾವ. The attitude of a slave -ಯ್ಯ. A (Vaishnava) devotee, *f* -ಗಿತ್ತಿ ದಾಸರ ಪದಗಳು Songs composed by Vaishnava devotees -ತ್ವ. Servitude, slavery.

ದಾಸಾಳ, ದಾಸವಾಳ, ದಾಸವಾಳ, *etc* f *n* The shoe-flower or China rose, *Hibiscus rosa sinensis*

ದಾಸರ, ದಾಸರಿ (*tb of* ದಾಸೇರ) *n* A Vaishnava religious mendicant. -ಹಾವು The boa.

ದಾಸೊಳ = ದಾಸಣ, *q v*

ದಾಸಿ s. *n* A female servant or slave

ದಾಸೋಹ (*fr* ದಾಸಃ ಅಹಂ I am a servant) s *n* Self-subjection, devotion

ದಾಸ್ತಾನ (*cf* ತೆಗೆಸ್ತಾನು) h *n.* A deposit, reserve, stock.

ದಾಹ s *n* Burning, internal heat 2, ardent desire 3, thirst -ಗೊಳ್ಳು To become thirsty -ನಿವಾರಣೆ, -ಶಮನ, -ಶಾಂತಿ Quenching desire or thirst

ದಾಳಾ, ದಾಳಿ (ಳ = ಟ *tb of* ಧಾಟಿ) *n* An impetuous assault, an attack, a rush; an inroad. -ಇಡು To make an assault; to rush up to ದಾಳಾದಾಳಿ.

ದಾಳಿಂಬ, ದಾಳಿಂಬೆ, *etc* (*tb. of* ದಾಡಿಮ, *q v*) *n* A pomegiannate

ದಿಕ್ಕು (*tb of* ದಿಶ್) *n* A point of the compass, direction. 2, refuge, protection, help -ದಿಕ್ಕಿಗೆ In every direction ದಿಕ್ಕಿಲ್ಲದೆ Refuge, *etc*, not existing ದಿಕ್ಕಿಲ್ಲದವ A helpless man ದಿಕ್ಕಾಪಾಲು. Dispersion in all directions, ruined condition -ಚಕ್ರ, ದಿಕ್ಚಕ್ರ The horizon, a mariner's compass.

ದಿಕ್ಪಾಲ, -ಕ s. *n* The regent or guardian of one of the quarters of the world.

ದಿಗಂತ s *n* The visible horizon

ದಿಗಂಬರ s *a* Sky-clothed, unclad naked *n*. A naked mendicant.

ದಿಗರು h *ad* Also, additionally *a*. Another. -ಜವಾಬು. Another or contradictory answer.

ದಿಗಿಲು k *n* Consternation, horror, alarm, fear.

ದಿಗಿಸು a. k. *v t* To let down, lower.

ದಿಗುಲು = ದಿಗಿಲು *q v*

ದಿಗ್ಗಜ s *n* An elephant of one of the eight quarters of the compass.

ದಿಗ್ಗನೆ k. *ad* Suddenly, all at once.

ದಿಗ್ದೇಶ s. *n*. Various regions, distant countries

ದಿಗ್ಬಂಧನ s. *n*. A general charm to keep off all evils

ದಿಗ್ಬಲಿ s *n* An offering to the regions of the sky

ದಿಗ್ಭ್ರಮೆ, ದಿಗ್ಭ್ರಾಂತಿ s. *n*. Consternation

ದಿಗ್ರೀ e *n*. Degree *n* Division or interval marked on a thermometer or barometer, *also* ಡಿಗ್ರೀ

ದಿಗ್ವಾಚಕ s *n*. A term denoting direction

ದಿಗ್ವಿಜಯ s *n* Universal conquest

ದಿಂಕು a. k. *n* A jump, leap. 2, gambol ದಿಂಕಿಸು To leap, jump.

ದಿಟ (*tb of* ದಿಷ್ಟ) *n* Truth. *ad* Certainly truly -ಪುಟ Courage, stout, robust -ಮಾತು. A true word

ದಿಟ್ಟ (*tb. of* ಧೃಷ್ಟ) *a* Bold, courageous, strong powerful -ಗಾರ A bold man. -ತನ Boldness

ದಿಟ್ಟಿ. *tb. of* ದೃಷ್ಟಿ, *q v* -ಕೊನೆ, -ಗೊನೆ A side-glance -ಗೊಳಿಸು To appear. -ಸು To see, to look at

ದಿಡ (*tb. of* ದೃಢ) *a* Firm, strong, *etc* *n* Firmness, strength.

ದಿಡ್ಡಿ f *n* A wicket, a sally-post, *also* -ಬಾಗಲು

ದಿಣ್ಣು k. *n* An eminence, a hillock

ದಿಂಡಿಗ k *n*. The tree *Anogeissus latifolia*, which yields a hard, white gum

ದಿಂಡು k *n*. A heap, a big stone, a bundle of wood or grass, a bale of cloth 2, the handle of a plough; a log. 3, the trunk of a tree 4, the centre of an orange, the core of a plantain tree. 5 thickness, strength pride, nutritiousness. -ಕ A stout man -ಕೈ A stout arm -ಮೈಯ್ಯಿ A stout, strong body -ಗೊಳ್ಳು, -ಪಡು, -ಬೀಳು. To become stout

ದಿಣ್ಣೆ (= ದಿನ್ನೆ, *q v*) k. *n* An eminence, a bank.

ದಿತಿ s. *n* N of a daughter of Daksha, wife of Kaśyapa

ದಿನ s *n* A day -ಗಟ್ಲೆ. Daily -ಕಳೆ, -ಗಳೆ To spend a day. -ಕೂಲಿ. Daily hire -ದಂತೆ, -ದ ಹಾಗೆ As usual -ದಿನ *rep*. Daily. -ದಿನಕ್ಕೆ Day by day, daily. -ಚರ್ಯೆ The daily observance of rites, an official journal -ಕರ, -ನಾಥ, -ಪ The sun. -ಪ್ರತಿ = ದಿನಂಪ್ರತಿ -ಮಾನ The length of a day ದಿನಂಪ್ರತಿ Daily -ವಹಿ A diary, day-book. -ವರ್ತಮಾನ, -ವಾರ್ತೆ, -ಸುದ್ದಿ Daily news.

ದಿನಸಿ (= ಜಿನಸು) f *n* Grain, *also* ದಿನಸು, ದಿನುಸು.

ದಿನಾ s *ad* Daily, *also* -ಗ, -ಗಲು, -ಲು

ದಿಬ್ಬ k *n* An eminence, a hillock, *cf* ದಿಣ್ಣೆ

ದಿನ್ನೆ = ದಿಣ್ಣೆ, *q. v* -ತಗ್ಗು. Hill and dale.

ದಿಬ್ಬಣ k *n* A nuptial procession 2, a wooden stopple

ದಿಮಾಕು h *n*. Haughtiness, inflation, arrogance pride

ದಿಂಬು k. n. A pillow for the head, *also* ತಲೆ- 2, the pericarp of a lotus.

ದಿಮ್ಮಗೆ, ದಿಮ್ಮನೆ k *ad* Strongly, loudly

ದಿಮ್ಮಿ k n. A log of wood 2, a bulb

ದಿಮ್ಮು 1 k n Giddiness. -ಹತ್ತು, -ಏರು Giddiness to come over one.

ದಿಮ್ಮು 2 k. v t To push, shove

ದಿವ s n. Heaven; the sky, air 2, day, a day -ರಾತ್ರಿ. Day and night.

ದಿವಸ (= ದಿನ, q v) s n A day -ಕಳೆ. = ದಿನಗಳೆ, q v -ಕ್ಕೆ ಹಾಕು To procrastinate -ದಿವಸ *rep* = ದಿನ ದಿನ. -ಹತ್ತು, -ಹಿಡಿ Days to be required (it takes ... days) -ವ್ಯಾಪಾರ = ದಿನಚರ್ಯೆ, q v

ದಿವಾಕರ s. n The sun.

ದಿವಾಣ, ದಿವಾನ h n A minister or chief officer of state 2, a royal hall, a court of justice 3, the sarkâr, *also* ದಿವಾನು

ದಿವಾನಾ h a Mad, foolish

ದಿವಾಭೀತಿ s n A person timid by day 2, an owl; a thief

ದಿವಾರಾತ್ರ, ದಿವಾರಾತ್ರಿ s. n Day and night

ದಿವಾಳಿ 1 *tb of* ದೀಪಾವಳಿ q v

ದಿವಾಳಿ 2 f n Bankruptcy -ಎತ್ತಿ ಹೋಗು, -ತೆಗೆ. To become bankrupt -ಕೋರ. A spendthrift, a bankrupt

ದಿವಿ s n Heavens, the sky 2, a day -ಜ A deity -ಜಪದ Svarga. -ನಾಯಕ Indra.

ದಿವ್ಯ s. a Divine heavenly, charming, beautiful -ಕಳೆ Divine lustre.

ದಿಶ್. = ದಿಕ್ಕು, q v ದಿಶಾಧಿಪ = ದಿಕ್ಪಾಲ The guardians are surarâja, agni, kâla, niruti, varuna, maruta, aithêsa, îsa

ದಿಶ, ದಿಶೆ s n A quarter or point of the compass, direction, region

ದಿಷ್ಟ s a Appointed, ordered, fixed *n.* Assignment, decree, fate, aim.

ದಿಷ್ಟಿ (*tb. of* ದೃಷ್ಟಿ, q v) n The eye, sight

ದೀಕ್ಷೆ s. n Preparation or consecration for a r . . . . dedication devotion, e. g ಪಿತೃ-, ಮಾತೃ-, ವಿವಾಹ-, ಶೈವ-, *etc.* ದೀಕ್ಷಿತ. Initiated, consecrated; a conductor of a sacrifice; a family N.

ದೀಟು k n Similarity, equality. 2, valuation -ಆಗಿರು, -ಗೊಳ್ಳು, -ಪಡು, -ಬೀಳು. To be equal

ದೀನ s. a Afflicted, miserable 2, dejected, downcast 3, poor, indigent 4, humble -ಗುಣ A humble disposition -ತನ, -ತೆ, -ತ್ವ, -ಭಾವ Humility ದೀನೋದ್ಧಾರಿ. A deliverer of the humble

ದೀಪ s n A lamp, a light. (2, *tb of* ದ್ವೀಪ -ದ್ರಾಕ್ಷೆ. Imported raisins) -ಕಚ್ಚು = -ಹಚ್ಚು. -ಆರಿಸು, -ಕಂತಿಸು -ಕಳೆ, -ತೆಗೆ, -ದೊತ್ತದು ಮಾಡು (*superstition*) To extinguish a lamp. -ದ ಕಡ್ಡಿ A match. -ಹಚ್ಚು. To light a lamp. -ಕಂಬ. = -ಸ್ತಂಭ, q. v -ದ ಮಲ್ಲಿ. A female image with a lamp-cup -ದರ್ಶನ Looking upon a lamp as in an adoring attitude -ಸ್ತಂಭ A lampstand. ದೀಪಾರತಿ A kind of lighted âratı ದೀಪಾವಳಿ (= ದಿವಾಳಿ, q v) A festival with nocturnal illuminations; *also* ದೀಪೋತ್ಸವ

ದೀಪ್ತ s a. Illuminated, bright. ದೀಪ್ತಿ. Brilliancy, light, lustre; a ray, flash

ದೀರ್ಘ s a Long (*as* space or time) 2, long, *as* a vowel -ಕಾಲ. A long time -ಕೋಶಿ. A cockle -ತೆ. Length, longness -ದರ್ಶಿ Seeing far wise, a seer -ದೃಷ್ಟಿ Far-seeing, far-sighted, shrewd, a sagacious man. -ದ್ವೇಷ. An old grudge. -ನಿದ್ರೆ, -ಶಯನ Death. -ರೋಗ A long illness -ಶಾಂತಿ Long-suffering, patience ದೀರ್ಘಾಯು, ದೀರ್ಘಾಯುಷ್ಯ Long life

ದೀವಟಿ, ದೀವಟಿಗೆ (*tb. of* ದೀಪವರ್ತಿಕ) n A torch, flambeau -ಗ, -ಯವ A torch-bearer -ಸಲಾಮು An honouring ceremony performed every evening by waving lighted torches before a noble personage or an idol.

ದೀವಿ *tb of* ದ್ವೀಪ, *q v.* -ಹಲಸು The breadfruit tree, *Artocarpus incisa*

ದೀವಿಗೆ (*tb of* ದೀಪಿಕೆ) *n.* A lamp 2, brightness, brilliancy.

ದು k. *A termination of the p. p, as* ಕುಡಿದು, ತಂದು, ನಡೆದು ನೆನೆದು, ಕೊಂದು, *etc.* 2, *tb of* ದ್ವಿ.

ದುಃ s. *pref* Evil, bad, difficult, hard.

ದುಃಖ s *n.* Unhappiness, pain, sorrow, grief, affliction, distress, misery; trouble, difficulty -ಕೊಡು To give trouble -ಗೊಳ್ಳು, -ಪಡು To be grieved, *etc.* -ಪಡಿಸು To cause trouble, *etc* -ಮಾಡು To feel unhappy; to grieve, *etc* -ಕರ Causing pain, sorrow, *etc.* -ಜೀವಿ. Living in pain or distress -ಶಮನ -ಶಾಂತಿ Allaying or cessation of pain grief, *etc*

ದುಃಖಿ s *n* Sorrowing, afflicted -ತ. Pained, distressed -ಸು To be unhappy, to grieve.

ದುಃಶಬ್ದ s. *n.* A bad sound or word

ದುಃಶೀಲ s *a.* Badly disposed, ill-natured, reprobate

ದುಃಸ್ಥಿತಿ s. *n.* Ill condition, unhappiness.

ದುಕಾನು h. *n* A shop -ದಾರ A shopkeeper

ದುಕೂಲ s. *n.* Woven silk, very fine cloth

ದುಗತ, ದುಗುಡ (*tb of* ದುರ್ಗ್ರಹ) *n.* Grief, care, anxiety uneasiness.

ದುಗ್ಗ. *tb. of* ದುರ್ಗ, *q v.*

ದುಗ್ಗಾಣಿ (*fr* ದು-ಕಾಣಿ) s *n* Two kâṇis, two kâsus

ದುಗ್ಧ s. *n.* Milk, sap ದುಗ್ಧಾಭಿಷೇಕ. Bathing with milk ದುಗ್ಧಾಬ್ಧಿ. The sea of milk

ದುಗ್ಧಿಕೆ s *n* A sort of *Asclepias* 2, a kind of gourd

ದುಗ್ಧೆ (*tb. of* ದುರ್ಗ್ರಹ) *n* Doubt, suspense 2, ill will; envy

ದುಡಕು = ದುಡುಕು, *q v*

ದುಡಿ k *v i* To labour, work, toil 2, to throb and pain, *as* a boil. *v. t.* To acquire by one's labour -ತ -ಸು. Acquisition, gain -ಮೆಗಾರ. An economist -ಸು. To cause to labour

ದುಡುಕು k. *v i.* To act rashly, violently or wickedly. *n* Rashness insolence, *also* -ತನ -ಬುದ್ಧಿ A rash mind

ದುತುಮ್ k *A sound of suddenly falling.* -ಪ್ರವೇಶ. Entering headlong upon a work -ನೆ. Suddenly.

ದುದುಮೆ = ದುಡಿಮೆ, *see* ದುಡಿ -ಗಾರ. An economist

ದುಡ್ಡು k. *n* A copper coin, ¼ of an Ana 2, money ದುಡ್ಡಾಸೆ Covetousness

ದುಂಟು k *n* Rocking, unevenness ದುಂಟಾಡು To rock, to be uneven, *as* a table, *etc*

ದುಂಡಗೆ, ದುಂಡಿಗೆ k *ad.* Roundly *a.* Round *n.* Roundness, *also* ದುಂಡನೆ, ದುಂಡನ್ನ, ದುಂಡಾನೆ.

ದುಂಡಿಗು k *n* A shrub from Brazil, used for hedges, *Jatropha curcas.*

ದುಂಡು k *n* Roundness. 2, a plain bracelet. ದುಂಡಿಸು To round, move circularly

ದುತ್ತಾರಿ h *n* Worked muslin

ದುತ್ತೂರ, -ರಿ (*tb of* ಧುಸ್ತೂರ, *q v.*) *n.* The thorn-apple

ದುದ್ದು k *n* The pulpy mass of a cucumber or pumpkin which contains the seeds

ದುಂದು k *n* Excessive expenditure, waste, prodigality ದುಂದವೃತ್ತನ A sumptuous dinner without occasion -ಮಾಡು To squander -ಗಾರ A spendthrift, prodigal. -ಗಾರತನ, -ಗಾರಿಕೆ Spendthriftness, prodigality

ದುಂದುಭಿ s. *n* The fifty-sixth year of the cycle. 2, a large kettle-drum.

ದುಪಟಿ, ದುಪ್ಪಟಿ, ದುಪ್ಪಟಿ (*tb of* ದ್ವಿಪಟ್ಟಿಕಾ) *n* A double cloth, a sheet.

ದುಬಾರಿ h. *a* Double, excessive -ಖರ್ಚು. Double expense -ಪ್ರತಿ A duplicate. -ತನ Prodigality

ದುಬಾಸಿ (*tb of* ದ್ವಿಭಾಷಿ) *n* An interpreter.

ದುಬ್ಬ .. *n* A very stout man, *f.* ದು..

ದುಮುಕು, ದುಮ್ಮಿಕ್ಕು k v.i To leap or jump down.

ದುಂಬು k. n Dust.

ದುಮ್ಮಾನ (tb. of ದುರ್ಮಾನ) n Distress, sorrow, grief

ದುಯಮ್ h. a Secondary subordinate.

ದುರ್, ದುಃ, ದುಷ್, ದುಸ್ (=ದುಃ) s pref Evil, bad, difficult, hard, etc

ದುರ a k n. A battle, war.

ದುರಂಗಿ (tb of ದ್ವಿರಂಗ) a. Double coloured, as cloth

ದುರಂಜಿ f. n. The custard-apple, *Anona squamosa*.

ದುರದೃಷ್ಟ s n Bad luck, misfortune.

ದುರಬೀನು h n A telescope

ದುರಭಿಪ್ರಾಯ s. n An evil intention

ದುರಭಿಮಾನ s. n. Offensive pride presumption ದುರಭಿಮಾನಿ Disagreeably proud

ದುರಭ್ಯಾಸ s n A bad practice or habit.

ದುರವಸ್ಥೆ s n A miserable condition, a bad situation

ದುರಸ್ತು (=ದುರುಸ್ತು) h a Right, fit, in good order. -ಮಾಡು To repair

ದುರಹಂಕಾರ s n. Offensive egotism, presumption

ದುರಾಗ್ರಹ s n Foolish obstinacy ದುರಾಗ್ರಹಿ. A head-strong person

ದುರಾಚರಣೆ s. n Bad behaviour, evil practices

ದುರಾಚಾರ s n Bad conduct, wickedness ದುರಾಚಾರಿ Loose, licentious.

ದುರಾತ್ಮ s n. A malevolent person; a rascal, scoundrel, f ದುರಾತ್ಮಿಕೆ.

ದುರಾಲಭ s a Difficult of attainment

ದುರಾಲೋಚನೆ s. a A bad thought or intention

ದುರಾಶೆ s n Bad hope or desire 2, groundless hope -ಗಾರ. A man of bad desire

ದುರಿಚ್ಛೆ s n. Bad desire

ದುರಿತ s. n Evil ways sin -ಹರ Removing sin.

ದುರೀಷಣೆ ' ' ' ,

ದುರುಕ್ತಿ s. n. Harsh, offensive speech, abuse.

ದುರುಸ್ತು.=ದುರಸ್ತು q v

ದುರುಳ (tb of ಧೂರ್ತ) n A cunning, dishonest or wicked man, f ದುರುಳೆ -ತನ Wickedness

ದುರ್ಗ (=ದುಗ್ಗ) s a. Difficult of access. n A stronghold, fort 2, a forest.

ದುರ್ಗತ s a Unfortunate, distressed, poor. ದುರ್ಗತಿ Ill condition, misfortune, misery, hell

ದುರ್ಗಂಧ s n. A bad smell, stink.

ದುರ್ಗಮ s. a. Difficult of access or attainment.

ದುರ್ಗಾಷ್ಟಮಿ s. n The eighth lunar day of the month of Âsvina, the birthday of Durgâ

ದುರ್ಗಿ.=ದುರ್ಗೆ, q. v. -ಬೇನೆ. Cholera

ದುರ್ಗುಣ s a An evil quality; a vicious propensity

ದುರ್ಗೆ ದುರ್ಗಾ s. n Daughter of Himavat and wife of Śiva

ದುರ್ಘಟ s. a Difficult, unattainable

ದುರ್ಜನ s n A bad man, a mischievous man, villain.

ದುರ್ಜಯ s a Invincible

ದುರ್ದರ್ಶ s a. Disagreeable to the sight, disgusting

ದುರ್ದಶೆ s n A bad situation, misfortune, calamity, *also* ದುರ್ದೆಸೆ

ದುರ್ದಿನ s. n. A dark, cloudy day, bad weather.

ದುರ್ದೈವ s n Hard fate, bad luck, unlucky destiny; misfortune, *also* -ಯೋಗ 2, a bad deity

ದುರ್ಧರ s a Difficult to be borne or suffered, irresistible, difficult, impracticable, dangerous.

ದುರ್ಧರ್ಷ s a Difficult of being assailed, inviolable; intolerable

ದುರ್ನಡತೆ s.-k. n Bad conduct.

ದುರ್ನಾಮ s. n. A bad name, piles.

ದುರ್ನಿಮಿತ್ತ s n. A bad omen. 2. a foul

] ' '

ದುರ್ನೀತಿ s n Bad conduct, impropriety, bad ethics

ದುರ್ನೆವ (tb. of ದುರ್ನಿಘ) n A bad excuse, poor pretence.

ದುರ್ಬಗೆ s -k. n Evil intention, wicked resolve.

ದುರ್ಬಲ s a Weak, feeble

ದುರ್ಬೀನು = ದುರಬೀನು, q v.

ದುರ್ಬುದ್ಧಿ s. n. Folly, silliness. 2, evil-mindedness

ದುರ್ಬೋಧನೆ, ದುರ್ಬೋಧೆ s. n. Evil counsel, bad, harmful teaching

ದುರ್ಭಯ s. n. Fear or painful apprehension of evil.

ದುರ್ಭರ s a Burdensome, intolerable

ದುರ್ಭಾಗ್ಯ s n Ill luck, lucklessness

ದುರ್ಭಾವ s n. Ill will, hostile feeling, hatred.

ದುರ್ಭಾಷಣೆ, ದುರ್ಭಾಷೆ s. n Bad, abusive speech, opprobrious language

ದುರ್ಭಿಕ್ಷ s n Scarcity of provisions dearth, famine. -ಬೀಳು A famine *etc* to come to pass

ದುರ್ಮತ s n A bad opinion, doctrine, or tenet

ದುರ್ಮತಿ s n. Evil-mindedness, malignity, foolishness. 2, the fifty-fifth year of the cycle

ದುರ್ಮನ, -ಸ್ಸು s n A bad disposition, evil mind. 2, bad advice.

ದುರ್ಮರಣ s. n. Any violent or unnatural death

ದುರ್ಮಾಂಸ s n Proud flesh that grows in a sore or wound

ದುರ್ಮಾರ್ಗ s. n Misconduct, offence, wickedness; *also* -ತನ. 2, a bad man

ದುರ್ಮುಖಿ s n The thirtieth year of the cycle of sixty

ದುರ್ಮೋಹ s n Bewildered, infatuated or enamoured state 2, ignorance, folly

ದುರ್ಯಶ s n. Ill repute, dishonour.

ದುರ್ಯೋಧನ s. n. N of the eldest son of Dhṛitarâshtra.

ದುರ್ಲಕ್ಷಣ s n A bad sign or symptom; a bad character, a vice.

ದುರ್ಲಕ್ಷ್ಯ s a Difficult to be observed; disagreeable to sight. n Inadvertence.

ದುರ್ಲಭ s a Difficult to be obtained; scarce, rare, excellent; dear

ದುರ್ವಚನ s. n A harsh expression, abusive language, insult.

ದುರ್ವಾಕ್ s n Evil speech, inelegant language.

ದುರ್ವಾರ s. a. Difficult to be repressed, irresistible

ದುರ್ವಾರ್ತೆ s. n Bad news, sad intelligence.

ದುರ್ವಾಸ, -ಸ್ಸು s n N of a ṛishi a. Unclothed

ದುರ್ವಾಸನೆ s. n. Bad smell, stink. 2, an evil recollection of past actions

ದುರ್ವಿದಗ್ಧ s. a Unskilled, stupid, wholly ignorant.

ದುರ್ವಿನೀತ s. a. Ill-trained, ill-mannered; stubborn

ದುರ್ವಿವಾದ s n A bad contest at law

ದುರ್ವಿಷಯ s. n A bad thing or affair

ದುರ್ವೃತ್ತ s n Bad conduct, mean practices a Vile, wicked.

ದುರ್ವೃತ್ತಿ s n Disreputable conduct. bad practices

ದುರ್ವ್ಯಯ s n Useless expense.

ದುರ್ವ್ಯಸನ s n An evil habit, bad desire. ದುರ್ವ್ಯಸನಿ. A man of evil habits; f ದುರ್ವ್ಯಸನೆ

ದುರ್ವ್ಯಾಪಾರ s n Evil action or operation.

ದುವ್ವಾಳಿ f n. Rapid course, a run -ಸು To make run

ದುಶ್. = ದುರ್, q v

ದುಶ್ಚಾಲಿ s. n A wicked, impious or immoral conduct -ತನ Wickedness, iniquity, immorality.

ದುಶ್ಚಿಹ್ನೆ s. n An inauspicious sign, an ill omen

ದುಶ್ಚೇಷ್ಟೆ s n Naughtiness

ದುಶ್ಶಕುನ s n. A bad omen

ದುಶ್ಶಾಲು s-f n Two shawls, a double shawl

ದುಶ್ಶಾಸನ (=ದುಃಶಾಸನ) s a Intractable. n N of a son of Dhritarâshtra

ದುಷ್ಕರ್ಮ s n An evil act, crime ದುಷ್ಕರ್ಮಿ. Sinful, wicked

ದುಷ್ಕಾಮ s. n. Inordinate passion, lust vice

ದುಷ್ಕಾಲ s n An evil time on account of sin, famine, *etc.*

ದುಷ್ಕೃತ್ಯ s n A misdeed, sin, crime

ದುಷ್ಟ s a. Corrupt bad, wicked, vicious depraved, noxious -ಗುಣ A wicked disposition -ತನ. Wickedness. -ಬುದ್ಧಿ Evil-minded; an evil mind, a N -ಮೃಗ A wild beast ದುಷ್ಟಾತ್ಮ Of a bad nature, wicked, an evil spirit

ದುಷ್ಪ್ರಯೋಗ s. n. Bad use, useless purpose, foul aim.

ದುಷ್ಫಲ s. n A bad fruit or result

ದುಸ್ = ದುರ್, *q. v*

ದುಸರಿಬಳ್ಳಿ n. A winding half shrubby plant, *Cocculus villosus*

ದುಸ್ತರ s a. Impassable, invincible

ದುಸ್ತು f n Dress, a suit of clothes

ದುಸ್ಸಂಗ s n Bad inclination. 2, bad company ದುಸ್ಸಂಗಿ. A person who associates with evil companions

ದುಸ್ಸಂತತಿ s n A bad progeny or family

ದುಸ್ಸಹ s a Intolerable, unbearable -ವಾಸ Bad association.

ದುಸ್ಸ್ವಪ್ನ s n An evil dream.

ದುಸ್ಸ್ವಭಾವ s n A bad disposition or nature.

ದುಹಿ (*tb of* ದ್ವಿ) n Discordance, hatred, ill-will.

ದುಹಿತೃ s n. A daughter, *tb.* ದುಹಿತೆ

ದುಹೇರ f. a Doubled, double, *cf.* ದುಬಾರಿ.

ದೂಗು k. v t To push, thrust, shove away or aside, throw out of, as out of a village, caste, *etc* ದೂಡಿಸು To cause to push, *etc*

ದೂಂಟು k v i To walk on one leg, hop

ದೂತ s n A messenger, envoy ambassador, *f.* ದೂತಿ -ಲಕ್ಷಣ. The characteristic mark of a messenger.

ದೂದಿ (*tb of* ತೂಲ) n Cleaned cotton. 2, silkcotton used as tinder

ದೂಪ *tb of* ಧೂಪ, *q v*

ದೂಮುರ (*tb of* ಧೂಮ್ರ) n Fine drizzling rain

ದೂರ s. a. Distant, far from, remote. n Distance, farness, remoteness, a long distance ದೂರಕ್ಕೆ To a distance; from afar -ಮಾಡು. To remove -ದರ್ಶಿ Far seeing, wise, a prophet. -ದೃಷ್ಟಿ. Far-sightedness, foresight, discernment.

ದೂರಿ h n. An axle-tree

ದೂರು (ರು=ಱು) k. v t To bear tales, to report evil of others, to blame, reproach, abuse, to slander n Blame, slander, calumny. -ಗೊಳ್ಳು To get blamed, *etc* -ಹೇಳು To tell tales, slander, blame, *etc.* -ತರು, -ಹೊರು To bring blame upon one's self

ದೂರ್ವೆ, ದೂರ್ವಾ s n The grass *Panicum dactylon.*

ದೂಲ (*tb of* ತುಲಾ) n A beam of timber

ದೂಷಕ s a Dishonouring, reviling, blaming. n A reviler, seducer, abuser, blasphemer

ದೂಷಣೆ s. n. Corrupting, contaminating, censuring, abusing, blame, guilt, sin -ಮಾಡು To abuse, blame, *etc* -ಹೇಳು To tell tales, *etc* -ಹೊಂದು To get blamed. ದೂಷಿಸು. To blame, censure, abuse, *etc.*

ದೂಷ್ಯ s a Censurable, condemnable, contemptible n Cloth, cotton, calico

ದೂಸ, ದೂಸು (*tb of* ದೂಷ್ಯ) n. Cloth. ದೂಸಿಗ A cloth merchant ದೂಸಿಗ ವಸರ. A cloth merchant's shop

ದೊಸರು a k n Reason, motive, cause, self-interest

ದೂಳಿ, ದೂಳು (*tb.* of ಧೂಳಿ) n Dust, powd-

ದೃಕ್ಕು (*tb of* ದೃಕ್) *n* An eye, seeing ದೃಕ್ಸಿದ್ಧಾಂತ The science of astronomical observation. ದೃಗ್ಗಣಿತ Calculations founded on observations of heavenly bodies

ದೃಢ s. *a*. Firm, strong solid, tenacious, compact 2, confirmed, established, certain, reliable. 3, powerful, mighty *n* Truth -ಚಿತ್ತ. A strong will -ಗೊಳ್ಳು To become firm. -ಪಡಿಸು To strengthen, confirm -ಬುದ್ಧಿ, -ಮನಸ್ಸು. A firm mind. ದೃಢಾಂಗ Firm-bodied, stalwart, *also* ದೃಢಾಂಗಿ ದೃಢೀಕರಣ Making firm, confirmation, an act of becoming a member of the Church of Christ

ದೃಶ (=ದೃಶ್) s *a*. Seeing, viewing *n* The eye ದೃಶ್ಯ Visible, to be looked at; beautiful -ಮಾಡು To show ದೃಶ್ಯಾ- Visible and invisible

ದೃಷ್ಟ s. *a*. Seen beheld, observed, visible, apparent, decided, known

ದೃಷ್ಟಾಂತ s *n* An example, illustration, instance, evidence. 2, a Śâstra science

ದೃಷ್ಟಿ (=ದಿಟ್ಟಿ, ದಿಷ್ಟಿ) s. *n* Seeing 2, sight, look, glance 3, the eye 4, intellect -ಇಡು. To look or aim at, to look after -ಕೊಡು To pay attention to, *etc* -ಗೆ ಬೀಳು To appear -ಗೋಚರ The range of the sight, in sight, visible -ದೋಷ A blast from an evil eye -ಸು. To see, look at.

ದೆಬ್ಬಾಳಿ f. *n* Greatness, pomp.

ದೆಬ್ಬೆ = ದಬ್ಬೆ, *q v*.

ದೆವ್ವ (*tb. of* ದೈವ) *n* A demon, evil spirit, phantom -ಚೇಷ್ಟೆ. The grimaces of one who is possessed. -ತಿಂಡಿ A glutton -ಬಡಿ A demon to strike (or possess) a person, *also* -ಹೊಡೆ. -ಬಿಡಿಸು To exorcise -ಸೋಕು The touch of an evil spirit. -ಹಿಡಿ A demon to possess a person

ದೆಸೆಂಬರ e *n* December (12th month of the year).

ದೆಸೆ (*tb of* ದಿಶೆ) *n* A point of the compass 2, (*tb of* ದಶೆ) condition, state. 3, luck *etc* ಅವನ ದೆಸೆಯಿಂದ On his account -ಗಾರ, -ವಂತ A fortunate man -ಗೆಡು Refuge *etc* to be lost.

ದೇಗಲ, ದೇಗುಲ (*tb of* ದೇವಕುಲ) *n* A temple ದೇಗುಲಿಗ An attendant on an idol

ದೇಟು, ದೇಂಟು f. *n*. A stem

ದೇಡ h *a*. One and a half.

ದೇಣಿ, ದೇಣಿಯ, ದೇಣೆ h *n*. Money due, a debt. 2, mercantile transactions. ದೇಣಾಲೇಣ. Lending and borrowing, mercantile transaction ದೇಣೆದಾರ A debtor

ದೇದೀಪ್ಯಮಾನ s. *a*. Brilliant, splendid

ದೇವ s. *a* Divine, celestial. *n*. A deity, god. 2, a king. 3, an honourific title, his majesty, his honour. ದೇವರು Your honour, *pl* ದೇವಗಳ್, ದೇವರು *The pl honourific form is used also of men, but when used of God the predicate is put in singl* -ಕಣಿಗಿಲು. A white sort of oleander -ಕಾರ್ಯ. Any act of worship, any religious rite -ಕುಸುಮ Cloves -ಖಾತ, -ಖಾತಕ. A natural pond -ಗಂಗೆ The celestial Ganges -ಗಣ A class of nakshatras -ತನ, -ತೆ, -ತ್ವ. Divinity, a deity, god -ತರು A celestial tree. -ತಾಯನ. A temple -ತಾರ್ಚನೆ, ದೇವಾರಾಧನೆ Divine worship. -ದತ್ತ God-given; N of the conch-shell of Arjuna, N of any one. -ದಾಯ, -ಮಾನ್ಯ. Lands allotted rent-free to pagodas -ದಾರ, -ದಾರು. A species of pine, *Pinus deodora* -ದಾಸ A servant of god, N., *f* -ದಾಸಿ -ದೂತ An angel -ನಾಗರಿ The character in which Samskrita is usually written -ನಾಳ A kind of reed. -ಪೂಜೆ Worship of gods -ಭೂಮಿ, -ಲೋಕ. Heaven -ಮಂದಿರ = ದೇವಾಲಯ. -ಮಾದಳ. A large kind of citron -ಮಾನುಷ A divine man, a harmless fellow. -ಮಾರ್ಗ The sky, ether

ಯಜ್ಞ The homa sacrifice -ಯಾನ The vehicle of a god. -ರಥ. The car of a deity -ರಾಜ Indra -ಲಿಪಿ A divine writing. -ವೈರಿ A râkshasa -ಸಭೆ An assembly of gods -ಸ್ತ್ರೀ A celestial nymph, *also* ದೇವಾಂಗನೆ. -ಸ್ಥಾನ A temple ದೇವತಾಂಶ A part of the deity divine ದೇವಾದ್ರಿ Mount Mêru ದೇವಾಧಿದೇವ A god above all other gods ದೇವಾಲಯ A temple, church, heaven -ಸ್ವ Property endowed to the service of temples.

ದೇವಕಿ s *n* Krishna's mother.

ದೇವಡಿ f. *n* A porch, the threshold, a house. -ಗ. An attendant upon an idol

ದೇವನ s. *n* Going, motion. 2, sport, play 3, a die. 4, grief, sorrow

ದೇವರ s *n* A husband's younger brother.

ದೇವರ್ಷಿ s *n* A heavenly rishi, *as* Nârada Atri, *etc*

ದೇವಲಿ, -ಕ s *n* An attendant on an idol

ದೇವಾಂಗ s *a* N of an emanation from Sadâsiva, held as the inventor of weaving. 2. a kind of cloth. -ದವರು A class of Śaiva weavers

ದೇವಿ 1 s *n* A goddess 2, Durgâ. 3, a queen, a princess. 4, the small-pox 5, *an honorific termination of fem names*. -ಪಂಡಿತ A vaccinator.

ದೇವಿ 2 h. *a* Giving ಲೇವಾ- Borrowing and lending.

ದೇವೇಂದ್ರ s. *n*. The chief of the gods Indra

ದೇಶ s *n* A place; a side, a country, district -ಕಾಲ. Place and time. -ಪರ್ಯಟನ, ದೇಶಾಟನ Travelling abroad. -ಭಾಷೆ The language of a country -ಭ್ರಷ್ಟ Expelled from a country -ಭ್ರಷ್ಟತ್ವ Expatriation -ಸ್ಥ Resident in a country; a class of Brâhmanas ದೇಶಾಚಾರ. The customs and manners of a country ದೇಶಾಧಿಪ, ದೇಶಾಧಿಪತಿ The ruler of a country. ದೇಶಾಂತರ Another or foreign country ದೇಶಾಭಿಮಾನ High opinion of one's country, patriotism ದೇಶಾಭಿಮಾನಿ. A person who has this opinion; a patriot

ದೇಶಾಯಿ = ದೇಸಾಯಿ, *q. v*

ದೇಶಾವರ, ದೇಶಾವಾರ s *n*. Begging alms from country to country, foreign countries. 2, alms. 3, imports

ದೇಶಿ s. *a* Belonging to a country. *n* The dialect of a country. 2, a certain raga -ಕ A guide, a teacher, a traveller, a stranger. ದೇಶೀಯ, ದೇಶ್ಯ Local, provincial, native

ದೇಸಾಯಿ f *n*. The head of a district, an hereditary officer

ದೇಸಿ (= ದೆಸಿ) a. k. *n* Beauty comeliness. -ಗಾರ An artist, *f* -ಗಾತಿ.

ದೇಸಿಗ *tb. of* ದೇಶಿಕ, *q v*

ದೇಹ s *n*. The body -ತ್ಯಾಗ Death. -ದಂಡನೆ Mortification of the body, corporal punishment -ಗುಣ, -ಧರ್ಮ. The constitution -ಧಾರಿ A living being; an individual -ಶುದ್ಧಿ. Bodily purification -ಸಾಧನೆ Bodily exercise, *as* bathing *etc* ದೇಹಾಂತ Death.

ದೇಹಿ s *a* Having a body, corporeal, embodied. *n*. A living man 2, the soul

ದೈತ್ಯ s *n* A demon, asura, râkshasa, *also* ದೈತೇಯ. -ಧ್ವಂಸಿ, -ವೈರಿ, ದೈತ್ಯಾರಿ. Vishnu -ಗುರು Sukra

ದೈನ್ಯ (*fr* ದೀನ) s. *n* Feebleness, depression, humbleness -ಪಡು. To be low spirited, to be humble. -ವೃತ್ತಿ Miserable subsistence, humble behaviour

ದೈವ (*fr*. ದೇವ) s. *a*. Divine. *n* A deity, god, *also* ದೈವತ. 2, destiny, fortune, fate 3, property, wealth 4, a demon or devil -ಕ Divine. -ಜ್ಞ An astrologer. -ಪರ Fatalistic. -ಗತಿ, -ಯೋಗ. Fortune, chance. -ಶಾಲಿ A fortunate person ದೈವಾಧೀನ Depending on deity, subject to fate; death

ದೈವಿಕ s. *a*. Divine, providential

[illegible]

ದೊಗೆ k. *v t* To dig or excavate with the nails, *etc*

ದೊಡ್ಡ k *a* Large, big, stout, thick, great, extensive, important, chief, loud, old, *as* -ಅಡವಿ, -ಕಲ್ಲು, -ಕೂಗು, -ಕೆಲಸ, -ತಪ್ಪು, -ತಾಳ್ಮೆ, -ದನ, -ದೊಣ್ಣೆ, -ದೊರೆ, -ನಾಯಿ, -ನೊಣ, -ಬೀದಿ, -ಬೆಟ್ಟ -ಮನೆ, -ಮರ, -ಮಾತು, -ಹೊಟ್ಟೆ, *etc* A large, big, *etc* ದೊಡ್ಡಕ್ಕ. The elder of the elder sisters ದೊಡ್ಡಣ್ಣ. The eldest of the elder brothers. ದೊಡ್ಡದು. A thing which is large -ತಂದೆ Father's elder brother; great aunt's husband. -ತಾಯಿ Mother's elder sister, great uncle's wife ದೊಡ್ಡಪ್ಪ = -ತಂದೆ -ನಡೆ A fast walk. -ನಿದ್ರೆ. Long sleep, death -ಮನಸ್ಸು A generous mind, generosity -ಮರದರಸಿನ. The tree turmeric -ಮಾರ್ಗ. A high road. -ರತ್ನಗಂಧಿ. The royal Gool-mohr, *Poinciana regia*. ದೊಡ್ಡವ A great, noble, old, rich, tall, *etc*, man, *f.* -ವಳು. ದೊಡ್ಡೊಕ್ಕಲು. A well-to-do inhabitant. -ತನ, -ತ್ವ, -ಸ್ತನ, -ಸ್ತಿಕೆ Exalted position, greatness dignity ದೊಡ್ಡಿತು That is large, *etc*

ದೊಡ್ಡಿ k. *n* A cow-pen, fold, stable, a stockade for impaling wild elephants, a settler's first house

ದೊಡ್ಡೆ k. *n* The bat used at tip-cat

ದೊಣ್ಣೆ k. *n* A cudgel, club, mace.

ದೊದ್ದೆ a. k. *n* A mass; a crowd, mob, tumult 2, indistinct speech.

ದೊಂದೆ k. *n* A bundle of sticks, grass, *etc.*, used as a torch, *diminutive* ದೊಂದಿ

ದೊನ್ನೆ k *n*. A leaf-cup.

ದೊಬ್ಬು (=ಡೊಬ್ಬು, *q v.*) k. *v. t* To shove, push, thrust, throw.

ದೊಂಬ (=ಡೊಂಬ, *q. v.*) f. *n*. A caste of tumblers, mountebank. -ಗಣೆ A tumbler's pole. ದೊಂಬರಾಟ. Tumbling.

ದೊಂಬಿ k *n* A crowd, mob; riotous mob, affray, quarrel -ಜಗಳ. A street quarrel -ದಾಸರ One of a company of stage players. -ಸಾಕ್ಷಿ A confused testimony. -ಗಾರ A rioter.

ದೊರಕಿಸು k *v. t* To cause to obtain, *etc.*

ದೊರಕು (= ದೊರೆ) k. *v i*. To be obtained, gained or found, to accrue *P. p* ದೊರಕಿ *Used impersonally with the dative case, as* ನಮಗೆ ದೊರಕುತ್ತದೆ. We get.

ದೊರಿ, ದೊರೆ 1. = ದೊರಕು, *q v P ps* ದೊರಿತು, ದೊರದು, ದೊರೆದು

ದೊರೆ 2. a k. *n* Resemblance, likeness, equality, propriety. 2, gain, advantage, use.

ದೊರೆ 3. (*tb of* ಧುರ್ಯ) *n*. A chief, a king, a master, a man of the ruling class, a gentleman -ತನ. Kingship, government, rule -ತನ ಮಾಡು To rule. -ಸಾನಿ. A lady

ದೋಟಿ k *n*. A pole with a hook for plucking fruit, *etc.*

ದೋಣಿ (= ಡೋಣಿ *tb. of* ದ್ರೋಣಿ) *n*. A boat

ದೋತರ, ದೋತ್ರ f *n* A Hindu-male's garment worn around the waist or over the shoulder -ಉಟ್ಟುಕೊಳ್ಳು To wear such a garment -ಹೊದ್ದುಕೊಳ್ಳು. To put on a garment

ದೋಬಿ f *n*. A washerman

ದೋಮೆ k *n* A musquito, a gnat

ದೋರ 1, **ದೋರೆ** 1 a k. *n*. Full-grown or mature state -ಗಾಯಿ A full-grown fruit

ದೋರ 2, **ದೋರೆ** 2 k *n* Thread. 2, a kind of bracelet

ದೋಲ s. *n*. Swinging, rocking. 2, a swing.

ದೋಲಿ (= ಡೋಲಿ), **ದೋಲೆ** s *n* A swing, a litter, palanquin. ದೋಲೋತ್ಸವ. The ceremony of swinging an idol

ದೋಷ s. *n* Fault, vice defect; a blemish; blame, reproach, badness, sin, morbid affection, disease; spots on the tongue foreboding death. -ಆಡು. To blame -ಇಡು To put fault or blame upon -ಹಚ್ಚು. To lay or bring reproach upon, to find fault with -ಕಾರಿ An evil-doer. -ಗ್ರಾಹಿ Fault-finding, censorious. -ಜ್ಞ A discerning wise man, a physician -ತ್ರಯ Vitiation of the three humours as wind, bile, and phlegm. -ಹರಣ Removing blemish ದೋಷಾಕರ. The moon, faulty ದೋಷಾರೋಪಣ Accusation.

ದೋಷಿ s. a Faulty, guilty sinful. -ಸು. Morbid affection to arise, as in fever

ದೋಷೆ s n Darkness, night. 2, the arm

ದೋಸೆ k n A flat, spongy cake of rice-flour, uddu, *etc.*

ದೋಸ್ತಿ h n Friendship. -ಗಾರ A friend.

ದೋಹದ, ದೋಹಳ s. n A longing of a pregnant woman, any morbid desire

ದೋಳು (= ಡೋಲು. *tb. of* ಢೋಲ) n A drum.

ದೌತು = ದವುತು, q v.

ದೌತಿ (= ದವತಿ, q v) f n. An inkstand

ದೌತ್ಯ (*fr.* ದೂತ) s n The function of a messenger

ದೌರಾತ್ಮ್ಯ (*fr.* ದುರಾತ್ಮ) s n Evil-mindedness, wickedness

ದೌರ್ಬಲ್ಯ s. n. Weakness, infirmity.

ದೌರ್ಭಾಗ್ಯ (*fr.* ದುರ್ಭಾಗ್ಯ) s n Ill-luck, misfortune

ದೌಲತು h n Wealth, affluence.

ದೌಷ್ಟ್ಯ (*fr.* ದುಷ್ಟ) s n Depravity, wickedness

ದೌಹಿತ್ರ (*fr* ದುಹಿತೃ) s n A daughter's son.

ದ್ಯಾವ. *tb. of* ದೇವ, q. v.

ದ್ಯು s n. A day. 2, the sky. -ನದಿ The celestial Ganges. -ಮುಖ Dawn, morning

ದ್ಯುತಿ, ದ್ಯೂತಿ s. n Brightness, brilliancy, lustre, light

ದ್ಯೂತ (= ಜೂಜು, *etc*) s n Gambling. -ಕಾರ A gambler

ದ್ಯೋತ s. n Shine, light, splendour. -ನ Shining enlightening seeing. ದ್ಯೋತಿಸು To shine, to appear

ದ್ರಮು e n A dram, a dose of liquor.

ದ್ರವ s n Dripping, flowing, liquid; fluidity. 2, moisture, essence, juice. 3, melting from pity or tenderness

ದ್ರವಿಡ s n N of a people and district on the east coast of the Dekhan Tamil -ಭಾಷೆ A family of languages in South-India, *as*: Tamil Telugu, Kannada, Malayâlam and Tulu

ದ್ರವಿಸು s v i To become liquid. v. t. To melt, *as* the mind

ದ್ರವ್ಯ s. n Substance, property, wealth, money. 2, a substance, thing 3, the receptacle of properties, *etc*, elementary substance. -ವಂತ, -ಸ್ಥ A wealthy man. ದ್ರವ್ಯಾನುಕೂಲ Help of money towards any business. ದ್ರವ್ಯಾಶೆ Covetousness

ದ್ರಾಕ್ಷೆ, ದ್ರಾಕ್ಷಿ s. n The vine 2, a grape, grapes -ಚಪ್ಪರ A vine-pandal. -ಪಾಕ An accomplished style of diction in poetry -ಬಳ್ಳಿ The grape vine -ರಸ Grape juice. -ಸರಾಯಿ. Wine. -ಹಣ್ಣು. A ripe grape

ದ್ರಾಬೆ (*tb of* ದ್ರಾಪ) n A blockhead. 2, wretchedness, feebleness 3, trash, rubbish 4, a wretched and poor person

ದ್ರಾವ s. n Liquefaction, distilling. -ಕ. A drug prepared by distillation.

ದ್ರಾವಿಡ (*fr* ದ್ರವಿಡ) s a Belonging to Dravida.

ದ್ರುತ s a Run, flown 2, melted, liquid. 3, quick, swift.

ದ್ರುಪದ s n King of the Pâñćâlas and father of Draupadî

ದ್ರೋಣ s n A trough, bucket, cup 2, a measure of capacity, equal to 4 âḍhakas. 3, Drônâćârya, the teacher of the Kurus and Pândavas

ದ್ರೋಣಿ (= ದೋಣಿ, q v) s n. A boat 2, a valley.

ದ್ರೋಹ s n. Injury mischief, treachery, [illegible]

Spiteful, treacherous, a traitor, betrayer, *as* ಗುರು-, ಪಿತೃ-, ಮಾತೃ-, ಮಿತ್ರ-, ಸ್ವಾಮಿ-, *etc.*

ದ್ರೌಪದಿ (*fr* ದ್ರುಪದ) s. *n* N. of the daughter of Drupada and wife of the five Pându princes

ದ್ವಂದ್ವ s *n* A pair couple 2, any pair of opposites, *as* right and wrong, heat and cold, *etc.* 3, strife, contest 4, doubt, uncertainty. 5, a form of compound (*g*) -ಯುದ್ಧ A duel, single combat.

ದ್ವಯ s. *a* Twofold, both, double *n.* A pair

ದ್ವಾದಶ s *a* Twelve. 2, the twelfth. ದ್ವಾದಶಿ The twelfth day of a lunar fortnight

ದ್ವಾಪರ, ದ್ವಾಪಾರ s. *n* The third of the four yugas of the world 2, doubt 3, war

ದ್ವಾರ s. *n* A door, gate. 2, a way, means, medium ದ್ವಾರಾ By means of through -ಪಟ್ಟ The threshold, the panel of a door -ಪಾಲ, -ಪಾಲಕ. A door-keeper. -ಬಂಧ A door-frame

ದ್ವಾರಕಾಪುರ, ದ್ವಾರಕೆ, ದ್ವಾರಾವತಿ s. *n.* Dvârakâ, the capital of Krishna

ದ್ವಿ s *a* Two -ಕರ್ಮ Two accusatives -ಗು. A grammatical compound -ಗುಣ Two-fold, double -ಗುಣಿಸು. To multiply by two -ಜ Twice-born, a man of the first three classes. a Brâhmana Kshatriya, or Vaiśya, a bird, a snake; a star, a house. -ಭಾಷಿ = ದುಬಾಸಿ, *q v.* *Cpds.* -ಮಾಸ, -ಮುಖ, *etc*

ದ್ವಿತೀಯ s *a* Second -ವಿವಾಹ A second marriage -ವಿಭಕ್ತಿ. The accusative ದ್ವಿತೀಯೆ. The 2nd of the lunar fortnight

ದ್ವಿತ್ವ s *n* Doubleness. 2, a pair, couple 3, reduplication of a consonant

ದ್ವಿಧಾ s. *ad* In a two-fold manner. -ಗತಿ. Duplicity.

ದ್ವಿಪ s *n.* An elephant (*lit drinking twice*).

ದ್ವಿಪದ s *n.* A biped *a* Two-footed

ದ್ವಿಪದಿ s. *n.* A kind of metre.

ದ್ವಿರದ s *n.* An elephant

ದ್ವಿರುಕ್ತಿ s. *n* Repetition, tautology

ದ್ವಿಸ್ವಭಾವ s *a* Having a double nature

ದ್ವೀಪ s *n.* An island, a sandbank ದ್ವೀಪಾಂತರ A foreign island. ದ್ವೀಪಿ. A tiger, leopard

ದ್ವೇಷ s *n* Hate, hatred, enmity, dislike ದ್ವೇಷಿ A hater, foe, enemy ದ್ವೇಷಿಸು To hate, dislike

ದ್ವೈತ s *n.* Duality dualism 2, dualism in philosophy, *as* of spirit and matter, *etc*

ದ್ವೈಧ s *n* Duplicity 2, disunion, dispute; doubt ದ್ವೈಧೀಭಾವ Duplicity, fraud, doubt

ದ್ವೈಪಾಯನ s *n.* The island-born Vyâsa

ದ್ವ್ಯಾಹಿಕ s *a* Returning every second day, *as* fever

ಧ

ಧ. The thirty-seventh letter of the alphabet. *In Kannada it occurs only in a few dêśya and tadbhava words.*

ಧಕಾರ s. *n* The letter ಧ.

ಧಗ f *n* Fire. [illegible] -ಧಗೆ [illegible] flaming, be[illegible] brill[illegible] [illegible]ing much -ಧಗನೆ. *rep* With a fierce glow *etc.* -ಧಗಿಸು To burn fiercely

ಧತ್ತೂರ (=ದತ್ತೂರ) s. *n* The white thorn-apple, *Datura alba*

[illegible] s *n* Property, wealth riches money. 2 wealth in cattle. [illegible]

Loss of property ಧನಂಜಯ Conquering wealth, fire, Arjuna -ಪಾಲ A guardian of treasure. Kubêra -ಬಲ Power of wealth -ಮದ Pride of wealth -ಲಕ್ಷ್ಮಿ Riches -ಲೋಭ Covetousness, avarice -ವಂತ A rich man. -ಹೀನ Poor ಧನಾಢ್ಯ Wealthy

ಧನಾಸರಿ s *n*. N of a tune.

ಧನಿ, -ಕ s *n* A rich man, an owner, master

ಧನಿಷ್ಠೆ s *n* The twenty-third lunar mansion

ಧನು, ಧನುರ್ (= ಧನುಸ್) s *n*. A bow. 2, the sign *Sagittarius*. ಧನುರ್ಧಾರಿ Bearing a bow. an archer ಧನುರ್ಬಾಣ A bow and arrow ಧನುರ್ಮಾಸ. The solar 9th month ಧನುರ್ವಾತ, ಧನುರ್ವಾಯು Tetanus, a disease which bends the body like a bow ಧನುರ್ವಿದ್ಯಾ. Archery. ಧನುರ್ವೇದ. The science of archery, N of a treatise on archery.

ಧನುಸ್ (= ಧನು, *q v*) s *n* A bow 2, the sign *Sagittarius* 2, an arc

ಧನ್ಯ s. *a*. Opulent, rich 2, fortunate, happy, blest, lucky. -ತೆ. Opulence; good fortune ಧನ್ಯೆ A fortunate woman; *Emblic myrobalan*

ಧನ್ಮಡಿ h *n* A rice-field, *also* ಧಾನ್ಮಡಿ

ಧನ್ವಂತರಿ s. *n* The sun 2, N. of a celebrated physician.

ಧಮನ, ಧಮನಿ s *n* A reed, pipe, tube

ಧಮ್ಮಿಲ್ಲ s. *n* A braided and ornamented hair of a woman

ಧರ s. *n* Holding, bearing, wearing, having, sustaining. 2, a mountain -ಣ Bearing holding, a support; a weight for gold

ಧರಣಿ s *n*. The earth, the ground. -ಜ, -ಜಾತ. A tree -ತಲ Earth's surface -ಪ, -ಪತಿ -ಪಾಲಕ, -ವರ, -ವಲ್ಲಭ, -ಈಶ, -ಈಶ್ವರ. A king. -ಧರ, -ಧೃ The serpent Sêsha, a mountain.

ಧರಾಧಿಪ, ಧರಾಧಿಪತಿ, ಧರಾಧೀಶ s *n*. A king

ಧರಿತ್ರಿ (= [illegible]

ಧರಿಸು s *v t*. To hold, bear, carry, to contain, to put on one's self, as clothes, *etc*, to obtain, get ಅವತಾರ- To become incarnate ಗರ್ಭ- To become pregnant

ಧರ್ಮ s *n* Ordinance law, duty, right justice, charity, liberality, a pious act 2, usage, custom 3, virtue, merit, good works, religion, piety 4, almsgiving; alms, gift 5, harmlessness 6, sacrifice. 7, nature. 8, the god of justice Yama -ಕರ್ತ The manager of a temple almshouse, *etc* -ಕೊಡು, -ಮಾಡು To give alms -ಬೇಡು. To ask for alms -ಕಾರ್ಯ Any pious act -ಗ್ರಂಥ A code of religious laws -ತ್ಯಾಗ. Apostacy -ತ್ಯಾಗಿ An apostate -ದೇವತೆ -ದೇವಿ Virtue personified as a woman -ನಿಷ್ಠೆ Devotion to religion or charity. -ಪತ್ನಿ A lawful wife. -ಬುದ್ಧಿ. Virtuousness, charitable disposition. -ಮಾರ್ಗ The path of virtue -ಜ, -ಪುತ್ರ, -ರಾಜ, -ರಾಯ Yudhishthira, Yama -ವಂತ A virtuous or pious man -ಶಾಲೆ A building for travellers, a poor-asylum, a school at which children are taught gratis. -ಶಾಸ್ತ್ರ A code of law, jurisprudence. -ಶೀಲ. Virtuous, pious -ಸತ್ರ An alms-house. -ಸ್ಥಲ N. of a place of pilgrimage in S. Canara. ಧರ್ಮಾತ್ಮ. A just and pious man ಧರ್ಮಾಧಿಕಾರಿ. A judge; the almoner of a prince ಧರ್ಮಾಧ್ಯಕ್ಷ. An administrator of laws, king. ಧರ್ಮಾರ್ಥ In charity, as a gift, gratis (*esp*. as ಧರ್ಮಾರ್ಥವಾಗಿ)

ಧರ್ಮಿ s *a* Virtuous, religious, just -ಷ್ಠ Most pious, very virtuous, *etc*

ಧವಲ, -ಳ s *a* White, dazzling 2, beautiful *n* A kind of camphor. ಧವಳೆ A white cow

ಧಾಟಿ s *n* Assault

ಧಾತ *tb. of* ಧಾತ್ರು, *q. v*

ಧಾತು s *n* Natural condition. 2, an [illegible]

tive matter, *as* earth, water, fire, air and ether or âkâša. 3, an essential ingredient of the body, *as* blood, marrow, *etc* 4, the organs of sense 5, a mineral, a metal, an ore 6, a grammatical root. 7, origin 8, strength 9, the pulse 10, the tenth year of the cycle of sixty. -ಕುಂದು, -ಗುಂದು Strength to decrease. -ನೋಡು To feel the pulse -ನಷ್ಟ, -ನಾಶನ Loss of strength. -ಪಾಠ A list of verbal themes. -ಪುಷ್ಟಿ. Nutrition or strength of the body -ಲಕ್ಷಣ. The state of the pulse. -ವಾದ Mineralogy.

ಧಾತೃ s. *n* A founder, maker, creator 2, Brahmâ.

ಧಾತ್ರಿ (= ದಾದಿ) s *n* A wet-nurse, foster-mother 2, the earth 3, *Emblic myrobalan*

ಧಾನ್ಯ s *n* Corn, grain; rice -ಧನ Property in grain ನವ-. Nine kinds of corn grown in India

ಧಾಮು s *n* A house, home. 2, the body. 3, radiance, light. 4, dignity.

ಧಾರ (= ದಾರ) s *n* Holding 2, a holder 3, streaming down, flowing, a violent shower, gush 4, a wave 5, a hole. 6, a thread. -ಕ A receptacle, box; a post -ಣ. The act of holding, bearing, undergoing, preserving, protecting, assuming, *etc*, keeping the mind collected, holding the breath suspended.

ಧಾರಣೆ (= ಧಾರಣ, *q. v.*) f. *n.* Rate, price. ಪೇಟೆ-. Market price.

ಧಾರಾಗೃಹೀತ s *n* A present received from the donor by pouring water over it; *also* ಧಾರಾದತ್ತ.

ಧಾರಾಳ s *n* Profusion; freedom from reserve, liberality, generosity ಧಾರಾಳಿ A liberal person. -ದ ಮಾತು, -ದ ನುಡಿ Eloquence

ಧಾರಿ s *aff.* A person who holds, wears, *etc.*

ಧಾರುಣಿ (*tb of* ಧಾರಿಣಿ) *n* The earth

ಧಾರೆ (= ಧಾರ) s. *n* The dropping of any liquid, a stream of water, a shower. 2, the pace of a horse. 3, the sharp edge of a sword or any cutting instrument

ಧಾರ್ಮಿಕ (*fr.* ಧರ್ಮ) s. *a.* Righteous, virtuous, religious. -ತನ Righteousness

ಧಾರ್ಷ್ಟ್ಯ (*fr* ಧೃಷ್ಣು) s *n* Impudence, violence.

ಧಾವಕ s. *a.* Washing, cleansing 2, running.

ಧಾವನ s *n.* Rubbing off, cleansing 2, running, flowing 3, attack, assault

ಧಾಷ್ಠು h. *n.* Boldness, courage, impudence 2, dread, awe

ಧಿಕ್ s *int.* Fie! shame! -ಕರಿಸು To reproach, censure, to treat scornfully -ಕಾರ Reproach, censure, disrespect.

ಧಿಷ್ಣ್ಯ s *a* Intelligent. *n* a thoughtful man. 2, Brahmâ. 3, a star.

ಧೀ s *n* Thought, understanding, intellect -ಮತ್ (*tb* ಧೀಮನ, ಧೀಮಂತ). Intelligent, wise, an intelligent man.

ಧೀರ s. *a* Firm, resolute, brave, daring 2, intelligent, prudent; sensible -ತನ, -ತೆ, -ತ್ವ. Firmness, energy, courage, resolution

ಧೀವರ s. *n.* A very intelligent man 2, a fisherman

ಧೀಶ s *n* A very intelligent man

ಧುನಿ s. *a* Sounding, roaring. *n.* A river

ಧುರ. = ದುರ, *q v*

ಧುರಂಧರ s *a* Bearing the yoke; laden with good qualities. *n.* A foreman, leader, chief 2, a man of business.

ಧುರ್ಯ (= ದೊರೆ, *q v*) s *a* Able to bear a yoke *n* A beast of burden 2, a leader, chief.

ಧೂಪ (= ದೂಪ) s *n.* Incense, frankincense, perfume. -ದೀಪನೈವೇದ್ಯ. The three essential constituents of idol-worship the burning of incense, the waving of lamps, and the offering of boiled rice, *etc* ಧೂಪಾರತಿ, ಧೂಪಾತಿ‍ೕ. A censer -ದ ಮರ The white dammer tree, *Vateria indica* -ಆಪಿ‍ಸು, -ತೋರು -ಎತ್ತು -ಹಾಕು To offer incense ಧೂಪಿಸು To incense, to perfume

ಧೂಮ s *n* Smoke, vapour -ಕೇತು A meteor, a comet. -ಪಾನ. Smoking tobacco -ಲ. Smoky -ಶಕಟ A railway carriage

ಧೂಮ್ರ s. *a* Smoke-coloured, grey, dark-red, dark, obscure -ಪತ್ರೆ. Tobacco. -ಪಾನ = ಧೂಮಪಾನ, *q v*

ಧೂರ್ಜಟಿ s. *n* Siva

ಧೂರ್ತ s. *a* Cunning, crafty, subtle *n*. A rogue, cheat 2, a passionate man; *f* ಧೂರ್ತೆ -ತ್ವ. Passion, wrath

ಧೂಲಿ, ಧೂಳಿ. = ದೂಳಿ, *q v*

ಧೃತರಾಷ್ಟ್ರ s *n* Dhritarâshtra. the oldest blind-born son of Vyâsa and the father of Duryôdhana. 2, a blind man. 3, a kind of bird

ಧೃತಿ s *n* Firmness, steadfastness, energy, courage. 2, pleasure -ಗೆಡು Courage to lose

ಥರ್ಮಾಮಿಟರ್ e *n*. Thermometer, an instrument for measuring temperature

ಧೇನು s. *n* A milch cow

ಧೈರ್ಯ (*f* ಧೀರ) s *n*. Firmness, steadiness, constancy 2, fortitude, courage -ಕುಗ್ಗು, -ಕುಂದು Courage, *etc*, to sink. -ಕೆಡು, -ಗೆಡು Courage to lose -ಗೊಳ್ಳು, -ತಾಳು, -ಪಡು, -ಮಾಡು To be encouraged, to take courage -ಗೊಳಿಸು, -ಪಡಿಸು. To encourage -ಬಿಡು To lose courage -ಗಾರ, -ವಂತ, -ಶಾಲಿ, -ಸ್ಥ A courageous man.

ಧೋರಣಿ s. *n* A vehicle in general. 2. aim, bent, tendency, manner, style, course ಧೋರಣೆ A good style of composition, disregard, inattention -ಗಾರ An inattentive man.

ಧೌತ s. *a*. Washed cleansed, bright. pure. -ವಸ್ತ್ರ Washed cloth.

ಧ್ಯಾನ s *n* Meditation, thought, reflection, heed 2, an abstract religious contemplation -ದಲ್ಲಿ ಬರು To come to the mind -ದೊಳಗೆ ಇಡು To consider, mind. -ಪರ Absorbed in meditation. -ಯೋಗ. Profound meditation, meditation and abstraction. ಧ್ಯಾನಿಸು To think of, contemplate, meditate, reflect upon, to counsel with one's self

ಧ್ರುವ s *a* Firm, immovable, fixed; constant, eternal *n* The polar star; the north pole. 2, the introductory stanza of a poem 3, N of a king, the son of ಉತ್ತಾನಪಾದ -ನಕ್ಷತ್ರ. The polar star -ಲೋಕ. The region of the polar star. -ವೃತ್ತ. A polar circle, arctic and antarctic -ಸ್ಥಾನ An extremity of the earth's axis

ಧ್ವಂಸ s *n* Destruction, loss.

ಧ್ವಜ s *n* A banner, flag, ensign -ಸ್ತಂಭ. A flag-staff.

ಧ್ವಜಿನಿ s *n* A standard-bearer, an arm

ಧ್ವನಿ s. *n* Sound, echo, noise, tone; a voice, a word 2, allusion, hint -ಗೈಯ್ಯು -ಗೊಡು -ಮಾಡು. To sound, roar, *etc* ಪ್ರತಿ- An echo.

ಧ್ವಾಂಕ್ಷ s *n* A crow, crane.

ಧ್ವಾನ s *n* Sound, noise; humming

ನ

ನ. The thirty-eighth letter of the alphabet.

ನಕಲಿ h *n*. Ridicule, joking, jesting, satire, mimicry *Cpds* -ಮಾತು, -ಚೇಷ್ಟೆ -ಗಾರ, -ಯವ. A buffoon, mimic

ನಕಲು h. *n* A copy, transcript -ತೆಗೆ, -ಮಾಡು. To copy.

ನಕಸಿ (= ನಕಾಸಿ, ನಕ್ಷೆ) h. *n* Ornamental representation, engraving, embroidery 2, a picture, a map, plan

ನಕಾರ s *n* The letter ನ 2, denying, denial ನಕಾರಿಸು To deny, decline.

ನಕಾರಿ f. *a* Inferior, bad, useless.

ನಕಾಸಿ = ನಕಸಿ, *q v.* -ತೆಗೆ, -ಮಾಡು. To carve, engrave, *etc*

ನಕುಲ s. *n*. The mungoose, *Viverra ichneumon*. 2, the fourth of the Pându princes

ನಕ್ಕಿ f *n* A ring of wire worn on fingers while playing upon a stringed instrument

ನಕ್ಕು k *v. t.* To lick, *also* ನೆಕ್ಕು 2 *p p of* ನಗು

ನಕ್ತ s *n*. Night 2, fasting on certain nights -ಂಚರ. A thief, an owl, a cat, a goblin

ನಕ್ರ s. *n*. A crocodile, alligator. -ಧ್ವಜ Krishna's son Pradyumna.

ನಕ್ಷೆ (= ನಕಸಿ, *etc*) h *n*. A map, picture

ನಕ್ಷತ್ರ s *n*. A star. 2, a constellation, lunar mansion -ಗತಿ The motion of the lunar mansions -ಬಾಣ A sky-rocket -ಮಂಡಲ, -ಲೋಕ The firmament ಜನ್ಮ- The star on which a man is born, natal star

ನಕ್ಷೆ = ನಕ್ಷೆ, *q v*

ನಖ, ನಖರ s *n* A nail of a finger or of a toe, a claw, talon

ನಗ 1 s *n*. An ornament, an article, a piece 2, a load of articles. 3, a ship.

ನಗ 2 s *n*. A mountain. 2, a tree. -ಜಾತೆ, -ಜೆ. Pârvatî.

ನಗದಿ h *n* Ready money *a* Fiscal, financial. -ಗುಮಾಸ್ತ A cashier

ನಗದು h. *n*. Ready money or cash.

ನಗರ s. *n* A town, city -ವಾಸಿ. A citizen -ಶೋಧಕ A town-watchman -ಶೋಧನ Inspection of a town

ನಗಾರ, ನಗಾರಿ h. *n* A large kettle-drum -ಖಾನೆ. A place where the instruments of a band are kept, a band-stand

ನಗು k. *v i*. To laugh, smile, to laugh at deride, to open (*P p* ನಕ್ಕು). *n*. A laugh, smile, laughter, derision. -ಮೊಗ. A smiling face

ನಗೆ (= ನಗು *n*) k. *n*. A laugh, *etc*.: blooming, *etc* -ಆಡು, ನಗಾಡು. To laugh. -ಗೇಡು. A laughing-stock. -ಮಾತು A joke -ಮುಖ, -ಮೋರೆ = ನಗುಮೊಗ, *q v.* -ಗಾರ. A joker, ridiculer

ನಗ್ಗಲು. = ನೆಗ್ಗಲು, *q v.*

ನಗ್ಗು k *v i* To become bruised, *as* a metal vessel *n*. A bruise in a metal vessel -ಬೀಳು To get bruised ನಗ್ಗಿ ಹೋಗು To go stooping

ನಗ್ನ s *a*. Naked, bare. *n* Šiva, nakedness.

ನಚ್ಚು 1. (= ನೆಚ್ಚು, *q v*) k. *v t* To confide, trust, put confidence in, believe. 2, to desire, love *n* Confidence, trust, faith, belief. 2, desire, love ನಚ್ಚಿಕೆ, ನೆಚ್ಚಿಗೆ (= ನೆಚ್ಚಿಕೆ, -ನೆಗೆ). Confiding, trust, *etc*

ನಚ್ಚು 2 k *n* Doubt. -ಮಾತು An unreliable word

ನಜರಾಣೆ, -ಕೆ h *n*. A forced tax levied on all the people, an unjust fine

ನಜರು h *n*. Favourable look, sight, a present to a superior -ಕಾಣಿಕೆ = ನಜರಾಣೆ. *q v.* -ಬಂದಿ. Temporary confinement.

ನಜರೇತು f n Nazaret, native place of Jesus Christ in Palestine

ನಜುಗು k v i To squash, crush, bruise, as dry ginger, pepper, etc

ನಜ್ಜು k n A crushed state. -ಗುಜ್ಜು. A completely crushed mass

ನಂಜು 1 k v t To take a little, eat a little of any thing as a relish

ನಂಜು 2 k. n. Poison, impurity of the blood; paralysis of the brain -ಗೊರಳ, ನಂಜುಂಡ, ನಂಜುಂಡೇಶ್ವರ, ನಂಜ Śiva -ಜೋಗಿ A dealer in antidotes -ರೋಗ. Paralysis of the brain.

ನಟ s n. An actor, dancer mime. 2, the tree *Colosanthes indica* -ನೆ A pantomime, a dance, hypocrisy ನಟಿ. An actress; an actor. ನಟಯಿಸು, ನಟಿಸು. To dance act

ನಟಿಕೆ k n The cracking of the finger or other joints

ನಟ್ಟ, ನಟ್ಟಿ k a Middle, central ನಟ್ಟಡವಿ The middle of a forest -ನಡು, -ನಡುವೆ The very middle ನಟ್ಟಿರುಳು Midnight ನಟ್ಟೆಲುವು. The backbone.

ನಟ್ಟವಿಗ, ನಟ್ಟುಗಾರ, ನಟ್ಟುವ s. n An actor 2, a dancing-master. f ನಟ್ಟುವಗಾತಿ, ನಟ್ಟವಿಗಿತ್ತಿ, ನಟ್ಟುವಿತಿ.

ನಟ್ಟು k n Grass, its wide spreading roots.

ನಡ 1 (= ನಡದು, ನಡೆದು) P p of ನಡೆ, in ನಡಕೊಳ್ಳು 2, (= ನಡೆ) walking etc. -ಸು = ನಡಿಸು

ನಡ 2 = ನಡು, q v. Cpds -ಕಟ್ಟು = ನಡು ಕಟ್ಟು, q v -ಗಂಘ, -ಪ್ರಾಯ, -ಬೀದಿ, -ಭಾಗ, -ರಾತ್ರಿ, -ಹಾದಿ, etc -ನಡುವೆ. The very midst

ನಡ 3, ನಡಕ k. n. Trembling.

ನಡಗು = ನಡುಗು, q v

ನಡತೆ k. n Walk, course, conduct, behaviour -ವಂತ A man of proper conduct, f -ವಂತೆ.

ನಡವಡಿಕೆ, ನಡವಳಿ, ನಡವಳಿಕೆ, ನಡಾವಳಿ, ನಡವಳಿತ k n Conduct, behaviour, custom, usage 2, proceedings.

ನಡವು = ನಡು 1, q. v. ನಡವಂತರ. Interval, interver [illegible]

ನಡವೆ k n The house-floor opposite the entrance-door

ನಡಾಂತರ. = ನಡವಂತರ s. ನಡವು, q. v

ನಡಾವಳಿ = ನಡವಳಿಕೆ, etc, q v

ನಡಿ (= ನಡೆ, q v) k. v i To walk, etc. -ಗೆ Pace, walk -ಸು To cause to walk, proceed, go, to carry on, to manage; to treat; to carry out, fulfil, as a promise, also ನಡಯಿಸು

ನಡು 1 (= ನಡು 2) k n The middle, centre, the waist, the flank of a horse, etc, also -ವು. -ಕಟ್ಟು A waist-band girdle -ಗಡ್ಡೆ. An island. Cpds. -ಗುಡ್ಡ, -ತಲೆ, -ತಿರುಬು, -ತೋಟ, -ದಟ್ಟಿ, -ನಾಡು, -ಬೀದಿ, -ಬೆಟ್ಟ, -ಬೆರಳು, -ಮನೆ, -ರಾಜ್ಯ, -ರಾತ್ರಿ, -ಹಗಲು, -ಹರೆಯ, etc. -ನಡುವೆ The very midst. -ವೆ. Between. -ವಂತರ = ನಡವಂತರ.

ನಡು 2 (= ನೆಡು, q v.) k v. t To plant fix firmly, etc

ನಡುಕ k n. Trembling shivering, tremor, fear

ನಡುಗು (= ನಡಗು) k. v i To tremble, shake shiver, quake.

ನಡೆ (= ನಡಿ) k v i To walk, to march; to go on proceed, to go, to be current, to continue, to come to pass to behave, conduct one's self to succeed, to be obedient to. (P ps ನಡದು, ನಡೆದು) -ಯಾಡು To walk about n Walking, going, walk, course, gait; march, going, conduct, behaviour; also ನಡತೆ 2, cattle -ಗೆಡಿಸು To cause to stop. -ನಡೆಗೆ. At every step. -ನುಡಿ. Conduct and speech -ಮಡಿ. A clean cloth to walk over -ವಾಹ. A self-moving chariot of the gods

ನಂಟ (= ನೆಂಟ, q. v) k n. A relative, etc. -ತನ, -ಸ್ತಿಕೆ. Relationship; also ನಂಟು (= ನೆಂಟು q v.)

ನತ್ತು 1 (= ನೆತ್ತು) k v. i. To stutter, stammer ನತ್ತಿ ಮಾತಾಡು To stammer.

ನತ್ತು 2 (= ಮೂತ್ತು) f. n A nose-jewel.

[illegible] s n Doubt, suspicion, uncertainty.

ನದ s n A river (*personified as male*), *f*. ನದಿ. 2, sounding ನದಿ. A river -ಪ್ರವಾಹ The current or flow of a river.

ನನ್.= ನಾನು *Gen* ನನ, ನನ್ನ, ನನ್ *Dat* ನನಗೆ, ನನಿಗೆ. *Acc* ನನ್ನ, ನನ್ನನು, ನನ್ನನ್ನು *Loc*. ನನಲಿ, ನನಲ್ಲಿ, ನನ್ನಲ್ಲಿ

ನನೆ 1. a k *v i*. To become wet, moist -ಸು, ನನಸು. To moisten.

ನನೆ 2 a k *n* A flower-bud, opening bud *v i* To bud -ಗೊಂಬು A branch with buds. -ಮೊಗ್ಗೆ. A bud and blossom.

ನಂದ s. *n* Happiness, joy 2, N of a cowherd who was the foster-father of Krishna. -ಕ Gladdening, the sword of Krishna

ನಂದನ s *n* Gladdening 2, a son. 3, a garden, grove, *also* -ವನ 4, twenty-sixth year of the cycle of sixty ನಂದನೆ A daughter

ನಂದಾದೀಪ, ನಂದಾದೀವಿಗೆ (*fr*. ನಂದದ ದೀಪ or ದೀವಿಗೆ) k.-s. *n*. An ever burning lamp; *cf* ನಂದು

ನಂದಿ s *n* Joy, delight 2, Śiva's bull. *a* Happy, gladdening. -ಬಟ್ಟಲಗಿಡ A shrub with fragrant white flowers, *Tabernaemontana coronaria*. -ಮಂಟಪ A kind of angular diagram -ವಾಹನ Śiva.

ನಂದು (= ನೊಂದು, *q v.*) *v i* To be extinguished, to go out, *etc* 2, to disappear, vanish ನಂದಿಸು. To extinguish, quench

ನಂದೆ s *n* Delight, felicity, prosperity 2, the first, sixth or eleventh day of a lunar fortnight

ನನ್ನ k. *pro Gen of* ನನ್, ನಾನು

ನನ್ನಿ k *n*. Truth, certainty 2, love, affection -ಮಾಡು To verify, prove

ನಪುಂಸಕ s. *n*. A hermaphrodite, a eunuch. 2, the neuter gender, *also* -ಲಿಂಗ.

ನಪ್ಪು k *n*. A bruise in a fruit or tree

ನಫರ h *n*. A mean wretch.

ನಫೆ h *n* Profit, gain -ಬಡ್ಡಿ (24 per cent) interest.

ನಬೀ h *n* A prophet the prophet Mahomed. ಇಸಾ-. Jesus Christ.

ನಭ, ನಭಸ್ s *n* The sky, atmosphere -ಸಂಗಮ A bird ನಭೋಜನ. A god. ನಭೋಮಂಡಲ The firmament, sky

ನಮ್ k *pro* We. *Gen* ನಮ್, ನಮ, ನಮ್ಮ. *Dat* ನಮಗೆ. *Acc* ನಮ್ಮನು, ನಮ್ಮನ್ನು. *Abl* ನಮ್ಮಿಂದ. *Loc*. ನಮ್ಮಲಿ. ನಮ್ಮಲ್ಲಿ.

ನಮನ s *n*. Bowing, obeisance.

ನಮಲು k *v t* To chew, masticate, to chew the cud *n*. Chewing the cud -ಹಾಕು. To chew the cud

ನಮಸ್ s *n* Bowing, a bow, salutation, obeisance -ಕರಿಸು To bow, make obeisance, adore -ಕಾರ. Obeisance reverence, adoration

ನಮಾಜು h *n*. Worship, divine service

ನಮಿಸು s. *v. t* To bow, to worship, adore

ನಮೂದು h *a*. Declared, shown, mentioned, recorded. -ಮಾಡು, ನಮೂದಿಸು To record, mention, show

ನಮೂನೆ h *n*. A specimen, sample, a model, a copy

ನಮೆ k *v i*. To grow lean or thin; to wear away; to become less, to be poor

ನಂಬರ e *n*. Number, a case, lawsuit -ದ ಕಟ್ಟು. The proceedings of a lawsuit ಮೂಲ- An original suit

ನಂಬಿಕೆ, ನಂಬಿಗ, ನಂಬುಗೆ k. *n* Confidence, trust, fidelity, faith, belief, faithfulness ನಂಬಿಗಸ್ತ A faithful man ನಂಬಿಗಸ್ತಿಕೆ Faithfulness trustworthiness. -ಉಳಿಸಿಕೊಳ್ಳು, -ಕಾದುಕೊಳ್ಳು To remain faithful

ನಂಬು k. *v. t*. To confide, trust, put confidence in, believe, to suppose -ವಿಕೆ = ನಂಬಿಕೆ ನಂಬಿಸು To cause to confide, to coax, persuade.

ನಂಬುಗೆ = ನಂಬಿಕೆ, *q v*

ನಮ್ಮ k. *pro*. (*pl. of* ನನ್) Our, ours

ನಮ್ಮಕ h. *n* Salt. -ಕೋಠಿ A salt factory

ನಮ್ರ s. *a* Bent, bowed 2, lowly, submissive, humble -ತೆ, -ತ್ವ, -ಭಾವ. Meekness, humility

ನಯ 1. k. *n* Softness, fineness, mildness, gentleness, cheapness -ಗಾರೆ. Smooth plaster -ನುಡಿ, -ಮಾತು. A gentle word -ಬಟ್ಟೆ. Fine cloth.

ನಯ 2. s *a* Guiding, leading. 2, fit, right, proper *n* Behaviour, conduct, way of life 2, prudent conduct, reason 3, polity, policy political economy 4, plan, principle. 5, opinion 6 right, justice -ಗುಣ A proper quality -ವಂತ, -ಶಾಲಿ A prudent man

ನಯನ s. *n* Guiding 2, the leading organ the eye -ಚ್ಛದ. An eyelid -ಜಲ, -ವಾರಿ ನಯನಾಶ್ರು, ನಯನೋದಕ. Tears. -ರೋಗ An eye-disease ಉಪ- Investiture with the brahmanical thread

ನರ 1 k *n*. A sinew nerve, muscle, a vein, artery -ಹುಲಿ = ನರೂಲಿ.

ನರ 2. s *n*. A man 2, Arjuna. -ಕವಿ, -ಗಬ್ಬಿಗ. A profane poet -ದೇವ, -ನಾಥ, -ಪತಿ, -ಪಾಲ, -ವರ, ನರಾಧಿಪ. A king. -ಪ್ರೇತ A ghost-like. lean man -ಬಲಿ A human sacrifice -ಭಕ್ಷಕ. A cannibal -ಮನುಷ್ಯ A human being. -ಲೋಕ. The earth, mortals. -ಕೇಸರಿ, -ಸಿಂಗ, -ಸಿಂಹ, -ಹರಿ Man-lion Vishnu in his fourth avatâra -ಶ್ರೇಷ್ಠ Best of men -ಹತ್ಯ Manslaughter ನರೇಂದ್ರ The lord of men a king.

ನರಕ s. *n* Hell, the Tartarus 2, a mass of filth. 3, N of a demon slain by Krishna; *also* ನರಕಾಸುರ -ಕೂಪ. A pit of filth -ಚತುರ್ದಶಿ A festival in the month of Âśvina to commemorate the destruction of Narakâsura -ಬಾಧೆ, -ಯಾತನೆ, -ವೇದನೆ The pains of hell ನರಕಾಧಿಪತಿ Yama

ನರಕು k *v. t.* To bruise *v i* To groan, *etc.*

ನರಟು k *v. i.* To become stunted in growth *n* Stunted growth 2, grumbling -ಗಾರ A discontented man, grumbler.

ನರಳು k *v. i.* To groan, moan

ನರಿ k. *n* A jackal, fox -ಕೂಗು The howl of jackals -ಚೆಂಡು A perennial creeping plant, *Lepidagathis cristata* -ನಾಲದ ಹುಲ್ಲು The plant *Hemionites cordifolia*, the common grass *Setaria glauca* -ಬುದ್ಧಿ Cunning

ನರು (ರು = ಱು) a k *n* Fragrance, scent, smell -ಗಂಪು Fragrance.

ನರುಗು k. *n* Grey colour: -ಗಂಬಳಿ. A cumbly with white and black stripes

ನರೂಲಿ k. *n* A wart, mole, *also* ನರಹುಲಿ

ನರೆ k *v. i* To become grey, *as* the hair *n* Grey hair, hoary age *Cpds* -ಕಂಬಳಿ, -ಕೂದಲು, -ಕೂದಲು, -ಗಡ್ಡ, -ಗೂಂಗಡಿ, -ತಲೆ, *etc.*

ನರ್ತಕ s *n* A dancer, *f.* ನರ್ತಕಿ.

ನರ್ತನ s *n*. Dancing. ನರ್ತಿಸು. To dance

ನರ್ಮ s. *n* Sport, play, pastime, joke, wit. -ದಾ, -ದೆ N. of a river -ಸಖ, -ಸಚಿವ An associate of a prince.

ನಲ್ a k *n* Goodness, fairness, loveliness, dearness *Cpds :* -ಗುಟುಕು, -ಗುದುರೆ, -ಗೆಳೆಯ, -ನುಡಿ, *etc* ನಲ್ಲ A good, dear man, a friend, *f.* ನಲ್ಲಳು

ನಲ 1 (= ನಲವು, ನಲಿ, ನಲಿವು, ನಲ್ಮೆ) a k *n* Pleasure, delight

ನಲ 2 s *n* A species of reed 2, N of a king and husband of Damayantî -ಕೂಬರ N of a son of Kubêra.

ನಲಗು (= ನಲುಗು) k *v. i.* To become rumpled, *as* cloth, paper, *etc*, to become flabby by heat; to droop *as* vegetables, *etc.*, to grow faint or feeble from sickness, *etc*

ನಲವು. = ನಲ 1, *q v*

ನಲಿ a k *v. i* To rejoice, to be pleased, to be fond of. *n.* (= ನಲ 1) Pleasure, *also* -ವು -ದಾಡು To be greatly delighted

ನಲಿನ s. *n* A lotus, a water-lily. -ಗರ್ಭ, -ಜ Brahmâ -ಬಾಂಧವ, -ಮಿತ್ರ, -ಸಖ The sun. -ವೈರಿ The moon. ನಲಿನಿ A lotus as *f*., a pond abounding in lotuses

ನಲುಗು.= ನಲಗು, *q v*.

ನಲ್ಮೆ a. k *n* Fondness, goodness, welfare, prosperity.

ನಲ್ಲ (*fr* ನಲ್) a k. *n* Goodness; beauty. 2, a good man *Cpds* -ತೈಲ -ಮುದ್ದು, -ರೂಪು, -ವಸ್ತು.

ನಲ್ವತ್ತು k *a* Forty. *also* ನಾಲ್ವತ್ತು

ನಲ್ಸು = ನಲ 1, *q v*.

ನವ 1. s. *a*. New, fresh modern -ತ. Freshness, novelty, = ನೌಕ

ನವ 2. s. *a* Nine -ಕ. Consisting of nine -ಖಂಡ. Nine fabulous continents. -ಗ್ರಹ The nine planets, namely Âditya, Sôma, Mangala, Budha Brihaspati, Šukra, Šani, Râhu, and Kêtu. -ಗ್ರಹದಾನ Nine-fold gifts to the nine planets. -ಗ್ರಹಶಾಂತಿ Propitiation of the nine planets. -ಜ್ವರ. A fever continuing for nine days -ದ್ವಾರ The nine outlets of the body. -ಧಾನ್ಯ. The nine grains: gôdivĕ, bhatta, uddu, hĕsaru, kadalĕ, tŏgari, hurali, avarĕ and ĕllu -ಮ The ninth -ಮಾಲಿಕೆ Arabian jasmine. -ಮಿ The ninth day of the lunar fortnight -ರಂಗ The middle hall of a temple -ರತ್ನ The nine precious gems vajra, vaidûrya, gômêdhika, pushyarâga, nîla, marakata, mânikya, vidruma, and mauktika -ರಸ The nine tastes or sentiments. -ರಾತ್ರಿ Nine nights a nine-days' feast of Durgâ, Indra, or Vishnu -ರಾಶಿಕ The double rule of three proportion (*arith*.) -ವಿಧ ಭಕ್ತಿ. Nine modes of devotion

ನವಕರ = ನವುಕರ.

ನವಂಬರ s *n* November (11th month of the year).

ನವಣೆ k. *n* The Italian millet, *Panicum italicum*

ನವನೀತ s *n* Fresh butter -ಜ Clarified butter.

ನವರು = ನವುರು, *q v*.

ನವಲ e *n*. A novel; a peculiar style of writing 2, novelty

ನವಸಾಗರ s *n* Sal ammoniac.

ನವರು.= ನವುರು, *q v*

ನವಸಿಗ k *n* A tormenter, molester

ನವಾಬ್ h *n* A Nabob.

ನವಾಯಿ h. *n* Novelty unusual beauty, grandeur. -ಕಾರ. A grandee -ತ Newly made· one of a class of Konkani speaking Mohammadans.

ನವಾರ h *n* A broad tape

ನವಿರು k *n* Hair 2, = ನವುರು *q v*

ನವಿಲು k. *n*. A peacock, pea-fowl; *also* ನವಿಲು -ಗರಿ A peacock's feathers -ಜುಟ್ಟು. A peacock's tuft

ನವೀನ s *a* New, fresh, excellent.

ನವುಕರ (= ನೌಕರ) h. *n* A servant, *also* ನವಕರ. ನವುಕರಿ Service.

ನವುಬತ್ತು h *n* A large kettle-drum

ನವುರು (= ನವರು) k *n*. That which is soft, thin, small *as* grass, hair, *etc*.

ನವುಲು k *n* The pea-fowl, *Pavo cristatus*

ನವೆ 1. (= ನವೆ *q v*) k *v i* To become thin *P ps* ನವದು. ನವೆದು

ನವೆ 2 k *n*. Itching, the itch -ಯಾಗು, -ಹತ್ತು. To itch, to get itch

ನಶಿಸು s *v. i* To vanish, to perish

ನಶೀಬು = ನಸೀಬು, *q v*

ನಶ್ವರ s *n* Perishing, vanishing, transient

ನಷ್ಟ s *a* Lost, vanished, perished *n* Loss; damage, ruin, destruction -ಜಾತಕ. The casting of a lost nativity. -ಜೀವಿ A sufferer from loss; a lost life -ದೃಷ್ಟಿ A blind man -ದ್ರವ್ಯ A lost thing -ಧನ. Lost riches. ನಷ್ಟೇಂದ್ರಿಯ Loss of one's organs of sense, impotency.

ನಸರಿ k *n* A good kind of honey

ನಸಿ 1 (= ನಮೆ, *etc*) k *v. i* To wear out, wane wither, decay 2, to faint.

3, to become poor. P ps. ನಸದು, ನಸಿದು

ನಸಿ 2. (tb. of ನಸ್ಯ = ನಸೆ, q v.) Snuff, also -ಪುಡಿ

ನಸಿಕು, ನಸಿಗು (= ನಸುಕು) k n. Dawn, twilight. ನಸಿಕಲೆ Early in the morning

ನಸೀಬು h n. Fortune, lot

ನಸೀಯತ್ತು h. n Chastisement.

ನಸು a k n. Minuteness, smallness, a little, a trifle -ಗತ್ತಲೆ Early dawn -ಗಾಳಿ. A light wind, breeze. -ಕುನ್ನಿ. A plant stinging like nettles, cowhage -ಗೆಂಪು. A tawny colour. -ನಗು. To smile. -ನಗೆ. A smile -ಬಿಳಿದು. Grey colour -ಲಜ್ಜೆ Modesty -ಸಯ್ರಣೆ. A little patience

ನಸುಕು = ನಸಿಕು, q v.

ನಸೂರಿ h n Slight fever. -ಬರು To be feverish

ನಸೆ s. n The nose 2, (= ನಸಿ 2) snuff, also -ಪುಡಿ ನಸ್ಯ Relating to the nose, snuff that produces sneezing

ನಳ. = ನಲ. q v

ನಳನಳಿಕೆ a. k n Softness, tenderness, beauty ನಳನಳಿಸು To be soft, tender, nice, bright.

ನಳಿಗೆ (tb of ನಲಕ) n A tube.

ನಳಿನ = ನಲಿನ, q v.

ನಳ್ಳಿ k. n. A crab.

ನಾ k pro 1, also ನಾಂ 2, four. -ಗಾಲು. Four feet. -ಗಾಲೋಟ A canter, a gallop

ನಾಕ s n Heaven, the sky, atmosphere; the abode of the gods

ನಾಕಾರಿ, ನಾಕಾರೆ = ನಕಾರಿ, q v

ನಾಕಿ s n A deity, god -ನಿಕರ. A multitude of gods.

ನಾಕು k. a. Four. 2, (f) an ant-hill -ಮಡಿ Four-fold.

ನಾಕ್ರಿಸ್ತ h. f. n A Non-christian, unbeliever

ನಾಖುಷಿ h n. Dissatisfaction, discontent, displea[illegible]

ನಾಕ್ಷತ್ರ s a Belonging to the stars, sidereal -ಮಾನ Sidereal computation of time

ನಾಗ s. n A snake, esp the Cobra capella. 2, a fabulous serpent-demon 3, an elephant. 4, any great man 5, fire, cloud, darkness 6, water. 7, lead. -ಕನ್ಯೆ A female of serpentine extraction. -ಕುಂಡಲ Śiva -ಕುಷ್ಠ A kind of leprosy. -ಕೇಸರ The tree *Mesua ferrea* -ದಂತಿ A species of sunflower, the Indian jalap -ಪಂಚಮಿ A feast on the 5th day of Śrâvana for the worship of serpent-images -ಪ್ರತಿಷ್ಠೆ Placing a stone-image of cobra for worship. -ಬೆತ್ತ A snake-coloured cane. -ಮಲ್ಲಿಗೆ A tall, shrubby plant, *Rhinacanthus communis* -ಮುರಿಗೆ. A serpentine bracelet -ರತ್ನ A jewel supposed to be found in the head of a cobra -ಲೋಕ The world of the serpent demons -ವಂದಿಗೆ. A shelf, peg, hook -ವರ್ಮ N of a Kannada poet. -ವಾಸ Abode of the Nâgas -ಶಯನ, -ಶಾಯಿ Vishnu. -ವೇಣಿ A woman with snake-like tresses. -ಸಂಪಿಗೆ A middle-sized flower-tree, *Mesua ferrea* -ಸ್ವರ A kind of pipe used by snake-players

ನಾಗರ 1. (= ನಾಗ, q v) s. n A snake, esp the cobra 2, an ornament with the image of a cobra, also -ಹೆಡೆ ನಾಗರು -ಕಾಟ. A disease of the skin; childlessness -ಪಂಚಮಿ = ನಾಗಪಂಚಮಿ. -ಹಾವು. The cobra.

ನಾಗರ 2. (fr. ನಗರ) s a. Belonging to a town, civic; polite, clever. n. A citizen. 2, = ದೇವನಾಗರಿ, q v. 3, dry ginger

ನಾಗರಿಕ, ನಾಗರೀಕ s a Town-bred, polite, clever n A townsman, a citizen, a cockney.

ನಾಗವಲಿ (tb of ನಾಗವಲ್ಲಿ) n Betel-nut the first chewing of betel-nut at a [illegible]

ನಾಗವಲ್ಲಿ (=ನಾಗವಲಿ, *q v*) s. *n* The betel creeper, *Piper betel* -ಹಚ್ಚಡ A cloth given to the son-in-law on the last day of his marriage

ನಾಗಾಶನ s *n*. A peacock 2, Garuda.

ನಾಗೇಂದ್ರ s *n* The serpent Śêsha

ನಾಚಿಕೆ k. *n*. Bashfulness, shame, modesty, decorum, grace -ಕೆಡು, -ಗೆಡು Shame or modesty to be lost -ಗೇಡಿ. A shameless person. -ಗೇಡಿತನ, -ಗೇಡು Shamelessness, impudence -ಗೊಳ್ಳು To feel ashamed -ಬಿಡು To give up shame.

ನಾಚು 1 k *v. i* To become ashamed or embarrassed. ನಾಚಿಸು To cause to be ashamed, to disgrace.

ನಾಚು 2 f *n*. A nautch, dance, dancing. -ಮಾಡು To dance, act

ನಾಜರು f. *n*. The sheriff of a law-court

ನಾಜೂಕು h *a* Delicate, soft, tender.

ನಾಟ h *n*. A stem or beam of wood.

ನಾಟಕ s. *n* A play, drama, dramatic representation -ಧಾರಿ, -ಪುರುಷ An actor, mime -ಶಾಲೆ A play-house, theatre.

ನಾಟಿ k *n* Young plants, *esp* of rice, fit for transplanting 2, transplanting. 3, (f) a kind of râga

ನಾಟು (=ನಡು) k *v i*. To get within, to be pierced or stuck into, *as* a thorn. *v t* To fix in the ground, plant; to pierce into *n* Planting, depth, *also* ನಾಟಿಕೆ -ಕೋಲು A planting stick ನಾಟಿಸು. To make plant

ನಾಟ್ಯ s *n*. Dancing, or dramatic representation -ಗಾರ. An actor. -ಗಾರ್ತಿ, -ಗಾತಿ. An actress -ಮಂದಿರ, -ರಂಗ A theatre.

ನಾಡದು k *n & ad* The day after tomorrow, *also* ನಾಡಿದು.

ನಾಡಾಡಿ, -ಗ k. *n* A rustic; a common [person

ನಾಡಿ s. *n*. The tubular stalk of any plant 2, any tubular organ, *as* an artery, a vein a nerve, *etc* 3, any pipe or tube 4 a fistulous sore. 5, the pulse 6, a period of twenty-four minutes, *also* -ಕೆ. 7, a juggling trick -ಆಡು, -ನಡೆ The pulse to beat. -ನಿಲ್ಲು The pulse to cease. -ನೋಡು To feel the pulse -ಪರೀಕ್ಷೆ Examining the pulse.

ನಾಡಿಗ k *n*. A village-superintendent 2, one of a caste so called in Canara, *f* -ಗಿತ್ತಿ. -ತನ. A nádiga's business.

ನಾಡು k *n*. A province, district, the country -ಗವುಡ The headman of a village -ಗಾದೆ A common proverb -ಶಾನಭೋಗ The accountant of a village

ನಾಡೆ a k. *ad* Further, moreover, much, excessively

ನಾಣ್ (=ನಾಚಿಕೆ, *etc*, *q v*) a. k. *n* Bashfulness, shame, modesty, *etc* 2, =ನಾಡು ನಾಣಿಲಿ. Shameless, a shameless person ನಾಣಿಲಿತನ Shamelessness -ಗೆಡಿಕ A shameless man. -ಗೆಡಿಸು To disgrace, reproach -ನುಡಿ. Popular report, common talk.

ನಾಣ್ಯ 1 k *n* Fineness, goodness, good quality, *as* that of cloth, grain, *etc*, honesty, truth -ಸ್ಥ, -ವಂತ. A trustworthy man

ನಾಣ್ಯ 2 f. *n* A coin, money. -ಪರೀಕ್ಷೆ. Assaying money. -ವಟ್ಟ The agio on money. -ವಾರು The detailed account of various coins

ನಾತ (=ನಾರು) k *n* Smell in general, a bad smell, stench -ಗೊಳ್ಳು, -ಬರು, -ಹಿಡಿ To smell, to stink

ನಾತು, *P. p of* ನಾರು, *q v*

ನಾಥ s *n* A protector; a master, ruler a husband -ವತ್ Dependent, subject

ನಾದ s *n* A sound, a tone in general 2, a note of music; *as* ಘಂಟಾ-, ವೀಣಾ-, ಕೊಳಲ-, ಸಿಂಹ-, *etc*.

ನಾದನಿ (*tb of* ನನಾಂದೃ) *n* A husband's sister, a brother's wife

ನಾದಾರಿ h. *n*. Insolvency, pauperism ನಾದಾರು Insolvent, a pauper

ನಾ-.ನಿ = ನಾದನಿ, *q v*.

ನಾದಿಸು s v i To sound

ನಾದು k. v t To knead, as dough etc. v i. To moisten, soak, to cool. ನಾದಿಸು To knead

ನಾದುರುಸ್ತು h. a Out of order, unrepaired, unmended.

ನಾದೇಯ s. a Aquatic ನಾದೇಯಿ A species of reed, *Calamus fasciculatus*, the orange-tree, the shoe-flower plant

ನಾನಾ s a Of different kinds, various, manifold, diverse ad. Variously, manifoldly. *Cpds* -ಕಾರ್ಯ, -ಕೆಲಸ, -ತರ, -ಪ್ರಕಾರ, -ಬಗೆ, -ರೀತಿ, -ವಿಧ, *etc* -ರೂಪ Various forms ನಾನಾರ್ಥ. Homonymous, a homonym.

ನಾನು 1 k *pro* I

ನಾನು 2 k v i To get wet, moist, damp *P ps* ನಾತು, ನಾದು

ನಾನೂರು k a Four hundred.

ನಾಂದಿ s n Joy, prosperity 2, eulogium or praise of a deity, a prayer recited at the opening of a religious ceremony or of a drama -ಮುಖ, -ಶ್ರಾದ್ಧ. A commemorative offering to the manes before any joyous occasion, *as* marriage, *etc*

ನಾಪಿತ s n A barber, *also* ನಾವಿಗ, ನಾಹಿಗ.

ನಾಭಿ s n The navel. 2, the nave of a wheel 3, the centre, focus, middle 4, a near relation

ನಾಮ s n A name 2, a noun. 3 the sectarian mark of Vaishnavas *ad* By name. 2, possibly -ಕೋಳಿ. The pigmy cormorant -ದ ಬೇರು. The country sarsaparilla, *Hemidesmus indicus* -ಕರಣ. The ceremony of naming a child. -ಧಾರಿ A Vaishnava; renowned -ಧೇಯ A name, title -ಪದ, -ವಾಚಕ A noun -ಸ್ಮರಣ Bearing in mind the name of a god -ಹಾಕು. To put on the Vaishnava marks, to cheat. ನಾಮಾಂಕಿತ. Renowned

ನಾಮಂಜೂರು h. n Disapproval. -ಮಾಡು Disallow, disapprove [a coward

ನಾಮರ್ದ h

ನಾಮಿ s. n Bending. 2, a N. for all vowels, except ಅ and ಆ. -ಕ. Having a name.

ನಾಮೋಷಿ h n. Disgrace, shame.

ನಾಮೆ h n A deed letters patent

ನಾಯ (*tb of* ನ್ಯಾಯ) n A lawsuit

ನಾಯಕ s. a Pre-eminent, chief n. A guide, leader, a chief, head, a general, commander, a husband, *f* ನಾಯಕಿ. -ತ್ವ Leadership -ವಾಡಿ A chief, headman, *as* of a caste, village, *etc*

ನಾಯಬ h n A deputy -ಸಿರಸ್ತೇದಾರ A native head clerk of a subordinate office

ನಾಯಿ k n A dog -ಕುನ್ನಿ, -ಮರಿ A puppy, whelp -ಕೊಡೆ. A mushroom -ಕೆಮ್ಮು, -ಗೆಮ್ಮು The hooping cough -ತುಲಸಿ The herb *Ocimum album* -ಪಾಡು, -ಬಾಳು A wretched, miserable existence -ಬೆಳೆಗಿಡ An annual herb, *Cleome viscosa* -ಬೇಲ The plant *Flacourtia sapida* -ಬೊಗಳು, -ಕೂಗು A dog to bark -ಯುಳ್ಳಿ. A bulbous plant, *Scilla indica*

ನಾಯಿಂದ (*tb of* ನಾಪಿತ) n. A barber

ನಾರಂಗ s n The orange tree, an orange

ನಾರದ s. n N of a devarshi -ವೀಣೆ Nârada's lute: a kind of lute.

ನಾರಾಗೋರ k n A very meagre man

ನಾರಾಚ s n A long arrow, a style to write with

ನಾರಾಯಣ (*fr* ನರ divine spirit and ಅಯನ pervading) s n. Brahmâ. 2, Vishnu, Krishna (*sometimes the deity who was before all worlds*) ನಾರಾಯಣಿ. Lakshmî, Durgâ

ನಾರಿ 1 k n A bow-string

ನಾರಿ 2 s n. A woman, wife

ನಾರಿಕೇರ, ನಾರಿಕೇಲ s n The cocoanut

ನಾರು 1. k n A fibre fibres of plants, ts

2, cloth made of hemp, or linen, *also* -ಮಡಿ. -ಸೀರೆ A female's linen garment -ಕಟ್ಟು Fibre-like pus to form in a sore -ಗ A dealer in fibres. -ಬೇರು Fibres and roots -ಹುಣ್ಣು. A guinea-worm.

ನಾರು 2 (ರು=ಱು) k. *n* Smell *v i* To smell, to stink *P ps.* ನಾರಿ, ನಾತು -ವ ಬೇಳೆ, ನಾರಂಬೇಳೆ A strong smelling herb, *Cleome pentaphylla.*

ನಾಲ 1. (=ನಾಳ) h. *n* A horse or bullock-shoe -ಗಾರ, -ಬಂದಿ One who shoes a horse or bullock.

ನಾಲ 2. h. *n.* A drain, gutter.

ನಾಲಾಯಖು h. *a.* Unfit, ineligible. *n* Demerit

ನಾಲಿ (=ನಾಳಿ) s. *n* A tubular stalk 2, a tube. 3, a period of 24 minutes

ನಾಲಿಗೆ k *n* The tongue 2, the clapper of a bell -ಕೆಡು. Appetite to be lost, a promise to fail -ತಪ್ಪು. A promise to break; a slip of the tongue -ತಿರುಗು To be able to speak fluently -ಪ್ರಮಾಣ. Confidence in one's words or promises -ಬೀಳು. To become unable to utter. -ಉಳಿಸು. To keep one's promise. -ವಾಸಿ Trustworthiness. -ಹೋಗು =-ಬೀಳು

ನಾಲಿಸು h *n* Complaint; censure, sneer, reprobation -ಮಾಡು. To disapprove, disparage

ನಾಲ್ಕು k. *a.* Four ನಾಲ್ಕಡಿ Four feet ನಾಲ್ಕನೆ Fourth. ನಾಲ್ಕಯಿದು. 9. ನಾಲ್ಕಷ್ಟು Four times as much ನಾಲ್ಕಾರು Four or six, several, some. -ಕೆಲಸ. Every kind of work. -ಜನ, -ಜನರು. All persons, every body. -ಜಾತಿ, -ವರ್ಣ The four castes -ದಿಕ್ಕು, -ದೆಸೆ The four points of the compass. -ಮಾಡು To divide into four. -ಮಾತು. Some words ನಾಲ್ಕೂಕಾಲು 4¼ ನಾಲ್ವತ್ತು Forty. ನಾಲ್ವರು. Four persons.

ನಾವಲಿಗ (*tb. of* ನಾಪಿಕ) *n* A barber.

ನಾವಾಡಿಗ f *n* A boatman, a helmsman

ನಾವಾರ (=ನವಾರ) h ... tape

ನಾವಿಕ s. *n.* A sailor, steersman, pilot.

ನಾವಿದ, ನಾವಿಂದ *tb. of* ನಾಪಿತ, *q. v.*

ನಾವು k *pro pl* of ನಾನು. We *See its decl. s.* ನಮ್ಮ.

ನಾವೆ s *n* A boat, ship, vessel. ನಾವ್ಯ. Navigable

ನಾಶ s. *n* Destruction, annihilation, ruin, loss, death -ಗೊಳಿಸು, -ಮಾಡು To destroy, ruin, kill -ಹೊಂದು To be ruined -ನ Destroying, *etc.*, ruin.

ನಾಷ್ಟ h *n.* Breakfast, luncheon

ನಾಸಾ s *n* The nose. ನಾಸಿ Snuff. ನಾಸಿಕ, ನಾಸೆ. A nose, a trunk.

ನಾಸ್ತಾ.=ನಾಷ್ಟ, *q v*

ನಾಸ್ತಿ s. It is not, there is not non-existence. -ಕ An atheist; an infidel. -ಕತನ, -ಕತೆ, -ಕತ್ವ, -ಕ್ಯ. Atheism, infidelity.

ನಾಳ (=ನಾಲ, *q v*) s *n* A pipe, tube. *etc.* 2, the clapper of a bell.

ನಾಳಿ. *tb. of* ನಾಡಿ, *q. v.*, *also* a water-channel, a weaver's shuttle

ನಾಳೆ k *ad* To-morrow

ನಿ. = ನಿರ್, ನಿಶ್, ನಿಷ್, ನಿಸ್, *q. v*

ನಿಃಶಂಕ s. *n* Fearless, without hesitation or fear ನಿಃಶಂಕೆ. Boldness, confidence.

ನಿಃಶಬ್ದ s. *a* Noiseless *n.* Silence, calm

ನಿಃಶೇಷ s *a* Without remainder, complete, entire.

ನಿಃಸಂಗ s *a* Unattached, indifferent; disinterested. *n* Unattachment, indifference

ನಿಃಸಂದೇಹ s *a* Doubtless, certain *n.* Certainty

ನಿಃಸಹಾಯ s. *a* Helpless, unassisted

ನಿಃಸಾರ s. *a* Sapless, insipid, worthless.

ನಿಕಟ s *a* Near, proximate *n.* Pith, sap

ನಿಕರ s. *n* A heap, a flock, multitude

ನಿಕಾ h *n.* A Mohammadan marriage

... s *n* Wish, de...

ನಿಕಾಯ s. n A heap, set, flock. 2, a house, dwelling.

ನಿಕಾಲಸು h a Plain, blunt, open, *as* a person, speech, *etc*

ನಿಕುಂಜ s n An arbour, thicket

ನಿಕುರುಂಬ s n A flock, multitude

ನಿಕೃತಿ s n Dishonest practice, deception, fraud.

ನಿಕೃಷ್ಟ s. a Drawn down, low, base, vulgar.

ನಿಕೇತನ s. n A house dwelling

ನಿಕ್ಕುವ a k n. Truth, certainty. *ad* Truly, certainly

ನಿಕ್ಷೇಪ s n Placing, a deposit, pledge, trust. 2 a hidden treasure. ನಿಕ್ಷೇಪಿಸು To deposit, to bury

ನಿಖಿಲ s a Complete, all entire

ನಿಗದಿ h. n Fixing *as* a hire, salary, *etc.*, decision -ಮಾಡು To fix, to decide

ನಿಗಮ s n. Insertion 2, a passage of the vêdas 3, the vêda, a sacred precept *a* Issued from, liberated, set free.

ನಿಗರ 1 (= ನಿಗುರು. *q v*) k *a* Straight, erect, *also* ನಿಗುರ -ಕಿವಿ An erect ear ನಿಗರಿಕೆ. Straightness

ನಿಗರ 2 (*tb of* ನಿಕರ) n The best of anything

ನಿಗರು. = ನಿಗುರು *q v*.

ನಿಗರ್ವ (= ನಿರ್ಗರ್ವ) s. *a* Prideless, humble *n* Humility. ನಿಗರ್ವಿ. A humble person

ನಿಗಾ, ನಿಗಾವಾನಿ, ನಿಗಾವ್ವ h n Care in looking after, tending, regard to.

ನಿಗುರು k v. i To be stretched forth, to spread, expand, to become erect, to rise; to swell, become proud n Expansion ನಿಗುರಿಸು To stretch forth, *etc*

ನಿಗೂಢ s *a* Hidden secret, profound, obscure

ನಿಗ್ರಹ್ಯ s. *a* Punishable.

ನಿಗೇವಾನಿ —

ನಿಗ್ಗರ (*tb of* ನಿಗ್ರಹ) n Coercion, compulsion

ನಿಗ್ಗವ a k n The tusks of an elephant ivory.

ನಿಗ್ರಹ s n Keeping in check, coercion, restraint, subjugation, humbling, punishing 2, rebuke, blame 3, aversion, dislike, a mental pain. ನಿಗ್ರಹಿಸು To restrain, subdue, keep in check, to punish. ನಿಗ್ರಹಿಸುವಿಕೆ. Keeping in check

ನಿಘಂಟು s n A vocabulary, dictionary

ನಿಘರ್ಷಣ s n Friction, grinding, trituration.

ನಿಚಯ s n A collection, a heap, assemblage

ನಿಚ್ಚ. *tb of* ನಿತ್ಯ, *q v*.

ನಿಚ್ಚಣಿ, -ಕೆ, -ಗೆ (*tb of* ನಿಃಶ್ರೇಣಿ) n A ladder.

ನಿಚ್ಚಯ *tb of* ನಿಶ್ಚಯ, *q v*.

ನಿಜ s. *a*. Innate. 2, own. 3, real, true, actual, genuine n Reality truth -ಗುಣ A truthful man -ಮಾರ್ಗ The proper way -ರೂಪ One's own shape -ಸಾಕ್ಷಿ. True evidence. -ಸ್ಥ = ನಿಜಗುಣ -ಮುಡಿ A moorah of 42 sheers

ನಿಜಾಮ h n Ruler the title of the native sovereign of Hyderabad

ನಿಟಿಲ s n. The forehead.

ನಿಟ್ಟು *abbr. of* ನಿಡಿದು (*in* ನಿಡು, *q v*) -ಸುರು A drawn out, deep sigh --ಬಿಡು To sigh deeply ನಿಟ್ಟೆಲುವು The spine ನಿಟ್ಟೋಟ A long run.

ನಿಡಿ 1. = ನಿಡು *q v* -ದು That which is long, length.

ನಿಡಿ 2 k. n A strong stifling smell, *as* that of tobacco, cayenne pepper, *etc* 2, scum, froth.

ನಿಡು a k n Length, extensiveness, bigness. *Cpds* -ಕತ, -ಗವಸೆ, -ಗೊಂಬು. -ಗೋಡು, -ಗೋಲು, -ಜಾಪ, -ಜಡೆ, -ನರ, -ನಿದ್ರೆ, -ಬತ್ತಳಿಕೆ, -ಬಲೆ, -ಬಾವಿ, -ಬೆರಳು, -ಮೊಬ್ಬೆ, -ಮೂಗು, -ಸರ, *etc*

ನಿತ್ಯ s *a.* Continual, perpetual, endless, eternal, everlasting, necessary, essential -ಕಟ್ಟಳೆ Daily observance. -ಕರ್ಮ A daily rites -ವಂತೆ. As usual. -ದರಿದ್ರ. An always poor man. -ತೆ, ತ್ವ. Eternity -ದಾನ Daily alms-giving. -ಶ್ರಾದ್ಧ. A daily śrâddha. ನಿತ್ಯಾತ್ಮ The eternal soul

ನಿತ್ರಾಣ (*tb of* ನಿಸ್ತ್ರಾಣ) *n* Weakness.

ನಿದರ್ಶನ s *n* An example or illustration 2, a view, vision; omen.

ನಿದಾನ 1 s *n* A first cause 2, end, termination. 3, pathology

ನಿದಾನ 2. *tb. of* ನಿಧಾನ. *q. v* -ವಂತ, -ಸ್ಥ, ನಿದಾನಿ. A patient man.

ನಿದೇಶ s *n* Command, instruction

ನಿದ್ದೆ *tb. of* ನಿದ್ರೆ, *q v.* -ಗಣ್ಣು. Sleepy eyes -ಮಾಡು To sleep -ಮೊಬ್ಬು Drowsiness. -ಎಚ್ಚರು To awake -ಹತ್ತು To be asleep -ಹೋಗು. To fall asleep.

ನಿದ್ರೆ (=ನಿದ್ದೆ) s. *n* Sleep, slumber. 2, sleepiness. -ಕೆಡು. Sleep to be spoiled -ಗೆಯ್, -ಮಾಡು To sleep -ಹತ್ತು = ನಿದ್ದೆಹತ್ತು [ರ್ಧನ.

ನಿಧನ s *n* End 2, death, loss. 3, = ನಿ

ನಿಧಾನ s *n* Laying aside 2, a receptacle, a treasure, wealth. 3, a place of rest 4, effort, work 5, slowness, patience, pausing -ಗೊಳ್ಳು -ವಡು. -ಬೀಳು, -ಮಾಡು, To consider, judge

ನಿಧಿ s *n.* A receptacle. 2, a treasure, wealth, a store 3, the ocean

ನಿನ್ k *pro* Thou, *also* ನೀನು. ನಿನ್ನ Thy. ನಿನ್ನದು. Thine.

ನಿಂತು = ನಿತ್ತು. *P p. of* ನಿಲ್ಲು, *q v*

ನಿಂದಿರು *See s.* ನಿಲ್ಲು, *q v*

ನಿಂದೆ s *n.* Blame, censure, reproach, abuse, scorn ನಿಂದಕ. A scorner ನಿಂದಿಸು To blame, abuse, *etc*

ನಿಂದ್ಯ s *a.* Blamable, despicable.

ನಿನ್ನ *pro Gen of* ನೀನು, *q v* Of thee, thine, thy [illegible] *Dat* ನಿನಗೆ *Abl.* ನಿನ್ನಿಂದ. *Loc.* [illegible]

ನಿನ್ನೆ k. *ad.* Yesterday *Instr.* -ಯಿಂದ *Dat* -ಗೆ. *Gen* -ಯ, ನಿನ್ನಿನ

ನಿಪಾತ s *n* Falling down dying, death; ruined state. 2, putting down as irregular or exceptional, *as* a word in a compound, exception 3, a particle (*g*). -ಮಾಡು. To destroy.

ನಿಪುಣ s *a* Perfect; accurate 2, clever, skilful. -ತನ, -ತೆ, -ತ್ವ Skilfulness, cleverness

ನಿಬದ್ಧ s *a* Bound, caught, fettered, confined. *n* A fixed rule.

ನಿಬಂಧನೆ s. *n* Binding, a rule, order.

ನಿಬಿಡ s. *a.* Thick, dense, tight. ನಿಬಿಡೀಕೃತ Made close, dense, *etc.*

ನಿಬ್ಬಣ k *n* A marriage festival. ನಿಬ್ಬಣಿಗ. A bridegroom's companion

ನಿಭಾಯಿಸು h. *v t* To endure, suffer, bear, succeed

ನಿಮಗ್ನ s. *a.* Immersed; sunk in, depressed

ನಿಮಂತ್ರಣ s *n* Invitation, *esp* to a śrâddha.

ನಿಮಾಜು = ನಮಾಜು, *q v*

ನಿಮಾನಿಮಿ h *a.* Exact, quite correct, *ad.* Exactly, *etc.*

ನಿಮಿತ್ತ, ನಿಮಿತ್ಯ s *n.* A mark, aim 2, sign; omen 3, cause, motive, reason. -ವಾಗಿ. Because of, on account of -ಗಾರ A fortune-teller

ನಿಮಿರು. = ನಿಗುರು, *q v*

ನಿಮಿರ್ಚು = ನಿಗುರಿಸು, *q v.*

ನಿಮಿಷ s *n.* Twinkling, winking, the twinkling of an eye, a moment 2, a minute.

ನಿಂಬ s *n* The Nimb-tree, *Azadirachta indica* -ತರು. The coral tree

ನಿಂಬೆ (=ಲಿಂಬೆ) k. *n* The acid lime, *Citrus medica.*

ನಿಮ್ಮ 1. (*pl of* ನಿನ್ನ) k. *pro* Your. -ದು Yours *Acc.* ನಿಮ್ಮನ್ನು *Abl* ನಿಮ್ಮಿಂದ *Dat* ನಿಮಗೆ *Loc* ನಿಮ್ಮಲ್ಲಿ

[illegible] 2 s. *n* Depth a slope [illegible] [illegible]. Deep. low.

ನಿಯತ s. *a* Checked; controlled 2, fixed, permanent. 3, certain. 4, positive *n* Restraint, a religious duty ನಿಯತಿ Restraint, restriction, rule 2, destiny, fate.

ನಿಯತ್ತು (*tb of* ನಿಯತ) *n* Truthfulness

ನಿಯಮ (=ನೇಮ) s *n* Ruling 2, a rule, law, precept, a regular practice, appointment 3 agreement, contract 4, any religious observance -ನಿಷ್ಠೆ. Regular and rigid observance of meritorious rites or works. ನಿಯಮಿತ. Regulated, prescribed, fixed ನಿಯಮಿಸು (=ನೇಮಿಸು). To restrain, subdue, to lay down a rule, to order, to appoint, fix, to nominate

ನಿಯಾಮಕ s *n* Guiding, governing. 2, a ruler. 3, a charioteer 4, a boatman, a pilot. 5, rule, order

ನಿಯಾಮಿಸು = ನಿಯಮಿಸು s ನಿಯಮ, *q. v*

ನಿಯುಕ್ತ s *a.* Fastened to, appointed; employed; assigned ನಿಯುಕ್ತಿ Injunction, order; charge

ನಿಯುತ s. *n* A great number.

ನಿಯೋಗ s *n.* Application, use, employment. 2, order, command 3, trust, business. ನಿಯೋಗಿ A functionary, a minister, a class of Brâhmanas ನಿಯೋಗಿಸು To assign, to employ, to command

ನಿಯೋಜನ s. *n.* Uniting, ordering, appointing to ನಿಯೋಜಿಸು. To assign, appoint, *etc*

ನಿರ್, ನಿಸ್, ನಿಷ್ (=ನಿಃ) s. *pref.* Certainty. 2 negation, privation. 3, out, without

ನಿರಕ್ಷರ s *a* Illiterate. -ಕುಕ್ಷಿ An illiterate person

ನಿರಖು h *n* Current price -ಪಟ್ಟಿ A price-current

ನಿರಂಕುಶ s *a* Unchecked, uncontrolled, self-willed

ನಿರಂಜನ s *a.* Unstained, untinged pure

ನಿರತ s. *a* Engaged or interested in

ನಿರತೆ (ರ=ಱ) k *n* Beauty, charm, elegan

ನಿರಂತರ s *a.* Having no interval, continuous, without interstices, compact, dense; uninterrupted, constant *ad* Continuously.

ನಿರಪರಾಧಿ s *n.* A faultless or guiltless person.

ನಿರಪಾಯ s *a* Imperishable, infallible.

ನಿರಪೇಕ್ಷೆ s. *n* Absence of desire or expectation.

ನಿರರ್ಥಕ s *a* Nonsensical, useless, unprofitable.

ನಿರವಧಿ s *a.* Unlimited, interminable.

ನಿರವಯವ s. *n.* Without limbs or members

ನಿರಶನ s. *n.* Fasting, a fast.

ನಿರಹಂಕಾರ s *n* Absence of selfishness.

ನಿರಹಂಕೃತ s. *a* Unselfish

ನಿರಾಕರಣ s. *n* Repudiation rejection ನಿರಾಕರಿಸು To put away, repudiate *etc*

ನಿರಾಕಾಂಕ್ಷೆ s. *n* Desirelessness

ನಿರಾಕಾರ s. *a.* Formless, shapeless, ugly, *also* ನಿರಾಕೃತಿ.

ನಿರಾಕ್ಷೇಪ s. *a* Unblamable, unobjectionable -ತೆ. Unobjectionableness

ನಿರಾಜಿ h. *a.* Furnished with kalâbatu, *as* a cloth

ನಿರಾಧಾರ s *n.* Groundlessness, poorness. *etc* ನಿರಾಧಾರಿ A poor person.

ನಿರಾಯಾಸ s *a* Not causing trouble, not requiring efforts, not fatiguing

ನಿರಾಶೆ s. *n* Hopelessness, despair.

ನಿರಾಶ್ರಯ s. *a.* Supportless, friendless, destitute.

ನಿರಾಹಾರ s. *n* Foodlessness, fasting. ನಿರಾಹಾರಿ. A fasting person.

ನಿರಾಳ (*tb of* ನಿರಾಕುಲ) *n* Doubtlessness, certainty, calmness. 2 the sky

ನಿರಿ 1 (ರಿ=ಱಿ) k *v. i* To be arranged, to be ready, *cf.* ನೆರೆ 3. *n* Orderly arrangement

ನಿರಿ 2., ನಿರಿಗೆ k. *n* Foldings the folds of a garment, *as* of a dôtra or

ನಿರಿಸು (ರಿ=ಱಿ.=ಇರಿಸು) a. k. *v. t.* To put down, to arrange, to adjust *n* Arrangement; display.

ನಿರೀಕ್ಷೆ s *n.* Looking towards, expectation, waiting for. ನಿರೀಕ್ಷಣ Looking at, expecting, a look ನಿರೀಕ್ಷಿಸು To look at, gaze at, to behold; to expect.

ನಿರೀಶ್ವರ s. *a.* Godless, atheistic. -ವಾದ Atheism -ವಾದಿ. An atheist.

ನಿರುಗೆ (ರು=ಱು) k *n.* Orderly arrangement, properness

ನಿರುಕ್ತ s *a.* Uttered, explained *n.* One of the vêdângas.

ನಿರುತ s *a* Undoubted; true *n* Undoubtedness, truth; unfailingness, rectitude [reposed

ನಿರುತ್ತರ s. *a* Without a reply; silenced

ನಿರುದ್ಯೋಗ s *a* Inactive, lazy, without employment ನಿರುದ್ಯೋಗಿ. One who is unemployed

ನಿರುಪದ್ರ, -ವ s *a.* Undisturbed; harmless, inoffensive *n* Undisturbedness

ನಿರುಪಮ, ನಿರುಪಮಾನ, ನಿರುಪಮಿತ s *a* Matchless, unequalled

ನಿರುಪಯುಕ್ತ s. *a.* Useless

ನಿರುಪಾಧಿ. -ಕ s *a* Free from cares or trouble

ನಿರುಪಾಯ s *a* Helpless, remediless

ನಿರೊಗ್ಗಿ s *n* Fame. 2 skilfulness.

ನಿರೂಪ s. *n.* An order, command; a written order. -ಣ, -ಣೆ Representing, investigation, determination, definition, sight, telling, narrating ನಿರೂಪಿಸು To order, to make known, to define ನಿರೂಪ್ಯಮಾಣ. Being defined, determined

ನಿರೋಗ s. *a* Free from sickness, healthy, well, *also* ನೀರೋಗ ನಿರೋಗಿ A healthy person, *also* ನೀರೋಗಿ

ನಿರೋಧ s *n* Shutting in, check, coercion, restraint, hindrance ನಿರೋಧಿಸು. To obstruct, to restrain, keep back

ನಿರೋಪ (*tb of* ನಿರೂಪ) *n* A message, permission to depart

ನಿರ್ಗತ s. *a.* Gone out, disappeared, extinct 2, freed from [ty.

ನಿರ್ಗತಿ s *n.* Helplessness, misery, pover-

ನಿರ್ಗಮ s *n* Going forth, setting out, receding, departure, *also* -ನ

ನಿರ್ಗರ್ವ = ನಿಗರ್ವ, *q v.*

ನಿರ್ಗುಣ s. *a* Without qualities *n* The supreme soul

ನಿರ್ಗುಂಡಿ s *n.* A shrub, the five-leaved chaste-tree, *Vitex negundo.*

ನಿರ್ಘೋಷ, -ಣ s. *n.* A loud sound, noise.

ನಿರ್ಜನ s *a.* Unpeopled, uninhabited, desolate [A god.

ನಿರ್ಜರ s *a.* Undecaying, immortal *n.*

ನಿರ್ಜಲ s. *a* Waterless, dry.

ನಿರ್ಜೀವ s. *n.* Lifelessness. *a* Lifeless, inanimate ನಿರ್ಜೀವಿ. A lifeless being

ನಿರ್ಣಯ s *n.* Decision, determination, precise definition 2, sentence, decree, verdict. 3, final settlement -ಮಾಡು, ನಿರ್ಣಯಿಸು To settle, decide, come to a decision, to give a verdict, to decree, order. ನೀತಿ- Justification (*Christ*) ಆಜ್ಞೆ-. Damnation (*Christ.*).

ನಿರ್ದಯ s. *a* Pitiless, unmerciful, unkind ನಿರ್ದಯೆ. Unmercifulness, cruelty.

ನಿರ್ದಿಷ್ಟ s. *a* Assigned, directed; described, ascertained

ನಿರ್ದುಷ್ಟ s. *n* Faultlessness.

ನಿರ್ದೇಶ s *n.* Pointing out, denoting; directing, order, command, direction, description. ನಿರ್ದೇಶಿಸು To point out, show, to specify, *etc.*

ನಿರ್ದೈವ s. *a* Luckless.

ನಿರ್ದೋಷ s. *a.* Faultless, guiltless, innocent. ನಿರ್ದೋಷಿ. A guiltless person.

ನಿರ್ಧನ (=ನಿಧನ) s *a* Poor. *n* Poverty.

ನಿರ್ಧರಿಸು s *v t.* To determine, ascertain, settle, make sure

ನಿರ್ಧಾರ s *n.* Particularizing, determining defining, settling, certainty judgment, *also* -

ನಿರ್ಧೂತ s. *a* Shaken off, removed.

ನಿರ್ನಾಮ s *a*. Nameless. 2, ruined. *n* Ruin.

ನಿರ್ನಿಮಿತ್ತ s *a* Causeless groundless. *n* Causelessness *ad* Causelessly.

ನಿರ್ಬಂಧ s. *n*. Restraining, hindrance, obstruction, *also* -ನ 2, force, violence 3, a rule -ಗೊಳಿಸು. To use force ನಿರ್ಬಂಧಿಸು. To restrain, hinder, to urge, force

ನಿರ್ಬಲ s. *a* Powerless *n*. Powerlessness.

ನಿರ್ಬಾಧ s. *n*. Freedom from trouble or annoyance.

ನಿರ್ಬುದ್ಧಿ s *a* Senseless, stupid. *n* Stupidity

ನಿರ್ಭಯ s. *a*. Fearless, secure. *n* Fearlessness, freedom from danger

ನಿರ್ಭಾಗ್ಯ s *n* Unluckiness *a* Unlucky.

ನಿರ್ಭೀತ s *a*. Fearless, undaunted. ನಿರ್ಭೀತಿ. Fearlessness

ನಿರ್ಮದ s *a* Sober; humble

ನಿರ್ಮರಣ s. *a* Deathless

ನಿರ್ಮಲ (= ನಿಮ್ಮಳ) s *a* Spotless stainless, virtuous, clean, pure, serene, shining, charming. -ಮಾಡು To clean, *as* a house, *etc* -ತೆ, -ತ್ವ Purity, cleanliness

ನಿರ್ಮಾಂಸ s *a* Fleshless, emaciated

ನಿರ್ಮಾಣ s. *n* Forming, making, creating, creation. -ಮಾಡು To produce, to create

ನಿರ್ಮಾತೃ s *n* A maker, creator.

ನಿರ್ಮಾಲ್ಯ s *n* Stainlessness, purity, the remains of an offering to an idol, *as* flowers *etc*

ನಿರ್ಮಿಸು s *v. t* To make, form, fabricate create.

ನಿರ್ಮುಕ್ತ s *a*. Set free, liberated

ನಿರ್ಮೂಲ s *a* Rootless, unfounded. *n*. Eradication, extirpation -ಮಾಡು To eradicate, extirpate. ನಿರ್ಮೂಲಿಸು To uproot, pluck out, extirpate.

ನಿರ್ಮೋಹ s *n* Absence of love.

ನಿರ್ಯಾಣ s. *n* Departure 2 disappearan[ce]

ನಿರ್ಯಾಸ s. *n* Exudation of trees, *as* juice, gum, resin, milk, *etc*

ನಿರ್ಲಕ್ಷ್ಯ s *n* Disregard, contempt.

ನಿರ್ಲಜ್ಜೆ s *n* Shamelessness, impudence.

ನಿರ್ಲೇಪ s *a* Stainless, spotless *n*. Spotlessness

ನಿರ್ಲೋಭ s *n* Unavariciousness, unselfishness ನಿರ್ಲೋಭಿ. Unselfish.

ನಿರ್ವಂಚನೆ s *n*. Fraudlessness. 2, sincerity; *also* ನಿರ್ವಂಚಕತ್ವ ನಿರ್ವಂಚಕ Sincere

ನಿರ್ವರ್ತಿಸು s *v. t* To complete finish.

ನಿರ್ವಹಿಸು s *v t* To carry out, to accomplish, effect

ನಿರ್ವಾಣ s. *a* Extinguished, liberated from existence *n* Extinction of life, the delivery of the individual soul from the body and further transmigration 2 death 3 highest felicity and reunion with the supreme soul 4, vacuity 5, immersion. 6, a kind of penance. 7, nakedness.

ನಿರ್ವಾಹ s *n* Extricating one's self out of, a way out, an escape 2, accomplishment, doing managing 3. supporting, subsisting on. 4 sufficiency, competent means of living -ಮಾಡು, ನಿರ್ವಾಹಿಸು To accomplish; to live frugally, to be content with what is absolutely necessary to sustain life. -ಸಾಗಿಸು. To obtain or supply the means of sustenance, to maintain -ಗಾರ An accomplisher

ನಿರ್ವಿಕಲ್ಪ s. *a* Changeless unalterable.

ನಿರ್ವಿಕಾರ s. *a* Unchangeable, immutable

ನಿರ್ವಿಘ್ನ s *a* Unobstructed *n* Absence of impediment, *also* -ತೆ -ನಾಯಕ. Ganêśa

ನಿರ್ವಿವಾದ s. *n*. Absence of contention

ನಿರ್ವಿಶೇಷ s *n* Absence of difference *a* Without distinction, indiscriminate

ನಿರ್ವಿಷ s *a* Poisonless, innocuous *n*.

ನಿರ್ವಿಷಯ s a Unattached to any object.

ನಿರ್ವೃತಿ (= ನಿವೃತ್ತಿ) s. n. Bliss, final emancipation

ನಿರ್ವೇಶ s. n Entering into. 2, expiation, atonement, also -ನ.

ನಿರ್ವ್ಯಸನ s. n Unconcernedness.

ನಿರ್ವ್ಯಾಜ s. a Without deceit, candid, honest plain. 2, without a pretext, cause or reason

ನಿರ್ಹೇತುಕ s a Causeless, reasonless

ನಿಲ (= ನಿಲು) k n Standing 2, the side-post of a door. 3, remainder, balance, also -ಬಾಕಿ -ಕಡೆ, -ಗಡೆ Attitude; leisure, patience; composure.

ನಿಲಕು. = ನಿಲುಕು, q. v.

ನಿಲಯ s. n An abode, residence. -ವಾನ್. A householder

ನಿಲವು (= ನಿಲ) k n. Standing 2, position 3, height. 4, cessation, leisure 5, a seat, place of abode. a High ನಿಲವಂಗಿ. A long garment

ನಿಲಿಸು = ನಿಲ್ಲಿಸು, q v.

ನಿಲು. = ನಿಲ, q v -ಕಡೆ = ನಿಲಕಡೆ Patience, composure, leisure -ಗಣ್ಣು A staring eye -ಗನ್ನಡಿ. A full-length mirror

ನಿಲುಕು k v t. To stretch one's self v i To reach; to stand upon one's tiptoes 2, to come within reach. 3, to begin.

ನಿಲುಂಬು a k v. t To heap up, amass v. i To crowd 2, to jump

ನಿಲುವಿಕೆ. = ನಿಲವು, q v

ನಿಲುವು. = ನಿಲವು, q v

ನಿಲ್ಲಿಸು k v t To cause to stand, stop, cease, stay, etc

ನಿಲ್ಲು k v. i. To stand, to stand up; to stop; to stay; to be, to wait, to remain, to stand or last, as colour, to remain without injury; to cease, as rain, to rest to endure, etc. P. ps. ನಿತ್ತು, ನಿಂತು [illegible] It stopped, [illegible] T [illegible] to stand, place, etc. ನಿಂದಿರು To stand, remain

ನಿವರು k. v t. To stroke or rub gently ನಿವರಿಸು. To cause to stroke.

ನಿವರ್ತನ s n. Accomplishment, turning back, ceasing ನಿವರ್ತಿಸು To turn away, repel, to leave off, remove

ನಿವಾರಣ s n Keeping back or off, warding off, averting, preventing, hindering, checking Cpds. ಅರಿಷ್ಟ-, ದಾಹ-, ದುಃಖ-, ಶ್ರಮ-. ನಿವಾರಿಸು To keep back, ward off, to avert.

ನಿವಾಸ s n. A resting-place, abode, dwelling.

ನಿವಾಸಿ s n An inhabitant -ಸು To dwell, reside.

ನಿವಾಳಿ f n The act of waving a thing in front of a person or idol to remove any evil. -ಮಾಡು, -ಸು. To wave anything to avert any evil

ನಿವೃತ್ತಿ s. n Return; disappearance, cessation, inactivity, leaving off, desisting from; abstinence, rest 2, felicity, bliss

ನಿವೇದನ s. n Communication, announcement; information, delivering, offering ನಿವೇದಿಸು. To make known, to present, offer. ನಿವೇದ್ಯ. An oblation, gift of food to an idol.

ನಿವೇಶ s n Entering, a settlement, a house, a camp

ನಿಶಾ 1 s. n. Night. -ಚರ Moving about by night, the moon, a thief. -ಟನ. An owl. -ದಿ. Evening -ನಾಥ, -ಪತಿ The moon. ನಿಶಾಂತ. Break of day; quiet; a house.

ನಿಶಾ 2. f. n. Intoxication -ಖೋರ A man taking intoxicants

ನಿಶಾನಿ h. n An ensign, flag, standard

ನಿಶಾಸ್ತ್ರವಾದ s. n Deism; natural religion

ನಿಶಿ 1, ನಿಶೆ (= ನಿಶಾ, q v) s n Night

ನಿಶಿ 2 h ad. Together with, along with

ನಿಶ್ಚಂಚಲ s [illegible] Fixed, firm, steady, also [illegible]

ನಿಶ್ಚಯ (=ನಿಚ್ಚಯ) s n Ascertainment, certain knowledge, conviction, certainty, determination, resolution, final decision design, purpose -ತಾಂಬೂಲ. The ceremony of betrothal -ಮಾಡು To ascertain, arrive at a decision, to resolve, to appoint ನಿಶ್ಚಯಿಸು To ascertain, to settle, to determine, resolve; to appoint

ನಿಶ್ಚಲ s a. Immovable invariable. 2, fixed. steady. n A mountain. 2, an ascetic 3, the earth

ನಿಶ್ಚಿತ s a Settled, decided, certain ನಿಶ್ಚಿತಾರ್ಥ A fixed matter; a certain kind of betrothal.

ನಿಶ್ಚಿಂತ s a Thoughtless, careless, unconcerned, free from care or anxiety ನಿಶ್ಚಿಂತೆ Thoughtlessness; freedom from anxiety, care.

ನಿಶ್ಚೇಷ್ಟೆ s. n Motionlessness, want of power

ನಿಶ್ಚೈತನ್ಯ s n Want of strength or power

ನಿಶ್ವಾಸ s n Inspiration, inhaling. ನಿಶ್ವಾಸೋಚ್ಛ್ವಾಸ. Inhaling and exhaling

ನಿಶ್ಶಂಕ = ನಿಃಶಂಕ, q v

ನಿಶ್ಶಬ್ದ = ನಿಃಶಬ್ದ, q v

ನಿಶ್ಶೇಷ. = ನಿಃಶೇಷ, q v

ನಿಶ್ಶ್ವಾಸ s n. Breathing out, expiration. 2, = ನಿಶ್ವಾಸ, q. v.

ನಿಷಾದ s n N. of a wild aboriginal tribe; a Hŏlĕya.

ನಿಷಿದ್ಧ s a. Prohibited, forbidden, prevented

ನಿಷೂದನ s n. Killing, destroying.

ನಿಷೇಧ s. n Prohibition, forbidding, hindering, negation, denial. -ರೂಪ The negative form of a verb ನಿಷೇಧಿಸು. To forbid

ನಿಷೇವಣ s. n. Waiting on, service, worship

ನಿಷ್ಕಪಟ s a Guileless n Guilelessness. also -ತನ -ತ್ವ, ನಿಷ್ಕಪಟಿ A guileless, candid person

ನಿಷ್ಕರುಣ s a Pitiless unmerciful, cruel. ನಿಷ್ಕರು [illegible]

ನಿಷ್ಕರ್ಷೆ s n Ascertainment, decision, settlement ನಿಷ್ಕರ್ಷಿಸು. To determine, settle.

ನಿಷ್ಕಲಂಕ s a. Stainless, spotless, sinless

ನಿಷ್ಕಾಪಟ್ಯ s n. Guilelessness.

ನಿಷ್ಕಾಮ s a. Desireless, disinterested, unselfish n. Absence of desire disinterestedness. ನಿಷ್ಕಾಮಿ. A person free from desire

ನಿಷ್ಕಾರಣ s. a Causeless, groundless

ನಿಷ್ಕುಟ s n The hollow of a tree. 2, a garden attached to a house

ನಿಷ್ಕೃತಿ s n. Expiation, compensation, discharge of a debt or obligation.

ನಿಷ್ಠ s a Staying on, grounded on, devoted to, practising. n. Intention, aim

ನಿಷ್ಠುರ. ನಿಷ್ಠೂರ (=ನಿಚ್ಚುರ) s a Hard, rough, harsh, unkind cruel, severe -ತನ, -ತೆ. -ತ್ವ Harshness. etc, severity cruelty.

ನಿಷ್ಠೆ s. n. Position; condition. 2, devotedness, uniform practice, religious duty, faith 3, excellence perfection 4, conclusion, the end of a drama, etc 5, death 6, certainty 7, trouble

ನಿಷ್ಪಕ್ಷಪಾತ s a. Impartial n. Impartiality

ನಿಷ್ಪಾಪ s a. Sinless, guiltless

ನಿಷ್ಪೇಷಣ s. n Grinding, pulverizing

ನಿಷ್ಪ್ರಯೋಜಕ s a Useless, needless

ನಿಷ್ಪ್ರಯೋಜನ s a Causeless, groundless, useless n. Uselessness

ನಿಷ್ಫಲ s a. Fruitless barren, unprofitable

ನಿಸರ್ಗ s n. Relinquishment, evacuation; 2, giving away. 3, the natural state

ನಿಸಿ k v t To squeeze between fingers

ನಿಸ್ತರಣ s n Going out, crossing over, passing time ನಿಸ್ತರಿಸು To spend,

ನಿಸ್ತ್ರಾರ್ತ *tb. of* ನಿಶ್ಚಿತಾರ್ಥ, *q v*

ನಿಸ್ತೂಕ s. *a* Weightless, light, pithless, weak. *n*. Weakness

ನಿಸ್ತೇಜ s *a* Devoid of energy, dull, impotent *n*. Want of brilliancy.

ನಿಸ್ಪೃಹ s *a*. Desireless, indifferent, content. *n*. Absence of covetousness, *also* -ತೆ.

ನಿಸ್ಸಂಶಯ s. *a*. Undoubted, unerring, certain

ನಿಸ್ಸಂಗ = ನಿಃಸಂಗ, *q v*

ನಿಸ್ಸತ್ವ s *a* Pithless, sapless. *n* Want of energy, weakness, *also* ನಿಃಸತ್ವ

ನಿಸ್ಸಂತಾನ s. *a* Childless, issueless, *also* ನಿಃಸಂತಾನ

ನಿಸ್ಸಂದೇಹ = ನಿಃಸಂದೇಹ, *q. v*

ನಿಸ್ಸಹಾಯ = ನಿಃಸಹಾಯ. *q v*

ನಿಸ್ಸಾರ (= ನಿಃಸಾರ, *q. v*) s *a* Sapless, insipid, pithless, worthless, vain *n* Saplessness, insipidity.

ನಿಳ್ಕು. = ನಿಲುಕು, *q v*

ನೀ k. *pro* Thou, *pl* ನೀವು *See its declension s*. ನಿನ್.

ನೀಗು k. *v t* To quit, leave, abandon, get rid of, to lose. to remove, take away, to squander.

ನೀಚ s *a* Low, base, vile, mean. -ತನ Meanness, vileness

ನೀಟ k. *n* Length -ಸಾಲು A long row

ನೀಟು k *n* Straightness 2, properness, neatness, beauty, tidiness -ಗಾರ. A tidy man, *f* -ಗಾತಿ.

ನೀಡು k *v t* To extend, stretch out, *as* fingers, arms, *etc* 2, to offer, present, give, to serve out, to put *n*. Extension, length. 2, presenting. *ad* Abundantly, much, further -ಮಾಡು To raise

ನೀತಿ s. *n* Leading, guidance, moral behaviour, political science, policy statesmanship, moral philosophy, ethics, prudence, acquisition. 2, righteousness, justification (*Christ*.). -ಗ A well-conducted, virtuous man -ಮಾರ್ಗ Moral conduct. -ವಂತ. A moral, just, prudent man -ವಿದ್ಯೆ, -ಶಾಸ್ತ್ರ The science of ethics or morals -ವಚನ, -ವಾಕ್ಯ, -ಮಾತು A moral saying

ನೀನು k *pro* Thou

ನೀರ್. = ನೀರು, *q v* ನೀರಡಿಕೆ Thirst ನೀರಡಿಸು. To be thirsty. ನೀರಣುಗ. The moon. -ಬೆಕ್ಕು, -ನಾಯಿ. An otter. -ದಾರಿ ನೀರಬಟ್ಟೆ A water passage. -ಮಾಡು To liquefy ನೀರಾಗು. To melt, *as* metals, sugar, *etc*. ನೀರಾಟ. Sporting in water. ನೀರಾಮೆ. A turtle ನಿರಾವರಿ, ನೀರಾವರಿಕೆ Abundance of water, soil fit for wet cultivation. ನೀರುಳ್ಳಿ The onion. ನೀರೆರೆ. To pour water ನೀರೆಸರು. A kind of plain pepper-water ನೀರೊತ್ತು The tide ನೀರೋಟ Stream, current.

ನೀರಜ s *n* A lotus 2, a pearl. 3, the garden plant *Costus speciosus a*. Free from impurity.

ನೀರಂಧ್ರ s. *a*. Coarse, thick.

ನಿರಲು = ನೇರಲು, *q v*.

ನಿರಾಂಜನ. = ನೀಲಾಂಜನ, *q v*

ನೀರು (= ನೀರ್) k *n*. Water. 2, the lustre of a gem ನೀರಿನವ. A waterman -ಕಟ್ಟು. To turn water. -ಕಾಗೆ, -ಗಾಗೆ. A kind of cormorant, shag, diver. -ಕಾಲುವೆ. A channel -ಕೊಕ್ಕರೆ A curlew -ಗಂಗಾಳ. A basin of water -ಗಣಿಗಿಲು The water hog-weed, *Barringtonia acutangula* -ಗಣ್ಣು. A water-spring. -ಕೋಳಿ. A water-fowl. -ಗೋಳಿಗಿಡ A small potherb, *Portulaca oleracea* -ಚೀಲ The bladder -ತೊಟ್ಟಿ. A water-trough -ದಗೆ Thirst. -ದಾರಿ A water-course. -ನಾಯಿ. The river-otter. -ನೆತ್ತಿ A water-shed, the crest of a hill adjoining cultivation -ಬಿಡು To let water -ಬೆಕ್ಕು. = ನೀರುನಾಯಿ, *q v* -ಬ್ರಹ್ಮಿ The Thyme-leaved Gratiola, *Herpestis monnieria*. -ಮಳೆ. Rain that brings water to fields, tanks, *etc*. -ವರಿ. Stream, current, water-cess. -ಹಕ್ಕಿ. The Indian or

Siberian crane, *Ardea sibirica*. -ಹಂದಿ. The skate fish. -ಹುಲ್ಲು. The water-reed, *Calamus fasciculatus*. -ಹಾವು. A water-snake. -ಹೊಗೆ. Fog arising from water; steam, vapour.

ನೀರೆ (ರೆ = ಱೆ) a. k. *n.* A damsel; a gay woman.

ನೀರ್. = ನೀರು, *q. v.* -ಕುಡಿ, -ಗುಡಿ. Water to drink. -ಗುಳ್ಳೆ. A water-bubble. -ಬಡಿಸು. To soak. -ಸೇದು. To draw water. -ಮಾನಸಿ. A mermaid, nymph. -ಹುಟ್ಟು. A paddle. -ಹೂವು. A lotus, *etc.*

ನೀಲ s. *a.* Dark-blue or black; dyed with indigo. 2, bad; vile. 3, slow, lazy. *n.* The sapphire. 2, N. of a monkey attendant on Râma. 3, sin, crime. 4, indigo. -ಕಂಠ, -ಕಂಧರ. A peacock; a quail; Śiva; N. -ಗಾರ. An indigo-dyer. -ಗಿರಿ. The Nilagiri hill. -ಮಣಿ. The sapphire. ನೀಲಾಂಬರಿ. N. of a râga.

ನೀಲಾಂಜನ s. *n.* A small lamp used for waving before an idol, *etc.*

ನೀಲಿ s. *n.* An indigo shrub, *Indigofera tinctoria*. 2, indigo, the dye. 3, a female evil spirit that speaks lies. -ಗಣ್ಣು. An eye with a bluish pupil. -ಗಾರ. An indigo-dyer. -ಮಾತು. A falsehood. -ವಾರ್ತೆ. A false report. ನೀಲೋತ್ಪಲ. The blue water-lily, *Nymphaea cyanea;* a blue lotus.

ನೀವಾರ f. *n.* Rice growing wild.

ನೀವಿ s. *n.* A cloth worn round a woman's waist. 2, capital, stock. 3, a wager, stake. 4, junction, union.

ನೀವು 1. k. *pro.* (*pl. of* ನೀನು) You. *See its decl. s.* ನಿಮ್ಮ.

ನೀವು 2. k. *v. t.* To rub softly, stroke down, *as* the hair, cloth, *etc.*

ನೀಸು (*tb. of* ನಯಿಸು) *v. t.* To manage; to fulfill.

ನೀಳ (= ನೀಡ.) k. *n.* Extension, length, height.

ನೀಳು (*cf.* ನೀಡು) a. k. *v. i.* To grow long, extend, [illegible]

ನು s. *int.* Now? what? indeed?

ನುಗ (= ನುಗ್ಗು) k. *v. t.* To powder.

ನುಗಿಚು k. *v. i.* To slip.

ನುಗ್ಗಿ. = ನುಗ್ಗೆ, *q. v.*

ನುಗ್ಗು 1. k. *v. i.* To force one's self into; to enter without permission, *as* a house, *etc.*; to creep into.

ನುಗ್ಗು 2. (= ನುಗ್ಗಿ, *q. v.*) k. *v. t.* To crush, powder, grind. *n.* Crushed or crumbled state. ನುಗ್ಗಾಗು. To be crushed to pieces, crumble.

ನುಗ್ಗೆ (= ನುಗ್ಗಿ) k. *n.* The horse-radish, *Moringa pterygosperma*. *Cpds.:* -ಕಾಯಿ, -ಗಿಡ, -ಬೀಜ, ಹೂವ, -ಸೊಪ್ಪು, *etc.*

ನುಂಗು k. *v. t.* To swallow; to devour

ನುಚ್ಚು (= ನುಗ್ಗು 2, *etc.*) k. *n.* Fragments, bits; grits of any grain. 2, wasting away, ruin, *etc.* ನುಚ್ಚಕ್ಕಿ. Broken rice. -ಗಂಜಿ. Ganji made of nuccu.

ನುಡಿ k. *v. i.* To utter; to speak; to say. *n.* A voice; speech; a word; a promise; a language. *Cpds.:* ಒಡೆ-, ಜಾಣ್ನು-, ಜವಳಿ-, ತಪ್ಪು-, ತೊದಲು-, ಬಲು-, ಬಿರು-, ಬಿರುಸು-, ಮರುವಾತು-, *etc.* -ಕೊಡು. To promise. -ಮೆಚ್ಚು. Assent by word. -ತ. Speech. -ಸು. To cause to utter, speak, *etc.*; to perform music upon, to play.

ನುಣ್ a. k. *n.* Smoothness, softness, gentleness; *also* ನುಣ್ಣು, ನುಣುಪು. -ಗಾರೆ, ನುಣುಗಾರೆ. Fine, smooth plaster. -ಜಗಲಿ. A soft seat. -ಅರಿಸಿನ. Fine turmeric. -ನುಡಿ, ನುಣ್ಣುಡಿ. A gentle word. -ಬೆಳಗು. A delicate lustre. -ಮಣಿ. A delicate gem. -ಮಾತು. = -ನುಡಿ, *q. v.* -ಮುತ್ತು. A fine pearl. ನುಣ್ಣಗೆ, ನುಣ್ಣನೆ. Smoothness, baldness. *a.* Smooth; bald. *ad.* Completely.

ನುಣ್ಪು. = ನುಣುಪು, *q. v.*

ನುತಿ s. *n.* Praise, eulogium; worship. -ಸು. To praise, *etc.*

ನುಂದು. = ನೊಂದು, *q. v.*

ನುರಿ (ರಿ = ಱಿ. = ನುಗ್ಗು 2, *q. v.*) k. *v. i.* To be [illegible] to be inured to, to become familiar with.

ನುರು (ರು=ಱು) k. n. The state of being harassed or exercised. -ಪಡಿ. Familiarity with, etc

ನುರುಕು (ರು=ಱು) k v. i To wane away. v t (=ನುಗ್ಗು 2) To reduce to powder, etc.

ನುರುಜು (ರು=ಱು) k. n Gravel.

ನುಲಿ k. v. t To twist, as a rope, etc, to wring, as clothes in washing; to curl, as the whiskers, etc 2, the intestines to gripe. n A twist, cord 2, griping pain in the intestines, also ನುಲಿಕೆ. ನುಲಿಸು To cause to twist.

ನುಲಿಕೆ, ನುಲಿಗೆ k n A twist, cord, thread, twine -ಮಾಡು. To twist. -ಅಗಣಿ, -ಯಗಣಿ The twisting pin that elevates or depresses the shaft of the oil-mill

ನುಸಿ 1 k n Powder, dust.

ನುಸಿ 2 k. n An insect that destroys cloth, grain, etc 2 an eye-fly, a gnat

ನುಸಿ 3 (=ನುಸುಳು) k. v. i To enter a door, etc. P ps. ನುಸಿದು, ನುಸ್ತು

ನುಸುಳು (=ನುಸಿ 3) k. v. i To enter a door, to get into, to retreat, hide one's self slink n Entering a door. 2, evasion, falsehood.

ನುಸ್ತು =ನುಸಿದು P p. of ನುಸಿ 3

ನೂಕು k. v. t To shove, push, to push away or aside; to push on, urge on. 2, to spend, as time. 3, to fare n Shoving, a push ನೂಕಿಸು To cause to push, etc

ನೂತನ s. a New, novel, recent; fresh, young, strange. -ಗಾರ A schemer.

ನೂತಿ (tb. of ಊತಿ) n. A cancerous disease.

ನೂರು (ರು=ಱು) k a A hundred. ನೂರನೆಯ Hundredth ನೂರಾಐವತ್ತು 150 ನೂರಾಇಪ್ಪತ್ತೈದು 125 ನೂರಾರು Fully a 100 -ಪಟ್ಟು, -ಮಡಿ. A hundred fold

ನೂಲು k. n Yarn, thread v t To make thre... -

...ಟಿಕೆ, -ಕಂಡಿಕೆ A ball of thread. -ಬಟ್ಟೆ. Cotton cloth -ಹುಣ್ಣಿಮೆ A festival on which the sacred thread is renewed.

ನೂಳದು k. ad. Much, exceedingly.

ನೃ s n Man -ಪ, -ಪತಿ, -ಪಾಲಕ A king. -ಪನೀತಿ. State policy -ಪೇಂದ್ರ. An excellent king. -ಹರಿ. Vishnu's incarnation of man-lion; also ನರಸಿಂಹ

ನೃತ್ಯ s n Dancing, pantomime.

ನೆಕ್ಕು (=ನಕ್ಕು) k v t. To lick ನೆಕ್ಕಿಸು. To cause to lick

ನೆಗಚು (=ನೆಗಸು) a k v. t. To cause to jump.

ನೆಗಡಿ k. n A cold, catarrh -ಬರು, -ಹಿಡಿ To catch cold.

ನೆಗತ k. n Leaping, jumping

ನಗಪು ನೆಗಹು a. k v. t. To raise, lift up. n Lifting up

ನೆಗಸು =ನೆಗಚು, q v

ನೆಗಳ್ (ಳ್=ೞ್) a. k. v t. To undertake, to engage in, to perform, do. v. i. To come, to be used

ನೆಗಳು 1. (ಳು=ೞು) a. k. v i To become manifest, well known, famous, to shine; to appear

ನೆಗಳು 2, ನೆಗಳೆ k n An alligator.

ನೆಗಳ್ತೆ a k n. Action, work, conduct 2, fame, accomplishment.

ನೆಗೆ k v i. To be purified, to be clear, to shine. 2, to jump up, to bound. 3, to rise, ascend v t To raise, lift up. P ps ನೆಗದು, ನೆಗೆದು ನೆಗೆತ Leaping

ನೆಗ್ಗಿಲು, ನೆಗ್ಗಿಲು k. n. The small caltrops, Tribulus lanuginosus, also -ಮುಳ್ಳು

ನೆಗ್ಗು 1 k. v i. To be curved or bent inward, to sink in to disappear; to get a bruise [troy.

ನೆಗ್ಗು 2 k v t. To crush, smash, destroy.

ನೆಚ್ಚು (=ನಚ್ಚು 1, q v) k. v t To believe, trust; to confide in. n. Confidence, trust, faith, reliance ನೆಚ್ಚಿಕೆ, -ಗೆ =ನಚ್ಚಿಗೆ s ನಚ್ಚು 1, q v.

ನೆಟ್ಟಗೆ, ನೆಟ್ಟನೆ k. a Straight, erect. ad ... ord ... -

ly, distinctly; well, in good health. ನೆಟ್ಟಗಾಗು. To become straight. -ಮಾಡು. To repair; to do well; to arrange.

ನೆಟ್ಟನ್ನ, ನೆಟ್ಟನ, ನೆಟ್ಟನೆ k. a. Straight, regular, proper, *etc. Cpds.:* -ಗೆರೆ, -ದಾರಿ, -ಮಾತು, *etc.*

ನೆಡು (= ನಡು 2, *etc., q. v.*) k. *v. t.* To fix firmly, plant, *etc. P. p.* ನೆಟ್ಟು.

ನೆಣ k. *n.* Fat, marrow.

ನೆಂಟ (= ನಂಟ, *q. v.*) k. *n.* A kinsman, relative. -ರುಇಷ್ಟರು, ನೆಂಟರಿಷ್ಟರು. Relations and other beloved ones. -ತನ, -ಸ್ತನ, -ಸ್ತಿಕೆ. Relationship.

ನೆಂಟು. = ನಂಟು, *q. v.*

ನೆತ್ತ (*tb. of* ನೇತ್ರ) *n.* The eye. 2, a die; a cowry used in gaming. 3, gambling. -ದ ಹಲಗೆ. A play-board. ನೆತ್ತದಾಟ. Playing at backgammon, *etc.* ನೆತ್ತಿಗ. A gambler.

ನೆತ್ತರು (= ನೆತ್ತ್ರು) k. *n.* Blood. -ಕುರು. A kind of bleeding boil.

ನೆತ್ತಿ k. *n.* The forehead; the crown of the head. -ಮುತ್ತು. A pearl in the head.

ನೆತ್ತ್ರು. = ನೆತ್ತರು, *q. v.*

ನೆನ. = ನೆನದು. *P. p. of* ನೆನೆ 1, *in* ನೆನಕೊಳ್ಳು.

ನೆನೆ 1. k. *v. i. & t.* To think, imagine; to think upon; to be mindful of; to wish; to remember; *also* ನೆನಸು. ನೆನಪು, ನೆನವು. Thought, reflection; recollection, remembrance. -ಪು ಇಡು, ನೆನಪಿಡು. To think about, remember. -ಪು ಇರು, ನೆನಪಿರು. To bear in mind. ನೆನಪರಿಕೆ. Recollection.

ನೆನೆ 2. k. *v. i.* To become wet. *P. ps.* ನೆನದು, ನೆನೆದು, ನೆಂದು. -ಯುವಿಕೆ. Becoming wet, *etc.* -ಹಾಕು. To put for soaking. -ಅಕ್ಕಿ, ನೆನೆಯಕ್ಕಿ. Soaked rice; a kind of sweetmeat. ನೆನಗಡಲೆ. Soaked kaḍale. -ಸು ನೆನಸು. To make wet, moisten.

ನೆಪ್ಪು (= ನೆನಪು, *etc.*) k. *n.* Recollection. 2, acquaintance.

ನೆಮ್ಮದಿ f. *n.* Serenity; comfort, happiness.

ನೆಮ್ಮು a. k. *v. i.* To lean on; to take for one's support. *n.* Leaning upon; a support. -ಗೆ. = ನಂಬಿಕೆ. ನೆಮ್ಮಿಸು. To charge with, attribute.

ನೆಯ್, ನೆಯು k. *v. t.* To weave; to entwine; *also* ನೆಯ್ಯು. ನೆಯಿಗೆ. Weaving; a web. -ಗೆಯವ, -ಕಾರ. A weaver.

ನೆಯ್ದಲೆ, ನೆಯ್ದಿಲೆ k. *n.* A water-lily.

ನೆರ 1. (= ನೆರೆ 1) k. *n.* Nearness; joining; assistance. *a.* Adjoining, coming near (to assist). -ನಾಡು. An adjoining district. -ಮನೆ (= ನೆರೆ-). A neighbouring house; next door. -ಯವ, -ಮನೆಯವ. A neighbour. -ಹೊರೆಯವರು. Next door and other neighbours.

ನೆರ 2. (ರ = ಱ) k. *n.* A vital point or organ; a secret. -ವಿ. Fullness, completeness.

ನೆರಕೆ (= ನೆರಿಕೆ) k. *n.* A fence of bamboos, *etc.*

ನೆರದು. = ನೆರೆದು. *P. p. of* ನೆರೆ, *q. v.*

ನೆರಪು, ನೆರಹು a. k. *v. t.* To bring together, join, collect, convene.

ನೆರವಣಿಗೆ (ರ = ಱ) a. k. *n.* Fullness; accomplishment; nicety; goodness.

ನೆರವಿ k. *n.* A union, mass, crowd, multitude, *etc.*

ನೆರವು 1. k. *n.* A mass. 2, an assistance, help.

ನೆರವು 2. (ರ = ಱ) k. *n.* Fullness, completeness. -ಏರಿಸು, ನೆರವೇರಿಸು. To fulfil, accomplish. ನೆರವೇರು. To be completed, fulfilled, *as* a word, work, *etc.*

ನೆರವೇರು. *See s.* ನೆರವು 2.

ನೆರಳು k. *n.* Shade; shadow; shelter.

ನೆರಿಕೆ. = ನೆರಕೆ, *q. v.*

ನೆರೆ 1. k. *v. i.* To join; to come together, assemble; to associate with. *P. ps.* ನೆರೆದು, ನೆರದು. *n.* Proximity, neighbourhood; union, company. -ಮನೆ. = ನೆರಮನೆ. -ಯವ. A neighbour. -ಊರು, ನೆರೆಯೂರು. A neighbouring village. -ಹಳ್ಳಿ. A neighbouring hamlet.

ನೆರೆ 3 (ರೆ=ಱೆ) k v i. To become entire, full complete, ready perfect, mature sufficient. P ps ನೆರದು, ನೆರೆದು. n. Completeness, maturity, etc 2, a flood ad. Completely, perfectly fully, exceedingly -ಜ್ಞಾನ Replete with wisdom.

ನೆಲ k n Ground, soil, land; floor, a country, kingdom, the earth ಜವುಗು- Swampy ground ತವರು- Rising ground -ಕಡಲೆ The earth-nut -ಕಲ A miser. -ಕಂಚಿ, -ಸಾರಂಗ A small shrub, *Naregamia alata* -ಗಟ್ಟು Pavement -ಗುಂಬಳ A creeper, *Ipomaea digitata* -ಗುಮ್ಮ. A kind of bird -ಗುಳ್ಳ A prickly nightshade -ತಾವರೆ -ದಾವರೆ The plant *Hibiscus mutabilis*. -ನೆಲ್ಲಿ. A small herb, *Phyllanthus madraspatensis*. -ಬೇವು The plant *Gentiana cherayta* -ಮನೆ. A cellar; a dungeon -ಮಾಳಿಗೆ A granary -ವರೆ (-ಅವರೆ) The plant *Cassia aborata* -ವಾಗು. To take root, to become a protection -ಸರಿ, -ಸಮಾನ. Level with the ground. -ಸಂಪಿಗೆ. A fragrant garden-flower, *Kaemferia rotunda* -ಸು To settle, to stay; to stand -ಹಲಸು The ananas -ಹಾದಿ A land-way ನೆಲಾವರೆ The Senna plant.

ನೆಲವು, ನೆಲಹು k n A net-work of rope in which pots etc are suspended

ನೆಲೆ k n Standing-place; a place of residence, an apartment of a house, place, ground footing; basis, certainty, certain knowledge, a mystery -ಕಟ್ಟು, -ಗಟ್ಟು. = ನೆಲಗಟ್ಟು, q v. -ಗಣ್ಣು A penetrating eye -ಗೆಡು. Ground to lose, etc -ಗೊಳ್ಳು To take footing; to take root, as plants, etc, to become settled -ಗೊಳಿಸು To place, establish, etc -ಮನೆ. An abode. -ಮಾಡ An upper story -ಯಾಗು. To get a firm footing, to be in use.

ನೆಲ್ಲಿ k. n The emblic myrobalan, *Phyllanthus emblica*

ನೆಲ್ಲು k. n. Paddy, rice in its husk -ಅಕ್ಕಿ, ನೆಲ್ಲಕ್ಕಿ Rice. -ಗದ್ದೆ. A paddy-field -ಹುಲ್ಲುಸರಿಗೆ A band of paddy straw

ನೆವ, ನೆವನ (tb of ನಿಭ) n A pretence, pretext, plea -ತೆಗೆ, -ಮಾಡು. To pretend. -ಹೇಳು To utter a pretext, to plead an excuse.

ನೆಸ (= ನೆಗೆ, q v) k. v i To jump about, etc 2 to give one's self airs P ps ನೆಸದು, ನೆಸೆದು, ನೆಸ್ತು. -ಆಟ, ನೆಸ್ಸಾಟ Jumping about ನೆಸ್ಸಾಡು To jump about

ನೆಳಲು (ಳ=ಱ). = ನೆರಳು q v

ನೇ = ನೇಯು, q v

ನೇಗಲಿ, ನೇಗಲು, ನೇಗಿಲು (tb. of ಲಾಂಗಲ) n. A plough -ಈಚು A plough-shaft. -ಸಾಲು A furrow -ಹೂಡು. To yoke oxen to a plough -ಹೊಡೆ To plough.

ನೇಗೆ. = ನೇಯಿಗೆ, etc, q v.

ನೇಜಿ k n Young plants, esp of rice, also ನಾಟಿ

ನೇಟು (= ನೀಟು, q v) k n Straightness, truth

ನೇಣು k n A cord, rope, a noose -ಹಾಕಿಕೊಳ್ಳು. To hang one's self

ನೇತು P p. of ನೇಲು, q v

ನೇತ್ರ s n A leader, leading 2, the eye -ತ್ರಯ Śiva -ವೈದ್ಯ An oculist. ನೇತ್ರಾಂಬು Tears ನೇತ್ರಾವತಿ. N. of a river in S Canara

ನೇಪಾಲ, ನೇಪಾಳ s n N of a country, Nepal. 2 = ಜಾಪಾಳ.

ನೇಮ (tb. of ನಿಯಮ, q v) n A rule, order, appointment -ಕ. Ruling, a rule; an appointment, etc -ತೆಗೆ. To lay down as a rule -ವಂತ = ನಿಯಮವಂತ

ನೇಮಣೂಕ, ನೇಮಣೂಕಿ s. n Appointment, allowance. stipend.

ನೇಮಿ s. n The circumference of a wheel.

ನೇಮಿಸು tb of ನಿಯಮಿಸು, q v

ನೇಯಿಗೆ (= ನೆಯಿಗೆ, q v) k. n. Weaving.

[illegible] = [illegible] q

ನೇರ k n Straightness, propriety, harmony; rightness, fitness, order ನೇರ ನೇರ rep. Quite proportionate, face to face.

ನೇರಿಮೆ a. k n. Propriety, rectitude. etc ನೇರಿಗ A Brâhmana, f ನೇರಿಗಳ್

ನೇರಲು. ನೇರಳೆ, ನೇರಿಲು (ರ=ಱ) k. n A common tree with purple berries, *Eugenia jambolana*

ನೇರೆ f n A breakfast

ನೇಲು k. v i To be suspended, to hang, swing, dangle P p. ನೇತು ನೇತಾಡು = ನೇಲು, q v

ನೇವರಿಸು k. v t. To make straight or smooth, to rub gently with the hand.

ನೇವಳ a. k. n A necklace of silver or gold, a girdle.

ನೇವುರ (tb of ನೂಪುರ) n An anklet.

ನೇಸರು (ರು=ಱು) a k n The sun. -ಗಲ್ಲು. Crystal.

ನೇಹ, ನೇಹ (tb of ಸ್ನೇಹ) n Love. -ಗಾರ. A male friend, f -ಗಾತಿ.

ನೈಚ್ಯ (fr. ನೀಚ) s n. Lowness, humility.

ನೈಜ (fr. ನಿಜ) s a. Real n. Reality, truth

ನೈಟ್ರೋಜನು e n Nitrogen, an element

ನೈಮಿತ್ತಿಕ s a Accidental, occasional

ನೈಮಿಷ s. a. Momentary. n N of a forest.

ನೈಮೇಯ (=ನಿಮಯ) s n Barter, exchange.

ನೈಯಾಯಿಕ s. n. A dialectician, logician.

ನೈರುತಿ (tb of ನೈರ್ಋತಿ) n The south-west quarter

ನೈರ್ಋತ s. a South-western n. The ruler of that quarter. ನೈರ್ಋತಿ The south-west quarter.

ನೈರ್ಮಲ್ಯ (fr ನಿರ್ಮಲ) s n Stainlessness purity [ness.

ನೈಲ್ಯ (fr ನೀಲ) s n Blueness; black-

ನೈವೇದ್ಯ (fr ನಿವೇದ್ಯ) s n. An offering of eatables to a deity -ಈ, -ಕೊಡು, -ಮಾಡು To p

ನೈಷ್ಠಿಕ (fr ನಿಷ್ಠೆ) s a Steady, firm, devoted -ತನ Constancy, steady adherence to rules, firm belief

ನೊಗ (tb of ಯುಗ) n A yoke -ಕಟ್ಟು, -ಹಾಕು To yoke.

ನೊಚ್ಚಗೆ k n Agreeableness or pleasant feeling when eating, hearing sweet words etc

ನೊಣ k n A fly -ಕಸ A common plant, *Plectranthos cordifolius*. -ಬ One of the Kuruba tribe

ನೊಣೆ k v t To clean the teeth with the tongue 2, (a k) to swallow

ನೊಂದಿಸು (=ನಂದಿಸು, ನುಂದಿಸು, q v) k v. t To extinguish, quench. ಬೆಂಕೀ-. To quench fire ದುಃಖ- To alleviate sorrow ದಾಹ-. To slake thirst

ನೊಂದು (=ನಂದು, ನುಂದು, q v) k v i To be extinguished, to go out

ನೊಯಿಸು = ನೋಯಿಸು q v

ನೊಯ್ಯು = ನೋ, q. v. P p ನೊಂದು

ನೊರಜು k. n. A gnat, eye-fly

ನೊರೆ k. n Foam, froth. -ಕಟ್ಟು, -ಗಟ್ಟು. Foam to be formed -ಬಾಯಿ A frothy mouth -ಹಾಲು Frothy milk fresh from the cow -ಹಪ್ಪಳ. A kind of rice-happala. -ಬೀಳು, -ಸೋರು. To foam at the mouth.

ನೊಸಲು k. n. The forehead. ನೊಸಲಕ್ಷರ, ನೊಸಲಬರಹ. The writ of destiny on the forehead. ನೊಸಲಬೊಟ್ಟು. A sandal mark on the forehead

ನೋ (=ನೊಯ್ಯು, ನೋಯು) k v. i. To feel pain, to ache, to be afflicted or grieved P p. ನೊಂದು.

ನೋಟ (fr. ನೋಡು) k. n. Viewing, beholding, a sight; a spectacle, a look, appearance, examination. -ಕ, -ಕಾರ, -ಗಾರ. A spectator, an eye-witness, an examiner a shroff

ನೋಟೀಸು e n Notice, information.

ನೋಡು k v. t To look, to view, behold; to look after, to examine, to consider; to take care, to see ರುಚಿ-. To taste. he pulse ಹಣಿಕಿ-. To peep ತಿರಿಗಿ- To look back ಎದುರು-. To wait, look for ನೋಡಿಸು To cause to look, *etc* -ವಿಕೆ Looking, *etc.*

ನೋತ (*p.* ನೋ) k *n.* Ache, pain

ನೋನು k. *v. t* To observe a vow or perform any meritorious act. *P. ps.* ನೋತು, ನೋಂತು.

ನೋಂಪಿ k *n* Any meritorious act of devotion, penance, or austerity.

ನೋಯು = ನೋ, *etc.*, *q v.* ನೋಯಿಸು To cause to suffer pain, to pain, afflict

ನೋರು h. *n* Fare, freight

ನೋವು (*p* ನೋ) k *n* Ache, pain, affliction -ಕೊಡು, -ಮಾಡು = ನೋಯಿಸು, *q v* ತಲೆ-. Headache ಹೊಟ್ಟೆ- Stomach-ache, colic

ನೌ s *n* A ship, boat. -ಕೆ A small ship.

ನೌಕರ = ನವುಕರ, *q v*

ನೌಲು. = ನವಿಲು, *q v*

ನ್ಯಗ್ರೋಧ s. *n.* The Indian fig or banyan tree *Ficus bengalensis.*

ನ್ಯಾಯ (= ನಾಯ) s *n.* Method, way, rule, manner, system, plan 2, fitness, right, justice, law, a lawful act 3, a lawsuit, dispute. 4, a logical argument, syllogism, logic. 5, an axiom. -ತೀರಿಕೆ A case, being settled (*also* -ತೀರುವಿಕೆ. Last judgment) -ತೀರಿಸು To decide a case, to judge. -ತೀರಿಸುವಿಕೆ. Deciding a case -ದ ಕಟ್ಟು A system of rules. -ಕಾರ A quarrelsome man -ನಿರ್ಣಯ A sentence or verdict. -ಪ್ರಮಾಣ A standard of law, decalogue, the ten commandments of God. -ಮಾರ್ಗ The way of justice. -ವಂತ, -ಸ್ಥ. A just man -ವಿಚಾರಕ A judge -ವಿಚಾರಣೆ Investigation of a lawsuit -ವಿಧಾಯಕ Legislative -ವಿಧಾಯಕಸಭೆ Legislative council -ಸಭೆ A court of justice. -ಸ್ಥಾನ A court, cutcherry. ನ್ಯಾಯಾಧಿಪತಿ, ನ್ಯಾಯಾಧೀಶ A judge. ನ್ಯಾಯಾಸನ. The judgment seat, bench.

ನ್ಯಾಸ s *n.* Depositing, consigning, a deposit pledge 2, certain religious ceremonies.

ನ್ಯೂನ s. *a.* Deficient, defective, wanting -ತೆ. Deficiency, want.

ಪ್

ಪ್. The thirty-ninth letter of the alphabet

ಪ k. *A letter used in reiteration, as* ಆಸ್ತಿ ಪಾಸ್ತಿ, ಕಲ್ಲು ಪಲ್ಲು ಕಾಯಿ ಪಾಯಿ, ಲೆಕ್ಕ ಪಕ್ಕ, ಸುಳ್ಳು ಪಳ್ಳು, *etc* 2, a k, *a letter to form the future tense and the present rel. part., as* ಇಪರ್, ಉದಯಿಪ, ಕಾಪ, ತಾಪ, ಪೋಪ, ಬರ್ಪ, ಮಾಳ್ಪ

ಪಕಳಿ f *n* A petal of a flower

ಪಕಾರ s. *n* The letter ಪ.

ಪಕಾಲಿ h *n* A double water-skin carried on a bullock

ಪಕೀರ. = ಫಕೀರ ,

ಪಕ್ಕ (*tb of* ಪಕ್ಷ) *n* A wing 2 the flank or side, a side, party, faction. 3, neighbourhood. 4, support. -ಡಿ The flank or side -ರಕ್ಕೆ, -ರಿಕ್ಕೆ (*tb of* ಪಕ್ಷರಕ್ಷೆ). The armour of horses or elephants. -ಶೂಲೆ. Pleurisy

ಪಕ್ಕನೆ (= ಫಕ್ಕನೆ) k *ad* Suddenly. -ನಗು. To burst out a laughing

ಪಕ್ಕಲೆ f *n* A kind of vessel.

ಪಕ್ಕಾ (*tb of* ಪಕ್ವ) *a* Mature, ripe, perfect; shrewd; accomplished. -ಖರಡೆ. The regular account compiled from the diary. -ಆದವ, -ದವ A shrewd, [illegible]

-ರಂಗು. Lasting colour. -ಸಿಪಾಯಿ An accomplished soldier -ಸೇರು A large measuring seru.

ಪಕ್ತಿ f n A manner, way, means 2, = ಪಕ್ಷ, q v

ಪಕ್ಕ 1 a k n Lying down, reposing. 2, a dormitory, the lair of wild beasts, a nest 3, a cow-pen. 4, closeness contact

ಪಕ್ಕ 2 = ಪಕ್ಷ, etc, q v n The side. 2, the page of a book.

ಪಕ್ವ (= ಪಕ್ಕಾ, q v) s. a. Cooked, baked 2 mature, ripe. 3, accomplished, perfect, fully developed, ready, shrewd, strong ಪಕ್ವಾನ್ನ Cooked food; a dish -ಮಾಡು To cook, to make fit. -ಆಗು To grow ripe or fit for use

ಪಕ್ಷ (= ಪಕ್ಕ, q v) s n. A wing, a feather 2, the side of anything, the flank. 3, a side, part, a party, faction 4, a follower, partisan 5. partiality 6 a case, an alternative, supposition (ಆ ಪಕ್ಷದಲ್ಲಿ, in that case, provided) 7, the half of a lunar month -ಮಾಡು. To be partial -ಹಿಡಿ To side with -ಪಾತ. Partiality -ಪಾತಿ A partisan -ಪ್ರಾಯಶ್ಚಿತ್ತ An expiatory act performed at the suklapaksha -ಭೇದ Partiality. -ಭೇದಮಾಡು. To be partial, to show partiality. ಪಕ್ಷಾಂತರ. Another way or manner. ಪಕ್ಷಾಪರ- Siding with another party ಪ್ರತಿ- Against, opposite (party)

ಪಕ್ಷಿ s. n A bird. 2, siding with -ಗೂಡು A bird's nest, a bird-cage -ರಾಜ. Garuda -ವಾಹನ Vishnu. -ಕೆಳಿಸು To espouse a side

ಪಕ್ಷ್ಮ s n A wing 2 an eye-lash. 3, the filament of a flower

ಪಗಡಿ h n A turban

ಪಗಡೆ 1 k n A frequently cultivated tree, *Mimusops elengi*

ಪಗಡೆ 2 f. n A mark on a die, a cowry for pl[…] 2, the play itself -ಯ ಕೋಟೆ. The centre of a dice-cloth *Cpds* -ಯ ಜೇಬಿ, -ಯ ಮನೆ, -ಯ ಸಾಲು, *etc* -ಯಾಟ. The pagadō-play

ಪಗಪಸ್ತಿ f a. Cautious, as in speech, painstaking -ಗಾರ A painstaking man

ಪಗದಿ k n Tribute. tax

ಪಗಲು, = ಹಗಲು, q v

ಪಗಾರ f. n Pay, salary

ಪಗಿಸು. = ಹಗಿಸು, q. v.

ಪಗಿಲ್ a. k v i. To be sticky, viscid, to adhere. 2, to be afflicted

ಪಗೆ = ಹಗೆ, q v.

ಪಂಕ 1 f n. A large fan, punka.

ಪಂಕ 2. s. n Mud, mire 2, sin. -ಜ, -ಜಾತ A lotus -ಜಗರ್ಭ -ಜನಾಭ Brahmâ -ಜವೈರಿ The moon -ಜಾಕ್ಷ, -ಜೋದರ Vishnu

ಪಂಕ್ತಿ s. n. A line, range, row, series 2, a row of people at a meal. 3, a flock, troop, a company. -ಗ್ರೀವ Râvana. -ಭೇದ. Partiality in serving guests. -ರಥ. Daśaratha *Cpds.* ರಾಜ-, ಸಭಾ-, *etc*

ಪಂಗ k. n A fork, a forked branch. -ನಾಮ A large forehead-mark --ಹಾಕು To deceive

ಪಂಗಡ k. a Apart, distinct. n. A party of people.

ಪಂಗು s a Lame, crippled

ಪಚಗಾಯಿಸು = ಪಚಾಯಿಸು, q v

ಪಚಡಿ = ಪಚ್ಚಡಿ, q v.

ಪಚನ ಪಚನ s n Cooking, roasting, maturing, digesting. 2, fire.

ಪಚಾರ f n. Reproach ಪಚಾರಿಸು. To reproach, chide, jeer

ಪಚ್ಚ 1 k. n. Greenness, an emerald. -ಕರ್ಪೂರ. Superior camphor -ನೆ Greenness

ಪಚ್ಚ 2. (tb of ಪ್ರಚ್ಛದ) n Dress, adorning, an ornament -ಡ, -ಪಡ (= ಪಚ್ಛದ) […] tton cloth used as a cover at night -ಪಡಿಸು To decorate, adorn

ಪಚ್ಚಡಿ (= ಪಚಡಿ) k. n A kind of pickles made of green vegetables.

ಪಚ್ಚೆ k. n A precious stone set in gold without soldering.

ಪಚ್ಚೀಸು h. a. Twenty-five 2, a kind of play.

ಪಚ್ಚುಗೆ k. n Privacy; consulting in private

ಪಚ್ಚೆ (= ಪಚ್ಚ) k. n Greenness. 2, yellowish colour 3, young sprouts, growing corn, *etc.*, and their colour. 4, freshness, unripeness, rawness. 5, an emerald. 6, N of a plant with fragrant ears, *also* -ತೆನೆಗಿಡ 7, any tatooed figure on the skin -ಕಾಯಿ ಗಿಡ. A climbing herb, *Cucumis pubescens.* -ತೋರಣ. A festoon of green leaves

ಪಜೀತಿ. = ಫಜೀತಿ, *q v*

ಪಜ್ಜೆ = ಹೆಜ್ಜೆ, *q v*

ಪಂಚ s. *a* Five. 2, incomparable *n* A jury -ಕ Made of five, a pack of five, *as* of paper. -ಕಜ್ಜಾಯ A sweet meat made of five ingredients, *as* avalakki, ĕllu, kadlĕ, kŏbari and bella. -ಕೋಣ. A pentagon. -ಘಾಯ The five wounds of Christ, *as* of hands, feet and heart. -ಗವ್ಯ. Five things from the cow milk, curds, ghee, urine and dung -ಗೌಡ Brâhmanas of Bengal and northern provinces -ತಂತ್ರ. N. of a collection of stories and fables in five chapters. -ತ್ವ. Fivefoldness; death. -ಪರ್ವ. Five days in a month on which Brâhmanas perform special worship -ಪಾಂಡವ The five sons of Pându, who are worshipped by peasants in the form of stones -ಪಾತ್ರೆ. A metal vessel -ಪ್ರಾಣ The five vital airs. -ಭೂತ. The five elements earth, fire, water, air and ether. -ಮ [illegible] a [illegible] dra, a cândâla -ಮಹಾಪಾತಕ -ಮಹಾ ಪಾಪ. The five heinous sins: killing a Brâhmana, *etc.* -ಮಹಾಯಜ್ಞ, -ಯಜ್ಞ Devotional acts performed in reference to the vêda, the gods, the manes of ancestors, men and all beings -ಮಹಾವಾದ್ಯ Five musical instruments: a horn, tabor, conch-shell, kettle-drum, and a gong. -ಮಿ The 5th day of the lunar fortnight; the ablative case -ಮುದ್ರೆ Five gestures of fingers made in presenting offerings, five sectarian marks of Śaivas -ರಂಗು = -ವರ್ಣ -ರಾತ್ರ N of doctrinal books of Vaishnava sects -ರಾಶಿ, -ರಾಶಿಕ The double rule of three. -ಲೋಹ. An alloy of 5 metals, viz gold, silver, copper, tin and iron -ವಕ್ತ್ರ. A lion, Śiva. -ವಟಿ. N. of a place where Râma resided. -ವರ್ಣ. The five colours white, black, red, yellow, and green, five letters or castes. -ವಾದ್ಯ. The bhêri, śankha, kahalĕ, gantĕ, and vîne -ವಿಷಯ. The five objects of sense: rasa, rûpa, gandha, śabda, and sparśa.

ಪಂಚಾಂಗ s. n. A calendar or almanac -ದವ An astrologer, a poor man -ಹೇಳು. To tell the things from an almanac, to tell verbosely.

ಪಂಚಾಮೃತ s n. The five nectarious substances milk, curds, ghee, honey, and sugar.

ಪಂಚಾಯಿತಿ h n. An assembly to settle a matter by arbitration; arbitration -ಫೈಸಲು An award of arbitrators. ಪಂಚಾಯಿತ. An arbitrator.

ಪಂಚಾಲ s. n. N of a tribe and their country in the north

ಪಂಚಾವಸ್ಥೆ s n Five states of humanity childhood, boyhood, youth, manhood, and old age.

ಪಂಚಾಶತ್ s. *a* Fifty. -ತಮ. Fiftieth ಪಂಚಾಶತ್ತಿನ ದಬ್ಬ Pentecost, the pouring down of the H[illegible] Spirit on the [illegible]sciples of Christ

ಪಂಚಾಳ s n One of the five classes of artificers goldsmiths carpenters, blacksmiths, braziers and stone-cutters. 2, a goldsmith

ಪಂಚಿ (= ಪಂಜಿ) f n A small dôtra

ಪಂಚೇಂದ್ರಿಯ s n The five organs of sense the eye, ear, nose, tongue and skin

ಪಂಛೇರು (fr. ಪಂಚ-ಸೇರು) s h n One-eighth of a maund

ಪಂಜರ s n A cage 2, a skeleton

ಪಂಜಾಬು (tb of ಪಂಚ-ಆಪ) n The Panjab.

ಪಂಜಿಕೆ f n The cotton-ball from which the thread is spun 2, an almanac. 3, a journal, a register.

ಪಂಜು f n A torch.

ಪಂಚೆ 1. k n A poor, weak person -ತನ Poverty.

ಪಂಜಿ 2. = ಪಂಚೆ, q v

ಪಟ (= ಪಟ್ಟ) s n Cloth 2, fine cloth, = ಪಟವೆ, q. v. 3, a veil, screen 4, a sheet, an expanse, vastness 5, a tablet or plate. 6, a thatch, roof. 7, a sail 8, a paper-kite 9, a picture 10 a basin for watering plants 11, a plat -ಕ Cotton cloth, a camp -ಕಾರ. A weaver, alum -ಕುಟಿ, -ಗೃಹ, -ವಾಸ A tent -ವಾಸಕ A perfumed powder -ಸ್ತಂಭ A mast

ಪಟಕ (tb of ಸ್ಫಟಿಕಾ) n Sulphate of alumina or alum, also ಪಟಿಕಾರ

ಪಟಕಾರು k n Tongs, pincers

ಪಟನೆ tb of ಪಠನ, q v.

ಪಟಲ s. n A roof, thatch. 2 a cover, veil 3, a basket 4, tb of ಪಟೋಲ

ಪಟವೆ s n Silk -ಕಾರ, -ಗಾರ A man who dyes silk yarn, makes silk tassels, etc.

ಪಟಾ f n. A stripe, streak. -ಪಟಿ Striped. -ಮುತ Striped as a tiger

ಪಟಾಕಿ, ಪಟಾಕ್ಷಿ h. n A cracker, squib

ಪಟಾಟೋಪ s n Ostentatious display of one's dress

ಪಟಾಣ h. n A Pathân, Afghân

ಪಟಾಲಮ್ f n A battalion regiment army.

ಪಟಾವಳಿ s n Stripes, lines. 2, woven silk -ಸೀರೆ. A sîrê with coloured stripes

ಪಟಿಕ = ಪಟಕ, q v 2, tb of ಸ್ಫಟಿಕ

ಪಟಿಂಗ f n An unprincipled fellow, a lecher, a prodigal, an adulterer -ತನ Unprincipledness, profligacy

ಪಟೀರ s n Sandal wood 2, the belly. 3, bamboo manna.

ಪಟು s a Sharp. 2, fierce, pungent, violent, active; strong, great 3, clever, skilful; crafty. 4, eloquent, talkative. -ಮಾಡು To kindle -ತ್ವ. Sharpness, cleverness, eloquence

ಪಟೇಲ h. n A village officer.

ಪಟೋಲ s. n A species of long cucumber, *Trichosanthes dioeca*, the snake-gourd; *also* ಪಡವಲ.

ಪಟ್ಟ s n. Cloth; silk. 2, a tablet, plate, a royal edict or grant 3 a frontlet with which a king is decorated at coronation, royalty, a royal throne, dignity, office -ಕಟ್ಟು To invest with dignity or authority (-ಕ್ಕೆ or) -ದ ಮೇಲೆ ಕುಳಿತುಕೊಳ್ಳು To come to the throne. -ಕ್ಕೆ ಕೂಡ್ರಿಸು To place on the throne -ದಿಂದ ತೆಗದುಹಾಕು, -ದಿಂದ ತಳ್ಳು To dethrone. -ದರಸಿ, -ದ ರಾಣಿ The queen. -ದಣೆ A throne. -ಆಗು, -ವಾಗು To be enthroned -ಏರು, -ವೇರು To ascend the throne -ಬದ್ಧ A king -ಮಹಿಷಿ. The queen -ವರ್ಧನ A vaidika Brâhmana of much reading -ಶಾಲೆ. A reading hall ಪಟ್ಟಾಭಿಷೇಕ. The coronation of a king, ordination of a priest.

ಪಟ್ಟಡಿ, ಪಟ್ಟಡೆ k. n An anvil -ಮನೆ A workshop

ಪಟ್ಟಣ (tb of ಪತ್ತನ) n. A town, city. ಪಟ್ಟಣಿಗ A townsman

ಪಟ್ಟಳೆ s n. A girth, martingale

ಪಟ್ಟಾ f. n A long broad sword; *also* -ಕತಿ.

ಪಟ್ಟಿ s n A stripe, line 2, a strip, slip strap, *as* of lace, cloth, a narrow and long piece, *as* of cloth, leather metal, wood, *etc*; a bar of iron, a rail for a railroad, a piece of timber of a door-frame, a squared rafter, joist, a female's zone, a dog's collar. 3 a roll of betel-leaves 4, a fold, *as* of a turban 5, a bed in gardens or fields 6, a roll of a general collection, a list of collection, subscription or contribution 7, pay, salary 8, a roll or list, *as* of names, *etc.* -ಚೋರ. A slanderer -ವೀಳ್ಯ = ಪಟ್ಟಿ No. 3 -ಹಾಕು. To collect money by subscription

ಪಟ್ಟಿಕೆ s. n. A tablet, a kind of necklace 2, a document 3, a bandage, ligature. 4, a frontlet.

ಪಟ್ಟು 1. k. *v. t.* To seize, catch, take hold of n. Hold; a firm grasp. 2, persistence; resolution, pertinacy. 3, an application to a swelling to allay pain. 4, a callous spot.

ಪಟ್ಟು 2 *P p of* ಪಡು 1, *q v* 2, (*fr.* ಪಡು 2) lying down. ಪಟ್ಟಿರಿಸು. To lay down, place.

ಪಟ್ಟು 3 k. n So much as, time, repetition

ಪಟ್ಟೆ 1. k n. The bark of trees. 2, plantain fibres folded up so as to hold snuff, *etc.*

ಪಟ್ಟೆ 2. (= ಪಟ್ಟಿ, *q. v*) s n The pate, *i. e.* a head without hair. 2, a stripe, *as* of colour. 3, a broad tape 4, a strap, girth, girdle 5, a zone, sash 6, a plat 7 the outer iron rim of a wheel 8, a roll of assessment -ಕಂಬಳಿ A striped kambly. -ತೆಗೆ. To shave the head in stripes -ಮಂಚ A cot with tape bottom

ಪಟ್ಟೆ 3 (= ಪಟ್ಟ No. 1) s n Silk, woven silk.

ಪಟ್ನ. = ಪಟ್ಟಣ, *q. v.*

ಪಠನ s. n. Reading, reciting ಪಠನಾಗಾರ A school. -ನಿಸು. To read, to recite; to study

ಪಡ 1 = ಪಡದು, ಪಡೆದು *P. p. of* ಪಡೆ, *in* ಪಡಕೊಳ್ಳು.

ಪಡ 2 (*tb of* ಪಟ) n. Cloth. 2, a thatch. -ಸಾಲೆ. A veranda, balcony.

ಪಡಗು (= ಪಡಗು, *q v*) a k. n A ship, *etc*

ಪಡಚ = ಪಡಿಚ, *q v.*

ಪಡದೆ (= ಪರದೆ) h. n. A curtain; a veil.

ಪಡಪೋಶಿ h n Inattention, carelessness.

ಪಡಮು f. n Coarse cotton used for bags, *etc.*

ಪಡಲು k. n A lying or falling down. ಪಡಲಿಡು. To fall down here and there.

ಪಡವಲ. = ಪಟೋಲ, *q. v.*

ಪಡವಲು. = ಪಡುವ, *q v.*

ಪಡಾವು h n. Wholesale merchandise. -ದಾರ A wholesale merchant.

ಪಡಿ 1. a. k. n. Manner, way 2, incurring, obtaining. -ಪಾಟು. Troubles

ಪಡಿ 2 k n A measure of capacity = ½ sheer.

ಪಡಿ 3. k n A leaf or panel of a door.

ಪಡಿ 4 k n. An allowance in food. -ತರ Daily allowance at a temple

ಪಡಿ 5. (*tb. of* ಪ್ರತಿ) n. Equality, likeness, comparison, par *ad.* Instead of, beside, against. -ಕಟ್ಟು. To produce equipoise -ಕಲ್ಲು. A stone used to produce equipoise. -ಗುಂಡು. A round stone used to break another one -ತೊತ್ತು. An extra servant -ಮುಖ *tb. of* ಪ್ರತಿಮುಖ -ಮೆಚ್ಚು. Doubt. -ಯಚ್ಚು A puncheon with which impressions are struck.

ಪಡಿಗ (*tb. of* ಪ್ರತಿಗ್ರಹ) n. A spitting-pot, spittoon.

ಪಡಿಚ (= ಪಡಚ) h. n Clearance (of a debt), consumption (of articles or provision), ruin.

ಪಡಿತಳ a. k. n. Effort, exertion. ಪಡಿತಳಿಸು To make effort.

ಪಡಿಯಾರ (*tb. of* ಪ್ರತಿಹಾರ) n. A door-keeper, *f.* -ತಿ

ಪಡಿಸು k v t To cause to incur, get, *etc* -ವಿಕೆ. Causing to get.

ಪಡು 1. (= ಪಡೆ 1) k v t To get, obtain; to catch, to incur, undergo, to experience feel, to suffer. *Affixed to the infinitive of verbs it gives them a passive signification, as* ಬರೆಯ-, ಬರೆಯಲ್- To be written *etc*

ಪಡು 2 a k. v. i To lie down, to go down, set, *as* the sun, to wear away, to die. *n* Setting: the west. -ಕಡೆ, -ಗಡೆ The western side. -ಪ, -ಪಲು The region of sun-set. the west.

ಪಡೆ 1 (= ಪಡು 1) k. v t. To get, to incur, undergo, to experience, to gain, obtain. 2, to beget, *esp.* to bear give birth to, *as* a mother. *P. ps* ಪಡದು, ಪಡೆದು. -ಯುವಿಕೆ, -ವಿಕೆ. Obtaining incurring, experiencing.

ಪಡೆ 2 k *n*. A multitude, force, army. -ಪತಿ, -ಪಳ್ಳಿ. A general. -ಯಿಲು A soldier.

ಪಡ್ಡಳಿ (*tb of* ಪ್ರತಿಹಾಸ) *n*. The sweet-scented oleander, *Nerium odorum*.

ಪಣ 1 f. *n*. Any tribe, a sectarian division. -ಕಟ್ಟು Caste rules.

ಪಣ 2 (= ಹಣ) s *n* Play, playing for a stake. 2, a stake at play, a wager. 3, wages, hire. 4, a fanam, a small coin. 5, a weight of two tolas. 6, price. 7, money, wealth. 8, business, trade. 9, a shop, stall. -ಕಟ್ಟು To wager.

ಪಣತೆ (*tb. of* ಪ್ರಣೀತ) *n*. A saucer-shaped lamp-cup.

ಪಣೆ k *n* A stick, bat. -ಚೆಂಡು A play with a bat and ball.

ಪಣಿ = ಹಣೆ, *q v* 2, tillage, a quarry.

ಪಂಡಿತ s *n* A Pandit, scholar, learned man, doctor, *f* -ಳು

ಪಣ್ಣು 1 a k *v t* To make ready, to array; to dress, to trim. ಪಣ್ಣಿಕೆ Arranging, equipping, an ornamental mark on the forehead. ಪಣ್ಣಿಸು. To cause to make ready.

ಪಣ್ಣು 2 = ಹಣ್ಣು, *q v*

ಪಣ್ಣೆಯ ...

ಪಣ್ಯ s *a*. Saleable, vendible. *n* An article of trade, wares. 2, a shop.

ಪತಂಗ s *n* A bird. 2 a grasshopper. 3, any flying insect, *esp* a moth. 4, the sun. 5, a sort of paper-kite. 6, an arrow.

ಪತಂಜಲಿ s *n* N of a muni, author of the yôga philosophy.

ಪತನ s *n* Falling down.

ಪತಾಕಿ s. *n*. A standard-bearer, an ensign. -ನಿ. An army.

ಪತಾಕೆ s *n* A flag, banner.

ಪತಿ s. *n* A master, owner. 2, a governor, ruler lord. 3, a husband. -ವ್ರತೆ A virtuous and faithful wife. -ಪತ್ನಿ Husband and wife.

ಪತಿತ s. *a*. Fallen, wicked. -ತ್ವ. Wickedness. -ಪಾವನ Purifier and restorer of the fallen.

ಪತ್ತಲ f. *n* A lower garment of females.

ಪತ್ತಳಿಕೆ (= ಬತ್ತಳಿಕೆ) s. *n*. A quiver.

ಪತ್ತಾರಿ h. *n* An examiner of tax money and measurer of public corn.

ಪತ್ತಿ s *n* Going, moving. 2, a footman. 3, a share of some joint concern. -ಗ, -ಗಾರ A partner.

ಪತ್ತಿಗೆ k *n* A hold a wall-shelf. 2, (*tb of* ಪತ್ರಿಕೆ) a sword-blade, a knife.

ಪತ್ತು 1. (= ಹತ್ತು 1 *q v*) a. k. *v i* To hold to, stick to *etc*. *n* Hold, adhesion. 2 a grapple in fight. 3, friendship. -ಪಟ The amount of frauds on government charged to a public functionary.

ಪತ್ತು 2 = ಹತ್ತು 2, *q v*

ಪತ್ತು 3 f *n* Credit, reputation.

ಪತ್ತೆ h *n* Tidings; trace, clue. -ಹಚ್ಚು, -ಹುಟ್ಟಿಸು. To trace. -ದಾರ. A detective. -ತೋರು Traces to appear.

ಪತ್ತೇಮಾರಿ f *n* A Pattimar.

ಪತ್ನಿ s *n* A wife. *Cpds*: ಗುರು-, ರಾಜ-, *etc*

ಪತ್ರ s. n A wing 2, a vehicle. 3, a leaf 4, a letter, note; a written paper or deed. 5, the leaf of a book, *also* -ಕ. 6, a knife. -ದ್ವಾರ. By means of a letter. -ಪುಟಿಕೆ. A basket of leaves ಪತ್ರಾಂಗ Sappan wood, red sanders. -ವ್ಯವಹಾರ Correspondence ಪತ್ರಾವಳಿ A plate made of leaves

ಪತ್ರಿ f. n. The coat of the nutmeg, mace. *a.* Having wings or leaves.

ಪತ್ರಿಕೆ s n. A letter, a leaf. ಜನ್ಮ-. A paper containing the horoscope.

ಪತ್ರೆ = ಪತ್ರಿ, *q v*

ಪಥ s n A path, way, road. ಪಥಿಕ. A traveller.

ಪಥ್ಯ s. *a* Proper, fit, suitable, as diet *n* Diet, dietetics -ಮಾಡು To observe dietetical rules -ಕರ Wholesome.

ಪದ 1 = ಹದ, *q. v*

ಪದ 2 s. *n* A step, footstep, a trace, mark 2, a verse-line, a verse, stanza 3, a footing, standpoint, position 4, an abode 5 an object 6, cause 7, an inflected word -ಗ A pedestrian, a foot-soldier -ಗತಿ Gait -ಚ್ಛೇದ. Parsing -ಪಾಠ. A peculiar method of reading and writing vedic texts. -ಪೂರ Expletive -ಪೂರಕ An expletive -ವಿನ್ಯಸ್ತಿ. The course of a verse -ಸಂಧಾನ. Combination of words or composing of verses. ಪದಾದಿ. The beginning of a word ಪದಾಂತ್ಯ. Final. ಪದಾಂತ್ಯಸಂಧಿ Euphonic coalition of a final letter with the letter of the next word.

ಪದಕ s *n* An ornamental breast-plate

ಪದಪು a. k *n* Zeal, pleasure, charm

ಪದರು 1. f. *n* A fold, *as* of cloth; a division, a thin layer of stone, a coat of an onion, scale of a fish 2, the lap, as protection, *as*· ಒಬ್ಬನನ್ನು ತನ್ನ ಪದರಿನಲ್ಲಿ ಇಟ್ಟುಕೊಳ್ಳು

ಪದರು 2 (ರು=ಱು) k *v. i* To be overhasty 2. to blabber ಪದರಾಡು, ಪದರು. To talk nonsense ಪದರಾಟ. Loquacity, haste.

ಪದವಿ s. *n.* A path, road. 2, situation, rank, office, wealth ದಿವ್ಯ-, ಮೋಕ್ಷ- Heaven.

ಪದಾಜಿ, ಪದಾತಿ s. *n* A footman, pedestrian

ಪದಾರ್ಥ s *n.* The meaning of a word. 2, a thing 3, a head, a category. 4, a dish of any vegetables, curry

ಪದಿ. = ಹದಿ, *q v.*

ಪದುಳ (= ಹದುಳ) a. k. *n* Well-being, welfare, safety. ಪದುಳಿಗ A happy man. ಪದುಳಿರು. To cheer up. ಪದುಳಿಸು To become well or happy, to feel refreshed.

ಪದೆ a k *v t* To desire, wish. *n* Desire, wish

ಪದೇ s *ad.* At a step -ಪದೇ At every step, on every occasion

ಪದ್ಧತಿ s *n* A way 2, manner, mode, usage, custom *Cpds* ಲೋಕ-, ಜನ-, ಶಾಸ್ತ್ರ, *etc.*

ಪದ್ಮ s *n.* A lotus, *Nelumbium speciosum.* 2, the water-lily. 3, a species of fragrant plant used in medicine 4, the moon. 5, a particular posture of the body in religious meditation. 6, thousand billions -ಗರ್ಭ, -ಜ, -ಭವ, -ಸಂಭವ Brahmâ. -ನಾಭ Vishnu -ಪತ್ರ *Costus speciosus.* -ಪಾಣಿ. Lakshmî, Pârvatî -ಪುರಾಣ. N. of a Purâna -ಬಂಧು, -ಸಖ. The sun -ಮುದ್ರೆ. A certain intertwining of the fingers in devotion, a sectarian mark on the forehead. -ರಾಗ Lotus coloured, a ruby ಪದ್ಮಾಕ್ಷ. Lotus-eyed, the seed of the lotus. ಪದ್ಮಾವತಿ N of a woman, the town Patna ಪದ್ಮಾಸನ. = ಪದ್ಮ No 5, *q v*

ಪದ್ಯ s *n.* A verse, metre, poetry.

ಪನಸ s. *n* The jack tree.

ಪನಿ. = ಹನಿ, *q. v*

ಪನಿವಾರ k *n* A sweet cake, fritter, *also* ಪನಿಯಾಣ.

ಪನೀರು f *n* Cheese.

ಪಂತ 1 (*tb. of* ಪಣಿತ) *n.* A bet wager. 2, a promise or vow, a challenge. -ಕ

ಟ್ಟು To bet, wager -ಮಾಡು, -ಹಾಕು To challenge vow -ಗಾರ. A wagerer

ಪಂತ 2 s n A learned man, Pandit, a schoolmaster.

ಪಂತಿ. tb. of ಪಂಕ್ತಿ, q v

ಪಂತು tb of ಪಂಥ, q v.

ಪಂತೋಜಿ f n A schoolmaster

ಪಂಥ s n A path, road

ಪಂದರು, ಪಂದಲ್ k n. A pandal, shed.

ಪಂದಿ. = ಹಂದಿ q. v

ಪಂದ (= ಹಂದೆ, q v) a k n A coward -ತನ Cowardice.

ಪನ್ನ 1. a k n Pride.

ಪನ್ನ 2 h. n The breadth of cloth

ಪನ್ನಗ s n A snake -ಭೂಷಣ Śiva -ಶಯನ Vishnu. ಪನ್ನಗಾಂತಕ, ಪನ್ನಗಾಶನ. Garuda

ಪನ್ನಂಗ (tb of ಪಲ್ಯಂಕ) n The canopy over a palanquin or couch, also ಪಲ್ಲಂಗ

ಪನ್ನತಿಕೆ a. k n Valour, courage.

ಪನ್ನಾಡೆ k n The web surrounding the lower part of a palm-tree leaf.

ಪನ್ನಿ k. n Boasting, self-conceit

ಪನ್ನೀರು k n. Rose-water; perfumed water.

ಪನ್ನೆ h n A funny way of trimming the whiskers

ಪನ್ನೇರಳು, -ಮರ k n A small tree with very fragrant flowers, *Guettarda speciosa*.

ಪಪ್ಪರಿಕೆ. = ಪರ್ಪರಿಕೆ, q v.

ಪಪ್ಪಳ. = ಹಪ್ಪಳ, q v.

ಪಪ್ಪಳಿ s n A chequered garment, the stuff called 'poplin".

ಪಪ್ಪಾಯಿ f n. The Papaya tree and [fruit

ಪಪ್ಪು k n Split pulse, almonds, *etc*

ಪಪ್ಪುಕೆ k n Beating bushes in hunting

ಪಂಪ a. k n Equal division.

ಪಂಪೆ (= ಹಂಪೆ, q v) s n The river, lake, or town of Pampâ or Hampĕ, *also* ಪಂಪಾಕ್ಷೇತ್ರ

ಪಂಬಲ್

ಪಯ = ಪಯಸ್, q v. ಪಯೋಧರ A cloud ಪಯೋಧಿ The ocean ಪಯೋನಿಧಿ, ಪಯೋಂಬುಧಿ The milk-sea

ಪಯಣ (tb of ಪ್ರಯಾಣ, q v) n A journey, *etc*

ಪಯಸ್ s n Water. 2 milk.

ಪಯಿರು, ಪಯ್ರು = ಪೈರು, q v.

ಪರ s. a Distant, remote. 2, ulterior, beyond 3 subsequent, next, future. 4, another different, foreign, alien 5, hostile 6 excellent, best, supreme. chief 7, intent upon, engrossed in n. A stranger. 2, final beatitude -ಕರ್ತೃ. Another agent. -ಕಾಯ. Another body. -ಕೀಯ Another's, a stranger. -ತಂತ್ರ Subject to another, dependent on -ತಂತ್ರತನ Dependence -ತೆ, Absoluteness, distinction, priority. -ತ್ರ Elsewhere, hereafter -ತ್ವ = ತೆ. Influence sway. -ತ್ವದಿಂದ Through -ದಾರ. Another's wife -ದೇಶ A foreign country -ದೇಶಸ್ಥ. A man from abroad. -ದೇಶಿ A foreigner, a poor wanderer, a wretch. -ನಿಂದೆ. Reviling others -ಪಕ್ಷ The side of an enemy. -ಪುರುಷ. A stranger. -ಬಲ A hostile army -ಬ್ರಹ್ಮ. The supreme soul -ಭಾಗ Excellence. -ಭಾಷೆ Foreign language. -ಮಂಡಲಿಕ. The ruler of another province -ಮತ. Heterodoxy, heresy. -ರಾಯ. Another or hostile king. -ರಾಷ್ಟ್ರ A hostile country, another kingdom -ಲೋಕ. The next world, future state, paradise, heaven. -ವಶ. Subject to another, dependant. -ವಶತೆ Dependence -ವಾದಿ. A controversialist, dissenter -ವಾಸ A foreign place or abode. -ವಾಸ ಮಾಡು To stay in a foreign place -ಸ್ತ್ರೀ = -ದಾರ -ಸ್ಥಲ. A foreign place -ಸ್ಥಾನ. Removing the baggage for a journey on an auspicious day to another house, when it is not convenient to start immediately. -ಸ್ವರ One

mutually, reciprocally. -ಸ್ವಾಧೀನ. = ಪರಾಧೀನ -ಹಿಂಸೆ Injuring others -ಹಿತ. Benevolent, benevolence ಪರಾತ್ಪರ. Higher than the highest ಪರಾರ್ಥ. The profit of another ಪರಾಶ್ರಯ Dependence. ಪರಾಶ್ರಿತ Dependant, subject. ಪರಾಹ್ಣ The afternoon.

ಪರಕಲು (ರ=ಐ) k. n. The state of being emaciated or lean

ಪರಕಾವಣೆ h n. Proving coin, shroffing, *also* ಪಾರಕಾವಣೆ.

ಪರಕಾಳೆ f. n. A long cloth.

ಪರಕು 1. = ಪರಳು.

ಪರಕು 2. h. n Distinction, difference; dissimilitude

ಪರಕೆ (= ಪರಕೆ, *q v*) a k n A benediction 2, a vow 3. a broom

ಪರಗಣೆ h. n. A district

ಪರಂಗಿ f n. A Frank; a European.

ಪರಚು (= ಪರಮು) k. v t. To scratch with the finger nails.

ಪರಜು (*tb. of* ಪರಂಜು) n The blade of a sword or knife, a sword 2, a sward-hilt

ಪರಂಜ್ಯೋತಿ s. n The supreme light. 2, God

ಪರಟಿ f n. A platter, pot, the blade of a hoe. 2, an enclosure around a house.

ಪರಡಿ f. n A kind of dish 2, the nape of the neck.

ಪರಡು 1. (= ಪರಡು) a k. v t To spread 2, to scrape out, to scratch v i To spread, extend.

ಪರಡು 2 a k n The ankle.

ಪರದ. = ಹರದ, q v

ಪರದೆ (= ಪಡದೆ) h n. A curtain, veil

ಪರದೈಸು f. n. Paradise, the garden of Eden; heaven.

ಪರಂತು f. ad But, yet, however.

ಪರಪು a k. v t. To spread about 2, to be divulged.

ಪರಭಾರಿ, ಪರಭಾರೆ f. ad Elsewise, in some other w... assignment transfer. -... deed of transfer.

ಪರಮ s. a Highest, most excellent, best, greatest. 2, extreme. n. The supreme soul -ಗತಿ. Final beatitude -ಜ್ಞಾನ. Supreme wisdom, knowledge of salvation (*Christ.*). -ಜ್ಞಾನಿ. A person of superior wisdom -ತ್ವ The highest end or aim. -ಪದ. Final beatitude. -ಪುರುಷ The supreme soul -ಹಂಸ. An ascetic of the highest order ಪರಮಾಣು. An atom. ಪರಮಾತ್ಮ The supreme soul, the soul of the universe, God. ಪರಮಾನಂದ Supreme felicity. ಪರಮಾನ್ನ. Best food, *as* rice boiled in milk with sugar ಪರಮಾರ್ಥ. Reality, truth. ಪರಮಾವಧಿ Utmost term or limit. ಪರಮೇಶ, ಪರಮೇಶ್ವರ Supreme lord. Śiva, Vishnu; Indra.

ಪರಮೆ (ರ=ಐ) a k n A black bee.

ಪರಂಪರ s a Successive, repeated. ಪರಂಪರೆ. A series, succession, order, race, lineage.

ಪರವರ್ಶಿ *tb. of* ಪರಾಮರ್ಶೆ, *q. v*

ಪರವಾ h. n Care, concern about; anxiety. -ಇಲ್ಲ. Never mind

ಪರವಾನಾ, ಪರವಾನೆ h. n. An order, pass, commission

ಪರಶು s n An axe -ಧರ, -ರಾಮ. Râma, the son of Jamadagni.

ಪರಸು. = ಹರಸು, q. v.

ಪರಸೆ (= ಪರಿಸೆ. *tb. of* ಪರಿಷದ್) n People assembled at an idol festival

ಪರಸ್ಮೈಪದ s n. The active transitive verb (*g.*).

ಪರಾಕು f. int. Attention! take heed! listen! n Carelessness, inattentiveness, forgetfulness.

ಪರಾಕ್ರಮ s. n. Heroism, valour, courage; power, strength 2, exertion, effort, enterprise. -ಶಾಲಿ A valorous man. -ವುಳ್ಳ, ಪರಾಕ್ರಮಿ. Powerful, valorous.

ಪರಾಗ s. n. The pollen of a flower. 2, dust, powder. 3, the nectar or honey of flowers.

sacrifice by faith, *Christ* ಪರಿಹರಿಸು To abandon, leave, reject, to take away, remove, set aside, remedy, to clear off, *as* a debt.

ಪರಿಹಾಸ, ಪರಿಹಾಸ್ಯ s *n* Jesting, joking, a jester, buffoon; *also* -ಕ. 2, mirth, sport; laughter, deriding, mockery.

ಪರೀಕ್ಷೆ s *n*. Investigation; examination, test, trial -ಆಗು. An examination to take place -ಕೊಡು. To undergo an examination; to pass an examination with success, *also* -ಪಾಸಾಗು. -ಗಾರ An examiner -ತೆಗೆ, -ಮಾಡು, ಪರೀಕ್ಷಿಸು. To inspect, examine, to investigate

ಪರೀಧಾವಿ = ಪರಿಧಾವಿ, *q v*

ಪರುಟವ, -ಣೆ (*tb. of* ಪ್ರಥಮನ್) *n* Spreading, prolixity; verbosity. ಪರುಟವಿಸು To spread about, to give details of

ಪರುವ (*tb of* ಪರ್ವ) *n* A yearly feast at which villagers take a common meal before an idol

ಪರುಷ s. *a*. Knotted, rough rugged; harsh, cruel, stern, rude. *n* A touch-stone, the philosopher's stone.

ಪರೆ 1 (= ಹರೆ, *q v*.) a. k. *v. t*. To spread, disperse *n* Extension, stretch.

ಪರೆ 2. k *n*. A scale, coat of an onion, a web on the eye, slough of a snake, a thin layer of stone, a spider's web; scab of a sore; scurf of the head

ಪರೆ 3. (ರೆ = ಱೆ) a k. *n*. A drum. 2, an eyelid 3, leanness, thinness, feebleness

ಪರೆಂಗಿ = ಪರಂಗಿ, *q v*

ಪರೆಯ (ರೆ = ಱೆ) k. *n* A Pariah.

ಪರೇಶ, ಪರೇಶ್ವರ s. *n*. The supreme lord

ಪರೋಕ್ಷ s *a* Invisible, imperceptible, absent. *n*. Invisibility.

ಪರೋಪಕಾರ s *n* Doing good to others, benevolence, charity ಪರೋಪಕಾರಿ A beneficient person

ಪರ್ಜನ್ಯ s. *n* A rain-cloud. 2, Indra. -ಜಪ A prayer for rain.

ಪರ್ಣ s *n* A leaf -ಕುಟಿ, -ಶಾಲೆ A hut made ... ಜನ, ಪರ್ಣಾಶನ, ಪರ್ಣಾಹಾರ Feeding on leaves.

ಪರ್ಪಟ = ಪಪ್ಪಟ, *q v* 2, = -ಕ

ಪರ್ಪಟಕ s. *n* A species of medicinal plant *Oldenlandia biflora*.

ಪರ್ಪರಿಕೆ (= ಪಪ್ಪರಿಕೆ) a k *n* Roughness, harshness.

ಪಪಾಟರ್ಕ f *n* A herb, *Mollugo cerviana*.

ಪಬ್ಬು (= ಹಬ್ಬು, *q v*) a. k. *v. i*. To spread, *etc*

ಪರ್ಯಟನ s *n* Roaming, wandering. -ಮಾಡು. To wander about.

ಪರ್ಯಂತ, -ರ s *n* Limit, border, edge, end. *ad* As far as, until unto.

ಪರ್ಯಯ s. *n* Going round; revolution of time 2, change, mutation

ಪರ್ಯವಸಾನ s *n*. End, conclusion, issue.

ಪರ್ಯಾಟನ = ಪರ್ಯಟನ, *q v*

ಪರ್ಯಾಪ್ತಿ s. *n* Obtaining 2, end, conclusion 3, competency. 4, satisfaction.

ಪರ್ಯಾಯ s. *n*. Revolution, course. 2, repetition 3, succession, turn 4, order, method; style, manner -ನಾಮ A synonym.

ಪರ್ಯುಷಿತ s *a*. Stale, not fresh -ಭೋಜನ Eating stale food. ಪರ್ಯುಷಿತಾನ್ನ. Stale rice

ಪರ್ಯೇಷಣೆ s *n*. Search, inquiry 2, service

ಪರ್ವ s. *n* A knot of a cane. 2, a section, chapter, book 3, a division of time the days of the four changes of the moon. 4, a festival -ಸಂಧಿ. The full and change of the moon.

ಪರ್ವತ s *n*. A mountain -ಕಾಕ A raven. -ನಾಥ The Himâlaya ಪರ್ವತಾರಿ Indra ಮೇರು- N. of a mountain.

ಪರ್ವು = ಪಬ್ಬು, *q v*

ಪಲ್ = ಹಲ್ಲು, *q. v* -ಗಿಂ To grin, show the teeth. -ಕಡಿ To gnash the teeth

ಪಲ 1, ಪಲವು (= ಹಲವು, *q v*) a k *a* Many, several, various. *Cpds* -ದಿವಸ, -ಬಗೆ, -ಮಾತು, -ರೂಪು, *etc* -ಬರ್,

ಪಲ 2 s *n.* A particular weight or measure

ಪಲಗೆ (=ಹಲಗೆ. *tb of* ಫಲಕ) *n.* A plank, a tabor; a shield

ಪಲಂಗ. *tb of* ಪರ್ಯಂಕ, *q v.*

ಪಲಹಾರ, ಪಲಾರ *tb of* ಫಲಾಹಾರ, *q. v.*

ಪಲಾಯನ s. *n* Fleeing, flight; a run. ಪಲಾಯಿತ Fled.

ಪಲಾವು h. *n.* The dish called Pulâo.

ಪಲಾಶ s. *n* The tree *Butea frondosa* 2, a leaf.

ಪಲಿತ s *a* Grey haired, old, aged *n* Grey hair, old age

ಪಲೆಸ್ತೀನು f. *n.* Palastine, the Holy Land.

ಪಲ್ಯ (=ಪಲ್ಯೆ, ಪಲ್ಲೆ) k. *n* Any garden green, any vegetable 2, a vegetable dish

ಪಲ್ಯಂಕ s. *n* A bedstead. 2, a palanquin.

ಪಲ್ಲ a. k *n* An elephant. 2, the black bee

ಪಲ್ಲಕ್ಕಿ (*tb of* ಪರ್ಯಂಕ, *q. v*) *n* A palanquin. 2, =ಪನ್ನಂಗ, *q. v., also* ಪಲ್ಲಂಗ.

ಪಲ್ಲಟ (*tb. of* ಪರ್ಯಾಯ) *n.* Inversion, irregularity, change, confusion. ಪಲ್ಲಟಿಸು To change places 2, to invert

ಪಲ್ಲವ s. *n* A sprout, shoot, young foliage. 2, a vocabulary 3, a refrain, *also* ಪಲ್ಲ. -ಪಾಣಿ. A hand like fresh shoot. ಪಲ್ಲವಿಸು. To sprout, to spread. ಪಲ್ಲವೋತ್ಸವ. A yearly feast at which young foliage is worshipped in a temple

ಪಲ್ಲಾ h. *n* A measure of capacity of 100 or 120 sêrs.

ಪಲ್ಲಿ (=ಹಲ್ಲಿ *q. v.*) k. *n.* A house-lizard.

ಪಲ್ಲೆ. =ಪಲ್ಯ, *etc q. v* 2, =ಹಲ್ಲೆ, *q v*

ಪವಡಿಸು (=ಪವಳಿಸು) f. *v. i.* To lie down, recline, repose.

ಪವಣ *tb. of* ಪ್ರಮಾಣ, *q. v.* ಪವಣ್ಣರಿ Exact proof or certainty

ಪವಣಿಗೆ k. *n.* Being threaded ಪವಣಿಸು. To thread, [illegible]

ಪವನ s. *n.* Winnowing. 2, wind, air. -ಜ, -ಸುತ Bhîma; Hanumat

ಪವಳ =ಹವಳ, *q. v.*

ಪವನು e *n.* A "pound" in money, gold sovereign.

ಪವಾಡ s. *n* A determination to effect an object, fanatical, pompous or marvellous words or acts.

ಪವಿತ್ರ s *a* Pure, clean, sinless, holy. *n* The kuśa grass, a ring made of it and put on the fourth finger 2, the sacrificial thread. 3, the middle finger. -ತೆ, -ತ್ವ Purity, cleanness; holiness ಪವಿತ್ರಾತ್ಮ The Holy Spirit.

ಪವುಜು =ಫೌಜು, *q v.*

ಪವುಂಚಿ h *n.* An ornament for the wrist of females

ಪವುತಿ h. *a* Deceased defunct

ಪವುಳಿ (=ಪೌಳಿ) f *n.* An enclosure; a rampart

ಪಶು s *n* Cattle, any domestic animal; a brute, beast, an ignorant person; a victim -ಪತಿ Śiva, a bull -ಪಾಲ. -ಪಾಲಕ. A herdsman -ತನ Brutishness.

ಪಶ್ಚಾತ್ s *ad* Behind, afterwards ಪಶ್ಚಾದ್ವಿವೇಕ Knowledge that comes after an act. ಪಶ್ಚಾತ್ತಾಪ. Sorrow, regret, repentance, remorse -ಗೊಳ್ಳು, -ಪಡು, -ಹುಟ್ಟು. To repent, regret.

ಪಶ್ಚಿಮ s. *a* Hindermost. 2, western *n.* The back; the west -ಘಟ್ಟ The western ghauts ಪಶ್ಚಿಮೋತ್ತರ North-west

ಪಸದನ *tb. of* ಪ್ರಸಾಧನ, *q v.*

ಪಸಂದು h *a.* Agreeable, comely, pleasing. -ಮಾಡು. To make pretty, nice; to approve

ಪಸರ =ಪ್ರಸರ, *q v.* ಪಸರಿಸು To spread, spread abroad

ಪಸಲೆ k. *n.* Young, green grass, pasturage.

ಪಸಾದ, ಪಸಾಯ. *tb. of* ಪ್ರಸಾದ, *q v*

ಪಸಾರಿ (*tb of* ಪ್ರಸಾರ) *n.* Things spread [illegible]

ಪಸಿ. = ಹಸಿ, q v.

ಪಸು a k. v. t. To divide, cut, to share. 2, = ಪಚ್ಚೆ. -ಗೆ Division, portion, share, arrangement

ಪಸುಬೆ (= ಹಸುಬೆ) a k n A long bag with an opening in the middle, also ಪಸುಂಬೆ. -ವೞ. A merchant

ಪಸುರು = ಹಸರು, q v

ಪಸುಳೆ (= ಹಸುಳೆ) a k n. A child -ತನ. Childhood

ಪಸೆ (= ಹಸೆ) a k. n. A bed, layer 2, a meaningless word.

ಪಸ್ಕ f. n Easter, passover; commemoration of the resurrection of Christ, also -ಹಬ್ಬ.

ಪಹರೆ (tb of ಪ್ರಹರ) n A period of three hours, watch, a watch or a guard -ಕಾಯು, -ಕೊಡು. To watch. -ತಿರುಗು. To go about on guard. -ಯವ A guard, sentinel.

ಪೞ = ಹೞ, q v

ಪೞಕ (ೞ = ಳ) k n Use, practice habit, custom ಪೞಕಿಸು To accustom, habituate, train, practise.

ಪೞಗು (ೞ = ಳ) k v. i. To become used to or familiar with, to be trained. ಪೞಗಿಸು. = ಪೞಕಿಸು, q v.

ಪೞಂಚು a. k. v t. To strike or dash against, also ಪೞಂಕು. n Opposition, resistance

ಪೞದಿ = ಪಳಿದ್ಯ, q v

ಪೞಯಿಗೆ, ಪೞವಿಗೆ (ೞ = ಳ tb. of ಪತಾಕೆ) a. k n A banner, flag

ಪೞಯಿಸು, ಪೞವಿಸು (tb of ಪ್ರಲಪಿಸು) v. i. To cry, lament.

ಪಳಿ 1 (ಳಿ = ೞಿ. = ಹಳಿ) a k. v t. To revile, scold n Blame, fault, rebuke.

ಪಳಿ 2. (ಳಿ = ೞಿ tb. of ಪ್ರತಿ, q v) n. Equality; counterpart, amends

ಪಳಿದ್ಯ (= ಪೞದಿ, q. v.) n Boiled and seasoned vegetables used as sauce

ಪಳು (= ಹಳುವ) a k n A forest 2, rubbish weeds.

ಪಳುಕು ([illegible]) n. Cry[illegible]

ಪಳೆ. = ಹಳೆ, q v

ಪಳ್ಳ (= ಹಳ್ಳ) a. k. n Depth 2, a pit 3, a stream

ಪಳ್ಳಿ (= ಹಳ್ಳಿ) k. n. A hamlet, village.

ಪಾಕ s n Cooking 2, maturity, ripeness; completion, accomplishment. 3, syrup. -ಮಾಡು. To cook -ಶಾಲೆ. A kitchen. -ಶಾಸ್ತ್ರ A book on cookery; cookery

ಪಾಕಿ 1 n A side of a roof 2, a cook

ಪಾಖಂಡಿ (= ಪಾಷಂಡಿ) s a Heterodox, heretic.

ಪಾಗ (tb. of ಪಾದ) n. The fourth part of a pana· 1 anĕ 2 kâsus, also ಹಾಗ.

ಪಾಗಾರ (tb of ಪ್ರಾಕಾರ) n. An encircling wall, fence, enclosure

ಪಾಗು h n. A kind of turban.

ಪಾಂಗು a. k n. Manner, form, shape, likeness.

ಪಾಚಕ s a Cooking, maturing; digestive n. A cook.

ಪಾಚಿ k n. Green stuff on stagnant water 2, milk, in children's language

ಪಾಚಿಕೆ s. n. A die used in playing.

ಪಾಚ್ಛ h n. A king, Pasha

ಪಾಜಿ h. a. Low, mean n. A scrub

ಪಾಂಚಾಲ (fr ಪಂಚಾಲ) s a Belonging to Pañcâla; the country or ruler of Pañcâlas ಪಾಂಚಾಲಿ, ಪಾಂಚಾಲೆ. Draupadî

ಪಾಟ 1. (fr ಪಾಡು) k n. Singing, a song.

ಪಾಟ 2 s n Breadth, expanse. 2, tb of ಪಾಠ, q v

ಪಾಟಲ s. a. Pale red. n. The trumpet flower, *Bignonia suaveolens*.

ಪಾಟಲಿಪುತ್ರ s. n. The capital of Magadha, Palibothra, the modern Patna

ಪಾಟವ (fr ಪಟು) s n Sharpness, acuteness, energy, harshness.

ಪಾಟೀ h n. A line, as drawn through a letter.

ಪಾಟಿ 1 (= ಪಾಟು) k. n Manner, shape, degree size fitness likeness 2, [illegible] sum.

ಪಾಟಿ 2 s. n A gang of workmen

ಪಾಟು (*fr.* ಪಡು, *q v*) k n Experiencing, obtaining, undergoing; feeling 2, (= ಪಾಡು) nature, manner, mode, fitness

ಪಾಠ s. n. Recitation 2, reading, study. 3, a lesson -ಒಪ್ಪಿಸು. To recite a lesson. -ಮಾಡು. To learn by heart; to teach. -ಕ A reader, a student, a teacher -ದೋಷ A false reading -ಶಾಲೆ A school, college ಪಾಠಾಂತರ. A variation of reading ಪಾಠಿ One who has read and studied. ಪಾಠಿಸು To recite; to learn.

ಪಾಡಗ (*tb of* ಪಾದಕಟಕ) n An anklet

ಪಾಡಿ k n A hamlet, village.

ಪಾಡು 1. (= ಹಾಡು 1, *q. v*) k. v. i To sing n. Singing, a song

ಪಾಡು 2. (= ಹಾಡು 2, *q. v*) k. n. Suffering, trouble, manner, mode, fitness; resemblance

ಪಾಡ್ಯ (*tb of* ಪ್ರತಿಪದ್) n. The first day of a lunar fortnight

ಪಾಣಿ s. n The hand; holding in hand -ಗ್ರಹಣ Marriage -ಮೂಲ The wrist

ಪಾಣಿನಿ s. n. N. of an eminent grammarian. [Pându

ಪಾಂಡವ s n. A descendant or son of

ಪಾಂಡಿತ್ಯ (*fr.* ಪಂಡಿತ) s. n Scholarship, learning, erudition; skill.

ಪಾಂಡು s. a. Yellowish white. n. Father of the five Pândavas. 2, jaundice, *also* -ರೋಗ

ಪಾಂಡುರ s a. Pale n Jaundice. 2, the white leprosy

ಪಾಂಡುರಂಗ s. n. N. of Krishna.

ಪಾಂಡ್ಯ s n. N. of a country and people in the Dekhan.

ಪಾತ s n. Falling, fall, a throw; a stroke, an attack; defect, fault a. Watched, protected.

ಪಾತಕ s n. Sin, crime. -ಪರಿಹರಿಸು Sin to be removed -ತನ. Sinful state -ಹಿಡಿ. To incur sin. ಪಾತಕ. A sinner.

ಪಾತರ (*tb. of* ಪಾತ್ರ, *q v*) n Performing, dancing. -ಗಿತ್ತಿ. A butterfly; a dancing girl, *also* -ದವಳು

ಪಾತಾಲ, ಪಾತಾಳ s. n One of the lower regions, the abode of the serpents and demons. -ಗಡ, -ಗರಡಿ, ಗರುಡ, -ಭೇದಿ. A hooked drag to catch things under water.

ಪಾತಿ k. n A basin round the foot of a tree, *etc* 2, a garden-bed

ಪಾತಿವ್ರತ್ಯ (*fr* ಪತಿವ್ರತಾ) s n Loyalty to a husband, conjugal fidelity

ಪಾತ್ರ (= ಪಾತರ, ಪಾತ್ರೆ) s n A drinking vessel, a goblet, cup, *etc.* 2, a vessel in general 3, a receptacle, a fit or worthy person, a recipient of punishment, blame, *etc.* 4 an actor. 5, a disguise 6, performing, dancing a Fit for. -ತೆ, -ತ್ವ Fitness, worthiness. -ದವಳು. A dancing girl.

ಪಾತ್ರೆ. = ಪಾತ್ರ, No. 1-2, *q. v.*

ಪಾಥೋದ, ಪಾಥೋಧರ s n A cloud.

ಪಾದ s. n A foot 2, *an honorific affix to proper names* 3, the foot of a mountain 4, the root of a tree 5, a verse-line. 6, a fourth part. -ಕಾಣಿಕೆ, -ಗಾಣಿಕೆ. A gift placed at the feet of a guru. -ಚಾರಿ. A footman. -ಜ. A Sûdra -ತೀರ್ಥ, ಪಾದೋದಕ Water in which the feet have been washed -ಪದ್ಮ. A lotus-like foot. -ಪೀಠ A foot-stool. -ಪೂಜೆ. Homage paid to the feet of a guru. -ಪೂರಣ. An expletive. -ರಕ್ಷೆ. A sandal, shoe.

ಪಾದರಸ f. n. Quicksilver, mercury

ಪಾದರಿ 1 (= ಪಾದ್ರಿ) f. n A padre or Christian minister or Catholic priest.

ಪಾದರಿ 2. *tb of* ಪಾಟಲ

ಪಾದುಕ, ಪಾದುಕೆ s. n. A wooden shoe; *also* ಪಾದು.

ಪಾದೆಮುಳ್ಳುಗಿಡ k. n. A perennial herb, *Polycarpea corymbosa*

ಪಾದ್ಯ s. n Water for washing the feet 2, washing the feet

ಪಾದ್ರಿ = ಪಾದರಿ, *q v*

ಪಾನ s *n*. Drinking. 2, a drink, beverage 3 a canal -ಕ. A draught, beverage, a beverage made of jaggory, sugar, *etc*. -ಗೋಷ್ಠಿ A drinking party -ಪಾತ್ರ, -ಭಾಜನ A drinking vessel. ಅನ್ನ- Meat and drink

ಪಾನಿ s *n* Water ಪಾನೀಯ. Drinkable, a drink. ಪಾನೀಯಶಾಲಿಕೆ A shed on the roadside for providing passengers with drinking water.

ಪಾನು f. *n* A leaf, the leaf of a book, the leaf of piper betel.

ಪಾಂಥ s. *n*. A traveller; *also* -ಸ್ಥ

ಪಾಪ 1 k. *n* A small child 2, a doll or puppet

ಪಾಪ 2 s. *a* Bad, wicked, sinful, *etc*. *n*. Sin, vice, crime, wickedness, guilt. 2, a bad state, misery. ಪಾಪ. O misery' -ಕ್ಷಮಿಸಿ ಬಿಡು, -ಮಾಫು ಮಾಡು To forgive sin -ಕರ್ಮ An evil deed -ಕ್ಷಯ, -ನಾಶನ. The destruction of sin. -ನಿವಾರಣ. Averting sin. -ನಿಷ್ಕೃತಿ Atonement for sin -ವಿಮೋಚನ. Liberation from sin -ಪರಿಹಾರ. Forgiveness of sin -ಹೊರು To bring sin upon one's self. ಪಾಪಾತ್ಮ. A sinner, a wicked person.

ಪಾಪಟೆ, ಪಾಪಡಿ, ಪಾಪರ (*tb. of* ಪರ್ಪಟ) *n*. The bitter apple, colocynth.

ಪಾಪಾಸು = ಪಾಪೋಸು, *q. v.*

ಪಾಪಿ s *a* Wicked, sinful *n* A sinner, criminal. -ಷ್ಠ. Most wicked, a sinner

ಪಾಪೆ (= ಪಾಪ 1) k *n*. A puppet, doll, an ensign; the pupil of the eye.

ಪಾಪೋಸು (= ಪಾಪಾಸು) h *n* A shoe or slipper.

ಪಾಮು (*tb*. ಪಾಮೆ) *n*. Herpes, scab.

ಪಾಮರ s. *a*. Low, vulgar, stupid *n*. A vulgar man, *f*. ಪಾಮರಿ -ತನ Lowness, rudeness, heathenism

ಪಾಯ್ (=ಹಾಯು) k *v. i* To jump over, to cross, leap, to step, advance, to butt, gore; to knock against *n*. Going ...

ಪಾಯ (*tb of* ಪಾದ) *n* Foot. -ಖಾನೆ. A privy. -ದಳ Infantry -ಪಟ್ಟಿ A badge of honour for the foot

ಪಾಯಸ (*fr* ಪಯಸ್) s. *a* Made of milk *n*. A dish of milk, rice, sugar, *etc*.

ಪಾಯಾ f *n* A foundation

ಪಾಯಿ. = ಪಾಯ, *q v* -ಜಾಮೆ Trowsers.

ಪಾಯಿದಾ, ಪಾಯಿದೆ h *n*. Advantage, profit

ಪಾರ s *n* The opposite bank of a river. 2, the limit of anything. *ad* Across, over, through -ಗಾಣಿಸು To cause to look through; to help to cross -ಗಾಣು To see the end of -ಮಾಡು To help out of ಪಾರಾಗು To be saved from, to get out of -ಗ Well versed in -ಗತ, -ಂಗತ Adept, proficient -ದರ್ಶಕ. Transparent.

ಪಾರಕಾವಣೆ. = ಪರಕಾವಣೆ, *q v*.

ಪಾರಜ ಪಾರದ s. *n* Quicksilver.

ಪಾರಣೆ s. *n*. Breakfast

ಪಾರಮಾರ್ಥಿಕ (*fr* ಪರಮಾರ್ಥ) s *a* Spiritual, real, true, spiritually-minded

ಪಾರಂಪರ್ಯ (*fr* ಪರಂಪರಾ) s. *n* Hereditary succession 2, tradition.

ಪಾರಲೌಕಿಕ (*fr* ಪರಲೋಕ) s. *a* Relating to the next world.

ಪಾರಾ = ಪಹರೆ, *q. v*

ಪಾರಾಯಣ s. *n* Reading through perusal, study

ಪಾರಾವತ (= ಪಾರಿವಾಣ, ಪಾರಿವಾಳ *etc.*) s *n*. A pigeon, dove

ಪಾರಾವಾರ s. *n* The further and nearer bank or shore 2, the ocean

ಪಾರಿಖತ್ತು h *n* A partition-deed; a deed relinquishing one's claim

ಪಾರಿಜಾತ, -ಕ s *n* The coral tree *Erythrina indica*

ಪಾರಿತೋಷಿಕ s *n*. A reward, present

ಪಾರಿಪ್ಲವ (*fr* ಪರಿಪ್ಲವ) s. *a*. Moving to and fro, shaking; unsteady.

ಪಾರಿಭಾಷಿಕ (*fr*. ಪರಿಭಾಷಾ) s *a* Common 2, technical, *as a term* [A dove.

... ತ) *n*.

ಪಾರಸಿ h. *a* Persian *n* A Parsee

ಪಾರು 1. k. *n* Looking to or after. -ಪತ್ಯ. Local administration, *as* of a temple, alms-house, *etc.* -ಪತ್ಯಗಾರ An officer in charge of a temple, a subordinate collector and magistrate.

ಪಾರು 2 *tb. of* ಪಾರ, *q v*

ಪಾರು 3 (ರು = ಱು = ಹಾರು, *q. v*) k *v i* To leap, jump, to run, to fly; to palpitate. *n* Running, flying, a kind of boat, a flying vehicle.

ಪಾರೆ = ಹಾರೆ, *q. v* 2, a crowbar, *also* ಪಾರೆಂಗಿ.

ಪಾರ್ಥ s. *n* A king. 2, Arjuna.

ಪಾರ್ಥವ s *n* Width; greatness immensity

ಪಾರ್ಥಿವ s. *n* A prince, king. 2, the nineteenth year in the cycle of sixty. 3, Šiva *a.* Terrestrial. 2, ruling or possessing earth

ಪಾರ್ವಣ (*fr* ಪರ್ವ) s *n* The general funeral ceremony offered to the deceased ancestors

ಪಾರ್ವತಿ (*fr* ಪರ್ವತ) s. *n* The daughter of Himavat, Durgâ -ನಂದನ Kârttikêya -ೀಶ, -ೀಶ್ವರ. Šiva

ಪಾರ್ಶ್ವ s *n* The part of the body below the arm-pit, the side, flank. -ವರ್ತಿ. An attendant -ವಾಯು. Partial paralysis -ಶೂಲೆ Pleurisy. ಎಡ- The left side ಬಲ- The right side.

ಪಾರ್ಷ್ಣಿ s. *n* The heel 2, the rear of an army

ಪಾಲಕ s. *n* A guardian; a ruler, king, *f.* -ಳು. ದಿಕ್-. The guardian of one of the quarters of the world

ಪಾಲಕಿ, ಪಾಲಕ್ಕಿ (*tb of* ಪಲ್ಯಂಕ) *n* A palanquin. -ಮೆರವಣಿಗೆ. A procession in a palanquin

ಪಾಲನ. ಪಾಲನೆ s. *n.* Guarding, protecting; keeping. -ಮಾಡು. = ಪಾಲಿಸು, *q v.*

ಪಾಲಿ s *n.* A line, row. 2, a dike, bridge. 3, a wall 4, a part. 5, a margin, edge 6, beginning. 7, the tip of the ear. 8, the lap. 9, green ginger.

ಪಾಲಿಸು s *v t* To guard, protect, nourish, to rule, to obey, *as* a command, to observe, *as* a rule, to present, give, *as* an order ದಯ- To grant, vouchsafe

ಪಾಲು 1 (= ಹಾಲು) a. k. *n* Milk -ಂಡೆ A kind of sweetmeat -ಕರೆ. To milk. -ಪಕ್ಕಿ A small owl

ಪಾಲು 2 k. *n* A division, a part, share, joint property. -ಗಾರ A partner in business, an associate; one who enjoys or suffers with another, *f.* -ಗಾರಳು, -ಗಾತಿ. -ಗಾರಿಕೆ. -ವಂತಿಗೆ. Partnership

ಪಾಲೆ k. *n* A large fruit tree, *Mimusops kauki.* 2, the blue jay 3, the lobe of the ear

ಪಾವಕ s *a* Purifying, pure, clear, apparent, manifest. *n.* Fire, a fire-poker. 2, religious custom

ಪಾವಟಿಗೆ f. *n.* A step, stair. -ಏರು. To ascend the steps -ಕಟ್ಟು. To erect steps

ಪಾವಡ, ಪಾವಡೆ (*tb. of* ಪ್ರಾವೃತ) *n* Cloth; a girl's petticoat, a woman's garment.

ಪಾವಡಿಗ. = ಹಾವಡಿಗ, *q v.*

ಪಾವನ s *a.* Purifying; pure, holy. *n* A means of purification penance; cow-dung, fire -ತೆ, -ತ್ವ. Purification

ಪಾವಲಿ, ಪಾವಲೆ f. *n* A quarter of a Rupee.

ಪಾವಸೆ (= ಪಾಸಿ, ಹಾವಸೆ, *q. v*) k. *n.* Algae produced on stagnant water, *etc.*, lichens upon stones, walls, *etc.*

ಪಾವು 1. = ಹಾವು, *q. v*

ಪಾವು 2 (*tb. of* ಪಾದ) *n.* A quarter.

ಪಾವುಗೆ *tb of* ಪಾದುಕ, *q v*

ಪಾವುಡ = ಪಾವಡ, *q. v.*

ಪಾಶ s. *n.* A tie, cord, rope, fetter, a noose, snare.

ಪಾಶಕ (= ಪಾಚಿಕೆ) s. *n* = ಪಾಶ, *q. v.* 2 a die used in playing

ಪಾಶಿ h. *n* A rope (for the gallows); hanging -ಕೊಡು, -ಹಾಕು To hang.

ಪಾಶುಪತ (*fr.* ಪಶುಪತಿ) s *a* Relating or sacred to Śiva *n* N. of a weapon, *also* ಪಾಶುಪತಾಸ್ತ್ರ

ಪಾಷಂಡ s. *n* Heresy 2, a heretic, *also* ಪಾಸಂಡಿ, ಪಾಷಂಡಿ

ಪಾಷಾಣ s. *n*. A stone, rock. 2, arsenic and other poisons -ಭೇದಿ The plant *Plectranthus scutellarioides*

ಪಾಸ್ e *n* A pass. -ಆಗು To pass. ಪರೀಕ್ಷೆ ಪಾಸಾಗು To pass an examination -ಮಾಡು To make pass

ಪಾಸಟಿ a k. *n* Likeness, resemblance

ಪಾಸಲೆ h. *n* Distance.

ಪಾಸೊಲೆ k *n* An earthen saucer-like vessel.

ಪಾಸಿ. = ಪಾಚಿ, ಹಾಸಿಗೆ, *q v*

ಪಾಸು = ಹಾಸು, *q v*

ಪಾಳ k. *n* An ingot or a bar of gold or silver.

ಪಾಳತಿ f *n* Spying, searching out, lying in wait. -ನೋಡು. To spy, lurk -ಗಾರ A spy

ಪಾಳಿ. = ಪಾಲಿ, *q v.*

ಪಾಳು. = ಹಾಳು, *q v*

ಪಾಳೆ, ಪಾಳೆಯ, ಪಾಳ್ಯ (*tb. of* ಪಾಲಯ) *n*. An encampment, camp, a settlement, hamlet -ಗಾರ A Poligar, a feudal chieftain

ಪಿಕ s. *n* The cuckoo, *Cuculus indicus*

ಪಿಕಲಕ್ಕಿ, ಪಿಕಲಾರಿ k. *n* The Madras bulbul

ಪಿಕಾಸು e. *n* A pickaxe.

ಪಿಕ್ಕಾ h *a*. Faint, pale, weak, pallid; poor

ಪಿಕ್ಕು. = ಹಿಕ್ಕು *q v.*

ಪಿಂಗ s *a* Reddish-brown, tawny. -ಳ. N. of a fabulous nâga, the 51st year of the cycle of sixty. -ಳಿ, -ಳೆ A kind of owl

ಪಿಂಗಾಣಿ f. *n* Crockery; porcelain, China ware -ಬಟ್ಟಲು A China cup, mug

ಪಿಂಗು = ಹಿಂಗು, *q. v*

ಪಿಚಕಾರಿ [illegible]

ಪಿಚಂಡ s *n* The belly. ಪಿಚಂಡಿ. The thigh

ಪಿಚಂಡಿ, ಪಿಚಾಡಿ h *n* The hinder parts; the heel-ropes, *as* of a horse -ಕಟ್ಟು. To pinion, to tie the hands from behind

ಪಿಚ್ಚಟ f. *a*. Pressed flat *n*. A cake. 2, an inflammation of the eyes.

ಪಿಚ್ಚೀಸು e. *n* Peach, a sweet stone-fruit.

ಪಿಚ್ಚು k *n* The rheum of the eye.

ಪಿಚ್ಚಿ k. *n* Deficiency in measure or weight. *Cpds* -ಮೊಳ -ಸೇರು.

ಪಿಚ್ಛಿಲ s *a* Slimy slippery, smeary. *n*. A miry place

ಪಿಚ್ಛಿಲೆ s. *n*. The silk-cotton tree, *Bombax heptaphyllum.*

ಪಿಚ್ಛೆ f *n* Scum of boiled rice. *etc* 2, the gum of the silk-cotton tree.

ಪಿಂಜ s. *a* Confused, confounded, bewildered. 2, injured *n* Injury. 2, power might

ಪಿಂಜರ s *a*. Tawny *n* Gold 2, yellow orpiment 3 a cage 4 a skeleton, *also* ಪಂಜರ. [cotton.

ಪಿಂಜಾರ h *n* A carder or comber of

ಪಿಂಜಿ s *n* A skein of cotton yarn

ಪಿಂಜು 1 (= ಹಿಂಜು, *q v*) a k *v t*. To divide. 2, to card cotton. *v i*. To go asunder, to be rent *as* cloth

ಪಿಂಜು 2. k *n*. A very tender fruit

ಪಿಟಕ s *n*. A basket, box, *also* ಪಿಟಿ. 2, a boil, blister

ಪಿಟೀಲು e *n*. A "fiddle", any stringed instrument.

ಪಿಡಗ f *n* Trouble, affliction, disease

ಪಿಡಿ (= ಹಿಡಿ) a k *v t* & *i* To seize, catch, grasp, *etc* 2, to begin *as* rain, *etc*, to be required, *as* time, *etc*, to hold, *as* in a sack, *etc*. *n* A seizing, hold 2, a grasp. 3, the fist 4, a handle, hilt 5, a female elephant. 6, a broom -ತೆ Seizure.

ಪಿಡುಗು a. k. *n* A thunderbolt. 2, = ಪಿಡ [illegible]

ಪಿಂಡ s n A lump, clod, ball 2, heap cluster 3, a bite, morsel. 4, a ball of boiled rice offered to the manes. -ಕ. Incense, myrrh. -ಜ Embryo-born men and beasts -ಪ್ರದಾನ The offering of pindas. ಪಿಂಡಾಂಡ. The body considered as identical with ಬ್ರಹ್ಮಾಂಡ ಪಿಂಡೋತ್ಪತ್ತಿ The formation of the fetus.

ಪಿಂಡಿ s n. A bundle, pack, mass. *Cpds* . -ಕಟ್ಟು, -ಹೊತ್ತುಕೊಳ್ಳು, -ಹೊರು, *etc.* ಕೆ A swelling, protuberance

ಪಿಂಡಿಸೊಪ್ಪು k n Deckanee hemp, *Hibiscus cannabinus.*

ಪಿಂಡು tb of ಪಿಂಡ, q. v

ಪಿಣ್ಯಾಕ f n An oil-cake. 2, incense.

ಪಿತ, ಪಿತರ. tb of ಪಿತೃ, q. v

ಪಿತರೌ s. n Mother and father parents.

ಪಿತಾಮಹ s. n. A paternal grandfather

ಪಿತೂರಿ h. n Revolt, plot, perfidy.

ಪಿತೃ (= ಪಿತ, ಪಿತರ) s. n. A father. -ಗಳು Forefathers, ancestors, the manes of the dead -ತರ್ಪಣ Oblations to the manes -ತಿಥಿ, -ದಿನ The death-day of a deceased parent. -ತ್ವ Fatherhood, paternity. -ಮೇಧ, -ಯಜ್ಞ. Obsequial offerings to the manes. -ಧನ Patrimony -ಪಕ್ಷ The dark half of the ಭಾದ್ರಪದ month. -ವನ. A cemetery -ವಿಯೋಗ The loss of a father

ಪಿತ್ತ s. n. Bile. 2 foolishness, irritability of temper -ಜ್ವರ. Bilious fever -ಭ್ರಮೆ. Biliousness, madness -ಲ Bilious; roguish behaviour. -ಲಾಟಿ. Trickery, deceit

ಪಿನೆಫೋರು e n. A pinafore, an apron worn by children to protect the front of the dress

ಪಿಂತು, ಪಿಂತೆ, ಪಿಂದು, ಪಿಂದೆ (= ಹಿಂದೆ, q. v) a. k. ad Afterwards, backwards, *etc.* 2, formerly

ಪಿಪೀಲಿಕ s. n. An ant.

ಪಿಪ್ಪಲ s n The holy fig-tree, *Ficus religiosa.*

ಪಿಯಾನೋ e n. A piano, a musical keyed instrument

ಪಿರಂಗಿ h n. A great gun or cannon 2, a Frank or European -ಗಾಡಿ A gun-carriage. -ಬಾಯಿ The muzzle of a gun

ಪಿರಿ (= ಹಿರಿ, q. v.) a. k. n Largeness, advanced age. -ದು. = ಹಿರಿದು.

ಪಿರಿಕೆ h n A range, division, jurisdiction.

ಪಿರಿಯಾದಿ = ಫಿರ್ಯಾದಿ, q v.

ಪಿರೆ (= ಪಿಟಿ) k. n. The posteriors.

ಪಿಲ್ಲಿ k n A silver ring worn by married women on the toe

ಪಿಶಾಚ s. n. A fiend, goblin, a devil, the devil. -ಕರ್ಮ, -ಕೆಲಸ. A devilish affair. -ಬುದ್ಧಿ Devilish mind.

ಪಿಶಿತ s. n. Flesh, meat. ಪಿಶಿತಾಶ, -ನ. Flesh-eating. a râkshasa

ಪಿಶುನ s. n. A betrayer, tale-bearer, backbiter, slanderer -ತನ, -ತ್ವ. Slander, scandal.

ಪಿಷ್ಟ s. a. Ground, pounded n. Flour, meal

ಪಿಸರು 1 h. n Foolish pride, arrogance. -ತೆಗೆ To scold, reprove.

ಪಿಸರು 2 k n Filth of the body, rheum of the eye.

ಪಿಸುಕು k. v t To squeeze, to knead; to shampoo.

ಪಿಸುರು. = ಪಿಸರು 1, 2, q v.

ಪಿಸ್ತೂಲು e n A 'pistol"

ಪಿಳಿ. = ಹಿಳಿ, q v.

ಪಿಳುಕು a k n. The lower part of an arrow; *also* ಪಿಳ್ಕು

ಪಿಳ್ಳ k. n A sound as that of a pipe. 2, = ಪಿಳ್ಳೆ, q v ಪಿಳ್ಳಂಗೋವಿ A pipe or flute.

ಪಿಳ್ಳೆ k n. A child, the young of animals

ಪೀಕ h n Spittle -ದಾನಿ. A spittoon

ಪೀಕು k. v t. To pull out, to wrest, tear. . ಕಾಟ. Trouble.

ಪೀಚು k. v. i. To squirt, syringe. n. Squirting. 2, shortness.

ಪೀಠ s. n. A stool. 2, the pedestal of an idol. 3, a basement. 4, a pulpit. ಪ್ರಸಂಗ- The Christian pulpit.

ಪೀಠಿಕೆ s. n. An introduction, preface. 2, a seat, bust.

ಪೀಡನ s. n. Squeezing, pressing, vexing, annoying, hurting, injuring.

ಪೀಡಿ h. n. A generation.

ಪೀಡೆ s. n. Pain, torment, affliction, trouble. 2, a plague, pest, devil. -ಪಡು, -ಹತ್ತು To suffer pain. -ಮಾಡು To give pain. -ಹೋಗು To be relieved of pain. ಪೀಡಿಸು. To torment, trouble, to squeeze. ಪೀಡಿತ Pressed, pained, hurt, injured.

ಪೀತ s. a. Yellow. 2, drunk, imbibed. n. A topaz, also -ಕಾಂತ. -ದಾರು A species of pine, *Pinus deodora*. ಪೀತಾಂಬರ. Clad in yellow: Vishnu or Krishna, a garment of yellow silk.

ಪೀನ s. a. Fat, fleshy, thick, plump, profuse.

ಪೀನಸ s. n. Cough, catarrh, purulent deflection in the nose.

ಪೀಪ, ಪೀಪಾಯಿ, ಪೀಪು f. n. A cask, barrel, tub.

ಪೀಯೂಷ s. n. Cow's milk during the first seven days of its calving. 2, nectar.

ಪೀರು. = ಹೀರು, q. v.

ಪೀಲಿ (= ಹೀಲಿ, q. v.) a. k. n. A peacock's feather.

ಪೀಲು f. n. The tree *Careya arborea*. 2, a flower. 3, an insect. 4, an atom.

ಪೀಳಿಗೆ f. n. A series of generations, pedigree, offspring, also ಪೀಡಿ.

ಪುಂ, ಪುಂಸ s. a. Male, masculine. -ತ್ವ, ಪುಂಸ್ತ್ವ Manhood, masculine gender.

ಪುಕಸಟ್ಟೆ. = ಪುಕ್ಕಟೆ, q. v.

ಪುಕಾರು h. n. Loud bawling, crying out.

ಪುಕ್ಕ 1 (tb. of ಪುಚ್ಛ, q. v.) n. The tail of a bird.

ಪುಕ್ಕ 2. k. ...

ಪುಕ್ಕಟೆ, ಪುಕ್ಕಸಟ್ಟೆ, ಪುಕ್ಸಟ್ಟೆ, ಪುಗಟೆ, ಪುಗಸಟ್ಟೆ, etc. f. ad. For nothing, gratis. a. Free, worthless. -ಬಾಯಿ A liar. -ಮನುಷ್ಯ. A good-for-nothing fellow. -ಹೋಗು To go for nothing.

ಪುಕ್ಕು k. n. Fear, timidity. -ತನ Cowardice, cf. ಪುಕ್ಕ 2.

ಪುಗು (= ಹೊಗು, q. v.) a. k. v. i. To enter in. n. Entering. ಪುಗಿಲ್. Entering, arrival.

ಪುಗುಳು (= ಹುಗುಳು) k. n. A blister, vesicle. 2, a sore in the mouth.

ಪುಗ್ಗು (= ಪುಗುರ್) h. n. Pride, arrogance.

ಪುಂಗವ s. n. A bull. 2, an eminent person.

ಪುಂಗಿ f. n. A sort of musical pipe.

ಪುಚ್ಚ (tb. of ಪುಚ್ಛ) n. A tail.

ಪುಚ್ಚವಣಿ (tb. of ಪರೀಕ್ಷಣ) n. Trial examination. 2, manliness, valour.

ಪುಚ್ಚಳಿ (ಳಿ = ಱಿ) a. k. n. Ruin, destruction.

ಪುಚ್ಛ s. n. A tail; the hinder part.

ಪುಂಜ 1 (= ಹುಂಜ) k. n. A cock.

ಪುಂಜ 2 s. n. A heap, mass, collection. ಪುಂಜಿಸು To be heaped.

ಪುಟ 1. k. n. Leaping up, jumping. -ಚೆಂಡು A kind of play. -ನೆಗೆ. To rise with a bounce. -ಹಾರು To bounce.

ಪುಟ 2. s. n. A fold. 2, a concavity. 3, a cup. 4, a basket made of leaves. 5, a folding. 6, a cover. 7, an eyelid. 8, a single application, as of fire, air etc., as in preparing medicine. 9, a casket. 10, the leaf of a book, a page. 11, a layer of mud in raising a wall. 12, a footprint. -ಕ್ಕೆ ಹಾಕು. To put into a crucible, to refine, as metal.

ಪುಟಾಣಿ f. n. Bengal gram soaked and parched.

ಪುಟಿ k. v. i. To bounce, to spring, ooze in jets, as water. -ಸು To cause to bounce. -ತ Clasped, folded, bound [illegible] reduced to powder, con-

ಪುಟ್ಟ k. n. Shortness, littleness, a short man a. Small. -ಡಿ. The small step of children. -ದು. That is small -ಮಗು A little child

ಪುಟ್ಟಿ k. n A basket 2, a (honey) comb.

ಪುಟ್ಟು 1 = ಹುಟ್ಟು, q. v

ಪುಟ್ಟು 2 k. n Salted dough baked in steam 2, a wooden ladle

ಪುಡಿ k n. Powder, dust, pollen. 2, a small packet of powder. -ಪುಡಿ ಮಾಡು To reduce to very fine powder

ಪುಳಜಿ k n A dust-like dry soil.

ಪುಣುಗು k n Civet. ಪುಣುಗಿನ ಬೆಕ್ಕು. The Indian civet cat

ಪುಂಡ f. a Turbulent, refractory. n. A free-booter; a rascal, rogue, a low man -ಗಾರ. A depraved man -ತನ, ಪುಂಡಾಟ, ಪುಂಡಾಟಿಕೆ. Refractoriness, lawlessness, brigandage, wickedness.

ಪುಂಡರೀಕ s. n A white lotus-flower. 2, a sectarial mark on the forehead. ಪುಂಡರೀಕಾಕ್ಷ. Lotus-eyed Vishnu or Krishna

ಪುಂಡಿ k n. The Deckanee hemp, *Hibiscus cannabinus*, red sorrel *Cpds* -ಕಡ್ಡಿ, -ಸಾರು, -ಸೊಪ್ಪು

ಪುಂಡು = ಪುಂಡ, q v

ಪುಂಡ್ರ s. n A red sugarcane 2, a sectarial mark.

ಪುಣ್ಯ s a Fine, bright, good, pure, right, righteous, virtuous, just, holy, prosperous, lucky. n. Virtue, moral merit, religious merit (real or erroneous) 2, a good, meritorious act 3, purity. 4, fame -ಕರ್ಮ, -ಕಾರ್ಯ. A virtuous act. -ಕಾಲ. An auspicious time -ಮಾರ್ಗ. The right way. -ಜೀವಿ, -ಮೂರ್ತಿ. A virtuous man. -ಲೋಕ Heaven. -ವಂತ A virtuous or fortunate man, a rich man -ಶರೀರ.= ಪುಣ್ಯವಂತ. -ಶೀಲ. Good, virtuous -ಶ್ಲೋಕ. Well spoken of, N of Nala -ಹೀನ. Virtueless -ಸಾಧನೆ ಮಾಡು. To persevere in good works ಪುಣ್ಯಾತ್ಮ Righteous, virtuous, pious

ಪುತ್ತಳಿ (tb. of ಪುತ್ರಿಕೆ) n A puppet, doll 2, a gold coin worth about four rupees; pure gold.

ಪುತ್ತು. = ಹುತ್ತು, q. v.

ಪುತ್ರ s. n A son, a child -ಜೀವ The wild olive, *Putranjiva roxburghii* -ವತಿ She who has a son. -ವಧು. A son's wife -ವಂತ One who has sons -ವಿರಹಿತ A sonless man -ಸಂತಾನ. Male progeny. -ಸ್ವೀಕಾರ. Adoption ಕ್ರಿಸ್ತನಲ್ಲಿ-- Adoption by God through Christ

ಪುತ್ರಿ, ಪುತ್ರಿಕೆ (= ಪುತ್ತಳಿ, q v) s. n A daughter 2, a puppet, doll.

ಪುದಿ (= ಹುದಿ, q v) a k. v i To enter into, etc , to combine 2, to be hidden

ಪುದಿನ f n. Mint, *Mentha sativa*

ಪುಡಿಂಗು e. n. Pudding, a dish of soft consistence, variously made

ಪುದು (= ಹುದು, q v.) a k n Union, holding in common -ವಾಳು To live together. -ವಾಳ್ತನ. Joint living or concern

ಪುದುಗು (= ಹುದುಗು, q v) a k. v. i To enter. v t. To hide, shelter.

ಪುದೆ a. k n. A quiver 2, a cover, a roof, thatch. 3, a bush, also ಪೊದೆ

ಪುದ್ಗಲ s. a. Beautiful n. The body. 2, the soul or individuality.

ಪುನಃ (= ಪುನರ್, ಪುನಹ, ಪುನಹಾ) s ad Further; again, back; in return. -ಪುನಹ Again and again, frequently.

ಪುನರಪಿ s. ad. Even again, also

ಪುನರಾಗಮನ s n Returning to the place set out from 2, second advent of Christ

ಪುನರುಕ್ತಿ s n Reiteration, repetition, tautology. ಪುನರುಕ್ತ. Reiterated, repetition.

ಪುನರುತ್ಥಾನ s. n Resurrection, esp of Jesus Christ from the dead

ಪುನರ್ಜನ್ಮ (ಪುನರ್ಜಲ್ಮ) s. n. Regeneration (*Chr.*), transmigration ಪುನರ್ಜಾತ Born again, regenerated

ಪುನರ್ದರ್ಶನ s. n Seeing again.

ಪುನರ್ನವ s n Becoming new again 2 a finger-nail

ಪುನರ್ನವೆ s n. Hogweed, *Boerhaavia procumbens*.

ಪುನರ್ಭವ s a Born again n New [birth

ಪುನರ್ಭೂ s a Born again n A virgin widow re-married.

ಪುನರ್ವಸು s n The seventh of the lunar asterisms.

ಪುನರ್ವಿವಾಹ s. n. Re-marriage.

ಪುನಹ, ಪುನಹಾ tb. of ಪುನಃ, q. v

ಪುನೀತ s a Made pure or clean

ಪುನ್ನಪುಂಸಕ s a Masculine and neuter

ಪುನ್ನಾಗ s n A distinguished man 2, a white elephant 3, a buffalo

ಪುಬ್ಬೆ (= ಹುಬ್ಬೆ. tb of ಪೂರ್ವ) n The eleventh of the lunar mansions

ಪುಯ್ಯಲ್ (=ಹುಯ್ಯಲು q v) k n. Lamentation 2, solicitation ಪುಯ್ಯಲಿಸು To lament; to solicit

ಪುರ 1. k n. A stream, brook, rivulet.

ಪುರ 2. s n A fortress, castle, a town, city 2. a house 3, the body -ದ್ವಾರ The gate of a city.

ಪುರಃ, ಪುರಸ್ s ad In front, in the presence of -ಸರ Going in advance

ಪುರಂದರ s n. Indra; Śiva -ದಾಸ N. of a Canarese poet -ವಿಟ್ಠಲ N of Krishna

ಪುರಸತ್ತು h. n. Leisure, interval, time, occasion 2, relief. -ಆಗು. To be at leisure

ಪುರಸ್ಕಾರ s n Reverence, honour. ಪುರಸ್ಕರಿಸು To honour, exalt

ಪುರಸ್ತಾತ್ s ad Before, in front of

ಪುರಾಣ s a Ancient, old, worn out n Legendary history, legend; a purâna, comprising the whole body of Hindu mythology, there are 18 acknowledged purânas, as ಅಗ್ನಿ-, ಪದ್ಮ-, ಬ್ರಹ್ಮ-, ಭವಿಷ್ಯತ್, ಲಿಂಗ-, ವಿಷ್ಣು-, ಶಿವ-. etc. -ಪುರುಷ. Vishnu, Râma, Śiva ಪುರಾಣಿ ... purâ ...

ಪುರಾತನ s a Old, ancient. 2 a man of the past age

ಪುರಿ 1 (=ಹುರಿ) k. v t To parch, as grain, pulse, etc 2, to roast, as coffee, etc

ಪುರಿ 2 (=ಹುರಿ) a. k n Twist, twine. string

ಪುರಿ 3 a k n Strength, courage.

ಪುರಿ 4 s n A castle, a town, city.

ಪುರುಡು 1 (= ಹುರುಡು q v.) a. k. n Rivalry, envy, jealousy, emulation

ಪುರುಡು 2. k n Uncleanness after childbirth

ಪುರುಷ s n. Mankind, a man, male, a person; a husband. 2, the soul. 3 Brahmâ -ತ್ವ Manhood; valour -ರತ್ನ A perennial herb, *Ionidium suffruticosum*. ಪುರುಷಾರ್ಥ. Any of the four objects of man, viz dharma, artha. kâma, and môksha ಪುರುಷೋತ್ತಮ. An excellent man ಯಜ್ಞ- Christ

ಪುರುಳಿ a k n. A young parrot

ಪುರುಳು (=ಹುರುಳು) k n. Fitness, meaning, power, strength.

ಪುರೋಗತಿ s n. Preceding, precedence.

ಪುರೋಭಾಗ s. n. The front part 2, forwardness obtrusiveness.

ಪುರೋಹಿತ s n The family-priest

ಪುರ್ಗು. = ಪುಗ್ಗು, q v.

ಪುರ್ಬು (=ಹುಬ್ಬು. tb. of ಭ್ರೂ) n An eyebrow, brow. ಪುರ್ಬಿಕ್ಕು To frown

ಪುಲಕ s n Bristling of the hairs occasioned by delight etc ಪುಲಕಿತ Thrilling with joy

ಪುಲಿ (= ಹುಲಿ, q v.) a. k n. A tiger

ಪುಲಿಂದ s n One of a barbarous tribe, f ಪುಲಿಂದಿನಿ.

ಪುಲ್ಲಿಂಗ s. n The masculine gender

ಪುಲ್ಲು = ಹುಲ್ಲು, q v

ಪುಲ್ಲೆ (= ಹುಲ್ಲೆ, q v) a k n. A deer

ಪುವ್ವು (=ಹೂ ಹೂವು q v.) a k n. A flower 2, a disease of the eye.

... her of ... 4, a

sword 5, the sky 6, water. -ಮೂಲ. A garden plant *Costus speciosus* ಪುಷ್ಕರಿಣಿ An artificial tank

ಪುಷ್ಕಲ s. *a*. Much, many, abundant, excellent, best

ಪುಷ್ಟ s *a* Nourished, well-fed, thriving, strong. ಪುಷ್ಟಿ Fatness, plumpness growth, thriving, strength, power, nourishment, support, backing aid. ಪುಷ್ಟಿಕರ Nourishing, strengthening ಪುಷ್ಟೀಕರಿಸು To nourish, strengthen

ಪುಷ್ಪ s *n* A flower, blossom -ಕ A flower, calx of brass, heat of the sun; a self-moving aerial car. -ಕೇತನ Kâma -ದಂತ. The elephant of the north-west quarter -ಫಲ The wood-apple tree, *Feronia elephantum* -ಮಾಲಿಕೆ, -ಮಾಲೆ. A garland of flowers -ಮಾಸ. The spring. -ವತ್, -ವಂತ Flowery -ವಾಟಿ, -ವಾಟಿಕೆ. A flower garden -ವಾಸನೆ The fragrance of flowers -ವೃಷ್ಟಿ. A shower of flowers ಸಮಯ. The spring ಪುಷ್ಪಿತ Flowered, blooming.

ಪುಷ್ಯ s. *n* Blossom 2, the 8th lunar mansion. 3, the month pausha (December-January) -ರಾಗ. A topaz

ಪುಸಲಾಯಿಸು h. *v. t* To cajole coax, wheedle, fawn ಪುಸಲಾಯಿಕ Cajoling, coaxing.

ಪುಸಿ (= ಹುಸಿ, *q v*) a k *v i*. To prove false, to lie. *v t* To bear no fruit *n*. A lie 2 bearing no fruit; not attaining ripeness, *as* fruits -ಗ. A liar

ಪುಸ್ತ s *a*. Smearing, anointing, writing -ಕ A book; a volume.

ಪುಸ್ತಿ *tb of* ಪುಷ್ಟಿ, *q v* 2, a paper of school-boys showing their progress in writing 3, a book or pack of paper to write upon

ಪುಳ (ಳ = ಟ). = ಹುಳ, *q v*

ಪುಳಿ (= ಹುಳಿ, *q v*) a k *n*. Acidity

ಪುಳುಕು (ಳು = ಟು = ಹುಳುಕು) k. *n* A pock-mark ... sore

ಪುಳ್ಳಿ (= ಹುಳ್ಳಿ) k. *n*. A small bit of very dry wood -ಮಾತು. A useless word

ಪೂ (= ಹೂ, *q. v*) a k *n* A flower, *etc*. *Cpds*. -ಗಣ, -ಗುಡಿ -ತೊಡಂಬೆ. -ತೋಟ, -ದೂಳು, -ಮರ, -ಮಾಲಿಕೆ, -ಮಾಲೆ, *etc*. -ವಾಗು. To blossom

ಪೂಗ s. *n*. The areca or betel-nut tree, *Areca catechu* ಪೂಗೀಫಲ A betel-nut.

ಪೂಜೆ 1. s *n* Honour, respect, reverence, adoration, worship. ಪೂಜಕ. A worshipper ಮೂರ್ತಿಪೂಜಕ An idolator ಪೂಜನ Reverencing, worshipping, worship ಪೂಜಾರಿ. The officiating Brâhmana or other person of a temple. ಪೂಜಿತ Honoured, respected, adored ಪೂಜಿಸು To honour, revere, worship, adore ಮೂರ್ತಿ- Idol-worship. ಸಾಂತ- Saint-worship

ಪೂಜಿ, ಪೂಜೆ 2. f. *a* A dot, the nasal sound, a cipher, *also* ಪೂಜ್ಯ.

ಪೂಜ್ಯ s. *a* Honourable, respectable, worshipful -ತೆ. Honourableness, venerableness ಪೂಜ್ಯಾರ್ಥ Honorific meaning.

ಪೂಟು 1 h *n* A bit, small portion. ಪೂಟಜ A summary arji

ಪೂಟು 2. e *n* Foot, a ameasure of space

ಪೂಡು (= ಹೂಡು, *q v*) a k. *v t* To unite, to put to, *etc*

ಪೂಣ್ a. k *v. i*. To begin *v t*. To admit, to promise; to challenge

ಪೂತ s *a* Made pure or clean, threshed, winnowed.

ಪೂತನಿ, ಪೂತನೆ s *n* N. of a female demon killed by Krishna

ಪೂತಿ s *n*. Purity, purification. 2, stench, fetor, civet

ಪೂತು a. k *int* Bravo! well done!

ಪೂರ (ಪೂರಾ) s. *n* Making full 2, a swelling of rivers, flood. *a* Full, complete, whole -ಣ. Filling, filling out, completing, accomplishing, fulfilling, completion, fulness, [illegible] ... cake, the ... [illegible] ... *r*eduation [illegible]

ಪೂರಯಿಸು. ಪೂರೈಸು s. v. t To fill, to fill up, complete, to accomplish, to effect, to fulfil, to blow, sound.

ಪೂರಾ (= ಪೂರ) s ad Fully, completely, wholly

ಪೂರಿ f n A thin cake of wheat-flour.

ಪೂರಿಸು. = ಪೂರಯಿಸು, q v.

ಪೂರ್ಣ h. a. Full, full of. 2, fulfilled, finished 3, complete, all, entire, perfect 4, strong, able -ತೆ Fulness, plenty -ಪಾತ್ರ A full cup, a measure of capacity, a ghee-vessel used at a hôma. -ಮಾಸಿ The day or night of full moon -ಮೆ The full moon. -ವಿರಾಮ. A full stop ಪೂರ್ಣಾಂಕ An integer

ಪೂರ್ತ s a. Full; complete n Fulness, completion 2, satisfaction ಪೂರ್ತಿ. Fulness; satiety, perfection

ಪೂರ್ತೆ tb of ಪೂರ್ತ, q v

ಪೂರ್ವ s. a Fore, first, previous to, earlier than 2, former, prior, preceding 3, initial. 4, ancient 5, eastern. 6, preceded by. n An ancestor 2, an ancient tradition; ancient times, former events. 3, east. -ಕ. Accompanied by, with, as ಮನಃ-, ವಿನಯ-. etc. -ಕಾಲ Former times -ಜ An elder brother. an ancestor. -ಜನ್ಮ A former birth -ದೇಶ An eastern country. -ಪಕ್ಷ The first part of an argument, proposition, thesis, the first half of a lunar month -ಪಕ್ಷಸಿದ್ಧಾಂತ. A demonstration that rests only on the proposition. -ಫಲ್ಗುನಿ. The 11th nakshatra. -ರಂಗ. The prelude of a drama -ರಾತ್ರಿ The first part of the night -ವಯಸ್ಸು Youth -ವಾಸರ. Yesterday

ಪೂರ್ವಣಿ s n Continuation of a series.

ಪೂರ್ವಾಪರ s. a Before and behind, antecedent and subsequent. n. Connection.

ಪೂರ್ವಾಭ[illegible] s [illegible] 25th [illegible]

ಪೂರ್ವಾಷಾಢೆ s. n. The 20th nakshatra.

ಪೂರ್ವಾಹ್ಣ s n. The forenoon.

ಪೂರ್ವಿಕ s. a Previous, former n An ancestor, forefather

ಪೂರ್ವೆ (= ಹುಬ್ಬೆ) s. n Tho 11th nakshatra.

ಪೂರ್ವೋಕ್ತ (ಪೂರ್ವ-ಉಕ್ತ) s a Aforesaid before mentioned.

ಪೂರ್ವೋತ್ತರ (ಪೂರ್ವ-ಉತ್ತರ) s. a North-eastern. 2, antecedent and subsequent.

ಪೂಲ h n A bridge

ಪೂವಡಿಗ, ಪೂವಳ k n A florist.

ಪೂಸು (= ಹೂಸು, q v) a k v t To smear, etc n. An unguent, smearing.

ಪೂಳು = ಹೂಳು, q. v.

ಪೃಚ್ಛೆ s n. Asking; a question, inquiry

ಪೃಥಕ್ s ad Separately. singly postp. Apart from, except, without -ಕರಣ Separating -ತ್ವ Separateness, diversity, individuality

ಪೃಥಿವಿ, ಪೃಥ್ವಿ s. n The earth. -ಜೆ. Sitâ -ಪತಿ, -ಪಾಲ A king.

ಪೃಥು s a. Broad, wide, spacious, numerous, important -ಕ = ಅವಲಕ್ಕಿ.

ಪೃಷ್ಟ s a Asked, questioned

ಪೃಷ್ಠ s n The back 2, the rear

ಪೆಗ್ಗ (= ಪೆಂಗ) k n A dolt, fool.

ಪೆಗ್ಗಡೆ, ಪೆರ್ಗಡೆ (= ಹೆಗ್ಗಡೆ) k. n. A headman; a chief, a superintendent.

ಪೆಂಗ k n A simpleton, fool, also ಪೆಗ್ಗ

ಪೆಚ್ಚು 1 = ಹೆಚ್ಚು, q v.

ಪೆಚ್ಚು 2. (= ಹುಚ್ಚು, q. v. tb. of ಪಿತ್ತ) n. Foolishness. -ತನ = ಹುಚ್ಚುತನ.

ಪೆಟಲುಪ್ಪು k n Saltpetre, also ಪೆಟ್ಲುಪ್ಪು

ಪೆಟಾರಿ f n A large box or chest (of rattan)

ಪೆಟ್ಟಣಿಗೆ k n. A road tamper

ಪೆಟ್ಟಲು k n A popgun

ಪೆಟ್ಟಿ, ಪೆಟ್ಟಿಗೆ (tb of ಪೇಟಿಕೆ) n. A box, chest, trunk, etc

[illegible] roke,

[illegible] -ತ

ಗು, -ತಿನ್ನು To be beaten -ಬೀಳು Blows to fall upon -ಮಣೆ = ಪೆಟ್ಟಣಿಗೆ -ಹತ್ತು To be hurt.

ಪೆಟ್ಲುಪ್ಪು k. *n*. Saltpetre, *also* ಪೆಟ್ಲುಪು.

ಪೆನ (=ಹೆಜ) a.k.*n* The back. *ad*. Backwards -ಮೆಟ್ಟು. To retreat; the back part.

ಪೆಡಸು k. *n*. Hardness; stiffness. 2, brittleness 3, harshness. 4, difficulty. -ಮಾತು. An offensive word.

ಪೆಣಗು (=ಹೆಣಗು) a k *v i* To wrangle, fight.

ಪೆಣೆ (=ಹೆಣೆ, *q v*.) a k *v. t*. To twist, twine, *etc* *n* Twining, union.

ಪೆಂಟೆ 1 (=ಹೆಂಟೆ) k *n* A clod; a lump

ಪೆಂಟೆ 2 f *n* A bundle.

ಪೆಂಡ (=ಹೆಂಣ್, ಹೆಂಡ) a. k. *n*. A female, woman -ತಿ (=ಹೆಂಡತಿ). A wife

ಪೆಂಡಾರಿ f *n*. A Pindaree, a freebooter, marauder

ಪೆಂಡಿ. = ಪೆಂಟೆ 2, *q v*.

ಪೆಂಡೆಯ f *n*. A badge of honour for the [foot.

ಪೆಣ್ಣು = ಹೆಣ್ಣು, *q v*. -ತನ A feminine character.

ಪೆದ್ದ = ಹುಚ್ಚ, *q v*.; *f*. ಪೆದ್ದಿ.

ಪೆನಶನು e *n* Pension, an allowance for past services. -ದಾರ. Pensioner.

ಪೆನಸಿಲು e *n*. Pencil

ಪೆಂತೆಕೊಸ್ತು e *n* Pentecost.

ಪೆಂಪು a k *n* Greatness, abundance; grandeur, sublimity.

ಪೆಬ್ರುವರಿ e *n* February (2nd month of the year).

ಪೆರ (ರ=ಱ.=ಪಱ) a k. *n* Hind part, backside *ad*. Backwards. -ಗು. The back side, afterwards.

ಪೆರೆ (ರೆ=ಱೆ =ಹೆರೆ, *q v*) a k *n* The crescent moon.

ಪೆರ್ a k *n*. Largeness, greatness. *Cpds*.: -ಗಿಚ್ಚು, -ಗೊನೆ, -ಗೊಣೆ, -ಜ್ವಾಲೆ, -ದೆರೆ, -ನಗೆ, -ನೊರೆ, -ಬಲೆ, -ಮಗ, -ಮಳೆ, *etc*

ಪೆರ್ಚಿಗೆ, ಪೆರ್ಚು. = ಹೆಚ್ಚಿಗೆ, ಹೆಚ್ಚು, *q v*

ಪೆಸರು (=ಹೆಸರು, *q. v*) a. k. *n* A name, fame.

ಪೆಳರು a. k *v. i* To tremble. *n* Fear, alarm. ಪೆಳರಿಸು. To alarm, frighten.

ಪೇಂಕುಳಿ a. k. *n*. A demon. 2, madness, fury

ಪೇಚಾಟ f *n* Trouble, difficulty, strait -ಪಡು, ಪೇಚಾಡು. To take pains, to be involved in trouble

ಪೇಟ h *n* A small kind of turban. 2, a basket, *also* -ಕ.

ಪೇಟೆ h *n* A pettah, market-town, bazaar

ಪೇಡ h. *n* A sweetmeat of milk and sugar; *also* ಪೇಡೆ

ಪೇತು k. *n* Confusion, a demon

ಪೇದಾ. ಪೇದೆ (=ಪ್ಯಾದೆ) h *n* A foot-soldier, a peon, a pawn at chess

ಪೇನು 1. e. *n*. A pen.

ಪೇನು 2 (=ಹೇನು) a. k. *n* A louse.

ಪೇಯ s. *a*. Drinkable. *n*. A drink, beverage

ಪೇರ್. = ಪೆರ್, *q. v*., *as*. -ಆನೆ, -ಆಲ, -ಆಮೆ, -ಓಟ, -ಓಲಗ, -ಪತ್ತು, *etc*

ಪೇರಣೆ f *n* A sword-dance -ಗ A dancer, actor.

ಪೇರಲ f *n* The guava, *Psidium guvava*

ಪೇರಿ f *n* Galloping

ಪೇರು 1 f *n* Difference in scales -ಕಟ್ಟು. To remove it.

ಪೇರು 2. = ಹೇರು, *q v*

ಪೇಲವ s. *a* Delicate, fine, tender, slender

ಪೇಲಾಗು e. *v. i*. To fail in an examination

ಪೇಲೆ f. *n*. A cup, bowl.

ಪೇಷ್ಕಾರ h. *n* A revenue officer.

ಪೇಷ್ವೆ h *n* The Peshwâ, the head minister of the Mahratta empire, *also* ಪೇಶವೆ.

ಪೇಳು. = ಹೇಳು, *q v*

ಪೈ f. *n*. A copper coin; a pie

ಪೈಕ f *n* Money, cash. 2, a division, set.

ಪೈಕಿ f. *ad*. Of, out of, from amongst

ಪೈಗಂಬರ h. *n*. A prophet

ಪೈಗಸ್ತಿ h. n. A superintendent, a patrole.

ಪೈಗು f. n. Pegu

ಪೈಂಗಲ (fr. ಪಿಂಗಲ) s n The 51st year of the cycle of sixty.

ಪೈಜಣ f. n. A small tinkling ornament for the feet

ಪೈಜಾರು h n A shoe

ಪೈಟಿ f. n A summerset

ಪೈಠಣ f. n N of a town ಪೈಠಣಿ Manufactured at Paithana. -ಸೀರೆ A kind of silk garment.

ಪೈತೃಕ s a Paternal. -ಧನ Patrimony

ಪೈತ್ಯ (tb of ಪಿತ್ತ) n Bilious humour, choler, foolishness, madness. -ಗಾರ A foolish man.

ಪೈಮಾಯಿಷಿ h n Surveying and measuring of lands

ಪೈರು (=ಪಯ್ರು) k n Green corn, growing corn, any green, growing crop.

ಪೈಲವಾನ h n An athlete, wrestler

ಪೈವಸ್ತು h. a Endorsement on a letter specifying the date of its receipt

ಪೈಶಾಚ (fr ಪಿಶಾಚ) s a Infernal, demoniacal n The lowest form of marriage

ಪೈಶುನ್ಯ (fr. ಪಿಶುನ) s. a Tale-bearing, backbiting, calumny

ಪೈಸ f n A copper coin, 4 pies, or 1 duddu 2, money

ಪೈಸಲು h n. Decision of a dispute, settlement of a debt, judgment. ಪೈಸಲಾತಿ Final settlement

ಪೈಸಾಲು h. n. Crop, harvest

ಪೊಕ್ಕುಳು = ಹೊಕ್ಕುಳು, q v

ಪೊಗದಿ k. n Tribute, tax.

ಪೊಗರು a k n. Shine, lustre, colour

ಪೊಗಳು = ಹೊಗಳು, q v

ಪೊಗು = ಹೊಗು, q v

ಪೊಗೆ (=ಹೊಗೆ q v) a k n Smoke v. i. To smoke.

ಪೊಂ. ಪೊ[illegible]

-ಕವಡಿ [illegible]

ಪೊಂಗಲು k n. Boiled rice mixed with milk and sugar -ಹಬ್ಬ A festival in honour of the sun entering the sign of Capricorn

ಪೊಂಗು a k v. i To boil over 2, to expand, blossom; to exult n Boiling over

ಪೊಟ್ಟಣ (= ಪೊಟ್ಲ. ಪೊಟ್ಲ tb of ಪುಟ) n A small cup or packet made of leaves paper, etc

ಪೊಟ್ಟರೆ (= ಪೊಟ್ರೆ) k n A hole in a tree

ಪೊಟ್ಟು (= ಹೊಟ್ಟು) k a Empty, useless n Chaff, husk

ಪೊಟ್ಟೆ (= ಹೊಟ್ಟೆ, q v) a k n The belly, etc

ಪೊಟ್ರೆ = ಪೊಟ್ಟರೆ, etc, q v

ಪೊಟ್ಲ = ಪೊಟ್ಟಣ, q v

ಪೊಡ 1. (tb of ಪುಟ) n A hollow formed by joining the palms of the hands -ಮುಡು, -ವಡು. To salute respectfully -ವಡಿಕೆ A respectful salutation

ಪೊಡ 2. (tb of ಸ್ಫುಟ) n Appearance, form, figure -ಕರಿಸು To come in sight, appear

ಪೊಡರು k v i To tremble, throb, quiver, to flash, shine

ಪೊಡರ್ಪು a k n Glitter, shine; glory, power. -ಗುಂದಿಸು. To cause lustre, etc, to decrease

ಪೊಡವಿ (tb of ಪೃಥ್ವಿ, q v) n The earth -ಪ, -ಪತಿ -ಯೊಡೆಯ A king.

ಪೊಡೆ 1 (=ಹೊಡಿ, ಹೊಡೆ, q v) a. k v t. To strike, smite, etc.

ಪೊಡೆ 2. = ಪೊಟ್ಟೆ, q v 2, a full ear of corn. 3, extension 4, pregnancy (of beasts) 5, a pouch formed by folding the front part of one's cloth

ಪೊಣರು a k v. i To join, couple 2, to fight. n Union, a couple 2, a fight ಪೊಣರ್ಕೆ. Fighting, a fight

ಪೊಣೆ (= ಹೊಣೆ q v) a k n Bond, bail, a surety.

[illegible] o be

[illegible] rice,

etc., to be overdone. *n* Flaming 2, the sun, time. -ಗಳೆ To spend time.

ಪೊದಕೆ (= ಹೊದಿಕೆ) k. *n* A cover, wrapper 2, a roof, thatch

ಪೊದರು (ರು = ಱು = ಹೊದರು, *q v*) a k *n* A bush, thicket

ಪೊದೆ 1. = ಹೊದೆ, *q v*.

ಪೊದೆ 2 k. *n* A quiver. 2 a thatch 3 a bush. 4, a bundle.

ಪೊನ್ (= ಪೊಂ. *q v*.) a k *n* Gold, *as* -ತಾವರೆ, -ತೆರೆ, -ತೊಡರು, *etc*

ಪೊಪ್ಪಿಳಿ k *n* A diffuse shrub yielding a yellow dye, *Morinda umbellata*

ಪೊಮ್ (= ಪೊಂ, *q v*) a k *n* Gold, *as* -ಬಿಸಿಲು, -ಬೆಟ್ಟು, -ಬೆತ್ತ, -ಬೆಸೆ *etc*.

ಪೊಂಪುಳಿ (ಳಿ = ೞಿ) k *n* Increase, growth, greatness.

ಪೊರ (ರ = ಱ = ಹೊರ, *q v*) a k *n* The outside. -ಮಡು To set out, start, to quit -ಗು, -ಗೆ = ಹೊರಗೆ

ಪೊರಕೆ k. *n* A broom.

ಪೊರಳು (= ಹೊರಳು, *q v*) a. k *v i* To roll, welter

ಪೊರಿಗೆ (ರಿ = ಱಿ = ಹೊರಿಗೆ) a k *n* Burden, business, work, *also* ಪೊರೆ

ಪೊರು (ರು = ಱು. = ಹೊರು, *q v*) a k. *v t* To bear, *as* a burden, *etc*.

ಪೊರೆ 1 (= ಹೊರೆ 1, *q v* ರೆ = ಱೆ) a. k. *n*. A load, *etc*

ಪೊರೆ 2 (= ಹೊರೆ 2) a k *v. t*. To nourish, cherish, invigorate, *etc*. 2, to join. *v. i* To be joined *n* Invigoration, refreshment: union

ಪೊರೆ 3 (= ಹೊರೆ 3) k. *n* A fold, layer, stratum.

ಪೊರೆ 4 (= ಹೊರೆ 4) a. k. *n*. Choking sensation while eating or drinking. -ಏರು To feel a choking sensation

ಪೊರ್ದು (= ಹೊದ್ದು) a k *v i* To join, to agree, to reach -ಗೆ (= ಹೊದ್ದಿಕೆ) Joining, contact, harmony, proximity

ಪೊಲ = ಹೊಲ, *q. v*

ಪೊಲಬು (= [illegible]) [illegible] A way, a manner.

ಪೊಲಸು = ಹೊಲಸು, *q v*.

ಪೊಲೆ = ಹೊಲೆ, *q v*. -ಯ. = ಹೊಲೆಯ, *f* ಪೊಲತಿ.

ಪೊಲ್ಲ (= ಹೊಲ್ಲ, *q v*) a. k *n* Meanness, *etc* *Cpds*. -ಮಾತು, -ಮೊಗ, -ವಾತೆ

ಪೊಸ = ಹೊಸ, *q v*

ಪೊಸಯಿಸು. ಪೊಸವಿಸು a k *v t*. To join; to apply to. 2, to churn, shake about

ಪೊಸೆ (= ಹೊಸ *q v*) a. k. *v. i* To shake, to rub 2, to twist, plait.

ಪೊಳಪು (= ಹೊಳಪು) a. k *n*. Radiance, brightness. 2, shaking, rolling; a swing

ಪೊಳಲು (= ಹೊಳಲು ಳ = ೞ) a k. *n*. A dwelling place a town, city.

ಪೊಳೆ 1 (= ಹೊಳೆ 1, *q. v*) a. k *v. i* To shine 2, to roll about

ಪೊಳೆ 2. (ಳೆ = ೞೆ. = ಹೊಳೆ 2) k. *n* A river. 2, a path, road

ಪೊಳ್ಳು (= ಹೊಳ್ಳು) k. *n* Hollowness; emptiness, trash, worthless stuff -ಕೂಗು A false report. -ಮಾತು A vain word. -ಸುದ್ದಿ A groundless report. -ಹಲ್ಲು A hollow tooth

ಪೋಕ, ಪೋಕರಿ k *n* A dissolute, profligate fellow, villain, rogue, prodigal. -ತನ The ways of a ಪೋಕರಿ.

ಪೋಗು = ಹೋಗು, *q v*

ಪೋಟ k *n* A coward. 2, = ಪೋಕ, *q. v*. -ತನ = ಪೋಕತನ.

ಪೋಟಿ k. *n* Competition, rivalry, *also* ಸ್ಪೋಟಾ- -ಗಾರ. A competitor.

ಪೋಟೆ (= ಪೊಟ್ಟರೆ, *q v*.) k. *n* A hole in a tree

ಪೋಡಿ f *n*. A slice, bit, *as* of a nut, *etc*.

ಪೋಡು k *n*. Combination. 2, splitting

ಪೋಣಿಸು k *v. t*. To couple, unite, string together, to thread, *as* a needle, *etc*

ಪೋತ, -ಕ s. *n*. The young of any animal.

ಪೋತರಿ *n*. The potherb *Basella lucida*

[illegible] e *n*. Photograph ([illegible])

ಪೋದ. *Rel. p p of* ಪೋಗು.

ಪೋಪ *Rel pres p. of* ಪೋಗು.

ಪೋಪನು e *n* The Pope, the head of the Roman Catholic Church.

ಪೋರ f *n* A child, a little boy. -ತನ. Childhood ಪೋರಿ A little girl

ಪೋರು = ಹೋರು 1. 2, *q v*

ಪೋಲಿ (=ಪೋಲು) k. *n* Ruin, destruction; waste, stray, profligacy, wickedness. 2, =ಪೋಕರಿ -ಮಾಡು To waste -ದನ Stray cattle. -ತನ = ಪೋಕರಿತನ, *q v*

ಪೋಲಿಕೆ s *n* A flat cake

ಪೋಲಿಸು. = ಹೋಲಿಸು, *q. v.*

ಪೋಲೀಸು e *n* Police. ಪೋಲೀಸಿನವ A policeman -ಕೆಲಸ. The duties of the police

ಪೋಲು (=ಪೋಲಿ) k *n.* Ruin, wasting, squandering 2,=ಹೋಲು. -ಮಾಡು To squander

ಪೋಲ್ಟೀಸು e. *n* Poultice, cataplasm, an application to sore part of the body.

ಪೋಷಣ, ಪೋಷಣೆ s *n.* Nourishing, cherishing, bringing up. ಪೋಷಕ. A nourisher, supporter. ಪೋಷಿತ Nourished, cherished, fostered. ಪೋಷಿಸು To nourish, cherish *etc*

ಪೋಷಾಕ, ಪೋಷಾಕು h *n* Apparel.

ಪೋಸ್ತಮಾಸ್ತರ್ e *n.* Postmaster.

ಪೋಳು = ಹೋಳು. *q v.*

ಪೌಜು (=ಪವುಜು, ಫೌಜು) h. *n* An army, *etc* -ದಾರ A native commander -ದಾರಿಕೆ. His office

ಪೌತಿ h. *n* Death. -ಆಸಾಮಿ A deceased person

ಪೌತ್ರ s. *n* A grandson, *f* ಪೌತ್ರಿ.

ಪೌರ (*fr.* ಪುರ) s *n* A townsman. 2, a species of fragrant grass

ಪೌರಾಣ (*fr* ಪುರಾಣ) s *a.* Relating to the past, old, ancient. ಪೌರಾಣಿಕ. = ಪುರಾಣಿಕ, *q v*

ಪೌರುಷ (*fr* ಪುರುಷ) s *a* Belonging to man *n* Manliness heroism power streng

ಪೌರೋಹಿತ (*fr* ಪುರೋಹಿತ) s *n* The office of a purôhita the family priest ಪೌರೋಹಿತ್ಯ. The office of a family-priest.

ಪೌರ್ಣಮಿ (*fr* ಪೂರ್ಣಮಾ) s *n* A day of full moon

ಪೌಲಿ s. *n* A sort of cake made of grain.

ಪ್ಯಾದೆ = ಪೇದೆ, *q v.*

ಪ್ರ s *pref* Before, forward, in front, forth, pre-eminently, excessively, very, much

ಪ್ರಕಟ s. *a.* Evident, clear, manifest; public, commonly known, published, notorious, visible -ಗೊಳಿಸು, -ಪಡಿಸು To make manifest -ಮಾಡು To publish. -ಣೆ, -ನೆ Notification, *also* -ಪತ್ರ ಪ್ರಕಟಿಸು. To manifest, to disclose, to publish, proclaim.

ಪ್ರಕರಣ s *n* Expounding discussion, explanation 2, a subject, department 3, a section, chapter. 4, occasion 5, a prologue, prelude. 6, a drama.

ಪ್ರಕಾಂಡ s *n* The stem or trunk of a tree 2, a branch

ಪ್ರಕಾರ s. *n* Sort, kind. 2, way, mode, manner. 3, similitude. *ad* According to, *etc* ಈ- Thus, in this way. ಆ- So, in that way.

ಪ್ರಕಾಶ s *n.* Brightness, brilliance lustre, splendour. 2, elucidation, manifestation, fame -ಗೊಳಿಸು To illuminate, make bright; to develop. -ಗೊಳ್ಳು To obtain lustre ಪ್ರಕಾಶಿತ Manifest displayed; enlightened. ಪ್ರಕಾಶಿಸು. To become manifest, to shine forth be full of lustre

ಪ್ರಕೃತಿ s *n* The original or natural form of anything 2, nature, character, constitution of the body; temperament 3, reality 4, the five elements. 5, the material world; Nature, as opposed to Purusha 6, work to be done 7, cause 8, a ... form of a word. ಪ್ರಕೃತ Made, accomplished, original, natural; real; the present moment

ಪ್ರಕೋಪ s n Violent anger, rage, provocation.

ಪ್ರಕ್ರಿಯೆ s. n. Conduct, manner, a rite. 2, precedence, prerogative, dignity

ಪ್ರಕ್ಷಾಲ, -ನ s. n. Washing, cleansing, bathing ಪ್ರಕ್ಷಾಲಿಸು To wash

ಪ್ರಕ್ಷೇಪಣ s. n Throwing, casting, depositing.

ಪ್ರಖ್ಯಾತ s a Celebrated, renowned, famous ಪ್ರಖ್ಯಾತಿ Celebrity, fame, praise.

ಪ್ರಗಲ್ಭ s. a Bold; resolute -ತೆ. Boldness, energy, resoluteness

ಪ್ರಗ್ರಹ s n Holding forth. 2, a rope, bridle, halter. 3, a captive.

ಪ್ರಚಂಡ s a Excessively violent, furious, fierce; intolerable; bold.

ಪ್ರಚಾರ s n Coming forth, becoming public, being in actual use, currency 2, conduct, behaviour, custom, usage. -ಗೊಳಿಸು. To make public.

ಪ್ರಚುರ s a. Much, many, plenteous, frequent, prevalent. -ತೆ. Increase, prevelance, publicity -ಪಡಿಸು To publish

ಪ್ರಚೋದನ s n Animating, exciting, directing. ಪ್ರಚೋದಿತ. Impelled, decreed, proscribed, commanded.

ಪ್ರಚ್ಛನ್ನ s. a. Covered, hidden; clothed. 2, private, disguised.

ಪ್ರಜಾಗರ s. n Waking, being awake.

ಪ್ರಜೆ s n Offspring 2, people, subjects ಪ್ರಜಾಪತಿ Lord of creatures, Brahmâ; a king, also ಪ್ರಜೇಶ್ವರ ಪ್ರಜೋತ್ಪತ್ತಿ. The raising up of progeny, the fifth year in the cycle of sixty

ಪ್ರಜ್ಞ s a Wise, intelligent, learned ಪ್ರಜ್ಞಾಚಕ್ಷುಸ್ The mental eye. ಪ್ರಜ್ಞಾ, ಪ್ರಜ್ಞೆ. Intellect, wisdom, also ಪ್ರಜ್ಞಾನ

ಪ್ರಜ್ವಲ, -ನ s. n. Blazing up, shining, kindling. ಪ್ರಜ್ವಲಿತ Being in flames, burning, shining ಪ್ರಜ್ವಲಿಸು To be in flames to shine.

ಪ್ರಣತ s. a. Bent forward, bowed, humble 2, skilful. ಪ್ರಣತಿ Salutation, obeisance

ಪ್ರಣಾಮ = ಪ್ರಣಾಮ, q v

ಪ್ರಣಯ s n. Confidence, familiarity; friendship, affection, kindness 2, affectionate solicitation. ಪ್ರಣಯಿ. A friend, lover, a lord, a petitioner, a humble servant.

ಪ್ರಣವ s n The mystic syllable ôm

ಪ್ರಣಾದ s n A loud noise expressing delight

ಪ್ರಣಾಮ s. n Prostration, obeisance.

ಪ್ರಣಿಧಾನ s. n Respectful conduct or behaviour towards 2, profound meditation 3, great effort, energy.

ಪ್ರಣಿಪಾತ s n. Falling at one's feet, salutation, obeisance.

ಪ್ರತಾಪ s n. Splendour, majesty, dignity 2, ardour, energy, valour -ನ. Burning, a particular hell.

ಪ್ರತಿ s. ad Towards, to, against, opposite, contra; before; on a par with, as, like, near, by, at on, in favour of, in each, at every, every, each, with regard to, on account of, according to; back. again, in lieu of, in return for, in the place of, instead of n. A copy -ಬರೆ, -ಮಾಡು To copy -ಒಂದು. Every one, each one -ಒಬ್ಬ. Every man, each man -ದಿನ, -ನಿತ್ಯ Day by day, daily, every day -ನಿಮಿಷ Every moment. -ವರ್ಷ Every year annually *For other cpds see below*

ಪ್ರತಿಕಾರ s n Retaliation, retribution; revenge. 2, counteraction, remedy, also ಪ್ರತೀಕಾರ

ಪ್ರತಿಕೂಲ s. a Contrary, adverse, inauspicious -ತೆ Opposition, hostility

ಪ್ರತಿಕೃತಿ s n Resistance, requital; revenge 2, an effigy, image.

ಪ್ರತಿಕ್ರಿಯೆ = ಪ್ರತಿಕಾರ, q v

ಪ್ರತಿಗ್ರಹ s n Receiving, accepting, [illegible]

ಪ್ರತಿಚ್ಛಾಯೆ s n A reflected image, picture, a shadow

ಪ್ರತಿಜ್ಞೆ s n Admission, consent; a solemn declaration, agreement, engagement, vow, promise, a vow, a statement, affirmation, a proposition -ಜ್ಞೆಯು -ಮಾಡು To make solemn declaration

ಪ್ರತಿಧ್ವನಿ s n. An echo. -ಕೊಡು, -ಮಾಡು To echo

ಪ್ರತಿನಿಧಿ s n. A substitute, representative, proxy, a deputy, vice-regent

ಪ್ರತಿಪಕ್ಷ s. n The opposite side or party. ಪ್ರತಿಪಕ್ಷಿ An opponent

ಪ್ರತಿಪತ್ತು (tb of ಪ್ರತಿಪದ್) n The first day of a lunar fortnight.

ಪ್ರತಿಪತ್ತಿ s n Perception, knowledge. 2, intellect. 3, statement 4, assent. 5 action 6 elevation; reputation

ಪ್ರತಿಪದ s. n A synonym, each word

ಪ್ರತಿಪದಿ s n The first day of a lunar fortnight 2, preferment. regard.

ಪ್ರತಿಪಾದನ s. n Explaining, declaring. 2, establishing, proving ಪ್ರತಿಪಾದಿಸು. To declare, to establish; to accuse. ಪ್ರತಿಪಾದ್ಯ Fit to be explained or proved

ಪ್ರತಿಪಾಲನ s n Protecting, cherishing nourishing ಪ್ರತಿಪಾಲಿಸು To protect, guard, to nourish

ಪ್ರತಿಫಲ s n. Reward, remuneration, retribution 2, reflection -ಕೊಡು To remunerate -ಹೊಂದು. To receive reward ಪ್ರತಿಫಲಿಸು To be rewarded

ಪ್ರತಿಬಂಧ s n An obstacle, hinderance, impediment -ಕ Obstructive hindering, an obstacle, a demon, devil -ನ. Obstructing impeding ಪ್ರತಿಬಂಧಿಸು To hinder, stop

ಪ್ರತಿಬಿಂಬ s n A reflection, an image, a picture, a shadow. ಪ್ರತಿಬಿಂಬಿಸು To be reflected, to reflect

ಪ್ರತಿಘಟ s [illegible]
ತಿಘಟನ [illegible]

ಪ್ರತಿಭೂ s. n A surety, security

ಪ್ರತಿಮಾನ s n A likeness, image, picture

ಪ್ರತಿಮೆ s n A likeness image; an idol

ಪ್ರತಿರವ s. n. Echo, also ಪ್ರತಿಧ್ವನಿ, ಪ್ರತಿಶಬ್ದ.

ಪ್ರತಿರೂಪ s n An image, representation, a picture a Similar, corresponding.

ಪ್ರತಿಲೋಮ s. a. Reverse. inverted, hostile, low, left, not right.

ಪ್ರತಿವಚನ, ಪ್ರತಿವಾಕ್ಯ s. n An answer, reply

ಪ್ರತಿವಾದ s. n A counter assertion. contradiction ಪ್ರತಿವಾದಿ An opponent, a defendant

ಪ್ರತಿಶಬ್ದ s. n Echo, also ಪ್ರತಿರವ

ಪ್ರತಿಷೇಧ s. n Forbidding, prohibition; denial, negation the negative mood -ಕ್ರಿಯೆ The negative mood (g) -ವಿಧಿ The imperative mood of prohibition.

ಪ್ರತಿಷ್ಠಾಲು s n. An illustrious person

ಪ್ರತಿಷ್ಠೆ s n. Setting up, honour, fame, pride, installation, as of a king, etc., consecration, as of a church, temple, idol, etc. -ವಂತ. An illustrious man ಪ್ರತಿಷ್ಠಿಸು. To establish; to set up, as an idol; to install consecrate

ಪ್ರತಿಹಸ್ತ s n A deputy. substitute, proxy

ಪ್ರತಿಹಾರ (= ಪ್ರತೀಹಾರ) s n. Repelling. 2, a door 3, a porter 4, juggling, disguise 5, a place near a town.

ಪ್ರತೀಕಾರ = ಪ್ರತಿಕಾರ, q v

ಪ್ರತೀಕ್ಷೆ s n Looking forward to, waiting for, expectation, hope ಪ್ರತೀಕ್ಷಿಸು To expect, wait for

ಪ್ರತೀಚಿ s n. Western quarter ಪ್ರತೀಚೀನ, ಪ್ರತೀಚ್ಯ Western

ಪ್ರತೀತ s a Gone towards; proved, known; convinced, pleased ಪ್ರತೀತಿ Going towards; definite perception, knowledge, conviction, faith, fame, delight.

ಪ್ರತುಮೆ. *tb* of ಪ್ರತಿಮೆ, *q. v*

ಪ್ರತ್ಯಕ್ಷ s. *a* Perceptible to the eye, visible, clear, distinct evident, real, cognizable by the senses. *n.* Ocular evidence, distinctness. *ad* Verily; distinctly. -ವಾಗು To appear. -ಪ್ರಮಾಣ The evidence of the senses, axiom -ತೆ Appearance. -ತೇ ಹಬ್ಬ Epiphany, in commemoration of the appearance of the star that led the magi to our Saviour at Bethlehem

ಪ್ರತ್ಯಗಾತ್ಮ s. *n* The individual soul

ಪ್ರತ್ಯಂತರ s *n.* Another copy

ಪ್ರತ್ಯಯ s. *n* Belief, conviction, trust, reliance, confidence. 2, certainty. 3, knowledge, apprehension intellect 4, idea notion 5, motive. 6, an oath, ordeal 7, a suffix or affix

ಪ್ರತ್ಯವಾಯ s. *n.* Decrease, privation, harm, separation

ಪ್ರತ್ಯಹ s *ad* Day by day, daily

ಪ್ರತ್ಯಾಬ್ದಿಕ s. *ad.* Yearly

ಪ್ರತ್ಯಾಮ್ನಾಯ s *ad* Instead of, in lieu of.

ಪ್ರತ್ಯಾಸಕ್ತಿ s *n* Great attachment or devotedness

ಪ್ರತ್ಯಾಸನ್ನ s *a* Near, proximate, imminent

ಪ್ರತ್ಯಾಹಾರ s *n.* Restraint of the organs of sense

ಪ್ರತ್ಯುತ್ತರ s. *n* An answer, reply, *also* ಪ್ರತ್ಯುಕ್ತಿ. -ವಾಗಿ ಹೇಳು To say in reply

ಪ್ರತ್ಯುತ್ಥಾನ s *n* Rising to welcome a visitor

ಪ್ರತ್ಯುಪಕಾರ s *n.* A return of a kindness

ಪ್ರತ್ಯುಷಸ್ s *ad* Every morning

ಪ್ರತ್ಯೇಕ s *a* Separate, different *ad.* Separately, severally ಪ್ರತ್ಯೇಕಿಸು. To separate

ಪ್ರಥಮ s *a* First, chief, principal, most, excellent *n* The third person (*g.*) ಪ್ರಥಮಾವಿಭಕ್ತಿ. The nominative case ಪ್ರಥಮೈಕವಚನ The nominative singular ಪ್ರಥಮೈಕಾದಶಿ The ಶುಕ್ಲ ಏಕಾದಶಿ in the month of ಆಷಾಢ

ಪ್ರದಕ್ಷಿಣ, ಪ್ರದಕ್ಷಿಣೆ s *n* Circumambulation of an object (*as* of an idol, person, *etc*, by way of reverence)

ಪ್ರದರ್ಶಕ s *a* Showing, exhibiting exhibiter. ಪ್ರದರ್ಶನ Showing pointing out, exhibiting, an example.

ಪ್ರದಾನ s *n* Giving away; an oblation; a gift, present, *also* ಪ್ರದ.

ಪ್ರದೇಶ s *n* A place, region, a country, district

ಪ್ರದೋಷ s. *a* Corrupt *n* Sin, *etc.* 2, the first part of the night, nightfall 3, a vrata in worship of Siva

ಪ್ರಧಾನ s. *a* Chief, main, principal, pre-eminent *n* A chief object. 2, intellect. 3, the minister of a king 4, the primary member of a compound (*g*) -ವಾಕ್ಯ. Principal sentence -ಯಾಜಕ. High priest (*Jewish*)

ಪ್ರಪಂಚ s *n* Development, diffusion, display, expansion, expanse 2, the visible world or universe 3, the business of life 4, manifoldness, diversity 5, error, illusion. -ಮಾಡು To carry on the business of life ಪ್ರಪಂಚಿಸು To spread, develop

ಪ್ರಪನ್ನ s. *n.* One who seeks for refuge.

ಪ್ರಪಾತ s *n* Rushing forwards 2, a steep rock, cliff, precipice 3, a waterfall

ಪ್ರಪಿತಾಮಹ s *n.* A paternal great-grandfather, *f.* -ಹಿ

ಪ್ರಪೌತ್ರ s *n* A great-grandson

ಪ್ರಫುಲ್ಲ s *a* Blown as a flower, covered with blossoms

ಪ್ರಬಂಧ s. *n.* A connection 2, a continuous series. 3, a connected discussion. 4, a literary composition, treatise

ಪ್ರಬಲ s *a* Predominant, strong; abounding with or in -ವಡಿಸು, ಪ್ರಬಲಿಸು To increase greatly

ಪ್ರಬುದ್ಧ s *a* Awake. 2, clever, wise, learned. -ಪ್ರಾಯ- Adult

ಪ್ರಬೋಧ s. n Awaking, vigilance, intellect, knowledge, wisdom, intelligence. -ನ Instructing ಪ್ರಬೋಧಿಸು. To instruct

ಪ್ರಭವ s. n Origin 2, the first year of the cycle. ಪ್ರಭವಿಸು To come into being; to become manifest

ಪ್ರಭಾವ s. n Strength, power. 2 majesty, glory 3, splendour

ಪ್ರಭಾವಳಿ s n. The halo around an idol

ಪ್ರಭು s a Powerful, mighty n A superior, master, lord. -ತೆ, -ತ್ವ Lordship, supremacy, power, rule

ಪ್ರಭೂತ s a Much. abundant. high, lofty n An oblation of rice, etc on the tenth day after the death of a person

ಪ್ರಭೆ, ಪ್ರಭಾ s. n. Light, splendour, radiance

ಪ್ರಮತ್ತ s. a Excited, wanton, drunken, impassioned. 2, careless, negligent

ಪ್ರಮಥ s. n An attendant on Śiva

ಪ್ರಮದ s n. Joy, rapture a Wanton; impassioned; careless. -ವನ A royal garden.

ಪ್ರಮಾಣ s. n Measure, scale, standard; quantity, extent, weight, limit 2, ground of assurance 3, proof. authority, support; testimony, evidence 4, an oath. 5, a correct notion. 6, statute, law, etc. 7, cause, motive. -ಮಾಡು. To swear -ವಾಗಿ ಹೇಳು To tell correctly -ವಾಕ್ಯ Authoritative statement; a formula used in taking an oath ಪ್ರಮಾಣಿಕ True, fair equitable. ಪ್ರಮಾಣಿಕತನ Truthfulness, honesty ಪ್ರಮಾಣಿಸು To discern, examine

ಪ್ರಮಾಥಿ s. n Stirring about. 2, the 13th year of the cycle

ಪ್ರಮಾದ s n Intoxication, madness, inadvertence, carelessness, a blunder, error, distress, misfortune

ಪ್ರಮಾದೀ... - The 47th ... of the cycle

ಪ್ರಮಿತ s. a Measured, understood; conformed, as by some rule ಪ್ರಮಿತಿ. Measure, true knowledge.

ಪ್ರಮುಖ s a. First, foremost, chief, principal. 2 at the end of cpds. headed by, accompanied by, and so on n A chief, a respectable man.

ಪ್ರಮೇಯ s a Demonstrable n. A subject, topic in general (= ವಿಷಯ)

ಪ್ರಮೋದ s n Joy, delight, happiness 2, the 4th year of the cycle. ಪ್ರಮೋದಿಸು To rejoice, be delighted.

ಪ್ರಮೋದೂತ tb. of ಪ್ರಮೋದ, q v.

ಪ್ರಯತ್ನ s n Great exertion, an effort; an endeavour, essay 2, difficulty. -ನಡಿಸು, -ಪಡು, -ಮಾಡು, ಪ್ರಯತ್ನಿಸು. To make effort, endeavour try

ಪ್ರಯಾಗ s. n. A sacrifice, a celebrated place of pilgrimage at (Allahabad) the confluence of ಗಂಗಾ and ಯಮುನಾ

ಪ್ರಯಾಣ s n Setting out, a journey march 2, departure, death -ಮಾಡು. To start, to journey, to die -ಸ್ಥ, ಪ್ರಯಾಣಿಕ. A traveller, a voyager

ಪ್ರಯಾಸ s. n Effort. exertion, endeavour, labour, pains, difficulty. -ಪಡು. To labour, take pains -ವಾಗು To be difficult. to require pains.

ಪ್ರಯುಕ್ತ s. a Used, employed, connected with; endowed with. occasioned by. prep On account of, as ಊಟದ-, ಕೆಲಸದ- ಪ್ರಯುಕ್ತಿ Use, employment, cause, result.

ಪ್ರಯುತ s n A million

ಪ್ರಯೋಗ s n Application, employment, use. 2, undertaking, beginning. 3, an order 4. a design, device, plan. 5, use, usage, practice 6 ceremonial form. 7, force or usual form (of a word). -ಮಾಡು, ಪ್ರಯೋಗಿಸು To use, employ, to throw, as an arrow

ಪ್ರಯೋಜಕ s. a. Useful, beneficial. n. A useful man

ಪ್ರಯೋಜನ s Application, use. 2, ... urpose,

object, intention, design 4, profit, gain, usefulness, advantage, benefit.

ಪ್ರಲಪನ s. n Speaking forth; prattling; crying, lamenting. ಪ್ರಲಪಿಸು. To speak, to lament, wail

ಪ್ರಲಯ (= ಪ್ರಳಯ) s n Dissolution, destruction 2, the destruction of the world at the end of a kalpa 3, the deluge of the Bible. -ಕಾಲ The time of universal destruction.

ಪ್ರಲಾಪ s n Senseless talk 2, prattling. 3, lamentation -ಸನ್ನಿ A sanni that produces delirium ಪ್ರಲಾಪಿಸು. To talk incoherently, to lament, wail

ಪ್ರವರ s n A family, lineage. 2, offspring. 3, one of the 49 *gôtras* 4, verbosity, prolixity.

ಪ್ರವರ್ತ s. a. Engaged in, occupied in. -ಕ Setting in motion, promoting, an originator, founder, a promoter, f -ಕಿ -ನ, -ನೆ Moving forwards, activity, action, business, course, proceeding, behaviour, conduct, way, manner ಪ್ರವರ್ತಿಸು To proceed, go on, to come to pass, to engage in, be occupied in, to act, to carry on, perform, *as* a business

ಪ್ರವರ್ಧ s. n Increasing, *also* -ನ Augmenting, increase. -ಮಾನ Growing, increasing. ಪ್ರವರ್ಧಿಸು. To grow, increase.

ಪ್ರವಹ s n. Flowing, streaming. 2, wind ಪ್ರವಹಿಸು To flow, to draw, *as* a carriage.

ಪ್ರವಾದ s n. Speaking forth, uttering; proclaiming, declaration; discourse, popular talk, rumour, report. -ನೆ Prophecy. ಪ್ರವಾದಿ A prophet (one who speaks by God's order) ಪ್ರವಾದಿಸು To prophesy, *also* -ನೆ ಹೇಳು.

ಪ್ರವಾಲ s. n. A young shoot 2, greenness 3, coral. -ಭಸ್ಮ. Ashes of coral, used medicinally

ಪ್ರವಾಸ s. n. Sojourning abroad; a temporary sojourn, a foreign abode. -ಮಾಡು To go abroad ಪ್ರವಾಸಿ. A sojourner abroad. -ನ Dwelling abroad, exile, banishment

ಪ್ರವಾಹ s. n A stream, current, flow, course. ಪ್ರವಾಹಿಸು. To stream, flow.

ಪ್ರವಿಷ್ಟ s a. Entered, gone into.

ಪ್ರವೀಣ s a Skilful, clever, proficient, conversant with, f. ಪ್ರವೀಣೆ. -ತೆ, -ತ. Skill, proficiency

ಪ್ರವುಢ *tb of* ಪ್ರೌಢ, q v

ಪ್ರವೃತ್ತಿ s n Proceeding, purging. 2, progress, advance 3, active life. 4, prevalence.

ಪ್ರವೃದ್ಧ s. a Grown up increased ಪ್ರವೃದ್ಧಿ. Growth, increase, prosperity

ಪ್ರವೇಣಿ s. n A braided hair.

ಪ್ರವೇಶ s n Entering into, entrance 2, commencement. -ಮಾಡು, ಪ್ರವೇಶಿಸು. To enter into, enter, go into, to interfere, *as* ಮನೆಗೆ-, ಮನೆಯಲ್ಲಿ-, ಮನೆಯನ್ನು-

ಪ್ರವ್ರಜನ, ಪ್ರವ್ರಜ್ಯೆ s. n Going abroad migration, wandering about, esp as a religious mendicant

ಪ್ರವ್ರಾಜಕ s. n A religious mendicant.

ಪ್ರಶಂಸೆ s n. Praise, eulogy ಪ್ರಶಂಸಿಸು. To praise, eulogize

ಪ್ರಶಮ s n Calmness, tranquility, peace, composure. ಪ್ರಶಮಿತ Appeased quenched

ಪ್ರಶಸ್ತ s n. Praised, extolled, commendable, admirable, excellent

ಪ್ರಶ್ನ s n. A question, query, interrogation, *also* ಪ್ರಶ್ನೆ. -ಕೇಳು. To ask a question -ಮಾಡು, -ಹಾಕು To question, ask. -ಚಿಹ್ನ. A sign of interrogation (?) ಪ್ರಶ್ನಾರ್ಥಕ Interrogative ಪ್ರಶ್ನೋತ್ತರ Questions and answers. a dialogue, catechism.

ಪ್ರಸಕ್ತಿ s n Connection, the topic of conversation; energy, effort. -ತೆಗೆ To take up, *as* a topic of conversation

ಪ್ರಸಂಗ s. n. Connection, intercourse, meeting. 2, topic, a subject of conversation; discussion, a sermon (*Chr*) 3, incident, event. 4, the fit time, season, an occasion. -ನಡಿಸು, -ಮಾಡು, -ಗೈಯು, ಪ್ರಸಂಗಿಸು. To discuss, to preach, proclaim ಪ್ರಸಂಗಿ A devotee, a discusser, a preacher -ಪೀಠ The Christian pulpit.

ಪ್ರಸನ್ನ s a. Clear, bright, tranquil, soothed, propitiated, pleased, gracious, propitious, kind, pleased with. -ತ Pleased. -ತೆ, -ತ್ವ, -ಭಾವ Clearness, favour, kindness, propitiousness

ಪ್ರಸರ s n Spreading, extending, extent, diffusion, dispersion 2, expansion 3, flow, current. 4, speed, force 5 affection. -ಣ Spreading; surrounding an enemy -ಣಶೀಲ Extensible ಪ್ರಸರಿಸು To be extended, to be diffused; to spread

ಪ್ರಸವ s n. Childbirth. 2, offspring 3, a flower. 4, fruit. 5, opening, budding. ಪ್ರಸವಿಸು To beget, bring forth.

ಪ್ರಸಾದ s n Clearness, brightness, purity. 2, calmness, repose, composure, good humour. 3, graciousness, propitiousness, favour, kindness. 4, sacrament, a pledge of grace (as the Lord's Supper and baptism) 5, anything presented to an idol 6, a free gift, gratuity -ನ Rendering clear, tranquillizing, gratifying, a gratuity -ನೆ. Service, worship

ಪ್ರಸಾದಿ s a Calming, showing favour. 2, come from a king, guru, *etc*, *as* a blessing. -ತ Purified, worshipped -ಸು To grant graciously.

ಪ್ರಸಾರ s n. Going forth, spreading, extending -ಣ Causing to go forwards, spreading, diffusing, expansion, increase, exhibiting, dissemination

ಪ್ರಸಿದ್ಧ s a. Accomplished, well known, renowned, famous, celebrated, public, adorned. -ಪಡಿಸು, -ಮಾಡು To make known . . .
-ಪತ್ರ . . .

ಪ್ರಸಿದ್ಧಿ s. n Accomplishment, celebrity, fame, publicity -ಗೆ ಬರು. To come to fame. -ಮಾಡು = ಪ್ರಸಿದ್ಧ ಮಾಡು, *q. v*

ಪ್ರಸೂತ s. a Begotten; born. ಪ್ರಸೂತಿ Birth, offspring ಪ್ರಸೂತೆ. A woman in childbed

ಪ್ರಸ್ತ (*tb of* ಪ್ರಶಸ್ತ) *n*. An auspicious ceremony, festive occasion, *as*. the ಉಪನಯನ-, ನಾಮಕರಣ-, ವಿವಾಹ-, *etc*

ಪ್ರಸ್ತಾಪ (*tb of* ಪ್ರಸ್ತಾವ) *n*. Speaking, saying, introduction, preface 2, beginning. 3, introducing a topic for conversation, the conversation on a topic, the topic itself, narration, news, affair, pursuit 4, occasion, opportunity; a favourable moment. -ನ = ಪ್ರಸ್ತಾಪನ ಪ್ರಸ್ತಾಪಿಸು. To introduce a topic and converse on it.

ಪ್ರಸ್ತಾರ s. n A plain 2, a jungle

ಪ್ರಸ್ತಾವ = ಪ್ರಸ್ತಾಪ, *q v* -ನೆ Introduction, preface, the prologue of a drama, introducing a topic for conversation, the conversation on a topic.

ಪ್ರಸ್ತುತ s a Praised, declared, said, ready, proximate. *n* A proposition *ad* At present

ಪ್ರಸ್ಥ s. n. Table-land. 2, a measure of four kudavas. *a* Going forth.

ಪ್ರಸ್ಥಾನ s n Going forth, a march, a journey, a method, system

ಪ್ರಸ್ರವ s. n A flow, stream, a fall of water, a cascade

ಪ್ರಹರ s. n. A watch, the eighth part of a day

ಪ್ರಹಸನ s n. Hearty laughter, mirth, mocking, sarcasm, satire; a farce

ಪ್ರಹ್ಲಾದ s n Pleasure, gladness, happiness 2, sound 3, N. of a daitya persecuted for his devotion to Vishnu.

ಪ್ರಳಯ = ಪ್ರಲಯ, *q v*

ಪ್ರಾಕ್ (*tb. of* ಪ್ರಾಚ್) *ad*. Before; formerly *a* Previous former

. . . Pr . . . -ation

ಪ್ರಾಕಾರ (=ಪಾಗಾರ, *q v*) s *n* A rampart, fence, enclosure.

ಪ್ರಾಕೃತ (*fr* ಪ್ರಕೃತಿ) s. *a* Original, natural, ordinary, common, uncultivated, vulgar, low, base; vernacular *n* Any provincial or vernacular dialect akin to Samskrita

ಪ್ರಾಕ್ಕು = ಪ್ರಾಕ್, *q v. tb of* ಪ್ರಾಚ್.

ಪ್ರಾಕ್ತನ s. *a* Former, prior. *n* Fate, destiny.

ಪ್ರಾಕ್ಪದ s. *n* The first member of a compound

ಪ್ರಾಗಾರಭ್ಯ (*fr* ಪ್ರಾಕ್-ಆರಭ್ಯ) s *a*. Beginning from the past time.

ಪ್ರಾಗುದಯ s. *a*. Rising in the east.

ಪ್ರಾಚೀನ s. *a* Former, prior, ancient, eastern *n*. The doings of former births and their consequences 2, a hedge, wall

ಪ್ರಾಜಾಪತ್ಯ (*fr* ಪ್ರಜಾಪತಿ) s. *n* A kind of marriage 2, a mode of penance

ಪ್ರಾಜ್ಞ s. *a*. Intelligent, wise, clever *n*. A learned man.

ಪ್ರಾಣ s. *n*. Breath, respiration. 2, air, wind 3, a vital air 4, life, vitality 5, the soul 6, strength, might -ಕೊಡು To offer one's life for the benefit of another, to die -ಗೆಳೆಯ, -ಮಿತ್ರ. A dearly loved friend -ತಕ್ಕೊಳ್ಳು (-ತೆಗೆ) To take away life, kill; to commit suicide. -ದಿಂದ ಹೋಗು To die, to go alive. -ಕಂಟಕ Danger of life, a dangerous man. -ಕಾಂತ -ನಾಥ, -ಪತಿ, -ವಲ್ಲಭ A dearly beloved husband -ಘಾತಕ Killing, money -ತ್ಯಾಗ Suicide. -ದಾನ The gift of life. -ನಷ್ಟ, -ಹಾನಿ Loss of life. -ಪ್ರತಿಷ್ಠೆ. The rite of bringing life to an idol -ಪ್ರಿಯ A dearly beloved man. -ಸಂಕಟ. Jeopardy of life. extreme distress. -ಸ್ನೇಹ. Very intimate friendship. -ಹತ್ಯ Murder -ಹಿಂಸೆ. Injury to life ಪ್ರಾಣಾಯಾಮ Restraint of breath during meditation

ಪ್ರಾಣಿ s *n* Any living creature, an animal, a person -ಕೋಟಿ. The animal kingdom

ಪ್ರಾತಃ, ಪ್ರಾತರ್ s. *ad* At daybreak ಪ್ರಾತಃಕಾಲ The early morning. ಪ್ರಾತಃಸ್ನಾನ Morning ablution. ಪ್ರಾತರ್ಭೋಜನ Breakfast

ಪ್ರಾತಿಭಾಸಿಕ (*fr* ಪ್ರತಿಭಾಸ) s *a* Existing only in appearance. 2, looking like.

ಪ್ರಾದೇಶ (*fr* ಪ್ರದೇಶ) s. *n* The span of the thumb and forefinger.

ಪ್ರಾಧಾನ್ಯ (*fr* ಪ್ರಧಾನ) s. *n*. Pre-eminence, supremacy, prevalence, ascendancy.

ಪ್ರಾಂತ, ಪ್ರಾಂತ್ಯ s *n* Edge, border; boundary. 2, a country; a region, a place.

ಪ್ರಾಪಂಚಿಕ s *a* Worldly, secular.

ಪ್ರಾಪ್ತ s *a* Attained to, obtained, got, acquired, fit, proper. ಪ್ರಾಪ್ತಿ. Attaining to, obtaining, acquisition, profit, advantage, lot, good luck ಪ್ರಾಪ್ತಿಸು To be obtained, to come to pass, to come to, to meet with

ಪ್ರಾಬಲ್ಯ s *n*. Powerfulness, prevalence

ಪ್ರಾಮಾಣಿಕ (*fr*. ಪ್ರಮಾಣ) s *a*. Authentic, credible, true, just *n* An upright, honest man -ತನ, -ತೆ, ಪ್ರಾಮಾಣ್ಯ Authenticity, credibility, truth, veracity, honesty.

ಪ್ರಾಯ s *n* Any period of life, age, prime of life -ತುಂಬು A period of age to be reached -ದವ A young man. -ಸಲ್ಲು Age to pass, decline -ಶಃ Generally, usually, to all appearances. -ಸ್ಥ A young man, *f* -ಸ್ಥಳು, -ಸ್ಥೆ.

ಪ್ರಾಯಶ್ಚಿತ್ತ s *n*. An expiation, atonement, penance, compensation 2, the atonement Christ made.

ಪ್ರಾರಬ್ಧ s *a* Begun *n* Fortune destiny

ಪ್ರಾರಂಭ s *n* Beginning, commencement. ಪ್ರಾರಂಭಿಸು. To begin, to commence.

ಪ್ರಾರ್ಥನೆ s n Requesting begging, a prayer, entreaty, request, application, petition 2, a vow. -ಕೂಟ Prayer-union -ವಾರ Prayer-week. -ಮಾಡು, ಪ್ರಾರ್ಥಿಸು To ask for, beg for, to petition anything, to pray to ಪ್ರಾರ್ಥಿತ Requested, asked for, prayed for

ಪ್ರಾವರಣ s. n A cover, cloak

ಪ್ರಾಶನ s. n Eating, feeding upon, drinking. ಪ್ರಾಶಿತ. Eaten, devoured, drunk ಪ್ರಾಶ್ಯ Eatable, edible.

ಪ್ರಾಸ s n Alliteration.

ಪ್ರಾಸಂಗಿಕ (fr. ಪ್ರಸಂಗ) s. a. Belonging to any topic, relevant, opportune, seasonable, occasional.

ಪ್ರಾಸಾದ (fr. ಪ್ರಸಾದ) s n. A temple, a palace

ಪ್ರಾಹ್ಣ s n Forenoon

ಪ್ರಿಯ s. a. Beloved, dear, valued, amiable, agreeable, desirable, loving, kind, affectionate. 2. dear, high in price. n Favour, love, a husband, lover; f. ಪ್ರಿಯೆ. -ಕರ. Giving pleasure -ತಮ. Most beloved; a lover -ವಾದಿ One who speaks kindly

ಪ್ರೀತ s a Pleased, joyful, dear

ಪ್ರೀತಿ s n. Gratification, satisfaction 2, grace, favour, kindness, affection, love -ಮಾಡು. To show affection, to love -ಇಡು To bestow love upon, *as* ಅವನಲ್ಲಿ or ಅವನ ಮೇಲೆ ಪ್ರೀತಿ ಇಡು. -ವಂತ, -ಶಾಲಿ A man full of love -ಸು. To love

ಪ್ರೇಕ್ಷೆ s n. Looking at, viewing, *also* ಪ್ರೇಕ್ಷಣ 2, a public show. 3, conception, intellect

ಪ್ರೇತ s. a Deceased n A dead person, a corpse. 2, a ghost. -ಕರ್ಮ Funeral rites. -ಬಲಿ Food offered to the departed spirit -ಸಂಸ್ಕಾರ The cremation of a corpse

ಪ್ರೇಮ s. n Lo[illegible] kindn[illegible] 2, joy pleasur[illegible] To show love ಪ್ರೇಮಿ Loving affectionate; a friend

ಪ್ರೇರಕ s n Urging, impelling, inciting, a pusher

ಪ್ರೇರಣೆ. = ಪ್ರೇರೇಪಣೆ, q v

ಪ್ರೇರಿತ s a Driven forwards, impelled, instigated, urged.

ಪ್ರೇರಿಸು = ಪ್ರೇರೇಪಿಸು, q v

ಪ್ರೇರೇಪಣೆ s n Pushing on, inciting, urging, instigating, direction, impulse ಪರಿಶುದ್ಧಾತ್ಮ- The prompting of the Holy Spirit ಪ್ರೇರೇಪಿಸು. To persuade, impel, urge on, stimulate, instigate

ಪ್ರೇಷಣ s n. Commissioning, ordering, directing.

ಪ್ರೇಷಿತ s a. Commissioned. sent forth, ordered, directed n An apostle

ಪ್ರೇಷ್ಯ s n A male servant, a messenger, f. ಪ್ರೇಷ್ಯೆ.

ಪ್ರೋಗ್ರಾಮು e n. Programme, an outline of the order of a performance or entertainment

ಪ್ರೊಟೆಸ್ಟಂಟ್ e a. Protesting (*against the doctrines and rites of the Church of Rome*). pertaining to Protestantism. n A Protestant (*opp. to Roman Catholic*) -ಕ್ರೈಸ್ತ. Protestant Christian -ಸಭೆ. Protestant church.

ಪ್ರೊಸೀಡಿಂಗ್ಸ್ e n Proceedings, course of measures or dealing.

ಪ್ರೋಕ್ತ s a Announced, declared, said.

ಪ್ರೋಕ್ಷಣ s. n. Sprinkling with water for purification 2, killing animals in sacrifice ಪ್ರೋಕ್ಷಿಸು To sprinkle

ಪ್ರೋತ್ಸಾಹ s n. Great effort, zeal, ardour. 2, stimulus. -ಗೊಳಿಸು, -ಪಡಿಸು To incite, inspirit, encourage ಪ್ರೋತ್ಸಾಹಿತ Stimulated, encouraged

ಪ್ರೌಢ (= ಪ್ರವೃದ್ಧ) s a Grown up, fully developed, mature, adult, proficient, grand, mighty, dignified -ತನ, -ತೆ. [illegible] ur maturity [illegible] gance. [illegible] ation, grandour, pomp, proficiency, self-confidence, zeal, enterprise, exertion. ಪ್ರೌಢಿಕೆ, ಪ್ರೌಢಿಮೆ Grandeur; proficiency

ಪ್ಲಕ್ಷ s n The waved-leaf fig-tree, *Ficus infectoria.*

ಪ್ಲವ s. n A float, raft. 2, the thirty-fifth year of the cycle of sixty

ಪ್ಲವಂಗ s n. The forty-first year of the cycle of sixty.

ಪ್ಲೀಹ s n The spleen 2, disease of the spleen.

ಪ್ಲುತ s a Floating, lengthened, protracted, as a vowel n A long vowel

ಪ್ಲ್ಯಾನಲ್ e. n Flannel.

ಫ್

ಫ್. The fortieth letter of the alphabet

ಫಕಾರ s n The letter ಫ

ಫಕೀರ (= ಪಕೀರ) h n. A Mahommadan mendicant.

ಫಕ್ಕನೆ = ಪಕ್ಕನೆ, q v

ಫಜೀತಿ, ಫಜೀತು h. n Disgrace, annoyance, harassment

ಫಡಪೋಸಿ. = ಪಡಪೋಸಿ, q v.

ಫಣ s. n The hood of the cobra ಫಣಾಮಣಿ. A hood-gem

ಫಣಿ s n A snake, a cobra. -ಧರ Śiva. -ವೇಣಿ. Braided hair resembling a snake

ಫನ h n Annihilation, ruin

ಫರಮಾನಾ, ಫರವಾನಾ h. n A royal mandate, order, a firman

ಫರಮಾಯಿಶಿ h a. Made to order. 2, very excellent.

ಫರಮಾಯಿಸು h v t. To order, direct, bid

ಫರಾಮೋಷಿ h n Forgetfulness, oversight; negligence.

ಫರಾರಿ h a. Absconded or emigrated 2, (f) a sail

ಫಲ s. n. Fruit; a fruit 2, produce, crop; profit, gain, benefit 3, offspring. 4, recompense, reward 5, one's own learning or merits 6, product, quotient. 7, final liberation 8, a tablet, board, *also* -ಕ. -ಕಾಲ. The fruit-season. -ಕೊಡು. To yield or produce fruit ಫಲವಾಗು. Fruit or gain to be produced -ಹಿಡಿ. To bear fruit. -ದಾನ A present of fruits. -ದಾಯಕ. One who rewards or retributes (*used of God*). -ಪೂರ್ಣ. Full of fruits -ಭರಿತ, -ವತ್ Laden with fruits, fruitful -ಶ್ರುತಿ. Advantage, profit -ಸಿದ್ಧಿ. A prosperous issue.

ಫಲಕ s n A board, plank 2, a slab, tablet 3, a shield.

ಫಲಾನ, ಫಲಾನೆ h. pro. Such a one.

ಫಲಾಫಲ s. n Profit and loss.

ಫಲಾಹಾರ (= ಪಲಹಾರ) s n Feeding on fruits, a slight repast

ಫಲಿತ s. a Bearing fruit ಫಲಿತಾರ್ಥ Result.

ಫಲಿಸು s. v i Fruit to grow, to grow, to bear fruit, become fruitful, to bear good or bad results, *also* ಫಲ-.

ಫಲೋದಯ s. n. Result, recompense, reward

ಫಲ್ಗುನ s n Arjuna

ಫಸಲಿ f. n The official revenue-year.

ಫಸಲು h. n. A crop, harvest.

ಫಾಜಿಲ್ h. n. Excess, surplus or spare, extra

ಫಾಯಿದಾ h n Advantage, profit

ಫಾಯಿಷ್ h a Published, proclaimed, notified.

ಫಾಲ್ಗುನ s. n N of the twelfth lunar month.

ಫಿದಿವಿ h n A servant

ಫಿರಕ h. n. A part, sub-division, a department

ಫಿರಿಯಾದಿ h n A complaint, suit -ದಾರ, A plaintiff, complainant -ಕೊಡು, -ಮಾಡು. To complain, to file a lawsuit

ಫರೋಕ್ತು h n Sale, selling.

ಫುಲ್ಲ s a Expanded, blown, *as* a flower, *also* ಫುಲ್ಲಿತ. n. A full blown flower.

ಫೇಣಾ, ಫೇಣಿ s. n. A kind of sweetmeat like vermicelli

ಫೇನ s. n Foam froth. ಫೇನಿಲ Foamy, frothy the soap plant, *Sapindus detergens.*

ಫೇರಿಸ್ತು h n A list, catalogue, roll

ಫೇಲಿ, ಫೇಲಿಕೆ, ಫೇಲೆ s n. Remnants of food, orts.

ಫೌಜು (= ಪೌಜು, *q. v*) h. n. An army, a body of troops

ಬ

ಬ. The forty-first letter of the alphabet

ಬಕ s n A heron, crane 2, a cheat, rogue. 3, N. of a rakshasa -ಪುಷ್ಪ The tree *Sesbana grandiflora* -ವಿಡಂಬನ. Hypocrisy

ಬಕರೆ, ಬಕ್ಕರೆ 1 k. n A potsherd

ಬಕರೆ 2. h n A goat, *also* ಬಕರಾ.

ಬಕಷಿ (= ಬಕ್ಷಿ) h. n. A general; the head of a department -ಗಿರಿ His employment

ಬಕಾರ s n The letter ಬ

ಬಕಾಸುರ = ಬಕ No 3, *q. v.* 2, a voracious eater.

ಬಕಾಳಭಾತು f. n Rice mixed with curds, butter, and milk

ಬಕುಳ (= ವಕುಲ) s n. The tree *Mimusops elengi*

ಬಕ್ಕ, ಬಕ್ಕಟ a. k. n. Bareness, voidness

ಬಕ್ಕರಿ f. n Bread -ಹಂಚು A platter for baking bread

ಬಕ್ಕುಡಿ, ಬಕ್ಕುಡೆ a. k n Agitation, amazement, alarm, grief

ಬಕ್ಕೆ k n Sweetness, goodness

ಬಕ್ಷಿ = ಬಕಷಿ, *q v*

ಬಕ್ಷೀಸು h n A present, gift.

ಬಖೇಡಿ h n Contention, a troublesome busine

ಬಗಬಗ k. n. Blazing, crackling of flames. -ನೆ ಉರಿ To blaze with a crackling noise, to burn *as* the eyes, *etc*

ಬಗಚು a. k. v. i To open the legs, to straddle.

ಬಗಡೆ f n Rice roughly cleaned 2, a species of pulse -ಯಕ್ಕಿ An inferior kind of rice

ಬಗರ h *prep* Without -ಬತ್ತಿ, -ಬದಲಿ. -ರಜಾ, -ಹುಕುಂ, *etc* Without—

ಬಗರಗೆ a k. n A temporary well 2, a kind of vessel.

ಬಗರಿ (= ಬೊಗರಿ, *q v*) f n A boy's spinning top

ಬಗರು k. v t To scratch with the nails or claws

ಬಗಲ h n. An Arab boat

ಬಗಲು h n The armpit, a side -ಚೀಲ A bag that is put over the shoulder

ಬಗಸಿಗೆ, ಬಗಸೆ k n The palms of the hands joined so as to form a cup.

ಬಗಳು = ಬಗುಳು, *q v*

ಬಗಿ k. v. t. To separate, to tear, to scratch 2 to scrape and remove ಬಗಿಸು To cause to scratch or scrape

ಬಗುಳು (= ಬೊಗಳು, *q. v*) k v i. To bark n Barking.

ಬಗೆ 1 k. v. t & i To think, to consider, ... pose

conjecture, to know. *P ps* ಬಗದು, ಬಗೆದು *n* Thought, concern, regard, notion, idea, intention, object, aim, the mind. -ಗುಂದು To get disappointed -ಗೆಡು To be bewildered, confused -ನೋಃ To grieve -ವಡೆ To think, reflect -ಹರಿ One's thought or purpose to proceed without any hindrance.

ಬಗೆ 2 (*cf* ಬಗಿ) k. *n* A division, kind, sort; a class, caste; a manner, mode, way. -ಬಗೆ. *rep* Different or various kinds. -ಹರಿ. To be settled -ಹರಿಸು. To settle.

ಬಗ್ಗ (*tb of* ವ್ಯಾಘ್ರ) *n*. A tiger

ಬಗ್ಗಡ k *n* Sediment, dregs, mud, mire.

ಬಗ್ಗನೆ k *ad* Quickly.

ಬಗ್ಗರಿ k *n* The thorax

ಬಗ್ಗು 1. a. k. *n* The crying, cooing, chirping, *etc*, of birds. ಬಗ್ಗಿಸು. To cry, coo, *etc*

ಬಗ್ಗು 2. k. *v t*. To bend, bow, to become submissive ಬಗ್ಗಿಸು To bend

ಬಗ್ಗೆ, ಬಗ್ಗೆಯ (*fr* ಬಗೆ 1, *n.*) k. *n*. The very thought or purpose *conj* On account of, for, with regard to. concerning.

ಬಂಕ (*tb of* ವಕ್ರ) a. k. *n* N. 2, a bend, a corner. ಬಂಕು To be crooked to bend.

ಬಂಕೆ k *n*. Gum, glue, resin.

ಬಂಗಡಬಳ್ಳಿ k *n* The creeper *Ipomaea biloba*

ಬಂಗಲೆ h. *n*. A bungalow.

ಬಂಗಾರ (=ಭಂಗಾರ *tb of* ಭೃಂಗಾರ) *n* Gold -ಕಾಯಿಮರ The Arnotto tree, *Bixa orellana*. -ದ ಮುಲಾಮು Gilt

ಬಂಗಾಳ s *n* The country Bengal ಬಂಗಾಳಿ A Bengalee ಬಂಗಾಳಿತನ, -ವಿದ್ಯೆ. Trickery.

ಬಂಗಿ 1 (*tb of* ಭಂಗಿ, *q v.*) *n* Appearance, likeness, similarity.

ಬಂಗಿ 2. (*tb of* ಭಂಗೆ) *n*. Hemp, a potion prepared from it. 2, a crazy person, crack

ಬಂಗು f. *n* A disease of the skin.

ಬಚಾವು h. *n*. Protection, deliverance, escape

ಬಚ್ಚ (*tb. of* ವತ್ಸ) *n*. A young one, a boy. -ಕಾಸೆ A cloth for boys

ಬಚ್ಚಲು k. *n* A drain from the bathroom, the bathing room -ಕುಣಿ. The bathroom pit -ಕೋಣೆ, -ಮನೆ. A bathroom.

ಬಚ್ಚಲೆ (ಬಸಲೆ) k *n* Spinage -ಬಳ್ಳಿ A small annual plant, *Portulaca quadrifida*.

ಬಚ್ಚು 1. ಬಚ್ಚಿಡು k *v t* To deposit, to put aside, conceal, hide, cover.

ಬಚ್ಚು 2. k *v i*. To grow lean

ಬಜಂತರಿ h *n* A musical instrument 2, a bajantari-player

ಬಜಾಯಿಸು h. *v. t* To beat, play a musical instrument. 2, to achieve, execute. ಬಜಾವಣೆ A musical performance.

ಬಜಾರ, ಬಜಾರು h. *n*. A market, the business of a market ಬಜಾರಿ Relating to a market; low, disreputable

ಬಜೆ (*tb of* ವಚೆ) *n*. An aromatic water-plant, *Acorus calamus*

ಬಜ್ಜರ. *tb of* ವಜ್ರ, *q v*

ಬಜ್ಜಿ (*tb of* ಭ್ರಜ್ಜಿ) *n*. A čatni made of roasted brinjals, chillis, *etc*

ಬಂಜರು h *n*. Waste land. -ಬೀಳು. To become waste -ಭೂಮಿ. =ಬಂಜರು

ಬಂಜೆ (*tb of* ವಂಧ್ಯೆ) *n* A childless woman 2, barrenness, sterility. -ಆಗು. To become barren, unproductive -ತನ Barrenness

ಬಟ (*tb of* ಭಟ) *n*. A brave warrior. -ತನ Bravery, valour. -ಮಾನ್ಯ. A free land granted to a Brâhmana

ಬಟವೆ f. *n*. A draw-purse

ಬಟಾ (=ಬಟ್ಟ) k *a* Void, empty. -ಬಯಲು. A wide, open plain, emptiness.

ಬಟವಾಡೆ h. *n* Distributing of wages

ಬಟಾಟೆ e. *n* A potato

ಬಟಾಣಿ h *n*. The common pea, *Pisum sativum*

ಬಟುವು (*tb of* ವೃತ್ತ) *n* Roundness, a circle

ಬಟ್ಟ 1. (=ಬಕ್ಕ, ಬಕ್ಕಟ) k. *n.* Bareness, voidness -ತಲೆ. A bald head. -ಬಯಲು = ಬಟಾಬಯಲು -ನೆ. Whirlingly

ಬಟ್ಟ 2 (*tb.* of ವೃತ್ತ) *n* A circle, disk; that is uniform, regular or beautiful. 2, a circular mark on the forehead *a* Round, circular. -ಕುದುರೆ. A chestnut horse -ಗಡಲೆ The round pea. -ಗೆ Roundness -ಗಿವಿ, -ದಲೆ, -ದೆಸೆ, -ಮುತ್ತು, -ಮೊಗ, *etc.* A round— ಬಟ್ಟನ್ನ Round, circular

ಬಟ್ಟ 3 (*tb of* ಭಟ್ಟ) *n.* A learned Brâhmana 2, a pûjâri 3, a panegyrist, bard

ಬಟ್ಟಲು (*tb. of* ವರ್ತುಲ) *n* A bowl, cup, basin, goblet

ಬಟ್ಟೆ 1. k *n* A rupture hernia.

ಬಟ್ಟೆ 2. h *n* A kiln, furnace, a spirit-still -ಇಳಿಸು To distil

ಬಟ್ಟು =ಬಟ್ಟ 2, *q v* 2, a round thing used for weighing

ಬಟ್ಟೆ 1 (*tb of* ವಾಟ) *n* A path, road, way -ಗಾಣು. To see a way -ಗೆಡು To lose the way

ಬಟ್ಟೆ 2 (*tb of* ವಸ್ತ್ರ) *n* Cloth

ಬಟ್ಲು =ಬಟ್ಟಲು, *q v.*

ಬಡ k *n.* Poorness, weakness; miserableness. humbleness. *a* Poor, weak; miserable, humble. *Cpds* -ಕುಟುಂಬ, -ಕೆಲಸ, -ಗಿಡ, -ವನ, -ನಂಟ, -ಪಾಪಿ -ಬಗ್ಗ. -ಮಂದಿ, *etc* -ವ A poor, miserable, weak man, *f* -ಪಳು, -ವೆ -ತನ, -ಸ್ತನ, -ಸ್ತಿಕೆ Thinness; poverty -ಕ, -ಕಲ A thin. feeble male. -ಕಲು. Weakness, thinness

ಬಡಗ. ಬಡಗು k *n* The north. *ad.* In the north.

ಬಡಗಿ (=ಬಡಾಯಿ, ಬಡಿಗ, ಬಡಿಗಿ, *q. v* *tb of* ವರ್ಧಕಿ) *n* A carpenter. -ತನ. Carpentry

ಬಡತ (=ಬಡಿತ) k *n* Beating: a stroke, blow

ಬಡಬಡ f *n* Gabble, prate. -ಮಾತಾಡು. To gabble, prate, babble

ಬಡಬಾಗ್ನಿ, ಬಡಬಾನಲ = ವಡವಾಗ್ನಿ, *q v.*

ಬಡಾಯಿ 1 = ಬಡಗಿ, *q v*

ಬಡಾಯಿ 2 h *n* Greatness vain pomp, bragging -ಕೋರ, -ಗಾರ A braggart -ಸು To become great, to grow, to increase.

ಬಡಿ (=ಬಡೆ) k *v t* To beat, strike, thresh, bang. 2, to sweep away. *n* Beating, a blow. -ಕೆ. Beating, *etc.*, trouble, *as* that of old age -ಗ One who serves up as a meal, one who beats -ದಾಟ Fighting, wrangling. -ದಾಡು. To fight wrangle -ಗಲ್ಲು. A stone-trap -ಮಣೆ A levelling plank -ಹೋರಿ A gelded bull

ಬಡಿಗ, ಬಡಿಗಿ. = ಬಡಗಿ. *q v*

ಬಡಿಗೆ k *n* A stick, staff, cudgel

ಬಡಿತ = ಬಡತ, *q. v*

ಬಡಿವಾರ f *n* Brag, bragging

ಬಡಿಸು k *v. t.* To help at meals serve up or out. 2, to cause to beat, *etc.*

ಬಡೆ 1 = ಬಡಿ, *q v* *P ps* ಬಡದು ಬಡೆದು ಬಡೆದಾಟ = ಬಡಿದಾಟ ಬಡೆದಾಡು = ಬಡಿದಾಡು

ಬಡೆ 2 k *n* A stick, pole.

ಬಡೆ 3 h *a* Great, big -ಸೋಪು Anise-seed.

ಬಡ್ಡ k *n* A blunt, dull fellow.

ಬಡ್ಡಿ (*tb of* ವೃದ್ಧಿ) *n.* Interest on money, usury. -ಏರು, -ಬೆಳೆಯು Interest to increase -ಕೊಡು, -ಗೆ ಕೊಡು. To lend money on interest. -ತೀರಿಸು To pay interest -ಹಿಡಿಯು. To charge interest.

ಬಡ್ಡು k. *n* Barrenness, vainness, bluntness, dullness. -ಆರಸು -ಕತ್ತಿ, -ಕುದುರೆ, -ಮನುಷ್ಯ, -ಹಸು. A dull, stupid —

ಬಣಗು a k *n.* A wretch, a poor person -ಕವಿ, -ತವಸಿ, -ದೈವ, -ಭಕ್ತ, -ಮಾನವ A poor, wretched— -ತನ Wretchedness.

ಬಣಜಿಗ, ಬಣಿಜಿಗ (*tb of* ವಣಿಜಕ) *n* A merchant a merchant caste -ತನ, [illegible]

ಬಣಾಬೆ, ಬಣಂಬೆ, ಬಣಾವೆ, ಬಣಿವೆ k. n A stack, rick

ಬಂಟ 1. (tb. of ವಂರ) n. A servant -ತನ. Servitude

ಬಂಟ 2. (=ಬಟ tb of ಭಟ) n. A warrior, soldier, a hero 2, the farmer-caste of the Tulu country

ಬಂಡ 1. k. n. Wool.

ಬಂಡ 2 (fr ಬಂಡು) f n A shameless, dishonourable, profligate man -ತನ Shamelessness, profligacy.

ಬಂಡ 3 (=ಷಂಡ) s. a Maimed, defective, impotent n A tailless ox.

ಬಂಡ 4. (tb of ಭಾಂಡ) n Capital, property, wealth

ಬಂಡಣ (tb of ಭಂಡನ) n A battle; war

ಬಂಡವಲ, ಬಂಡವಾಲ, ಬಂಡವಾಳ (tb of ಭಾಂಡ) n. Capital, funds, stock, store, cf. ಬಂಡ 4

ಬಂಡಾಯ, ಬಂಡಾಯಿ f n Quarrelling, revolt.

ಬಂಡಾರ =ಭಂಡಾರ, q v.

ಬಂಡಿ k. n A wheel. 2, a bandy, cart, carriage. -ಯವ, -ಯಾಳು A driver, cartman

ಬಂಡು 1 a. k n Honey 2, the pollen of flowers

ಬಂಡು 2 (=ಬಂಡ 2) f n. Shamelessness, impudence, obscenity, lewdness 2, awkwardness, trouble, disgrace ಬಂಡಾಟ. A disgraceful position; a very awkward or troublesome affair, etc. -ಚಿತ್ರ, -ವದ, -ಬಾಳು, -ಮಾತು. A shameless or obscene—. -ತನ.=ಬಂಡತನ, q. v

ಬಂಡೆ k. n A rock, block or slab of stone

ಬಣ್ಣ (tb of ವರ್ಣ) n Colour, paint -ಎದ್ದು, -ವಿಡು, -ಹಾಕು To dye, paint -ಏರು To become brighter -ಕಟ್ಟು. To fix a colour -ಗಾರ A dyer, a painter. -ಣೆ =ವರ್ಣನೆ, q v. -ಸರ A necklace of gold beads, corals, etc

ಬಣ್ಣಿಸು (tb of ವರ್ಣಿಸು) v t. To colour, paint 2, ...

ಬತನ್ e. n A button, a knob to fasten the dress.

ಬತ್ತ 1 (=ಭತ್ತ) f. n Paddy, rice in the husk -ಭರಣ. Paddy and other articles of food.

ಬತ್ತ 2 h. n Batta, an allowance beyond pay, extra allowance.

ಬತ್ತಲು (fr ಬತ್ತು) k n Dried fruit.

ಬತ್ತಲೆ (=ಬೆತ್ತಲೆ) k n. Bareness, nakedness.

ಬತ್ತಳಿಕೆ (=ಪತ್ತಳಿಕೆ, q v.) f. n A quiver

ಬತ್ತಾಸು h. n A kind of sweetmeat

ಬತ್ತಿ (tb of ವರ್ತಿ) n. A wick, the wick of a lamp, a candle, a cigar. -ಕೊಡು. To cheat -ಸೇದು To smoke a cigar.

ಬತ್ತು k. v i To grow dry, as a stream, to dry up, as water; to grow lean, to fade, wither. n Drying up, etc

ಬತ್ತೇರಿ e. n. A battery.

ಬತ್ಲೆರ್ e n A butler: a servant who has charge of the table.

ಬದ =ಬದುವು, q v

ಬದಕು =ಬದುಕು, q v.

ಬದಗು k n Drudgery. ಬದಗ A servant.

ಬದನಾಮಿ h n. Ignominy, infamy

ಬದನೆ k. n The brinjal or egg-plant, *Solanum melongena*.

ಬದರಿ s n The jujube tree, *Zizyphus jujuba* 2, the cotton plant. -ಕಾಶ್ರಮ N of a hermitage in the Himâlaya

ಬದರಿಕೆ h. n. A convoy, guard on the road.

ಬದಲು h. n. Changing, change, alteration, exchange, retaliation. a. Other ad. Instead of ಬದಲಾಗು To change, be changed. -ಕೊಡು. To give in exchange or as a substitute. -ಮಾಡು. To change, alter -ಮಾತು A word in reply; a contradiction -ಹೇಳು To reply. ಬದಲಾಬದಲಿ, ಬದಲಾವಣೆ Exchange, interchange ಬದಲಾಯಿಸು, ಬದಲಿಸು. To change, to alter, make differ ಬದಲಿ A substitute

..1 .. n. Mud ... ..lu-

ಬದಿ 2 k *n.* The side, flank; nearness, vicinity. ಬದಿಗೆ ಮಾಡು To put to one side. -ಎಲು A rib.

ಬದುಕು (=ಬದ್ಕು) k. *v. i.* To live, be alive, to subsist, to live by; to revive, return to life *n* Leaving, life, livelihood, property, things, goods -ಬಾಳು *dpl.* -ಮಾಡು. To carry on a business. ಬದುಕಿಸು To cause to live or subsist, to save from death, to bring to life

ಬದುವು (=ಬದ) k *n* A raised bank in fields a low ridge.

ಬಡ್ಡ (*tb. of* ಬದ್ಧ, *q. v.*) *a* Firm, true *ad* Firmly, certainly

ಬಡ್ಡಿಕೆ (*tb. of* ಬಂಧಕ) *n* A band, tie 2, comparing anything with a standard *as* weights, *etc.* ಬಡ್ಡಿಸು To compare anything with a standard, to be bound or obstructed.

ಬದ್ದು f. *n* A hole in the ground into which children play marbles

ಬದ್ಧ (=ಬಡ್ಡ) s *a.* Bound, tied, fastened, fettered checked, connected, confined, constructed, firm, true. -ಪ್ರಕೃತಿ A constitution subject to costiveness. -ಮುಷ್ಟಿ Close-fisted, covetous, miserly -ವಿರುದ್ಧ, -ವೈರ Deadly hatred.

ಬಧಿರ s *a* Deaf -ತ್ವ Deafness

ಬನ. *tb. of* ವನ, *q v*

ಬನಪು k. *n* A large timber tree, *Terminalia tomentosa.*

ಬನಾತು h. *n.* Broad-cloth, woollen.

ಬನಾಯಿಸು h. *v t* To make, fabricate. ಬನಾವಣೆ, ಬನಾವು Making, bringing about. 2, mutual agreement

ಬನಿ h *n.* Substance, *as* of grain, milk, *etc*

ಬನಿಯನ್ h *n* A waistcoat with short sleeves

ಬಂತು k (*3rd pers sing neut. past of* ಬರು) *v i* It came.

ಬಂತೆ =ಬೊಂದೆ, *q v.*

ಬಂದ [illegible]
etc [illegible]

security. -ದಮರ The wild mangosteen

ಬಂದಗಿ h *n* Slavery

ಬಂದಣಿಕೆ (*tb of* ವಂದಾಕ) *n* The parasitical plant *Epidendrum tesselatum.*

ಬಂದನೆ *tb of* ಬಂಧನ, *q. v.*

ಬಂದರ h *n.* A port, a port-town; a landing place.

ಬಂದಿ s *n* A captive or prisoner 2, an obstacle, stop; confinement. 3, a tie, an armlet, a neck-ornament of females 4, plunder, booty. -ಯುವ. -ವಾನ A prisoner -ಖಾನೆ A prison.

ಬಂದು (*tb of* ಬಂಧ) *n* Any tie bond, fetter, confinement -ಕಟ್ಟು Well regulated or compact state -ಮಾಡು To close, shut

ಬಂದೂಕು h. *n* A musket, a matchlock

ಬಂದೋಬಸ್ತು, ಬಂದೋಬಸ್ತು h *n* Settlement, well-ordered or firm condition; order, security, safety

ಬಂಧ (=ಬಂದ ಒಂದು) s *n.* Binding, a bond, tie, chain, fetter, imprisonment, check, agreement, a border. -ಕ A binder, hindrance, a pledge -ನ. Binding, fastening, confinement, bondage, imprisonment, a bond, chain fetter. ಬಂಧಿಸು To bind, tie, fetter, confine, to bind on one's self, to connect, to inflict punishment. chastise

ಬಂಧು s *n.* Connection, relationship 2, a kinsman, relation, relative. 3, a friend. -ಜನ. Kinsfolk, relations. -ತೆ, -ತ್ವ Relationship, affinity -ಬಳಗ Kinsfolk.

ಬಂಧುರ s *a.* Uneven, wavy 2, bent, crooked. 3, pleasing, beautiful *n* A goose

ಬಂಧ್ಯ =ವಂಧ್ಯ, *q v.*

ಬನ್ನ (*tb. of* ಭಂಗ, *q v.*) *n* Sufferings, *etc.* -ಬಡಿಸು To cause to suffer discomfiture -ಬಡು To suffer ruin

ಬನ್ನಿ 2 k n A prickly tree, *Acacia ferruginea*

ಬಬ್ಬುಳಿ (*tb of* ಬಬ್ಬೂರ) n The thorny Babool tree, *Acacia arabica*

ಬಭ್ರು s a. Brown. n. A large kind of mungoose. -ವಾಹನ. N. of a son of Arjuna

ಬಂಪು k n A vegetable mucilage used as soap

ಬಂಬಲ್ a k n. A heap, mass, swarm.

ಬಂಬು k. n. A hollow bamboo

ಬಯ್ 1. (= ಬಯ್ಯು) k. n The evening. -ತನಕ. Till evening. -ಸಾರಿ Evening time

ಬಯ್ 2 = ಬಯ್ಯು, q v

ಬಯಕೆ (= ಬಯಿಕೆ) k. n Longing, wish, desire, hope, a desired object 2, a deposit, trust

ಬಯಲು, ಬಯ್ಲು k. n. An open space, field or plain. 2, publicity, conspicuousness, distinction, a vacuity; disappearance, vanity, uselessness ಬಯಲಾಗು, ಬಯಲಿಗೆ ಬರು ಬಯಲಿಗೆ ಬೀಳು To come to light, to become public; to become fruitless -ಪಡಿಸು, ಬಯಲಿಗೆ ಹಾಕು To make public, or show -ಕಡೆ A public privy -ಭೂಮಿ An open plain, a public privy -ಸೀಮೆ An open country, a plain.

ಬಯಸು, ಬಯಿಸು k. v. t To desire, wish, to long for. -ವಿಕೆ. Desiring.

ಬಯಿ k. n. An open spot, a parting. 2, = ಬಯ್ಯು -ತಲೆ. Parting of the hair between the sides of the head

ಬಯಿಕೆ, ಬಯ್ಕೆ. = ಬಯಕೆ, q v

ಬಯ್ಯು (= ಬಯ್ 1) k n The evening, evening-twilight.

ಬಯ್ನು k n The bastard sago tree, *Caryota urens*

ಬಯ್ಯು k. v. t To abuse, revile, to use bad language. ಬಯ್ದಾಟ = ಬಯ್ಯು ಬಯ್ಗುಳು Reviling, abuse, bad language, cursing.

ಬಯ್ರಿಗೆ f. n A kind of gimlet.

ಬಯ್ಲು = ಬಯ. . .

ಬರ 1 (ರ = ಐ) k. n Dryness, dearth, famine, drought, scarcity, hollowness, ruin. -ಗಾಲ. A time of famine. -ಬರು, -ಬೀಳು, -ಏರು. A famine to happen.

ಬರ 2 (*tb of* ವರ) n Limit *ad* Up to, [till.

ಬರ 3 = ಬರದು, ಬರೆದು P p *of* ಬರೆ, *as in* ಬರಕೊಳ್ಳು. -ವಣಿಗೆ. Writing -ಇಕೆ, -ಹ. Writing; writ, scripture, written letters.

ಬರಕತ್ತು h n Success, successfulness; overplus.

ಬರಖಾಸ್ತು h. a. Risen, broken up, *as* an assembly.

ಬರಗು k n A kind of grain, *Paspalum frumentaceum* 2, a kind of hill-grass used for writing pens 3, Indian millet.

ಬರಟಿ (ರ = ಐ) k. n. Dried cow-dung

ಬರಡು (ರ = ಐ) k. n. Bareness, vainness, barrenness, dullness -ಕೆಲಸ. Useless work. ಬರಡ A useless man. ಬರಡೆಮ್ಮೆ A barren buffalo.

ಬರಣಿ f. n A small box, casket, China jar.

ಬರತರಫ h. a Dismissed, discharged. n Dismissal.

ಬರತಿ. *tb of* ಭರ್ತಿ, q v

ಬರದು = ಬರೆದು P. p. *of* ಬರೆ, q. v.

ಬರಲು (ಬಱಲ್) k. n A broom 2, (ರ = ಐ) bareness -ಮಾಡು To make bare, *as* trees.

ಬರವಸ = ಭರವಸ, q v

ಬರಾಬರ್ h a Equal; correct; proper, fit. ಬರಾಬರಿ Equality, evenness.

ಬರಾಯಿಸು h v t To fill or enter (items into a book)

ಬರಾವರ್ದ್ h n A monthly statement of payable amounts. 2, a list of public servants.

ಬರಿ 1. k. n The side flank.

ಬರಿ 2 = ಬರೆ, q v.

ಬರಿ 3. (ರಿ = ಱಿ) k. n. Bareness, nakedness; emptiness; soleness, worthlessness, uselessness -ಕಷ್ಟ. Nothing but trouble -ಕೊಬ್ಬು. Nothing but fat -ಗಂಟು. An empty bundle. -ಗಾಲು. A naked foot ಬರಿದು, ಬರಿದು Empty, vain, idle. -ದು ಮಾಡು. To empty, as a box ಬರಿದೆ. Vainly, for nothing idly -ಕರ್ಮ. Mere sin. -ಗುಲ್ಲು. A useless noise. -ಬಾಯಿ. A person who only speaks but does not act -ಮಾತು Mere words -ಮಾಯೆ Nothing but tricks -ಸುಳ್ಳು A barefaced liar. -ಹೊಟ್ಟೆ An empty stomach.

ಬರಿಸು k. v. t. To cause to come etc 2, to cause to write

ಬರು k v i To come, to arrive. 2, to accrue, fall to one's share, to come into and be in the possession of, to become an acquisition. 3, to be a matter of possibility 4, to be under control. 5, to be becoming, fit, suitable, useful, proper, or advisable, to be allowed 6 to suffice for. P p. ಬಂದು Imp ಬಾ, pl. ಬನ್ನಿ, ಬನ್ನಿರಿ, ಬರ್ರಿ rel part ಬರುವ, ಬರ್ಪ, ಬಪ್ಪ, ಬಹ ಬರಗೊಡು. To allow to come ಬರ ಬರ More and more, in course of time ಬರಬರುತ್ತ In course of time, by and by, etc ಬರಮಾಡು. To make come, to recover, as money, etc ಬರೋಣ Coming, arrival ಬಂದು ಹೋಗು. To come and go. ಬರುತ್ತಾ ಬರುತ್ತಾ = ಬರಬರುತ್ತಾ -ವಿಕೆ, ಬರವು = ಬರೋಣ. Neg. ಬಾರದ, ಬಾರದೆ

ಬರೆ 1. (=ಬರಿ) k. v t. To write, draw P. p ಬರದು, ಬರೆದು

ಬರೆ 2 = ಬರಿ 3, q v. 2, dry soil -ಸೂಲು, -ಸೆರೆ, -ಪೆಟ್ಟಿಗೆ, -ಬಯ್ಯು, -ಮಾತು, -ಹಾಲು A mere —.

ಬರ್ಚಿ h. n A sort of spear.

ಬರ್ದು a k v i To die. n Death 2, increase, greatness, skill. -ಗ A proficient man. -ಗೆ. Death

ಬರ್ಫ h. n Snow; hoar-frost, ice

ಬರ್ಬರ s n A man of low origin, a non ... Bab ...

ಬಬ್ಬೂರ (=ಬಬ್ಬುಲ) s. n The thorny Babool tree.

ಬರ್ಮ (tb of ಬ್ರಹ್ಮ) n Burma

ಬರ್ಲು = ಬರಲು, q. v

ಬರ್ಹಿ s n A peacock, also -ಣ -ಷ್ಠ A species of fragrant grass, Andropogon muricatus, the resin of Pinus longifolia

ಬಲ್ (=ಬಲು, q v.) a. k n. Strength, firmness, greatness Cpds -ಅಡವಿ, -ಎತ್ತು, -ಗತ್ತಲೆ, -ಗಿಚ್ಚು, -ಗೆಯ್ಮೆ, -ಬಂಡಿ, -ಬರ, -ಬಲ, -ಬಿಸಿ, -ಮನೆ, -ಮರ, -ಮರೆ, -ಮುಡಿ, -ಮೊನೆ, -ಸೋನೆ, etc -ಬಂಟ, ಬಲ್ಲಳ, ಬಲ್ಲಾಳ A very valorous man ಬಲ್ಲಾಳ್ತನ. Great valour

ಬಲ 1 k n. The right (not the left), right side Cpds. -ಕಡೆ -ಗಣ್ಣು, -ಗಾಲು, -ಗೆಯ್ಮೆ, -ತೊಡೆ, -ಮಂಕ, -ಪಾಗ.

ಬಲ 2 s n Power, strength, might vigour, force. 2, violence, severity, daring. 3, help, influence 4, bulkiness. 5, forces, troops, an army 6, body, form -ಕರ Strengthening -ಗಾರ A powerful man. -ಗುಂದು To decrease in strength. -ಗೊಳ್ಳು To get strength. -ಕಾಯಿಸು -ಗೊಳಿಸು, -ಪಡಿಸು To strengthen -ದೇವ, -ಭದ್ರ, -ರಾಮ. N of Krishna's elder brother. -ರಾಕ್ಷಸಿ An under-shrub Paeonia odorata. -ವಂತ A powerful, mighty man, force, violence -ಶಾಲಿ Strong, vigorous. -ಹೀನ. Weak, infirm -ಹೀನತೆ, -ಹೀನತ್ವ Weakness, infirmity. ಬಲಾಢ್ಯ. Strong, powerful ಬಲಾತ್ಕಾರ Doing anything by force, force, violence, compulsion. ಬಲಾತ್ಕಾರ ಮಾಡು, ಬಲಾತ್ಕರಿಸು To do by force, act with violence to compel. ಬಲಾಬಲ Strength and weakness, relative, importance and insignificance ಬಲಿಷ್ಠ. Very strong or powerful

ಬಲಿ 1 (cf ಬಲ್) k v. i To increase, grow, to become abundant, strong, big, tight, or full grown v t. To ... ಬಲಿದು

ಬಲಿ 2. s n. Tax tribute. 2, an oblation or religious offering. 3, boiled rice 4, N. of a daitya 5, a soldier 6 a crow -ಇಕ್ಕು, -ಕೊಡು To present a bali, to sacrifice -ಗಲ್ಲು A stone on which a bali is kept -ತಿನ್ನು To eat a bali -ಹಾಕು To offer a bali -ಪೀಠ. An altar

ಬಲು (=ಬಲ್, q. v.) k n Strength, firmness, greatness, etc. Cpds -ಕಲಹ, -ಗುದ್ದು, -ಗೆಲಸ, -ಗೋಪ, -ಜಾಣ, -ತಂತ್ರ, -ದರ್ಪ, -ಸೈನ್ಯ, -ಧನ, -ಸುಡಿ, -ಬೊಬ್ಬೆ, -ಯೋಚನೆ, -ಸಂತೋಷ, -ಹಾನಿ, etc -ಮೆ, -ಹು. Strength, power, vigour, ability, firmness, force, violence, compulsion, also ಬಲ್ಮೆ

ಬಲೆ k n A net. -ಗಾರ A fisherman.

ಬಲ್ಯ=ಬಲ್ಲೆ, q v

ಬಲ್ಲ k n A man who possesses ability, skill or erudition, a man who knows 2, (used as a rel pres p) knowing, etc -ವ, ಬಲ್ಲಾತ A man who knows -ತನ, -ಂದ, -ವಿಕೆ Ability, knowledge good sense ಬಲ್ಲಿದ. A man who is strong, able or clever. ಬಲ್ಲೆ. I know.

ಬಲ್ಲೆ, ಬಲ್ಲೆಯು f. n A spear, lance, javelin

ಬವ s n. The first karana of the day

ಬವಕೆ = ಬಯಕೆ, q v

ಬವಣೆ, ಬವಳಿ (tb of ಭ್ರಮಣಿ) n. Vertigo; confusion

ಬವನಾಸಿ f. n. A mendicant's vessel for receiving alms

ಬವರ f n Battle, war 2, tb of ಭ್ರಮರ. ಬವರಿಗ. A warrior

ಬವರಿ (tb of ಭ್ರಮರಿ) n. Turning, swinging revolving -ಸು To move about.

ಬವರು = ಬಿಸರು, q v.

ಬಸದಿ (=ಬಸ್ತಿ tb. of ವಸತಿ) n. A Jaina temple

ಬಸರಿ k n The waved-leaved fig-tree, *Ficus infectoria.*

ಬಸರು. = ಬಸುರು, q v

ಬಸಲೆ (=ಬಸಳೆ) k. n The plant *Basella cordifolia* 2, ...

ಬಸವ (tb of ವೃಷಭ) n A bull; its stone-image worshipped by the Lingâytas. Basava 2, N of the founder of the Lingâyta sect. 3, a shameless fellow, f. ಬಸವಿ ಬಸವನ (ಕೊಂಬಿನ or ಕೋಡಿನ) ಹುಳ A snail ಬಸವೇಶ್ವರ. The bull on which Śiva rides. its stone-image, the founder of the Lingâyta sect

ಬಸಳೆ (=ಬಸಲೆ) k. n The Malabar nightshade, *Basella alba*

ಬಸಿ k v t To drip, trickle, ooze v t To pour off the water from boiled rice, etc, to strain P. ps ಬಸಿದು, ಬಸ್ತು ಬಸ್ತ ಗಂಜಿ ಬಸ್ತ ಸಾರು. Conjee or broth strained from boiled rice or vegetables.

ಬಸುಮ tb of ಭಸ್ಮ, q v.

ಬಸುರು (=ಬಸರು ರು=ಱು) k n The belly, the womb, pregnancy -ಕಂತ್ತು Diarrhœa ಬಸುರಾಗು To be pregnant. ಬಸುರಿ A pregnant woman

ಬಸೆ (tb of ವಶೆ) n A barren cow 2, (tb of ವಸೆ) fat 3, (k) a stubble

ಬಸ್ತಿ. = ಬಸದಿ, q v

ಬಸ್ತು h n. A bale of goods; a packet of letters

ಬಹ a k Pres rel part. of ಬರು ಬಹುದು (= ಬರುವದು) It will come, etc. it is possible, permitted, it may, etc

ಬಹನೆ h. n. A false plea, pretext

ಬಹಲಿ, ಬಹಲು h. n Establishment in an office -ಬರತರಫ Appointment and dismissal

ಬಹಳ (=ಬಾಳ. tb of ಬಹಲ) a Abundant, copious, much, many n Abundance -ಮಾಡಿ Usually, likely, probably, almost, nearly

ಬಹಾದೂರ್ h n A title of honour given to the nobles of the court or to persons of respectable station

ಬಹಿರ್ s ad Out outside; out-of-doors; except, apart, also ಬಹಿಸ್ ಬಹಿರಂಗ. The outside, publicity, notoriety ಬಹಿರಂಗಕ್ಕೆ ತರು, ಬಹಿರಂಗ ಪಡಿಸು, -ಮಾಡು ... public ... ...

ವಾಗು. To become public -ದೇಶೆ, -ಭೂಮಿ. A public necessary voiding excrement -ಮುಖ. Indifferent to, averse from -ವಾಸ An upper garment ಬಹಿಷ್ಕರಿಸು To expel, to excommunicate. ಬಹಿಷ್ಕಾರ. Expulsion, exclusion (from caste, *etc*), excommunication

ಬಹು s *a*. Much, abundant, many, large, great, mighty -ತರ. More, very numerous, for the greater part, chiefly, frequently, often. -ತೇಕ Many a one, several -ತ್ವ Abundance, plurality, majority -ಧಾನ್ಯ The twelfth year in the cycle of sixty -ನಾಯಕತ್ವ Polyarchy -ಪಾದ The Indian fig-tree -ಭಾಷಣ Talkativeness, garrulity. -ಭಾಷಿ A great talker. -ಮಾನ Respectability dignity, great respect or regard for, honourable reception, a present -ಮೂತ್ರ. Diabetes. -ವಚನ The plural number -ವರ್ಣ. Many coloured -ವಿಧ. Manifold, various -ವ್ರೀಹಿ A relative or adjective compound

ಬಹುದು (*fr.* ಬಹ) k *d v*. It is possible; it is becoming, fit, suitable, or advisable, it is allowed, it may (one may), *e g*. ಓದ-, ಬರ-, ಮಾಡ-, ಹೇಳ-, ಹೋಗ-, *etc*

ಬಹುಲ, ಬಹುಳ s *a*. Abundant, manifold, many; frequent 2, spacious, ample, comprehensive *n* Abundance, frequency, *also* -ತೆ, -ತ್ವ 2, the dark fortnight of a lunar month

ಬಹುಶಃ, ಬಹುಶಾ (*tb. of* ಬಹುಶಸ್) *ad* Much, generally speaking, for the most part

ಬಳಕು = ಬಳುಕು, *q v*

ಬಳಕೆ (= ಬಳಿಕೆ ಳ=ೞ) k *n* Use, custom, practice; exercise, familiarity, familiar intercourse

ಬಳಗ k *n*. A multitude, troop, *etc* 2, the family circle, relations.

ಬಳಚು ... k ... smea...

ಬಳಪ k *n* A whitish pot-stone, *Lapis ollaris*, frequently used (as a substitute for slate pencil, *etc*) in writing

ಬಳಲು (ಳ=ೞ) k *v. i* To become weary, fatigued, to droop fade, to be cast down, distressed 2, to become slack or loose, to dangle slip *n* The state of being loose. ಬಳಲಿಕೆ, ಬಳಲ್ಕೆ. Weariness, fatigue, distress. ಬಳಲಿಸು. To exhaust, weary

ಬಳಸು 1 a. k. *v i*. To go round, to wander about, to turn round, *as* in serving dinner 2, to be wrapped up 3, to surround 4 to be in one's company. *n* Surrounding. 2, circuitousness, *as* of a road 3, one round or turn, *as* of a rope, dôtra, sîre *etc*, a turn in serving up dinner

ಬಳಸು 2 (ಳ=ೞ) k. *v. t* To use, to spend, *as* time, *also* ಬಳಿಸು

ಬಳಿ 1 (ಳ=ೞ) k. *n* A way, road. 2, a place, spot 3, vicinity, nearness, company. 4, way, mode, proper course 5, race, lineage 6, succeeding time *prep* After afterwards further, and. -ಗೆ To, towards near ಬಳಿಯು, ಬಳಿಯಲ್ಲಿ Near, by, beside -ಸಲು To follow -ವಳಿ. Different ways, presents to one's daughter other than those given at the time of marriage

ಬಳಿ 2 (ಳ=ೞ) k *n* A gift, present.

ಬಳಿ 3 (ಳ=ೞ) k *v t*. To sweep wipe off with the hand. 2, to apply, *as* lime, mud, *etc*. to a wall, cow-dung to the floor, ointment to the body, *etc*, to besmear, to anoint *P ps* ಬಳಿದು, ಬಳದು

ಬಳಿಕ k *prep* After, afterwards, further, *also* ಬಳಿಯ

ಬಳಿಕೆ = ಬಳಕೆ, *q. v*.

ಬಳಿದು k *n* Slopeness, gradual ascent.

ಬಳುಕು (= ಬಳಕು) k. *v i* To shake, tremble, to bend

... 1 k. T... rease,

ಬಳೆ 2. (*tb. of* ವಲಯ) *n.* A ring; an armlet, bracelet, arm-ring. 2 a bangle. -ಗಾರ, -ಯವ A bracelet-maker or vendor, *f* -ಗಾತಿ. -ಮಲಾರ A bundle of glass bangles strung on a string. ಬಳೆಯುಪ್ಪು A sort of salt

ಬಳ್ಳ k. *n* A measure of capacity

ಬಳ್ಳಿ (*tb. of* ವಲ್ಲಿ) *n* A creeper, vine. -ಮಾವು. A kind of mango tree. -ಮಿಂಚು Lightning in zigzag

ಬಳ್ಳು k *n* A jackal.

ಬಾ 1. k *Imp sing of* ಬರು Come'

ಬಾ 2 (= ಬಾಯು) k *v i.* To swell, tumefy *P. ps* ಬಾದು, ಬಾತು.

ಬಾಕ (*tb. of* ಭಾಕ್ಷ) *n* A glutton, *also* ಹೊಟ್ಟೆ- -ತನ Gluttony, *f.* ಬಾಕಿ.

ಬಾಕಿ h *n* Remainder, balance; debt *a.* Remaining -ದಾರ One who is in arrears

ಬಾಕು h *n* A dagger. 2, a bend, curve. 3, a bench. -ಡ The husband of a pariah woman.

ಬಾಕುಳ, ಬಾಕುಳಿ k. *n* Excessive desire. 2, a covetous person

ಬಾಗಲ, ಬಾಗಲು = ಬಾಗಿಲು, *q. v*

ಬಾಗವಾನ h. *n.* A gardener, a seller of vegetables and flowers.

ಬಾಗಾಯತಿ, ಬಾಗಾಯತು h *n* Garden-land, a garden

ಬಾಗಿ k. *n* The tree *Calosanthes indica*

ಬಾಗಿನ (*tb of* ವಾಯನ) *n.* A present, gift

ಬಾಗಿಲು (= ಬಾಗಲ, *etc, q v*) k *n* A door, gate door-way. ಬಾಗಿಲವ A doorkeeper, warder -ವಾಡ An up-stair-house over a gate, a door-frame

ಬಾಗು k. *v. i* To bend, bow, incline, stoop *n* A bend, curve, a bow ಬಾಗಿಸು. To cause to bend, *etc.*

ಬಾಗುಳ *tb. of* ವ್ಯಾಕುಲ, *q v.*

ಬಾಗೆ k. *n* The tree *Acacia seeressa.*

ಬಾಂಕಿ h *n.* A kind of bugle.

ಬಾಂಗಿ h *n* A pole with slings, attached to the cr... ages across the shoulder, the package so carried 2, the bangy post.

ಬಾಚಣಿಗೆ k *n.* A comb -ಹಲ್ಲು. The tooth of a comb.

ಬಾಚಿ 1. k *n* A bodice, a coat of mail.

ಬಾಚಿ 2. (*tb of* ವಾಶಿ) *n* An adze

ಬಾಚು 1. k. *v t* To comb. ಬಾಚಿಸು To cause to comb

ಬಾಚು 2. k *v. t* To scrape together with the hand, *etc*, and gather up, *as* sweepings, *etc*, to spoliate.

ಬಾಜಾ (*tb of* ವಾದ್ಯ) *n* Playing upon musical instruments, instrumental music, a musical instrument -ಬಜಂತರಿ Music played upon all instruments ಬಾಜಿಸು To sound, to play a musical instrument

ಬಾಜಾರ, ಬಾಜಾರು (= ಬಜಾರ, *etc, q. v*) h *n.* A bazaar market. ಬಾಜಾರಿ Of market, a prostitute

ಬಾಜು h *n* A side, either side of the body, verge; party -ಆಗು To go aside -ಬಂದ A bracelet.

ಬಾಜೆ. = ಬಾಜಾ, *q. v.*

ಬಾಜೀ h. *a* Miscellaneous. -ಬಾಬು. A miscellaneous head in accounts.

ಬಾಟೆ h *n.* A road.

ಬಾಡಿಗೆ (*tb. of* ಭಾಟಕ) *n* Hire; rent, fare -ಗೆ ಕೊಡು To hire out -ಯವ A man who has hired -ಎತ್ತು, -ಕುದುರೆ, -ಬಂಡಿ, -ಮನೆ, *etc* A hired—.

ಬಾಡು 1 k *v i* To wither, fade, *as* shrubs, *etc.*, to grow dry, *as* wounds; to become weak, to pine away, to be downcast or sad ಬಾಡಿಸು To cause to fade, *etc*, to eat any pungent food to excite appetite

ಬಾಡು 2 k *n* Flesh.

ಬಾಣ s. *n* A shaft, arrow; a rocket 2, an asura -ಎಸೆ, -ಬಿಡು, -ಹೊಡೆ. To shoot an arrow -ಗಾರ A maker of fireworks, an archer

ಬಾಣತಿ, ಬಾಣಂತಿ f. *n.* A lying-in-...

ಬಾಣಲಿ, ಬಾಣಲೆ (*tb of* ಭ್ರಾಷ್ಟ್ರ) *n* A frying pan, *also* ಬಾಳ್ಳಿ.

ಬಾಣಸ (*tb of* ಮಹಾನಸ) *n* A kitchen, cookery ಬಾಣಸಿ, ಬಾಣಸಿಗ. A cook, *f.* -ಗಿತಿ

ಬಾಂಡು e. *n.* A bond. 2, a musical band.

ಬಾತಮಿ h *n.* Intelligence, news. -ದಾರ An intelligencer, correspondent

ಬಾತು. = ಬಾದು *P. p of* ಬಾ *and* ಬಾಯು, *q v.*

ಬಾತು f *n.* A duck, *also* -ಕೋಳಿ.

ಬಾದರಾಯಣ s *n* Vyâsa

ಬಾದಶಹ, ಬಾದಶಾಹ h *n.* A Mohammadan or foreign king

ಬಾದಾಮು, ಬಾದಾಮಿ f *n.* An almond ಬಾದಾಮಿ ಎಣ್ಣೆ Almond-oil

ಬಾಧಿ f. *n* Weight, load 2, a patron

ಬಾದು h *a.* Deducted *n* Deduction.

ಬಾಧ್ಯ (*tb of* ಬಾಂಧವ) *n* A relative, relation 2, a man who has a right to, an heir 3, a right to possession. 4, property, inheritance -ತನ, -ತೆ, -ತ್ವ, -ಸ್ತಿಕೆ A right or claim to possession; heirship. -ಸ್ಥ The rightful owner, an heir

ಬಾಧ = ಬಾಧೆ, *q v* -ಕ An oppressor troubler.

ಬಾಧೆ s. *n.* Pain, suffering, grief, sorrow, annoyance trouble, opposition, hindrance, objection, a contradiction, injury, hurt -ಪಡಿಸು, ಬಾಧಿಸು To oppress, harass, pain torment. trouble, vex. -ಪಡು To suffer distress, *etc*

ಬಾನ a. k *n* The sky 2 a pile of earthen pots or of cowdung-cakes. -ಉ Cloudiness. ಬಾನಿ, ಬಾನೆ A large earthen pot

ಬಾಂದಿ h *n* A female slave

ಬಾಂದು f *n.* A dam, a heap of stones *etc* used as a landmark -ಕಲ್ಲು. A landmark-stone

ಬಾಪು 1. k. *n.* Boiled-rice.

ಬಾಪು 2. h *n.* A father

ಬಾಪುರಿ, ' ~ - ' '

ಬಾಬತು h *n* An article item, a point of view.

ಬಾಬು h *n.* An article, item, *cf* ಬಾಬತು

ಬಾಯಾರು *See s* ಬಾಯಿ.

ಬಾಯಿ 1 k *n* The mouth, the mouth of a vessel, bag, drain, *etc*, the head of a drum 2, the edge of any cutting instrument -ಕಟ್ಟು To shut the mouth; to restrain the appetite -ಕೂಡು The growth of teeth to be complete, as of cattle, to become conformable. -ಗೆ ಕೊಡು To give something for the mouth, *as* betel-nut, *etc* -ಗೆಬರು To come to one's mouth, *as* words in speaking -ಗೆ ಬಂದ ಹಾಗೆ ಬಯ್ಯು. To abuse inconsiderately -ಗೆ ಬೀಳು To fall into the mouth (of people, wild animals, *etc.*) -ಗೆ ಹಾಕು To put into the mouth, to bribe. -ಜೊಲ್ಲು Saliva -ತಪ್ಪು A slip of the tongue. -ತೆರೆ, -ಬಿಚ್ಚು To open the mouth -ಪಾಠ Learning by heart -ಪಾಠವಾಗು To be learned by heart. -ಪಾಠ ಮಾಡಿಕೊಳ್ಳು To learn by heart -ಬಡಕ. One who talks much and foolishly; *f* -ಬಡಕಿ -ಬಡುಕೊಳ್ಳು To beat one's mouth from fear or grief -ಬಿಡು. To open one's mouth, to humble one's self, to speak beg, to divulge *as* a secret, to crack, burst -ಮಾಡು To use abusive language, chide. -ಮಾತು. A mere word, a vain word, an oral tradition -ಯಿಲ್ಲದವ. A dumb man. ಬಾಯಾರ, ಬಾಯಾರೆ Much to one's heart's content, *as in* ಬಾಯಾರ ಮಾತಾಡು ಬಾಯಾರು. To become thirsty ಬಾಯಾರಿಕೆ Thirst. -ಸವಿ. Savouriness. -ಹಾಕು To put the mouth into anything *as* dogs, to utter, speak.

ಬಾಯಿ 2 f *n.* A term of respect for one's mother or an elderly female 2, an affix of respect to names of females

ಬಾಯು (= ಬಾ 2, *q v*) k *v. i.* To swell.

ಬಾರಿ 1 (*tb. of* ಭಾರಿ) *n* Weightiness, importance, greatness, abundance, valuableness

ಬಾರಿ 2 h *n.* A time, turn; a season, year. -ಬಾರಿಗೆ Again and again, repeatedly, frequently

ಬಾರಿ 3 h *n* The slope at the side of a great well for bullocks to run down in drawing up water

ಬಾರಿಸು 1. k *v t.* To cause to tremble, to set in rapid motion

ಬಾರಿಸು 2 (ರಿ=ಱ = ಬಾಜಿಸು) k *v. t* To sound or play a musical instrument

ಬಾರಿಸು 3 (=ವಾರಿಸು) f. *v. t* To ward off, restrain, remove

ಬಾರು 1 k *n* A strap of leather, thong.

ಬಾರು 2. h *n* A charge (of a gun) ಬಾರ ಕೋತು Infantry barracks. ಬಾರಿನವ. A foot-soldier -ಮಾಡು To load a gun

ಬಾರು 3 *tb of* ಭಾರ, *q v* -ಮಾಡು To fill into a book (*as* items)

ಬಾರೋಮೆಟರ್ e. *n.* A barometer, an instrument to measure the weight of the atmosphere

ಬಾರ್ಲಿ e. *n.* Barley

ಬಾಲ s. *a* Young, infantine, newly risen, *as* the sun, waxing, *as* the moon, *etc* 2, childish, ignorant. *n* A child, infant, a boy 2, the young of an animal 3, a colt, foal 4, a tail. 5, the cuscus grass. -ಕೇಲಿ. Children's play -ಗೋಪಾಲ. Krishna -ಗ್ರಹ Convulsions of children -ಚಂದ್ರ The waxing moon -ಚಿಕ್ಕಿ A comet. -ತನ, -ತ್ವ Childhood, boyhood -ಬೋಧು The Dêvanâgari character -ಬೋಧೆ, -ಬೋಧನೆ, ಬಾಲೋಪದೇಶ. Instruction for the young, catechism. -ಭಾಷೆ Children's language -ಮೆಣಸು. Cubeb, *Piper cubeba* -ರಕ್ಷೆ A preservative or charm for children -ಲೀಲೆ Juvenile pastime. -ಶಯ್ಯೆ A cradle -ಶಿಕ್ಷೆ Punishment, or instruction of children -ಹತ್ಯೆ Infanticide.

ಬಾಲಕ s. *a* Young. *n.* A child, infant, a boy, *f* ಬಾಲಕಿ.

ಬಾಲಿಕೆ, ಬಾಲೆ s. *n* A girl

ಬಾಲ್ಯ, ಬಾಲ್ಯಾವಸ್ಥೆ s *n.* Childhood, infancy youth

ಬಾವ ((*tb. of* ಭಾಮ) *n* A sister's husband -ನಂಟ The relative, *as* a sister's husband. ಬಾವಮೈದುನ A wife's or husband's brother

ಬಾವಟೆ. = ಬಾವುಟೆ, *q v.*

ಬಾವನ್ನ a. k *n* Sandalwood 2 (h.) fifty-two.

ಬಾವಲಿ 1 k *n.* A bat, the flying fox.

ಬಾವಲಿ 2. f *n* A gold ornament worn on the tip of the ear 2, a doll

ಬಾವಳಿಸು (*tb. of* ವ್ಯಾಕುಲಿಸು) *v i.* To be confused, bewildered

ಬಾವಿ (*tb of* ವಾಪಿ) *n* A well.

ಬಾವು k *n* A swelling, abscess

ಬಾವುಗ k. *n.* A male cat.

ಬಾವುಟ (= ಬಾವಟೆ) h. *n* A flag.

ಬಾವುಲಿ. = ಬಾವಲಿ, *q. v*

ಬಾಷ್ಪ s *n* Tears, *also* -ಜಲ

ಬಾಸಣೆ a. k. *n* Covering. -ಸು. To cover

ಬಾಸಿಗ f *n* A chaplet of flowers, an ornament of pith worn on the forehead of the bridegroom

ಬಾಸು h *n* Stench.

ಬಾಸುಂಡೆ, ಬಾಸುಳ k. *n.* A wale or mark caused by a blow or stroke

ಬಾಸೆ (*tb. of* ಭಾಷೆ *q v.*) *n* Speech, a promise, an oath -ಕೊಡು. To promise, swear -ಗಳ್ಳ -ಗೆಡುಕ, -ಯಿಲ್ಲದ. A promise-breaker -ವಂತ Faithful, one who keeps a promise

ಬಾಹ. *Pres rel. part of* ಬರು, *q v*

ಬಾಹಿರ (*fr.* ಬಹಿರ) s *a* Outer, external; excluded from, devoid of *n* A foreigner, an outcast; *f.* -ಗಿತ್ತಿ

ಬಾಹು s. *n* The arm; the upper arm. -ಜ A Kshatriya -ಪುರಿ, ಬಾಪುರಿ A bracelet -ಮೂಲ. The armpit -ಯು.

ದ್ಧ A close fight, wrestling -ರಕ್ಷೆ. An armour

ಬಾಹುಲ್ಯ s n. Abundance, plenty

ಬಾಹ್ಯ s a Outer, external; cf. ಬಹಿರ n An outcast

ಬಾಳ (tb of ಬಾಲ) n A boy. 2, the cuscus-grass 3, (tb. of ಫಾಲ) the forehead

ಬಾಳ. = ಬಹಳ, q. v.

ಬಾಳಕ (ಳ = ಬಿ) = ಬಾಳುಕ, q v

ಬಾಳಬಂದು. tb of ಬಾಲಬಂಧು.

ಬಾಳು 1 k. n A sword, knife

ಬಾಳು 2 (ಳು = ಬು) k. v. i. To live, to be alive, to subsist, to live by, to live happily, to be preserved, as fruit, etc. 2, to be worth, sell for. n Living, life, livelihood, property P p ಬಾಳಿ, ಬಾಳ್ದು ಬಾಳಿಕೆ, ಬಾಳುವಿಕೆ, ಬಾಳ್ಕೆ, ಬಾಳ್ವನ, ಬಾಳ್ತೆ, ಬಾಳ್ವಿಕೆ, ಬಾಳ್ವೆ. Living, livelihood, profession, household

ಬಾಳುಕ (ಳು = ಬು) k n Sliced vegetables dried and fried

ಬಾಳೆ 1. k. n. The plantain or Banana, the plantain tree. -ಕಾಯಿ. An unripe plantain. -ಗೊನೆ A bunch of plantains -ತೋಟ A plantain garden -ಹಣ್ಣು A ripe plantain

ಬಾಳೆ 2. a. k n. A sea-fish.

ಬಿಕ tb. of ಭಿಕ್ಷು, q v -ನಾಸಿ An avaricious person

ಬಿಕರಿ (tb of ವಿಕ್ರಯ) n Selling, sale. -ದಾರ A seller, vendor.

ಬಿಕನ tb of ಭಿಕ್ಷೆ, q v.

ಬಿಕಾರಿ h n A beggar poor person -ತನ Poverty, wretchedness

ಬಿಕ್ಕಟ್ಟು. = ಇಕ್ಕಟ್ಟು, q v.

ಬಿಕ್ಕಲು. = ಬಿಕ್ಕು, q. v ಬಿಕ್ಕಲ. A stammerer, stutterer -ಮಾತು A faltering word.

ಬಿಕ್ಕಳಿಕೆ k n. Hiccough

ಬಿಕ್ಕು k. v i To sigh, pant; to sob in crying, to hiccough, to falter, stammer stutter n Sobbing, stammering

ಬಿಕ್ಕಳಿ k n. Throwing up, vomiting. -ಸು. To throw up, vomit.

ಬಿಕ್ಕೆ 1 k. n N. of a small forest tree with eatable fruit, Gardenia gummifera.

ಬಿಕ್ಕೆ 2. tb of ಭಿಕ್ಷೆ, q v

ಬಿಗಡಾಯಿಸು f. v i To be out of order, as one's health, to disagree, as the mind ಬಿಗಡಾವು Disagreement.

ಬಿಗಿ k v. t To bind, fasten, to tighten, to compress, to restrain, as desire; to amass firmly v. i To be tight, stiff or full. 2. to become proud n. Tightness tension, firmness, well-ordered condition. 2, a girth for horses. 3, pride -ಯಾಗು. To become tight -ಯೊಳಗೆ ಇಡು To keep under control. -ಮಾಡು To tighten, to order, enact, to behave arrogantly. -ತ Tightening, tightness -ಸು To cause to fasten, tighten

ಬಿಗುರ್ a k v i To be afraid; to get amazed n Fear, amazement.

ಬಿಗುವು, ಬಿಗುಹು (= ಬಿಗಿ, q v) k. n Tightness, etc

ಬಿಂಕ (cf. ಬಿಗಿ n) k n Pride, pompousness

ಬಿಂಕು k. n Dishonesty, guile

ಬಿಂಗ ಬಿಂಗು (tb of ಭೃಂಗ) n Talc mica

ಬಿಚಾನ h n. A mattress, mat. ಬಿಚಾಯಿಸು. To spread. as a bed, etc

ಬಿಚ್ಚಗಿಸು. ಬಿಚ್ಚಳಿಸು k v t To extend, spread, amplify.

ಬಿಚ್ಚರಿಕೆ, ಬಿಚ್ಚಳಿಕೆ a. k. n. Expansion, extension, spreading.

ಬಿಚ್ಚು k v t. To loosen, untie, open, undo, as a bundle, etc.; to lay open, as the mind, etc, to solve, to draw, as a sword v i. To become loose or open, as a tie, to be cracked or broken n. Loosening, unfolding ಬಿಚ್ಚಿಸು To cause to loosen, etc. ಬಿಚ್ಚಿ ಹೇಳು. To tell plainly. -ಕತ್ತಿ A ...lled up palmyra-leaf put in the ear-holes of women

ಬಿಜಯ (*tb. of* ವಿಜಯ) *n.* Going, coming; *also* ಬಿಜ. -ಂಗೆಯ್ಯು, -ಮಾಡು. To walk, to go, to come.

ಬಿಜಾಗರಿ f *n.* A jointed hinge, jummers.

ಬಿಜ್ಜಣ, ಬಿಜ್ಜಣಿಗೆ (*tb. of* ವ್ಯಜನ) *n* A fan.

ಬಿಜ್ಜಲ, ಬಿಜ್ಜೆ 1. a k. *n* Greatness

ಬಿಜ್ಜು k *n* A voracious bird, *Putta's paradoxurus* 2, ruin

ಬಿಜ್ಜೆ 2. (*tb of* ವಿದ್ಯೆ) *n* Knowledge, science -ವಳ Ganêśa -ವೆಣ. Sarasvatî

ಬಿಟ್ಟಿ (*tb of* ವಿಷ್ಟಿ) *n* Compulsory and unpaid labour press-service, *also* -ಕೆಲಸ -ಗಂಟು A load carried without hire; that which is worthless, money obtained without labour -ಮಾಡು. To perform bitti -ಯೂಟ. A meal obtained gratis -ಹಿಡಿ To exact forced labour

ಬಿಟ್ಟು. P p *of* ಬಿಡು, *q. v*

ಬಿಡತೆ k *n.* Interval; space; cessation; leisure

ಬಿಡದಿ k. *n.* Lodgings provided for visitors

ಬಿಡಯ 1 = ಬಿಡಿಯ, *q. v*

ಬಿಡಯ 2 k *n* A mass, flock, swarm 2, anger, wrath

ಬಿಡವು = ಬಿಡತೆ, *q v*

ಬಿಡಾರ k *n* A halting place, a dwelling place, lodgings.

ಬಿಡಿ (= ಬಿಡು, *q v*) k. *a.* Loose, separated -ಕಟ್ಟಿಗೆ Loose pieces of wood. -ಬಿಟ್ಟು 1. Looseness, laxity, freedom -ಹೂ. A plucked flower

ಬಿಡಿಕು k. *n.* Separation, a crack

ಬಿಡಿಕೆ k *n* Interval.

ಬಿಡಿತೆ = ಬಿಡತೆ, *q. v.*

ಬಿಡಿಯ (= ಬಿಡಯ, ಬಿಡೆ) f. *n.* Respect, regard, consideration, deference for 2, shame, bashfulness, *also* -ತನ.

ಬಿಡಿಸು k. *v t* To loosen, to cause to leave, to remove, to cast out, to liberate, to [illegible]

etc ಅರಳಿಯನ್ನು-, ಪಾರಿಯನ್ನು-, ದೆವ್ವನ್ನು-, ಹುಚ್ಚು ತಿಳುವಿಕೆಯನ್ನು-, ನಾಚಿಕೆಯನ್ನು-, *etc*

ಬಿಡು k *v t* To let loose to discharge, throw, *as* an arrow, to emit, *as* breath; to let drop, to let on, to let down, *as* a rope, to let hang down, to set to, to quit, leave, to abandon, give up, to leave out, to set aside, to take off, *as* from the price, to quit, *as* a debt, to leave off *as* work, to allow, let; to spare or let live, to let grow, to drive. *as* a horse, *etc*, to send *as* a servant, *etc*, to put forth, *as* leaves, flowers, *etc* *v i* To be loosened; to cease, stop, to halt, to settle, to go away *P. p* ಬಿಟ್ಟು ಬಿಡು, *esp in common language, is often joined to a P p. to lay stress upon its meaning or to express the completion of an action, e g* ಮಾರಿ-, ಹೇಳಿ-, ಹೋಗಿ-, ಮಾಡಿ-, ಹೊಡದು-, ಕೊಟ್ಟು-, ಬಿಟ್ಟ-, *etc* *n* (= ಬಿಡಿ) Loosening, looseness, freedom *etc* -ಗಡೆ Release, freedom, liberty. -ಗಂಡಿ A flood-gate. -ಗೊಳು To scatter about -ತಲೆ, -ದಲೆ A head of dishevelled hair. -ಬಾಯಿ. An open mouth

ಬಿಡುಕು = ಬಿಡಿಕು, *q v.*

ಬಿಡುವು, ಬಿಡುವಿಕೆ. ಬಿಡುಹು k. *n* Leaving, giving up, *etc*

ಬಿಡೆ = ಬಿಡಯ, ಬಿಡಿಯ, *q. v*

ಬಿಣ್ಪು a k *n* Largeness, stoutness, hugeness, gravity. 2, a metrically long syllable

ಬಿತ್ತನೆ, ಬಿತ್ತಿಗೆ k. *n* Sowing seeds.

ಬಿತ್ತರ. *tb of* ವಿಸ್ತಾರ, *q. v* ಬಿತ್ತರಿಸು. = ವಿಸ್ತರಿಸು. *q v*

ಬಿತ್ತರಿಗೆ f *n.* A throne

ಬಿತ್ತಿ. *tb of* ಭಿತ್ತಿ 2, support.

ಬಿತ್ತು 1. k. *v. t* To put seeds, sow. *n.* Seed, a seed ಬಿತ್ತಿಸು. To cause to sow

ಬಿತ್ತು 2. *Third p sing of the imp of* [illegible]

ಬಿತ್ತೆಗ f. n A clever, well-educated and polite man

ಬಿದರು (=ಬಿದಿರು) k. n The bamboo, *Bambusa arundinacea*. -ಅಕ್ಕಿ, ಬಿದರಕ್ಕಿ. Bamboo seed. -ತಟ್ಟಿ A bamboo-screen.

ಬಿದಿಗೆ (*tb of* ದ್ವಿತೀಯ) n A crescent new moon, the second day of a lunar fortnight.

ಬಿದಿರು 1 a. k v. t. To scatter about, to open, *as* the mouth, to unfold, *as* the wings, to loosen, untie, to throw about v. i To be spread about.

ಬಿದಿರು 2 ಬಿದುರು = ಬಿದರು, q. v. -ಗೆಣ್ಣು. A bamboo knot -ಮೆಳೆ A bamboo bush -ಮೊಳೆ A bamboo shoot.

ಬಿದ್ದಣ, ಬಿದ್ದನ a. k n. An invitation to dinner; a banquet, a feasting.

ಬಿದ್ದನ a k n A guest 2, a relative

ಬಿದ್ದು P p. of ಬೀಳು, q v

ಬಿನುಗು k n A low, base, mean person -ನುಡಿ Whispering words.

ಬಿಂದಿಗೆ f n A metal water-vessel.

ಬಿಂದು s n. A drop 2, a dot, mark 3, a cypher or dot

ಬಿನ್ನ 1 = ಬಿನ್ನಹ, q. v -ಮಾಡು To invite (for dinner) -ವತ್ತಳೆ. A petition.

ಬಿನ್ನ 2 *tb of* ಭಿನ್ನ, q v

ಬಿನ್ನಗೆ. ಬಿನ್ನನೆ k. ad Silently.

ಬಿನ್ನಣ = ಬಿನ್ನಾಣ. q. v ಬಿನ್ನಣಿ A learned man, a proficient.

ಬಿನ್ನಹ, ಬಿನ್ನಪ (*tb of* ವಿಜ್ಞಾಪನ) n Respectful petition -ಮಾಡು, ಬಿನ್ನಯಿಸು ಬಿನ್ನವಿಸು. To make a humble petition.

ಬಿನ್ನಾಣ (*tb of* ವಿಜ್ಞಾನ) n. Knowledge, skill, dexterity; art, device. -ಗಾರ. A clever man; *f.* -ಗಾತಿ, ಬಿನ್ನಾಣಿ

ಬಿಂಬ s. n A disk, ball. 2, a mirror. 3, a reflection, an image. 4. a rainbow 5, the fruit of *Momordica monadelpha* ಬಿಂಬಿಸು. To be reflected

ಬಿಮ್ಮಗೆ. ಬಿಮ್ಮನೆ k ad Firmly, tightly, loudly, powerfully

ಬಿರ P [illegible]

ಬಿರಕು, ಬಿರವು = ಬಿರಿಕು, q v

ಬಿರಡೆ k n. A peg to tighten the strings of musical instruments, a cork

ಬಿರತು, ಬಿರದು P p of ಬಿರಿ q v

ಬಿರನೆ (ರ=ಱ) k. ad Swiftly, quickly

ಬಿರಸು (ರ=ಱ) k n Hardness, roughness, coarseness, harshness, briskness 2, a rocket, cracker *Cpds*. -ಗೂದಲು, -ಬಟ್ಟೆ, -ಬಾಣ, -ಮನುಷ್ಯ, -ಮಾತು, -ಹುಲ್ಲು *etc*

ಬಿರಾಜೆ f n A grain, *as* of gunpowder

ಬಿರಾದಾರಿ h n A band, company, herd

ಬಿರಿ 1. k v. i To burst; to be rent asunder, to split open, cra k. to break away, to burst forth; to expand, open blossom. blow P ps ಬಿರಿತು, ಬಿರಿದು, ಬಿರತು, ಬಿರದು

ಬಿರಿ 2 (ರಿ=ಱಿ) k n Firmness; tightness, *as* of a door. [crack

ಬಿರಿಕು (= ಬಿರಕು) k. n. A cleft, fissure,

ಬಿರಿದು = ಬಿರುದು, q v

ಬಿರಿಸು. = ಬಿರಸು, q v

ಬಿರು (ರು=ಱು) k n. Hardness, roughness; vehemence, swiftness -ಗಾಳಿ A hurricane -ನಡೆ. A brisk walk -ನುಡಿ A harsh word. -ನೋಟ An unkind look -ಮಳೆ A heavy rain -ಬಿಸಿಲು A great heat of the sun

ಬಿರುದು (*tb of* ವಿರುದ) n. Praise 2, a badge of honour 3, distinction, valour ಬಿರುದ. A brave man

ಬಿರುಸು = ಬಿರಸು, q v

ಬಿಲ s n A hole, cavity, a gap, chasm.

ಬಿಲಪಾರ k n The Coromandel ebony-tree, *Diospyros melanoxylon*.

ಬಿಲ್ಕುಲ್ f ad. Never, by no means (*always negat*) -ಮಾಡ ಬೇಡ. Never do it

ಬಿಲ್ಲು k n A bow. ಬಿಲ್ಲವ A bow-man; N of a low caste in Canara, a toddy-drawer -ಗಾರ = ಬಿಲ್ಲವ. ಬಿಲ್ಲೆಸಗೆ. A bow-shot

ಬಿಲೆ h n The breast-plate of a belt, [illegible]

ಬಿಲ್ವ s n A thorny tree, the Bael tree, *Aegle marmelos, also* -ಪತ್ರ.

ಬಿಸದಳ (*tb of* ವಿಸ್ಮಯ) n Surprise, wonder.

ಬಿಸಲು = ಬಿಸಿಲು, *q. v.*

ಬಿಸಾಡು k. v t To throw away P p. ಬಿಸಾಟು

ಬಿಸಿ (= ಬಿಸು 1) k. n. Heat. a Hot *Cpds* -ಕಾಫಿ, -ಚಾ, -ನೀರು, -ನೆತ್ತರು, -ಬೆಲ್ಲ, -ಮಾಂಸ, *etc*

ಬಿಸಿಲು k n The heat and glare of the sun, sunshine -ಕುದುರೆ, -ತೊರೆ The mirage. -ತಪ್ಪರ A screen to keep off the sun.

ಬಿಸು 1 = ಬಿಸಿ, *q v* -ಸುಯ್ಯು. To sigh hotly

ಬಿಸು 2 (= ಬೆಸೆ) k v t To unite firmly, solder. -ಗೆ Soldering, composition.

ಬಿಸುಡು (*cf.* ಬಿಸಾಡು) k. v. t To throw, fling away carelessly or heedlessly, to leave apruptly P. p ಬಿಸುಟು

ಬಿಸ್ಕೀಟು e n Biscuit, a kind of sweet cake

ಬಿಳಗಾರ k n Borax

ಬಿಳಪು = ಬಿಳುಪು, *q v*

ಬಿಳಲು (ಳ = ಬಿ) k. n A pendent root, as that of the banian tree

ಬಿಳಿ, ಬಿಳೆ k n Whiteness a. White, *also* ಬಿಳಿಯ, ಬಿಳೀ. -ಕಾಗದ, -ಗಡ್ಡ, -ಗಂಬಳಿ, -ಗೂದಲು, -ಗೆಣಸು, -ತಾವರೆ, -ಬಣ್ಣ, -ಮೆಣಸು, -ಬೋಳ, *etc* A white— -ಗೆಂಪು Pale red, pink -ಜಾಲಿ *Acacia leucophlaea.* -ದು. That which is white, the colour white, *also* ಬಿಳಪು, ಬಿಳುಪು. -ಮತ್ತಿ The timber tree *Terminalia paniculata.* -ಮಂದಾರ A flower plant, *Bauhinia acuminata*

ಬಿಳವಾರ k. n A large forest tree, *Albizzia odoratissima*

ಬೀ a. k v t. To cease, to fail, to perish. P. p ಬೀತು -ಕಲ್. Ending

ಬೀಗ 1 k n A lock, pad-lock -ದ ಕೈ A key -ದ ಮರ. The tree *Elaeocarpus lanceaefolius* -ಮುದ್ರೆ, A seal upon a (closed) door

ಬೀಗ 2 k n A relative by marriage. -ತನ A relationship by marriage, *f* -ತಿ.

ಬೀಗು a. k. v i To swell 2, to be elated 3, to retreat n. A swelling.

ಬೀಜ s n Seed (of plants, *etc*), seed-corn, grain. 2, source, origin. 3, algebra -ಗಾಣು. To be sown with seed -ವರಿ The amount of seed required for a land -ಕೋಶ. The pericarp of a flower. -ಕೋಶಿ A pod, legume -ಗಣಿತ Algebra -ಪೂರ. The citron. ಬೀಜಾಕ್ಷರ. The principal syllable of a mantra ಬೀಜಾವಾಪ. Sowing seed

ಬೀಟಿ, ಬೀಟೆ 1. k. n The blackwood tree, *Dalbergia latifolia.*

ಬೀಟೆ 2 k n A chink, crack, crevice -ಬೀಳು To crack

ಬೀಡಿ h. n. A small sheroot, cigarette.

ಬೀಡು 1. a. k. n Leave, halting. 2, a halting place, camp. abode, house ಬೀಡಾಗು, -ಗೊಳ್ಳು, -ಬಿಡು. To encamp ಬೀಡಾರ A halting place, a house, lodging. ಬೀಡಿಕೆ Halting, a halting place, a camp

ಬೀಡು 2. k n A waste, uncultivated land. 2, a pile heap -ಬಿಡು To let remain waste ಬೀಡಾಗು, -ಬೀಳು To become waste

ಬೀದಿ (*tb of* ವೀಥಿ) n A street, road -ಜಗಳ A street quarrel. -ವರಿ. To run at one's pleasure, a run *ad libitum*

ಬೀಮು e n. Beam, main timber 2, (f) insurance. -ಪತ್ರ. A policy of insurance.

ಬೀಫು e. n Beef, the flesh of an ox

ಬೀಬಿ h. n. A Mussalman lady. -ಸಾಹೇಬ A lady, a wife.

ಬೀಭತ್ಸ s. a Loathsome, disgusting, hideous, detesting n. Disgust

ಬೀರ (*tb. of* ವೀರ 1, *q. v*) n A hero, *etc*, *f.* ಬೀರಿ 2, N 3, heroism.

ಬೀರು 1 e. n. A bureau. 2, beer.

ಬೀರು 2 (ರು = ಱು) k v. t To fling, throw, *as* a stone, stick, *etc.* 2, to give liberally *n* Flinging. 2, spending profusely

ಬಿಲ್ಲು e *n* A bill, an account, note

ಬೀಸಣಿಗೆ (*fr.* ಬೀಸು) a k *n.* A fan

ಬೀಸಿಗೆ (*tb of* ವಿಂಶತಿ) *a* Twenty

ಬೀಸು k *v t* To swing, whirl, wave; to mill, grind, to cast. *v i* To fan, to blow, *as* the wind *n* Swinging, *etc* ಬೀಸಾಡು To fling, throw. -ವ ಕಲ್ಲು, -ಗಲ್ಲು A millstone.

ಬೀಳು 1. (ಳು = ೞು) k *v i* To fall, to happen; to turn out, to become to slip 2, to go to ruin, to die *P p* ಬಿದ್ದು, *pers n sing.* ಬಿತ್ತು. ಜಾರಿ-. To slip ಉಪಯೋಗಕ್ಕೆ-, ಪ್ರಯೋಜನಕ್ಕೆ-. To be of use ಹೆಸರು. To be named; to lose reputation ಕ್ರಯ-. To cost, to fall in price. ಬಿದ್ದುಕೊಳ್ಳು To lie down ಬಿದ್ದು ಬಿದ್ದು ನಗು. To wallow from laughter. ಬೀಳಗೆಡಹು. To fell ಬೀಳ ಸದೆ, -ಹೊಡೆ To beat down. ಬೀಳಿಸು To cause to fall, to knock down. -ವಿಕೆ. Falling, a fall

ಬೀಳು 2 (ಳು = ೞು = ಬೀಡು 2, *q v*) k *n* A waste, *etc* 2, badness 3 prostration 4, leaving -ಕೆಡವು To leave fallow. -ಭೂಮಿ A waste -ಕೊಡು, ಬೀಳ್ಕೊಡು. To give leave to go -ಕೊಳ್ಳು, ಬೀಳ್ಕೊಳ್ಳು To take leave to go

ಬೀಳಲು, ಬೀಳಿಲು. = ಬಿಳಲು, *q v.*

ಬುಕಣಿ h. *n* Powder

ಬುಕ್ಕ f *n* The heart. 2, a goat, *also* ಬುಕ್ಕೆ 3, = ಬುಕ್ಕಿ.

ಬುಕ್ಕಿ f *n* A fragrant powder, *also* ಬುಕ್ಕಿಟ್ಟು

ಬುಗಡಿ, ಬುಗುಡಿ f *n.* A female's ear-ornament

ಬುಗರಿ (= ಬೊಗರಿ) f. *n* A spinning top 2, (k) the porcher tree, *Hibiscus populneoides*

ಬುಗುಡು k *n* A swelling, protuberance

ಬುಗ್ಗೆ . . .

ಬುಜ. *tb. of* ಭುಜ, *q v.* 2, *tb. of* ಭೂರ್ಜ -ಪತ್ರೆ Birch bark

ಬುಜ್ಜಯಿಸು f *v. t.* To cajole, flatter, persuade

ಬುಟಿ h *n* A flower or other figure worked or painted -ದಾರ Decorated with flowery work

ಬುಟ್ಟಿ, ಬುಟ್ಟೆ k *n* A basket 2, an untrimmed object

ಬುಡ (*tb of* ಬುಧ್ನ) *n* The bottom of anything, the foot, *as* of a tree; the roof *as* of the tongue, *etc* *Cpds* ಮರದ-, ಕಿವಿಯ-, ನಾಲಿಗೆಯ-, ಗಿಡದ-, ಸತ್ಯದ-, ಪ್ರೀತಿಯ-, *etc* -ಕಟ್ಟು. A clan, family

ಬುಡಮೆ, ಬುಡುಮೆ k *n.* A sort of cucumber

ಬುಡುಬುಡಿಕೆ k *n.* A small rattle-drum. 2, untruth -ಯವ A fantastically dressed Mahratta mendicant with a rattle-drum.

ಬುಡ್ಡಿ k. *n* An ink-bottle

ಬುಡ್ಡು k. *n* Roundness, curvedness. ಬುಡ್ಡ A bandy-legged man, *f* ಬುಡ್ಡಿ.

ಬುತ್ತಿ (*tb of* ಭುಕ್ತಿ) *n* Food (*prepared for a journey*), travelling provisions. -ಗಂಟು. A bundle of travelling provisions

ಬುದ್ದಣಿಗೆ, ಬುದ್ದಲಿ f. *n* A skin bottle for oil, ghee, *etc*

ಬುದ್ಧ s *a* Known, understood, wise. *n.* A learned man 2, Buddha, a Buddhist ಬುದ್ಧಾವತಾರ The ninth incarnation of Vishnu

ಬುದ್ಧಿ s. *n* Perception, intelligence, intellect judgment, wisdom, sense; knowledge, opinion. notion view, idea, purpose. *int* (*in accosting*) Well' right' -ಹೇಳು. To advise, instruct exhort -ಪೂರ್ವಕ Purposely -ಬಲ. The power of intellect -ವಂತ, -ವಾನ An intelligent, sensible man, *f* -ವಂತಳು, -ವಂತೆ -ವಂತಿಕೆ = ಬುದ್ಧಿ -ವಿಕಾರ [illegible] of intellect -ಶಾಲಿ An . . . = ಬು . . .

ಬಲ, q v -ಹೀನ Ignorant, foolish, stupid, a stupid man, f -ಹೀನಳು, -ಹೀನೆ ಬುದ್ಧೀಂದ್ರಿಯ. The perceptive organ of sense, as eye, ear, nose, tongue and skin. ಕಾಕ-. Insolent notions

ಬುದ್ಬುದ s. n A bubble

ಬುಧ s. n The planet Mercury. -ವಾರ Wednesday

ಬುಧ್ನ = ಬುಡ q v.

ಬುಧ್ಯಾ s ad Purposely, designedly

ಬುನಗು, ಬುನುಗು f n. The rear

ಬುನಾದಿ h n Foundation, as of a building.

ಬುಂದಿ h n. Fried granules of gram-flour -ಲಡು. Sweetmeat of such granules

ಬುಂದು h. n A coffee-berry, also ಬುನ್ನು

ಬುಭುಕ್ಷೆ s. n Appetite, hunger. ಬುಭುಕ್ಷಿತ. Hungry, needy.

ಬುರಕಿ h n. A veil, a cloth covering

ಬುರಗಲು, ಬುರುಗಲು k n. Parched rice

ಬುರಡೆ, ಬುರುಡೆ (ರ=ಱ) k n A gourd-bottle, calabash, an inkstand, a snuff-box, the skull; dim ಬುರಡಿ. 2, a lie, untruth. -ಮನುಷ್ಯ. A liar -ಮಾತು A lie -ಹೊಡೆ To utter lies.

ಬುರುಗು a k n Foam, scum.

ಬುರುಜು h n A bastion 2, a drawn play at chess

ಬುರುನು k n Roundness. -ಗಾಲು. A round, beautiful heel. -ಮೊಗ A round, handsome face

ಬರುವೆ k n Mud, mire

ಬುರ್ಮ f. n A gimlet, a small borer

ಬುಸಾರ್ಸು h a Nasty, worthless 2, decayed, spoiled -ಮನುಷ್ಯ. A worthless man

ಬುರ್ನಿಸು f n A kind of felt.

ಬುಲಾಕು h. n A jewel worn by women in the centre of their nostrils.

ಬುಲ್ಬುಲ್ h n The Indian nightingale, Pycnonotus.

ಬುಲ್ಲಯಿಸು, ಬುಲ್ಲವಿಸು h v t. To coax, beguile, to fondle v i To be elated. ಬುಲ್ಲವಣೆ. Flattering, coaxing, elation

ಬುಸ f n. Chaff, refuse, rubbish

ಬುಸು k. n. Hissing, snoring -ಗುಟ್ಟು. To puff, hiss

ಬೂಕು e n Book -ಬೈಂಡರ್ The book-binder.

ಬೂಚಿ k. n A worm, insect.

ಬೂಚು f. n. A stopple, a cork.

ಬೂಜು, ಬೂಜೆ (=ಬೂಷ್ಟು) k. n Mould, mildew, mustiness. -ಗಟ್ಟು. Mould to form -ಹಿಡಿ. To be mouldy

ಬೂಟಕ k n Trickery, deceit, a lie, falsehood, also -ತನ, ಬೂಟಾಟ

ಬೂತ tb. of ಭೂತ, q v -ಗನ್ನಡಿ A magnifying glass, microscope

ಬೂತು a k n Obscenity 2, an obscene man. 3, (e) a boot -ಗ. A shameless man.

ಬೂದಿ (tb of ಭೂತಿ) n. Ashes; ash-colour -ಗುಂಬಳ The white gourd. -ಬಡಕ. A man who smears his body with ashes -ಗನಕಸ. An ash-coloured herb, Aerva lanata -ಬಣ್ಣ. Ash-colour -ಬಾಳೆ A kind of plantain -ಹುಣ್ಣಿವೆ The Hôli feast.

ಬೂಪು = ಬೂದಿ, q. v

ಬೂಂದು = ಬುಂದು, q v.

ಬೂಮಿ tb of ಭೂಮಿ, q. v

ಬೂರಗ, ಬೂರುಗ k n. The silk-cotton tree, Bombax.

ಬೂಷ್ಟ = ಬೂಜು, q. v.

ಬೂಸ f. n N for cerial grains, grasses, and esculent culms.

ಬೃಹತ್ s a Great, large, vast -ಕುಕ್ಷಿ. Corpulent ಬೃಹದಾರಣ್ಯ A large forest.

ಬೃಹಸ್ಪತಿ s n The planet Jupiter -ವಾರ Thursday

ಬೆಕ್ಕಸ a k n Astonishment, surprise.

ಬೆಕ್ಕು k n. A cat. Cpds : ಕಾಡು-, ನೀರು-, ಪುಣುಗಿನ-, ಮಂಟ-, etc ಬೆಕ್ಕಿನ ಹೆಜ್ಜೆ A wind-

[illegible]

cat's eye -ಮಾಳಿಗೆ An opening in the mâligĕ for the egress of smoke

ಬೆಗಡು a k n. Amazement, fear -ಗೊಳಿಸು To frighten

ಬೆಂ (ಬೆನ್) k. n The back -ಗಾವಲ Body-guard. -ಗೊಡು. To flinch retreat.

ಬೆಂಕಿ k. n Heat, fire -ಕಡ್ಡಿ. A match -ಪೆಟ್ಟಿಗೆ A match-box -ಬೀಳು Fire to fall upon -ಮಾಡು To make a fire. -ಯಾಗು To become very angry. -ಹಚ್ಚು, -ಹತ್ತಿಸು, -ಹಾಕು To set fire, to kindle -ಹತ್ತು Fire to kindle

ಬೆಚ್ಚಗೆ, ಬೆಚ್ಚನೆ k n Heat, warmth a Hot, warm. ad Warmly -ಮಾಡು. To make warm, to beat soundly, to give a bribe

ಬೆಚ್ಚರ a k n. Haste, speed 2, bewilderment. 3, straying ad. Quickly.

ಬೆಚ್ಚು k. v i To be frightened, scared, to fear. n. Fear, dread, a scare-crow. -ಬೀಳು To be seized with alarm

ಬೆಜ್ಜ (tb of ವೇಧ) n A bore, hole, as in a gem. etc, the eye of a needle, etc

ಬೆಜ್ಜರ (=ಬೆಚ್ಚರ) k n. Fear.

ಬೆಂಚು e n A bench

ಬೆಂಚೆ a. k n. A small pond.

ಬೆಟ್ಟ 1 k n A big hill, mountain -ದ ಕುರುಬ. A class of Kurubas. -ತೊರೆ A mountain-stream -ಬೇಗೆ Wild fire in hills -ಹೆಬ್ಬಾವು A rock-snake

ಬೆಟ್ಟ 2 (=ಬಿಟ್ಟ) k n Firmness, hardness, as of metal -ಬೇಸಗೆ A severe hot season -ಬೆಸಗೆ A firm soldering or union. -ನೆ Harshly, fiercely

ಬೆಟ್ಟಿ (=ಬೆಟ್ಟ 2) k n A rude person a Hard. -ಚಿನ್ನ. Hard, brittle gold -ಬೆಸಳ A kind of crustacean articulate. -ತು That is hard, firm, etc.

ಬೆಟ್ಟು 1 a k. v t To strike forcibly into, to impress, stamp, coin n. A tool for making impressions.

ಬೆಟ್ಟು 2 (=ಬಟ್ಟು) f. n. A finger, toe -ಮ [illegible] cra[illegible]

ಬೆಟ್ಟೆ = ಬೆಟ್ಟ 2 q v ಬೆಟ್ಟಡಿಕೆ. A hard, round areca-nut. -ಚಿನ್ನ, -ಬೆಳ್ಳಿ Hard, brittle gold silver

ಬೆಡಗು, ಬೆಡಂಗು a. k n. Novelty, beauty, grace pleasantness 2, showiness. airs ಬಡಗ. A showy man

ಬೆಣಚೆ, ಬೆಣಚು k n Quartz, white spar, also -ಕಲ್ಲು

ಬೆಣೆ k n A peg, plug, a cork

ಬೆಂಡು k n The white corky wood of the bendu kasa, cork pith ಬೆಂಡಾಗು To become like mere pith, to faint -ಕಸ A tall annual plant, Aeschynomene indica -ಬತ್ತಾಸು A porous kind of sweetmeat so named.

ಬೆಂಡೆ k. n The esculent okra or edible Hibiscus, Hibiscus esculentus. also -ಕಾಯಿ

ಬೆಂಡೇಕು k n A large timber tree, Lagerstrœmia lanceolata.

ಬೆಣ್ಣೆ k. n. Butter -ಗರುಗಗಿಡ A shrubby plant, Sida rhombifolia -ಗಳ್ಳ. Krishna -ಗಾರಿಗೆ A kind of soft cake fried in ghee

ಬೆತ್ತ (tb of ವೇತ್ರ) k. n A cane rattan

ಬೆತ್ತಲೆ = ಬತ್ತಲೆ, q v.

ಬೆದ k. n Heat, also ಬೆದೆ ad Hotly. fiercely -ಬೆದ Very fiercely

ಬೆದಕು k v t To seek, search for, look for 2, to strike with the claws n Search

ಬೆದರು (ರು=ಱು) k. v. i To be agitated, confounded, alarmed, frightened, to fear. n. Alarm, fright 2, a scare-crow, also ಬೆದರಿಕೆ. ಬೆದರಿಸು. To alarm, frighten ಬೆದರಿಸುವಿಕೆ. Frightening.

ಬೆದೆ k. n Sowing, sowing seed, seed 2, heat -ಗಾಲ. Sowing season -ಮಳೆ Rain at the sowing season

ಬೆನ್ k n. The back ಬೆಂತಟ್ಟು To pat one's back, encourage, persuade ಬೆನ್ನಟ್ಟು, ಬೆನ್ನತ್ತು To follow, pursue. ಬೆನ್ನಸ್ಥಿ. The back-bone ಬೆನ್ನೀ. To [illegible]. ಬೆನ್ನೀ [illegible]

ಬೆಂದು *P p of* ಬೇ 1, *q v.*

ಬೆನ್ನು (= ಬೆನ್) k *n.* The back. ಬೆನ್ನಾಗು To become accustomed to carry loads, *as* a bullock, horse, *etc*; the back to get sore, *as* of an ox, horse, *etc* ಬೆನ್ನಾಸರೆ. Support, help. ಬೆನ್ನಿ ಸವನು A younger brother; a follower -ಕೊಡು To flee, retreat -ಬೀಳು. To follow, to take refuge -ಹಂಚು. A ridge tile -ಹತ್ತು To follow pursue. -ಹುರಿ, ಬೆನ್ನೆಲುಬು The spine

ಬೆಪ್ಪ k. *n.* A confused, stupid man -ಳ Alarm, fear

ಬೆಪ್ಪು k. *n* Wandering of mind, confusion

ಬೆಬ್ಬಳ, ಬೆಬ್ಬಳೆ a k *n* Alarm 2, confusion, distress.

ಬೆಮ್ = ಬೆಸ್, *q v* ಬೆಂಬತ್ತು (= ಬೆನ್ನಟ್ಟು) To pursue -ಬಲ (= ಬೆನ್-ಬಲ) Rear-force help, aid -ಬಳಿ. Following, company, association -ಬಳಿಸು To follow -ಭಾಗ The back part of the body, the ridge of a building. -ಬಿಡಿ (-ಹಿಡಿ) To follow. -ಬಿಡು To withdraw

ಬೆಮರು (= ಬೆವರು, *q v.*) k *v i* To perspire. *n.* Sweat. -ವಿಕೆ. Perspiring

ಬೆಮೆ *tb of* ಭ್ರಮೆ, *q v* 2, desire -ಗೊಳ್ಳು To become confused -ಗೊಳಿಸು. To confuse

ಬೆಯಿಸು = ಬೇಯಿಸು, *q v*

ಬೆರಕೆ (= ಬೆರಿಕೆ *fr* ಬೆರೆ 1) k *n* Mingling, mixture, combination 2, touch, contamination

ಬೆರಗು 1 (ರ = ಱ) k. *n.* Amazement, astonishment, alarm 2, confusion of mind ಬೆರಗಾಗು To become amazed

ಬೆರಗು 2 k *n.* Haste, speed. 2, rudeness

ಬೆರಟು, ಬೆರಂಟು k. *v t* To scratch with the nails, claws, *etc*

ಬೆರಲು, ಬೆರಳು k. *n* A finger, a toe, the tip of an elephant's trunk ಬೆರಳಾಡಿಸು To move a finger about -ಗಿಣ್ಣು A finger knuckle.

ಬೆರಸು (= ಬೆರಿಸು) k. *v t* To mix, mingle, join *v. i.* T...

ad. Together with, combined with, with.

ಬೆರಿಕೆ. = ಬೆರಕೆ, *q v* *Cpds* -ಜಾತಿ, -ಮಣ್ಣು, -ಮನುಷ್ಯ, -ಹುಲ್ಲು, *etc*

ಬೆರಿಸು = ಬೆರಸು, *q v*

ಬೆರೆ 1. k. *v. i* To be joined, mingled, or mixed, to associate, *etc* *P ps* ಬೆರೆದು, ಬೆರದು, ಬೆರತು

ಬೆರೆ 2 (ರೆ = ಱೆ) k *v i* To become stiff, *as* from cold, rain, death, *etc.* 2, to be proud or conceited. *P ps* ಬೆರೆದು ಬೆರದು, ಬೆರತು.

ಬೆಲಪತ್ರೆ. *tb of* ಬಿಲ್ವಪತ್ರೆ, *q v*

ಬೆಲೆ k. *n.* Price, cost. -ಕೊಡು. To pay for -ಗಾಣು To be sold for -ತಗ್ಗು. Price to fall -ಬರು Price to fetch. -ಬೀಳು Price to cost, price to fall

ಬೆಲ್ಲ k *n* Coarse, dark sugar, jaggory.

ಬೆಳ್ಳೊಟ್ಟೆ f *n* A shrub with yellow flowers *Mussaenda frondosa*

ಬೆವರು 1 (= ಬೆಮರು) k. *v i.* To perspire, sweat *n* Perspiration, sweat; *also* -ನೀರು. -ಗುಳ್ಳೆ, -ಸಾಲೆ. The prickly heat

ಬೆವರು 2. k *v. t* To take away, *as* rubbish 2, to stir a heap of grain, in sifting

ಬೆವಸಾಯ *tb. of* ವ್ಯವಸಾಯ, *q. v.*

ಬೆಸ (*tb of* ವಿಧ) *n* Making; act of worship, an order, injunction; asking, inquiry. -ಕೈ, -ಗೈ To perform, to worship, to obey -ಗೊಳ್ಳು. To ask, demand, to solicit -ಸು. To order, to declare, to request

ಬೆಸಗೆ (= ಬೆಸಿಗೆ) k *n* Soldering -ಹಾಕು. To solder

ಬೆಸಡ = ಬೆಸ್ತ, *q. v.*

ಬೆಸನ (*tb of* ವಿಧಾನ) *n.* Order, command 2, *tb of* ವ್ಯಸನ, *q v* ಬೆಸಸೀ To order

ಬೆಸಲ್ a. k *n.* Birth, bringing forth ಬೆಸಲಾಗು. To bring forth

ಬೆಸಿ (*tb of* ವಿಷಮ) *a* Odd, not even

...

ಬೆಸೆ 1. k. v. t. To solder, to unite firmly. v. i. To be in use. 2, to be proud. *P. ps.* ಬೆಸೆದು, ಬೆಸದು, ಬೆಸ್ತು.

ಬೆಸೆ 2. k. n. A stroke with a whip, *etc.*, a blow. 2, a bow for dressing cotton.

ಬೆಸ್ತ k. n. A fisherman.

ಬೆಳ್ (*fr.* ಬಿಳಿದು) a. k. n. Whiteness. *Cpds.* -ಗದಿರು, -ಗಾಡು, -ಗೊಡೆ, -ದಿಂಗಳು (ಬೆಳದಿಂಗಳು moonlight), -ತೊನ್ನು (white leprosy), -ನೊರೆ, -ಮಿಂಚು, -ಮೃಗ, -ಮುಗಿಲು, ಬೆಳ್ಳಕ್ಕಿ (the white heron), ಬೆಳ್ಳಾನೆ, ಬೆಳ್ಳುಳ್ಳಿ (garlic), *etc.*

ಬೆಳಕು k. n. Light, a lamp. ಬೆಳಕರೆ. To dawn. -ಬಿಡು. To stand out of the light. -ಮಾಡು. To light. ಬೆಳಕಿಂಡಿ A window.

ಬೆಳಗು k. v. i. To shine, become bright. *v. t.* To cause to shine, to manifest, to kindle; to scour, polish. *n.* Shine, lustre, the dawn. ಬೆಳಗಿಸು To lighten, to cause to scour. ಬೆಳಗನಕ. Till dawn. ಬೆಳಗಂಜಾವ The period of dawn. ಬೆಳಗಾಗು To dawn. ಬೆಳಗಾತ, ಬೆಳಗಾನಾ At dawn. -ಮುಂಜಾನೆ At day-break. -ವಿಕೆ Shining.

ಬೆಳತಿಗೆ, ಬೆಳಂತಿಗೆ k. n. Whiteness, brightness. -ಅಕ್ಕಿ. White rice.

ಬೆಳಲ k. n. The wood-apple tree, *Feronia elephantum.*

ಬೆಳವ k. n. A wild pigeon.

ಬೆಳವಲ, ಬೆಳವಲು = ಬೆಳಲ, *q. v.*

ಬೆಳವಾರ k. n. An outcast, low man.

ಬೆಳಸು (= ಬೆಳಿಸು, ಬೆಳೆಸು) k. v. t. To cause to grow, to raise, *as* a crop, to rear, foster; to increase. *n.* Growth, a crop of corn, *etc.*

ಬೆಳಗ್ಗೆ, ಬೆಳಗ್ಗೆ (*fr.* ಬೆಳಗು) k. *ad.* When it dawns, at dawn.

ಬೆಳಿಸು = ಬೆಳಸು, *q. v.*

ಬೆಳೆ k. v. i. To grow, *as* corn, grass, trees, *etc.*; to increase. v. t. To grow, raise, as a crop. P. ps. ಬೆಳೆದು, ಬೆಳೆದು. n. Growth, a crop of corn, *etc.* 2, seedlings. -ಗೇಡು A failure of crops. -ನೆಡು To plant seedlings. -ಬಿತ್ತು, -ಇಡು To plant, sow. -ಮಾಡು To raise a crop. -ಯುವಿಕೆ Growing, *etc.* ಬೆಳವಣಿಗೆ, ಬೆಳುವಣಿಗೆ, ಬೆಳವಿಗೆ Growing, growth, increase.

ಬೆಳ್ಪು = ಬಿಳುಪು, *q. v.*

ಬೆಳ್ಳಗೆ, ಬೆಳ್ಳನ್ನ, ಬೆಳ್ಳಾನೆ k. a. White.

ಬೆಳ್ಳವಾರ, ಬೆಳ್ಳಾರ k. n. A snare, noose.

ಬೆಳ್ಳಿ k. n. Silver.

ಬೇ 1 (= ಬೇಯು) k. v. i. To be burnt; to be cooked, boiled, to burn with a fever, grief, *etc.* *P. p.* ಬೆಂದು.

ಬೇ 2. k. v. t. To beg with an humble, pitiable voice. *P. p.* ಬೇತು. -ಕರೆ. A crying beggar.

ಬೇ 3 h. *pref.* Without, dis-, un-, *as* -ಅದಬು. Insult. -ಆಬುರು Defamation, dishonour. -ಖಬರ್. Careless, stupid. -ಚಿರಾಕು. Untenanted, desolate, *as* a house. -ನಾಮಿ Nameless, fictitious.

ಬೇಕು (*fr.* ಬೇಡು) k. *3rd pers. sing.* It is wished, desired, requested, it is necessary, it is wanted, it is due, it must, he, she, thou, you, they are desirable, *etc.* ಬೇಕಿಲ್ಲ *for* ಬೇಡ. ಬೇಕಾಗು To be desired, necessary, *etc.* ಬೇಕನ್ನು. To say "it is wished or desired" "it is desirable", *etc.* ನಾನು ಬೇಕೆಂತ (intentionally) ಬಡಿದೆನೋ? ಬೇಕಂತ (purposely) ತಪ ಮಾಡಿದನು.

ಬೇಕೂಬ, ಬೇಖೂಬ h. a. Foolish, silly. *n.* A fool, *see s.* ಬೇ 3.

ಬೇಗ (*tb. of* ವೇಗ) n. Speed. *ad.* Speedily, quickly. -ನೆ Quickly. -ಮಾಡು To hasten.

ಬೇಗಡೆ f. n. Talc mineral, mica, a thin plate of tin covered with some colouring substance.

ಬೇಗಾರಿ h. n. Compulsory labour without wages.

ಬೇಗು (= ಬೇಹು, *q. v.*) k. n. Spying. -ಗಾರ = ಬೇಹುಗಾರ.

ಬೇಗೆ k. n. Fire, heat, wild fire in jungles. -ಬೀಳು, -ಹತ್ತು. Wild fire to break out

ಬೇಂಕು e. n. A bank, place where money is deposited ಬೇಂಕಿನವ. A dealer in money

ಬೇಜಾ h. a. Meaningless, groundless, bad.

ಬೇಜಾರು h. n. Weariness (from fatigue, pain, etc), annoyance.

ಬೇಟೆ (=ಬೇಂಟೆ) k. n. Hunting, the chase 2, game. -ಯಾಡು To hunt. -ಗಾರ A hunter

ಬೇಡ 1 -ರವ k. n. A huntsman, a tribe of forest people living by the chase, f -ತಿ

ಬೇಡ 2. (abbr. of ಬೇಡವದು, neg of ಬೇಡು, contrary of ಬೇಕು) k. def. v. It is not wished, desired requested, it is not desirable, required or necessary, it is not wanted, it is not due, it must not, he, she, you, they (are) not desirable, etc. Hon pl ಬೇಡರಿ ಬೇಡಿ ಬೇಡವೆನ್ನು, ಬೇಡೆನ್ನು To forbid, etc; to refuse etc. ಬೇಡಾಗು To be undesirable, etc

ಬೇಡಿ h n A chain, fetter

ಬೇಡು k. v. t. To wish, to beg, pray, entreat, request -ವಿಕೆ, ಬೇಡಿಕೆ Asking, begging, entreating

ಬೇಂಟೆ = ಬೇಟೆ, q. v.

ಬೇತಾಳ (tb of ವೇತಾಲ) n A ghost, goblin, demon

ಬೇತು h n Plan, scheme, purpose, design

ಬೇನೆ k. n. Pain, sickness, disease -ಬರು Pain or disease to be brought on. -ಬೀಳು. To become sick -ಯವ A sick man. Cpds. ಕಾಲು-, ತಲೆ-, ಹೆರುವ-, ಹೊಟ್ಟೇ-.

ಬೇಪಾರ tb. of ವ್ಯಾಪಾರ, q. v.

ಬೇಫಾಮು h n Heedlessness, negligence, indifference

ಬೇಬಂದು h a Confused n Disorder, etc.

ಬೇಯು. = ಬೇ, etc. P. p. ಬೆಂದು. -ವದು. Boiling. ಬೇಯಿಸು To boil up, to prepare, as food by boiling; to bake, as bread; to pain, afflict

ಬೇರ tb of ವ್ಯಾಪಾರ, q. v. -ಮಾಡು. To traffic

ಬೇರೀಜು m. n. The total assessment of a land, village, etc

ಬೇರು k. n. A root. -ಗ A root seller -ಕೀಳು, ಬೇರಿಂದಿಗೆ ಕೀಳು. To uproot, eradicate -ಗೊಲೆ Utter ruin ಬೇರೂರು To take root, be established, to spring up, originate ಬೇರಿನ ವಲ್ಲಿ Roots used for curry -ಬಿಡು. To begin to root

ಬೇರೆ (ರ=ಱ) k. a. Separate, apart, different, other, else. ad Separately, further. -ಬೇರೆ rep Separate, different, one by one, various --ಇಡು, --ಇರಿಸು To place separately -ಮಾಡು To separate, to change, alter -ಯಾಗು To become separate or changed. ಬೇರೊಂದು Another thing, something else, another. ಬೇರೊಬ್ಬ. Another man, another.

ಬೇರ್ಪಡು (fr. ಬೇರೆ) k. v. i. To be separated. ಬೇರ್ಪಡಿಸು To distinguish, to separate.

ಬೇಲ (= ಬೆಳಲ) k. n. The wood-apple tree.

ಬೇಲಿ k. n. A hedge, fence. -ಕಟ್ಟು, -ನಾಟು, -ಹಾಕು To put a fence

ಬೇವಸ (fr ಬೇ) k. n. Grief, anxiety.

ಬೇವಾರಸು h. a. Without heir or owner, unclaimed.

ಬೇವು k. n. The neem tree or margosa tree, Melia azadirachta

ಬೇಷು h. a. Good, proper, well.

ಬೇಸಗೆ, = ಬೇಸಿಗೆ, q. v.

ಬೇಸತ್ತು P. p. of ಬೇಸರು, q. v.

ಬೇಸರ, ಬೇಸರಿಕೆ, ಬೇಸರು (ರ=ಱ) k. n. Weariness, fatigue, disgust, vexation. v. i. To grow weary or fatigued, to be disgusted. P. p. ಬೇಸತ್ತು -ಗೊಳ್ಳು, -ಪಡು, ಬೇಸರಾಗು To get tired of, feel [illegible]

ಬೇಸಾಯ (*tb. of* ವ್ಯವಸಾಯ, *q v*) *n.* Agriculture -ಮಾಡು, -ಸಾಗಿಸು To cultivate -ಗಾರ A farmer

ಬೇಸಿಗೆ (= ಬೇಸಗೆ, *tb of* ವೈಶಾಖ) k *n* The hot season -ಕಾಲ The hot weather

ಬೇಸು. = ಬೇಯಿಸು, *q. v*

ಬೇಹು (= ಬೇಗು, *q v*) k *n* Spying -ಗಾರ, ಬೇಹಪ, ಬೇಹಿನವ A spy

ಬೇಹುಷಾರು h. *n.* Want of attention or care. 2, indisposition.

ಬೇಳ್, ಬೇಳುವೆ a k *n.* Bewilderment, confusion, madness ಬೇಳಾಗು To grow bewildered.

ಬೇಳಂಬ k *n* Desire, extreme anxiety

ಬೇಳು a. k *v t* To offer into fire, *as* ghee, animals *etc*

ಬೇಳೆ 1 k *n* Split pulse, *as of* ಕಡ್ಲೆ-, ತೊಗರಿ-, ಹೆಸರು-, *etc.* 2, the half of a ಪಾಗ (=)

ಬೇಳೆ 2. k *n.* A common potherb, *Chenopodium album*

ಬೈ. = ಬಯ್ಯು *q v.*

ಬೈಕ (*tb. of* ಭೈಕ್ಷ) *n.* Charity, alms

ಬೈಗಳು = ಬಯ್ಗಳು, *s.* ಬಯ್ಯು, *q. v.*

ಬೈತನಕ k. *ad* Till evening.

ಬೈಬಲು f. *n* The Bible, the name given to the book that contains the Christian sacred Scriptures, Word of God

ಬೈರಾಗಿ (*tb. of* ವೈರಾಗಿ) *n* One of a class of mendicants

ಬೈಲು = ಬಯಲು, *q v.*

ಬೈಸಿಕಲ್ e. *n* A bicycle, two-wheeled veloceped

ಬೈಸಿಕೆ h *n* Sitting down and rising in alternation (as an exercise or punishment at school)

ಬೈಸು = ಬಯಸು *q. v.*

ಬೊಕ್ಕ 1 k *ad* With a turn or bend -ಬೀಳಲು, -ಬೀಳಲು. Headlong, flatwise -- ಬೀಳು To fall headlong.

ಬೊಕ್ಕ 2 (= ಬೊಚ್ಚು 2) f *n.* A toothless man *a* Bare, uncovered. -ಬಾಯಿ. A too

ಬೊಕ್ಕಣ k *n* A pocket in a coat, a betel pouch, horse's gram bag. 2, *tb of* ಭಕ್ಷಣ

ಬೊಕ್ಕಸ h *n* A coffer, treasury (*as* of a king, rich man or temple). -ದ ಮನೆ A treasury. -ದವನು. A treasurer

ಬೊಕ್ಕೆ k. *n* A pimple blister. boil 2, any round small hole made by rats, *etc*

ಬೊಗರಿ (= ಬುಗರಿ) k *n.* A spinning top

ಬೊಗಸೆ (= ಬಗಸ, *q v*) k *n* The palms of the hands joined like a cup

ಬೊಗಳು, ಬೊಗುಳು (= ಬಗುಳು, *q v*) k. *v t* To bark, clamour.

ಬೊಗ್ಗು (= ಬಗ್ಗು, *q v*) k. *v t* To bend. stoop ಬೊಗ್ಗಿ ನೋಡು To stoop down and look ಬೊಗ್ಗಿಸು To cause to bend ಬೊಗ್ಗಿ ಹಾಕು To humble

ಬೊಂಕು k. *v. i. & t.* To lie or speak falsely, deny

ಬೊಚ್ಚು 1 k *a* Wool, fine hair, down.

ಬೊಚ್ಚು 2. = ಬೊಕ್ಕ 2, *q v.*

ಬೊಜ್ಜ (*tb of* ಭೋಜ್ಯ) *n* A feast *etc.* the last Śrâddha ceremony performed for a deceased relative.

ಬೊಜ್ಜು k *n* A pot-belly

ಬೊಟ್ಟು (= ಬೆಟ್ಟು, *q. v*) f. *n* A finger; a toe 2 a small quantity, drop. 3, (*tb of* ವೃತ್ತ) a circular mark (of sandal paste, *etc*) on the forehead.

ಬೊಡ್ಡಿ, ಬೊಡ್ಡೆ = ಬಡ್ಡಿ, *q v*

ಬೊಡ್ಡೆ (*tb of* ಬುಧ್ನ, *q v*) *n* The trunk of a tree

ಬೊಂಡುಳ k *n* An annual herb, *Physalis indica*

ಬೊಂತೆ f *n* A cloth made of quilted rags -ಗಳ್ಳಿ A large leafless shrub. the triangular spurge, *Euphorbia antiquorum.*

ಬೊಬ್ಬಡೆ k *n* Rind, bark.

ಬೊಬ್ಬುಳಿ 1 (*tb of* ಬಬ್ಬರ) *n.* The thorny Babool tree, *Acacia arabica*

ಬೊಬ್ಬೆ k *n.* An outcry, shout, bawl, yell, a great noise; loud sound ಬೊಬ್ಬಾಟ Bawling, *etc* -ಕೊಡು, -ಮಾಡು, -ಹಾಕು, -ಹೊಡೆ, ಬೊಬ್ಬಿಡು To bawl, shout, *etc.*

ಬೊಂಬೆ (=ಗೊಂಬೆ) k *n.* An image, figure, a puppet, doll, an idol. -ಯಾಟ A puppet-show -ಕಟ್ಟು To curse by sorcery

ಬೊಮ್ಮ *tb. of* ಬ್ರಹ್ಮ, *q v*

ಬೊರಲು k *n.* A broom

ಬೊಳ = ಬಳ 3, *q v.*

ಬೋಕಿ k *n* A potsherd.

ಬೋಗ *tb. of* ಭೋಗ, *q v*

ಬೋಗಣಿ. ಬೋಗುಣಿ f. *n* A metal vessel.

ಬೋಗಾರ (*tb of* ವ್ಯೋಕಾರ) *n* A blacksmith. 2, a coppersmith.

ಬೋಡ k *n* A toothless man, *f* ಬೋಡಿ. ಬೋಡು Toothlessness.

ಬೋಣಿ. ಬೋಣಿಗೆ h *n* The first sale of goods at dawn, handsel

ಬೋಂಡಾ f *n.* A fried cake made of horse gram salt, chillies, *etc*

ಬೋದಿಗೆ k *n* The cornice or capital of a column or pillar

ಬೋದು k. *n* Luxuriance in growth, rank fruits (as badanĕ, savutĕ, *etc.*) without substance or taste.

ಬೋದುಗೆ = ಬೋದಿಗೆ, *q v*

ಬೋದೆಹುಲ್ಲು k *n.* The Roussa or ginger grass, *Andropogon martini*

ಬೋಧ. ಬೋಧೆ s *n* Making known, instruction, awakening. 2, understanding, perception, knowledge. -ಕ. Instructing, an instructor, teacher, preacher, indicating, signifying. -ನ, -ನೆ Making known, explaining, instructing, teaching, instruction, admonition. ಕ್ರಿಸ್ತ- Christian teaching ವಿಶ್ವಾಸ-. Dogmatics. ದುರ್-. Bad advice ಸು-. Good advice ಬೋಧಿತ Explained, instructed. ಬೋಧಿಸು To make known, explain, teach, instruct.

ಬೋನ 1. k *n* Boiled rice, food. -ಗಿತಿ A female cook

ಬೋನ 2. f *n* A metal vessel for culinary purposes, *cf* ಬೋಸಿ. [trap

ಬೋನು k. *n.* A trap ಇಲಿ-. A rat-

ಬೋನುಸು e *n* A bonus, an extra dividend to shareholders out of accumulated profits

ಬೋಯಿ h *n* A class of palanquin-bearers and fishermen.

ಬೋಯಿಲರ್ e. *n* Boiler, a vessel in which the steam is generated.

ಬೋರಲ, -ಲು (=ಬೋರ್ಲ) k *ad.* Upside down, topsyturvy -ಬೀಳು. To fall on the face, to be upset -ಹಾಕು To put (*as* a vessel) upside down

ಬೋರೆ 1 k *n.* A hill, hillock, a swelling

ಬೋರೆ 2. (*tb of* ಬದರಿ) *n* The jujube-tree and its fruit 2, chestnut colour. -ಕಾಯಿ An unripe jujube. -ಹಣ್ಣು Its fruit

ಬೋರ್ಲ. = ಬೋರಲ, *q v.*

ಬೋವ = ಬೋಯಿ, *q v.* 2, a foreman. -ತನ Leadership

ಬೋಸರ f. *n* False courtesy, flattery ಬೋಸರಿಸು To flatter, coax

ಬೋಸಿ = ಬೋನ, *q v.*

ಬೋಳ (ಳ = ಱ) k *n.* A man with a bald or shaven head. *a* Bald, shaven, uncovered -ಪತ್ರಿ A roadside plant, *Erigeron asteroides.* -ತಲೆ, -ಮಂಡೆ. A shaven or bald head -ಮಾಳಿಗೆ. The flat roof of a house without a balustrade ಬೋಳಿ. A shaven widow ಬೋಳಿಸು To shave (*esp* the head). ಬೋಳಿಸಿಕೊಳ್ಳು To have one's head shaved. ಬೋಳು A bald, bare, roofless, leafless, treeless state. *Cpds.* -ತಲೆ, -ಬೆಟ್ಟ, -ಮನೆ, -ಮರ, -ಮುಂಡೆ, *etc.*

ಬೋಳಯಿಸು, ಬೋಳಯ್ಸು, ಬೋಳವಿಸು k. *v t.* To coax, caress, fondle, court.

ಬೌದ್ಧ (*fr* ಬೋಧ, ಬುದ್ಧ) s *a* Relating to intellect. *n.* A Buddhist, a Buddha -ಧರ್ಮ. The religion of Buddha. -ಮಾರ್ಗ. The Buddhistic

ಬ್ರಹಸ್ಪತಿ *tb of* ಬೃಹಸ್ಪತಿ, *q v.*

ಬ್ರಹ್ಮ (=ಬೊಮ್ಮ) s *n* Brahma, the first deity of the Hindu triad, the creator. 2, a vedic text. 3, the vedas. 4, religious knowledge 5, liberation from further existence 6, the soul of the universe 7, the supreme soul 8, a Brâhmana. -ಕಲ್ಪ The age of Brahmâ -ಚರ್ಯ Religious studentship, abstinence, chastity -ಚಾರಿ A young Brâhmana student, a bachelor -ಜ್ಞಾನ. Knowledge of the soul of the universe -ಜ್ಞಾನಿ. One who possesses that knowledge. -ತಿ =-ಹತ್ಯ. -ತ್ವ Brahmanhood -ದಾರು. The Indian mulberry tree. *Morus indica*, the tree *Ficus religiosa* -ಪುತ್ರ N of a river, a vegetable poison -ರಂಧ್ರ. An aperture in the crown of the head through which the soul is said to escape at death -ರಾಕ್ಷಸ. A fiend of the Brâhmanas -ಲೋಕ. The heaven of Brahmâ -ವರ್ಚಸ Divine splendour or glory. -ವಿದ್ಯೆ The vêda and vêdânta -ವೀಣೆ. A sort of lute -ವೃಕ್ಷ The tree *Butea frondosa* -ಸಾಯುಜ್ಯ Union with Brahmâ -ಸೂತ್ರ The sacrificial thread, the vêdânta sûtra. -ಸ್ವ Property belonging to Brâhmanas. -ಹತ್ಯ Killing a Brâhmana. ಬ್ರಹ್ಮಾಂಜಲಿ Joining the hollowed hands in token of homage while repeating the vêda ಬ್ರಹ್ಮಾಂಡ. The universe, a great quantity, excess ಬ್ರಹ್ಮಾಂಡಪುರಾಣ. N of a Purâna ಬ್ರಹ್ಮಾಮ್ಲಿಕೆ The monkey-bread tree, *Adansonia digitata* ಬ್ರಹ್ಮಾರ್ಪಣ. Dedicating to Brahmâ *as* ceremonies of a śrâddha. ಬ್ರಹ್ಮಿ The plant *Aloe perfoliata*. ಬ್ರಹ್ಮೇತಿ =ಬ್ರಹ್ಮಹತ್ಯ) ಬ್ರಹ್ಮೇತಿಗಾರ. A killer of a Brâhmana ಬ್ರಹ್ಮೋಪದೇಶ Instruction in mantras *esp.* the gâyatrî

ಬ್ರಾಂದಿ e *n* Brandy.

ಬ್ರಾಹ್ಮ s *a* Brahmanical. *n* A Brâhmana. 2, a form of marriage -ಣ Brahmanical, a Brâhmana or priest, *f* ಬ್ರಾಹ್ಮಣಿ; a portion of the vêda containing the sacrificial ritual with legends and old stories -ಣತ್ವ -ಣಿಕೆ, -ಣ್ಯ Brahmanhood

ಬ್ರಾಹ್ಮಿ s. *n.* The personified energy of Brahmâ. 2, Brahmâ's wife. 3, the moon-plant, *Asclepias acida* -ಮುಹೂರ್ತ (*tb of* ಬ್ರಾಹ್ಮ್ಯಮುಹೂರ್ತ). The hour preceding sun-rise, dawn

ಭ

ಭ The forty-second letter of the alphabet.

ಭಕಾರ s. *n* The letter ಭ

ಭಕುತಿ *tb of* ಭಕ್ತಿ. *q v*

ಭಕ್ತ s *a* Attached to devoted to *n* A follower of, worshipper, votary, *f.* -ಳು, ಭಕ್ತೆ. -ವತ್ಸಲ Kind to worshippers

ಭಕ್ತಿ (=ಭಕುತಿ) s *n* Devotion, devotedness, loyalty, loving faith; love, homage worship -[illegible] A devoted m[illegible] faith -ರಸ. Sense of devotion. -ವಂತ A pious, religious man -ಹೀನ Devoid of devotion or piety, *etc*, a man lacking in devotion, *f* -ಹೀನಳು -ಹೀನೆ. -ಹೀನತೆ Devotionlessness, *etc.*

ಭಕ್ಷ್ಯ s *n* Eating, an eatable, food, drink. -ಕ. An eater, voracious, gluttonous. -ಕಾರ. A baker -ಕಾರಿ A glutton -ಣ Eating, an eatable, *esp* a sweetmeat. ಭಕ್ಷಿಸು To eat, [illegible] ke.

ಭಗ s n The sun 2, fate, good fortune 3, dignity, glory 4, strength 5, effort 6, radiance 7, love. 8, knowledge 9, law, religion 10, final emancipation. -ನ್ದರ A carbuncle -ವತ್ Venerable, a deity -ವತಿ Durgâ, Pârvatî -ವದ್ಗೀತ N of an episode in the Mahâbhârata. -ವಂತ. A god

ಭಗಿನಿ s. n A sister. -ಜ A sister's son

ಭಗೀರಥ s n N of a king who brought down the Ganges

ಭಗೇಂದ್ರ (tb. of ಭಗಂದರ) n A carbuncle

ಭಗ್ನ s a Broken, defeated, destroyed, disheartened, disappointed -ಮನಸು. Discouragement, disappointment -ಮಾನಸ Discouraged, disappointed.

ಭಂಗ s n. Breaking 2, a break 3, fall downfall, ruin 4, defeat, overthrow, distress, trouble 5, disappointment 6, flight. 7, bowing, a bend. 8, a wave 9, falsehood, deceit, fraud -ಪಡಿಸು To ruin, defeat, etc -ಪಡು To be ruined, defeated, troubled, disappointed, etc -ಶ್ಲೇಷ. A kind of pun in rhetoric.

ಭಂಗಾರ tb of ಬಂಗಾರ, q. v.

ಭಂಗಿ s n Breaking, a wave 2, irony, wit, pretext, fraud 3, a way, manner mode -ಸು To break, ruin, destroy

ಭಂಗುರ s a Frail, changeful, variable. 2, crooked n. A bend

ಭಂಗೆ (= ಬಂಗಿ, q v) s n The common hemp plant, *Cannabis sativa*

ಭಜನ, ಭಜನೆ s n Adoring, adoration, worship devotion. 2, dividing (arith) ಭಜಕ A worshipper, votary. ಭಜಿಸು To adore, worship

ಭಂಜಕ s n A breaker, destroyer. ಭಂಜನ Destroying; routing, afflicting ಭಂಜಿಸು. To break, to humiliate

ಭಟ (= ಬಟ) s. n A warrior, soldier a hero

ಭಟ್ಟ (= ಬಟ್ಟ 3) s. n Any learned man, doctor or philosopher. *used also as a* title 2, a l

ಭಂಟಾಕಿ, ಭಂಪಾಕಿ s n. The egg-plant, *Solanum melongena*

ಭಂಡ (= ಬಂಡ 2) s n A jester, buffoon, a mimic. 2, N of a mixed caste ಭಂಡು = ಬಂಡು.

ಭಂಡಾರ (tb of ಭಾಂಡಾಗಾರ, q v) n A store-room, magazine, treasury ಭಂಡಾರಿ A treasurer, storekeeper.

ಭಂಡಿ s n Bengal madder, *Rubia munjista*.

ಭಂಡಿಲ s. a Fortunate, prosperous n Fortune, welfare. 2, a messenger 3, an artizan

ಭದ್ರ s a. Good, well. 2, favourable, gracious 3, pleasant. 4, safe, secure, firm, strong, as a cloth or rope. n. Happiness, welfare, good fortune 2, a bull -ಕಾಲಿ, -ಕಾಳಿ. Pârvatî, Durgâ -ದಾಯಕ The bestower of welfare -ದಾರು. A sort of pine, *Pinus deodora*. -ಪದೆ N. of the 3rd and 4th asterisms -ಮಂಟಪ A nuptial shed -ಮುಸ್ತಕ, -ಮುಸ್ತೆ A kind of sedge, *Cyperus hexastachyus*. -ಶ್ರೀ Sandalwood

ಭದ್ರಾ s. n N of the second, seventh and twelfth days of the lunar fortnight -ಕರಣ The act of shaving ಭದ್ರಾಸನ A splendid seat, a posture in devotion

ಭದ್ರಾಕ್ಷ s. n A kind of seed used as beads.

ಭದ್ರೆ s n The 7th astrological division of the day.

ಭಯ s n Fear, alarm, dread, dismay. fright, terror, danger, risk. -ಆಸ್ಪದ Reason for fear -ಗೊಳ್ಳು To become afraid, alarmed -ಗೂಳ್ಳಿಸು -ಪಡಿಸು To frighten -ಂಕರ Fear-causing; fearful terrible -ತಟ್ಟು Fear to seize -ಪಡು. To fear, to be alarmed. -ಭಕ್ತಿ Fear and devotion -ತ್ರಸ್ತ Trembling for fear. -ದ್ರುತ Fleeing for fear -ಧ್ವನಿ A voice expressing fear. -ಭೀಷ Put to flight in terror [illegible] Confused [illegible]

A man in fear, *f.* -ಸ್ಥೆ, -ಸ್ಥಳು ಭಯಾನಕ Fearful, terrible, fear, terror. ಭಯಾತುರ Alarmed ಭಯಾರ್ತಿ Alarm.

ಭರ s *n.* Bearing, upholding, supporting. 2, a burden, load weight 3, a large quantity, multitude, plenty 4, desire 5, exacerbation 6, haste -ಕ್ಕೆ ಬೀಳು To be irritated. -ಭರನೆ. *rep* In great haste. -ಣ. Bearing, supporting, maintaining, wages, hire, filling, filling stuff

ಭರಣಿ = ಬರಣಿ, *q v* 2, the second nakshatra.

ಭರತ s *n* An actor, dancer 2 N of a muni 3, N. of one of Daśaratha's sons and Râma's younger brother 4, N of a monarch 5, the flux of the ocean, flow -ಇಳಿತ Flow and ebb. -ಖಂಡ, -ವರ್ಷ India

ಭರದ್ವಾಜ s. *n* A sky-lark 2, N of a rishi

ಭರವಸ f. *n.* Confidence, trust. 2, quickness. -ಇಡು. To believe, trust.

ಭರಿತ s *a* Full, filled, full of

ಭರ್ತ, ಭರ್ತಾರ *tb of* ಭರ್ತೃ, *q v*

ಭರ್ತಿ (= ಭರತಿ) s *n* Loaded state, *as of* a cart, vessel, bag, *etc.* 2, the flux of the ocean

ಭರ್ತೃ (= ಭರ್ತ, ಭರ್ತಾರ) s *n.* A cherisher, supporter, a master, a husband, a chief. -ದಾರಕ. A crown prince, *f* -ದಾರಿಕೆ.

ಭಲ, ಭಲರೆ, ಭಲಾ f. *int.* Fine! well done! bravo!

ಭಲ್ಲ s *n* A kind of pointed arrow.

ಭಲ್ಲಾತಕ s. *n.* The marking-nut tree, *Semecarpus anacardium*

ಭಲ್ಲುಕ, ಭಲ್ಲೂಕ s *n* A bear.

ಭವ s *n* Becoming, existing. existence 2, birth, origin 3, transmigration 4, life. 5, the world 6, welfare. -ದೂರ Far from the world and its misery -ಬಂಧನ. -ಪಾಶ Fetters of wo

The ocean of transmigration. ಭವಾಂತರ Another existence

ಭವತ್ s. *n* Present time. 2, you, your honour ಭವತಿ Your ladyship, lady. ಭವದೀಯ. Your, your honour's

ಭವನ s *n* Existing, production, birth 2, a house dwelling, mansion 3, a field.

ಭವಾನಿ s. *n* Pârvati, Śiva's wife

ಭವಿ s *n* Living: a living being 2, a worldling. -ಸು To produce.

ಭವಿಷ್ಯ s *a.* To be about to become, future, imminent -ತ್ Future, futurity, future time, the future tense -ಕಾಲ Future time, the future tense.

ಭಸ್ಮ (= ಬಸುಮ) s. *n* Ashes, any metallic oxide -ಪುಟ. Application to fire in order to make ashes ಭಸ್ಮಾಸುರ N. of a demon.

ಭಳರೆ, ಭಳಿರೆ = ಭಲ, *q v*

ಭಾಗ s. *n* A fraction, a part, portion, share, a division 2, lot luck 3 a place, region ಮುಂ- The front part ಹಿಂ- The hind part ಭಾಗಾಕಾರ, ಭಾಗಹಾರ Division (*arith.*)

ಭಾಗವತ (*fr.* ಭಗವತ್) s. *n* A worshipper of Vishnu or Krishna 2 N of a Purâna *also* -ಪುರಾಣ 3, the manager of a dramatic performance

ಭಾಗಿ s *a* Having a share, *n* A partner; a co-heir 2, a possessor. ಭಾಗಿಸು To divide (*esp arith*)

ಭಾಗೀರಥಿ s *n.* The Ganges

ಭಾಗ್ಯ s *n* Lot, luck fate, fortune 2, good fortune, welfare, riches. -ಲಕ್ಷ್ಮಿ Goddess of good fortune, welfare, riches -ವಂತ, -ಶಾಲಿ A lucky, fortunate or rich man -ಹೀನ A luckless or poor man ದೌರ್- Ill-luck ಸೌ- Good luck

ಭಾಜಕ s. *n* A divisor (*arith*) ಭಾಜನ Dividing, division, a vessel. a receptacle: a recipient a fit, clever (*arith*)

ಭಾಣ s. n. A kind of dramatic entertainment

ಭಾಂಡ s. n. Any vessel, pot, pan, cup, plate, dish, *etc* 2, any implement, instrument 3, horse trappings, harness 4, goods, wares 5, mimicry, buffoonery -ಗಾರ (= ಭಂಡಾರ, *q v.*). A store-room store-house; a treasury.

ಭಾದ್ರ (*fr.* ಭದ್ರ) s n The month Bhâdra (August-September), *also* -ಪದ.

ಭಾನು s. n. Light. 2, the sun -ಜ. The planet Saturn -ಭಾಮೆ. The sun's wife -ಮತ್ Luminous, splendid -ಮತಿ Duryôdhana's wife -ವಾರ Sunday

ಭಾಪು h *int* Hurrah! well done! -ಭಾಪುರೆ *rep*

ಭಾಮ s n Passion, anger. 2, splendour, the sun 3, a sister's husband.

ಭಾಮಿನಿ s. n A passionate woman; a woman -ಷಟ್ಪದಿ N. of a metre.

ಭಾಮೆ s. n A wife; a woman

ಭಾಯಿ h *aff* Person, fellow, man, chap; brother.

ಭಾರ s. n Bearing 2, a burden, load. 3, heaviness, weight 4, gravity, importance, influence. 5, heavy work, labour, toil -ಧರಿಸು, -ಹೊತ್ತುಕೊಳ್ಳು To take up a burden bear the responsibility

ಭಾರತ (*fr* ಭರತ) s. n A descendant of Bharata 2, India 3 N. of the Mahâbhârata in Kannada. -ನಿಘಂಟು. N of a small vocabulary to it. -ವರುಷ India.

ಭಾರತಿ s. n. Sarasvati. 2, one of the styles of dramatic composition 3, a learned man -ಕ An actor

ಭಾರದ್ವಾಜ (*fr* ಭರದ್ವಾಜ) s *a* Coming from Bharadvâj *n.* N of a rishi. 2, a sky-lark

ಭಾರಿ s n Bearing, a bearer, abundance. *a* Heavy -ಕ A porter

ಭಾರ್ಗವ (*fr.* ಭೃಗು) s *a* Coming from Bhrigu *n* ... descendant of ... planet Venus 2, Paraśurâma -ವಾರ Friday

ಭಾರ್ಯೆ, ಭಾರ್ಯಾ s. n. A wife

ಭಾವ 1. (*tb. of* ಭಾವುಕ) *n* A brother-in-law, sister's husband -ಮೈದನ, -ಮೈದುನ A wife's brother

ಭಾವ 2 s. n. Becoming, existence, appearance 2, origin 3, state, condition 4, truth 5, manner of being, nature, innate property, temperament disposition 6, affection feeling, emotion, passion 7, sentiment, idea, thought, supposition, conjecture, intention 8, meaning, sense 9, the soul, heart, mind. 10, behaviour, action 11, an abstract idea 12, the eighth year in the cycle of sixty -ಚೇಷ್ಟೆ Emotion -ಜ, -ಜಾತ Kâma, love -ಜ್ಞ Knowing the heart or aim of others. -ನ, -ನೆ Reverencing, treating with respect, imagining, fancying, supposing, thinking, imagination, fancy, reflection, thought, (*in med.*) saturating any powder with fluid. -ಬೋಧಕ Indicating a feeling or passion -ವಚನ, -ವಾಚಕ An abstract verbal noun. -ಮಾಡು = ಭಾವಿಸು ಭಾವಾರ್ಥ The simple meaning of a word; the obvious purport of a phrase, letter, affair, *etc*

ಭಾವಿ s *a* About to come, future *n.* The future tense, *also* -ಕಾಲ. -ಕ. Full of feeling or sentiment; a prophet -ತ Obtained; manifested, conceived, imagined, thought about, happy, well. -ಸು To conceive, imagine, fancy, to think, consider, to think of, meditate on (*with acc.*, *as* ದೇವರನ್ನು ಭಾವಿಸು)

ಭಾಷಣ s. n Speaking speech, talk

ಭಾಷಾಂತರ s. n A translation -ಮಾಡು, ಭಾಷಾಂತರಿಸು To translate [talk.

ಭಾಷಿ s. n A speaker. -ಸು. To speak,

ಭಾಷೆ (= ಬಾಸೆ) s n Speech language ... dialect 2, ... promise ...

-ಅಳಿ, -ಮೀರು. To break a promise -ಆಡು To speak a language -ಇಡು To swear -ಈ, -ಕೊಡು, -ನುಡಿ To promise -ಕೇಡು, -ಗೇಡು. A promise to be broken -ಮುಟ್ಟಿಸು, -ಸಲಿಸು. To fulfill a promise -ವಂತ. Faithful -ಹಿಡಿ, -ತೊಡು To make a promise

ಭಾಷ್ಯ s. n An exposition, gloss, commentary -ಕಾರ A commentator, expounder

ಭಾಸ s n Light, lustre 2, a vulture 3, a cock -ಮಾನ Shining, appearing, lustre, brightness

ಭಾಸುರ s a Shining, splendid 2, terrible n. Splendour, beauty 2 a hero. -ತರ Uncommonly splendid or beautiful

ಭಾಸ್ವರ s. n. The sun 2, a N

ಭಿಕ್ಷ, ಭಿಕ್ಷೆ s. n Begging. 2, alms 3, wages. 4, service -ಇಕ್ಕು To give alms. -ಬೇಡು. To beg. -ಗಾರ A beggar ಭಿಕ್ಷಾಟನ. Mendicancy ಭಿಕ್ಷಿಸು. To beg alms ಭಿಕ್ಷು A beggar, a religious mendicant. ಭಿಕ್ಷುಕ A male mendicant, *f.* ಭಿಕ್ಷುಕಿ

ಭಿತ್ತಿ s n A bit, fragment, piece 2, a rent, fissure. 3, a wall partition 4, an asylum

ಭಿಂದಿಪಾಲ s. n A short javelin, *also* ಭಿಂಡಿಪಾಲ

ಭಿನ್ನ s a. Broken, split, fractured, torn, rent, disunited, expanded, destroyed 2, separated, distinct, other, different, deprived of. n A fragment, bit. -ಕರ್ತೃ, -ಕರ್ತೃಕ. A causative agent -ಭಾವ Another mind. incongruity of state -ಭಿನ್ನ Various. -ಭೇದ Difference. -ವೃತ್ತ A metrical fault -ಶಬ್ದ A faulty term ಭಿನ್ನಾ- Separate and not separate ಭಿನ್ನಿಸು To break split, to loosen, to alter, change

ಭಿಲ್ಲ s n A wild mountain race

ಭಿಷಜ್, ಭಿಷಜ s n A physician

ಭೀಕರ

ಭೀತ s. a Frightened, alarmed afraid ಭೀತಿ Fear, alarm, apprehension, dread, danger

ಭೀಮ s a Fearful, dreadful. n. Bhîma the second son of Pându, *also* -ಸೇನ 2, a strong man, hero -ನದಿ, -ರಥಿ N. of a river

ಭೀರು s. a. Timid, cowardly, shy -ತ್ವ Timidity, cowardice

ಭೀಷ್ಮ s a Terrible, fearful n Fear, horror 2 the grand-uncle of the Pândavas -ಕ. N of Rukminî's father, Damayanti's father.

ಭುಕ್ತ s a Enjoyed, eaten -ಗೃಹ A dining-room. ಭುಕ್ತಿ Enjoyment, fruition, possession, food, the daily motion of a planet -ಮುಕ್ತಿ. Fruition and final emancipation

ಭುಜ (=ಬುಜ) s n The arm. -ಕೀರ್ತಿ An epaulet-like ornament for the upper arm -ಗ, -ಂಗ A snake -ಗಶಯನ Vishnu -ಬಲ Strength of arm. ಭುಜಾಗ್ರ. The shoulder

ಭುಜಿಸು, ಭುಂಜಿಸು s v t To eat, to enjoy, to suffer, experience

ಭುವನ s n A living creature 2, the world, the earth 3, water 4, the sky -ಮಾತೆ Pârvatî, Lakshmî ಭುವನಸಾಕ್ಷಿ The sun

ಭುವಸ್, ಭುವರ್ s. n The atmosphere, sky ಭುವರ್ಲೋಕ The space between earth and heaven

ಭೂ s n Being 2, the earth 3, land ground, earth, as a substance 4, a country, district -ಕಂಪ, -ಕಂಪನ. An earthquake -ಗತ Destroyed -ಗತ ಮಾಡು. To destroy -ಗೋಲ, -ಗೋಳ The terrestrial globe earth -ಗೋಲವಿದ್ಯೆ, -ಗೋಲಶಾಸ್ತ್ರ Geography -ಚಕ್ರ The earth's orbit, the equator, an umbrella attached to a throne -ಚರ. Moving on earth, a man -ಛಾಯೆ Darkness -ಜಾತೆ Sîtâ -ತಲ The [illegible] landed of the earth. -ದೇವ. A Brâhmana -ನಾಗ An earth-worm -ನಾಥ -ವ, -ಪತಿ, -ಪಾಲ, -ಪಾಲಕ, -ಭುಜ್. A king -ಪ್ರದಕ್ಷಿಣ Going round the earth. -ಭಾರ A wicked man. -ರಚನೆ. The composition of a soil. -ರುಹ A tree. -ಲೋಕ, -ಮಂಡಲ. The terrestrial globe -ಶಿರ. A cape -ಸಾರ. The strength of a soil. -ಸುರ A Brâhmana -ಸ್ಥಾಪನೆ Putting in the ground, as money. -ಸ್ಥಿತಿ Landed property.

ಭೂತ s. a. Become, produced 2, past, gone, former. 3, got, obtained 4, right, fit n Past time, the past, the past tense. 2, a living being, creature. 3, a goblin, demon, a ghost. 4, an element, as earth, water, fire, air, ether 5, in law fact, matter of fact -ಕಾಲ, -ಕಾಲಕ್ರಿಯೆ The past time, past tense -ಗಣ The aggregate of beings; a class of demons. -ಗ್ರಹ. The bhûta-imp. -ಚಿಕಿತ್ಸೆ The science of administering antidotes for demoniacal possessions -ದಯೆ Universal benevolence -ಪಂಚಕ The aggregate of the five elements. -ಬಲಿ. An offering to demons -ವಿದ್ಯೆ Demonology. -ನಾಥ, -ಪತಿ, ಭೂತಾಧಿಪ Śiva. -ಶಂಕೆ Doubt arising from demons -ಸೇವೆ. Demonolatry ಭೂತಾತ್ಮ The vital principle, the individual soul. ಭೂತಾರ್ಥ. A matter of fact, fact ಭೂತಾವೇಶ A demoniac possession ಭೂತೇಶ Lord of beings, Śiva.

ಭೂತಿ s n Being, existence, birth. 2, well-being, wealth, riches. 3, power, dignity 4, ashes -ಕ The plant *Gentiana chirayta,* lemon grass

ಭೂಮಿ (=ಬೂಮಿ) s n The earth. 2, soil, ground, a country, land estate; a place, site in general -ವ, -ಪತಿ, -ಪಾಲ, -ಪಾಲಕ, -ವಲ್ಲಭ, ಭೂಮಿನಾಥ, ಭೂಮೀಶ್ವರ. A king.

ಭೂರಿ s a. Much many numerous n Gold. 2, a [illegible]

present at any festival or funeral; *also* -ದಕ್ಷಿಣೆ

ಭೂಷಣ s n Decorating, ornament, decoration, embellishment; a trinket, *etc* ಭೂಷಿತ Decorated, adorned ಭೂಷಿಸು. To decorate, adorn, to praise. ಭೂಷೆ An ornament, jewel.

ಭ್ರುಕುಟಿ s. n. A frown

ಭೃಗು s n N of a rishi 2, Venus 3, a cliff, slope -ವಾರ Friday.

ಭೃಂಗ s. n The large black bee 2, the bird *Cuculus melanoleucus.* 3, woody Cassia, *Laurus cassia*

ಭೃಂಗಾರ (=ಭಂಗಾರ) s n. A vase used at a king's inauguration or at a marriage 2, gold.

ಭೃತ s a Borne, carried, *also* -ಕ. ಭೃತಿ. Support, wages, hire, capital ಭೃತ್ಯ A servant, minister. ಭೃತ್ಯತೆ. Servitude. ಭೃತ್ಯೆ Service, hire, wages

ಭೆಟ್ಟಿ. =ಭೇಟಿ, q v. -ತಕ್ಕೊಳ್ಳು To visit -ಯಾಗು To meet, encounter; a visit to take place.

ಭೇಟಿ (=ಭೆಟ್ಟಿ, q v.) h n. Meeting, an interview, visit -ಗೆ ಬರು To come to visit -ಕೊಡು. To favour one with a visit. -ಮಾಡಿಸು To introduce -ಮಾಡು To visit

ಭೇದ s n. Breaking, dividing 2, division, separation, portion 3, discrimination 4, distinction, difference, variety 5, change, modification 6, dissension, disunion, disagreement. 7, creating divisions (among confederates) 8, an opponent -ಬುದ್ಧಿ. Idea of a difference. -ಕ Breaking; distinguishing. -ನ Separating, loosening

ಭೇದಿ s. n. A destroyer, loosening the bowels, purging -ಕಟ್ಟು To stop purging -ಸು To break, split, to distinguish, to separate, to destroy, to disclose; to be broken, as the heart, to separate ಭೇದ್ಯ. Breakable frangible [illegible]

ಭೇರಿ s n. A kettle-drum

ಭೇಷಜ s. n A remedy, medicament. 2, (=ಡಂಭ) hypocrisy, deceit -ಗಾರ, A hypocrite

ಭೈರವ (fr ಭೀರು) s a Formidable, awful, terrific. n A form of Śiva ಭೈರವಿ N. of a tune

ಭೋಕ್ತೃ, ಭೋಕ್ತಾರ (tb of ಭೋಕ್ತೃ) n An enjoyer eater feeder, enjoying eating ಭೋಕ್ತವ್ಯ Fit to be enjoyed

ಭೋಗ s n Enjoyment, eating, use, application 2, possessing, protecting 3 perception of sorrow or joy 4, pleasure, 5, feasting a banquet 6, money, wealth 7 fullness -ಸ್ಥಳ, -ಭೂಮಿ A place of enjoyment ಭೋಗಿ Enjoying, using suffering; an enjoyer a happy person, a voluptuary, a king a barber, -ಸಾಡು. ಭೋಗಿಸು, To eat, to enjoy, to experience, feel suffer ಭೋಗ್ಯ Enjoyable ಭೋಗ್ಯಾಧಿ, A pledge which may be used by the mortgagee until redeemed ಭೋಗ್ಯಾಧಿ ಪತ್ರ A mortgage-deed.

ಭೋಜನ s n The act of enjoying, eating, a meal, food -ಮಾಡು To eat -ದಕ್ಷಿಣೆ Money-presents to Brâhmanas at a meal. ಭೋಜನಾರ್ಥ On account of a meal ಭೋಜನಾರ್ಥಿ A stranger who asks for a meal ಭೋಜ್ಯ Eatable, food, a dainty. ಪ್ರಭು- The Lord's Supper

ಭೋರನೆ k ad Swiftly, quickly

ಭೋಷ್ಯ s n Decorum decency, honour

ಭೌತಿಕ (fr ಭೂತ) s a Relating to existing beings, material

ಭೌಮ (fr ಭೂಮಿ) s. a Earthly, terrestrial n. The planet Mars -ವಾರ, Tuesday

ಭ್ರಂಶ s n. Falling off declining, losing, straying from

ಭ್ರುಕುಟಿ (= ಭ್ರುಕುಟಿ) s n A frown

ಭ್ರಮ, ಭ್ರಮೆ s n Roaming about, whirling, going round, a whirl a whirlpool, giddiness, dizziness confusion, perplexity mistake misconception, delusion -ಗೊಳ್ಳು To become confused or bewildered ಭ್ರಮಿಸು, To roam about, wander, to be confused, perplexed to act foolishly ಭ್ರಮಣ, ಭ್ರಮಣೆ Roaming whirling, revolution, wavering, staggering unsteadiness, confusion, giddiness dizziness

ಭ್ರಮರ s. n The large black bee, *Bombinatrix glabra* 2, giddiness, vertigo

ಭ್ರಷ್ಟ s a Fallen, ruined, lost, strayed from fallen (as from dignity, power, caste, virtue) depraved vicious -ತ್ವ, -ತೆ Depravity, viciousness wickedness

ಭ್ರಾತೃ s n A brother -ಜ -ಪುತ್ರ -ವ್ಯ A brother's son. ಭ್ರಾತೃತ್ವ Fraternal

ಭ್ರಾಂತ s a. Whirled round 2 confused, perplexed, bewildered -ತೆ Confusion bewilderment ಭ್ರಾಂತಿ Roaming etc. confusion perplexity bewilderment mistake, delusion, false idea. ಭ್ರಾಂತಿಗೊಳ್ಳು, -ಪಡು To be confused

ಭ್ರೂ s n. An eyebrow, the brow -ಕುಟಿ = ಭ್ರುಕುಟಿ q v.

ಮ್

ಮ್. The forty-third letter of the alphabet

ಮಕರ - . . . shi

zodiac. *Capricornus* -ಕುಂಡಲ A kind of ear-ornament -ತೋರಣ A mortar- . . . -kara-like . . . gurus.

and kings. -ಧ್ವಜ. Kâma. -ಮಾಸ. The tenth solar month. -ಸಂಕ್ರಮಣ, -ಸಂಕ್ರಾಂತಿ. The sun's passage from *Sagittarius* into *Capricornus*.

ಮಕರಂದ s. *n.* The nectar of flowers; honey.

ಮಕರಿ, -ಕೆ s. *n.* Figures drawn with fragrant pigments on the breast, arm, neck, *etc.*

ಮಕಾರ s. *n.* The letter ಮ. 2, dishonour.

ಮಕುಟ (=ಮುಕುಟ) s. *n.* A crown, crest, diadem. -ವರ್ಧನ. A crowned sovereign.

ಮಕ್ಕ, ಮಕ್ಕಾ f. *n.* Mecca.

ಮಕ್ಕರಿ k. *n.* A basket plaited of stout bamboo slits.

ಮಕ್ಕಳು k. *n.* Children; *pl. of* ಮಗ, ಮಗಳು, ಮಗು, *etc.*, *q. v.* ಮಕ್ಕಳಾಟಿಕೆ, ಮಕ್ಕಳಾಟಿಗೆ. Children's play. -ಮರಿಗಳು. *dpl.* ಮೊಂ-. Grand-children.

ಮಕ್ತಾ h. *n.* A copy. -ಕಾಂಮಕ್ತಾ. An exact copy.

ಮಕ್ಕಿಗದ್ದೆ k. *n.* Rice-field above the level of a valley.

ಮಕ್ಷಿಕ s. *n.* A fly; a bee.

ಮಖ s. *n.* A sacrifice.

ಮಖಮಲ್ಲು h. *n.* Velvet.

ಮಖೆ = ಮಘೆ, *q. v.*

ಮಗ k. *n.* A son; a male; *f.* -ಳು. *Pl.* ಮಕ್ಕಳು. ಮಗನ-, ಮೊಂ-. A grandson. ಸಾಕು-. An adopted son.

ಮಗಚು, ಮಗುಚು k. *v. i.* To turn round; to return (*as in* ಮಗಚಿ ಬಂದನು). 2, to fall upside down. *v. t.* To turn, *as* the leaf of a book. 2, to turn upside down, overthrow. 3, to grind, whet.

ಮಗಟ f. *n.* A silk or linen cloth with borders worn during pûja or meal and considered ceremonially clean.

ಮಗಧ s. *n.* N. of South Behâr. 2, its inhabitant.

ಮಗಿಮಾವು s. *n.* The monkey-bread tree, Baobab, *Adansonia digitata*.

ಮಗು, -ವು (*cf.* ಮಗ) k. *n.* An infant, child; *pl.* ಮಕ್ಕಳು. -ತನ. Childhood.

ಮಗುಳು (ಳು=ಱು) a. k. *v. i.* To turn round, to be turned upside down; to recede, retreat; to happen. ಮಗುಳೆ. Again. ಮಗುಳೆ ಮಗುಳೆ. *rep.* Again and again.

ಮಗ್ಗ k. *n.* A weaver's loom. -ದ ಕುಣಿ, -ಗುಂಡಿ. A hole in which a weaver puts his feet when at work. -ದವ. A weaver.

ಮಗ್ಗಲು, ಮಗ್ಗಿಲು (= ಮಗ್ಗುಲು) k. *n.* Side; the side. ಮಗ್ಗಲುಹಾಸಿಗೆ. A coverlet.

ಮಗ್ಗಾರೆ k. *n.* The thorny shrub *Vangueria spinosa.*

ಮಗ್ಗಿ k. *n.* Multiplication-table. -ಗುಣಿತ. Multiplication.

ಮಗ್ಗು a. k. *v. i.* To become pale or sallow; to grow dim, *as* gold; to wither; to vanish away, disappear; to grow dirty or rusty; to perish. 2, to roar. *n.* Subjection, submission.

ಮಗ್ಗುಲು. = ಮಗ್ಗಲು, *q. v.*

ಮಗ್ನ s. *a.* Plunged, immersed; sunk into; absorbed. -ತೆ. The state of absorption, despondency.

ಮಘೆ s. *n.* The 10th nakshatra.

ಮಂಕಣಿ f. *n.* A frame-work set on beasts for carrying pitchers, *etc.*

ಮಂಕು k. *n.* Dimness, want of lustre (*as of* pearls, gold, *etc.*); obscurity of intellect, silliness, stupidity. ಮಂಕ. A stupid fellow; *f.* ಮಂಕಿ. -ಬೀಳು, ಮಂಕಾಗು. To become stupid, *etc.* -ತನ, ಮಂಕಾಟ. Silly behaviour. -ತಬ್ಬು. = -ಹಿಡಿ, *q. v.* -ಬುದ್ಧಿ. A dull understanding. -ಮರುಳು. *dpl.* -ಮಳೆ. A furious, heavy rain. -ಹಿಡಿ. To become perplexed or stupid.

ಮಂಗ (*tb. of* ಮರ್ಕ) *n.* A monkey. -ಚೇಷ್ಟೆ. Apish grimaces. -ಬಾವು. Mumps. -ತನ, -ನಾಟ, ಮಂಗಾಟ. Apish behaviour. ಮಂಗೇಶ. Hanumat; N.

ಮಂಗರಬಳ್ಳಿ, ಮಂಗರೋಳಿ k. *n.* A climbing shrub with eatable stem, *Vitis quadrangularis.*

ಮಂಗಲ, ಮಂಗಳ s. *a.* Fortunate, auspicious, prosperous, beautiful, pleasing. *n.* Good fortune, success, prosperity, welfare, happiness. 2, a good omen, an auspicious prayer, benediction; lines at the opening or end of a poem in praise of a deity. 3, any lucky object. 4, any happy event, as marriage, *etc.* 5, the planet Mars. -ಕಷ್ಟ Trouble arising from Mars. -ಕಾರ್ಯ A festive occasion. -ಪ್ರದ Bestowing welfare or prosperity. -ವಾರ Tuesday. -ಸೂತ್ರ A marriage badge worn round the neck by a wife. ಮಂಗಲಾಚರಣ. Benediction; lines at the beginning or close of a poem in praise of a deity. ಮಂಗಳಾರತಿ. Waving of a burning lamp, the lamp so waved. ಮಂಗಳಾಶಾಸನ Benediction. ಮಂಗಳೂರು N. of a sea-port in South-Canara.

ಮಂಗಾರೆ k. *n.* The thorny shrub *Vangueria spinosa.*

ಮಚ್ಚ, ಮಚ್ಚೆ k. *n.* A black speck or scar, mole, freckle. 2, a piece of gold or silver kept for a sample or test.

ಮಚ್ಚರ. *tb.* of ಮತ್ಸರ, *q. v.* ಮಚ್ಚರಿಸು. To be envious, jealous, selfish, to grudge.

ಮಚ್ಚು 1 = ಮೆಚ್ಚು, *q. v.*

ಮಚ್ಚು 2. k. *n.* A bill-hook for cutting bushes *etc.*, *also* -ಕತ್ತಿ.

ಮಜಕೂರು h. *a.* Above mentioned, current. *n.* Affair, concern, an oral communication, the contents of an epistle.

ಮಜಬೂತು h. *a.* Strong, firm, fast.

ಮಜಲು h. *n.* A stage, halting place, a day's journey. -ಗದ್ದೆ. A paddy-field yielding two crops, generally higher than ಬೈಲುಗದ್ದೆ and lower than ಬೆಟ್ಟು-ಗದ್ದೆ.

ಮಜಾ, ಮಜಾಕು h. *n.* Flavour, taste.

ಮಜ ... The ... of a labourer ... hi ...

ಮಜ್ಜ s. *n.* The marrow of bones. 2, the pith of plants. -ಸಾರ, ಮಜ್ಜಾಸಾರ Pith, substance, that is most important, flatulence.

ಮಜ್ಜನ s. *n.* Bathing, ablution, water for bathing. -ಗೃಹ, -ಶಾಲೆ A bath-room.

ಮಜ್ಜಿಗೆ k. *n.* Buttermilk. 2, whey. -ನೀರು Buttermilk mixed with water. -ಪಲ್ಯ The yellow wood-sorrel, *Oxalis corniculata.* -ಪಳದ್ಯ A kind of sour sauce. -ಹುಲ್ಲು The lemon grass *Andropogon schoenanthus.*

ಮಂಚ (*fr.* ಮಲಗು) k. *n.* A bedstead, cot, bed. 2, an elevated shed.

ಮಂಚಿಕೆ, ಮಂಚಿಗೆ k. *n.* A stand in a field, jungle, *etc.*, for watching the crops or the chase, *etc.*

ಮಂಜರಿ s. *n.* A cluster of blossoms; a flower-bud, a sprout, sprig, stalk; *also* -ಕೆ. ಶಬ್ದ- A cluster or glossary of words, a dictionary.

ಮಂಜಳ k. *n.* Indian saffron, turmeric.

ಮಂಜಾಡಿ (*tb.* of ಮಂಜಿಷ್ಠ) *n.* The red seeds of the red-wood tree which are used in weighing gold and diamond.

ಮಂಜಿ k. *n.* The bow-string hemp, *Sanseviera zeylanica.* 2, a coasting boat.

ಮಂಜಿಷ್ಠೆ s. *n.* The Bengal madder, *Rubia munjista.*

ಮಂಜೀರ k. *n.* An anklet. 2, a post round which the string of a churning stick passes.

ಮಂಜು 1. k. *n.* Dew, fog, coldness, coolness, dimness of sight, obscurity. 2, a N. -ಕಾಲ The cold season. ಮಂಜ N. of Śiva or of any male, *f.* ಮಂಜಿ.

ಮಂಜು 2, **ಮಂಜುಲ** s. *a.* Beautiful, lovely, charming, pleasing, sweet, melodious.

ಮಂಜೂರು h. *n.* Approval, confirmation; sanction. *a.* Approved, confirmed. -ಮಾಡು. To approve, sanction, con-

ಮಟ. *tb. of* ಮಠ, *q. v.*

ಮಟ್ಟ 1. (ಮಟ್ಟಸ) k. *n.* Levelness, equality, regularity, exactness. 2, a carpenter's level. 3, (= ಮಟ್ಟು) measure, extent, limit. -ಗೋಲು. A mason's level. -ಸ. Levelness, evenness, smoothness. -ಸ ಮಾಡು. To make even or smooth. -ಮೊದಲು. At the very beginning. -ಪಲಿಗೆ. A carpenter's ruler.

ಮಟ್ಟ 2. k. *n.* Shortness; abating, *as* wind, rain, fever, price, *etc.*; inferiority. 2, a pony. -ಜಾತಿ. An inferior caste. -ತರ. An inferior kind.

ಮಟ್ಟ 3. k. *n.* Illusion, phantom, ruin. -ಮಾಯ. *veil.* Perfect disappearance.

ಮಟ್ಟಿ (*tb. of* ಮೃದ್) *n.* Earth, clay.

ಮಟ್ಟು (= ಮಟ್ಟ 1, No. 3) k. *n.* Measure; extent, height; bound, limit. ಮಟ್ಟಿಗೆ. Till, until, as far as. ಎಷ್ಟು ಮಟ್ಟಿಗೆ. How far? *Cpds.:* ತಕ್ಕ-, ಕೈಲಾದ-, ಸಾಕಾದ-, *etc.* ಅಷ್ಟು-, ಅಷ್ಟರ-. So far as that. ಇಷ್ಟು-, ಇಷ್ಟರ-. So far as this. ಈ ದಿನದ-. Until this day.

ಮಟ್ಟೆ 1. k. *n.* A bough of the palm, *etc.* 2, the fibrous coat of a cocoanut.

ಮಟ್ಟೆ 2. f. *n.* The bucket of a bullock-draw-well.

ಮಠ s. *n.* A hut, cottage; a hermitage; a residence of a guru; a convent, monastery; a temple; a school. *Cpds.:* ಓದುವ-, ಗುರು-, ಗೋಸಾಯಿ-, ಜಂಗಮ-, ಸನ್ಯಾಸಿ-, *etc.*

ಮಡ. = ಮಡಿ 4, *q. v.*

ಮಡಕಿ f. *n.* A much cultivated annual pulse, *Phaseolus aconitifolius.*

ಮಡಕೆ 1. = ಮಡಿಕೆ 1, *q. v.*

ಮಡಕೆ 2. (= ಮಡಿಕೆ 2) k. *n.* A pot; a water-jar.

ಮಡಗು k. *v. t.* To lay down, place, put (*cf.* ಮಲಗು); to take into one's service; to procure, *as* a horse, *etc.* 2, to hide.

ಮಡತ a. k. *n.* Folding, a fold.

ಮಡದಿ k. *n.* A woman. 2, a wife.

ಮಡಪು k. *n.* A fold, as of cloth, betel-leaf, *etc.*

ಮಡಲು k. *n.* Thick foliage; a thicket, bush; a bough of the cocoanut tree. ಮಡಲಿಸು. To spread, run, as a creeper; to prevail, increase.

ಮಡಿ 1. k. *n.* A fold. 2, the pouch-like fold in front part of the garment to put in eatables, *etc.*; *also* ಮಡಲು. 3, the bed of a garden. 4, fold, times, *as:* ಇಂ-, ಮೂಂ-, ನಾಲ್-, *etc.* *v. t.* To bend; to fold.

ಮಡಿ 2. k. *v. i.* To die, perish.

ಮಡಿ 3. k. *n.* A washed, clean cloth. 2, purity. -ದೋತ್ರ. A washed, clean dôtra.

ಮಡಿ 4. (= ಮಡ) k. *n.* The heel, *in* ಹಿಮ್ಮಡಿ.

ಮಡಿಕೆ 1. (= ಮಡಕೆ 1) k. *n.* A fold; fold, times. 2, the warp ready for the loom. 3, a kind of harrow or rake.

ಮಡಿಕೆ 2. = ಮಡಕೆ 2, *q. v.*

ಮಡಿವಳ, ಮಡಿವಾಳ (*fr.* ಮಡಿ 3) k. *n.* A washerman. -ಗಿತ್ತಿ. A washer-woman. -ಹಾಗಲಬಳ್ಳಿ. A climbing herb, *Momordica dioica*; *also* ಮಡಿಹಾಗಲಬಳ್ಳಿ.

ಮಡಿಸು (*fr.* ಮಡಿ 1) k. *v. t.* To bend, fold, fold up. ಮಡಿಸಿದ ವಸ್ತ್ರ. A folded cloth.

ಮಡು, ಮಡುವು k. *n.* Deep water; a pool.

ಮಡೆ k. *n.* A small dam or dike.

ಮಡ್ಡ k. *n.* A stupid man. -ತನ. Stupidity.

ಮಡ್ಡಿ 1. (= ಮಡ್ಡು) k. *n.* Dregs, lees, *as* of oil, ghee, *etc.* 2, = ಕಲಗಚ್ಚು.

ಮಡ್ಡಿ 2. k. *n.* A tree yielding a soft gum, *Ailanthus malabarica.*

ಮಡ್ಡಿ 3. k. *n.* A stupid, dull person. 2, awkwardness, rudeness. -ಕಾಗದ. A coarse paper. -ಗಾರೆ. Rough plaster. -ತನ. Stupidity, rudeness.

ಮಡ್ಡು = ಮಡ್ಡಿ 1, *q. v.*

ಮಣಿ, -ವು (= ಮಣು) f n A measure of capacity · a maund, quarter = 28 lbs.

ಮಣಕ k. n A young cow or buffalo -ನೆ Quickly

ಮಣಲು = ಮಳಲು, q v.

ಮಣಿ 1 k v. i To bend, bow, to make obeisance n A bend, bow, an obeisance -ಕಟ್ಟು. The wrist. -ಸು To cause to bend

ಮಣಿ 2 s n A jewel, gem, precious stone 2, an ornament in general 3, a bed -ತೊಂಡೆ ಬಳ್ಳಿ. A creeping herb, *Bryonia scabrella* -ಗಾರ A jeweller. *Cpds*.. -ದರ್ಪಣ, -ದೋಷ, -ಪೀಠಿಕೆ, *etc* -ಶಿಲೆ A reddish mineral used for medicinal purposes.

ಮಣಿಯ k n Superintendence of temples, mathas, palaces, *etc* -ಗಾರ A maniya-officer, superintendent

ಮಣು. -ವು. = ಮಣ, q v.

ಮಣೆ k n. A stool, low bench, seat

ಮಣೆಯ = ಮಣಿಯ, q v 2, a religious performance or vow. -ಕಟ್ಟಿಸು, -ಹಾಕಿಸು To have this maneya performed. -ಗಾರ. = ಮಣಿಗಾರ, q. v.

ಮಂಟ = ಮಟ, q. v. -ಬೆಕ್ಕು A wild cat, tree-cat.

ಮಂಟಪ s n A halting place for travellers, a temporary shed erected on festive occasions (*as* marriage, munji, *etc*), a sacrificial shed, a structure for carrying about an idol

ಮಂಡ s. n The scum on the surface of any liquid, cream, barm, gruel. 2, the castor-oil plant 3, the head.

ಮಂಡಕ = ಮಂಡಿಗೆ, q v

ಮಂಡನ s n. Adorning, ornament

ಮಂಡಪ. = ಮಂಟಪ, q v. ಮಂಡಪಿಗೆ. A small shed, shop

ಮಂಡಲ s n A disk (of the sun or moon), a circle, globe, ball, orb; a halo. 2, the visible horizon. 3, a dist[illegible]

mu[illegible]

period of forty-eight days -ಹಾವು A kind of snake. -ಕ. White leprosy

ಮಂಡಲಿ, ಮಂಡಳಿ s. n A circle, orb 2, a multitude, company, congregation 3, whirling 4, a kind of snake -ಸು. To whirl, turn round, to be amassed -ಕ, ಮಂಡಲೇಶ್ವರ A ruler, prefect, superintendent.

ಮಂಡಿ 1 k n The knee -ಇಡು, -ಊರು, -ಹಾಕು, -ಹೂಡು To kneel. -ಕಾಲು = ಮಂಡಿ 1.

ಮಂಡಿ 2 h n A wholesale shop, warehouse

ಮಂಡಿ 3 f n Gout or rheumatism of the thigh

ಮಂಡಿಗೆ (*tb of* ಮಂಡಕ) n A sugared cake of wheaten flour

ಮಂಡಿಸು k v i To sit down, to be set or turned towards, *as* the eye

ಮಂಡೂಕ s. n. A frog. -ಪರ್ಣಿ. Bengal madder, *Rubia munjista*

ಮಂಡೂರ s n Rust of iron, scoriae. -ಭಸ್ಮ Calcined iron

ಮಂಡೆ (*tb of* ಮಂಡ) n The head -ನೋವು Headache. -ಸುತ್ತು A turban.

ಮಣ್ಣು k. n Earth, clay, mud, soil, ground. ಮಣ್ಣಡಿಕೆ The Sepistan plum, *Cordia myxa* ಮಣ್ಣಾಗು To become earth, be soiled; to be ruined ಮಣ್ಣಾಸೆ. Desire after landed property. -ಕೂಡಿಸು, -ಕೊಡು. To bury. -ಗಡ್ಡೆ. A clod of earth -ಗೋಡೆ. A mud wall -ಪಾತ್ರೆ An earthen vessel -ಪಾಲು. Destruction, death -ಮುಕ್ಕು To get disappointed -ಮಾಡು To bury -ಹಾಕು To put earth (into a person's mouth, i e. to deceive and ruin him). -ಹುಳ, ಮಣ್ಣುಣಿ An earth-worm.

ಮತ s a Thought, considered, intended. n A thought idea, an opinion, view, a doctrine, creed, sect, design. -ದ್ವೇಷ Sectarian enmity -ಭ್ರಷ್ಟ. Fallen from one's creed, an apostate. -ವಿಚಾರ Examination of a creed. -ಸಿ[illegible]

[illegible] -ಸ್ಥ.

[illegible] ಮತಾ

ಚಾರ. The customs of a sect. ಕ್ರೈಸ್ತ-. Christianity. ಹಿಂದು-. Hinduism.

ಮತಲಬು h. n. Purpose; purport, *as* of a document.

ಮತಾಪು, ಮತಾಬು h. n. A kind of fire-work.

ಮತಿ s. n. Mind; understanding, intellect, will, judgment. 2, thought, idea, opinion. 3, counsel, advice. 4, wish, inclination, purpose. -ಗೆಡು. To lose one's wits; to be perplexed; to become stupid. -ಭ್ರಷ್ಟ. Devoid of sense; foolish. -ವಂತ, -ವಾನ್. A sensible, clever man. -ಶೂನ್ಯ, -ಹೀನ. Stupid.

ಮತ್ಕುಣ s. n. A bug; a flea.

ಮತ್ತ 1. s. a. Intoxicated, drunk. 2, mad, furious. 3, lustful, wanton. 4, delighted. 5, proud. -ತ್ವ. Intoxication; *also* -ತೆ.

ಮತ್ತ 2, ಮತ್ತಂ (= ಮತ್ತೂ, ಮತ್ತೆಯೂ) a. k. *conj.* Again, further, moreover, and.

ಮತ್ತಿ 1. k. n. A freckle, mark.

ಮತ್ತಿ 2. k. n. N. of several species of timber trees of the genus *Terminalia*.

ಮತ್ತು 1. k. *conj.* Other, again, further, besides, and. ಮತ್ತಿನ. Of another, different. ಮತ್ತಿಷ್ಟು. Twice as much. ಮತ್ತೂ. = ಮತ್ತ2. ಮತ್ತೆಲ್ಲಿ. Where else? anywhere else. ಮತ್ತೆಲ್ಲಿಯೂ. At or to any other place. ಮತ್ತೇನು. What else? what more? ಮತ್ತೇನೂ. Any other thing. ಮತ್ತೊಂದು, *etc. See s.* ಮತ್ತೆ. ಮತ್ತ್ಯಾಕೆ. For what other reason? ಮತ್ತ್ಯಾರು. Who else? who more? ಮತ್ತ್ಯಾವ. What other thing? *etc.* ಮತ್ತ್ಯಾವಾಗಾದರೂ. At any other time.

ಮತ್ತು 2. (*tb. of* ಮತ್ತ, ಮದ) n. Intoxication; pride.

ಮತ್ತೆ (= ಮತ್ತು, *q. v.*) k. *ad.* Other, else, again, further, besides, afterwards, and. ಮತ್ತೊಂದು. Another—, a different—; another thing, *etc.* ಮತ್ತೊಬ್ಬ. Ano[illegible] *f.* ಮತ್ತೊಬ್ಬಳು[illegible] ಮತ್ತೊಮ್ಮೆ. A[illegible]

ಮತ್ಯ s. n. Exercise of knowledge. ಏಕ-. Concord.

ಮತ್ಸರ (= ಮಚ್ಚರ, *q. v.*) s. a. Envious, grudging, jealous. 2, selfish, greedy. n. Envy, grudge; jealousy, hostility; greediness; anger; *also* -ಭಾವ, -ಬುದ್ಧಿ. -ಗೊಳ್ಳು, -ಪಡು, ಮತ್ಸರಿಸು. To be envious.

ಮತ್ಸ್ಯ s. n. A fish. -ಧ್ವಜ. Kâma. -ಪುರಾಣ. One of the 18 purâṇas. -ಸಂಘಾತ. A shoal of young fry. ಮತ್ಸ್ಯಾವತಾರ. N. of Vishṇu's first incarnation.

ಮಥನ s. n. Stirring; churning; rubbing, friction; crushing; injury, trouble. ಮಥನಿಸು, ಮಥಿಸು. To churn; to discuss; to quarrel.

ಮದ 1. (= ಮದಿವೆ, ಮದುವೆ, *q. v.*) k. n. A wedding, marriage. -ಮಕ್ಕಳು. The bride and bridegroom. -ಮಗ, -ಲಿಗ, -ಲಿಂಗ, -ವಣಿಗ, -ವಳಿಗ. A bridegroom. -ಮಗಳು, -ಲಗಿತ್ತಿ, -ವಣಿಗಿತ್ತಿ, -ವಳಿಗೆ. A bride. -ವನ. A husband.

ಮದ 2. s. n. Intoxication. 2, madness. 3, ardent passion, love, lust; lasciviousness. 4, delight. 5, pride, conceit. 6, bloom of youth. 7, honey. 8, musk. *Cpds.:* ಅಸ್ತ್ರ-, ಅಘ್ರ-, ಧನ-, ಯೌವನ-, ವಿದ್ಯಾ-, *etc.* -ಏರಿಸು, -ಬೇರಿಸು. To raise intoxication, *etc.* -ಏರು. To be intoxicated; to be ruttish, proud or furious. -ಗಜ. An elephant in rut. ಮದಾಂಧ, ಮದಾಂಧಕ. Blinded by passion. ಮದೋನ್ಮತ್ತ. Intoxicated with passion or pride.

ಮದಗ, ಮದಗು k. n. A sluice, flood-gate.

ಮದಡು k. n. Dullness, stupidity. ಮದಡ. A stupid man.

ಮದತು (= ಮದ್ದತು) h. n. Aid, help.

ಮದನ (= ಮದ 2, *q. v.*) s. a. Intoxicating; exhilerating. n. Passion, lust. 2, an intoxicated, mad, haughty man. 3, Kâma. 4, the thorn-apple, *Datura metel.* 5, bees' wax. -ಕೈ. Ornamental supports of the [illegible] of a house; a [illegible]

ಮದರಂಗ, -ಗಿ s. n The Henna plant, *Lawsonia alba*.

ಮದರಿ (*tb. of* ಮಧುರೆ) n. N of a town in the Tamil country where red cloths are made. -ರುಮಾಲು A red turban

ಮದಿಪು (*fr* ಮತಿ) s n. Estimation, valuation, rating.

ಮದಿರೆ, ಮದಿರಾ s n Spirituous liquor ಮದಿರಾಗೃಹ. A tavern.

ಮದಿವೆ, ಮದುವೆ k n Wedding, marriage -ಮಾಡಿ ಕೊಡು To give away as wife -ಮಾಡಿ ಕೊಳ್ಳು To marry. -ಮಾಡಿಸು To cause to be married -ಮಾಡು To perform a marriage -ಆಗು, -ಯಾಗು To be married. *Cpds* -ಚಪ್ಪರ, -ಮನೆ, -ಸಿಬ್ಬಣ.

ಮದಿಸು (*fr* ಮದ) s. v. i To be proud. 2, to grow fat or plump

ಮದು. = ಮದ 1, *q v*

ಮದುರೆ *tb of* ಮಧುರೆ, *q v*

ಮದೋದ್ಧತ s a Arrogant, haughty

ಮದ್ದತು, ಮದ್ದತ್ತು (= ಮದತು) h. n Aid, help; succour

ಮದ್ದಲೆ, ಮದ್ದಳೆ (*tb of* ಮರ್ದಲ) n A kind of drum, a tabor

ಮದ್ದು 1 (= ಮದುರ್) k n Any drug, medicine, whether a powder pill, or fluid, a remedy. 2, gunpowder ಮದ್ದಿನ ಚೀಲ A powder bag

ಮದ್ದು 2. (*tb of* ಮತ್ತು) f n Intoxication, madness, an intoxicant. -ಗುಣಿಕೆ. The thorn-apple ಮದ್ದಾನೆ An elephant in rut

ಮದ್ಯ s. a. Intoxicating, gladdening n Any intoxicating drink, spirituous liquor. -ಪ, -ಪಾಯಿ. A drinker -ಪಾನ. Drinking of intoxicating liquor

ಮದ್ರಾಸು f n Madras

ಮಧು s a Sweet, pleasant n Honey, the nectar of flowers 2, ambrosia, milk. 3, mead, spirituous liquor 4, liquorice. 5, the black bee 6, spring the vernal season. -ಕ, -ವಲ್ಲಿ. Th[illegible] of [illegible] receiving a guest. -ಪರ್ಣಿ. The creeper *Cocculus cordifolius* -ಪಾನ. Spirituous liquor, sipping it -ಪ್ರಿಯ The black bee; a voluptuary -ಮಿತ್ರ, -ಪ A bee. -ರ. Sweet; pleasant, pleasing, melodious, sweetness; a kind of sugar, the red sugar-cane -ರತ್ವ Sweetness -ರಸ Honey

ಮಧುರೆ s n Madura in the Tamil country. 2, the plant *Anethum sowa* -ರಂಗು A purple colour from that town

ಮಧ್ಯ s a Middle, central; intermediate 2, middling 3, right, just n. The middle, midst, centre. 2, the waist. -ರಾತ್ರಿ -ರಾತ್ರೆ. Midnight. -ರೇಖೆ, -ರೇಷೆ The equator -ವರ್ತಿ. A mediator. -ಸ್ತ, -ಸ್ಥ Central mediation, a mediator, arbitrator, *also* -ಸ್ತಗಾರ. -ಸ್ಥಾನ. A middle place, the waist -ಸ್ತಿಕೆ Mediation mediatorship (*Christ in the work of redemption*).

ಮಧ್ಯಮ s. a. Middle, central; intermediate, middling, moderate. n A middle condition or quality, mediocrity. 2, the waist. 3, the second person, *also* -ಪುರುಷ

ಮಧ್ಯಾಹ್ನ s n Midday. noon -ಮಲ್ಲಿಗೆ. The marvel of Peru or four-o'clock flower, *Mirabilis jalappa*.

ಮನ (= ಮನಸು, ಮನಸ್ಸು q v. *tb of* ಮನಸ್) n Mind *etc.* -ಕೆ ತರು To take to heart. -ಕೆ ಬರು. To enter the mind, to be agreeable -ಕ್ಲೇಶ Mental affliction. -ಗಾಣು. To observe, apprehend. -ಗುಂದು. To grieve, grief, sorrow. -ಗೆಡಿಸು. To spoil the intentions (of another) -ಗೆಡು The mind to be spoiled or altered -ಗೊಡು. To pay attention -ಂಗೊಳಿಸು. To fascinate, charm. -ಂಗೊಳ್ಳು To be fascinated, charmed -ತಟ್ಟು, -ದಟ್ಟು. To touch the mind, be known -ದೊಳಗೆ ಇಡು To [illegible] ಬಗು To [illegible] ಬಟ್ಟು To apply one's (whole) mind to. -ಮುರಿ. Inclination to disappear. -ವರಿ. To know the mind. -ವರಿಕೆ. Knowledge. -ದಾರೆ. With one's whole mind. -ವಿಡು. To feel a desire for. -ವಿಳಿ. To be discouraged, humbled. -ವುಕ್ಕು. To be elated. -ವೆರಗು. To make hearty obeisance. -ವೊಲಿ. To rejoice; to long for. -ವೊಲಿಸು. To gain one's favour. -ಸೋಲು. To suffer a mental defeat. -ಮಾರಿ. A fool. ಮನಃಪೂರ್ವಕ. With the whole *mind* or heart; deliberately. ಮನಃಶುದ್ಧಿ. Sincerity. ಮನಃಸಾಕ್ಷಿ (= ಮನಸ್ಸಾಕ್ಷಿ). Conscience. ಮನೋಗತ. Notion, wish. ಮನೋಗತಿ. The heart's desire; the speed of thought. ಮನೋಜಯ. Conquering the mind; pleasing, agreeable. ಮನೋಜ್ಞ. Pleasing, lovely, charming; a wise man; *f.* ಮನೋಜ್ಞೆ. ಮನೋದುಃಖ. Heart-ache, anguish. ಮನೋದೃಢ. Firm in mind; firmness of mind. ಮನೋಧರ್ಮ. A faculty of the mind, *as* thought, memory, *etc.* ಮನೋನಿಗ್ರಹ. Restraining and governing the mind. ಮನೋರಂಜಕ. Pleasing, lovely. ಮನೋರಂಜನ. Pleasantness; diversion, sport. ಮನೋರಥ. A wish, desire, purpose; a desired object. -ಸಿದ್ಧಿ. The fulfilment of a wish. ಮನೋರಮ. Attractive, pleasing, agreeable. ಮನೋವಾಕ್ಕಾಯ. Mind, word and body. ಮನೋವಿಕಾರ. Passion or emotion of the mind, bewilderment, *etc.* ಮನೋವೃತ್ತಿ. = ಮನೋಧರ್ಮ, *q. v.* ಮನೋವೇಗ. The speed of thought. ಮನೋವ್ಯಥೆ. Mental pain, anguish. ಮನೋವ್ಯಾಪಾರ. Mental operation. ಮನೋಹರ. Captivating, attractive, delightful, charming, beautiful.

ಮನನ s. *a.* Thoughtful, careful. *n.* Thought; understanding; knowledge; meditation.

ಮನವಿ, ಮನವೆ s. *n.* A petition, request, solicitation.

ಮನಸು, ಮನಸ್ಸು (= ಮನ *q. v. tb. of* ಮನಸ್) *n.* Mind, intellect, conscience, will; the mind; the heart. 2, intention, design, purpose; will, wish; desire; liking, choice. ಮನಸಿಗಾಗು. To be suitable for one's mind. ಮನಸಿಗೆ ತರು. = ಮನಕೆ ತರು. ಮನಸಿಗೆ ಬರು. = ಮನಕೆ ಬರು. ಮನಸಿನಲ್ಲಿಟ್ಟುಕೊಳ್ಳು. To keep in mind, remember, *etc.* ಮನಸಿಗೆ ಹತ್ತು. To remain in the mind. ಮನಸಿಗೆ ಹಿಡಿ. To touch the mind; to retain in the mind. ಮನಸಿಡು. = ಮನವಿಡು. ಮನಸಿನ ಮೇಲೆ ತೆಕ್ಕೊಳ್ಳು. To mind, attend to diligently. ಮನಸಿನೊಳಗೆ ಬರು. To enter the mind. -ಕರಗು. The heart to melt. -ಕೂಡು. Opinions to agree. -ಕೆಡು, -ಗೆಡು. = ಮನಗೆಡು. -ತಿರುಗಿಸು. To change the mind, repent. -ನೋಯು. The mind to be pained. -ನೋಯಿಸು. To pain the mind. -ಬರು. To desire, list. -ಬಂದ ಹಾಗೆ ಮಾಡು. To do as one pleases, *etc.* -ಬಿಚ್ಚು. To open ones mind. -ಬಿಚ್ಚಿ ಮಾತಾಡು. To speak out one's thoughts. -ಮಾಡು. To make up one's mind; to resolve. -ಹಾಕು. To engage in. -ಹೇಸು. The mind to feel disgust. ಮನಸ್ಕರಿಸು. To be inclined, to will. ಮನಸ್ಕಾರ. Full perception; perfect consciousness. ಮನಸ್ತಾಪ. Mental pain, agony; remorse, regret.

ಮನಸ್ವಿ s. *a.* According to one's inclination. 2, capricious, fanciful.

ಮನು s. *n.* Man, mankind; the father of mankind; one of the 14 successive progenitors or sovereigns of the earth, to the 1st of them is ascribed the code of Manu. -ಜ. A man; *f.* -ಜೆ. -ಸ್ಮೃತಿ. The code of Manu.

ಮನುಷ್ಯ s. *n.* A man; *f.* ಮನುಷ್ಯಳು, ಮನುಷ್ಯೆ. -ತ್ವ. Manhood. -ಧರ್ಮ. The duty of man. -ಮಾತ್ರ. A mere man.

ಮನೆ k. *n.* A habitation, abode; a house; an apartment, room. *Cpds.:* ಚಪ್ಪರಗರ-, ದೀವಿಗೆ-, ಮಲಗುವ-, ಮೀಯುವ-, ಸಜ್ಜೆಯ-, ಹೆತ್ತ-, *etc.* -ಕೆಲಸ. Domestic work. -ಖರ್ಚು. Household expenses. -ತನ. Household, household-life. -ತನ ಮಾಡು. To keep house, to support a family. -ತನದವ -ತನಸ್ತ. A householder, a worthy honourable man -ತೊತ್ತು A house-maid -ದೇವ, -ದೈವ A household deity -ಬದುಕು, -ವಾರ್ತೆ Household affairs, domestic property. -ಮಾಡಿಕೊಳ್ಳು. To settle -ಮಾಡು To build a house. -ಮಾರು. *etc* House and its appendages -ಮುಟ್ಟು. To reach the house; the furniture of a house. -ಮುರುಕ. One who ruins a house. -ಮುರುಕತನ Ruining a house. -ಯಜಮಾನ. The master of a house, *f* -ಯಜಮಾನಳು, -ಯಜಮಾನಿ -ಯವ. An inmate of a house; *f.* -ಯವಳು, *pl.* -ಯವರು, *also* the master of a house (*in the wife's language*), *f.* -ಯವಳು, -ಯಾಕೆ -ಯಾಳು. A domestic servant.

ಮಂತನ, ಮಂತಾನ = ಮನೆತನ, *q v.*

ಮಂತರ *tb. of* ಮಂತ್ರ, *q v.*

ಮಂತು (*tb. of* ಮಂಥ) *n* Churning. 2, a churning-stick 3, a fault, an offence

ಮಂತ್ರ s. *n* A vedic verse of prayer. 2, a magical formula incantation, charm, spell 3, secret consultation; counsel, secret plan -ಗಾರ, -ವಾದಿ. A magician conjurer -ಜ್ಞ A learned Brahmana, a priest; a secret agent. -ತಂತ್ರ. Spells and devices. -ಭೇದ Breach of counsel, a particular magical incantation -ವಾದಿ. A magician, conjurer -ಶಾಸ್ತ್ರ Magical science ಮಂತ್ರಾಕ್ಷತೆ Akshatĕ consecrated by mantras ಮಂತ್ರಾಲೋಚಕ. A councillor ಮಂತ್ರಾಲೋಚನ A private consultation ಮಂತ್ರಾಲೋಚನ ಸಭೆ A council

ಮಂತ್ರಿ s *n.* A king's councillor, minister. 2, a conjurer. -ಕ. A magician -ತನ -ತ್ವ Ministership -ಸು To counsel advice, to enchant with spells or charms.

ಮಂಥ

ting

-ದಂಡ -ನ Churning, kindling fire by friction

ಮಂದ s. *a.* Slow, idle lazy, apathetic 2, dull, heavy, stupid, silly, foolish. 3, little, dim, faint, *as* light, *etc.*; mild, *as* a smile, low, *as* a tone, gentle *as* breeze, feeble, *as* digestion, thick, *as* a cloth, plank wall, curds, *etc.* *n.* Indigestion. 2 the planet Saturn -ಕಾರಿ Causing indigestion -ಗತಿ A slow motion, *also* -ಗಮನ -ಗಾಮಿ Marching slowly. -ಜ. A lotus -ತ್ವ Slowness, dulness, stupidity. -ಬುದ್ಧಿ, -ಮತಿ. Stupidity, dulness. -ಮಾರುತ A gentle breeze, *also* ಮಂದಾನಿಲ ಮಂದಾಕ್ಷ. Weak-eyed; bashfulness -ಸ್ಮಿತ, -ಹಾಸ A smile ಮಂದಾಗ್ನಿ Weakness of digestion. ಮಂದಾಸನ A wooden chest ಮಂದೋಷ್ಣ. Lukewarm. tepid, gentle heat

ಮಂದಟ್ಟು (*fr.* ಮನ-ತಟ್ಟು) k *n.* Knowledge.

ಮಂದರ s *n* N of a mountain with which the ocean was churned by the gods and asuras *also* ಮಂದರಾಚಲ. *a* Large, bulky, thick

ಮಂದಾಕಿನಿ s *n* The Ganges

ಮಂದಾರ s *n* The Coral tree, *Erythrina indica* 2, a white species of swallow-wort, *Calotropis gigantea.*

ಮಂದಿ k. *n* Persons, people. *Cpds* ಅನೇಕ-, ಒಕ್ಕೀ-, ಬಹು-, ಸಾವಿರ- ಹೆಚ್ಚು- -ವಾಳ. Impertinence, arrogance

ಮಂದಿರ s. *n* A habitation, house. ದೇವ-. A temple ರಾಜ- A palace

ಮಂದು k *n* A hamlet of the Todas on the Nilagiri

ಮಂದೆ s. *n* A flock of sheep or goats, herd of cattle 2, a fold pen.

ಮಂದೈಸು f *v. i.* To thicken, coagulate. to form a mass, to become pleasing.

ಮನ್ನ f *n* Manna, the (bread-like) food miraculously supplied to the Israelites in the wilderness

... ation,

reveri-

kindly

ಮನ್ನಾ h. *a* Forbidden, stopped *n* Prohibition, stoppage -ಆಗು. To be stopped, to cease -ಮಾಡು To stop, prohibit

ಮನ್ನಿಸು (*fr.* ಮನ್ನಾ) h *v t* To bear with, overlook, excuse, pardon.

ಮನ್ಮಥ s. *n.* Love, Kâma 2, the wood-apple tree, *Feronia elephantum*

ಮನ್ಯು s. *n* Anger, wrath, fury 2, sorrow, distress.

ಮನ್ಯೆ s. *n* The nape of the neck.

ಮನ್ವಂತರ (*fr* ಮನು) s *n* A Manu's age comprising 71 great yugas

ಮಬ್ಬು k. *n.* Darkness; gloom, dimness, drowsiness, dulness, stupidity -ಕಣ್ಣು Dim sight -ಗತ್ತಲೆ Sable darkness ಮಬ್ಬಿಗ An Asura, Râkshasa.

ಮಮ s. *pro* Of me, mine -ಕಾರ Attachment, love, selfishness -ತೆ. Love, tenderness, affection, selfishness, pride, arrogance

ಮಮ್ಮು k. *n* Food (*in children's language*)

ಮಯ್, ಮಯಿ (= ಮೈ, *q. v*) k *n* The body -ಗಡ, -ಸಾಲ Money lent without document or interest.

ಮಯ s *a.* Made of, consisting of, full of. *n.* N of an asura.

ಮಯಿದುನ = ಮಯ್ದುನ, *q. v*

ಮಯೂರ s *n* A peacock 2, a species of flower, cock's comb, *Celosia cristata, also* -ಶಿಖೆ -ಕ -ಕಂಠ, -ತುತ್ಥ Blue vitriol -ಗಮನ, -ಧ್ವಜ. Shanmukha

ಮಯ್ದುನ (= ಮಯಿದುನ, ಮೈದುನ) k *n.* A husband's or wife's brother; a sister's husband, a maternal uncle's son.

ಮಯ್ಲಿ (= ಮೈಲಿ) h. *n* Impurity, dirt 2, pox (the small-, chicken-, vaccine-) -ಏಳು Pox to break out -ತೆಗಿಸು. To have (a person) vaccinated -ತೆಗೆ To vaccinate -ಹಾಲು Vaccine matter -ಗೆ, ಮಯ [illegible] dirtiness, [illegible]

ಮರ k. *n* A tree, wood, timber. -ಅವುಡಲ A hedge-shrub, *Jatropha curcas* -ಕಟ್ಟು To draw toddy -ಕಬ್ಬು A hard kind of sugar-cane -ಕಾಲು, -ಗಾಲು A stilt, a wooden leg, a corn or salt measure -ಕುಟಕ, -ಕುಟಪಕ್ಷಿ, -ಕುಟಿಗ, -ಗಡಕ. The wood-pecker. -ಕೆಲಸ Carpentry. -ಗಾಣ A wooden oil-mill -ಗಿಣಿ A tree parrot which cannot talk -ಗೊರಡು A log of wood. -ದಣಬೆ A tree-mushroom -ದರಸಿನ, -ದರಿಸಿನ A species of Curcuma -ಪಟ್ಟಿ. A carpenter's work-board -ಬೆಕ್ಕು. The Bondar, *Paradoxurus bondar.* -ಮೆಣಸು The *Pimento* tree, *Pimenta acris* -ಹುಣಿಸೆ. The hog-plum, *Spondias mangifera*

ಮರ. = ಮರು 1, *q. v*

ಮರಕತ s. *n* An emerald

ಮರಕಳಿಸು (ರ = ಱ) k *v t* To ruminate, chew the cud, *as* an animal.

ಮರಗ f. *n.* Mint, *Mentha sativa.*

ಮರಗಿ, ಮರಗೆ k *n* A wooden basin; a sort of bucket.

ಮರಗು = ಮರುಗು, *q. v.*

ಮರಣ s *n.* Dying, death. -ಕಾಲ The time of death. -ಪಡಿಸು To kill -ಪಡು, -ಪಾಗು, -ಹೊಂದು To die. -ವೇದನೆ, -ಸಂಕಟ The agony of death -ಶಾಸನ A last will. ಮರಣಾಂತ Ending in death.

ಮರತು, ಮರದು = ಮರೆದು (ರ = ಱ). *P p. of* ಮರೆ, *q v* ಮರವು = ಮರವು, *q v.*

ಮರಲು 1 k *v i.* To turn, to retreat, return, to occur or do again ಮರಳಿ Again, back

ಮರಲು 2 k *n* Sand, gravel. 2 flower

ಮರವಳಿ k *n.* The produce of trees -ಗುತ್ತಿಗೆ. Renting such produce.

ಮರವು 1. ಮರವೆ 1 a k. *n* Intoxication, madness, bewilderment, torpor ಮರಸು To become furious

ಮರವು 2 ಮರವೆ 2 (ರ = ಱ) k *n* Hiding, secrecy, forgetting, forgetfulness, [illegible]

ಮರಸುತ್ತು f n. A screw

ಮರಹುವ್ಕ್ಕತು. = ಮರಾಮತ್, q v

ಮರಳು 1. = ಮರಲು 1, q v

ಮರಳು 2. = ಮರಲು 2 q v

ಮರಳು 3. k. v. i To bubble up, boil fiercely ಮರಳಿಸು To cause to bubble up, etc.

ಮರಳು 4 = ಮರುಳು q v

ಮರಾಟ (tb of ಮಹಾರಾಷ್ಟ್ರ) n Mahratta, a Mahratta man ಮರಾಟಿ Belonging to Mahratta, a Mahratta person, also ಮರಾಟಿಯವ, f. ಮರಾಟಿಯವಳು.

ಮರಾಮತ್ತು h n Repairs, as of roads houses, tanks, etc. -ಇಲಾಖೆ The public works department

ಮರಾಲ, ಮರಾಳ s n A flamingo, a goose a Soft, tender

ಮರಿ (ರಿ = ಱಿ) s. n. The young of any animal, a young child, a pupil, a shoot, sapling. ಕೋಳೀ-. A chicken -ಈ, -ಕೊಡು, -ಹಾಕು To bring forth young, to yean -ಗುದುರೆ A colt -ಗೋಗಿಲೆ A young cuckoo. -ಜೇಡ ಹುಳ A young spider -ಮಕ್ಕಳು (pl. of ಮರಿಮಗ) Great grand-children. -ಮಗ. A great grand-son -ಮಗಳು A great grand-daughter. -ಮಾಡು To hatch as fowls.

ಮರಿಸು = ಮರಸು, q v

ಮರಿಗೆ = ಮರಗೆ, q v

ಮರಿಯಾದೆ. tb of ಮರ್ಯಾದೆ, q v

ಮರೀಚಿಕೆ s. n Mirage

ಮರು 1 (ರು = ಱು) k a Other, next, following second; again, opposite. n Forgetfulness -ಕಳಿಸು To return, as fever -ಚಲ A third or last born child -ದಿನ, -ದಿವಸ The next day. -ಮಾತು. An answer -ವಸಲ An antagonist enemy

ಮರು 2 s n A sandy desert -ಭೂಮಿ. = ಮರು-

ಮರುಕ (ರ = ಱ) k n. Sorrow, grief, affection, love, allurement, infatuation

ಮರುಕುಳಿ k. n Bewilderment. 2, a forgetful man.

ಮರುಗ (tb of ಮರುವಕ) n. A kind of Ocimum 2, sweet marjoram

ಮರುಗು (ರು = ಱು) k. v i. To burn, be very hot, to fret, grieve; to be distressed.

ಮರುತ, ಮರುತ್ತು (tb of ಮರುತ್) n Wind 2, the god of the wind.

ಮರುವ, -ಕ = ಮರುಗ, q v

ಮರುಳ (ಜಡ) k n A kind of plant. 2, a mad, foolish man; f ಮರುಳಿ.

ಮರುಳು (= ಮರಳು) k n Bewilderment, confusion, foolishness, stupidity; fury madness, frenzy. ಮರುಳ A fool. ಮರುಳಾಗು To become mad, confused ಮರುಳಾಟ Confusion madness, etc -ಗೊಳ್ಳು. To become mad, etc Cpds. -ನಾಯಿ -ನುಡಿ, -ಮಾತು, etc -ತನ. Madness, frenzy

ಮರೆ (ರೆ = ಱೆ) k v. t & v i To forget 2, to be forgotten. P ps ಮರೆತು ಮರೆದು, ಮರೆದು n. Disappearance, secrecy, concealment, cover, veiling, a screen, shelter. refuge -ನಿಲು To stand out of one's light -ಬೀಳು To take refuge, to seek shelter. -ಮಾಡು To hide -ಮೊಗ A veiled face -ಯಾಗು, -ಗೊಳ್ಳು. To disappear. -ಹೊಗು To resort to, to go for protection.

ಮರ್ಕಟ s n A monkey, ape. ಮರ್ಕಟಿ. The Molucca bean, cowhage.

ಮರ್ಜಿ h n Will, pleasure opinion, disposition; manner, way.

ಮರ್ಡಿ k. n. A hill

ಮರ್ತಬಾ h. n Rank, station, dignity

ಮರ್ತ್ಯ s n A mortal, man a Mortal. -ಲೋಕ. The earth

ಮರ್ದನ s. n Crushing, grinding, pounding. rubbing, pressing -ಮಾಡು, ಮರ್ದಿಸು. To crush, grind, pound, to rub, to destroy.

ಮರ್ದಲ = ಮದ್ದಳೆ q v

ಮರ್ಮ s. n. A vital part. 2, a secret, mystery, secret meaning; secret purpose, a secret quality. -ತಿಳಿ, -ಹಿಡಿ, -ಸಿಕ್ಕು To find out a secret. -ಜ್ಞ. A discerning man. ಮರ್ಮಿ. A mysterious person.

ಮರ್ಮರ s. n. A rustling sound, murmur.

ಮರ್ಯಾದೆ (= ಮರಿಯಾದೆ) s. n. A limit, border. 2, the bounds of morality, moral law, rule of decency; propriety of conduct, reverential demeanour, respect, civility. -ಮಾಡು, -ತೋರಿಸು, -ಕೊಡು. To show respect, etc. Cpds.: ಕುಲದ-, ಗ್ರಾಮ-, ದೇಶದ-.

ಮಲ 1. (= ಮರು, q. v.) k. a. Other, next, second, etc. -ಚಲ. A third or last child. -ತಂದೆ A step-father. -ತಮ್ಮ A step-mother's son. -ತಾಯಿ. A step-mother. -ಮಾಸ An intercalary month.

ಮಲ 2. = ಮಲೆ 1, q. v. -ನಾಡು. A hilly country. -ವಾರು, -ಯಾಳ. Malabar.

ಮಲ 3. s. n. Excretions of the body, dirt, filth, excrement, etc., dregs, dross of metal. 2, moral impurity, sin. 3, original sin. -ಕಟ್ಟು, -ಬದ್ಧ Constipation. -ನಾಗರು, -ರೋಗ Epilepsy. -ಪೃಷ್ಠ The fly-leaf of a book. -ವಿಸರ್ಜನೆ, -ಶುದ್ಧಿ, -ಶೋಧನೆ Evacuation of the bowels, a purgative. -ತೆ, -ತ್ವ Dirtiness, impurity.

ಮಲಕು 1. k. n. A round ornament of glass beads, corals, etc. 2, a kind of necklace.

ಮಲಕು 2. k. n. Bringing up again in rumination. -ಹಾಕು. To chew the cud.

ಮಲಗು k. v. i. To recline, lie down, repose, rest. 2, to incline, bend, as paddy-ears, etc. n. A pillow, cushion. ಮಲಗಿಸು To cause to lie down, or recline, to place; to lay down, etc.

ಮಲಫೂಫ h. n. Enclosure, as of a letter.

ಮಲಮಲು h. n. Muslin.

ಮಲಯ s. n. N. of a hill-range in Malabar, Malabar country. -ಪರ್ವತ. Malabar mountain. -ಪವನ Malabar air. ಮಲಯಾಳ The Malayâlam country.

ಮಲರ್ (= ಮರಲು 2, q. v.) Sand. 2, a flower. -ಪುಡಿ The pollen of flowers.

ಮಲಾಮತು h. n. A difficulty, strait, trouble.

ಮಲಾಮು h. n. Ointment, plaster.

ಮಲಾರ s. n. A cluster or string of glass bracelets.

ಮಲಿನ (fr. ಮಲ 3) s. a. Dirty, filthy, unclean. 2, sinful, vile. 3, dark, obscure (as the intellect), dull, rusty (as learning, etc.). -ಚಿತ್ತ, -ಬುದ್ಧಿ. A depraved or dull mind. -ತೆ, -ತ್ವ Filthiness, impurity.

ಮಲುಕು = ಮಲಕು, q. v.

ಮಲೆ 1. (= ಮಲ 2, ಮಲಯ) k. n. A mountain. -ಯಾಳ = ಮಲಯಾಳ, q. v.

ಮಲೆ 2. a. k. v. t. To oppose, fight against. v. i. To be refractory, to be haughty, insolent. ಮಾರ್-. To rebel.

ಮಲ್ಲ k. n. A wrestler, boxer; an athlete. a. Strong, stout, good. -ಯುದ್ಧ. A wrestling match. -ರಂಗ. A palaestra. ಮಲ್ಲಾಡು. To struggle or strive. ಮಲ್ಲಾಟ Mutual strife.

ಮಲ್ಲಳಿ (ಳ = ಱ) a. k. n. Turning round. 2, bewilderment, alarm, fear. 3, the black bee. 4, a crowd.

ಮಲ್ಲಿ 1, ಮಲ್ಲಿಗೆ (tb. of ಮಲ್ಲಿಕಾ) n. A cultivated flower shrub, Jasminum sambac. Varieties: ಆಡವಿಯ-, ಕದರು-, ಕಸ್ತೂರಿ-, ಕೋಲು-, ದುಂಡು-, ಸಂಜೆ-, ಹಸರು-.

ಮಲ್ಲಿ 2. s. n. A female image of metal with a lamp-cup, also ದೀಪದ-.

ಮಲ್ಲಿಕಾರ್ಜುನ s. n. N. of Śiva and of a linga.

ಮವುಜು h. n. A plantain.

ಮವುಜೆ h. n. A village.

ಮಶಕ s. n. A gnat, musquito, a bug.

ಮಶೀನು e. n. A machine (= ಯಂತ್ರ).

ಮಶೀತಿ, ಮಶೀದಿ (=ಮಸೀದಿ) h *n*. A mosque

ಮಷಾಲು h *n* A torch. ಮಷಾಲ್ಜಿ. A torch-bearer, a menial servant of an office

ಮಷಿ. = ಮಸಿ *q v*.

ಮಷ್ಕರಿ h *n* Obstinacy, stubbornness

ಮಷ್ಟು = ಮುಷ್ಟಿ 1 *q v*

ಮಸಕ 1. a k *n*. Great agitation passion; wrath, rage.

ಮಸಕ 2, ಮಸಕು (= ಮಸ್ಕು) k *n*. Duskiness; a dusky colour, *etc*, impurity

ಮಸಗು a k *v i* To expand, develop; to be displayed, agitated, enraged *v t*. To display, exhibit. 2, to rub, whet

ಮಸಣ, ಮಸಾಣ (*tb of* ಶ್ಮಶಾನ, *q v*) *n*. A cemetery, *also* -ಗಾಡು, -ವಟ್ಟಿಗೆ, -ವಟ್ಟಿ

ಮಸರು = ಮೊಸರು, *q v*

ಮಸಲತು h. *n* Planning, scheming, a plan, plot, counsel, clever contrivance.

ಮಸಾರೆ (ಭೂಮಿ) f. *n* A kind of good red soil.

ಮಸಾಲಾ, ಮಸಾಲೆ f *n* Seasoning drugs, spicery -ವಡೆ A kind of spiced cake

ಮಸಿ (= ಮಷಿ) s *n* Ink, soot, lampblack, charcoal -ಕುಡಿಕೆ, -ಪಾತ್ರೆ. An inkstand. -ಬಟ್ಟೆ. A rag used in lifting pots from the fire -ಯಾಗು. To become charcoal (*said of buried money*)

ಮಸೀದಿ = ಮಶೀತಿ, *etc.*, *q v*.

ಮಸುಕು = ಮಸಕು, *q v*

ಮಸುಳು a. k *v i* To grow dim, faint, to become pale, *etc* ಮಸುಳಿಸು To cause to grow dim, *etc*

ಮಸೂದೆ h. *n* A sketch, a draft.

ಮಸೂರ, ಮಸೂರಿ h *n*. A sort of pulse or lentil, *Ervum hirsutum* ಮಸೂರಿಕೆ Pustules, small-pox, a musquito-curtain, a cushion

ಮಸೆ k *n* Whetting, sharpness. 2, a sli

To rub to grind, whet, sharpen, to rub off *P ps* ಮಸದು, ಮಸೆದು ಮಸ್ತು

ಮಸ್ಕರಿ h *n*. A good-for-nothing fellow

ಮಸ್ಕು = ಮಸಕ 2, *q v*.

ಮಸ್ತಕ s *n* The head, skull; the top of anything

ಮಸ್ತಿ h. *n* Intoxication, pride. 2, fatness, rut. ಮಸ್ತು Intoxicated; fat, bulky, abundant, plentiful, intoxication; abundauce, plenty.

ಮಸ್ತಿಷ್ಕ s *n* The brain.

ಮಸ್ಲತು = ಮಸಲತು, *q v*

ಮಸ್ಲೀನು h *n* Muslin, *also* ಮಲಮಲು

ಮಹ = ಮಹಾ, *q v*

ಮಹಜರು h *n* A general affidavit, a certificate sig.ed by all present at a transaction

ಮಹತ್ (= ಮಹಾ) s *a* Great, mighty, strong, big, large. 2, abundant, much. 3, high, lofty, noble; excellent -ತಮ. Greatest, mightiest -ತರ. Greater, the oldest, most respectable ಮಹತ್ವ ಮಹತ್ವತೆ. Greatness, majesty mightiness, *etc* ಮಹರ್ಷಿ. A great rishi

ಮಹತಾಪು, ಮಹತಾಬು (= ಮತಾಪು) f *n*. A kind of fire-work

ಮಹತ್ತು. *tb of* ಮಹತ್, *q v*

ಮಹಂತ. *tb of* ಮಹತ್, *q v*

ಮಹಮದ, ಮಹಮ್ಮದ h. *n*. Mahomed, a Mahomedan

ಮಹಲು. = ಮಹಾಲು *q v*.

ಮಹಸೂಲು h. *n* Public revenue, private income from land -ದಾರ A receiver of taxes

ಮಹಳ *tb of* ಮಹಾಲಯ, *q v*

ಮಹಾ (= ಮಹ, ಮಹತ್ತು, ಮಹತ್. *q v*) s *a* Great, mighty. -ಕಾಲ Siva, a fierce man. -ಕಾಲಿ. -ಕಾಳಿ. Durgâ. -ಖರ್ವ Ten kharvas -ಜನ. The populace, respectable men -ತಲ The 6th of the lower worlds -ದಾನ N of certain valuable gifts to priests. A large kettle-drum -ನವಮಿ. The 9th or last day of the navarâtri festival. -ನುಭಾವ Worthy, pre-eminent, a gentleman -ಪದ್ಮ. Ten padmas a million of millions. -ಪಾತಕ. A heinous crime -ಪುರುಷ An eminent personage -ಪ್ರಲಯ The total annihilation of the universe -ಪ್ರಾಣ. An aspirate, a vital air -ಫಲ. Great fruit, the citron. -ಭಾರತ. N of a great epic poem. -ಭಾಷ್ಯ Patanjali's great commentary on Pâṇini's grammar. -ಭೂತ A primary element. -ಮನಸ್ High-minded, liberal, magnanimous. -ಮಾಯೆ Great illusion Durgâ -ಮೇರು The great Mêru -ರಥ. A great chariot, great warrior -ರಾಜ An emperor, a word of respectful compellation -ರಾಣಿ. An empress. -ರಾಷ್ಟ್ರ A great realm, the Mahratta country -ರೌರವ One of the 21 hells. -ಋುದ. Ten arbudas. -ಲಕ್ಷ್ಮಿ. The Śakti or wife of Nârâyana -ಶಯ. The ocean; an honorific title, high-minded, magnanimous -ಸಾಗರ The great ocean

ಮಹಾತ್ಮ s a High-souled, noble-minded, generous, eminent, mighty. n. A noble-minded man. ಮಹಾತ್ಮೆ Noble-mindedness, a noble-minded woman.

ಮಹಾಂತ s. n. Abundance. 2, an eminent man

ಮಹಾಲಯ (= ಮಹಲು) s. n. A great dwelling, palace, temple. 2, (= ಮಹಳ) the latter fortnight of the bhâdrapada month; the śrâddha performed at that time

ಮಹಾಲು (= ಮಹಲು, ಮಹಾಲಯ) h. n A palace, hall 2, a subdivision of a talook or district

ಮಹಿ s a Great, large n Greatness 2, the earth, soil -ತಲ The earth's surface. -ಧರ A mountain -ಕಾಂತ -ಪ, -ಪತಿ, [illegible] A king. -ಮಂಡಲ. The whole earth.

ಮಹಿಮೆ s n Greatness, grandeur, majesty, glory; might, power, energy -ಪಡಿಸು To glorify, magnify -ಕೊಡು To give glory, etc ಮಹಿಮಾಕರ. A mine of glory, glorious.

ಮಹಿಷ s n A male buffalo ಮಹಿಷಿ. A buffalo-cow ಮಹಿಷಾಸುರ N. of an asura slain by Durgâ

ಮಹೇಂದ್ರ s n Great Indra, regent of the east quarter -ಜಾಲ. Indra's net trick, cheating, illusion, jugglery, sorcery.

ಮಹೇಶ, ಮಹೇಶ್ವರ s. n. A great lord, Śiva, f ಮಹೇಶ್ವರಿ

ಮಹೋತ್ಪಾತ s. n A meteor, comet.

ಮಹೋತ್ಸವ s. n A great festival

ಮಹೋತ್ಸಾಹ s n Great effort. a. Very energetic, persevering.

ಮಹೋದಯ s n Great happiness. 2, a very auspicious day

ಮಹೋದರ s n. Dropsy

ಮಹೋನ್ನತ s a Very high, lofty

ಮಹೋಪದ್ರವ s n. Great distress.

ಮಹೋಲ್ಲಾಸ s. n Great delight.

ಮಹೌಷಧ s n A very efficacious remedy.

ಮಳಲು k n Sand, gravel. ಮಳಲೇರಿ. A sand-bank

ಮಳಿಗೆ f n. A warehouse, shop

ಮಳೆ (ಳೆ = ಟಿ) k n Rain. -ಕಾಲ, -ಗಾಲ. The rainy season -ಗರೆ, -ಸುರಿ. To rain· -ಗುರುತು Signs of rain -ನೀರು Rainwater. -ಬಿಡು. Rain to cease. -ಬಿಲ್ಲು. A rainbow. -ಹನಿ. A rain-drop. -ಹಿಡಿ Rain to set in

ಮಾ 1 tb of ಮಹಾ, q v. -ಗೆಲಸ Great work. -ಕಾಳಿ, -ತಾಯಿ. Durgâ

ಮಾ 2 k n. Great emotion -ಮಸಕ. Great agitation or activity.

ಮಾಂಸ s. n. Flesh, meat, the pulp of fruit -ಗ್ರಂಥಿ. A gland, wen -ಜೀವಿ, -ಭಕ್ಷಕ, ಮಾಂಸಾಹಾರಿ Carnivorous, a flesh-eater. [illegible] Fleshy lusty, muscular, strong. [illegible] Animal food ಮಾಂಸಿಕ A butcher -ಭಕ್ಷಕ. A cannibal ಗೋ- Beef

ಮಾಕರಿಸು k v i To reveal secrets

ಮಾಗಣಿ 1 k n A garden-herb, *Coleus barbatus*.

ಮಾಗಣಿ 2 h n A division of a talook

ಮಾಗಧ (*fr*. ಮಗಧ) s *a*. Relating to Magadha *n* A bard, minstrel ಮಾಗಧಿ. The Magadha language; a sort of jasmin, *Jasminum auriculatum*

ಮಾಗಾಯಿ k *n* A small ear-ornament of females.

ಮಾಗಿ, ಮಾಗೆ (*tb. of* ಮಾಘ) *n*. The cold season, *also* -ಕಾಲ

ಮಾಗು k *v i* To ripen fully, *as* fruit; to be mature *as* a medicine ಮಾಗಿಸು. To cause to ripen, *etc*

ಮಾಘ (= ಮಾಗಿ, ಮಾಗೆ) s *n* The 11th lunar month (January-February) -ಸ್ನಾನ. A bath in that month

ಮಾಂಗಲ್ಯ (*fr* ಮಂಗಲ) s *a* Auspicious *n* An auspicious or festive ceremony 2, prosperity, welfare. -ಸೂತ್ರ = ಮಂಗಲಸೂತ್ರ.

• ಮಾಚಿ k *n* A species of plant -ಪತ್ರೆ, ಪತ್ರೆ A common weed, *Artemisia maderaspatana*

ಮಾಜಿ h *a* Gone by, passed away, late, former

ಮಾಜು k. *v t* To cause to disappear, to hide, conceal, efface *n* Dissimulation, deceit, fraud

ಮಾಜುಂ h. *n* An intoxicating preparation of the hemp plant.

ಮಾಟ (*fr*. ಮಾಡು) k *n* Making, doing; a work, business, undertaking. 2, a manner, way 3, handsomeness beauty. 4 trickery, jugglery, magic, sorcery -ಕೂಟ Good execution finish -ಗಾರ A sorcerer, *f* -ಗಾತಿ. -ಗಾರಿಕೆ Sorcery

ಮಾಡ 1 (= ಮಾಡು 2) k *n* A hole or niche in a wall 2, a kind of litter.

ಮಾಡ 2 (= ಮಾಡು 3 *cf* ಮಾಳಿಗೆ) f *n* A large ... *also* ಮಾಡಿ. 3, a gable roof -ಹಾಗಲಬಳ್ಳಿ. A climbing herb, *Momordica dioica*

ಮಾಡು 1. k. *v. t* To do, make, perform, accomplish, effect, prepare, construct, build, execute, to cultivate, *as* a field, *etc*. *P. p.* ಮಾಡಿ. *Cpds* ಅಡಿಗೆ-, ಅಪಮಾನ-, ಅರಿಕೆ-, ಉಪವಾಸ-, ಕೆಲಸ-, ಕೇಡು-, ಜೀವನ-, ದಾನ-, ಪಕ್ಷ-, ಪರೀಕ್ಷೆ-, ಪೂಜೆ-, ಪ್ರೀತಿ-, ಮೋಸ-, ಯುದ್ಧ-, ವರ್ತಕತನ-, ವಶ-, ಸೇವೆ-, ಸ್ತೋತ್ರ-, ಸ್ನಾನ-, ಸ್ನೇಹ-, ಹಗೆ-, *etc* ಮಾಡಗೊಡು To allow to do, *etc* ಮಾಡೇ-. *rep* To do certainly ಮಾಡುವಿಕೆ Doing. *etc*. ಮಾಡಿಸು To cause to make, do, perform, *etc* ಮಾಡಿಸುವಿಕೆ Causing to make, *etc*

ಮಾಡು 2. = ಮಾಡ 1, *q v*

ಮಾಡು 3. = ಮಾಡ 2, *q v*

ಮಾಣಿಕ (*tb. of* ಮಾಣಿಕ್ಯ) *n* A ruby. 2, redness.

ಮಾಣು k *v i* To stop, cease, subside, be checked, to desist, cease from, give over 2, to be healed, cured *P p* ಮಾಣ್ದು. ಮಾಣಿಸು To cause to stop, *etc*

ಮಾಂಡಲಿಕ s. *a* Provincial. *n*. The governor of a province

ಮಾತಂಗ s *n* A man of the lowest rank; an outcast, *f*. ಮಾತಂಗಿ

ಮಾತಾಮಹ s. *n* A maternal grandfather, *f* ಮಾತಾಮಹಿ.

ಮಾತು 1 k *n* A word, a saying, a language, a promise slander, rumour. ಮಾತಾಟ. Talking, talk, garrulity ಮಾತಾಡು. To speak, converse. ಮಾತಾಳಿ A talkative man -ಕೊಡು To promise -ಗಳ್ಳ A cheat, liar -ಕೇಳು. To listen to words -ತಪ್ಪಿಸು, -ತಿರಿಗಿಸು, -ಮುರಿ To break a promise. -ತಪ್ಪು. A promise to be broken. -ಮಾಡು. To make an oral agreement. -ಹಿಡಿ To lay hold of a word, to catch one by his word -ದೂರಿಸು To accuse -ಗ, -ಗಾರ A talkative man -ಗಾರತನ,

ಮಾತು 2 *tb of* ಮಾತೃ, *q. v* -ಶ್ರೀ A word of respect for one's mother or an elderly female. -ಲ. A thorn-apple, a maternal uncle -ಲಾನಿ His wife.

ಮಾತುಬರಿ h. *a* Respectable, trustworthy. honest *n.* Trustworthiness, respectability.

ಮಾತುಲಂಗ, ಮಾತುಲುಂಗ s *n.* The citron.

ಮಾತೃ (= ಮಾತು 2, *q. v* , ಮಾಡಿರಿ, *etc*) s. *n* A measurer 2, a mother; *also* ಮಾತೆ. -ಕ. Maternal, fostered. -ಕೆ A mother, the original of a copy -ವಿಯೋಗ The separation from a mother -ಷ್ವಸೃ. A maternal aunt. -ಸೇವೆ. Waiting on a mother. -ಹತ್ಯ Matricide

ಮಾತ್ರ s. *n* Measure, quantity, size, bulk. 2, the whole, the only thing 3, a minute portion, particle. 4, a prosodical instant *ad* As much as; nothing but, mere, only none but *Cpds* ಅದು-, ಇದು-, ಇಷ್ಟು-, ನೀನು-, ಅವನು-, ಒಂದು-, ಹಡಗ-. Only that, *etc* ಸ್ವಲ್ಪ-. Just a little.

ಮಾತ್ರೆ (= ಮಾತ್ರ *n* , *q v.*) s *n* Measure, *etc* 2, a pill

ಮಾತ್ಸರ್ಯ (*fr.* ಮತ್ಸರ) s. *n.* Envy, jealousy, malice

ಮಾದ s *n* Drunkenness, stupor 2, joy, delight 3, pride, passion. 4, *tb of* ಮಹಾದೇವ.

ಮಾದಲ, ಮಾದಾಳ (*tb. of* ಮಾತುಲಂಗ) *n* The citron tree, *Citrus medica.*

ಮಾದಿಗ (*tb. of* ಮಾತಂಗ) *n.* A cobbler, chuckler, an outcast.

ಮಾದಿರಿ, ಮಾದ್ರಿ (*tb of* ಮಾತೃಕೆ) *n.* The original 2, a pattern, specimen sample.

ಮಾದೇವ. *tb of* ಮಹಾದೇವ, *q v.*

ಮಾದೃಶ s. *ad* Like me, resembling me

ಮಾಧವ (*fr.* ಮಧು) s *a.* Sweet *n.* Honey, mead 2, the month vaiśâkha (April-May) 3 spring 4 Vishnu.

ಮಾಧುರ್ಯ s. *n.* Sweetness; pleasantness 2, kindness, amiability

ಮಾಧ್ವ s. *a* Belonging to Madhva's doctrine, *n* An adherent of Madhva; sweetness

ಮಾನ 1. s *n.* Measure, dimension, a measure; rule, standard 2, half a sêru. 3, likeness, resemblance. -ಅಕ್ಕಿ, ಮಾನಕ್ಕಿ. A measure of rice.

ಮಾನ 2 s. *n* Opinion; conception. 2, conceit, arrogance, pride. 3, regard for others, honour, respect, reverence; dignity respectability 4, indignation, caprice -ಕಳೆ, -ತೆಗೆ To disgrace -ಕಾಯು To protect honour. -ಕೊಡು, -ಮಾಡು To honour. -ಗೇಡಿ A dishonourable person -ಗೇಡಿತನ. Disgracefulness -ಗೇಡು Disgrace -ತೋರಿಸು. To show respect. -ನಷ್ಟ Defamation. -ಹೊಂದು. To receive honour -ಭಂಗ Loss of honour, humiliation. -ಮರ್ಯಾದೆ Reputation, respect, regard -ವಂತ, -ಸ್ಥ A respectable man *f.* -ವತಿ -ವಂತೆ. -ಸ್ಥಾನ. The private parts. -ಹಾನಿ Dishonour. -ಹೀನ Disgraceful.

ಮಾನವ s *a* Human. *n* A man ಮಾನವಿ A woman; human

ಮಾನಸ (*fr* ಮನಸ್) s *a* Mental; ideal. *n* The mental powers, the mind. 2, N of a lake. ಮಾನಸಾಂತರ Change of mind, repentance (*for sins, Chr*). ಮಾನಸಿಕ. Mental.

ಮಾನಸಿಕ (*fr* ಮಾಣು) k *n* Stopping, cessation.

ಮಾನಾಯ s *n.* Fees in grain given to a measurer of a village produce.

ಮಾನಿ s *n* A respectable person, *f.* -ನಿ -ಷ್ಠ. Very highly honoured. -ಸು To honour

ಮಾನುಷ, ಮಾನುಷ್ಯ s *a* Human. *n* Humanity

ಮಾನೆ (= ಮಾನ 1) s *n.* A copy to write from a model -ತಿದ್ದು. To draw the pen over the [illegible]

ಮಾಂತ್ರಿಕ (*fr.* ಮಂತ್ರ) s *n* An enchanter, conjurer, sorcerer

ಮಾಂಡು k *v. t* To stop, ward off, check

ಮಾಂದ್ಯ (*fr.* ಮಂದ) s *n* Slowness, laziness 2 torpor, apathy, weakness 3, indisposition, apepsy

ಮಾನ್ಯ s *a* Respectable, honourable, acceptable *n* A ruler 2, honour, a privilege. 3, land either liable to a trifling quit-rent or free from tax. 4 a complimentary form of address in letters -ಗಾರ. One holding a mânya, an incumbent

ಮಾಪ f. *n.* Measure. -ಣ, ಮಾಪಿ. Measuring ಮಾಪಿ ಜಿನಸು Articles of capacity

ಮಾಫಕು h. *a* Conformable, suitable

ಮಾಫ್, ಮಾಫಿ h *a* Pardoned, gratis. *n* Remission (as of tax, *etc*), pardon, excusing

ಮಾಮಲ, ಮಾಮಲೆ h *n* The office of a Mâmaledâra -ದಾರ A subordinate collector of the revenues of a talook.

ಮಾಮಸಕ k *n* Bustling activity, great zeal, ardour.

ಮಾಮೂಲು h *a* Usual, ordinary *n.* Custom, usage, prescription -ಪ್ರಕಾರ ನಡೆ To act according to an established custom

ಮಾಯ (*tb. of* ಮಾಯೆ, *q. v.*) *n* *Also* disappearance, vanishing -ಕ = ಮಾಯಿಕ -ಕ ಮಾಡು To conceal, to cheat -ವಾಗು To vanish. -ಕಾರ, -ಗಾರ A deceiver; a juggler -ಪಾಶ The fetters of illusion -ವಾದ Falsehood -ವಾದಿ A liar -ವಿದ್ಯೆ Jugglery, witchcraft ಮಾಯಾದೇವಿ Buddha's mother, Durgâ ಮಾಯಾವಿ Illusory, magical, a conjurer, juggler.

ಮಾಯಿ 1 s *a* Illusory, unreal, deceptive *n.* A juggler, a cheat 2, deceit -ಕ. Illusory, deceitful, a juggler

ಮಾಯಿ 2 h *n* A mother

ಮಾಯು 1 k *v i.* To be healed *P. p* ಮಾ...

ಮಾಯು 2. s. *n* Sounding crying. 2, gall, bile

ಮಾಯೆ (= ಮಾಯ) s *n* Art 2, illusion, trick deceit deception, fraud, jugglery, sorcery 3, phantasm, phantom. 4, idealism, unreality

ಮಾರ, ಮಾರಣ s. *n* Killing slaughter. destruction 2, a magical ceremony for the purpose

ಮಾರನೆ (ರ = ಱ) k *a.* Other, following, next -ದಿನ -ದಿವಸ The next day

ಮಾರಾಟ. *See s* ಮಾರು 2

ಮಾರಾಮಾರಿ h. *n* Mutual fighting or beating.

ಮಾರಿ (*cf.* ಮಾರ) s *n* Killing. 2, a plague, epidemic, pestilence, the cholera 3 the goddess of death; Durgâ, *also* -ಅಮ್ಮ -ಕುತ್ತ, -ಜಡ, -ರೋಗ The cholera -ಕಾ A plague, pestilence, *etc*

ಮಾರೀಚ s *n* N. of a râkshasa

ಮಾರೀಫತ್ತು h *n* Trust, charge, instrumentality *prep* By means of, through.

ಮಾರು 1 k *n* A fathom

ಮಾರು 2 (ರು = ಱು) k *v t.* To barter, sell. *v i.* To be sold, to be exchanged *P p* ಮಾರಿ ಮಾರಾಟ Exchange, barter, sale. ಮಾರಾಡು To sell

ಮಾರು 3. (ರು = ಱು) k. *n* The state of being other, different, next, change, exchange, barter, sale. 2, hostility ಮಾರಡಿ An opponent, enemy ಮಾರನೆ Following, subsequent. ಮಾರನೆ ದಿನ. The next day. ಮಾರವ. A seller. ಮಾರುತ್ತರ. A reply ಮಾರುತ್ತರ ಕೊಡು. To reply ಮಾರುಳಿ Another affair

ಮಾರ್ = ಮಾರು 3, *q v* -ಕಟ್ಟು A market -ದನಿ. An echo -ನುಡಿ. To answer, a reply. -ನಡೆ Equality, likeness, another force. -ಪೊಡವು, -ಪೊಳವು. A reflection. -ಪೊಳೆ To be reflected -ಬಡ್ಡಿ Compound interest. -ಬಲ. opposing force -ಮಲೆ. To oין,

ಮಾರ್ಗ (*fr* ಮೃಗ) s *n* Search 2, a road, way, track. 3, a channel, canal 4, mode, manner, usage, custom, style. -ಕ್ರಮಣ. Journying -ವಿದ. A knower of the right way. -ಶೀರ್ಷ N of the 9th lunar month. ಅಡ್ಡ- A cross road ದುರ್-, ದುರ್ಮಾರ್ಗ ತನ. Immorality, wickedness ಸನ್- Good conduct ಸನ್ಮಾರ್ಗಕ್ಕೆ ಬರು To reform. -ಕಾಣು. To find the road. -ಸ್ಥ, ಮಾರ್ಗಿಗ A traveller

ಮಾರ್ಚಿ e *n* March (*3rd month of the year*)

ಮಾರ್ಜಿನ್ e *n* Margin

ಮಾರ್ಜನ s *n* Cleansing, scouring, washing. ಮಾರ್ಜನಿ A broom

ಮಾರ್ಜಾರ s *n* A cat, *also* ಮಾರ್ಜಾಲ

ಮಾರ್ತಂಡ, ಮಾರ್ತಾಂಡ s. *n* The sun

ಮಾರ್ಪು (*cf* ಮಾರು 3, *q v*) k *n* Exchange, change ಮಾರ್ಪಾಟು. Change ಮಾರ್ಪಾಗು ಮಾರ್ಪಾಟವಾಗು To change.

ಮಾಲವ (= ಮಾಳವ) s *n*. N of a country, Malva

ಮಾಲಾ = ಮಾಲಿ, *q v* -ಕಾರ A florist.

ಮಾಲಿ s. *n* Wearing a garland. 2, a gardener. -ಕ A florist, *f*. -ನಿ -ಕೆ A garland, a necklace, a collection of things arranged, *as* ನವ-, ಪುಷ್ಪ-, ರಾಗ-

ಮಾಲಿನ್ಯ (*fr* ಮಲಿನ) s *n*. Uncleanness, impurity, sinfulness 2 obscurity

ಮಾಲಿಸು k *v i* To look obliquely, to leer *v t* To bend to one side, *as* a post, *etc*

ಮಾಲೀಕ k *n* An owner, master

ಮಾಲೀಸು h. *n*. Grooming (of a horse)

ಮಾಲು 1. k *v. i*. To bend *n* Sloping, a slope, descent. -ಕಣ್ಣು A squint-eye.

ಮಾಲು 2 h. *n*. Property, goods, wares -ದಾರ A man of property an owner

ಮಾಲೂರ f. *n* The bacl tree, *Aegle marmelos*. 2, the wood-apple tree, *Feronia elephantum*

kha s *n* A w[illegible] garland, a chaplet, Vish necklace; [illegible] -, a row, a series -ಗಾರ. A florist, *f*. -ಗಾತಿ ಜಪ-. A rosary. ಮುಕ್ತಾ-. A pearl necklace. ಹೂ-. A wreath of flowers

ಮಾವ (*tb. of* ಮಾಮ) *n* A father-in-law. ಸೋದರ- A maternal uncle

ಮಾವಟಿಗ, ಮಾವತ, ಮಾವಂತ s. *n* An elephant driver, mahaut.

ಮಾವಿ h. *a* Yellowish green

ಮಾವು k *n* The mango the mango tree, *Mangifera indica* *Cpds* ಮಾವಿನಕಾಯಿ, ಮಾವಿನಗಿಡ, ಮಾವಿನ ಹಣ್ಣು, *etc*

ಮಾವುತ. = ಮಾವಟಿಗ, *q. v*.

ಮಾಷ s *n* A bean; a kind of pulse, *Phaseolus radiatus*. 2, a weight of gold = 11 grs troy

ಮಾಸ s *n* The moon, a month of thirty days. -ಗಟ್ಟಲೆ. A monthly practice, monthly -ಮಾಸ Every month.

ಮಾಸರ s *n* A meal of parched barley soaked with sour milk 2, rice gruel

ಮಾಸವಳ, ಮಾಸವಳ್ಳ, ಮಾಸಾಳು (*tb of* ಮಹಸ್) *n* A great man, hero, leader

ಮಾಸಿಕ (*fr* ಮಾಸ) s. *a* Monthly -ಶ್ರಾದ್ಧ. A monthly śrâddha

ಮಾಸು (= ಮಾಜು, *q. v.*) k *v i* To grow dim; to become dusky, foul, dirty. *v t* To dirty, soil. *n*. Filth, dirt ಮಾಸಲು Impurity, dirtiness

ಮಾಹಾತ್ಮ್ಯ (*fr*. ಮಹಾತ್ಮ) s. *n*. High-mindedness. 2, greatness, majesty, dignity 3, a legend

ಮಾಹಿತು h. *n*. Experience, observation, knowledge.

ಮಾಹೆ h *n*. A month -ವಾರಿ A monthly settlement, monthly accounts

ಮಾಹೇಶ, ಮಾಹೇಶ್ವರ s *n* Relating to Śiva ಮಾಹೇಶ್ವರಿ Pârvatî, Durgâ.

ಮಾಳ f. *n* A plain, a tract of ground. 2, a bed of the sea

ಮಾಳವ = ಮಾಲವ, *q v*

ಮಾಳಿ f.*n*. A washerman. 2, a female gardener

ಮಾಳಿಗೆ (*tb. of* ಮಾಲಿಕೆ) *n*. An upstair house with a flat roof, a flat roof -ಮನೆ. A house with a flat roof.

ಮಿಕ್ಕು 1. *P p of* ಮಿಗು, *q v*

ಮಿಕ್ಕು 2 (= ಮಿಗು) k *i t* To increase, exceed, to remain *n.* Excess, remainder, rest ಮಿಕ್ಕಾಗು To remain

ಮಿಗ *tb of* ಮೃಗ, *q v*

ಮಿಗು (= ಮಿಕ್ಕು 1) k *v i* To grow great, abundant, to exceed, to be in excess, to remain, to go beyond, surpass *P p* ಮಿಕ್ಕಿ, ಮಿಕ್ಕು -ತೆ, ಮಿಗತೆ. Surplus, remnant, rest. ಮಿಗಲು, ಮಿಗಿಲು Greatness, abundance, excellence, excess, remainder, rest ಮಿಗಿಲಾಗು To surpass, excel, to remain ಮಿಗಿಸು To cause to be left or remain

ಮಿಗೆ a k. *ad* Abundantly, much, further, well.

ಮಿಜಾಕು h *n.* Airs and affectation, high notions and fancies

ಮಿಂಚು 1. (= ಮಿಗು, *etc.*, *q v*) k. *i. i* To become great, to excel, exceed, to expire, *as* a period, to pass beyond reach, to behave proudly.

ಮಿಂಚು 2 k *v i* To shine, sparkle, glitter; to flash, lighten. *n.* Shine, lustre, brightness, lightning -ಗಲ್ಲು Talc -ಬಳ್ಳಿ The heart-pea -ಮಾಡು, ಮಿಂಚಿಸು To cause to shine, to furnish, polish. -ಹುಳ A glow-worm

ಮಿಟಕಿಸು, ಮಿಟಕು k *i i* To twinkle, blink, to stare

ಮಿಟಲ (= ಮಿಟ್ಲೆ) k. *n.* N. of a plant.

ಮಿಟಿ k *n* Blinking, staring. -ನೋಡು To look at in a blinking and inquisitive manner -ಮಿಟಿ ಸ್ವರ್ಗ. A svarga without attractions and happiness.

ಮಿಟ್ಟನೆ (*fr.* ಮಿಡುಕು) k *ad* In a sorrowful manner. -ಮಿಡುಕು To be greatly grieved.

ಮಿಟ್ಟೆ k. *n.* Jutting out, rising ground, a hill -ತಗ್ಗು Hills and dales -ನೆಲ. Rising ground.

ಮಿಟ್ಲೆ (= ಮಿಟಲ) k. *n* -ಗಿಡ A small craggy tree with rough leaves *Ehr. can.*

ಮಿಠಾಯಿ h *n* Sweetmeat -ಗಾರ A confectioner

ಮಿಡಿ 1. (= ಮಿಟು) k *v. i* To strike, fillip 2, to toss up with the thumb, *as* a Rupee

ಮಿಡಿ 2 a. k. *v i* To leap, bounce, hop; to move about rapidly, to shed, as tears *n* Springing, bouncing, hopping.

ಮಿಡಿ 3 k. *n* A very young and unripe fruit -ಕಾಯಿ An unripe fruit.

ಮಿಡಿಚೆ, ಮಿಡಿತ k. *n.* A grasshopper, locust

ಮಿಡುಕು a k. *v i* To grieve, *etc* 2, to become conscious, lively or vigorous, be alive 3, to move. 4, to urge on *n* Grieving 2, animation, liveliness; activity, strength, vigour

ಮಿಣುಕು, ಮಿಣುಕು (= ಮಿಂಚು 2, *q v*) k. *v. i.* To glitter *n* Glittering -ಹುಳ. A glow-worm

ಮಿಣಿ k *n* A rope of twisted leather straps

ಮಿಂಡ k. *n.* A paramour, lover. 2, a hero, *f.* ಮಿಂಡಿ.

ಮಿಣ್ಣೆ k *n* A small wooden or metal spoon 2 a small drinking vessel

ಮಿತ s *a.* Measured, limited, moderate, scanty, frugal, sparing, brief

ಮಿತಿ s. *n.* Measure, limit, moderation; accurate knowledge -ಮೀರಿ. *dpl.* -ತಪ್ಪಿ ಹರಿ To overflow its bounds, *as* a river. -ತಪ್ಪಿ ಹೋಗು To go beyond limits -ಇಲ್ಲದ Boundless, immeasurable.

ಮಿತ್ರ s. *n.* A friend associate. 2, an ally. 3 the sun, *f* ಮಿತ್ರಳು, ಮಿತ್ರೆ. -ಘ್ನ Treacherous. -ಜ್ಞ. Thankful to a friend -ತ್ವ. Friendship, intimacy. -ದ್ರೋಹ. Betrayal of a friend -ದ್ರೋಹಿ. A treacherous friend. -ಭೇದ. Breach of friendship. -ಲಾಭ. Acquisition of friends

ಮಿಥುನ s *n.* A pair couple 2, the

ಮಿಥ್ಯಾ (= ಮಿಥ್ಯೆ) s. *ad.* Falsely; untruly, *etc* *a* False, sham, untrue -ತ್ವ Falsity, untruth -ದೃಷ್ಟಿ Heresy -ಪವಾದ A false accusation -ಮತಿ A false opinion. -ವಾದಿ. A liar

ಮಿಥ್ಯೆ (= ಮಿಥ್ಯಾ) s *n* Untruth, falsehood, fraud

ಮಿದಿ k. *v t* To pound; to kill, to rub, grind -ಸು. To cause to pound, *etc*

ಮಿದು. *tb of* ಮೃದು, *q v.*

ಮಿದುಳು, ಮಿದುಳು (*tb. of* ಮೇದಸ್) *n* Marrow, the brain

ಮಿನಹು h. *ad* Till, until.

ಮಿನಾಹಿ h. *n.* Dismissing, discharging, abolishing.

ಮಿನಿಕೆ k *n* A climbing herb, the melon vine, *Cucumis melo*

ಮಿನುಕು, ಮಿನುಗು (= ಮಿಣುಕು, *q. v*) k *v. i* To glitter, shine. 2, to murmur *n.* Glitter, lustre

ಮಿಂದು *P. p of* ಮೀಯು, *q v*

ಮಿರಾಸಿ h. *n.* A hereditary title to periodical gifts of money, coin, *etc* -ದಾರ A holder of a mirâsi title

ಮಿರುಗು (ರ=ಱ = ಮಿನುಕು, *q. v*) k *v i* To glitter, flash, sparkle, shine *n.* Glitter, shine, lustre

ಮಿಲನ s *n* Mixing with, union contact. ಮಿಲಾಕತ್ತು Mingling, mixing; a meeting, interview. ಮಿಲಾಯಿಸು To mix, mingle; to join, to introduce ಮಿಲಾವಣೆ Mixing ಮಿಲಿತ, ಮಿಳಿತ Mixed, united, combined.

ಮಿಲ್ಲ್ಯನ್ e *n* A million, 10 times 100,000

ಮಿಶ್ರ s. *a* Mixed, mingled, combined, manifold, diverse. *n* Mixture -ಣ Mixing, union, combination ಮಿಶ್ರಿತ Mixed, blended

ಮಿಶ್ಯನ್ e *n* Mission, propagation of the Gospel -ಕಾರ್ಯ, -ಕೆಲಸ M work -ವಾರ್ತೆ, -ವರ್ತಮಾನ. M. news -ಸಂಘ M. society, *as* Basle German Mission, London Mis[illegible] -ಸೂತ್ರ M. p[illegible]

Christians. ಮಿಶ್ಯನೇರಿ A missionary, *also* ಮಿಷನೇರಿ.

ಮಿಸಕು = ಮಿಸುಕು, *q. v.*

ಮಿಸಲು f. *n* Official inspection (*as* of troops, peons, horses, *etc*)

ಮಿಸಿ e. *n* Miss, an unmarried lady, *also* -ಯವರು, -ಯಮ್ಮನವರು.

ಮಿಸುಕು k. *v i* To move, stir, to quiver, throb, swing, *etc* -ಆಡು, ಮಿಸುಕಾಡು To move, stir about.

ಮಿಸುನಿ a k. *n* Gold

ಮಿಹಿರ s *n* The sun.

ಮಿಳಿ k. *n* A leather rope, a strap

ಮಿಳಿರು a. k. *v i.* To move about, swing, wave, roll, *etc.* 2, to prosper, flourish *n* Moving to and fro

ಮಿಳ್ಳಿ, ಮಿಳ್ಳೆ (= ಮಿಣ್ಣೆ, *q v*) k *n* A small drinking vessel made of any metal

ಮೀ. = ಮೀಯು, *q v*

ಮೀಟು 1. k. *v. i* To strike the wires of a lute or guitar with the finger 2 to raise with a lever. *n.* Eminence, greatness, excess, beauty

ಮೀಟು 2. f. *n.* Salt -ಮೋಳಿ. A salt manufactory.

ಮೀಣ k *n* Bathing, bath

ಮೀಂಟು = ಮೀಟು 1, *q v*

ಮೀನ s *n* A fish. 2, the *Pisces* of the zodiac -ಕಂಡ, -ಗಂಡ. The calf of the leg

ಮೀನು (*tb of* ಮೀನ) *n* A fish. 2, a star. *Varieties* ಕರಿಯ-, ಕಿರು-, ಕೆಂಪು-, ಕೇರೆ-, ಚಳಿಯ-, ಜೊರ-, ಬಳ್ಳಿ-, ಹಾವು-, ಹುಲ್ಲು-, *etc* -ಬೇಟೆ Fishing. -ಗಾರ. A fisherman ಮೀನಾಕ್ಷಿ A fish-eyed woman; N

ಮೀಮಾಂಸ (*tb of* ಮೀಮಾಂಸೆ) *n.* Reflection, examination, discussion. 2, a philosophical system

ಮೀಯು (= ಮೀ) k *v i* To take a bath, to bathe *P ps.* ಮಿಂದು, ಮೀದು. ಮೀಯಿಸು To bathe.

[illegible]

out of reach, etc, to be elated, lofty, to act proudly P ps ಮಿಾರಿ, ಮಿಾರದ- ಆಣೆ- To violate an oath ಮಿತಿ- To exceed the limits ಹೊತ್ತು- Time to pass

ಮಿಾಸ e. n Mass, re-sacrificing of Christ in the Roman Catholic Church

ಮಿಾಸಲು k. n Anything set apart for a purpose, anything untouched or undefiled, dedicated or vowed. -ಕಾಣಿಕೆ. A present for a particular purpose Cpds. -ನೀರು, -ಹಸು, -ಹಾಲು, -ಎಮ್ಮೆ etc -ಕಟ್ಟು To set apart

ಮಿಾಸೆ f n A mustache, the mustaches -ತಿದ್ದು, -ತಿಕ್ಕು. To trim the mustaches -ಕಟ್ಟು To defy, challenge

ಮುಕ್ k. a Three ಮುಕ್ಕಟ್ಟು. Three obstacles or ties ಮುಕ್ಕಣ್ಣ. (Three-eyed) Siva. ಮುಕ್ಕರಿ. A cow that calves every third year ಮುಕ್ಕಾಣಿ Three-sixty-fourths ಮುಕ್ಕಾಲು Three feet, a tripod, three-fourths, a copper coin worth three kāsus

ಮುಕುಟ s n A crown, crest diadem.

ಮುಕುತಿ. tb. of ಮುಕ್ತಿ, q v

ಮುಕುಂದ s n Vishnu

ಮುಕುರ s n A mirror

ಮುಕುಲ s n An opening bud

ಮುಕ್ಕ (tb of ಮೂರ್ಖ) n A common word of abuse, f. ಮುಕ್ಕಿ

ಮುಕ್ಕಳಿಸು = ಮುಕ್ಕುಳಿಸು, q v.

ಮುಕ್ಕು 1 k v t. To eat voraciously, greedily, to gobble ಮುಕ್ಕ A gobbler

ಮುಕ್ಕು 2. k n A small break, a small fragment. 2 pride, arrogance

ಮುಕ್ಕುರಿ k. n Straining in pain or distress

ಮುಕ್ಕುರು a k v t. To come upon, to inclose. n Coming or falling upon covering.

ಮುಕ್ಕುಳಿ k. n A mouthful for rinsing. -ಸು To rinse the mouth with water, to [illegible]

ಮುಕ್ತ s a Loosened let loose, set free, quitted, released, liberated emancipated. ಮುಕ್ತಾವಳ A pearl ಮುಕ್ತಾವಳಿ A pearl necklace

ಮುಕ್ತಾಯ s. n Completing, conclusion, end -ಗೊಳಿಸು, -ಮಾಡು To complete, finish, execute

ಮುಕ್ತಿ s. n Release, setting free. 2 freedom 3, final liberation, final beatitude 4, salvation (Chr). -ಪದ -ಮಾರ್ಗ The way to emancipation -ಸಾಧನೆ A means of obtaining mukti

ಮುಖ (= ಮೊಗ) s. n The mouth. 2, the face, a direction, quarter, facing 3, the fore-part, front. 4, the head, tip of anything. 5, edge, surface 6, opening, entrance; beginning. 7, means, expedient a Chief, best -ಚಿವ್ಲಾಡಿಸು, -ತಿರುವು To frown -ದಾಕ್ಷಿಣ್ಯ Kindness, etc, shown in a person's presence. -ಭಂಗಿತ Putting to shame. -ಭಾವ The expression of the countenance. -ಮಜ್ಜನ, -ಮಾರ್ಜನ Washing the face -ರೋಮಿ. A cockroach -ವೀಣೆ A kind of pipe. -ಸ್ತುತಿ Flattery ಮುಖಾಮುಖಿ Face to face -ಬಿಚ್ಚಿ ಮಾತಾಡು. To speak out openly -ದಿಂದ, ಮುಖಾಂತರ, ಮುಖಾಂತ್ರ By means of, through.

ಮುಖಮಲು h. n Velvet

ಮುಖರ s a Garrulous, noisy. -ತೆ. Garrulity.

ಮುಖ್ಯ s a Principal. chief, primary; first eminent, first-rate, most excellent n The chief, a leader, guide 2, a principal thing -ತೆ, -ತ್ವ Preeminence superiority -ಪ್ರಾಣ Hanumat -ಮುಖ್ಯ The various, chief. -ಸ್ಥ A leader, chief, f ಮುಖ್ಯಸ್ಥಳು.

ಮುಗಸು = ಮುಗಿಸು, q v.

ಮುಗಳು = ಮುಗುಳು, q v

ಮುಗಿ k. v. i To contract or close, as a flower. 2, to end terminate, to be completed, accomplished i t To [illegible] saluting).

P. ps ಮುಗದು, ಮುಗಿದು. -ಯುವಿಕೆ. Closing, joining; ending -ಸು To finish, close

ಮುಗಿಲು k. *n* A cloud, the sky.

ಮುಗು = ಮೂಗು, *q. v.* -ದಾರ. The cord put through an ox's nose.

ಮುಗುವಳಿ k. *n* A settlement about salary, rent, *etc*

ಮುಗುಳು (*tb. of* ಮುಕುಲ) *v i.* To bud, sprout. *n* A bud, opening bud ಮುಗುಳಾಗು. To bud

ಮುಗುಳಿ k. *n* A thorny tree, the *Acacia suma*

ಮುಗ್ಗರಿಸು, ಮುಗ್ರಿಸು k *v i.* To stumble, [trip.

ಮುಗ್ಗು 1 k *v. i* To be interrupted in going to stumble, to fall, to sink. *n* A pitfall, *as in* ತಗ್ಗು-

ಮುಗ್ಗು 2 k *v i* To be musty or mouldy. *n.* An offensive smell, mouldiness, mustiness -ನಾತ. A mouldy smell. -ಹಿಡಿ To become musty ಮುಗ್ಗಲು Mustiness, mouldiness.

ಮುಗ್ಧ s *a.* Perplexed, stupid, ignorant, foolish, silly, artless, innocent -ತನ, -ಭಾವ Stupidity, simplicity ಮುಗ್ಧೆ. An artless woman

ಮುಂ, ಮುಙ್ (= ಮುಂದು, ಮುನ್ನು, *etc*, *q. v*) k *n* That which is before, in front of, or preceding, following, *etc* -ಕೊಳ್ಳು. To move on, advance -ಗಟ್ಟು An offset at the foot of a wall -ಗಡ. Advance in money or kind -ಗಡೆ. The front side, *etc* -ಗತ್ತಲೆ The darkness just after sunset or just before sunrise. -ಗಾಣು To have foresight. -ಗಾರು, -ಗಾರೆ ಮಳೆ The first rains -ಗಾರು ಬೆಳೆ The first crop -ಗಾಲು The fore legs (of quadrupeds), the upper part of the foot -ಗುರುತು. Foreboding, prognosis -ಗುರುಳು. A front lock. -ಗೆಡೆ. To fall on the face -ಗೈ. The forearm. -ಗೋಪ Momentary anger

ಮುಂಗಿ, ಮುಂಗಿ [illegible] The mungoose

ಮುಚ್. = ಮು, *q v* ಮುಚ್ಚಂಜೆ Dawn, noon and evening.

ಮುಚ್ಚಲಿಕೆ h *n* A final agreement in writing.

ಮುಚ್ಚಲು k *n.* A winnowing fan, used by children as a toy. 2, = ಮುಚ್ಚಳ, *see* s ಮುಚ್ಚು.

ಮುಚ್ಚು k *v t* To close, shut, to shut up, to cover; to conceal *v i.* To close, shut (*as in* ಮುಚ್ಚಿಕೊಳ್ಳು) *n.* Shutting, closing. -ಗಲ್ಲು The stone cover of a gutter -ಮರೆ. Secrecy. ಮುಚ್ಚಳ. A cover, lid ಮುಚ್ಚಿಕೆ Shutting, closing; ceiling.

ಮುಚ್ಛೆ. *tb of* ಮೂರ್ಛೆ, *q v*

ಮುಜರಾ h *n* Deduction, remission 2, respect, bow or salâm -ಮಾಡು To make all allowance.

ಮುಜಾಕು h *n* Matter, consequence.

ಮುಂ, ಮುಞ್. = ಮುನ್. ಮುಂಚಿತ Beforehand, previous. ಮುಂಚು. To precede, to exceed, to outdo, surpass, excel; the preceding, previous or prior state; former time, *etc* ಮುಂಚೆ Previously, formerly, first, before, earlier than, ere ಮುಂಜಾನೆ, ಮುಂಜಾವು Early morning

ಮುಂಜ, ಮುಂಜಿ s. *n.* A sort of grass, *Saccharum munja* 2, the investiture of a boy with the sacred thread

ಮುಟ್ಟಾಮುಟ್ಟಿ. *tb of* ಮುಷ್ಟಾಮುಷ್ಟಿ. *q v*

ಮುಟ್ಟಿ *tb. of* ಮುಷ್ಟಿ, *q. v.*

ಮುಟ್ಟಿಸು k *v. t* To cause to touch, to apply to, to cause to reach, deliver, *as* a letter, *etc*, to apply or lay out, *etc*; to kindle, *as* a light

ಮುಟ್ಟು 1. k *v t.* To touch; to come in contact with *v i* To reach, arrive, *as* a letter, place (*with Dat*), to be laid out expended, *as* money, *etc* *n* Touch, contact. 2, hindrance ಮುಟ್ಟು. As far as, till, up to ಬೇರು ಮುಟ್ಟ [illegible] To pluck up by the root -[illegible] ಮು[illegible] ಸಾಧಿಸು. To finish [illegible]

ತಲೆ ಮುಟ್ಟ ಮುಣುಗು. To immerse completely ಮುಟ್ಟಗೋಲು A stoppage-pole, total pillage. ಮುಟ್ಟಗೋಲು ಹಾಕು. To pillage

ಮುಟ್ಟು 2 k. n An implement, tool, utensils furniture

ಮುಟ್ಟುವಳಿ k n Expenses, outlay, as of money, grain, etc

ಮುಡಿ 1 k v i To bind or tie the hair of the head, to fasten in it, as flowers n A knot bundle, a braid of hair 2 unshaved hair on account of a vow to an idol 3 a hollow ring of brass used as a charm. 4, a kind of crown for idols -ಕಟ್ಟು. To tie up in a bundle of straw, hair braided round the head -ಒಳಿ = ಮುಡಿ 2 -ವಾಳ, -ವಾಳ A kind of fragrant grass, *Andropogon schoenanthus.* -ಸು. To fasten in the hair-knot as flowers

ಮುಡಿ 2 a k i. t. To end, come to an end n End [ಹೂವು-

ಮುಡು. P p of ಮುಡಿ 1, in ಮುಡುಕೊಳ್ಳು, as

ಮುಡುಕು, ಮುಡುಗು k. i i To bend, shrink, become crooked, distorted v t To bend, distort. n. Bending, distorting; a curve, an angle

ಮುಡುಪು k. n. A bundle, money-bag as one dedicated to an idol

ಮುಡುಹು a k n The shoulder, shoulder-blade.

ಮುಣಗು, ಮುಣೆಗು, ಮುಣುಗು k v i To sink, to be drowned, to dip, bathe, to set, as the sun, to be ruined n An immersion, dip ಮುಣಗಿಸು, ಮುಣೆಗಿಸು, ಮುಣುಗಿಸು. To immerse, dip, plunge, to drown, to ruin

ಮುಂಡ s. a. Shaved, bald. 2, hornless 3, blunt 4, mean. n The trunk of a lopped tree, pollard. 2, a headless body 3 a bald head 4, a barber. 5, myrrh -ಕ. The lopped trunk of a tree, the head. -ನ Tonsure, shaving -ಮೋಡು To cover the head, as a wid

ಮುಂಡಾಸ. ಮುಂಡಾಸು h n. A turban. -ಸುತ್ತು To wind a turban.

ಮುಂಡಿ s. a Shaven, bald, shorn n A barber 2, a pestle without a ferrule

ಮುಂಡಿಗೆ (tb. of ಮುಂಡಕ) n A stem, post pillar 2, a wooden bar

ಮುಂಡು 1. k n Kissing, fondling ಮುಂಡಾಡು To kiss, fondle

ಮುಂಡು 2 k n A short cloth, used as a garment

ಮುಂಡು 3 (tb of ಮುಂಡ) n A headless body -ಗಳ್ಳಿ. The leafless milk-hedge, *Euphorbia antiquorum,* the triangular spurge -ಮುಳಕ The Bengal kite, a kind of duck

ಮುಂಡೆ k. n. A widow -ಮುಸುಕು A widow's veil

ಮುತ್ತುಗ, ಮುತ್ತುಲ, ಮುತ್ತುಗ k n The bastard teak, *Butea frondosa*

ಮುತ್ತಂಡೆ, ಮುತ್ತಾತ. See s ಮುತ್ತು 2

ಮುತ್ತಿಗೆ k n Covering, surrounding, a siege, blockade. -ಇಕ್ಕು =-ಹಾಕು. -ತೆಗೆ To raise a siege -ಹಾಕು To lay siege to, to besiege -ಬೀಳು. To be besieged

ಮುತ್ತು 1 k i t To inclose; to cover; to encompass, surround, shut in, to besiege, to attack i i. To swarm. as bees etc

ಮುತ್ತು 2 (= ಮುದಿ) k n Old age. oldness. ಮುತ್ತಜ್ಜ ಮುತ್ತಂದೆ, ಮುತ್ತಪ್ಪ, ಮುತ್ತಾತ A great grandfather. ಮುತ್ತಜ್ಜಿ, ಮುತ್ತಮ್ಮ, ಮುತ್ತವ್ವ A great grandmother ಮುತ್ತೈದೆ A respectable woman whose husband is alive ಮುತ್ತೈದೆತನ. Being a muttaidĕ. ಮುತ್ತಯ್ಯ = ಮುತ್ತಜ್ಜ

ಮುತ್ತು 3 (= ಮುದ್ದು, q. v) k n A kiss -ಇಡು ಮುತ್ತಿಡು, -ಕೊಡು To kiss.

ಮುತ್ತು 4. (tb of ಮುಕ್ತಿ) n A pearl ಮುತ್ತಿನ ಚಿಪ್ಪು. An oyster

ಮುತ್ಸದ್ದಿ h n An accountant, clerk

ಮುದ s n Joy, pleasure, delight.

ಮುದಕ (= ಮುದುಕ, q. v) k n An old

ಮುವಡು. = ಮುದುಡು, q v

ಮುದಿ (= ಮುತ್ತು2, ಮುದು, q v) k a. Old n Advanced age, etc -ಎತ್ತು, -ಕಾಗ, -ಗೂಬೆ, -ಡೊಂಬ, etc An old—. -ತನ. Old age. -ತಿ An old woman

ಮುದು. = ಮುತ್ತು2, ಮುದಿ, q v -ಕ = ಮುದಕ

ಮುದುಡು, ಮುದುರು (= ಮುದಡು) k. v i To bend: to shrink, contract, shrivel up, as flowers, etc, to wrinkle, as hide, skin, etc. v. t To bend; to draw in, as a limb, to crumple, as cloth paper, to fold, as a mat; to pull up; to draw aside.

ಮುದ್ಗರ s n. A mace, rod

ಮುದ್ದತು, ಮುದ್ದತ್ತು h n A space of time, term.

ಮುದ್ದಾಮ್, ಮುದ್ದಾಮು h. ad. Expressly, positively a Own. -ಆಳು, -ಮನುಷ್ಯ Own servant

ಮುದ್ದು (= ಮುತ್ತು3, q v.) k. n. A kiss, love, affection, an object of love a Dear, affectionate. ಮುದ್ದಾಡು. To kiss mutually. ಮುದ್ದಿಕ್ಕು, ಮುದ್ದಿಡು, -ಕೊಡು To kiss -ಗೂಸು, -ಮಗು A dear child. -ತನ Pleasantness, charm -ಮಗ A dear son -ಮೊಗ A sweet face -ಗೈಯು, -ಮಾಡು To fondle, caress. -ನುಡಿ, -ಮಾತು A fondle, pleasant, sweet word

ಮುದ್ದೆ k. n A ball, roundish lump, a clod. 2, râgi-porridge. 3, a weaver's pegstand -ಪಲ್ಲೆ Vegetable porridge -ಬೆಲ್ಲ. A lump of jaggory

ಮುದ್ದೈ h. n A plaintiff, complainant, prosecutor (law). -ಅಲೆ A defendant

ಮುದ್ರೆ s. n A seal, signet, seal-ring 2, a stamp, print; a seal of lac. 3, a coin 4, stamp, cast, air. -ಕೋಲು A wooden seal. -ಯುಂಗರ A seal-ring -ಒತ್ತು, -ಮಾಡು, -ಹಾಕು To seal -ಕೀಳು, -ಬಿಚ್ಚು, -ತೊಡೆ. To unseal ಮುದ್ರಾಕ್ಷರ Type, print. ಮುದ್ರಾಕ್ಷರಶಾಲೆ A printing office ಮುದ್ರಿತ ಮುದ್ರಿತ Stamped, printed ಮುದ್ರಿಕೆ A seal, seal-ring, an impress, dedication to a deity at the end of a poem or book ಮುದ್ರಿಸು To seal, to stamp, to print, to coin, to seal up

ಮುನ್ (= ಮುಂ, q v) k a. Three. n That which is before. ad. Before. -ತಿಳುಹು. To inform beforehand -ದಲೆ The forehead -ದರಿ. To proceed. -ತೋರು. To appear or show beforehand, to show the way. -ನೀರು The ocean -ನೂರು 300. -ನೇಸರು The dawn.

ಮುನಸೀಫು h n. A native, subordinate civil judge

ಮುನಾಸಬು h a. Right, proper, fit due. n. Discretion.

ಮುನಿ 1 k v i. To become angry, to be displeased n Anger; also -ಪು, -ಸು.

ಮುನಿ 2. s. n An ascetic, a sage, saint; a devotee; a monk, a Buddha 2, a male devil. ಮುನೀಂದ್ರ, ಮುನೀಶ್ವರ. A great sage

ಮುನಿಷಿ h n A writer 2, a teacher of language.

ಮುನಿಸು s n. Anger, wrath, passion, rage, enmity. -ತಿಳಿ Anger to calm down -ಹರಿ Anger to cease -ಗಾರ An angry man.

ಮುಂತು = ಮುಂದು q v. ಮುಂತಾಗು To be the first of a series ಮುಂತೆ. = ಮುಂದೆ, q v ಮುಂತಾದ. Etc ಮುಂತಿಟ್ಟು. In the presence of.

ಮುಂದು (= ಮುಂತು) k. n The front part or side; following, succeeding; the state of being first, before, or future. ಮುಂದಕ್ಕೆ ಮಾಡು To shut, as a door ಮುಂದಕ್ಕೆ ಹಾಕು To place in front; to put off, delay. ಮುಂದರಿ. To go before, to surpass, to go forward, to know beforehand, to be far-seeing. ಮುಂದಾಗು. To go to the front, excel. ಮುಂದಿಕ್ಕು ಮುಂದಿಡು, ಮುಂದಿರಿಸು. To put in front, to put forward, extend -ಗಡೆ. The front, in front; to the front, forwards. -ಗೆಡು. Prospects to be ruined; to be at a loss, to despair.

-ಗೊಳ್ಳು To take the lead, to remember. -ಮಾಡು To put to the front to bring forward -ಸರಿ To rush forward; to advance. ಮುಂದಾಟಿ. A leather rope for cart ಮುಂದೆ (=ಮುಂತೆ) Before, in front of, forward, first in the first instance, further, thereafter, hereafter, in future ಮುಂದೆ ಬರು To come or arrive first, to happen in future

ಮುಂದೆ k. n A jar-like brass vessel.

ಮುಂಪೋರು. *See* s. ಮುನ್.

ಮುನ್ನ (=ಮುನ್, ಮುಂದು. *q v*) ಮುನ್ನರಿ To know beforehand. ಮುನ್ನಾದಿನ, ಮುನ್ನಾದಿವಸ. The day before. ಮುನ್ನೋರ್ವ A predecessor

ಮುನ್ನೂರು (-ಱು) *See* s ಮುನ್

ಮುಪ್. = ಮು, *q. v* ಮುಪ್ಪಾಗ Three-fourths of a pana (3 anês and 6 kâsus)

ಮುಪ್ಪು k n. Old age

ಮುಮ್ = ಮುನ್. *q v* -ಬಾಗಲು. The front door -ಬೆಳಕು Moon's light in the Śukla paksha before it is full -ಭಾರ Weight in the front part (of a cart) -ಮಡಿ. Threefold, three times -ಮಡಿಸು To treble, to do thrice as much

ಮುಮುಕ್ಷು s a Desirous of freeing. n A person desirous of mukti

ಮುಯ್ಯಿ k n Return, recompense, retaliation, punishment 2, a gift, present -ಮಾಡು To present an object at a marriage -ಗೆ ಮುಯ್ಯಿಕೊಡು, -ಗೆ ಮುಯ್ಯಿ ತೀರಿಸು To repay (*in a good or bad sense*), to revenge

ಮುರ 1 = ಮುರಪು, *q. v.*

ಮುರ 2 s. n Encompassing, surrounding. n A daitya slain by Krishna -ರಿಪು, ಮುರಾರಿ. Vishnu, Krishna.

ಮುರಕ, ಮುರಕು. = ಮುರುಕು, *q. v*

ಮುರದಾರಸಿಂಗಿ h n Sulphate of copper; or semi-vitrified oxide of lead.

ಮುರಲಿ, ಮುರಳಿ k n A flute, pipe -ಧ-

ಮುರವು (= ಮುರ. ಮುರುವು) k n An ear- or nose-ring.

ಮುರಿ 1 k *v i.* To bend, be bent, to grow crooked, to turn, to wind, to stretch one's self (with windings of the limbs) n A bend, curve, winding 2, a ring worn on the wrist 3, a pad of wool laid under the saddle of an ox

ಮುರಿ 2 (ರಿ = ಱಿ) k. n. A fragment, piece *v t* To break, to break off, to crush, to break down, defeat, destroy, to break up, to do away *v i* To break to lose strength, to be impaired, *etc* *P ps* ಮುರಿದು. ಮುರಿದು -ಸು To cause to break crush, to get changed *as* a coin -ಯುವಿಕೆ Breaking

ಮುರಿಕೆ, ಮುರಿಗೆ, ಮುರಿವು k n Bending, twisting -ಬಳೆ. A twisted bracelet.

ಮುರು (= ಮುರವು 2) k n Turning, a turn -ದಲೆ The turning point in a cross-road -ವು = ಮುರವು

ಮುರುಕು (ರು=ಱು) k n A fragment. bit, *as* of bread, sweetmeat, *etc.* 2, frowning, making grimaces, foppishness, showiness

ಮುರುಟು (= ಮುದುಡು, *q. v*) k *v i* To be bent, shrink, shrivel n. Shrinking, shrivelling

ಮುರುಡಿ k n A shrub or small tree. *Helicteres isora.*

ಮುರುಸು (= ಮೊರಡು) k n. Roughness. ruggedness, unevenness ಮುರಚಿಸು To pluck out by twisting.

ಮುರುವ (ರು = ಱು) k n A maimed or imbecile man

ಮುರುವು = ಮುರವು, *q v*

ಮುರ್ಗಿನಹುಳಿ k n The mate mangosteen, *Garcinia purpurea*

ಮುಲಾಜು. ಮುಲಾಜೆ h n. Respect, regard for.

ಮುಲಾಮು = ಮಲಾಮು, *q v* 2, a gilding or plating

ಮುಲುಕು k *v. i* To groan, *as* when lifting a heavy load, to strain. 2, to

ಮುಲ್ಕಿ f *n* Revenue *a* Relating to revenue 2, native, indigenous

ಮುಲ್ಲ h. *n* A Mahomedan jurist or theologian, a schoolmaster. -ಶಾಸ್ತ್ರ. The Koran.

ಮುಲ್ಲಂಗಿ =ಮೂಲಂಗಿ, *q. v.*

ಮುವ್ವತ್ತು k *n.* Thirty. ಮುವ್ವರು. Three persons.

ಮುಶಲ s *n.* A pestle, club

ಮುಷ್ಕರ k *n* Stubbornness, obstinacy, insolence. -ಹಿಡಿ To be obstinate.

ಮುಷ್ಕೀಲು h. *a.* Difficult, hard. *n.* A difficulty.

ಮುಷ್ಟಿ s *n.* The closed hand, fist. 2, a hilt or handle of a sword, *etc.* -ಗೆಯ್ಯು, -ಹಿಡಿ To clench the fist -ಬಂಧ Clenching the fist; a handful. -ಯುದ್ಧ. A fight with fists. ಮುಷ್ಟಾ-. Fisticuffs.

ಮುಸಕು =ಮುಸುಕು, *q v*

ಮುಸಡಿ, ಮುಸಗು. =ಮುಸುಡಿ, *q v.*

ಮುಸರೆ k. *n* Boiled rice considered to be unclean -ಗಡಿಗೆ, -ಪಾತ್ರೆ A pot in which anything has been boiled

ಮುಸಲ, -ಮಾನ h. *n.* A Mussulmân. -ಮತ. Mohammedanism

ಮುಸಾಫರ h *n.* A traveller ಮುಸಾಫರಿ Relating to travellers -ಬಂಗಲೆ. A travellers' bangalow

ಮುಷಿ s *n* A crucible

ಮುಸು k *n* A black ape, *also* -ವ

ಮುಸುಕು (=ಮುಸಕು) k *v t* To cover, to hide, to veil, shroud *v i* To come or fall upon, as flies, *etc.*, to swarm *n* Covering, a cover, a veil. -ಇಡು, -ಹಾಕು. To put on a veil.

ಮುಸುಟೆ h. *n* The elephant-creeper, *Argyreia speciosa*

ಮುಸುಡಿ, ಮುಸುಡು (=ಮುಸಡಿ, *q v*) k *n* The face, the snout, muzzle

ಮುಸುಂಡಿ k. *n* A crooked, rude person, a coward -ತನ Crookedness, cowardice

ಮುಸುರು (ರು=ಱು) k *v t.* To cover, to hide, to swarm, crowd *n* A cover, veil. -ಗಟ್ಟು A cover to form

ಮುಸುವ k *n* A large and black kind of ape, *also* ಮುಸು

ಮುಸ್ತ s *n* A species of grass, *Cyperus rotundus*, *also* ಮುಸ್ತೆ.

ಮುಸ್ತಾಭ s. *n* The grass, *Cyperus hexastachyus.*

ಮುಸ್ತೈದು h *a* Prepared, ready ಮುಸ್ತೈದಿ Preparation, things prepared

ಮುಹುರ್, ಮುಹುಃ s *ad.* In or for a moment, repeatedly, again and again.

ಮುಹೂರ್ತ 1. s *n* A moment instant. 2, the fit time 3, the twelfth part of a day and night ಮುಹೂರ್ತಿಕ An astrologer

ಮುಹೂರ್ತ 2. (*tb. of* ಮೂರ್ತ) *n* A sitting posture -ಗೊಳ್ಳು. To sit down

ಮುಳಗು =ಮುಳುಗು, *q v*

ಮುಳಿ 1 k *v i* To grow passionate angry, *etc* -ಯಿಸು To enrage. -ಸು Anger, passion

ಮುಳಿ 2. k. *n.* A cause.

ಮುಳುಗು (ಳು=ೞು =ಮುಣುಗು, ಮುಳಗು, *etc*) k *v i.* To sink under water, to sink; to immerse one's self, dive, to set *as* the sun, *etc.* to be ruined. ಮುಳುಗಿಸು To immerse, to dip, plunge, to bathe, to ruin

ಮುಳುವು a. k. *n* Ruin. loss

ಮುಳ್ಳು k. *n.* A thorn, a pointed thing, a sting, spur, the hand of a clock; the tongue of a balance, *etc* ಮುಳ್ಳೇಳು Horripilation to take place. -ಕಲ್ಲು Thorns and stones -ಗಳ್ಳಿ. The prickly pear, *Opuntia dillenii* -ಗೆಣಸು A prickly kind of yam, *Dioscorea tomentosa* -ಗೋರಟೆ, -ಗೋರಂಟೆ A small prickly shrub, *Barleria prionitis* -ಬೇಲಿ A thorny hedge -ಮುತ್ತಗ The tree *Andersonia rohitaka* -ಮುಸ್ತ A spinous shrub, *Canthium parviflorum* -ಮೊನೆ. The point of a thorn [illegible]

[illegible]

common cucumber, *Cucumis sativus* -ಸೇವಂತಿಗೆ A kind of white rose, *Rosa glandulifera* -ಹಂದಿ, ಮುಳ್ಳಿಕ್ಕಿ A porcupine. -ಕಂತು, -ಚುಚ್ಚು, -ನಾಟು, -ಬಯ್ಯು. A thorn to prick

ಮೂ (= ಮೂರು) k *a* Three *Cpds.* -ಗಾವುದ -ಜಗ, -ಲೋಕ, -ವಲೆ. -ನೂರು. 300 -ವತ್ತು 30 -ವತ್ತೊಂದು. 31. -ವರು. Three persons

ಮೂಕ s *a.* Dumb, speechless, silent, mute *n.* A dumb man, *f.* ಮೂಕಿ. -ತೆ Dumbness, silence

ಮೂಕಾಂಬೆ k. *n* N of Śiva's śakti.

ಮೂಕೆ k. *n* The taper pole or shaft of a carriage

ಮೂಕುತಿ = ಮೂಗುತಿ, *q v*

ಮೂಗ *tb of* ಮೂಕ, *q. v* -ತನ, -ತೆ. Dumbness.

ಮೂಗು k *n* The nose, a forepart, a bill or beak. the nozzle of a vessel ಮೂಗ್ಗರಕ A man whose nose is cut off, *f.* ಮೂಗ್ಗರಕಿ. ಮೂಗಿಲಿ A musk-rat -ದಾಣ, -ದಾರ, -ನೇಣು, ಮೂದಾಣ The cord put through an ox's nose -ಕಟ್ಟು, -ಮುಚ್ಚು. To stop the nose. ಮೂಗಿನ ರಂಧ್ರ, ಮೂಗಿನ ಸೊಳ್ಳೆ. ಮೂಗಿನ ಹೊಳ್ಳೆ. The nostril. -ತಿ -ಬೊಟ್ಟು A nose-jewel.

ಮೂಜುವರಿ ಮೂಜೂರಿ h *n* Refractoriness

ಮೂಟೆ k *n.* A bundle of grain, cloth, *etc*, a pack bale.

ಮೂಡ, ಮೂಡಲು, ಮೂಡ್ಲ (= ಮೂಡು) k *n.* The east -ಗಡೆ Eastward ಮೂಡಣ Eastern. -ಗಿರಿ N of a mountain or person ಮೂಡಲ್ಲರಿ To dawn

ಮೂಡಿಗೆ k *n* A quiver.

ಮೂಡು k *v i* To rise, to originate, to be born. to become visible, to come about ಮೂಡಿಸು. To cause to rise, *etc.*

ಮೂಡೆ (= ಮುಡಿ) k *n* A straw-bundle containing rice, pulse or rāgi.

ಮೂಢ s. *a.* Perplexed, stupid, dull, silly. [illegible]

n. An ignorant man, fool, *etc* -ತನ, -ತ್ವ, -ತೆ. Stupidity, folly, ignorance. -ಜನ Ignorant people -ಭಕ್ತಿ A blind faith. ಮೂಢಾತ್ಮ. A foolish, ignorant person.

ಮೂತಿ k *n* The face, mouth, snout, beak.

ಮೂತ್ರ s. *n* Urine -ಕಟ್ಟು -ಕೃಚ್ಛ್ರ, -ಬಂಧ Stoppage of urine, strangury. -ಶಂಕೆ Making water ಬಹು-. Diabetes. ಮೂತ್ರಿಸು. To discharge urine

ಮೂದಲೆ k *n.* Confronting and upbraiding, taunt. ಮೂದಲಿಸು. To confront, and upbraid, taunt.

ಮೂಬದಲು, ಮೂಬದಲೆ f *n.* Exchange, barter, sums lent and paid on running accounts.

ಮೂರು (ರು = ಱು) k *a* Three ಮೂರ ಡಿಗ Agni ಮೂರನೆಯ Third. ಮೂರನೆಯವ A third man. ಮೂರವಸರ = -ಹೊತ್ತು. -ನಾಮ. Three sectarian marks of a Vaishnava's forehead. -ನಾಲ್ಕು. Three or four - ಮೂರು Three and three, each three -ಮೂರ್ತಿ = ತ್ರಿಮೂರ್ತಿ, *q v.* -ಲೋಕ. The three worlds -ವರ್ಣ Three letters or colours, *etc* ಮೂರುವರೆ Three and a half -ಸಂಜೆ. Evening-twilight, nightfall. -ಹೊತ್ತು Morning, noon, and evening ಮೂರೂ ಕಾಲು Three and a quarter

ಮೂರ್ಖ s. *a.* Stupid, foolish, silly, ignorant. *n* A fool, blockhead -ತನ, -ತೆ, -ತ್ವ Stupidity, foolishness, ignorance

ಮೂರ್ಛನ s *n.* Stupefying 2, fainting, stupor 3, vehemence 4, rising of sounds, intonation 5, a semi-tone in the musical scale ಮೂರ್ಛಿತ Stupefied, fainted, fainting ಮೂರ್ಛಿಸು To faint away, swoon. ಮೂರ್ಛೆ. Fainting, loss of consciousness; swoon, hallucination. ಮೂರ್ಛೆಗೊಳ್ಳು, -ಬೀಳು, -ಹಿಡಿ, -ಹೊಂದು. To faint away -ತಿಳಿ. To recover from fainting. -ರೋಗ

ಮೂರ್ತ. = ಮುಹೂರ್ತ 2, q v

ಮೂರ್ತಿ s n A solid body, a material form, visible shape; matter, substance, embodiment, incarnation. 2, an image, idol, figure, form. -ಗೊಳ್ಳು. To assume a form, to sit down. -ಪೂಜಕ. An idol-worshipper. -ಪೂಜೆ. Idol-worship -ಮತ್ Material embodied, corporeal, personified.

ಮೂರ್ಧ s. n The forehead, the head -ನ್ಯ. Cerebral, as a letter. ಮೂರ್ಧಾಭಿಷಿಕ್ತ. Inaugurated, installed; a consecrated king; a Kshatriya.

ಮೂಲ s n The basis, ground-work, beginning. 2, root, origin, cause, means 3. the original. 4, capital, stock. 5, the 19th lunar asterism 6, termination, ruin. -ಕಾರಣ. The first cause -ಗಾರ. The proprietor of a land. -ಗಂಟು -ಧನ, -ಬಂಡವಲ Capital, principal -ಗೇಣಿ Permanent rent or tenancy. -ನಿವಾಸಿ An aboriginal -ಬಲ An original force. -ರೋಗ, -ವ್ಯಾಧಿ. Piles. -ಸ್ಥಾನ The place of origin -ಸ್ಥಾಪಕ The founder ಮೂಲಿವರ್ಗ. Proprietary right of a land

ಮೂಲಕ (= ಮುಲ್ಲಂಗಿ, ಮೂಲಂಗಿ) s. a Rooted in springing from prep On account of n An esculent root, radish

ಮೂಲಂಗಿ (tb. of ಮೂಲಕ) n The radish, *Raphanus sativus*

ಮೂಲಿಕ s. a. Primary. ಮೂಲಿಕೆ A root, Ceylon leadwort ಮೂಲಿಗ. A vendor of medicinal roots

ಮೂಲೆ k. n. A corner, an angle, a point of the compass. -ಗೆ ಮುಟ್ಟಾಗಿ ಹೋಗು To be ruined.

ಮೂವತ್ತು k. a Thirty

ಮೂಷಕ s. n. A thief, a mouse, a rat, *also* ಮೂಷಿಕ

ಮೂಸು k v. t. To smell. ಮೂಸಿ ನೋಡು To test by the smell

ಮೂಸೆ (tb of ಮೂ... A crucible ... a mould

ಮೂಳ (ಳ = ಐ) k n. An earless man 2, a man who has lost any limb, a fool, brute, f. ಮೂಳಿ, *also* a widow.

ಮೂಳೆ k n A bone

ಮೃಗ (= ಮಿಕ, ಮಿಗ) s. n. A wild beast. 2, any animal in general, as a cow. 3, a deer, antelope, game in general. -ಜಲ, -ತೃಷ್ಣೆ Mirage -ಶಿರ, -ಶಿರಸ್, -ಶೀರ್ಷ The fifth lunar mansion -ಪತಿ, ಮೃಗೇಂದ್ರ A lion, a tiger -ತನ, -ಭಾವ. Brutishness.

ಮೃಜೆ s. n Wiping, cleansing

ಮೃತ s. a. Dead, deceased, mortal n. Death, *also* ಮೃತಿ -ವಾಗು To die -ತಿಥಿ. The death-day on which srâddha is performed -ಪತ್ರ. A written will -ಸಂಸ್ಕಾರ Obsequies -ಸಂಜೀವ Revival of the dead, N of a plant. -ಸ್ನಾನ Ablution after a funeral

ಮೃತ್ತಿಕೆ s. n. Earth, clay

ಮೃತ್ಯು s. n Death. 2, Yama. ಮೃತ್ಯುಂಜಯ Overcoming death, Śiva.

ಮೃದಂಗ s n A sort of tabour

ಮೃದು (= ಮಿದು, ಮೆದು, q v) s. a Soft, tender, flexible, pliant 2, mild, gentle, weak; slow. n Softness, mildness, gentleness -ತರ Uncommonly mild. -ಯಾನ Slow walk. -ವಾಕ್ಯ, -ಶಬ್ದ, ಮೃದೂಕ್ತಿ. A gentle word. -ಸ್ಮಿತ A gentle smile

ಮೃನ್ಮಯ s. a. Earthen.

ಮೃಷೆ s n. Untruth. ಮೃಷಾ. Falsely; uselessly.

ಮೃಷ್ಟ s a Clean, pure, dressed, savoury. ಮೃಷ್ಟಾನ್ನ Delicate food, dainties

ಮೆಕ್ಕಾ = ಮಕ್ಕಾ, q. v

ಮೆಕ್ಕೆ k n A climbing herb, *Cucumis trigonus.*

ಮೆಚ್ಚು k v. i. To assent, agree to, approve, be pleased with, to like n. Assent, approbation, what is pleasant, satisfaction, pleasure. -ತಕ್ಕ What is praiseworthy ಮೆಚ್ಚಿಕೆ, ಮೆಚ್ಚು

ಗೆ, ಮೆಚ್ಚುವಿಕೆ. Assent, approbation, approval, liking, pleasure. ಮೆಚ್ಚಿಸು. To cause to assent, *etc.*; to please.

ಮೆಜಿಸ್ಟ್ರೇಟು e. *n.* Magistrate, a justice of the peace.

ಮೆಟ್ಟಿಗೆ (= ಮೆಟ್ಲು) k. *n.* A step, stair; steps, stairs.

ಮೆಟ್ಟು 1. k. *v. t.* To step, pace, walk; to tread or trample on; to put on, *as* slippers. ಮೆಟ್ಟಿಸು. To cause to step, *etc.*

ಮೆಟ್ಟು 2. k. *n.* A step of the foot. 2, a step of a stringed instrument. 3, a sandal, shoe. 4, the step of a stair. ಮೆಟ್ಟಕ್ಕಿ. A platter filled with rice on which the bridegroom has to stand at a certain part of the marriage ceremonies. -ಗಲ್ಲು. A stair.

ಮೆಟ್ರು k. *n.* The throat. -ಗಟ್ಟು. Glandular swelling of the throat.

ಮೆಟ್ಲು k. *n.* A step, stair.

ಮೆಣಸು k. *n.* Black pepper, chilli. ಮೆಣಸಿನ ಕಾಯಿ. Chilli, Cayenne pepper. ಮೆಣಸಿನ ಬಳ್ಳಿ. The black pepper vine. ಮೆಣಸಿನ ಕಾಳು. A corn of black pepper.

ಮೆತ್ತಗೆ, ಮೆತ್ತಿಗೆ (*tb. of* ಮೃದು) *n.* Softness. *a.* Soft, pliant, *etc.* *ad.* Softly; slowly. ಮೆತ್ತನೆ, ಮೆತ್ತನ್ನ, ಮೆತ್ತಾನೆ. Soft, *etc.*

ಮೆತ್ತು k. *v. t.* To coat walls with chunam or mud; to plaster, lay on, press into. ಮೆತ್ತಿಗೆ, ಮೆತ್ತನೆ. Plastering; plaster. -ಮಾಡು. To plaster.

ಮೆತ್ತೆ k. *n.* Bedding; a mattress.

ಮೆದಡು, ಮೆದಳು, ಮೆದುಳು (*tb. of* ಮೇದಸ್) *n.* Marrow; the brain.

ಮೆದು. *tb. of* ಮೃದು, *q. v.*

ಮೆದೆ k. *n.* A heap, pile, stack, *esp. of* straw. 2, silliness. -ಒಟ್ಟು, -ಮೆದೊಟ್ಟು, -ಹಾಕು. To pile, stack.

ಮೆಂತೆ (*tb. of* ಮೇಥಿ) *n.* Fenugreek, *Trigonella foenum graecum.*

ಮೆಯ್ (= ಮೈ, *q. v.*) k. *n.* The body; side, [illegible] the b[illegible]

wasted away. -ಕೊಡು. To present one's self, to apply the body (or shoulders) to. -ಗರೆ. To hide one's self. -ಗಲಿ. A valiant person. -ಗಳ್ಳ (= ಮೈಗಳ್ಳ). A lazy man. -ಗಳ್ಳತನ. Laziness. -ಗಾವಲು. A body-guard. -ಗುಂದು. To become lean or emaciated. -ಜೋಡು. A coat of mail. -ತಡವು. To stroke the body, caress. -ತುಂಬ. All over the body; through the whole body. -ತುಂಬು. The body to become stout and strong. -ತೊಡಿಗೆ. Apparel of the body. -ದೋರು. To appear one's self; to show; to exhibit valour. -ನೋತ, -ನೋವು. Pain in the body. -ಬರು. To become stout and strong. -ಬಗ್ಗು. To bend the body, *as* in work. -ಮರವು, -ಮರತೆ. Unconsciousness; swoon; inadvertence. -ಮರೆ. To swoon, faint; to be careless. -ಮೇಲೆ ಬರು. To fall upon; to attack. -ಮೇಲೆ ಹಾಕು. To put upon; to burden on. -ಮೇಲೆ ಬೀಳು. To attack. -ಉರಿ. The body to burn; burning heat of the body. -ರಕ್ಷೆ. Taking care of one's body. -ಯಿಕ್ಕು. To make obeisance, to prostrate; salutation, obeisance. -ಮುಂಗು. To imbibe, absorb. -ಸಾಲ. A loan without pledge or mortgage. -ಸಾಲಪತ್ರ. A simple bond. -ಸಿರಿ. Beauty, comeliness. -ಹತ್ತು. To act upon the body, *as* food, medicine, *etc.*

ಮೆರವಣಿಗೆ (ರ = ಱ) k. *n.* A great display; a public procession.

ಮೆರುಗು k. *n.* Shine, lustre.

ಮೆರೆ 1. (ರ = ಱ) k. *v. i.* To shine; to gleam, glitter; to appear. 2, to display, exhibit, parade. *P. ps.* ಮೆರದು, ಮೆರೆದು. *n.* Shine, lustre; ostentation. ಮೆರಸು, ಮೆರೆಸು. To cause to shine; to display; to exhibit.

ಮೆರೆ 2. k. *v. i.* To wander, roam about. ಮೆರಸು. To spread abroad, *as a* secret.

[illegible] tend- [illegible] smile.

ಮೆಲ್ಲಡಿ A slow pace. ಮೆಲ್ನುಡಿ. A gentle voice or word

ಮೆಲಕು, ಮೆಲುಕು (*fr* ಮೆಲ್ಲು) k. *n* Rumination 2, the lower jaw -ಹಾಕು, ಮೆಲಕಾಡು, ಮೆಲಕಾಡಿಸು. To chew the cud

ಮೆಳು = ಮೆಲ್ಲು *q. v.*

ಮೆಲ್ಲ, ಮೆಲ್ಲಕೆ, ಮೆಲ್ಲಗೆ, ಮೆಲ್ಲನೆ (*fr* ಮೆಲ್. *tb of* ಮೃದು) *ad* Gently, slowly, deliberately. ಮೆಲ್ಲ- Very gently or slowly

ಮೆಲ್ಲು (=ಮೆಲು) k *v t.* To chew, masticate, mumble, eat. *P p* ಮೆದ್ದು.

ಮೆಹರ್ಬಾನಿ h. *n* Condescension, favour

ಮೆಳೆ k *n* A bush, clump, thicket.

ಮೆಳ್ಳ k. *n* Rolling; looking obliquely, squinting. -ಗಣ್ಣು A squint-eye. ಮೆಳ್ಳ A squint-eyed man -ನೋಟ. Oblique vision.

ಮೆಸ್ಸೀಯಾ e *n.* Messiah, the Anointed One or Christ, the Saviour

ಮೇ 1 = ಮೇಯು, *q v.*

ಮೇ 2 e *n* May (*the 5th month of the year*)

ಮೇ 3 = ಮೇಲೆ, *q. v.* -ಗಡೆ The upper side -ಗಾಟು. The main guard -ಗಾಲು The instep -ಗಾವಲು Guard, supervision -ಗೈ. The back of the hand

ಮೇಕು 1. k *n* Rivalry

ಮೇಕು 2. h. *n* A peg, tent-pin nail

ಮೇಕೆ k *n* A she-goat

ಮೇಖಲೆ s *n* A girdle, zone 2 a sword-belt

ಮೇಗು, ಮೇಗೆ k *n.* The upper side, surface *ad* Upwards.

ಮೇಘ s. *n* A cloud -ಗರ್ಜನೆ, -ಘೋಷ, -ಧ್ವನಿ -ನಾದ Thunder -ಜ್ಯೋತಿ, -ವಹ್ನಿ Lightning -ದ್ವಾರ The sky. -ಮಂಡಲ. The atmosphere -ಕವಿ, -ಮುಸುಕು, -ಮುಚ್ಚು Clouds to collect and overspread. -ವರ್ಣ. Ash-colour

ಮೇಚಕ s *a* Dark-blue *n.* Dark-blue colour.

ಮೇಜು h *n* A table, dinner. ಮೇಜವಾನಿ. Ente[illegible] hospitably.

ಮೇಜೋಡು k *n.* A pair of stockings

ಮೇಟಿ 1 k *n* A chief, head 2, a head-servant 3, the plough-tail

ಮೇಟಿ 2 (*tb. of* ಮೇಢಿ) *n* A pillar, post.

ಮೇಡು k *n.* Height, a hillock.

ಮೇಣ (*tb. of* ಮದನ) *n.* Bees' wax, oily dirt, gum, resin -ದ ಬತ್ತಿ. A wax-candle. -ದ ಗೊಂಬೆ A wax-doll

ಮೇಣಿ (=ಮೇಟಿ) k. *n* The plough-tail. -ಪಾಲು. The share of the crop given to the person who assisted in ploughing.

ಮೇಣು k *ad* Upwards, further, besides

ಮೇದ 1, ಮೇದರ k *n.* A basket- and mat-maker.

ಮೇದ 2 = ಮೇದಸ್, *q v*

ಮೇದಕ s *n* Spirituous liquor

ಮೇದಸ್ (= ಮಿದುಡು, ಮಿದುಳು) s *n.* Fat, marrow, brain

ಮೇದಿನಿ s *n* The earth, land. -ಪಾಲ, ಮೇದಿನೀಶ A king

ಮೇಧ s. *n* A sacrifice (*as* ಅಶ್ವ-, ನರ-, ಪಶು-) -ವಾನ್. An intelligent, wise man. ಮೇಧಾವಿ Intelligent, wise, a learned man

ಮೇನ f *n* A kind of palankeen.

ಮೇಯು (= ಮೇ 1) k *v. i.* To graze, eat grass feed *P p* ಮೇದು ಮೇಯಿಸು To graze, feed

ಮೇರು s *n* N of a fabulous mountain said to be in the middle of Jambudvîpa

ಮೇರೆ (*tb of* ಮರ್ಯಾದೆ) *n* A boundary, limit, verge, an end, the bounds of propriety, manner, extent, rate. 2, sphere, region. 3, devotion. ಈ-, ಇದೇ- In this manner -ಕಟ್ಟು To fix boundaries -ಕಲ್ಲು A boundary-stone -ತಪ್ಪು, -ದಾಟು, -ಮೀರು To exceed bounds. -ಒತ್ತು. To encroach upon another's boundary. ಮಿತಿ ಮೇರೆ ಇಲ್ಲದ Immoderate

ಮೇಲ್ (= [illegible]) k [illegible] -[illegible]. To be[illegible] higher, superior *etc.* -ಉಡೆ. The upper garment. -ಕಟ್ಟು An awning, a canopy. -ಕಡೆ On the top, above, upon -ಗಾವಲಿ Control superintendence -ತರ A superior kind -ದವಡೆ. The upper jaw -ಬರಹ A superscription -ಬೀಳು. To rush upon. -ಭಾಗ The upper part. -ಮಾಡು To turn upwards -ಮಾಳಿಗೆ An upper story -ಮುಚ್ಚಳ, -ಮುಚ್ಚಿಗೆ A lid, a thatch, roof -ಮೇಲೆ One upon or after the other -ಲೋಕ Heaven -ವಟ್ಟು. An awning. -ವರಿ To rush upon. -ವಿಚಾರಕ An overseer, superintendent -ವಿಚಾರಣೆ Overseership, superintendence. -ಸೀಮೆ. The country on the Ghauts. -ಸೆರಗು The skirts of a woman's garment

ಮೇಲಿ (=ಮೇಳ) s *n* Meeting, assembly, *etc* 2, a set of singers 3, a concourse of people, a fair

ಮೇಲು k. *n*. That which is above, top-part, upper part, the surface, superior position *a* Future, following. *prep* Over, above, on. *ad*. Upwards, afterwards, after, farther ಯಾತರ ಮೇಲಿಂದ? On what account? why? ಮೇಲಾಟ. Outbidding ಮೇಲಾಡು To outbid. ಮೇಲಿನ ದಿನ The next day. ಮೇಲಿಂದ ಮೇಲೆ One after the other again and again, continually. -ಗೊಳ್ಳು, -ಪಡು To be successful -ಜಾತಿ A high caste -ತುಟಿ. The upper lip. -ನೋಟ A fine sight -ಪಂಕ್ತಿ An upper line -ಬರು To prosper. -ಬೀಳು To outbid, to fall upon. -ಮಾಡು To turn upward, to do a kindness -ಮಾಳಿಗೆ =ಮೇಲ್ಮಾಳಿಗೆ, *q. v.* -ಮುದ್ದೆ The earth put on a ceiling or a flat roof -ವಿಳಾಸ The address on a letter -(ಉ)ಸುರು. A pant. -ಹೊದಿಕೆ. An upper garment ಮೇಲೋಗರ Vegetables; vegetable sauce

ಮೇಲೆ k *prep* Above, over; on, upon *ad* Upwards, afterwards, more, fart[h]
-ಇಡ.

move up and down. -ಬೀಳು To fall upon, to begin to quarrel, to compete with impertinence -ಹಾರಿಸು To toss up ಮೇಲೆತ್ತು, ಮೇಲೆಬ್ಬಿಸು To lift up ಮೇಲೇರು. To ascend, mount. ಆ- After that ಇನ್ನು- Hereafter

ಮೇವು k *n* Grazing, pasturage. feed

ಮೇಷ s *n* A ram 2, the sign of the zodiac *Aries*.

ಮೇಸು =ಮೇಯಿಸು, *q v.*

ಮೇಸ್ತ್ರಿ f. *n*. A head workman

ಮೇಹ s *n*. Urine 2, urinary disease, *also* -ರೋಗ.

ಮೇಹನತು h *n* Exertion, pains. -ಮಾಡು. To take pains

ಮೇಳ =ಮೇಲ, *q v.* k. *n*. 4, mirth, merriment, jest, sport, fun. 5, a musical instrument. 6, a band of musicians. -ಗಾರ, -ದವ. A musician -ಯಿಸು, -ವಿಸು, ಮೇಳಿಸು. To meet combine, to join, assemble. -ನ, -ವ Union, harmony, chorus -ವಣೆ A chorus, a dance with music ಮೇಳಿಗೆ. An assembly.

ಮೈ (=ಮಯಿ, *q v*) k. *n*. The body *etc* -ಗಳ್ಳ A lazy man, sluggard. -ಗಳ್ಳತನ Laziness -ಸಾಲ. *See s* ಮಯಿ

ಮೈತ್ರ (*fr* ಮಿತ್ರ) s *a*. Friendly. *n* Friendship, goodwill, intimacy. 2 a friend, *also* ಮೈತ್ರ್ಯ.

ಮೈದಾನ h *n*. A plain, a level tract

ಮೈನ h. *n*. The Goravanka, a kind of jay.

ಮೈನಾಕ s *n* N. of a mountain

ಮೈಲಿ, ಮೈಲಿಗೆ, ಮೈಲೆ (=ಮಯ್ಲಿ, *q v*) f. *n*. Filth, pollution, dirtiness

ಮೈಲು e *n* A mile. -ಕಲ್ಲು A milestone

ಮೊಕ *tb of* ಮುಖ, *q v*

ಮೊಕದ್ದಮೆ h. *n* An affair, matter, a case, civil or criminal

ಮೊಕರರು, ಮೊಕರರಾರು h. *a* Settled, fixed, certain. *n*. An appointment -ಮಾಡು. To appoint

mpari-

ಮೊಕಾಮು, ಮೊಕ್ಕಾಮು h *n* A stage; encamping, a place of residence.

ಮೊಕೋಬ h *n*. A kind of scented snuff

ಮೊಕ್ಕಳ a. k. *n* A heap, mass, assemblage.

ಮೊಕ್ತಾ (*tb of* ಮುಖತಾ) *prep* In front, before, face to face

ಮೊಕ್ತಿಯಾರ್ h *a*. Absolute, free *n* Independence, an agent, attorney. -ನಾಮೆ. A power of attorney.

ಮೊಕ್ತೇಸರ h *n* A headman, a chief officer, a trustee, *as* of a temple.

ಮೊಗ. *tb of* ಮುಖ, *q v* -ಗೆಡಿಸು. To put to shame in a person's front. -ಗೊಡು To turn the face towards one. -ಚಿಟ್ಲಿಸು, -ಸಿಂಡ್ರಿಸು To frown. -ವಡ, -ವಾಡ A head-stall for horses, a mask, a muzzle. -ವರಿಕೆ Acquaintance, intimacy. -ಸಾಲೆ A front verandah, portico.

ಮೊಗಚು. = ಮಗಚು, *q v*.

ಮೊಗಲ h. *n* A Mogul.

ಮೊಗಸು k *v. i* To exert one's self *v t* To cover, to attack. *n* Desire

ಮೊಗಳು k. *n*. The ridge of a roof.

ಮೊಗು = ಮಗು, *q v*

ಮೊಗುಮ್ h. *a* General, undefined, implied.

ಮೊಗೆ 1. k *v t* To take (water with a vessel out of a tank, *etc.*) 2, to lade out, scoop, bale

ಮೊಗೆ 2. k *n* A small earthen vessel.

ಮೊಗ್ಗರ (= ಮೊಕ್ಕಳ, *q v.*) a k *n*. A mass, heap, a body, force.

ಮೊಗ್ಗು, ಮೊಗ್ಗೆ k *n* A bud, blossom

ಮೊಚ್ಚೆ f. *n* A shoe

ಮೊಟಕು k. *n*. A bit, piece, *as* of a pencil, *etc.* -ಬೆರಳು A little finger. -ಹಾದಿ A short road

ಮೊಟ್ಟು k *v. t* To rap one's head with the knukles of the fist *n*. A rap with the knuckles of the fist

ಮೊಟ್ಟೆ 1 k *n*. An egg

ಮೊಟ್ಟೆ 2 k. *n* A [illegible] bundle

ಮೊಡವಿ, ಮೊಡವೆ k *n* A small pimple in the face

ಮೊಣ (= ಮೊಳ) k. *n* A projecting joint. -ಕಾಲು The knee. -ಕಾಲುಕಣ್ಣು. The hollow on each side of the knee. -ಕಾಲುಚಿಪ್ಪು The knee-pan. -ಕಾಲು ಊರು, -ಕಾಲು ಬಗ್ಗಿಸು To kneel. -ಕೈ, -ಗೈ The elbow

ಮೊಂಡ. *tb of* ಮುಂಡ. *q. v*. -ಕೈ A maimed hand. -ಕತ್ತಿ, -ಗತ್ತಿ, -ಚೂರಿ A blunt knife. -ಗುದ್ದಲಿ A blunt hoe. -ಬೀಳು, -ಹೋಗು. To be obstinate, refractory

ಮೊಂಡು k *n*. Stupid obstinacy, *esp* in dunning; *also* ಮೊಂಡಾಟ, ಮೊಂಡುತನ ಮೊಂಡ An obstinate man.

ಮೊತ್ತ k *n*. A heap mass, a multitude, flock, *etc*, a collection

ಮೊದಲು k. *n* The state of being first, preceding, prior, the chief thing, the beginning, the base, the principal or capital. *ad* At the beginning, first, *etc.*, for the first time. -ಕಾರಣ. The first cause -ಗೊಳ್ಳು. To begin. -ತರ. The best sort. -ಮಾಡು. To begin. ಮೊದಲನೇ First, *etc* ಮೊದಲನೇದು That which is the first, the first. ಮೊದಲನೆಯದ. The first. ಮೊದಲಾಗು To become first of a series. ಮೊದಲಿಗ. A headman. ಮೊದಲಿನ. Preceding, prior ಮೊದಲಿನಷ್ಟು As much as in former times. ಮೊದಲಿನಂತೆ As before. ಮೊದಲೆ. At first, first of all. -ಹಿಡಿದು ಮಾತಾಡು To speak out fully.

ಮೊದ್ದು k *n* A block, log of wood 2, stupidity, bluntness ಮೊದ್ದ. A male blockhead, *f.* ಮೊದ್ದಿ

ಮೊನೆ 1 k *n* A point, an extremity, end, sharpness 2, courage -ಗಾರು A tongue used to make wire -ಕೆಡು, -ಗೆಡು To become blunt. -ಇಡು, -ತಿವಿ, -ಮಾಡು To make pointed -ಗಾರ. A bold man.

[illegible]

ಮೊನ್ನೆ k *ad* The day before yesterday, the other day, lately -ಮೊನ್ನೆ *rep.* Lately.

ಮೊಬಲಗು h *n* Sum, money.

ಮೊಬ್ಬು = ಮಬ್ಬು, *q v*

ಮೊಮ್ಮಗ k. *n* A grand-son ಮೊಮ್ಮಗಳು A grand-daughter. ಮೊಮ್ಮಕ್ಕಳು Grand-children.

ಮೊರ (ರ=ಐ) k. *n* A bamboo fan used for winnowing corn, *etc*

ಮೊರಡಿ, ಮೊರಡು 1. k *n* A hill, hillock.

ಮೊರಡು 2 = ಮುರುಡು *q. v*

ಮೊರಲೆ, ಮೊರವೆ (ರ=ಐ) k. *n* A large tree, bearing a kind of almonds, *Buchanania latifolia*

ಮೊರೆ 1 (ರೆ=ಐ) k *v. i* To roar, *as* the sea, tiger *etc*, to clamour, bawl, complain *n.* Roaring, wailing, lamentation 2, complaint -ಇಡು, -ಇಟ್ಟುಕೊಳ್ಳು. To cry loud; to wail, to complain, to beseech fervently ಮೊರತ Roar- ing, *etc.*

ಮೊರೆ 2. k. *v. i.* To hum, buzz, to sound, to murmur, to bubble *n* Humming.

ಮೊಲ k *n* A hare, a rabbit

ಮೊಲೆ k. *n* The female breast -ಕೂಸು, -ಗುನ್ನಿ A puppy -ಕೂಸು, -ಗೂಸು, -ಮೊಗು A suckling -ತುದಿ, -ತೊಟ್ಟು The nipple -ಉಣ್ಣು -ತಿನ್ನು To suck the breast -ಕೊಡು, -ಊಡು. To suckle, give the breast -ಬಿಡಿಸು. To wean

ಮೊಲ್ಲೆ k *n* A kind of jasmine, *Jasminum multiflorum*

ಮೊಸರು k *n* Curds. -ಕಡಿ. To churn the turned milk -ಸೋಸು. To strain curds ಮೊಸರನ್ನ Boiled rice mixed with curds

ಮೊಸಳೆ k *n* An alligator, crocodile -ಮಡುವು. A lake abounding with alligators

ಮೊಹತರ್ಫ f. *n* A tax on artizans.

ಮೊಹರ ... mol

ಮೊಹರಮ್ h. *n.* An annual Mussulman festival commemorating the death of two heroes, called *Hassan* and *Hoossein*, Moharam

ಮೊಹರಾ h *n.* A leader, chief, *cf.* ಮೊಹರ.

ಮೊಹರಿ 2. h *n* A little channel to carry off water

ಮೊಹರು h *n* A seal, a seal-ring.

ಮೊಹಸಲೆ h. *n* Restraint put on a person to prevent his escape or to enforce the payment of a demand; arrest

ಮೊಳ (=ಮೊಣ ಳ=ಐ) k *n* A projecting joint, a cubit -ಕಾಲು (=ಮೊಣಕಾಲು) The knee -ಕೈ (=ಮೊಣಕೈ). The elbow

ಮೊಳಕೆ, ಮೊಳಕೆ k *n.* A germ, bud, sprout

ಮೊಳಗು (ಳ=ಐ) a k *v. i.* To sound, to roar, to thunder *n* Thunder. 2, the plant *Marsilea quadrifolia*

ಮೊಳಸು k *n* Germination, *etc.*

ಮೊಳೆ k. *v. i.* To grow, shoot forth, sprout, bud, shoot, to appear *P ps.* ಮೊಳತು, ಮೊಳಿತು *n* A germ, bud, sprout. 2, a pin, nail, spike, wedge, peg, stake 3, the core of a boil. 4, piles ಕಬ್ಬಿಣದ- An iron nail ಮರದ- A wooden peg

ಮೋಕ್ಷ (=ಮುಕ್ತಿ1) s *n* Liberation, deliverance, release. 2, liberation from individual existence (*Hindu*); salvation, final beatitude (*Chr.*) 3, death -ಕಾಲ The time of liberation. -ಧರ್ಮ. Law of emancipation. *Cpds.* -ಪದವಿ, -ಮಾರ್ಗ, -ಶಾಸ್ತ್ರ, *etc.* -ಸಾಧನ Means of emancipation -ಕರ್ತ, -ದಾಯಕ ಪ್ರಭು Jesus Christ

ಮೋಖಾಫು h *n.* Abolishment, cessation; adjournment or recess, *as* of a court

ಮೋಚಕ s. *n* Final emancipation. -ಕ. A deliverer, liberator

ಮೋಚಿ h *n.* A shoemaker

ಮೋಂಡು k *v. i.* To become a widow. ... boot.

ಮೋಜು h. n. Play, sport. -ಗಾರ. A sportive man.

ಮೋಟನ s n Crushing 2, disgrace

ಮೋಟು k. n Stumpiness, maimedness; the stump of a tree, stubbles. ಮೋಟ An aimless or dwarfish man, f ಮೋಟಿ -ಮರ A branchless trunk -ಗಿವಿ, -ಕೈ. A maimed ear, arm. -ಬಾಲ A stumpy tail. ಮೋಟಗಾರ, ಮೋಟು ಮನುಷ್ಯ. A foolish man

ಮೋಡ k n A cloud, a cloudy weather -ಕಟ್ಟು, -ಕವಿ, -ಮುಸುಕು, -ವಾಗು To be cloudy or lowering.

ಮೋಡಿ 1 k. n A kind of craft or enchantment to try the ability of another -ಗಾರ A performer of môdi ರಾಜ-. Royal grandeur

ಮೋಡಿ 2 f n. A running hand, the business character, as in Marâtti 2, a kind of drug 3, a style, fashion (of speech, etc)

ಮೋತಿ 1. k n The face, snout

ಮೋತಿ 2. (tb of ಮುಕ್ತಾ) n A pearl

ಮೋತಿ 3. h n A petty grocer. -ಖಾನೆ. A granary

ಮೋತೆ k n. The leaf-like spathe over the flowers of the plantain, the cocoanut, etc

ಮೋದ s. n. Delight, gladness. 2, fragrance -ಕ Causing delight; a small, round sweetmeat. ಮೋದಿಸು To rejoice.

ಮೋದಂಡ s. n Undefined state.

ಮೋದು a. k. v t. To strike, beat, smite. n. A swelling caused by a blow, a hard boil

ಮೋನ (tb of ಮೌನ) n Silence. 2, asceticism.

ಮೋಪು k n Heaviness, as of a load, severeness, as of a wound, firmness, as of grasping 2, timber of a building, as beams, rafters, pillars, doors, etc.

ಮೋರಿ f. n A little water channel

ಮೋರೆ (ರೆ=ಱೆ) k n. The face. -ಗಂಟು. A frown. -ಗಂಟಿಡು, -ಗಂಟು ಹಾಕು. To frown -ತಪ್ಪಿಸಿಕೊಳ್ಳು To abscond. -ತೋರಿಸು To show one's self -ತಗ್ಗಿಸು, -ಬಗ್ಗಿಸು. To hang down the face.

ಮೋರ್ಚಾ h n Fortifications

ಮೋರ್ಚಿಂಗು h n A jew's-harp

ಮೋಷ s. n. Robbery, theft -ಕ. A robber, thief.

ಮೋಸ k. n Deceit, fraud, trick, duping, hypocrisy; blunder, fault; danger, peril; loss. ಅವನ ಪ್ರಾಣಕ್ಕೆ ಮೋಸ ವಿಲ್ಲ There is no danger to his life. -ಗೊಳಿಸು, -ಮಾಡು. To cheat, deceive. -ಗೊಳ್ಳು, -ಬೀಳು, -ಹೋಗು. To be deceived. -ಗಾರ A deceiver; f -ಗಾತಿ.

ಮೋಸಬಿ, ಮೋಸಮೆ h. n Responsibility

ಮೋಸಲೆ = ಮೊಸಲೆ, q v.

ಮೋಹ s n. Delusion, bewilderment; ignorance, folly, enamoured state, fascination 2, affection, fondness, love 3, a magical art -ಗೊಳಿಸು. To bewilder; to fascinate, charm. -ಗೊಳ್ಳು To become stupefied, to be fascinated, etc -ನ. Bewildering, charming, fascinating, temptation, seduction

ಮೋಹರ a k n. A mass, host, army. ಮೋಹರಿಸು. To become plentiful, to array, as troops.

ಮೋಹಿ s a Fascinating, charming -ತ. Deluded, beguiled, fascinated -ನಿ A fascinating woman -ಸು To faint; to be fascinated, to love; to desire

ಮೋಹು = ಮೋದು, q v.

ಮೋಳೆ k n A small hole in the banks of rice-fields, a fissure. 2, a pile, heap (of salt-earth).

ಮೌಂಜಿ s n The Brahmanical girdle made of muṅja grass -ಬಂಧನ. Investiture with it.

ಮೌಢ್ಯ (fr. ಮೂಢ) s. n. Stupidity, folly.

ಮೌನ (fr ಮುನಿ) s. n Silence, stillness -ಗೊಳ್ಳು To become silent. -ಗೊಳಿಸು.

To silence. -ತ್ವ. Silence. -ವ್ರತ. A vow of silence. ಮೌನಿ (= ಮುನಿ). A silent person.

ಮೌರಿ s. *n.* A clarionet.

ಮೌಲವಿ h. *n.* A Mussalman priest.

ಮೌಲಿ, ಮೌಳಿ s. *n.* The head, top. 2, a crown, crest.

ಮೌಲ್ಯ s. *n.* Price, value, cost.

ಮ್ಲಾನ s. *a.* Withered, faded; languid; feeble, weak; dejected, melancholy. -ತೆ. Witheredness; languor.

ಮ್ಲೇಚ್ಛ, ಮ್ಲೇಂಛ s. *n.* A non-Aryan, barbarian, outcast. -ದೇಶ. A foreign or barbarous country.

ಯ್

ಯ್. The forty-fourth letter of the alphabet. *For words beginning with* ಯ *not found here, see s.* ಎ.

ಯಕಾರ s. *n.* The letter ಯ.

ಯಕ್ಕು. = ಎಕ್ಕು, *q. v.*; *also:* to beat soundly.

ಯಕ್ಷ s. *n.* N. of certain demi-gods attending on Kubêra; *f.* ಯಕ್ಷಿಣಿ. -ಗಾನ. A kind of dramatic composition. -ಧೂಪ. The resin of *Shorea robusta.* -ಪ, -ರಾಜ್. Kubêra. ಯಕ್ಷಿಣಿ (= ಜಕ್ಕಿಣಿ). A female Yaksha; Kubêra's wife; a female fiend; sorcery done with that fiend's help. ಯಕ್ಷಿಣಿಗಾರ. A sorcerer. ಯಕ್ಷಿಣಿವಿದ್ಯೆ. Sorcery.

ಯಕ್ಷ್ಮರೋಗ. = ಕ್ಷಯರೋಗ, *q. v.*

ಯಜಮಾನ (= ಎಜಮಾನ) s. *n.* A householder; the master of a house; the head of a family, caste, *etc.*; a respectable, elderly man. (*pl.*) -ರು. A wife's name for her husband. -ತನ. ಯಜಮಾನಿಕೆ. The position of a Yajamâna. -ಗಿತ್ತಿ, -ತಿ, ಯಜಮಾನಿ. A mistress; a wife.

ಯಜು. *tb. of* ಯಜುಸ್, *q. v.*

ಯಜುಸ್ s. *n.* A sacrificial prayer or formula. 2, the yajurvêda. ಯಜುರ್ವೇದ. The sacrificial vêda.

ಯಜ್ಞ s. *n.* A sacrifice. -ಮಾಡು. To sacrifice [illegible] -ಕುಂಡ [illegible] the sa[illegible] fire. -ದೀಕ್ಷೆ. Initiation into sacrificial rites. -ಪಶು. A sacrificial victim. -ಪುರುಷ, ಯಜ್ಞೇಶ್ವರ. Fire, Agni; Vishṇu. -ಸೂತ್ರ, ಯಜ್ಞೋಪವೀತ. A sacrificial thread. -ಪುರುಷ. Agni; Jesus Christ.

ಯತನ. = ಯತ್ನ, *q. v.*

ಯತಿ s. *n.* Restraint, control. 2, an ascetic, devotee; a religious mendicant. 3, a pause (*in music*). 4, caesura (*in prosody*). ಯತೀಂದ್ರ. A great ascetic.

ಯತ್ಕಿಂಚಿತ್, ಯತ್ಕಿಂಚಿತ s. *ad.* Whatsoever, somewhat.

ಯತ್ನ (= ಎತ್ನ, ಯತನ) s. *n.* Effort, exertion; energy, diligence, perseverence; pains, care; effort for; eagerness; help. -ನಡಿಸು, -ಮಾಡು, ಯತ್ನಯಿಸು, ಯತ್ನಿಸು, ಯತ್ನೈಸು. To make effort, take pains.

ಯಥಾ s. *ad.* In which manner, as, like as, like. -ಕಾಮ. At pleasure. -ಕಾಲ In due time. -ಗತಿ. As usual, as before. -ಪೂರ್ವ, -ಪ್ರಕಾರ. As before, as previously. -ಪ್ರತಿ. A true copy. -ಪ್ರಯೋಗ. Common usage or custom. -ಮತಿ. According to opinion; to the best of one's judgment. -ಯಥ. Properly, suitably; by degrees. -ಯೋಗ್ಯ. Rightly, suitably. -ವತ್. Becomingly, properly, truly. -ವಿಧಿ. According to [illegible] ly. [illegible] the [illegible] According to law. -ಸ್ಥಾನ. Proper place; in regular order, properly, suitably. -ಸ್ಥಿತಿ. As usual, as on previous occasions.

ಯಥಾರ್ಥ s. a. True, real, genuine, right. ad. Truly, justly, suitably. n. Truth, etc. -ತ್ವ. Truthfulness, veracity, propriety.

ಯಥೇಷ್ಟ (fr. ಯಥಾ-ಇಷ್ಟ) s. ad. According to wish or desire; plentifully, copiously. ಯಥೇಚ್ಛೆ. A suitable wish or desire. = ಯಥೇಷ್ಟ.

ಯದಾ s. ad. When; since, as.

ಯದು s. n. N. of an ancient hero and his race.

ಯದೃಚ್ಛೆ s. n. Self-will, wilfulness, independence; accident, chance.

ಯದ್ವಾ s. conj. Or, else, whether. -ತದ್ವಾ. Disorderly; disorder, confusion.

ಯಂತ್ರ s. n. Any instrument, machine, engine, apparatus. 2, a band, fastening. 3, restraint. 4, an amulet, charm; a diagram of a mystical or astrological nature. -ಕಟ್ಟು. To tie an amulet. -ಕ. A machinist. -ಕಲೆ. The mechanical art.

ಯಮ s. n. Keeping in check; restraint; self-control. 2, the god of the infernal regions, punisher of the dead. 3, a pair; a twin. 4, the south-quarter. -ನಿಯಮ. Self-imposed restraint. -ದಿಕ್ಕು. The south. -ದೂತ, ಯಮನಾಳು. Messenger of death. -ಪಟ್ಟ, -ಪುರ, -ಪುರಿ, -ಲೋಕ. Yama's region, hell. -ಬಾಧೆ, -ಯಾತನೆ. The torture inflicted by Yama, hell-torments.

ಯಮಕ s. n. Restraint; a religious obligation. 2, a twin, pair. 3, a kind of play upon words or paronomasia. a. Two-fold, doubled.

ಯಮಲ s. n. A pair. 2, twin; also ಯಮಳಿ. 3, the number two.

ಯಮುನೆ s. n. N. of a river.

ಯಯಾತಿ s. n. N. of the fifth monarch of the lunar race.

ಯವ s. n. Barley, *Hordeum hexastichon*; also -ಕ. -ಕ್ಷಾರ. Saltpetre, nitre, nitrate of potash.

ಯವನ s. n. A Greek; a Mahomedan; a foreigner. -ದೇಶ. Bactria; Turkissthân, Arabia.

ಯವಾರ (tb. of ವ್ಯವಹಾರ) n. A law-suit; quarrel.

ಯವೆ. tb. of ಯವ, q. v.

ಯವ್ವನ. tb. of ಯೌವನ, q. v.

ಯಶ, ಯಶಸ್ (tb. ಯಶಸ್ಸು) s. n. Honour, glory, fame, reputation; beauty, splendour. ಯಶಸ್ಕರ, ಯಶಸ್ವಿ. Famous, glorious. ಯಶೋವಂತ. A famous man.

ಯಶೋದೆ s. n. Krishṇa's foster-mother. 2, N. of a female.

ಯಾ (= ವಾ, q. v.) s. conj. Or.

ಯಾಕೆ k. pro. Why? wherefore? ಯಾಕಾಗಬಲ್ಲದು? (i. e. ಯಾಕೆ ಆಗ ಒಲ್ಲದು?)

ಯಾಗ s. n. A sacrifice; also ಯಜ್ಞ.

ಯಾಗಸ್ಸು f. n. A stone cutter's chisel.

ಯಾಚನೆ, ಯಾಜ್ಞೆ s. n. A petition, request; begging. ಯಾಚಕ, ಯಾಚನಕ. A petitioner, beggar. ಯಾಚಿಸು. To ask, beg, request.

ಯಾಜಕ s. n. A sacrificer; a priest. ಪ್ರಧಾನ-. A high priest. ಮಹಾ ಪ್ರಧಾನ-. Christ. ಯಾಜನ. Assisting at a sacrifice.

ಯಾಜ್ಞವಲ್ಕ್ಯ s. n. N. of the author of a code of law.

ಯಾತ 1. (= ಏತ) k. n. A picotta.

ಯಾತ 2. s. n. The driving of an elephant with a goad. 2, going, motion.

ಯಾತಕ್ಕೆ k. pro. Why? for what?

ಯಾತನ, ಯಾತನೆ s. n. Requital, retaliation. 2, acute pain, torment, anguish, agony, pain, as of hell.

ಯಾತರ k. pro. Of what? ಯಾತರಿಂದ. From what? ಯಾತರದು. Of what it (is). ಯಾತರವ. Of what (is) he?

ಯಾತು s. n. A traveller, wayfarer. 2, an evil spirit, demon. 3, witchcraft, torture.

ಯಾತ್ರೆ (= ಜಾತ್ರೆ, q. v.) s. n. Going, travel; expedition. 2, going on a pilgrimage, pilgrimage. 3, a car-festival; a festive procession. 4, support of life, maintenance. ಕಾಶೀ-, ತಿರುಪತಿ-, ಶ್ರೀರಂಗ-, ಸೇತು-. Pilgrimage to Benares, Tirupati, Shrîrangam, Râmêśvaram, etc.

ಯಾದ (tb. of ಯಾದಸ್) n. A large aquatic animal, sea-monster.

ಯಾದವ (fr. ಯದು) s. n. A descendant of Yadu; Kṛishṇa.

ಯಾದಾಸ್ತು h. n. A memorandum, rough note. [scrap.

ಯಾದಿ h. n. Remembrance; a memo-

ಯಾದೃಶ s. pro. (int.) Which or what like? which? what?

ಯಾನ s. n. Going. 2, a conveyance or vehicle of any kind.

ಯಾನೆ f. a. Another. conj. Alias, or.

ಯಾಂತ್ರಿಕ s. a. Relating to instruments or machines.

ಯಾಪನ s. n. Delay, procrastination; loitering. 2, maintenance, support.

ಯಾಪಾರ (tb. of ವ್ಯಾಪಾರ, q. v.) n. Trade, traffic.

ಯಾಮ (= ಜಾವ) s. n. Going; motion, course. 2, a night-watch, eighth part of a day.

ಯಾಯಾವರ (tb. ಯಾಯಾವಾರ) n. Wandering; a vagrant mendicant; alms.

ಯಾರು k. pro. (pl. of ಯಾವ, q. v.) Who?

ಯಾಲಕ್ಕಿ (= ಏಲಕ್ಕಿ, q. v.) f. n. Cardamoms.

ಯಾವ k. (int.) pro. What? which? ಯಾವ್ಯಾವ (= ಯಾವ ಯಾವ). Whichever. -ನು. Who? which man? -ಲ್ಲಿ. Where? whither? -ಳು, ಯಾವಾತೆ. Which woman? ಯಾವಾಗ, ಯಾವಾಗ್ಗೆ. When? ಯಾವಾಗಲಾದರೂ. At any time, whensoever. ಯಾವಾಗಲು, ಯಾವಾಗಲೂ, ಯಾವಾಗ್ಲೂ. Always, ever.

ಯಾವಜ್ಜೀವ s. ad. Throughout life.

ಯಾವತ್ತು (tb. of ಯಾವತ್) [illegible] All the whole.

ಯಾವಾಗ, ಯಾವಾಗ್ಗೆ. See s. ಯಾವ.

ಯಿ, ಯೀ. For Kannaḍa words with these initials, see s. ಇ and ಈ.

ಯಿಂಗಡಿಸು = ಇಂಗಡಿಸು, q. v.

ಯುಕುತಿ tb. of ಯುಕ್ತಿ, q. v.

ಯುಕ್ತ s. a. Yoked, endowed with, having, possessed of, adopted, fitted, fit, suitable, right; moderate; intent on; engaged in; proved, inferred; f. ಯುಕ್ತೆ, ಯುಕ್ತಳು. ಯುಕ್ತಾಯುಕ್ತ. Suitable and unsuitable.

ಯುಕ್ತಿ (= ಯುಕುತಿ) s. n. Combination, union. 2, application, practice. 3, appliance, means, plan, scheme, expedient, trick, contrivance, device, ingenuity. 4, skill, art, tact. 5, suitableness, propriety, fitness; the secret, key, etc. 6, argument, inference. 7, connection of events in a plot (in drama). -ತೆಗೆ. To take hold of a device. -ಹುಡುಕಿ ತೆಗೆ. To make an invention. -ವಂತ, -ಶಾಲಿ. An ingenious or clever man. -ಸಾಧ್ಯ. Attainable by expedients, etc. -ಸಾಮರ್ಥ್ಯ. The power of expedients, etc. ಕಪಟ-, ಕು-. A sly scheme.

ಯುಗ (= ನೊಗ) s. n. A yoke. 2, a pair, couple. 3, a lustrum. 4, the period of a year (see ಯುಗಾದಿ). 5, one of the 4 ages of the world. ಯುಗಾದಿ. The beginning of a year, a new year's first day (its feast); also ಯುಗಾದಿಹಬ್ಬ.

ಯುಗಲ, ಯುಗ್ಮ s. n. A pair, couple.

ಯುದ್ಧ s. n. A war, battle, fight, combat. -ನಡೆ. A war to happen. -ಮಾಡು. To make war; to fight. -ಭೂಮಿ, -ರಂಗ. A battle-field. ದೊಣ್ಣೆ-. A fight with cudgels. ಮಲ್ಲ-. Boxing. -ಸ್ಥ. A warrior.

ಯುಧಿಷ್ಠಿರ s. n. N. of the eldest of the Pâṇḍu princes.

ಯುವ s. a. Young, youthful. n. A youth, young man; f. -ತಿ. 2, the ninth year in the Hindu cycle. -ರಾಜ. An heir apparent to a prince.

ಯೂಥ s. *n.* A flock, herd; a troop. -ನಾಥ, -ಪ. The leader of a herd, *as* of elephants.

ಯೂಪ s. *n.* A post to which the sacrificial victim is tied; *also* -ಸ್ತಂಭ. 2, a column erected in honour of a victory.

ಯೆಂಗಿ. *tb. of* ವ್ಯಂಗ್ಯ. -ಹಾಕು. To cheat.

ಯೆಹೂದ್ಯ f. *n.* A Jew, Hebrew or Israelite.

ಯೆಹೋವ f. *n.* Jehovah, God as revealed to men by His Word (*lit.* the Self-existent and Eternal). -ದಯೆ. The grace of Jehovah.

ಯೇಸು f. *n.* Jesus, the Saviour of the world. -ವಿನ ಶಿಷ್ಯ. A Christian. -ವಿತ. A Jesuit, one to counterinfluence the Reformation; a crafty person. -ವಿತರ ಬೋಧನೆ. The teachings of the Jesuits.

ಯೋಗ s. *n.* Yoking, union, contact; connection; mixture; arrangement; manner, means; an expedient, plan; charm, magic. 2, work, business; performance. 3, fitness, propriety. 4, accession of property. 5, conjunction (of stars); an auspicious moment; good luck. 6, a period of time. 7, a constellation. 8, etymology. 9, construction. 10, an aphorism. 11, abstract contemplation, meditation. 12, N. of a system of philosophy. 13, the body. 14, a remedy. -ಕ್ಷೇಮ. Well-being; welfare. -ಧ್ಯಾನ. Contemplation (of the Deity). -ನಿದ್ರೆ. A state between sleep and wakefulness. -ವಂತ, -ಶಾಲಿ. A lucky man. -ವಾಹ. A letter on the top of another. ಯೋಗಾಕ್ಷರ. A compound consonant. ಯೋಗಾಭ್ಯಾಸ. Practice of the yôga.

ಯೋಗಿ (=ಜೋಗಿ) s. *n.* A yôgi; an ascetic; a devotee; *f.* -ನಿ.

ಯೋಗ್ಯ s. *n.* Useful, serviceable, fit, suitable, proper; able. *n.* A useful, worthy man; *f.* -ಳು. -ತನ, -ತೆ. Suitableness, fitness; ability.

ಯೋಚನ, ಯೋಚನೆ (*tb. of* ಯೋಜನ) *n.* Application of the mind, consideration, reflection, (sorrowful) thought. ಯೋಚಿಸು. To deliberate, reflect, think; to consider, ponder; to ascertain.

ಯೋಜನ (=ಯೋಚನ) s. *n.* Junction; application. 2, a measure of distance (= about 9 English miles). 3, grammatical construction (*g.*). 4, abstraction. ಯೋಜಿಸು. To deliberate; to approve, assent.

ಯೋಧಕ s. *n.* A warrior, soldier.

ಯೋನಿ s. *n.* The womb; birth, origin; family, race. -ಜ. Viviparous.

ಯೌವನ (*fr.* ಯುವ. = ಜವ್ವನ, ಯವ್ವನ) s. *n.* Youth; prime of life, manhood. *a.* Juvenile. -ಸ್ಥ. A young man; *f.* ಯೌವನಿ. ಯೌವನಾವಸ್ಥೆ. Youthfulness.

ರ

ರ. The forty-fifth letter of the alphabet.

ರಕಮು h. *n.* An item; an amount; a dose; a piece. -ವಾರು. Piece by piece.

ರಕಾರ s. *n.* The letter ರ.

ರಕ್ಕಸ. *tb. of* ರಾಕ್ಷಸ, *q. v.* *f.* ರಕ್ಕಸಿ. *tb. of* ರಾಕ್ಷಸಿ.

ರಕ್ಕೆ. *tb. of* ರೆಕ್ಕೆ, *q. v.*

ರಕ್ತ s. *a.* Coloured, dyed. 2, red; loving, dear, lovely. *n.* Blood. 2, saffron. 3, vermilion. -ಕಮಲ. A red lotus-flower. -ಕಾಸ. Cough with homoptysis. -ಕುಷ್ಠ. Red leprosy. -ಚಂದನ. Red sandal, *Pterocarpus santolinus*.

-ತೆ Redness. -ಪವಳ, -ಬೋಳ Gum-myrrh, aloes -ಪುಷ್ಪ. A red flower -ಭೇದಿ ರಕ್ತಾತಿಸಾರ The dysentery. -ಮಂಡಲ A red-ringed snake

ರಕ್ತಾಕ್ಷಿ s. n A buffalo. 2, the fifty-eighth year in the cycle of sixty.

ರಕ್ಷ, ರಕ್ಷಕ s. n A guardian, protector, saviour 2, the only Saviour Jesus Christ ರಕ್ಷಣ, ರಕ್ಷಣೆ Watching, tending, protecting, preserving, saving, salvation in Christ ರಕ್ಷಾಪತ್ರ. A book-cover. ರಕ್ಷಾಬಂಧ The binding of thread around the wrist as a preservative (against evil spirits, *etc*). ರಕ್ಷಿಸು To guard, protect, preserve, save, keep, tend; to save (*from sin by Christ's atonement*).

ರಕ್ಷಸ್ = ರಾಕ್ಷಸ, *q v*

ರಕ್ಷೆ s. n. Protecting, protection, care, a preservative, a mark of ashes on the forehead, a charm, amulet. -ಕಟ್ಟು, -ಗಟ್ಟು To tie an amulet -ಬಳೆ. An amulet-ring ಅಂಗ- A coat. ಪಾದ-. A sandal ಶಿರೋ-. A turban ರಕ್ಷ್ಯ. Proper to be guarded, protected, *etc*

ರಗತ h n Abundance, profusion, masses, lots, heaps; throng

ರಗಡೆ f. n A grinding stone

ರಗಳೆ (*tb of* ರಘಟೆ) n Vain words, gabble. 2, a never-ending business, prolixity.

ರಘು s. n N of an ancient king. -ವಂಶ His race or family *also* -ಕುಲ, N of a poem (by Kâlidâsa) -ನಂದನ. -ನಾಥ, -ರಾಮ, -ವರ, -ವೀರ, -ಸುತ Râma

ರಂಕ s. *a* Indigent, poor n A beggar

ರಂಗ (= ರಂಗು, *q v*) s. n. Colour paint, hue 2, a stage, arena, circus 3, a place of assembly; an assemblage of spectators 4, a battle-field 5, dancing, acting, fun. 6, splendour, glow. -ನಾಥ Vishnu. -ಭೂಮಿ An arena, theatre -ವಲಿ, -ವಲ್ಲಿ. Ornamen[illegible]

various powders on the floor -ಸ್ವಾಮಿ Vishnu; N ರಣ-, ಯುದ್ಧ-. The battle-field ರಂಗಿಸು To be coloured, to be excited.

ರಂಗಳಿಸು f *v t* To press and rub fine, as small articles

ರಂಗಾರಿ h n. A dyer.

ರಂಗು *tb of* ರಂಗ, *q v* -ಮಹಲು A saloon, drawing-room

ರಂಗೋಲೆ. *tb. of* ರಂಗವಲಿ, *q. v*

ರಚನೆ s. n Making, forming, formation, creation, arranging; arrangement, disposition performance; embellishment, composition, a literary production ರಚಿತ Made, formed, produced, planned, composed, *etc* ರಚಿಸು To make, form, construct, compose, array, *etc*

ರಚ್ಚೆ (= ರಟ್ಟು 2) k. n. Crying aloud (of children), noisy clamour 2, report, publication

ರಜ = ರಜಸ್, *q v* -ವಂದಿ Acceptable; a compromise, composition deed

ರಜಕ s. n. A washerman, *f.* ರಜಕಿ

ರಜತ s *a*. White, silver-coloured; pure -ಗಿರಿ, -ಪರ್ವತ, -ಶೈಲ, ರಜತಾಚಲ, ರಜತಾದ್ರಿ N. of a mountain -ಭಸ್ಮ. Calcined silver

ರಜನಿ s n Night. 2, Durgâ. -ಕರ -ಚರ, -ಪತಿ, -ಪಾಲ. The moon

ರಜಪುತ್ರ, ರಜಪೂತ (*tb. of* ರಾಜಪುತ್ರ, *q. v.*) n A Rajpoot

ರಜಸ್, ರಜಸ್ಸು (= ರಜ, *q. v*) s. n. Gloom. dimness. 2 dust, powder 3, the pollen of flowers 4, passion, foulness.

ರಜಾ h. n. Leave, permission 2, leave of absence.

ರಜ್ಜು s n A rope, cord string.

ರಂಜಕ s. *a* Colouring. 2 gladdening, rejoicing, pleasing (see ಮನೋ-) 3, powder. 4, the train of powder to a mine. ರಂಜನ Colouring, de-[illegible] shine, to appear; to be beautiful; to be affected, excited; to be pleased.

ರಟ್ಟು 1. k. *n.* A coarse, thick cloth. 2, the cover of a book; its binding.

ರಟ್ಟು 2. = ರಟ್ಟೆ, *q. v.*

ರಡ್ಡಿ *tb. n.* A Reḍḍi: a title of a caste of Telugu cultivators.

ರಣ s. *n.* Noise. 2, battle, war, combat. 3, joy, delight. -ಗಲಿ. A hero in war. -ಗಾಳೆ A war-trumpet. -ಪದ್ದು. A vulture. -ಹೇಡಿ. A coward in battle. -ಭೂಮಿ, -ಮಂಡಲ, -ರಂಗ. A battle-field. -ಭೇರಿ. A war-drum. -ವಾದ್ಯ. Martial music. -ವೀರ, -ಶೂರ. A warrior. ರಣಾಗ್ರ. The front of a battle. ರಣಾಂಗಣ. A battle-field; war, battle.

ರಂಟೆ k. *n.* A small plough.

ರಂಡೆ k. *n.* A widow. 2, the plant *Salvinia cucullata.* -ತನ. Widowhood.

ರತ s. *a.* Pleased, satisfied; delighted with; intent on; devoted to, engaged in. *n.* Pleasure.

ರತಿ 1. s. *n.* Pleasure. 2, love, affection. 3, Kâma's wife; *also* -ದೇವಿ.

ರತಿ 2. f. *n.* A small weight.

ರತ್ನ s. *n.* A jewel, gem, precious stone; a pearl. 2, any precious thing. -ಕಂಬಳಿ, -ಗಂಬಳಿ. A figured carpet. -ಗಂಧಿ. A shrub with showy flowers, the peacock's pride, *Caesalpinia pulcherrima.* -ನಗರಿ, -ಪುರಿ. N. of a town. -ಪರೀಕ್ಷೆ. Jewel-testing. -ಗರ್ಭ. The sea; Kubêra. -ಗರ್ಭೆ. The earth. -ಮಾಲೆ. A jewel necklace; N. of a work.

ರಥ s. *n.* A carriage, car, chariot. 2, a warrior. 3, the body. 4, the foot. 5, a limb, member. 6, pleasure, desire. -ಶಾಲೆ. A carriage-shed. -ಸಪ್ತಮಿ. A feast on the 7th day of the eleventh lunar month. ರಥಾರೋಹ, ರಥಾರೋಹಣ. Mounting a chariot; the ceremony of placing an idol on a car. ರಥಿಕ. The owner of a carriage; a charioteer. ರಥೋತ್ಸವ. A car-festival. ಮನೋ-. Wish, desired object.

ರದ್ದು h. *a.* Null and void, cancelled, repealed. -ಮಾಡು. To repeal, cancel. -ಆಗು, -ಪಡು. To be repealed.

ರಂಧ್ರ s. *n.* A split, fissure, opening, hole, cavity; a defect, fault, flaw. ರಂಧ್ರಿಸು. To bore a hole.

ರನ್ನ. *tb. of* ರತ್ನ, *q. v. Cpds.:* -ಗನ್ನಡಿ, -ಜಗಲಿ, -ದೊಡವು, -ಪಲ್ಲಕಿ, -ವಣೆ, *etc.*

ರಪಣ s. *n.* A kind of weapon.

ರಫ, ರಫ್ಫು h. *n.* Darning. -ಗಾರ. A darner. -ಮಾಡು. To darn.

ರಫ್ತು f. *n.* Exportation. -ಆಗು. To be exported.

ರಭಸ s. *n.* Violence, vehemence, haste, speed. 2, passion, anger. 3, pleasure. 4, a loud cry, clamour.

ರಮಣ s. *a.* Pleasing, agreeable, delightful. *n.* A lover; a husband; pleasure. ರಮಣಿ. A wife. ರಮಣೀಯ. Pleasing, agreeable, delightful, lovely. ರಮಾ-. Vishṇu.

ರಮಾ, ರಮೆ s. *n.* A wife; a woman; Lakshmî. ರಮಾಧವ, ರಮಾಪತಿ. Vishṇu. ರಮಿಸು. To rejoice, play.

ರಂಪ k. *n.* Clamour.

ರಂಪಿಗೆ k. *n.* A shoemaker's awl.

ರಂಬೆ k. *n.* A twig, small bough.

ರಂಭೆ s. *n.* The plantain tree, *Musa sapientum.* 2, N. of an Apsaras.

ರಮ್ಯ s. *a.* Enjoyable, pleasant, delightful, beautiful.

ರಯಾತ, ರಯಿತ (= ರೈತ) h. *n.* A subject; a tenant; a ryot. ರಯತಾಪಿ. Peasantry.

ರವ s. *n.* A cry, shriek, yell, howl, roar; sound, noise. -ಣ. Crying, sounding; jesting; a camel. ರವಿಸು. To cry, *etc.*

ರವಳಿ a. k. *n.* Cry, clamour. -ಗೆ. A small bamboo basket. -ಸು. To vociferate.

ರವಾನೆ h. *n.* Despatch; a pass, permit, passport. -ಮಾಡು, ರವಾನಿಸು. To send on, despatch, transmit.

ರವಿ s n. The sun. 2, a mountain. 3, wealth. -ಕಾಂತ A sort of crystal. -ಕುಲ. The solar race of kings -ವಾರ Sunday.

ರವೆ (tb of ಲವ) n A grain, granule, a particle of anything, hail, grits -ಅಷ್ಟು, ರವಷ್ಟು. A little, trifle.

ರಶೀತಿ, ರಶೀದಿ e n A receipt.

ರಶ್ಮಿ s. n. A rope. 2, a ray of light. 3, an eyelash

ರಸ s n The sap or juice of plants, syrup. 2, essence 3, any liquid. 4, ghee; water, milk, etc 5. sauce, seasoning 6, quicksilver 7, resin. 8, constituent fluid of the body 9, taste, savour, relish 10, passion, desire 11, pleasure, charm, grace, sweetness, spirit wit, joy, etc 12, style 13. sentiment, feeling, pathos -ಕರ್ಪೂರ Sublimate of mercury -ಘುಟಿಕೆ. A pill made with quicksilver -ಜ್ಞ An alchemist -ದಾಳಿ. A fine sort of sugarcane -ಬಾಳೆ A plantain of a sweet flavour -ಭಸ್ಮ Calx or oxide of mercury -ವತ್, -ವತ್ತು Tasteful well-flavoured, tasty -ವರ್ಗ All condiments (as pepper, salt etc). -ವಾದ Metallurgy; alchemy. -ವಾದಿ. An alchemist -ಸಿದ್ಧಿ. Skill in alchemy -ಸಿಂದೂರ A sort of factitious cinnabara. ನವ-. The nine sentiments of poetry, as ಶೃಂಗಾರ, love, ವೀರ, heroism, ಕರುಣ, tenderness, ಅದ್ಭುತ, surprise, ಹಾಸ್ಯ, mirth; ಭಯಾನಕ, terror, ಬೀಭತ್ಸ, disgust; ರೌದ್ರ, anger; ಶಾಂತ, tranquillity.

ರಸಾತಲ s n The lower world, one of the 7 regions under the earth.

ರಸಾಭಾಸ s n. The unsuitable manifestation of a sentiment. 2, disorder, confusion

ರಸಾಯನ s n. An elixir, any medicinal compound 2, alchemy, chemistry. 3, boiled fruit-juice mixed with sugar, mil[illegible]

ರಸಾಲ s n The mango tree 2, the sugarcane; also ರಸದಾಳಿ

ರಸಿಕ s. a Tasty, savoury. 2, graceful, elegant 3, spirited witty. 4, having a liking for -ತನ, -ತ್ವ Tastefulness, sapidity, affection, taking pleasure in.

ರಸುಮೆ. tb of ರಶ್ಮಿ, q. v

ರಸ್ತಾಳೆ (tb of ರಸದಾಳಿ) n A fine sort of sugarcane.

ರಸ್ತು h. n. Grain stored up for an army

ರಸ್ತೆ h n A road way.

ರಹ (= ರಹಸ್ಯ) s. n Wonderfulness, a marvel. 2, way, method.

ರಹಣೆ s. n. Dancing, pantomime; manner.

ರಹದಾರಿ h. n Passage to and fro; traffic; a passport.

ರಹಸ್ಸು (= ರಹ) s. n Solitude, privacy, a secret, mystery. ರಹಸ್ಯ. Secret, private, mysterious, a secret, a mystery.

ರಹಾಟ = ರಾಟಣ, q v

ರಹಿತ s a Left, abandoned 2, deprived of, void or destitute of, without -ತೆ The state of being without.

ರಾಕಟೆ f. n A golden circular ornament worn by females on their hair-tresses

ರಾಕಾ, ರಾಕೆ s. n. The full moon

ರಾಕ್ಷಸ (= ರಕ್ಕಸ, q. v) s. n. An evil being or demon, a goblin 2, a form of marriage -ಕೃತ್ಯ A cruel deed -ವೈದ್ಯ Harsh medical treatment ರಾಕ್ಷಸಿ (= ರಕ್ಕಸಿ). A female demon

ರಾಗ s n Colour, hue. 2, affection, emotion, feeling 3, love, sympathy, joy, pleasure. 4, greediness, envy 5, anger 6, loveliness 7, a musical note, a tune, music -ತೆಗೆ To begin to sing. -ದ್ವೇಷ Hatred from anger or envy. -ನುಡಿಸು To make music. -ಮಾಡು, -ಹಾಡು, -ಹೇಳು To [illegible] -ಮಾಲೆ. A piano, harmonium; *also* -ಮಾಲಿಕೆ ಪೆಟ್ಟಿಗೆ.

ರಾಗಟಿ. = ರಾಕಟಿ, *q. v.*

ರಾಗಿ 1. k. *n.* Raggy, a sort of grain, *Eleusine coracana.* -ಯಂಬಲಿ. Raggy gruel. -ರೊಟ್ಟಿ. R. bread. -ಹಿಟ್ಟು. R. meal; its porridge.

ರಾಗಿ 2. s. *a.* Coloured; red; given up to passion; full of love; fond of. *n.* A painter; a lover. -ಸು. To be coloured; to be very fond of.

ರಾಘವ (*fr.* ರಘು) s. *n.* A descendant of Raghu. 2, Râmaċandra; *also* ರಾಘವೇಂದ್ರ.

ರಾಜ (= ಅರಸು, ರಾಯ, *q. v.*) s. *n.* A king, sovereign, prince, chief; an excellent man; a master. 2, a Kshatriya. -ಕ. A petty king; what comes from a king. -ಕನ್ನಿಕೆ. A (virgin) princess. -ಕಾರ್ಯ. State affairs. -ಕೀಯ. Royal, kingly. -ಕುಮಾರ. A prince. -ಕುರು. A carbuncle. -ಕುಲ. A royal family. -ಗೃಹ, -ಭವನ, -ಮಂದಿರ. A palace. -ಚಿಹ್ನ, -ಚಿಹ್ನೆ, -ಲಕ್ಷಣ, -ಸದನ. Insignia of royalty. -ಚೂಡಾಮಣಿ. The best of kings. -ತ್ವ. Kingship, royalty. -ತರು. The tree *Cassia fistula*; the plant *Pterospermum acerifolium.* -ಧರ್ಮ. A king's duties; a virtue fit for a king. -ಧಾನಿ. A capital. -ನೀತಿ. Royal politics. -ಪಟ್ಟ. A royal tiara. -ಪತ್ನಿ. A queen. -ಪದವಿ. Kingship. -ಪುತ್ರ. A prince; a Rajpoot. -ಪೂಜಿತ. Excellent (*an honorific term*). -ಬೀದಿ, -ಬಾಟೆ, -ಮಾರ್ಗ. A high road, main road. -ಮರ್ಯಾದೆ. Respect shown to a king or to superiors. -ಮಾನ್ಯ. Excellent. -ಮುದ್ರೆ. A royal signet. -ಯೋಗ. An easy mode of meditation. -ಯೋಗ್ಯ. Princely. -ಋಷಿ. A royal saint. -ವಂಶ. A royal family. -ವಿದ್ಯೆ. State policy. -ವೈದ್ಯ. A royal physician; an excellent practice of medicine. -ಶಾಸನ. A royal edict. -ಶಿರೋಮಣಿ, -ಶಿರೋಮಣಿ. The first of kings. -ಶೇಖರ. The chief of kings; Śiva; N. of a king. -ಶೇಖರವಿಲಾಸ. N. of a Kannaḍa poem. -ಶ್ರೀ. A term of courtesy. -ಸಭೆ. A royal assembly, a court of justice. -ಸೂಯ. A great sacrifice at a king's coronation. -ಸೇವೆ. King's service. -ಹಂಸ. A flamingo. -ಹುಣ್ಣು. Scrofula. ರಾಜಾಜ್ಞೆ. A royal decree. ರಾಜಾಧಿರಾಜ. A king of kings.

ರಾಜಿ 1. s. *n.* A strip, line, row.

ರಾಜಿ 2. h. *a.* Willing, ready. *n.* Full consent, willingness, agreement, content. -ನಾಮೆ. A deed of resignation (of an office, claim, *etc.*), an acquittance. -ಮಾಡು. To bring to terms. -ಯಾಗು. To consent, acquiesce.

ರಾಜಿಕ, ರಾಜೀಕ s. *a.* Relating to a king. *n.* A lord, noble person.

ರಾಜಿತ s. *a.* Illuminated; adorned.

ರಾಜಿಸು s. *v. i.* To shine, glitter. *v. t.* To make radiant.

ರಾಜೀವ s. *n.* A species of fish. 2, a lotus. 3, water. -ನೇತ್ರ. Vishṇu. -ಮಿತ್ರ, -ಸಖ. The sun.

ರಾಜೇಂದ್ರ s. *n.* A king of kings.

ರಾಜ್ಞಿ (= ರಾಣಿ) s. *n.* A queen.

ರಾಜ್ಯ s. *n.* A kingdom, empire, country, government. 2, administration of government. 3, kingship. -ಗೆಯ್ಯು, -ಮಾಡು, -ನಾಳು. To rule. -ಭಾರ. Rule, reign. -ಭಾರ ಮಾಡು. To exercise government. -ಶ್ರೀ. An empire; an honorific term. ರಾಜ್ಯಾಧಿಪತಿ. A ruler, king. ರಾಜ್ಯಾಭಿಷೇಕ. Coronation.

ರಾಟಣ, ರಾಟವಾಣ, ರಾಟವಾಳ, ರಾಟೆ, ರಾಟ್ಣ (*th. of* ಅರಘಟ್ಟ) *n.* A machine for drawing water; a spinning wheel; a wheel of any machine. 2, a whirling machine. ರಾಟಿಸು. To wind upon a reel.

ರಾಡಿ s. *n.* A mass of mud. *a.* Foul, turbid.

ರಾಣಿ (*th. of* ರಾಜ್ಞಿ) *n.* A queen. 2, a wife. -ರಾಜ್ಯ. A queen's government. -ವಾಸ. A queen's apartment.

ರಾತಲು h *n* A weight of 12 or 16 ounces, a pound

ರಾತೀಪು ರಾತೀಬು h *n* A nutritive and fattening diet; a regular quantity of food

ರಾತ್ರಿ s *n*. Night. -ಕಾಲ Night-time. -ಪತಿ -ಮಣಿ, ರಾತ್ರೀಶ The moon. ಅರ್ಧ-, ಸಮ- ನಡು-, ಮಧ್ಯ-. Midnight ಶಿವ- An annual festival in honour of Śiva's birth -ಭೋಜನ The Lord's Supper instituded by Christ

ರಾದಾರಿ = ರಹದಾರಿ *q v*.

ರಾದ್ಧ s *a* Accomplished; prepared, obtained. ರಾದ್ಧಾಂತ. A demonstrated truth, dogma.

ರಾಧೆ s *n*. N. of the foster-mother of Karna 2, N of Krishna's favourite wife

ರಾಪ f. *n*. Astringent property, *as* juice of fruits.

ರಾಬ್ತಿ h *n* Custom usage. -ಬೀಳು. To become familiar.

ರಾಮ s *a* Pleasing, lovely, charming 2, white, pure *n*. N. of Vishnu's 7th incarnation, *also* -ಚಂದ್ರ. -ಗುಳ್ಳ. The plant *Solanum jacquini* -ತುಳಸಿ The herb *Ocimum album* -ದೂತ Hanumat -ಪುರ N. of several places -ಫಲ The bullock's heart (a fruit) -ಸೇತು. Adam's bridge. ಪರಶು-. Vishnu's 6th incarnation. ಬಲ- Krishna's elder brother ರಾಮಾನುಜ A Vaishnava teacher of the twelfth century ರಾಮಾಯಣ. An epic poem by Vâlmîki describing the adventures of Râma. ರಾಮಾಯಣಪಾರಾಯಣ. Reading the Râmâyana ರಾಮೇಶ್ವರ N of a place between Ceylon and Coromandel coast

ರಾಯ *tb of* ರಾಜ, *q v* -ಬಹಾದರ್. A title of honour -ಭಾರಿ An embassador. -ಭಾರ, -ಭಾರಿಕೆ Government, ruling; ambassadorship. -ಬೋಗಿ A large shrub, *Webera corymbosa*

ರಾಯಸ s. *n*. Secretaryship in native government 2, a letter from a su

ರಾವಣ s *n*. Roaring, N of the ruler of Lankâ (Ceylon) slain by Râma.

ರಾವು (*tb. of* ರಾಹು) *n* The daitya Râhu. 2 a startle -ಗಣ್ಣು. The evil eye. -ತಟ್ಟು, -ಬಡಿ A horror to touch. -ತೆಗೆ. To wave an offering before a person to remove evil influences.

ರಾವುತ (*tb of* ರಾಹುತ) *n* A horseman.

ರಾಶಿ s *n* A heap, mass, pile, quantity. 2, a sign of the zodiac. *a*. Exceedingly much -ಚಕ್ರ An astrological diagram. -ಮಾಡು, -ಹಾಕು To pile heap up

ರಾಷ್ಟ್ರ s *n* A kingdom, realm, empire a district ಮಹಾ- The Mahratta country

ರಾಸ s *n*. Uproar, noise. 2, a rustic dance, *as* of Kṛishna and gôpis, *also* -ಕ್ರೀಡೆ.

ರಾಸಿ *tb. of* ರಾಶಿ, *q v*. -ಮೋಹ Excessive passion -ಮಾಡು. To heap up

ರಾಸ್ನೆ s *n*. The thorny shrub *Mimosa octandra*

ರಾಹು s *n* N of a demon supposed to swallow the sun and moon and thus cause eclipses 2, the ascending node of the moon 3 a startling event, *as* an eclipse, *etc*

ರಾಹುತ = ರಾವುತ, *q v*.

ರಾಳ f. *n* Resin in general -ದ ಮರ. The white dammer tree. *Vateria indica*

ರಿಕಾಪು h. *n* A stirrup.

ರಿಕಾಮಿ f. *n* Empty, vacant, unemployed.

ರಿಕಾರ್ಡು e *n* Record.

ರಿಕ್ಕಟ k. *n*. Silence *ad* Silently.

ರಿಕ್ತ s. *a* Empty, poor, vain, worthless ರಿಕ್ತೆ A poor woman.

ರಿಖಾನೆ h *n* A column in a form -ದ ರಾಯಿಸು To fill up the columns of a tabular form

ರಿಂಗಣ s. *n*. Crawling, creeping 2 dancing. 3, slipping; deviating

ರಿಜಿಸ್ಟ್ರಾರು e *n* A registrar, *as* of assur-

ರಿಣ. *tb. of* ಋಣ, *q. v.*

ರಿಪು s. *n.* An enemy, foe.

ರಿಯಾಯಿತಿ h. *n.* Protection; leniency, indulgence. -ಮಾಡು. To make an exception, treat leniently.

ರಿವಾಜು h. *n.* Usage, custom.

ರಿಸಾಲು h. *n.* A troop of horses.

ರೀತಿ s. *n.* A course. 2, way, method, mode, manner, fashion; usage. 3, style, diction.

ರೀಪು f. *n.* A wooden lath, reeper.

ರುಕ್ಮ s. *a.* Bright, radiant. *n.* Gold. -ಕಾರಕ. A goldsmith. ರುಕ್ಮಾಂಗದ. N. of a king.

ರುಕ್ಮಿಣಿ s. *n.* N. of a daughter of king Bhīshmaka and wife of Kṛishṇa.

ರುಚಕ s. *a.* Agreeable, pleasing. 2, tonic, stomachic. *n.* The citron.

ರುಚಿ s. *n.* Light, lustre. 2, wish, will; taste for. 3, taste, flavour, relish, savour, appetite. -ಕಾಣು, -ನೋಡು. To taste, try. -ಹತ್ತು. To be tasty or agreeable. -ಕರ. Savoury, tasty. -ಕೊಡು. To impart a flavour. -ಸು. To be savoury or tasty; to be agreeable, *as* a word.

ರುಚಿರ s. *a.* Bright, beautiful; sweet, pleasant, nice.

ರುಜನ s. *n.* Sickness; toil, fatigue; *cf.* ರೋಗ-.

ರುಜು h. *n.* Signature; proof. -ಮಾಡು. To sign; to prove. -ವಾತು. Proved; proof, evidence. ಕೇಳಿಕೇ ರುಜುವಾತು. Hearsay evidence. ಸಂಗತ್ಯಾನುಸಾರ ರುಜುವಾತು. Circumstantial evidence.

ರುಣ. *tb. of* ಋಣ, *q. v.*

ರುಂಡ s. *n.* A headless trunk; a skull. -ಮಾಲೆ. A wreath of skulls.

ರುತು. *tb. of* ಋತು, *q. v.*

ರುದ್ರ s. *n.* Crying, howling. 2, N. of the god of tempests. 2, Śiva. -ಗಂಟು. A peculiar knot of a Śaiva's sacrificial thread. -ಭೂಮಿ. A place of burial or cremation. -ಮಂತ್ರ. -ಸೂಕ್ತ. N. of a ṛigvêda hymn. -ವೀಣೆ. A kind of lute. ರುದ್ರಾಭಿಷೇಕ. Anointing a liṅga reciting -ಸೂಕ್ತ. ರುದ್ರಾವತಾರ. Śiva's incarnation; excitement, rage, fury. ರುದ್ರಾಕ್ಷ, ರುದ್ರಾಕ್ಷಿ. The berry of *Elaeocarpus ganitrus* tree.

ರುಧಿರೋದ್ಗಾರಿ s. *n.* Spitting blood; the fifty-seventh year in the cycle of sixty.

ರುಪಾಯಿ. = ರೂಪಾಯಿ, *q. v.*

ರುಬರೂಬು. = ರೂಬರೂ, *q. v.*

ರುಬ್ಬು k. *v. t.* To grind. *n.* Grinding.

ರುಮಾಲ, ರುಮಾಲು h. *n.* A turban. 2, a handkerchief; *also* ಶ್ಯ-.

ರುವಿ, ರುವ್ವಿ (*tb. of* ರೂಪ್ಯ) *n.* A pie, kâsu.

ರುಷಿ. *tb. of* ಋಷಿ, *q. v.*

ರುಷಿತ s. *a.* Enraged, angry.

ರುಸುಮು h. *n.* Fees, dues, commission.

ರುಳಿ f. *n.* A silver chain worn on the legs by women.

ರೂ k. *n.* Repetition of words and sentences. -ಹಾಕು. To repeat them frequently, to commit them to memory.

ರೂಕ್ಷ್ಯ s. *n.* Emaciation; harshness, cruelty.

ರೂಡಿ. *tb. of* ರೂಢಿ, *q. v.*

ರೂಢ s. *a.* Commonly known, popular, conventional. -ನಾಮ. A common noun.

ರೂಢಿ (= ರೂಡಿ) s. *n.* Rise; origin. 2, custom, usage, common currency, general use; a popular use of words (*opposed to etymological meaning*). -ಬೀಳು, -ಯಾಗು. To become common. -ಮಾಡು. To practice. -ಮಾತು, -ಶಬ್ದ. A common word.

ರೂಢಿಸು s. *v. i.* To be commonly known and used; to become famous. 2, to improve, accumulate.

ರೂಪ (= ರೂಪು, ರೂಹು) s. *n.* Any form, figure, shape; an image. 2, an inflected form (*g.*). 3, shapeliness, beauty. 4, feature, character. 5, kind, sort. 6, a single specimen, type, pattern. 7, mode. -ವಂತ. A handsome man; *f.* -ವಂತಳು, -ವಂತೆ, -ವತಿ. -ಹೀನ. Ugly. ರೂಪಾಂತರ. A change of form, transfiguration, *as* of Christ. -ತಳೆಯಿಸು, -ಧರಿಸು, -ಮಾಡಿಕೊಳ್ಳು. To assume a form. ರೂಪಿಸು. To form, mould, figure; to represent, show, point out.

ರೂಪಕ **s.** *a.* Figurative. *n.* A metaphor. 2, a form, figure, image. 3, a drama, play; a dramatic composition or performance.

ರೂಪಾಯಿ (*tb. of* ರೂಪ್ಯ) **s.** *n.* A rupee. -ತೂಕ. A rupee's weight, tola.

ರೂಪು. *tb. of* ರೂಪ, *q. v.*

ರೂಪ್ಯ **s.** *a.* Handsome. 2, stamped. *n.* A stamped coin; silver.

ರೂಬರೂ, ರೂಬರೂಬು h. *ad.* Face to face.

ರೂಲು e. *n.* A rule; a line.

ರೂಹು. *tb. of* ರೂಪ, *q. v.*

ರೆಕ್ಕೆ (ರೆ = ಱೆ) k. *n.* A wing. -ಯುಳಿ. A winged ant. -ಬಡಿ, -ಯಾಡಿಸು. To shake the wings.

ರೆಟ್ಟೆ (ರೆ = ಱೆ) k. *n.* The arm; the upper part of the arm; *also* ರಟ್ಟೆ.

ರೆಪ್ಪೆ (ರೆ = ಱೆ) k. *n.* An eyelid. -ಹಾಟು. The twinkling of an eye. -ಬಡಿ, -ಹಾಕು. To wink.

ರೆಂಬೆ (= ರಂಬೆ) k. *n.* A twig.

ರೆಳ್ಳು k. *n.* A reed used to write with, *Saccharum sara.*

ರೇಕ f. *n.* Emptying, evacuating, leaving; purging. 2, doubt.

ರೇಕು k. *n.* A thin plate of metal. 2, the petal of a flower.

ರೇಕೆ (*tb. of* ರೇಖೆ, *q. v.*) *n.* A line.

ರೇಖೆ (= ರೇಕೆ) s. *n.* A line; a streak, stripe; a row; drawing. 2, the first meridian. 3, a small quantity. ರೇಖಾಂತ. Longitude. ರೇಖಾಗಣಿತ. Geometry.

ರೇಗು k. *v. i.* To be aroused, excited; to become angry. ರೇಗಿಸು. To irr[illegible]

ರೇಚಕ **s.** *n.* Purging; expiration. 2, a purge.

ರೇಜಿಗೆ f. *n.* Disgust.

ರೇಡು. = ರೇತಿ, *q. v.*

ರೇಣು **s.** *n.* Dust. 2, the pollen of a flower. -ಕ. A Yaksha. -ಕೆ. The mother of Paraśurâma.

ರೇತಿ **h.** *n.* Sand. -ದಾನಿ. A sandbox.

ರೇಫ **s.** *n.* A burr: the letter ರ. 2, passion. *a.* Low, vile.

ರೇವಡಿ f. *n.* A kind of sweetmeat. 2, discomfiture. -ಗಿಡ. A wiry thorny shrub, *Capparis divaricata.*

ರೇವತಿ s. *n.* N. of the twenty-seventh nakshatra. 2, N. of Balarâma's wife.

ರೇವಲ್ಚಿನ್ನಿ f. *n.* The perennial plant *Rhubarb, Rheum palmatum.*

ರೇವು k. *n.* A landing place, beach, port.

ರೇವೆ f. *n.* Fine gravel; the grit of sugar.

ರೇಷ್ಮೆ, ರೇಶ್ಮೆ, ರೇಶಿಮೆ *etc.* h. *n.* Silk. *a.* Silken. -ಹುಳ. The silk-worm.

ರೈ **s.** *n.* Wealth; gold; lustre. -ವತ. Rich, wealthy; N. of a king or a mountain.

ರೈಟರ್ e. *n.* A writer.

ರೈತ. = ರಯತ, *q. v.*

ರೊಕ್ಕ **f.** *n.* Cash, ready money; change; money in general. ಚಿಲ್ಲರೆ-. Small change.

ರೊಚ್ಚು, ರೊಚ್ಚೆ, ರೊಜ್ಜು **k.** *n.* Mud, mire, foul water.

ರೊಟ್ಟಿ f. *n.* Bread; a cake of bread. -ಗಿಡ. A spreading herb, *Malva rotundifolia.*

ರೊದ್ದ k. *n.* The left. -ಕೈ. The left hand.

ರೊಂಡಿ k. *n.* The haunch.

ರೊಂಡೆ k. *n.* Mud.

ರೊಪ್ಪ (ರೊ = ಱೊ) k. *n.* A fold.

[illegible] k. *n.* Teasing [illegible] 2, (e.)

ರೋಕ s. *n.* Light. 2, a hole, cavity. 3, buying for cash.

ರೋಗ s. *n.* Sickness, disease, malady; *cf.* ರುಜಿನ. -ದಲ್ಲಿ ಬೀಳು. To fall sick. -ಚಿಹ್ನ, -ಲಕ್ಷಣ. The symptoms of a disease. -ಪರೀಕ್ಷೆ. Examination of a disease. -ರಾಜ. Consumption. -ರುಜಿನ. *dpl.* -ಶಾಂತಿ. Cure of a malady. -ಸ್ಥ. A sick man. -ಹರ. Curative. -ಹಾರಿ. Curing, curative; a physician. ರೋಗಿ. Sick, ill; a sick person. ರೋಗಿಷ್ಟ. One who is sickly.

ರೋಚಕ s. *a.* Sapid, tasty, savoury. *n.* A stimulant, stomachic. 2, hunger, appetite.

ರೋಜ 1. e. *n.* A rose.

ರೋಜ 2, ರೋಜಾ h. *n.* Fast, a fast.

ರೋಜು h. *n.* A day; service, work; a day's wages. -ಗಾರ. A workman, servant. -ಗಾರಿ, -ಗಾರಿಕೆ. Work; wages; earning. -ನಾಮೆ. A diary, ledger-book.

ರೋಡ್ e. *n.* A road.

ರೋಡು (ರೊ = ಬೊ) s. *v. i.* To be foolish. ರೋಡಾಡು. To laugh at with grimaces; to deride.

ರೋಡೆ (= ರೋಸು, *q. v.*) k. *n.* Dirt, filth, any nasty thing.

ರೋದನ s. *n.* Weeping, wailing. ರೋದಿಸು. To weep, wail.

ರೋಧ s. *n.* Checking; restraint, obstruction, prohibiting. *See* ನಿ-, ವಿ-, *etc.*

ರೋಮ (= ಲೋಮ) s. *n.* The hair on the body; wool, down, bristles, feathers. -ಕೂಪ. A pore of the skin. -ರಾಜಿ. A row of hair. -ವಿಕಾರ, -ಹರ್ಷ. Horripilation; bristling of hair; thrill, shudder; *also* ರೋಮಾಂಚ.

ರೋಮನ್ e. *a.* Pertaining to Rome. -ಕಥೋಲಿಕ್. Roman Catholic. -ಕಥೋಲಿಕ ಮತ. Roman Catholicism. -ಕಥೋಲಿಕ ಆಚಾರ. R. Catholic ceremonies.

ರೋಷ s. *n.* Anger, rage, wrath. -ಣ. Angry, passionate.

ರೋಷನ್ h. *n.* Lighting, illumination.

ರೋಸು (= ರೋಡೆ) k. *n.* Dirt, filth. *v. i.* To feel disgusted.

ರೋಹಣ s. *n.* Rising, ascending; *see* ಆ-.

ರೋಹಿಣಿ s. *n.* Rising. 2, N. of the fourth or ninth nakshatra. 3, N. of Daksha's daughter, Balarâmâ's mother. 4, a young girl. -ಸುತ. The planet Mercury; Balarâma.

ರೋಹಿತ s. *a.* Red. *n.* A kind of deer.

ರೌದ್ರ (*fr.* ರುದ್ರ) s. *a.* Rudra-like; violent, terrible, formidable. *n.* Ardour, passion, anger, fury. -ತೆ. Fierceness, formidableness.

ರೌದ್ರಿ s. *n.* The fifty-fourth year of the cycle of sixty.

ರೌರವ (*fr.* ರುರು) s. *a.* Dreadful, terrible. *n.* One of the hells; *also* -ನರಕ.

ಱ

ಱ. The forty-sixth letter of the alphabet; *now out of use and represented by* ರ.

ಲ್

ಲ್. The forty-seventh letter of the alphabet.

ಲಕಡಿ h. *n.* Wood.

ಲಕಲಕ f. *n.* Glitter, flash. *ad.* Brightly, brilliantly.

ಲಕಾರ s. *n.* The letter ಲ.

ಲಕುಚ s. *n.* A kind of bread-fruit tree, *Artocarpus lacucha.*

ಲಕ್ಕೋಟು, ಲಕೋಟೆ h. *n.* The envelope of a letter; a closed letter.

ಲಕ್ರಾ f. *n.* A kind of pigeon.

ಲಕ್ಕಿ k. *n.* The shrub *Vitex negundo*; *also* -ಲಿ.

ಲಕ್ಷ s. *n.* A mark, sign, token. 2, a butt, aim. 3, appearance, show, pretence. 4, a lac, one hundred thousand. 5, (= ಲಕ್ಷ್ಯ *n.* No. 2) attention, regard, consideration. -ಕೊಡು. To give heed, pay attention to, to mind, aim at. -ಗಟ್ಟಲೆ. By lacs. -ದೊಳಗೆ ಇಡು. To consider, regard. -ದೊಳಗೆ ಬರು. To come under observation, to be perceived. ಲಕ್ಷಾಧಿಕಾರಿ, ಲಕ್ಷಾಧಿಪತಿ, ಲಕ್ಷೇಶ್ವರ. A millionaire. ಲಕ್ಷಾಂತರ. A lac and more, very much. ಲಕ್ಷಾವಧಿ. By lacs, very much, very many. ಲಕ್ಷಿಸು, ಲಕ್ಷೀಕರಿಸು. To distinguish; to aim at; to consider, regard; to behold, notice, know.

ಲಕ್ಷಣ s. *n.* A distinctive mark, token, characteristic; character, attribute. 2, a favourable sign; handsomeness. 3, a symptom, *as* of a disease. 4, a definition. 5, aim, scope, object. -ಗೇಡಿ. An unlucky person. -ವಂತ. A lucky or handsome man. ಲಕ್ಷಣೆ. An ellipsis, metonymy.

ಲಕ್ಷ್ಮಣ s. *a.* Having signs. 2, lucky, fortunate. *n.* N. of Rāma's younger [illegible]

ಲಕ್ಷ್ಮೀ s. *n.* Good fortune, prosperity, wealth, happiness. 2, beauty, loveliness. 3, N. of the goddess of fortune and beauty, Vishṇu's wife. -ಕರ. Causing prosperity. -ಕಾಂತ, -ಪತಿ, -ರಮಣ, -ವಲ್ಲಭ, -ವರ. Vishṇu. -ವಂತ. A wealthy man.

ಲಕ್ಷ್ಯ s. *a.* To be marked; to be aimed at. *n.* An aim, object, butt, a feature. 2, attention, consideration, regard, care for. -ಕೊಡು. = ಲಕ್ಷಕೊಡು. -ಮಾಡು, -ಕ್ಕೆ ತರು. To mark, mind. -ದಲ್ಲಿ ಇಡು. = ಲಕ್ಷದೊಳಗೆ ಇಡು. -ಸಿದ್ಧಿ. Proof derived from examples.

ಲಗಡಿಸು h. *v. t.* To beat, flog.

ಲಗತ h. *n.* Enclosure, appendage. -ಮಾಡು. To append, enclose. ಲಗತು. Adjoining.

ಲಗಬಗೆ f. *n.* Haste, bustle. ಲಗುಬಗೆ, ಲಗೆಬಗೆ. Hastily.

ಲಗಾಂ (= ಲಗಾಮು) h. *n.* The bit of a bridle; a bridle.

ಲಗಾಟಿ s. *n.* A wicked woman.

ಲಗಾಡಿ. = ಲಿಗಾಡು, *q. v.*

ಲಗಾಮು. = ಲಗಾಂ, *q. v.*

ಲಗಾವು f. *n.* Union, connection. 2, application. -ಮಾಡು. To make applicable to, *as* provisions of law. ಲಗಾಯಿಸು. To join; to beat; to eat.

ಲಗು (*tb. of* ಲಘು, *q. v.*) *a.* Light. *n.* Alleviation. *ad.* Quickly, swiftly. -ಬಿಗು. The state of being easy or difficult. -ಲಗು. Very quickly.

ಲಗ್ಗೆ (*tb. of* ಲಂಘ) *n.* Ascending, scaling; an assault, attack. -ಆಗು. To be scaled. -ಮಾಡು, -ಹತ್ತು, -ಹೋಗು. To scale.

ಲಗ್ನ s. *n.* Attached; joined, united; auspicious. *n.* The time of the [illegible] ...ical sign; [illegible] time for action; *also* ಸು-, ಶುಭ-. 2, marriage. 3, the rising of the sun, planets, *etc.* -ಕಾಲ. An auspicious moment; the marriage-time. ಜನ್ಮ-. A natal star. -ಪತ್ರಿಕೆ. A paper on which the time of celebrating a wedding is noted down; a letter of invitation for a wedding. ಮದುವೆ-. A marriage ceremony.

ಲಘಿಮೆ s. *n.* Lightness. 2, smallness. 3, frivolousness. 4, meanness. ಲಘಿಷ್ಠ. Lightest, smallest.

ಲಘು (=ಲಗು) s. *a.* Quick, swift, fleet. 2, light, easy. 3, little, small, slight, trivial, trifling, insignificant. 4, weak, low; mean, frivolous. 5, soft, gentle. *ad.* Quickly. -ಕೆಲಸ. A trifling business. -ತ್ವ. Quickness; lightness; levity; incivility, disrespect; frivolity. -ಶಂಕೆ. Making water. -ಹಸ್ತ. Light-handed, expert.

ಲಂಕಿಣಿ s. *n.* A female demon of Laṅka.

ಲಂಕೆ, ಲಂಕಾ s. *n.* The capital of Râvaṇa in Ceylon; Ceylon.

ಲಂಗ h. *n.* A skirt.

ಲಂಗರ್, ಲಂಗರ h. *n.* An anchor. -ಬಿಡು. To cast anchor. -ಎತ್ತು. To weigh anchor.

ಲಂಗೋಟಿ h. *n.* A piece of cloth covering the privities.

ಲಂಘನ s. *n.* Jumping; leaping over, crossing. 2, transgression; offence. 3, ascending; assaulting; capture. 4, fasting, abstinence. ಲಂಘಿಸು. To leap, spring; to overstep; to ascend, *etc.*

ಲಜ್ಜೆ, ಲಜ್ಜಾ s. *n.* Shame, bashfulness; perplexity. ಲಜ್ಜಾವತಿ. A modest woman; a prickly shrub *Mimosa pudica.* ಲಜ್ಜಾಳು, ಲಜ್ಜಾಶೀಲ, ಲಜ್ಜಿತ. Bashful, modest, shameful. ಲಜ್ಜಾಹೀನ. Shameless, impudent.

ಲಂಚ, ಲಂಚೆ s. *n.* A present, bribe. ಲಂಚ ಗಿಂಚ, -ಸಂಚ. *red.* -ಕೊಡು, -ಹಾಕು. To bribe. -ತಿನ್ನು, -ತೆಗೆ. To take bribes. -ಕೋರ, -ಗಾರ, -ಗುಳಿ. A receiver of bribes.

ಲಟಕಟಿಸು f. *v. i.* To grow agitated; to be restless; to be alarmed.

ಲಟಾಪಟ f. *n.* Altercation, coming to blows.

ಲಟ್ಟ h. *n.* A stick; a club. *a.* Stout, thick. -ಣಿಗೆ. A roller; a rolling-pin. ಲಟ್ಟಿಸು. To roll out, *as* dough.

ಲಡಾಯಿ h. *n.* Fighting; a fight; war.

ಲಡಿ h. *n.* A string, *as* of pearls.

ಲಡ್ಡ s. *n.* A wretch, villain.

ಲಡ್ಡು 1. k. *n.* Pithlessness, weakness. -ಆಗು, ಲಡ್ಡಾಗು. To become pithless, *as* wood. -ಸೌದೆ. Pithless firewood.

ಲಡ್ಡು 2. f. *n.* A sweetmeat-ball; *also* ಲಡ್ಡುಕ, ಲಡ್ಡಿಗೆ, ಲಡ್ಡುಗೆ.

ಲಂಡ. *tb. of* ಲಡ್ಡ. 2, (=ಲದ್ದಿ) excrement.

ಲತೆ s. *n.* A creeper. 2, a plant in general. 2, a branch. ಲತಾಗೃಹ. A creeper-house, arbour. ಲತಾಂಗಿ. A woman of delicate form. ಲತಿಕೆ. A small creeper.

ಲತ್ತೆ f. *n.* A kick; a blow. -ಕೊಡು, -ಹಾಕು. To kick; to give a blow.

ಲದ್ದಿ h. *n.* The dung of elephants, horses, camels, *etc.*

ಲಪನ s. *n.* Speaking, talk. 2, the mouth. ಲಪಿತ. Spoken, said; speech.

ಲಪ್ಪಟ್ಟಿ s. *n.* A cloth for wrapping round the head.

ಲಬ್ಧ s. *a.* Obtained, got, gained, acquired. 2, obtained, *as* a quotient. -ನಾಶ. Loss of any thing acquired.

ಲಬ್ಧಿ s. *n.* Gaining, acquisition. 2, gain, profit. 3, quotient (*arith.*).

ಲಬ್ಬೆ h. *n.* A caste of Mahomedans.

ಲಭ್ಯ s. *a.* Acquirable, obtainable; attainable. 2, suitable, proper, fit. ಲಭಿಸು. To be gained or obtained, *etc.*

ಲಂಪಟ s. *a.* Covetous, greedy; desirous; addicted to. -ತನ, -ತೆ. Greediness; lewdness.

ಲಂಪು k. *n.* Weariness, fatigue.

ಲಂಬ s. a. Hanging down, pendulous, dangling. 2, hanging upon. 3, long; spacious. n. Length. 2, a perpendicular (*geom.*). -ನ. Hanging down; a necklace.

ಲಂಬಾಡಿ, ಲಂಬಾಣಿ h. n. A Lumbadee, a migratory caste trading in salt, grain, *etc.*

ಲಂಬಿ s. a. Hanging down, pendent; resting on. -ಸು. To hang down or from, to dangle. v. t. To lengthen, expand (*as* words, time, *etc.*).

ಲಂಬೋದರ s. a. Pot-bellied. n. Gaṇêśa.

ಲಯ s. n. Clinging, adherence. 2, a dwelling; rest, repose. 3, melting away; dissolution; extinction, destruction; disappearing. 4, time or pause in music. -ನ. Rest, repose; a place of rest.

ಲಲನ s. n. Playing, sporting. 2, lolling the tongue.

ಲಲನೆ s. n. A woman, wife. 2, the tongue.

ಲಲಾಟ s. n. The forehead. -ರೇಖೆ. Destiny written on the forehead. ಲಲಾಟಾಕ್ಷ. Śiva.

ಲಲಾಮ s. n. A mark; sign. 2, a banner, flag. 3, greatness, dignity. 4, beauty. 5, an ornament. 6, an eminent person. 7, a horse.

ಲಲಿತ s. a. Sported; wanton, voluptuous; lovely, beautiful; simple; soft, gentle; pleasant, sweet. n. Sport; beauty, grace. 2, simplicity, artlessness. -ವೃತ್ತ, ಲಲಿತೆ. One of the ragaḷĕ metres.

ಲಲ್ಲೆ s. n. Caressing; love, affection; a kiss. -ಗೆಯ್ಯು. To caress; to kiss; *also* ಲಲ್ಲಯಿಸು.

ಲವ s. n. Cutting; plucking. 2, a fragment, piece, bit, a little. 3, a moment, instant. 4, wool, hair. 5, N. of a son of Râma.

ಲವಂಗ s. n. The clove tree, *Myristica caryophyllata*, cloves. -ಪಟ್ಟೆ. Cinnamon [illegible] leaves of *Laurus cassia*. -ವಾಸನ ಹುಲ್ಲು. A grass with fragrant roots, *Panicum cimicinum*.

ಲವಡಿ h. n. A female slave; a strumpet.

ಲವಣ s. n. Salt. 2, N. of a Daitya. a. Saline, briny, salt. -ಭಸ್ಮ. Calcined salt. -ಸಮುದ್ರ, ಲವಣೋದಧಿ. Ocean.

ಲವಣೆ s. n. Stooping, bending, winding. 2, flash, shine. ಲವಣಿಸು. To wind; to shine, flash.

ಲವಲವಿಕೆ f. n. Ardent desire, longing. ಲವಲವಿಸು. To desire ardently.

ಲವುಡಿ. = ಲವಡಿ, q. v. 2, an iron club.

ಲಶುನ s. n. Garlic.

ಲಷ್ಕರು h. n. An army; a cantonment. 2, a lascar.

ಲಸತ್ s. a. Shining, glittering; skilful, clever. -ವಚನ. A clever word. ಲಸಿತ. Played, sported; come to light; skilled.

ಲಹರಿ 1. s. n. A large wave, billow; a waving line.

ಲಹರಿ 2. h. n. Intoxication.

ಲಳಿ s. n. Liveliness; enthusiasm, animation, cheerfulness; dexterity.

ಲಳಿಗೆ. = ನಳಿಗೆ, q. v.

ಲಳ್ಳಿ (= ನಳ್ಳಿ, q. v.) k. n. A crab.

ಲಾಕ್ಷ, ಲಾಕ್ಷೆ s. n. Lac, sealing wax.

ಲಾಕ್ಷಣಿಕ (fr. ಲಕ್ಷಣ) s. a. Distinguished, characteristic; technical. n. A distinguished teacher.

ಲಾಖಿ h. a. Red, crimson.

ಲಾಗ f. n. A summerset. -ಹಾಕು, -ಹೊಡೆ. To make a summerset, to tumble.

ಲಾಗವತು, ಲಾಗವಾತು f. n. Expense, cost.

ಲಾಗಾಯಿತು h. n. Beginning, commencement. a. From the beginning.

ಲಾಗು (= ಲಾಗ) f. n. A leap, jump; a summerset. 2, excess. 3, catch, hold; an aim.

ಲಾಘವ (fr. ಲಘು) s. n. Quickness, swiftness, lightness, levity, dexterity, [illegible] light.

ಲಾಂಗಲ s. *n.* A plough. 2, the palm tree.

ಲಾಂಗೂಲ s. *n.* A tail.

ಲಾಚಾರು h. *a.* Helpless, poor. -ತನ, ಲಾಚಾರಿ. Helplessness.

ಲಾಜ, ಲಾಜೆ s. *n.* Parched grain.

ಲಾಂಛನ s. *n.* A mark, sign; a stain, stigma. ಲಾಂಛಿತ. Furnished with; marked, characterised.

ಲಾಟ s. *a.* Old, worn, spoiled. *n.* N. of a people. 2, repetition of words in the same sense.

ಲಾಟೀನು e. *n.* A lantern.

ಲಾಟು e. *n.* A lot.

ಲಾಡಿ f. *n.* A cord. 2, a strap. 3, a tape.

ಲಾಡು. = ಲಡ್ಡು 2, *q. v.*

ಲಾತು. = ಲತ್ತೆ, *q. v.*

ಲಾಂದರ. = ಲಾಟೀನು, *q. v.*

ಲಾಭ s. *n.* Gain, advantage, profit; emolument. -ನಷ್ಟ. Profit and loss. ಲಾಭಿಸು. To gain, to profit.

ಲಾಮಚ, ಲಾಮಂಚ (*tb. of* ಲಾಮಜ್ಜ) *n.* The cuscus-grass, *Andropogon muricatus.*

ಲಾಯ (*fr.* ಲಯ) s. *n.* A stable.

ಲಾಯಖ್ h. *a.* Fit, proper; merited, qualified; excellent. ನಾ-. Unfit, *etc.*

ಲಾಲನ, ಲಾಲನೆ s. *n.* Caressing, fondling, dandling. ಲಾಲಿತ. Caressed, fondled, *etc.* ಲಾಲಿಸು. To caress, fondle; to listen kindly, accept favourably; to attend to.

ಲಾಲಸ s. *n.* Louging, ardent desire. *a.* Ardently desirous.

ಲಾಲಾ, ಲಾಲಾಜಲ s. *n.* Saliva, spittle.

ಲಾಲಿ k. *n.* A lullaby sung to children. -ಹಾಡು. To sing lullaby.

ಲಾಲೆ. = ಲಾಲಾ, *q. v.*

ಲಾವ s. *n.* Cutting; plucking. 2, a sort of quail. -ಕ್ಕಿ. The red spur-fowl.

ಲಾವಕ s. *n.* A reaper. 2, a snake-catcher and [illegible]. 3, a quail. -ತನ. Tale-bea[illegible]

ಲಾವಂಚ. = ಲಾಮಚ, *q. v.*

ಲಾವಣಿ f. *n.* A list of soldiers or public servants.

ಲಾವಣೆ f. *n.* A ballad. 2, a collection, throng.

ಲಾವಣ್ಯ (*fr.* ಲವಣ) s. *n.* Saltness. 2, beauty, loveliness, charm. -ವಂತ. A handsome man; *f.* -ವಂತಳು, -ವತಿ, -ವಂತೆ.

ಲಾವಿಗೆ, ಲಾವ್ಗೆ. = ಲಾವಕ, *q. v.*

ಲಾಳ (*tb. of* ನಾಲ) *n.* A tube; a stalk. 2, a kind of reed used for pens. 3, (= ನಾಲ 1) a horse shoe.

ಲಾಳಿ (= ನಾಳಿ, *etc.*) f. *n.* A weaver's shuttle.

ಲಿಖಿತ s. *a.* Written, drawn. *n.* Writing, a document or composition. ಲಿಖಿಸು. To write.

ಲಿಗಾಡು f. *n.* A trouble, perplexity. 2, compensation for damages.

ಲಿಂಗ s. *n.* A mark, sign, emblem; a characteristic. 2, a proof, evidence. 3, Śiva, *as* worshipped. 4, an idol. 5, gender (*g.*). -ತೊಂಡೆಬಳ್ಳಿ. A climbing herb, *Bryonia laciniosa.* -ಪ್ಪ. N.; *f.* -ವ್ವ. -ತ್ರಯ. The three genders (*g.*). -ಧಾರಕ, -ವಂತ, -ಧಾರಿ. A Liṅgavanta. -ಧರಿಸು, -ಕಟ್ಟಿಕೊಳ್ಳು. To put on the liṅga. ಗುರು-. A spiritual guide. -ಜಂಗಮ. A mendicant Liṅgâita priest. ಲಿಂಗಾಯತ, ಲಿಂಗಾಯಿತ. = ಲಿಂಗಧಾರಕ, *q. v.* ಲಿಂಗಾನುಶಾಸನ. The rules of grammatical gender. ಲಿಂಗಿ. An ascetic; a Liṅgavanta.

ಲಿಪಿ s. *n.* Smearing; painting, drawing, writing. 2, written characters, the letters. 3, a writing, document, letter. -ಕ, -ಕಾರ. A writer, scribe. ಲಿಪ್ತ. Smeared; stained; poisoned.

ಲಿಫಾಫೆ h. *n.* An envelope, cover.

ಲಿಂಬೆ (*tb. of* ನಿಂಬೆ) *n.* The acid lime, *etc.*

ಲೀನ s. *a.* Clung to, attached to; resting on, entered into. 2, dissolved, melted; absorbed; united with. 3, vanished. -ತೆ. The state of being hidden, absorbed, [illegible]

ಲೀಲಾವತಿ s. n. A beautiful woman. 2, N. of a treatise.

ಲೀಲೆ, ಲೀಲಾ s. n. Play, sport, amusement, pastime. 2, wanton sport. 3, sportive appearance, sham, child's play. 4, air, mien. 5, grace, beauty. 6, a story about a deity's sports. *Cpds.:* ಕೃಷ್ಣ-, ದೇವರ-, ಶಿವ-, ಬಾಲ-, *etc.*

ಲುಕಸಾನು, ಲುಕ್ಸಾನು h. n. Loss; damage. -ಆಗು, -ಬೀಳು. To suffer damage or loss.

ಲುಂಗಿ h. n. A cloth tied by males round the loins.

ಲುಚ್ಚಾ f. n. Dissolute, mean, base, low. -ಗಿರಿ, -ತನ. Dissoluteness, meanness. -ಮನುಷ್ಯ. A base fellow.

ಲುಟಾಯಿಸು f. *v. t.* To plunder, pillage.

ಲುಪ್ತ s. *a.* Broken; deprived of; omitted; elided; obsolete.

ಲುಬ್ಧ s. *a.* Desiring; covetous, greedy. -ಕ. A miser; the sixth nakshatra. -ತ್ವ. Avariciousness.

ಲುಳಿ a. *tb. n.* Agility, briskness, quick motion.

ಲೂಟಿ f. *n.* Robbing; booty, spoil. 2, misbehaviour, mischief. -ಗಾರ. A mischievous fellow.

ಲೂತಿ, ಲೂತೆ s. *n.* A cutaneous disease.

ಲೆಕ್ಕ (*tb. of* ಲೇಖಾ) *n.* Reckoning, numbering, calculation; arithmetic; a sum; an account; a number. 2, estimation, regard. -ಇಡು. To keep account. -ಕೊಡು. To give an account. -ಮಾಡು. To count, reckon up. -ನೋಡು, -ಪರಿಶೋಧಿಸು. To examine an account. ಲೆಕ್ಕಾಚಾರ (= ಲೆಕ್ಕ). Accounts, transaction. ಲೆಕ್ಕಿಸು. To count, reckon up; to esteem, regard.

ಲೆಕ್ಕಣಿ, ಲೆಕ್ಕಣಿಕೆ. *tb. of* ಲೇಖನಿ, *q. v.*

ಲೆತ್ತ. = ನೆತ್ತ, *q. v.* -ಪಗಡೆ. Lĕtta and pagaḍĕ.

ಲೇಖ s. *n.* A writing, writ, letter, document, etc. -ಕ. A writer, copyist; a cl

ಕ. A letter-carrier. ಲೇಖಾಸಂಪಾದಕ. An accountant general. -ನಿ, -ನಿಕೆ (= ಲೆಕ್ಕಣಿ). A *reed-pen, pen.* ಲೇಖಿಸು. To write.

ಲೇಖೆ (= ರೇಖೆ, *q. v.*) s. *n.* A scratch. 2, a writ.

ಲೇಡಿ e. *n.* A lady.

ಲೇಣಾ, ಲೇಣಿ h. *n.* Borrowing. ಲೇಣಿಗಾರ. A borrower. -ದೇಣಿ. Borrowing and lending.

ಲೇಪ, ಲೇಪನ s. *n.* Besmearing, daubing. 2, salve; plaster, mortar, chunam, white-wash, *etc.* ಲೇಪಿಸು. To smear, besmear, anoint, *etc.*

ಲೇಫು f. *n.* A mattress, bed.

ಲೇವಡಿ h. *n.* Derision, mockery.

ಲೇವಾ. = ಲೇಣಾ, *q. v.* -ದೇವಿ. Borrowing and lending.

ಲೇವ್ಯ f. *n.* A Levite, one of the tribe of Levi (*Jewism*).

ಲೇಶ s. *n.* A particle, atom, bit, small quantity; smallness. -ಮಾತ್ರ. Only a little.

ಲೇಸು k. *n.* Goodness, excellence; well-being, welfare; pleasantness; beauty; propriety, fitness; reality.

ಲೇಹ s. *n.* Licking, tasting, sipping. 2, a lambative, linctus. -ನ. Licking. ಲೇಹ್ಯ. A lambative, emulsion.

ಲೈಲಾಮು h. *n.* Auction. -ಗಾರ, -ದಾರ. Auctioneer.

ಲೈಸೆನ್ಸು e. *n.* License, permission.

ಲೊಚಗುಟ್ಟು k. *v. i.* To lap, *as dogs, etc.*; to smack in tasting.

ಲೊಟಕಲೆ, ಲೊಟಗರೆ k. *n.* Gabbling, jabbering. *v. i.* To gabble, jabber.

ಲೊಟಗು k. *v. t.* To scold.

ಲೊಟ್ಟೆ k. *n.* A smack with the tongue. 2, emptiness, hollowness. 3, a lie, fib. -ಹೊಡೆ. To smack the tongue; to lie.

ಲೊಪ್ಪ. = ಲಪ್ಪ, *q. v.*

ಲೊಳಳೆ, ಲೊಳ್ಳೆ k. *n.* Saliva.

ಲೋಕ s. n. The wide world, sky; the world; any place, region, country. 2, mankind, folk, man, people. 3, common life or practice. 4, sight, regard. -ಕರ್ತ. The Creator of the world. -ತ್ರಯ. The three worlds: heaven, earth, and lower regions. -ಜನ. An inhabitant of the world; a worldling. -ನಾಥ. Lord of lords; a king. -ನೇತ್ರ. The sun, moon. ಪರ-, ಸ್ವರ್ಗ-. Heaven, the place of the ransomed souls. ಇಹ-, ಈ-. This world. *Cpds.:* -ನಡತೆ, -ಪದ್ಧತಿ, -ಪಾಲ, -ಪ್ರಸಿದ್ಧಿ, -ರಕ್ಷಕ, -ರೀತಿ, -ರೂಢಿ, -ಮರ್ಯಾದೆ, -ವಾದ, -ವಿರುದ್ಧ, -ವ್ಯವಹಾರ, ಲೋಕಾಚಾರ. -ನ. Seeing, viewing. ಲೋಕಾಂತರ. Another world; a future life. ಲೋಕಾಲೋಕ. The visible and invisible world. ಲೋಕೋಪಕಾರ. A public charity.

ಲೋಚನ s. n. The eye. -ಗೋಚರ. Perceptible.

ಲೋಟಾ h. n. An earthen pot.

ಲೋಟು f. n. Pushing, disturbance, annoyance.

ಲೋಡು f. n. A long bolster to recline upon.

ಲೋಪ s. n. Cutting off; deprivation, want; ellipsis. 2, omission, dropping or falling out; annulling; elision (*g.*), *as:* ಅಕ್ಷರ-, ಪದ-, ಪ್ರತ್ಯಯ-, ವಿಭಕ್ತಿ-, ವಾಕ್ಯ-. The dropping of—, *etc.* ಲೋಪಿಸು. To omit, drop, elide.

ಲೋಬಾನ h. n. Frankincense, olibanum.

ಲೋಭ s. n. Eager desire, cupidity, avarice, greed; *also* -ತ್ವ. 2, affection, favour. ಲೋಭಿ. Greedy, covetous, avaricious; a greedy, *etc.* person. -ತನ, -ತ್ವ. Greediness, stinginess.

ಲೋಮ s. n. The hair of the body. -ಶ. Hairy. -ಹರ್ಷ, -ಹರ್ಷಣ. The bristling of the hair, horripilation.

ಲೋರಬು. = ಲೋಳಿ, *q. v.*

ಲೋಲ s. a. Moving hither and thither, shaking; agitated, alarmed; unsteady, restless; changeable, fickle. 2, longing for. *n.* Joy. -ತೆ. Fickleness; cupidity. ಲೋಲುಪ. Very eager, greedy after, covetous. ಲೋಲುಪಾಪ್ತಿ, ಲೋಲುಪತೆ, ಲೋಲುಪತ್ವ, ಲೋಲುಪ್ತಿ. Eager desire; greediness, desire, lust.

ಲೋವೆ k. n. A sloping fixture to a flat roof.

ಲೋಷ್ಟ s. n. A lump, clod; *also* -ಕ.

ಲೋಹ s. n. Any metal; iron; copper. 2, a weapon. 3, aloe wood. -ಕಾಂತ. A loadstone, magnet. -ಕಾರ. A blacksmith. -ಕಿಟ್ಟ. Rust of iron. -ದ್ರುತಿ. Steel drops. -ಭಸ್ಮ. Calcined metal. -ಮಂಡೂರ. Manganese. -ಮಾರ್ಗ. A railway. ಲೋಹಾಭಿಸಾರ, ಲೋಹಾಭಿಹಾರ. Lustration of arms.

ಲೋಹಿತ s. a. Red. *n.* The colour red.. 2, blood. 3, copper. 4, auger. 5, an axe. -ಕ. A ruby. -ಚಂದನ. Saffron.

ಲೋಳಿ, ಲೋಳು k. n. Mucilage, mucus. albumen, gelatine; *also* ಲೋಳೆ. -ಸರ. The aloe, *Aloe littoralis* or *perfoliata.*

ಲೋಳೆ k. n. Saliva; tenacious mucus, phlegm.

ಲೌಕಿಕ (*fr.* ಲೋಕ) s. a. Worldly, mundane; popular, general; vulgar, common; secular, not sacred. *n.* A man of the world; a secular business. -ವ್ಯಾಪಾರ. Common practice.

ಲೌಕೀಕ. *tb. of* ಲೌಕಿಕ, *q. v.* -ಕೆಲಸ. A secular business.

ಲೌಭ್ಯ (*fr.* ಲೋಭ) s. n. Cupidity, avarice.

ವ್

ವ್. The forty-eighth letter of the alphabet.

ವ k. *A syllable used to form the pres. or fut. rel. part. and future tense, as:* ಮಾಡುವ, ಹೇಳುವ, ಇರುವ, *etc.* ಮಾಡುವನು, ಇರುವನು, ಕೊಡುವನು, *etc.*

ವಂಶ s. *n.* A bamboo. 2, a flute. 3, the spine. 4, a lineage, race, family; a dynasty. 5, an assemblage. 6, the Sal tree, *Shorea robusta.* -ಜ. Belonging to the family of. -ನಾಶಕ, ವಂಶಾಂತಕ. The last of a family, or race. -ಪರಂಪರೆ. Lineage, descent; progeny. -ವೃಕ್ಷ. Genealogical tree. -ಸ್ಥ. One of a (good) family. ವಂಶಾವಳಿ. The line of a family, genealogy, pedigree. ವಂಶೋದ್ಧಾರಕ. A deliverer or preserver of a family.

ವಕಾರ s. *n.* The letter ವ.

ವಕಾಲತ್ತು h. *n.* The duties of a Vakil. -ನಾಮೆ. A power of attorney.

ವಕೀಲ h. *n.* A lawyer, pleader; an envoy.

ವಕುಲ, ವಕುಳ (= ಬಕುಳ) s. *n.* The tree *Mimusops elengi.*

ವಕ್ಕಣೆ (*tb. of* ವ್ಯಾಖ್ಯಾನ) *n.* Comment; statement. 2, the address to a letter or petition. ಚಮತ್ಕಾರದ-. A subtle style. ವಕ್ಕಣಿಸು. To explain, state.

ವಕ್ತವ್ಯ s. *a.* Proper to be said; blamable; accountable, responsible; dependent, subject. *n.* A precept, sentence; speaking, censure.

ವಕ್ತಾರ (*tb. of* ವಕ್ತೃ) *n.* A speaker; an orator. *a.* Eloquent, loquacious.

ವಕ್ತ್ರ s. *n.* The mouth; the face.

ವಕ್ರ s. *a.* Crooked, winding, curved, bent, curly; retrograde. 2, cunning, dishonest; evasive, ambiguous. 3, cr... -2. Crook... -ತ್ವ ... ness. m... grade motion. -ನಾಸಿಕ. An owl. -ಬುದ್ಧಿ. A crooked mind. -ಭಾವ. Crookedness; cunning. -ರೇಖೆ. A curved line. ವಕ್ರೋಕ್ತಿ. Indirect speech, evasive reply; insinuation; sarcasm.

ವಕ್ಷ (*tb. of* ವಕ್ಷಸ್) *n.* The breast; *also* -ಸ್ಥಲ.

ವಗೈರೆ h. *prep. Et caetera,* and the rest.

ವಗ್ರಹ, ವಗ್ರಾಹ (*tb. of* ಅವಗ್ರಾಹ) *n.* Drought.

ವಂಕ. *tb. of* ವಕ್ರ, *q. v.* ವಂಕಿ. A kind of curved armlet; a hook.

ವಂಕುಡಿ k. *n.* A dagger.

ವಂಗ s. *n.* Bengal proper; its inhabitant. 2, tin. 3, lead. -ಭಸ್ಮ. Calx of tin.

ವಂಗಡ a. k. *n.* An assemblage, multitude.

ವಚನ s. *n.* Speaking. 2, a speech, word, expression, utterance, sentence; a promise. 3, a text, aphorism, rule. 4, grammatical number (*g.*). -ಕೊಡು. To promise. -ಕಡೆಗಾಣಿಸು, -ನೆರವೇರಿಸು. To fulfil a promise. -ತ್ರಯ. The three numbers (*g.*): singular, dual, and plural. -ದೋಷ. A slip of the tongue. -ಭ್ರಷ್ಟ. One who has broken his promise. -ಸ್ಥ. A trustworthy man. ವಚನೀಯ. Fit or proper to be spoken. ವಚನೀಯತೆ. Rumour, report, scandal.

ವಜೆ. = ಬಜೆ, *q. v.*

ವಜನು h. *n.* Weight. -ದಾರ. Weighty; influential; an influential man. ವಜನಿ. Of weight.

ವಜಾ h. *a.* Subtracted. *n.* Subtraction; deduction; removal. -ಮಾಡು. To subtract, *etc.* -ವಟ್ಟಿ. Making up and settling of accounts.

ವಜೀರ h. *n.* A vizier, prime minister.

... severe.

... s. 2, a

diamond. 3, a strong glue. -ಕಾಯ, -ದೇಹ. One who has a very robust and hardy body. -ಗಾರೆ. A durable plaster. -ಜ್ವಾಲೆ. Lightning. -ಪಾಣಿ. Indra. -ಮುಷ್ಟಿ. A hard fist; a weapon of the athlete. -ಶುಂಠ. A stupid man.

ವಂಚಕ s. *a.* Deceitful, crafty. *n.* A deceiver, rogue, cheat. -ತ್ವ. Fraud. ವಂಚನ, ವಂಚನೆ. Cheating, tricking, defrauding; fraud, deceit; illusion. ವಂಚಿಸು. To deceive, cheat.

ವಟ s. *n.* The banyan or Indian fig-tree, *Ficus indica.* 2, (= ಬಡೆ) a kind of fried cake; *also* -ಕ.

ವಠಾರ (= ಬಠಾರ) f. *n.* The compound round a house. 2, a lodge, room.

ವಟು s. *n.* A boy, lad. 2, a Brahmachâri, a religious student.

ವಟ್ಟ (= ಬಟ್ಟ, *q. v.*) h. *n.* Discount: a deduction made by money-changers or money-lenders in their own favour.

ವಡಬಾಗ್ನಿ, ವಡವಾಗ್ನಿ s. *n.* Submarine fire; *also* ವಡಬಾಗ್ನಿ, ವಡವಾನಲ, ವಡವಾಮುಖ.

ವಡವೆ. = ಒಡವೆ, *q. v.*

ವಡಿ k. *n.* Heat.

ವಡಿಗ k. *An affix of nouns to intimate a person's trade or employment, as:* ಹೂ-. A florist.

ವಡೆ (*tb. of* ವಟ) *n.* A fried cake made of pulse.

ವಣಿಗ k. *An affix of masc. nouns to express fondness or habit, as:* ಲಂಚ-. A person fond of bribes. ಮಾತು-. A talkative person. ವಣಿಗೆ, *neut., as* ಮೊರ-, ಚಿಳಿ-, *etc.*

ವಣಿಜ s. *n.* A merchant, trader. 2, trade, merchandise.

ವತನ h. *n.* A hereditary estate. -ದಾರ. Its holder.

ವತಿ (= ವಂತೆ) s. *fem. affix.* She who possesses. *n.* Asking, begging.

ವತ್ಸ s. *n.* A calf; a child, boy; a son; *f.* ವತ್ಸೆ. 2, a year (= -ರ). -ಕ. A little calf; the medicinal plant, *Wrightia antidysenterica.*

ವತ್ಸನಾಭಿ s. *n.* A strong poison taken from aconite.

ವತ್ಸರ s. *n.* A year.

ವತ್ಸಲ s. *a.* Affectionate, kind, loving; fond of. -ತೆ, -ತ್ವ. Affection, tenderness.

ವದ s. *n.* Speaking. 2, speaking well or sensibly. ವದಾನ್ಯ. Eloquent; affable; liberal. ವದಾವದ. Talkative; eloquent.

ವದನ s. *n.* Speaking. 2, the mouth, face.

ವಧ. = ವಧೆ, *q. v.*

ವಧು, ವಧೂ s. *n.* A bride, young wife. ವಧೂವರ. Bride and bridegroom.

ವಧೆ s. *n.* Slaughter, murder. ವಧಿಸು. To kill, slay.

ವನ (= ಬನ) s. *n.* A wood, forest; a garden. 2, a residence. -ಗಜ. A wild elephant. -ಚರ. Living in a forest. -ದೇವತೆ. A sylvan deity. -ಧಿ, -ನಿಧಿ. The ocean. -ಪಶು. A wild beast. -ಪಾಲ, -ಪಾಲಕ. A gardener. -ಪ್ರಿಯ. The cuckoo. -ಪ್ರಸ್ಥ (*cf.* ವಾನಪ್ರಸ್ಥ). Retiring into a forest, living as an anchorite. -ಮಲ್ಲಿಕೆ. Wild jasmine. -ವಾಸ. Living in a wood. -ವಾಸಿ, -ಸ್ಥ. A hermit, ascetic. ವನಸ್ಪತಿ. A large tree bearing fruit but apparently having no blossoms; any tree; vegetable kingdom. ವನಾಂತರ. The interior of a forest; a forest.

ವನಾಶ್ರಯ s. *n.* Living in a forest.

ವನಿತೆ s. *n.* A wife. 2, a woman in general.

ವಂತ. *tb. of* ವತ್. *An affix used to form masc. derivatives, as:* ಬುದ್ಧಿ-, ಧನ-, ಧರ್ಮ-; *f.* ವಂತೆ, ವಂತಳು.

ವಂತಿ (= ಬಂತು, *q. v.*) k. *n.* A turn, time.

ವಂತಿಕೆ s. *n.* A public subscription. -ಎತ್ತು, -ಹಾಕು. To subscribe.

ವಂತೆ (*tb. of* ವತಿ) *Fem. affix of* ವಂತ, *q. v.*

ವಂದನ, ವಂದನೆ s n Soliciting 2, praising 3, obeisance, reverence, worship, adoration. 4, a festoon -ಗೆಯ್ಯು To reverence, salute respectfully.

ವಂದಿ s n A praiser bard ವಂದಿತ. Praised, extolled -ಸು To praise, eulogise, to show honour, to worship. ವಂದ್ಯ Laudable, praiseworthy; adorable.

ವಂಧಿ. = ಬಂಧಿ, q v.

ವಪನ s n Sowing seed 2, shaving.

ವಪುಸ್ s n A form, figure, body.

ವಪೆ s n A hollow 2, fat, marrow.

ವಪ್ರ s. n A sown field 2, a rampart, mudwall, mound; a bank, a ditch

ವಮನ s. n. Vomiting 2, an emetic

ವಯ, ವಯಸು, ವಯಸ್ಸು (tb. of ವಯಸ್) n Youth, prime of life. 2, age, time of life ವಯೋಧಿಕ An old man ವಯೋವೃದ್ಧ. Advanced in age

ವಯಿನ (tb. of ವಹನ) n. A way, means

ವಯ್ಯಾರ (tb. of ವಿಹಾರ = ಒಯ್ಯಾರ, q v) n. Parade, showiness, dandyism, coquetry, also ವಯ್ಯಾರಿ. A showy person

ವಯ್ಯಾಳಿ (tb. of ವಾಹ್ಯಾಳಿ) n An excursion on horseback, ride, a procession of idols carried by people

ವಯ್ವಾಟ f n Administration, despatch, business, use, practice, also ವಹಿವಾಟು

ವರ s n Choice, election. 2, a boon, blessing, favour, talent, a gift; a reward 3, a dowry 4, charity. 5, a lover, bridegroom, a husband a Desirable; valuable, best, most excellent -ಕವಿ. A gifted poet -ದಕ್ಷಿಣೆ A present made to the bridegroom on account of the bride. -ಪ್ರಸಾದ An eminent favour. -ಸಾದೃಶ್ಯ Likeness (in form) of the bride to the bridegroom -ಕೇಳು To entreat a favour -ಕೊಡು To confer a boon

ವರಕು h. [illegible]

ವರಂಡ s n. A veranda, portico 2, (e) warrant, right authority to do a certain act

ವರದಿ (tb. of ವಾರ್ತಾ; cf ವರ್ತಮಾನ) n Tidings, report, intelligence -ಕೊಡು To report

ವರಸೆ (= ವರಿಸೆ) k. n A line row, lineage, race, family.

ವರಹ, ವರಹಾ (tb. of ವರಾಹ) n A boar 2, a gold coin with a boar-stamp, a pagoda. -ಕಟ್ಟು, -ಕೂರ್ಚ. A brush, made of a hog's bristles

ವರಾಟ s n A cowry, *Cypraea moneta* (used as a coin, $\frac{1}{80}$ of a pana).

ವರಾಡ f n A public subscription, tax. -ಎತ್ತು, -ಹಾಕಿಕೊಳ್ಳು To make a subscription.

ವರಾತ, ವರಾತು h n Urging for payment.

ವರಿ 1 (fr ವರ) s. n Tax, cess; levy -ಎತ್ತು, -ತೆಗೆ. To raise taxes -ಕೊಡು -ತೆರು. To pay taxes.

ವರಿ 2 (= ವರೆ) k n Limit -ಗೆ Up to, till, until; as far as ಈ- Up to this.

ವರಿಸು s v t. To choose, espouse, elect, desire, claim; also ವರಯಿಸು

ವರಿಸೆ. = ವರಸೆ, q v

ವರುಣ s. n N. of the god of heavens and waters 2, the regent of the western quarter.

ವರುಷ. tb of ವರ್ಷ, q v. -ವರುಷ, ವರುಷಾನು- rep Every year, for years

ವರೂಥ s. n Protection, armour, shield. 2, a multitude, assemblage, army 3, a chariot

ವರೆ (= ವರಿ) f n. Limit, boundary prep. Until, as far as. -ಗೆ Until, as far as, up to

ವರ್ಗ s. n A division, class tribe society, family 2, any classified group of words or consonants, heading, category 3, a section, chapter 4, a sphere, province 5 a school-class 6, the square of a number 7, trans- [illegible] ledger.

[illegible] -ವರ್ಗ

ಲ. Square root. ವರ್ಗಾಕ್ಷರ. A classified consonant. ವರ್ಗೀಯ. Belonging to a class of consonants.

ವರ್ಚಸ್ s. n. Vigour. 2, lustre, brilliancy. 3, form, figure, shape. ವರ್ಚಸ್ವಿ. Full of lustre.

ವರ್ಜ, -ನ s. n. Excluding, avoiding, leaving; exclusion. 2, hurting, injury. ವರ್ಜನೀಯ, ವರ್ಜ್ಯ. Avoidable; improper. ವರ್ಜಿತ. Excluded, avoided. ವರ್ಜಿಸು. To avoid, leave, abandon, *etc.*

ವರ್ಣ s. n. Exterior, form, figure. 2, colour, hue, dye, paint; lustre. 3, dress. 4, gold. 5, a sort, kind, class, race, tribe, caste. 6, a letter of the alphabet. 7, property, quality. 8, a musical mode. -ಕ. A mask; colour; a syllable; a bard; a poetical diction. -ನ, -ನೆ. Description, explanation, pointing out qualities; praise, panegyric. -ನೆ ಮಾಡು. To describe, *etc.* -ಮಾಲೆ. The alphabet. -ಸಂಕರ. A mixture of castes. ವರ್ಣಾಶ್ರಮ. Caste and order. ವರ್ಣಾಶ್ರಮಧರ್ಮ. Their duties. ವರ್ಣಿಸು. To depict, delineate, write, describe; to praise.

ವರ್ತಕ s. n. A trader, merchant. -ತನ. Traffic, trade. -ಮಾಡು. To trade.

ವರ್ತನ, ವರ್ತನೆ s. n. Moving about. 2, proceeding, conduct; practice, employment, use. 3, abiding; living. 4, living on; livelihood, subsistance; earnings, wages. 5, occupation, profession; commerce. 6, appointment.

ವರ್ತಮಾನ s. a. Present, existing. n. The present tense. 2, news, tidings, notice. -ಕಾಲ. The present time, present tense; *also* -ಕ್ರಿಯೆ. -ಪತ್ರ. A newspaper.

ವರ್ತಿ s. n. Moving, going; behaving, acting. 2, the wick of a lamp; *also* -ಕೆ. 3, a swelling, rupture. -ಸು. To move, go; to conduct one's self; to take place, occur; to enter upon; to stay; abide.

ವರ್ತುಲ s. a. Round, circular. n. A circle. 2, a kind of pulse, pea.

ವರ್ಧ s. n. Increasing, augmenting. -ಕ. Increasing, strengthening; cutting. -ಕಿ. A carpenter. -ನ. Increasing, growing; increase, growth; prosperity; success; strengthening; a restorative; cutting. -ನಿ. A broom, brush. ವರ್ಧಂತಿ. (= ಒರ್ಧಂತಿ, q. v.) A birthday, nativity. -ಮಾನ. Increasing, growing, thriving; prosperous; the castor-oil plant; Burdwan. ವರ್ಧಿತ. Grown, *etc.* ವರ್ಧಿಸು. To increase, grow, thrive.

ವರ್ಮ s. n. A coat of mail. 2, a bulwark, shelter, defence. 3, = ಮರು.

ವರ್ಯ s. a. Eligible; eminent, best.

ವರ್ವರ. = ಬರ್ಬರ, q. v.

ವರ್ಷ (= ಒರುಷ, ವರುಷ, *etc.*, q. v.) s. n. Rain. 2, a year. -ಕಾಲ, -ತು. The rainy season. -ಗಂತಿ. (A cow, *etc.*) calving yearly. -ಣ. Raining. -ಧಾರೆ. A stream of rain. ವರ್ಷಾವಧಿ. Yearly. ವರ್ಷಾಯುತು, ವರ್ಷಾಕಾಲ. = -ಕಾಲ. ವರ್ಷಾಂತರ. Another year; some years. ವರ್ಷಾಶನ. Annual allowance.

ವಲಯ s. n. A bracelet, armlet; a girdle, zone. 2, a circle, boundary; enclosure.

ವಲಸೆ (= ಒಲಸೆ, q. v.) k. n. Flight, emigration. -ತೆಗೆ. (People) to leave a village *en masse.*

ವಲೀಕ s. n. The eaves of a roof.

ವಲ್ಕಲ s. n. A garment made of bark.

ವಲ್ಮೀಕ s. n. An ant-hill. 2, swelling.

ವಲ್ಲಭ s. n. A lover, husband, friend; f. ವಲ್ಲಭೆ. A wife, beloved female.

ವಶ s. n. Subdued, tamed. n. Power, control, charge, custody, subjection, submission. -ಆಗು. To become subject to. -ಮಾಡು, ವಶೀಕರಿಸು. To subdue. ವಶಂವದ. Submissive, compliant. ವಶೀಕರಣ. Subjugating, enchanting.

ವಶ್ಯ. Controllable, subdued; docile, humble, tame, a decoy.

ವಸಡಿ, ವಸಡು (=ಒಸಡು, q v) k. n. The gums.

ವಸತಿ s. n Dwelling, a dwelling place, house, abode 2, comfort, commodity, convenience.

ವಸನ s n Clothing, clothes, dress 2, a dwelling, residence

ವಸಂತ s. n. Spring. 2 a kind of râga 3, (=ಓಕುಳಿ) saffron water -ಕಾಲ, -ಋತು. The vernal season. -ದೂತ. The cuckoo -ದೂತಿ, -ದೂತಿಕೆ. The creeper *Gaertnera racemosa* -ಮಂಟಪ A shed erected for recreation during the hot season ವಸಂತೋತ್ಸವ. A festive occasion on which vasanta (ôkali) is sprinkled.

ವಸಲೀನು e n Vasaline

ವಸಾರೆ h n A veranda 2, a perfume.

ವಸಿಷ್ಠ s n. N of a rishi.

ವಸಿಸು s. v. i. To dwell, live, abide

ವಸೀಲು h n. Support, patronage. -ದಾರ A patron.

ವಸು s. a Good, wealthy; chief n Excellence 2, light, fire, agni 3, wealth; a gem, etc. 4, N of a deity. -ಕಾಂತಿ The moon-plant *Asclepias acida* -ಧೆ, -ಮತಿ The earth

ವಸೂಲು h n. Collection, revenue, also ವಸೂಲಾತಿ. -ಮಾಡು To collect, as revenue, etc. -ಬಾಕಿ. A balance of revenue due

ವಸೆ s n The marrow of the flesh.

ವಸ್ತಾದ h n A teacher of wrestling, dancing, etc.

ವಸ್ತಿ s n Abiding, staying; an abode; the people, population 2, the abdomen 3, the ends or skirt of a cloth

ವಸ್ತು s. n A real substance 2, object; a thing in general, an article, substance, wealth, goods 3, essential property. -ಕ. Real. faithful ... An ...

ವಸ್ತ್ರ s. n Cloth, clothes, garment dress, a cloth -ಗಾಳು. Sifting through a cloth -ಗಲಿತ, -ಗಾಲಿತ Strained through a cloth -ದಾನ A gift of clothes -ಹೀನ Destitute of or without clothes.

ವಹ, ವಹನ s n Bearing, carrying, conveying 2, any vehicle or means of conveyance. 3, a road, way. 4, a raft

ವಹವಾ = ವಾಹವಾ, q v

ವಹಿ f. n. A stitched book -ಕ. A bearer.

ವಹಿಲ s. n. Quickness, agility ad. Quickly

ವಹಿವಾಟು = ವಯ್ವಾಟ, q v

ವಹಿಸು s v t. To bear, sustain, to carry; to appropriate to one's self, to proceed; to become current.

ವಹ್ನಿ s. n. Fire 2, lead-wort, *Plumbago zeylanica*

ವಳ k An affix of nouns implying profession e. g ತೋಟ-. A gardener. ಮಡಿ-. A washerman. ಅಡು-. A cook

ವಳಿ 1 k An affix for forming neuter nouns e g. ನಡ-, ಕಲು-, ಹುಟ್ಟು-, etc

ವಳಿ 2 s. n. A wave, a wrinkle.

ವಳಿತ s n. A circle, district, dependency

ವಳ್ಳಿ k. Fem. form of ವಳ.

ವಾ conj s Or

ವಾಃ = ವಾಹವಾ, q v.

ವಾಕರಿ = ಓಕರಿ, etc, q. v

ವಾಕ್ = ವಾಕ್ಕು, ವಾಚ್ -ಕಲಹ. Quarrel, dispute -ಚಾತುರ್ಯ Cleverness of speech. -ಜಾಲಲ್ಯ. Rattle, gabble -ಪಟುತ್ವ. Eloquence. -ಪಂಡಿತ, -ಪ್ರೌಢ. Proficient in speech or language -ಪೌರುಷ Power in using big words.

ವಾಕೆ f n A wrist ornament

ವಾಕ್ಕು (tb. of ವಾಕ್) n Speech, language 2, Sarasvati.

ವಾಕ್ಯ s. n Speech, saying, a word 2, ... -ಬಂ ... poetical

composition. -ಮಾಲೆ. A sentence. ವಾಕ್ಯಾನ್ವಯ. The connection of words in a sentence. ವಾಕ್ಯಾರ್ಥ. The meaning of a sentence; a lecture. ವಾಕ್ಯಾಲಂಕಾರ. An expletive.

ವಾಗ್. = ವಾಕ್, q. v. ವಾಗಾಡಂಬರ. A vain display of words. ವಾಗೀಶ. A master of language; an eloquent man. ವಾಗೀಶ್ವರ. Brahmâ. ವಾಗೀಶ್ವರಿ. Sarasvati. ವಾಗ್ಜಾಲ. Prate, gabble; eloquence. ವಾಗ್ದತ್ತ, ವಾಗ್ದಾನ. A promise. ವಾಗ್ದೇವತೆ, ವಾಗ್ದೇವಿ. Sarasvati, muse. ವಾಗ್ವೀರಣೆ. Good style of composition. ವಾಗ್ಬಲ. The power of speech. ವಾಗ್ವಾದ. Quarrel, dispute. ವಾಙ್ಮಾಧುರ್ಯ. Sweetness of speech. ವಾಙ್ಮೂಲ. Deposition.

ವಾಗ್ಮಿ s. a. Loquacious, talkative, eloquent. n. An eloquent man.

ವಾಚ್ (= ವಾಕ್, ವಾಗ್) s. n. Speech; language; discourse; a word. 2, Sarasvati. ವಾಚಕ. Reading; declaratory; verbal; a speaker, reader. ವಾಚಕಶಕ್ತಿ. Reading power. ವಾಚಾಟ, ವಾಚಾಲ. Talkative, loquacious; wrangle.

ವಾಚೆ s. a. Speaking, uttering; a word, an attribute. 2, a speaker, minister. -ಕ. Verbal, oral; news, tidings. -ಸು. To speak, say, *etc.*

ವಾಚ್ಯ s. a. To be spoken; blamable, censurable. 2, attributive, declinable. n. A predicate (*g.*). 2, the voice of a verb (*g.*). ವಾಚ್ಯಾವಾಚ್ಯ. Proper and improper to be said.

ವಾಜ s. n. Strength, energy. 2, speed. 3, vegetable food. 4, ghee.

ವಾಜಿ s. a. Strong, powerful; swift. n. A horse. -ಕರ. A mule. -ನಿ. A mare.

ವಾಜಿಬಿ, ವಾಜೀಮ h. a. Fit, proper, right.

ವಾಂಛೆ s. n. Wish, desire. ವಾಂಛಿತ. Wished, desired, longed for. ವಾಂಛಿಸು. To wish, desire.

ವಾಟ 1. = ಓಟ, q. v.

ವಾಟ 2. k. n. A slope, incline.

ವಾಟ 3. s. n. An enclosure; a court-yard; a compound, [illegible]. 2, a road, way. 3, course, procedure.

ವಾಡಬ, ವಾಡವ s. n. Submarine fire. 2, the lower regions. ವಾಡಬಾನಲ, ವಾಡವಾಗ್ನಿ, ವಾಡವಾನಲ. The fire of the lower regions.

ವಾಡಿಕೆ k. n. Usage, custom, practice.

ವಾಡೆ. = ಓಡೆ, q. v.

ವಾಣಿ s. n. Sound, speech; voice. 2, Sarasvati. 3, a Banyan. 4, an oilman. 5, weaving; a weaver's loom. -ಜ. A merchant, Banyan. -ಜ್ಯ, -ಜತನ. Traffic, trade. -ನಿ. A shrewd or passionate woman.

ವಾತ s. n. Wind, air, breeze. 2, rheumatism, gout. -ಗುಲ್ಮ. Acute gout. -ಧಾತು, -ನಾಡಿ. One of the (three) arteries near the wrist. -ರೋಗ. = ವಾತ No. 2. ವಾತಾಶನ, ವಾತಾಶಾಪಾರಿ. A serpent; a tiger.

ವಾತ್ಸಲ್ಯ (*fr.* ವತ್ಸಲ) s. n. Tender fondness, love. *Cpds.:* ಬಾಲ-, ಮಾತೃ-, ದಾಸ-, ದೇಶ-.

ವಾದ s. n. Talking. 2, sound; playing on a musical instrument. 3, discourse. 4, disputation, debate, dispute; controversy. 5, explanation. 6, a plaint. 7, report. -ವಿವಾದ. Argument and disputation. ವಾದಿ. A disputant; a plaintiff; an expounder. ವಾದಿಪ್ರತಿವಾದಿ. A plaintiff and a defendant. -ಸು. To dispute; to debate.

ವಾದ್ಯ s. n. Any musical instrument. -ಬಾರಿಸು. To play upon it.

ವಾನ (*fr.* ವನ) s. a. Relating to a forest. -ಪ್ರಸ್ಥ. A Brâhmaṇa of the third order: a hermit, anchorite.

ವಾನರ s. n. A monkey.

ವಾಂತಿ s. n. Vomiting; an emetic. -ಭೇದಿ, -ಭ್ರಾಂತಿ. Cholera.

ವಾಪಸು h. *ad.* Back, in return.

ವಾಪಿ s. n. A sowing machine. 2, a well.

ವಾಮ s. *ad.* Beautiful, pleasing, lovely. *a.* Reverse, adverse opposite. 2, left, not right. 3, [illegible]. 4, short

ವಾಮಾಂಗಿ A wife (who is the left side of her husband)

ವಾಮನ s a Short, dwarfish n A dwarf 2 Vishṅu in his 5th incarnation -ಪುರಾಣ. A purâna about this incarnation. ವಾಮನಾವತಾರ = ವಾಮನ No 2.

ವಾಯ (*tb of* ವ್ಯಾಜ) *n* Deceit, lie, pretext 2 (s) wearing, sewing.

ವಾಯನ s *n* Presents of cocoanuts, sweetmeats, *etc* offered to a deity by a Brâhmana married woman

ವಾಯವ್ಯ s *a* Windy *n* The north-west quarter.

ವಾಯಸ s *n* A crow. ವಾಯಸಿ. The plant *Solanum indicum*

ವಾಯಿದೆ h. *n* Period, a term fixed for payment, instalment -ಚೀಟು Notice of demand of the assessment to be paid within a given time -ಗೇಣಿ Tenancy for a stipulated period.

ವಾಯು s *n* Wind, air, the god of wind 2, a vital air 3, flatulence, rheumatism, gout -ಪಂಚಕ. The set of five vital airs. -ನಂದನ, -ಪುತ್ರ, -ಸುತ Bhîma, Hanumat -ವಿಳಂಗ. A plant of which the seed is used as a vermifuge, *Erycibe paniculata* -ವೇಗ. The velocity of wind -ಸಖ, -ಸಖಿ Fire.

ವಾರ 1. k *n* A landlord's half share of the produce of a field as rent 2, = ಓರ.

ವಾರ 2 s *n* A turn, time. 2, a day of the week, a recurring day for furnishing a meal to poor males 3, a moment, occasion. -ದನ್ನ Food obtained by poor males in rotation -ಶೂಲೆ Unpropitious day for a journey, *etc* ಶ್ರೀ- Good-Friday.

ವಾರಗಿತ್ತಿ = ಓರಗಿತ್ತಿ, *q v*

ವಾರಣ s. *n*. Warding off, keeping off; removing, protecting, resisting, opposition 2, armour 3, an elephant 4, an embankment -[illegible] off, [illegible]

ವಾರಣಾಸಿ, ವಾರಾಣಸಿ s. *n*. The town Benares.

ವಾರವಾಣ s *n*. A bodice; a quilted jacket, armour.

ವಾರಸು h *n* Heritage, the proprietorship of it, claim, title -ದಾರ An inheritor, heir. -ಪತ್ರ An assignment ಬೇ- Ownerless, unclaimed

ವಾರಿ 1 f. *prep*. By, according to, for, *also* ವಾರು

ವಾರಿ 2. s *n* Water. -ಚರ Aquatic -ಜ A lotus -ಜರಿಪು, -ಜವೈರಿ. The moon -ಜಭವ, -ಜಾಸನ Brahmâ -ಜಾಕ್ಷ. Vishnu. -ಧಿ The ocean -ಧಿಕನ್ಯೆ. Lakshmî. -ವಾಹ A cloud.

ವಾರಿಸು 1. s. *v t*. To ward off, keep back, stop, remove.

ವಾರಿಸು 2 = ವಾರಸು, *q v*.

ವಾರು = ವಾರಿ 1 *q v*

ವಾರುಣ (*fr* ವರುಣ) s *a* Of Varuna ವಾರುಣಿ The west

ವಾರೆ (= ಓರೆ, *q v*.) k *n* Declivity, sloping

ವಾರ್ತ s *n*. Welfare. 2, chaff 3, (= ವಾರ್ತೆ) news ವಾರ್ತಿಕ A reporter, teacher, a critical gloss

ವಾರ್ತೆ s *n* Livelihood, profession. 2, tidings, rumour, news, intelligence 3, knowledge. 4, meanness *Cpds* · ವ-ನೆ-, ಮಿಶನ್-, ಡಾಕ್-

ವಾರ್ಧಕ (*fr* ವೃದ್ಧಿ) s *n* Increase. 2 old age; *also* ವಾರ್ಧಕ್ಯ. -ಷಟ್ಪದಿ. N. of a metre

ವಾರ್ಯ s *a*. To be warded off. 2, eligible desirable.

ವಾರ್ಷಿಕ (*fr*. ವರ್ಷ) s. *a*. Annual.

ವಾಲ s. *n* Hair. 2, tail. 3, the cuscus-grass -ಖಿಲ್ಯ. A certain divine personage.

ವಾಲಕ s *n*. A bracelet 2, a finger-ring. 3, the cuscus-grass. 4, a tail

ವಾಲಗ (= ಓಲಗ, *q v*. *tb*. *of* ವಾಲಕ) *n* Service *etc* 2 [illegible] [illegible] Angada

ವಾಲೀ h. n. A protector, patron; a master.

ವಾಲು (= ವಾಲು 1) k. v. i. To bend; to slope.

ವಾಲುಕೆ s. n. Sand, gravel. 2, a species of cucumber. ವಾಲುಕಾಸ್ತಂಭ. A cloud of drifting sand.

ವಾಲೆ. = ಓಲೆ, q. v.

ವಾಲ್ಮೀಕ, ವಾಲ್ಮೀಕಿ s. n. N. of the author of the Râmâyaṇa.

ವಾವಿ, ವಾವೆ (tb. of ಜಾಮಿ) n. Affinity, relationship.

ವಾಶಿ s. n. Singing, crying; a war-cry; voice. 2, an adze.

ವಾಸ s. n. Dwelling; a dwelling-place, habitation; site, abode. 2, (= -ನೆ) scent, trace. 3, dress, clothes; as in ಕಟ್ಟು-, ವಟಿ-. -ಯೋಗ್ಯ. Fit to reside in. -ಸ್ಥಲ, -ಸ್ಥಾನ. A place of residence.

ವಾಸನೆ s. n. Smell, odour, scent; fragrance, flavour. 2, inclination, desire. -ನೋಡು. To smell. ದುರ್-. A stink. ಸು-. Aroma.

ವಾಸರ 1. = ಓಸರ, q. v.

ವಾಸರ 2. s. n. A day. -ಪತಿ, -ಮಣಿ. The sun.

ವಾಸಿ 1. s. n. An inhabitant. a. Abiding, dwelling; clothed, as: ಗ್ರಾಮ-, ನಗರ-, ವನ-, ಸಹ-.

ವಾಸಿ 2. (tb. of ವಾಚಿ) n. The state of being so and so much; as: ಅರ-, ಕಾಲು-, ಮುಕ್ಕಾಲು-, etc. 2, an improved state (as of health, etc.), relief, ease; superiority, preference; as in ಕಾಯಿದೆ-, ಹೆಸರು-, etc. 3, moderation (in price, etc.), as in ಧಾರಣೆ-. 4, excess, interest, as in ತಲೆ-.

ವಾಸಿತ s. a. Perfumed, scented.

ವಾಸಿಸು s. v. i. To dwell, reside. 2, to smell, be fragrant, be perfumed. v. t. To smell.

ವಾಸುಕಿ s. n. N. of a serpent.

ವಾಸುದೇವ s. n. N. of Vishṇu or Krishṇa.

ವಾಸ್ತವ, ವಾಸ್ತವಿಕ (fr. ವಸ್ತು) s. a. Substantial; real, true substantiated, demonstrated. ವಾಸ್ತವ್ಯ. Real, true; fit for habitation; an inhabitant.

ವಾಸ್ತು s. n. The site or foundation of a house. 2, a habitation. -ಪುರುಷ. The tutelary deity of a house. -ಶಾಂತಿ. = ಗೃಹಶಾಂತಿ. -ಪೂಜೆ. The ceremony before beginning to build a house.

ವಾಹ s. n. Bearing, conveying, carrying; as in ಪ್ರ-, ವಿ-. 2, a porter, carrier. 3, a vehicle. -ಕ. Bearing, conveying; a porter; a driver; a horseman. -ನ. A vehicle, chariot, carriage.

ವಾಹವಾ h. int. Bravo! capital! excellent!

ವಾಹಿ s. n. Bearing, carrying. -ನಿ. A river; an army. -ನೀಪತಿ. A general. -ಸು. To cause to bear.

ವಾಳ s. n. A tail. 2, a tumour. 3, aff. = ವಳ.

ವಿ s. pref. Apart from, asunder; off; away; various; manifold.

ವಿಂಶತಿ s. a. Twenty.

ವಿಕಟ s. a. Large; formidable, hideous, ugly; horrible; crooked, perverse.

ವಿಕರಾಲ s. a. Very terrible; hideous.

ವಿಕರಿಸು s. v. t. To alter, change (arith.).

ವಿಕಲ s. a. Defective, incomplete. 2, decayed, impaired. 3, confused, confounded. -ತೆ, -ತ್ವ. Confusion, agitation; sorrow.

ವಿಕಲ್ಪ s. n. Alternative, option. 2, uncertainty; indecision, doubt. 3, error. 4, suspicion; an evil thought. ವಿಕಲ್ಪಿಸು. To form differently.

ವಿಕಸನ s. n. Bursting, blossoming, expanding; cf. ವಿಕಾಸ.

ವಿಕಾರ s. n. Change, modification, abnormity. 2, change for the worse, disease. 3, perturbation, passion, excitement. Cpds.: ಧ್ವನಿ-, ನಿದ್ರಾ-, ಮುಖ-, ರೋಮ-, etc. ಮನೋ-, ಬುದ್ಧಿ-. Perversion of understanding. ವಿಕಾರಿ. Changing; an ugly person; the thirty-third year in the cycle of sixty

ವಿಕಾಶ, ವಿಕಾಸ s n Opening, expanding, blowing, budding 2, expanse, sky 3, appearance, display, manifestation

ವಿಕಿರ, ವಿಕೀರಣ s n Scattering about (as boiled rice at a Śrâddha).

ವಿಕೀರ್ಣ s a Scattered, dispersed, spread about, filled with, famous

ವಿಕೃತ s a. Changed; disfigured, ugly; afflicted, unnatural; estranged, strange n. Change, a disorder. ವಿಕೃತಿ Change from a natural or healthy state. 2, the twenty-fourth year in the cycle of sixty

ವಿಕ್ರಮ s n Stepping or going beyond; a step stride 2, heroism, prowess 3 = ವಿಕ್ರಮಾದಿತ್ಯ, q. v. 4, the fourteenth year in the cycle of sixty -ಶಕ The era of Vikramâditya -ಶಾಲಿ A valorous person ವಿಕ್ರಮಾದಿತ್ಯ, ವಿಕ್ರಮಾರ್ಕ. N of a king of Ujjayini.

ವಿಕ್ರಯ s n Sale, selling ವಿಕ್ರಯಿಸು. To sell, vend. ವಿಕ್ರೀತ Sold ವಿಕ್ರೇಯ. Saleable.

ವಿಕ್ಷಿಪ್ತ s a Thrown away; scattered; bewildered

ವಿಕ್ಷೇಪ s. n. Throwing away, rejecting, scattering, confusion, a side-glance

ವಿಖ್ಯಾತ s a Renowned, famous, celebrated ವಿಖ್ಯಾತಿ Fame, celebrity.

ವಿಖ್ಯಾಪನ s n. Making known, announcing, publishing, acknowledging, confessing, exposition

ವಿಗಡ tb of ವಿಕಟ, q v.

ವಿಗತ s. a Gone, departed, disappeared, devoid of, obscured.

ವಿಗಲಿತ, ವಿಗಳಿತ s a Flowed away, trickled, dropped fallen, liquefied

ವಿಗ್ರಹ s n. Shape, form, an image, idol. 2, the body 3, separation, analysis, a division, portion 4, encounter, conflict, war ವಿಗ್ರಹಾರಾಧಕ An idolator ವಿಗ್ರಹಾರಾಧನೆ. Idolwor[illegible]

ಪ್ರಾಣಪ್ರತಿಷ್ಠೆ ಮಾಡು. To perform the rite of bringing life into an idol

ವಿಘಟಿಕೆ s. n The sixtieth part of a ghatikâ

ವಿಘಾತ, ವಿಘಾತಿ s n. Destruction; a blow, opposition. prevention, obstacle

ವಿಘ್ನ s n. An obstacle, impediment, hindrance, opposition. 2, any trouble -ರಾಜ, ವಿಘ್ನೇಶ್ವರ Ganêśa

ವಿಂಗಡ (tb. of ವಿಘಟ) n Separating, disuniting, separation, parting. ವಿಂಗಡಿಸು To separate, to disunite

ವಿಚಕ್ಷಣ s. a. Far-sighted, discerning, wise, clever. ವಿಚಕ್ಷಣೆ. A clever woman; cleverness, skill

ವಿಚಲ s. a. Moving about, unsteady.

ವಿಚಾರ s n Deliberation, consideration, examination, trial 2, discrimination, judgment decision. 3, subject, topic. 4, doubt, perplexity, anxiety, trouble -ಕ An investigator, judge. -ಗೇಡಿ. A fool. -ಗೇಡಿತನ Foolishness. -ಮಾಡು. To inquire into, to reflect -ಪರ Thoughtful, inquisitive -ವಂತ. A thoughtful or considerate man, *also* ವಿಚಾರಿ. -ಣೆ Deliberation, examination, investigation, the exercise of judgment ನ್ಯಾಯ- The trial of a lawsuit. -ಣೆಯಾಗು, -ಣೆ ನಡೆ. A trial to take place -ಣೆಕರ್ತ. A judge, a manager, superintendent -ಣೆ ಮಾಡು, ವಿಚಾರಿಸು To examine, try, inquire; to ask, to reflect

ವಿಚಿತ್ರ s a Variegated; wonderful, surprising.

ವಿಚ್ಛಿತ್ತಿ s. n Separating; cutting off, interruption, cessation, destruction, loss, pause in a verse, limit

ವಿಚ್ಛಿನ್ನ s a Cut asunder, severed, divided, broken off, interrupted, violated, destroyed, variegated.

ವಿಚ್ಛೇದ s n. Separation, cutting off; interruption, termination, disappearance, a section, dissension

ವಿಜಯ s. n. Conquest, victory. 2, the twenty-seventh year of the cycle of sixty. -ದಶಮಿ. The tenth day of dasarâ festival. -ನಗರ. N. of a town. -ರಾಘವ. Râma. -ಲಕ್ಷ್ಮಿ, -ಶ್ರೀ. = ಜಯಲಕ್ಷ್ಮೀ.

ವಿಜಾತ s. a. Of a mixed origin; generated; wild, refractory. ವಿಜಾತಿ. A different kind or caste; a low caste. ವಿಜಾತೀಯ. Of a different kind, of mixed origin.

ವಿಜಾಪುರ s. n. N. of a town.

ವಿಜೃಂಭಣ s. n. Gaping; expanding, exhibiting; displaying, budding; pastime, sport; extravagance. ವಿಜೃಂಭಿಸು. To gape; to expand, display, *etc.*

ವಿಜ್ಞಪ್ತಿ. = ವಿಜ್ಞಾಪನೆ, *q. v.*

ವಿಜ್ಞಾನ s. n. Understanding; discerning; intelligence, knowledge, science, learning. ವಿಜ್ಞಾನಿ. Learned, proficient.

ವಿಜ್ಞಾಪನೆ s. n. A petition, solicitation, representation, humble intimation; application. -ಮಾಡು, ವಿಜ್ಞಾಪಿಸು. To request, state respectfully; to represent, submit.

ವಿಟ s. n. A libertine; a rogue, cheat. -ಚೇಷ್ಟೆ, -ತನ, -ತ್ವ. Lewdness.

ವಿಟಂಕ s. n. A dove-cot.

ವಿಟ್ಠಲ, ವಿಠಲ s. n. Vishṇu as worshipped at Paṇḍharapur.

ವಿಡಂಗ. = ವಾಯುವಿಳಂಗ, *s.* ವಾಯು, *q. v.*

ವಿಡಂಬನ s. n. Imitation, copying, disguise, masquerade; simulation; imposture, deception, fraud. 2, displaying, showing. 3, ridiculing, mocking. 4, vexation.

ವಿಡಾಯ, ವಿಡಾಯಿ s. n. Grand display, pomp.

ವಿಡೂರ, ವಿಡ್ಡೂರ f. n. Enmity, annoyance.

ವಿತಂಡ, ವಿತಂಡೆ s. n. Cavil, frivolous argument; criticism.

ವಿತತ s. a. Broa[illegible] [illegible] expanded; accomplished, c[illegible] n. A string[illegible] instrument. ವಿತತಿ. Stretching out; extension; a collection, multitude; a cluster.

ವಿತರಣ s. n. A gift, donation. 2, giving up. 3, liberality.

ವಿತರ್ಕ s. n. Argument, discussion, conjecture; opinion; deliberation; doubt.

ವಿತಲ s. n. The second of the seven lower regions.

ವಿತಾನ s. n. Stretching out, expansion. 2, an awning, canopy.

ವಿತ್ತ s. a. Known. 2, found, gained, acquired. n. Property, wealth. 2, power. -ವಣಿಜ. A shroff. ವಿತ್ತೇಹಾ. Desire of wealth.

ವಿದ s. n. Knowing; a knower.

ವಿದರ್ಭ s. n. N. of a district in Bengal, the modern Berar proper. -ಜೆ. Damayanti; Rukmiṇi.

ವಿದಲ s. a. Split, rent; opened, blown (as a flower). n. Cuttings, chips.

ವಿದಾರಣ s. n. Splitting, rending, killing; war.

ವಿದಾರಿ s. n. Tearing asunder. 2, the plant *Balatas paniculata.* -ಸು. To split, rend.

ವಿದಿಕ್ಕು (*tb. of* ವಿದಿಶ್) n. An intermediate point of the compass.

ವಿದಿತ s. a. Known, understood; informed; represented. n. Knowledge; information; thought.

ವಿದುರ s. a. Knowing, intelligent. n. N. of the younger brother of Dhṛitarâshṭra and Pâṇḍu.

ವಿದ್ವಾಂಸ s. n. A wise man; a scholar; *f.* ವಿದುಷಿ.

ವಿದೂರ s. n. Remote; devoid of, without.

ವಿದೂಷಕ s. n. An abuser; a jester, buffoon.

ವಿದೇಶ s. n. Foreign country.

ವಿದೇಹ s. a. Bodiless. n. Mithilâ, Tirhut; its people.

ವಿದ್ದೆ. = ವಿಡೆ, *q. v.*

[illegible] *tb. of* [illegible] n. [illegible]

ವಿದ್ಯಮಾನ s a. Being known, existing, actual, real

ವಿದ್ಯಾ (= ವಿದ್ಯೆ, q v) s n. Knowledge, etc -ಗುರು, -ದಾತೃ A teacher. -ದಾನ Giving of knowledge, teaching. -ಧನ. Wealth of learning. -ಧರ Knowledge-holder, a genius, a N., f -ಧರಿ -ಭ್ಯಾಸ Study. -ಲಯ -ಶಾಲೆ A school -ವಂತ A learned man, f -ವಂತಳು, -ವಂತೆ -ವಾಲಿ. A learned person. -ಸಾಧನೆ Acquisition of knowledge -ಸಾಫಲ್ಯ Profit of knowledge. -ಹೀನ Ignorant, uninstructed. -ರ್ಥಿ A student, pupil, disciple

ವಿದ್ಯುತ್ s n. Lightning

ವಿದ್ಯುಲ್ಲತ s n. Zigzag lightning.

ವಿದ್ಯೆ (= ವಿದ್ಯೆ, ವಿದ್ಯಾ) s. n Knowledge, learning science, an art, magical skill. ದೇವ- Theology. ಕ್ರಿಸ್ತ- Christology. ಶಿಲ್ಪ- Architecture

ವಿದ್ರಧಿ s n An internal abscess

ವಿದ್ರವ, ವಿದ್ರಾವ s. n. Flight, retreat, panic, liquefaction.

ವಿದ್ವತ್, ವಿದ್ವತ್ತ್ವ s n Learning, erudition ವಿದ್ವಜ್ಜನ. A scholar, philosopher ವಿದ್ವತ್ಸಭೆ, ವಿದ್ವತ್ಸಮೂಹ. An assembly of scholars.

ವಿದ್ವಾನ್ = ವಿದ್ವಾಂಸ, q. v

ವಿದ್ವಾಂಸ (tb of ವಿದ್ವಸ್) a. Learned. n A wise man, scholar.

ವಿದ್ವೇಷ s. n. Enmity, hatred, contempt ವಿದ್ವೇಷಿ. An enemy

ವಿಧ s n Form, manner, kind, sort; fold -ವಿಧ rep. -ವಿಧವಾಗಿ. Variously

ವಿಧವತೆ s n. Widowhood ವಿಧವಾ, ವಿಧವೆ. A widow.

ವಿಧಾನ s n Arranging, disposing; arrangement; action 2, a rule, precept, a law, ordinance, a regulation, sacred text 3 a rite, ceremony 4, a form, mode, manner -ಪೂರ್ವಕ. According to rule.

ವಿಧಾ[illegible] n.

ವಿಧಿ s n. A rule, formula, precept, injunction, a vedic text. 2, an order, ordinance, statute. 3. a rite, ceremony. 4, a method, manner. 5, fate, destiny. -ಕ್ರಿಯೆ, -ರೂಪ The imperative (g). -ಪ್ರಕಾರ. According to rule. -ವತ್. In due form. ವಿಧಿಸು To prescribe, order, ordain, appoint, allot.

ವಿಧುರ s a. Separated 2 agitated, troubled; adverse. n Separation; adversity 2, a widower

ವಿಧೃತ s a Kept apart. 2, seized, held, taken, assumed.

ವಿಧೆ = ವಿಧ, q. v

ವಿಧೇಯ s a Arrangeable, governable, submissive, obedient -ತೆ, -ತ್ವ Obedience, docility.

ವಿಧ್ಯರ್ಥ s n The imperative (g)

ವಿಧ್ವಂಸ s n. Ruin destruction 2, aversion, enmity 3, insult, offence.

ವಿನತ, ವಿನಮಿತ s. a Bowed down, humble, modest ವಿನತಿ. Bowing down, humility. modesty.

ವಿನಮತಿ s. a Bending down bowing ವಿನಮಿಸು To make obeisance. ವಿನಮ್ರ Humble, modest.

ವಿನಯ s n Leading, guidance, gentlemanlike bearing, good behaviour, condescension, humility; reverence, courtesy ಠಕ್ಕು-, ಸಕ್ಕ- Pretended modesty -ವಾಗಿ ನಡೆ To behave modestly -ಪೂರ್ವಕ With reverence, etc ವಿನಯಿತ A well-behaved man

ವಿನಹ, ವಿನಹಾ (tb. of ವಿನಾ) ad Without, except

ವಿನಾಡಿ s n. A period of twenty-four [seconds

ವಿನಾಯಕ s. n. Ganêśa. 2. a leader a Anarchical.

ವಿನಾಯಿತಿ h. n Exemption as from passing an examination ವಿನಾಯಿಸು To except, exempt [illegible]. To be exempted.

[illegible] on, ruin.

ವಿನಿಮಯ s. n. Exchange, barter. 2, deposit, security.

ವಿನಿಯೋಗ s. n. Unyoking. 2, assignment, distribution (as of eatables). 3, application, use, employment. 4, a business. ವಿನಿಯೋಗಿಸು. To assign; to use.

ವಿನೀತ s. a. Well-trained, educated, well-behaved; modest, gentle; lovely, handsome. ವಿನೀತಿ. Good behaviour.

ವಿನುತಿ s. n. Praise. ವಿನುತ, ವಿನೂತ. Praised.

ವಿನೋದ s. n. Diversion, sport, play. 2, interesting pursuit, pleasure. 3, jesting, joking. -ಗಾರ. A playful man; one fond of jesting. ವಿನೋದಿಸು. To play, sport; to be delighted.

ವಿಂಧ್ಯ, ವಿಂಧ್ಯಾಚಲ, ವಿಂಧ್ಯಾದ್ರಿ s. n. N. of a mountain range.

ವಿನ್ಯಾಸ s. n. Depositing; a deposit; arranging, distributing; disposition; a receptacle. 2, gesticulation.

ವಿಪಕ್ಷ s. n. An opponent, adversary, enemy; a rival. 2, a syllogism.

ವಿಪತ್ಕಾಲ s. n. Adversity.

ವಿಪತ್ತಿ, ವಿಪತ್ತು (tb. of ವಿಪದ್) n. Adversity, calamity, misfortune, disaster.

ವಿಪರೀತ s. a. Reversed, adverse, contrary; uncommon, unusual; different; disagreeable. -ಕೆಲಸ. An unusual act. -ಕಾಲ. An adverse time.

ವಿಪರ್ಯಯ. ವಿಪರ್ಯಾಯ s. n. Reverse, contrariety; perverseness; opposition; misfortune; exchange, barter; error, mistake; also ವಿಪರ್ಯಾಸ.

ವಿಪಲ s. n. A moment, instant.

ವಿಪಾಕ s. n. Cooking; ripening, maturity; result; calamity, distress.

ವಿಪಿನ s. n. A wood, forest, grove.

ವಿಪುಲ s. a. Large, great, broad, wide; spacious; ample; profound.

ವಿಪ್ಪತ್ತು. = ವಿಪತ್ತಿ, q. v.

ವಿಪ್ರ s. n. A poet. 2, a Brâhmaṇa.

ವಿಪ್ರತಿಷಿದ್ಧ s. a. C... prohibit...

ವಿಪ್ರತಿಸಾರ s. n. Repentance.

ವಿಪ್ರಯೋಗ s. n. Disjunction, separation.

ವಿಪ್ರಲಬ್ಧ s. a. Cheated; hurt; afflicted.

ವಿಪ್ರಲಾಪ s. n. Prattling; wrangling, quarrel.

ವಿಫಲ s. a. Fruitless, useless.

ವಿಬುಧ s. n. A learned or wise man.

ವಿಬೋಧ s. n. Awaking; intelligence; wisdom. 2, absence of mind.

ವಿಭಕ್ತ s. a. Divided. 2, parted separated. -ಕುಟುಂಬ. A divided family. ಸಹೋದರರು. Divided brothers.

ವಿಭಕ್ತಿ s. n. A division, partition. 2, a portion, part. 3, inflection of the cases of a noun or pronoun. -ಪಾಠ. A table of inflection of cases.

ವಿಭಜನ s. n. Division (arith.), separation, partition. ವಿಭಜಿಸು. To divide (arith.).

ವಿಭವ s. n. Display; greatness, glory, dignity; power; wealth; magnanimity. 2, the second year in the cycle of sixty.

ವಿಭಾಗ s. n. Division, separation; partition, part, share; distribution. -ಪತ್ರ, -ಸಾಧನ. A deed of partition. ವಿಭಾಗಿಸು. To divide, distribute. ವಿಭಾಜ್ಯ. Divisible, portionable.

ವಿಭಾವ s. n. Discrimination, judgment. 2, a friend. -ನ. Clear perception, discrimination.

ವಿಭಾಷೆ s. n. A foreign language. 2, an alternative, option.

ವಿಭಾಸೆ s. n. Light, lustre.

ವಿಭೀತ, -ಕ s. a. Fearless. n. The tree *Terminalia bellerica*.

ವಿಭೀಷಣ s. a. Terrifying, formidable. n. N. of Râvaṇa's younger brother.

ವಿಭು s. a. Omnipresent; excellent, eminent, supreme. n. A master, lord, ruler. -ತ್ವ. Might, power; ownership.

ವಿಭೂತಿ s. n. Great power; might, dominion; di... ...

-ಧರಿಸು, -ಹಚ್ಚು. To put ashes on the forehead

ವಿಭೂಷಣ s *n* Decoration; an ornament. ವಿಭೂಷಿತ. Adorned, decorated.

ವಿಭೇದ s *n* Breaking asunder, separating; a variety, kind ವಿಭೇದಿಸು To divide piece, to become different, to alter.

ವಿಭ್ರಮ, -ಣ s. *n*. Roaming about, error, doubt apprehension, hurry, confusion, bewilderment, flurry ವಿಭ್ರಮಿಸು. To be confused, bewildered

ವಿಭ್ರಾಂತಿ s *n* Confusion, bewilderment, hurry, flurry

ವಿಮತ s *a* Disagreed, dissenting *n* A different religion -ಸ್ಥ. A man of a different religion

ವಿಮನಸ್ಕ s *a* Displeased, sad, heartbroken; perplexed -ತ Sad, melancholy

ವಿಮಯ (ವಿನೀಮಯ) s *n*. Exchange, barter

ವಿಮರ್ದ s *n* Grinding, pounding, trituration, *also* -ನ

ವಿಮರ್ಶ, ವಿಮರ್ಶೆ s *n* Investigation, inquiry.

ವಿಮಲ s. *a* Stainless, spotless, pure -ತ್ವ. Stainlessness, purity -ಮತಿ. Pure-minded.

ವಿಮಾತೃ s *n* A step-mother. -ಜ Her son.

ವಿಮಾನ s *n* A measure 2 a chariot of the gods going through the skies, a baloon

ವಿಮುಕ್ತ s. *a* Let loose, liberated. ವಿಮುಕ್ತಿ Liberation, release, final emancipation

ವಿಮುಖ s *a* Averted; turned away from, disinclined

ವಿಮೆ h *n* Insurance -ಕಂಪನಿ I company -ಪತ್ರ. I policy

ವಿಮೋಕ್ಷ s. *n*. Liberation, release, final emancipation

ವಿಮೋಚನ, ವಿಮೋಚನೆ s *n*. Liberating, es

ಜ

giveness of sin (*through Christ*) ವಿಮೋಚಿಸು To liberate, set free, to save

ವಿಯೋಗ s *n* Separation, disunion, loss, death *Cpds* ಪಿತೃ-, ಮಾತೃ-, ಭಾರ್ಯಾ-, *etc*

ವಿರಕ್ತ s. *a*. Disaffected, indifferent. 2, free from passion or affection. *n*. One who is free from worldly affections or passions ವಿರಕ್ತಿ Absence of affections or passions, indifference apathy ವಿರಕ್ತಿ ಪಡು, -ಬರು, -ಹುಟ್ಟು. To be indifferent

ವಿರಚನೆ s. *n*. Arrangement; compiling, contrivance, composition ವಿರಚಿಸು To arrange, construct, compile, *etc*.

ವಿರಂಚಿ, ವಿರಿಂಚಿ s *n*. Brahmâ.

ವಿರತ s *a* Stopped, ceased, rested ವಿರತಿ Cessation, end; indifference.

ವಿರಲ s *a* Thin, delicate, loose, wide, apart, rare, scarce, remote -ತೆ, -ತ್ವ Rareness, *etc*.

ವಿರಸ s *a* Juiceless, sapless, tasteless, insipid, unenergetic. -ಮಾಡು. To offend -ಹುಟ್ಟು. To become offended.

ವಿರಹ s *n* Separation, loneliness, want of, abandonment, cessation -ಅಗ್ನಿ, -ಜ್ವರ, -ತಾಪ, -ವೇದನೆ Ardour of love in separated lovers

ವಿರಹಿತ s *a*. Absent from, bereft of, deserted, devoid of, destitute of, free from without

ವಿರಳ. = ವಿರಲ, *q v*

ವಿರಾಗ s. *n* Passionlessness.

ವಿರಾಜ s. *n* Shining, splendour, beauty. -ಮಾನ Shining, splendid, handsome. ವಿರಾಜಿಸು To shine, be brilliant, *etc*.

ವಿರಾಟ, -ಪುರುಷ s *n*. The first progeny of Brahmâ, *also* ವಿರಾಟ್ಪುರುಷ

ವಿರಾಮ s *n* Cessation rest, stoppage, pause 2, end, conclusion -ಚಿಹ್ನೆ. A sign of pause

ವಿರುದ್ಧ s *a* Opposed, hindered ob-
, reverse,
.ble; pro-

hibited *n* Opposition, hostility. ವಿರುದ್ಧಾರ್ಥ Contrary meaning

ವಿರೂಪ s *a* Deformed, misshapen ugly, monstrous *n* Deformity, *also* -ತೆ ವಿರೂಪಾಕ್ಷ Śiva

ವಿರೇಕ, ವಿರೇಚನ s *n* Purging of the bowels 2. a purgative

ವಿರೋಚನ s *n* Shining. 2 the sun: the moon, the fire 3 Bali's father

ವಿರೋಧ s. *n* Opposition obstruction hindrance restraint, contradiction, contrariety. contrast inconsistency hostility enmity. ಮತ- Opposed to a religious sect ಶಾಸ್ತ್ರ- Opposed to scripture ವಿರೋಧಿ An enemy, opponent, the twenty-third year of the cycle of sixty. ವಿರೋಧಿಕೃತ್. The forty-fifth year of the cycle. ವಿರೋಧಿಸು To oppose, hinder. obstruct to hate *i. t* To be opposed

ವಿಲಕ್ಷಣ s. *a*. Other, different, extraordinary, strange, odd, novel *n* Oddness. strangeness.

ವಿಲಂಬ s *a* Hanging down, pendulous *n* Slowness, delay; *also* -ನ.

ವಿಲಂಬಿ s *a* Depending pendulous. slow. *n*. The thirty-second year of the cycle of sixty -ಸು. To hang down; to protract.

ವಿಲಯ s *n* Dissolution, destruction

ವಿಲಸಿತ s *a* Flashing, shining, brilliant, splendid. ವಿಲಸಿತ Shining, sportive; a gleam, flash; sport [ing.

ವಿಲಾಪ s. *n* Lamentation. crying, weep-

ವಿಲಾಯತಿ h *n*. Europe; a foreign country. *a* Foreign, European

ವಿಲಾಸ s. *n*. A label, address on a letter, *also* ಮೇಲ್ವಿಲಾಸ 2, sport, pastime, amusement, coquetry 3 grace elegance, charm -ವಾಸ A pleasure-house. ವಿಲಾಸಿ Sportive, playful, a sensualist ವಿಲಾಸಿನಿ. A coquettish woman.

ವಿಲೆ h *n* A class head, order, arrangement -ವಾರಿ Assorting; classifying, distribution, settlement -- ಮಾಡು. To order

ವಿಲೇಪನ s *n* Besmearing, anointing. ವಿಲೇಪಿತ Smeared over ವಿಲೇಪಿಸು. To smear over, *etc*

ವಿಲೋಚನ s. *n* The eye

ವಿಲೋಭನ s *a* Beguiling allurement, attraction, temptation. ವಿಲೋಭಿಸು To allure, tempt

ವಿಲೋಮ s *a* Reverse contrary opposite *n* Reverse order

ವಿಲೋಲ s. *a* Shaking, tremulous fickle, unsteady. *n* Tremor, rolling. -ತೆ Tremulousness

ವಿವಕ್ಷೆ s. *n* Meaning, sense, intention purpose, wish ವಿವಕ್ಷಿಸು To wish to say, to intend

ವಿವರ s *n* Expansion, specification, detailed account, particulars 2, an interval, a breach -ಣೆ. Explanation, exposition, interpretation, description, detail -ಪತ್ರಿಕೆ A statement of particulars ವಿವರಿಸು To explain, interpret; to detail specify

ವಿವರ್ಜಿಸು s. *i. t* To leave, abandon

ವಿವರ್ಣ s *a* Colourless, pale. pallid, ignorant

ವಿವರ್ಧನ s *n* Increase. growth

ವಿವಾದ s. *n* A dispute, quarrel, controversy, debate, contest, contention

ವಿವಾಹ s *n* Marriage, matrimony. -ಮಾಡಿಕೊಳ್ಳು To marry. -ವಾಗು. To become married -ಮಾಡಿಕೊಡು To give away in marriage ಪುನರ್-. Widow-marriag.

ವಿವಿಧ s. *a*. Diverse, manifold, various

ವಿವೇಕ s. *n*. Discrimination, discernment, judgment, *also* -ತೆ 2 true knowledge 3. discretion. 4, discussion, investigation. ವಿವೇಕಿ. Discriminating prudent, a discriminator ವಿವೇಕಿಸು To discriminate, decide

ವಿವೇಚನೆ s *n* Discriminating *n* Investigation

ವಿಶಂಕೆ s. *n* Suspicion, doubt, fear.

ವಿಶದ s. *a*. Clear, pure bright; white, evident, obvious -ತ್ವ Clearness. ವಿಶ ... [illegible]

ವಿಶಾಖೆ s. *n*. The sixteenth lunar asterism.

ವಿಶಾರದ s *a* Skilled in, conversant with 2, confident, bold

ವಿಶಾಲ s *a*. Large wide, broad, extensive -ತೆ Expansion, magnitude

ವಿಶಿಷ್ಟ s *a*. Distinguished, endowed with, superior, excellent. 2, without a rest, all

ವಿಶುದ್ಧ s. *a*. Clean, pure, pious, rectified, accurate ವಿಶುದ್ಧಿ Purity; rectitude.

ವಿಶೇಷ s. *n*. Discrimination 2, difference, distinction, speciality, peculiarity, particularity 3, a defining word (*g*). 4, a sort, variety, species kind, *etc*. 5, peculiar merit *a* Extraordinary, singular, much, more -ಧೂಪ. Resin of *Boswallia thurifera* -ಕ. Distinguishing, characteristic, an attribute, predicate -ಣ. Distinguishing, discriminative; distinction, discrimination, an attribute, adjective (*g*) -ವಾಗಿ. Especially ವಿಶೇಷಿಸು To distinguish; to particularise, specify. ವಿಶೇಷ್ಯ. Distinguished, a noun; the subject of a predicate (*g*), *also* -ಪದ

ವಿಶ್ರಮ, -ಣ s *n* Rest, repose, pause, stop, *also* ವಿಶ್ರಾಮ. ವಿಶ್ರಮಿಸು. To rest, repose.

ವಿಶ್ರಾಂತ s *a* Rested, reposed, calm, composed

ವಿಶ್ರಾಂತಿ s *n*. Rest, repose. -ಹಿಡಿಕೊಳ್ಳು -ಗೊಳ್ಳು, -ತೀರಿಸು To take rest. -ದಿವಸ The Sabbath-day.

ವಿಶ್ರುತ s *a* Renowned, famous

ವಿಶ್ವ s. *a* All, every, much, many. *n*. The universe, world -ಕರ್ತ The creator. -ಕರ್ಮ The architect of the gods; a minister. -ದಾತ The giver of all. -ನಾಥ, -ಪತಿ, ವಿಶ್ವೇಶ್ವರ Śiva, a N. ವಿಶ್ವಂಭರ Supporting the universe, Vishnu -ರೂಪ Universal, omnipresent ... The ur ...

ವಿಶ್ವಸನ (= ವಿಶ್ವಾಸ) s *n*. Trusting, confiding ವಿಶ್ವಸನೀಯ. Trustworthy ವಿಶ್ವಸಿಸು = ವಿಶ್ವಾಸಿಸು, *q v*

ವಿಶ್ವಾಮಿತ್ರ s *n* N of a Kshatriya who became a Brâhmana

ವಿಶ್ವಾವಸು s. *n* N of one of the gandharvas 2, the thirty-ninth year in the cycle of sixty

ವಿಶ್ವಾಸ s *n*. Trust, confidence, faith, reliance; hope, affection, love 2, a secret ಕ್ರಿಸ್ತರ-. The faith of Christians -ಪ್ರಮಾಣ The creed -ಬೋಧನ. Dogmatics -ಇಡು To believe, place confidence in. -ಘಾತ, -ಘಾತಕ Breach of trust -ಘಾತಕ A traitor, *f*. -ಘಾತಕಿ -ತನ Trustworthiness. ವಿಶ್ವಾಸಿ Trusting confiding, trustworthy, honest, a trustworthy person ಅವಿಶ್ವಾಸಿ. An unbeliever. ವಿಶ್ವಾಸಿಸು. To trust, believe, confide in, to love

ವಿಷ s *n* Poison, venom, anything bitter, bitterness. 2, intoxication -ಇಕ್ಕು To administer poison. -ಇಳಿಸು. To dispel poison -ಏರು Poison to take effect -ಕಾರಕ Poisonous -ಜಿತ. An ichneumon -ವ Elephantiasis -ಪುಚ್ಛ A scorpion -ವೃಕ್ಷ. A cloud, a forest, a snake -ಭಿಷಜ್, -ವೈದ್ಯ. A poison-doctor. -ಹರ. Antidotal.

ವಿಷಮ s *a*. Uneven, rough. 2, unequal, irregular 3, odd 4, different 5, coarse, cross 6, disagreeable, troublesome 7, unusual 8, adverse. *n* Unevenness *etc* -ಜ್ವರ, -ಶೀತಜ್ವರ An unremittent fever -ಬುದ್ಧಿ A crooked mind -ಸಂಖ್ಯೆ. An odd number ವಿಷಮಿಸು. To become abnormal, *as* a fever.

ವಿಷಯ s *n*. An object or organ of sense, any thing perceptible by the senses 2 an affair, business 3, concern respect, regard, reference, subject, subject-matter. 4, a region, field, sphere, scope, range, reach ... ic ವಿಷ ... , a materialist. -ದಲ್ಲಿ, -ವಾಗಿ, -ಕ್ಕೆ Respecting, concerning, about. -ಲಂಪಟ Addicted to worldly objects

ವಿಷಾದ s n Dejection, despondency, lassitude, sadness, fear

ವಿಷು s a Various, manifold. n The fifteenth year in the cycle of sixty 2, = ವಿಷುವ, q v

ವಿಷುವ, -ತ್ s n The equinox

ವಿಷೂಚಿ s n A kind of spasmodic cholera

ವಿಷ್ಣು s. n The second deity of the Hindu triad -ಕ್ರಾಂತಿ A small creeping herb, *Evolvulus alsinoides* -ಪದ The sky -ಪದಿ The Ganges. -ರಥ, -ವಾಹನ Garuda

ವಿಸಂವಾದ s n False assertion, deception, disagreement

ವಿಸಂಧಿ s. n Absence of euphony.

ವಿಸರ್ಗ s. n Emission, dismissal, getting rid of, separation, the aspirate marked by two dots (ಃ)

ವಿಸರ್ಜನೆ s n. Sending forth, letting go; relinquishing, abandoning, getting rid of; voiding, donation, gift. ವಿಸರ್ಜಿಸು To get rid of, reject, relinquish

ವಿಸರ್ಪ s n. Erysipelas, a kind of itch; elephantiasis -ಣ Spreading, itching

ವಿಸೃಷ್ಟ s a Let go, emanated, created.

ವಿಸ್ತರ, ವಿಸ್ತಾರ s n. Spreading; extension, diffuseness, prolixity; minute detail. 2, vastness, expanse. 3, a layer, a seat 4, abundance ವಿಸ್ತರಿಸು, ವಿಸ್ತಾರಿಸು To spread out, extend, amplify, detail.

ವಿಸ್ತೀರ್ಣ s a. Spread about; expanded, broad, large, vast, roomy, wide. n Extent, area

ವಿಸ್ಮಯ s n Wonder, surprise, amazement. -ಗೊಳ್ಳು, -ಪಡು, ವಿಸ್ಮಯಿಸು To be astonished, surprised, *etc* ವಿಸ್ಮಿತ Surprised, astonished, perplexed

ವಿಸ್ಮರಣ s. n Forgetting, oblivion ವಿಸ್ಮೃತಿ Forgetfulness, oblivion, unmindfulness

ವಿಸ್ರಾವ s n Floating forth, trickling.

ವಿಹರಣ s n Going about. 2, pastime, pleasure

ವಿಹಾರ s n. Walking for pleasure, taking an airing, roaming. 2, sporting, pastime, pleasure 3, a Buddhist or Jaina temple 4, a pleasure-garden. ವಿಹರಿಸು ವಿಹಾರಿಸು. To take away; to ramble, roam, to sport, play

ವಿಹಿತ s a. Regulated, settled, suitable, fit, proper

ವಿಹೀನ s a Destitute; devoid of, free from, without. *Cpds* ಕುಲ-, ಗತಿ-, ನೀತಿ-, ರಸ-, *etc.* -ತೆ, -ತ್ವ Being wholly free from.

ವಿಹ್ವಲ s a. Agitated, alarmed, confused, distressed

ವಿಳಂಗ = ವಿಡಂಗ, q v

ವೀಕ್ಷೆ s. n Looking at, sight. ವೀಕ್ಷಿಸು To see, behold, observe

ವೀಜ = ಬೀಜ, q v 2, a king's attendant.

ವೀಜನ s. n. Fanning, a fan.

ವೀಟಿ = ವೀಳಿ, *etc.*, q v.

ವೀಣೆ s. n. The Indian lute -ಗಾರ. A lutanist

ವೀತ s a Gone, accepted, liked, quiet, tame 2, set free, exempted. -ರಾಗ Free from passions, calm. -ಶೋಕ. Free from sorrow

ವೀಧಿ (= ಬೀದಿ, q v) s. n. A row, line. 2, a road, street

ವೀರ s a Heroic, mighty, robust n A hero, warrior, champion, prowess; valour -ಕಂಕಣ. A warrior's wrist ornament. -ಕೆಲಸ, -ಗೆಲಸ A heroic act -ತನ, -ತ್ವ Heroism, prowess. -ಭದ್ರ. N of a great hero -ರಾಘವ Râmachandra; N. -ಲಕ್ಷ್ಮಿ, -ಶ್ರೀ The glory of valour -ವೈಷ್ಣವ. A follower of Râmânuja. -ಸೇನ N. of Nala's father -ಶೈವ. A Lingavanta. ವೀರಾಸನ Kneeling on one knee.

ವೀರಣ k *n* A double drum used at weddings. *etc* 2 (s) a fragrant grass

ವೀರ್ಯ s *n* Vigour, strength, energy. 2, heroism, prowess courage -ವಂತ, -ಶಾಲಿ. A vigorous man

ವೀಸ k *n.* A sixteenth, $\frac{1}{16}$ of a hana -ಬಡ್ಡಿ Interest at one-sixteenth.

ವೀಳೆ, ವೀಳೆಯ, ವೀಳ್ಯ, ವೀಳ್ಯೆ (*tb of* ವೀಟಿ, *q.v*) *n.* The betel plant, *Piper betel*, the leaf of *Piper betel*

ವು, ವೂ *For Kannada words with these initials see s.* ಉ, ಊ

ವೃಕ s. *n.* A wolf. 2, a jackal. ವೃಕೋದರ Bhima.

ವೃಕ್ಷ s *n* A tree; a shrub. -ಭೇದಿ A hatchet -ರುಹೆ, ವೃಕ್ಷಾದನಿ. A parasitical plant ವೃಕ್ಷಾವಲ್ಲ The hog-plum, *Spondias mangifera*

ವೃಜಿನ s *a* Crooked, curved 2, wicked, wrong 3, sin, vice. 4, distress

ವೃತ್ತ s *a.* Turned. 2. round, circular. 3, existed, happened; past; gone, done, fixed. *n* Event news 2, practice occupation 3, action, conduct 4, a circle, circumference 5, metre, a verse. -ಶಾಲಿ, -ಸಂಪನ್ನ ಸು- Well-behaved; a man of good conduct ವೃತ್ತಾಂತ Occurrence, event, tidings, rumour, report; a tale story, a subject

ವೃತ್ತಿ s *n* State, condition. 2, course, conduct, practice, profession, employment; livelihood, maintenance, inâm land. 3, use, currency. 4, style in composition. 5, comment, exposition, gloss. 6, a hedge. *Cpds.* ಅಕ್ಷರ-, ಅರ್ಥ-, ನಿ-, ಪರಿ-, ಪ್ರ-, ಮನೋ-, *etc*

ವೃತ್ರ s. *n* Darkness 2, N of a demon.

ವೃಥಾ s. *ad.* Unnecessarily, uselessly, fruitlessly. *a.* Vain, useless

ವೃದ್ಧ s *a.* Grown up 2, old, aged, ancient. 3, large. 4 wise. *n* An old man. *f* ವೃದ್ಧೆ. -ತ್ವ. ವೃದ್ಧಾಪ್ಯ. Old

ವೃದ್ಧಿ s *n* Increase, increment, growth 2, an assemblage 3. prosperity, success, advancement. 4, profit, gain 5, money-lending, usury, interest (= ಬಡ್ಡಿ) 6, lengthening of a vowel, augment (*g*) -ಜೀವ. A usurer. -ಜೀವನ Living by usury

ವೃಂದ s *n.* A multitude, flock ವೃಂದಾವನ. A little tower-form erection of clay or stone in which Krishna's worshippers plant and preserve the tulasi

ವೃಶ್ಚಿಕ s. *n* A scorpion. 2, the zodiacal sign *Scorpio* -ಮಾಸ The month when the sun is in *Scorpio*.

ವೃಷ s *n* A rainer 2, a bull, the sign *Taurus* -ಕೇತು Karna's son. -ಧ್ವಜ. Śiva, Ganapati

ವೃಷಭ s *n* A bull 2, the zodiacal sign *Taurus* -ಧ್ವಜ, -ವಾಹನ. Śiva. -ಮಾಸ. The month when the sun is in *Taurus*

ವೃಷಿ s *n* A seat of a religious student or ascetic

ವೃಷ್ಟಿ s. *n* Rain, shower

ವೆಕ್ಕಸ a. k *n.* Roughness, harshness; unkindness, unpleasantness

ವೆಕ್ತ *tb of* ವ್ಯಕ್ತ *q v*

ವೆಗ್ಗಳ a k *n* Abundance, excess -ತನ. ವೆಗ್ಗಳಿಕೆ. Excessiveness, muchness. ವೆಗ್ಗಳಿಸು To become much, to increase, to be actuated by impulse

ವೆಂಕ, ವೆಂಕಟ s. *n.* N. of an idol of Vishnu on the hill at Tirupati -ಗಿರಿ, ವೆಂಕಟಾಚಲ. A fort on that hill ವೆಂಕಪ್ಪ, ವೆಂಕಟೇಶ N. ವೆಂಕಟರಮಣ. Vishnu

ವೆಂಗ್ಯ (*tb of* ವ್ಯಂಗ್ಯ) *n.* Crookedness, perverseness

ವೆಚ್ಚ (*tb. of* ವ್ಯಯ) *n.* Spending, expenditure, outlay, disbursement -ಮಾಡು, ವೆಚ್ಚಿಸು. To spend. -ವಾಗು. To be spent. -ಹತ್ತು, -ಹಿಡಿ Expense to be required

ವೆತ್ಯಾಸ. *tb of* ವ್ಯತ್ಯಾಸ, *q. v*

ವೆವಸಾಯ *tb. of* ವ್ಯವಸಾಯ, *q v.*

ವೆವಹಾರ *tb of* ವ್ಯವಹಾರ, *q v*

ವೆಸನ *tb. of* ವ್ಯಸನ, *q v*

ವೇಗ (=ಬೇಗ, *q v*) s. *n* Impetus. 2, speed, quickness; velocity 3, activity, energy, force -ತನ, -ತ್ವ. Haste, violence -ಶಾಲಿ An active person ವೇಗಾಯಿಲ. A courier, an express, *also* ವೇಗಿ

ವೇಡೆ, ವೇಡೆಯ (*tb. of* ವೇಷ್ಟ) *n* Enclosing, surrounding, an enclosure, fence. ವೇಡಯಿಸು To surround, enclose.

ವೇಣಿ s. *n* A braid of hair. 2, conflux of rivers. 3, a stream, current.

ವೇಣು s *n* A bamboo 2, a flute, fife. -ಗೋಪಾಲ. Krishna playing a flute

ವೇತನ, ವೇತೆ s. *n.* Wages, livelihood

ವೇತಾಲ s. *n* A goblin, demon.

ವೇತ್ತ (*tb. of* ವೇತ್ತೃ) s. *n* A knower, sage -ತೆ. Knowledge

ವೇದ s *n* Knowledge 2, the vêda, the three vêdas· rigvêda, yajurvêda. and sâmavêda -ಪಾರಾಯಣ Reciting the vêda -ಬಾಹ್ಯ Not founded on the vêda. -ಮೂರ್ತಿ An honorific title prefixed to a learned Brâhmana's name -ವಿತ್, -ವಿದ್. Conversant with the vêda -ವ್ಯಾಸ N. of Bâdarâyana -ಶಾಸ್ತ್ರಸಂಪನ್ನ. Versed in the vêdas and śâstras; an epithet of a learned Brâhmana, *also* -ಪಾರಗ. ವೇದಾಂಗ. N of certain works which are auxiliary to or part of the vêdas. ವೇದಾಂತ. An Upanishad, N of a philosophical system. ವೇದಾಂತಶಾಸ್ತ್ರ. The vêdânta philosophy ವೇದಾಭ್ಯಾಸ. Study of the vêda ವೇದೋಕ್ತ. Declared in the vêdas. ವೇದೋಕ್ತ ಆಶೀರ್ವಾದ A mode of blessing in a letter from a Brâhmana. ಸದ್ವೇದ The Bible

ವೇದನ s. *n.* Knowledge, perception 2, pain, torment, agony.

ವೇದಿ 1. s. *n.* A learned Brâhmana, a teacher.

ವೇದಿ 2, ವೇದಿಕೆ s *n.* A raised place prepared for sacrifice, an altar, pulpit

ವೇದಿಸು s. *v. t.* To make known 2, to afflict, trouble

ವೇದೆ = ವೇದನೆ, *q. v*

ವೇದ್ಯ s *a.* Known

ವೇಧ (*tb of* ವೇಧಸ್) *n* An arranger, Brahmâ. 2, boring a hole

ವೇಲೆ = ವೇಳೆ, *q v*

ವೇಶ s. *n.* Entrance, ingress. 2, an abode. 3, dress, disguise -ನ Access ವೇಶ್ಯೆ. A harlot, *also* -ಸ್ತ್ರೀ, ವೇಶ್ಯಾಸ್ತ್ರೀ.

ವೇಷ s *n.* Dress, apparel. 2, disguise, hypocrisy, falsity 3, ornament. -ಗಾರ A masquerader, a hypocrite. -ಧಾರಿ One who is disguised, a hypocrite. -ಸ್ತ್ರೀ. The guise of a woman -ಧರಿಸು, -ಹಾಕು To disguise one's self.

ವೇಷ್ಟನ s. *n* Surrounding, a wrapper, a turban, diadem, a girdle; a cover

ವೇಷ್ಟಿ s. *n* A dôtra. -ತ Surrounded, wrapped up -ಸು To surround, encircle, wrap round.

ವೇಸ *tb. of* ವೇಷ, *q v*

ವೇಳೆ, ವೇಳ್ಯ (*tb of* ವೇಲೆ, *q. v*) *n* Time, season. 2, opportunity, leisure, convenience 3, tide. -ಕಳೆ. To spend time -ಯಾಳು A watchman

ವೈಕಲ್ಯ s. *n* Imperfection, deficiency, defect (*as·* ಅಂಗ-, ಇಂದ್ರಿಯ-, ಬುದ್ಧಿ-); incompetency, agitation, flurry

ವೈಕುಂಠ s. *n* Vishnu or Krishna 2, the heaven of Vishnu -ಯಾತ್ರೆ Death

ವೈಖರಿ s *n.* Articulate utterance, the faculty of speech

ವೈಖಾನಸ s. *n.* A Brâhmana of the third order. a hermit. 2, N. of a sect of Vaishnavas -ಸೂತ್ರ Their scriptures

ವೈಚಕ್ಷಣ್ಯ (*fr* ವಿಚಕ್ಷಣ) s *n* Proficiency, skill.

ವೈಚಿತ್ರ್ಯ (*fr.* ವಿಚಿತ್ರ) s *n* Variety, manifoldness, surprise.

[illegible] s *n* [illegible]

ವೈಡೂರ್ಯ s. *n.* A gem of a dark colour, *Lapis lazuli.*

ವೈಣಿಕ s. *n.* A flutist.

ವೈತರಣಿ s. *n.* The river of hell.

ವೈದಗ್ಧ್ಯ (*fr.* ವಿದಗ್ಧ) s. *n.* Cleverness, skill, wit; cunning.

ವೈದಿಕ (*fr.* ವೇದ) s. *a.* Vedic, scriptural, sacred. *n.* A religious mendicant. -ಜೀವನ, -ವೃತ್ತಿ. Living as a religious mendicant.

ವೈದೀಕ. *tb. of* ವೈದಿಕ, *q. v.* 2, the day of performing a śrâddha.

ವೈದೇಹ, -ಕ s. *n.* A trader, merchant.

ವೈದ್ಯ (*fr.* ವೇದ) s. *a.* Vedic. 2, medical. *n.* A doctor, physician; medical practice. -ತನ. Medical science. -ನಾಥ. Śiva; N. of a poet. -ಶಾಸ್ತ್ರ. The science of medicine. -ಮಾಡು. To practice as a doctor.

ವೈಧವ್ಯ s. *n.* Widowhood.

ವೈಧೇಯ (*fr.* ವಿಧೇಯ) s. *a.* Foolish, [ignorant.

ವೈನತೇಯ s. *n.* Garuḍa.

ವೈಪರೀತ್ಯ (*fr.* ವಿಪರೀತ) s. *n.* Contrariety, adverseness, reverse.

ವೈಭವ, ವೈಭೋಗ s. *n.* Power, greatness, grandeur, glory, wealth.

ವೈಮನಸ್ಯ (*fr.* ವಿಮನಸ್) s. *n.* Great sadness or sorrow. 2, hostility of feeling towards.

ವೈಮಲ್ಯ s. *n.* Spotlessness, purity.

ವೈಮೇಯ (*fr.* ವಿಮಯ) s. *n.* Barter, exchange.

ವೈಯಾಕರಣ s. *a.* Grammatical. ವೈಯಾಕರಣಿ. A grammarian.

ವೈಯಾರ. = ವಯ್ಯಾರ, *q. v.*

ವೈರ (*fr.* ವೀರ) s. *n.* Heroism. 2, enmity, malice, spite. -ತನ, -ತ್ವ. Enmity, hostility. ವೈರಿ. An enemy, foe.

ವೈರಾಗ್ಯ s. *n.* Passionlessness; absence of worldly desires. ವೈರಾಗಿ. An ascetic or devotee.

ವೈಲಕ್ಷಣ್ಯ (*fr.* ವಿಲಕ್ಷಣ) s. *n.* Contrariety, dis[illegible]

str[illegible]

ವೈವರ್ತ (*fr.* ವಿವರ್ತ) s. *n.* Revolution, change of existence.

ವೈವಸ್ವತ (*fr.* ವಿವಸ್ವತ್) s. *n.* Vivasvat's son Yama. 2, the Manu of the present period. 3, the present period.

ವೈವಾಹ, ವೈವಾಹಿಕ (*fr.* ವಿವಾಹ) s. *a.* Relating to marriage.

ವೈಶಂಪಾಯನ s. *n.* N. of a sage; Vyâsa.

ವೈಶಾಖ s. *n.* The second month of the lunar year (April-May).

ವೈಶೇಷಿಕ (*fr.* ವಿಶೇಷ) s. *a.* Particular, characteristic. *n.* N. of a philosophical system founded by Kaṇâda.

ವೈಶ್ಯ s. *n.* A man of the third caste; *f.* ವೈಶ್ಯೆ.

ವೈಶ್ವದೇವ s. *n.* A daily offering to all deities.

ವೈಶ್ವಾನರ s. *n.* Agni, fire.

ವೈಷಮ್ಯ s. *n.* Inequality, oddness. 2, calamity, distress. 3, injustice.

ವೈಷ್ಣವ s. *n.* Relating to Vishṇu. *n.* A follower of Vishṇu.

ವೈಸಿಕ (*tb. of* ವೈಶಿಕ) *n.* Deceit, fraud.

ವೈಹಾಸಿಕ (*fr.* ವಿಹಾಸ) s. *n.* A comic actor, buffoon.

ವೊ & ವೋ k. *For Kannada words with these initials not found below, see s.* ಒ & ಓ.

ವ್ಯಕ್ತ s. *a.* Manifest, apparent, clear, evident; specific. -ಪಡಿಸು. To make clear, show. -ತರ. Very plain. ವ್ಯಕ್ತಿ. Clearness, distinctness, discrimination; indication; individuality; an individual; an entity.

ವ್ಯಗ್ರ s. *a.* Distracted, perplexed, agitated. 2, zealous, occupied. -ತೆ. Perplexity, confusion; zeal.

ವ್ಯಂಗ s. *a.* Limbless; deformed, crippled.

ವ್ಯಂಗ್ಯ s. *a.* Sarcastic, allusive. *n.* Sarcasm; insinuation; crookedness, perversity, impropriety. ವ್ಯಂಗ್ಯಾರ್ಥ. [illegible]. Covert

[illegible]

ವ್ಯಂಜನ s. n. A consonant 2, a mark, sign. 3, seasoning, condiment. -ಸಂಧಿ Euphony of consonants (*g.*).

ವ್ಯತಿ s. *a.* Different -ಕ್ರಮ Transgressing, violating, reverse, opposition, crime, sin, misfortune -ರಿಕ್ತ. Surpassing, separate, different from, without, except; withdrawn -ರೇಕ. Separateness, difference, distinction; exception, contrast, negative inference -ಹಾರ Barter, exchange, reciprocity

ವ್ಯತೀತ s. *a.* Passed away, gone.

ವ್ಯತೀಪಾತ s. *n.* Deviation from right any portent or prodigy indicating calamity *as* a comet, *etc.*, one of the astronomical yôgas

ವ್ಯತ್ಯಾಸ (=ವೆತ್ಯಾಸ) s. *n.* Reverse order variation, difference ವ್ಯತ್ಯಸ್ತ. Reversed; contrary

ವ್ಯಥೆ s. *n.* Disquietude, perturbation, pain, agony, sorrow, distress, anguish, alarm, fear ವ್ಯಥಿತ Distressed, afflicted, troubled. ವ್ಯಥಿಸು. To be afflicted

ವ್ಯಭಿಚಾರ s. *n.* Going astray, following improper courses, profligacy; adultery, anomaly -ಮಾಡು To commit adultery ವ್ಯಭಿಚರಿಸು To go astray; to adulterate ವ್ಯಭಿಚಾರಸ್ಥ, ವ್ಯಭಿಚಾರಿ An adulterer, *f.* ವ್ಯಭಿಚಾರಳು, ವ್ಯಭಿಚಾರಿಣಿ

ವ್ಯಯ s. *n.* Decay; decline 2, spending, expense, outlay, squandering, waste. 3, the twentieth year of the cycle of sixty.

ವ್ಯರ್ಥ s. *a.* Useless, unprofitable, fruitless, vain, unmeaning.

ವ್ಯವಕಲನ s. *n.* Subtraction, deduction.

ವ್ಯವಧಾನ s. *n.* Intervention, separation; a screen, partition, interval, space, covering, leisure

ವ್ಯವಸಾಯ s. *n.* Resolve 2, endeavour, exertion, activity, energy, industry, perseverance. 3, a trade, business. 3, cultivation, agriculture. -ಗಾರ A farmer -ಮಾಡು. To cultivate, farm. ವ್ಯವಸಾಯಿ. A diligent man

ವ್ಯವಸ್ಥೆ s. *n.* Adjusting; arrangement. 2, settlement, decision, decree, rule 3, an affirmation; a state, course, condition -ಮಾಡು. To lay down a law.

ವ್ಯವಹಾರ s. *n.* Conduct, action, process; procedure, affair; work, business, dealing, traffic, commerce, a lawsuit, quarrel, usage, habit, custom, *also* ವ್ಯವಹರಣ. -ಕಾಲ A mundane period. ವ್ಯವಹಾರಿ. A trader; litigant ವ್ಯವಹಾರಿಕ. Customary, usual, common ವ್ಯವಹರಿಸು To be in use; to deal in, to traffic, trade, to litigate, contend ವ್ಯವಹರ್ತೃ. A plaintiff, litigant.

ವ್ಯಷ್ಟಿ s. *n.* Individuality

ವ್ಯಸನ (=ವೆಸನ) s. *n.* Violation; ill-luck 2, a vice, vicious habit. 3, grief, sorrow. -ಕರ Grievous -ಪಡು. To grieve ವ್ಯಸನಿ Addicted to a vice, of vicious habits, a sorrowful person.

ವ್ಯಸ್ತ s. *a* Separated, divided, dispersed 2, different, various 3, troubled, confused, deranged. -ಪದ. A simple word (*g.*).

ವ್ಯಾಕರಣ s. *n.* Grammar, grammatical analysis. -ಕಾರ, -ಜ್ಞ A grammarian.

ವ್ಯಾಕುಲ s. *a* Confounded, perplexed; troubled. *n.* Anxious thought, grief. -ತೆ. Perplexity; grief. ವ್ಯಾಕುಲಿತ. Perplexed; grieved. ವ್ಯಾಕುಲಿಸು. To be perplexed, to grieve

ವ್ಯಾಕೃತಿ s. *n.* Analysing 2, grammar. 3, change of form. 4, a way, form.

ವ್ಯಾಖ್ಯಾನ (= ವಕ್ಕಣೆ) s. *n* Explanation, exposition; comment, interpretation; description, *also* ವ್ಯಾಖ್ಯೆ ವ್ಯಾಖ್ಯಾನಿ A commentator, annotator, *as* ಬೈಬಲ್ ವ್ಯಾಖ್ಯಾನಿ, ಶಾಸ್ತ್ರ-

ವ್ಯಾಘಾತ s. *n* Contradiction; inconsistency

ವ್ಯಾಘ್ರ s. *n.* A tiger.

ವ್ಯಾಜ s n Deceit, fraud, craft, disguise, pretence -ನಿಂದೆ Disguised reproach.

ವ್ಯಾಜ್ಯ s n A contest, quarrel, dispute, a law-suit -ಗಾರ A litigant, a party in a suit (*law*). -ತೀರಿಸು To settle a dispute -ಮಾಡು, -ಹಾಡು. To quarrel; to litigate, sue. -ದ ಹೇತು The cause of action (*law*).

ವ್ಯಾಧ s. n. A hunter, fowler

ವ್ಯಾಧಿ s. n Sickness, disease -ತ Sick, [ill.

ವ್ಯಾನ s n. One of the vital airs.

ವ್ಯಾಪಕ s. a. Pervading, diffusive, widely spreading n An intimate associate. ಸರ್ವ-. All-pervading ವ್ಯಾಪನ. Pervading, penetrating ವ್ಯಾಪಿಸು. To reach through, pervade, cover, fill.

ವ್ಯಾಪಾರ s. n. Occupation, business trade profession. 2, exertion practice 3, work, affair, operation, transaction. 4, trade, traffic -ಸಾಪಾರ. *reit* -ನಡಸು, -ಮಾಡು. To do a work; to trade -ಗಾರ, -ಸ್ಥ, ವ್ಯಾಪಾರಿ A tradesman, dealer, merchant ಮನೋ-. Mental operation. ಸದ್-. An excellent practice

ವ್ಯಾಪ್ತಿ s n Pervasion, permeation 2, universality. 3, obtaining, acquiring 4, occupation, work ವ್ಯಾಪ್ತ Pervaded, pervading, filled up, full, overspread

ವ್ಯಾಮ s n. A fathom 2, sickliness.

ವ್ಯಾಮೋಹ s. n Bewilderment. 2, inordinate affection, carnal desire.

ವ್ಯಾಯಾಮ s n Athletic exercise, exercise of the body in general.

ವ್ಯಾಲ s. n A snake 2, a beast of prey. 3, a villain, rogue -ಗ್ರಾಹಿ A snake-catcher -ಶಾಯಿ Vishnu

ವ್ಯಾವಹಾರಿಕ (*fr.* ವ್ಯವಹಾರ) s. a Practical, active, judicial, legal, customary. n Use.

ವ್ಯಾವೃತ್ತಿ s n Separation from. 2, exception removal 3 ... 4, re...

ವ್ಯಾಸ s n Distribution severality. detail, diffusion, extension, the diameter of a circle 2, Vyâsa, the original arranger of the vêdas. -ಪೀಠ. A kind of stool for placing a reading book

ವ್ಯಾಸಂಗ s n. Assiduous application to

ವ್ಯಾಹಾರ s n Utterance, speech, a word; a humorous speech.

ವ್ಯುತ್ಕ್ರಮ s. n Transgression, disorder, confusion

ವ್ಯುತ್ಪತ್ತಿ s n Production, origin, derivation, etymology 2, scholarship, proficiency, learning. ಕಾವ್ಯ-. Proficiency in poetry. ಶಾಸ್ತ್ರ-. Proficiency in śâstras

ವ್ಯುತ್ಪನ್ನ s a Produced, derived, taught, quite proficient in, learned

ವ್ಯುತ್ಪಾದನ s. n Tracing (words) back to a root. ವ್ಯುತ್ಪಾದಿಸು To derive from a root

ವ್ಯೂಹ s n A mass, flock; an army; military array. -ಕಟ್ಟು, -ಮಾಡು To array

ವ್ಯೋಕಾರ s n A blacksmith 2, a coppersmith

ವ್ಯೋಮ s. n The sky, ether, atmosphere. -ಕೇಶ Śiva. -ಗಂಗೆ, The heavenly Ganges.

ವ್ರಜ s n A road 2, a flock, herd. 3, a cowpen, cattle-shed

ವ್ರಣ s. n A wound sore. boil, bruise.

ವ್ರತ s n Rite, observance 2, any religious act, a vow -ಭಂಗ The breach of a vow. -ಭ್ರಷ್ಟ Deviated from one's vow. -ಸ್ಥ One who keeps a vow. -ಹೀನ. One who neglects his vow ವ್ರತಿ An ascetic ಪತಿವ್ರತೆ A chaste woman. [outlay

ವ್ರಯ (*tb of* ವ್ಯಯ) n Expenditure,

ವ್ರಾತ್ಯ s n One of the three first classes who has lost caste through nonobservance of the samskaras, an ... d man.

ಶ

ಶ. The forty-ninth letter of the alphabet. *It does not occur in pure Kannada.*

ಶಂಸನ s. n. Saying, reciting, praising ಶಂಸಿತ Said, praised ಶಂಸೆ. Speech praise, *cf.* ಪ್ರ-

ಶಕ s n. An era, epoch. -ವರುಷ, ಶಕಾಬ್ದ A year of the śaka year, *esp* of ಶಾಲಿವಾಹನ.

ಶಕಟ (= ಚಕ್ಕಡಿ) s n A cart, waggon

ಶಕಾರ s. n. The letter ಶ

ಶಕುನ s. n A bird. 2, an omen, prognostic ಅಪ-, ಕೆಟ್ಟ- ದುಃ- A bad omen ಶುಭ- A good omen. -ನೋಡು To consult an omen ಶಕುನಿ A bird; a kite, N of the maternal uncle of the Kauravas

ಶಕುಂತಲೆ s. n. N of the daughter of an Apsaras, the heroine of a celebrated drama

ಶಕ್ತಿ s. n Strength, power, ability, capacity, faculty, regal power, the energy of a deity personified as his wife ಬಿಂಬ-, ವಿಗ್ರಹ-. The inherent power of an idol. -ಉಪದ್ರ, -ಕಾಟ, -ಚೇಷ್ಟೆ. A plague occasioned by a village goddess. -ಪೂಜೆ Śakti-worship. *Cpds.*: ಔಷಧ-, ಜ್ಞಾನ-, ಬುದ್ಧಿ-, ವಿಶ್ವಾಸ- *etc* -ಮಾನ, -ವಂತ. Strong, mighty, able. -ಹೀನ Powerless, impotent ಶಕ್ತ. Strong, mighty, able, capable, clever, intent.

ಶಕ್ಯ s. a Able, possible, practicable, ಶಕ್ಯಾರ್ಥ. Admissible meaning, meaning conveyed by a word

ಶಕ್ರ s a Powerful, strong. n Indra 2, Vishnu -ಚಾಪ, -ಧನುಸ್, -ಶರಾಸನ. The rainbow.

ಶಂಕರ s a Causing happiness n Śiva, a N. ಶಂಕರಾಚಾರ್ಯ. N of a celebrated scholar

ಶಂಕು s n A pin, peg, a stake, post, pillar. 2, a dart. 3, the trunk of a lopped tree 4, the pin of a dial. 5, a surveyor's compass. -ಯಂತ್ರ A sun-dial.

ಶಂಕೆ s. n. Doubt, uncertainty, scruple, suspicion, misgiving, fear, alarm 2, presumption. ಗಾಳಿ-, ದೆವ್ವ-, ಭೀತಿ-, ಭೂತ-, ವಾಯು- An evil spirit ಅಲ್ಪ-, ಜಲ-, ಮೂತ್ರ-. Making water ಶಂಕಿಸು To doubt, hesitate; to fear; to suspect. ಶಂಕಿತ Doubted, doubtful, alarmed; scrupulous, suspicious

ಶಂಖ s. n A shell, conch-shell 2, the cheek-bone. 3, one of Kubêra's treasures -ಪಾಲ. N. of a serpent. -ಪಾಷಾಣ. White oxide of arsenic -ಪುಷ್ಪಬಳ್ಳಿ A climbing herb with blue or white flowers, *Clitoria ternatea* -ಮುದ್ರೆ The seal of a conch. -ವಾದ್ಯ. A conch-shell blowing as a horn

ಶಚಿ s n N of Indra's wife; *also* -ದೇವಿ -ಪತಿ, -ಪಾಲ Indra

ಶಠ s. a Wicked bad, dishonest n A rogue, knave, a fool, roguery. -ತ್ವ Wickedness, roguery; foolishness.

ಶತ s. n. A hundred. -ಕೋಟಿ. A hundred crores -ಘ್ನಿ. A cannon -ತಮ. The hundredth -ದ್ರು The river Sutlej -ದ್ರೋಹಿ. One who is guilty of a hundred acts of treason -ಧಾರ A thunder-bolt -ಪದಿ. A centipede. -ತಾರೆ, -ಭಿಷಜ್, -ಭಿಷೆ N. of a nakshatra. -ಮಾನ A century, a hundred-fold. -ಮೂಲಿಕೆ, ಶತಾವರಿ. The shrub *Asparagus racemosus*

ಶತ್ರು s n An enemy, foe, adversary. -ಘ್ನ N of Râma's youngest brother. -ತನ, -ತ್ವ, -ಭಾವ Enmity.

ಶನಿ s n. The planet Saturn. 2, a wicked person [illegible]

ಶ್ಚರ The planet Saturn -ವಾರ. Saturday

ಶಪಥ s *n* An imprecation, curse 2, an oath, ordeal, swearing

ಶಪನ s *n* Cursing 2, an oath ಶಪಿಸು To curse to abuse

ಶಬ (*tb of* ಶವ, *q v*) *n*. A corpse. 2, clothes. 3, all sorts of beasts.

ಶಬಗಸ್ತು h. *n*. Nocturnal procession

ಶಬರ s *n* N. of a wild mountaineer tribe, *f* ಶಬರಿ 2, a sort of deer. 3, N of a demon -ಶಂಕರ Śiva

ಶಬ್ದ s. *n*. Sound, noise 2, a word -ಖಂಡ A chapter on words -ಖಂಡನ Verbal criticism -ಚೋರ A plagiarist. -ಜ್ಞ. A philologist grammarian -ಮಂಜರಿ N of a Kannada vocabulary. -ಮಣಿದರ್ಪಣ. N. of a Kannada grammar -ಶಾಸ್ತ್ರ A grammar -ಸಂಗ್ರಹ A vocabulary ಶಬ್ದಾನುಶಾಸನ N of a Kannada grammar in Sanskrit ಶಬ್ದಾರ್ಥ The meaning of a word. ಶಬ್ದಾಲಂಕಾರ Rhetorical use of words. ಶಬ್ದಾವಯವ The component parts of a term. ನಿಶ್ಶಬ್ದ Noiseless, still

ಶಮ s. *n* Quiet, tranquillity, rest, calm 2, quietude, stillness, absence of passion -ದಮ Quietism and self-command -ಥ. Quiet, tranquillity. -ನ. Appeasing, tranquilizing, soothing, tranquillity; cessation, end *Cpds* ತಾಪ-, ದುಃಖ-, ದಾಹ-, ರೋಗ-, *etc* ಶಮಿತ. Appeased, allayed, calmed. ಶಮಿಸು. To be appeased, alloyed, calmed, to cease, to appease, pacify, soothe, *etc*

ಶಮಿ s *n*. A legume, pod 2, the tree *Mimosa suma* 3, calm, tranquil

ಶಂಬರ s. *n* N of a demon and of a daitya 2, water. 2, a cloud.

ಶಂಬಲ (= ಸಂಬಳ) s. *n*. Provisions for a journey

ಶಂಭು s *a* Causing happiness *n* A happy prosperous man 2, Brahmâ 3, ...

ಶಯನ s. *n* Lying down, reposing, sleeping. 2 sleep 3, a couch, bed. -ಗೃಹ, -ಸ್ಥಾನ, ಶಯ್ಯಾಗೃಹ A dormitory. ಶಯನಿಸು To lie down, repose, sleep. ಶಯಾಳು. Sleepy, slothful. ಶಯ್ಯೆ A couch, bed, sleeping, sleep.

ಶರ s *n* A sort of reed or grass *Saccharum sara* 2, an arrow. 3, cream 4, water, a lake 5, sound, noise.

ಶರಣ s. *n* A protector, preserver 2, protection, help, refuge. 3 a refuge, asylum. 4, a house. 5, a devotee. ಶರಣಾಗತ Come for protection, a refugee ಶರಣಾಗತಿ. Coming for protection. ಶರಣಾರ್ಥಿ A person seeking protection, a form of salutation ಶರಣು ಹೇಳು To take refuge ಶರಣು ಹೋಗು To seek refuge. ಶರಣ್ಯ. Dependent, poor, helpless, protection, defence, a protector.

ಶರತ್ಕಾಲ, ಶರದ್, ಶರದೃತು, ಶರದೆ s. *n* [Autumn.

ಶರಧಿ s *n* The ocean

ಶರಭ s. *n* A fabulous animal

ಶರಾರತಿ h *n* Wickedness, outrage. ಶರಾರು. Hurtful, mischievous

ಶರೀರ s *n*. The body. -ತ್ಯಾಗ. Suicide -ದಂಡನೆ Corporal punishment. -ಧರ್ಮ. The functions of the body -ಪ್ರಕೃತಿ, -ಗುಣ Constitution of the body -ಸಂಬಂಧ Affinity ಶರೀರಾಂತ, ಶರೀರಾವಸಾನ. Death ಪುಣ್ಯ-. A blessed body ಸ್ಥೂಲ-. The gross material body ಸೂಕ್ಷ್ಮ- The atomic body. ಪಿತ್ತ- A bilious habit ಸ್ವರ್ಗೀಯ- A glorified body. -ಸಂಬಂಧಿ A relative -ದಂಡಿಸಿ ತಿನ್ನು. To live by hard labour. ಶರೀರಿ. Embodied, a sentient being

ಶರೆ = ಸೆರೆ, *q v*.

ಶರ್ಕರೆ s. *n* A potsherd. 2, a pebble, gravel 3, candied sugar

ಶರ್ಮ s *n* Happiness, delight 2, refuge 3, an ending of a Brâhmana's name.

ಶರ್ವರಿ s *n* Night. -ಪತಿ The moon.

... also ಶಲ.

ಲಭ s. n. A grasshopper, a locust.

ಲಾಕೆ s n A dart, spike shaft, a thin bar

ಲ್ಯ 1. s. n A stake, pin, splinter 2, a dart, javelin, a pike, an arrow 3, N. of the maternal uncle of Pândavas

ಲ್ಯ 2, ಶಲ್ಲೆ (tb of ಚೇಲ) n Thin muslin cloth, a shawl

ವ s. n A corpse. -ಸಂಸ್ಕಾರ Cremation or interment of a corpse.

ಶ, -ಕ s. n A hare, rabbit. -ಧರ, ಶಶಾಂಕ The moon

ಶಿ s n The moon -ಕಲೆ, -ಖಂಡ, -ರೇಖೆ, -ಲೇಖೆ The digit of the moon -ಕಾಂತ The moon-stone.

ಸ್ತ s a Said 2, praised. 3, best, happy 4, struck.

ಸ್ತ್ರ s n. A weapon, a sword, knife 2, steel -ಜೀವಿ, -ಧಾರಿ, ಶಸ್ತ್ರಾಜೀವಿ A soldier. -ಯುದ್ಧ A sword-fight -ವಿದ್ಯೆ The science of arms -ವೈದ್ಯ A surgeon, surgery ಶಸ್ತ್ರಾಭ್ಯಾಸ Military exercise ಶಸ್ತ್ರಾಸ್ತ್ರ Arms and missile weapons.

ಹಬಾಸು (=ಶಾಬಾಸು) h int Bravo! well done! [town

ಹರ, ಶಹರು h. n. A city or large town

ಹಾಣೆ h. a. Sagacious, clever

ಹಾಮೃಗ h.-s. n. An ostrich.

ಾಕ s n Any vegetable, vegetable food 2 power strength

ಾಕಿನಿ s. n. A female demon attendant on Durgâ

ಾಕ್ತ, ಶಾಕ್ತೇಯ s. a Relating to Sakti n A worshipper of Sakti

ಾಕ್ಯ s. n Buddha, also -ಮುನಿ, -ಸಿಂಹ.

ಾಖಾ, ಶಾಖೆ s n. The branch of a tree, etc, branch in general 2, an arm 3, a section of a book. 4, a sect, party ಶಾಖಾಚರ, ಶಾಖಾಮೃಗ A monkey. -ನಗರ A suburb

ಶಾಟಿ, ಶಾಟೆ f. n Cloth. garment, a petticoat ಸ್ನಾನ- A bathing cloth.

ಶಾಠ್ಯ s. n Villainy dishonesty, deceit

ಶಾಣ 1. f. n. A cl - -

ಶಾಣ 2 s. n. Sharpening, whetting. 2, a whetstone. [garment.

ಶಾಣ 3 s a Hempen ಶಾಣಿ A hempen garment.

ಶಾತ s. a Whetted, sharp 2, thin, weak n Happiness -ಕುಂಭ. Gold

ಶಾದಿ h. n Marriage.

ಶಾನಭಾಗ, ಶಾನಭೋಗ, ಶಾನಭೋಗ f. n. A village clerk. -ತನ The business of a village clerk

ಶಾನೆ (tb. of ಸೇನೆ) a Much, many.

ಶಾಂತ s. a. Appeased, calmed, hushed, tranquil, calm, satisfied, extinguished, mild, gentle, meek. -ಮನುಷ್ಯ. A meek man -ತನ -ತೆ, -ತ್ವ. Calmness, meekness. -ಪಡಿಸು To pacify, etc.

ಶಾಂತನವ s n Bhîshma, son of Santanu

ಶಾಂತಿ s. n Quietness. calmness, peace; serenity, mildness, quietism, stoicism; rest, repose; appeasing, soothing, any expiatory or propitiatory rite for averting evil ತಾಪ-. Allaying of distress ದಾಹ-. Quenching thirst. ರೋಗ-. The curing of a disease. -ಕಾಯಿ. The nut of *Termalia belerica* -ಪಡಿಸು. To appease, etc -ಪರ್ವ N. of the 12th book of the Mahâbhârata

ಶಾಪ s. n. Curse, cursing. 2, abuse 3, an oath. -ಕೊಡು, ಶಾಪಿಸು (= ಶಪಿಸು) To curse -ಗ್ರಸ್ತ Seized by a curse. -ರಹಿತ Void of curse -ಮುಕ್ತಿ, -ಮೋಕ್ಷ, -ವಿಮುಕ್ತಿ. -ವಿಮೋಚನೆ. Deliverance from a curse.

ಶಾಬಾಸು = ಶಹಬಾಸು, q v

ಶಾಬ್ದ s. a Sounding, verbal, oral ಶಾಬ್ದಿಕ Wordy, a philologist grammarian

ಶಾಮ tb of ಶ್ಯಾಮ, q. v.

ಶಾಮಕ s a Appeasing, curing

ಶಾಮಿಲು h a. Including, extending to ಶಾಮಿಲಾತು A tract of land attached to an estate

ಶಾಯಿ h n. Ink. -ದಾನಿ, -ದವತಿ, -ಬುರುಡೆ An inkstand

ಶಾಯಿದಿ h n A witness at law, wit- [illegible]

ಶಾರದ s a Autumnal 2, fresh, new. 3, able, clever ಶಾರದಾ, ಶಾರದೆ. Sarasvati, intelligence

ಶಾರೀರ. ಶಾರೀರಕ s. a Corporeal, bodily, embodied. ಶಾರೀರಾಗ್ನಿ The gastric-juice.

ಶಾಂರ್ಗ s. n A bow -ಧನ್ವ, -ಧರ. Vishnu

ಶಾರ್ದೂಲ s n A tiger

ಶಾರ್ವರಿ s n. The thirty-fourth year of the cycle of sixty

ಶಾಲಗ್ರಾಮ s n A black stone worshipped as sacred to Vishnu

ಶಾಲಿ s. a Endowed with, possessing, having, as ಗುಣ-, ಜಯ-, ಬುದ್ಧಿ-, ಧೈರ್ಯ-, ಯುದ್ಧ-, etc

ಶಾಲಿವಾಹನ s n N. of an ancient king and institutor of the era so called -ಶಕ. The era of Śālivāhana

ಶಾಲು, ಶಾಲುವೆ h n. A woollen shawl -ಜೋಡು, -ಜೋಡಿ. A pair of shawls ಕಾಶ್ಮೀರ-. Cashmere shawl ಕಂಬಳೀ- = ಶಾಲು.

ಶಾಲೆ s n A hall, a room, a house. 2, a school. ಅಶ್ವ- A horse-stable ಆಯುಧ-. An arsenal armoury ಪಾಕ-. A kitchen ಪಾಠ- A school ವಿದ್ಯಾ- A college, etc

ಶಾಲ್ಮಲಿ s. n The silk-cotton tree.

ಶಾವಿಗೆ = ಸಾವಿಗೆ, q v

ಶಾಶ್ವತ s. a. Eternal, perpetual permanent. -ಕೆಲಸ A lasting work -ಚೇರೀಜು. A permanent assessment.

ಶಾಸನ s. n Ruling, government, training, punishing 2, discipline 3, an order, a precept 4, a charter edict a deed. -ಮಾಡು To punish

ಶಾಸ್ತ್ರ s n. An order, rule. 2. a religious or scientific treatise, scripture, institutes of a religion. 3, a book -ಜ್ಞ A scientist Cpds ಕ್ಷೇತ್ರ-, ಗಣಿತ-, ಧರ್ಮ-, ವೇದಾಂತ-, -ಪದ್ಧತಿ, -ಪಾರ, -ವಿಧಿ, -ಸಿದ್ಧಿ, -ಸಿದ್ಧಾಂತ, etc -ವ್ಯುತ್ಪತ್ತಿ. Perfect conversancy with the śāstras ನೀತಿ- The sience of ethicks ಶಿಲ್ಪ- A worl man; a teacher of the Śāstras. ಶಾಸ್ತ್ರೋಕ್ತ. Declared by the Śāstras

ಶಿಂಶಪೆ, ಶಿಂಶುಪೆ f. n The tree Dalbergia sisu.

ಶಿಕಸ್ತು h. a Folding, as of paper.

ಶಿಕಾರಿ h n. Hunting, the chase -ಮಾಡು, -ಹೋಗು To hunt. -ಗಾರ, -ಯವ. A hunter.

ಶಿಕ್ಕ. = ಸಿಕ್ಕ, q. v

ಶಿಕ್ಷಕ s n. A teacher instructor

ಶಿಕ್ಷಣ s. n. Learning, knowledge 2, training

ಶಿಕ್ಷೆ, ಶಿಕ್ಷಾ s. n Study. 2 teaching, instruction 3, punishment -ಅನು ಭೋಗಿಸು, -ತಾಳು, -ತಿನ್ನು. To suffer punishment -ಕೊಡು, -ಮಾಡು To punish -ರಕ್ಷೆ. Chastising and protecting ಶಿಕ್ಷಿಸು. To teach; to check discipline, to chastise punish

ಶಿಖಂಡಿ s n. A peacock. 2 N. of a son of Drupada born as a female. 3, an hermaphrodite

ಶಿಖರ s n A point, top, summit, the peak of a mountain ಶಿಖರಿ. Pointed; a mountain, a cover; a forest

ಶಿಖಿ s. a. Crested tufted n A peacock 2, a comet. 3, a crest helmet. 4, a lock of hair. -ಪಿಂಛ A peacock's feather

ಶಿಖೆ, ಶಿಖಾ s. n. A point, peak. top. 2, a crest, tuft, plume, a lock of hair on the head, the acme. 3, a flame, a ray of light ಶಿಖಾಮಣಿ. A crest-gem, pre-eminent (at the end of Cpds.).

ಶಿತಾರು h. n A cithara; a stringed instrument.

ಶಿಥಿಲ s a Loose, lax, not rigid, out of repair. 2, inert, feeble n. Looseness, laxity -ತೆ, -ತ್ವ Laxity, languor.

ಶಿಪಾರಸು h n. Recommendation, patronage.

ಶಿಪಿ s. n. A ray of light -ವಿಷ Leprosy

ಬೆ f n A legume, pod

', ಶಿರಸ್ (= ಶಿರಸ್ಸು) s n The head, skull ಶಿರದಲಿ ಧರಿಸು, ಶಿರಸಾವಹಿಸು To accept with pleasure, to honour highly ಶಿರಶ್ಛೇದ. Decapitation. ಶಿರಸ್ತ್ರ, ಶಿರಸ್ತ್ರಾಣ. A helmet -ಸ್ನಾನ A bath of the whole body. ಶಿರೋಭ್ರಮಣ. Vertigo giddiness ಶಿರೋಮಣಿ A crest-jewel, a distinguished person. ಶಿರೋರೋಗ, ಶಿರೋಬೇದನೆ, ಶಿರೋವ್ಯಥೆ, ಶಿರೋವ್ಯಾಧಿ. Headache

ಸ್ತೆದಾರ h. n. The native head clerk in a collector's office or in a court

ಸ್ಸು (lb of ಶಿರಸ್).= ಶಿರ, q v

ಬಕು h n Balance in hand -ಬಾಕಿ. Balance left.

, ಶಿಲಾ s n. A stone, a rock ಶಿಲಾಜತು, ಶಿಲಾಜತ್, ಶಿಲಾಧಾತು Bitumen; red chalk, etc. ಶಿಲಾವರ್ಷ, ಶಿಲಾವೃಷ್ಟಿ Hail ಶಿಲಾಶಾಸನ. An edict or inscription on a stone.

ಬೆ (=ಸಿಲುಬೆ, q v.) f. n. A cross 2, sorrow, grief -ಕರ್ತ, -ಸ್ವಾಮಿ Jesus Christ ಶಿಲುಬಿಸು To crucify, also ಶಿಲುಬೆಗೆ ಹಾಕು, ಶಿಲುಬೆಯಲ್ಲಿ ಜಡಿ.

ಲ್ಪ s. n An art, any manual or mechanical art -ಕೆಲಸ Artisanship -ಕ, -ಗಾರ An artisan, mechanic -ವಿದ್ಯೆ. Handicraft, art -ಶಾಲೆ A workshop -ಶಾಸ್ತ್ರ. Mechanics ಶಿಲ್ಪಿ An artificer, artist, artisan, also ಶಿಲ್ಪಿಕ, ಶಿಲ್ಪಿಗ

ವ s a. Auspicious, happy. n. Bliss, happiness 2, Śiva. 3, virtue, etc. -ಕ A post, peg. -ಕಾರಿ One who causes happiness. -ಗಣ Śiva's followers -ದಾನ. Buttermilk -ಗಂಗೆ N. of a village in Mysore. -ಪುರ Kailâsa. -ಪ್ರಾಣಿ, -ಭಕ್ತ A Lingavanta. -ರಕ್ತಬಳ್ಳಿ, -ಶಕ್ತಿಬಳ್ಳಿ A scandent plant, *Gloriosa superba* -ರಾತ್ರಿ, -ರಾತ್ರೆ. A festival held in honour of Śiva -ಶರಣ A Jangama; a Lingavanta *Other cpds* -ಮೂರ್ತಿ, -ಯೋಗ, -ಲಿಂಗ, -ಲೀಲೆ, -ಲೋಕ, -ಸೂತ್ರ. ಶಿವಾಲಯ A temple dedicated

ಶಿವಾಯಿ h. ad Besides; except, extra.

ಶಿವಿಕೆ (= ಶಿಬಿಕೆ) f n. A palanquin, litter.

ಶಿಶಿರ s a Cool, cold. n Coolness, cold 2, the cold season, also -ಋತು. -ಕರ The moon. ಶಿಶಿರೋಪಚಾರ Kind treatment with cooling articles

ಶಿಶು s n A child, infant, the young of any animal -ತ್ವ. Infancy, childhood

ಶಿಷ್ಟ s a Disciplined, trained; obedient, learned; eminent, noble. 2, remaining n A learned man 2, remainder. -ಪಾಲಕ A guardian of the virtuous ಶಿಷ್ಟಾಚಾರ. The custom of good people.

ಶಿಷ್ಯ s n. A pupil, disciple -ತನ, -ತ್ವ Pupilage ಕ್ರಿಸ್ತನ- A disciple of Christ

ಶಿಸ್ತು h n Aim 2, assessment, tax 3, decoration. -ಗಾರ A fop, a lewd man, f -ಗಾತಿ -ಗಾರಿಕೆ Lewdness

ಶೀ = ಸೀ, q. v

ಶೀಘ್ರ s a Quick, speedy. ಶೀಘ್ರಂ. Quickly, swiftly. -ಗಾಮಿ A camel.

ಶೀತ s a Cold, chilly 2, idle, lazy. 3, damp. n Cold, dampness -ಕರ, -ರಶ್ಮಿ The moon -ಜ್ವರ Ague -ಶಿವ A kind of fennel

ಶೀತಲ s a Cold, chilly, cool.

ಶೀತಲೆ s n Small-pox

ಶೀಮೆ = ಸೀಮೆ, q v

ಶೀರೆ. = ಸೀರೆ, q v

ಶೀರ್ಣ s a Withered; rotten, slender, shattered, injured.

ಶೀರ್ಷ (= ಶಿರಸ್, q v) s. n The head -ಕ A helmet, turban

ಶೀಲ s n Disposition, character, habit. 2, practice, conduct 3, good disposition or character good nature, etc., virtue, also -ಸ್ವಭಾವ 4, form, beauty *At the end of cpds* possessed of, disposed to, as ಕಾರ್ಯ-, ಧರ್ಮ-, ಗುಣ-, ವಿವೇಕ-, ಬುದ್ಧಿ-, etc -ವಂತ, ಸು- A man of good conduct -ವೃದ್ಧ Very

[illegible]

ಶೀಳು. = ಸೀಳು, q. v.

ಶುಕ s. n. A parrot. 2, a mango tree. 3, a son of Vyâsa. 4, an ascetic. -ಪಂಜರ. A parrot's cage. -ವಾಣಿ. The prate of a parrot.

ಶುಕ್ತ s. a. Acid; harsh. n. Sour gruel.

ಶುಕ್ತಿ s. n. An oyster-shell. -ಜ. A pearl.

ಶುಕ್ರ s. a. Bright; white. n. The planet Venus. -ವಾರ. Friday. ಶುಕ್ರಾಚಾರ್ಯ. The preceptor of the Asuras.

ಶುಕ್ಲ (= ಶುಕ್ರ) s. a. Bright; white. n. The light half of a solar month. 2, the third year in the cycle of sixty. -ತ್ವ. Whiteness. -ಪಕ್ಷ. = ಶುಕ್ಲ n. No. 1. -ಪಾಡ್ಯ. The first day of -ಪಕ್ಷ.

ಶುಚಿ s. a. Clean, pure. 2, virtuous, innocent; honest, true; accurate. n. Purity, virtue, etc. -ಕರ. Purifying. -ತನ, -ತ್ವ. Cleanness, purity.

ಶುಂಠ f. n. A blockhead, dolt.

ಶುಂಠಿ s. n. Dry ginger.

ಶುಂಡ, ಶುಂಡೆ (= ಸುಂಡಿಲು) s. n. An elephant's trunk, proboscis.

ಶುದ್ಧ s. a. Purified, clean, pure. 2, stainless, true, fair, honest, holy. 3, correct, right. 4, simple, mere, only, alone. ad. Nothing but; wholly. n. Purity, etc. -ಕಳ್ಳ. A downright thief. -ಗೊಳಿಸು, ಶುದ್ಧೀಕರಿಸು. To purify. -ಪಡುವಲು. Due west. -ಮಾಡು. To make clean. -ಲೋಭಿ. A complete miser. -ಸುಳ್ಳು. A pure lie. -ತೆ, -ತ್ವ. Purity, etc. -ಪತ್ರಿಕೆ.=ಶುದ್ಧಿಪತ್ರ. -ಪ್ರತಿ. A fair copy. -ಭಕ್ತಿ. True devotion. -ಮನಸ್ಸು. A pure mind. ಶುದ್ಧಾಚಾರ. Virtuous conduct. ಶುದ್ಧಾಶುದ್ಧ. Pure and impure.

ಶುದ್ಧಿ s. n. Purity, cleanness, holiness. 2, purification, cleansing. 3, goodness; clearance; correction; accuracy; truth. -ಪತ್ರ. An errata list.

ಶುಭ s. a. Bright. 2, auspicious, lucky, right, virtuous. n. Good luck; welfa[illegible]il. joy. [illegible] auspicious ceremony. -ಕೃತ್. The thirty-sixth year in the cycle of sixty. -ನಕ್ಷತ್ರ. A favourable star. ಶುಭಮಸ್ತು. May it be auspicious. -ವಾರ್ತೆ. Good news, gospel. -ಶಕುನ. A good omen. ಶುಭಾಚಾರ. Good conduct.

ಶುಭ್ರ s. a. Shining, bright. 2, white. -ವಸ್ತ್ರ. A white cloth.

ಶುಲ್ಕ (= ಸುಂಕ) s. n. Toll, duty. 2, a dower. 3, gain. ಕನ್ಯಾ-. The price given for a wife. ಗುರು-. The teacher's fee.

ಶುಶ್ರೂಷಣೆ, ಶುಶ್ರೂಷೆ s. n. Service; reverence.

ಶುಷ್ಕ s. a. Dried, dry; shriveled; useless; fruitless, vain. -ವಾದ. Useless talk. ಶುಷ್ಕೋಪಚಾರ. Vain compliments.

ಶೂಕ s. n. The awn of barley. -ಧಾನ್ಯ. Bearded grain.

ಶೂಕರ. = ಸೂಕರ, q. v.

ಶೂದ್ರ s. n. A man of the fourth caste; f. ಶೂದ್ರಳು, ಶೂದ್ರಿ, ಶೂದ್ರೆ. -ತ್ವ. The state or condition of a śûdra.

ಶೂನ್ಯ (= ಸೊನ್ನೆ) s. a. Empty, void, hollow; vacant. 2, utterly destitute, without. 3, ruined. 4, bare. n. A void, blank; a cypher; a desert. 2, a zero. 3, the anusvára. 4, vacuity. 5, sorcery. -ಮಾಡು. To injure by sorcery. -ಕೀಳು, -ತೆಗೆ. To remove the effects of sorcery. -ಗಾರ. A sorcerer; f. -ಗಾತಿ. -ವಾದಿ. An atheist; a Buddhist. -ದ ಬೊಂಬೆ. An effigy.

ಶೂರ s. n. A hero, warrior, mighty man. -ತನ, -ತೆ, -ತ್ವ. Heroism, etc.

ಶೂರಣ (= ಸೂರಣ) s. n. An esculent root, *Amorphophallus campanulatus*, Telinga potato.

ಶೂರ್ಪ s. n. A van; a sifting fan. -ಕರಣ. Winnowing, sifting. -ಕರ್ಣ. An elephant; Gaṇêśa. -ಣಖಿ, -ಣಖೆ. N. of the sister of Râvaṇa; any monstrous [illegible]

ೂಲ s n A spear, pike, lance; the trident of Śiva, *also* ತ್ರಿ-. 2, any acute pain, colic

ೂಲೆ (= ಶೂಲ No. 2) s n. A sharp pain, colic, headache ಹೊಟ್ಟೆ-. The colic. ಪಕ್ಕ-, ಪಾರ್ಶ್ವ-. Pain in the sides, pleurisy. ಹೃದಯ-, ಎದೆ-. An aching heart.

ೃಂಖಲ s n A chain, fetter. 2, a girdle, zone

ೃಂಗ s n A horn, a mountain peak, height, supremacy. 2, N. of a ṛishi ಶೃಂಗಿ. Horned; peaked, a mountain, a deer

ೃಂಗಾರ s n Decoration, embellishment, beauty. -ಮಾಡು, ಶೃಂಗರಿಸು, ಶೃಂಗಾರಿಸು To ornament, decorate.

ೃಂಗೇರಿ s. n N of a village and matha on the ghâts

ೆಟ್ಟಿ = ಸೆಟ್ಟಿ, q v.

ೆರೆ = ಸೆರೆ, q v

ೇಕದಾರ h n The native collector of the revenue of a division of villages

ೇಖರ s. n A chaplet, crest, diadem. 2, a chief

ೇಲೆ (= ಸೇಲೆ *tb. of* ಚೇಲ) n Cloth, a garment.

ೇದು. = ಸೇದು, q v

ೇರು = ಸೇರು, q. v

ೇರುವೆ. = ಸೇರುವೆ, q. v

ೇಷ s n. Remaining. 2, remainder, rest 2, N of the thousand-headed serpent -ಗಿರಿ N. ಶೇಷೆ. Rice thrown on the heads of a wedding couple as an auspicious rite

ೈತ್ಯ (*fr*. ಶೀತ) s n Coldness, coolness, dampness; chilliness. -ಪದಾರ್ಥ A cooling thing, *as* an orange, *etc* ಶೈತ್ಯೋಪಚಾರ. Presenting a tired guest with cool drinks

ೈಲ s. *a* Stony, rocky. *n* A mountain

ೈವ (*fr*. ಶಿವ) s *a* Relating to Śiva *n* A worshipper of Śiva. -ಪುರಾಣ. N. of Śiva purâṇa

ಶೋಕ s n Sorrow, grief, mourning. -ಪಡು, -ಮಾಡು, ಶೋಕಿಸು To mourn, lament ಶೋಕಾಗ್ನಿ. Deep sorrow or distress

ಶೋಧ s n Search inquiry, scrutiny. -ಕ Purificatory, a purifier, refiner, an inquirer, seeker, searcher, examiner, scrutinizer, a tempter -ನ, -ನೆ Search, research, examination, cleaning, cleansing, purifying, trial, temptation correction, clearing away faults, the refining of metals ಶೋಧಿತ Cleansed, *etc* ಶೋಧಿಸು To purify, cleanse, to correct; to strain, sift, filter, to refine, clean, to examine, investigate, search

ಶೋಫ s. n Swelling, tumefaction

ಶೋಭಕೃತ್ s n The thirty-seventh year in the cycle of sixty

ಶೋಭ s. n. Brilliance, lustre -ನ. Handsome, auspicious, lustre, brilliance, any auspicious ceremony, *as* a marriage, *also* -ನಪ್ರಸ್ಥ ಶೋಭಾಯಮಾನ. Beautiful, splendid. ಶೋಭಿಸು To shine be splendid, look beautiful ಶೋಭೆ Light, lustre, splendour; beauty, elegance, comeliness

ಶೋಷಣ s. n Drying up; draining, withering, exhaustion. ಶೋಷಿತ. Dried up, exhausted ಶೋಷಿಸು. To dry up, to become dry, to make dry.

ಶೌಚ (*fr* ಶುಚಿ) s. n Purification 2, easing nature. 3, evacuation, excrement ಶೌಚಾಚಾರ Practice of purification -ಕ್ಕೆ ಹೋಗು To go to stool

ಶೌರ್ಯ (*fr* ಶೂರ) s n Heroism, prowess, might, courage, *also* -ತೆ -ವಂತ. A hero, valiant man.

ಶ್ಮಶಾನ (= ಮಸಣ) s n A cemetery, burning or burial ground, *also* -ಭೂಮಿ ಶ್ಮಶಾನಿ. Kâli or Durgâ

ಶ್ಯಾನಭೋಗ. = ಶಾನಬೋಗ, q v

ಶ್ಯಾಮ (= ಶಾಮ) s *a* Dark-blue. -ತೆ Blackness -ಕ, ಶ್ಯಾಮಾಕ (= ಸಾವೆ) A kind of edible grain, *Panicum frumentaceum also* -ಅಕ್ಕಿ.

ಶ್ರದ್ಧೆ, ಶ್ರದ್ಧಾ s. n. Faith, belief, trust, confidence. 2, reverence; hope; wish. ಶ್ರದ್ಧಾಭಕ್ತಿ. Faith and devotion. ಶ್ರದ್ಧಾಳು. Faithful.

ಶ್ರಮ, ಶ್ರಮೆ s. n. Exertion, labour, toil, taking pains. 2, exercise, drill. 3, weariness, fatigue. 4, distress; annoyance. 5, penance. -ಗೊಳಿಸು. To fatigue, annoy. -ಗೊಳ್ಳು. To be fatigued, wearied. -ತಕ್ಕೊಳ್ಳು. To take pains. -ಪಡಿಸು. To weary. -ಪಡು, -ಪೀಳು. To be wearied; to suffer. -ಗಾರ. A hard working man. ಕ್ರಿಸ್ತನ. Christ's passion. -ವಾರ. Week of passions of Christ. -ಣ. Labouring; an ascetic; a Buddhist mendicant.

ಶ್ರಯ (tb. of ಶ್ರಾಯ) n. Improvement of land by cultivation. -ಸಾಗುವಳಿ. Farming land on a rent less than its original value. -ಪಟ್ಟೆ. -ಚೀಟು. A lease on such terms.

ಶ್ರವ s. n. Hearing, listening. 2, the ear. -ಣ. Hearing; the ear; the twenty-second lunar asterism; a goldsmith's pincers. ಶ್ರವಣೇಂದ್ರಿಯ. The organ of hearing.

ಶ್ರಾದ್ಧ (fr. ಶ್ರದ್ಧಾ) s. n. An anniversary ceremony performed to the manes of the nearest relatives. -ಕರ್ತೃ. Its performer. -ದೇವ. Yama.

ಶ್ರಾಂತ s. a. Tired, fatigued, exhausted. 2, calm, tranquil. ಶ್ರಾಂತಿ. Fatigue, exhaustion.

ಶ್ರಾವಕ s. n. A hearer; a pupil. 2, a particular class of Jainas.

ಶ್ರಾವಣ s. a. Audible. n. N. of the fifth lunar month.

ಶ್ರೀ s. n. Prosperity, well-being; success; wealth, riches. 2, dignity, majesty, fame. 3, beauty, loveliness; splendour, lustre. 4, Lakshmî, the wife of Vishṇu. 5, any virtue or excellence. 6, decoration. 7, an honorific prefix. -ಗಂಧ. Sandalwood. -ತಾಳಿ, -ತಾಳೆ. The talipot or fan-palm, Corypha umbraculifera. -ತುಳಸಿ. The holy basil. -ಧರ. Vishṇu or Kṛishṇa. -ನಿವಾಸ. Vishṇu. -ಪತಿ. A king. -ಪರ್ಣೀ. The shrub Gmelina arborea. -ಮತ್, -ಮತು. Prosperous, famous; an honorific title. -ಮಂತ. A nobleman, rich man. -ಮಂತರಾಜಶ್ರೀ. A general term of courtesy. -ಮುಖ. The seventh year in the cycle of sixty. -ಮುದ್ರೆ. The five seals used by Mâdhvas. -ರಂಗ. Kṛishṇa; N. of a town near Trichinopoly. -ರಂಗಪಟ್ಣ. N. of a town near Mysore. -ವೈಷ್ಣವ. A Vaishṇava of the Viśishṭhâdvaita sect. -ಶುಕ್ರವಾರ. Good-Friday. -ಹರ್ಷ. N. of a Saṁskṛita poet.

ಶ್ರುತ s. a. Heard; reported; understood. n. Traditional learning, a śâstra, the vêda. -ಪಡಿಸು. To let know, tell. ಶ್ರುತಿ. Hearing; an ear; oral account, news; the vêda; any vedic text; a sort of drone. ಶ್ರುತಿಕಟು. Harsh to the ear. -ಗಾರ. A drone-player. ಶ್ರುತಿಬಾಹ್ಯ. Contrary to vêdas. ಶ್ರುತಿಶಿರಸ್. The vêdânta.

ಶ್ರೇಣಿ s. n. A line, row, range. 2, a multitude, troop.

ಶ್ರೇಯಸ್ s. a. Best, preferable. n. Virtue, moral merit. 2, good fortune, bliss. 3, final beatitude. ಶ್ರೇಯೋವಂತ, ಶ್ರೇಯಸ್ವಿ. A prosperous man.

ಶ್ರೇಷ್ಠ s. a. Best, excellent, very eminent, far better; most prosperous; senior. -ತನ, -ತೆ, -ತ್ವ. Superiority, excellence. ಶ್ರೇಷ್ಠಿ (= ಸೆಟ್ಟಿ). The head of a tribe or company.

ಶ್ರೋತ್ರ s. n. The ear; also ಶ್ರೋತ್ರೇಂದ್ರಿಯ.

ಶ್ರೋತ್ರಿಯ s. n. A Brâhmaṇa versed in the vêdas.

ಶ್ಲಾಘನೆ, ಶ್ಲಾಘೆ s. n. Flattery; praise; boasting. -ಮಾಡು, ಶ್ಲಾಘಿಸು. To praise. ಶ್ಲಾಘ್ಯ. Praiseworthy, respectable.

ಶ್ಲೇಷ s. n. A figure of speech in rhetoric, connecting words of a double [illegible] ಅಲಂಕಾರ.

ಷ್ಮ s. n. Phlegm, rheum. -ರೋಗ. A phlegmatic disease -ಶರೀರ A phlegmatic constitution

ೇಕ s n. Any verse or stanza 2. kind of metre 3, celebrity fame. ಪುಣ್ಯ-, ಉತ್ತಮ- Well-spoken of, a amous person

ಪಚ s n. A man of low caste, a Candála.

ುರ s. n A father-in-law, f ಷ್ವಶ್ರು.

ಸನ s. n. Breathing, respiration

ಶ್ವಾನ s. n. A dog.

ಶ್ವಾಪದ s. n. A beast of prey.

ಶ್ವಾಸ s. n Breath, respiration; air, wind, hard breathing. -ಆಡಿಸು To breathe. -ಎಳೆ. To inhale. -ಧಾರಣೆ Suspension of breath -ಬಿಡು To exhale

ಶ್ವೇತ s a White n Silver -ಕುಷ್ಠ White leprosy. -ಕೇತು N of a sage and of a king -ರೋಗ A kind of venereal affection

ಷ

. The fiftieth letter of the alphabet. *It does not occur in pure Kannada*

ಾರ s n. The letter ಷ

ಕ್ಕ h n Doubt, suspicion; blemish, [fault

ತ, ಷಡ್ s a Six. ಷಟ್ಕರ್ಮ The six duties of a Brâhmana, *as* ಯಜನ, sacrificing; ಯಾಜನ, officiating at sacrifices made by others; ಅಧ್ಯಯನ, studying the vêdas; ಅಧ್ಯಾಪನ, teaching vêdas, ದಾನ, bestowing alms; ಪ್ರತಿಗ್ರಹ, receiving alms. ಷಟ್ಕೋಣ. A hexagon ಷಟ್ಪದಿ N of a Kannada metre. ಷಡಂಗ Six-membered, the six vedângas ಷಡಂಗಕಷಾಯ A decoction of six medicinal ingredients. ಷಡರಿ Six enemies ಕಾಮ, ಕ್ರೋಧ, ಲೋಭ, ಮೋಹ, ಮದ, ಮತ್ಸರ ಷಡಿಂದ್ರಿಯ. The six indriyas ಷಡ್ವಿಷಯ The six objects of sense, *as* ಶಬ್ದ, ಸ್ಪರ್ಶ, ರೂಪ, ರಸ, ಗಂಧ, ಜ್ಞಾನ ಷಡ್ಗುಣ. Six-fold, an aggregate of six qualities

ಜ s. a Six-born. n. N of the fourth note of music

ದರ್ಶನ s n The six recognised systems of philosophy mîmâmsâ (by Jaimini), vêdânta (by Bâdarâyana), nyâya (by Gautama), vaiśêshika (by Kanâda), sânkhya (by Kapila), and yôga by Patañj i)

ಷಡ್ರಸ s n The six tastes madhura, katu, amla, tuvara, tikta, and lavana

ಷಡ್ವರ್ಗ, ಷಡ್ವೈರಿ. = ಷಡರಿ, q v

ಷಂಡ s. n A multitude, collection, group, heap, flock -ಕ A eunuch.

ಷರತ್ತು h n A wager, bet 2, agreement, condition

ಷರಬತ್ತು h n A sweet drink so called

ಷರಾ h n. Remark, *nota-bene.*

ಷರಾಬು h n Spirituous liquor

ಷರಾಯಿ h n Trousers

ಷಷ್ಟಿ s a Sixtieth. 2, = ಷಷ್ಠ. ಷಷ್ಟಿ. Sixty, = ಷಷ್ಟಿ.

ಷಷ್ಠ s a Sixth ಷಷ್ಠಿ The sixth day of a lunar fortnight

ಷಾಪು e n A shop.

ಷಾಲು. = ಶಾಲು, q v

ಷಿಕಮಿ h n A subordinate tenure whose revenue is paid through the proprietor

ಷುರು h a Begun n Beginning, commencement.

ಷೋಕಿ, ಷೋಕು f n Voluptuousness. -ದಾರ A voluptuous man

ಷೋಡಶ s a. Sixteenth 2 sixteen ಷೋಡಶೋಪಚಾರ. Sixteen ways of doing homage (to idols) or civility (to men). -ಸಂಸ್ಕಾರ. Sixteen ceremonies to be performed from birth to death

ಸ್

ಸ್. The fifty-first letter of the alphabet.

ಸಂ = ಸಮ್ q v.

ಸಂಯಮ s n Restraint, check. 2, humanity, forbearance 3, a religious vow -ನ. Restraining, checking. ಸಂಯಮಿ. An ascetic

ಸಂಯುಕ್ತ s a. United; attached, blended, endowed with

ಸಂಯೋಗ s. n. Connection, junction, union, association, conjunction ಸಂಯೋಗಿಸು. To join, mix

ಸಂರಕ್ಷಕ s n A guardian ಸಂರಕ್ಷಣೆ. Protecting, guarding, preserving; saving ಸಂರಕ್ಷಿಸು To guard, protect, save.

ಸಂಲಾಪ s. n Talking, friendly conversation, chat

ಸಂವತ್ಸರ s n A year. ಚಾಂದ್ರಮಾನ-. The lunar year ಸೌರಮಾನ-. The solar year

ಸಂವರಣೆ (tb. of ಸಂಭರಣ) n Preparing, preparation, procuring ಸಂವರಿಸು To make ready, prepare

ಸಂವಾದ s n Conversation dialogue, discussion, communication, report ಸಂವಾದಿಸು To speak with, converse; to discuss.

ಸಂವಿಧಾನ s n. Disposition, performance, plan, minding

ಸಂವೇದ s n. Perception, consciousness, understanding. ಸಂವೇದಿಸು To know, learn

ಸಂಶಯ s n Uncertainty, doubt, scruple, suspicion 2, difficulty, risk -ಗೊಳ್ಳು -ತಕ್ಕೊಳ್ಳು, -ತೆಗೆ To waver, to become suspicious -ಪಡು, -ಬೀಳು -ಮಾಡು, ಸಂಶಯಿಸು. To doubt, suspect

ಸಂಶ್ರಯ s. n. Refuge. shelter protectio

ಸಂಸರ್ಗ s. n. Close union, close contact, association; intercourse, acquaintance.

ಸಂಸಾರ s n Secular life, the affairs of life, worldly illusion; a household; a family, a wife -ತಾಪತ್ರಯ Family-cares -ನಡಿಸು, -ಮಾಡು, -ಸಾಗಿಸು. To manage the affairs of life, to keep house -ಭಾರ The weight of affairs of life -ವಿಮೋಚನ Emancipation from the world ಸಂಸಾರಿ Worldly secular. ಸಂಸಾರಿಕ One who has a family.

ಸಂಸಿದ್ಧಿ s n Complete accomplishment, perfection 2, nature

ಸಂಸೃಷ್ಟ s a. Conjoined, united, common to all, re-united (as kinsmen) ಸಂಸೃಷ್ಟಿ Union, combination, a re-united kinsman, co-partner.

ಸಂಸೆ tb of ಸಂಶಯ, q v

ಸಂಸ್ಕಾರ s n Refinement. 2, conception, idea. 3, any faculty, instinct. 4, preparation, consecration, dedication 5, a sanctifying or purificatory rite or ceremony, as ಗರ್ಭಾಧಾನ, ಜಾತಕರ್ಮ, ನಾಮಕರಣ ಚೌಲ, ಉಪನಯನ, ವಿವಾಹ, etc 6, funeral obsequies. ಸಂಸ್ಕರಿಸು. To prepare, refine, to sanctify, consecrate ಸಂಸ್ಕೃತ Refined, polished; consecrated, the Samskrita language.

ಸಂಸ್ತುತ s. a Praised; lauded. ಸಂಸ್ತುತಿ Praise, eulogy

ಸಂಸ್ಥಾನ s. n A collection, conformation 2 any place, a station, presidency 3, a royal city, a capital, a state, government. ಸಂಸ್ಥಾನಿಕ, ಸಂಸ್ಥಾನಾಧಿಪತಿ A ruler, chief

ಸಂಸ್ಥಾಪನ s n Confirm... establish... ...ion.

ಸ್ಥಿತಿ s. n Standing with; contiguity, duration. 2, abiding; situation, condition 3, standing still; death

ಸ್ಪರ್ಶ s. n. Mutual contact. 2, perception, sense

ಸ್ಮರಣ, ಸಂಸ್ಮರಣೆ s. n. Remembering, recollecting.

ಹತಿ s n Close combination; compactness; an assemblage.

ಹರ s n Destroying, destruction ಸಂಹರಿಸು To destroy, annihilate

ಹರ್ಷ s. n Thrill of delight, joy, pleasure.

ಹಾರ s. n Destruction, annihilation; cf ಸಂಹರ. ಸಂಹಾರಿಸು. = ಸಂಹರಿಸು. q v.

ಹಿತೆ s n. A compilation, compendium. 2, any arranged collection of texts, the hymnical text of the vêdas

ತಿ tb. of ಶಕ್ತಿ, q v

ರ್ಮಕ s. n Transitive n The transitive verb.

ಲ s a All, whole, entire. n. Every thing, the whole.

ಲಾತಿ h n European woollen cloth

ಾರ s n. The letter ಸ

ಾಲ s. n. Good time. a Seasonable ad. Betimes.

ುಟುಂಬ s a With family or wife 2, all sorts together

ೇಶ s a Having hair, hairy ಸಕೇಶಿ. An unshaven widow.

ಕ್ಕರೆ (tb of ಶರ್ಕರೆ) n. Sugar ಕಲ್ಲು-, ಖಂಡ- Sugar-candy. -ಕಂಚಿ. The large citron -ಕಡ್ಡಿ A sugar stick.

ಕ್ತ s. a Attached to; diligent, attentive ಸಕ್ತಿ. Attachment, contact; severity. ಸಕ್ತ Hard; harsh, oppressive.

ಕ್ರೆ. = ಸಕ್ಕರೆ, q. v.

ಖ, ಸಖಿ s. n An associate, companion ಸಖಿತ್ವ, ಸಖ್ಯ Friendship, intimacy

ಗಟು f n. The whole in a lump; an average

ಗಣಿ, ಸಗಣಿ s. n. Cowdung

ಸಗಾಟ, ಸಗಾಟಿಕೆ s n Great friendship

ಸಗುಣ s. a Virtuous, worldly.

ಸಗೋತ್ರ s. n. A kinsman 2, race, lineage.

ಸಗ್ಗ tb. of ಸ್ವರ್ಗ, q v

ಸಗ್ಗಿಗ (tb of ಸ್ವರ್ಗಿ) n A deity.

ಸಂಕ f. n A bridge

ಸಂಕಟ s a Narrow, strait n A strait, difficulty, trouble, hardship, affliction, distress -ಗೊಳ್ಳು, -ಪಡು, -ಬೀಳು, -ಪಾಗು To suffer distress ಪ್ರಾಣ-. The agony of death, any great difficulty Other cpds ಅನ್ನ-, ದಾಹ-, ಜನ-, ಮರಣ-.

ಸಂಕರ s n Union, confusion, unlawful mixture 2, a mixed caste, also ಜಾತಿ- 3, sweepings, dust 4, a double sack 5, tb. of ಶಂಕರ

ಸಂಕರ್ಷಣ s n. Contracting, shortening, attracting. 2, Baladêva.

ಸಂಕಲನ s. n. Addition (arith) ಸಂಕಲಿತ. Added, addition (arith).

ಸಂಕಲಿಕೆ s n. A pair of wedding garments.

ಸಂಕಲೆ (tb. of ಶೃಂಖಲೆ) n. A chain, fetter.

ಸಂಕಲ್ಪ s n. Will, volition, purpose, resolution, vow. 2, wish. 3, thought, fancy, consideration 4, mind, soul 5, declaration of purpose. ದೇವರ- The will of God -ಮಾಡು, ಸಂಕಲ್ಪಿಸು. To will, purpose, resolve, to wish for.

ಸಂಕೀರ್ತನ, ಸಂಕೀರ್ತನೆ s n. Lauding, praising, glorification.

ಸಂಕುಚಿತ s. a. Contracted, shrivelled up, wrinkled

ಸಂಕುಲ s a Crowded together, confused; filled with n A crowd, throng. -ತೆ. Confusion, perplexity.

ಸಂಕೇತ s n Gesture, hint, a sign, token, symbol; convention, engagement. -ಸ್ಥಲ An appointed place. ಸಂಕೇತಾಕ್ಷರ. A secret writing. Cpds. ಕೈ-, ಬಾಯಿ-.

ಸಂಕೋಚ s n Shrinking, contraction, abridgment, dimin[illegible]n. 2, reserve repression -ಪಡು, ಸಂಕೋಚಿಸು. To shrink, close, to hesitate, doubt. -ಮಾಡು. To abridge -ಗಾರ A hesitator

ಸಂಕೋಲೆ (*tb of* ಶೃಂಖಲ, *q v*) *n* A chain. -ಬೀಳು To be fettored. -ಹಾಕು To fetter.

ಸಂಕ್ರಮಣ s *n*. Transition, progress, passage 2, the sun's passage from one sign of the zodiac to another 3, the day on which the sun so passes, *also* ಸಂಕ್ರಾಂತಿ

ಸಂಕ್ರಾಮ s. *n* Difficult passage 2 a causeway

ಸಂಕ್ಲೇಶ s *n* Affliction, pain, torment

ಸಂಕ್ಷಿಪ್ತ s. *a*. Abridged, abbreviated; concise, compact.

ಸಂಕ್ಷೇಪ s *n* Abridgment, abbreviation, conciseness, brevity, an epitome. ಸಂಕ್ಷೇಪವಾಗಿ Briefly. ಸಂಕ್ಷೇಪಿಸು To abridge, shorten.

ಸಂಖ್ಯೆ, ಸಂಖ್ಯಾ s *n*. Numeration. 2, an account, sum. 3, number, a numeral ಸಂಖ್ಯಾತ Reckoned, numbered ಅಸಂಖ್ಯಾತ Innumerable ಸಂಖ್ಯಾಪೂರಣ. Ordinal number ಸಂಖ್ಯಾವಾಚಕ, ಸಂಖ್ಯಾವಾಚಿ. A numeral

ಸಂಗ s. *n*. Union, contact, intercourse, association -ಮಾಡು To associate with ದುರ್ಜನ-, ದುಃ- Bad company ಸಜ್ಜನ-, ಸತ್-. Good company. ನಿಃ-. Absence of attachment

ಸಂಗಡ (*tb of* ಸಂಘಾತ) *prep*. Together with, with, by, in presence. -ಕರಕೊಂಡು ಹೋಗು, -ತಕ್ಕೊಳ್ಳು, -ತೆಗೆದುಕೊಂಡು ಹೋಗು To take (somebody or something) with (one's self) ಸಂಗಡಿ, ಸಂಗಡಿಗ. A companion, friend ಸಂಗಡಿಸು To assemble, to crowd, *etc.*

ಸಂಗತ s. *a* Joined, united, assembled. 2, proper, seasonable, applicable, fitted for. *n* Union; association.

ಸಂಗತಿ s *n* Union, association, company. 2, occurrence, affair, matter, [illegible] To [illegible] into society -ಹಿಡಿ To keep company with. ಸಂಗತ್ಯಾನುಸಾರ According to circumstances

ಸಂಗಮ s *n* Meeting, union, junction, association, intercourse. 2, the confluence of two rivers.

ಸಂಗರ s *n* Agreement, assent 2, a day and night 3, devouring. 4, war, battle 5, trouble, pain

ಸಂಗಳಿಸು s *v i* To be joined, mixed. 2, to be brought about, to come to pass, occur.

ಸಂಗಾತ (*tb. of* ಸಂಘಾತ) *n*. Union, company *prep* With, together with. ಸಂಗಾತಿ A companion, friend. -ಬಿಡು To give up connection with a person

ಸಂಗೀತ s. *a* Sung together. *n*. Symphony, a concert, chorus -ಗಾರ A singer, a music-master -ವಿದ್ಯೆ, -ಶಾಸ್ತ್ರ. The science of music -ಸ್ವರ. The notes of the musical scale.

ಸಂಗ್ರಹ s. *n* Seizing, grasp, taking hold of 2, reception, gathering, collection, heap, store, a compilation, a totality. 3, an abridgment, summary 4, a catalogue 5, a store-room -ಮಾಡು To collect, lay up in store ಸಂಗ್ರಹಿಸು To gather acquire, amass, to abridge, to include, comprehend ಮದುವೆಗೆ ಸಂಗ್ರಹ ಮಾಡು To provide necessaries for a wedding

ಸಂಗ್ರಾಮ s *n* A battle, war, fighting

ಸಂಘ s. *n*. A combination, gathering, multitude, crowd, group, a commitee.

ಸಂಘಟನ, ಸಂಘಟನೆ, ಸಂಘಟ್ಟನ s. *n* Union; junction, being effected, collision, friction ಸಂಘಟಿಸು. To occur, happen, to be effected, to strike against.

ಸಂಘರ್ಷ, ಸಂಘರ್ಷಣ s. *n* Rubbing, grinding, friction, collision, emulation

ಸಂಘಾತ (= ಸಂಗಡ, ಸಂಗಾತ, *q v*) s *n* Union, association 2, a mass, heap, assemblage, cluster. ಸಂಘಾತಿ. A com-[illegible]

ಚರಾಚರ s a. Animate and inanimate, universal n. The universe

ಚಿವ s n A companion 2, a counsellor, minister.

ಚೇತನ s. a Sentient, animate, living.

ಚೇಲ s a Clothed, dressed -ಸ್ನಾನ. Ablution in one's garments

ಚ್ಚಿದಾನಂದ s. n Existence, thought and joy (*of the universal soul—vedantic*)

ಜಾ h n Punishment.

ಜಾತಿ, ಸಜಾತೀಯ s a Of the same caste or tribe.

ಜೀವ s a Alive, animate.

ಜ್ಜ s. a Covered. 2, trimmed. 3, prepared, ready 4, armed. n Equipment, harness

ಜ್ಜನ s a Respectable, virtuous, good n. A good or virtuous man -ಸಂಗ Good company. ಸಜ್ಜನಿಕೆ Goodness = ಸೌಜನ್ಯ.

ಜ್ಜರಸ *tb of* ಸರ್ಜರಸ, *q v*

ಜ್ಜೆ, ಸಜ್ಜು. *tb. of* ಸಜ್ಜ, *q v*

ಜ್ಜಿಗೆ (= ಸೊಜ್ಜಿಗೆ, ಸೋಜಿ) f. n Wheaten flour rolong. 2, a dish made of it.

ಜ್ಜೀಕಾರ (*tb of* ಸರ್ಜಿಕಾಕ್ಷಾರ) n. Country alkali, carbonate of soda.

ಜ್ಜೆ 1. k n The grain *Holcus spicatus*.

ಜ್ಜೆ 2. (*tb of* ಶಯ್ಯಾ) n A place of rest 2, an upper story. -ಮನೆ A sleeping apartment

ಂಚ 1. = ಸಂಚು, *q. v*

ಂಚ 2 (*tb of* ಸಂಚಯ) n That is accumulated or saved (*as* money, grain, *etc*)

ಂಚಕಾರ (*tb. of* ಸತ್ಯಂಕಾರ) n Advance, earnest money, pledge, deposit

ಂಚಯ s. n Heaping up, collection, heap, store, quantity -ನ Putting up or saving, taking the ashes of a cremated body and throwing in a river. -ಮಾಡು, ಸಂಚಯಿಸು. To collect, put up

ಂಚರ ಸಂಚರಣ s. n Travelling, going about, motion [illegible] move about, roam, wander. ಸಂಚಾರ. Roaming, wandering, passage, progress, course, a passage ಸಂಚಾರ ಮಾಡು = ಸಂಚರಿಸು, *q. v* ಸಂಚಾರಿ A wanderer, traveller. ದೇಶ-, ಭೂ-. Foreign travel.

ಸಂಚಿ f. n A sack, bag

ಸಂಚಿಕೆ f. n A section or part of a book.

ಸಂಚಿತ s a. Heaped up, amassed, collected, saved. 2, filled with. *Cpds* -ಕರ್ಮ, -ದ್ರವ್ಯ, -ಪುಣ್ಯ

ಸಂಚು k n An expedient, means; an artifice, a trick, intrigue, skill ಒಳ-. A secret plot, intrigue. -ನಡಿಸು, -ಮಾಡು. To intrigue -ಗಾರ A spy; *f* -ಗಾತಿ, -ಗಾತಿರ್.

ಸಂಜೀವನ s n. Remaining alive 2, bringing to life, an animating process, an elixir. ಸಂಜೀವಿನಿ A plant that restores to life ಸಂಜೀವಿಸು To remain alive, to resuscitate

ಸಂಜೆ (*tb. of* ಸಂಧ್ಯಾ) n Evening -ಗತ್ತಲೆ, -ಹೊತ್ತು. Evening twilight

ಸಂಜ್ಞಾ, ಸಂಜ್ಞೆ s. n Sense; knowledge, thought, mind 2, a sign, token, signal, symbol, gesture, hint. 3, a title, term ಸಂಜ್ಞಾಕ್ಷರ. An initial letter

ಸಟುಕ = ಸಟ್ಟುಗ, *q v*.

ಸಟೆ (*tb. of* ಶಠೆ) n Falsehood, lying, cheating, villainy, *also* -ಪಟೆ. [illegible] -ಮಾತು, -ಪಟೆಮಾತು. A lie -ಗಾರ A liar

ಸಟ್ಟುಗ k n A spoon, ladle.

ಸಡಗರ k n. Agitation, eagerness, joy; festivity, festive display 2, excellence, beauty. ಸಡಗರಿಸು To grow agitated, elated or joyful, to adorn

ಸಡಲು, ಸಡಿಲು (= ಸಡ್ಲು, *q v*) k. a. Loose, slack, relaxed or lax ಸಡಲಾಗು. To become lax -ಮಾಡು, ಸಡಿಲಿಸು. To slacken, loosen -ಬಿಡು To relax; to give liberty

ಸಡ್ಡಕ f. n A brother-in-law, the husband of a man's wife's sister.

ಸಡ್ಡೆ 1. f. n A sowing machine used with the hand.

ಸಡ್ಡೆ 2. (tb of ಶ್ರದ್ಧೆ) n Respect, honour, esteem, attention, heed. -ಮಾಡು To respect, etc, cf ಅ-

ಸಡ್ಲು = ಸಡಲು, q v

ಸಣಬು (tb of ಶಣ) n Hemp, *Cannabis sativa.*

ಸಂಡಿಗೆ (tb of ಷಡಂಶ) n. A thin crisp cake made of the flour of any grain mixed with or without chillies, salt, *etc.*, dried and roasted or fried.

ಸಣ್ಣ (tb of ಸನ್ನ) a Small, little, tiny, fine, thin, delicate, slender. *Cpds* -ಅಕ್ಕಿ, -ಅರಿವೆ, -ಕೆರೆ, -ಗೋದಿ, -ನೆಗ್ಗಿಲು, -ಹನಿ, -ಹುಡುಗ, -ಹುಡುಗಿ, *etc* -ದೊಡ್ಡ. Small and big. -ದು. That is small; a small thing -ಧ್ವನಿ. A low voice. -ನಡು. A slender waist -ಮಾತು. An insignificant or mean word. -ಮೋರೆ. A dejected face. -ವ A boy, f -ವಳು. -ಗೆ, -ನೆ. Small, fine, *etc* ಸಣ್ಣಾಗು To be small, low.

ಸಣ್ಗ f n. A garment of coarse silk.

ಸತ್ (= ಸದು, *etc.*) s. a. Being; real, true. 2, virtuous, good, right; excellent. -ಕರ್ಮ, -ಕಾರ್ಯ. A good or virtuous action. -ಕೀರ್ತಿ. Great fame -ಕುಲ. A good family -ಕೃತಿ, -ಕ್ರಿಯೆ. A good composition; a virtuous act. -ಕ್ರೈಸ್ತ. A true Christian -ಪಾತ್ರ A worthy or virtuous person. -ಪುಣ್ಯ A real merit. -ಪುತ್ರ A virtuous son -ಪುರುಷ. A virtuous man; a respectable person. -ವಿಶ್ವಾಸ True, living faith -ಸಂಗ, -ಸಹವಾಸ. Good company.

ಸತತ s. a Constant, perpetual, eternal. *ad* Always

ಸತವು (tb of ಸತ್ವ) n. Strength, firmness.

ಸತಿ s n. A faithful wife. 2, a wife.

ಸತುವು (tb of ಸತ್ವ) n Strength, etc 2 pewter, zinc.

ಸತ್ಕಾರ s. n. Hospitality, respect; care, attention -ಮಾಡು, ಸತ್ಕರಿಸು. To receive hospitably, to treat kindly; to welcome.

ಸತ್ತಾ (= ಸತ್ತೆ 2) s n Existence, authority, sway, power, might.

ಸತ್ತಿಗೆ (tb. of ಛತ್ರಿಕೆ) n An umbrella

ಸತ್ತು P. p. of ಸಾಯು

ಸತ್ತೆ 1. k n Rubbish, dirt, stuff, trash

ಸತ್ತೆ 2 = ಸತ್ತಾ q v

ಸತ್ಯ s. a True, real, sincere, honest, truthful faithful n Truth, sincerity reality, a fixed rule 2, a promise, oath -ತನ, -ತೆ, -ತ್ವ Truth, sincerity, veracity -ಪ್ರತಿಜ್ಞೆ, -ಪ್ರಮಾಣ. A sincere vow or oath. -ವಚನ A true word, a sincere promise. -ಲೋಕ The highest of the seven worlds. -ಯುಗ. The first of the four yugas -ವಂತ, -ಶಾಲಿ A faithful, honest man. -ವಾದಿ A truth-speaking man. ಸತ್ಯಾಚರಣೆ Observance of truth. ಸತ್ಯಾನೃತ. Truth and lie; commerce

ಸತ್ರ s n A sacrifice, an oblation; liberality, wealth 2, a place of refuge -ಶಾಲೆ An alms-house.

ಸತ್ವ s. n. Essence, life 2, breath; mind 3, a substance 4, nature. 5, goodness, truth; strength, energy, power -ಗುಣ The quality of purity or goodness, generosity, valour. -ವಂತ, -ಶಾಲಿ A powerful man. -ಹೀನ A weak man

ಸತ್ವರ s. a. Quick, speedy.

ಸದ್ = ಸತ್, q. v. -ಗತಿ. Felicity, fortune -ಗುಣ. A good quality. -ಗುರು A true guru -ಧರ್ಮ. A good religion, justice, virtue -ಭಕ್ತ. A true devotee. -ಭಕ್ತಿ. True devotion. -ಭಾವ Reality, goodness, amiability -ವೃತ್ತಿ Good conduct. -ವ್ಯವಹಾರ. -ವ್ಯಾಪಾರ Good occupation or transaction

ಸದನ s n A seat. 2, an abode, house. 3, exhaustion

[illegible] s. [illegible], truly pure - [illegible] Truly [illegible] devotedness.

ದರ್ h n. The highest court of law. 2, a state-room -ಅದಾಲತ್. A zillah court -ಅಮೀನ. A subordinate judge

ದರ f. n Familiarity, friendliness, facility.

ದರಹು, ಸದರಿ h. a Afore-said, above-mentioned

ದರು = ಸದರ್, q. v

ದಸ್ (tb ಸದಸ್ಸು) s. n. An assembly, meeting. 2, a set ಸದಸ್ಯ An assessor, member.

ದಾ s ad. Always, at all times, continually, ever, also -ಕಾಲ -ಚರಣ, -ಚಾರ Good manners, a good custom -ಚಾರಿ A virtuous person -ನಂದ, -ಶಿವ Always happy: N of Śiva.

ದಾಪ, ಸದಾಬು f. n The strong-smelling rue, *Ruta graveolens*

ದೃಶ s a Like, similar, same, fit, proper. -ತೆ, -ತ್ವ. Likeness, similarity

ದೆ a. k v t To bruise, crush, to strike, beat v. i To be reduced to powder n Trash, rubbish, stuff.

ದ್ದು 1. k. v i. To cease, stop (*used only in the imperative*)

ದ್ದು 2. *tb. of* ಶಬ್ದ, *q. v*

ದ್ಯ, ಸದ್ಯಾ (*tb of* ಸದ್ಯಸ್) *ad.* Today, this moment, now; at once, on the spot, presently. [*Domini.*

ನ್ h n An age or period, year, *anno*

ನಕ, ಸನತ್ಕುಮಾರ, ಸನತ್ಸುಜಾತ s n Ns of Brahmâ's sons.

ನದು s n A grant, diploma, charter, patent. ಸನದಿ Held by a grant.

ನಾತನ s a Eternal; ancient n A hautboy

ನಾಥ s a. Having a master. 2, possessing, having

ನಾದಿ h. n A clarion, hautboy

ನಿ, *tb of* ಶನಿ, *q v*

ನೀನು h. n A bayonet.

ಂತ (*fr* ಸತ್ = ಶಾಂತ) s. n. A saint. a. Venerable, respected. 2, gentle, calm, soft -ಆರಾಧನೆ -ಸೇವೆ Saints' worship. -ಯಿಸ. -ಯಿಸು, -ವಿಸು. To appease, allay, pacify, calm, soothe, comfort, console

ಸಂತತ s a Continuous, lasting, eternal

ಸಂತತಿ s n Lineage, offspring, progeny. ಸ್ತ್ರೀ- The female line ಪುರುಷ-. The male line [burnt up.

ಸಂತಪ್ತ s a. Inflamed, hot, glowing,

ಸಂತರ್ಪಣೆ s n. A sumptuous meal

ಸಂತಸ *tb. of* ಸಂತೋಷ, *q. v*

ಸಂತಾನ (= ಸಂತತಿ) s n Progeny, offspring, a child -ವೃದ್ಧಿ Increase of progeny -ಅಳಿದು ಹೋಗು, ನಿಃಸಂತಾನವಾಗು A generation to perish to be childless.

ಸಂತಾಪ s. n Great heat 2, affliction, pain, anguish, distress. 3, remorse, penitence, resentment. -ಪಡಿಸು To afflict, torment -ಪಡು, ಸಂತಾಪಿಸು To be distressed or afflicted

ಸಂತು k. *3rd pers sing of the imperf of* ಸಲ್ಲು

ಸಂತುಷ್ಟ s a. Satisfied, contented, well-pleased, delighted ಸಂತುಷ್ಟಿ. Satisfaction, contentment

ಸಂತೃಪ್ತಿ s. n Complete satisfaction, satiety

ಸಂತೆ 1 (*tb of* ಸಂಸ್ಥಾ) n A mass, crowd. 2, a fair or market -ಕಟ್ಟು, -ಕೂಡು, -ನೆರೆ A market to convene -ಹರಿ A market to disperse

ಸಂತೆ 2 f n. A lesson -ಹೇಳು To tell a santĕ repeatedly

ಸಂತೋಷ (= ಸಂತಸ) s. n. Satisfaction. 2, happiness, delight, joy, pleasure. -ಕೊಡು To give joy. -ಗೊಳಿಸು, -ಪಡಿಸು To please, gladden gratify. -ಪಡು, ಸಂತೋಷಿಸು. To feel happy or glad -ಕರ Causing joy, *etc*, pleasing. -ಪುರುಷ A cheerful man -ಬಾಷ್ಪ. Tears of joy. -ದಿಂದಿರು, -ದಲ್ಲಿರು To be pleased cheerful

ಸಂದಣಿ (*tb of* ಸಂಧಾನ) n A collection, crowd, flock, throng -ಸು (v. i). To collect, meet, crowd, flock

ಸಂದರ್ಭ s. n. Convenience, opportunity, leisure. 2, affair, matter. -ಆಗು, -ಬೀಳು, ಸಂದರ್ಭಿಸು. To be opportune or convenient.

ಸಂದರ್ಶನ s. n. Seeing, sight, vision; meeting; an interview, visit. -ಕೊಡು, -ತೆಗೆದುಕೊಳ್ಳು. To visit.

ಸಂದಾಯ k. n. Payment of what is due. -ಆಗು. To be paid up. -ಮಾಡು. To pay.

ಸಂದಿ. = ಸಂದು 2, q. v.

ಸಂದಿಗ್ಧ s. a. Obscure; dubious, doubtful, uncertain.

ಸಂದಿಸು s. v. t. To join; to fasten; to tie; to fix. v. i. To associate one's self to. 2, to occur, happen.

ಸಂದು 1. P. p. of ಸಲ್ಲು, q. v. -ಹೋಗು. To die.

ಸಂದು 2. (= ಸಂದಿ. tb. of ಸಂಧಿ) n. Juncture; a joint; a nook, corner; a lane; a cleft, gap, crack, opening. -ಹೊಬ್ಬು. Opportunity, convenience; a junction of two roads. -ಕೊಡಿಸು. Tor abbet. -ಬಳ್ಳಿ. A climbing herb, *Vitis quadrangularis*. -ವಾತ. Rheumatism of the joints. -ಬಿಡು. To leave a space. -ಬೀಳು. To crack; to be patched. -ಹಾಕು. To patch. -ಸೇರುವೆ. Exact joinery.

ಸಂದೂಕ, ಸಂದೂಕು h. n. A large box, chest.

ಸಂದೇಶ s. n. Information, tidings; a message.

ಸಂದೇಹ s. n. Doubt, uncertainty; scruple; risk, danger. -ಗೊಳ್ಳು, -ಪಡು, ಸಂದೇಹಿಸು. To doubt, suspect. -ತೀರಿಸು. To remove a doubt.

ಸಂಧಾನ (= ಸಂದಣೆ, q. v.) s. n. Junction; combination; alliance, league; peace; reception. ಲೌಕಿಕ-. Bribe.

ಸಂಧಿ (= ಸಂದಿ, ಸಂದು, q. v.) s. n. Conjunction, union. 2, alliance, peace. 3, euphonic junction of letters (g.). 4, a joint. 5, a critical juncture. 6, a breach, gap, hole; a chapter. 7, an interval. -ವಾತ (= ಸಂದುವಾತ). Rheumatism. -ಸಾರಾಂಶ. Contents of [illegible]

ಸಂಧ್ಯಾಕಾಲ. Evening time, evening. ಸಂಧ್ಯಾರಾಗ. Twilight; evening. ಸಂಧ್ಯಾವಂದನ. Morning and evening adoration. ಸಂಧ್ಯೆ = ಸಂಜೆ, etc., q. v.

ಸನ್ನದ್ಧ s. a. Armed; arrayed, prepared; provided, ready.

ಸನ್ನಹ, ಸನ್ನಾಹ s. n. Preparation, military array. 2, armour, mail.

ಸನ್ನಿ. tb. of ಸನ್ನಿಪಾತ, q. v.

ಸನ್ನಿಕರ್ಷ, -ಣ s. n. Approximation, nearness, vicinity.

ಸನ್ನಿಧ s. n. Proximity, vicinity, nearness. ಸನ್ನಿಧಾನ, ಸನ್ನಿಧಿ. Proximity, nearness, presences; *Cpds.*: ಅಪ್ಪಂದಿರ-, ದೇವರ-, ಧೊರೆಗಳ-, *etc.*

ಸನ್ನಿಪಾತ s. n. Falling down; collision. 2, combined derangement of the three humours (wind, bile, and phlegm).

ಸನ್ನೆ 1. (tb. of ಸಂಜ್ಞೆ, q. v.) n. A sign, hint.

ಸನ್ನೆ 2. -ಕೋಲು k. n. A lever.

ಸನ್ನ್ಯಾಸ s. n. Laying aside, resignation, abandonment of all worldly possessions and earthly affections, asceticism. ಸನ್ನ್ಯಾಸಿ. An ascetic, religious mendicant.

ಸನ್ಮತ s. n. Approbation, sanction. ಸನ್ಮತಿ. A good understanding.

ಸನ್ಮಾನ s. n. Respect, honour. -ಮಾಡು. To honour. ಸನ್ಮಾನಿಸು. To respect, honour.

ಸನ್ಮಾರ್ಗ s. n. The right way; a virtuous conduct. -ಸ್ಥ. A man of good conduct.

ಸನ್ಯಾಸ, ಸನ್ಯಾಸಿ. tb. of ಸನ್ನ್ಯಾಸ, ಸನ್ನ್ಯಾಸಿ, q. v.

ಸಫಾಯಿ h. n. Polish, gloss; smoothness; cleanness, neatness, elegance.

ಸಪಿಂಡ s. n. A kinsman. ಸಪಿಂಡಿ. Offering of a ball of rice to a deceased relative. ಸಪಿಂಡೀಕರಣ. Performing the said rite for a deceased relative.

ಸಪ್ತ s. a. Seven. -ಋಷಿ, ಸಪ್ತರ್ಷಿ. The constellation *Ursa major*; seven great rishis. -ದಶ. The seventeenth. *Cpds.*: [illegible] ಲೋಕ, -ತಿ.

Seventy. -ಮ The seventh. ಸಪ್ತಮಿ The seventh case, locative; the seventh day of the lunar fortnight -ವಿಭವಿಭಕ್ತಿ The seven kinds of case-terminations

ಸಪ್ಪಗೆ, ಸಪ್ಪನೆ (= ಚಪ್ಪಗೆ, q v) k n Flatness, dulness, insipidness a Flat, dull, effectless ad Flatly, insipidly.

ಸಪ್ಪಂಗ f. n The suppan or brasiletto, *Caesalpinia sappan.*

ಸಪ್ಪಳ k n A sound, noise -ಮಾಡು. To make a sound or noise.

ಸಪ್ಪು (= ಸೊಪ್ಪು, q v) k n Foliage, leaves

ಸಪ್ಪೆ (= ಚಪ್ಪೆ, q. v) k a Insipid, dull, dejected, inert. n Flatness, insipidness, spiritlessness -ಪಥ್ಯ Diet without salt and acids.

ಸಫಲ s a Fruitful, productive, successful -ತೆ, -ತ್ವ Fruitfulness, productiveness

ಸಫೇದು h. a White

ಸಬಕಾರ (ಸಬ್ಬು) f n. Soap

ಸಬಗ. = ಸೊಬಗ, q v

ಸಬಬು h. n Cause, reason, motive

ಸಬರ k n A pack-saddle for bullocks

ಸಬಲ s. a Powerful, strong.

ಸಬಳ s. n. A spear, lance, pike.

ಸಬ್ಬಕ್ಕಿ. ಸಬ್ಬು f. n Sago

ಸಬ್ಬತು f n Sabbath, day of rest and Divine worship.

ಸಬ್ಬವ s n Mirth, jest, fun -ಕಾರ A jester, buffoon

ಸಬ್ಬಸಿಗೆ f n. A sort of fennel, *Anethum panmorium*

ಸಬ್ಬಿಗೆ, ಸಬ್ಬೆ k n A slender branch of a tree

ಸಬ್ಬು (= ಸಬಕಾರ) f n Soap 2, sago

ಸಭೆ s n An assembly, congregation, meeting; a company, a community. ಕ್ರೈಸ್ತ- The Christian church -ಮಾಡು. To constitute an assembly. -ಕೂಡು An assembly to meet *Cpds* ಧರ್ಮ-, ನ್ಯಾಯ-, ರಾಜ-, ವಿದ್ಯಾ-. ಸಭಾಕಂಪ. Bashfulness in the public assembly ಸಭಾಜನ Courtesy, politeness, civility, persons of an assembly ಸಭಾಧ್ಯಕ್ಷ, ಸಭಾನಾಯಕ, ಸಭಾಪತಿ The president or chairman of an assembly ಸಭಾಮನೆ A meeting house ಸಭಾಪರ್ವ N of the 2nd book of the Mahâbhârata. ಸಭಾಮಂಟಪ An audience hall, council-chamber. ಸಭಾಸದ. A member of any society.

ಸಭ್ಯ s. n Fit or suitable for an assembly, well-bred, decent, civilized, gentle n A polite man -ತನ, -ತ್ವ Politeness, refinement

ಸಮ್ s *prep.* Con, with, along with *ad.* Greatly, thoroughly, well

ಸಮ s. a Even, level, flat 2, same equal, like, similar 3, straight, upright, honest, just, good, fit, proper, right, perfect n Identity of objects compared -ಗೊಳಿಸು To put in order. -ಮಾಡು To make even or equal, to put in order, to make proper. -ಕಾಲ The same time, simultaneous -ಚಿತ್ತ Even-minded, indifferent. -ಚ್ಛೇದ Common denominator (*arith*) -ಜಾತಿ Homogeneous. -ತೆ, -ತ್ವ Evenness, equality, fairness, justness. -ದೃಷ್ಟಿ Impartiality -ಭಾಗ An equal share. -ಭಾವ Of like nature, sameness, equability. -ಭೂಮಿ. Level ground. -ರಾತ್ರಿ Midnight -ರೇಖೆ A straight line.

ಸಮಗ್ರ s a All, entire, whole. a Totality, *also* -ತೆ, -ತ್ವ

ಸಮಜಾಯಿಷಿ, ಸಮದಾಯಿಷಿ h. n Persuading, appeasing, peace ಸಮಜಾಯಿಸು, ಸಮದಾಯಿಸು To persuade, satisfy, appease, calm, quiet

ಸಮನಿಸು a. k. v. i To be acquired, found, or got, to come about, to occur v. t To prepare

ಸಮಂತ s a. Universal, entire n Limit, term. ಸಮಂತಾತ್. All round.

ಸಮಂತು s. *ad* In that way, so, thus

ಸಮಭಿಹಾರ s n Repetition, reiteration

ಸಮಯ s. n Proper time opportunity occasion. time; leisure. 2, conventional usage -ಸಂಕಟ A difficulty -ತಪ್ಪು ಹೋಗು An opportunity to be lost -ಕ್ಕೆ ಬರು. To come in time, to be opportune ಸಮಯಕ್ಕೆ. In due time or season ಸಮಯಾಧೀನ Dependant on circumstances ಸಮಯೋಚಿತ Seasonable, opportune.

ಸಮರ s. n Conflict, battle, war -ರಂಗ ಸಮರಾಂಗ A battle field ಸಮರೋಚಿತ Fit for war

ಸಮರು (ರು = ಱು) k t. t. To trim, to adjust the contents of a corn-measure.

ಸಮರ್ಥ s. a Proper fit capable competent. 2 strong powerful. able 3 having the same sense -ತೆ -ತ್ವ -ನ Adequacy, capability ability ಸಮರ್ಥಿಸು. To make fit or ready

ಸಮರ್ಪಕ s a Suiting, worthy of conformable

ಸಮರ್ಪಣ, ಸಮರ್ಪಣೆ s. n Presenting offering ಸಮರ್ಪಿಸು To present. offer to deliver

ಸಮಲ s. a Dirty, impure. n Ordure

ಸಮವಾಯ s n. Close union. intimate relation. ಸಮವಾಯಿ. Closely connected; inseparable cause ಸಮವಾಯಿ ಕಾರಣ Material cause.

ಸಮಷ್ಟಿ s n Totality

ಸಮಸು (= ಸವಿಸು) k t. t To make wear away

ಸಮಸ್ತ s a All whole, entire n The whole.

ಸಮಸ್ಯೆ s. n Giving part of a stanza by a person to be completed by another as a trial of skill

ಸಮಾಖ್ಯಾ ಸಮಾಖ್ಯೆ s n Report fame renown 2 a term 3 a document of convention signed by all concerned

ಸಮಾಗಮ s n Meeting, encounter union junction. company

ಸಮಾಚಾರ s n Upright conduct, usage 2. news, accounts, intelligence -ತೆಗೆ To inquire about. -ಪತ್ರ A newspaper

ಸಮಾಜ s. n A meeting. assembly, congregation a society, club.

ಸಮಾಧಾನ s n Satisfaction, relief calm. peace. 2 removal of an objection. -ಗೊಳಿಸು, -ಪಡಿಸು, -ಮಾಡು To satisfy, to comfort appease, etc -ಹೊಂದು To be contented ಜಗಳ ಸಮಾಧಾನವಾಗು A quarrel to be appeased. ಜ್ವರ ಸಮಾಧಾನವಾಗು. Fever to abate.

ಸಮಾಧಿ s. n. A grave tomb. 2, deep meditation, silence -ಸ್ಥ Absorbed in meditation

ಸಮಾನ s a. Same alike similar uniform 2 common n An equal, a friend. 2 one of the vital airs. -ಕಾಲಿಕ, -ಕಾಲೀನ. Contemporaneous. simultaneous. -ತ್ವ Sameness likeness -ಸ್ಥ An equal.

ಸಮಾಪನ ಸಮಾಪ್ತಿ s n Accomplishment, completion. conclusion finish, end ಸಮಾಪ್ತ Finished, etc -ಮಾಡು. To finish.

ಸಮಾರಂಭ s n. Enterprise, beginning 2 a festival

ಸಮಾರಾಧನೆ s. n. Worship service 2, a festive or religious entertainment to Brâhmanas ಸಮಾರಾಧಿಸು To worship. serve.

ಸಮಾವರ್ತನೆ s n Completing. fulfilling. 2 (the ceremony of) a student's returning home after finishing his religious studies

ಸಮಾಸ s. n Composition of words, a compound word 2 whole, totality 3. contraction abridgment, brevity ಸಮಾಸಿಸು. To compound.

ಸಮಾಹೃತ s a Compiled; contracted 2. accepted. received ಸಮಾಹೃತಿ. Compilation abridgment

ಸಮಾಳಿಸು f t t. To manage, control

ಸಮಿತ s a Limited, met n Conflict ಸಮಿತಿ Meeting; conflict. sameness

ಸಮಿಧ s n Fuel. also (tb) ಸಮಿದು

ಸಮೀಕರಣ s. n. Reducing of fractions to a common denominator, equation. ಸಮೀಕರಿಸು To equalise

ಸಮೀಪ s. a. Near, close by, at hand n. Proximity, vicinity. ಸಮೀಪಿಸು To come near, approach

ಸಮುಖ s. a. Talkative, eloquent.

ಸಮುಚಿತ s. a. Suitable, proper, appropriate, worthy.

ಸಮುಚ್ಚಯ s. n. Accumulation, aggregation 2, conjunction of words or sentences (g.) ಸಮುಚ್ಚಯಿಸು To join words or sentences ಸಮುಚ್ಚಾಯಕ Conjoining ಸಮುಚ್ಚಾಯಕಾವ್ಯಯ A conjunction (g.).

ಸಮುದಯ, ಸಮುದಾಯ s. n. Rise, ascent 2, a collection, mass, multitude quantity. 3, the whole, totality 4, combination

ಸಮುದ್ರ s. n. The sea, ocean -ದ ಉಪ್ಪು, -ಲವಣ Sea-salt -ಫಲ An evergreen tree, *Barringtonia racemosa* -ವಹ್ನಿ. Submarine fire.

ಸಮೂಲ s. a. Along with the root -ವಾಗಿ. *ad.* With the roots, completely.

ಸಮೂಹ s. n. A collection, assemblage, multitude, quantity -ಗೊಳ್ಳು. To be assembled.

ಸಮೃದ್ಧ s. n. Thriving, prospering 2, rich, full 3, complete ಸಮೃದ್ಧಿ Increase, profusion; plenty, wealth

ಸಮೆ 1 = ಸವೆ, q. v.

ಸಮೆ 2 f. n. A lamp-stand

ಸಮೇತ s. a. Come together, united with, furnished with, having.

ಸಂಪಗೆ (= ಸಂಪಿಗೆ tb. of ಚಂಪಕ) n. A tall flower-tree *Michelia champaca*, bearing fragrant flowers

ಸಂಪತ್ತಿ, ಸಂಪತ್ತು, ಸಂಪದ (tb. of ಸಂಪದ್) n. Prosperity, welfare, luck, wealth, riches, excess, abundance

ಸಂಪನ್ನ s. a. Prosperous accomplished, acquired, possessed of, endowed with -ಗೃಹಸ್ಥ A worthy householder -ತೆ. Prosperity, accomplishment, attainment, ability

ಸಂಪರ್ಕ s. n. Mixing together, union, contact, touch

ಸಂಪಾದನೆ s. n. Gaining, acquiring, getting, attaining, gain, acquisition ಸಂಪಾದಿಸು To acquire, obtain, get. ಸಂಪಾದ್ಯ Gain, acquisition

ಸಂಪಿಗೆ = ಸಂಪಗೆ, q. v. -ಮರ The sampigĕ tree -ಹೂ. A s. flower

ಸಂಪೀಡನ s. n. Compression, paining, punishment, pain.

ಸಂಪು = ಸೊಂಪು, q. v.

ಸಂಪುಟ s. n. A casket, box, *also* -ಕ

ಸಂಪೂರ್ಣ s. a. Full, complete; all, whole, entire -ತನ, -ತೆ, -ತ್ವ, ಸಂಪೂರ್ತಿ. Perfection, completeness

ಸಂಪ್ರತಿ s. n. The present time *ad.* Now, at present

ಸಂಪ್ರದಾನ s. n. Gift, donation. 2, the dative case.

ಸಂಪ್ರದಾಯ s. n. Tradition, traditional belief or usage, custom, usage ಸಂಪ್ರದಾಯಿ. A member of a sect.

ಸಂಪ್ರಾಪ್ತಿ s. n. Attainment, acquisition, gaining -ಸು. To be got, found ಅ-. Failure, missing

ಸಂಬಂಧ (= ಸಮ್ಮಂಧ, q. v.) s. n. Connection, relationship, relation, a relation, relative 2, the genitive case -ಕ, ಸಂಬಂಧಿ, ಸಂಬಂಧೀಕ A relation, a friend. ಸಂಬಂಧಿಸು To be related, to join

ಸಂಬರ (= ಸಂಬಾರ, q. v. tb. of ಸಂಭಾರ) n. Seasoning ingredients, as pepper, cloves, nutmeg, *etc.* -ಕಾಗೆ The crow pheasant

ಸಂಬಳ s. n. Pay, salary -ಕ್ಕೆ ಇಡು To take (any body) into one's employ for pay. -ತಕ್ಕೊಳ್ಳು To receive pay -ನಿಷ್ಕರ್ಷೆ ಮಾಡು, -ಮೊಕರರಾರು ಮಾಡು. To fix a salary -ದವ A paid servant; a retainer, *also* -ಗಾರ

ಸಂಬಾರ. = ಸಂಬರ, q. v.

ಸಂಬಾಳಿಸು s *v t* To manage 2, to support, to take care of 3, to last.

ಸಂಬುದ್ಧಿ s *n* Perfect knowledge. 2, calling to, the vocative case

ಸಂಬೆ k. *n* The sword-bean, *Canavalia ensiformis* -ನೆಲ್ಲು A superior kind of rice

ಸಂಬೋಧನ s *n*. The vocative case. 2, instructing, addressing ಸಂಬೋಧಿಸು To instruct, advise

ಸಂಬ್ರಾಣಿ f *n* The Java almond, *Canarium commune*

ಸಂಭವ s *n*. Birth, origin 2, cause; possibility, probability. ಸಂಭವಿಸು To occur, to take place, happen.

ಸಂಭಾರ s *n*. Preparation provision; apparatus, necessaries, ingredient, wealth.

ಸಂಭಾವನೆ s. *n* Fitness, adequacy, ability 2, idea, fancy 3, regard, esteem 4, worship, honour. 5, a present. 6, value, price ಸಂಭಾವಿತ. Esteemed, honourable, a respectable man ಸಂಭಾವಿಸು. To honour, esteem, greet ಸಂಭಾವ್ಯ Suitable, possible, probable; respectable.

ಸಂಭಾಷಣೆ s *n* Conversation, discourse, conference, *also* ಸಂಭಾಷೆ -ಮಾಡು To converse with.

ಸಂಭೋಗ s *n* Enjoyment, pleasure, delight, fruition ಸಂಭೋಗಿ A sensualist -ಮಾಡು, ಸಂಭೋಗಿಸು To enjoy.

ಸಂಭ್ರಮ s. *n*. Whirling about, hurry, confusion, zeal, rapture, pleasure, grandeur, pomp. ಸಂಭ್ರಮಿಸು To be confused; to be in rapture

ಸಮ್ಮ *tb of* ಚರ್ಮ, *q v*. -ಗಾರ A shoemaker, *f* -ಗಾತಿ

ಸಮ್ಮತ *a* Agreed, assented to, esteemed, considered *n* Consent; approval. 2, opinion ಸಮ್ಮತಿ. Agreement, permission, consent, assent, approval; esteem, regard, order ಸಮ್ಮತಿಸು To agree, consent to

ಸಮ್ಮ [illegible]

ಸಮ್ಮಂಧ. *tb of* ಸಂಬಂಧ, *q. v.*

ಸಮ್ಮಾನ (= ಸನ್ಮಾನ, *q. v*) s. *n*. Honour ಸಮ್ಮಾನಿಸು To honour

ಸಮ್ಮಾರ್ಜನ, ಸಮ್ಮಾರ್ಜನೆ s *n* Cleaning, scouring, sweeping, purefying 2, smearing with cow-dung ಸಮ್ಮಾರ್ಜನಿ A brush, broom ಸಮ್ಮಾರ್ಜಿಸು To clean, sprinkle, to smear with cow-dung.

ಸಮ್ಮಿಶ್ರ s *a* Commingled, mixed, blend- [ed.

ಸಮ್ಮುಖ s. *n* Facing, confronting, meeting, presence. *ad* In front of.

ಸಮ್ಮೇಳ s *n* Union, a large concourse of people. 2, a double drum -ನ Coming together, mixure

ಸಮ್ರಾಜ್ s *n* A sovereign lord

ಸಯ್ 1 (= ಸೈ) k *n* Straightness, rectitude propriety. *v i* To cease, to be quieted

ಸಯ್ 2. ಸಯಿ 1 k *int*. Indeed. aye, of course, well said, correct

ಸಯಿ 2. h. (= ಸಹಿ) *n* Signature -ಹಾಕು To sign.

ಸಯಿಸು. = ಸಹಿಸು, *q v*.

ಸಯ್ತು, ಸಯ್ಪು a k *n* Cessation, rest, quiet, silence 2, rectitude propriety,

ಸಯ್ರಣೆ (= ಸೈರಣೆ *tb. of* ಸಹನ) *n* Patience, endurance, bearing ಸಯ್ರಿಸು (= ಸೈರಿಸು, ಸಹಿಸು) To suffer, endure, to be patient to put up with

ಸರ್ h *pref*. The chief, principal. superintendent.

ಸರ 1 (*tb of* ಸ್ವರ, *q v*) *n*. Sound, *etc*

ಸರ 2. (= ಸರಸ್) s *n* A lake, pond, pool.

ಸರ 3 s *n* A string 2 a piece of timber put across a roof.

ಸರ 4 f *n*. A sudden rush, a fit of delirium -ತಪ್ಪು Many mistakes -ಬಟ್ಟೆ Disorderliness, falsehood, lie. -ಮಗ್ಗಿ. A chief multiplication-table.

ಸರಕಾರ h. *n* The government of a state, the supreme power, the state -ಖಾತೆ. [illegible] Govern- [illegible] money

ಕು 1 h v i To move on, slip aside; o give place, yield ಸರಕಿಸು To ush aside

ಕು 2 k. n Goods, things, commodities, cargo, valuable articles, as loths, rice, etc

ಗಸ್ತು = ತಬಗಸ್ತು, q. v

ಗುಣಿಕೆ k n A loop with a running not, a noose

ಂಜಾಮು h n Materials, apparatus, ools, etc.

ತಿ, ಸರದಿ (= ಸತಿF, q. v tb. ಸರತ್) n. A ime, a turn, rotation -ಯ ಮೇಲೆ. By turns

ದಾರ h n A chieftain, a prince or eader, an officer

ದಿ h n Coldness, dampness (as of limate, air, etc); morbid cold

ದು. P p. of ಸರಿ 1, q v

ಪಣಿ, ಸರಪಳಿ (tb of ಸರ್ಪಣ) n A bain 2, a necklace

ಫರಾಜು f n The regard or kindness shewn by a superior to an inferior

ಬರಾಯಿ h n Providing supplies on a journey; supplies

ಲ (= ಸರಳ) s a Straight, right, ionest sincere, simple, upright. -ಬ ಡ್ಡಿ Simple interest. -ತ, -ತ್ವ Straightness, honesty.

ಸ್ (= ಸರಸಿ) s n A lake, pond

ಸ s a Succulent, juicy; fresh; tasty, pirited, piquant, witty charming ?, cheap n Piquancy, wit, fun, oke ಗಂಡಹೆಂಡರ- Dalliance of husband and wife -ಆಡು, -ವಾಡು. To port. -ಕೇಲಿ Jocose play -ಮಾತು ಸರಸೋಕ್ತಿ. A jocose expression -ಗಾರ, ಸರಸಿ. A jocose person

ಸಿ s n A pond. -ಜ A lotus -ಜಮಿತ್ರ, -ಜಸಖ. The sun -ಜಾತ, -ರುಹ. A otus.

ಸ್ವತಿ s. n. The goddess of speech and eloquence and wife of Brahmâ 2, speech 3, a river. -ಪೂಜೆ. The worship of Sarasvatî -ವೀಣೆ A kind of lute

ಸರಹದ್ದು f n Frontier, boundary

ಸರಳ = ಸರಲ, q v.

ಸರಳು k n An iron rod, bar 2, an arrow

ಸರಳಿ f n. The notes of the gamut.

ಸರಾಗ f a Unobstructed, easy. -ಮಾರ್ಗ An easy road

ಸರಾಫ h n A shroff, banker, a cashkeeper

ಸರಾಯು, ಸರಾಯಿ f. n Spirituous liquor. -ಬಟ್ಟಿ A spirit-still

ಸರಾಸರಿ h. ad. Anyhow, on an average, approximately. n Average

ಸರಾಳ (fr ಸರಲ) s n Going uninterruptedly. without difficulty.

ಸರಿ 1 k v i. To move, go, to move aside, to slide, slip, to run over v t To shove in 2, to put in proper order n Sliding; a precipice, ravine.

ಸರಿ 2 k. n Fitness, propriety, rightness; correctness, evenness, similarity a. Fit, proper, right, correct, even, reasonable ad Indeed, in truth -ಕಟ್ಟನ, Equality of position. -ಕ, -ಛಕ -ಗ A man of equal position -ಗಟ್ಟು. To make equal -ಗೂಡು To agree with -ಗೆ ಸರಿ ಮಾಡು To requite, repay. -ನೋಡು To compare, to examine -ಬರು To become right, to suit -ಬೀಳು To become right; to agree with, suit -ಬೆಸ Even and odd -ಮಗ A grown up son; f -ಮಗಳು -ಮಾಡು. To adjust; to compare, to make even. -ಮಾಡಿ ನೋಡು To compare -ಯಾಗು. To become equal, fit or right. -ರಾತ್ರಿ Midnight ಸರಿಯಾಗಿ Properly, rightly, correctly. -ಯೋ ಸರಿ Very proper indeed -ಸಮ, -ಸಮಾನ. Quite equal. -ಹಗಲು. Noon -ಹೊತ್ತು. Exact time. -ಹೊಂದು. To become fit or equal -ಹೋ- ... Resemblance

ಸರಿ 3 a k. *n.* Rain. 2, a heap

ಸರಿ 4. (ರಿ=ಱ) k *n.* Paste, gum, glue

ಸರಿಗೆ f *n* A necklace of females. 2, a wire. 3, =ಜರಿ 2, *q v*

ಸರಿಸ a k *n* Straightness, exactness; measure, equality.

ಸರಿಸು k *v t.* To move aside. ಸರಿಸಾಡು. To move about

ಸರುಕು =ಸರಕು 2, *q v.*

ಸರೆ. =ಸರಾಯಿ, *q. v* -ಗಾರ A liquor-manufacturer.

ಸರೋಜ s *n.* A lotus -ರಿಪು The moon. -ಸಖ The sun.

ಸರೋವರ s. *n.* A lake, pond

ಸರ್ಕಾರ. =ಸರಕಾರ, *q v*

ಸರ್ಗ s *n* Abandonment 2, creation 3, the universe. 4, a chapter, section

ಸರ್ಜ s *n* A timber tree, *qatica robusta* -ರಸ. Resin

ಸರ್ತಿ, ಸರ್ದಿ. =ಸರತಿ, *q. v*

ಸರ್ಪ s *n* A snake, serpent -ಯಾಗ Serpent-sacrifice -ರಾಜ Vâsuki ಸರ್ಪಾರಿ A peacock, Garuda ನಾಗ- A hooded serpent.

ಸರ್ಲೆ, -ಹಕ್ಕಿ k *n.* A water-fowl, the teal

ಸರ್ವ s *a* All, every, whole, entire, complete -ಗತ All-pervading, omnipresent -ಜಿತ್, -ಜಿತು All-conquering, the 21st year of the cycle. -ಜ್ಞ. All-knowing, all-wise -ಜ್ಞತೆ -ಜ್ಞತ್ವ Omniscience -ತ್ರಾಣಿ Almighty -ಧಾರಿ. The 22nd year of the cycle -ನಾಮ A pronoun -ನಿಯಾಮಕ. All-controlling -ಪ್ರಕಾರ Every way. -ಭಕ್ಷಕ Omnivorous. -ಮಂಗಲ. All-auspicious -ಮಂಗಳೆ Durgâ, Pârvati -ಮಯ. Universal -ಲೋಕ The universe -ವ್ಯಾಪಕ All-pervading. -ಶಕ್ತಿ. All might, almighty. -ಸಾಧಾರಣ Common to all. -ಸಾಮರ್ಥ್ಯ. All power -ಸಿದ್ಧಿ Universal success. The whole body ಸರ್ವಾಧಿಕಾರ. Universal rule. ಸರ್ವಾಪರಾಧ All offences ಸರ್ವಾಪರಾಧಿ One who is guilty of all sorts of transgressions ಸರ್ವಾರ್ಥ. All matters, all objects. ಸರ್ವಾರ್ಥಸಿದ್ಧಿ. Universal success. ಸರ್ವೇಶ Lord of all; the universal monarch

ಸರ್ವತ್ರ s *ad* Everywhere, always 2, all

ಸರ್ವಥಾ s. *ad* In all ways, by all means; entirely, wholly; assuredly, certainly, exceedingly, at all times

ಸರ್ವದಾ s *ad.* Always at all times.

ಸರ್ವಸ್ವ s. *n.* The whole of one's property

ಸಲ k *n* A time

ಸಲಗ k *n* The leader of a herd

ಸಲವು k *n* Cause account ಸಲವಾಗಿ. On account of, for

ಸಲಪೆ k. *n.* Washing and bleaching new cotton cloth

ಸಲಹಾ, ಸಲಹೆ (=ಸಲ್ಲಾ, *q v*) h. *n* Counsel

ಸಲಹು k *v t* To foster, preserve, bring up, take care of -ವಿಕೆ Fostering

ಸಲಾಡು f *n* Salad, raw herbs dressed with vinegar, oil, *etc* -ಎಣ್ಣೆ. S oil

ಸಲಾಮ್, ಸಲಾಮು h *n* Safety, peace 2, a mode of salutation expressive of respects or thanks. -ಮಾಡು To salute, complement, to greet -ಹೇಳು. To tell one's compliments or thanks.

ಸಲಾಕಿ, ಸಲಾಕೆ (*tb of* ಶಲಾಕೆ) *n* An iron rod or bar.

ಸಲಿಕೆ 1 (*fr.* ಸಲು, *q. v*) k *n* Paying, payment

ಸಲಿಕೆ 2 =ಸಲಾಕಿ, *q. v* *n.* A crowbar; a kind of spade

ಸಲಿಗೆ k *n* Familiarity, freedom, indulgence.

ಸಲು. =ಸಲ್ಲು *q. v* ಸಲಿಸು =ಸಲ್ಲಿಸು, *q v.*

ಸಲುವಳಿ k. *n* Fitness, propriety, currency. -ಕ್ರಯ. A just price -ಮಾತು A proper word

'1 k *ad* Currently; constantly, properly, well

!2 (= ಸಲಿಕೆ, *q v*) k *n* Payment 2, product -ಮಾಡು To find an area ಯಡಿ. A cubic foot

ಾ (= ಸಲಾಮ, *etc*, *q v*.) h. *n* Counsel 2, peace, truce.

ಾಪ (= ಸಂಲಾಪ) s. *n*. Conversation, familiar discourse. ಸಲ್ಲಾಪಿಸು To discourse

ಸು k *v t*. To fulfil, to give, grant, to show; to pay; to spend

ಲ್ಲ k. *v i* To accrue, pass be current (*as* money, *etc*), to be in use; to pass by general consent, be valid or fit, to depart from life, to be given, be paid or liquidated. 2, to be famous. *P p* ಸಂದು ಸಲ್ಲದು It is unfit, improper, *etc* ಸಲ್ಲದವ A useless man

ವ *tb of* ಸಮ, *q v*. -ನು To be equal -ನೆ. Quite equal, in the very same manner

ವಟು (= ಸೌಟು) k. *n* A ladle, spoon.

i t & i. To dirty, or be dirty, *as* clothes.

ವರಿ f. *n* Pincers.

ವಣಿಸು (= ಸವರಿಸು *tb. of* ಸಂವರಿಸು) *v t* To prepare, get ready, arrange. ಮೀಸೆ ಸವಣಿಸಿಕೊಳ್ಳು To trim one's mustaches

ವತಿ (*tb of* ಸವತ್ನಿ) *n* A second or rival wife -ತಾಯಿ A step-mother. -ಮಗ. A step-son. -ಮತ್ಸರ Jealousy between rival wives.

ವದೆ = ಸವುದೆ, ಸೌದೆ, *q. v*

ವನಿಸು k *v. i*. To be acquired; to occur.

ವಯಸ್ಕ s. *n*. Coeval, contemporary *n* A coeval, a contemporary, friend.

ವರಿಸು = ಸವಣಿಸು, *q v*.

ವರು 1 k *v. t* To cut off branches of a tree, *etc* 2, to chip ಸವರಿಸು To cause to cut off branches, to cause to chip.

ಸವರು 2 k *v. t* To rub in or apply to, *as* water, oil, *etc* ಸವರಿಸು. To have applied to.

ಸವರು 3 (ರು = ಱು) k. *v t* To trim (*as* the hair *etc*), to measure even with the striker

ಸವರ್ಣ s *n* The letter ಸ 2, the homogen *a*. Belonging to the same class of letters, homogeneous.

ಸವಾ h. *a*. One and a quarter. -ಸೇರು. 1¼ sheer

ಸವಾರ h *n* A man on horseback, horseman, rider

ಸವಾರಿ h. *n*. Riding upon the back of any animal or in a carriage, riding *Cpds* -ಎತ್ತು, -ಕುದುರೆ, -ಬಂಡಿ, *etc*., ಕುದುರೆ-, ಬಂಡಿ-, *etc*

ಸವಾಲು h. *n* A question, inquiry.

ಸವಿ 1 (= ಸವೆ) k. *v i* To wear away, to pass, *as* time

ಸವಿ 2 k. *v t* To taste, to eat. *a* Savoury, sweet or nice *n* Taste; sweetness; ambrosia -ಗಾಣು, -ತಕ್ಕೊಳ್ಳು, -ನೋಡು To taste, to be pleased -ಗಾರ A witty man *Cpds*. -ತುಟಿ, -ತುತ್ತು, -ನೀರು. -ನೋಟ, -ನುಡಿ, -ಮಾತು, -ಮಾವು -ಹಣ್ಣು *etc* -ಯೂಟ A delicious meal. -ಹತ್ತು. To have a pleasing taste.

ಸವಿಸ್ತಾರ s *a* Detailed *ad* Minutely.

ಸವುಟು (= ಸೌಟು) k *n* A spoon, ladle.

ಸವುತೆ (= ಸೌತೆ) k *n* A kind of cucumber, *Cucumis utilissimus*, *also* -ಕಾಯಿ.

ಸವುದೆ (= ಸವದೆ, ಸೌದೆ) f. *n* Firewood. fuel

ಸವುಳು (= ಸೌಳು) k *n* Brackishness *a*. Brackish *Cpds*: -ನೀರು, -ನೆಲ, -ಪದಾರ್ಥ, -ಮಣ್ಣು.

ಸವೆ (= ಸವಿ) k *v. i*. To be spent, to wear away, be wasted, to pass away 2, to be made ready.

ಸವ್ಯ s *a* Left 2, southern 3, reversed, contrary -ಪಹಾರ Intercourse

[illegible] k *a* Still motionless

ಸಸಿ 1 (*tb of* ಸಸ್ಯ) *n* Corn a young, plant

ಸಸಿ 2. k. *v t.* To pull out, as corn 2, to dress cotton

ಸಸಿನ a k *n.* Straightness rectitude. ಸಸಿನೆ Straightly, properly, nicely

ಸಸ್ಯ s *n* Corn, grain, fruit ಸಸ್ಯಾವಳಿ All sorts of corn or grain

ಸಹ s *ad.* With, together, also, too *also* ಸಹಾ. -ಕಾರ Acting with, co-operation, assistance -ಕಾರಿ. One who co-operates with another, an assistant associate -ಗಮನ, -ಮರಣ A woman's burning herself with her husband's dead body -ಚರಿ, -ಚಾರಿ A wife -ಜಾತ A brother, innate -ದೇವ The youngest of the Pândava princes, *f* -ದೇವಿ, *also* the ash-coloured flea-bane. -ಧರ್ಮಿಣಿ A lawful wife -ಭೋಜನ Eating together. ಸಹಾಧ್ಯಾಯಿ A fellow-student

ಸಹಜ s *a* Innate, inherent, natural 2, true, proper -ಗುಣ Inherent nature -ದೋಷ. An offence easily accounted for.

ಸಹನ, ಸಹನೆ s *n* Enduring, endurance, patience, toleration -ಶೀಲ Of a patient disposition

ಸಹವಾಸ s *n* Companionship; intercourse ಸಹವಾಸಿ A companion, friend

ಸಹಸಾ s *ad.* On a sudden, suddenly; at once. 2, by no means

ಸಹಸಿ s *a* Powerful, strong mighty. -ಗ A powerful man.

ಸಹಸ್ರ s *n* A thousand -ಕಾಲ Many years -ನಾಮ The thousand names of any deity. -ಕರ, -ಕಿರಣ, -ಪಾದ. The sun ಸಹಸ್ರಾಧಿಪತಿ A chief of a district ಸಹಸ್ರಾವಧಿ By thousands.

ಸಹಾಯ s *n* Aid, help, assistance, succour. -ಕೊಡು, -ಮಾಡು To help, aid -ಗಾರ A helper.

ಸಹಿ (= ಸಯಿ, *q. v.*) h *n.* Signature

ಸಹಿತ s *a* Accompanied by possessed of, along with with

ಸಹಿಸು (= ಸಯ್ರಿಸು *q v.*) s *v t* To bear, endure, *etc.*

ಸಹೃದಯ s *a.* Good-hearted, amiable, sincere.

ಸಹೋದರ s *n* A brother, *f* ಸಹೋದರಿ

ಸಹ್ಯ s *a* Endurable, sufferable *n.* Health, a healthy man. 2, wish 3, adequacy

ಸಾಂಯಾತ್ರಿಕ s *n.* A merchant trading by sea

ಸಾಂವತ್ಸರ, ಸಾಂವತ್ಸರಿಕ (*fr* ಸಂವತ್ಸರ) s. *a.* Yearly, annual *n* An astrologer.

ಸಾಂಸರ್ಗಿಕ (*fr* ಸಂಸರ್ಗ) s *a.* Contagious (*as* a disease)

ಸಾಂಸಾರಿಕ (*fr* ಸಂಸಾರ) s *a* Worldly

ಸಾಂಸಿದ್ಧಿಕ s. *a* Natural innate

ಸಾಕಲ್ಯ (*fr* ಸಕಲ) s *n* Totality, completeness; all -ವಚನ. A complete perusal

ಸಾಕಾರ s *a.* Having form, figurate. *n* A definite shape.

ಸಾಕು 1. k *v t* To bring up, foster, rear, feed, protect, preserve. *n* Bringing up, fostering -ತಂದೆ. A foster-father -ತಾಯಿ. A foster-mother -ತೆಗೆ To adopt. -ಮಗ, ಸಾಕಿದ ಮಗ. A foster or adopted son ಸಾಕಿದ ಕುರಿ ಮರಿ A foster lamb. ಸಾಕುವ ದಾದಿ A wet nurse. ಸಾಕಿಸು To cause to bring up, *etc*

ಸಾಕು 2 k *n* Sufficiency *a* Sufficient, enough. *int* Enough! *v i* It is enough (*imperat only*). ಸಾಕಾಗು To become sufficient, to become disgustful -ಮಾಡು To make sufficient, to give up with disgust. ಸಾಕಷ್ಟು As much as is wanted

ಸಾಕ್ಷಾತ್ s. *ad.* Visibly, evidently, manifestly. openly; truly, certainly. ಸಾಕ್ಷಾತ್ತರಿಸು. To see with one's own eyes ಸಾಕ್ಷಾತ್ಕಾರ Perception with one's own eyes -ಕೃತ್ Made manifest

ಸಾಕ್ಷಿ s *n* Evidence testimony. 2, [illegible] -ಯವನು,

ಗಾರ, -ದಾರ. A witness -ಜಾಬಿತೆ, -ವ
ೃ. A list of witnesses. -ವಾಙ್ಮೂಲ A
eposition of a witness ಅಪ-, ಅಬದ್ಧ-,
'ಳ್ಳ-, ತಪ್ಪು-, ಸುಳ್ಳು- A false witness
ಮಃ-, ಲೋಕ- The sun. ಮನಃ-, ಅಂತ
ಾತ್ಮ- Conscience.

ಗ = ಸಾಗು q v.

ಗಡೆ k. n The forest tree *Sleichera*
ijuga.

ಗರ 1. k n Extending and bending
ɔıwards -ಬೀಳು. To extend and
end forwards

ಗರ 2 s. n The ocean.

ಗವಳಿ = ಸಾಗುವಳಿ, q. v.

ಸು k. v. t. To carry on, perform,
ɔ conduct (*as* affairs), to manage
ıs a household), to convey; to nour-
sh (*as* the belly) 2, to cultivate.

ಗು 1. k v i To move forward (*as* a
hip, person, *etc*), to proceed, ad-
ance (*as* work, *etc*), to continue in
ime; to be brought about. ಸಾಗ ಕಳು
ಹಿಸು To send on, to accompany a
hort distance ಸಾಗ ಹಾಕು To carry
n, to send on

ಗು 2 k. n. Cultivation, tillage -ಆ
ಗು Cultivation to take place -ಬೀಳು
Cultivation to be abandoned -ಮಾಡು
To cultivate

ಗು 3. k. v i. To lengthen, extend
ಸಾಗ ಬಡಿ To elongate (*as* iron by
hammering)

ಗುವಳಿ (= ಸಾಗವಳಿ) k. n Cultivation
ಮಾಡು To cultivate. -ಯಾಗು. To
be cultivated.

ಂಕ್ರಾಮಿಕ (*fr* ಸಂಕ್ರಾಮ) s a. Contagious (*as* disease)

ಂಖ್ಯ (*fr* ಸಂಖ್ಯಾ) s a Relating to
number or calculation; deliberating,
easoning n N. of a philosophical
system *also* -ಶಾಸ್ತ್ರ.

ಂಗ (*fr* ಸ-ಅಂಗ) s. a Having members;
complete, finished, perfect ಸಾಂಗೋ
ಪಾಂಗ With all its members and parts

ಸಾಂಗ್ಯಾಣಿ s n A flat circular stone with a hole in the middle used in gymnastic exercises.

ಸಾಚಾ h. a. True, real 2, a mould or matrice

ಸಾಜ. *tb of* ಸಹಜ, *q v*

ಸಾಟಿ k n Likeness a. Like, equal

ಸಾಟೀನ್ = ಸಾತೀನು, *q v*

ಸಾಟೆ h. n Exchange, barter -ವ್ಯಾಪಾರ Bartered merchandise.

ಸಾಣೆ, ಸಾಣಿ (*tb of* ಶಾಣ) n A grindstone, whet-stone, *also* -ಕಲ್ಲು -ಗೊಡು, -ಹಿಡಿ. To grind, sharpen, *as* a knife -ಗ, -ಗಾರ A sharpener of tools

ಸಾಣಿಗೆ f n A sieve, strainer. -ಹಾಕು To sift, strain [cloth

ಸಾತೀನು e. n Satin, a species of silk

ಸಾತ್ವಿಕ, ಸಾತ್ವೀಕ s a Real, substantial, natural, genuine, true, honest, sincere, good, amiable, gentle. -ತನ, -ತ್ವ Honesty, sincerity, *etc*.

ಸಾದರ s. n Respect, love.

ಸಾದರು h a Arrived, come; issued.

ಸಾದಾ. = ಸಾಧಾ, q. v

ಸಾದಿಲವಾರು h n Any contingent charge (*as* of an office, stationery)

ಸಾದು 1. k. n. The black colour with which females mark their foreheads.

ಸಾದು 2 = ಸಾಧು, *q v*

ಸಾದೃಶ್ಯ s n Likeness, resemblance, a protrait, a likeness

ಸಾಧಕ s. n. Exercise, practice 2, a skilful man; a practiser -ಮಾಡು, To practice. ಗರಡೀ-. Practice in arms generally ಕತ್ತೀ-. Sword exercise.

ಸಾಧನ, ಸಾಧನೆ s n A means, expedient, an instrument, agent, an implement, utensil, ingredient 2, exercise, practice. 3, a document -ಸಂಪತ್ತು Materials and means -ಮಾಡು To practice, to recover

ಸಾಧಾ (= ಸಾದಾ) s a Plain, simple, mere pure. *etc*. -ಬಟ್ಟೆ A plain dress -ಬಟ್ಟೆ A plain cloth -ಬಡತನ. Mere poverty

ಸಾಧಾರಣ s a Common, general, universal. 2, middling, ordinary. n The forty-fourth year of the cycle -ತಃ Generally. -ರೀತಿ. Ordinary manner.

ಸಾಧಿತ s. a Accomplished, succeeded; recovered, subdued. 2, derivative

ಸಾಧಿಸು s. v t To effect, perform do, complete, settle to substantiate, prove 2, to recover 3, to obtain, to acquire. 4, to subdue; to master 5, to charge (upon another) ತಪ್ಪು-. To prove an offence ವಿದ್ಯೆ-. To master an art or science

ಸಾಧು s. a. Virtuous, mild, tame or gentle (*used also of beasts*) 2, fit, right. n. A good or honest man, a saint -ಜನ. A good person.

ಸಾಧ್ಯ s a. Practicable, feasible, possible. 2, subduable. 3, curable n Accomplishment. 2, a thing to be proved.

ಸಾಧ್ವಿ s. n. A chaste or virtuous woman; a faithful wife

ಸಾನಂದ s a Delighted n Joy, happiness.

ಸಾನಿ h. n A companion, colleague, *also a fem affix, e. g* ದೊರೆ-, ನಾಯಕ-, *etc*

ಸಾನು f n A table-land. 2, a summit.

ಸಾನುಕೂಲ s a Suitable, favourable

ಸಾನುನಯ s. a. Courteous, kind, polite

ಸಾನುಭವ s n. Fruition, experience.

ಸಾನುಮತ, ಸಾನುಮತಿ s. n. Approbation, assent

ಸಾಂತ 1 = ಸಂತ, q. v.

ಸಾಂತ 2 *tb of* ಶಾಂತ. q. v. -ಪ್ಪ. N of a man, *f.* -ಮ್ಮ, -ವ್ವ

ಸಾಂತ್ವ s n Consolation, comforting, conciliation -ನ. Consoling; friendly salutation and enquiry

ಸಾನಿ ... (*tb* ...) s n Nearness, vicini...

ಸಾಫ = ಸಾಫು, q. v.

ಸಾಫಲ್ಯ s n Fruitfulness, profit, success.

ಸಾಫು h a. Clean; pure; smooth, plain, clear, simple. n. Utter ruin.

ಸಾಬ್ = ಸಾಹೇಬ, q. v

ಸಾಬೀತು, ಸಾಬೂತು h a. Proved, established

ಸಾಮ s n Calming, soothing, conciliation, gentleness 2, negotiation. -ವೇದ N. of one of the four vêdas

ಸಾಮಗ್ರಿ s. n Wholeness 2, a collection of materials, apparatus, goods, effects -ಸನ್ನಾಹ Preparation of materials.

ಸಾಮತಿ (*tb of* ಸಾಮ್ಯತೆ) n Likeness; a comparison, simile

ಸಾಮಂತ s. a. Neighbouring n A neighbour 2, a feudatory chief, a leader.

ಸಾಮರ್ಥ್ಯ s. n. Force, capacity, power, ability, capability, strength, energy. ಬುದ್ಧಿ-. Intellectual power ವಿದ್ಯಾ-. Distinction in science

ಸಾಮಾಜಿಕ s. a Relating to an assembly n. A member of an assembly

ಸಾಮಾನ, ಸಾಮಾನು h n Instruments, apparatus, furniture, goods, things, articles. ಅಡಿಗೇ-. Materials for cooking, cooking utensils ಕಬ್ಬಿಣದ-, ಕಮ್ಮಾರ-. A smith's tools.

ಸಾಮಾನ್ಯ s. a Common, general. 2, vulgar, ordinary, low n Generality. 2, kind, sort. -ಗುಣ A common temper. -ಧರ್ಮ A general duty.

ಸಾಮೀಪ್ಯ s n. Nearness.

ಸಾಮು h. n Gymnastics feats of strength

ಸಾಮುದ್ರಿಕೆ s. n Palmistry

ಸಾಮೆ (*tb of* ಶ್ಯಾಮಕ, q v) *see* ಶ್ಯಾಮು.

ಸಾಮೋಪಚಾರ s. n A mild, conciliating measure.

... remedy, ... ation

ಪ್ರತ s. n. The present time. ad. At resent, now.

ಪ್ರದಾಯ (fr ಸಂಪ್ರದಾಯ) s. n Custom, ractice, tradition. ಸಾಂಪ್ರದಾಯಿಕ. raditionary

ಬ (fr. ಸ-ಅಂಬ) s n Śiva. -ಶಿವ. Śiva ong with Amba

ಬ್ರಾಜ್ಯ. tb. of ಸಾಮ್ರಾಜ್ಯ, q v

ಬ್ರಾಣಿ tb of ಸಾಮ್ರಾಣಿ, q v.

್ಯ s n Likeness, a comparison, mile, harmony. 2, (tb of ಸ್ವಾಮ್ಯ) es paid for the performance of me ceremonies. -ತೆ. Equality, sameess.

ಮ್ರಾಜ್ಯ s. n Universal sovereignty, npire

ಮ್ರಾಣಿ (= ಸಾಂಬ್ರಾಣಿ) s. n. Benzoin. a kind of perfume.

ು. tb. of ಸಹಾಯ, q. v.

ಯಂ, -ಕಾಲ s. n. Evening, eventide

ಯರು h. n Excise, custom

ಯು k. v i. To die, decease, depart om life. P. p. ಸತ್ತು. 2, power to e lost, as that of a limb, etc. ಸತ್ತು ತ್ತು ಉಳಿ, ಸತ್ತು ಸತ್ತು ಬದುಕು To reover from a dangerous illness.

ಯುಜ್ಯ s. n. Intimate union, absorpon into the divine essence.

1 k n Scaffolding

2 s n Essence, substance; the ssential part of anything, the matter a speech, etc, real truth 2, arrow, pith 3, the sap of trees, ectar 4, strength, power; vigour. , a summary, epitome 6, a verct. a. Excellent, real, sound ಅಸಾರ-. Real and vain ಅ-, ನಿಃ-. ithless, juiceless. ಭೂ-. The strength a soil.

ಕ s a Cathartic, laxative. ಉತ್-. xpelling.

ಗ, ಸಾರಂಗ s. n The spotted antelope, a deer. 2, the ćâtaka bird , a large bee.

ಸಾರಂಗಿ f. n. A kind of fiddle.

ಸಾರಟಿ s. n A chariot, gig.

ಸಾರಣಿ s n. A drain, channel.

ಸಾರಣಿಗೆ (tb of ಚಾಲನಿ) n A sieve, strainer.

ಸಾರಣೆ k n Smearing, smoothing (with cow-dung, etc), also ಸಾರವಣೆ. Cpds ಕೋಟೆ-, ಗೋಡೆ-, ಮನೆ-, ಶಾಲಾ-, ಸಗಣೆ-.

ಸಾರಥಿ s n A coachman. -ತನ, ಸಾರಥ್ಯ. Charioteering, driving.

ಸಾರವಾನ h. n A camel-driver 2, (s.) a scholar.

ಸಾರಸ (fr ಸರಸ್) s n The Indian crane. 2, a goose. 3, a lotus. 4, Yama. 5, a mountain. 6, weariness 7, a sharp man 8, a girdle or zone.

ಸಾರಾಂಶ s n Essence, substance, scope, purport, an abstract, epitome.

ಸಾರಾಯಿ, ಸಾರಾಯಿ (= ಸರಾಯ, etc, q. v) k. n. Spirituous liquor, gin. -ಅಂಗಡಿ. A gin shop -ಗುತ್ತಿಗೆ A tax levied on the sale of spirituous liquors, a liquor shop

ಸಾರಿ, ಸಾರೆ k. n A time, turn, time.

ಸಾರಿಗೆ k. n A piece of land.

ಸಾರಿಸು k v. t. To smear, smooth, clean

ಸಾರು 1 (ರ = ಱ) k. v. t. To cry out, proclaim, publish. ಸಾರಿಸು. To cause to proclaim, publish.

ಸಾರು 2. (ರ = ಱ) k. n Sauce, broth, pepper-water Cpds.. ಬೇಳೆ-, ಮೆಣಸು-, ತಿಳಿ-, ಸಪ್ಪೆ-, ಹುಣಿಸೇ-.

ಸಾರೂಪ್ಯ s n Sameness, resemblance, conformity.

ಸಾರ್ಚು (fr. ಸಾರಿಸು) k v i. To go near, approach. 2, to apply to, to put.

ಸಾರ್ಥ (fr. ಸ-ಅರ್ಥ) s a. Significant, important, useful, wealthy. n A caravan -ಕ Important, useful, advantageous, fruitful

ಸಾರ್ವ s a. Relating to all, general -ಕಾಲ Continually -ಜನಿಕ Universal, public. -ತ್ರಿಕ Suited to all places, general -ಭೌಮ Comprising the whole world; a universal monarch, emperor

ಸಾಲ್, ಸಾಲು h n A year. -ಗುಜಸ್ತಾ The past year -ಮುಜಕೂರು The present year -ವಾರ್ Annual

ಸಾಲ k n. Debt. -ಕೇಳು To ask for a loan, to demand payment of a debt. -ಕೊಡು To lend -ತೀರಿಸು. To discharge a debt -ತೆಗೆದುಕೊಳ್ಳು, -ಮಾಡು To borrow. -ಬಿಡು. To quit a debt. -ಬಡಕ, -ವಣಿಗ. A contractor of debts. ವೆಚ್ಚ-. A loan without security ಬಡ್ಡೀ-. loan on interest. -ತೀರಿಸು, -ಮುಟ್ಟಿಸು, -ಸಲ್ಲಿಸು, -ಪರಿಹರಿಸು. To pay a debt -ಗಾರ A creditor, a debtor

ಸಾಲಗ್ರಾಮ. = ಶಾಲಗ್ರಾಮ, q. v.

ಸಾಲದು (neg of ಸಾಲು) k. v. i It is not enough, it is insufficient ಸಾಲದೆ ಇರು To be deficient ಸಾಲದೆ ಹೋಗು. To be insufficient.

ಸಾಲಾಮಿಸ್ರಿ f n Salep, the tubers of *Orchis mascula*

ಸಾಲಾವಳಿ k n. Fitness, suitableness

ಸಾಲಿಗ k. n. A debtor. 2, a creditor 3, (fr ಸಾಲೆ) a weaver

ಸಾಲಿಗ್ರಾಮ. = ಶಾಲಗ್ರಾಮ, q. v

ಸಾಲು 1. k. v. i To be sufficient or enough, suffice.

ಸಾಲು 2 k n A line, row, range, a furrow. -ಇಡು, -ಕಟ್ಟು To put in rows, to arrange ಸಾಲಾಗಿ. In a row.

ಸಾಲು 3. = ಸಾಲ್, q v

ಸಾಲೆ (tb of ಶಾಲೆ, q. v.) n. A school -ಗೆ ಹಾಕು To put to school, -ಬರೆ. To study at school. -ಸ್ಥಾಪಿಸು, -ಹಾಕು. To establish a school. ಧರ್ಮ- An alms-house ಪಡ- An (inclosed) veranda; an out-house

ಸಾಲೋಕ್ಯ s. n Abiding in the same heaven with the deity

ಸಾವಕಾರ (= ಸಾವುಕಾರ) h. n A banker, ... a rich man ...

ಸಾವಕಾಶ f n Leisure, an interval; slowness a Leisurely, slow -ಗತಿ Slow manner

ಸಾವಧಾನ (fr ಸ-ಅವಧಾನ) s n Attention, carefulness, due heed a Attentive, careful, cautious

ಸಾವಂತ = ಸಾಮಂತ, q v

ಸಾವಂತಿಗೆ f n The garden-flower, *Chrysanthemum indicum*

ಸಾವಯವ (fr. ಸ-ಅವಯವ) s a. Composed of parts

ಸಾವರಿಸು f v t To recruit one's spirits.

ಸಾವಿಗೆ (tb. of ಶಾವಿಗೆ) n Macaroni, vermicelli.

ಸಾವಿತ್ರಿ s. n A cluster of solar rays 2 a N of Brahmâ's wife 3, N of Umâ

ಸಾವಿರ (tb. of ಸಹಸ್ರ, q v) n A thousand ಸಾವಿರಾರು A great number, thousands

ಸಾವು k n. Death. 2, a corpse -ನೋವು Death-pangs -ಹುಟ್ಟು Death and birth

ಸಾವುಕಾರ = ಸಾವಕಾರ, ಸಾಹುಕಾರ, q v

ಸಾವೆ (tb of ಶ್ಯಾಮಕ) n The grain *Panicum frumentaceum*.

ಸಾವೇರಿ s n N. of a tune

ಸಾಷ್ಟಾಂಗ (fr ಸ-ಅಷ್ಟ-ಅಂಗ) s n A mode of humble prostration by which eight parts of the body viz the hands, breast forehead knees and feet are made to touch the ground. -ನಮಸ್ಕಾರ, -ಪ್ರಣಾಮ Such a salutation -ಎರಗು, -ಬೀಳು, -ಮಾಡು. To prostrate as above

ಸಾಸ tb of ಸಾಹಸ, q v.

ಸಾಸವಿ, ಸಾಸವೆ, ಸಾಸಿವೆ, ಸಾಸುವೆ (tb of ಸರ್ಷಪ) n. Mustard, *Sinapis dichotoma* -ಕಾಳು Mustard seed.

ಸಾಸಿಗ tb. of ಸಾಹಸಿಗ, q v.

ಸಾಸಿರ. tb. of ಸಹಸ್ರ, q v

ಸಾಹಜಿಕ (fr ಸಹಜ) s. a Natural, coexistent

ಸಾಹಸ s n Boldness, daring, courage, effort, valour, power -ಗಾರ, -ವಂತ, ... A bold daring etc, man.

ಂತ್ಯ s n Association 2, literary ɔmposition, poetry 3, a collection f materials or implements.

ರುಕಾರ = ಸಾಪಕಾರ, q v

ೇಬ (=ಸಾಬ್) h n A lord or ıaster, a gentleman, sır, etc

ೀರಿಮೃಗ s. n. A porcupine.

ಹ s n A lion. 2, the sign of the odiac *Leo*. 3, a hero -ನಾದ. A ar-cry. -ಳ. Ceylon ಸಿಂಹಾಸನ A hrone ಸಿಂಹಿ A lioness

ತ s n Sand, a sand-bank, *also* ಸಿಕತೆ

ುರ, ಸಿಕಾರಿ (= ಶಿಕಾರಿ, q v) h n Hunt-ng, game. -ಖಾನೆ A menagerie, viary

h. n. The royal seal, a coining die.

ಟಿ, ಸಿಕ್ಕಣಿಗೆ k n A comb.

ು k v i. To be caught; to fall into he hands of to get among, to be ound, to be obtained or got 2, to nsert n Entanglement, intricacy, mpediment, obstacle, trouble. -ಬಿಡಿ ು To disentangle -ಬೀಳು, ಸಿಕ್ಕಿಬೀ ು, ಸಿಕ್ಕಿಕೊಳ್ಳು. To fall into a snare, to e caught ಸಿಕ್ಕಿಸು. To insert, to ause to be caught, to entangle ಸಿಕ್ಕಿ ಕೊಳ್ಳು. To hold or tuck anything ınder the arms, *etc.*

k v. t. To split; to tear or rend. ಗಸು, ಸಿಗಿಸು To get split.

ು = ಸಿಕ್ಕು, q v

ುರು a k. n. A splinter, shiver, ind.

ು k n. Shame, decency, modesty, imidity, disgust ಸಿಗ್ಗಾಗು To feel ishamed. ಸಿಗ್ಗಾಳಿ A bashful person.

ಗ, tb. of ಸಿಂಹ, q v

ಗರ, ಸಿಂಗಾರ tb. of ಶೃಂಗಾರ, q. v

ಗಳೀಕ k. n A black monkey

ು k n. Anger, passion, wrath, rage ಸಿಟ್ಟಾಗು To get angry, *etc* ಸಿಟ್ಟಿಗೆ ಬ್ಬಿಸು. To provoke to wrath. -ಇಳಿ Anger, *etc.* to abate -ಗೊಳ್ಳು To become angry -ತೀರಿಸು. To revenge one's self. -ತಡಕೊಳ್ಳು, -ನುಂಗು To keep down or suppress one's anger -ಬರು. Anger, *etc* to come. -ಬಿಡು To forsake anger -ಮಾಡು To become angry with -ಹಿಡಿ. To grow angry -ಗಾರ. A passionate or angry man ಸಿಟ್ಟೆಬ್ಬಿಸು. To enrage, *cf* ಸಿಟ್ಟಿಗೆಬ್ಬಿಸು

ಸಿಡಿತ (*fr.* ಸಿಡಿ 2.) k n Headache 2, jumping about from pride.

ಸಿಡಿ 1 k. a Small, fine -ಮಳೆ, -ಸೋನೆ Drizzling rain

ಸಿಡಿ 2 k n A hook-machine on which men are suspended in the air by a hook passed through the sinews of the back. -ಪೂಜೆ, -ಹಬ್ಬ The swinging feast

ಸಿಡಿ 3 k v i To fly about; to be spattered, *as* mud, *etc*, to snap, *as* parched grain; to start; to bounce. n Scattering, spattering. 2, a spring trap 3, fear, perplexity -ಮಿಡಿ. Alarm, consternation. -ಸು To spatter, bespatter.

ಸಿಡಿ 4 h n A ladder, a staircase.

ಸಿಡಿಲು, ಸಿಡ್ಲು k n A thunder-bolt, shaft of lightning.

ಸಿಡುಕು k v t To chide, scold n Peevishness, wrath. -ಮೋರೆ A peevish face. ಸಿಡುಕ A peevish man, *f.* ಸಿಡುಕಿ

ಸಿಡುಬು k n. The small-pox -ಮಾಡು, -ಹಾಕು. To vaccinate -ಮೋರೆ A pock-marked face.

ಸಿಂಡು k n A fetid smell

ಸಿಂಡ್ರಿಸು k v. t. To frown

ಸಿತ s a White. n Whiteness -ಶೂಕ. Barley ಸಿತಾಬ್ಜ, ಸಿತಾಂಬುಜ A white lotus

ಸಿದ್ದ tb. of ಸಿದ್ಧ, q v.

ಸಿದ್ದಾಯ s. n. Tribute; revenue.

ಸಿದ್ದಿ f n An Abyssinian.

ಸಿದ್ದಿಗೆ, ಸಿದ್ದೆ f n. A leather-bottle.

ಸಿದ್ಧ s a Accomplished, finished, perfected 2, successful. 3, established-ed, demonstrated, proved 4, valid, primitive (*g*) 5, ready, decided, settled. 5, thoroughly prepared, dressed, matured; ripened 6, sanctified, emancipated, eminent *n*. A semi-divine being; an inspired sage or seer; a saint -ಮಾಡಿಸು. To have made ready -ಮಾಡು To prove, to decide, to prepare. -ತೆ Perfection; validity (*as* of a rule). -ಧಾತು. Ore; a primitive verbal theme (*g*.). -ರಸ Quicksilver ಸಿದ್ಧಾನ್ನ. Cooked food

ಸಿದ್ಧಾಂತ s. *n* Established truth, conclusion, dogma, axiom, a theorem -ಮಾಡು To prove, demonstrate. ಸಿದ್ಧಾಂತಿ. An astrologer or astronomer

ಸಿದ್ಧಾರ್ಥ s. *n*. N. of the fifty-third year in the cycle of sixty.

ಸಿದ್ಧಿ s. *n*. Accomplishment, fulfilment, perfection 2, success. 3, proof, validity 4, certainty; determination 5 solution of a problem 6, preparation, readiness 7, a supernatural faculty. 8, good effect, advantage -ಗೆ ಒಯ್ಯು, -ಗೆ ತರು To bring to completion, to accomplish -ಗೆ ಹೋಗು To be fulfilled. -ಸು. To be accomplished, to prepare

ಸಿದ್ಧೇಶ, ಸಿದ್ಧೇಶ್ವರ s. *n* N. of Śiva

ಸಿಧ್ಮ s *n*. A kind of leprosy, *also* -ಟೆ

ಸಿಂದೂರ s. *n*. Red lead, minium.

ಸಿಂಧು s *n*. The river Indus. 2, the sea, ocean -ದೇಶ The country of Sindh. -ನದಿ The river Indus -ಲವಣ Rock-salt.

ಸಿಪಾಯಿ h. *n*. A native soldier, a policeman, a belted peon.

ಸಿಪ್ಪು (= ಚಿಪ್ಪು) k *n* An oyster-shell

ಸಿಪ್ಪೆ k *n*. The skin of fruits and vegetables

ಸಿಬಂದಿ, ಸಿಬ್ಬಂದಿ h. *n* An establishment of clerks, peons and servants.

ಸಿಬ್ಬ = ಸಿಧ್ಮ, *q v*

ಸಿಂಪ[illegible] (= ಸಿ[illegible]ಸು) s [illegible] sp[illegible] be -mink[illegible]

ಸಿಂಪಿ s *n*. An oyster-shell

ಸಿಂಪಿಗ (= ಚಿಪ್ಪಿಗ *fr* s ಸಿವ್) *n*. A tailor. -ನಹುಲ್ಲು. A common grass, *Panicum crus corvi*.

ಸಿಂಬಡಿಸು. = ಸಿಂಪಡಿಸು, *q v*.

ಸಿಂಬಳ k. *n* The mucus of the nose. -ತೆಗೆ. To blow the nose.

ಸಿಂಬಿ k *n* A coil of straw for setting a vessel on the ground. 2, the coil of a snake -ಸುತ್ತು To coil.

ಸಿರಿ *tb of* ಶ್ರೀ, *q v* -ಕನ್ನೆ The sunflower -ಕಾಳಗಿಡ. A strong smelling herb, *Gynandropsis pentaphylla*. -ವಂತ A wealthy man

ಸಿರ್ಕಾ h *n* Vinegar.

ಸಿರ್ಕ. = ಸಿಕ್ಕು, *q v*.

ಸಿಲುಕು 1 (= ಸಿಕ್ಕು, *q v*.) k. *v. i* To be entangled, caught. *n* Troublesomeness, *also* ಸಿಲ್ಕು

ಸಿಲುಕು 2. h *n* Balance in hand, *also* ಸಿಲ್ಕು.

ಸಿಲುಬೆ (= ಶಿಲುಬೆ) h *n*. A crucifix, cross.

ಸಿಲುವು k *n* Thin, *as* boards, paper, transparent, *as* water.

ಸಿವಂಗಿ k. *n* The hyena

ಸಿವಡು k *n* A bundle of straw or grass 2, a pad put under a load or vessel, *also* ಸಿವುಡಿ

ಸಿವಿಲ್ e *a* Civil.

ಸಿಹಿ = ಸೀ, *q. v*.

ಸಿಳ್ಳು 1 k *n* Whistling -ಹಾಕು. To whistle

ಸಿಳ್ಳು 2. k *n* Rheum of the eye

ಸಿಳ್ಳೆ k *n*. A bifurcation, fork

ಸೀ 1 k *n* Sweetness -ಕರಣೆ The pulp of ripe mangoes mixed with sugar. -ಗೆಣಸು The Goa potato, *Dioscorea aculeata*. -ನೀರು. Drinking water. -ವಲ್ಯ, -ಸಾರು A vegetable dish without tamarind. -ಮೊಸರು Fresh curds.

ಸೀ 2. k *v. i* To be scorched, burnt, parched [illegible] A parched [illegible] -ಕಾ[illegible] Parched or burnt state. -ಕು. Anything burnt in the bottom of a vessel in cooking.

ಸೀಕು e. a. Sick. -ಮನೆ. A sick house.

ಸೀಗಡಿ f. n. A very small kind of fish.

ಸೀಗೆ k. n. A climbing prickly shrub, *Acacia concinna*, the pods of which are used like soap. -ಕಾಯಿ. Its pod. -ಬಳ್ಳಿ. Its creeper.

ಸೀಂಟು k. v. i. To slide along on the posteriors.

ಸೀತಳ f. n. Combined derangement of the three humours.

ಸೀತಾಫಲ f. n. The custard-apple.

ಸೀತಾಳ, -ಳೆ f. n. The chicken-pox.

ಸೀತೆ s. n. N. of the wife of Râma. ಸೀತಾಪತಿ, ಸೀತಾರಾಮ. Râma.

ಸೀನು k. n. Sneering; a sneer. v. i. To sneeze. *P. p.* ಸೀತು.

ಸೀಪು (= ಚೀಪು 1) k. v. t. To suck.

ಸೀಬೆ h. n. The guava. -ಹಣ್ಣು. Its fruit.

ಸೀಬು k. n. The bamboo-slit. 2, bamboo twigs put on roofs of houses.

ಸೀಮಂತ s. n. Parting of hair on each side of the head. 2, a ceremony performed during the time of a woman's first pregnancy. -ಪುತ್ರ. A first-born son; *f.* -ಪುತ್ರಿ.

ಸೀಮೆ s. n. A boundary, frontier, landmark. 2, a country. -ಕೋಳಿ. A duck; a goose. -ಯಕ್ಕಿ. Sago. -ಯಗಸೆ. The ring-worm shrub, *Cassia alata*. -ಯೆಣ್ಣೆ. Kerosene oil. -ಸುಣ್ಣ. Chalk.

ಸೀಯಾಳ k. n. A tender coçoa-nut.

ಸೀರ (ರ = ಱ) k. n. A streak, stripe.

ಸೀರಣಿ k. n. A small chisel.

ಸೀರಣಿಗೆ k. n. A comb.

ಸೀರು 1. k. v. t. To louse. n. A nit.

ಸೀರು 2. (ರು = ಱು) a. k. v. i. To become angry. n. Raging, fierceness. ಸೀರನಾಯಿ. A wild dog.

ಸೀರೆ (*tb. of* ಚೀರ) n. A female's garment.

ಸೀವಣ್ಣಿ. *tb. of* ಶ್ರೀಪರ್ಣೀ, *q. v.*

ಸೀವರಿಸು a. k. v. t. To hiss, puff; to show disgust.

ಸೀಸ, ಸೀಸವು s. n. Lead.

ಸೀಸೆ h. n. A bottle, flagon.

ಸೀಳು k. v. i. To split, to be cleft, to be rent. v. t. To split, rend. n. A split, fragment, piece.

ಸು s. *pref. implying* good, well, excellent, excellently; excessive, excessively, much, readily, *etc.* -ಕರ. Practicable, feasible; doing well. -ಕಾಲ. A time of plenty. -ಕೀರ್ತಿ. Good report. -ಕುಮಾರ. A beautiful youth (*f.* -ಕುಮಾರಿ); tender, delicate. -ಕೃತ. Well made; virtuous, pious; a virtuous act; virtue; fortune; auspiciousness; reward. -ಕ್ಷೇಮ. Perfect health. -ಗತಿ. A fine gait; a good condition. -ಗಂಧ. Fragrant; fragrance. -ಗಂಧತೈಲ. Scented oil. -ಗಂಧಮುಸ್ತೆ. Indian spikenard. -ಗಂಧರಾಜ. The tuberose, *Polianthes tuberosa*. -ಗಂಧಿ. Sweet-smelling; a kind of fragrant flower-grass. -ಗಂಧಿಬೇರು. The country sarsaparilla. -ಗಮ. Easy, practicable; plain, intelligible. -ಗುಣ. A good quality. -ಗುಣಿ. A person of good qualities. -ಚರಿತ. Well conducted, well behaved. -ಚಿತ್ತ. Good mind. -ಜನ. A gentleman. -ಜನತೆ, -ಜನತ್ವ. Gentlemanliness. -ಜ್ಞಾನ. Understanding, knowledge. -ಜ್ಞಾನಿ. A wise person. -ತಲ. One of the lower regions. -ದರ್ಶನ. Good looking; Vishṇu's discus. -ದಿನ. An auspicious day. -ದೇಶ. A good country. -ಧರ್ಮ. Justice, virtue. -ನಾಮ. A good name. -ನೀತ. Well-behaved, polite. -ನೀತಿ. Good manners, good policy. -ಪರ್ಣ. Garuḍa. -ಪ್ರತಿಷ್ಠೆ. Installation, consecration. -ಪ್ರಭಾತ. An auspicious dawn; a morning prayer. -ಪ್ರಲಾಪ. Eloquence. -ಪ್ರಸನ್ನ. Well-pleased, gracious. -ಪ್ರಸಾದ. Great propitiousness. -ಫಲ. Very fertile, profitable; good fruit; good reward. -ಬುದ್ಧಿ. Good understanding. -ಬೋ

ಥನೆ Good instruction -ಭಗ. Very fortunate, prosperous, amiable. -ಭಟ. A valiant man, a good servant -ಭಾನು. The 17th year of the cycle. -ಭಾಷಿತ Well-spoken, eloquent, an elegant composition. -ಭಿಕ್ಷ Abundance of food or provisions -ಮಂಗಲ Very auspicious -ಮಂಗಲಿ A woman whose husband is alive. -ಮತಿ. Benevolence, kindness, kindly disposed. -ಮನ Very charming, one who has a good mind -ಮನಸ್. Good-minded, well-pleased, a learned man -ಮಾನ, ಸುಮ್ಮಾನ Joy delight. -ಮಿತ್ರ. A good friend; N -ಮಿತ್ರೆ Lakshmana's mother -ಮುಖ. A handsome face, lovely, pleasing. -ಮೇರು The mountain Mêru -ರಕ್ಷಿತ Safe and sound -ರಸ. Juicy, sweet -ಲಕ್ಷಣ. An auspicious mark, a grace, fortunate -ಲಗ್ನ. An auspicious time -ಲಲಿತ Very pleasing, pure -ಲಾಲಿಸು To listen to very kindly. -ಲೋಚನ. Fine-eyed, spectacles. -ವರ್ಣ Gold, a gold coin -ವರ್ಣಕಾರ A goldsmith -ವಾರ್ತೆ. Good news, gospel. -ವಾಸ, -ವಾಸನೆ Fragrance -ವಾಸಿನಿ. A term of courtesy for a respectable woman whose husband is alive (*cf* -ಮಂಗಲಿ) -ವಿಚಾರ Good thoughts -ವಿಶೇಷ Good tidings, news. -ವ್ರತ Strict in observing a vow. -ವ್ರತೆ A virtuous wife -ಶಿಕ್ಷಿತ Well-trained, disciplined skilful. -ಶಿಕ್ಷೆ. Good training. -ಶೀಲ Well-disposed, good temper. -ಶೀಲೆ. A good-tempered female, N -ಶೀಲತೆ. Good morals; amiability. -ಶ್ರುತ Well heard. -ಷಿರ. Perforated, hollow, a hole, a wind-instrument -ಷುಪ್ತಿ Deep sleep. -ಸಾಧ್ಯ Easily attainable -ಸೂತ್ರ. Easily, without obstruction. -ಸ್ಥಲ An excellent place -ಸ್ಥಿತಿ Good condition, well-being, welfare -ಸ್ಥಿರ Very firm or steady. -ಸ್ವಪ್ನ. A [illegible]
[illegible]

Salutary, beneficial, satisfied -ಹೃದ್. Cordial, friendly, a good man. -ಹೃದಯ Goodhearted, well-disposed

ಸುಕಾಣಿ. = ಚುಕಾಣಿ *q. v.*

ಸುಕ್ಕು k *n* Shrinkage, a wrinkle. fold. *v. i.* To shrink, shrivel

ಸುಖ s. *n* Happiness, pleasure, delight, joy, comfort, ease. *a.* Happy, joyful, agreeable, suitable. -ಕರ Causing happiness, done easily. -ಕೊಡು. To give pleasure -ದಿಂದ ಇರು To be happy -ಪಡಿಸು. To make happy -ಗೊಳ್ಳು, -ಪಡು, --ಭೋಗಿಸು To feel happy. -ದ, -ಪ್ರದ Giving happiness. -ದುಃಖ Pleasure and pain. -ರೂಪ. Well happy ಸುಖಾಸನ A comfortable seat ಸುಖಿ. Happy, joyful, comfortable, a happy man ಸುಖಿಸು. To feel pleasure

ಸುಗಿ a. k. *v. i* To tear off; to plunder.

ಸುಗಿ k. *n.* Harvest, *esp.* the time of reaping the corn and grain 2 plenty. -ಕಾಲ The season of gathering crop.

ಸುಗ್ಗು k. *n.* Rice parched ground and mixed with jaggory and cocoanut. ಸುಗ್ಗಿ ಸುಂಡೆ A ball of ಸುಗ್ಗು.

ಸುಗ್ರೀವ s. *n* N. of a monkey-king

ಸುಂಕ (*tb of* ಶುಲ್ಕ) *n* Toll, duty, customs. -ದವ A publican, *also* ಸುಂಕಿಗ

ಸುಂಕು 1. a. k *n.* A fold, curl. 2, = ಸೊಂಕು, *q v*

ಸುಂಕು 2 (*tb of* ಶೂಕ) *n* An awn

ಸುಚಿ. *tb of* ಶುಚಿ, *q v*

ಸುಟ್ಟ k *a.* Clever, able, powerful

ಸುಟ್ಟು k *P p. of* ಸುಡು, *q v.* -ರೆ A whirlwind; *also* -ರೆ ಗಾಳಿ.

ಸುಡು k *v t* To burn, to roast; to bake, to fire off, to consume. *v i* To burn, to be very hot; to feel heated, to be consumed. *P p* ಸುಟ್ಟು. *n* Burning [illegible] ಸುಟ್ಟು ಮಾಂಸ [illegible] ಮಾಡಿಬಿಡು

To destroy by fire. -ಗರ *Ignis fatuus* -ಗಾಡು A cemetery -ಗಾಡು ಮಾತು. A disagreeable word

ಸುಂಟರ, ಸುಂಟುರ k. *n* A cyclone, hurricane, *also* -ಗಾಳಿ

ಸುಂಟಿ (*tb. of* ಶುಂಠಿ) *n.* Dry ginger, the common ginger. [ಸುಂಡಿಲಿ.

ಸುಂಡ (*tb of* ಶುಂಡ) *n* A musk rat; *also*

ಸುಂಡಲು, ಸುಂಡಿಲು (= ಸೊಂಡಲು, *etc* *tb of* ಶುಂಡಾರ) *n* An elephant's trunk

ಸುಂಗು k. *v. i* To evaporate ಸುಂಗಿಸು To cause to evaporate

ಸುಣ್ಣ (*tb. of* ಚೂರ್ಣ) *n.* Chunam, lime, quicklime -ದ ಗೂಡು A lime-kiln -ಪಾದ. The basement of a pillar.

ಸುತ s *a* Begotten. *n* A son, *f.* ಸುತೆ.

ಸುತರಾಮ್ s *ad* Altogether, utterly; never.

ಸುತ್ತ, ಸುತ್ತಲು, ಸುತ್ತಮುತ್ತಲು (*cf.* ಸುತ್ತು) k. *prep.* About, round about, surrounding, all around -ಬರು To come round about. -ನೋಡಿ ಕಾರ್ಯ ಮಾಡು To do a thing with circumspection ಸುತ್ತಾಲೆ The surrounding wall of a temple

ಸುತ್ತಿಗೆ k *n* A hammer

ಸುತ್ತು k. *v t* To surround, put around, inwrap, to roll up, wrap up. *v. i* To go around, to walk about *n* Enclosure, expansion; a coil, roll, cheeroot, a walk round, a turn *a* Circuitous, round. -ಅಳತೆ, ಸುತ್ತಳತೆ. Compass, circumference -ಮುತ್ತಲು. = ಸುತ್ತ, *q. v.* ಸುತ್ತಿಕೊಂಡು ಹೋಗು. To wind up, to go round about ಸುತ್ತಿ ಕೊಂಡು ಬೀಳು. To reel and fall ಸುತ್ತಿ ನೋಡು To go round and look ತಲೆ-. To feel giddy -ಹಾಕು. To surround -ಎಕೆ. Turning round ಸುತ್ತಿಸು. To cause to roll or wind.

ಸುದಾ s. *ad* Along with, also, even; *also* ಸುಧಾ.

ಸುದಾಮ s *n.* A liberal man 2, N. of a poor Brâhmana

ಸುದ್ದಿ (*tb of* ಶುದ್ಧಿ) *n* News, tidings, intelligence, rumour, talk

ಸುಧಾರಣೆ s. *n* A civilized or enlightened state, revising, *as* a work 2, rest, forbearance, shift.

ಸುಧಾರಿಸು s *v. t* To adjust, to train, to finish; to polish; to civilise, enlighten 2, to rest, to manage or get through *v. i* To be civilised or enlightened

ಸುಧೆ (ಸುಧಾ) s *n.* Nectar, ambrosia, milk, juice 2, lime, mortar 3, the emblic myrobalan.

ಸುನತಿ h *n.* Circumcision

ಸುನಾಯಾಸ s. *ad* Without trouble or difficulty, easily.

ಸುನಾವಣೆ h *n.* Reading and explaining ಸುನಾಯಿಸು To explain, tell

ಸುಂದರ s *a.* Beautiful, handsome, charming, agreeable -ತೆ Beauty.

ಸುಪ್ತ s *a.* Slept, asleep, numbed. ಸುಪ್ತಿ. Sleep, numbness

ಸುಪ್ಪತ್ತಿಗೆ f. *n* A sleeping mattress.

ಸುಬ h. *n* A province. -ದಾರ The chief native officer of a talook.

ಸುಬ್ಬ (*tb of* ಶುಭ್ರ) *n.* The serpent âdiśêsha 2, N. -ರಾಯ. N

ಸುಬ್ಬಲು k *n* Roughness

ಸುಬ್ರಹ್ಮಣ್ಯ s *n* Kârttikêya, N. of a place of pilgrimage in S Canara

ಸುಭದ್ರೆ (ಸುಭದ್ರಾ) s *n.* N of Krishna's sister and Arjuna's wife.

ಸುಮಾರ, ಸುಮಾರು h. *n.* Conjecture or guess 2, nearness, aboutness. 3, moderateness, tolerableness. *a.* Middling, ordinary *ad* About

ಸುಂಬಳ 1. = ಸಿಂಬಳ, *q. v*

ಸುಂಬಳ 2 f. *n.* White arsenic, *also* -ಕಾರ

ಸುಮ್ಮಗ, ಸುಮ್ಮನೆ k *ad* Quietly silently; causelessly, for nothing, uselessly. *a* Quiet silent -ಕೊಡು To give gratis -ಬರು. To come without any particular business, to come often. -ಇರಿಸು, ಸುಮ್ಮನಿರಿಸು. To silence ಸುಮ್ಮಗಿರು, ಸುಮ್ಮನಿರು To be silent, (*imp. 2nd pers*) be silent

ಸುಯಿ k *v i.* To breathe, to sigh *n* Breath, a sigh *also* -ಲು

ಸುರ s n A god, deity. -ಗಿರಿ. The mountain Mêru. -ಗುರು Brihaspati -ಚಾಪ, -ಧನು A rainbow -ಪ, -ಪತಿ, -ರಾಜ, -ವರ Indra -ಪುರ Indra's capital -ರಿಪು, ಸುರಾರಿ A god's enemy.

ಸುರಗಿ k n N of a tree with very fragrant flowers 2, (tb of ಕ್ಷುರಿಕೆ) a sword

ಸುರಂಗ f. n. A hole made by burglars in a house-wall, etc; a mine.

ಸುರಟಿ s n. N. of a tune.

ಸುರಣ f n An esculent root Arum campanulatum

ಸುರತ s. n. N of Surat a Playful, tender

ಸುರಪರ್ಣಿ s. n. The tree Rottlera tinctoria; also ಸುರಹೊನ್ನೆ.

ಸುರಭಿ s a Agreeable 2, fragrant n. The cow of plenty. 2, a wise man. 3, mint, Mentha sativa.

ಸುರಮು = ಸುರುಮು, q v.

ಸುರಳಿ (= ಸುರುಳಿ) k. n. A coil, roll. ಮಾತಿನ-. Many words.

ಸುರಳಿತ f a Straight and smooth, fair and flowing, plain

ಸುರಿ 1. k v i To flow, pour, drop, as tears, blood, rain, etc. v t To pour, drop, shoot out, etc ಸುರಿಸು To cause to flow, etc. -ಯುವಿಕೆ Flowing, etc -ವು. To pour

ಸುರಿ 2. (ರಿ = ಱ) k v t To drink with a supping noise.

ಸುರು. = ಶುರು q. v

ಸುರುಟು k v. i. To become shrivelled, to coil or roll up

ಸುರುಮು h. n A collyrium for the eyes 2, sulphuret of antimony

ಸುರುಳಿ = ಸುರಳಿ. q. v

ಸುರೆ (ಸುರಾ) s. n. Spirituous liquor, toddy ಸುರಾಪಾನ Drinking of spirituous liquor

ಸುರ್ಕು k. v t To shrivel, contract, to curl n Shrivelling, shrinking, a wrinkle; a curl -ಸುರು (-ಮಸುರು) [illegible]

[illegible]

ಸುಲಂಗಿ (tb. of ಶೂಲಿಕೆ) n A mining crow-bar. 2, a spike for peeling cocoanuts

ಸುಲ್ತಾನ h n A sultan ಸುಲತಾನಿ Relating to a sultan. ಸುಲತಾನಿ ಹಣ A kind of coin

ಸುಲಭ s a Easy, attainable, feasible -ಹೇಳು. To be easy.

ಸುಲಾವಣೆ. = ಸುನಾವಣೆ, q v

ಸುಲಿ k. v. t To strip off, to peel, to skin. 2 to plunder, rob P ps ಸುಲಿದು, ಸುಲಿದು -ಗೆ Plundering, robbery, pillage, booty -ಗೆ ಮಾಡು, ಸುಲುಕೊಳ್ಳು. To plunder, rob.

ಸುವ್ವಿ k n A chorus used by women at marriages, when pounding rice, etc

ಸುಸ್ತಿ, ಸುಸ್ತು h n Slowness, delay, laziness -ಮಾಡು. To delay, loiter -ಗಾರ. A lazy man

ಸುಳಿ (ಳಿ = ಱಿ) k v i To turn round, whirl, revolve, to coil, to wander, roam, to move, to walk, to be unsteady, to waver, flicker. n Whirling, waving, motion, a whirl-pool 2, the tender leaf of a plantain, cocoa or areca-nut tree. 3, deception, fraud. -ಹಾಕು, (-ದು ಆಡು). To move about -ಗುಂಡಿ A whirl-pool -ನೆತ್ತಿ. The fontanelle

ಸುಳಿವು, ಸುಳುವು (ಳಿ ಳು = ಱಿ ಱು) k n. Motion, waving. 2, a glimpse, slight notice or sign

ಸುಳುವು (tb. of ಸುಲಭ) n Facility, fine workmanship, ingenuity, cheapness

ಸುಳ್ಳು k n Falsehood, untruth, lie, also -ಮಾತು ಸುಳ್ಳ A liar ಸುಳ್ಳಾಡು To lie. ಸುಳ್ಳಾಸೆ. False hopes. -ಕಥೆ A fable. -ಗಾರ A liar. -ಚಾಡಿ Calumny, false accusation -ತನ. Falsification -ನಿಮಿತ್ತ, -ನೆವನ A false plea -ಮನುಷ್ಯ A fraudulent man. -ಮುಚ್ಚು To hide a lie -ಸಾಕ್ಷಿ. A false witness. -ಹೇಳು. To lie.

ಸೂಕ್ತ s. n A vedic hymn 2, a good word a. Well spoken.

ಸೂಕ್ಷ್ಮ s a Subtile. minute, atomic, [illegible] [illegible]tle, artful, ly. n. An atom. -ಕಾರ್ಯ, -ಕೆಲಸ. A lelicate work. -ದೃಷ್ಟಿ. Sharp sight. ಬುದ್ಧಿ. Acute intellect. -ಶರೀರ. The ubtile body.

ಚನೆ s. n. Indication, intimation, iinting. 2, hint, information. 3, n index, summary. -ಆಗಿ ಹೇಳು. To ell briefly. ಸೂಚಿಸು. To point out, ndicate, intimate, hint; to show.

ಚಿ (tb. ಶೂಚಿ) s. n. A needle. 2, a rristle, quill. 3, an index, list.

ಜಿ. tb. of ಶೂಚಿ, q. v. -ಕಣ್ಣು. The eye of a needle. -ಕಲ್ಲು. A magnet. -ತೂ ತು, -ತೂಬು. = ಸೂಜಿಕಣ್ಣು.

ಟಿ k. n. Smartness, quickness.

ಟೆ f. n. A torch of wisps, etc.

ಡಿ k. n. A sheaf or bundle of grass; ilso ಸೂಡು n., q. v.

ಡು a. k. v. t. To put on the head, tc., as flowers, etc.; to receive. n. A bundle; also ಸೂಡಿ, q. v.

ತ s. n. A charioteer. 2, a bard.

ತಕ s. n. Impurity from childbirth, nenses or death.

ತಿ s. n. Birth; offspring, progeny.

ತ್ರ s. n. A thread, string. 2, a precept, rule, law, canon, decree. 3, art, spring (as of a piece of mechanism). -ಧಾರ. A stage-director; also ಧಾರಕ, -ಧಾರಿ.

ದ s. n. Cooking; a cook. ಸೂದಾಗಾರ. A kitchen.

ನಗಿ, ಸೂನಂಗಿ (tb. of ಶೂಲಿಕೆ) n. A pike for peeling cocoanuts; also ಶುಲಂಗಿ.

ನು s. n. A son; a child.

ಪ s. n. Soup, broth, sauce. 2, a cook. ಕಾರ. A cook. -ಶಾಸ್ತ್ರ. Cookery; a book on cookery.

ರಣ. = ಸುರಣ, q. v.

ರು. = ಚೂರು, q. v.

ರುಳು a. k. n. An oath. v. i. To wear; also ಸೂರುಳಿಸು.

ರೆ (ರೆ = ಱೆ) k. n. Plundering, pillaging; plunder, spoil. -ಕೊಡು. To lavish, squander. -ಗಾರ. A plunderer. -ಮಾಡು. To plunder. -ಯಾಗು, -ಹೋಗು. To be plundered.

ಸೂರ್ಯ s. n. The sun. -ಕಾಂತ. Crystal. -ಕಾಂತಿ. Sun-shine; the sun-flower. -ಗ್ರಹಣ. A solar eclipse. -ಬಿಂಬ, -ಮಂ ಡಲ. The disk of the sun. -ವಂಶ. The solar race. ಸೂರ್ಯಾಸ್ತ, ಸೂರ್ಯಾಸ್ತ ಮಯ, ಸೂರ್ಯಾಸ್ತಮಾನ. Sun-set. ಸೂ ರ್ಯೋದಯ. Sun-rise. -ಸಂಕ್ರಮಣ. The sun's passage from one sign of the zodiac to another.

ಸೂಲ (tb. of ಸೂತ) n. Child-bearing; bringing forth. -ಗಾತಿ, -ಗಿತ್ತಿ. A midwife.

ಸೂಸಕ a. k. n. A forehead-jewel, trinket.

ಸೂಸಲು k. n. A kind of dish; also -ಕ ಡುಬು.

ಸೂಸು a. k. v. i. To issue, as breath, etc.; to flow, drop, shower, as water, rain. v. t. To spread, scatter or sprinkle about, as water, etc. n. Sprinkling.

ಸೂಳು 1. a. k. n. A loud sound, noise.

ಸೂಳು 2. (ಳು = ೞು) a. k. n. A time, turn; a season. ಸೂಳಾಯ್ತ. A herald.

ಸೂಳೆ (tb. of ಶೂಲೆ) n. A harlot, whore. -ಗಾರ. A whoremonger. -ಗಾರಿಕೆ. Whoredom.

ಸೃಜಿಸು. = ಸೃಷ್ಟಿಸು, q. v. 2, to let go.

ಸೃಷ್ಟ s. a. Created, made. -ಕೆ, -ನೆ. Making, fabrication, forgery, falsehood. -ಪತ್ರ. A forged document. ಸೃಷ್ಟಿ. Creation; emanation; nature; natural property. ಸೃಷ್ಟಿಕರ್ತ. A creator. ಮೃಷ್ಟಿಸೃಷ್ಟಿ. A creation in which the deity is inherent in all the parts. ಸೃಷ್ಟಿಸು. To create, produce, make.

ಸೆಕೆ, ಸೆಖೆ (tb. of ಶಿಖಿ) n. Heat. -ನಾಡು. A hot country.

ಸೆಜ್ಜೆ 1. k. n. A cultivated grass, *Holcus spicatus*.

ಸೆಜ್ಜೆ 2. (= ಸಜ್ಜೆ. tb. of ಶಯ್ಯ) n. A bed.

ಸೆಟಿ k. v. i. To bend.

ಸೆಟ್ಟಿ (tb. of ಶ್ರೇಷ್ಠ) n. A title for a banker, merchant; the head of a caste.

ಸೆಡೆ k. v. i. To grow bulky, to get puffed up. 2, to become stiff, *as* limbs, *etc.* 3, to bend, shrink. 4, to fear. ಸೆಡಕು. Pride, haughtiness. ಸೆಡವು. The state of being crooked or bent, pride.

ಸೆಣಸು a. k. v. i. To be envious or jealous. n. Anger, wrath.

ಸೆರಗು (ರ=ಱ) k. n. The loose end of a garment, cover, protection. ಸೆರಗೊಡ್ಡು. To stretch the end of one's garment as a sign of humble petition.

ಸೆರೆ 1. k. n. The hollowed palm of the hand, a handful.

ಸೆರೆ 2. (ರೆ=ಱೆ) k. n. Confinement, captivity; a prison, hold. -ಬಿಡಿಸು. To release from prison. -ಯಾಗು. To become a prisoner. -ಹಾಕು. To imprison. -ಹಿಡಿ. To take prisoner.

ಸೆರ್ಟಿಫಿಕೇಟು e. n. A certificate, testimonial.

ಸೆಲೆ a. k. n. Sound; echo. 2, a spring, fountain.

ಸೆಳೆ 1. a. k. n. A twig, stick, rod.

ಸೆಳೆ 2. k. v. t. To cane, beat or flog.

ಸೆಳೆ 3. k. v. t. To draw, drag, pull. v. i. To draw up, *as* a limb. n. Pulling the current of a stream, *also* -ತ, ಸೆಳವು.

ಸೇಕ (= ಸೆಕೆ, q. v.) f. n. Heat. 2, fomentation. 3, sprinkling, effusion.

ಸೇಕಡಾ h. a. Per hundred.

ಸೇಗುಡಿ k. n. N. of a medicinal plant.

ಸೇಚನ s. n. Sprinkling, shedding; effusion. 2, a bucket.

ಸೇಡು k. n. Bending, shrinking, contraction.

ಸೇಡು (= ಸಿಟ್ಟು, q. v.) k. n. Anger, *etc.*

ಸೇತು, ಸೇತುವೆ s. n. A bridge; a mound, dike.

ಸೇದು k. v. t. To draw up water; to pull in (a string), to snuff, to draw in (*as* breath); to smoke (as a pipe, [illegible]
[illegible]

ಸೇನ h. n. A revenue officer of a village. -ಬೋವ (= ಶಾನಭೋಗ) A village clerk.

ಸೇನಾ, ಸೇನೆ s. n. A host, army. ಸೇನಾಧಿಪತಿ, ಸೇನಾನಾಯಕ, ಸೇನಾನಿ, ಸೇನಾಪತಿ. A commander, general.

ಸೇಬು h. n. An apple.

ಸೇರು k. v. i. To go to, to approach, to reach, to belong to, to enter, to be included, to join, to meet, to agree to, to be in harmony; to agree with, *as* food, to be agreeable. *P. p.* ಸೇರಿ. n. Meeting, *etc.* -ವಿಕೆ. Joining, *etc.* ಸೇರಿಸು. To join, to put together, to put into; to make enter, to insert, to assemble.

ಸೇರು 2. f. n. A seer, a measure of weight or capacity.

ಸೇರುವೆ, ಸೇರ್ವೆ k. n. Connection, company, a herd of cattle. -ಗಾರ. One in charge of a cattle-pound.

ಸೇಲೆ. *tb. of* ಚೇಲ, *q. v.*

ಸೇವಗೆ, ಸೇವಿಗೆ k. n. Macaroni.

ಸೇವಂತಿಗೆ s. n. A kind of jasmine, *Jasminum auriculatum.*

ಸೇವೆ s. n. Service, attendance, worship, homage, devotion, use, practice. -ಮಾಡು. To serve. ಸೇವಕ. A servant, attendant, a worshipper, *f.* ಸೇವಕಳು. ಸೇವನೆ. Service; devotion, using, taking, enjoying. ಸೇವನ ಮಾಡು. To use, enjoy, take. ಸೇವಿಸು. To serve, honour, worship, to enjoy, use. ಸೇವಾವೃತ್ತಿ. The functions of service. *Cpds.*: ಆತ್ಮ-, ದೇವರ-, ಭೂತದ-, ಮಾಂಸದ-, ಮುಂತಿರ-, ಸೈತಾನನ-, *etc.*

ಸೇಸೆ (*tb. of* ಶೇಷ) n. The remains of flowers, raw rice and other offerings made to an idol. 2, raw rice thrown on the heads of a married couple.

ಸೈ (= ಸರಿ, q. v.) k. n. Straightness; rectitude, propriety.

ಸೈತಾನ h. n. Satan, the devil. -ಬುದ್ಧಿ, -ಭಾವ. Devilish disposition.

ಸೈತ್ಯ (*tb. of* ಶೈತ್ಯ) n. Catarrh.

ಸೈನಿಕ [illegible] Military, [illegible] A soldier.

ಸೈಂಧವ (*fr* ಸಿಂಧು) s. *n* A native of Sindh 2, a kind of rock-salt *a* Marine, aquatic

ಸೈನ್ಯ (*fr* ಸೇನಾ) s *n* An army

ಸೈರಣೆ, ಸೈರಿಸು = ಸಯ್ರಣೆ, ಸಯ್ರಿಸು, *q v*

ಸೈರಂಧ್ರಿ (*tb* ಸೈರೇಂಧ್ರಿ) s *n* A female attendant, a toilet woman

ಸೊಕ್ಕು k *v i* To become mad or intoxicated, to get bewildered or confused; to be proud or arrogant. *n* Infatuation; stupefaction, pride, arrogance. ಸೊಕ್ಕಿಳಿ. To be humbled ಸೊಕ್ಕೇರು. Pride to arise

ಸೊಗಡು a. k *n*. A sharp smell 2, touch.

ಸೊಗಯಿಸು, ಸೊಗಸು k *v. i.* To shine, look beautiful. be pleasant ಸೊಗಸು. Shine, beauty, charm; happiness, pleasure, delight, glee, gaiety -ಗಾರ A beau, gay man -ಗುಂದು Pleasure to be less

ಸೊಂಕು a k. *v. i.* To touch, come near, to infect, taint *n* Touch, contact, infection. -ರೋಗ An infectious disease

ಸೊಟ್ಟ, ಸೊಟ್ಟು k *n* Crookedness, curvedness. -ಗಾಲು A bandy-leg -ಗೈ A crump hand -ಬಾಯಿ, -ಮೋರೆ A wry mouth or face. ಸೊಟ್ಟಗೆ Crookedly.

ಸೊಡರು, ಸೊಡಲು k. *n*. A lamp

ಸೊಣೆ k *v i* To point at a person, as a sign of mockery

ಸೊಂಟ k *n* The hip, loins, waist

ಸೊಂಡಲು, ಸೊಂಡಿಲು ಸೊಂಡ್ಲು (= ಸುಂಡಲು, *q v* *tb. of* ಶುಂಡಾರ) *n*. An elephant's trunk

ಸೊಂಡಿಲಿ (*tb* *of* ಶುಂಡ) *n* The musk shrew, *also* ಸುಂಡಿಲಿ.

ಸೊಂಡೆ k *n* The plant *Solanum pubescens*

ಸೊತ್ತು 1 (= ಜೊಟ್ಟು) k *n*. Crookedness

ಸೊತ್ತು 2. (*tb of* ಸ್ವತ್ವ) *n* Property goods

ಸೊನೆ k *n*. The juice that exudes from a stalk, twig, etc

ಸೊನ್ನ (*tb of* ಸ್ವರ್ಣ) *n*. Gold -ಗಾರ A goldsmith. ಸೊನ್ನಾರ Gilt, gilding

ಸೊನ್ನೆ (*tb. of* ಶೂನ್ಯ) *n* The anusvāra. 2, a cypher or zero 3, (*tb of* ಸ್ವರ್ಣ) Gold -ವರದ A dealer in gold.

ಸೊಪ್ಪು 1 k. *n* Slackness, weakness. *v t.* To repress, check ಸೊಪ್ಪಾಗು To slacken (*as* cloth, lips, *etc*); to pine, grow weak.

ಸೊಪ್ಪು 2 k *n* Foliage, a vegetable, herb, greens -ಗುಟ್ಟು. To beat the bush for game. ಸದೆ Leaves and litter.

ಸೊಪ್ಪೆ k *n* The straw of millet.

ಸೊಬಗು (*tb of* ಸುಭಗ) *n* Beauty, charm, loveliness, *etc* ಸೊಬಗ. A beautiful man, *f* ಸೊಬಗಿ

ಸೊಂಪು (= ಸಂಪು) k. *n* Beauty, elegance, charm, grace ಸೊಂಪಗೆ Nicely, beautifully.

ಸೊರಗು k *v i* To wither, languish, to grow lean or meagre.

ಸೊರಟು k *n* The state of being contracted, shrivelled *as* a leaf, or crooked *as* a bamboo

ಸೊರೆ 1. = ಸೋರೆ, *q v.*

ಸೊರೆ 2. k. *n* The milk collected in the udder of a cow or buffalo -ಬಿಡು To let down that milk

ಸೊರ್ಕು = ಸೊಕ್ಕು, *q v*

ಸೊಲಗೆ ಸೊಲಿಗೆ k *n*. A measure of capacity = ¼ of a kudava or balla

ಸೊಲ್ಲು k *v. i.* To say, speak *n* A word ಸೊಲ್ಲಿಸು To be said

ಸೊಸೆ (*tb. of* ಸ್ನುಷೆ) *n* A daughter-in-law.

ಸೊಳ್ಳೆ k *n*. A nostril. 2 a musquito ಮೂಗಿನ- A nostril. ಕಣ್ಣು-. An eye-fly

ಸೋ (= ಸೋವು) k *v t.* To drive off, scare away

ಸೋಕು. = ಸೊಂಕು, *q v*

ಸೋಗು (*tb of* ಯೋಗ) *n* A disguise, mask -ತೆಗೆದು ಕೊಳ್ಳು, -ಮಾಡು To assume a disguise -ಹಾಕು To disguise one's self.

ಸೋಗೆ k. *n*. The peculiar leaf of palms. sugar-cane *etc* 2, a peacock's tail.

3, a rudder *Cpds.* ಅಡಿಕೇ- ಕಬ್ಬಿಣ-, ತಾಳೇ-, ತೆಂಗಿನ-

ಸೋಜಿ f *n* Meal ground coarse. grits of wheat, rolong

ಸೋಜಿಗ (= ಚೋಜಿಗ, *q v tb of* ಚೋದ್ಯ) *n*. Surprise, wonder; a wonder.

ಸೋಟೆ k *n*. The lower part of the cheek. -ಸುಲಿ To pinch it

ಸೋಡ f *n*. Letting go freely, acquittance -ಪತ್ರ A bill of divorce

ಸೋಡಿ f. *n* Remission of a debt, *etc.*, the sum remitted 2, release from bondage, freedom.

ಸೋತು *P. p of* ಸೋಲು, *q. v*

ಸೋದರ s. *a* Co-uterine. *n* An own brother -ಅತ್ತೆ, ಸೋದರತ್ತೆ A father's sister, a mother's brother's wife. -ಮಾವ. A maternal uncle -ಅಳಿಯ A nephew, sister's son.

ಸೋನೆ a k *n*. An incessant drizzle.

ಸೋಪಸ್ಕರ s. *n*. Materials, provision. ಸೋಪಸ್ಕಾರ A measure or means.

ಸೋಪಾನ s *n*. Stairs, steps. -ಕಟ್ಟು. A staircase

ಸೋಪು k *n*. Anise-seed, *Pimpinella anisum*

ಸೋಬತಿ f *n* A companion, fellow. ಸೋಬತು. Company, society.

ಸೋಬಾನೆ (*tb of* ಶೋಭನ) *n*. A festive song

ಸೋಮ s *n* A climbing plant, *Sarcostema viminalis*, its juice 2, nectar 3, the moon 4, Śiva -ನಾದ Śiva, N. -ಣ್ಣ, -ಪ್ಪ, -ಯ್ಯ. N. -ಯಾಗ. A sôma sacrifice -ಯಾಜಿ A sôma sacrificer, a title among Brâhmanas -ವಂಶ. The lunar dynasty -ವಾರ Monday. -ಸೂತ್ರ A sluice for conveying the water bathed to an idol or linga ಸೋಮೇಶ, ಸೋಮೇಶ್ವರ Śiva or his representation N of a Kannada poet

ಸೋಮಾರಿ k. *n* A sluggard, idler -ತನ. Laziness -ಕೆಲಸ Lazy work.

ಸೋ[illegible] f [illegible] st[illegible]

ಸೋರು k. *v i* To drop, drip, trickle, ooze, flow, to leak (*P p* ಸೋರಿ). *n*. Dropping, leaking ಸೋರುವ ಮನೆ. A leaking house. ಸೋರಿಸು To cause to drop or flow

ಸೋರುಪ್ಪು f. *n* Nitre saltpetre.

ಸೋರೆ (= ಸೊರೆ 1) k. *n*. The bottle gourd *Cpds*. ಕೈ-, ತೀ-, ಹಾಲು-, -ಬುಳ್ಳಿ, -ಬುರುಡೆ A calabash.

ಸೋಲು k. *v. i*. To be defeated or overcome, to lose, forfeit, fail. 2, to be captivated allured. (*P p.* ಸೋತು). *n* Defeat, loss; *also* ಸೋಲುವಿಕೆ, ಸೋಲ, ಸೋಲುವೆ. -ಗೆಲವು Defeat and success. ಸೋಲಿಸು. To defeat, vanquish.

ಸೋಲೆ k *n*. The slough of a snake, coa of an onion

ಸೋವು 1. (= ಸೋ, *q v*) a. k. *v. t* To drive off, *etc.*

ಸೋವು 2. k. *n* Trace, mark, sign.

ಸೋಸು 1 *tb. of* ಶೋಧಿಸು, *q. v*

ಸೋಸು 2 (*tb of* ಸಹಿಸು) *v t* To endure, bear, suffer

ಸೌಕರ್ಯ (*fr.* ಸುಕರ) s *n*. Easiness of performance.

ಸೌಖ್ಯ (*fr* ಸುಖ) s *n*. Pleasure, happiness, ease, comfort, enjoyment. -ದಿಂದ ಇರು To be happy, *etc*

ಸೌಗಂಧ (*fr* ಸುಗಂಧ) s. *a* Sweet-scented, fragrant.

ಸೌಜನ್ಯ (*fr.* ಸುಜನ) s *n*. Goodness, generosity, kindness, benevolence; friendship.

ಸೌಜ್ಞೆ *tb. of* ಸಂಜ್ಞೆ.

ಸೌದೆ (= ಸವದೆ, ಸವುದೆ, *q. v.*) f. *n* Firewood -ಒಟ್ಟು A stack of wood -ಹೊರೆ A faggot

ಸೌಧ (*fr* ಸುಧಾ) s. *n* A plastered mansion, a palace.

ಸೌಂದರ, ಸೌಂದರ್ಯ (*fr* ಸುಂದರ) s. *n* Beauty, loveliness, elegance. -ಶಾಲಿ A beautiful person

ಸೌಭದ್ರ (*fr* ಸುಭದ್ರಾ) s. *n*. Abhimanyu, [illegible]

ಭಾಗ್ಯ (fr ಸುಭಗ) s. n. Good fortune, ood luck, blessedness, beauty, harm; the state of wifehood -ವತಿ. . married and unwidowed woman.

ಮ್ಯ (fr. ಸೋಮ) s. a Handsome, leasing, mild, calm, gentle n. The planet Mercury. 2, the 43rd ear of the cycle -ರೂಪ A pleasing orm. -ವಾರ Wednesday.

ರ (fr. ಸೂರ) s n. The planet Saturn , a solar month. a Solar -ಮಾನ. solar measurement of time. -ಮಾಸ solar month. -ಮಾಸವರ್ಷ. A solar ear

ರಾಷ್ಟ್ರ (fr. ಸುರಾಷ್ಟ್ರ) s. a. Relating to urat. n Surat 2, N. of a tune

ಲಭ್ಯ (fr ಸುಲಭ) s n Easiness of cquisition, facility.

ಳು = ಸವುಳು, q v

ದ s n. Kârttikêya, the god of war. , a learned man. -ಪುರಾಣ. N. of a urâna

ಧ s. n The shoulder 2, a large ranch. 3, a section, chapter. 4, a roop. 5, a prince; a wise man

ನ s. n. Slipping, tripping, tottering; falling or deviating from; an rror, mistake, blunder dropping, hock, collision ಸ್ಖಲಿತ Stumbled, nsteady, erring.

ನ s n The breast of a woman, udder. ವ, -ಂಧಯ A male infant.

ನಯಿತ್ನು, ಸ್ತನಿತ s n Thunder.

ಬಕ s. n A cluster, bunch. 2, uantity, multitude

ಬ್ಧ s. a Fixed, stiff, rigid, immovable, motionless, numb, paralyzed, enseless, dull. -ತ್ವ Fixedness, immoility.

ಬು tb of ಸ್ತಂಭ, q. v.

ಭ s n Fixedness, stiffness 2, a illar, column, post; a stem, trunk. , numbness, stupor, paralysis, stupiity 4, stoppage -ನ. Fixing irmly, paralysing, [illegible]; arrest ing, stopping, etc ಸ್ತಂಭಿಸು To fix firmly, stop.

ಸ್ತವ, ಸ್ತವನ s n. Praising, praise, a hymn ಸ್ತವನೀಯ Praiseworthy

ಸ್ತಿಮಿತ s a Still, motionless, steady, fixed, immovable. 2, tender; wet, moist

ಸ್ತುತಿ s n Praise, eulogy; commendation, adulation ಆತ್ಮ- Self-praise. ಮುಖ- Flattery, ಸ್ತುತ್ಯ. Laudable, praiseworthy. -ಪಾಠಕ A panegyrist, bard -ಸು To praise, laud, to praise in song

ಸ್ತೂಪ s n. A heap or pile of earth; a Buddhist monument.

ಸ್ತೇಯ s n. Theft, robbery. ಸ್ತೇಯಿ. A thief, robber

ಸ್ತೋಕ s. a. Little, small. n A tail 2, offspring -ಕ The câtaka bird.

ಸ್ತೋತ್ರ s. n Praise, eulogium, a hymn of praise, ode

ಸ್ತೋಮ s. n. Praise 2, an oblation. 3, a multitude, a heap, collection, mass. [prayer.

ಸ್ತೌತ್ಯ (fr. ಸ್ತುತಿ) s. n. Praise, etc. 2

ಸ್ತ್ರೀ s. n A woman, female -ಜಾತಿ The female sex. -ಬುದ್ಧಿ A fickle, effeminate mind. -ಲಿಂಗ The feminine gender -ವಾಚಕ A feminine noun.

ಸ್ಥಲ, ಸ್ಥಳ s n Ground, land. 2, a place, spot, site, locality 3, stead, place, lieu 4, station -ಪಲ್ಲಟ Transfer, confusion of places. -ವಂತಿಗ, ಸ್ಥಳೀಕ A resident -ವಾರ (= ತಳವಾರ) A watchman, beadle. -ವಾಸ Place of residence

ಸ್ಥಾನ s n Standing, state a place, spot, site 2, situation, position; office, rank 3, an abode, house. 4, an object -ಭ್ರಷ್ಟ Displaced, out of place. ಸ್ಥಾನಾಂತರ Another place ಸ್ಥಾನಿಕ. Local, a paid-servant in a temple who assists the pûjâri. ಸ್ಥಾನೀಯ Local

ಸ್ಥಾಪಕ s. n An establisher, founder. ಸ್ಥಾಪನ, ಸ್ಥಾಪನೆ Establishing, founding instituting, appointing ಪುನಃಸ್ಥಾಪನ The Reformation ಸ್ಥಾಪನೆ ಮಾಡು To establish ಸ್ಥಾಪಿತ Established, founded. ಸ್ಥಾಪಿಸು To establish, set up, found, institute, to place, set, lay.

ಸ್ಥಾಯಿ s a Situated, fixed, stationary, enduring, constant, lasting, steady, firm -ಭಾವ A fixed condition of mind or body

ಸ್ಥಾಲಿ s n. A pot, pan, kettle, boiler.

ಸ್ಥಾವರ s. a Standing still, fixed, stationary, firm, immovable, real -ಸೊತ್ತು. Real estate -ಜಂಗಮ Immovable and movable.

ಸ್ಥಿತಿ s n. Situation, state, position, condition, good condition, station rank, good manners, property, wealth. -ಗತಿ State and course of life -ವಂತ. A wealthy man -ಸ್ಥಾಪಕ Elastic, elasticity. ಸ್ಥಿತ. Situated, fixed, settled, steady.

ಸ್ಥಿರ s a Firm, steady, permanent, durable, lasting immovable still; constant, faithful certain, sure, firm, strong -ಗೊಳಿಸು, -ಪಡಿಸು. To confirm strengthen -ಜೀವಿ Long-lived -ತನ, -ತೆ -ತ್ವ. Firmness, stability, steadfastness -ಬುದ್ಧಿ Steadiness of mind -ವಾರ Saturday. ಸ್ಥಿರಾಯು. Long-lived

ಸ್ಥೂಲ s. a Stout, bulky, thick, fat, corpulent; clumsy, coarse, stupid -ದೇಹ, -ಶರೀರ The material body -ಬುದ್ಧಿ Dulness -ಸೂಕ್ಷ್ಮ. Mighty and subtile.

ಸ್ಥೈರ್ಯ (fr ಸ್ಥಿರ) s n Firmness, steadiness, resolution, constancy, hardness, solidity, calmness, patience.

ಸ್ನಾತ s a. Bathed, immersed, deeply engaged. n. An initiated householder, also -ಕ

ಸ್ನಾನ s. n. Bathing, ablution. 2. baptism. -ಮಾಡು To bathe ಕಂಠ- Bathing all but the head ಆತ್ಮ- Receiving the Holy Spirit ... Re... ...

ಸ್ನಾಯು s. n. A sinew, tendon muscle.

ಸ್ನಿಗ್ಧ s a. Oily, greasy, fat, sticky, viscid smooth, moist, cooling, tender 2, attached, lovely.

ಸ್ನೇಹ s n Tenderness, love, affection, fondness, friendship -ಬೀಳು Friendship to originate -ಮಾಡು. To court friendship, to love ಸ್ನೇಹಿಸು To love ಸ್ನೇಹಿತ A friend, f. -ಳು.

ಸ್ಪಂದ, -ನ s n Throbbing, moving, motion.

ಸ್ಪರ್ಧೆ s. a Rivalry; envy, jealousy; competition ಸ್ಪರ್ಧಿಸು To rival, envy.

ಸ್ಪರ್ಶ s. n Touching, touch, contact; the sense of touch. -ಮಾಡು, ಸ್ಪರ್ಶಿಸು To touch

ಸ್ಪಷ್ಟ s a Distinct, clear, plain, intelligible, true, real.

ಸ್ಪೃಹತೆ, ಸ್ಪೃಹೆ s n Desire, wish; envy. ನಿ- Freedom from desire or envy

ಸ್ಫಟಿಕ s. n Crystal, quartz ಸ್ಫಟಿಕೆ. Alum.

ಸ್ಫುಟ s a Burst open, clear, plain, evident

ಸ್ಫುರಣ s n Trembling, vibration, rising to mind, suggesting itself ಸ್ಫುರಿಸು. To rise to mind, suggest itself.

ಸ್ಫೋಟ, ಸ್ಫೋಟಕ s n. A swelling, boil, tumour, pimple, small-pox. ಸ್ಫೋಟನ Breaking, cracking, disclosing

ಸ್ಮರಣ s n Recollection, reminiscence; remembrance; memory. 2, tradition ಸ್ಮರಿಸು To remember, recollect, bear in mind, be mindful of, to call upon God

ಸ್ಮಾರ್ತ (fr. ಸ್ಮೃತಿ) s a Relating to memory 2, recorded in the smriti n A Brâhmana belonging to the advaita vêdânta creed 2, any act enjoined by the smriti

ಸ್ಮೃತಿ s. n. Remembrance, memory recollection. 2, the body of tradi... ... aw-book. ...

ೀರ s. n. A smile, gentle laugh

ಂದನ s n. A car. 2, water. 3, a river. 4, air, wind.

ಲ s n. A wife's brother.

ಜ s n A chaplet, garland.

ವ (= ಸ್ರವ, q. v) s. n. Flowing, streaming, trickling 2, a spring, fountain, also -ಣ

s a Own, one's own. 2, native, natural, proper. n. Self. Cpds · -ಕಾರ್ಯ, -ಕ್ಷೇತ್ರ, -ಗ್ರಾಮ, -ಜನ, -ಜಾತಿ, -ದೇಶ, ಧರ್ಮ, -ಪ್ರಯೋಜನ, -ಬುದ್ಧಿ, -ರೂಪ, ಹೀನ, -ಹಸ್ತ, etc

ಕೀಯ s. a. Own, one's own, belonging to one's self. -ಜನ. A relative; own persons

ಚ್ಛ s a. Pellucid, white; pure; clear ತನ, -ತೆ Purity, clearness.

ಚ್ಛಂದ s. n. One's own will, own choice a. Self-willed, spontaneous ಸ್ವಚ್ಛಂದಿ Self-willed, wilful.

ತಃ (tb of ಸ್ವತಸ್) ad By one's self, of one's own accord. -ಪ್ರಮಾಣ. Self-evident.

ತಂತ್ರ s n. Self-dependence, independence, freedom. a. Independent, free, self-willed, unruly. -ದಿಂದ ಇರು. To be independent. -ತನ, -ತ್ವ Independence

ಶಾ = ಸ್ವತಃ, q. v

ತೇವ s a Of one's self; by itself.

ಧಾ, ಸ್ವಧೆ s. n One's own condition or nature 2, custom, usage 3, oblation offered to pitris

ದನ s. n. Tasting, eating

ತ್ತು (tb. of ಸ್ವತ್ವ) n Property, wealth.

ಂತ (tb of ಸ್ವ, q. v) a Own, proper, peculiar, etc -ಗಾರ A proprietor.

ಪ್ನ s. n. Sleep 2, a dream, dreaming. ಒಳ್ಳೇ-, ಸು-. A pleasant dream ಕೆಟ್ಟ-, ದುಃ-. A bad dream

ಭಾನು s. n. The 47th year of the cycle a. Selfish.

ಸ್ವಭಾವ s n Natural state, natural temper, nature, innate disposition. Cpds -ಗುಣ, -ನಡತೆ, -ಬುದ್ಧಿ, -ಲಕ್ಷಣ. etc. ಸ್ವಭಾವಿಕ = ಸ್ವಾಭಾವಿಕ, q v

ಸ್ವಯಂ s n. Self. a. Of one's own self. -ವರ The election of a husband by a virgin girl who was not married in time. -ಕೃತ. Self-made, natural, spontaneous -ಪಾಕ. Cooking for one's self -ಪಾಕಿ. A cook -ಭೂ. Selfexistent; Brahmâ. ಸ್ವಯಮೇವ. Of one's own accord.

ಸ್ವಯಾರ್ಜಿತ. = ಸ್ವಾರ್ಜಿತ, q. v.

ಸ್ವಯಿರ tb. of ಸ್ವೈರ, q v

ಸ್ವರ s. n Sound, noise, voice. 2, tone, music, a note of the musical scale 3, a vowel. 4, an accent. -ಧಾತು. A verbal theme ending in a vowel -ಭಂಗ Hoarseness -ಸಂಧಿ. Junction of vowels.

ಸ್ವರೂಪ s. n One's own form, features; natural state or appearance. a. Similar, like, identical. -ನಾಶನ, -ಭಂಗ. Disgrace.

ಸ್ವರ್ಗ s n Heaven, paradise. 2, happiness, joy. -ಲೋಕ. The celestial region. -ಸ್ಥ A deity, dead. ಸ್ವರ್ಗೀಯ. Heavenly, celestial

ಸ್ವರ್ಣ s. n Gold, a gold coin. -ಮಯ. Consisting of gold

ಸ್ವಲ್ಪ (its tb ಸ್ವಲ್ಪು) s. a Very small; little, minute, trifling; very few. -ಸ್ವಲ್ಪ rep. -ದಿವಸ A few days. -ದೂರ. Not far. -ಹೊತ್ತು. A little while.

ಸ್ವಸ್ತಿ s n. Welfare, health, blessing. int May it be well! hail! -ವಾಚನ Invocation of blessings

ಸ್ವಸ್ಥ s a Well, healthy, comfortable. n Well-being, health; also -ತೆ ad. At ease, in health.

ಸ್ವಹಸ್ತ s. n. One's own hand 2, handwriting, signature.

ಸ್ವಾಗತ s. n. Welcome, welcoming a. Come of one's self

ಸ್ವಾತಂತ್ರ್ಯ (*fr* ಸ್ವತಂತ್ರ) s *n* Independence, free will.

ಸ್ವಾತಿ s *n* The star *Arcturus*.

ಸ್ವಾದ s *n*. Taste, flavour, liking, relishing, enjoyment. ಸ್ವಾದಿಸು To be pleasant to the taste, to taste.

ಸ್ವಾಧೀನ s *a*. Self-dependent, independent 2, in one's own power or subjection 3 at the control of, under. -ಮಾಡು. To subject, to take possession of; to control, *also* -ಮಾಡಿಕೊಳ್ಳು.

ಸ್ವಾಧ್ಯಾಯ s. *n*. Repeating to one's self

ಸ್ವಾನುಭವ s *n* One's own personal experience.

ಸ್ವಾಭಾವಿಕ (*fr*. ಸ್ವಭಾವ) s *a* Natural, peculiar. constitutional, spontaneous

ಸ್ವಾಮಿ s *n* A proprietor, owner. 2, a master, lord, sovereign, a guru, a learned Brâhmana. -ತನ, -ತ್ವ Lordship, ownership. -ದ್ರೋಹ. Treachery to a master. -ದ್ರೋಹಿ. A traitor -ಭಕ್ತಿ Devotedness to a master ರಕ್ಷಾ-, ಕ್ರಿಸ್ತ-. Christ

ಸ್ವಾಮ್ಯ s *n* Supremacy, dominion

ಸ್ವಾರಸ್ಯ (*fr*. ಸ್ವರಸ) s *n* Possession of natural pathos, fire, *etc*, goodness

ಸ್ವಾರ್ಜಿತ s *a* Self-acquired; *also* ಸ್ವಯಾರ್ಜಿತ

ಸ್ವಾರ್ಥ s. *n* One's own advantage or interest, self-interest. selfishness -ಪರ. Self-interested, selfish -ಬುದ್ಧಿ. Selfishness

ಸ್ವಾಶ್ರಿತ s *a*. Self-dependent.

ಸ್ವಾಸ್ತ್ಯ (*fr* ಸ್ವ-ಅಸ್ತಿ) s *n* Land exem[pt] from tax or liable for a trifli[ng] quit-rent

ಸ್ವಾಸ್ಥ್ಯ (*fr* ಸ್ವಸ್ಥ) s *n* Self-relian[ce], resoluteness, firmness 2, sound stat[e] of health, prosperity, happiness contentment.

ಸ್ವಾಹಾ s *n* Agni's wife *int*. An e[x]clamation made at oblations. Ha[il] blessing!

ಸ್ವೀಕರಿಸು s *v t* To make one's ow[n], adopt, accept, to embrace *as* a fai[th], to admit, assume.

ಸ್ವೀಕಾರ s *n* Making one's own. appr[o]priation, taking, adoption. ಪು[ತ್ರ]- Adoption of a son

ಸ್ವೀಯ s *a* Own, peculiar, characte[r]istic.

ಸ್ವೇಚ್ಛೆ, ಸ್ವೇಚ್ಛೆ s. *n*. One's own wi[sh] or will, self-will, wilfulness.

ಸ್ವೇದ s *n* Sweat, perspiration. [-ಜ] Insects, vermin, *etc*. produced [by] sweat

ಸ್ವೈರ (= ಸ್ವಯಿರ) s. *a*. Self-will[ed], wilful. *n* Wilfulness, self-will

ಹ

ಹ The fifty-second letter of the alphabet.

ಹಂಸ s *n* A goose, swan, flamingo -ಕ An anklet. -ಪಾದ A caret. -ರಥ, -ವಾಹನ. Brahmâ

ಹಕಾರ s *n* The letter ಹ

ಹಕೀಕತು h *n* Account, statement; -[illegible], facts.

[illegible] h *n* A physician.

ಹಕ್ಕರಿಕೆ (ರಿ = ಱ) k. *n*. The plant *ch[ry]sopogon aciculatus*

ಹಕ್ಕಲ, ಹಕ್ಕಲು k *n* Gleanings (of cor[n]) ಹಕ್ಕಲಾಯು, ಹಕ್ಕಲಾರಿಸು To glean.

ಹಕ್ಕಳೆ k *n* An incrustation or scab

ಹಕ್ಕಿ (*tb of* ಪಕ್ಷಿ) *n* A bird. -ಕೂದ[ಲು] The plumage of a bird. -ಗರಿ [A] quill -ಗೂಡು. A bird's nest.

[illegible] f. *n*. Sleight of hand

ು 1. k. n. Dry mucus or rheum; a :ab.

ು 2. h. n. Right, title; a just right r claim. -ದಾರ. The holder of a ight. -ದಾರಿ, -ದಾರಿಕೆ. = ಹಕ್ಕು.

; k. n. A place for reposing, etc.; a ed.

. = ಹಗೆಯ, q. v.

ರ. = ಹಗುರ, q. v.

ರಣ k. n. Vain talk, chatter, babble. ಾರ. A babbler.

ರು k. n. The dandruff of the head. , a split of a bamboo.

ಲು k. n. The daytime; a day. ad. y day. -ಗಳ್ಳ. A day-robber. -ರಾತ್ರಿ, ಇರುಳು. Day and night. -ಬತ್ತಿ. A ind of firework.

ಸು k. n. Gum, resin.

ುರ, ಹಗುರು k. a. Light; easy; mean. ಮಾಡು. To make light. -ತನ. Lightess.

k. n. Hatred, enmity. -ತೀರಿಸು, ಸಾಧಿಸು. To revenge one's self. -ಗೊ ಳ್ಳು, -ಮಾಡು. To hate. -ಗಾರ, -ಯವ. .n enemy. -ತನ. Hatred.

ಯ, ಹಗೇವು (= ಹಗ) k. n. A subteraneous granary.

(tb. of ಪ್ರಗ್ರಹ) n. A rope or cord. pds.: ನೂಲಿನ-, ನಾರಿನ-, etc.

ು k. n. Low ground.

ಕಾರ. tb. of ಅಹಂಕಾರ, q. v.

ಗೆ. = ಹಂಗು, q. v.

ಗರಲು, ಹಂಗರು k. n. An evergreen hrub, Dodonaea viscosa.

ಗಾಮಿ h. a. Temporary. ಹಂಗಾಮು. 'he season, time, as for business or nything. -ಉದ್ಯೋಗ. A temporary mployment.

ಗಾಮು h. n. Uproar, tumult, riot; n assault. -ಮಾಡು, -ನಡಿಸು. To make n assault.

ಗು k. n. An obligation, indebtedness; egard. ಹಂಗಾಳು, ಹಂಗಿಗ. A man under bligation. ಹಂಗಿಸು. To remind a erson of neglecting his obligation.

ಹಂಗುಳಿ, -ಗೆ k. n. A stool.

ಹಚ್ಚನೆ (= ಪಚ್ಚನೆ) k. n. Greenness. a. Green; yellowish. ad. Greenly.

ಹಚ್ಚಡ (= ವಚ್ಚಡ, q. v.) k. n. A stout cotton cloth; a bed sheeting.

ಹಚ್ಚು k. v. t. To apply to; to put to; to join, affix, attach; to fix. 2, to use or employ. 3, to kindle, light. 4, to mince; cf. ಕೊಚ್ಚು. ಬೆಂಕಿ-. To set fire to. ಹಚ್ಚಿಸು. To kindle, light; to cause to apply to; to have planted; to put or join to.

ಹಚ್ಚೆ k. n. Cane or ratan; tattoo. 2, a bamboo split. -ಚುಚ್ಚು. To tattoo. -ತಿಲಕ, -ಬೊಟ್ಟು. A tattooed mark on the forehead.

ಹಜಂ h. n. Concealment. 2, digestion.

ಹಜಾಮು h. n. A barber. -ತ್. Shaving.

ಹಜಾರ h. n. A hall, pavilion.

ಹಜೂರು h. n. The presence of a superior authority, as collector, judge, etc. 2, the principal collector's office; also -ಕಚೇರಿ.

ಹಂಚಿಕೆ 1. k. n. Sharing, dividing, distributing. -ಗಾರ, ಹಂಚಿಗ. A divider.

ಹಂಚಿಕೆ 2. k. n. A means, plan, expedient. -ತೆಗೆ, -ಮಾಡು. To devise a plan. -ಗಾರ. A contriver, etc.

ಹಂಚು 1. k. v. t. To divide, share, distribute.

ಹಂಚು 2. k. n. A tile. 2, a potsherd. ಬೆನ್ನು-. A ridge tile. ಹಂಚಿನ ಮನೆ. A house with a tiled roof.

ಹಂಜರ 1. (= ವಂದರು, ಹಂದರ) k. n. A pandal.

ಹಂಜರ 2. (ರ = ಱ) k. n. A bamboo split.

ಹಂಜಿ (= ಪಂಜಿಕೆ, q. v.) f. n. A roll of cotton.

ಹಟ (tb. of ಹಠ) n. Obstinacy, stubbornness; obstinate insisting upon. -ಗಾರ, -ಮಾರಿ, -ವಾದಿ. An obstinate person. -ತನ. Importunity. -ವಾಗಿರು, -ಹಿಡಿ. To be obstinate. -ಸಾಧಿಸು. To persevere in obstinacy.

ಹಟ್ಟಿ k. n. A fold, cow-pen. -ಕಾರ. A herdsman.

ಹಟ್ಟು (tb. of ಪಟ್ಟು) n. Woven silk. -ಗಾರ. A silk-weaver.

ಹಠ (= ಹಟ, q. v.) s. n. Violence, force. 2, obstinacy. -ಯೋಗ. A mode of contemplation. ಹಠಾತ್. By force, forcibly, suddenly. ಹಠಾತ್ಕಾರ. Suddenness.

ಹಡಗ, ಹಡಗು k. n. A ship, sailing vessel. -ದ (ಹಡಗಿನ) ರೇವು. A harbour. -ನಡಿಸು. To steer a vessel. -ದವರು, ಹಡಗಿನವರು. Mariners, sailors.

ಹಡದಿ, ಹಡದೆ k. n. An annual allowance of grain or money to washermen, barbers, etc.

ಹಡಪ k. n. A betel-nut pouch. 2, a barber's bag. -ಗಾರ. A barber; also ಹಡಪಿಗ.

ಹಡಲಗೆ, ಹಡಲಿಗೆ (= ಅಡ್ಲಿಗೆ) k. n. A flat round basket.

ಹಡಿ. = ಪಡೆ, q. v.

ಹಡಿಕೆ k. n. A disagreeable smell, stench. -ನಾತ. Stench. -ನಾರು. To stink.

ಹಡುಕು (= ಹಡಿಕೆ) k. n. A bad smell.

ಹಡೆ (= ಪಡೆ, q. v.) k. v. t. To get, obtain, etc.; to bear, give birth to.

ಹಡ್ಲು k. n. Mud. a. Uncultivated. -ಗದ್ದೆ. An uncultivated paddy-field.

ಹಣ (tb. of ಪಣ 2.) n. Money; wealth. 2, an old coin equal to As. 4-8. -ಗಾರ, -ವಂತ, -ಪುಳ್ಳವ. A rich man. -ದ ನೋಟ. Shroffing. -ಕಟ್ಟು. To pay taxes. -ಮುರಿಸು, -ಮುರಿಸು. To change money.

ಹಣಕು k. v. i. To look slyly, pry, peep; also ಹಣಿ+ನೋಡು.

ಹಣತೆ (tb. of ಪ್ರಣೀತ). = ಪಣತೆ, q. v.

ಹಣಾ k. n. Beating. -ಹಣಿ. Mutual beating. -ಹಣಿಜಗಳ. A quarrel with mutual beating.

ಹಣಿ k. v. t. To beat thin, sharpen by beating, as a sickle. -ತ. Beating; a blow.

ಹಣಿಕು. = ಹಣಕು, q. v.

[illegible] k. n. A comb. 2, one of the [illegible]sters of fruits, as of plantains.

ಹಣೆ k. n. The forehead. 2, the lair of wild beasts. -ಗೆ ಗಟ್ಟಿಸಿ ಕೊಳ್ಳು, -ಗೆ ಬಡಕೊಳ್ಳು. To affix to one's forehead, i. e. to use (*said contemptuously*). -ಬರಹ. Destiny, fortune.

ಹಂಡಬಂಡ *reit. n.* A certain colour of a pigeon.

ಹಂಡಾ, ಹಂಡೆ f. n. A large metal pot or boiler.

ಹಣ್ಣ, ಹಣ್ಣ k. n. The sunflower, *Heliotropium indicum.*

ಹಣ್ಣು k. n. A ripe fruit; ripeness. -ಗಾಯಿ. A ripe pod vegetable. -ಮುದುಕ. A very old man; *f.* -ಮುದುಕಿ. -ಹಂಪಲು. *reit.* -ಸಿಪ್ಪೆ. The rind or peel of a fruit. ಹಣ್ಣಿನ ರುಚಿ. The taste of a fruit.

ಹಣ್ಣೆ. = ಹಣ್ಣ 2, q. v. 2, the kitchen herb *Celosia albida.*

ಹತ್ *interj. for* angry reproof.

ಹತ s. a. Struck; killed; wounded; ruined; disappointed. -ಕ. Miserable. -ವಾಗಿ ಹೋಗು. To die, perish. ಹತಾಹತಿ. Mutual striking.

ಹತ್ತ k. a. Close. 2, all. *ad.* Closely 2, together. -ಕಟ್ಟು. To tie tightly, a[s] a necklace, etc. -ಕಾಸು. To hea[t] thoroughly. -ಬಡಿ. To beat all (fruits off (from a tree). -ಸೇದು. To drav[w] tightly.

ಹತ್ತಡಿ (= ಹತ್ತಿ) k. n. A carpenter's plane

ಹತ್ತರ k. n. Nearness, proximity. *a[d].* Near, close by, by; *also* ಹತ್ತಿರ, ಹತ್ತಿರೆ

ಹತ್ತಿ k. n. Cotton in the pod; cotton i[n] general. -ಕಾಯಿ. An unripe cotto[n] pod. -ಕಾಳು, -ಬೀಜ. Cotton seed. -[ಹ]ಡಿಸು. To pluck cotton; to dress cotto[n]. -ಬೆಳೆ. A cotton crop.

ಹತ್ತು 1. k. v. i. To stick to; to join; t[o] apply to; to touch; to reach, as [a] shore. 2, to be reached, arrived a[t], found as a road, etc. 3, to be re[-]quired; to suffice. 4, to begin. 5, t[o] take root. 6, to ascend, climb, moun[t] n. Joining, etc.; climbing, scalin[g] ಹತ್ತಗೊಡು. To let mount. ಹತ್ತಿಸು. T[o] ply; to cause to climb; to kindle, :ht, *as* fire, a light. ಹತ್ತಿಸರಿಗೆ ಬರು. · be nearly done up, *as* rice in oking; to be on death-bed. ಹತ್ತೊ ,. To press firmly; to suppress, *as* ughter.

,2. k. *a.* Ten. -ಅವತಾರ. Vishṇu's ı incarnations. ಹತ್ತೊಂಬತ್ತು. 19.

,3. (= ಹೊತ್ತು) k. *v. i.* To be kindled. to be burnt in cooking.

s. *n.* Killing, slaying; murder..

ರ h. *n.* A weapon, instrument.

= ಹತ್ತರ, *q. v.*

= ಹತ್ತಡಿ, *q. v.*

k. *n.* Properness, proper way; the npered state, *as* of any food, *etc.*; ırpness; *also* -ನ. -ಕೆಡು, -ಗೆಡು. To e the proper state, *etc.* (*used of food, 'n, crop, etc.*). -ಗೆಯ್ಯು, -ಮಾಡು. To ıke fit for use, *etc.* -ವಿಡು. To nper, sharpen. -ವಿಳಿಸು. To reduce proper state.

:. k. *v. t.* To lay stone or brick .*ps.* ಹದಿದು, ಹದ್ದು). *n.* A layer of me or brick.

:. (= ಹತ್ತು, *q. v.*) k. *a.* Ten. -ನಾರು. xteen. -ನಾಲ್ಕು. Fourteen. -ನೆಂಟು. ghteen. -ನೇಳು. Seventeen. -ನೈದು. fteen. -ಮೂರು. Thirteen.

ು k. *n.* An unripe fruit. 2, way, ınner.

ಗು k. *v. i.* To bend.

ಳ (= ಪದುಳ, *q. v.*) a. k. *n.* Well-ing; steadiness. ಹದುಳಿಗ. A happy ın. ಹದುಳಿಸು. To be well; to be othed; to feel refreshed.

, 1. k. *n.* A kite; a hawk; a vulture.

, 2. h. *n.* A limit, border. -ತಪ್ಪು, ಡು. To violate borders. -ಬಸ್ತು. De-ırcation of boundaries.

, 3. *P. p. of* ಹದಿ, *q. v.*

k. *a.* Ten. ಹನ್ನೆರಡು. Twelve. ನ್ನೊಂದು. Eleven.

; s. *n.* Slaughter, destruction; hurt-g, injuring.

ಹನಿ k. *n.* A drop. *v. i.* To fall in drops. -ಸು. To pour, *as* water, *etc.*

ಹನುಮ, ಹನುಮಂತ (*tb. of* ಹನುಮತ್) *n.* N. of a monkey-chief, the ally of Râmacandra.

ಹಂತ k. *n.* A stair, step; a flight of steps.

ಹಂತಿ (*tb. of* ಪಂಕ್ತಿ) *n.* A line, row.

ಹಂದರ (= ಹಂಜರ, *q. v.*) k. *n.* A pandal, temporary shed.

ಹಂದಿ k. *n.* A pig, hog, swine. ಕಾಡು-. A wild hog. -ಕೀರ. The small screech-owl. -ಕೋರೆ. A boar's tusk. -ತನ. Piggishness.

ಹಂದು k. *v. i.* To move shake. ಹಂದಾಡು. To move about.

ಹಂದೆ k. *n.* A coward.

ಹಪ್ತೆ h. *n.* An instalment. 2, a week.

ಹಪ್ಪಳ (= ಪಪ್ಪಳ) f. *n.* A very thin cake.

ಹಬಸಿ h. *n.* An Abyssinian.

ಹಬೆ (= ಹವೆ, *q. v.*) f. *n.* Vapour, heat. 2, *tb. of* ಪ್ರಭೆ.

ಹಬ್ಬ (*tb. of* ಪರ್ವ) *n.* A festival, feast, holiday. -ಆಚರಿಸು, -ಮಾಡು. To celebrate a feast. -ಗುಳ್ಳ. The Indian night-shade, *Solanum indicum.*

ಹಬ್ಬು k. *v. i.* To spread, extend, *etc.*; to spread, *as* a creeper. *n.* The state of being spread. -ಗೆ, -ವಿಕೆ. Spreading, extention, vastness. ಹಬ್ಬಿಸು. To cause to spread.

ಹಬ್ಬೆ k. *n.* Cane, ratan, *Calamus rotang.*

ಹಮಾಮು h. *a.* All, together. -ಜೀನಸು. All kinds of articles.

ಹಮಾಲ h. *n.* A bearer (of a palanquin, *etc.*); a porter.

ಹಮೀರ (= ಅಮೀರ, *q. v.*) h. *n.* An emir, nobleman. *a.* Excellent.

ಹಮೇಷಾ h. *ad.* Always, ever.

ಹಂಬಲ, ಹಂಬಲು k. *n.* Ardent desire; look-out; solicitous thought. ಹಂಬಲಿಸು. To desire, to long for, crave for; to mind, heed.

ಹಂಬು k. *n.* A creeper.

ಹಮ್ಮುದ a. k. n. Fainting, stupor, torpor. ಹಮ್ಮೈಸು. To faint, swoon.

ಹಮ್ಮಿಣಿ (= ಹಿಮ್ಮಣಿ) n. A long and narrow money-bag.

ಹಮ್ಮು k. n. Pride, conceit. -ಗಾರ. A proud man.

ಹಯ s. n. A horse. -ಗ್ರೀವ, -ವದನ. N. of a form of Vishṇu. -ಜ್ಞತೆ. Horsemanship. -ಪ್ರಾಸ. A kind of alliteration.

ಹಯನು, ಹಯ್ನು, ಹಯ್ಯು s. n. Milk and all that is made of milk, as curds, butter, etc.

ಹಯಿಲು k. n. Bewilderment.

ಹರ 1. k. n. Broadness, breadth. 2, spreading. 3, flying, etc. -ಗಲ, -ಗೋಲು. A basket-boat lined with leather; also ಹರಿಗೋಲು.

ಹರ 2. s. n. Conveying, carrying; seizing; removing; a seizer, etc. 2, Śiva. Cpds.: ಪ್ರಾಣ-; ಮನೋ-; ಪಾತಕ-; etc.

ಹರಕತ್ತು h. n. Opposition, hindrance.

ಹರಕಾರ. = ಹರಿಕಾರ, q. v.

ಹರಕು (= ಹರುಕು. ರ = ಱ) k. n. A tatter, rag. a. Torn, rent; old. -ಅರಿವೆ, -ಬಟ್ಟೆ, -ವಸ್ತ್ರ. A rag. -ಪುಸ್ತಕ. A torn book. -ಮಾತು. An incoherent speech. ಹರಕ. A man in rags.

ಹರಕೆ k. n. A blessing. 2, a vow. -ಕೊಡು. To bless. -ಮಾಡು, -ಹರಸು. To vow. -ತೀರಿಸು, -ಸಲ್ಲಿಸು. To fulfil a vow. -ಮುರಿ, -ತಪ್ಪಿಸು. To break a vow.

ಹರಗು k. v. t. To clean (a field) by removing the grass, weeds, etc. ಹರಗಣೆ. Removing superfluous standing corn.

ಹರಟೆ k. n. Idle talk, jabber, babble. -ಕೋರ, -ಗಾರ. A babbler. ಹರಟು. To talk idly, prate, blabber.

ಹರಡಿ, ಹರಡು 1. k. n. The ankle; the wrist. 2, a wrist-let of gold and coral beads.

ಹರಡು 2. k. v. t. To spread; to scratch, claw. v. i. To spread.

ಹರಡೆ k. n. The ink-nut.

ಹರಣ 1. s. n. Taking, removing. 2, stealing; withholding.

ಹರಣ 2. tb. of ಪ್ರಾಣ, q. v. -ಕೊಡು, -ಹೊಯ್ಯು. To restore life. -ಪಡೆ. To obtain life.

ಹರತಾಳ. tb. of ಹರಿತಾಲ, q. v.

ಹರತ (ರ = ಱ) k. n. Sharpness.

ಹರದ a. k. n. A trader, merchant. ಹರದಿಕೆ, ಹರದು. Trade, traffic.

ಹರದಾರಿ (fr. ಹರಿ 1) k. n. A distance of three English miles.

ಹರದು. P. p. of ಹರೆ 1, q. v.

ಹರವರಿ k. n. Manifestation; display.

ಹರವಸ (tb. of ಪರವಶ) n. Loss of self-control.

ಹರವಿ (= ಹರಿವಿ) k. n. An earthen water-vessel.

ಹರವು, ಹರಹು k. v. i. To spread. v. t. To spread out. n. Spreading, extension.

ಹರಸು (= ಹರಿಸು, q. v.) k. v. t. To bless. 2, to make a vow.

ಹರಳು k. n. A pebble, stone, grit. 2, the castor-oil plant, Palma christi. ಹರಳೆಣ್ಣೆ. Castor-oil.

ಹರಾಮು h. a. Unlawful; wicked, wrong; vile. -ಕುದುರೆ. A restive horse.

ಹರಿ 1. k. v. i. To run; to flow; to creep, proceed; to disappear, as trouble. n. A run, flowing; cf. ಹರ 1. -ಕಾರ. A runner, courier; a hawker; a spy. -ಗಲು, -ಗೋಲು. A wicker boat lined with leather. -ವು. Streaming; current. ಹರಿದಾಡು. To creep or move about. ಹರಿದಾರಿ. = ಹರದಾರಿ, q. v. -ನಾಳ, -ನಾಳಿಗೆ. A gutter, channel.

ಹರಿ 2. (ರಿ = ಱ) k. v. t. To tear, rend, break, slit, etc.; to pluck. v. i. To cut, as a knife. 2, to be torn or rent. n. Tearing. -ಗಲ್ಲು. A split stone.

ಹರಿ 3 a k. v i To spread, disperse

ಹರಿ 4. s a Green, yellow. n. The sun 2, the moon 3, India 4, Vishnu, Krishna. 5, Brahmâ 6, a lion. -ಕಥೆ. Any puranic story related with music and singing. -ದಾಸ One who relates such a story. -ದ್ವಾರ A place of pilgrimage on the Ganges -ನಾಮ Vishnu's name. -ನೀಲ Sapphire -ವಂಶ. Krishna's family -ವಾಸ Vishnu's day the eleventh lunar day; a day of fasting. -ಪೀಠ, -ವಿಷ್ಟರ. A throne -ಬುವ್ವ A ceremony on the fourth day of a marriage -ಭಕ್ತ. A worshipper of Vishnu ಹರಿಶ್ಚಂದ್ರ N. of a king of the solar dynasty. -ಹರ. Śiva.

ಹರಿಕಾರ. See s. ಪರಿ 1.

ಹರಿಕೆ. = ಹರಕೆ, q v.

ಹರಿಣ s n A deer, antelope. ಹರಿಣಿ A doe

ಹರಿತಾಲ (= ಹರತಾಳ. ಅರದಳ) s n. Sulphuret of arsenic, yellow orpiment.

ಹರಿಬ k n. A host, assemblage. 2, business, affair, concern

ಹರಿಯಣ, ಹರಿಯಾಣ, ಹರಿವಾಣ k n. A metal dish of any kind

ಹರಿವಿ = ಹರವಿ, q v.

ಹರಿವೆ (ರ=ಱ) k. n. A common potherb, *Amarantus oleraceus* [bless.

ಹರಿಸು 1 (= ಹರಸು, q v.) k v t. To

ಹರಿಸು 2 s v. t To take away, divide.

ಹರೀತಕಿ s. n The yellow myrobalan tree, *Terminalia chebula*

ಹರುಕು = ಹರಕು, q v.

ಹರುವು k n. A way, means, expedient.

ಹರುಷ tb of ಹರ್ಷ, q. v

ಹರೆ 1. (= ಪರೆ, ಹರಿ) k v i. To spread, to disperse. P ps ಹರದು, ಹರೆದು

ಹರೆ 2. k. v i. To begin to shine, dawn n Dawn ಮೂಡಲ- (The sun) to dawn in the east

ಹರೆಯ (tb of ಪ್ರಾಯ) n The time of youth, prime of life. ಹರೇತನ. Youth. -ದವ, ಹರೇದವ A young man, f -ದವಳು, ಹರೇದವಳು

ಹರ್ಷ s n Bristling, thrilling 2, rapture, delight, joy, pleasure, gladness -ಣ. Gladdening, delightful ಹರ್ಷಾಶ್ರು Tears of joy. ಹರ್ಷೋತ್ಸವ Abundance of joy ಹರ್ಷಿಸು. To rejoice, exult, be glad or pleased

ಹಲ್ 1. (= ಹಲ್ಲು, q v) k n. A tooth. -ಕಡಿ To gnash the teeth -ಕುರು. A gumboil.

ಹಲ್ 2. s. n A consonant. ಹಲಂತ Ending in a consonant -ಸಂಧಿ Euphony of consonants

ಹಲ 1 = ಪಲ 1, ಹಲವು, q v -ಬರು, -ವರು. Many or several persons.

ಹಲ 2 (= ಪಲ 2, q v) s. n. A particular weight

ಹಲ 3. s. n A plough -ದಂಡ. The shaft of a plough

ಹಲಕು k n The lower part of the cheek. 2, a kind of harrow. v. t To climb a tree.

ಹಲಗೆ (tb. of ಫಲಕ) n A plank, board. 2 a shield -ಸೇರುವೆ. A ceiling of boards

ಹಲಚಿ f n. Flatness. -ಮೂಗಿನವ. A flat-nosed man.

ಹಲದಿ = ಹಳದಿ, q v.

ಹಲವು k. a Much, many, some. -ಕೆಲವು Some, several -ಪ್ರಕಾರ, -ಬಗೆ Various kinds. -ಮಕ್ಕಳು. Many children -ಮಕ್ಕಳ ತಾಯಿ, -ಮಕ್ಕಳ ಬಳ್ಳಿ The shrub *Asparagus sarmentosus*. -ನುಡಿ, -ಮಾತು Very verbose

ಹಲಸಂದಿ. = ಅಲಸಂದಿ, q. v.

ಹಲಸು (tb. of ಪನಸ) n. The jack tree; also ಹಲಸಿನ ಮರ ಹಲಸಿನ ಹಣ್ಣು A jack fruit.

ಹಲಾಕು h a Oppressed, overcome, ruined, lost

ಹಲಾಯಿಸು h v. t To shake, agitate.

ಹಲಾಯುಧ s n. N. of Balarâma. 2, Râmačandra

ಹಲಾಲ್ಖೋರ h. n. A sweeper, scavenger.

ಹಲಾಹಲ s. *n.* A deadly poison.

ಹಲಿಗೆ. = ಹಲಗೆ, *q. v.*

ಹಲಿವೆ, ಹಲುಬೆ, ಹಲುವೆ k. *n.* A kind of rake or harrow.

ಹಲುಬು a. k. *v. i.* To lament.

ಹಲ್ಕಾ h. *a.* Light; unimportant, trifling, inferior, vulgar; *also* ಹಲ್ಕಿ.

ಹಲ್ಲಕಲ್ಲೋಲ. = ಅಲ್ಲಕಲ್ಲೋಲ, *q. v.*

ಹಲ್ಲಗೆಸು a. k. *v. i.* To go on, advance.

ಹಲ್ಲಾ h. *n.* An attack, onset; scaling a fort. -ಏರು, -ಹತ್ತು. To scale, *as* a fort.

ಹಲ್ಲಿ k. *n.* The small house-lizard, *Lacerta gecko.*

ಹಲ್ಲು (= ಹಲ್) k. *n.* A tooth, a step of a ladder; a spoke of a wheel. -ಕಡಿ, -ತಿನ್ನು. To gnash the teeth. -ಕಡ್ಡಿ. A tooth-pick. -ಕಿರಿ. To grin. -ಕುರು. A gumboil. -ನೋವು, -ಬೇನೆ, -ಶೂಲೆ. The toothache. -ಪುಡಿ. Tooth-powder. ಹಾಲ-, ಮೊಳೆ-. Milk teeth. -ಪೋಗವು. The lacker of the teeth.

ಹಲ್ಲೆ 1. k. *n.* The lobe of the ear. 2, a horse or bullock-shoe.

ಹಲ್ಲೆ 2. k. *n.* The seed or pod of the climbing shrub *Entada monastachya.*

ಹಲ್ಲೆಲೂಯಾ f. *int.* Halelujah (*Hebr.*): 'Praise ye the Lord'. *n.* A song of praise.

ಹಲ್ಲೋಲಕಲ್ಲೋಲ (= ಅಲ್ಲೋಲಕಲ್ಲೋಲ, *q. v.*) k. *n.* Tumult; tossing, *as* the sea, waves, *etc.*

ಹವಣು (*tb. of* ಪ್ರಮಾಣ, *q. v.*) *n.* Measure, proper measure, fitness, *etc.*; making ready, preparing. ಹವಣಿಕೆ. Due consideration; contemplation; thought; desire. ಹವಣಿಸು. To make ready, prepare, arrange; to think; to desire.

ಹವನ s. *n.* An oblation, sacrifice.

ಹವಳ (*tb. of* ಪ್ರವಾಲ) *n.* Coral. -ಕ್ರಿಮಿ, -ದ ಹುಳ. The coral polyp. -ಬಂಡೆ. A coral rock. -ಸರಗಂಧಕ. A kind of sulphur.

ಹವಾ. = ಹವೆ, *q. v.*

ಹವಾಲೆ [illegible] h. *n.* Transfer, *as* of a debt.

ಹವಾಲು, ಹವಾಲೆ h. *n.* Charge, trust, care. ಹವಾಲದಾರ, ಹವಾಲುದಾರ, ಹವಾಲ್ದಾರ. A native officer in the army.

ಹವಿಸ್ s. *n.* Any thing offered as oblation.

ಹವೀಕ. = ಹೈಗ, *q. v.*

ಹವುದಾ. = ಹೌದಾ, *q. v.*

ಹವುದು (= ಅಹುದು, ಹೌದು, *q. v.*) k. ((*v. i.*) *ad.* Yes; it is so.

ಹವುರ. = ಹೌರ, *q. v.*

ಹವೆ h. *n.* Air, wind; weather; climate; *also* ಹವಾ.

ಹವೇಲಿ h. *n.* A large house, villa.

ಹವ್ಯ s. *n.* Oblation. *a.* Fit for oblation. -ಕವ್ಯ. Oblations to the gods and the manes of ancesters.

ಹವ್ಯಾಸ h. *n.* Desire, lust.

ಹವ್ವನೆ, ಹವ್ವನೆ k. *ad.* Suddenly.

ಹಸ 1. (*tb. of* ಪಶು) *n.* A cow. -ಕರ. A cow and a calf.

ಹಸ 2, ಹಸಿತ s. *n.* Laughing, smiling; a laugh; *also* ಹಸನ. ಹಸನ್ಮುಖ. A smiling face.

ಹಸನ, ಹಸನು k. *n.* Good state or order; tillage; purity. -ಗೆಡು. Beauty to be lost. -ಮಾಡು. To till; to clean.

ಹಸರ್, ಹಸರು (= ಹಸುರು) k. *n.* Green colour, greenness; freshness; tenderness; young, green grass. -ಕಾಯಿ. An unripe fruit. -ಬಣ್ಣ. Green colour. -ರತ್ನ. Emerald. -ಹಾವು. A kind of green snake. -ವಾಣಿ, ಹಸವಾರ್ಣಿ, ಹಸರಾಣಿ. Vegetables of trade.

ಹಸಿ 1. k. *n.* Greenness; freshness, rawness. *a.* Green, fresh, moist, *etc.* -ಅಕ್ಕಿ, -ಯಕ್ಕಿ. Raw rice. -ಕಟ್ಟಿಗೆ. Green wood. -ಹಿಟ್ಟು, ಹಸಿಟ್ಟು. Raw flour of râgi. -ಬಿಸಿ. Slightly boiled. -ಮಾಂಸ. Raw flesh. -ಕಾಯಿ. A green unripe fruit.

ಹಸಿ 2. k. *v. i.* To hunger, crave food. *P. p.* ಹಸಿದು, ಹಸ್ತು. -ವು, -ವೆ. Hunger.

ಹಸಿ 3. = ಅಸಿ 2, *q. v.* -ಕಲ್ಲು. The lower part of a grinding-stone.

[illegible] 1. [illegible] A toll ([illegible] table, *etc.*) [illegible] officials from the vendors.

ಹಸಿಗೆ 2 k n. Sharing of the produce between the landlord and cultivator

ಹಸಿಬೆ, ಹಸುಬೆ (= ಪಸುಬೆ, q v) k n A long bag with an opening in the middle, carried on the shoulder or on a beast, a wallet

ಹಸು 1 k a Young, fresh, tender. -ಗೂಸು. A tender infant. -ಮಕ್ಕಳು. Young children.

ಹಸು 2. (= ಹಸ 1, q. v. tb of ಪಶು) n. A cow.

ಹಸುಕು k n A sharp smell

ಹಸುಬೆ = ಹಸಿಬೆ, q. v.

ಹಸುರು. = ಹಸರು, q. v.

ಹಸುಳ, ಹಸುಳೆ (= ಪಸುಳೆ, q v) k n A child. -ತನ. Childhood.

ಹಸೆ (= ಪಸೆ, q v) k n. A bed, a decorated seat or place.

ಹಸ್ತ s n. The hand. 2, an elephant's trunk. 3, a cubit. -ಕ. A mate, associate. -ಕಂಕಣ, -ಕಡಗ A bracelet -ಕೌಶಲ, -ಕೌಶಲ್ಯ, -ಲಾಘವ. Sleight of hand, legerdemain -ಗತ Come to hand, procured, obtained. -ಗುಣ. Luck. -ದೋಷ A slip of the hand -ಪರೀಕ್ಷೆ. Examination (of the lines on the palms) of the hand -ಲಾಘವ Dexterity, sleight of hand. ಹಸ್ತಾಕ್ಷರ. Autograph signature, handwriting. ಹಸ್ತಾಂತರ. That is in hand, as capital, a treasury. ಹಸ್ತೋದಕ. Water poured upon the hand prior to a meal

ಹಸ್ತಿ s. n An elephant. -ದಂತ Ivory -ನಾಪುರ The ancient Delhi

ಹಳ (ಳ = ೞ) k. a. Old. n Oldness. 2, weeds. -ಗನ್ನಡ = ಹಳೆಗನ್ನಡ, s ಹಳೆ, q v. -ಬ An old man, an old servant

ಹಳಚು a k v l To strike against

ಹಳತು, ಹಳದು (ಳ = ೞ) k n That is old

ಹಳದಿ f. a. Yellow, greenish, yellow n. Turmeric, *Curcuma longa*

ಹಳಮೆ (ಳ = ೞ) k n Antiquity; a tradition

ಹಳವಂಡ, ಹಳಹಳಿ f n Inquietude, painful restlessness. ಹಳವಳಿಸು To become unquiet and anxious

ಹಳಸು (ಳ = ೞ) k v i To spoil, become old ಹಳಸಲು That which is spoiled

ಹಳಿ 1, ಹಳುಕು k n. A bit, piece, lump

ಹಳಿ 2. (= ಪಳಿ 1. ಳಿ = ೞಿ) k v t. To revile, scold, rebuke, scorn. n. Blame, rebuke, calumny, also -ವು

ಹಳುವು (ಳು = ೞು) k. n. A forest, jungle.

ಹಳೆ (= ಹಳ) k. a. Old, ancient, antique. -ಕನ್ನಡ, -ಗನ್ನಡ, -ಕರ್ನಾಟಕ. Ancient Kannada -ಚಿಂದಿ. An old rag. -ದು. That is old -ನೀರು Stale water -ಬ. = ಹಳಬ s ಹಳ. -ಪೈಕ. One of a class of Shûdras. -ಮಗ. A house slave. -ಮಾತು, -ವಾತು. A tradition, legend -ನಾಣ್ಯ An ancient coin.

ಹಳ್ಳ (= ಪಳ್ಳ) k n Depth a pit, hole in the ground, low ground, a stream, rivulet

ಹಳ್ಳಿ k n. A hamlet, village -ಗಾಡಿನವ. A rustic. -ಗಾಡು A hamlet without civilisation. -ಗಾರ A villager

ಹಾಕು k v. t To put, to put on, to lay out, plan, plant, to sow, to pour; to cast or throw; to bring forth, to apply, perform, *used also pleonastically, as:* ಕಟ್ಟಿ-, ತಿಂದು-, ಒಡದು-, *etc.* ಕಿತ್ತು-. To pluck out. ಕೊಯಿದು-. To cut off. ಚೀಟು- To cast lots ತೆಗೆದು- To take out ದೊಬ್ಬಿ-. To push away. ಹಾಕಿಸು To cause to put, *etc* -ವಿಕೆ. Putting, throwing.

ಹಾಗ f. n One anè and two kâsus; one-fourth ಹಾಗೂವೀಸ. 1 ano 5½ kâsus.

ಹಾಗಲ k n A winding plant with bitter fruit, *Momordica charantia, cf* ಮಡ- -ವಾಡಿ. N. of a place

ಹಾಗೆ k. ad In that manner, thus, so; like; as; likewise, so that, for nothing ಹಾಗೂ. So also, likewise, also ಹಾಗೇ, ಹಾಗೆಯೇ. Even so.

ಹಾಂಗೆ = ಹಾಗೆ, q v.

ಹಾಜರ್, ಹಾಜರು h a Present; ready ಹಾಜರು. Presence. -ಜವಾಬು. A ready answer, a repartee -ಜಾಮೀನು A bail for presenting a person. -ಪಟ್ಟಿ

A muster roll ಗೈರ- Absent.

ಹಾಡು k v. t & i. To sing. n Singing (*also* ಹಾಡಿಕೆ), a song -ಗಾರ A singer, minstrel. ಧ್ವನಿ ಎತ್ತಿ- To sing aloud. ಸ್ವರ ತಗ್ಗಿಸಿ- To sing lowly -ಹಾಡು To sing a song

ಹಾಡು 2. k n. Manner, mode. 2, suffering, trouble

ಹಾಣಾಹಾಣಿ k n. Mutual beating

ಹಾತು f. n. A hand -ಬೇಡಿ. A handcuff.

ಹಾದರ k n. Adultery; fornication -ಗಳ್ಳ. An adulterer. -ಗಿತ್ತಿ. An adulteress. -ತನ Adultery

ಹಾದಿ k n A road, way. -ಕಾರ. A traveller -ಖರ್ಚು. Travelling expenses -ನಡೆ. To walk on a road. -ನೋಡು. To look out for, wait for. -ಬಾಕ. A beggar at the roadside. -ಯವ, -ಹೋಕ. A wayfarer. -ತಪ್ಪಿ ಹೋಗು To go astray.

ಹಾದು *P p. of* ಹಾಯು. *q v.*

ಹಾನಿ s. n. Loss, decrease, damage, harm, destruction, hurt. -ಹೊರಕು. To suffer loss

ಹಾಯ್, ಹಾಯಿ k n. A sail 2, crossing, course, way a. Nice, pleasant. -ಗಡ. A fording place -ಹೋರು. To be agreeable.

ಹಾಯು (= ಪಾಯ್, *q v*) k v t. To assault, to butt i. i To step or pass over; to cross, leap, to go, flow *P. ps* ಹಾಯಿದು, ಹಾದು. ಹಾದಾಟ Mutual butting; fording ಹಾವಾಡು To butt with horns, to cross

ಹಾರ s n. A string of pearls, a necklace. 2 taking, conveying, captivating, charming, *also* -ಕ.

ಹಾರಯಿಸು (= ಆರಯಿಸು, *q v*) k v. t. To look for, to desire, *also* ಹಾರಯ್ಸು ಹಾರಯ್ಕೆ Wish, desire

ಹಾರವಾಣ (*tb. of* ಪಾರಾವತ) n. A dove, *etc*

ಹಾರು 1 k v. t. To look for. 2, to desire. ಹಾರನ, ಹಾರುವ ಹಾರ- A Brāhmaṇa; *f.* -ವಿತಿ, ಹಾರ್ತಿ

ಹಾರು 2. (ರು = ಱು) k. v. i. To leap up; to jump, spring, to run, to fly; to fly about; to cross by jumping ಹಾರ ತೆಗೆ, ಹಾರ ಬಡಿ To open (a door) completely. ಹಾರಾಡು, ಹಾರ್ಯಾಡು To fly about, run about. ಹಾರಿಸು To cause to jump, *etc.* -ಎಕೆ, ಹಾರಿಕೆ Jumping ಹಾರಿ ಹಾರಿ ಬೀಳು To fall upon in a passion

ಹಾರೆ f n. A crowbar -ಕಾಲು. The spoke of a wheel.

ಹಾಲವಕ್ಕಿ f. n. A small bird the cry of which is said to be ominous

ಹಾಲಹವಾಲು h n Distressful condition; fatigue, humour, *etc.*, a grievance.

ಹಾಲಿ f. *ad* At present, now, current.

ಹಾಲಿವಾಣ f. n. The coral tree 2, a dove

ಹಾಲು 1. k. n Milk, the white juice of a cocoanut or any plant 2, (e) a ball -ಅನ್ನ, ಹಾಲನ್ನ Milk and boiled rice. ಹಾಲಿನವ. A milkman. ಹಾಲುಣ್ಣೆ. A wart -ತೆನೆ The cream of milk. -ಬೆಳ್ಳಿ Pure silver -ವಕ್ಕಿ = ಹಾಲವಕ್ಕಿ. ಮೊಲೇ- Breast-milk -ಮೊಸರು. Excellent curds ಹಾಲೋಗರ. Rice boiled with milk.

ಹಾಲು 2 = ಹಾಲಿ, *q v*

ಹಾಲುವಾಣ. = ಹಾಲಿವಾಣ *q v.*

ಹಾಲೆ k. n The tree *Mimusops kauki.* 2, the lobe of the ear

ಹಾವ f n. Gestures, dalliance, airs -ಭಾವ Gesticulation.

ಹಾವಸೆ k n. The aquatic plant. *Vallisneria octandra*

ಹಾವಳಿ k. n. Trouble, harass, annoyance, molestation, havoc.

ಹಾವಿಗೆ (*tb. of* ಪಾದುಕ) n. A wooden shoe.

ಹಾವು k. n A snake, serpent. -ಗಾರ. = ಹಾವಡಿಗ, ಹಾವಾಡಿಗ. A snake-charmer ಹೆಬ್ಬಾವು A boa. ಪೊರೆ ತೆಗೆದ- A serpent which has cast its slough. ಹಾವಿನ ಹಾಡೆ. A serpent's fang -ಮೀನು A kind of muscle shell -ಮೆಕ್ಕೆ. Colocynth, *Citrullus colocynthis.* -ರಾಣಿ A kind of skink.

ಹಾವುಗೆ. = ಪಾವಿಗೆ, *q v.*

ಹಾಸ s *n.* Laughing, laughter, derision. -ಕ A laugher, buffoon, *cf.* ಹಾಸ್ಯ

ಹಾಸರ. = ಹೇಸರ, *q v.*

ಹಾಸಲ್ ಕಲಂ h. *n* Essence; abstract *ad* Briefly, shortly.

ಹಾಸಲು, ಹಾಸಿಲು h. *n.* Postage, custom, [toll, duty.

ಹಾಸು 1. k. *v. t* To spread, to lay *n.* A bed. 2, the warp. 3, a chequered cloth -ಗಲ್ಲು A slab, *also* ಹಾಸಿಗಲ್ಲು ಹಾಸಿಕ್ಕು To prepare the warp. -ಗೆ That is spread, a bed, cover, *also* ಹಾಸಿಕೆ.

ಹಾಸು 2 *tb of* ಪಾಶ, *q v*

ಹಾಸೆ k *n.* A beautiful seat.

ಹಾಸ್ಯ s *n.* Laughter, jest, amusement. 2, ridicule, derision *a* Laughable ridiculous. -ಗಾರ A gester, buffoon. -ರಸ Sense of humour ಹಾಸ್ಯಾಸ್ಪದ A laughing-stock.

ಹಾಹಾ s *int* of grief, surprise, pain. -ಕಾರ, -ರವ. A general lamentation.

ಹಾಳಿ k. *n.* A sheet of glass. 2, a division of paddy land.

ಹಾಳತ, ಹಾಳಿತ (ಳ, ಳಿ = ೞ, ೞಿ) k. *n.* Propriety, fitness; due proportion.

ಹಾಳು (ಳು = ೞು) k *n* Ruin, desolation, destruction, a waste ಹಾಳ. A miserable being. -ಬೀಳು, ಹಾಳಾಗು. To go to ruin, to be destroyed -ಗೋಡೆ. A dilapidated wall. -ಬಾವಿ. An unused well -ಭೂಮಿ Waste land. -ಮಣ್ಣು A sterile soil. -ಮನೆ. A house in ruins -ಮಾಡು To ruin, to destroy, to waste. -ಸ್ಥಲ. A desolate place. -ಹರಟೆ Idle, useless talk. ಹಾಳೂರು A deserted village

ಹಿಂಸಾ, ಹಿಂಸೆ s *n.* Injury, hurt 2 molesting, tormenting 3, killing, slaughter. ಜೀವ-, ಪ್ರಾಣ- Murder, a violent assault ಹಿಂಸಕ A murderer, persecutor; injurious, hurtful, savage. ಹಿಂಸಕ ಪ್ರಾಣಿ A beast of prey. ಹಿಂಸಿಸು To hurt, harm, wound, injure; to kill, slay, destroy.

ಹಿಕಮತ್ತು h. *n.* Skill, cunning, art, trick -ಗಾರ A clever or cunning man

ಹಿಕ್ಕಟ್ಟು k *n.* The backside, *as* of a ship, lateness, *as* of rain

ಹಿಕ್ಕಲು k *n.* A small branch-channel in gardens.

ಹಿಕ್ಕು k *v t* To comb

ಹಿಕ್ಕೆ k *n* The dung of goats, sheep, *etc.* 2, (f) hiccough.

ಹಿಗ್ಗಾಮುಗ್ಗಾ h *ad* Backwards and for- [wards

ಹಿಗ್ಗು k. *v i.* To separate, extend 2, to grow elated, begin to rejoice. ಹಿಗ್ಗಲಿಸು, ಹಿಗ್ಗಿಸು To separate, straddle, to open, *as* the mouth of a bag, to slacken

ಹಿಂ, ಹಿಮ್ k. *ad* Behind, after. -ಗಟ್ಟು, -ಗಡೆ. The backside, place behind -ಗತ್ತಲೆ The early dawn, darkness after moonset -ಗಾರಿ, -ಗಾರು The latter rain, *also* -ಗಾರ ಮಳೆ -ಗಾರು ಪೈರು. The second crop -ಗಾಲು The hind leg of a quadruped

ಹಿಂಗು 1. (= ಪಿಂಗು) k. *v i* To go back, retreat; to fail 2, to be imbibed

ಹಿಂಗು 2 s *n.* Asafoetida

ಹಿಂಗುಲ. ಹಿಂಗೂಲಕ (= ಇಂಗಲಿಕ) s. *n.* Vermilion

ಹಿಜರಿ h *n.* The Mahomedan era.

ಹಿಂಚು k. *v i* To be behind *ad.* Behind -ಮುಂಚು = ಹಿಂದು ಮುಂದು

ಹಿಂಚೆ = ಹಿಂದೆ, *q v.*

ಹಿಂಜರಿ k *v i.* To retreat, withdraw, recoil, to backslide

ಹಿಂಜು k *v. t* To separate, disentangle

ಹಿಟ್ಟು (*tb. of* ಪಿಷ್ಟ) *n* Flour, meal. 2, porridge 3, food. -ಬಟ್ಟೆ Food and raiment -ಬಳಪ A soft kind of pot-stone. -ಬೀಸು To grind flour -ಗಾಳಿಸು To sift flour -ಕುಟ್ಟು To beat flour. -ಕಲಸು. To mix flour. ಹಿಟ್ಟಡಿಗೆ A cake.

ಹಿಡ *P. p. of* ಹಿಡಿ -ಕೊಳ್ಳು To seize, lay hold on. -ತ Grasping, seizing; parsimony

ಹಿಡಿ 1. (= ಪಿಡಿ, *q. v.*) k. *v. t.* To seize, catch, take hold of; to hold, take possession, *as* of a country. 2, to restrain, *as* the breath, *etc.* 3, to undertake, begin. 4, to find out, discover. 5, to stop, *as* pay. *v. i.* To be attacked by insects. 2, to cost. 3, to fit, suit. 4, to be possessed by evil spirits. 5, to be absorbed, *as* colours. 6, to be affected by disease or pain. 7, to take up time. ಅಮಲು-. To be intoxicated. ಉಳುಕು-. To be sprained. ಬೂಜು-, ಬೂಷ್ಟು-. To grow mouldy. ದಾರಿ-. To take a road; begone! ಕೈ-. To marry; to uphold. -ದು ಕೊಂಡು ಬರು. To bring by force. -ಕೊಂಡು ಹೋಗು. To take away by force. -ತ. = ಹಿಡತ, *q. v.* -ಸು. To cause to seize, *etc.*

ಹಿಡಿ 2. k. *n.* A hold; a handful, grasp. 2, a handle, hilt. 3, a broom. -ಕ, ಕೆ. A handle, hilt; the fist. -ಗಲು. A broom. -ತುಂಬ. A handful. -ಯಾಳು. A captive.

ಹಿಡಿಂಬ s. *n.* N. of a râkshasa slain by Bhima.

ಹಿಡುವಳಿ k. *n.* Possession, ownership (of land). -ದಾರ. A possessor.

ಹಿಣಿ, ಹಿಣಿಲು k. *n.* A bullock's hump. 2, a bow-string. 3, a braid of hair.

ಹಿಂಟೆ (= ಹೆಂಟೆ) k. *n.* A lump, clod.

ಹಿಂಡಿ k. *n.* The refuse of oil-seed, an oil-cake. 2, a chutney of *Emblic myrobalan.*

ಹಿಂಡು 1. k. *v. t.* To press, squeeze out; to wring, *as* a wet cloth; to pinch, *as* the ears; to extract, *as* milk; to harass.

ಹಿಂಡು 2. (*tb. of* ಷಂಡ) *n.* A multitude, flock, herd. *Cpds.:* ಆನೆಗಳ-, ಕುರಿಗಳ-, ಪಶುಗಳ-, *etc.* -ಗಟ್ಟು, -ಗೂಡು. To form a herd, to come together in crowds.

ಹಿತ s. *a.* Suitable; advantageous, beneficial, useful; salutary, wholesome, agreeable. 2, friendly, kind. *n.* Advantage, profit, benefit, welfare. -ಕರ, -ಕಾರಕ. Beneficial. -ಕಾರಿ. Doing services, befriending. -ವಂತ, -ವಾದಿ. A benefactor, friend. -ಶತ್ರು. A secret enemy. -ಶತ್ರುತ್ವ. Secret enmity. ಹಿತಾವಹ. Salutary, salubrious. ಹಿತೋಪದೇಶ. Friendly advice, good counsel; N. of a popular work.

ಹಿತ್ತಲು k. *n.* A back-yard.

ಹಿತ್ತಳೆ, ಹಿತ್ತಾಳೆ, ಹಿತ್ತಾಳಿ k. *n.* Brass.

ಹಿದುಕು k. *v. t.* To peel soaked pulse.

ಹಿಂ, ಹಿನ್. = ಹಿಂದೆ, *q. v.* -ತಿರುಗು, -ದಿರುಗು. To turn back; to return. -ತಿರುಗಿಸು (*v. t.*). To turn back, *etc.* -ತೆಗೆ, -ದೆಗೆ. To draw back, flinch.

ಹಿಂದ. = ಹಿಂದು, *q. v.* -ಗಡೆ. Afterwards.

ಹಿಂದಟ್ಟು k. *v. t.* To follow, pursue.

ಹಿಂದು 1. k. *n.* That which is behind, (*in place*), back, previous or past; past time. *ad.* Behind, *etc.* ಹಿಂದಕ್ಕೆ ಮುಂದಕ್ಕೆ. Backwards and forwards. ಹಿಂದಟ್ಟು. To follow, pursue. ಹಿಂದಾಗು. To be behind, flinch. ಹಿಂದಾಡು. To speak behind a person. -ಗಡೆ. A place that is behind; subsequent time. -ಗಳೆ. To flinch; to transgress. -ಗೊಳ್ಳು. To follow. -ಮುಂದು. That is behind and in front. -ಮುಂದು ನೋಡು. To be cautious; to hesitate.

ಹಿಂದು 2. (*tb. of* ಸಿಂಧು) *n.* A Hindoo. -ಜನ. Hindoos. -ದೇಶ, -ಸ್ಥಾನ. India. -ಸ್ಥಾನಿ. The Hindustani language.

ಹಿಂದೆ (= ಹಿಂ, ಹಿಂದು 1, *q. v.*) k. *n.* Past time. *prep.* Behind, after, at the back, backwards; in former times, ago; later on, afterwards. -ಬೀಳು. To lag behind; to be less in use. -ಆಡು, -ಯಾಡು. To backbite. -ಹತ್ತು, -ಹೋಗು. To follow.

ಹಿಂದೋಲ s. *n.* A swing, hammock.

ಹಿಪ್ಪಲಿ (*tb. of* ಪಿಪ್ಪಲಿ) *n.* Long pepper, *Piper longum.* -ನೇರಳೆ. The mulberry, *Morus indica.*

ಹಿಪ್ಪಿ, ಹಿಪ್ಪೆ k. *n.* The refuse after the juice has been squeezed out

ಹಿಂ, ಹಿನ್[6] = ಹಿಂದು 1, q v ಹಿಂಬಲ Help, refuge. -ಬಳೆ. A wrist-ornament worn behind the kadaga -ಬಳಿ. The rear. -ಭಾರ. Weight in the back part (of a cart). -ಬಾಲ. The tail, hind part, following. -ಬಾಲ ಮಾಡು, -ಬಾಲಿಸು. To follow. -ಭಾಗ The back part. -ಮಡಿ. The heel -ಮೆಟ್ಟು. To step backwards.

ಹಿಮ s a Cold, frosty n. Frost, ice, snow, dew, cold. -ಕರ, -ಕಿರಣ. The moon -ವತ್. Snowy, icy. -ಗಿರಿ, -ವತ್, ಹಿಮಾಚಲ, ಹಿಮಾದ್ರಿ, ಹಿಮಾಲಯ The Himâlaya mountain.

ಹಿಮ್ಮಣಿ. = ಹಮ್ಮಿಣಿ, q v

ಹಿಮ್ಮತ್ತು h n Protection, patronage, aid

ಹಿಯ್ಯಾಳಿ = ಹೀಯಾಳಿ, q v

ಹಿರಣ್ಯ s. n Gold. 2, wealth, riches. ಹಿರಣ್ಮಯ Golden -ಕಶಿಪು. N. of a daitya king killed by Narasimha -ಗರ್ಭ Brahmâ. ಹಿರಣ್ಯಾಕ್ಷ. Brother of ಹಿರಣ್ಯಕಶಿಪು.

ಹಿರಿ 1. k a Great, elder, senior. -ತನ. Dignity, greatness -ದು. That is big, older, superior, etc. -ಮಗ The eldest son -ಯ. An elder, senior -ಯರು. Elders, ancestors

ಹಿರಿ 2. k. v. t To break up, pull to pieces, to pull out of, to unsheathe v i. To be broken, to fall out of.

ಹಿರೆ. = ಹಿರಿ 1, q v.

ಹಿಸಕು, ಹಿಸಿಕು, ಹಿಸುಕು k v t To squeeze, press, as a fruit, to knead, to shampoo

ಹಿಸಾಬು h n. Calculation, an account. 2, practical arithmetic

ಹಿಸಿ k v. i. To burst (as a jack fruit), to crack (as a wall)

ಹಿಸ್ಸೆ h n. A share, part. -ದಾರ. A shareholder

ಹಿಳಲು (= ಹಿಣಿಲು) k. n. A bullock's hump. [ಹೆಸಗೆ

ಹಿಳಿಗೆ (tb of ಪಿಟಕ) n. A basket; cf

ಹಿಳ್ಳು, ಹಿಳ್ಳೆ k. n. A shoot, rootlet. -ಒಡೆ. Shoots to break forth

ಹೀಗಳಿ, ಹೀಗಳೆ k v t To scoff, revile. -ಯುವಿಕೆ. Scoffing.

ಹೀಗೆ, ಹೀಂಗೆ k. ad In this manner, thus, so, like -ಯೂ. Even in this manner. -ಯೇ In this very manner. ಹೀಗಿರಲಿಕ್ಕೆ, ಹೀಗಿರುವಲ್ಲಿ. While, thus.

ಹೀಚು (= ಪಿಂಜು 2, q. v) k. n. A fruit newly come out of blossom, also ಈಚು

ಹೀಜು = ಈಜು, q v

ಹೀನ s a Deprived of, devoid of, without, bereft of, deficient, faulty, mean, base, vile, low. -ಕೆಲಸ A base act. *Cpds* : ಕುಲ-, ಜಾತಿ-, ಬುದ್ಧಿ-, ಭಾಗ್ಯ-, ಮತಿ-, ಮಾನ-, ರಾಜ್ಯ-, ಲಜ್ಜಾ-, *etc.* -ಜಾತಿ. Low-born, a low caste. -ತನ, -ತೆ, -ತ್ವ. Baseness; meanness. -ದಶೆ. Miserable state -ಸ್ವರ A bad voice. ಹೀನಾಯ. Want, dishonour. -ಯಿಸು, -ಯ್ಸು, ಹೀನೈಸು. To despise, degrade, disesteem

ಹೀಬ್ರೂ f n. A Jew. 2, the Hebrew language

ಹೀಯಾಳಿ (= ಹಿಯ್ಯಾಳಿ) k. n. Scoffing, sneer, rough or cruel treatment, a despicable person. -ಸು. To scoff, sneer, to upbraid, cf ಹೀಗಳಿ.

ಹೀರು k v t To suck up, absorb, as water, etc , to drink P. p ಹೀರಿ.

ಹೀರೆ k. n The vegetable *Luffa acutangula*. -ಕಾಯಿ Its fruit.

ಹೀಲಿ a k n A peacock's tail

ಹುಕುಂ, ಹುಕ್ಕುಂ h. n A command, order. -ನಾಮೆ. A written order, decree.

ಹುಕ್ಕಾ h. n. A smoking apparatus, hooka. -ಕುಡಿ, -ಸೇದು To smoke the hooka.

ಹುಗಳು = ಹುಗುಳು, q v.

ಹುಗಿ k v t To inter, bury. ಹುಗಿತ. Burying ಹುಗಿಸು. To cause to bury.

ಹುಗುಳು (= ಪುಗುಳು, ಹುಗಳು) k n A blister, boil, sore.

ಹುಗ್ಗಿ k. n Boiled rice mixed with any split pulse and salted or sweetened to taste, as [illegible]

ಹುಚ್ಚು (= ಪೆಚ್ಚು, q. v. tb. of ಪಿತ್ತ) n. Foolishness, folly, madness. ಹುಚ್ಚ. A fool; f. ಹುಚ್ಚಿ. ಹುಚ್ಚಾಟ. Silly conduct. Cpds.: -ಕೆಲಸ, -ಕೋಪ, -ಗಾಳಿ, -ತಿಳುವಳಿಕೆ, -ನಾಯಿ, -ಪ್ರೀತಿ, -ಬುದ್ಧಿ, -ಮಳೆ, etc. -ಹತ್ತು. Foolishness to seize. -ಮಾಡು. To make a fool of. -ಮೋರೆ ಮಾಡು. To put on a frightful look. ಹುಚ್ಚೋಟ. A rash run. -ತನ. Madness.

ಹುಜತ್ತು h. n. Perverse wrangling, objecting or making difficulties. -ಗಾರ, ಹುಜತ್ತಿನವ. A perverse objector.

ಹುಂಜ 1, ಹುಂಜು k. n. A cock. -ದಡಿ. A kind of border of a cloth.

ಹುಂಜ 2. f. n. A quantity of cotton yarn. -ಕೋಡು. A twist, skein.

ಹುಟ್ಟ 1. (= ಹುಟ್ಟು 1, n. q. v.) ಹುಟ್ಟಾ. From one's very birth. ಹುಟ್ಟಾವಳಿ. = ಹುಟ್ಟುವಳಿ, q. v.

ಹುಟ್ಟ 2. k. n. A (honey) comb.

ಹುಟ್ಟಿಸು k. v. t. To create, produce, originate.

ಹುಟ್ಟು 1. k. v. i. To arise, originate, come into existence, be born, be produced. n. Birth, origin; produce; family. -ಕುರುಡ. A male born blind; f. -ಕುರುಡಿ. -ಗುಣ. A natural disposition. -ಬುದ್ಧಿ. Instinct. -ಮನೆ. The house in which one has been born. ಹುಟ್ಟುವಳಿ (= ಹುಟ್ಟಾವಳಿ). Produce, as of a garden, field, etc.; the amount of an assessment. -ವಿಕೆ. Coming into existence. ಹುಟ್ಟೂರು. A birth-place.

ಹುಟ್ಟು 2. k. n. A wooden spoon; a paddle.

ಹುಡಕು. = ಹುಡುಕು, q. v.

ಹುಡಗ. = ಹುಡುಗ, q. v. ಹುಡಗಿ. = ಹುಡುಗಿ, q. v.

ಹುಡಿ (= ಪುಡಿ) k. n. Powder; dust; snuff. -ಮಣ್ಣು. Fine earth, dust. -ಮಾಡು. To reduce to powder. -ಯಾಗು. To be powdered.

ಹುಡಿಗಿ. = ಹುಡುಗಿ, q. v.

ಹುಡುಕು (= ಹುಡಕು) k. v. t. To seek, search for, search out, find. 2, to search, examine.

ಹುಡುಗ (= ಹುಡಗ) k. n. A boy. 2, a child. -ತನ, ಹುಡುಗು. Childhood; boyishness, childishness; also ಹುಡುಗಾಟ, ಹುಡುಗಾಟಿಕೆ.

ಹುಡುಗಿ k. n. A girl. -ತನ. Girlhood.

ಹುಡುಗು k. v. t. To sweep n. Sweeping. -ಮಾಡು. To sweep.

ಹುಣಸೆ, ಹುಣಿಸಿ, ಹುಣಿಸೆ k. n. The tamarind, Tamarindus indica. Cpds.: -ಕಾಯಿ, -ಗಿಡ, -ಬೀಜ, -ಮರ, -ಹಣ್ಣು, -ಹುಳಿ. -ಬೀಜದ ಹುರಳು. A fried preparation of tamarind seeds.

ಹುಣಿಮೆ. = ಹುಣ್ಣಿಮೆ, q. v.

ಹುಂಡಿ 1. k. n. A hamlet.

ಹುಂಡಿ 2. f. n. A bill of exchange; also -ಕಾಗದ, -ಚೀಟು.

ಹುಣ್ಣಿಮೆ, ಹುಣ್ಣಿವೆ (tb. of ಪೂರ್ಣಿಮೆ) n. Full moon.

ಹುಣ್ಣು k. n. A sore, ulcer, abscess. ಅರಸ-, ರಾಜ-. A carbuncle. -ಹಿಡಿ, -ಹತ್ತು. A sore to break out. ಹುಣ್ಣಿನಲ್ಲಿ ಕೀವು ಸೋರು. An ulcer to discharge matter.

ಹುತ್ತ, ಹುತ್ತು k. n. A white-ant hill. -ಗಾಲು. A kind of elephantiasis.

ಹುದುಗ k. n. A cover. ಹುದುಗು. To be covered; to hide, conceal one's self.

ಹುದ್ದೆ h. n. An office, post. -ದಾರ. An officer. -ದಾರಿ. The business of an officer.

ಹುನ್ನರ f. n. An art; power of skill, scheme.

ಹುಬ್ಬು (tb. of ಭ್ರೂ) n. The eye-brow. -ಗಂಟು. A frown. -ಗಂಟಿಕ್ಕು, -ಗಂಟು ಹಾಕು. To frown.

ಹುಬ್ಬೆ (tb. of ಪೂರ್ವೆ) n. The eleventh of the lunar mansions.

ಹುಮ್ಮಸ್ಸು f. n. Pride, arrogance.

ಹುಯಿ k. v. t. To beat. P. p. ಹುಯಿದು, ಹೊಡು.

ಹುಯಿಲು, ಹುಯ್ಯಲು k. n. Vociferation. -ಇಡು, ಹುಯಿಲಿಡು, ಹುಯ್ಯಲಿಕ್ಕು. To roar out.

ಹುರ. = ಹುರಿ 1, q. v. 2, (= ಪುರು) roughness. -ಒರಟ. Roughness. -ಕೆಲಸ.

Parched corn or pulse -ಹುರುಳು Roughness of the skin, a kind of herpes; itches -ವಳಿಸು To be parched.

ಹುರಮಂಜಿ = ಹುರುಮಂಜಿ, *q v*

ಹುರಳಿ (= ಹುಳಿ್) k *n* Horse-gram, *Dolichos uniflorus* -ಕಟ್ಟು ತಿನ್ನಿಸು. To give (a horse) gram

ಹುರಿ 1 (=ಉರಿ 1) k. *v t.* To roast, parch, *as* grain, pulse, *etc* *n* Parching -ಯಕ್ಕಿ, ಹುರ್ಯಕ್ಕಿ Parched rice. -ಗಡಲೆ, -ಗಡ್ಲೆ Parched (Bengal) gram -ಸಕ್ಕರೆ A kind of sugar.

ಹುರಿ 2 k *n.* Twist, cord, twine, a twisting -ಕಳಚು, -ಬಿಚ್ಚು. To untwist a thread ಮಾಡು. To twist.

ಹುರಿ 3. k. *n* Strength, courage, valour. 2, the spine -ಗೂಡಿಸು, -ಗೊಳಿಸು, -ದುಂಬಿಸು, -ಮಾಡು. To encourage. -ದುಂಬು To be courageous, to encourage.

ಹುರುಕು. = ಹುರುಕು, *q v.*

ಹುರುಗು k. *n* Rivalry; envy, jealousy, emulation -ಮಾಡು, ಹುರುಡಿಸು To rival, envy. ಹುರುಡಿಗ An envious man.

ಹುರುಮಂಜಿ (= ಹುರಮಂಜಿ) h *n* A particular kind of red ochre

ಹುರುಳಿ, ಹುಳಿ್. = ಹುರಳಿ, *q v*

ಹುರುಳು (= ಪುರುಳು, *q v*) k. *n.* Meaning, power, use; service ಇದರಲ್ಲಿ ಏನು ಹುರುಳಿಲ್ಲ There is no use in this, *etc.*

ಹುಲಬು, ಹುಲುಬು k *v i* To come to light, to be detected

ಹುಲಸು = ಹುಲಿಸು, *q. v.*

ಹುಲಿ k *n* A tiger. -ಯುಗುರು A tiger's claws, a scandant plant, *Gloriosa superba* (= ಕೋಳಿಕುಟುಮ). -ಯ ಚರ್ಮ, -ಯತೊಗಲು A tiger's skin ಹೆಣ್ಣು- A tigress ಹೆಬ್ಬುಲಿ. A royal tiger

ಹುಲಿಗಿಲಿ, ಹುಲಿಗಿಲು k *n* The Indian beech *Pongamia glabra*

ಹುಲಿವೆ k *n* The timber tree, *Terminalia paniculata*

ಹುಲಿಸು, ಹುಲುಸು k. *v. i.* To increase, thrive, grow *n.* Increase in bulk. richness, *as* of a crop

ಹುಲ್ಲು k *n.* Grass, straw, hay. -ಕಡ್ಡಿ. A piece of straw. -ಗದ್ದೆ. A paddy-field overgrown with grass. -ಗಾವಲು. Pasture land. -ತುಳಿಸು To tread out corn with oxen. -ಬಡಿ To thrash corn. -ಬಣವೆ, -ಮೆದೆ A stack of straw. -ಮೇಯು To eat grass graze *as* cattle -ಚಾಪೆ A grass mat -ಮನೆ A thatched house. -ಮೂಟೆ, ಹುಲ್ಲಡಕ A heap of straw. ಹುಲ್ಲೊಕ್ಕಲ್. Bullocks treading thrashed straw

ಹುಲ್ಲೆ k *n* An antelope or deer

ಹುವ್ವ (= ಹೂ, ಹೂವು, *q v.*) k *n* A flower

ಹುಷಾರ, ಹುಷಾರು h *a.* Smart, sharp, attentive, alert, watchful, fresh ಹುಷಾರಿ. Smartness, intelligence -ಇರು. To be alert

ಹುಸಿ (= ಪುಸಿ) k *v. i* To become untrue or false. *n* A falsehood, lie; *also* -ನುಡಿ, -ಮಾತು -ಗಾಯಿ An unripe fruit. -ಗುಂಡು A missed shot. -ನಗೆ A pretended or gentle smile -ಹೂ A flower that drops without producing fruit

ಹುಳ (ಳ = ೞ) k. *n* A worm, insect in general. -ಕು = ಹುಳುಕು, *q. v.*

ಹುಳಿ 1 k. *n* Acidity, sourness. 2, leaven *a.* Sour, acid. *v i* To be sour. *Cpds* -ನೀರು, -ಪದಾರ್ಥ, -ಪಲ್ಯ, -ಮರ, -ಮಾವು, -ರಸ, -ಸೊಪ್ಪು -ಹಣ್ಣು, *etc* -ಹಿಡಿ. To turn sour

ಹುಳಿ 2. (ಳ = ೞ) k *v. i.* To get worm-eaten, rot, decay.

ಹುಳು (= ಹುಳ ಳು = ೞು) -ಕಲು Decayed state -ಕು (= ಹುಳಕು) Decay, rottenness, decayed, unsound, corrupt -ಕು ನೀತಿ Base precepts -ಕು ಮನಸ್ಸು. A corrupt mind -ಕು ಮರ A rotten tree -ಕು ಮೋರೆ A pock-marked face. -ಕು ಹಲ್ಲು. A carious tooth.

ಹೂ 1 (= ಹುವ್ವ) k. *n* A flower, blossom. -ಗಣ್ಣು. Albugo -ಗಾಯ. A slight wound. -ಚೆಂಡು A bouquet. -ಏಂಗಣ The Indian shot, *Canna indica.* -ಗ A fl w r r t n -ಗಣ್ಣು ' n light colour. -ಬಾಣ. A kind of firework. -ಬಿಡು. To begin to blossom. -ಬಿಸಲು. A moderate evening sunshine. -ಗಾರ, -ವಡಿಗ, -ವಾಡಿಗ. A florist. -ಮಾಲೆ. A chaplet or garland of flowers; *also* -ಹಾರ.

ಹೂ 2. k. *A particle expressing consent or assent:* yes, well.

ಹೂಂ s. *int.* of reproach, menace, *etc.* -ಕರಿಸು. To cry out angrily.

ಹೂಜ, ಹೂಜೆ 1. (=ಕೂಜೆ, *q. v.*) h. *n.* A goglet, jug.

ಹೂಜೆ 2. k. *n.* Envy, jealousy. -ಗಾರ. A jealous man; *f.* -ಗಾತಿ.

ಹೂಟ k. *n.* A plan, means, expedient, scheme. 2, yoking. -ಗಾರ. A schemer; contriver.

ಹೂಡು k. *v. t.* To join, unite; to yoke; to put oxen, horses, *etc.* to carts or plough; to arrange, make ready.

ಹೂಡೆ k. *n.* A circular bastion-like structure of stones for defence.

ಹೂಣ s. *n.* A barbarian, Hun; a European. *Cpds.:* -ಭಾಷೆ, -ಶಕ.

ಹೂಣಿಗ a. k. *n.* A bold man. -ತನ. Bravery.

ಹೂಣು k. *v. t.* To bury; *also* ಹೂಳಿಸು. ಹೂಣುವ ಸ್ಥಳ. A burial ground.

ಹೂನು, ಹೂಂಹು. = ಹೂ 2, *q. v.*

ಹೂರಣ, ಹೂರ್ಣ (*tb. of* ಪೂರ್ಣ) *n.* The stuffing of cakes. -ಹೋಳಿಗೆ. A stuffed cake.

ಹೂಲಿ 1. k. *n.* N. of a straggling shrub.

ಹೂಲಿ 2. f. *n.* A commotion, alarm. -ಎಬ್ಬಿಸು. To raise an alarm.

ಹೂವು. = ಹೂ, *q. v.*

ಹೂಸು k. *v. t.* To daub, smear. 2, to break wind downwards. *n.* A fart.

ಹೂಳು (ಳು = ಱು) k. *v. t.* To cover; to bury; *also* ಹೂಣು. *v. i.* To sink into, as a foot, *etc.* -ವ ಭೂಮಿ, -ವ ಸ್ಥಳ. A burial place.

ಹೃದ್ (ಹೃತ್) s. *n.* The heart, mind. -ರೋಗ, ಹೃಚ್ಛೂಲ. Heart-ache. -ಕಂಪ. Heart-throb; anxiety. -ತಾಪ. Mental distress. -ಗತ. Conceived; believed, cherished. ಹೃದಯ. The heart; the mind, soul, seat of thought and feeling; breast, chest, bosom. ಹೃದಯಭೇದಕ. Heart-rending. ಹೃದಯಾಳು. Kind, affectionate.

ಹೆಕ್ಕತ್ತು k. *n.* The nape of the neck.

ಹೆಕ್ಕಳ a. k. *n.* Abundance. 2, conceit, pride; *cf.* ಹಗ್ಗಳ. ಹೆಕ್ಕಳಿಸು. To get proud.

ಹೆಕ್ಕು k. *v. t.* To pick up, take up one by one. 2, to comb.

ಹೆಗ k. *n.* Largeness. -ಗಚ್ಚು. A strong band or knot. ಹೆಗ್ಗಡೆ. A headman, chief; *f.* -ಗಡತಿ. -ಗಣ. A very large rat, bandicoot. -ಗಣಬೋನು. A bandicoot trap. -ಗ್ಗತ್ತು. = ಹೆಕ್ಕತ್ತು, *q. v.* -ಗಾಡು (-ಕಾಡು). A thick forest. -ಗಾಣ. A large oil-mill of stone. -ಗುಂಟೆ. A weeding plough. -ಗುರುತು. A prominent mark. -ಗೊಂಬೆ. A main branch of a tree. -ಗೋರಟೆ. Globe amaranth, *Gomphrena globosa.*

ಹೆಗಲು k. *n.* The shoulder. -ಬಡಿಕ. A ruthless man.

ಹೆಗ್ಗು (= ಎಗ್ಗು, *q. v.*) k. *n.* Blame, fault, censure, *etc.*

ಹೆಂ. = ಹೆಣ್ಣು, *q. v.* -ಗೂಸು (-ಕೂಸು). A female child.

ಹೆಂಗಸು (*fr.* ಹೆಂ-ಕೂಸು) k. *n.* A female; a woman. 2, a wife; *pl.* ಹೆಂಗಸರು.

ಹೆಂಗೆ. = ಹ್ಯಾಗೆ, *q. v.*

ಹೆಚ್ಚರ. = ಎಚ್ಚರ, *q. v.*

ಹೆಚ್ಚಳ k. *n.* Pride, conceit, elation; excess. -ಗೊಳ್ಳು, -ಪಡು, ಹೆಚ್ಚಳಿಸು. To become elated, to rejoice.

ಹೆಚ್ಚಿಗೆ 1. k. *n.* Increase, growth; excess, superfluity. *a.* Extra, beyond what is expected. *ad.* Greatly, much, more. -ತೆಗೆದುಕೊಳ್ಳು. To take more than is due. -ಮಾಡು. To increase; exalt.

ಹೆಚ್ಚಿಗೆ 2. k. *n.* A small flat basket.

ಹೆಚ್ಚು 1. k. *v. i.* To become more, increase, thrive, grow, swell. *n.* Increase, growth; largeness: excess;

superfluity, surplus, excess, *etc.* *a.* More, excessive. ಹೆಚ್ಚಿಸು. To cause to increase, *etc*, to multiply, increase. -ಕಡಿಮೆ. Difference, variation, more or less, about. -ಆಗು To augment, increase, to abound, become too much. -ಗಾರಿಕೆ Exaltation. -ಗುಣಿಸು To multiply -ಗೆ (= ಹೆಚ್ಚಿಗೆ). Increase, growth. -ಗೊಳ್ಳು To increase -ಮಾಡು To increase (*v t.*). -ವಿಕೆ. Increasing -ಹೆಚ್ಚು. More and more.

ಹೆಚ್ಚು 2 k. *v. t* To mince, *as* vegetables, *etc.*

ಹೆಚ್ಚೆ = ಹಚ್ಚೆ, *q v*

ಹೆಜ್ (= ಹೆಗ್ಗ್) k. *n* Largeness -ಜೇನು. Superior honey.

ಹೆಜ್ಜೆ. (= ಪಜ್ಜೆ) k *n* A foot-step, a foot-print, track. 2, the foot -ಇಡು, -ಹಾಕು To walk -ಯ ಹಿಡಿ. To track, follow by the foot-steps.

ಹೆಂಚು (= ಹಂಚು, *q v*) k *n.* A tile

ಹೆಟ್ಟ k *n.* A bush-harrow. 2, dregs of castor-oil 3, a clod

ಹೆಟ್ಟಿಗೆ k. *n.* A stout beam 2, (f) a dovecot

ಹೆಟ್ಟು (= ಪೆಟ್ಟು, *q v*) k *v t* To beat, box, give a blow. 2, to insert, put, *as* a morsel into the mouth

ಹೆಟ್ಟೆ k *n* A lump of earth, clod

ಹೆಡ k *n.* The back, rear -ಕಟ್ಟು. Hind-binding, to pinion, *also* -ಗುಡಿ ಕಟ್ಟು -ತಲೆ The back of the head -ಮುರಿಕೆ, -ಮುರಿಗೆ. Pinioning. -ಮುರಿಗೆ ಕಟ್ಟು To pinion.

ಹೆಡಕು k *n* The back of the neck

ಹಡಿಗೆ, ಹೆಡಿಗೆ (*tb of* ಪಿಟಕ) *n.* A basket.

ಹೆಡೆ (*tb of* ಸ್ಫಟಿ) *n* The expanded hood of a serpent

ಹೆಡ್ಡ k *n.* A dull, stupid man, fool *a* Dull, foolish. -ತನ, ಹೆಡ್ಡು. Stupidity ಹೆಡ್ಡಾಳು A stupid, foolish person

ಹೆಣ k. *n* A corpse, a carcass -ದತ್ತು, -ಮೋರೆ A good-for-nothing fellow; a coward. -ಹೂಳು. To bury a corpse -ಗಾಡು A cemetery

ಹೆಣಗು k *v i* To wrangle, quarrel, fight, strive ಹೆಣಗಾಟ Quarrel, fight ಹೆಣಗಾಡು, = ಹೆಣಗು, *q. v.* ಹಣಗಿಸು To cause to fight.

ಹೆಣಿಗೆ k *n* Plaiting; that is plaited.

ಹೆಣೆ k. *v. t* To intertwine, plait, *as* mats, *etc.*, to braid *as* the hair, to knit, *as* nets, to rattan, *as* a chair *n.* Joining together, plait, braid. -ಕೊಳ್ಳು. To intertwine, to plait. -ಕಟ್ಟು To tie cattle in a row for treading corn.

ಹೆಂಟೆ k *n* A lump of earth, a clod. 2, an unburnt brick. 3, a bush-harrow.

ಹೆಂಡ 1 k *n* A female, a wife, *also* -ತಿ. *Pl* ಹೆಂಡರು, ಹೆಂಡಂದಿರು, ಹೆಂಡಿರು. ಹೆಂಡರು ಮಕ್ಕಳು Wife and children.

ಹೆಂಡ 2. k *n.* Spirituous liquor, toddy. ಈಚಲ- Date toddy. ತೆಂಗಿನ-. Cocoanut toddy. ತಾಳೇ- Palmyra toddy.

ಹೆಂಡೆ k *n* Cowdung 2, = ಹೆಂಟೆ

ಹೆಣ್ಣಿಗ k *n* A coward. -ತನ. Cowardice.

ಹೆಣ್ಣು k *n.* A female, a woman *a.* Female, feminine *Cpds* -ಆಡು, -ಆಳು. -ಒಂಟೆ, -ಕಪ್ಪೆ, -ಕರ, -ಕರಡಿ, -ಕುದುರೆ (mare), -ಕೂಸು, -ಕೋಳಿ (hen), -ಗುಬ್ಬಿ (hen-sparrow), -ಚಿಗರಿ -ತೋಳ, -ದೇವತೆ, -ನರಿ, -ನಾಯಿ (bitch), -ಸಿಂಹ (lioness), -ಹಂದಿ (sow), -ಹುಲಿ (tigress). -ಮಕ್ಕಳು Female children, women ಹೆಣ್ಣಾನೆ, ಹೆಣ್ಣಾಡೆ, ಪೆಣ್ಣೊಂಟೆ A female goat, *etc*

ಹೆತ್ತಪ್ಪ, ಹೆತ್ತಯ್ಯ, ಹೆತ್ತಾತ k *n.* A grandfather ಹೆತ್ತಮ್ಮ. A grandmother.

ಹೆತ್ತು *P p of* ಹೆರು.

ಹೆದ್ k *a.* Large, big -ದನಿ. A loud voice. -ದರೆ An extensive barren tract -ದಾರಿ. A high-road -ದಿಂಡಿ (-ತಿಂಡಿ), -ದಿನಿ (-ತಿನಿ) Much food, an omnivorous person -ದಿನಿ ಉಣ್ಣು To eat voraciously [illegible] glutton

ಹೆದರು (ರು = ಱು) k. v. i. To be alarmed or frightened, to fear. n. Fear, alarm, fright. ಹೆದರದವ. A courageous man. ಹೆದರಿಕೆ. Fear. ಹೆದರಿಸು. To frighten.

ಹೆದೆ a. k. n. A bow-string.

ಹೆಡ್ಡ k. n. A lever used in moving a car.

ಹೆಪ್ಪು 1. k. n. Any thing put into milk to cause it to turn or curdle. -ಗಟ್ಟು, ಹೆಪ್ಪಾಗು. To be turned, *as* milk. -ಇಡು, -ಕೊಡು, -ಹಾಕು. To curdle or turn milk.

ಹೆಪ್ಪು 2. k. n. Sod, sward, grass, turf.

ಹೆಬ್ k. a. Large, big. -ಬಲಸು (-ಹಲಸು). The jungle jack, *Artocarpus pubescence*. -ಬಾಗಿಲು. The principal gate or door. -ಬಾರ, -ಬಾರುವ (-ಹಾರ, -ಹಾರುವ). The head Brâhmaṇa of a caste. -ಬಾವು (-ಹಾವು). The boa. -ಬುಲಿ (-ಹುಲಿ). The royal tiger. -ಬೆಟ್ಟು, -ಬೆರಳು, -ಬೊಟ್ಟು. The thumb; the great toe.

ಹೆಮ್ k. a. Large, big. -ಮರ. A large tree; a lofty tree producing a fragrant resin, *Ailanthus malabarica*. -ಮಾರಿ. A wicked woman; Durga. -ಮುಗುಳು. A garden plant, *Spilanthes acmella*.

ಹೆಮ್ಮೆ k. n. Greatness, etc.; pride, vanity. -ಗಾರ. A proud man. -ಗೊಳಿಸು (-ಕೊಳಿಸು). To elate.

ಹೆರ (ರ = ಱ) k. *pro.* Another, other. -ಗೆ. Outside. -ರು. Others.

ಹೆರಲು, ಹೆರಳು k. n. A braid of hair. -ಹಾಕು. To braid the hair.

ಹೆರು 1. (ರು = ಱು) k. v. t. To bear, bring forth, give birth to. *P. p.* ಹೆತ್ತು. ಹೆತ್ತವರು. Parents. ಹೆರಿಗೆ, ಹೆರುವಿಕೆ. Bringing forth, delivery.

ಹೆರು 2. (ರು = ಱು) k. v. i. To thicken, congeal, *as* clarified butter. *P. p.* ಹೆತ್ತು. ಹೆತ್ತುಪ್ಪ. Congealed ghee.

ಹೆರೆ 1. k. v. t. To scrape, *as* a fruit, the floor [illegible]

ಹೆರೆ 2. [illegible]

ಹೆರೆ 3. (ರೆ = ಱೆ) a. k. n. The crescent, the moon.

ಹೆಸರು 1. k. n. A name; fame, celebrity. -ಗೊಳ್ಳು, -ಪಡು, -ಸಂಪಾದಿಸು, -ಹೊಂದು, ಹೆಸರಾಗು, ಹೆಸರಿಗೆ ಬರು. To get a name, become famous. ಹೆಸರಿಗೆ ಮಾತ್ರ. In name only. -ಇಡು, ಹೆಸರಿಡು. To name. -ಪಡೆ. To get a name. -ವಾಸಿ. Fame, reputation. -ಹೋಗು. A name to go; to become noted.

ಹೆಸರು 2. (ರು = ಱು) k. n. Green gram, *Phaseolus mungo*.

ಹೆಳಲು (= ಹೆರಳು) k. n. A braid of hair.

ಹೆಳವ (ಳ = ೞ) k. n. A lame man, cripple; *f.* ಹೆಳವಿ.

ಹೇ s. *A voc. particle*: Oh! ho! -ಕರಿಸು. To neigh.

ಹೇಗೆ k. *ad.* How?

ಹೇಟೆ, ಹೇಂಟೆ k. n. A hen.

ಹೇಡಿ k. n. A timid person, coward. -ತನ. Cowardice. ರಣ-. A coward in battle.

ಹೇತಿ s. n. A weapon. 2, light; flame.

ಹೇತು s. n. Motive; cause, ground, reason, purpose; proof; logic; sophistry. -ಕ. Causal, instrumental; cause. ಜಗಳಕ್ಕೆ-, ವ್ಯಾಜ್ಯಕ್ಕೆ-, ಸಾವಿಗೆ-, *etc.* The cause of a quarrel, *etc.*

ಹೇನು k. n. A louse. -ಸೀರು. A nit. -ಎತ್ತು. To pick out lice.

ಹೇಮ 1. s. n. Gold.

ಹೇಮ 2. s. n. Winter; *also* ಹೇಮಂತ. -ಪರ್ವತ, ಹೇಮಾದ್ರಿ. The mountain Méru.

ಹೇಯ s. a. To be gone; to be avoided. n. Dislike.

ಹೇರಳ k. n. Largeness, greatness, abundance. a. Much, many; *also* ಹೇರಾಳ.

ಹೇರಾಸಿ k. n. Abundance.

ಹೇರು (ರು = ಱು) k. v. t. To lift up and put upon; to load, lade; to pile up. n. A load; a bullock-load.

ಹೇರಂಳ k. n. A kind of bitter orange.

[illegible] s. [illegible] ceremonies, each [illegible] 2, the dung of men, dogs *etc.* -ಮನುಷ್ಯ A filthy man -ಮಾತು. A loathsome word

ಹೇವ a k. *n* Disgust, repugnance 2, shame, modesty. ಹೇವರಿಸು To recoil, shrink

ಹೇವಿಲಂಬಿ (*tb of* ಹೇಮಲಂಬ) *n* N. of the thirty-first year of the cycle.

ಹೇಷ, ಹೇಷಾ s *n* Neighing, braying.

ಹೇಷ್ಯ (*tb of* ಏಷ್ಯತ್) *n* A portent, an ill-omen

ಹೇಸರ (*tb. of* ವೇಸರ) *n* A mule.

ಹೇಸು k. *v. i.* To feel aversion, have a dislike, to recoil *n* = ಹೇಸಿಕೆ. -ತನ. Nastiness ಹೇಸಿ A disgustful female. ಹೇಸಿಕೆ, ಹೇಸಿಗೆ. Aversion, disgust; nastiness, a nasty, disagreeable object, filthy, nasty, loathsome ಹೇಸಿಕೆಗಿಡ A prickly shrub, *Lantana aculeata* ಹೇಸಿಕೆಗೊಳಿಸು, ಹೇಸಿಕೆ ಮಾಡು To soil, dirty

ಹೇಳಿಗೆ (= ವೇಳಿಗೆ *tb of* ಪೇಟಕಾ) *n* A basket, a snake-basket

ಹೇಳು (ಳು = ಱು) k *v t & v. i.* To say, speak, to name, to mention; to narrate, relate, to tell, to order, command. ಹೇಳಿ ಕಳಿಸು, ಹೇಳಿ ಕಳುಹಿಸು To send word, to let know. ಹೇಳ ಕೂಡದ ಕೆಲಸ A shameful business ಹೇಳಿಕೊಡು To instruct, communicate. ಹೇಳಿತೀರದ. Unspeakable ಹೇಳಿಕೊಟ್ಟ ಮಾತು A communicated word ಊಟಕ್ಕೆ-. To invite to a meal ಹೇಳಿಸು. To cause to say, *etc* -ವಿಕೆ, ಹೇಳಿಕೆ, ಹೇಳ್ವಿಕೆ. Saying, telling ಹೇಳಿಕೇ ಮಾತು Rumour, hearsay.

ಹೈಗ (*tb of* ಪದ್ಯಕ) *n* A class of Smârta Brâhmanas

ಹೈಡ್ರೊಜಿನ್ e *n.* Hydrogen, a highly inflammable gas

ಹೈನು = ಪಯ್ನು, *q v.*

ಹೈಮಂತ (*fr* ಹೇಮಂತ) s. *a* Wintery, cold *n* The winter season

ಹೈರಾಣು h. *n.* Distressful condition, bewilderment, confusion, trouble, harass -ಮಾಡು, [illegible]

ಹೈರೊಗ್ಲಿಫಿಕ್ಸ್ e *n* Hieroglyphics; the symbolic writing of the ancient Egyptians and Mexicans

ಹೈರೋಡ್ e *n* A high-road.

ಹೊ = ಹೋ 2, *q. v*

ಹೊಕ್ಕಳು, ಹೊಕ್ಕುಳು (ಳು = ಱು) k *n.* The navel 2, the perpendicular dash put under a letter to make it aspirate -ಮಾಡು, -ಸೀಳು To make this dash, *as* ದ *into* ಧ [loom.

ಹೊಕ್ಕು k *n* A boil 2, the woof of a

ಹೊಕ್ಕು. *P p of* ಹೊಗು, *q v* -ಬಳಕೆ. Familiar intercourse

ಹೊಗರು a. k. *n* Shine, lustre, effulgence.

ಹೊಗಳು (= ಪೊಗಳು ಳು = ೞು) k *v. t* To praise *n* Praise, renown ಹೊಗಳಿಕೆ Praise, flattery. ಹೊಗಳಿಸು To cause to praise

ಹೊಗು k *v i* To enter *P p* ಹೊಕ್ಕು. ಹೊಗಿಸು To cause to enter ಹೊಗಗೊಡು, ಹೊಗಗೊಡಿಸು To allow to enter

ಹೊಗೆ k *v i.* To smoke 2, to look sullen *n* Smoke; steam, vapour -ಕಟ್ಟು. Soot -ಕೊಡು. To apply smoke to; to give a thin coating of gold or silver -ಬಂಡಿ A railway carriage. -ಬತ್ತಿ, -ಸುತ್ತು A cheeroot, cigar -ಸೊಪ್ಪು Tobacco -ಹಡಗ A steam-ship -ಹಾಕು To smoke, produce smoke -ಸೂರು, -ಹಿಡಿ To become black from smoke.

ಹೊಂ, ಹೊನ್ k *n.* Gold. -ಗಟ್ಟು (-ಕಟ್ಟು). A golden ferrule. -ಗರಿ A gold-coloured feather. -ಗಳಸ (-ಕಳಸ) A gold penacle -ಗೆಲಸ (-ಕೆಲಸ). Work in gold.

ಹೊಂಗರ, ಹೊಂಗರಕ k *n.* The Indian coral tree, *Erythrina indica.*

ಹೊಂಗು a k *v i* To swell, rise up, *as* the sea, to be elated; to exult.

ಹೊಂಗೆ k. *n* The Indian beech, *Pongamia glabra*

ಹೊಚ್ಚು k. *v. t* To put on, *as* tiles, to [illegible] put on

,7

ಹೊಂಚು k. *v. t.* To look after; to spy, lurk; to lie in wait, be on the look-out. *n.* Lying hid. -ಗಾರ. A spy. -ಜಾಗ. An ambush. -ವಿಕೆ. Being on the look-out for, lurking.

ಹೊಟ್ಟು k. *n.* Chaff; husk of rice or corn; a pod without its contents. -ಕೇರು. To winnow. -ಗುಟ್ಟು (-ಕುಟ್ಟು). To speak nonsense.

ಹೊಟ್ಟೆ k. *n.* The belly; the body of a vessel. ಡೊಳ್ಳು-. Potbellied. -ಉರಿ, -ಕಿಚ್ಚು, ಹೊಟ್ಟೆಚ್ಚರಿ. Envy. -ಕಟ್ಟು. To restrain the appetite; to live frugally; to be constipated. -ಕಳತ. Purging. -ಕಳಿ, -ವ್ಯೂಡಿಸು. The bowels to purge. -ಖರ್ಚು. Expense for food. -ಗೆ ಹಾಕು. To give to eat. -ತುಂಬು. To fill the belly. -ನೋವು, -ಬೇನೆ, -ಶೂಲೆ. Colic. -ಬಾಕ. A glutton. -ಬಾಕತನ. Gluttony. -ಯ ಮೇಲೆ ಬಡಿ. To take away the means of sustenance. -ಯೊಳಗೆ ಬೆಂಕಿ ಬೀಳು. Envy or sorrow to be produced. -ಯೊಳಗೆ ಹಾಕು. To keep to one's self, conceal and forgive. -ಯೊಳಗಿನ ಮಾತು. A covert expression. -ಹೊರೆ. To support life.

ಹೊಡ. = ಹೊಡದು, ಹೊಡೆದು. *P. p. of* ಹೊಡೆ, *in* ಹೊಡಕೊಳ್ಳು.

ಹೊಡಕೆ k. *n.* The elephant grass.

ಹೊಡಗು k. *n.* A hole.

ಹೊಡಿ, ಹೊಡೆ 1. k. *v. t.* To strike, beat, lash, flog, smite; to cast, *as* a stone; to shoot, *as* an arrow; to drive cattle, cart, *etc.*; to drive away, beat off; to devour. *P. ps.* ಹೊಡದು, ಹೊಡೆದು. ಕೊಳ್ಳೆ-. To sack, plunder. ಗಂಟೆ-. To strike the hour, ring a bell. ಗಾಳಿ-. The wind to blow. ಗುಡಾರ-. To pitch a tent. ತಲೆ-. To behead. ಮಳೆ-. Rain to fall. ಹೊಡತ. Beating; a stroke, blow. ಹೊಡತಾ-. To beat severely. ಹೊಡದಾಟ. Beating. ಹೊಡ ದಾಡು. To beat mutually.

ಹೊಡೆ 2. k. *n.* The pri[illegible] [illegible]op-be[illegible], in a [illegible]

ಹೊಡೆ 3. k. *n.* An ear of corn. 2, the calyx of the kêdagĕ.

ಹೊಣೆ k. *n.* Bond, bail; a bondsman, surety. -ಕೊಡು. To give bail. -ಗಾರ. A surety. -ನಿಲ್ಲು, -ಯಾಗು. To stand security for.

ಹೊಂಡ k. *n.* A pit, hole; a pond.

ಹೊಂಡೆ f. *n.* The small tree, *Cerbera-odollam.*

ಹೊತ್ತಾರೆ k. *n.* Day-break. *ad.* At day-break.

ಹೊತ್ತಗೆ, ಹೊತ್ತಿಗೆ. *tb. of* ಪುಸ್ತಕ, *q. v.*

ಹೊತ್ತು 1. (=ಹತ್ತು 3) k. *v. i.* To be kindled, catch fire. 2, to be burnt at the bottom of a cooking vessel. ಹೊತ್ತಿಸು. To kindle, light.

ಹೊತ್ತು 2. k. *n.* The sun; time; a time of the day. -ಆಗು. To be time. -ಕಳೆ. To spend time. -ಗೊತ್ತು ಮಾಡು. To fix a time. -ಮಾಡು. To delay. -ಮೀರು. Time to be passed. -ಮುಳುಗು. The sun to set. -ಮೂಡು, -ಹುಟ್ಟು. The sun to rise. -ಸಾಧಿಸು. To await an opportunity. -ಹೋಗು. Time to pass. -ಹೊತ್ತಿಗೆ. From time to time. ಹೊತ್ತುಂಟೆ. At day-break, early.

ಹೊತ್ತು 3. k. *P. p. of* ಹೊರು, *q. v.*

ಹೊದಕೆ k. *n.* A cover, covering, wrapper. 2, a thatch, roof.

ಹೊದರು 1. k. *n.* The hollow of a tree.

ಹೊದರು 2. (ರು = ಱು) k. *n.* A bush. 2, a mass; a host; a herd.

ಹೊದಿ. = ಹೊದೆ, *q. v.* -ಸು. To put on, cover, *etc.* -ಕೆ. = ಹೊದಕೆ, *q. v.*

ಹೊದೆ 1. (= ಹೊದಿ) k. *v. t.* To put on; to put over; to wrap round; to cover. *P. ps.* ಹೊದದು, ಹೊದೆದು, ಹೊದ್ದು. ಹೊದ್ದುಕೊಳ್ಳು. To put on one's self. ಹೊದ್ದಿಸು. To put on.

ಹೊದೆ 2. = ಪೊದೆ, *q. v.*

ಹೊದ್ದಿಕೆ k. *n.* Union; concord. 2, a cover, wrapper; *cf.* ಹೊದಕೆ.

[illegible] a. k. [illegible] To join; to g[illegible] near.

[illegible] n. k. [illegible] A [illegible]

ಹೊಂತ (*tb* of ಪಂಥ) *n.* A path, way. -ಗಾರ A clever, able man.

ಹೊಂದಿಕೆ k *n* Fitness, intimacy, attachment, friendship

ಹೊಂದಿಸು k *v t* To join (*as limbs for greeting*), to attach, to collect, to make fit, *as* price.

ಹೊಂದು k. *v t.* To obtain, get, procure, acquire; to experience, to suffer *v i.* To touch, to go nigh, approach, to join, to agree, befit, suit.

ಹೊನ್ನು, (ಹೊನ್) k *n.* Gold; a gold coin; ½ of a varaha. ಹೊನ್ನಗನ್ನೆ. A common weed, used as a potherb, *Alternanthera sessilis.*

ಹೊನ್ನೆ k. *n.* The tree *Terminalia tomentosa.* 2, a large timber-tree yielding a red dye

ಹೊಪ್ಪೆ k. *n* A natural division in some fruits. 2, a large timber tree yielding a red dye.

ಹೊಮ್ = ಹೊನ್ನು -ಬಳಿ. To gild -ಬಾಳೆ A kind of plantain

ಹೊಮಿಯೊಪಥಿ f *n* Homoeopathy

ಹೊಮ್ಮು k *v i* To rise, break out, run over, come forth 2, to be thick, rank

ಹೊಯಿ (= ಹೊಯ್ಯು, *q v.*) k. *v t* To beat, cast, to pour. *n* Beating, a stroke, blow -ಗಡುಬು. A cake made by pouring the dough into a vessel -ಸು. To cause to beat cast or pour. -ದಾಟ. Mutual beating. -ದಾಡು To beat mutually. -ತ, -ಲು, ಹೊಯ್ಲು. Beating, a stroke blow

ಹೊಯಿಗೆ k. *n* Sand.

ಹೊಯಿಲು, ಹೊಯ್ಲು (= ಹುಯಿಲು) k *n.* Calling out 2, the current of a stream.

ಹೊಯ್ಯು (= ಹೊಯಿ. *q. v.*) k. *v t* To beat, strike, smite; to kill, to cast, pour, to drive (*as* ಕೈ-, ತಲೆ-, ನೀರು-), *etc.* *n* A stroke, blow. ಉಚ್ಚೆ- To void urine.

ಹೊರ 1 (ರ = ಱ) k. *n.* The outside. *a* Outside, out… [illegible]

-ಕಡೆ, -ಗಡೆ. The outside, a public privy, evacuation of bowels -ಗು. The outside. -ಗೆ Outside, without -ಗಾಗು To be excluded -ಗಿಕ್ಕು, -ಗಿಡು. To put outside. -ಬರು. To come out -ಮಾಡು. To expel. -ತರು To divulge, bring out. -ಚೆಲ್ಲು To pour out; to be spilt. -ನೂಕು. To push out. -ಪಡಿಸು To make public -ಪಡು. To become public. -ಬೀಳು. To come out, to become public. -ಮಗ್ಗಲು The outside. -ಮೈ The outside -ವಡು. To set out, start. -ಹೊಮ್ಮು. To rise; to come forth. -ಹೊರಡು To go forth.

ಹೊರ 2 *P p.* of ಹೊರೆ, *in* ಹೊರಕೊಳ್ಳು -ಕ One who nourishes, *as* ಹೊಟ್ಟೆ ಹೊರಕ.

ಹೊರಜೆ k *n* A stout long rope

ಹೊರಡು (*fr* ಹೊರ ರ = ಱ) k *v i* To go out, to come forth, to set out, sally forth; to start. *P p* ಹೊರಟು. ಹೊರಡಿಸು. To cause to start ಹೊರಡುವಿಕೆ. Starting ಹೊರಟು ಹೋಗು To set out.

ಹೊರತು (*fr* ಹೊರ ರ = ಱ) k *prep* Except, without -ಮಾಡು. To except, exempt.

ಹೊರಸು k. *n.* A cot, couch 2, a kind of pigeon.

ಹೊರಳಿ a. k. *n.* A heap, mass

ಹೊರಳು k *v i* To roll, to wallow, welter ನಾಲಗೆ-, ಮಾತು- To be retracted, *as* a word or promise ಹೊರಳಾಡು To roll about. ಹೊರಳಿಸು. To cause to roll *etc*, to roll about

ಹೊರಳೆ k *n* A nostril 2, money accounts transferred from one head to another

ಹೊರಿಕೆ k *n.* The scale or coat of an onion, a layer

ಹೊರಿಗೆ (ರಿ = ಱಿ) k. *n* Business, work.

ಹೊರಿಸು k. *v. i* To have one's self nourished *v t* To cause to nourish, *cf.* ಹೊರಿಸು s ಹೊರು

ಹೊರು (ರು = ಱು) k *v t* To bear, carry on the head, to take upon one's self, [illegible]

ಹೊತ್ತುಕೊಳ್ಳು. To take upon one's self; to put on. ಹೊತ್ತುಕೊಂಡು ಹೋಗು. To carry, bear, sustain. ಸಾಲವ-. To be in debt. ಹೊರೇ-. To carry a load. ಹೊರಿಸು. To put on; to cause to carry; to lay on, impose; to impute; *as:* ಅಪರಾಧ-, ತಪ್ಪು-, ದೋಷ-, *etc.*

ಹೊರೆ 1. (*fr.* ಹೊರು. ರ = ಱ) k. *n.* A load, burden. -ಗಾರ, -ಯಾಳು. A porter, carrier. ಸೌದೆ-. A faggot. ಹುಲ್ಲು-. A bundle of grass.

ಹೊರೆ 2. k. *v. t.* To nourish, invigorate, foster, support, preserve. *n.* Spirit, courage. ಹೊಟ್ಟೆ-. To sustain the belly.

ಹೊರೆ 3. k. *n.* The slough of a serpent; a coat of a plantain tree; a fold. 2, a web of cloth. 3, neighbourhood, vicinity, *as in* ನೆರೆ-.

ಹೊರೆ 4. (= ಪೊರೆ 4) k. *n.* Choking sensation. -ಹೊಗು. To feel a choking sensation.

ಹೊರ್ತು. = ಹೊರತು, *q. v.*

ಹೊಲ k. *n.* A plough-field; a corn-field. -ಬಿತ್ತು. To sow a field. -ಮಾಡು. To till the ground. -ದ ಪೈರು, -ದ ಬೆಳೆ. A crop. -ಹಸಗು. To weed a field.

ಹೊಲಗೆ. = ಹೊಲಿಗೆ, *q. v.*

ಹೊಲತಿ k. *n.* A low-caste woman.

ಹೊಲಬು a. k. *n.* A way; a manner, mode. -ಗೆಡು. To become bewildered.

ಹೊಲಸು k. *n.* Nastiness; nasty matter, filth; dirtiness. *a.* Nasty. -ತನ. Nastiness, obscenity. -ನುಡಿ, -ಮಾತು. An obscene word.

ಹೊಲಿ k. *v. t.* To sew, stitch. -ಗೆ. Sewing; needle-work. -ಗೇ ಬಿಚ್ಚು. To open a seam. -ಗೇ ಹಾಕು. To put a seam.

ಹೊಲೆ k. *n.* Pollution, defilement; impurity; meanness, *etc.* -ಗೇರಿ. A place where outcasts or Hŏlĕyas live. ಹೊಲೆಯ. A low-caste man, a Hŏlĕya; *f.* ಹೊಲತಿ. -ಯಾಳು. A low-caste servant. -ೕ ಕೂಗು. Obscene discourse.

ಹೊಲ್ಲ a. k. *n.* Meanness, impropriety. *a.* V[illegible]

ಹೊಸ k. *a.* New, novel; fresh, recent. *Cpds.:* -ತುಪ್ಪ, -ನೀರು, -ಬೆಣ್ಣೆ, -ರೊಟ್ಟಿ, -ಬರ, -ಹುಕುಮ್, *etc.* -ತು, -ದು. That which is new, fresh, *etc.* -ಬ. A new man; *f.* -ಬಳು. -ತಾಗಿ, ಹೊಸ್ತಾಗಿ. Newly, recently.

ಹೊಸಕು, ಹೊಸಗು k. *v. t.* To rub anything between the hands or with the foot.

ಹೊಸಗೆ, ಹೊಸಿಗೆ k. *n.* Report, news, tidings. 2, joy. -ಹೇಳು. To relate news.

ಹೊಸತಿಲು, ಹೊಸ್ತಿಲು k. *n.* A threshold. -ದಾಟು. To cross the threshold.

ಹೊಸೆ (= ಪೊಸೆ) k. *v. t.* To twist, plait, make rope. 2, To churn.

ಹೊಸ್ತು. = ಹೊಸತು, *q. v.*

ಹೊಳಕು a. k. *v. i.* To appear, be manifest.

ಹೊಳಪು, ಹೊಳವು k. *n.* Radiance, lustre, brightness. ಹೊಳಪಿಸು. To furbish, scour.

ಹೊಳಲು (= ಪೊಳಲು. ಳ = ೞ) k. *n.* A town.

ಹೊಳೆ 1. k. *v. i.* To be radiant or bright; to shine, glitter. ಹೊಳಿಸು. = ಹೊಳಪಿಸು, *q. v.*

ಹೊಳೆ 2. (ಳೆ = ೞೆ) k. *n.* A river. -ಹಳ್ಳ, *dupl.* -ೕ ಕಟ್ಟು. A water-dam. -ದಾಟು, -ಹಾಯು. To cross a river.

ಹೊಳ್ಳು. = ಪೊಳ್ಳು, *q. v.*

ಹೊಳ್ಳು (= ಹೊರಳು, *q. v.*) k. *v. i.* To roll, *etc.* ಹೊಳ್ಳಿಸು. To cause to roll; to roll.

ಹೊಳ್ಳೆ (= ಸೊಳ್ಳೆ) k. *n.* A nostril.

ಹೋ 1. k. *int.* *A particle used in stopping, rejoicing or in sorrow.*

ಹೋ 2. k. *abbr. of* ಹೋಗುವ. -ಕ. Goer, *as* ದಾರಿಹೋಕ, ದಾವಹೋಕ, *etc.* -ಗಾಲ. going time; death.

ಹೋ 3. k. *n.* *A particle of calling or surprise.*

ಹೋಕು k. *n.* A defect, fault, flaw. -ಮಾಡು. To maim. -ಹೋಗು. To be frustrated.

ಹೋಕೆ k *n* A way, passage 2, impudence, hypocrisy 3, debauchery.

ಹೋಗು k. *v i* To go, go off or away, proceed 2, to be lost, disappear, to die. *P p* ಹೋಗಿ *Rel p. p* ಹೋದ -ಗೊಡು, -ಬಿಡು To allow to go ಹೋಗಿ ಬರು To go and come ಹೋಗಿಬಿಡು To go away ಕೊಂಡು-, ತೆಗೆದು ಕೊಂಡು- To carry off. ಹೋಗಲಾಡಿಸು, ಹೋಗಾಡಿಸು To make away with, to dissipate destroy ಹೋಗಲಾಡು To let go, to lose ಹೋಗಾಡು To throw away. dissipate, squander; to quit -ವಿಕೆ Going exit ಹೋಯಿತು. *3rd pers sing imp of* ಹೋಗು.

ಹೋಟೆ a. k. *n* The hollow of a tree, emptiness

ಹೋತ, ಹೋತು k *n.* A he-goat

ಹೋತೃ s *n.* An offerer of an oblation

ಹೋಬಳಿ k *n* A division of a talook. -ದಾರ. A chief of armed peons. -ಶಾನ ಬೋಗ. A village accountant.

ಹೋಮ s. *n.* A burnt-offering, a sacrifice. -ಕುಂಡ A fireplace prepared for an oblation, *also* -ಶಾಲೆ ಹೋಮಾಗ್ನಿ A sacrificial fire.

ಹೋರಿ k *n* A young bull, a he-buffalo. -ಕರ A he-calf ಬೀಜದ-, ಕಾಯಿ- An uncastrated bull. ಬೀಜ ಒಡೆದ- A castrated bull

ಹೋರು 1 k *v. t.* To wrestle, to fight to altercate. ಹೋರಾಟ Mutual fight, strife, altercation ಹೋರಾಡು To wrestle, fight, wrangle

ಹೋರು 2 k. *n.* A hole.

ಹೋರೆ (ರೆ = ಱೆ) k. *n* Business, work

ಹೋಲು k. *v i* To be like, resemble. -ವಿಕೆ, -ವೆ, ಹೋಲಿಕೆ Resemblance, likeness, similarity ಹೋಲಿಕೆ ಮಾಡು, ಹೋಲಿಸು. To make analogous, to compare

ಹೋಹ (= ಹೋಗುವ) a. k *Rel. pres. part of* ಹೋಗು.

ಹೋಳಿ f *n* The hôli festival in desecration of cupid when his effigy is burnt, *also* -ಹಬ್ಬ.

ಹೋಳಿಗೆ (*tb of* ಪೋಲಿಕಾ) *n.* A cake in general.

ಹೋಳು (ಳು = ಟು) k. *n.* A split piece, slice

ಹೌದಾ (=ಹವುದಾ, *q v.*) f *n* An uncovered chair upon an elephant. 2, a reservoir

ಹೌದು (= ಹವುದು, *q. v*) k *ad* Yes ಹೌದೇ, ಹೌದೇನೇ Is it so? ಹೌದೇನೋ Whether is it so? ಹೌದೋ ಅಲ್ಲವೋ Is it or is it not?

ಹೌರ = ಹವುರ. *q v*

ಹೌಸ h *n* Ambition, lust

ಹ್ಯಾಗೆ, ಹ್ಯಾಂಗೆ k *ad.* In what manner? how? ಹ್ಯಾಗಂದರೆ That is to say, namely ಹ್ಯಾಗಾದರೂ, ಹ್ಯಾಗೂ, ಹ್ಯಾಂಗಾದರೂ, ಹ್ಯಾಂಗೂ Somehow, in one way or another, however, at all events.

ಹ್ರಸ್ವ s *a.* Short, small. *n.* A short vowel

ಹ್ರಾಸ s *n* Loss, detriment. 2, decrease, decline

ಳ

ಳ The fifty third letter of the alphabet

ೞ

ೞ The fifty-fourth letter of the alphabet. *At present it is obsolete and represented by* ಳ.

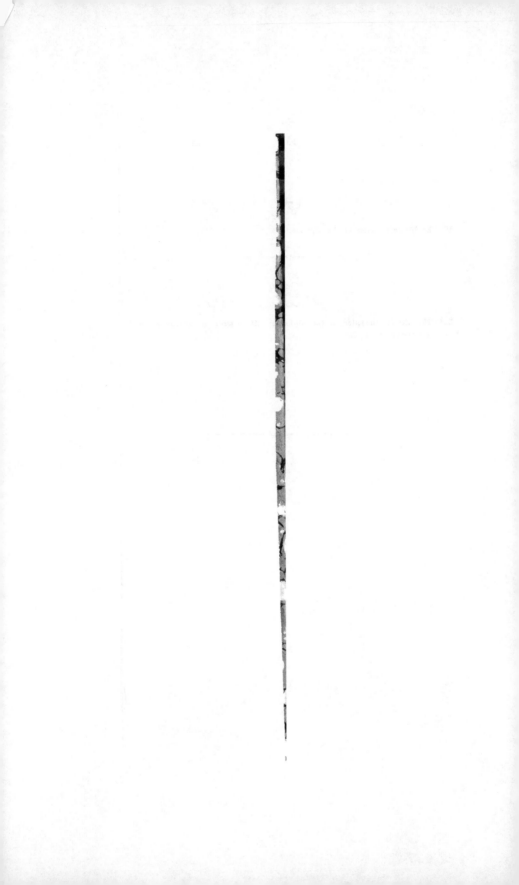

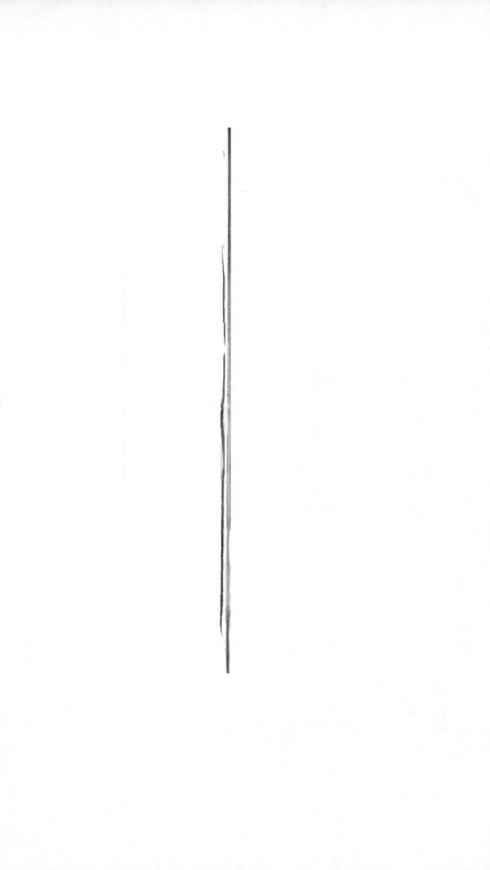

Lightning Source UK Ltd.
Milton Keynes UK
UKHW02f1842150218
317967UK00003B/129/P

9 781375 94887